STRATEGIC MANAGEMENT
Concepts and Cases

Arthur A. Thompson, Jr.
A. J. Strickland III

Both of the University of Alabama

Tenth Edition

Irwin
McGraw-Hill

Boston, Massachusetts   Burr Ridge, Illinois   Dubuque, Iowa
Madison, Wisconsin   New York, New York   San Francisco, California   St. Louis, Missouri

Irwin/McGraw-Hill

A Division of The **McGraw·Hill** *Companies*

STRATEGIC MANAGEMENT: CONCEPTS AND CASES

Copyright ©1998 by The McGraw-Hill Companies, Inc. All rights reserved. Previous edition(s) ©1978, 1981, 1984, 1987, 1990, 1992, 1993, 1995, and 1996 by Richard D. Irwin, a Times Mirror Higher Education Group, Inc. company. Printed in the United States of America. Except as permitted under the United States Copyright Act of 1976, no part of this publication may be reproduced or distributed in any form or by any means, or stored in a database or retrieval system, without the prior written permission of the publisher.

This book is printed on acid-free paper.

1 2 3 4 5 7 8 9 0 DOW/DOW 9 0 9 8 7 (US edition)
1 2 3 4 5 7 8 9 0 DOW/DOW 9 0 9 8 7 (International edition)

ISBN 0-256-23738-7

Vice president and editorial director: *Michael W. Junior*
Publisher: *Craig S. Beytien*
Senior sponsoring editor: *John E. Biernat*
Senior developmental editor: *Laura Hurst Spell*
Marketing manager: *Ellen Cleary*
Senior project manager: *Mary Conzachi*
Production supervisor: *Scott Hamilton*
Designer: *Ellen Pettengell/Michael Warrell*
Compositor: *Shepard Poorman Communications*
Typeface: *10.5/12 Times Roman*
Printer: *R.R. Donnelley & Sons Company*

Library of Congress Cataloging-in-Publication Data

Thompson, Arthur A., (date)
    Strategic management : concepts and cases / Arthur A. Thompson, A.J. Strickland. — 10th ed.
        p. cm.
    Includes a collection of "35 cases, 22 of which are freshly written and 13 of which are . . . carryovers from the two previous editions"—Pref.
    "Also includes an enhanced Strat-Tutor software supplement of chapter self-tests and case preparation guides for student use"—-Pref.
    Includes index.
    ISBN 0-256-23738-7
    1. Strategic planning.   2. Strategic planning—Case studies.
I. Strickland, A. J. (Alonzo J.)   II. Title.
HD30.28.T53   1998
658.4'012—dc21   97-31064

INTERNATIONAL EDITION

Copyright © 1998. Exclusive rights by The McGraw-Hill Companies, Inc. for manufacture and export. This book cannot be re-exported from the country to which it is consigned by McGraw-Hill. The International Edition is not available in North America.

When ordering this title, use ISBN 0-07-115577-5.

http://www.mhhe.com

To Hasseline and Kitty

PREFACE

enth editions are something of a milestone in the evolution of a textbook. For potential adopters they signal effective pedagogy and sustained market acceptance. For authors they impose responsibilities to recast presentations, inject added disciplinary coherence, and move the subject matter to a new plateau of clarity and understanding. We've tried to live up to these responsibilities, attacking this revision with renewed vigor and endeavoring to do our level best to fully satisfy the market's legitimate yearning for a teaching/learning package that squarely targets what every student needs to know about crafting, implementing, and executing business strategies. If we have done the job we think we have, you will find that this tenth edition package reflects continuous improvement along all fronts.

The chapters have undergone major revision in some cases and extensive fine-tuning in others; the most outstanding change is the thoroughness with which the resource-based view of the firm has been incorporated into the presentations of both crafting and implementing strategy. There's an exciting and very teachable collection of 34 cases, 22 of which are freshly written and 12 of which are popular and timely carryovers from the two previous editions. The tenth edition package also includes an enhanced Strat-Tutor software supplement of chapter self-tests and case preparation guides for student use, a fresh version of the companion global simulation—*The Business Strategy Game*, a comprehensively updated readings book with 34 new selections, and a full array of instructional aids for adopters. This tenth edition is our best ever, we think—and by a more than modest margin.

CONTENT FEATURES OF THE TENTH EDITION

New concepts, analytical tools, and methods of managing continue to surface at rates that mandate important edition-to-edition changes in content and emphasis. In the interval since the last revision, the conceptual underpinning and articulation of the resource-based view of the firm has blossomed. While SWOT analysis and the emphasis on building and nurturing core competencies have always pointed to the importance of careful internal strength-weakness assessment in crafting strategy, recent contributions to the literature make it clear that there's much more to the resource-based view of the firm than is implied in a simple weighing of company strengths and weaknesses. We have made a concerted attempt throughout this tenth edition to drive home the strategy-making, strategy-implementing relevance of strengthening a company's resource complement and upgrading its competencies and competitive capabilities to match market realities and create competitive advantage. This edition gives balanced treatment to the thesis that a company's strategy must be matched both to its external market circumstances and to its resources and competitive capabilities. Hence, you'll find the resource-based view of the firm prominently integrated into the coverage of crafting business strategy (Chapters 2 and 4) and crafting diversification strategies (Chapters 7 and 8). You'll also find that Chapters 9 and 10 have a strong resource-based perspective regarding the role of core competencies, competitive capabilities, and organizational resources in implementing and executing strategy.

In addition to the exceptionally thorough resource-based orientation, we've incorporated important new material on cooperative strategies, collaborative alliances, and competing in "high velocity" market environments where the pace of change (from whatever source) places special demands on a company to adapt its strategy and its resource capabilities to rapidly unfolding events. Once again, there's front-to-back coverage of global issues in strategic management, prominent treatment of ethical and social responsibility issues, and margin notes in every chapter that highlight basic concepts, strategic management principles, and kernels of wisdom. Extensive rewriting to sharpen the presentations in every chapter has allowed us to include the new material and still cover everything in less than 365 pages—something that readers and adopters ought to welcome, given the jam-packed content of the course.

Specific Chapter Modifications and Content Improvements

While the overall chapter organization continues to parallel that of the last several editions, we've made a number of noteworthy changes in chapter content and topical emphasis:

- Chapters 1 and 2 contain fresh presentations on the importance of a clear, motivating strategic vision, stretch objectives, and rapid adaptation of strategy to newly unfolding market conditions and customer expectations. We continue to place strong emphasis on how and why a company's strategy emerges from (*a*) the deliberate and purposeful actions of management and (*b*) as-needed reactions to unanticipated developments and fresh competitive pressures. The material in Chapter 1 underscores even more strongly that a company's strategic plan is a collection of strategies devised by different managers at different levels in the organizational hierarchy and builds a case for why all managers are on a company's strategy-making, strategy-implementing team. The worldwide organizational shift to empowered employees and managers makes it imperative for company personnel to be "students of the business" and skilled users of the concepts and tools of strategic management.

- Together, the material in Chapter 3, "Industry and Competitive Analysis" and Chapter 4, "Evaluating Company Resources and Competitive Capabilities," create the understanding for why managers must carefully match company strategy both to industry and competitive conditions and to company resources and capabilities. The role of Chapter 3 is to set forth the now familiar analytical tools and concepts of industry and competitive analysis and demonstrate the importance of tailoring strategy to fit the circumstances of a company's industry and competitive environment. The role of Chapter 4 is to establish the equal importance of doing solid company situation analysis as a basis for matching strategy to organizational resources, competencies, and competitive capabilities.

- Chapter 4 has been thoroughly overhauled and contains a full-blown discussion of all the concepts and analytical tools required to understand why a company's strategy must be well matched to its internal resources and competitive capabilities. The roles of core competencies and organizational resources and capabilities in creating customer value and helping build competitive advantage have been given center stage in the discussions of company resource strengths and weaknesses. SWOT analysis has been recast as a tool for assessing a company's resource strengths and weaknesses. There are new sections on determining the competitive value of specific company resources and assets and on selecting the competencies and capabilities having the biggest competitive advantage potential. The standard tools of value-chain analysis, strategic cost analysis, benchmarking, and competitive strength assessments, however, continue to have a prominent role in the methodology of evaluating a company's situation—they are an essential part of understanding a company's relative cost position and competitive standing vis-à-vis rivals.

- Chapter 5 contains a major new section on using cooperative strategies to build competitive advantage. Chapter 6 features a new section on competing in industry situations characterized by rapid-fire technological change, short product life-cycles, frequent moves by competitors, and/or rapidly evolving customer requirements and expectations. It also includes more extensive discussions of strategic alliances to enhance a company's competitiveness in both high velocity markets and in global markets.

- We continue to believe that global competition and global strategy issues are best dealt with by integrating the relevant discussions into each chapter rather than partitioning the treatment off in a separate chapter. The globalization of each chapter, a prominent feature of the two previous editions, is carried over and strengthened in this edition, plus we've added more illustration capsules to highlight the strategies of non-U.S. companies.

- We have recast our analytical treatment of corporate diversification strategies in Chapters 7 and 8, eliminating much of the attention formerly given to drawing business portfolio matrixes and, instead, putting the analytical emphasis on (1) assessing industry attractiveness, (2) evaluating the company's competitive strength in each of its lines of business, (3) appraising the degree of strategic fits among a diversified company's different businesses, and (4) appraising the degree of *resource fit* among the different businesses. You'll find a very strong resource-based view of the firm in the recommended methodology for evaluating the pros and cons of a company's diversification strategy. Chapter 8 continues to incorporate analytical use of the industry attractiveness/business strength portfolio matrix because of its conceptual soundness and practical relevance, but we have abandoned coverage of the flawed growth-share matrix and the little-used life-cycle matrix.

- The three-chapter module (Chapters 9–11) on strategy implementation features a solid, compelling conceptual framework structured around (1) building the resource strengths and organizational capabilities needed to execute the strategy in competent fashion; (2) developing budgets to steer ample resources into those value-chain activities critical to strategic success; (3) establishing strategically appropriate policies and procedures; (4)

instituting best practices and mechanisms for continuous improvement; (5) installing information, communication, and operating systems that enable company personnel to carry out their strategic roles successfully day-in and day-out; (6) tying rewards and incentives tightly to the achievement of performance objectives and good strategy execution; (7) creating a strategy-supportive work environment and corporate culture; and (8) exerting the internal leadership needed to drive implementation forward and to keep improving on how the strategy is being executed.

- The eight-task framework for understanding the managerial components of strategy implementation and execution is explained in the first section of Chapter 9. The remainder of Chapter 9 focuses on building an organization with the competencies, capabilities, and resource strengths needed for successful strategy execution. You'll find welcome coverage of what it takes for an organization to build and enhance its competencies and capabilities, develop the dominating depth in competence-related activities needed for competitive advantage, and forge arrangements to achieve the necessary degree of collaboration and cooperation both among internal departments and with outside resource providers. There is much-expanded treatment of the task of building resource strengths through collaborative alliances and partnerships. We've continued the coverage initiated in the last two editions concerning the pros and cons of outsourcing noncritical activities, downsizing and delayering hierarchical structures, employee empowerment, reengineering of core business processes, and the use of cross-functional and self-contained work teams. The result is a powerful treatment of building resource capabilities and structuring organizational activities that ties together and makes strategic sense out of all the revolutionary organizational changes sweeping through today's corporations. So far, the efforts of companies across the world to organize the work effort around teams, reengineer core business processes, compete on organizational capabilities (as much as on differentiated product attributes), and install leaner, flatter organization structures are proving to be durable, fundamental additions to the conventional wisdom about how to manage and valuable approaches for improving the caliber of strategy execution.

- As before, Chapter 10 surveys the role of strategy-supportive budgets, policies, reward structures, and internal support systems and explains why the benchmarking of best practices, total quality management, reengineering, and continuous improvement programs are important managerial tools for enhancing organizational competencies in executing strategy. Chapter 11 continues to deal with creating a strategy-supportive corporate culture and exercising the internal leadership needed to drive implementation forward. There's coverage of strong versus weak cultures, low performance and unhealthy cultures, adaptive cultures, and the sustained leadership commitment it takes to change a company with a problem culture, plus sections on ethics management and what managers can do to improve the caliber of strategy execution.

- There are 17 new or revised illustration capsules.

The use of margin notes to highlight basic concepts, major conclusions, and "core" truths was well received in earlier editions and remains a visible feature of this edition. The margin notes serve to distill the subject matter into concise principles, bring the discussion into sharper focus for readers, and point them to what is important.

Diligent attention has been paid to putting life into the explanations and to improving clarity and writing style. We've tried to take dead aim on creating a text presentation that is crisply written, clear and convincing, interesting to read, comfortably mainstream, and as close to the frontiers of theory and practice as a basic textbook should be.

THE CASE COLLECTION IN THE TENTH EDITION

The 34 cases in this edition include 22 new cases not appearing in any of our previous editions, 8 cases from the ninth edition, and 4 carryover cases from the eighth edition. We've tried to strike a good balance between fresh cases, previously used cases that are still timely and very much on-target with respect to the issues, and proven favorites. To highlight the close linkage between the cases and strategic management concepts, we have grouped the cases under five chapter-related and topical headings. In the Section A grouping are five cases spotlighting the role and tasks of the manager as chief strategy-maker and chief strategy-implementer; these cases—America Online, Ben & Jerry's Homemade, Intel, The Fudge Cottage, and Cineplex Odeon (B)—provide convincing demonstration of why the discussions in Chapters 1 and 2 are relevant to a company's long-term market success. Section B contains a 13-case grouping where the central issues deal with analyzing industry and competitive situations and crafting business-level strategy; these cases call upon students to apply the text material in Chapters 3–6. In Section C are four cases involving strategy assessments and strategy-making in diversified companies that make nice follow-ons to the coverage in Chapters 7 and 8. There are nine cases in Section D, all revolving around the managerial challenges of implementing strategy and giving students an opportunity to apply the concepts presented in Chapters 9–11. Section E contains three cases highlighting the links between strategy, ethics, and social responsibility.

The case line-up in this tenth edition reflects our steadfast preference for cases that feature intriguing products and companies and that are capable of sparking both student interest and lively classroom discussions. At least 19 of the cases involve high-profile companies, products, or people that students will have heard of, know about from personal experience, or can easily identify with. The America Online, Intel, and Acer Computer cases will provide students with insight into the special demands of competing in industry environments where technological developments are an everyday event, product life-cycles are short, and competitive maneuvering among rivals comes fast and furious. At least 16 of the cases involve situations where company resources and competitive capabilities play as much a role in the strategy-making, strategy-implementing scheme of things as do industry and competitive conditions. Indeed, we made a special effort to ensure that the cases selected for this edition demonstrated the relevance of the resource-based view of the firm. Scattered throughout the lineup are 11 cases concerning non-U.S. companies, globally competitive industries, and/or cross-cultural situations; these cases, in conjunction with the globalized content of the text chapters, provide ample material for linking the study of strategic management tightly to the ongoing globalization of the world economy—in proper keeping with AACSB standards. You'll also find 5 cases where the central figures are women, 9 cases dealing with the strategic problems of family-owned or relatively small entrepreneurial businesses, and 18 cases involving public companies about which students can do further research in the library or on the Internet. Six of the cases (America Online, Ben & Jerry's, Callaway Golf, Nintendo vs. SEGA, Bama Pie, and Food Lion) have videotape segments that either are available from the publisher or can be ordered from other sources.

The case researchers whose work appears in this edition have done an absolutely first-class job of preparing cases that contain valuable teaching points, that illustrate the important kinds of strategic challenges managers face, and that allow students to apply the tools of strategic analysis. We believe you will find the tenth edition's collection of 34 cases exceptionally appealing, eminently teachable, and very suitable for drilling students in the use of the concepts and analytical treatments in Chapters 1 through 11. It is an unusually attractive and stimulating case lineup from beginning to end.

COMPANY WEB SITE ADDRESSES AND USE OF THE INTERNET

Following Chapter 11 and prior to Case 1, we have once again included "A Guide to Case Analysis" that gives students positive direction in what case method pedagogy is all about and offers suggestions for approaching case analysis. To this discussion, we have added a section on how to use the Internet and various online services to (1) do further research on an industry or company, (2) obtain a company's latest financial results, and (3) get updates on what has happened since the case was written. The information available on the Internet is exploding at a rapid-fire pace. We think students will find our list of information-laden Web sites and the accompanying suggestions of how to use the various search engines a time-saving and valuable assist in running down the information they are interested in. To further facilitate student use of the Internet, we have included company Web site addresses at appropriate locations in the cases themselves. Alternatively, students can link directly to company Web sites by going to the student section of the Web page for the text (*www.mhhe.com/thompson*).

THE STRAT-TUTOR SOFTWARE SUPPLEMENT FOR STUDENTS

Available with the tenth edition is a second-generation software option called Strat-Tutor that is, in effect, a full-fledged, computer-assisted, interactive study guide for the whole text. Strat-Tutor has two main sections:

- A series of self-tests that students can use to measure their comprehension, chapter-by-chapter, of the material presented in the text.
- Study questions for each of the 34 cases in the tenth edition, plus a set of custom-designed case preparation guides for 17 of the cases that lead students through the needed analysis, provide number-crunching assistance, and tutor students in use of the concepts and tools presented in the chapters.

The Self-Testing Feature

The test section of Strat-Tutor contains (1) a 25-question self-test for each text chapter, (2) a 50-question self-exam covering the material in Chapters 1–6, and (3) a 50-question self-exam covering the material in Chapters 7–11. The 11 chapter tests consist of an assortment of true-false, fill-in-the-blank, and challenging multiple answer questions that cover the text presentation rather thoroughly. These tests were deliberately made demanding (given their "open book" nature) so as to require careful reading and good comprehension of the material. When the student completes each test, Strat-Tutor automatically grades the answers, provides a test score, posts the test score in the student's personal "grade book," indicates the questions with wrong answers, and directs students to the text pages where the correct answers can be found. Questions incorrectly answered can be attempted as many times as needed to arrive at the right answer. In addition, we created conventional (single-answer) multiple-choice tests covering Chapters 1–6 (50 questions) and Chapters 7–11 (50 questions) that students can use to prepare for in-class exams given by the instructor.

Used properly and in conjunction with each other, we think these tests will provide students with a welcome and effective way to gauge their readiness for the course instructor's own examinations on the 11 chapters. *None of the questions on* Strat-Tutor *correspond to those on the instructor's test bank.*

The Study Questions and Case Preparation Guides

We've all experienced poor and uneven student preparation of cases for class discussion. Sometimes it's because of inadequate effort, but more often it is because of confusion over exactly what analysis to do and/or inexperience in using the tools of strategic analysis to arrive at solid recommendations. To give students some direction in what to think about in preparing a case for class, Strat-Tutor provides study questions for all 34 cases in the tenth edition. To help them learn how to use the concepts and analytical tools properly, there's an interactive guide (not a solution!) for use in preparing 17 of the cases. Each study guide has been tailored to fit the specific issues/problems and analytical requirements posed by the case. We have scrupulously avoided creating one generic study guide because cases in strategic management cut across a broad range of issues/problems and entail diverse analytical requirements (strategy analysis in single-business situations is fundamentally different from strategy analysis of diversified companies; cases where the spotlight is on developing a strategy are fundamentally different from cases where the main issues revolve around strategy implementation and execution).

The Strat-Tutor case preparation guides provide:

- *Study questions* to trigger the process of thinking strategically and to point students toward the analysis needed to arrive at sound recommendations.

- A *series of interactive screens that coach students in the use of whatever analytical tools are appropriate*—whether it be five-forces analysis, strategic group mapping, identification of key success factors, SWOT analysis, value chain analysis, competitive strength assessments, construction of a business portfolio matrix, industry attractiveness assessments, or strategic fit matchups.

- *Follow-on questions* to prod students to think clearly about what conclusions flow from their analysis.

- *Calculations* of financial ratios, compound average growth rates, common-size income statements and balance sheets, and any other statistics useful in evaluating industry data, company financial statements, and company operating performance.

- *What-iffing capability* that allows students to readily develop projections of company financial performance (when such projections are germane to the case).
- *Reminders* of strategy principles and generic strategic options to help students arrive at a set of pragmatic action recommendations.
- *Printouts* of the work done (to serve as notes students can use in the class discussion).

The interactive design of the case preparation guides keeps the ball squarely in the student's court to do the analysis, to decide what story the numbers tell about a company's situation and performance, and to think through the options to arrive at recommendations. Strat-TUTOR is thus not a crutch or "answer-file" for the cases; rather, it is a vehicle for using the PC to tutor students in strategic thinking and helping students learn to correctly apply the tools and concepts of strategic management. We've endeavored to design the case preparation guides to coach students in how to think strategically about business problems/issues, to drill them in the methods of strategic analysis, and to promote sound business judgment. You can be assured that the case notes students develop with the aid of Strat-TUTOR will represent their work, not ours.

To decide whether Strat-TUTOR makes sense as a requirement or recommended option in your course, we suggest booting up the accompanying Strat-TUTOR disk and perusing one or two of the chapter tests and case preparation guides to get a feel for the caliber of the software and its fit with your instructional approach. Strat-TUTOR uses a Windows format (familiar to most students) and is very user-friendly; the software must be used on computers equipped with either Windows 3.1x or Windows95 (or 98).

Students can download free demos of the self-test for Chapter 1 and the case preparation guide for Ben & Jerry's Homemade at the Web site for the tenth edition (*www.mhhe.com/thompson*). If they are satisfied with the value-added offered by the sample test and preparation guide, they can use a credit card to purchase the full software package at the Web site (in the event you decide to make use of Strat-TUTOR optional rather than to require it as part of the official course package).

THE BUSINESS STRATEGY GAME OPTION

There's a freshly revised edition of *The Business Strategy Game* to accompany this text. It has two major new features and an assortment of refinements that make it a welcome upgrade over the version introduced in 1996. This fifth-generation version is the product of excellent feedback and suggestions from users, a couple of new ideas on our part, and reworked programming—and represents an ongoing effort to continuously improve the simulation.

The Business Strategy Game has five features that make it an uncommonly effective teaching–learning aid for strategic management courses: (1) the product and the industry—producing and marketing athletic footwear is a business that students can readily identify with and understand, (2) the industry environment is global—providing students with up-close exposure to what global competition is like and the kinds of strategic issues that managers in global industries have to address, (3) the realistic quality of the simulation exercise—we've designed the simulation to be as faithful as possible to real world markets, competitive conditions, and revenue-cost-profit relationships, (4) the wide degree of strategic freedom students have in managing their companies—we've gone to great lengths to make the game free of bias as concerns one strategy versus another, and (5) the five-year planning and decision-making capability it incorporates as an integral part of the exercise of running a company. These features, wrapped together as a package, provide an exciting and valuable bridge between concept and practice, the classroom and real-life management, and reading conventional wisdom about management and learning-by-doing.

The Value a Simulation Adds

Our own experiences with simulation games, along with hours of discussions with users, have convinced us that simulation games are *the single best exercise available* for helping students understand how the functional pieces of a business fit together and giving students an integrated, capstone experience. First and foremost, the exercise of running a simulated company over a number of decision periods helps develop students' business judgment. Simulation games provide a live case situation where events unfold and circumstances change as the game progresses. Their special hook is an ability to get students personally involved in the subject matter. *The Business Strategy Game* is very typical in this respect. In plotting their competitive strategies each decision period, students learn about risk-taking. They have to respond to changing market conditions, react to competitors' moves, and choose among alternative courses of action. They get valuable practice in reading the signs of industry change, spotting market opportunities, evaluating threats to their company's competitive position, weighing the tradeoffs between higher profits now and higher profits later, and assessing the long-term consequences of short-term decisions. They chart a long-term direction, set strategic and financial objectives, and try out different strategies in pursuit of competitive advantage. They become active strategic thinkers, planners, analysts, and decision makers. By having to live with the decisions they make, students experience what it means to be accountable for decisions and responsible for achieving satisfactory results. All this serves to drill students in responsible decision making and improve their business acumen and managerial judgment.

Second, students learn an enormous amount from working with the numbers, exploring options, and trying to unite production, marketing, finance, and human resource decisions into a coherent strategy. They begin to see ways to apply knowledge from prior courses and figure out what really makes a business tick. The effect is to help students integrate a lot of material, look at decisions from the standpoint of the company as a whole, and see the importance of thinking strategically about a company's competitive position and future prospects. Since a simulation game is, by its very nature, a hands-on exercise, the lessons learned are forcefully planted in students' minds—the impact is far more lasting than what is remembered from lectures. Third, students' entrepreneurial instincts blossom as they get caught up in the competitive spirit of the game. The resulting entertainment value helps maintain an unusually high level of student motivation and emotional involvement in the course throughout the term.

About the Simulation

We designed *The Business Strategy Game* around athletic footwear because producing and marketing athletic footwear is a business students can readily understand and because the athletic footwear market displays the characteristics of many globally competitive industries—fast growth, worldwide use of the product, competition among companies from several continents, production located in low-wage locations, and a marketplace where a variety of competitive approaches and business strategies can co-exist. The simulation allows companies to manufacture and sell their brands in North America, Europe, and Asia, plus there's the option to compete for supplying private-label footwear to North American chain retailers. Competition is head-to-head—each team of students must match their strategic wits against the other company teams. Companies can focus their branded marketing efforts on one geographic market or two or all three or they can deemphasize branded sales and specialize in private-label production (an attractive strategy for low-cost producers). Low-cost leadership, differentiation strategies, best-cost producer strategies, and focus strategies are all viable competitive options. Companies can position their products in the low end of the market, the high end, or stick close to the middle on price, quality, and service; they can have a wide or narrow product line, small or big dealer networks, extensive or limited advertising. Company market shares are based on how each company's competitive effort stacks up against the efforts of rivals. Demand conditions, tariffs, and wage rates vary among geographic areas. Raw materials used in footwear production are purchased in a worldwide commodity market at prices that move up or down in response to supply-demand conditions. If a company's sales volume is unexpectedly low, management has the option to liquidate excess inventories at deep discount prices.

The company that students manage has plants to operate, a workforce to compensate, distribution expenses and inventories to control, capital expenditure decisions to make, marketing and sales campaigns to wage, sales forecasts to consider, and ups and downs in exchange rates, interest rates, and the stock market to take into account. Students must weave functional decisions in production, distribution, marketing, finance, and human resources into a cohesive action plan. They have to react to changing market and competitive conditions, initiate moves to try to build competitive advantage, and decide how to defend against aggressive actions by competitors. They must endeavor to maximize shareholder wealth via increased dividend payments and stock price appreciation. Each team of students is challenged to use their entrepreneurial and strategic skills to become the next Nike or Reebok and ride the wave of growth to the top of the worldwide athletic footwear industry. The whole exercise is representative of a real world competitive market where companies try to outcompete and outperform rivals—things are every bit as realistic and true to actual business practice as we could make them.

There are built-in planning and analysis features that allow students to (1) craft a five-year strategic plan, (2) gauge the long-range financial impact of current decisions, (3) do the number-crunching to make informed short-run versus long-run tradeoffs, (4) assess the revenue-cost-profit consequences of alternative strategic actions, and (5) build different strategy scenarios. Calculations at the bottom of each decision screen provide instantly updated projections of sales revenues, profits, return on equity, cash flow, and other key outcomes as each decision entry is made. The sensitivity of financial and operating outcomes to different decision entries is easily observed on the screen and on detailed printouts of projections. With the speed of today's personal computers, the relevant number-crunching is done in a split-second. The game is designed throughout to lead students to decisions based on "My analysis shows . . ." and away from the quicksand of decisions based on "I think," "It sounds good," "Maybe, it will work out," and other such seat-of-the-pants approaches.

The Business Strategy Game is programmed to work on any PC capable of running Windows 3.1x, Windows95 (or 98), or Windows NT, and it is suitable for both senior-level and MBA courses. The game accommodates a wide variety of disk drives, monitors, and printers and runs quite nicely on a network.

Features of the New Version

In preparing this latest version, we've benefited enormously from the experiences and advice of both adopters and players. We've listened carefully, implemented many suggestions of users, programmed in numerous behind-the-scenes refinements that users have requested, and added a couple of new features. You'll find this newest incarnation of *The Business Strategy Game* to be meaningfully better for players and game administrators in several respects:

- **The New Demand Forecasting Feature.** The biggest change is the addition of a demand forecasting model that allows each company to project the number of branded pairs it is likely to sell in each geographic market, given its contemplated marketing effort and given the overall competitive effort it expects to encounter from rival companies. We think players will be thrilled to have a tool that is capable of projecting the upcoming year's branded sales volumes (usually within 5 percent of what actually happens, *provided that they accurately anticipate the competitive effort of rivals*).

- **The New Inventory Liquidation Option.** A second new feature is that companies are given the option to liquidate any excess inventories at deep discount prices, thereby clearing their warehouses of unwanted stocks of unsold branded or private-label shoes.

- **Assorted Fine-Tuning.** We have further tweaked the relationships among decision variables and the interactions among the determinants of company competitiveness to mirror market realities in the athletic footwear business ever more closely. A few minor changes have been made in the Footwear Industry Report and the Administrator's Report. We have executed a number of behind-the-scenes programming changes to make the simulation an easier-to-administer exercise from a technical perspective.

- **The Irwin/McGraw-Hill Web Site.** We now have the capability to provide users with immediate downloads of software upgrades at the Web site for this text (*www.mhhe.com/thompson*), plus offer some online technical support (including answers to FAQs)—all in addition to the technical support via e-mail and telephone that has been and continues to be in place. Should you encounter any glitches, the procedure for downloading software upgrades is painless and automatic, allowing you to proceed without having to reinstall the software or restart the simulation.

At the same time, we have retained the array of new features and improvements introduced in the previous version: the celebrity endorsements feature, the optional executive compensation feature, the extensive on-screen decision support calculations and what-iffing capability, the much improved five-year strategic plan format, and the added scoring flexibility. As before, instructors have numerous ways to heighten competition and keep things lively as the game progresses. There are options to raise or lower interest rates, alter certain costs up or down, and issue special news flashes announcing new tariff levels, materials cost changes, shipping difficulties, or other new considerations to keep business conditions dynamic and "stir the pot" a bit as needed. The built-in scoreboard of company performance keeps students constantly informed about where their company stands and how well they are doing. Rapid advances in PC technology continue to cut processing times—

it should take no more than 45 minutes for you or a student assistant to process the results on an older PC and well under 30 minutes if you have a PC with a Pentium 120 or faster chip.

A separate instructor's manual for *The Business Strategy Game* describes how to integrate the simulation exercise into your course, provides pointers on how to administer the game, and contains step-by-step processing instructions. Should you encounter technical difficulties or have questions, the College New Media department at Irwin/McGraw-Hill can provide quick assistance via a toll-free number.

READINGS BOOKS OPTION

For instructors who want to incorporate samples of the strategic management literature into the course, a companion *Readings in Strategic Management* containing 43 selections is available. Thirty-four of the 43 readings are new to this latest edition. All 43 selections are quite readable, and all are suitable for seniors and MBA students. Most of the selections are articles reprinted from leading journals; they add in-depth treatment to important topic areas covered in the text and put readers at the cutting edge of academic thinking and research on the subject. Some of the articles are drawn from practitioner sources and stress how particular tools and concepts relate directly to actual companies and managerial practices.

To make the close linkage between the selected readings and the 11 chapters of text material readily apparent to students, we have grouped the readings into five categories. Six articles examine the role of the manager as chief strategist and chief strategy-implementer and expand on the topics covered in Chapters 1 and 2. Eleven articles concern strategic analysis and strategy formation at the business unit level and add more range and depth to the material presented in Chapters 3–6. There are five articles dealing with strategy in diversified companies that are very appropriate for use with Chapters 7 and 8. Seventeen of the readings relate to various aspects of strategy implementation and execution, making them suitable complements for the material in Chapters 9–11. Four of the articles focus on strategy, values, and ethics.

In tandem, the readings package provides an effective, efficient vehicle for reinforcing and expanding the text-case approach. It is an exceptionally solid lineup of recently published articles.

TENTH EDITION INSTRUCTOR'S PACKAGE

A full complement of instructional aids is available to assist adopters in using the tenth edition successfully. A two-volume *Instructor's Manual* contains suggestions for using the text materials, various approaches to course design and course organization, a sample syllabus, alternative course outlines, a thoroughly revised and expanded set of 940 multiple-choice and essay questions, a comprehensive teaching note for each case, plus six classic cases from previous editions. There is a computerized test bank for generating examinations, a set of color transparencies depicting the figures and tables in the 11 text chapters, and a PowerPoint presentation package for use in classrooms equipped with computer screen projection capability. The 3½-inch PowerPoint disks can also be used to make black-and-white overheads in the event you use an overhead projector to support your lectures. The PowerPoint package includes over 500 visuals that thoroughly cover the material presented in the 11 chapters, thus providing plenty to select from in creating support for your classroom lectures (we deliberately created enough visuals for each chapter to give you an ample number of choices in putting together a presentation that fits both your preferences and time constraints). To help instructors enrich and vary the pace of class discussions of cases, there are video supplements for use with the America Online, Ben & Jerry's, Callaway Golf, Nintendo vs. SEGA, Bama Pie, and Food Lion cases. There's a special instructor-only section at the text Web site (*www.mhhe.com/thompson*) that allows you to download many of the instructor support materials.

In concert, the textbook, the three companion supplements, and the comprehensive instructor's package provide a complete, integrated lineup of teaching materials. The package provides exceptional latitude in course design, allows you to capitalize on the latest computer-assisted instructional techniques, arms you with an assortment of visual aids, and offers rich pedagogical options for keeping the nature of student assignments varied and interesting. We've endeavored to equip you with all the text materials and complementary resources you need to create and deliver a course that is very much in keeping with contemporary strategic management issues and that wins enthusiastic student approval.

ACKNOWLEDGMENTS

We have benefited from the help of many people during the evolution of this book. Students, adopters, and reviewers have generously supplied an untold number of insightful comments and helpful suggestions. Our intellectual debt to those academics, writers, and practicing managers who have blazed new trails in the strategy field will be obvious to any reader familiar with the literature of strategic management.

We are particularly indebted to the case researchers whose casewriting efforts appear herein and to the companies whose cooperation made the cases possible. To each one goes a very special thank you. The importance of timely, carefully researched cases cannot be overestimated in contributing to a substantive study of strategic management issues and practices. From a research standpoint, cases in strategic management are invaluable in exposing the generic kinds of strategic issues that companies face, in forming hypotheses about strategic behavior, and in drawing experienced-based generalizations about the practice of strategic management. Pedagogically, cases about strategic management give students essential practice in diagnosing and evaluating strategic situations, in learning to use the tools and concepts of strategy analysis, in sorting through various strategic options, in crafting strategic action plans, and in figuring out successful ways to implement and execute the chosen strategy. Without a continuing stream of fresh, well-researched, and well-conceived cases, the discipline of strategic management would quickly fall into disrepair, losing much of its energy and excitement. There's no question, therefore, that first-class case research constitutes a valuable scholarly contribution.

The following reviewers provided insightful suggestions and advice regarding ways to make the tenth edition better: David Aviel, California State University, Hayward; Maria A. Corso, State University of New York at Oswego; David Flynn, Hofstra University; J. Leslie Jankovich, San Jose State University; Eveann Lovero Lewis University; and Vince Luchsinger, University of Baltimore.

We are also indebted to James Boulgarides, Betty Diener, Daniel F. Jennings, David Kuhn, Kathryn Martell, Wilbur Mouton, Bobby Vaught, Tuck Bounds, Lee Burk, Ralph Catalanello, William Crittenden, Stan Mendenhall, John Moore, Will Mulvaney, Sandra Richard, Ralph Roberts, Thomas Turk, Gordon VonStroh, Fred Zimmerman, S.A. Billion, Charles Byles, Gerald L. Geisler, Rose Knotts, Joseph Rosenstein, James B. Thurman, Ivan Able, W. Harvey Hegarty, Roger Evered,

Charles B. Saunders, Rhae M. Swisher, Claude I. Shell, R. Thomas Lenz, Michael C. White, Dennis Callahan, R. Duane Ireland, William E. Burr, II, C.W. Millard, Richard Mann, Kurt Christensen, Neil W. Jacobs, Louis W. Fry, D. Robley Wood, George J. Gore, and William R. Soukup. These reviewers were of considerable help in directing our efforts at various stages in the evolution of the text.

Naturally, as custom properly dictates, we are responsible for whatever errors of fact, deficiencies in coverage or presentation, and oversights that remain. As always, we value your recommendations and thoughts about the book. Your comments regarding coverage and contents will be most welcome, as you will your calling our attention to specific errors. Please fax us at (205) 348-6695, e-mail us at athompso@cba.ua.edu, or write us at P.O. Box 870225, Department of Management and Marketing, The University of Alabama, Tuscaloosa, AL 35487-0225.

Arthur A. Thompson, Jr.
A. J. Strickland

CONTENTS

3 INDUSTRY AND COMPETITIVE ANALYSIS 68

Illustration Capsule:

4 EVALUATING COMPANY RESOURCES AND COMPETITIVE CAPABILITIES 103

Illustration Capsules:

5 STRATEGY AND COMPETITIVE ADVANTAGE 134

6   MATCHING STRATEGY TO A COMPANY'S SITUATION 174

7   STRATEGY AND COMPETITIVE ADVANTAGE IN DIVERSIFIED COMPANIES 213

*Cases for which there are case preparation exercises on Strat-Tutor.

Section E: Strategy, Ethics, and Social Responsibility

I

THE CONCEPTS AND TECHNIQUES OF STRATEGIC MANAGEMENT

PART

1

THE STRATEGIC MANAGEMENT PROCESS

An Overview

T his book is about the managerial tasks of crafting, implementing, and executing company strategies. *A company's strategy is the "game plan" management has for positioning the company in its chosen market arena, competing successfully, pleasing customers, and achieving good business performance.* Strategy consists of the whole array of competitive moves and business approaches that managers employ in running a company. In crafting a strategic course, management is saying that "among all the paths and actions we could have chosen, we have decided to go in this direction and rely upon these particular ways of doing business." A strategy thus entails managerial choices among alternatives and signals organizational commitment to specific markets, competitive approaches, and ways of operating.

Managers devise company strategies because of two very compelling needs. One is the need to *proactively shape* how a company's business will be conducted. Passively allowing strategy to drift along as the by-product of ongoing business approaches, occasional proposals for improvement, and periodic adjustments to unfolding events is a surefire ticket for inconsistent strategic actions, competitive mediocrity, and lackluster business results. Rather, it is management's responsibility to exert entrepreneurial leadership and commit the enterprise to conducting business in a fashion shrewdly calculated to produce good performance. A strategy provides a roadmap to operate by, a prescription for doing business, a game plan for building customer loyalty and winning a sustainable competitive advantage over rivals. The second need is that of molding the independent decisions and actions initiated by departments, managers, and employees across the company into a *coordinated, companywide* game plan. Absent a strategy, managers have no framework for weaving many different action initiatives into a cohesive whole, no plan for uniting cross-department operations into a team effort.

Crafting, implementing, and executing strategy are thus core management functions. Among all the things managers do, nothing affects a company's ultimate success or failure more fundamentally than how well its management team charts the company's

> "Cheshire Puss," she [Alice] began . . . "would you tell me, please, which way I ought to go from here?"
>
> "That depends a good deal on where you want to get to," said the Cat.
>
> **Lewis Carroll**
>
> Without a strategy the organization is like a ship without a rudder, going around in circles.
>
> **Joel Ross and Michael Kami**
>
> My job is to make sure the company has a strategy and that everybody follows it.
>
> **Kenneth H. Olsen**
> *Former CEO, Digital Equipment Corporation*

long-term direction, develops competitively effective strategic moves and business approaches, and implements what needs to be done internally to produce good day-in/day-out strategy execution. Indeed, *good strategy and good strategy execution are the most trustworthy signs of good management.* Managers don't deserve a gold star for designing a potentially brilliant strategy, but failing to put the organizational means in place to carry it out in high-caliber fashion—weak implementation and execution—undermines the strategy's potential and paves the way for shortfalls in customer satisfaction and company performance. Competent execution of a mediocre strategy scarcely merits enthusiastic applause for management's efforts either. To truly qualify as excellently managed, a company must exhibit excellent execution of an excellent strategy. Otherwise, any claim of talented management is suspect.

> *Competent execution of a well-conceived strategy is not only a proven recipe for organizational success, but also the best test of managerial excellence.*

Granted, good strategy combined with good strategy execution doesn't *guarantee* that a company will avoid periods of so-so or even subpar performance. Sometimes it takes several years for management's strategy-making/strategy-implementing efforts to show good results. Sometimes blue-chip organizations with showcase practices and reputable managers have performance problems because of surprisingly abrupt shifts in market conditions or internal miscues. But neither the "we need more time" reason nor the bad luck of unforeseeable events excuses mediocre performance year after year. It is the responsibility of a company's management team to adjust to unexpectedly tough conditions by undertaking strategic defenses and business approaches that can overcome adversity. Indeed, the essence of good strategy making is to build a market position strong enough and an organization capable enough to produce successful performance despite unforeseeable events, potent competition, and internal difficulties. The rationale for using the twin standards of good strategy making and good strategy execution to determine whether a company is well managed is therefore compelling: The better conceived a company's strategy and the more competently it is executed, the more likely the company will be a solid performer and a competitive success in the marketplace.

THE FIVE TASKS OF STRATEGIC MANAGEMENT

The strategy-making, strategy-implementing process consists of five interrelated managerial tasks:

1. *Forming a strategic vision of what the company's future business makeup will be and where the organization is headed*—so as to provide long-term direction, delineate what kind of enterprise the company is trying to become, and infuse the organization with a sense of purposeful action.
2. *Setting objectives*—converting the strategic vision into specific performance outcomes for the company to achieve.
3. *Crafting a strategy to achieve the desired outcomes.*
4. *Implementing and executing the chosen strategy efficiently and effectively.*
5. *Evaluating performance and initiating corrective adjustments in vision, long-term direction, objectives, strategy, or implementation in light of actual experience, changing conditions, new ideas, and new opportunities.*

Figure 1.1 displays this process. Together, these five components define what we mean by the term *strategic management.* Let's examine this five-task framework in enough detail to set the stage for all that follows in the forthcoming chapters.

FIGURE 1.1   The Five Tasks of Strategic Management

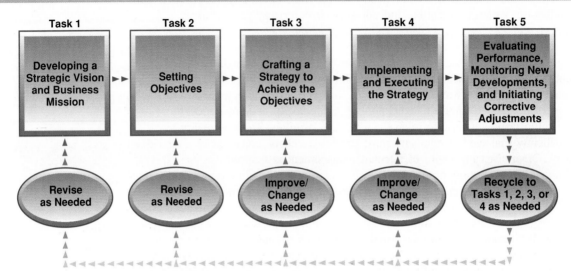

Developing a Strategic Vision and Business Mission

Very early in the strategy-making process, company managers need to pose the issue of "What is our vision for the company—where should the company be headed, what kind of enterprise are we trying to build, what should the company's future business makeup be?" Drawing a carefully reasoned conclusion about what the company's long-term direction should be pushes managers to take a hard look at the company's present business and form a clearer sense of whether and how it needs to change over the next 5 to 10 years. Management's views about "where we plan to go from here—what businesses we want to be in, what customer needs we want to satisfy, what capabilities we're going to develop" charts a course for the organization to pursue and creates organizational purpose and identity.

What a company is currently seeking to do for its customers is often termed the company's *mission*. A mission statement is useful for putting the spotlight on what business a company is presently in and the customer needs it is presently endeavoring to serve. But just clearly setting forth what a company is doing today doesn't speak to the company's future or incorporate a sense of needed change and long-term direction. There is an even greater managerial imperative to consider what the company will have to do to meet its customers' needs tomorrow and whether and how the company's business makeup will have to evolve for the company to grow and prosper. Thus, managers are obligated to look beyond the present business mission and think strategically about the impact of new technologies on the horizon, changing customer needs and expectations, the emergence of new market and competitive conditions, and so on. They have to make some fundamental choices about where they want to take the company and form a vision of the kind of enterprise they believe the company needs to become. In other words, management's concept of the *present* company mission has to be supplemented with a concept of the company's *future* business makeup, product line, and customer base. The faster a company's business environment is changing, the more that coasting along with the status quo is an invitation to disaster and the greater the managerial imperative to consider what the enterprise's future strategic path should be in light of changing conditions and emerging market opportunities.

Management's view of the kind of company it is trying to create and the kind of business position it wants to stake out in the years to come constitutes a *strategic vision* for the company. In the event a company's mission statement not only sets forth a clear definition of the present business but also indicates where the company is headed and what its business will become in the years ahead, then the concepts of company mission (or mission statement) and strategic vision merge into one and the same—in other words, a strategic vision and a future-oriented business mission amount to essentially the same thing. In practice, actual company mission statements tend to exhibit more concern with "what our business is now" than with "what our business will be later," so the conceptual distinction between company mission and strategic vision is relevant. Forming a strategic vision of a company's future is a prerequisite to effective strategic leadership. A manager cannot succeed as an organization leader or a strategy maker without first having drawn some soundly reasoned conclusions about where the enterprise needs to head, the changes in business makeup that are called for, and the organizational capabilities it will take to meet future customer needs and compete successfully. With a clear, well-conceived strategic vision, a manager has a beacon to truly guide managerial decision making, a course for the organization to follow, and a basis for shaping the organization's strategy and operating policies.

> *A strategic vision is a roadmap of a company's future—the direction it is headed, the business position it intends to stake out, and the capabilities it plans to develop.*

Some examples of company mission and vision statements are presented in Illustration Capsule 1.

Setting Objectives

The purpose of setting objectives is to convert managerial statements of strategic vision and business mission into specific performance targets, something the organization's progress can be measured by. Successful managers set company performance targets that require stretch and disciplined effort. The challenge of trying to achieve bold, aggressive performance targets pushes an organization to be more inventive, to exhibit some urgency in improving both its financial performance and its business position, and to be more intentional and focused in its actions. Setting objectives that require real organizational stretch helps build a firewall against complacent coasting and low-grade improvements in organizational performance. As Mitchell Leibovitz, CEO of Pep Boys–Manny, Moe, and Jack, puts it, "If you want to have ho-hum results, have ho-hum objectives."

Objective setting is required of *all* managers. Every unit in a company needs concrete, measurable performance targets that contribute meaningfully toward achieving company objectives. When companywide objectives are broken down into specific targets for each organizational unit and lower-level managers are held accountable for achieving them, a results-oriented climate builds throughout the enterprise. There's little if any internal confusion over what to accomplish. The ideal situation is a team effort where each organizational unit strives to produce results in its area of responsibility that contribute to the achievement of the company's performance targets and strategic vision.

> *Objectives are yardsticks for tracking an organization's performance and progress.*

From a companywide perspective, two very distinct types of performance yardsticks are required: those relating to *financial performance* and those relating to

ILLUSTRATION CAPSULE 1   Examples Of Company Mission and Vision Statements

McDonald's Corporation

McDonald's vision is to dominate the global foodservice industry. Global dominance means setting the performance standard for customer satisfaction while increasing market share and profitability through our Convenience, Value, and Execution Strategies.

Otis Elevator

Our mission is to provide any customer a means of moving people and things up, down, and sideways over short distances with higher reliability than any similar enterprise in the world.

Microsoft Corporation

One vision drives everything we do: A computer on every desk and in every home using great software as an empowering tool.

Avis Rent-a-Car

Our business is renting cars. Our mission is total customer satisfaction.

The Body Shop

We aim to achieve commercial success by meeting our customers' needs through the provision of high quality, good value products with exceptional service and relevant information which enables customers to make informed and responsible choices.

American Red Cross

The mission of the American Red Cross is to improve the quality of human life; to enhance self-reliance and concern for others; and to help people avoid, prepare for, and cope with emergencies.

Eastman Kodak

To be the world's best in chemical and electronic imaging.

Ritz-Carlton Hotels

The Ritz-Carlton Hotel is a place where the genuine care and comfort of our guests is our highest mission.

We pledge to provide the finest personal service and facilities for our guests who will always enjoy a warm, relaxed yet refined ambience.

The Ritz-Carlton experience enlivens the senses, instills well-being, and fulfills even the unexpressed wishes and needs of our guests.

Intel

Intel supplies the computing industry with chips, boards, systems, and software. Intel's products are used as "building blocks" to create advanced computing systems for PC users. Intel's mission is to be the preeminent building block supplier to the new computing industry worldwide.

Compaq Computer

To be the leading supplier of PCs and PC servers in all customer segments.

Long John Silver's

To be America's best quick service restaurant chain. We will provide each guest great tasting, healthful, reasonably priced fish, seafood, and chicken in a fast, friendly manner on every visit.

Bristol-Myers Squibb

The mission of Bristol-Myers Squibb is to extend and enhance human life by providing the highest quality health and personal care products. We intend to be the preeminent global diversified health and personal care company.

strategic performance. Achieving acceptable financial results is crucial. Without adequate profitability, a company's pursuit of its vision, as well as its long-term health and ultimate survival, is jeopardized. Neither shareowners nor lenders will continue to sink additional monies into an enterprise that can't deliver satisfactory financial results. Even so, the achievement of satisfactory financial performance, by itself, is not enough. Attention also has to be paid to a company's strategic well-being—its competitiveness and overall long-term business position. Unless a company's performance reflects improving competitive strength and a stronger long-term market position, its progress is less than inspiring and its ability to continue delivering good financial performance is suspect.

The need for both good financial performance and good strategic performance calls for management to set financial objectives and strategic objectives. *Financial objectives* signal commitment to such outcomes as earnings growth, an acceptable return on investment (or economic value added—EVA), dividend growth, stock price appreciation (or market value added—MVA), good cash flow, and creditworthiness.[1] *Strategic objectives*, in contrast, direct efforts toward such outcomes as winning additional market share, overtaking key competitors on product quality or customer service or product innovation, achieving lower overall costs than rivals, boosting the company's reputation with customers, winning a stronger foothold in international markets, exercising technological leadership, gaining a sustainable competitive advantage, and capturing attractive growth opportunities. Strategic objectives serve notice that management not only intends to deliver good financial performance but also intends to improve the organization's competitive strength and long-range business prospects.

Both financial and strategic objectives ought to be time-based—that is, involve both near-term and longer-term performance targets. Short-range objectives focus organizational attention on the need for immediate performance improvements and outcomes. Long-range objectives serve the valuable purpose of prompting managers to consider what to do *now* to put the company in position to perform well over the longer term. As a rule, when trade-offs have to be made between achieving long-run objectives and achieving short-run objectives, long-run objectives should take precedence. Rarely does a company prosper from repeated management actions that put better short-term performance ahead of better long-run performance.

Examples of the kinds of strategic and financial objectives companies set are shown in Illustration Capsule 2.

Crafting a Strategy

A company's strategy represents management's answers to such gut business issues as whether to concentrate on a single business or build a diversified group of businesses, whether to cater to a broad range of customers or focus on a particular market niche, whether to develop a wide or narrow product line, whether to pursue a competitive advantage based on low cost or product superiority or unique organiza-

---

[1]Economic value added (EVA) is profit over and above the company's cost of debt and equity capital. More specifically, it is defined as operating profit less income taxes less the cost of debt less an allowance for the cost of equity capital. For example, if a company has operating profits of $200 million, pays taxes of $75 million, pays interest expenses of $25 million, has shareholders' equity of $400 million with an estimated equity cost of 15 percent (which translates into an equity cost of capital of $60 million), then the company's EVA is $200 million minus $75 million minus $25 million minus $60 million, or $40 million. The EVA of $40 million can be interpreted to mean that the company's management has generated profits well in excess of the benchmark 15 percent equity cost needed to justify or support the shareholder investment of $400 million—all of which represents wealth created for the owners above what they could expect from making investment of comparable risk elsewhere. Such companies as Coca-Cola, AT&T, and Briggs & Stratton use EVA as a measure of their profit performance.

Market value added (MVA) is defined as the amount by which the total value of the company has appreciated above the dollar amount actually invested in the company by shareholders. MVA is equal to a company's current stock price times the number of shares outstanding less shareholders' equity investment; it represents the value that management has added to shareholders' wealth in running the business. For example, if a company's stock price is $50, there are 1,000,000 shares outstanding, and shareholders' equity investment is $40 million, then MVA is $10 million ($50 million in market value of existing shares minus $40 million in equity investment); in other words, management has taken the shareholders' investment of $40 million in the company and leveraged it into a current company value of $50 million, creating an additional $10 million in shareholder value. If shareholder value is to be maximized, management must select a strategy and long-term direction that maximizes the market value of the company's common stock. In recent years, MVA and EVA have gained widespread acceptance as valid measures of a company's financial performance.

ILLUSTRATION CAPSULE 2   Strategic And Financial Objectives Of Well-Known Corporations

Banc One Corporation
To be one of the top three banking companies in terms of market share in all significant markets we serve.

Domino's Pizza
To safely deliver a hot, quality pizza in 30 minutes or less at a fair price and a reasonable profit.

Ford Motor Company
To satisfy our customers by providing quality cars and trucks, developing new products, reducing the time it takes to bring new vehicles to market, improving the efficiency of all our plants and processes, and building on our teamwork with employees, unions, dealers, and suppliers.

Exxon
To provide shareholders a secure investment with a superior return.

Alcan Aluminum
To be the lowest-cost producer of aluminum and to outperform the average return on equity of the Standard and Poor's industrial stock index.

General Electric
To become the most competitive enterprise in the world by being number one or number two in market share in every business the company is in. To achieve an average of 10 inventory turns and a corporate operating profit margin of 16% by 1998.

Bristol-Myers Squibb
To focus globally on those businesses in health and personal care where we can be number one or number two through delivering superior value to the customer.

Atlas Corporation
To become a low-cost, medium-size gold producer, producing in excess of 125,000 ounces of gold a year and building gold reserves of 1,500,000 ounces.

3M
To achieve annual growth in earnings per share of 10% or better, on average; a return on stockholders' equity of 20-25%; a return on capital employed of 27% or better; and have at least 30% of sales come from products introduced in the past four years.

An organization's strategy consists of the actions and business approaches management employs to achieve the targeted organizational performance.

tional capabilities, how to respond to changing buyer preferences, how big a geographic market to try to cover, how to react to new market and competitive conditions, and how to grow the enterprise over the long-term. A strategy thus reflects managerial choices among alternatives and signals organizational commitment to particular products, markets, competitive approaches, and ways of operating the enterprise.

Crafting a winning strategy needs to be a top-priority managerial task in every organization. To begin with, there is a compelling need for managers to be proactive in shaping *how* the company's business will be conducted. It is management's responsibility to exert strategic leadership and commit the enterprise to going about its business in one fashion rather than another. Without a strategy, managers have no prescription for doing business, no roadmap to competitive advantage, no game plan for pleasing customers or achieving objectives. Such a lack is a surefire ticket for organizational drift, competitive mediocrity, and lackluster performance. Moreover, there is an equally compelling need to mold the business decisions and competitive actions taken across various parts of the company into a coordinated, compatible *pattern*. A company's activities necessarily involve the efforts and decisions of many divisions, departments, managers, and employees. All the actions and initiatives being taken in such areas as production, marketing, customer service, human resources, information systems, R&D, and finance need to be mutually supportive if a *companywide* game plan that makes good business sense is to emerge. Absent a company strategy, managers have no framework for weaving many different decisions into a cohesive whole and no overarching business rationale that unites departmental operations into a team effort.

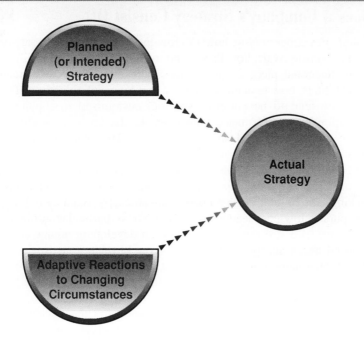

Strategy making brings into play the critical managerial issue of *how* to achieve the targeted results in light of the organization's situation and prospects. Objectives are the "ends," and strategy is the "means" of achieving them. The hows of a company's strategy are typically a blend of (1) deliberate and purposeful actions and (2) as-needed reactions to unanticipated developments and fresh competitive pressures.[2] As illustrated in Figure 1.2, strategy is more than what managers have carefully plotted out in advance and *intend* to do as part of some grand strategic plan. New circumstances always emerge, whether important technological developments, rivals' successful new product introductions, newly enacted government regulations and policies, widening consumer interest in different kinds of performance features, or whatever. Future business conditions are sufficiently uncertain that managers cannot plan every strategic action in advance and pursue a preplanned or *intended strategy* without any need for alteration. Company strategies end up, therefore, being a composite of planned actions and business approaches (intended strategy) and as-needed reactions to unforeseen conditions ("unplanned" or "adaptive" strategy responses). Consequently, *strategy is best looked upon as being a combination of planned actions and on-the-spot adaptive reactions to freshly developing industry and competitive events.* The strategy-making task involves developing a game plan, or intended strategy, and then adapting it as events unfold. A company's actual strategy is something managers must shape and reshape as events transpire outside and inside the company. It is normal, therefore, for a company's actual strategy to differ from management's

Strategy is both proactive (intended) and reactive (adaptive).

---

[2]Henry Mintzberg and J. A. Waters, "Of Strategies, Deliberate and Emergent," *Strategic Management Journal*, 6 (1985), pp.257–72.

planned strategy as new strategy features are added and others subtracted to react and adapt to changing conditions.

What Does a Company's Strategy Consist Of?

Company strategies concern *how*: how to grow the business, how to satisfy customers, how to outcompete rivals, how to respond to changing market conditions, how to manage each functional piece of the business and develop needed organizational capabilities, how to achieve strategic and financial objectives. The hows of strategy tend to be company-specific, customized to a company's own situation and performance objectives. In the business world, companies have a wide degree of strategic freedom. They can diversify broadly or narrowly, into related or unrelated industries, via acquisition, joint venture, strategic alliances, or internal start-up. Even when a company elects to concentrate on a single business, prevailing market conditions usually offer enough strategy-making latitude that close competitors can easily avoid carbon-copy strategies—some pursue low-cost leadership, others stress particular attributes of their product or service, and still others concentrate on developing unique capabilities to meet the special needs and preferences of narrow buyer segments. Some compete only locally or regionally, others compete nationally, and others compete globally. Hence, descriptions of the content of company strategy necessarily have to cut broadly across many aspects of the business to be complete.

Company strategies are partly visible and partly hidden to outside view.

Figure 1.3 depicts the kinds of actions and approaches that reflect a company's overall strategy. Because many are visible to outside observers, most of a company's strategy can be deduced from its actions and public pronouncements. Yet, there's an unrevealed portion of strategy outsiders can only speculate about—the actions and moves company managers are considering. Managers often, for good reason, choose not to reveal certain elements of their strategy until the time is right.

To get a better understanding of the content of company strategies, see the overview of McDonald's strategy in Illustration Capsule 3 on page 12.

Strategy and Entrepreneurship. Crafting strategy is an exercise in entrepreneurship and *outside-in* strategic thinking. The challenge is for company managers to keep their strategies closely matched to such *outside drivers* as changing buyer preferences, the latest actions of rivals, new technological capabilities, the emergence of attractive market opportunities, and newly appearing business conditions. Company strategies can't end up being well matched to the company's present and future environment unless managers exhibit first-rate entrepreneurship in studying market trends, listening to customers, enhancing the company's competitiveness, and steering company activities in whatever new directions are dictated by market conditions and customer preferences. Good strategy making is therefore inseparable from good business entrepreneurship. One cannot exist without the other.

Strategy-making is fundamentally a market-driven and customer-driven entrepreneurial activity— venturesomeness, business creativity, an eye for spotting emerging market opportunities, keen observation of customer needs, and an appetite for risk-taking are inherent to the task of crafting company strategies.

A company encounters two dangers when its managers fail to exercise strategy-making entrepreneurship. One is a stale strategy. The faster a company's business environment is changing, the more critical it becomes for its managers to be good entrepreneurs in diagnosing shifting conditions and instituting whatever strategic adjustments are indicated. Coasting along with a status quo strategy tends to be riskier than making modifications. Managers with weak entrepreneurial skills are usually risk-averse and disinclined to embark on a different strategic course so long as they believe the present strategy can produce acceptable results for a while

FIGURE 1.3   Understanding a Company's Strategy—What to Look For

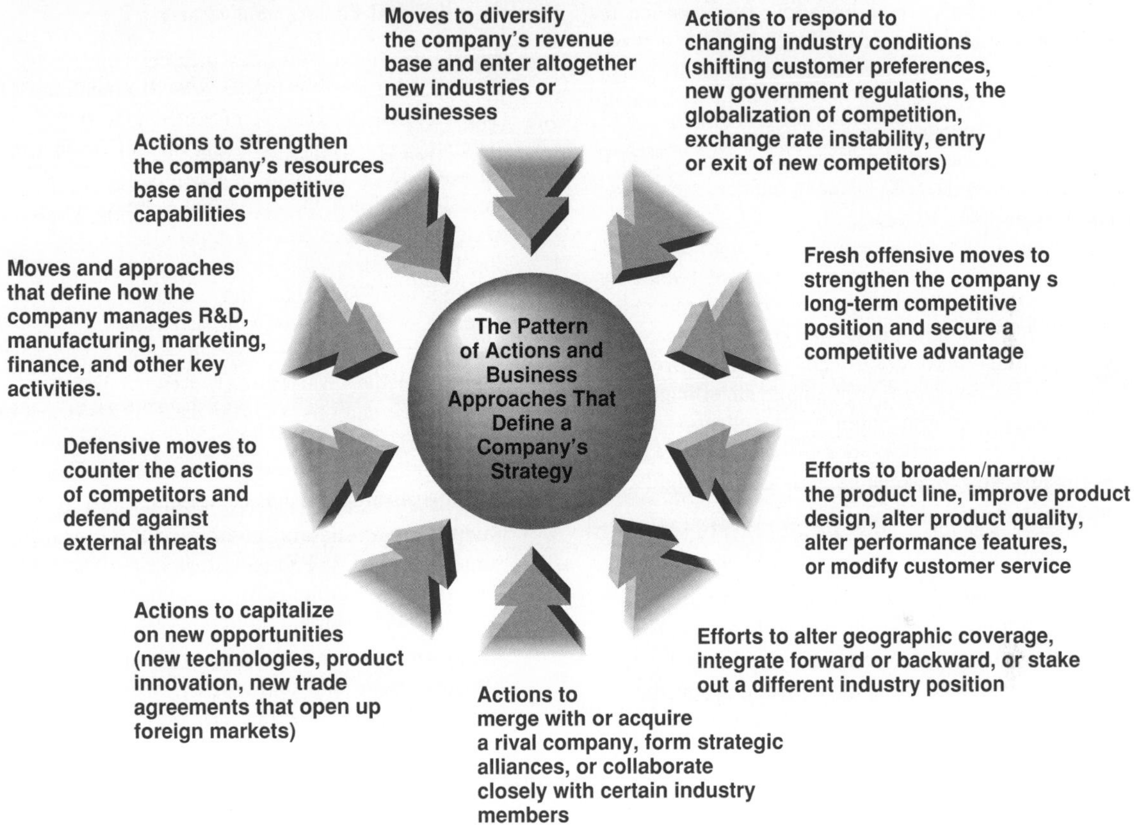

Moves to diversify
the company's revenue
base and enter altogether
new industries or
businesses

Actions to respond to
changing industry conditions
(shifting customer preferences,
new government regulations, the
globalization of competition,
exchange rate instability, entry
or exit of new competitors)

Actions to strengthen
the company's resources
base and competitive
capabilities

Moves and approaches
that define how the
company manages R&D,
manufacturing, marketing,
finance, and other key
activities.

The Pattern
of Actions and
Business
Approaches That
Define a
Company's
Strategy

Fresh offensive moves to
strengthen the company s
long-term competitive
position and secure a
competitive advantage

Defensive moves to
counter the actions
of competitors and
defend against
external threats

Efforts to broaden/narrow
the product line, improve product
design, alter product quality,
alter performance features,
or modify customer service

Actions to capitalize
on new opportunities
(new technologies, product
innovation, new trade
agreements that open up
foreign markets)

Actions to
merge with or acquire
a rival company, form strategic
alliances, or collaborate
closely with certain industry
members

Efforts to alter geographic coverage,
integrate forward or backward, or stake
out a different industry position

longer. They are prone to misread market trends and put too little weight on subtle shifts in customers' needs and behavior. Often, they either dismiss the signs of impending developments as unimportant ("we don't think it will really affect us") or else move so slowly in taking actions that the company is habitually late in responding to market change. There's pervasive resistance to bold strategic change, a wariness of deviating very far from the company's tried-and-true business approaches unless absolutely forced to. Strategies that grow increasingly out of touch with market and customer realities weaken a company's competitiveness and performance.

The second danger of failing to exercise strategy-making entrepreneurship is inside-out strategic thinking. Managers with deficient entrepreneurial skills or an entrepreneurially cautious nature usually focus most of their time and energy inwardly—on solving internal problems, improving organizational processes and procedures, and taking care of daily administrative chores. The strategic actions they do decide to initiate tend to be heavily dictated by inside considerations—what is philosophically comfortable, what is acceptable to various internal political coalitions, and what is safe, both organizationally and career-wise. Often, outside considerations end up being compromised to accommodate internal considerations, resulting in strategies that are as much a reflection of inwardly focused strategic thinking as of the need to respond to changing external market and customer conditions. Inside-out strategies, while not disconnected from external developments, nearly always fall short of being truly market-driven and customer-driven,

Good strategy making is more outside-in than inside-out.

ILLUSTRATION CAPSULE 3   A Strategy Example: McDonald's

In 1997 McDonald's was the leading food service retailer in the global consumer marketplace, with a strong brand name and systemwide restaurant sales approaching $35 billion. Two-thirds of its 22,000-plus restaurants were franchised to nearly 5,000 owner/operators around the world. Sales had grown an average of 6 percent in the United States and 20 percent outside the United States over the past 10 years. McDonald's food quality specifications, equipment technology, marketing and training programs, operating systems, site selection techniques, and supply systems were considered industry standards throughout the world. The company's strategic priorities were continued growth, providing exceptional customer care, remaining an efficient and quality producer, offering high value and good-tasting products, and effectively marketing McDonald's brand on a global scale. McDonald's strategy had eight core elements:

Growth Strategy

- Penetrate the market not currently served by adding 2,500 restaurants annually (an average of 8 per day), some company-owned and some franchised, with about two-thirds outside the United States. Establish a leading market position in foreign countries ahead of competitors.

- Promote more frequent customer visits via the addition of attractive menu items, low-price specials, Extra Value Meals, and children's play areas.

Franchising Strategy

- Grant franchises only to highly motivated, talented entrepreneurs with integrity and business experience and train them to become active, on-premise owners of McDonald's (no franchises were granted to corporations, partnerships, or passive investors).

Store Location and Construction Strategy

- Locate restaurants on sites offering convenience to customers and profitable growth potential. The company's research indicated that 70 percent of all decisions to eat at McDonald's were made on the spur of the moment, so its goal was to pick locations that were as convenient as possible for customers to visit. In the United States, the company supplemented its traditional suburban and urban locations with satellite outlets in food courts, airports, hospitals, universities, large shopping establishments (Wal-Mart, The Home Depot), and service stations; outside the United States, the strategy was to establish an initial presence in center cities, then open freestanding units with drive-thrus outside center cities.

- Reduce site costs and building costs by using standardized, cost-efficient store designs and by consolidating purchases of equipment and materials via a global sourcing system.

- Make sure restaurants are attractive and pleasing inside and out and, where feasible, provide drive-thru service and play areas for children.

Product Line Strategy

- Offer a limited menu.

- Improve the taste appeal of the items offered (especially sandwich selections).

- Expand product offerings into new categories of fast food (chicken, Mexican, pizza, adult-oriented sandwiches, and so on) and include more items for health-conscious customers.

- Do extensive testing to ensure consistent high quality and ample customer appeal before rolling out new menu items systemwide.

---

once again setting the stage for weakened competitiveness, impaired ability to exercise industry leadership, and underperformance.

How boldly managers embrace new strategic opportunities, how much they emphasize outinnovating the competition, and how often they champion actions to improve organizational performance are good barometers of their entrepreneurial spirit. Entrepreneurial strategy-makers are inclined to be first-movers, responding quickly and opportunistically to new developments. They are willing to take prudent risks and initiate trailblazing strategies. In contrast, reluctant entrepreneurs are risk-averse; they tend to be late-movers, hopeful about their chances of soon catching up and alert to how they can avoid whatever "mistakes" they believe first-movers have

Store Operations

- Enforce stringent standards regarding food quality, store and equipment cleanliness, restaurant operating procedures, and friendly, courteous counter service.
- Develop new equipment and production systems that improve the ability to serve hotter, better-tasting food, faster and with greater accuracy.

Sales Promotion, Marketing, and Merchandising

- Enhance the McDonald's image of quality, service, cleanliness, and value globally via heavy media advertising and in-store merchandise promotions funded with fees tied to a percent of sales revenues at each restaurant.
- Use Ronald McDonald to create greater brand awareness among children and the Mc prefix to reinforce the connection of menu items and McDonald's.
- Project an attitude of happiness and interest in children.

Human Resources and Training

- Offer wage rates that are equitable and nondiscriminatory in every location; teach job skills; reward both individual and team performance; create career opportunities; have flexible work hours for student employees.

- Hire restaurant crews with good work habits and courteous attitudes and train them to act in ways that will impress customers; promote promising employees quickly.
- Provide proper training on delivering customer satisfaction and running a fast-food business to franchisees, restaurant managers, and assistant managers. (Instructors at Hamburger University campuses in Illinois, Germany, England, Australia, and Japan annually train over 5,000 students in 22 languages.)

Social Responsibility and Community Citizenship

- Take an active community role—support local charities and community projects; help create a neighborhood spirit; promote educational excellence.
- Sponsor Ronald McDonald Houses (at year-end 1995, there were 168 houses in 12 countries providing a home-away-from-home for families of seriously ill children receiving treatment at nearby hospitals).
- Promote workforce diversity, voluntary affirmative action, and minority-owned franchises (over 25% of McDonald's franchisees were females and minorities).
- Adopt and encourage environmentally friendly practices.
- Provide nutritional information on McDonald's products to customers.

Source: Company annual reports.

made. They prefer incremental strategic change over bold and sweeping strategic moves.

In strategy-making, all managers, not just senior executives, must take prudent risks and exercise entrepreneurship. Entrepreneurship is involved when a district customer service manager, as part of a company's commitment to better customer service, crafts a strategy to speed the response time on service calls by 25 percent and commits $15,000 to equip all service trucks with mobile telephones. Entrepreneurship is involved when a warehousing manager contributes to a company's strategic emphasis on total quality by figuring out how to reduce the error frequency on filling customer orders from one error every 100 orders to one error every 100,000. A sales manager exercises strategic entrepreneurship by deciding to run a special promotion and cut sales prices by 5 percent to wrest market share away from rivals. A manufacturing manager exercises strategic entrepreneurship in deciding, as part of a companywide emphasis on greater cost competitiveness, to source an important component from a lower-priced South Korean supplier instead of making it in-house. Company strategies can't be truly market- and customer-driven unless the strategy-related activities of managers all across the company have an outside-in entrepreneurial character aimed at boosting customer satisfaction and achieving sustainable competitive advantage.

Why Company Strategies Evolve   Frequent fine-tuning and tweaking of a company's strategy, first in one department or functional area and then in another, are quite normal. On occasion, quantum changes in strategy are called for—when a competitor makes a dramatic move, when technological breakthroughs occur, or when crisis strikes and managers are forced to make radical strategy alterations very quickly. Because strategic moves and new action approaches are ongoing across the business, an organization's strategy forms over a period of time and then reforms as the number of changes begin to mount. Current strategy is typically a blend of holdover approaches, fresh actions and reactions, and potential moves in the planning stage. Except for crisis situations (where many strategic moves are often made quickly to produce a substantially new strategy almost overnight) and new company start-ups (where strategy exists mostly in the form of plans and intended actions), it is common for key elements of a company's strategy to emerge piece by piece as events transpire and the enterprise seeks to improve its position and performance.

A company's strategy is dynamic, forming in bits and pieces and then reforming as managers see avenues for improvement or a need to adapt business approaches to changing conditions.

Rarely is a company's strategy so well crafted and durable that it can go unaltered for long. Even the best-laid business plans must be adapted to shifting market conditions, altered customer needs and preferences, the strategic maneuvering of rival firms, the experience of what is working and what isn't, emerging opportunities and threats, unforeseen events, and fresh thinking about how to improve the strategy. This is why strategy-making is an ongoing process and why a manager must reevaluate strategy regularly, refining and recasting it as needed.

However, when managers decide to change strategy so fast and so fundamentally that their business game plan undergoes major overhaul every year, they are almost certainly guilty of poor entrepreneurship, faulty situation analysis, and inept "strategizing." Quantum changes in strategy may well be needed occasionally, especially in crisis situations or during unusually rapid periods of industry change, but they cannot be made on a regular basis without creating a zigzag market wake, generating undue confusion among customers and employees, and undermining performance. Well-crafted strategies normally have a life of at least several years, requiring only minor tweaking to keep them in tune with changing circumstances.

Strategy and Strategic Plans   Developing a strategic vision and mission, establishing objectives, and deciding on a strategy are basic direction-setting tasks. They map out where the organization is headed, its short-range and long-range performance targets, and the competitive moves and internal action approaches to be used in achieving the targeted results. Together, they constitute a *strategic plan*. In some companies, especially those committed to regular strategy reviews and the development of explicit strategic plans, a document describing the company's strategic plan is circulated to managers and employees (although parts of the plan may be omitted or expressed in general terms if they are too sensitive to reveal before they are actually undertaken). In other companies, the strategic plan is not put in writing for widespread distribution but rather exists in the form of oral understandings and commitments among managers about where to head, what to accomplish, and how to proceed.

Organizational objectives are the part of the strategic plan most often spelled out explicitly and communicated to managers and employees. Some companies spell out key elements of their strategic plans in the company's annual report to shareholders or in statements provided to the business media, while others deliberately refrain from candid public discussion of their strategies for reasons of competitive sensitivity.

However, strategic plans seldom anticipate all the strategically relevant events that will transpire in upcoming months and years. Unforeseen events, unexpected opportunities or threats, plus the constant bubbling up of new proposals encourage managers to modify planned actions and forge "unplanned" reactions. Postponing the recrafting of strategy until it's time to work on next year's strategic plan is both foolish and unnecessary. Managers who confine their strategizing to the company's regularly scheduled planning cycle (when they can't avoid turning something in) have a wrongheaded concept of what their strategy-making responsibilities are. Once-a-year strategizing under "have-to" conditions is not a prescription for managerial success.

Implementing and Executing the Strategy

The managerial task of implementing and executing the chosen strategy entails assessing what it will take to make the strategy work and to reach the targeted performance on schedule—the managerial skill here is being good at figuring out what must be done to put the strategy in place, execute it proficiently, and produce good results. Managing the process of implementing and executing strategy is primarily a hands-on, close-to-the-scene administrative task that includes the following principal aspects:

- Building an organization capable of carrying out the strategy successfully.
- Developing budgets that steer resources into those internal activities critical to strategic success.
- Establishing strategy-supportive policies and operating procedures.
- Motivating people in ways that induce them to pursue the target objectives energetically and, if need be, modifying their duties and job behavior to better fit the requirements of successful strategy execution.
- Tying the reward structure to the achievement of targeted results.
- Creating a company culture and work climate conducive to successful strategy implementation and execution.
- Installing information, communication, and operating systems that enable company personnel to carry out their strategic roles effectively day in and day out.
- Instituting best practices and programs for continuous improvement.
- Exerting the internal leadership needed to drive implementation forward and to keep improving on how the strategy is being executed.

The strategy implementer's aim must be to create strong "fits" between the way things are done internally to try to execute the strategy and what it will take for the strategy to succeed. The stronger the methods of implementation fit the strategy's requirements, the better the execution and the better the odds that performance targets will be achieved. The most important fits are between strategy and organizational capabilities, between strategy and the reward structure, between strategy and internal support systems, and between strategy and the organization's culture (the latter emerges from the values and beliefs shared by organizational members, the company's approach to people management, and ingrained behaviors, work practices, and ways of thinking). Fitting the ways the organization does things internally to what is needed for strategic success helps unite the organization behind the accomplishment of strategy.

The strategy-implementing task is easily the most complicated and time-consuming part of strategic management. It cuts across virtually all facets of managing and must be initiated from many points inside the organization. The strategy-implementer's agenda for action emerges from careful assessment of what the organization must do differently and better to carry out the strategic plan proficiently. Each manager has to think through the answer to "What has to be done in my area to carry out my piece of the strategic plan, and how can I best get it done?" How much internal change is needed to put the strategy into place depends on the degree of strategic change, how far internal practices and competencies deviate from what the strategy requires, and how well strategy and organizational culture already match. As needed changes and actions are identified, management must see that all the details of implementation are attended to and apply enough pressure on the organization to convert objectives into results. Depending on the amount of internal change involved, full implementation can take several months to several years.

> *Strategy implementation is fundamentally an action-oriented, make-it-happen activity—developing competencies and capabilities, budgeting, policy making, motivating, culture building, and leading are all part of the process.*

Evaluating Performance, Monitoring New Developments, and Initiating Corrective Adjustments

It is always incumbent on management to evaluate the organization's performance and progress. It is management's duty to stay on top of the company's situation, deciding whether things are going well internally, and monitoring outside developments closely. Subpar performance or too little progress, as well as important new external circumstances, call for corrective actions and adjustments. Long-term direction may need to be altered, the business redefined, and management's vision of the organization's future course narrowed or broadened or radically revised. Performance targets may need raising or lowering in light of past experience and future prospects. Strategy may need to be modified because of shifts in long-term direction, because new objectives have been set, because some elements are not working well, or because of shifting market conditions and customer preferences.

> *A company's vision, objectives, strategy, and approach to implementation are never final; evaluating performance, monitoring changes in the surrounding environment, and making adjustments are normal and necessary parts of the strategic management process.*

Likewise, one or more aspects of implementation and execution may not be going as well as intended. Budget revisions, policy changes, reorganization, personnel changes, revamped activities and work processes, culture-changing efforts, and revised compensation practices are typical managerial actions that may have to be taken to hasten implementation or improve strategy execution. *Proficient strategy execution is always the product of much organizational learning.* It is achieved unevenly—coming quickly in some areas and proving nettlesome in others. Progress reviews, ongoing searches for ways to continuously improve, and corrective adjustments are thus normal.

WHY STRATEGIC MANAGEMENT IS A PROCESS, NOT AN EVENT

The march of external and internal events guarantees that a company's vision, objectives, strategy, and implementation approaches will have to be revisited, reconsidered, and eventually revised. This is why the task of evaluating performance and initiating corrective adjustments is both the end and the beginning of the strategic management *cycle*. Evaluating and adjusting means that prior strategy-related decisions and actions are subject to modification as conditions in the surrounding environment change and ideas for improvement emerge. The choice of whether to continue or change the company's vision, objectives, strategy, and implementation approaches always presents itself. Strategic management is thus an ongoing, never-ending *process*, not a start-stop event that once done can be safely put aside for a while. Managers have everpresent responsibility for detecting when new developments require a strategic response and when they don't. It is their job to track progress, spot problems early, monitor the winds of market and customer change, and initiate adjustments.

Characteristics of the Process

Although forming a strategic vision, setting objectives, crafting a strategy, implementing and executing the strategic plan, and evaluating performance portray what strategic management involves, actually performing these five tasks is not so cleanly divided into separate, neatly sequenced compartments. There is much interplay and recycling among the five tasks, as shown in Figure 1.1. For example, considering what strategic actions to take raises issues about whether and how the strategy can be satisfactorily implemented. Deciding on a company mission and vision shades into setting objectives (both involve directional priorities). Objective setting entails considering current performance, the strategy options available to improve performance, and what the organization can really achieve when pushed and challenged. Deciding on a strategy is entangled with decisions about long-term direction and whether objectives have been set in all the key financial and strategic areas. Clearly, the direction-setting tasks of developing a mission, setting objectives, and crafting strategy need to be integrated and done as a package, not individually.

> *Strategic management is a process; the boundaries between the five tasks are conceptual, not fences that prevent some or all of them being done together.*

Second, the five strategic management tasks are not done in isolation from a manager's other duties and responsibilities—administering day-to-day operations, dealing with crises, going to meetings, reviewing information, handling people problems, and taking on special assignments and civic duties. Thus, while the job of managing strategy is the most important managerial function insofar as organizational success or failure is concerned, it isn't all managers must do or be concerned about.

Third, crafting and implementing strategy make erratic demands on a manager's time. Change does not happen in an orderly or predictable way. Events can build quickly or gradually; they can emerge singly or in rapid-fire succession; and their implications for strategic change can be easy or hard to diagnose. Hence the task of reviewing and adjusting the strategic game plan can take up big chunks of management time in some months and little time in other months. As a practical matter, there is as much skill in knowing *when* to institute strategic changes as there is in knowing what to do.

Last, the big day-in, day-out time-consuming aspect of strategic management involves trying to get the best strategy-supportive performance out of every individual and trying to perfect the current strategy by refining its content and execution. Managers usually spend most of their efforts improving bits and pieces of the current strategy rather than developing and instituting radical changes. Excessive changes in strategy can be disruptive to employees and confusing to customers, and they are usually unnecessary. Most of the time, there's more to be gained from improving execution of the present strategy. Persistence in making a sound strategy work better is often the key to managing the strategy to success.

WHO PERFORMS THE FIVE TASKS OF STRATEGIC MANAGEMENT?

An organization's chief executive officer, as captain of the ship, is the most visible and important strategy manager. The title of CEO carries with it the mantles of chief direction setter, chief objective setter, chief strategy maker, and chief strategy implementer for the total enterprise. Ultimate responsibility for *leading* the tasks of formulating and implementing a strategic plan for the whole organization rests with the CEO, even though other senior managers normally have significant *leadership* roles also. What the CEO views as strategically important usually is reflected in the company's strategy, and the CEO customarily puts a personal stamp of approval on big strategic decisions and actions.

Vice presidents for production, marketing, finance, human resources, and other key departments have important strategy-making and strategy-implementing responsibilities as well. Normally, the production VP has a lead role in developing the company's production strategy; the marketing VP oversees the marketing strategy effort; the financial VP is in charge of devising an appropriate financial strategy; and so on. Usually, senior managers below the CEO are also involved in proposing key elements of the overall company strategy and developing major new strategic initiatives, working closely with the CEO to hammer out a consensus and coordinate various aspects of the strategy more effectively. Only in the smallest, owner-managed companies is the strategy-making, strategy-implementing task small enough for a single manager to handle.

But managerial positions with strategy-making and strategy-implementing responsibility are by no means restricted to CEOs, vice presidents, and owner-entrepreneurs. Every major organizational unit in a company—business unit, division, staff plant, support group, or district office—normally has a leading or supporting role in the company's strategic game plan. And the manager in charge of that organizational unit, with guidance from superiors, usually ends up doing some or most of the strategy making for the unit and deciding how to implement whatever strategic choices are made. While managers farther down in the managerial hierarchy obviously have a narrower, more specific strategy-making/strategy-implementing role than managers closer to the top, *every manager is a strategy maker and strategy implementer for the area he/she supervises.*

Every company manager has a strategy-making, strategy-implementing role—it is flawed thinking to view strategic management as solely a senior executive responsibility.

One of the primary reasons why middle- and lower-echelon managers are part of the strategy-making/strategy-implementing team is that the more geographically scattered and diversified an organization's operations are, the more unwieldy it becomes for senior executives at the company's headquarters to craft and implement all the necessary actions and programs. Managers in the corporate office seldom know enough about the situation in every geographic area and operating unit to direct every move made in the field. It is common practice for top-level managers to grant some strategy-making responsibility to managerial subordinates who head the organizational subunits where specific strategic results must be achieved. Delegating a strategy-making role to on-the-scene managers charged with implementing whatever strategic moves are made in their areas fixes accountability for strategic success or failure. When the managers who implement the strategy are also its architects, it is hard for them to shift blame or make excuses if they don't achieve the target results. And, having participated in developing the strategy they are trying to implement and execute, they are likely to have strong buy-in and support for the strategy, an essential condition for effective strategy execution.

In diversified companies where the strategies of several different businesses have to be managed, there are usually four distinct levels of strategy managers:

- The chief executive officer and other senior corporate-level executives who have primary responsibility and personal authority for big strategic decisions affecting the total enterprise and the collection of individual businesses the enterprise has diversified into.

- Managers who have profit-and-loss responsibility for one specific business unit and who are delegated a major leadership role in formulating and implementing strategy for that unit.

- Functional area heads and department heads within a given business unit who have direct authority over a major piece of the business (manufacturing, marketing and sales, finance, R&D, personnel) and whose role it is to support the business unit's overall strategy with strategic actions in their own areas.

- Managers of major operating units (plants, sales districts, local offices) who have on-the-scene responsibility for developing the details of strategic efforts in their areas and for implementing and executing their piece of the overall strategic plan at the grassroots level.

Single-business enterprises need no more than three of these levels (a business-level strategy manager, functional-area strategy managers, and operating-level strategy managers). In a large single-business company, the team of strategy managers consists of the chief executive, who functions as chief strategist with final authority over both strategy and its implementation; the vice presidents and department heads in charge of key activities (R&D, production, marketing, finance, human resources, and so on); plus as many operating-unit managers of the various plants, sales offices, distribution centers, and staff support departments as it takes to handle the company's scope of operations. Proprietorships, partnerships, and owner-managed enterprises, however, typically have only one or two strategy managers since in small-scale enterprises the whole strategy-making/strategy-implementing function can be handled by just a few key people.

Managerial jobs involving strategy formulation and implementation abound in not-for-profit organizations as well. In federal and state government, heads of local, district, and regional offices function as strategy managers in their efforts to respond to the needs and situations of the areas they serve (a district manager in Portland may need a slightly different strategy than a district manager in Orlando). In municipal government, the heads of various departments (fire, police, water and sewer, parks and recreation, health, and so on) are strategy managers because they have line authority for the operations of their departments and thus can influence departmental objectives, the formation of a strategy to achieve these objectives, and how the strategy is implemented.

Managerial jobs with strategy-making/strategy-implementing roles are thus the norm rather than the exception.[3] The job of crafting and implementing strategy touches virtually every managerial job in one way or another, at one time or another. Strategic management is basic to the task of managing; it is not something just top-level managers deal with.

Is Strategy-Making an Individual Responsibility or a Group Task?

Many companies today are involving teams of managers and key employees in strategy-making exercises, partly because many strategic issues cut across traditional functional and departmental lines, partly to tap into the ideas and problem-solving skills of people with different backgrounds, expertise, and perspectives, and partly to give a greater number of people an ownership stake in the strategy that emerges and win their wholehearted commitment to implementation. Frequently, these teams include line and staff managers from different disciplines and departmental units, a few handpicked junior staffers known for their ability to think creatively, and near-retirement veterans noted for being keen observers, telling it like it is, and giving sage advice. And it is not uncommon for these teams to involve customers and suppliers in assessing the future market situation and deliberating the various strategy options. One of the biggest causes of flawed strategy is insufficient focus on what customers really need and want; another is not seeing the company as part of a wider environment and recognizing the value of reaching out and collaborating closely with key suppliers and customers (and maybe even select competitors) to gain competitive advantage.[4]

Electronic Data Systems recently conducted a yearlong strategy review involving 2,500 of its 55,000 employees that was coordinated by a core of 150 managers and staffers from all over the world.[5] J.M. Smucker, a maker of jams and jellies, formed a team of 140 employees (7 percent of its 2,000-person workforce) who spent 25 percent of their time over a six-month period to seek ways to rejuvenate the company's growth; the team, which solicited input from all employees, came up with 12 initiatives to double the company's revenues over the next five years. Nokia Group, a Finland-based telecommunications company, involved 250 employees in a recent strategy review of how different communications technologies were converging, how this would impact the company's business, and what strategic responses were needed.

Broad participation in a company's strategy-creating exercises is usually a strong plus.

Involving teams of people to dissect complex situations and find market-driven, customer-driven solutions is becoming increasingly necessary in many businesses. Not only are many strategic issues too big or too complex for a single manager to handle but they often are cross-functional and cross-departmental in nature, requiring the contributions of many disciplinary experts and the collaboration of managers from different parts of the organization to decide upon sound strategic actions. The notion that an organization's strategists are at the top and its doers are in the ranks below needs to be cast aside; very often, key pieces of strategy

---

[3]The strategy-making, strategy-implementing roles of middle managers are thoroughly discussed and documented in Steven W. Floyd and Bill Wooldridge, *The Strategic Middle Manager* (San Francisco: Jossey-Bass Publishers, 1996), Chapters 2 and 3.

[4]See James F. Moore, *The Death of Competition* (New York: HarperBusiness, 1996), Chapter 3.

[5]"Strategic Planning," *Business Week*, August 26, 1996, pp. 51–52.

originate in the middle and lower ranks of the organization, with senior managers endorsing what emerges from below and providing the resources necessary for implementation.

Is There a Role for Full-Time Strategic Planners?

If senior and middle managers have the lead roles in strategy making and strategy implementing in their areas of responsibility, supplemented by multidisciplinary strategy teams and broad employee participation in some circumstances, is there any need for full-time strategic planners or staffers with expertise in strategic analysis? The answer is perhaps in a few companies, but even then a planning staff's role and tasks should consist chiefly of helping to gather and organize information that strategy makers decide they need, providing administrative support to line managers in revising their strategic plans, and coordinating the process of higher-level executive review and approval of the strategic plans developed for all the various parts of the company. A strategic planning staff can help line managers and strategy teams crystallize the strategic issues that ought to be addressed; in addition, they can provide data, conduct studies of industry and competitive conditions as requested by the strategy makers, and develop assessments of the company's strategic performance. But strategic planners should not make strategic decisions, prepare strategic plans (for someone else to implement), or make strategic action recommendations that usurp the strategy-making responsibilities of line managers or self-directed work teams in charge of operating units or particular activities.

When strategic planners are asked to go beyond providing staff assistance and actually prepare a strategic plan for management's consideration, any of four adverse consequences may occur. One, weak managers will gladly turn tough strategic problems over to strategic planners to do their strategic thinking for them—a questionable outcome because it deludes managers into thinking they shouldn't be held responsible for crafting a strategy for their own organizational unit or for acting on strategic issues related to their areas of responsibility.

Two, planners, however expert they may be in strategic analysis and writing snappy reports, can't know as much about all the ins and outs of the situation as on-the-scene managers who are responsible for staying on top of things in their assigned area on a daily basis. This puts planning staffers at a severe disadvantage in devising sound action recommendations and taking into account the practical difficulties of implementing what they recommend.

Three, giving planners responsibility for strategy making and line managers responsibility for implementation makes it hard to fix accountability for poor results. Planners can place the blame for poor results on weak implementation; line managers can claim the problem rests with bad strategy.

Four, when line managers see no urgency in or have no ownership stake in the strategic agenda proposed by the planning staff, there's a big risk they will give it lip service, perhaps make a few token implementation efforts, and then let most of the planners' recommendations die through inaction. Handing the strategy-making function off to a strategic planning staff runs the risk that line managers and senior executives will not see the urgency or necessity of following through on what is proposed. Skepticism or disagreement over planners' recommendations breeds inaction. Absent strong concurrence with the actions recommended by planners, their work is likely to fall through the cracks—and strategic planning exercises come to be seen

Strategic Management Principle

Strategy making is a job for line managers, not a staff of planners—the doers should be the strategy makers.

as an unproductive bureaucratic activity. Such outcomes raise the chances that a company will drift along with no strong top-down strategic direction and with fragmented, uncoordinated strategic decisions. The hard truth is that strategy making is not a staff function.

All four consequences are unacceptable. Strategizing efforts get a bum rap as ineffective, line managers don't develop the skills or the discipline to think strategically about the business, and the company encounters much bigger risk of a strategy-making vacuum. On the other hand, when people are expected to be the chief strategy makers and strategy implementers for the areas they head, their own strategy and implementation efforts end up being put to the test. They quickly see the necessity of having a workable strategic plan (their annual performance reviews and perhaps even their future careers with the organization are at risk if their strategies prove unsound and they fail to achieve the target results!). When responsibility for crafting strategy is lodged with the same people charged with implementing strategy, there's no question who is accountable for results. Furthermore, pushing authority for crafting and implementing the strategy down to the people closest to the action puts decision making in the hands of those who *should* know best what to do. Broad participation gives more organizational members experience in thinking strategically about the business and in crafting and implementing strategies. People who consistently prove incapable of crafting and implementing good strategies and achieving target results have to be moved to less responsible positions.

The Strategic Role of the Board of Directors

Since lead responsibility for crafting and implementing strategy falls to key managers, the chief strategic role of an organization's board of directors is to exercise oversight and see that the five tasks of strategic management are done in a manner that benefits shareholders (in the case of investor-owned enterprises) or stakeholders (in the case of not-for-profit organizations). Recent increases in the number of stockholder lawsuits and the escalating costs of liability insurance for directors and officers have underscored that corporate board members do indeed bear ultimate responsibility for the strategic actions taken. Moreover, holders of large blocks of shares (mutual funds and pension funds), regulatory authorities, and the financial press are all calling for board members, especially outside directors, to be more active in their oversight of company strategy.

It is standard procedure for executives to brief board members on important strategic moves and to submit the company's strategic plans to the board for official approval. But directors rarely can or should play a direct, hands-on role in formulating or implementing strategy. Most outside directors lack industry-specific experience; their company-specific knowledge is limited (especially if they are relatively new board members). Boards of directors typically meet once a month (or less) for six to eight hours. Board members can scarcely be expected to have detailed command of all the strategic issues or know the ins and outs of the various strategic options. They can hardly be expected to come up with compelling strategy proposals of their own to debate against those put forward by management. Such a hands-on role is unnecessary for good oversight. The immediate task of directors is to be *supportive critics*, exercising their own independent judgment about whether proposals have been adequately analyzed and whether proposed strategic actions

---

Strategic Management Principle

A board of directors' role in the strategic management process is to critically appraise and ultimately approve strategic action plans but rarely, if ever, to develop the details.

appear to have greater promise than available alternatives.[6] If executive management is bringing well-supported strategy proposals to the board, there's little reason for board members to aggressively challenge and try to pick apart everything put before them—asking perceptive and incisive questions is usually sufficient to test whether the case for the proposals is compelling and to exercise vigilant oversight. However, if the company is experiencing gradual erosion of profits and market share, and certainly when there is a precipitous collapse in profitability, board members have a duty to be proactive, expressing their concerns about the validity of the strategy, initiating debate about the company's strategic path, having one-on-one discussions with key executives and other board members, and perhaps directly intervening as a group to alter both the strategy and the company's executive leadership.

The real hands-on role of directors is to evaluate the caliber of senior executives' strategy-making and strategy-implementing skills. The board is always responsible for determining whether the current CEO is doing a good job of strategic management (as a basis for awarding salary increases and bonuses and deciding on retention or removal). In recent years, at Apple Computer, General Motors, IBM, American Express, Kmart, W.R. Grace, and Compaq Computer, company directors concluded that top executives were not adapting their company's strategy fast enough and fully enough to the changes sweeping their markets. They pressured the CEOs to resign, and installed new leadership to provide the impetus for strategic renewal. Boards must also exercise due diligence in evaluating the strategic leadership skills of other senior executives in line to succeed the CEO. When the incumbent CEO retires, the board must elect a successor, either going with an insider (frequently nominated by the retiring CEO) or deciding that an outsider is needed to perhaps radically change the company's strategic course.

Hence, the strategic role of the board of directors is twofold: (1) to continuously audit the validity of a company's long-term direction and strategy, typically giving top executives free rein but always monitoring, offering constructive critiques, and standing ready to intervene if circumstances require, and (2) to evaluate the strategic leadership skills of the CEO and other insiders in line to succeed the incumbent CEO, proactively making personnel changes whenever the organization's performance is deemed not to be as good as it should be. Board oversight and vigilance is therefore very much in play in the strategy arena.

THE BENEFITS OF A "STRATEGIC APPROACH" TO MANAGING

The message of this book is that doing a good job of managing inherently requires good strategic thinking and good strategic management. Today's managers have to think strategically about their company's position and about the impact of changing conditions. They have to monitor the external situation closely enough to know when to institute strategy changes. They have to know the business well enough to know what kinds of strategic changes to initiate. Simply said, the fundamentals of strategic

---

[6]For a good discussion of the role of the board of directors in overseeing the strategy-making, strategy-implementing process, see Gordon Donaldson, "A New Tool for Boards: The Strategic Audit," *Harvard Business Review* 73, no.4 (July–August 1995), pp. 99–107.

management need to drive the whole approach to managing organizations. The chief executive officer of one successful company put it well when he said:

> In the main, our competitors are acquainted with the same fundamental concepts and techniques and approaches that we follow, and they are as free to pursue them as we are. More often than not, the difference between their level of success and ours lies in the relative thoroughness and self-discipline with which we and they develop and execute our strategies for the future.

The advantages of first-rate strategic thinking and conscious strategy management (as opposed to freewheeling improvisation, gut feel, and hoping for luck) include (1) providing better guidance to the entire organization on the crucial point of "what it is we are trying to do and to achieve"; (2) making managers more alert to the winds of change, new opportunities, and threatening developments; (3) providing managers with a rationale for evaluating competing budget requests for investment capital and new staff—a rationale that argues strongly for steering resources into strategy-supportive, results-producing areas; (4) helping to unify the numerous strategy-related decisions by managers across the organization; and (5) creating a more proactive management posture and counteracting tendencies for decisions to be reactive and defensive.

The advantage of being proactive is that trailblazing strategies can be the key to better long-term performance. Business history shows that high-performing enterprises often initiate and lead, not just react and defend. They launch strategic offensives to outinnovate and outmaneuver rivals and secure sustainable competitive advantage, then use their market edge to achieve superior financial performance. Aggressive pursuit of a creative, opportunistic strategy can propel a firm into a leadership position, paving the way for its products/services to become the industry standard. High-achieving enterprises are nearly always the product of astute, proactive management, rather than the result of lucky breaks or a long run of good fortune.

TERMS TO REMEMBER

In the chapters to come, we'll be referring to *mission, vision, objectives, strategy, strategic plan*, and other terms common to the language of strategy again and again. In practice, these terms generate a lot of confusion—managers, consultants, and academics often use them imprecisely and sometimes interchangeably. No single, common vocabulary exists. To cut down on the confusion and promote precise meaning, we're going to incorporate the following definitions throughout our presentation.

Strategic vision—a view of an organization's future direction and business makeup; a guiding concept for what the organization is trying to do and to become.

Organization mission—management's customized answer to the question "What is our business and what are we trying to accomplish on behalf of our customers?" A mission statement broadly outlines the organization's activities and present business makeup. Whereas the focus of a strategic vision is on a company's future, the focus of a company's mission *tends* to be on the present. (If the statement of mission speaks as much to the future path the organization intends to follow as to the present organizational purpose, then the mission statement incorporates the strategic vision and there's no *separate* managerial need for a vision.)

Financial objectives—the targets management has established for the organization's financial performance.

Strategic objectives—the targets management has established for strengthening the organization's overall business position and competitive vitality.

Long-range objectives—the results to be achieved either within the next three to five years or else on an ongoing basis year after year.

Short-range objectives—the organization's near-term performance targets; the amount of short-term improvement signals how fast management is trying to achieve the long-range objectives.

Strategy—the pattern of actions and business approaches managers employ to please customers, build an attractive market position, and achieve organizational objectives; a company's actual strategy is partly planned and partly reactive to changing circumstances.

Strategic plan—a statement outlining an organization's mission and future direction, near-term and long-term performance targets, and strategy.

Strategy formulation—the entire direction-setting management function of conceptualizing an organization's mission, setting performance objectives, and crafting a strategy. The end product of strategy formulation is a strategic plan.

Strategy implementation—the full range of managerial activities associated with putting the chosen strategy into place, supervising its pursuit, and achieving the targeted results.

On the following pages, we will probe the strategy-related tasks of managers and the methods of strategic analysis much more intensively. When you get to the end of the book, we think you will see that two factors separate the best-managed organizations from the rest: (1) superior strategy making and entrepreneurship, and (2) competent implementation and execution of the chosen strategy. There's no escaping the fact that the quality of managerial strategy making and strategy implementing has a significant impact on organization performance. A company that lacks clear-cut direction, has vague or undemanding objectives, has a muddled or flawed strategy, or can't seem to execute its strategy competently is a company whose performance is probably suffering, whose business is at long-term risk, and whose management is lacking. In short, the better conceived a company's strategy and the more proficient its execution, the greater the chances the company will be a leading performer in its markets and truly deserve a reputation for talented management.

SUGGESTED READINGS

Andrews, Kenneth R. *The Concept of Corporate Strategy,* 3rd ed. Homewood, Ill.: Richard D. Irwin, 1987, chap. 1.

Collins, James C., and Jerry I. Porras. "Building Your Company's Vision." *Harvard Business Review* 74, no.5 (September–October 1996), pp. 65–77.

Farkas, Charles M., and Suzy Wetlaufer. "The Ways Chief Executive Officers Lead," *Harvard Business Review* 74 no. 3 (May–June 1996), pp. 110–22.

Hamel, Gary. "Strategy as Revolution," *Harvard Business Review* 74 no. 4 (July–August 1996), pp. 69–82.

Lipton, Mark. "Demystifying the Development of an Organizational Vision." *Sloan Management Review* (Summer 1996), pp. 83–92.

Mintzberg, Henry. "Rethinking Strategic Planning: Pitfalls and Fallacies." *Long Range Planning* 27, no. 3 (1994), pp. 12–19.

———."Rethinking Strategic Planning: New Roles for Planners." *Long Range Planning* 27, no. 3 (1994), pp. 22–29.

———. "Crafting Strategy." *Harvard Business Review* 65, no. 4 (July–August 1987), pp. 66–75.

Porter, Michael E. "What Is Strategy?" *Harvard Business Review* 74, no. 6 (November–December 1996), pp. 61–78.

Yip, George S. *Total Global Strategy: Managing for Worldwide Competitive Advantage.* Englewood Cliffs, N.J.: Prentice-Hall, 1992, chap. 1.

THE THREE STRATEGY-MAKING TASKS

Developing a Strategic Vision, Setting Objectives, and Crafting a Strategy

2

In this chapter, we take a more in-depth look at the three strategy-making tasks: developing a strategic vision and business mission, setting performance objectives, and crafting a strategy to produce the desired results. We also examine the kinds of strategic decisions made at each management level, the major determinants of a company's strategy, and four frequently used managerial approaches to forming a strategic plan.

DEVELOPING A STRATEGIC VISION AND MISSION: THE FIRST DIRECTION-SETTING TASK

Early on, a company's senior management has to look to the future and address the issue of "where do we go from here—what customer needs and buyer segments do we need to be concentrating on, what should the company's business makeup be 5 to 10 years down the road?" Management's views and conclusions about the organization's future course, the customer focus it should have, the market position it should try to occupy, and the business activities to be pursued constitute a *strategic vision* for the company. A strategic vision indicates management's aspirations for the organization, providing a panoramic view of "what businesses we want to be in, where we are headed, and the kind of company we are trying to create." It spells out a direction and describes the destination.

The last thing IBM needs right now is a vision. (July 1993) What IBM needs most right now is a vision. (March 1996)

> **Louis V. Gerstner, Jr**
> *CEO, IBM Corporation*

How can you lead if you don't know where you are going?

> **George Newman**
> *The Conference Board*

Management's job is not to see the company as it is . . . but as it can become.

> **John W. Teets**
> *CEO, Greyhound Corporation*

A strategy is a commitment to undertake one set of actions rather than another.

> **Sharon M. Oster**
> *Professor, Yale University*

ILLUSTRATION CAPSULE 4   Delta Airlines' Strategic Vision

In late 1993, Ronald W. Allen, Delta's chief executive officer, described the company's vision and business mission in the following way:

> . . . we want Delta to be the **Worldwide Airline of Choice**.
>
> Worldwide, because we are and intend to remain an innovative, aggressive, ethical, and successful competitor that offers access to the world at the highest standards of customer service. We will continue to look for opportunities to extend our reach through new routes and creative global alliances.
>
> Airline, because we intend to stay in the business we know best—air transportation and related ser-

vices. We won't stray from our roots. We believe in the long-term prospects for profitable growth in the airline industry, and we will continue to focus time, attention, and investment on enhancing our place in that business environment.

> Of Choice, because we value the loyalty of our customers, employees, and investors. For passengers and shippers, we will continue to provide the best service and value. For our personnel, we will continue to offer an ever more challenging, rewarding, and result-oriented workplace that recognizes and appreciates their contributions. For our shareholders, we will earn a consistent, superior financial return.

Source: *Sky Magazine*, December 1993, p. 10.

Why Have a Mission or Strategic Vision?

A clear and entrepreneurially astute strategic vision is a prerequisite to effective strategic leadership. A manager cannot function effectively as either leader or strategy maker without a future-oriented concept of the business—what customer needs to work toward satisfying, what business activities to pursue, and what kind of long-term market position to build vis-à-vis competitors. Forming a strategic vision is thus not a wordsmithing exercise to create a catchy company slogan; rather, it is an exercise in thinking strategically about a company's future, forming a viable concept of the company's future business, and putting the company on a strategic path that management is deeply committed to. It is an exercise in coming up with a coherent and powerful picture of what the company's business can and should be 5 or 10 years hence. When management's strategic vision conveys something substantive about what business position it intends for the company to stake out and what course the company is going to follow, then the vision is truly capable of *guiding* managerial decision making, *shaping* the company's strategy, and *impacting* how the company is run. Such outcomes have *real managerial value*. Illustration Capsule 4 presents Delta Airlines' strategic vision.

Effective strategy making begins with a concept of what the organization should and should not do and a vision of where the organization needs to be headed.

Strategic Visions Chart a Company's Future   The term *strategic vision* is inherently more future oriented than the oft-used terms *business purpose* or *mission statement*. The statements of mission or business purpose that most companies include in their annual reports tend to deal more with the present ("What is our business?") than with the organization's aspirations and long-term direction (where we are headed, what new things we intend to pursue, what we want our business makeup to be in 5 to 10 years, what kind of company we are trying to become, and what sort of long-term market position we aspire to achieve). However, a here-and-now-oriented purpose/mission statement highlighting the boundaries of the company's current business is a logical vantage point from which to look down the road, decide what the enterprise's future business makeup and customer focus need to be, and chart a strategic path for the company to take. As a rule, strategic visions should have a time horizon of a decade or more.

Strategic Visions Are Company-Specific, Not Generic   Strategic visions and company mission statements ought to be highly personalized—unique to the organization for which they were developed. There's nothing unusual about companies in the same industry pursuing significantly, even radically, different strategic paths. For example, the current mission and future direction of a globally active New York bank like Citicorp has little in common with that of a locally owned hometown bank even though both are in the banking industry. IBM, with its mainframe computer business, its line-up of personal computers, and its software and services business, is not on the same long-term strategic course as Compaq Computer (which concentrates on PCs and servers), even though both are leaders in the personal computer industry. *The whole idea behind developing a strategic vision/mission statement is to set an organization apart from others in its industry and give it its own special identity, business emphasis, and path for development.*

Generically worded statements, couched in everything-and-everybody language that could apply just as well to many companies and lines of business, are not managerially useful—they paint no mental picture of where the company is destined and offer no guidance to managers in deciding which business activities to pursue and not to pursue, what strategies make the best sense, or how to operate the company. Nor do they communicate useful information about a company's long-term direction and future business makeup to employees and investors. Ambiguous or vaguely worded mission/vision statements may have some public relations value, but they don't help managers manage. *The best vision statements are worded in a manner that clarifies the direction in which an organization needs to move.*

> *Visionless companies are unsure what business position they are trying to stake out.*

The Mission or Vision Is Not to Make a Profit   Sometimes companies couch their business purpose or mission in terms of making a profit. This is misguided—profit is more correctly an *objective* and a *result* of what the company does. The desire to make a profit says nothing about the business arena in which profits are to be sought. Missions or visions based on making a profit are incapable of distinguishing one type of profit-seeking enterprise from another—the business and long-term direction of Sears are plainly different from the business and long-term direction of Toyota, even though both endeavor to earn a profit. A company that says its mission/business purpose/strategic vision is to make a profit begs the question "What will we do to make a profit?" To understand a company's business and future direction, we must know management's answer to "make a profit doing what and for whom?"

The Elements of a Strategic Vision   There are three distinct pieces to the task of forming a strategic vision of a company's business future:

- Defining what business the company is *presently* in.
- Deciding on a *long-term* strategic course for the company to pursue.
- Communicating the vision in ways that are clear, exciting, and inspiring.

Defining a Company's Present Business

Coming up with a strategically insightful definition of what business an organization is presently in is not as simple as it might seem. Is IBM in the computer business (a product-oriented definition) or the information and data-processing business (a customer service or customer needs type of definition) or the advanced electronics business (a technology-based definition)? Is America Online in the computer services business, the information business, the business of connecting people to the Internet, the on-line content business, or the entertainment business? Is AT&T in the long-distance business or the telephone business or the telecommunications business? Is Coca-Cola in the soft-drink business (in which case management's strategic attention can be concentrated on outselling and outcompeting Pepsi, 7UP, Dr Pepper, Canada Dry, and Schweppes) or is it in the beverage business (in which case management also needs to think strategically about positioning Coca-Cola products to compete against other fruit juices, ready-to-drink teas, bottled water, sports drinks, milk, and coffee)? Whether to take a soft-drink perspective or a beverage perspective is not a trivial question for Coca-Cola management—only partly because Coca-Cola is also the parent of Minute Maid and Hi-C juice products. With a beverage industry vision as opposed to a soft-drink focus, Coca-Cola management can better zero in on how to convince young adults to get their morning caffeine fix by drinking Coca-Cola instead of coffee.

A company's business is defined by what needs it is trying to satisfy, by which customer groups it is targeting, and by the technologies it will use and the functions it will perform in serving the target market.

Incorporating What, Who, and How Into the Business Definition   To arrive at a strategically revealing business definition, three elements need to be incorporated:[1]

1. Customer needs, or *what* is being satisfied.
2. Customer groups, or *who* is being satisfied.
3. The technologies used and functions performed—*how* customers' needs are satisfied.

Defining a business in terms of what to satisfy, who to satisfy, and how the organization will go about producing the satisfaction produces a comprehensive definition of what a company does and what business it is in. Just knowing what products or services a firm provides is never enough. Products or services per se are not important to customers; a product or service becomes a business when it satisfies a need or want. Without the need or want there is no business. Customer groups are relevant because they indicate the market to be served—the geographic domain to be covered and the types of buyers the firm is going after.

Technology and functions performed are important because they indicate *how* the company will satisfy the customers' needs and how much of the industry's production-distribution chain its activities will span. For instance, a firm's business can be *fully integrated*, extending across the entire range of industry activities that must be performed to get a product or service in the hands of end users. Major international oil companies like Exxon, Mobil, BP, Royal Dutch Shell, and Chevron lease drilling sites, drill wells, pump oil, transport crude oil in their own ships and pipelines to their own refineries, and sell gasoline and other refined products through their own networks of branded distributors and service station outlets. Their operations cover all stages of the industry's entire production-distribution chain.

Other firms stake out *partially integrated* positions, participating only in selected stages of the industry. Goodyear, for instance, both manufactures tires and operates a chain of company-owned retail tire stores, but it has not integrated backward into

[1]Derek F. Abell, *Defining the Business: The Starting Point of Strategic Planning* (Englewood Cliffs, N.J.: Prentice-Hall, 1980), p. 169.

rubber plantations and other tire-making components. General Motors, the world's most integrated manufacturer of cars and trucks, makes between 60 and 70 percent of the parts and components used in assembling GM vehicles. But GM is moving to outsource a greater fraction of its parts and systems components, and it relies totally on a network of independent, franchised dealers to handle sales and service functions. Still other firms are *specialized*, concentrating on just one stage of an industry's total production-distribution chain. Wal-Mart, Home Depot, Toys-R-Us, Lands' End, and The Limited are essentially one-stage firms. Their operations focus on the retail end of the production-distribution chain; they don't manufacture the items they sell. Delta Airlines is a one-stage enterprise; it doesn't manufacture the airplanes it flies, and it doesn't operate the airports where it lands. Delta has made a conscious decision to limit its business activities to moving travelers from one location to another via commercial jet aircraft.

An example of a company that does a pretty good job of covering the three bases of what, who, and how is Russell Corporation, the largest U. S. manufacturer of athletic uniforms:

> Russell Corporation is a vertically integrated international designer, manufacturer, and marketer of athletic uniforms, activewear, better knit shirts, leisure apparel, licensed sports apparel, sports and casual socks, and a comprehensive line of lightweight, yarn-dyed woven fabrics. The Company's manufacturing operations include the entire process of converting raw fibers into finished apparel and fabrics. Products are marketed to sporting goods dealers, department and specialty stores, mass merchandisers, golf pro shops, college bookstores, screen printers, distributors, mail-order houses, and other apparel manufacturers.

The concepts that McDonald's uses to define its business are a limited menu, good-tasting fast-food products of consistent quality, fast and accurate service, value pricing, exceptional customer care, convenient locations, and global market coverage. McDonald's business mission is built around "serving a limited menu of hot, tasty food quickly in a clean, friendly restaurant for a good value" to a broad base of fast-food customers worldwide (McDonald's serves approximately 30 million customers daily at 20,000-plus restaurants in over 90 countries).

Trying to identify needs served, target market, and functions performed in a single, snappy sentence is a challenge, and many firms' business definitions/mission statements fail to illuminate all three bases explicitly. The business definitions of some companies are thus better than others in terms of how they cut to the chase of what the enterprise is really about and the strategic position it is trying to stake out.[2]

A Broad or Narrow Business Definition?   Merck, one of the world's foremost pharmaceutical companies, has defined its business broadly as "providing society with

---

[2]For a more extensive discussion of the challenges of developing a well-conceived vision, as well as some in-depth examples, see James C. Collins and Jerry I. Porras, "Building Your Company's Vision," *Harvard Business Review* 74, no.5 (September–October 1996), pp. 65–77; Robert A. Burgelman and Andrew S. Grove, "Strategic Dissonance," *California Management Review* 38, no. 2 (Winter 1996), pp. 8–25; and Ron McTavish, "One More Time: What Business Are You In?" *Long Range Planning* 28, no. 2 (April 1995), pp. 49–60. For a discussion of some of the alternative ways a company can position itself in the marketplace, see Michael E. Porter, "What Is Strategy," *Harvard Business Review* 74, no. 6 (November–December 1996), pp. 65–67. Porter argues that the three basic strategic positions are based on (a) the range of customer needs to be served, (b) the variety of products to be offered (anywhere along the spectrum of one to many), and (c) the means by which customers are accessed—the terms Porter uses are needs-based positioning, variety-based positioning, and access-based positioning. For an empirical study of executive success in formulating and implementing a company vision and the difficulties encountered, see Laurie Larwood, Cecilia M. Falbe, Mark Kriger, and Paul Miesing, "Structure and Meaning of Organizational Vision," *Academy of Management Journal*, 38, no. 3 (June 1995), pp. 740–69.

superior products and services—innovations and solutions that satisfy customer needs and improve the quality of life." Such broad language, however, offers no practical strategic guidance. With such a definition Merck could pursue limitless strategic paths—developing innovative computer software, producing and marketing uniquely satisfying snack foods, manufacturing very appealing sports utility vehicles, or providing tax preparation services—businesses well outside its capabilities and actual intent. Trying to go in several business directions at once may be tempting and even fashionable, but it risks lack of business focus and dilution of effort. Few businesses fail because they are clearly focused on one market opportunity; many do badly because they try to pursue too many things at once.

To have managerial value, strategic visions, business definitions, and mission statements must be narrow enough to pin down the company's real arena of business interest. Consider the following definitions based on broad-narrow scope:

Broad Definition	Narrow Definition
• Beverages	• Soft drinks
• Children's products	• Toys
• Furniture	• Wrought-iron lawn furniture
• Global mail delivery	• Overnight package delivery
• Travel and tourism	• Ship cruises in the Caribbean

Broad-narrow definitions are relative to a company's business focus and intent, however. Being in "the furniture business" is probably too broad a concept for a company intent on being the largest manufacturer of wrought-iron lawn furniture in North America. On the other hand, toys has proved too narrow a scope for a growth-oriented company like Toys-R-Us, which, with its desire to capitalize on the potential of providing parents with more of what their children need, has ventured beyond toys and opened Kids-R-Us stores containing a wide selection of children's apparel and Books-R-Us stores specializing in children's books and reading programs. The U.S. Postal Service operates with a broad definition, providing global mail-delivery services to all types of senders. Federal Express, however, operates with a narrow business definition based on handling overnight package delivery for customers who have unplanned emergencies and tight deadlines.

Diversified companies have broader missions and business definitions than single-business enterprises.

Diversified firms, understandably, employ more sweeping business definitions than single-business enterprises. For example, Times Mirror Corp. describes itself broadly as a media and information company (which covers a lot of ground) but then goes on to pin down its business arenas in fairly explicit terms:

> Times Mirror is a media and information company principally engaged in newspaper publishing; book, magazine and other publishing; and cable and broadcast television.

Mission Statements for Functional Departments   There's also a place for mission statements for key functions (R&D, marketing, finance) and support units (human resources, training, information systems). Every department can benefit from a consensus statement spelling out its contribution to the company mission, its principal role and activities, and the direction it needs to be moving. Functional and departmental managers who think through and debate with subordinates and higher-

---

ILLUSTRATION CAPSULE 5   Intel's Bold Decision to Radically Alter Its Strategic Vision

Sometimes there's an order-of-magnitude change in a company's environment that dramatically alters its future prospects and mandates radical revision of its direction and strategic course—Intel's Chairman Andrew Grove calls such occasions "strategic inflection points." Grove and Intel encountered such an inflection point in the mid-1980s. At the time, memory chips were Intel's principal business, and Japanese manufacturers, intent on dominating the memory chip business, were cutting their prices 10 percent below the prices charged by Intel and other U.S. memory chip manufacturers; each time U.S. companies matched the Japanese price cuts, the Japanese manufacturers responded with another 10 percent price cut. Intel's management explored a number of strategic options to cope with the aggressive pricing of its Japanese rivals—building a giant memory chip factory to overcome the cost advantage of Japanese producers, investing in R&D to come up with a more advanced memory chip, and retreating to niche markets for memory chips that were not of interest to the Japanese. Grove concluded that none of these options offered much promise and that the best long-term solution was to abandon the memory chip business even though it accounted for 70 percent of Intel's revenue.

Grove then proceeded to commit Intel's full energies to the business of developing ever more powerful microprocessors for personal computers (Intel had invented microprocessors in the early 1970s but had recently been concentrating on memory chips because of strong competition and excess capacity in the market for microprocessors).

Grove's bold decision to withdraw from memory chips, absorb a $173 million write-off in 1986, and go all out in microprocessors produced a new strategic vision for Intel—becoming the preeminent supplier of microprocessors to the personal computing industry, making the PC the central appliance in the workplace and the home, and being the undisputed leader in driving PC technology forward. Grove's vision for Intel and the strategic course he subsequently charted has produced spectacular results. Today, 85 percent of the PCs have "Intel inside," and Intel was one of the five most profitable U.S. companies in 1996, earning after-tax profits of $5.2 billion on revenues of $20.8 billion.

---

ups what their unit needs to focus on and do have a clearer view of how to lead the unit. Three examples from actual companies indicate how a functional mission statement puts the spotlight on a unit's organizational *role* and *scope*:

- The mission of the human resources department is to contribute to organizational success by developing effective leaders, creating high-performance teams, and maximizing the potential of individuals.
- The mission of the corporate claims department is to minimize the overall cost of liability, workers compensation, and property damage claims through competitive cost containment techniques and loss prevention and control programs.
- The mission of corporate security is to provide services for the protection of corporate personnel and assets through preventive measures and investigations.

Deciding on a Long-Term Strategic Vision for the Company

Coming to grips with what a company's business can and should be 5 or 10 years down the road is something of a daunting task. It requires rational analysis of what the company should be doing to get ready for the changes coming in its present business and to capitalize on newly developing market opportunities. It also requires good entrepreneurial instincts, creativity, and an intuitive sense of what the company is capable of when pushed and challenged. Management's strategic vision ought to be realistic about the market, competitive, technological, economic, regulatory, and societal conditions the company is likely to encounter, and it ought to be realistic about the company's resources and capabilities. A strategic vision is not supposed to be a pipe dream or a fantasy about the company's future. Indeed, it has got to be compelling enough to shape the company's actions and energize its strategy.

The entrepreneurial challenge in developing a strategic vision is to think creatively about how to prepare a company for the future.

Often, the driving consideration is how best to position the enterprise to be successful in light of emerging developments and changes on the horizon. Alertness to the winds of change lessens the chances of the company becoming trapped in a stagnant or declining business or letting attractive new growth opportunities slip away because of inaction. Good entrepreneurs and strategists have a sharp eye for shifting customer wants and needs, new technological developments, openings to enter attractive foreign markets, and other important signs of growing or shrinking business opportunity. They attend quickly to users' problems and complaints with the industry's current products and services. They listen intently when a customer says, "If only . . . " Such clues and information tidbits stimulate them to think creatively and strategically about ways to break new ground. Appraising new customer-market-technology opportunities ultimately leads to entrepreneurial judgments about which fork in the road to take and what kind of strategic position to stake out in the marketplace. It is the strategy maker's job to evaluate the risks and prospects of alternative paths and make direction-setting decisions to position the enterprise for success in the years ahead. *A well-chosen vision and long-term business mission prepare a company for the future.*

Many successful organizations need to change direction not to survive but to maintain their success.

Communicating the Strategic Vision

How to communicate the strategic vision down the line to lower-level managers and employees is almost as important as the strategic soundness of the organization's business concept and long-term direction. One-way communication is seldom adequate, however; conversations with employees that allow for give-and-take discussion work best. People have a need to believe that the company's management knows where it's trying to take the company, where the company's markets are headed, and what changes lie ahead. When management can paint a picture of the company's future path in words that inspire employees and arouse a committed organizational effort, then the strategic vision serves as a powerful motivational tool—the simple, clear, lofty mission of the International Red Cross is a good example: "to serve the most vulnerable." Bland language, platitudes, and dull motherhood-and-apple-pie-style verbiage must be scrupulously avoided—they can be a turn-off rather than a turn-on. Managers need to communicate the vision in words that induce employee buy-in, build pride, and create a strong sense of organizational purpose. People are proud to be associated with a company pursuing a worthwhile strategic course and trying to be the world's best at something competitively significant and beneficial to customers. Hence, expressing the strategic vision in engaging language that reaches out and grabs people, that creates a vivid image in their heads, and that provokes emotion and excitement has enormous motivational value; it lifts thoughts above and beyond the daily routine of the business.

A well-articulated strategic vision creates enthusiasm for the future course management has charted and poses a challenge that inspires and engages members of the organization.

Having an exciting business cause energizes the company's strategy, brings the workforce together, galvanizes people to act, stimulates extra effort, and gets people to live the business instead of just coming to work.[3] In organizations with a just-revised vision and long-term direction, it is particularly important for executives to provide a compelling rationale for the new strategic path and why the company must

---

[3]Tom Peters, *Thriving on Chaos* (New York: Harper & Row, Perennial Library Edition, 1988), pp. 486–87; and Andrall E. Pearson, "Corporate Redemption and The Seven Deadly Sins," *Harvard Business Review* 70, no. 3 (May–June 1992), pp. 66–68.

NovaCare is a health care company specializing in providing patient rehabilitation services on a contract basis to nursing homes. Rehabilitation therapy is a $12 billion industry, of which 35 percent is provided contractually. In 1996 NovaCare was an $800 million company with 17,000 employees at 2,300 sites in 43 states. The company stated its business mission and vision as follows:

NovaCare is people committed to making a difference . . . enhancing the future of all patients . . . breaking new ground in our professions . . . achieving excellence . . . advancing human capability . . . changing the world in which we live.

We lead the way with our enthusiasm, optimism, patience, drive, and commitment.

We work together to enhance the quality of our patients' lives by reshaping lost abilities and teaching new skills. We heighten expectations for the patient and family. We rebuild hope, confidence, self-respect, and a desire to continue.

We apply our clinical expertise to benefit our patients through creative and progressive techniques. Our ethical and performance standards require us to expend every effort to achieve the best possible results.

Our customers are national and local health care providers who share our goal of enhancing the patients' quality of life. In each community, our customers consider us a partner in providing the best possible care. Our reputation is based on our responsiveness, high standards, and effective systems of quality assurance. Our relationship is open and proactive.

We are advocates of our professions and patients through active participation in the professional, regulatory, educational, and research communities at national, state, and local levels.

Our approach to health care fulfills our responsibility to provide investors with a high rate of return through consistent growth and profitability.

Our people are our most valuable asset. We are committed to the personal, professional, and career development of each individual employee. We are proud of what we do and dedicated to our Company. We foster teamwork and create an environment conducive to productive communication among all disciplines.

NovaCare is a company of people in pursuit of this Vision.

Source: Company annual report and website.

begin to stake out a different future business position. Unless people understand how a company's business environment is changing and why a new course is being charted, a new vision and long-term business mission does little to win employees' commitment and wholehearted cooperation. Employee failure to understand or accept the need for redirecting organizational efforts often produces resistance to change and makes it harder to move the organization down a newly chosen path. Hence, explaining and justifying the new strategic vision in persuasive terms that everyone can understand and agree with is a necessary step in getting the organization redirected and ready to move along the new course.

Well-worded vision statements give employees a larger sense of purpose—so that they see themselves as "building a cathedral" rather than "laying stones."

The best-worded mission statements and visions of a company's future are simple and easy to grasp; they convey unmistakable meaning, generate enthusiasm for the firm's future course, and elicit personal effort and dedication from everyone in the organization. They have to be presented and then repeated over and over as a worthy organizational challenge, one capable of benefiting customers in a valuable and meaningful way—indeed, it is crucial that the mission/vision stress the payoff for customers, not the payoff for stockholders. It goes without saying that the company intends to profit shareholders from its efforts to provide real value to its customers. A crisp, clear, often-repeated, inspiring strategic vision has the power to turn heads in the intended direction and begin a new organizational march. When this occurs, the first step in organizational direction-setting is successfully completed. Illustration Capsule 6 is a good example of an inspiration-oriented company vision and mission.

A well-conceived, well-worded strategic vision/mission statement has real managerial value: (1) it crystallizes senior executives' own views about the firm's long-term direction and future business makeup; (2) it reduces the risk of visionless management and rudderless decision making; (3) it conveys an organizational purpose that arouses employee buy-in and commitment and that motivates employees to go all out and contribute to making the vision a reality; (4) it provides a beacon lower-level managers can use to form departmental missions, set departmental objectives, and craft functional and departmental strategies that are in sync with the company's direction and strategy; and (5) it helps an organization prepare for the future.

ESTABLISHING OBJECTIVES: THE SECOND DIRECTION-SETTING TASK

Setting objectives converts the strategic vision and directional course into specific performance targets. Objectives represent a managerial commitment to achieving specific outcomes and results. They are a call for action and for results. Unless an organization's long-term direction and business mission are translated into specific performance targets and managers are pressured to show progress in reaching these targets, vision and mission statements are likely to end up as nice words, window dressing, and unrealized dreams of accomplishment. The experiences of countless companies and managers teach that *companies whose managers set objectives for each key result area and then press forward with actions aimed directly at achieving these performance outcomes typically outperform companies whose managers exhibit good intentions, try hard, and hope for the best.*

Objectives represent a managerial commitment to achieving specific performance targets within a specific time frame.

For objectives to function as yardsticks of organizational performance and progress, they must be stated in *quantifiable* or measurable terms and they must contain a *deadline for achievement.* They have to spell out *how much* of *what kind* of performance *by when.* This means avoiding generalities like "maximize profits," "reduce costs," "become more efficient," or "increase sales," which specify neither how much or when. As Bill Hewlett, cofounder of Hewlett-Packard, once observed, "You cannot manage what you cannot measure . . . And what gets measured gets done."[4] Spelling out organization objectives in measurable terms and then holding managers accountable for reaching their assigned targets within a specified time frame (1) substitutes purposeful strategic decision making for aimless actions and confusion over what to accomplish and (2) provides a set of benchmarks for judging the organization's performance and progress.

What Kinds of Objectives to Set

Objectives are needed for each *key result* managers deem important to success.[5] Two types of key result areas stand out: those relating to *financial performance*

---

[4]As quoted in Charles H. House and Raymond L. Price, "The Return Map: Tracking Product Teams," *Harvard Business Review* 60, no. 1 (January–February 1991), p. 93.

[5]The literature of management is filled with references to *goals* and *objectives.* These terms are used in a variety of ways, many of them conflicting. Some writers use the term goals to refer to the long-run outcomes an organization seeks to achieve and the term objectives to refer to immediate, short-run performance targets. Some writers reverse the usage, referring to objectives as the desired long-run results and goals as the desired short-run results. Others use the terms interchangeably. And still others use the term goals to refer to broad organizationwide performance targets and the term objectives to designate specific

and those relating to *strategic performance*. Achieving acceptable financial performance is a must; otherwise the organization's financial standing can alarm creditors and shareholders, impair its ability to fund needed initiatives, and perhaps even put its very survival at risk. Achieving acceptable strategic performance is essential to sustaining and improving the company's long-term market position and competitiveness. Representative kinds of financial and strategic performance objectives are listed below:

Strategic Management Principle

Every company needs both strategic objectives and financial objectives.

Financial Objectives	Strategic Objectives
• Growth in revenues	• A bigger market share
• Growth in earnings	• Quicker design-to-market times than rivals
• Higher dividends	• Higher product quality than rivals
• Wider profit margins	• Lower costs relative to key competitors
• Higher returns on invested capital	• Broader or more attractive product line than rivals
• Attractive economic value added (EVA) performance[6]	• A stronger reputation with customers than rivals
• Strong bond and credit ratings	• Superior customer service
• Bigger cash flows	• Recognition as a leader in technology and/or product innovation
• A rising stock price	• Wider geographic coverage than rivals
• Attractive and sustainable increases in market value added (MVA)[7]	• Higher levels of customer satisfaction than rivals
• Recognition as a "blue chip" company	
• A more diversified revenue base	
• Stable earnings during periods of recession	

Illustration Capsule 7 presents the strategic and financial objectives of four well-known enterprises.

---

targets set by operating divisions and functional departments to support achievement of overall company performance targets. In our view, little is gained from semantic distinctions between goals and objectives. The important thing is to recognize that the results an enterprise seeks to attain vary as to both organizational scope and time frame. Nearly always, organizations need to have companywide performance targets and division/department performance targets for both the near-term and long-term. It is inconsequential which targets are called goals and which objectives. To avoid a semantic jungle, we use the single term *objectives* to refer to the performance targets and results an organization seeks to attain. We use the adjectives *long-range* (or long-run) and *short-range* (or short-run) to identify the relevant time frame, and we try to describe objectives in words that indicate their intended scope and level in the organization.

[6]Economic value added (EVA) is profit over and above the company's weighted average after-tax cost of capital; specifically, it is defined as operating profit less income taxes less the weighted average cost of capital. Such companies as Coca-Cola, AT&T, Briggs & Stratton, and Eli Lilly use EVA as a measure of the profit performance. For more details on EVA, consult footnote 1 in Chapter 1.

[7]Market value added (MVA) is defined as the amount by which the total value of the company has appreciated above the dollar amount actually invested in the company by shareholders. MVA is equal to a company's current stock price times the number of shares outstanding less shareholders' equity investment; it represents the value that management has added to shareholders' wealth in running the business. If shareholder value is to be maximized, management must select a strategy and long-term direction that maximizes the market value of the company's common stock.

ILLUSTRATION CAPSULE 7   Examples Of Corporate Objectives: McDonald's, 3M Corp., Anheuser-Busch, and McCormick & Company

McDonald's

- To achieve 100 percent total customer satisfaction . . . everyday . . . in every restaurant . . . for every customer.

Anheuser-Busch

- To make all of our companies leaders in their industries in quality while exceeding customer expectations.
- To achieve a 50% share of the U.S. beer market.
- To establish and maintain a dominant leadership position in the international beer market.
- To provide all our employees with challenging and rewarding work, satisfying working conditions, and opportunities for personal development, advancement, and competitive compensation.
- To provide our shareholders with superior returns by achieving double-digit annual earnings per share growth, increasing dividends consistent with earnings growth, repurchasing shares when the opportunity is right, pursuing profitable international beer expansions, and

generating quality earnings and cash flow returns.

3M Corporation

- 30 percent of the company's annual sales must come from products fewer than four years old.

McCormick & Company

- To achieve a 20 percent return on equity.
- To achieve a net sales growth rate of 10 percent per year.
- To maintain an average earnings per share growth rate of 15 percent per year.
- To maintain total debt-to-total capital at 40 percent or less.
- To pay out 25 percent to 35 percent of net income in dividends.
- To make selective acquisitions which complement our current businesses and can enhance our overall returns.
- To dispose of those parts of our business which do not or cannot generate adequate returns or do not fit our business strategy.

Source: Company annual reports.

Strategic Objectives versus Financial Objectives: Which Take Precedence?   Even though an enterprise places high priority on achieving both financial and strategic objectives, what if situations arise where a trade-off has to be made? Should a company under pressure to pay down its debt elect to kill or postpone investments in strategic moves that hold promise for strengthening the enterprise's future business and competitive position? Should a company under pressure to boost near-term profits cut back R&D programs that could help it achieve a competitive advantage over key rivals in the years ahead? The pressures on managers to opt for better near-term financial performance and to sacrifice or cut back on strategic initiatives aimed at building a stronger competitive position become especially pronounced when (1) an enterprise is struggling financially, (2) the resource commitments for strategically beneficial moves will materially detract from the bottom line for several years, and (3) the proposed strategic moves are risky and have an uncertain competitive or bottom-line payoff.

Strategic objectives need to be competitor-focused, often aiming at unseating a rival considered to be the industry's best in a particular category.

Yet, there are dangers in management's succumbing time and again to the lure of immediate gains in profitability when it means paring or forgoing strategic moves that would build a stronger business position. A company that consistently passes up opportunities to strengthen its long-term competitive position in order to realize better near-term financial gains risks diluting its competitiveness, losing momentum in its markets, and impairing its ability to stave off market challenges from ambitious rivals. The business landscape is littered with ex-market leaders who put more emphasis on boosting next quarter's profit than strengthening long-term market position. The danger of trading off long-term gains in market position for near-term gains in bottom-line performance is greatest when a profit-conscious market leader has competitors who invest relentlessly in gaining market share, striving to become big and strong enough to outcompete the leader in a head-to-head market battle. One need look no further than Japanese companies' patient and persistent strategic efforts to gain market ground on their more profit-centered American and European rivals to appreciate the pitfall of letting short-term financial objectives dominate. The surest path to protecting and sustaining a company's profitability quarter after quarter and year after year is for its managers to pursue strategic actions that strengthen the company's competitiveness and business position.

> **Strategic Management Principle**
>
> *Building a stronger long-term competitive position benefits shareholders more lastingly than improving short-term profitability.*

The Concept of Strategic Intent

A company's strategic objectives are important for another reason—they indicate *strategic intent* to stake out a particular business position.[8] The strategic intent of a large company may be industry leadership on a national or global scale. The strategic intent of a small company may be to dominate a market niche. The strategic intent of an up-and-coming enterprise may be to overtake the market leaders. The strategic intent of a technologically innovative company may be to pioneer a promising discovery and create a whole new vista of products that change the way people work and live—as many entrepreneurial companies are now trying to do with the Internet.

> **Basic Concept**
>
> A company exhibits strategic intent *when it relentlessly pursues an ambitious strategic objective and concentrates its competitive actions and energies on achieving that objective.*

The time horizon underlying a company's strategic intent is *long term*. Ambitious companies almost invariably begin with strategic intents that are out of proportion to their immediate capabilities and market positions. But they set aggressive long-term strategic objectives and pursue them relentlessly, sometimes even obsessively, over a 10- to 20-year period. In the 1960s, Komatsu, Japan's leading earthmoving equipment company, was less than one-third the size of Caterpillar, had little market presence outside Japan, and depended on its small bulldozers for most of its revenue. But Komatsu's strategic intent was to eventually "encircle Caterpillar" with a broader product line and then compete globally against Caterpillar. By the late 1980s, Komatsu was the industry's second-ranking company, with a strong sales presence in North America, Europe, and Asia plus a product line that included industrial robots and semiconductors as well as a broad selection of earthmoving equipment.

Often, a company's strategic intent takes on a heroic character, serving as a rallying cry for managers and employees alike to go all out and do their very best. Canon's strategic intent in copying equipment was to "Beat Xerox." Komatsu's motivating battle cry was "Beat Caterpillar." When Yamaha overtook Honda in the motorcycle

---

[8]The concept of strategic intent is described in more detail in Gary Hamel and C. K. Pralahad, "Strategic Intent," *Harvard Business Review* 89, no. 3 (May–June 1989), pp. 63–76; this section draws upon their pioneering discussion. See, also, Michael A. Hitt, Beverly B. Tyler, Camilla Hardee, and Daewoo Park, "Understanding Strategic Intent in the Global Marketplace," *Academy of Management Executive*, 9, no. 2 (May 1995), pp. 12–19. For a discussion of the different ways that companies can position themselves in the marketplace, see Michael E. Porter, "What Is Strategy?" *Harvard Business Review* 74, no. 6 (November–December 1996), pp. 65–67.

market, Honda responded with "Yamaha wo tsubusu" ("We will crush, squash, slaughter Yamaha"). The strategic intent of the U.S. government's Apollo space program was to land a person on the moon ahead of the Soviet Union. Throughout the 1980s, Wal-Mart's strategic intent was to "overtake Sears" as the largest U.S. retailer (a feat accomplished in 1991). Netscape's running battle with Microsoft over whose Internet browser software will reign supreme prompted employees to hang "Beat Microsoft" banners in Netscape's offices. In such instances, strategic intent signals a deep-seated commitment to winning—unseating the industry leader or remaining the industry leader (and becoming more dominant in the process) or otherwise beating long odds to gain a significantly stronger business position. Small, capably managed enterprises determined to achieve ambitious strategic objectives exceeding their present reach and resources often prove to be more formidable competitors than larger, cash-rich companies with modest strategic intents.

The Need for Long-Range and Short-Range Objectives

Objective setting should result in both long-range and short-range performance targets. Absent an impending crisis or pressing reason to bolster a company's long-term position and future performance, managers are prone to focus on the near term and place a higher priority on what has to be done to hit this year's numbers. The trouble with giving too high a priority to short-term objectives, of course, is the potential for managers to neglect actions aimed at enhancing a company's long-term business position and sustaining its capacity to generate good results over the long term. Setting bold, long-range performance targets and then putting pressure on managers to show progress in achieving them helps balance the priorities between better near-term results and actions calculated to ensure the company's competitiveness and financial performance down the road. A strong commitment to achieving long-range objectives forces managers to begin taking actions *now* to reach desired performance levels *later*. (A company that has an objective of doubling its sales within five years can't wait until the third or fourth year of its five-year strategic plan to begin growing its sales and customer base!)

By spelling out the near-term results to be achieved, short-range objectives indicate the *speed* at which management wants the organization to progress as well as the *level of performance* being aimed for over the next two or three periods. Short-range objectives can be identical to long-range objectives anytime an organization is already performing at the targeted long-term level. For instance, if a company has an ongoing objective of 15 percent profit growth every year and is currently achieving this objective, then the company's long-range and short-range profit objectives coincide. The most important situation where short-range objectives differ from long-range objectives occurs when managers are trying to elevate organizational performance and cannot reach the long-range/ongoing target in just one year. Short-range objectives then serve as stairsteps or milestones.

How Much Stretch Should Objectives Entail?

As a starter, objectives should be set high enough to produce outcomes at least incrementally better than current performance. But incremental improvements are not necessarily sufficient, especially if current performance levels are subpar. At a minimum, a company's financial objectives must aim high enough to generate the resources to execute the chosen strategy proficiently. But an "enough-to-get-by" mentality is not the way to approach objective setting. Arriving at an appropriate set of performance targets requires considering what performance is possible in light of external conditions, what performance other comparably situated companies are achieving, what performance it will take to please shareholders, what performance is required for long-term competitive success, and what performance the organization is capable of achieving when pushed. Ideally, objectives ought to serve as a managerial tool for truly *stretching an organization to reach its full poten-* *tial;* this means setting them high enough to be *challenging*—to energize the organization and its strategy.

> *Company performance targets should require organizational stretch.*

However, there is a school of thought that objectives should be set boldly and aggressively high—above levels that many organizational members would consider "realistic." The idea here is that *more* organizational creativity and energy is unleashed when stretch objectives call for achieving performance levels well beyond the reach of the enterprise's immediate resources and capabilities. One of the most avid practitioners of setting bold, audacious objectives and challenging the organization to go all out to achieve them is General Electric, arguably the world's best-managed corporation. Jack Welch, GE's CEO, believes in setting stretch targets that seem "impossible" and then challenging the organization to go after them. Throughout the 1960s, 1970s, and 1980s, GE's operating margins hovered around 10 percent and its sales-to-inventory ratio averaged about five turns per year. In 1991, Welch set stretch targets for 1995 of at least a 16 percent operating margin and 10 inventory turns. Welch's letter to the shareholders in the company's 1995 annual report said:

> 1995 has come and gone, and despite a heroic effort by our 220,000 employees, we fell short on both measures, achieving a 14.4 percent operating margin and almost seven turns. But in stretching for these "impossible" targets, we learned to do things faster than we would have going after "doable" goals, and we have enough confidence now to set new stretch targets of at least 16 percent operating margin and more than 10 turns by 1998.

GE's philosophy is that setting very aggressive stretch targets pushes the organization to move beyond being only as good as what is deemed doable to being as good as it possibly can be. GE's management believes challenging the company to achieve the impossible improves the quality of the organization's effort, promotes a can-do spirit, and builds self-confidence. Hence, a case can be made that objectives ought to be set at levels *above* what is doable with a little extra effort; there's merit in setting stretch targets that require something approaching a heroic degree of organizational effort.

Objectives Are Needed at All Organizational Levels

For strategic thinking and strategy-driven decision making to permeate organization behavior, performance targets must be established not only for the organization as a whole but also for each of the organization's separate businesses, product lines, functional areas, and departments. Only when each unit's strategic and financial objectives support achievement of the company's strategic and financial objectives is the objective-setting process sufficiently complete to conclude that each part of the organization knows its strategic role and that the various organizational units are on board in helping the whole organization move down the chosen strategic path.

The Need for Top-Down Objective-Setting To appreciate why a company's objective-setting process needs to be more top-down than bottom-up, consider the following example. Suppose the senior executives of a diversified corporation establish a corporate profit objective of $5 million for next year. Suppose further, after discussion between corporate management and the general managers of the firm's five different businesses, each business is given a stretch profit objective of $1 million by year-end (i.e., if the five business divisions contribute $1 million each in profit, the corporation can reach its $5 million profit objective). A concrete result has thus been agreed on and translated into measurable action commitments at two levels in the managerial hierarchy. Next, suppose the general manager of business unit X, after some analysis and discussion with functional area managers, concludes that reaching the $1 million profit objective will require selling 100,000 units at an average price of $50 and producing them at an average cost of $40 (a $10 profit margin times 100,000 units equals $1 million profit). Consequently, the general manager and the manufacturing manager settle on a production objective of 100,000 units at a unit cost of $40; and the general manager and the marketing manager agree on a sales objective of 100,000 units and a target selling price of $50. In turn, the marketing manager breaks the sales objective of 100,000 units into unit sales targets for each sales territory, each item in the product line, and each salesperson. It is logical for organizationwide objectives and strategy to be established first so they can *guide* objective setting and strategy making at lower levels. Top-down objective setting and strategizing steer lower-level units toward objectives and strategies that take their cues from those of the total enterprise.

A top-down process of setting companywide performance targets first and then insisting that the financial and strategic performance targets established for business units, divisions, functional departments, and operating units be directly connected to the achievement of company objectives has two powerful advantages. One, it helps produce *cohesion* among the objectives and strategies of different parts of the organization. Two, it helps *unify internal efforts* to move the company along the chosen strategic course. If top management, in the interest of involving a broad spectrum of organizational members, allows objective setting to start at the bottom levels of an organization without the benefit of companywide performance targets as a guide, then lower-level organizational units have no basis for connecting their performance targets to the company's. Letting organizationwide objectives be the product of whatever priorities and targets bubble up from below simply leaves too much room for the objectives and strategies of lower-level organizational units to be uncoordinated with each other and lacking in what makes good business sense for the company as a whole. Bottom-up objective setting, with little or no guidance from above, nearly always signals an absence of strategic leadership on the part of senior executives.

CRAFTING A STRATEGY: THE THIRD DIRECTION-SETTING TASK

Organizations need strategies to guide *how* to achieve objectives and *how* to pursue the organization's business mission and strategic vision. Strategy making is all about *how*—how to achieve performance targets, how to outcompete rivals, how to achieve sustainable competitive advantage, how to strengthen the enterprise's long-term business position, how to make management's strategic vision for the company a reality. A strategy is needed for the company as a whole, for each business the company is in, and for each functional piece of each business—R&D, purchasing, production, sales and marketing, finance, customer service, information systems, and so on. An organization's overall strategy emerges from the *pattern of actions already initiated and the plans managers have for fresh moves*. In forming a strategy out of the many feasible options, a manager acts as a forger of responses to market change, a seeker of new opportunities, and a synthesizer of the different moves and approaches taken at various times in various parts of the organization.[9]

The strategy-making spotlight, however, needs to be kept trained on the important facets of management's game plan for running the enterprise—those actions that determine what market position the company is trying to stake out and that underpin whether the company will succeed. Low-priority issues (whether to increase the advertising budget, raise the dividend, locate a new plant in country X or country Y) and routine managerial housekeeping (whether to own or lease company vehicles, how to reduce sales force turnover) are not basic to the strategy, even though they must be dealt with. Strategy is inherently action-oriented; it concerns what to do and when to do it. Unless there is action, unless something happens, unless somebody does something, strategic thinking and planning simply go to waste and, in the end, amount to nothing.

An organization's strategy evolves over time. The future is too unknowable for management to plan a company's strategy in advance and encounter no reason for changing one piece or another as time passes. Reacting and responding to unpredictable happenings in the surrounding environment is a normal and necessary part of the strategy-making process. There is always something new to react to and some new strategic window opening up—whether from new competitive developments, budding trends in buyer needs and expectations, unexpected increases or decreases in costs, mergers and acquisitions among major industry players, new regulations, the raising or lowering of trade barriers, or countless other events that make it desirable to alter first one then another aspect of the present strategy.[10] This is why the task of crafting strategy is never ending. And it is why a company's actual strategy turns out to be a blend of managerial plans and intentions and as-needed reactions to fresh developments.

While most of the time a company's strategy evolves incrementally, there are occasions when a company can function as an industry revolutionary by creating a rule-breaking strategy that redefines the industry and how it operates. A strategy can challenge fundamental conventions by reconceiving a product or service (like creating a single-use, disposable camera or a digital camera), redefining the marketplace (the growing potential for electronic commerce on the Internet is allowing companies to market their products anywhere at any time rather than being restricted to making their products available at particular locations during normal shopping times), or redrawing industry boundaries (consumers can now get their credit cards from Shell Oil or General Motors, or have their checking account at Charles Schwab, or get a home mortgage from Merrill Lynch, or get a family-style meal for takeout at the Boston Market or the supermarket).[11]

Basic Concept

An organization's strategy deals with the game plan for moving the company into an attractive business position and building a sustainable competitive advantage.

A company's **actual strategy** *usually turns out to be both more and less than the* **planned strategy** *as new strategy features are added and others are deleted in response to newly emerging conditions.*

---

[9]Henry Mintzberg, "The Strategy Concept II: Another Look at Why Organizations Need Strategies," *California Management Review* 30, no. 1 (Fall 1987), pp. 25–32.

[10]Henry Mintzberg and J. A. Waters, "Of Strategies, Deliberate and Emergent," *Strategic Management Journal*, 6 (1985), pp.257–72.

[11]For an in-depth discussion of revolutionary strategies, see Gary Hamel, "Strategy as Revolution," *Harvard Business Review* 74, no. 4 (July–August 1996), pp. 69–82.

The Strategy-Making Pyramid

As we emphasized in the opening chapter, strategy making is not just a task for senior executives. In large enterprises, decisions about what business approaches to take and what new moves to initiate involve senior executives in the corporate office, heads of business units and product divisions, the heads of major functional areas within a business or division (manufacturing, marketing and sales, finance, human resources, and the like), plant managers, product managers, district and regional sales managers, and lower-level supervisors. In diversified enterprises, strategies are initiated at four distinct organization levels. There's a strategy for the company and all of its businesses as a whole (*corporate strategy*). There's a strategy for each separate business the company has diversified into (*business strategy*). Then there is a strategy for each specific functional unit within a business (*functional strategy*)—each business usually has a production strategy, a marketing strategy, a finance strategy, and so on. And, finally, there are still narrower strategies for basic operating units—plants, sales districts and regions, and departments within functional areas (*operating strategy*). Figure 2.1 shows the strategy-making pyramids for a diversified company and a single-business company. In single-business enterprises, there are only three levels of strategy (business strategy, functional strategy, and operating strategy) unless diversification into other businesses becomes an active consideration. Table 2.1 highlights the kinds of strategic actions that distinguish each of the four strategy-making levels.

Corporate Strategy

Corporate strategy is the overall managerial game plan for a diversified company. *Corporate strategy extends companywide—an umbrella over all a diversified company's businesses. It consists of the moves made to establish business positions* in different industries and the approaches used to manage the company's group of businesses. Figure 2.2 depicts the core elements that identify a diversified company's corporate strategy. Crafting corporate strategy for a diversified company involves four kinds of initiatives:

Basic Concept

Corporate strategy *concerns how a diversified company intends to establish business positions in different industries and the actions and approaches employed to improve the performance of the group of businesses the company has diversified into.*

1. *Making the moves to establish positions in different businesses and achieve diversification.* In a diversified company, a key piece of corporate strategy is how many and what kinds of businesses the company should be in—specifically, what industries should the company participate in and whether to enter the industries by starting a new business or acquiring another company (an established leader, an up-and-coming company, or a troubled company with turnaround potential). This piece of corporate strategy establishes whether diversification is based narrowly in a few industries or broadly in many industries and whether the different businesses will be related or unrelated.

2. *Initiating actions to boost the combined performance of the businesses the firm has diversified into.* As positions are created in the chosen industries, corporate strategy making concentrates on ways to strengthen the long-term competitive positions and profitabilities of the businesses the firm has invested in. Corporate parents can help their business subsidiaries be more successful by financing additional capacity and efficiency improvements, by supplying missing skills and managerial know-how, by acquiring another company in the same industry and merging the two operations into a stronger business, and/or by acquiring new businesses that strongly complement existing businesses. Management's overall strategy for improving companywide performance usually involves pursuing rapid-growth strategies in the most

FIGURE 2.1   The Strategy-Making Pyramid

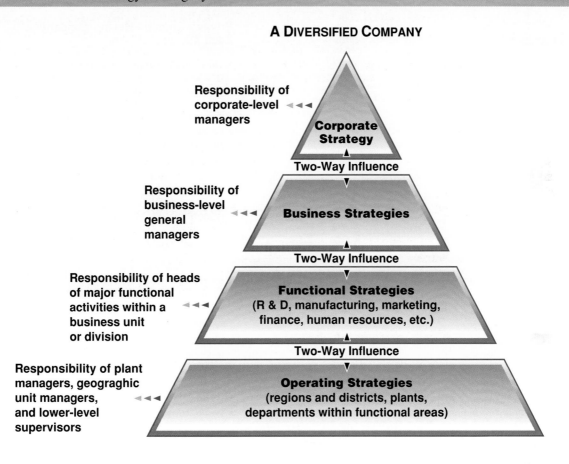

TABLE 2.1 How the Strategy-Making Task Tends to Be Shared

Strategy Level	Lead Responsibility	Primary Strategy-Making Concerns at Each Managerial Level
• Corporate strategy	• CEO, other key executives (decisions are typically reviewed/approved by boards of directors)	• Building and managing a high-performing portfolio of business units (making acquisitions, strengthening existing business positions, divesting businesses that no longer fit into management's plans) • Capturing the synergy among related business units and turning it into competitive advantage • Establishing investment priorities and steering corporate resources into businesses with the most attractive opportunities • Reviewing/revising/unifying the major strategic approaches and moves proposed by business-unit managers
• Business strategies	• General manager/head of business unit (decisions are typically reviewed/approved by a senior executive or a board of directors)	• Devising moves and approaches to compete successfully and to secure a competitive advantage • Forming responses to changing external conditions • Uniting the strategic initiatives of key functional departments • Taking action to address company-specific issues and operating problems
• Functional strategies	• Functional managers (decisions are typically reviewed/approved by business-unit head)	• Crafting moves and approaches to support business strategy and to achieve functional/departmental performance objectives • Reviewing/revising/unifying strategy-related moves and approaches proposed by lower-level managers
• Operating strategies	• Field-unit heads/lower-level managers within functional areas (decisions are reviewed/approved by functional area head/department head)	• Crafting still narrower and more specific approaches/moves aimed at supporting functional and business strategies and at achieving operating-unit objectives

promising businesses, keeping the other core businesses healthy, initiating turnaround efforts in weak-performing businesses with potential, and divesting businesses that are no longer attractive or that don't fit into management's long-range plans.

3. *Pursuing ways to capture the synergy among related business units and turn it into competitive advantage.* When a company diversifies into businesses with related technologies, similar operating characteristics, common distribution channels or customers, or some other synergistic relationship, it gains competitive advantage potential not open to a company that diversifies into totally unrelated businesses. Related diversification presents opportunities to transfer skills, share expertise or facilities, and leverage a common brand name, thereby reducing overall costs, strengthening the competitive-

FIGURE 2.2   Identifying the Corporate Strategy of a Diversified Company

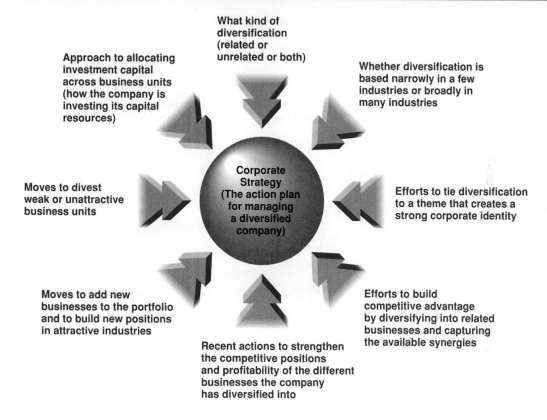

ness of some of the company's products, or enhancing the capabilities of particular business units—any of which can represent a significant source of competitive advantage and provide a basis for greater overall corporate profitability.

4. *Establishing investment priorities and steering corporate resources into the most attractive business units.* A diversified company's different businesses are usually not equally attractive from the standpoint of investing additional funds. This facet of corporate strategy making involves channeling resources into areas where earnings potentials are higher and away from areas where they are lower. Corporate strategy may include divesting business units that are chronically poor performers or those in an increasingly unattractive industry. Divestiture frees up unproductive investments for redeployment to promising business units or for financing attractive new acquisitions.

Corporate strategy is crafted at the highest levels of management. Senior corporate executives normally have lead responsibility for devising corporate strategy and for choosing among whatever recommended actions bubble up from lower-level managers. Key business-unit heads may also be influential, especially in strategic decisions affecting the businesses they head. Major strategic decisions are usually reviewed and approved by the company's board of directors.

Business Strategy

The term *business strategy* (or business-level strategy) refers to the managerial game plan for a single business. It is mirrored in the pattern of approaches and moves crafted by management to produce successful performance in *one specific*

FIGURE 2.3   Identifying Strategy for a Single-Business Company

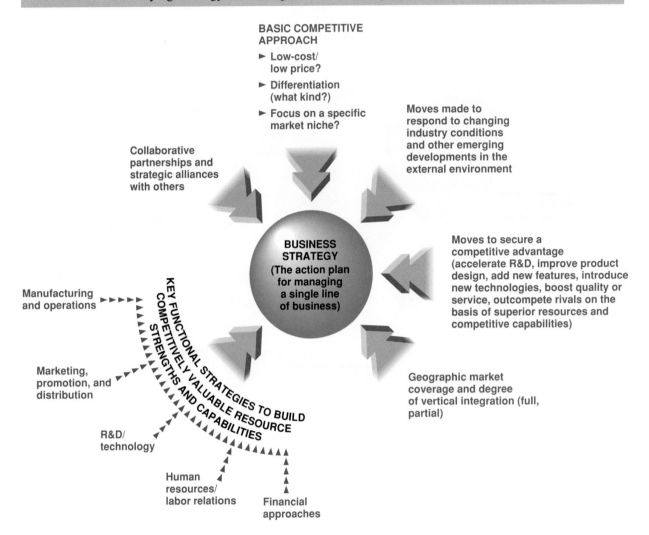

BASIC COMPETITIVE
APPROACH
► Low-cost/
  low price?
► Differentiation
  (what kind?)
► Focus on a specific
  market niche?

Moves made to
respond to changing
industry conditions
and other emerging
developments in the
external environment

Collaborative
partnerships and
strategic alliances
with others

Moves to secure a
competitive advantage
(accelerate R&D, improve product
design, add new features, introduce
new technologies, boost quality or
service, outcompete rivals on the
basis of superior resources and
competitive capabilities)

BUSINESS
STRATEGY
(The action plan
for managing
a single line
of business)

KEY FUNCTIONAL STRATEGIES TO BUILD
COMPETITIVELY VALUABLE RESOURCE
STRENGTHS AND CAPABILITIES

Manufacturing
and operations

Marketing,
promotion, and
distribution

R&D/
technology

Human
resources/
labor relations

Financial
approaches

Geographic market
coverage and degree
of vertical integration (full,
partial)

Basic Concept

Business strategy *concerns the
actions and the approaches
crafted by management to
produce successful performance
in one specific line of business;
the central business strategy
issue is how to build a stronger
long-term competitive position.*

line of business. The core elements of business strategy are illustrated in
Figure 2.3. For a stand-alone single-business company, corporate strategy
and business strategy are one and the same since there is only one business
to form a strategy for. The distinction between corporate strategy and
business strategy is relevant only for diversified firms.

*The central thrust of business strategy is how to build and strengthen the
company's long-term competitive position in the marketplace.* Toward this
end, business strategy is concerned principally with (1) forming responses
to changes under way in the industry, the economy at large, the regulatory
and political arena, and other relevant areas, (2) crafting competitive moves
and market approaches that can lead to sustainable competitive advantage,
(3) building competitively valuable competencies and capabilities, (4) uniting the strategic initiatives of functional departments, and (5) addressing specific
strategic issues facing the company's business.

Clearly, business strategy encompasses whatever moves and new approaches
managers deem prudent in light of market forces, economic trends and develop-

ments, buyer needs and demographics, new legislation and regulatory requirements, and other such broad external factors. *A good strategy is well-matched to the external situation;* as the external environment changes in significant ways, then adjustments in strategy are made on an as-needed basis. Whether a company's response to external change is quick or slow tends to be a function of how long events must unfold before managers can assess their implications and how much longer it then takes to form a strategic response. Some external changes, of course, require little or no response, while others call for significant strategy alterations. On occasion, external factors change in ways that pose a formidable strategic hurdle—for example, cigarette manufacturers face a tough challenge holding their own against mounting efforts to combat smoking.

What separates a powerful business strategy from a weak one is the strategist's ability *to forge a series of moves and approaches capable of producing sustainable competitive advantage.* With a competitive advantage, a company has good prospects for above-average profitability and success in the industry. Without competitive advantage, a company risks being outcompeted by stronger rivals and locked into mediocre performance. Crafting a business strategy that yields sustainable competitive advantage has three facets: (1) deciding what product/service attributes (lower costs and prices, a better product, a wider product line, superior customer service, emphasis on a particular market niche) offer the best chance to win a competitive edge; (2) developing skills, expertise, and competitive capabilities that set the company apart from rivals; and (3) trying to insulate the business as much as possible from the effects of competition.

> *A business strategy is powerful if it produces a sizable and sustainable competitive advantage; it is weak if it results in competitive disadvantage.*

A company's strategy for competing is typically both offensive and defensive—some actions are aggressive and amount to direct challenges to competitors' market positions; others aim at countering competitive pressures and the actions of rivals. Three of the most frequently used competitive approaches are (1) striving to be the industry's low-cost producer (thereby aiming for a cost-based competitive advantage over rivals); (2) pursuing differentiation based on such advantages as quality, performance, service, styling, technological superiority, or unusually good value; and (3) focusing on a narrow market niche and winning a competitive edge by doing a better job than rivals of serving the special needs and tastes of niche members.

Internally, business strategy involves taking actions to develop the capabilities and resource strengths needed to achieve competitive advantage. Successful business strategies usually aim at building strong competencies and competitive capabilities in one or more activities crucial to strategic success and then using them as a basis for winning a competitive edge over rivals. A *distinctive competence* is something a firm does especially well in comparison to rival companies. It thus represents a source of competitive strength. Distinctive competencies can relate to R&D, mastery of a technological process, manufacturing capability, sales and distribution, customer service, or anything else that is a competitively important aspect of creating, producing, or marketing the company's product or service. *A distinctive competence is a basis for competitive advantage because it represents expertise or capability that rivals don't have and cannot readily match.*

> *Having superior internal resource strengths and competitive capabilities is an important way to outcompete rivals.*

On a broader internal front, business strategy must also aim at uniting strategic initiatives in the various functional areas of business (purchasing, production, R&D, finance, human resources, sales and marketing, distribution, and customer service). Strategic actions are needed in each functional area to *support* the company's competitive approach and overall business strategy. Strategic unity and coordination across the various functional areas add power to the business strategy.

Business strategy also extends to action plans for addressing any special strategy-related issues unique to the company's competitive position and internal situation (such as whether to add new capacity, replace an obsolete plant, increase R&D funding for a promising technology, reduce burdensome interest expenses, form strategic alliances and collaborative partnerships, or build competitively valuable competencies and capabilities). Such custom tailoring of strategy to fit a company's specific situation is one of the reasons why companies in the same industry employ different business strategies.

Lead responsibility for business strategy falls in the lap of the manager in charge of the business. Even if the business head does not personally wield a heavy hand in the business strategy-making process, preferring to delegate much of the task to others, he or she is still accountable for the strategy and the results it produces. The business head, as chief strategist for the business, has at least two other responsibilities. The first is seeing that supporting strategies in each of the major functional areas of the business are well conceived and consistent with each other. The second is getting major strategic moves approved by higher authority (the board of directors and/or corporate-level officers) if needed and keeping them informed of important new developments, deviations from plan, and potential strategy revisions. In diversified companies, business-unit heads may have the additional obligation of making sure business-level objectives and strategy conform to corporate-level objectives and strategy themes.

Functional Strategy

The term *functional strategy* refers to the managerial game plan for a particular functional activity, business process, or key department within a business. A company's marketing strategy, for example, represents the managerial game plan for running the marketing part of the business. A company's new product development strategy represents the managerial game plan for keeping the company's product lineup fresh and in tune with what buyers are looking for. A company needs a functional strategy for every competitively relevant business activity and organizational unit—for R&D, production, marketing, customer service, distribution, finance, human resources, information technology, and so on. Functional strategies, while narrower in scope than business strategies, add relevant detail to the overall business game plan by setting forth the actions, approaches, and practices to be employed in managing a particular functional department or business process or key activity. They aim at establishing or strengthening specific competencies and competitive capabilities calculated to enhance the company's market position and standing with its customers. The primary role of a functional strategy is to *support* the company's overall business strategy and competitive approach. Well-executed functional strategies give the enterprise competitively valuable competencies, capabilities, and resource strengths. A related role is to create a managerial roadmap for achieving the functional area's objectives and mission. Thus, functional strategy in the production/manufacturing area represents the game plan for *how* manufacturing activities will be managed to support business strategy and achieve the manufacturing department's objectives and mission. Functional strategy in the finance area consists of *how* financial activities will be managed in supporting business strategy and achieving the finance department's objectives and mission.

Lead responsibility for conceiving strategies for each of the various important business functions and processes is normally delegated to the respective functional

Basic Concept

Functional strategy *concerns the managerial game plan for running a major functional activity or process within a business—R&D, production, marketing, customer service, distribution, finance, human resources, and so on; a business needs as many functional strategies as it has strategy-critical activities.*

department heads and activity managers unless the business-unit head decides to exert a strong influence. In crafting strategy, the manager of a particular business function or activity ideally works closely with key subordinates and touches base with the managers of other functions/processes and the business head often. If functional or activity managers plot strategy independent of each other or the business head, they open the door for uncoordinated or conflicting strategies. Compatible, collaborative, mutually reinforcing functional strategies are essential for the overall business strategy to have maximum impact. Plainly, a business's marketing strategy, production strategy, finance strategy, customer service strategy, new product development strategy, and human resources strategy should be in sync rather than serving their own narrower purposes. Coordination and consistency among the various functional and process/activity strategies are best accomplished during the deliberation stage. If inconsistent functional strategies are sent up the line for final approval, it is up to the business head to spot the conflicts and get them resolved.

Operating Strategy

Operating strategies concern the even narrower strategic initiatives and approaches for managing key operating units (plants, sales districts, distribution centers) and for handling daily operating tasks with strategic significance (advertising campaigns, materials purchasing, inventory control, maintenance, shipping). Operating strategies, while of limited scope, add further detail and completeness to functional strategies and to the overall business plan. Lead responsibility for operating strategies is usually delegated to frontline managers, subject to review and approval by higher-ranking managers.

Even though operating strategy is at the bottom of the strategy-making pyramid, its importance should not be downplayed. For example, a major plant that fails in its strategy to achieve production volume, unit cost, and quality targets can undercut the achievement of company sales and profit objectives and wreak havoc with the whole company's strategic efforts to build a quality image with customers. One cannot reliably judge the strategic importance of a given action by the organizational or managerial level where it is initiated.

Frontline managers are part of an organization's strategy-making team because many operating units have strategy-critical performance targets and need to have strategic action plans in place to achieve them. A regional manager needs a strategy customized to the region's particular situation and objectives. A plant manager needs a strategy for accomplishing the plant's objectives, carrying out the plant's part of the company's overall manufacturing game plan, and dealing with any strategy-related problems that exist at the plant. A company's advertising manager needs a strategy for getting maximum audience exposure and sales impact from the ad budget. The following two examples illustrate how operating strategy supports higher-level strategies:

- A company with a low-price, high-volume business strategy and a need to achieve low manufacturing costs launches a companywide effort to boost worker productivity by 10 percent. To contribute to the productivity-boosting objective: (1) the manager of employee recruiting develops a strategy for interviewing and testing job applicants that is thorough enough to weed out all but the most highly motivated, best-qualified candidates; (2) the manager of information systems devises a way to use office technology to boost the productivity of office workers; (3) the employee compensation manager

Basic Concept

Operating strategies concern how to manage frontline organizational units within a business (plants, sales districts, distribution centers) and how to perform strategically significant operating tasks (materials purchasing, inventory control, maintenance, shipping, advertising campaigns).

devises a creative incentive plan to reward increased output by manufacturing employees; and (4) the purchasing manager launches a program to obtain new efficiency-increasing tools and equipment in quicker, less costly fashion.

- A distributor of plumbing equipment emphasizes quick delivery and accurate order-filling as keystones of its customer service approach. To support this strategy, the warehouse manager (1) develops an inventory stocking strategy that allows 99.9 percent of all orders to be completely filled without back-ordering any item and (2) institutes a warehouse staffing strategy that allows any order to be shipped within 24 hours.

Uniting the Strategy-Making Effort

The previous discussion underscores that *a company's strategic plan is a collection of strategies* devised by different managers at different levels in the organizational hierarchy. The larger the enterprise, the more points of strategic initiative it has. Management's direction-setting effort is not complete until the separate layers of strategy are unified into a coherent, supportive pattern. Ideally the pieces and layers of strategy should fit together like the pieces of a picture puzzle. Unified objectives and strategies don't emerge from an undirected process where managers set objectives and craft strategies independently. Indeed, functional and operating-level managers have a duty to work in harmony to set grassroots performance targets and invent frontline strategic actions that will help achieve business objectives and increase the power of business strategy.

Objectives and strategies that are unified from top to bottom of the organizational hierarchy require a team effort.

Harmonizing objectives and strategies piece by piece and level by level can be tedious and frustrating, requiring numerous consultations and meetings, periodic strategy review and approval processes, the experience of trial and error, and months (sometimes years) of consensus building and collaborative effort. The politics of gaining strategic consensus and the battle of trying to keep all managers and departments focused on what's best for the total enterprise (as opposed to what's best for their departments or careers) are often big obstacles in unifying the layers of objectives and strategies and producing the desired degree of cooperation and collaboration.[12] Broad consensus is particularly difficult when there is ample room for opposing views and disagreement. Managerial discussions about an organization's mission and vision, long-term direction, objectives, and strategies often provoke heated debate and strong differences of opinion.

Consistency between business strategy and functional/operating strategies comes from the collaborative efforts of functional and operating-level managers to set performance targets and invent strategic actions in their respective areas of responsibility that contribute directly to achieving business objectives and improving the execution of business strategy.

Figure 2.4 portrays the networking of objectives and strategies through the managerial hierarchy. The two-way arrows indicate that there are simultaneous bottom-up and top-down influences on missions, objectives, and strategies at each level. Furthermore, there are two-way influences across the related businesses of a diversified company and across the related processes, functions, and operating activities within a business. These vertical and horizontal linkages, if man-

---

[12]Functional managers are sometimes more interested in doing what is best for their own areas, building their own empires, and consolidating their personal power and organizational influence than they are in cooperating with other functional managers to unify behind the overall business strategy. As a result, it's easy for functional area support strategies to conflict, thereby forcing the business-level general manager to spend time and energy refereeing functional strategy conflicts and building support for a more unified approach.

FIGURE 2.4 The Networking of Strategic Visions, Missions, Objectives, and Strategies in the Strategy-Making Pyramid

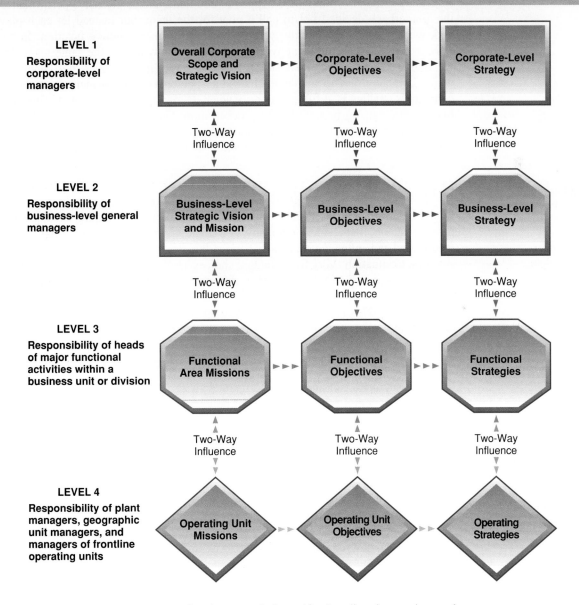

aged in a way that promotes coordination, can help unify the direction-setting and strategy-making activities of many managers into a mutually reinforcing pattern. The tighter that coordination is enforced, the tighter the linkages in the missions, objectives, and strategies of the various organizational units. Tight linkages safeguard against organizational units straying from the company's charted strategic course.

As a practical matter, however, corporate and business strategic visions, objectives, and strategies need to be clearly outlined and communicated down the line before much progress can be made in direction setting and strategy making at the functional and operating levels. Direction and guidance need to flow from the corporate level to the business level and from the business level to functional and grassroots operating levels. The strategic disarray that occurs in an organization when senior managers don't exercise strong top-down direction setting and strategic leadership is akin to what would happen to a football team's offensive performance if the quarterback decided not to call a play for the team, but instead let each player pick whatever play he thought would work best at his respective position. In business, as in sports, all the strategy makers in a company are on the same team. They are obligated to perform their strategy-making tasks in a manner that benefits the whole company, not in a manner that suits personal or departmental interests. A company's strategy is at full power only when its many pieces are united. This means that the strategizing process has to proceed more from the top down than from the bottom up. Lower-level managers cannot do good strategy making without understanding the company's long-term direction and higher-level strategies.

THE FACTORS THAT SHAPE A COMPANY'S STRATEGY

Many situational considerations enter into crafting strategy. Figure 2.5 depicts the primary factors that shape a company's strategic approaches. The interplay of these factors and the influence that each has on the strategy-making process vary from situation to situation. Very few strategic choices are made in the same context—even in the same industry, situational factors differ enough from company to company that the strategies of rivals turn out to be quite distinguishable from one another rather than imitative. This is why carefully sizing up all the various situational factors, both external and internal, is the starting point in crafting strategy.

Societal, Political, Regulatory, and Citizenship Considerations

What an enterprise can and cannot do strategywise is always constrained by what is legal, by what complies with government policies and regulatory requirements, and by what is in accord with societal expectations and the standards of good community citizenship. Outside pressures also come from other sources—special-interest groups, the glare of investigative reporting, a fear of unwanted political action, and the stigma of negative opinion. Societal concerns over health and nutrition, alcohol and drug abuse, environmental pollution, sexual harassment, corporate downsizing, and the impact of plant closings on local communities have caused many companies to temper or revise aspects of their strategies. American concerns over jobs lost to foreign imports and political debate over how to cure the chronic U.S. trade deficit are driving forces in the strategic decisions of Japanese and European companies to locate plants in the United States. Heightened consumer awareness about the hazards of saturated fat and cholesterol have driven most food products companies to phase out high-fat ingredients and substitute low-fat ingredients, despite the extra costs.

Societal, political, regulatory, and citizenship factors limit the strategic actions a company can or should take.

Factoring in societal values and priorities, community concerns, and the potential for onerous legislation and regulatory requirements is a regular part of external situation analysis at more and more companies. Intense public pressure and adverse media coverage make such a practice prudent. The task of making an organization's strategy socially responsible means (1) conducting organizational activities within the bounds of what is considered to be in the general public interest; (2) responding positively to emerging societal priorities and expectations; (3) demonstrating a willingness to take action ahead of regulatory confrontation; (4) balancing stockholder interests against the larger interests of society as a whole; and (5) being a good citizen in the community.

FIGURE 2.5 Factors Shaping the Choice of Company Strategy

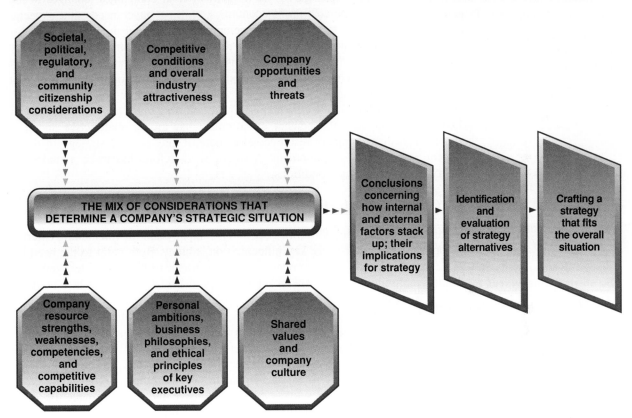

STRATEGY-SHAPING FACTORS EXTERNAL TO THE COMPANY

Societal, political, regulatory, and community citizenship considerations

Competitive conditions and overall industry attractiveness

Company opportunities and threats

THE MIX OF CONSIDERATIONS THAT DETERMINE A COMPANY'S STRATEGIC SITUATION

Conclusions concerning how internal and external factors stack up; their implications for strategy

Identification and evaluation of strategy alternatives

Crafting a strategy that fits the overall situation

Company resource strengths, weaknesses, competencies, and competitive capabilities

Personal ambitions, business philosophies, and ethical principles of key executives

Shared values and company culture

STRATEGY-SHAPING FACTORS INTERNAL TO THE COMPANY

Corporate social responsibility is showing up in company mission statements. John Hancock, for example, concludes its mission statement with the following sentence:

> In pursuit of this mission, we will strive to exemplify the highest standards of business ethics and personal integrity; and shall recognize our corporate obligation to the social and economic well-being of our community.

At Union Electric, a St. Louis-based utility company, the following statement is official corporate policy:

> As a private enterprise entrusted with an essential public service, we recognize our civic responsibility in the communities we serve. We shall strive to advance the growth and welfare of these communities and shall participate in civic activities which fulfill that goal—for we believe this is both good citizenship and good business.

Competitive Conditions and Overall Industry Attractiveness

An industry's competitive conditions and overall attractiveness are big strategy-determining factors. A company's strategy has to be tailored to the nature and mix of competitive factors in play—price, product quality, performance features, service, warranties, and so on. When competitive conditions intensify significantly, a company must respond with strategic actions to protect its position. Competitive weakness on the part of one or more rivals may signal the need for a strategic offensive.

Furthermore, fresh moves on the part of rival companies, changes in the industry's price-cost-profit economics, shifting buyer needs and expectations, and new technological developments often alter the requirements for competitive success and mandate reconsideration of strategy. The industry environment, as it exists now and is expected to exist later, thus has a direct bearing on a company's best competitive strategy option and where it should concentrate its efforts. *A company's strategy can't produce real market success unless it is well-matched to the industry and competitive situation.* When a firm concludes its industry environment has grown unattractive and it is better off investing company resources elsewhere, it may begin a strategy of disinvestment and eventual abandonment. A strategist, therefore, has to be a student of industry and competitive conditions.

The Company's Market Opportunities and External Threats

The particular business opportunities open to a company and the threatening external developments that it faces are key influences on strategy. Both point to the need for strategic action. A company's strategy needs to be deliberately aimed at capturing its best growth opportunities, especially the ones that hold the most promise for building sustainable competitive advantage and enhancing profitability. Likewise, strategy should be geared to providing a defense against external threats to the company's well-being and future performance. For strategy to be successful, it has to be well matched to market opportunities and threatening external developments; this usually means crafting offensive moves to capitalize on the company's most promising market opportunities and crafting defensive moves to protect the company's competitive position and long-term profitability.

Company Resource Strengths, Competencies, and Competitive Capabilities

One of the most pivotal strategy-shaping internal considerations is whether a company has or can acquire the resources, competencies, and capabilities needed to execute a strategy proficiently. An organization's resources, competencies, and competitive capabilities are important strategy-making considerations because of (1) the competitive strengths they provide in capitalizing on a particular opportunity, (2) the competitive edge they may give a firm in the marketplace, and (3) the potential they have for becoming a cornerstone of strategy. The best path to competitive advantage is found where a firm has competitively valuable resources and competencies, where rivals do not have matching or offsetting resources and competencies, and where rivals can't develop comparable capabilities except at high cost and/or over an extended period of time.

Even if an organization has no outstanding competencies and capabilities (and many do not), managers still must tailor strategy to fit the enterprise's particular resources and capabilities. It is foolish to develop a strategic plan that cannot be executed with the resources and capabilities a firm is able to assemble. In short, *strategy must be well-matched to a company's resource strengths and weaknesses and to its competitive capabilities.* Experience shows that winning strategies aim squarely at capitalizing on a company's resource strengths and neutralizing its resource deficiencies and skills gaps. An organization's resource strengths make some strategies and market opportunities attractive to pursue; likewise, its resource deficiencies, its gaps in important skills and know-how, and the weaknesses in its present competitive market position make the pursuit of certain strategies or opportunities risky (or even out of the question). Consequently, what resources, competencies, and capabilities a company has and how competitively valuable they are is a very relevant strategy-making consideration.

The Personal Ambitions, Business Philosophies, and Ethical Beliefs of Managers

Managers do not dispassionately assess what strategic course to steer. Their choices are often influenced by their own vision of how to compete and how to position the enterprise and by what image and standing they want the company to have. Both casual observation and formal studies indicate that managers' ambitions, values, business philosophies, attitudes toward risk, and ethical beliefs have important influences on strategy.[13] Sometimes the influence of a manager's personal values, experiences, and emotions is conscious and deliberate; at other times it may be unconscious. As one expert noted in explaining the relevance of personal factors to strategy, "People have to have their hearts in it."[14]

The personal ambitions, business philosophies, and ethical beliefs of managers are usually stamped on the strategies they craft.

Several examples of how business philosophies and personal values enter into strategy making are particularly noteworthy. Ben Cohen and Jerry Greenfield, cofounders and major stockholders in Ben and Jerry's Homemade Ice Cream, have consistently insisted that the company's strategy be supportive of social causes of their choosing and incorporate a strong social mission. Japanese managers are strong proponents of strategies that take a long-term view and that aim at building market share and competitive position. In contrast, some U.S. and European executives have drawn criticism for overemphasizing short-term profits at the expense of long-term competitive positioning because of pressures to meet investors' quarterly and annual earnings expectations. Japanese companies also display a quite different philosophy regarding the role of suppliers. Their preferred supplier strategy is to enter into long-term partnership arrangements with key suppliers because they believe that working closely with the same supplier year after year improves the quality and reliability of component parts, facilitates just-in-time delivery, and reduces inventory carrying costs. In U.S. and European companies, the traditional strategic approach has been to play suppliers off against one another, doing business on a short-term basis with whoever offers the best price and promises acceptable quality.

---

[13]The role of personal values, individual ambitions, and managerial philosophies in strategy making has long been recognized and documented. The classic sources are William D. Guth and Renato Tagiuri, "Personal Values and Corporate Strategy," *Harvard Business Review* 43, no. 5 (September–October 1965), pp. 123–32; Kenneth R. Andrews, *The Concept of Corporate Strategy*, 3rd ed. (Homewood, Ill.: Richard D. Irwin, 1987), chap. 4; and Richard F. Vancil, "Strategy Formulation in Complex Organizations," *Sloan Management Review* 17, no. 2 (Winter 1986), pp. 4–5.

[14]Andrews, *The Concept of Corporate Strategy,* p. 63.

Attitudes toward risk also have a big influence on strategy. Risk-avoiders are inclined toward "conservative" strategies that minimize downside risk, have a quick payback, and produce sure short-term profits. Risk-takers lean more toward opportunistic strategies where visionary moves can produce a big payoff over the long term. Risk-takers prefer innovation to imitation and bold strategic offensives to defensive moves to protect the status quo.

Managerial values also shape the ethical quality of a firm's strategy. Managers with strong ethical convictions take pains to see that their companies observe a strict code of ethics in all aspects of the business. They expressly forbid such practices as accepting or giving kickbacks, badmouthing rivals' products, and buying political influence with political contributions. Instances where a company's strategic actions run afoul of high ethical standards include charging excessive interest rates on credit card balances, employing bait-and-switch sales tactics, continuing to market products suspected of having safety problems, and using ingredients that are known health hazards.

The Influence of Shared Values and Company Culture on Strategy

An organization's policies, practices, traditions, philosophical beliefs, and ways of doing things combine to create a distinctive culture. Typically, the stronger a company's culture the more that culture is likely to shape the strategic actions it decides to employ, sometimes even dominating the choice of strategic moves. This is because culture-related values and beliefs are so embedded in management's strategic thinking and actions that they condition how the enterprise responds to external events. Such firms have a culture-driven bias about how to handle strategic issues and what kinds of strategic moves it will consider or reject. Strong cultural influences partly account for why companies gain reputations for such strategic traits as leadership in technological advance and product innovation, dedication to superior craftsmanship, a proclivity for financial wheeling and dealing, a desire to grow rapidly by acquiring other companies, having a strong people orientation and being a good company to work for, or unusual emphasis on customer service and total customer satisfaction.

A company's values and culture can dominate the kinds of strategic moves it considers or rejects.

In recent years, more companies have articulated the core beliefs and values underlying their business approaches. One company expressed its core beliefs and values like this:

> We are market-driven. We believe that functional excellence, combined with teamwork across functions and profit centers, is essential to achieving superb execution. We believe that people are central to everything we will accomplish. We believe that honesty, integrity, and fairness should be the cornerstone of our relationships with consumers, customers, suppliers, stockholders, and employees.

Wal-Mart's founder, Sam Walton, was a fervent believer in frugality, hard work, constant improvement, dedication to customers, and genuine care for employees. The company's commitment to these values is deeply ingrained in its strategy of low prices, good values, friendly service, productivity through the intelligent use of technology, and hard-nosed bargaining with suppliers.[15] At Hewlett-Packard, the

---

[15]Sam Walton with John Huey, *Sam Walton: Made in America* (New York: Doubleday, 1992); and John P. Kotter and James L. Heskett, *Corporate Culture and Performance* (New York: Free Press, 1992), pp. 17 and 36.

company's basic values, known internally as "the HP Way," include sharing the company's success with employees, showing trust and respect for employees, providing customers with products and services of the greatest value, being genuinely interested in providing customers with effective solutions to their problems, making profit a high stockholder priority, avoiding the use of long-term debt to finance growth, individual initiative and creativity, teamwork, and being a good corporate citizen.[16] At both Wal-Mart and Hewlett-Packard, the value systems are deeply ingrained and widely shared by managers and employees. Whenever this happens, values and beliefs are more than an expression of nice platitudes; they become a way of life within the company and they mold company strategy.[17]

LINKING STRATEGY WITH ETHICS

Strategy ought to be ethical. It should involve rightful actions, not wrongful ones; otherwise it won't pass the test of moral scrutiny. This means more than conforming to what is legal. Ethical and moral standards go beyond the prohibitions of law and the language of "thou shalt not" to the issues of *duty* and the language of "should do and should not do." Ethics concerns human duty and the principles on which this duty rests.[18]

Every strategic action a company takes should be ethical.

Every business has an ethical duty to each of five constituencies: owners/shareholders, employees, customers, suppliers, and the community at large. Each of these constituencies affects the organization and is affected by it. Each is a stakeholder in the enterprise, with certain expectations as to what the enterprise should do and how it should do it.[19] Owners/shareholders, for instance, rightly expect a return on their investment. Even though investors may individually differ in their preferences for profits now versus profits later, their tolerances for greater risk, and their enthusiasm for exercising social responsibility, business executives have a moral duty to pursue profitable management of the owners' investment.

A company's duty to employees arises out of respect for the worth and dignity of individuals who devote their energies to the business and who depend on the business for their economic well-being. Principled strategy making requires that employee-related decisions be made equitably and compassionately, with concern for due process and for the impact that strategic change has on employees' lives. At best, the chosen strategy should promote employee interests as concerns compensation, career opportunities, job security, and overall working conditions. At worst, the chosen strategy should not disadvantage employees. Even in crisis situations where adverse employee impact cannot be avoided, businesses have an ethical duty to minimize whatever hardships have to be imposed in the form of workforce reductions, plant closings, job transfers, relocations, retraining, and loss of income.

A company has ethical duties to owners, employees, customers, suppliers, the communities where it operates, and the public at large.

The duty to the customer arises out of expectations that attend the purchase of a good or service. Inadequate appreciation of this duty led to product liability laws and a host of regulatory agencies to protect consumers. All kinds of strategy-related

---

[16]Kotter and Heskett, *Corporate Culture and Performance*, pp. 60–61.

[17]For another example of the impact of values and beliefs, see Richard T. Pascale, "Perspectives on Strategy: The Real Story behind Honda's Success," in Glenn Carroll and David Vogel, *Strategy and Organization: A West Coast Perspective* (Marshfield, Mass.: Pitman Publishing, 1984), p. 60.

[18]Harry Downs, "Business Ethics: The Stewardship of Power," working paper provided to the authors.

[19]Ibid.

ethical issues still abound, however. Should a seller voluntarily inform consumers that its product contains ingredients that, though officially approved for use, are suspected of having potentially harmful effects? Is it ethical for the makers of alcoholic beverages to sponsor college events, given that many college students are under 21? Is it ethical for cigarette manufacturers to advertise at all (even though it is legal)? Is it ethical for manufacturers to stonewall efforts to recall products they suspect have faulty parts or defective designs? Is it ethical for supermarkets and department store retailers to lure customers with highly advertised "loss-leader" prices on a few select items, but then put high markups on popular or essential items?

A company's ethical duty to its suppliers arises out of the market relationship that exists between them. They are both partners and adversaries. They are partners in the sense that the quality of suppliers' parts affects the quality of a firm's own product. They are adversaries in the sense that the supplier wants the highest price and profit it can get while the buyer wants a cheaper price, better quality, and speedier service. A company confronts several ethical issues in its supplier relationships. Is it ethical to purchase goods from foreign suppliers who employ child labor and/or pay substandard wages and/or have sweatshop working conditions in their facilities? Is it ethical to threaten to cease doing business with a supplier unless the supplier agrees not to do business with key competitors? Is it ethical to reveal one supplier's price quote to a rival supplier? Is it ethical to accept gifts from suppliers? Is it ethical to pay a supplier in cash? Is it ethical *not* to give present suppliers advance warning of the intent to discontinue using what they have supplied and to switch to components supplied by other enterprises?

A company's ethical duty to the community at large stems from its status as a citizen of the community and as an institution of society. Communities and society are reasonable in expecting businesses to be good citizens—to pay their fair share of taxes for fire and police protection, waste removal, streets and highways, and so on, and to exercise care in the impact their activities have on the environment, on society, and on the communities in which they operate. For example, is it ethical for a liquor firm to advertise its products on TV at times when these ads are likely to be seen by children and people under the age of 21? Is it ethical for liquor firms to even advertise on TV at any time? Some years ago, an oil company was found to have spent $2 million on environmental conservation and $4 million advertising its virtue and good deeds—actions that seem deliberately manipulative and calculated to mislead. A company's community citizenship is ultimately demonstrated by whether it refrains from acting in a manner contrary to the well-being of society and by the degree to which it supports community activities, encourages employees to participate in community activities, handles the health and safety aspects of its operations, accepts responsibility for overcoming environmental pollution, relates to regulatory bodies and employee unions, and exhibits high ethical standards.

Carrying Out Ethical Responsibilities   Management, not constituent groups, is responsible for managing the enterprise. Thus, it is management's perceptions of its ethical duties and of constituents' claims that drive whether and how strategy is linked to ethical behavior. Ideally, managers weigh strategic decisions from each constituent's point of view and, where conflicts arise, strike a rational, objective, and equitable balance among the interests of all five constituencies. If any of the five constituencies conclude that management is not doing its duty, they have their own avenues for recourse. Concerned investors can protest at the annual shareholders' meeting, appeal to the board of directors, or sell their stock. Concerned employees can unionize and

---

ILLUSTRATION CAPSULE 8   Harris Corporation's Commitments to Its Stakeholders

Harris Corporation is a major supplier of information, communication, and semiconductor products, systems, and services to commercial and governmental customers throughout the world. The company utilizes advanced technologies to provide innovative and cost-effective solutions for processing and communicating data, voice, text, and video information. The company had sales of $3.6 billion in 1996, and it employs nearly 23,000 people. In a recent annual report, the company set forth its commitment to satisfying the expectations of its stakeholders:

Customers—For customers, our objective is to achieve ever-increasing levels of satisfaction by providing quality products and services with distinctive benefits on a timely and continuing basis worldwide. Our relationships with customers will be forthright and ethical, and will be conducted in a manner to build trust and confidence.

Shareholders—For shareholders, the owners of our company, our objective is to achieve sustained growth in earnings-per-share. The resulting stock-price appreciation combined with dividends should provide our shareholders with a total return on investment that is competitive with similar investment opportunities.

Employees—The people of Harris are our company's most valuable asset, and our objective is for every employee to be personally involved in and share the success of the business. The company is committed to providing an environment that encourages all employees to make full use of their creativity and unique talents; to providing equitable compensation, good working conditions, and the opportunity for personal development and growth which is limited only by individual ability and desire.

Suppliers—Suppliers are a vital part of our resources. Our objective is to develop and maintain mutually beneficial partnerships with suppliers who share our commitment to achieving increasing levels of customer satisfaction through continuing improvements in quality, service, timeliness, and cost. Our relationships with suppliers will be sincere, ethical, and will embrace the highest principles of purchasing practice.

Communities—Our objective is to be a responsible corporate citizen. This includes support of appropriate civic, educational, and business activities, respect for the environment, and the encouragement of Harris employees to practice good citizenship and support community programs. Our greatest contribution to our communities is to be successful so that we can maintain stable employment and create new jobs.

Source: 1988 Annual Report.

---

bargain collectively, or they can seek employment elsewhere. Customers can switch to competitors. Suppliers can find other buyers or pursue other market alternatives. The community and society can do anything from staging protest marches and urging boycotts to stimulating political and governmental action.[20]

A management that truly cares about business ethics and corporate social responsibility is proactive rather than reactive in linking strategic action and ethics. It steers away from ethically or morally questionable business opportunities (for example, in late 1996, Anheuser-Busch announced it would no longer run its beer commercials on MTV). It won't do business with suppliers that engage in activities the company does not condone. It produces products that are safe for its customers to use. It operates a workplace environment that is safe for employees. It recruits and hires employees whose values and behavior match the company's principles and ethical standards. It acts to reduce any environmental pollution it causes. It cares about how it does business and whether its actions reflect integrity and high ethical standards. Illustration Capsule 8 describes Harris Corporation's ethical commitments to its stakeholders.

---

[20]Ibid.

Tests of a Winning Strategy

What are the criteria for weeding out candidate strategies? How can a manager judge which strategic option is best for the company? What are the standards for determining whether a strategy is successful or not? Three tests can be used to evaluate the merits of one strategy over another and to gauge how good a strategy is:

1. *The Goodness of Fit Test*—A good strategy is tailored to fit the company's internal and external situation—without tight situational fit, there's real question whether a strategy appropriately matches the requirements for market success.

2. *The Competitive Advantage Test*—A good strategy leads to sustainable competitive advantage. The bigger the competitive edge that a strategy helps build, the more powerful and effective it is.

3. *The Performance Test*—A good strategy boosts company performance. Two kinds of performance improvements are the most telling of a strategy's caliber: gains in profitability and gains in the company's competitive strength and long-term market position.

Strategic options that clearly come up short on one or more of these tests are candidates to be dropped from further consideration. The strategic option that best meets all three tests can be regarded as the best or most attractive strategic alternative. Once a strategic commitment is made and enough time elapses to see results, these same tests can be used to determine whether the chosen strategy qualifies as a winning strategy. The more a strategy fits the situation, builds sustainable competitive advantage, and boosts company performance, the more it qualifies as a winner.

Strategic Management Principle

A winning strategy must fit the enterprise's situation, build sustainable competitive advantage, and improve company performance.

There are, of course, some additional criteria for judging the merits of a particular strategy: completeness and coverage of all the bases, internal consistency among all the pieces of strategy, clarity, the degree of risk involved, and flexibility. These criteria are useful supplements and certainly ought to be looked at, but they can in no way replace the three tests posed above.

APPROACHES TO PERFORMING THE STRATEGY-MAKING TASK

Companies and managers go about the task of developing strategic plans differently. In small, owner-managed companies, strategy making usually occurs informally, emerging from the experiences, personal observations and assessments, verbal exchanges and debates, and entrepreneurial judgments of a few key people at the top—with perhaps some data gathering and number-crunching analysis involved. Often, the resulting strategy exists mainly in the entrepreneur's own mind and in oral understandings with key subordinates, but is not reduced to writing and laid out in a formal document called a strategic plan.

Large companies, however, tend to develop their strategic plans more formally (occasionally using prescribed procedures, forms, and timetables) and in deeper detail. There is often considerable data gathering, situational analysis, and intense study of particular issues, involving the broad participation of managers at many organizational levels and numerous meetings to probe, question, sort things out, and hammer out the pieces of the strategy. The larger and more diverse an enterprise, the more managers feel it is better to have a structured process with timetables, studies and debate, and written plans that receive official approval from up the line.

Along with variations in the organizational process of formulating strategy are variations in how managers personally participate in analyzing the company's situation and deliberating what strategy to pursue. The four basic strategy-making styles managers use are:[21]

The Master Strategist Approach   Some managers take on the role of chief strategist and chief entrepreneur, singlehandedly exercising *strong* influence over assessments of the situation, over the strategy alternatives that are explored, and over the details of strategy. This does not mean that the manager personally does all the work; it means that the manager personally becomes the chief architect of strategy and wields a proactive hand in shaping some or all of the major pieces of strategy. Master strategists act as strategy commanders and have a big ownership stake in the chosen strategy.

The Delegate-It-to-Others Approach   Here the manager in charge delegates pieces and maybe all of the strategy-making task to others, perhaps a group of trusted subordinates, a cross-functional task force, or self-directed work teams with authority over a particular process or function. The manager then personally stays in touch with how the strategy deliberations are progressing, offers guidance when appropriate, smiles or frowns as trial balloon recommendations are informally run by him/her for reaction, and reserves final approval until the strategy proposals are formally presented, considered, modified (if needed), and deemed ready for implementation. While strategy delegators may leave little of their own imprint on individual pieces of the strategy proposals presented for approval, they often must still play an integrative role in bringing the separate strategy elements devised by others into harmony and in fleshing out any pieces not delegated. They also must bear ultimate responsibility for the caliber of the strategy-making efforts of subordinates, so their confidence in the business judgments of those to whom strategy-making tasks are delegated must be well placed. This strategy-making style allows for broad participation and input from many managers and areas, plus it gives managers some flexibility in picking and choosing from the smorgasbord of strategic ideas that bubble up from below. The big weakness of delegation is that its success depends heavily on the business judgments and strategy-making skills of those to whom the strategy-making tasks are delegated—for instance, the strategizing efforts of subordinates may prove too short-run oriented and reactive, dealing more with how to address today's problems than with positioning the enterprise and adapting its resources to capture tomorrow's opportunities. Subordinates may not have either the clout or the inclination to tackle changing major components of the present strategy.[22] A second weakness of chartering a group of subordinates to develop strategy is that it sends the wrong signal: Strategy development isn't important enough to warrant a big claim on the boss's personal time and attention. Moreover, a manager can end up too detached from the process to

---

[21]This discussion is based on David R. Brodwin and L. J. Bourgeois, "Five Steps to Strategic Action," in Glenn Carroll and David Vogel, *Strategy and Organization: A West Coast Perspective* (Marshfield, Mass.: Pitman Publishing, 1984), pp. 168–78.

[22]For a case in point of where the needed strategy changes were too big for a chartered group of subordinates to address, see Thomas M. Hout and John C. Carter, "Getting It Done: New Roles for Senior Executives," *Harvard Business Review* 73 no. 6 (November–December 1995), pp. 140–44.

exercise strategic leadership if the group's deliberations bog down in disagreement or go astray, either of which set the stage for rudderless direction setting and/or ill-conceived strategy.

The Collaborative Approach   This is a middle approach whereby the manager enlists the help of key peers and subordinates in hammering out a consensus strategy. The strategy that emerges is the joint product of all concerned, with the collaborative effort usually being personally led by the manager in charge. The collaborative approach is well suited to situations where strategic issues cut across traditional functional and departmental lines, where there's a need to tap into the ideas and problem-solving skills of people with different backgrounds, expertise, and perspectives, and where it makes sense to give as many people as feasible a participative role in shaping the strategy that emerges and help win their wholehearted commitment to implementation. Involving teams of people to dissect complex situations and find market-driven, customer-driven solutions is becoming increasingly necessary in many businesses. Not only are many strategic issues too far-reaching or too involved for a single manager to handle but they often are cross-functional and cross-departmental in nature, thus requiring the contributions of many disciplinary experts and the collaboration of managers from different parts of the organization to decide upon sound strategic actions. A valuable strength of this strategy-making style is that the group of people charged with crafting the strategy can easily include the very people who will also be charged with implementing it. Giving people an influential stake in crafting the strategy they must later help implement is not only motivational but also means they can be held accountable for putting the strategy into place and making it work—the oft-used excuse of "It wasn't my idea to do this" won't fly.

The Champion Approach   In this style, the manager is interested neither in a big personal stake in the details of strategy nor in the time-consuming task of leading others through participative brainstorming or a collaborative "group wisdom" exercise. Rather, the idea is to encourage individuals and teams to develop, champion, and implement sound strategies on their own initiative. Here important pieces of company strategy originate with the "doers" and the "fast-trackers." Executives serve as judges, evaluating the strategy proposals needing their approval. This approach works well in large diversified corporations where the CEO cannot personally orchestrate strategy making in each of many business divisions. For headquarters executives to capitalize on having people in the enterprise who can see strategic opportunities that they cannot, they must delegate the initiative for strategy making to managers at the business-unit level. Corporate executives may well articulate general strategic themes as organizationwide guidelines for strategic thinking, but the key to good strategy making is stimulating and rewarding new strategic initiatives conceived by a champion who believes in the opportunity and badly wants the blessing to go after it. With this approach, the total strategy ends up being the sum of the championed initiatives that get approved.

These four basic managerial approaches to forming a strategy illuminate several aspects about how companies arrive at a planned strategy. When the manager in charge personally functions as the chief architect of strategy, the choice of what strategic course to steer is a product of his/her own vision about how to position the enterprise and of the manager's ambitions, values, business philosophies, and entrepreneurial judgment about what moves to make next. Highly centralized strategy making works fine when the manager in charge has a powerful, insightful vision of where to head and how to get there. The primary weakness of the master strategist approach is that the caliber of the strategy depends so heavily on one person's strategy-making skills and entrepreneurial acumen. It also breaks down in large enterprises where many strategic initiatives are needed and the strategy-making task is too complex for one person to handle alone.

Of the four basic approaches managers can use in crafting strategy, none is inherently superior—each has strengths and weaknesses and each is workable in the "right" situation.

On the other hand, the group approach to strategy making has its risks too. Sometimes, the strategy that emerges from group consensus is a middle-of-the-road compromise, void of bold, creative initiative. Other times, it represents political consensus, with the outcome shaped by influential subordinates, by powerful functional departments, or by majority coalitions that have a common interest in promoting their particular version of what the strategy ought to be. Politics and the exercise of power are most likely to come into play in situations where there is no strong consensus on what strategy to adopt; this opens the door for a political solution to emerge. The collaborative approach is conducive to political strategic choices as well, since powerful departments and individuals have ample opportunity to try to build a consensus for their favored strategic approach. The big weakness of a delegate-it-to-others approach is the potential lack of sufficient top-down direction and strategic leadership.

The strength of the champion approach is also its weakness. The value of championing is that it encourages people at lower organizational levels to be alert for profitable market opportunities, to propose innovative strategies to capture them, and to take on responsibility for new business ventures. Individuals with attractive strategic proposals are given the latitude and resources to try them out, thus helping renew an organization's capacity for innovation and growth. On the other hand, a series of championed actions, because they spring from many places in the organization and can fly off in many directions, are not likely to form a coherent pattern or result in a clear strategic direction for the company as a whole without some strong top-down leadership. With championing, the chief executive has to work at ensuring that what is championed adds power to the overall organization strategy; otherwise, strategic initiatives may be launched in directions that have no integrating links or overarching rationale. Another weakness of the championing approach is that top executives will be more intent on protecting their reputations for prudence than on supporting sometimes revolutionary strategies, in which case innovative ideas can be doused by corporate orthodoxy.[23] It is usually painful and laborious for a lowly employee to champion an out-of-the-ordinary idea up the chain of command.

All four styles of handling the strategy-making task thus have strengths and weaknesses. All four can succeed or fail depending on whether they are used in the right circumstances, on how well the approach is managed, and on the strategy-making skills and judgments of the individuals involved.

KEY POINTS

Management's direction-setting task involves charting a company's future strategic path, setting objectives, and forming a strategy. Early on in the direction-setting process, managers need to address the question of "What is our business and what will it be?" Management's views and conclusions about the organization's future

[23]See Hamel, "Strategy as Revolution," pp. 80–81.

course, the market position it should try to occupy, and the business activities to be pursued constitute a *strategic vision* for the company. A strategic vision indicates management's aspirations for the organization, providing a panoramic view of "what businesses we want to be in, where we are headed, and the kind of company we are trying to create." It spells out a direction and describes the destination. Effective visions are clear, challenging, and inspiring; they prepare a firm for the future, and they make sense in the marketplace. A well-conceived, well-said mission/vision statement serves as a beacon of long-term direction, helps channel organizational efforts along the path management has committed to following, builds a strong sense of organizational identity, and creates employee buy-in.

The second direction-setting step is to establish *strategic* and *financial* objectives for the organization to achieve. Objectives convert the business mission and strategic vision into specific performance targets. The agreed-on objectives need to spell out precisely how much by when, and they need to require a significant amount of organizational stretch. Objectives are needed at all organizational levels.

The third direction-setting step entails forming strategies to achieve the objectives set in each area of the organization. A corporate strategy is needed to achieve corporate-level objectives; business strategies are needed to achieve business-unit performance objectives; functional strategies are needed to achieve the performance targets set for each functional department; and operating-level strategies are needed to achieve the objectives set in each operating and geographic unit. In effect, an organization's strategic plan is a collection of unified and interlocking strategies. As shown in Table 2.1, different strategic issues are addressed at each level of managerial strategy making. Typically, the strategy-making task is more top-down than bottom-up. Lower-level strategies should support and complement higher-level strategy and contribute to the achievement of higher-level, companywide objectives.

Strategy is shaped by both outside and inside considerations. The major external considerations are societal, political, regulatory, and community factors; competitive conditions and overall industry attractiveness; and the company's market opportunities and threats. The primary internal considerations are company strengths, weaknesses, and competitive capabilities; managers' personal ambitions, philosophies, and ethics; and the company's culture and shared values. A good strategy must be well matched to all these situational considerations. In addition, a good strategy must lead to sustainable competitive advantage and improved company performance.

There are essentially four basic ways to manage the strategy formation process in an organization: the master strategist approach where the manager in charge personally functions as the chief architect of strategy, the delegate-it-to-others approach, the collaborative approach, and the champion approach. All four have strengths and weaknesses. All four can succeed or fail depending on how well the approach is managed and depending on the strategy-making skills and judgments of the individuals involved.

| SUGGESTED READINGS | Campbell, Andrew, and Laura Nash. *A Sense of Mission: Defining Direction for the Large Corporation.* Reading, Mass.: Addison-Wesley, 1993. |

Campbell, Andrew, and Laura Nash. *A Sense of Mission: Defining Direction for the Large Corporation.* Reading, Mass.: Addison-Wesley, 1993.

Collins, James C. and Jerry I. Porras. " Building Your Company's Vision." *Harvard Business Review* 74, no.5 (September–October 1996), pp. 65–77.

Drucker, Peter. "The Theory of the Business." *Harvard Business Review* 72, no. 5 (September–October 1994), pp. 95–104.

Hamel, Gary, and C. K. Prahalad. "Strategic Intent." *Harvard Business Review* 67, no. 3 (May–June 1989), pp. 63–76.

———. "Strategy as Stretch and Leverage." *Harvard Business Review* 71, no. 2 (March–April 1993), pp. 75–84.

Hamel, Gary. "Strategy as Revolution," *Harvard Business Review* 74 no. 4 (July–August 1996), pp. 69–82.

Hammer, Michael, and James Champy. *Reengineering the Corporation.* New York: HarperBusiness, 1993, chap. 9.

Ireland, R. Duane, and Michael A. Hitt. "Mission Statements: Importance, Challenge, and Recommendations for Development." *Business Horizons* (May–June 1992), pp. 34–42.

Kahaner, Larry. "What You Can Learn from Your Competitors' Mission Statements." *Competitive Intelligence Review* 6 no. 4 (Winter 1995), pp. 35–40.

Lipton, Mark. "Demystifying the Development of an Organizational Vision." *Sloan Management Review* (Summer 1996), pp. 83–92.

McTavish, Ron. "One More Time: What Business Are You In?" *Long Range Planning* 28, no. 2 (April 1995), pp. 49–60.

Mintzberg, Henry. "Crafting Strategy." *Harvard Business Review* 65, no. 4 (July–August 1987), pp. 66–77.

Porter, Michael E. "What Is Strategy?" *Harvard Business Review* 74, no. 6 (November–December 1996), pp. 61–78.

Wilson, Ian. "Realizing the Power of Strategic Vision." *Long Range Planning* 25, no.5 (1992), pp. 18–28.

3

INDUSTRY AND COMPETITIVE ANALYSIS

Crafting strategy is an analysis-driven exercise, not a task where managers can get by with opinions, good instincts, and creative thinking. Judgments about what strategy to pursue need to flow directly from solid analysis of a company's external environment and internal situation. The two biggest considerations are (1) industry and competitive conditions (these are the heart of a single-business company's "external environment") and (2) a company's competitive capabilities, resources, internal strengths and weaknesses, and market position.

Figure 3.1 illustrates what is involved in sizing up a company's situation and deciding on a strategy. The analytical sequence is from strategic appraisal of the company's external and internal situation to identification of issues to evaluation of alternatives to choice of strategy. Accurate diagnosis of the company's situation is necessary managerial preparation for deciding on a sound long-term direction, setting appropriate objectives, and crafting a winning strategy. Without perceptive understanding of the strategic aspects of a company's macro- and microenvironments, the chances are greatly increased that managers will concoct a strategic game plan that doesn't fit the situation well, that holds little prospect for building competitive advantage, and that is unlikely to boost company performance.

This chapter examines the techniques of *industry and competitive analysis*, the term commonly used to refer to assessing the strategically relevant aspects of a company's *macroenvironment* or *business ecosystem*. In the next chapter, we'll cover the methods of *company situation analysis* and see how to appraise the strategy-shaping aspects of a firm's immediate *microenvironment*.

THE METHODS OF INDUSTRY AND COMPETITIVE ANALYSIS

Industries differ widely in their economic characteristics, competitive situations, and future profit prospects. The economic and competitive character of the trucking industry bears little resemblance to that of discount retailing. The economic and competitive traits of the fast-food business have little in common with those of providing Internet-related products or services. The cable-TV business is shaped by industry and competitive conditions radically different from those in the soft-drink business.

FIGURE 3.1   How Strategic Thinking and Strategic Analysis Lead to Good Strategic Choices

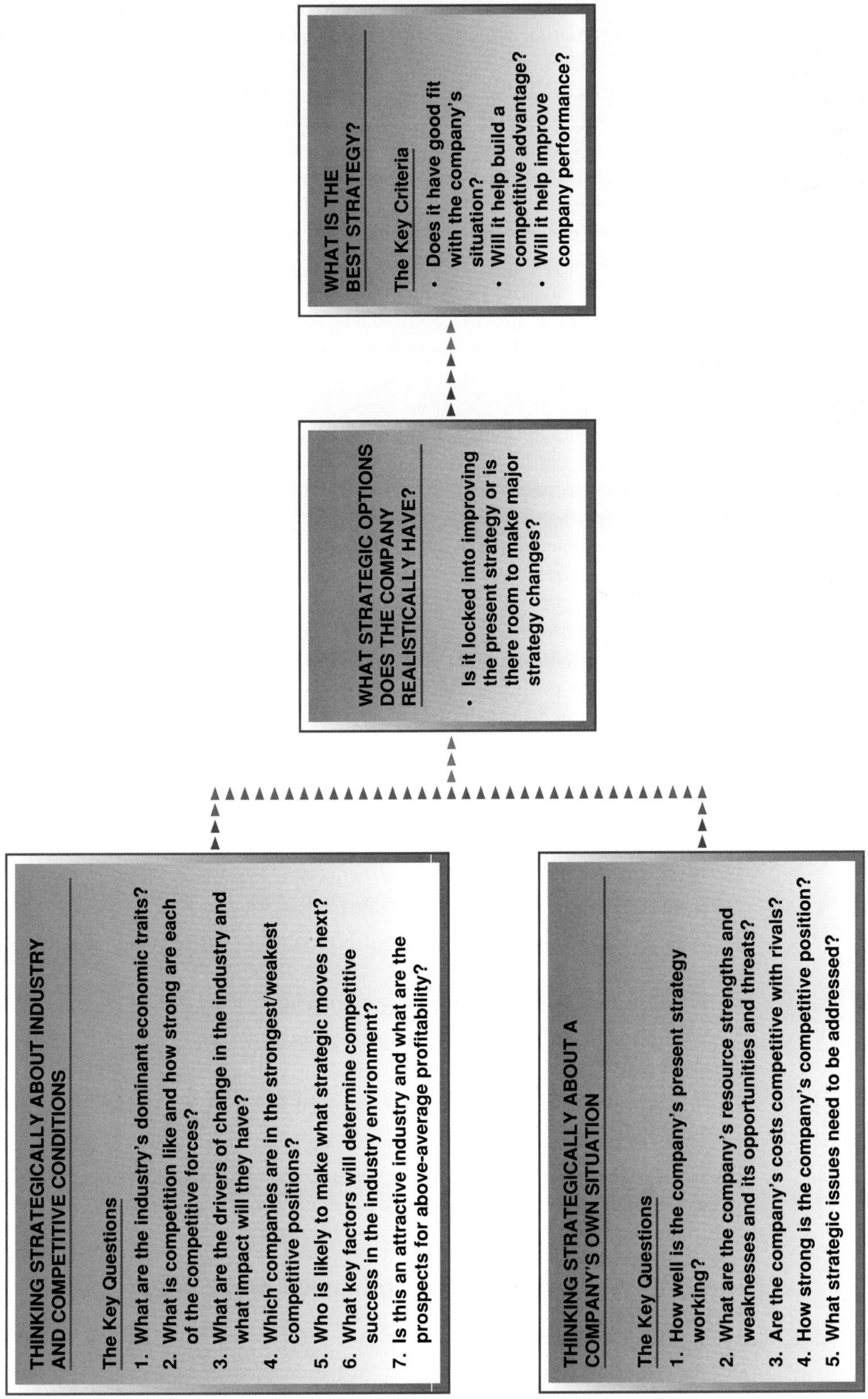

THINKING STRATEGICALLY ABOUT INDUSTRY AND COMPETITIVE CONDITIONS

The Key Questions

1. What are the industry's dominant economic traits?
2. What is competition like and how strong are each of the competitive forces?
3. What are the drivers of change in the industry and what impact will they have?
4. Which companies are in the strongest/weakest competitive positions?
5. Who is likely to make what strategic moves next?
6. What key factors will determine competitive success in the industry environment?
7. Is this an attractive industry and what are the prospects for above-average profitability?

THINKING STRATEGICALLY ABOUT A COMPANY'S OWN SITUATION

The Key Questions

1. How well is the company's present strategy working?
2. What are the company's resource strengths and weaknesses and its opportunities and threats?
3. Are the company's costs competitive with rivals?
4. How strong is the company's competitive position?
5. What strategic issues need to be addressed?

WHAT STRATEGIC OPTIONS DOES THE COMPANY REALISTICALLY HAVE?

• Is it locked into improving the present strategy or is there room to make major strategy changes?

WHAT IS THE BEST STRATEGY?

The Key Criteria

• Does it have good fit with the company's situation?
• Will it help build a competitive advantage?
• Will it help improve company performance?

The economic character of industries varies according to a number of factors: the overall size and market growth rate, the pace of technological change, the geographic boundaries of the market (which can extend from local to worldwide), the number and sizes of buyers and sellers, whether sellers' products are virtually identical or highly differentiated, the extent to which costs are affected by economies of scale, and the types of distribution channels used to access buyers. Competitive forces can be moderate in one industry and fierce, even cutthroat, in another. Moreover, industries differ widely in the degree of competitive emphasis put on price, product quality, performance features, service, advertising and promotion, and new product innovation. In some industries, price competition dominates the marketplace while in others the competitive emphasis is centered on quality or product performance or customer service or brand image/reputation. In other industries, the challenge is for companies to work cooperatively with suppliers, customers, and maybe even select competitors to create the next round of product innovations and open up a whole new vista of market opportunities (as we are witnessing in computer technology and telecommunications).

Managers are not prepared to decide on a long-term direction or a strategy until they have a keen understanding of the company's strategic situation— the exact nature of the industry and competitive conditions it faces and how these conditions match up with its resources and capabilities.

An industry's economic traits and competitive conditions and how they are expected to change determine whether its future profit prospects will be poor, average, or excellent. Industry and competitive conditions differ so much that leading companies in unattractive industries can find it hard to earn respectable profits, while even weak companies in attractive industries can turn in good performances.

Industry and competitive analysis uses a tool kit of concepts and techniques to get a clear fix on key industry traits, the intensity of competition, the drivers of industry change, the market positions and strategies of rival companies, the keys to competitive success, and the industry's future profit outlook. This tool kit provides a way of thinking strategically about any industry and drawing conclusions about whether the industry represents an attractive investment for company funds. It entails examining a company's business in the context of a much wider environment. Industry and competitive analysis aims at developing probing, insightful answers to seven questions:

1. What are the industry's dominant economic features?
2. What competitive forces are at work in the industry and how strong are they?
3. What are the drivers of change in the industry and what impact will they have?
4. Which companies are in the strongest/weakest competitive positions?
5. Who's likely to make what competitive moves next?
6. What key factors will determine competitive success or failure?
7. How attractive is the industry in terms of its prospects for above-average profitability?

The answers to these questions build understanding of a firm's surrounding environment and, collectively, form the basis for matching its strategy to changing industry conditions and competitive realities.

Question 1: What Are the Industry's Dominant Economic Features?

Because industries differ significantly in their character and structure, industry and competitive analysis begins with an overview of the industry's dominant economic features. As a working definition, we use the word *industry* to mean a group of firms whose products have so many of the same attributes that they compete for the same buyers. The factors to consider in profiling an industry's economic traits are fairly standard:

- Market size.
- Scope of competitive rivalry (local, regional, national, international, or global).
- Market growth rate and where the industry is in the growth cycle (early development, rapid growth and takeoff, early maturity, mature, saturated and stagnant, declining).
- Number of rivals and their relative sizes—is the industry fragmented with many small companies or concentrated and dominated by a few large companies?
- The number of buyers and their relative sizes.
- The prevalence of backward and forward integration.
- The types of distribution channels used to access buyers.
- The pace of technological change in both production process innovation and new product introductions.
- Whether the product(s)/service(s) of rival firms are highly differentiated, weakly differentiated, or essentially identical.
- Whether companies can realize economies of scale in purchasing, manufacturing, transportation, marketing, or advertising.
- Whether certain industry activities are characterized by strong learning and experience effects such that unit costs decline as *cumulative* output (and thus the experience of "learning by doing") grows.
- Whether high rates of capacity utilization are crucial to achieving low-cost production efficiency.
- Resource requirements and the ease of entry and exit.
- Whether industry profitability is above/below par.

Table 3.1 provides a sample profile of the economic character of the sulfuric acid industry.

An industry's economic features are important because of the implications they have for strategy. For example, in capital-intensive industries where investment in a single plant can run several hundred million dollars, a firm can spread the burden of high fixed costs by pursuing a strategy that promotes high utilization of fixed assets and generates more revenue per dollar of fixed-asset investment. Thus commercial airlines try to boost the revenue productivity of their multimillion-dollar jets by cutting ground time at airport gates (to get in more flights per day with the same plane) and by using multi-tiered price discounts to fill up otherwise empty seats. In industries characterized by one product advance after another, companies must spend enough time and money on R&D to keep their technical prowess and innovative capability abreast of competitors—a strategy of continuous product innovation becomes a condition of survival.

An industry's economic features help frame the window of strategic approaches a company can pursue.

In industries like semiconductors, strong *learning/experience* effects in manufacturing cause unit costs to decline about 20 percent each time *cumulative* production volume doubles. With a 20 percent experience curve effect, if the first

TABLE 3.1   A Sample Profile of the Dominant Economic Characteristics of the Sulfuric Acid Industry

Market Size: $400–$500 million annual revenues; 4 million tons total volume.

Scope of Competitive Rivalry: Primarily regional; producers rarely sell outside a 250-mile radius of plant due to high cost of shipping long distances.

Market Growth Rate: 2–3 percent annually.

Stage in Life Cycle: Mature.

Number of Companies in Industry: About 30 companies with 110 plant locations and capacity of 4.5 million tons. Market shares range from a low of 3 percent to a high of 21 percent.

Customers: About 2,000 buyers; most are industrial chemical firms.

Degree of Vertical Integration: Mixed; 5 of the 10 largest companies are integrated backward into mining operations and also forward in that sister industrial chemical divisions buy over 50 percent of the output of their plants; all other companies are engaged solely in the production of sulfuric acid.

Ease of Entry/Exit: Moderate entry barriers exist in the form of capital requirements to construct a new plant of minimum efficient size (cost equals $10 million) and ability to build a customer base inside a 250-mile radius of plant.

Technology/Innovation: Production technology is standard and changes have been slow; biggest changes are occurring in products—1–2 newly formulated specialty chemicals products are being introduced annually, accounting for nearly all of industry growth.

Product Characteristics: Highly standardized; the brands of different producers are essentially identical (buyers perceive little real difference from seller to seller).

Scale Economies: Moderate; all companies have virtually equal manufacturing costs but scale economies exist in shipping in multiple carloads to same customer and in purchasing large quantities of raw materials.

Learning and Experience Effects: Not a factor in this industry.

Capacity Utilization: Manufacturing efficiency is highest between 90–100 percent of rated capacity; below 90 percent utilization, unit costs run significantly higher.

Industry Profitability: Subpar to average; the commodity nature of the industry's product results in intense price-cutting when demand slackens, but prices firm up during periods of strong demand. Profits track the strength of demand for the industry's products.

Basic Concept

When strong economies of learning and experience result in declining unit costs as cumulative production volume builds, a strategy to become the largest-volume manufacturer can yield the competitive advantage of being the industry's lowest-cost producer.

1 million chips cost $100 each, by a production volume of 2 million the unit cost would be $80 (80 percent of $100), by a production volume of 4 million the unit would be $64 (80 percent of $80), and so on. When an industry is characterized by sizable economies of experience in its manufacturing operations, a company that first initiates production of a new-style product and develops a successful strategy to capture the largest market share gains sustainable competitive advantage as the low-cost producer.[1] The bigger the experience-curve effect, the bigger the cost advantage of the company with the largest *cumulative* production volume, as shown in Figure 3.2.

Table 3.2 presents some additional examples of how an industry's economic traits are relevant to managerial strategy making.

---

[1]There are a large number of studies of the size of the cost reductions associated with experience; the median cost reduction associated with a doubling of cumulative production volume is approximately 15 percent, but there is a wide variation from industry to industry. For a good discussion of the economies of experience and learning, see Pankaj Ghemawat, "Building Strategy on the Experience Curve," *Harvard Business Review* 64, no. 2 (March–April 1985), pp. 143–49.

FIGURE 3.2   Comparison of Experience Curve Effects for 10 Percent, 20 Percent, and 30 Percent Cost Reductions for Each Doubling of Cumulative Production Volume

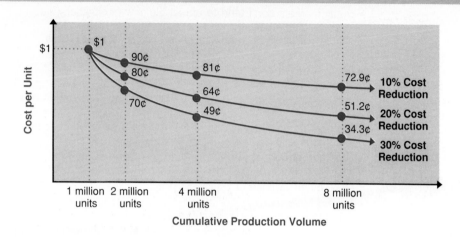

Question 2: What Is Competition Like and How Strong Are Each of the Competitive Forces?

An important part of industry and competitive analysis is to delve into the industry's competitive process to discover the main sources of competitive pressure and how strong each competitive force is. This analytical step is essential because managers cannot devise a successful strategy without understanding the industry's competitive character.

The Five-Forces Model of Competition   Even though competitive pressures in various industries are never precisely the same, the competitive process works similarly enough to use a common analytical framework in gauging the nature and intensity of competitive forces. As Professor Michael Porter of the Harvard Business School has convincingly demonstrated, *the state of competition in an industry is a composite of five competitive forces:*[2]

1. The rivalry among competing sellers in the industry.
2. The market attempts of companies in other industries to win customers over to their own *substitute* products.
3. The potential entry of new competitors.
4. The bargaining power and leverage suppliers of inputs can exercise.
5. The bargaining power and leverage exercisable by buyers of the product.

Porter's *five-forces model*, as depicted in Figure 3.3, is a powerful tool for systematically diagnosing the chief competitive pressures in a market and assessing how

[2]For a thoroughgoing treatment of the five-forces model by its originator, see Michael E. Porter, *Competitive Strategy: Techniques for Analyzing Industries and Competitors* (New York: Free Press, 1980), chapter 1.

TABLE 3.2 Examples of the Strategic Importance of an Industry's Key Economic Features

Economic Feature	Strategic Importance
• Market size	• Small markets don't tend to attract big/new competitors; large markets often draw the interest of companies looking to acquire competitors with established positions in attractive industries.
• Market growth rate	• Fast growth breeds new entry; growth slowdowns spawn increased rivalry and a shake-out of weak competitors.
• Capacity surpluses or shortages	• Surpluses push prices and profit margins down; shortages pull them up.
• Industry profitability	• High-profit industries attract new entrants; depressed conditions encourage exit.
• Entry/exit barriers	• High barriers protect positions and profits of existing firms; low barriers make existing firms vulnerable to entry.
• Product is a big-ticket item for buyers	• More buyers will shop for lowest price.
• Standardized products	• Buyers have more power because it is easier to switch from seller to seller.
• Rapid technological change	• Raises risk factor; investments in technology facilities/equipment may become obsolete before they wear out.
• Capital requirements	• Big requirements make investment decisions critical; timing becomes important; creates a barrier to entry and exit.
• Vertical integration	• Raises capital requirements; often creates competitive differences and cost differences among fully versus partially versus nonintegrated firms.
• Economies of scale	• Increases volume and market share needed to be cost competitive.
• Rapid product innovation	• Shortens product life cycle; increases risk because of opportunities for leapfrogging.

strong and important each one is. Not only is it the most widely used technique of competition analysis, but it is also relatively easy to understand and apply.

The Rivalry among Competing Sellers   The strongest of the five competitive forces is *usually* the jockeying for position and buyer favor that goes on among rival firms. In some industries, rivalry is centered around price competition—sometimes resulting in prices below the level of unit costs and forcing losses on most rivals. In other industries, price competition is minimal and rivalry is focused on such factors as performance features, new product innovation, quality and durability, warranties, after-the-sale service, and brand image.

Competitive jockeying among rivals heats up when one or more competitors sees an opportunity to better meet customer needs or is under pressure to improve its performance. *The intensity of rivalry among competing sellers is a function of how vigorously they employ such tactics as lower prices, snazzier features, expanded customer services, longer warranties, special promotions, and new product introductions.* Rivalry can range from friendly to cutthroat, depending on how frequently and how aggressively companies undertake fresh moves that threaten rivals' profitability. Ordinarily, industry rivals are clever at adding new wrinkles to their product offer-

FIGURE 3.3   The Five-Forces Model of Competition: A Key Analytical Tool

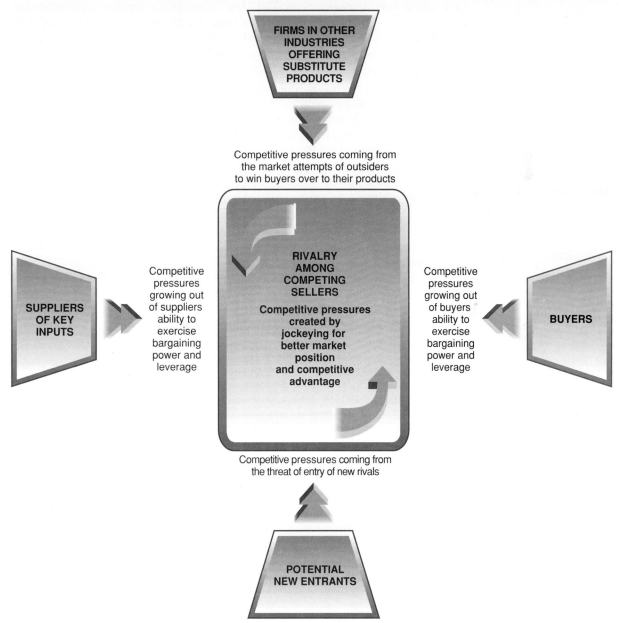

Source: Adapted from Michael E. Porter, "How Competitive Forces Shape Strategy," *Harvard Business Review* 57, no. 2 (March–April 1979), pp. 137–45.

ings that enhance buyer appeal, and they persist in trying to exploit weaknesses in each other's market approaches.

Whether rivalry is lukewarm or heated, every company has to craft a successful strategy for competing—ideally, one that *produces a competitive edge over rivals* and strengthens its position with buyers. The big complication in most industries is that *the success of any one firm's strategy hinges partly on what offensive and defensive maneuvers its rivals employ and the resources rivals are willing and able to put behind their strategic efforts*. The "best" strategy for one firm in its maneuvering for competitive advantage depends, in other words, on the competitive capabilities and strategies of rival companies. Thus, whenever one firm makes a strategic move, its rivals often retaliate with offensive or defensive countermoves. This pattern of action and reaction makes competitive rivalry a "war-games" type of contest conducted according to the rules of fair competition. Indeed, from a strategy-making perspective, *competitive markets are economic battlefields*, with the ebb and flow of the competitive battle varying with the latest strategic moves of the players. In practice, the market outcome is almost always shaped by the strategies of the leading players.

Principle of Competitive Markets

Competitive jockeying among rival firms is a dynamic, ever-changing process as firms initiate new offensive and defensive moves and emphasis swings from one blend of competitive weapons and tactics to another.

Not only do competitive contests among rival sellers assume different intensities but the kinds of competitive pressures that emerge from cross-company rivalry also vary over time. The relative emphasis that rival companies put on price, quality, performance features, customer service, warranties, advertising, dealer networks, new product innovation, and so on shifts as they try different tactics to catch buyers' attention and as competitors launch fresh offensive and defensive maneuvers. Rivalry is thus dynamic; the current competitive scene is ever-changing as companies act and react, sometimes in rapid-fire order and sometimes methodically, and as they swing from one mix of competitive tactics to another.

Regardless of the industry, several common factors seem to influence the tempo of rivalry among competing sellers:[3]

1. *Rivalry intensifies as the number of competitors increases and as competitors become more equal in size and capability*. Up to a point, the greater the number of competitors, the greater the probability of fresh, creative strategic initiatives. In addition, when rivals are more equal in size and capability, they can usually compete on a fairly even footing, making it harder for one or two firms to "win" the competitive battle and dominate the market.

2. *Rivalry is usually stronger when demand for the product is growing slowly*. In a rapidly expanding market, there tends to be enough business for everybody to grow. Indeed, it may take all of a firm's financial and competitive resources just to keep up with buyer demand, much less steal rivals' customers. But when growth slows or when market demand drops unexpectedly, expansion-minded firms and/or firms with excess capacity often cut prices and deploy other sales-increasing tactics, thereby igniting a battle for market share that can result in a shakeout of the weak and less efficient firms. The industry then consolidates into a smaller, but individually stronger, number of sellers.

3. *Rivalry is more intense when industry conditions tempt competitors to use price cuts or other competitive weapons to boost unit volume*. Whenever fixed costs account for a large fraction of total cost, unit costs tend to be lowest at or near full capacity since fixed costs can be spread over more units of production. Unused capacity imposes a significant cost-increasing penalty because there are fewer units

---

[3]These indicators of what to look for in evaluating the intensity of intercompany rivalry are based on Porter, *Competitive Strategy*, pp. 17–21.

carrying the fixed cost burden. In such cases, if market demand weakens and capacity utilization begins to fall off, the pressure of rising unit costs often pushes rival firms into secret price concessions, special discounts, rebates, and other sales-increasing tactics, thus heightening rivalry. Likewise, when a product is perishable, seasonal, or costly to hold in inventory, competitive pressures build when one or more firms decide to dump excess supplies on the market.

4. *Rivalry is stronger when customers' costs to switch brands are low.* The lower the costs of switching, the easier it is for rival sellers to raid one another's customers. High switching costs, however, give sellers a more protected customer base and work against the efforts of rivals to promote brand-switching.

5. *Rivalry is stronger when one or more competitors is dissatisfied with its market position and launches moves to bolster its standing at the expense of rivals.* Firms that are losing ground or in financial trouble often react aggressively by introducing new products, boosting advertising, discounting prices, acquiring smaller rivals to strengthen their capabilities, and so on. Such actions can trigger a new round of maneuvering and a more hotly contested battle for market share.

6. *Rivalry increases in proportion to the size of the payoff from a successful strategic move.* The more rewarding an opportunity, the more likely some firm will aggressively pursue a strategy to capture it. The size of the payoff varies partly with the speed of retaliation. When competitors respond slowly (or not at all), the initiator of a fresh competitive strategy can reap benefits in the intervening period and perhaps gain an advantage that is not easily surmounted. The greater the benefits of moving first, the more likely some competitor will accept the risk and try it.

7. *Rivalry tends to be more vigorous when it costs more to get out of a business than to stay in and compete.* The higher the exit barriers, the stronger the incentive for existing rivals to remain and compete as best they can, even though they may be earning low profits or even incurring losses.

8. *Rivalry becomes more volatile and unpredictable the more diverse competitors are in terms of their visions, strategic intents, objectives, strategies, resources, and countries of origin.* A diverse group of sellers often contains one or more mavericks willing to rock the boat with unconventional moves and market approaches, thus generating a livelier and less predictable environment. Attempts by cross-border rivals to gain stronger footholds in each other's domestic markets boosts the intensity of rivalry, especially when foreign rivals have lower costs or very attractive products.

9. *Rivalry increases when strong companies outside the industry acquire weak firms in the industry and launch aggressive, well-funded moves to transform their newly acquired competitors into major market contenders.* A concerted effort to turn a weak rival into a market leader nearly always entails launching well-financed strategic initiatives to dramatically improve the competitor's product offering, excite buyer interest, and win a much bigger market share. If these actions are successful, they put pressure on rivals to counter with fresh moves of their own.

Two facets of competitive rivalry stand out: (1) the launch of a powerful competitive strategy by one company intensifies the pressures on the remaining companies and (2) the character of rivalry is shaped partly by the strategies of the leading players and partly by the vigor with which industry rivals use competitive weapons to try to outmaneuver one another. In sizing up the competitive pressures created by rivalry among existing competitors, the strategist's job is to identify the current weapons and tactics of competitive rivalry, to stay on top of which tactics are most and least successful, to understand the "rules" that industry rivals play by, and to decide whether and why rivalry is likely to increase or diminish in strength.

Judgments about how much pressure cross-company rivalry is going to put on profitability is the key to concluding whether and why the rivalry among existing sellers is fierce, strong, moderate, or attractively weak. Competitive rivalry is considered intense when the actions of competitors are driving down industry profits, moderate when most companies can earn acceptable profits, and weak when most companies in the industry can earn above-average returns on investment. Chronic outbreaks of cutthroat competition among rival sellers make an industry brutally competitive.

The Competitive Force of Potential Entry   New entrants to a market bring new production capacity, the desire to establish a secure place in the market, and sometimes substantial resources.[4] Just how serious the competitive threat of entry is in a particular market depends on two classes of factors: *barriers to entry* and the *expected reaction of incumbent firms to new entry*. A barrier to entry exists whenever it is hard for a newcomer to break into the market and/or economic factors put a potential entrant at a disadvantage. There are several types of entry barriers:[5]

1. *Economies of scale*—Scale economies deter entry because they force potential competitors either to enter on a large-scale basis (a costly and perhaps risky move) or to accept a cost disadvantage (and lower profitability). Trying to overcome scale economies by entering on a large-scale basis at the outset can result in long-term overcapacity problems for the new entrant (until sales volume builds up), and it can so threaten the market shares of existing firms that they retaliate aggressively (with price cuts, increased advertising and sales promotion, and similar blocking actions). Either way, a potential entrant is discouraged by the prospect of lower profits. Entrants may encounter scale-related barriers not just in production, but in advertising, marketing and distribution, financing, after-sale customer service, raw materials purchasing, and R&D as well.

2. *Inability to gain access to technology and specialized know-how*—Many industries require technological capability and skills not readily available to a newcomer. Key patents can effectively bar entry as can lack of technically skilled personnel and an inability to execute complicated manufacturing techniques. Existing firms often carefully guard know-how that gives them an edge. Unless new entrants can gain access to such proprietary knowledge, they will lack the capability to compete on a level playing field.

3. *The existence of learning and experience curve effects*—When lower unit costs are partly or mostly a result of experience in producing the product and other learning curve benefits, new entrants face a cost disadvantage competing against firms with more know-how.

4. *Brand preferences and customer loyalty*—Buyers are often attached to established brands. Japanese consumers, for example, are fiercely loyal to Japanese brands of motor vehicles, electronics products, cameras, and film. European consumers have traditionally been loyal to European brands of major household appliances. High brand loyalty means that a potential entrant must build a network of distributors and

[4]Michael E. Porter, "How Competitive Forces Shape Strategy," *Harvard Business Review* 57, no. 2 (March–April 1979), p. 138.

[5]Porter, *Competitive Strategy*, pp. 7–17.

dealers, then be prepared to spend enough money on advertising and sales promotion to overcome customer loyalties and build its own clientele. Establishing brand recognition and building customer loyalty can be a slow and costly process. In addition, if it is difficult or costly for a customer to switch to a new brand, a new entrant must persuade buyers that its brand is worth the costs. To overcome the switching-cost barrier, new entrants may have to offer buyers a discounted price or an extra margin of quality or service. All this can mean lower profit margins for new entrants—something that increases the risk to start-up companies dependent on sizable, early profits.

5. *Resource requirements*—The larger the total dollar investment and other resource requirements needed to enter the market successfully, the more limited the pool of potential entrants. The most obvious capital requirements are associated with manufacturing plant and equipment, distribution facilities, working capital to finance inventories and customer credit, introductory advertising and sales promotion to establish a clientele, and cash reserves to cover start-up losses. Other resource barriers include access to technology, specialized expertise and know-how, and R&D requirements, labor force requirements, and customer service requirements.

6. *Cost disadvantages independent of size*—Existing firms may have cost advantages not available to potential entrants. These advantages can include access to the best and cheapest raw materials, patents and proprietary technology, the benefits of learning and experience curve effects, existing plants built and equipped years earlier at lower costs, favorable locations, and lower borrowing costs.

7. *Access to distribution channels*—In the case of consumer goods, a potential entrant may face the barrier of gaining access to consumers. Wholesale distributors may be reluctant to take on a product that lacks buyer recognition. A network of retail dealers may have to be set up from scratch. Retailers have to be convinced to give a new brand display space and a trial period. The more existing producers tie up distribution channels, the tougher entry will be. To overcome this barrier, potential entrants may have to "buy" distribution access by offering better margins to dealers and distributors or by giving advertising allowances and other incentives. As a consequence, a potential entrant's profits may be squeezed unless and until its product gains enough acceptance that distributors and retailers want to carry it.

8. *Regulatory policies*—Government agencies can limit or even bar entry by requiring licenses and permits. Regulated industries like cable TV, telecommunications, electric and gas utilities, radio and television broadcasting, liquor retailing, and railroads feature government-controlled entry. In international markets, host governments commonly limit foreign entry and must approve all foreign investment applications. Stringent safety regulations and environmental pollution standards are entry barriers because they raise entry costs.

9. *Tariffs and international trade restrictions*—National governments commonly use tariffs and trade restrictions (antidumping rules, local content requirements, and quotas) to raise entry barriers for foreign firms. In 1996, due to tariffs imposed by the South Korean government, a Ford Taurus cost South Korean car buyers over $40,000. The government of India requires that 90 percent of the parts and components used in Indian truck assembly plants be made in India. And to protect European chipmakers from low-cost Asian competition, European governments instituted a rigid formula for calculating floor prices for computer memory chips.

Whether an industry's entry barriers ought to be considered high or low depends on the resources and competencies possessed by the pool of potential entrants. Entry barriers are usually steeper for new start-up enterprises than for companies in other industries or for current industry participants looking to enter new geographic markets. Indeed, the most likely entrants into a geographic market are often enterprises looking to expand their market reach. A company already well established in one geographic market may have the resources, competencies, and competitive capabilities to hurdle the barriers of entering an attractive new geographic market. In evaluating the potential threat of entry, one must look at (1) how formidable the entry barriers are for each type of potential entrant—new start-up enterprises, candidate companies in other industries, and current industry participants aiming to enter additional geographic markets and (2) how attractive the profit prospects are for new entrants. High profits act as a magnet to potential entrants, motivating them to commit the resources needed to hurdle entry barriers.[6]

Even if a potential entrant has or can acquire the needed competencies and resources to attempt entry, it still faces the issue of how existing firms will react.[7]

Principle of Competitive Markets

The threat of entry is stronger when entry barriers are low, when there's a sizable pool of entry candidates, when incumbent firms are unable or unwilling to vigorously contest a newcomer's efforts to gain a market foothold, and when a newcomer can expect to earn attractive profits.

Will they offer only passive resistance, or will they aggressively defend their market positions using price cuts, increased advertising, new product improvements, and whatever else will give a new entrant (as well as other rivals) a hard time? A potential entrant can have second thoughts when financially strong incumbent firms send clear signals that they will stoutly defend their market positions against newcomers. It may also turn away when incumbent firms can leverage distributors and customers to retain their business.

The best test of whether potential entry is a strong or weak competitive force is to ask if the industry's growth and profit prospects are attractive enough to induce additional entry. When the answer is no, potential entry is a weak competitive force. When the answer is yes and there are entry candidates with enough expertise and resources, then potential entry adds to competitive pressures in the marketplace. The stronger the threat of entry, the more that incumbent firms are driven to fortify their positions against newcomers.

One additional point: The threat of entry changes as the industry's prospects grow brighter or dimmer and as entry barriers rise or fall. For example, the expiration of a key patent can greatly increase the threat of entry. A technological discovery can create an economy of scale advantage where none existed before. New actions by incumbent firms to increase advertising, strengthen distributor-dealer relations, step up R&D, or improve product quality can raise the roadblocks to entry. In international markets, entry barriers for foreign-based firms fall as tariffs are lowered, as domestic wholesalers and dealers seek out lower-cost foreign-made goods, and as domestic buyers become more willing to purchase foreign brands.

Competitive Pressures from Substitute Products   Firms in one industry are, quite often, in close competition with firms in another industry because their products are good substitutes. The producers of eyeglasses compete with the makers of contact lenses. The producers of wood stoves compete with such substitutes as kerosene heaters and

---

[6]When profits are sufficiently attractive, entry barriers fail to deter entry; at most, they limit the pool of candidate entrants to enterprises with the requisite competencies and resources and with the creativity to fashion a strategy for competing with incumbent firms. George S. Yip, "Gateways to Entry," *Harvard Business Review* 60, no. 5 (September–October 1982), pp. 85–93.

[7]Porter, "How Competitive Forces Shape Strategy," p. 140, and Porter, *Competitive Strategy*, pp. 14–15.

portable electric heaters. The sugar industry competes with companies that produce artificial sweeteners and high-fructose corn syrup. The producers of glass bottles and jars confront strong competition from manufacturers of plastic containers, paperboard cartons, and metal cans. Aspirin manufacturers compete against the makers of substitute types of pain relievers. Newspapers compete with television in providing news (television has taken over as the preferred source of late-breaking news) and with Internet sources in providing sports results, stock quotes, and job opportunities. Just how strong the competitive pressures are from substitute products depends on three factors: (1) whether attractively priced substitutes are available, (2) how satisfactory the substitutes are in terms of quality, performance, and other relevant attributes, and (3) the ease with which buyers can switch to substitutes.

Readily available and attractively priced substitutes create competitive pressure by placing a ceiling on the prices an industry can charge for its product without giving customers an incentive to switch to substitutes and risking sales erosion.[8] This price ceiling, at the same time, puts a lid on the profits that industry members can earn unless they find ways to cut costs. When substitutes are cheaper than an industry's product, industry members come under heavy competitive pressure to reduce their prices and find ways to absorb the price cuts with cost reductions.

The availability of substitutes inevitably invites customers to compare quality and performance as well as price. For example, ski boat manufacturers are facing strong competition from jet skis because water sports enthusiasts are finding that jet skis have exciting performance features that make them satisfying substitutes. The users of glass bottles and jars constantly weigh the performance trade-offs with plastic containers, paper cartons, and metal cans. Competition from substitute products pushes industry participants to heighten efforts to convince customers their product has superior attributes.

Another determinant of the strength of competition from substitutes is how difficult or costly it is for the industry's customers to switch to a substitute.[9] Typical switching costs include the extra price premium if any, the costs of additional equipment that may be required, the time and cost in testing the substitute's quality and reliability, the costs of severing old supplier relationships and establishing new ones, payments for technical help in making the changeover, and employee retraining costs. If switching costs are high, sellers of substitutes must offer a major cost or performance benefit in order to entice the industry's customers away. When switching costs are low, it's much easier for sellers of substitutes to convince buyers to change over to their products.

Principle of Competitive Markets

The competitive threat posed by substitute products is strong when substitutes are readily available and attractively priced, buyers believe substitutes have comparable or better features, and buyers' switching costs are low.

As a rule, then, the lower the price of substitutes, the higher their quality and performance, and the lower the user's switching costs, the more intense the competitive pressures posed by substitute products. Good indicators of the competitive strength of substitute products are the rate at which their sales and profits are growing, the market inroads they are making, and their plans for expanding production capacity.

The Power of Suppliers   Whether the suppliers to an industry are a weak or strong competitive force depends on market conditions in the supplier industry and the

---

[8]Porter, "How Competitive Forces Shape Strategy," p. 142, and Porter, *Competitive Strategy*, pp. 23–24.
[9]Porter, *Competitive Strategy*, p. 10.

significance of the item they supply.[10] Supplier-related competitive pressures tend to be minimal whenever the items supplied are standard commodities available on the open market from a large number of suppliers with ample capability. Then it is simple to obtain whatever is needed from a list of capable suppliers, perhaps dividing purchases among several to promote competition for orders. In such cases, suppliers have market power only when supplies become tight and users are so eager to secure what they need that they agree to terms more favorable to suppliers. Suppliers are also relegated to a weak bargaining position whenever there are good substitute inputs and switching is neither costly nor difficult. For example, soft-drink bottlers can check the bargaining power of aluminum can suppliers on price or delivery by using more plastic containers and glass bottles.

Suppliers also tend to have less leverage to bargain over price and other terms of sale when the industry they are supplying is a *major* customer. In such cases, the well-being of suppliers is closely tied to the well-being of their major customers. Suppliers then have a big incentive to protect and enhance their customers' competitiveness via reasonable prices, exceptional quality, and ongoing advances in the technology and performance of the items supplied.

On the other hand, when the item accounts for a sizable fraction of the costs of an industry's product, is crucial to the industry's production process, and/or significantly affects the quality of the industry's product, suppliers have great influence on the competitive process. This is particularly true when a few large companies control most of the available supplies and have pricing leverage. Likewise, a supplier (or group of suppliers) has bargaining leverage the more difficult or costly it is for users to switch to alternate suppliers. Big suppliers with good reputations and growing demand for their output are harder to wring concessions from than struggling suppliers striving to broaden their customer base or more fully utilize their production capacity.

Principle of Competitive Markets

The suppliers to a group of rival firms are a strong competitive force whenever they have sufficient bargaining power to put certain rivals at a competitive disadvantage based on the prices they can command, the quality and performance of the items they supply, or the reliability of their deliveries.

Suppliers are also more powerful when they can supply a component more cheaply than industry members can make it themselves. For instance, most producers of outdoor power equipment (lawnmowers, rotary tillers, snowblowers, and so on) find it cheaper to source small engines from outside manufacturers rather than make their own because the quantity they need is too little to justify the investment, master the process, and capture scale economies. Specialists in small-engine manufacture, by supplying many kinds of engines to the whole power equipment industry, obtain a big enough sales volume to fully realize scale economies, become proficient in all the manufacturing techniques, and keep costs low. Small-engine suppliers, then, are in a position to price the item below what it would cost the user to self-manufacture but far enough above their own costs to generate an attractive profit margin. In such situations, the bargaining position of suppliers is strong *until* the volume of parts a user needs becomes large enough for the user to justify backward integration into self-manufacture of the component. The more credible the threat of backward integration into the suppliers' business becomes, the more leverage users have in negotiating favorable terms with suppliers.

There are a couple of other instances in which the relationship between industry members and suppliers is a competitive force. One is when suppliers, for one reason

---

[10]Ibid., pp. 27–28.

or another, cannot provide items of high or consistent quality. For example, if a manufacturer's suppliers provide components that have a high defect rate or that fail prematurely, they can so increase the warranty and defective goods costs of the manufacturer that its profits, reputation, and competitive position are seriously impaired. A second is when one or more industry members form close working relationships with key suppliers in an attempt to secure lower prices, better quality or more innovative components, just-in-time deliveries, and reduced inventory and logistics costs; such benefits can translate into competitive advantage for industry members who do the best job of managing their relationships with key suppliers.

The Power of Buyers   Just as with suppliers, the competitive strength of buyers can range from strong to weak. Buyers have substantial bargaining leverage in a number of situations.[11] The most obvious is when buyers are large and purchase much of the industry's output. Typically, purchasing in large quantities gives a buyer enough leverage to obtain price concessions and other favorable terms. Retailers often have negotiating leverage in purchasing products because of manufacturers' need for broad retail exposure and favorable shelf space. Retailers may stock one or even several brands but rarely all available brands, so competition among sellers for the business of popular or high-volume retailers gives such retailers significant bargaining leverage. In the United States and Britain, supermarket chains have sufficient leverage to require food products manufacturers to make lump-sum payments to gain shelf space for new products. Motor vehicle manufacturers have significant bargaining power in negotiating to buy original-equipment tires not only because they buy in large quantities but also because tire makers believe they gain an advantage in supplying replacement tires to vehicle owners if their tire brand is original equipment on the vehicle. "Prestige" buyers have a degree of clout in negotiating with sellers because a seller's reputation is enhanced by having prestige buyers on its customer list.

> **Principle of Competitive Markets**
>
> *Buyers are a strong competitive force when they are able to exercise bargaining leverage over price, quality, service, or other terms of sale.*

Even if buyers do not purchase in large quantities or offer a seller important market exposure or prestige, they may still have some degree of bargaining leverage in the following circumstances:

- *If buyers' costs of switching to competing brands or substitutes are relatively low*—Anytime buyers have the flexibility to fill their needs by switching brands or sourcing from several sellers, they gain added negotiating room with sellers. When sellers' products are virtually identical, it is relatively easy for buyers to switch from seller to seller at little or no cost. However, if sellers' products are strongly differentiated, buyers may be less able to switch without sizable changeover costs.

- *If the number of buyers is small*—The smaller the number of buyers, the less easy is it for sellers to find alternatives when a customer is lost. The prospect of losing a customer often makes a seller more willing to grant concessions of one kind or another.

- *If buyers are well informed about sellers' products, prices, and costs*—The more information buyers have, the better bargaining position they are in.

- *If buyers pose a credible threat of backward integrating into the business of sellers*—Retailers gain bargaining power by stocking and promoting their

---

[11]Ibid., pp. 24–27.

own private-label brands alongside manufacturers' name brands. Companies like Campbell's soup, Anheuser-Busch, Coors, and Heinz have integrated backward into metal can manufacturing to gain bargaining power in buying cans from otherwise powerful metal can manufacturers.

- *If buyers have discretion in whether they purchase the product*—The buying power of personal computer manufacturers in purchasing from Intel and Microsoft is greatly muted by the critical importance of Intel chips and Microsoft software in making personal computers attractive to PC users. Or, if consumers are unhappy with the sticker prices of new motor vehicles, they can delay purchase or buy a used vehicle instead.

One last point: all buyers of an industry's product are not likely to have equal degrees of bargaining power with sellers, and some may be less sensitive than others to price, quality, or service. For example, apparel manufacturers confront significant customer power when selling to retail chains like Wal-Mart or Sears, but they can command much better prices selling to small owner-managed apparel boutiques. Independent tire retailers have less bargaining power in purchasing replacement tires than do motor vehicle manufacturers in purchasing original-equipment tires and they are also less quality sensitive—motor vehicle manufacturers are very particular about tire quality and tire performance because of the effects on vehicle performance.

Strategic Implications of the Five Competitive Forces   The five-forces model thoroughly exposes what competition is like in a given market—the strength of each of the five competitive forces, the nature of the competitive pressures comprising each force, and the overall structure of competition. As a rule, the stronger the collective impact of competitive forces, the lower the combined profitability of participant firms. The most brutally competitive situation occurs when the five forces create market conditions tough enough to impose prolonged subpar profitability or even losses on most or all firms. The structure of an industry is clearly "unattractive" from a profit-making standpoint if rivalry among sellers is very strong, low entry barriers are allowing new rivals to gain a market foothold, competition from substitutes is strong, and both suppliers and customers are able to exercise considerable bargaining leverage.

A company's competitive strategy is increasingly effective the more it provides good defenses against the five competitive forces, alters competitive pressures in the company's favor, and helps create sustainable competitive advantage.

On the other hand, when competitive forces are not strong, the structure of the industry is "favorable" or "attractive" from the standpoint of earning superior profits. The "ideal" environment from a profit-making perspective is where both suppliers and customers are in weak bargaining positions, there are no good substitutes, entry barriers are relatively high, and rivalry among present sellers is only moderate. However, even when some of the five competitive forces are strong, an industry can be attractive to those firms whose market position and strategy provide a good enough defense against competitive pressures to preserve their ability to earn above-average profits.

To contend successfully against competitive forces, managers must craft strategies that (1) insulate the firm as much as possible from the five competitive forces, (2) influence competitive pressures to change in directions that favor the company, and (3) build a strong, secure position of advantage. Managers cannot expect to develop winning competitive strategies without first identifying what competitive pressures exist, gauging the relative strength of each, and gaining a deep and profound understanding of the industry's whole competitive structure. The five-forces model is a powerful tool for gaining this understanding. Anything less leaves strategy makers short of the competitive insights needed to craft a successful competitive strategy.

Question 3: What Are the Drivers of Change in the Industry and What Impact Will They Have?

An industry's economic features and competitive structure say a lot about the character of industry and competitive conditions but very little about how the industry environment may be changing. All industries are characterized by trends and new developments that gradually or speedily produce changes important enough to require a strategic response from participating firms. The popular hypothesis about industries going through evolutionary phases or life-cycle stages helps explain industry change but is still incomplete.[12] The life-cycle stages are strongly keyed to changes in the overall industry growth rate (which is why such terms as rapid growth, early maturity, saturation, and decline are used to describe the stages). Yet *there are more causes of industry change than an industry's position on the growth curve.*

> *Industry conditions change because important forces are driving industry participants (competitors, customers, or suppliers) to alter their actions;* **the driving forces** *in an industry* **are the** major underlying causes *of changing industry and competitive conditions.*

The Concept of Driving Forces   While it is important to judge what growth stage an industry is in, there's more value in identifying the factors causing fundamental industry and competitive adjustments. Industry and competitive conditions change *because forces are in motion that create incentives or pressures for change.*[13] The most dominant forces are called driving forces because they have the biggest influence on what kinds of changes will take place in the industry's structure and environment. Driving forces analysis has two steps: identifying what the driving forces are and assessing the impact they will have on the industry.

The Most Common Driving Forces   Many events can affect an industry powerfully enough to qualify as driving forces. Some are one of a kind, but most fall into one of several basic categories.[14]

- *Changes in the long-term industry growth rate*—Shifts in industry growth up or down are a force for industry change because they affect the balance between industry supply and buyer demand, entry and exit, and how hard it will be for a firm to capture additional sales. An upsurge in long-term demand attracts new entrants to the market and encourages established firms to invest in additional capacity. A shrinking market can cause some companies to exit the industry and induce those remaining to close their least efficient plants and retrench.

- *Changes in who buys the product and how they use it*—Shifts in buyer demographics and new ways of using the product can alter the state of competition by forcing adjustments in customer service offerings (credit, technical assistance, maintenance and repair), opening the way to market the industry's product through a different mix of dealers and retail outlets, prompting producers to broaden/narrow their product lines, bringing

---

[12]For more extended discussion of the problems with the life-cycle hypothesis, see Porter, *Competitive Strategy*, pp. 157–62.

[13]Porter, *Competitive Strategy*, p. 162.

[14]What follows draws on the discussion in Porter, *Competitive Strategy*, pp. 164–83.

different sales and promotion approaches into play. Mushrooming popularity of the Internet at home and at work is creating new opportunities for electronic shopping, on-line brokerage services, e-mail services, bulletin board services, data services, and Internet-provider services. The changing demographics generated by longer life expectancies are creating growth markets for residential golf resorts, retirement planning services, mutual funds, and health care.

- *Product innovation*—Product innovation can shake up the structure of competition by broadening an industry's customer base, rejuvenating industry growth, and widening the degree of product differentiation among rival sellers. Successful new product introductions strengthen the market position of the innovating companies, usually at the expense of companies who stick with their old products or are slow to follow with their own versions of the new product. Industries where product innovation has been a key driving force include copying equipment, cameras and photographic equipment, golf clubs, electronic video games, toys, prescription drugs, frozen foods, personal computers, and personal computer software.

- *Technological change*—Advances in technology can dramatically alter an industry's landscape, making it possible to produce new and/or better products at lower cost and opening up whole industry frontiers. Technological developments can also produce significant changes in capital requirements, minimum efficient plant sizes, vertical integration benefits, and learning or experience curve effects. For instance, the pace of technological developments in electronic commerce via the Internet is fast changing the way business is conducted in many industries (stock trading, software sales and distribution, and mail-order retailing, to name a few) and is ushering in "the Information Age."

- *Marketing innovation*—When firms are successful in introducing new ways to market their products, they can spark a burst of buyer interest, widen industry demand, increase product differentiation, and/or lower unit costs— any or all of which can alter the competitive positions of rival firms and force strategy revisions. The Internet is becoming the vehicle for all kinds of marketing innovations.

- *Entry or exit of major firms*—The entry of one or more foreign companies into a market once dominated by domestic firms nearly always shakes up competitive conditions. Likewise, when an established domestic firm from another industry attempts entry either by acquisition or by launching its own start-up venture, it usually applies its skills and resources in some innovative fashion that pushes competition in new directions. Entry by a major firm often produces a "new ball game" with new key players and new rules for competing. Similarly, exit of a major firm changes the competitive structure by reducing the number of market leaders (perhaps increasing the dominance of the leaders who remain) and causing a rush to capture the exiting firm's customers.

- *Diffusion of technical know-how*—As knowledge about how to perform an activity or execute a manufacturing technology spreads, any technically based competitive advantage held by firms originally possessing this know-how erodes. The diffusion of such know-how can occur through scientific journals, trade publications, on-site plant tours, word-of-mouth among suppliers and customers, and the hiring away of knowledgeable employees. It can also occur when the possessors of technological know-how license others to use it for a royalty fee or team up with a company interested in turning the technology into a new business venture. Quite often, technological know-how can be acquired by simply buying a company that has the wanted skills, patents, or manufacturing capabilities. In recent years technology transfer across national boundaries has emerged as one of the most important driving forces in globalizing markets and competition. As companies in more countries gain access to technical know-how, they upgrade their manufacturing capabilities in a long-term effort to compete head-on against established companies. Examples include automobiles, tires, consumer electronics, telecommunications, and computers.

• *Increasing globalization of the industry*—Industries move toward globalization for any of several reasons. One or more nationally prominent firms may launch aggressive long-term strategies to win a globally dominant market position. Demand for the industry's product may pop up in more and more countries. Trade barriers may drop. Technology transfer may open the door for more companies in more countries to enter the industry arena on a major scale. Significant labor cost differences among countries may create a strong reason to locate plants for labor-intensive products in low-wage countries (wages in China, Taiwan, Singapore, Mexico, and Brazil, for example, are about one-fourth those in the United States, Germany, and Japan). Firms with world-scale volumes as opposed to national-scale volumes may gain important cost economies. Multinational companies with the ability to transfer their production, marketing, and management know-how from country to country at very low cost can sometimes gain a significant competitive advantage over domestic-only competitors. As a consequence, global competition usually shifts the pattern of competition among an industry's key players, favoring some and hurting others. Such occurrences make globalization a driving force in industries (1) where scale economies are so large that rival companies need to market their product in many country markets to gain enough volume to drive unit costs down, (2) where low-cost production is a critical consideration (making it imperative to locate plant facilities in countries where the lowest costs can be achieved), (3) where one or more growth-oriented companies are pushing hard to gain a significant competitive position in as many attractive country markets as they can, and (4) based on natural resources (supplies of crude oil, copper, and cotton, for example, are geographically scattered all over the globe).

• *Changes in cost and efficiency*—Widening or shrinking differences in the costs and efficiency among key competitors tends to dramatically alter the state of competition. The low-cost economics of e-mail and faxing has put mounting competitive pressure on the relatively inefficient and high-cost operations of the U.S. Postal Service—sending a one-page fax is cheaper and far quicker than sending a first-class letter. In the electric power industry, sharply lower costs to generate electricity at newly constructed combined-cycle generating plants has put older coal-fired and gas-fired plants under the gun to lower their production costs to remain competitive; moreover, solar power and windpower companies have been forced to aggressively pursue technological breakthroughs to get the costs down far enough to survive against the much-improved cost and efficiency of combined-cycle plants.

- *Emerging buyer preferences for differentiated products instead of a commodity product (or for a more standardized product instead of strongly differentiated products)*—Sometimes growing numbers of buyers decide that a standard "one-size-fits-all" product at a budget price is a better bargain than premium-priced brands with lots of snappy features and personalized services. Such a development tends to shift patronage away from sellers of more expensive differentiated products to sellers of cheaper look-alike products and to create a market characterized by strong price competition. Pronounced shifts toward greater product standardization can so dominate a market that rival producers are limited to driving costs out of the business and remaining price competitive. On the other hand, a shift away from standardized products occurs when sellers are able to win a bigger and more loyal buyer following by introducing new features, making style changes, offering options and accessories, and creating image differences with advertising and packaging. Then the driver of change is the contest among rivals to cleverly outdifferentiate one another. Competition evolves differently depending on whether the market forces are increasing or decreasing the emphasis on product differentiation.

- *Regulatory influences and government policy changes*—Regulatory and governmental actions can often force significant changes in industry practices and strategic approaches. Deregulation has been a potent procompetitive force in the airline, banking, natural gas, telecommunications, and electric utility industries. Governmental efforts to reform Medicare and health insurance have become potent driving forces in the health care industry. In international markets, host governments can drive competitive changes by opening up their domestic markets to foreign participation or closing them off to protect domestic companies.

- *Changing societal concerns, attitudes, and lifestyles*—Emerging social issues and changing attitudes and lifestyles can instigate industry change. Growing antismoking sentiment has emerged as the major driver of change in the tobacco industry. Consumer concerns about salt, sugar, chemical additives, saturated fat, cholesterol, and nutritional value have forced food producers to revamp food-processing techniques, redirect R&D efforts into the use of healthier ingredients, and compete in coming up with healthy, good-tasting products. Safety concerns have transformed products with safety features into a competitive asset in the automobile, toy, and outdoor power equipment industries, to mention a few. Increased interest in physical fitness has spawned whole new industries in exercise equipment, mountain biking, outdoor apparel, sports gyms and recreation centers, vitamin and nutrition supplements, and medically supervised diet programs. Social concerns about air and water pollution have forced industries to add expenses for controlling pollution into their cost structures. Shifting societal concerns, attitudes, and lifestyles usually favor those players that respond quicker and more creatively with products targeted to the new trends and conditions.

- *Reductions in uncertainty and business risk*—A young, emerging industry is typically characterized by an unproven cost structure and uncertainty over potential market size, how much time and money will be needed to surmount technological problems, and what distribution channels to emphasize. Emerging industries tend to attract only risk-taking entrepreneurial companies. Over time, however, if the industry's pioneers succeed and uncertainty about the product's viability fades, more conservative firms are usually enticed to enter the market. Often, these later entrants are larger, financially strong firms looking to invest in attractive growth industries. Lower business risks and less industry uncertainty also affect competition in international markets. In the early stages of a company's entry into foreign markets, conservatism prevails and firms limit their downside exposure by using less risky strategies like exporting, licensing, and joint ventures to accomplish entry. Then, as experience accumulates and perceived risk levels decline, companies move more boldly, constructing plants and making acquisitions to build strong competitive positions in each country market and beginning to link the strategies in each country to create a global strategy.

The many different *potential driving forces* explain why it is too simplistic to view industry change only in terms of the growth stages model and why a full understanding of the *causes* underlying the emergence of new competitive conditions is a fundamental part of industry analysis.

The task of driving forces analysis is to separate the major causes of industry change from the minor ones; usually no more than three or four factors qualify as driving forces.

However, while many forces of change may be at work in a given industry, no more than three or four are likely to qualify as *driving* forces in the sense that they will act as *the major determinants* of why and how the industry is changing. Thus, strategic analysts must resist the temptation to label everything they see changing as driving forces; the analytical task is to evaluate the forces of industry and competitive change carefully enough to separate major factors from minor ones.

The Link between Driving Forces and Strategy Sound analysis of an industry's driving forces is a prerequisite to sound strategy making. Without keen awareness of what external factors will produce the biggest potential changes in the company's business over the next one to three years, managers are ill prepared to craft a strategy tightly matched to emerging conditions. Similarly, if managers are uncertain about the implications of each driving force or if their views are incomplete or off-base, it's difficult for them to craft a strategy that is responsive to the driving forces and their consequences for the industry. So driving forces analysis is not something to take lightly; it has practical strategy-making value and is basic to the task of thinking about where the business is headed and how to prepare for the changes.

Managers can use environmental scanning to spot budding trends and clues of change that could develop into new driving forces.

Environmental Scanning Techniques One way to try to detect future driving forces early on is to systematically monitor the environment for new straws in the wind. *Environmental scanning* involves studying and interpreting the sweep of social, political, economic, ecological, and technological events in an effort to spot budding trends and conditions that could become driving forces. Environmental scanning involves time frames well beyond the next one to three years—for example, it could involve judgments about the demand for energy in the year 2010, what kinds of household appliances and computerized electronic controls will be in the "house of the future," how people will communicate over long distances 10 years from now, or what will happen to the income levels and purchasing habits of retired people in the 21st century if average life expectancies continue to increase. Environmental scanning thus attempts to spot first-of-a-kind happenings and new ideas and approaches that are catching on and to extrapolate their implications 5 to 20 years into the future. *The purpose and value of environmental scanning is to raise the consciousness of managers about potential developments that could have an important impact on industry conditions and pose new opportunities or threats.*

Environmental scanning can be accomplished by monitoring and studying current events, constructing scenarios, and employing the Delphi method (a technique for finding consensus among a group of knowledgeable experts). Environmental scanning methods are highly qualitative and subjective. The appeal of environmental scanning, notwithstanding its speculative nature, is that it helps managers lengthen their planning horizon, translate vague inklings of future opportunities or threats into clearer strategic issues (for which they can begin to develop strategic answers), and think strategically about future developments in the surrounding environment.[15] Companies that undertake formal environmental scanning include General Electric, AT&T, Coca-Cola, Ford, General Motors, Du Pont, and Shell Oil.

Question 4: Which Companies Are in the Strongest/Weakest Positions?

The next step in examining the industry's competitive structure is to study the market positions of rival companies. One technique for revealing the competitive positions of industry participants is *strategic group mapping*.[16] This analytical tool is a bridge between looking at the industry as a whole and considering the standing of each firm separately. It is most useful when an industry has so many competitors that it is not practical to examine each one in depth.

Strategic group mapping is a technique for displaying the competitive positions that rival firms occupy in the industry.

Using Strategic Group Maps to Assess the Competitive Positions of Rival Firms A strategic group consists of those rival firms with similar competitive approaches and positions in the market.[17] Companies in the same strategic group can resemble one another in any of several ways: They may have comparable product line breadth, be vertically integrated to much the same degree, offer buyers similar services and technical assistance, use essentially the same product attributes to appeal to similar types of buyers, emphasize the same distribution channels, depend on identical technological approaches, and/or sell in the same price/quality range. An industry contains only one strategic group when all sellers pursue essentially identical strategies and have comparable market positions. At the other extreme, there are as many strategic groups as there are competitors when each rival pursues a distinct competitive approach and occupies a substantially different competitive position in the marketplace.

Strategic group analysis helps pinpoint a firm's closest competitors.

---

[15]For further discussion of the nature and use of environmental scanning, see Roy Amara and Andrew J. Lipinski, *Business Planning for an Uncertain Future: Scenarios and Strategies* (New York: Pergamon Press, 1983); Harold E. Klein and Robert U. Linneman, "Environmental Assessment: An International Study of Corporate Practice," *Journal of Business Strategy* 5, no. 1 (Summer 1984), pp. 55–75; and Arnoldo C. Hax and Nicolas S. Majluf, *The Strategy Concept and Process* (Englewood Cliffs, N.J.: Prentice-Hall, 1991), chapters 5 and 8.

[16]Porter, *Competitive Strategy,* Chapter 7.

[17]Ibid., pp. 129–30.

The procedure for constructing a strategic group map and deciding which firms belong in which strategic group is straightforward:

- Identify the characteristics that differentiate firms in the industry—typical variables are price/quality range (high, medium, low), geographic coverage (local, regional, national, global), degree of vertical integration (none, partial, full), product line breadth (wide, narrow), use of distribution channels (one, some, all), and degree of service offered (no-frills, limited, full service).

- Plot the firms on a two-variable map using pairs of these differentiating characteristics.

- Assign firms that fall in about the same strategy space to the same strategic group.

- Draw circles around each strategic group, making the circles proportional to the size of the group's respective share of total industry sales revenues.

This produces a two-dimensional *strategic group map* such as the one for the retail jewelry industry portrayed in Illustration Capsule 9.

Several guidelines need to be observed in mapping the positions of strategic groups in the industry's overall strategy space.[18] First, the two variables selected as axes for the map should *not* be highly correlated; if they are, the circles on the map will fall along a diagonal and strategy makers will learn nothing more about the relative positions of competitors than they would by considering just one of the variables. For instance, if companies with broad product lines use multiple distribution channels while companies with narrow lines use a single distribution channel, then looking at broad versus narrow product lines reveals just as much about who is positioned where as looking at single versus multiple distribution channels—one of the variables is redundant. Second, the variables chosen as axes for the map should expose big differences in how rivals position themselves to compete. This, of course, means analysts must identify the characteristics that differentiate rival firms and use these differences as variables for the axes and as the basis for deciding which firm belongs in which strategic group. Third, the variables used as axes don't have to be either quantitative or continuous; rather, they can be discrete variables or defined in terms of distinct classes and combinations. Fourth, drawing the sizes of the circles on the map proportional to the combined sales of the firms in each strategic group allows the map to reflect the relative sizes of each strategic group. Fifth, if more than two good competitive variables can be used as axes for the map, several maps can be drawn to give different exposures to the competitive positioning relationships present in the industry's structure. Because there is not necessarily one best map for portraying how competing firms are positioned in the market, it is advisable to experiment with different pairs of competitive variables.

What Can Be Learned from Strategic Group Maps One thing to look for is whether *industry driving forces and competitive pressures favor some strategic groups and hurt others*.[19] Firms in adversely affected strategic groups may try to shift to a more favorably situated group; how hard such a move is depends on whether entry barriers into the target strategic group are high or low. Attempts by rival firms to enter a new strategic group nearly always increase competition. If certain firms are known to be trying to

---

[18]Ibid., pp. 152–54.

[19]Ibid., pp. 130, 132–38, and 154–55.

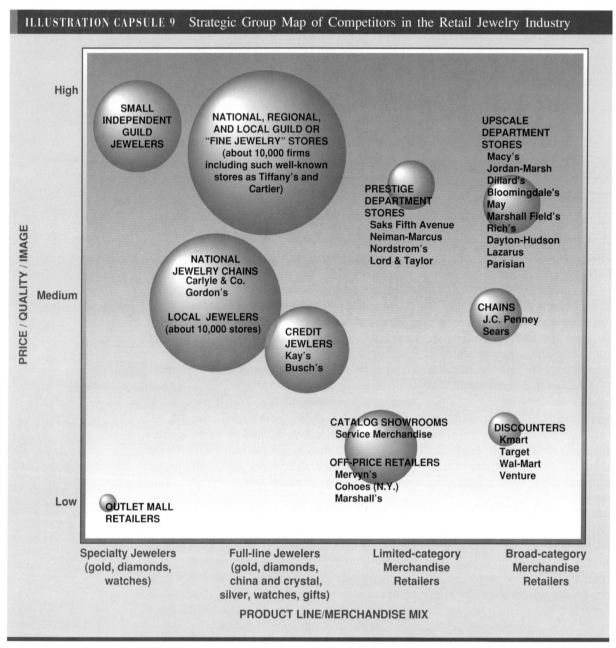

ILLUSTRATION CAPSULE 9   Strategic Group Map of Competitors in the Retail Jewelry Industry

Note: The sizes of the circles are roughly proportional to the market shares of each group of competitors.

change their positions on the map, then attaching arrows to the circles showing the targeted direction helps clarify the picture of competitive jockeying among rivals.

Another consideration is whether *the profit potential of different strategic groups varies due to the competitive strengths and weaknesses in each group's market position.* Differences in profitability can occur because of differing degrees of bargaining leverage with suppliers or customers, differing degrees of exposure to competition from substitute products outside the industry, differing degrees of competitive rivalry within strategic groups, and differing growth rates for the principal buyer segments served by each group. Driving forces and competitive forces do not affect each strategic group evenly.

Generally speaking, *the closer strategic groups are to each other on the map, the* stronger competitive rivalry among member firms tends to be. Although firms in the same strategic group are the closest rivals, the next closest rivals are in the immediately adjacent groups.[20] Often, firms in strategic groups that are far apart on the map hardly compete at all. For instance, Tiffany's and Wal-Mart both sell gold and silver jewelry, but the prices and perceived qualities of their products are much too different to generate any real competition between them. For the same reason, Timex is not a meaningful competitive rival of Rolex, and Subaru is not a close competitor of Lincoln or Mercedes-Benz.

Some strategic groups are usually more favorably positioned than other strategic groups.

Question 5: What Strategic Moves Are Rivals Likely to Make Next?

Unless a company pays attention to what competitors are doing, it ends up flying blind. A company can't expect to outmaneuver its rivals without monitoring their actions, understanding their strategies, and anticipating what moves they are likely to make next. As in sports, scouting the opposition is essential. The strategies rivals are using and the actions they are likely to take next have direct bearing on a company's own best strategic moves—whether it needs to defend against specific actions taken by rivals or whether rivals' moves provide an opening for a new offensive thrust.

Successful strategists take great pains in scouting competitors—understanding their strategies, watching their actions, sizing up their strengths and weaknesses, and trying to anticipate what moves they will make next.

Understanding Competitors' Strategies   The best source of information about a competitor's strategy comes from examining what it is doing and what its management is saying about the company's plans (Figure 2.3 indicates what to look for in identifying a company's business strategy). Additional insights can be gotten by considering the rival's geographic market arena, strategic intent, market share objective, competitive position on the industry's strategic group map, willingness to take risks, basic competitive strategy approach, and whether the competitor's recent moves are mostly offensive or defensive.[21] Good sources for such information include the company's annual report and 10-K filings, recent speeches by its managers, the reports of securities analysts, articles in the business media, company press releases, information searches on the Internet, rivals' exhibits at international trade shows, visits to the company's Web site, and talking with a rival's customers, suppliers, and former employees. Many companies have a competitive intelligence unit that gathers information on rivals and makes it available on the company's intranet.

It is advantageous to know more about your competitors than they know about you.

---

[20]Strategic groups act as good reference points for firms' strategies and for predicting future strategies and the evolution of an industry's competitive structure. See Avi Fiegenbaum and Howard Thomas, "Strategic Groups as Reference Groups: Theory, Modeling and Empirical Examination of Industry and Competitive Strategy," *Strategic Management Journal* 16 (1995), pp. 461–76. For a study of how strategic group analysis helps identify the variables that lead to sustainable competitive advantage, see S. Ade Olusoga, Michael P. Mokwa, and Charles H. Noble, "Strategic Groups, Mobility Barriers, and Competitive Advantage," *Journal of Business Research* 33 (1995), pp. 153–64.

[21]For a discussion of legal ways of gathering competitive intelligence on rival companies, see Larry Kahaner, *Competitive Intelligence* (New York: Simon & Schuster, 1996).

Gathering competitive intelligence on rivals can sometimes tread the fine line between honest inquiry and illegal behavior, subterfuge, and unethical conduct, however. For example, calling rivals to get information about prices, the dates of new product introductions, or wage and salary levels is legal, but misrepresenting one's company affiliation is unethical. Pumping rivals' representatives at trade shows is ethical only if one wears an accurate name tag like everyone else. In an effort to learn more about a competitor's strategic plans, Avon in 1991 was able to secure discarded materials about its biggest rival, Mary Kay Cosmetics, by having its personnel search through the garbage dumpsters outside MKC's headquarters.[22] When MKC officials learned of the action and sued, Avon claimed it did nothing illegal (a 1988 Supreme Court case ruled that trash left on public property—in this case, a sidewalk—was anyone's for the taking). Avon even produced a videotape of its removal of the trash at the MKC site. Avon won—but the legality of Avon's action does not mean that what it did was ethical.

Table 3.3 provides an easy-to-apply classification scheme for profiling the objectives and strategies of rival companies. Such profiles, along with a strategic group map, provide a working diagnosis of the strategies and recent moves of rivals and are readily supplemented by whatever additional information is available about each competitor.

Evaluating Who the Industry's Major Players Are Going to Be   It's usually obvious who the *current* major contenders are, but these same firms are not necessarily positioned most strongly for the future. Some may be losing ground or be ill equipped to compete in the future. Smaller companies may be moving into contention and poised for an offensive against larger but vulnerable rivals. Long-standing contenders for market leadership sometimes slide quickly down the industry's ranks; others end up being acquired. Today's industry leaders don't automatically become tomorrow's.

The company that consistently has more and better information about its competitors is better positioned to prevail, other things being equal.

Whether a competitor is favorably or unfavorably positioned to gain market ground depends on why there is potential for it to do better or worse. Usually, how securely a company holds its present market share is a function of its vulnerability to driving forces and competitive pressures, whether it has a competitive advantage or disadvantage, and whether it is the likely target of offensive attack from other industry participants. Pinpointing which rivals are poised to gain market position and which seem destined to lose market share helps a strategist anticipate what kinds of moves they are likely to make next.

Predicting Competitors' Next Moves   This is the hardest yet most useful part of competitor analysis. Good clues about what moves a specific company may make next come from studying its strategic intent, monitoring how well it is faring in the marketplace, and determining how much pressure it is under to improve its financial performance. The likelihood of a company continuing with its present strategy usually depends on how well it is doing and its prospects for continued success with its current strategy. Content rivals are likely to continue their present strategy with only minor fine-tuning. Ailing rivals can be performing so poorly that fresh strategic moves, either offensive or defensive, are virtually certain. Aggressive rivals with ambitious strategic intent are strong candidates for pursuing emerging market opportunities and exploiting weaker rivals.

Since managers generally operate from assumptions about the industry's future and beliefs about their own firm's situation, insights into the strategic thinking of

---

[22]Kahaner, *Competitive Intelligence*, pp. 84–85.

TABLE 3.3 Categorizing the Objectives and Strategies of Competitors

Competitive Scope	Strategic Intent	Market Share Objective	Competitive Position/Situation	Strategic Posture	Competitive Strategy

• Local
• Regional
• National
• Multicountry
• Global
	• Be the dominant leader
	• Overtake the present industry leader
	• Be among the industry leaders (top 5)
	• Move into the top 10
	• Move up a notch or two in the industry rankings
	• Overtake a particular rival (not necessarily the leader)
	• Maintain position
	• Just survive
		• Aggressive expansion via both acquisition and internal growth
		• Expansion via internal growth (boost market share at the expense of rival firms)
		• Expansion via acquisition
		• Hold on to present share (by growing at a rate equal to the industry average)
		• Give up share if necessary to achieve short-term profit objectives (stress profitability, not volume)
			• Getting stronger; on the move
			• Well-entrenched; able to maintain its present position
			• Stuck in the middle of the pack
			• Going after a different market position (trying to move from a weaker to a stronger position)
			• Struggling; losing ground
			• Retrenching to a position that can be defended
				• Mostly offensive
				• Mostly defensive
				• A combination of offense and defense
				• Aggressive risk-taker
				• Conservative follower
					• Striving for low cost leadership
					• Mostly focusing on a market niche
					  —High end
					  —Low end
					  —Geographic
					  —Buyers with special needs
					  —Other
					• Pursuing differentiation based on
					  —Quality
					  —Service
					  —Technological superiority
					  —Breadth of product line
					  —Image and reputation
					  —More value for the money
					  —Other attributes

Note: Since a focus strategy can be aimed at any of several market niches and a differentiation strategy can be keyed to any of several attributes, it is best to be explicit about what kind of focus strategy or differentiation strategy a given firm is pursuing. All focusers do not pursue the same market niche, and all differentiators do not pursue the same differentiating attributes.

rival company managers can be gleaned from their public pronouncements about where the industry is headed and what it will take to be successful, what they are saying about their firm's situation, information from the grapevine about what they are doing, and their past actions and leadership styles. Another thing to consider is whether a rival has the flexibility to make major strategic changes or whether it is locked into pursuing its same basic strategy with minor adjustments.

Managers who fail to study competitors closely risk being blindsided by "surprise" actions on the part of rivals.

To succeed in predicting a competitor's next moves, one has to have a good feel for the rival's situation, how its managers think, and what its options are. Doing the necessary detective work can be tedious and time-consuming since the information comes in bits and pieces from many sources. But scouting competitors well enough to anticipate their next moves allows managers to prepare effective countermoves (perhaps even beat a rival to the punch!).

Question 6: What Are the Key Factors for Competitive Success?

An industry's *key success factors* (KSFs) are those things that most affect the ability of industry members to prosper in the marketplace—the particular strategy elements, product attributes, resources, competencies, competitive capabilities, and business outcomes that spell the difference between profit and loss. *Key success factors concern what every industry member must be competent at doing or concentrate on achieving in order to be competitively and financially successful.* KSFs are so important that all firms in the industry must pay them close attention—they are the *prerequisites* for industry success. The answers to three questions help identify an industry's key success factors:

An industry's key success factors concern the product attributes, competencies, competitive capabilities, and market achievements with the greatest direct bearing on company profitability.

- On what basis do customers choose between the competing brands of sellers?
- What must a seller do to be competitively successful—what resources and competitive capabilities does it need?
- What does it take for sellers to achieve a sustainable competitive advantage?

In the beer industry, the KSFs are full utilization of brewing capacity (to keep manufacturing costs low), a strong network of wholesale distributors (to gain access to as many retail outlets as possible), and clever advertising (to induce beer drinkers to buy a particular brand). In apparel manufacturing, the KSFs are appealing designs and color combinations (to create buyer interest) and low-cost manufacturing efficiency (to permit attractive retail pricing and ample profit margins). In tin and aluminum cans, because the cost of shipping empty cans is substantial, one of the keys is having plants located close to end-use customers so that the plant's output can be marketed within economical shipping distances (regional market share is far more crucial than national share). Table 3.4 provides a shopping list of the most common types of key success factors.

Determining the industry's key success factors is a top priority. At the very least, managers need to understand the industry situation well enough to know what is more important to competitive success and what is less important. They need to know what kinds of resources are valuable. Misdiagnosing the industry factors critical to long-term competitive success greatly raises the risk of a misdirected strategy—one that overemphasizes less important competitive targets and under-emphasizes more important competitive capabilities. On the other hand, a company with perceptive understanding of industry KSFs can gain sustainable competitive advantage by training its strategy on industry KSFs and devoting its energies to being better than rivals on one or more of these factors. Indeed, *key success factors represent golden opportunities for competitive advantage*—companies that stand out on a particular KSF enjoy a stronger market position for their efforts. Hence using one or more of the industry's KSFs as *cornerstones* for the company's strategy and trying to gain sustainable competitive advantage by excelling at one particular KSF is a fruitful approach.[23]

Strategic Management Principle

A sound strategy incorporates efforts to be competent on all industry key success factors and to excel on at least one factor.

Key success factors vary from industry to industry and even from time to time within the same industry as driving forces and competitive conditions change. Only rarely does an industry have more than three or four key success factors at any one time. And even among these three or four, one or two usually outrank the others in importance. Managers, therefore, have to resist the temptation to include factors that

---

[23]Some experts dispute the strategy-making value of key success factors. Professor Ghemawat claims that the "whole idea of identifying a success factor and then chasing it seems to have something in common with the ill-considered medieval hunt for the *philosopher's stone,* a substance which would transmute everything it touched into gold." Pankaj Ghemawat, *Commitment: The Dynamic of Strategy* (New York: Free Press, 1991), p.11.

TABLE 3.4 Common Types of Key Success Factors

Technology-Related KSFs

Scientific research expertise (important in such fields as pharmaceuticals, medicine, space exploration, other "high-tech" industries)

Technical capability to make innovative improvements in production processes

Product innovation capability

Expertise in a given technology

Capability to use the Internet to disseminate information, take orders, deliver products or services

Manufacturing-Related KSFs

Low-cost production efficiency (achieve scale economies, capture experience curve effects)

Quality of manufacture (fewer defects, less need for repairs)

High utilization of fixed assets (important in capital intensive/high fixed-cost industries)

Low-cost plant locations

Access to adequate supplies of skilled labor

High labor productivity (important for items with high labor content)

Low-cost product design and engineering (reduces manufacturing costs)

Flexibility to manufacture a range of models and sizes/take care of custom orders

Distribution-Related KSFs

A strong network of wholesale distributors/dealers (or electronic distribution capability via the Internet)

Gaining ample space on retailer shelves

Having company-owned retail outlets

Low distribution costs

Fast delivery

Marketing-Related KSFs

Fast, accurate technical assistance

Courteous customer service

Accurate filling of buyer orders (few back orders or mistakes)

Breadth of product line and product selection

Merchandising skills

Attractive styling/packaging

Customer guarantees and warranties (important in mail-order retailing, big-ticket purchases, new product introductions)

Clever advertising

Skills-Related KSFs

Superior workforce talent (important in professional services like accounting and investment banking)

Quality control know-how

Design expertise (important in fashion and apparel industries and often one of the keys to low-cost manufacture)

Expertise in a particular technology

An ability to develop innovative products and product improvements

An ability to get newly conceived products past the R&D phase and out into the market very quickly

Organizational Capability

Superior information systems (important in airline travel, car rental, credit card, and lodging industries)

Ability to respond quickly to shifting market conditions (streamlined decision making, short lead times to bring new products to market)

Superior ability to employ the Internet and other aspects of electronic commerce to conduct business

More experience and managerial know-how

Other Types of KSFs

Favorable image/reputation with buyers

Overall low cost (not just in manufacturing)

Convenient locations (important in many retailing businesses)

Pleasant, courteous employees in all customer contact positions

Access to financial capital (important in newly emerging industries with high degrees of business risk and in capital-intensive industries)

Patent protection

have only minor importance on their list of key success factors—the purpose of identifying KSFs is to make judgments about what things are more important and what things are less important. To compile a list of every factor that matters even a little bit defeats the purpose of concentrating management attention on the truly critical factors.

Question 7: Is the Industry Attractive and What Are Its Prospects for Above-Average Profitability?

The final step of industry and competitive analysis is to use the answers to the previous six questions to draw conclusions about the relative attractiveness or unattractiveness of the industry, both near term and long term. Important factors for company managers to consider include:

- The industry's growth potential.
- Whether competition currently permits adequate profitability and whether competitive forces will become stronger or weaker.
- Whether industry profitability will be favorably or unfavorably impacted by the prevailing driving forces.
- The company's competitive position in the industry and whether its position is likely to grow stronger or weaker (being a well-entrenched leader or strongly positioned contender in an otherwise lackluster industry can still produce good profitability; on the other hand, having to fight an uphill battle against much stronger rivals can make an otherwise attractive industry unattractive).
- The company's potential to capitalize on the vulnerabilities of weaker rivals (perhaps converting an unattractive *industry* situation into a potentially rewarding *company* opportunity).
- Whether the company is insulated from, or able to defend against, the factors that make the industry unattractive.
- How well the company's competitive capabilities match the industry's key success factors.
- The degrees of risk and uncertainty in the industry's future.
- The severity of problems/issues confronting the industry as a whole.
- Whether continued participation in this industry adds to the firm's ability to be successful in other industries in which it may have interests.

As a general proposition, *if an industry's overall profit prospects are above average, the industry can be considered attractive*. If its profit prospects are below average, it

A company that is uniquely well situated in an otherwise unattractive industry can, under certain circumstances, still earn unusually good profits.

is unattractive. However, it is a mistake to think of industries as being attractive or unattractive *to all industry participants and all potential entrants*. Attractiveness is relative, not absolute, and conclusions one way or the other are in the eye of the beholder—industry attractiveness *always* has to be appraised from the standpoint of a particular company. Industries unattractive to outsiders may be attractive to insiders. Industry environments unattractive to weak competitors may be attractive to strong competitors. Companies on the outside may look at an industry's environment and conclude that it is an unattractive business for them to get into; they may see more profitable opportunities elsewhere, given their particular resources and competencies. But a favorably positioned company already in the industry may survey the very same business environment and conclude that the industry is attractive because it has the resources and competitive capabilities to take sales and market share away from weaker rivals, build a strong leadership position, and earn good profits.

An assessment that the industry is fundamentally attractive suggests that current industry participants employ strategies that strengthen their long-term competitive positions in the business, expanding sales efforts and investing in additional facilities and capabilities as needed. If the industry and competitive situation is relatively unattractive, more successful industry participants may choose to invest cautiously, look for ways to protect their long-term competitiveness and profitability, and perhaps acquire smaller firms if the price is right; over the longer term, strong companies may consider diversification into more attractive businesses. Weak companies in unattractive industries may consider merging with a rival to bolster market share and profitability or, alternatively, begin looking outside the industry for attractive diversification opportunities.

ACTUALLY DOING AN INDUSTRY AND COMPETITIVE ANALYSIS

Table 3.5 provides a *format* for presenting the pertinent findings and conclusions of industry and competitive analysis. It embraces all seven questions discussed above and leads would-be analysts to do the strategic thinking and evaluation needed to draw conclusions about the state of the industry and competitive environment.

Two things should be kept in mind in doing industry and competitive analysis. One, the task of analyzing a company's external situation is not a mechanical, formula-like exercise in which facts and data are plugged in and definitive conclusions come pouring out. Strategic analysis always leaves room for differences of opinion about how all the factors add up and what future industry and competitive conditions will be like. There can be several appealing scenarios about how an industry will evolve, how attractive it will be, and how good the profit outlook is. However, while no methodology can guarantee a conclusive diagnosis, it doesn't make sense to shortcut strategic analysis and rely on opinion and casual observation. Managers become better strategists when they know what analytical questions to pose, have the skills to read clues about which way the winds of industry and competitive change are blowing, and can use situation analysis techniques to find answers and identify strategic issues. This is why we concentrated on suggesting the right questions to ask, explaining concepts and analytical approaches, and indicating the kinds of things to look for.

Two, sweeping industry and competitive analyses need to be done every one to three years; in the interim, managers are obliged to continually update and reexamine their thinking as events unfold. There's no substitute for being a good student of industry and competitive conditions and staying on the cutting edge of what's happening in the industry. Anything else leaves a manager unprepared to initiate shrewd and timely strategic adjustments.

KEY POINTS

Thinking strategically about a company's external situation involves probing for answers to the following seven questions:

1. *What are the industry's dominant economic traits?* Industries differ significantly on such factors as market size and growth rate, the geographic scope of competitive

TABLE 3.5   Sample Form for an Industry and Competitive Analysis Summary

1. **Dominant Economic Characteristics of the Industry Environment** (market size and growth rate, geographic scope, number and sizes of buyers and sellers, pace of technological change and innovation, scale economies, experience curve effects, capital requirements, and so on)

2. **Competition Analysis**
   - Rivalry among competing sellers (a strong, moderate, or weak force/weapons of competition)

   - Threat of potential entry (a strong, moderate, or weak force/assessment of entry barriers)

   - Competition from substitutes (a strong, moderate, or weak force/why)

   - Power of suppliers (a strong, moderate, or weak force/why)

   - Power of customers (a strong, moderate, or weak force/why)

3. **Driving Forces**

4. **Competitive Position of Major Companies/Strategic Groups**
   - Favorably positioned/why

   - Unfavorably positioned/why

5. **Competitor Analysis**
   - Strategic approaches/predicted moves of key competitors

   - Whom to watch and why

6. **Key Success Factors**

7. **Industry Prospects and Overall Attractiveness**
   - Factors making the industry attractive

   - Factors making the industry unattractive

   - Special industry issues/problems

   - Profit outlook (favorable/unfavorable)

rivalry, the number and relative sizes of both buyers and sellers, ease of entry and exit, whether sellers are vertically integrated, how fast basic technology is changing, the extent of scale economies and experience curve effects, whether the products of rival sellers are standardized or differentiated, and overall profitability. An industry's economic characteristics are important because of the implications they have for crafting strategy.

2. *What is competition like and how strong are each of the five competitive forces?* The strength of competition is a composite of five forces: the rivalry among competing sellers, the presence of attractive substitutes, the potential for new entry, the leverage major suppliers have, and the bargaining power of customers. The task of competition analysis is to understand the competitive pressures associated with each force, determine whether these pressures add up to a strong or weak competitive force in the marketplace, and then think strategically about what sort of competitive strategy, given the "rules" of competition in the industry, the company will need to employ to (a) insulate the firm as much as possible from the five competitive forces, (b) influence the industry's competitive rules in the company's favor, and (c) gain a competitive edge.

3. *What are the drivers of change in the industry and what impact will they have?* Industry and competitive conditions change because forces are in motion that create incentives or pressures for change. The most common driving forces are changes in the long-term industry growth rate, changes in buyer composition, product innovation, entry or exit of major firms, globalization, changes in cost and efficiency, changing buyer preferences for standardized versus differentiated products or services, regulatory influences and government policy changes, changing societal and lifestyle factors, and reductions in uncertainty and business risk. Sound analysis of driving forces and their implications for the industry is a prerequisite to sound strategy making.

4. *Which companies are in the strongest/weakest competitive positions?* Strategic group mapping is a valuable, if not necessary, tool for understanding the similarities, differences, strengths, and weaknesses inherent in the market positions of rival companies. Rivals in the same or nearby strategic group(s) are close competitors whereas companies in distant strategic groups usually pose little or no immediate threat.

5. *What strategic moves are rivals likely to make next?* This analytical step involves identifying competitors' strategies, deciding which rivals are likely to be strong contenders and which weak contenders, evaluating their competitive options, and predicting what moves they are likely to make next. Scouting competitors well enough to anticipate their actions helps prepare effective countermoves (perhaps even beat a rival to the punch) and allows managers to take rivals' probable actions into account in designing their own company's best course of action. Managers who fail to study competitors closely risk being blindsided by "surprise" actions on the part of rivals. A company can't expect to outmaneuver its rivals without monitoring their actions and anticipating what moves they may make next.

6. *What key factors will determine competitive success or failure?* Key success factors are the particular strategy elements, product attributes, competitive capabilities, and business outcomes that spell the difference between profit and loss and, ultimately, between competitive success or failure. KSFs point to the things all firms in an industry must be competent at doing or must concentrate on achieving in order to be competitively and financially successful—they are the *prerequisites* for good performance in the industry. Frequently, a company can gain sustainable competitive advantage by training its strategy on industry KSFs and devoting its energies to being distinctively better than rivals at succeeding on these factors. Companies that only dimly perceive what factors are truly crucial to long-term competitive success are less likely to have winning strategies.

7. *Is the industry attractive and what are its prospects for above-average profitability?* The answer to this question is a major driver of company strategy. An assessment that the industry and competitive environment is fundamentally attractive typically suggests employing a strategy calculated to build a stronger competitive position in the business, expanding sales efforts, and investing in additional facilities and capabilities as needed. If the industry is relatively unattractive, outsiders considering entry may decide against it and look elsewhere for opportunities, weak companies in the industry may merge with or be acquired by a rival, and strong companies may restrict further investments and employ cost-reduction strategies and/or product innovation strategies to boost long-term competitiveness and protect their profitability. On occasion, an industry that is unattractive overall is still very attractive to a favorably situated company with the skills and resources to take business away from weaker rivals.

Good industry and competitive analysis is a prerequisite to good strategy making. A competently done industry and competitive analysis provides the understanding of a company's macroenvironment needed for shrewdly matching strategy to the company's external situation.

SUGGESTED READINGS

D'Aveni, Richard A. *Hypercompetition.* New York: Free Press, 1994, chaps. 5 and 6.

Ghemawat, Pankaj. "Building Strategy on the Experience Curve*." Harvard Business Review* 64, no. 2 (March–April 1985), pp. 143–49.

Kahaner, Larry. "What You Can Learn from Your Competitors' Mission Statements." *Competitive Intelligence Review* 6 no. 4 (Winter 1995), pp. 35–40.

Langley, Ann. "Between 'Paralysis by Analysis' and 'Extinction by Instinct.'" *Sloan Management Review* (Spring 1995), pp. 63–75.

Linneman, Robert E., and Harold E. Klein. "Using Scenarios in Strategic Decision Making." *Business Horizons* 28, no. 1 (January–February 1985), pp. 64–74.

Porter, Michael E. "How Competitive Forces Shape Strategy." *Harvard Business Review* 57, no. 2 (March–April 1979), pp. 137–45.

———. *Competitive Strategy: Techniques for Analyzing Industries and Competitors.* New York: Free Press, 1980, chap. 1.

———. *Competitive Advantage.* New York: Free Press, 1985, chap. 2.

Yip, George S. *Total Global Strategy: Managing for Worldwide Competitive Advantage.* Englewood Cliffs, N.J.: Prentice-Hall, 1992, chap. 10.

Zahra, Shaker A., and Sherry S. Chaples. "Blind Spots in Competitive Analysis." *Academy of Management Executive* 7, no. 2 (May 1993), pp. 7–28.

EVALUATING COMPANY RESOURCES AND COMPETITIVE CAPABILITIES

4

I n the previous chapter we described how to use the tools of industry and competitive analysis to assess a company's external situation. In this chapter we discuss the techniques of evaluating a company's resource capabilities, relative cost position, and competitive strength versus rivals. Company situation analysis prepares the groundwork for matching the company's strategy *both* to its external market circumstances and to its internal resources and competitive capabilities. The spotlight of company situation analysis is trained on five questions:

1. How well is the company's present strategy working?
2. What are the company's resource strengths and weaknesses and its external opportunities and threats?
3. Are the company's prices and costs competitive?
4. How strong is the company's competitive position relative to its rivals?
5. What strategic issues does the company face?

To explore these questions, four new analytical techniques will be introduced: SWOT analysis, value chain analysis, strategic cost analysis, and competitive strength assessment. These techniques are basic strategic management tools because they expose the company's resource strengths and deficiencies, its best market opportunities, the outside threats to its future profitability, and its competitive standing relative to rivals. Insightful company situation analysis is a precondition for identifying the strategic issues that management needs to address and for tailoring strategy to company resources and competitive capabilities as well as to industry and competitive conditions.

Organizations succeed in a competitive marketplace over the long run because they can do certain things their customers value better than can their competitors.

Robert Hayes, Gary Pisano, and David Upton

The greatest mistake managers make when evaluating their resources is failing to assess them relative to competitors'.

David J. Collis and Cynthia A. Montgomery

Only firms who are able to continually build new strategic assets faster and cheaper than their competitors will earn superior returns over the long term.

C. C. Markides and P. J. Williamson

QUESTION 1: HOW WELL IS THE PRESENT STRATEGY WORKING?

In evaluating how well a company's present strategy is working, a manager has to start with what the strategy is (see Figure 2.3 in Chapter 2 to refresh your recollection of the key components of business strategy). The first thing to pin down is the company's competitive approach—whether it is (1) striving to be a low-cost leader or stressing ways to differentiate its product offering and (2) concentrating its efforts on serving a broad spectrum of customers or a narrow market niche. Another strategy-defining consideration is the firm's competitive scope within the industry—how many stages of the industry's production-distribution chain it operates in (one, several, or all), what its geographic market coverage is, and the size and makeup of its customer base. The company's functional strategies in production, marketing, finance, human resources, information technology, new product innovation, and so on further characterize company strategy. In addition, the company may have initiated some recent strategic moves (for instance, a price cut, newly designed styles and models, stepped-up advertising, entry into a new geographic area, or merger with a competitor) that are integral to its strategy and that aim at securing an improved competitive position and, optimally, a competitive advantage. The strategy being pursued can be further nailed down by probing the logic behind each competitive move and functional approach.

While there's merit in evaluating the strategy from a qualitative standpoint (its completeness, internal consistency, rationale, and suitability to the situation), the best quantitative evidence of how well a company's strategy is working comes from studying the company's recent strategic and financial performance and seeing what story the numbers tell about the results the strategy is producing. The two best empirical indicators of whether a company's strategy is working well are (1) whether the company is achieving its stated financial and strategic objectives and (2) whether it is an above-average industry performer. Persistent shortfalls in meeting company performance targets and weak performance relative to rivals are reliable warning signs that the company suffers from either a malfunctioning strategy or less-than-competent strategy execution (or both). Sometimes company objectives are not explicit enough (especially to company outsiders) to benchmark actual performance against, but it is nearly always feasible to evaluate the performance of a company's strategy by looking at:

The stronger a company's financial performance and market position, the more likely it has a well-conceived, well-executed strategy.

- Whether the firm's market share ranking in the industry is rising, stable, or declining.
- Whether the firm's profit margins are increasing or decreasing and how large they are relative to rival firms' margins.
- Trends in the firm's net profits, return on investment, and economic value added and how these compare to the same trends in profitability for other companies in the industry.
- Whether the company's overall financial strength and credit rating is improving or on the decline.
- Trends in the company's stock price and whether the company's strategy is resulting in satisfactory gains in shareholder value (relative to the MVA gains of other companies in the industry).
- Whether the firm's sales are growing faster or slower than the market as a whole.

- The firm's image and reputation with its customers.
- Whether the company is regarded as a leader in technology, product innovation, product quality, customer service, or other relevant factor on which buyers base their choice of brands.

The stronger a company's current overall performance, the less likely the need for radical changes in strategy. The weaker a company's financial performance and market standing, the more its current strategy must be questioned. Weak performance is almost always a sign of weak strategy or weak execution or both.

QUESTION 2: WHAT ARE THE COMPANY'S RESOURCE STRENGTHS AND WEAKNESSES AND ITS EXTERNAL OPPORTUNITIES AND THREATS?

Sizing up a firm's resource strengths and weaknesses and its external opportunities and threats, commonly known as *SWOT analysis*, provides a good overview of whether a firm's business position is fundamentally healthy or unhealthy. SWOT analysis is grounded in the basic principle that *strategy-making efforts must aim at producing a good fit between a company's resource capability and its external situation*. A clear view of a company's resource capabilities and deficiencies, its market opportunities, and the external threats to the company's future well-being is essential. Otherwise, the task of conceiving a strategy becomes a chancy proposition indeed.

Identifying Company Strengths and Resource Capabilities

A *strength* is something a company is good at doing or a characteristic that gives it enhanced competitiveness. A strength can take any of several forms:

- *A skill or important expertise*—low-cost manufacturing know-how, technological know-how, a proven track record in defect-free manufacture, expertise in providing consistently good customer service, skills in developing innovative products, excellent mass merchandising skills, or unique advertising and promotional know-how.
- *Valuable physical assets*—state-of-the-art plants and equipment, attractive real estate locations, worldwide distribution facilities, natural resource deposits, or cash on hand.
- *Valuable human assets*—an experienced and capable workforce, talented employees in key areas, motivated employees, managerial know-how, or the collective learning and know-how embedded in the organization and built up over time.
- *Valuable organizational assets*—proven quality control systems, proprietary technology, key patents, mineral rights, a base of loyal customers, a strong balance sheet and credit rating, a company intranet for accessing and exchanging information both internally and with suppliers and key customers, computer-assisted design and manufacturing systems, systems for conducting business on the World Wide Web, or e-mail addresses for many or most of the company's customers.
- *Valuable intangible assets*—brand-name image, company reputation, buyer goodwill, a high degree of employee loyalty, or a positive work climate and organization culture.

- *Competitive capabilities*—short development times in bringing new products to market, build-to-order manufacturing capability, a strong dealer network, strong partnerships with key suppliers, an R&D organization with the ability to keep the company's pipeline full of innovative new products, organizational agility in responding to shifting market conditions and emerging opportunities, or state-of-the-art systems for doing business via the Internet.

- *An achievement or attribute that puts the company in a position of market advantage*—low overall costs, market share leadership, having a better product, wider product selection, stronger name recognition, or better customer service.

- *Alliances or cooperative ventures*—partnerships with others having expertise or capabilities that enhance the company's own competitiveness.

Company strengths thus have diverse origins. Sometimes they relate to fairly specific skills and expertise (like know-how in researching consumer tastes and buying habits or training customer contact employees to be cordial and helpful) and sometimes they flow from different resources teaming together to create a competitive capability (like continuous product innovation—which tends to result from a combination of knowledge of consumer needs, technological know-how, R&D, product design and engineering, cost-effective manufacturing, and market testing). The regularity with which employees from different parts of the organization pool their knowledge and expertise, their skills in exploiting and building upon the organization's physical and intangible assets, and the effectiveness with which they collaborate can create competitive capabilities not otherwise achievable by a single department or organizational unit.

Basic Concept

A company is positioned to succeed if it has a good complement of resources at its command.

Taken together, a company's strengths—its skills and expertise, its collection of assets, its competitive capabilities, and its market achievements—determine the complement of *resources* with which it competes. These resources, in conjunction with industry and competitive conditions, are big drivers in how well the company will be able to perform in a dynamic competitive marketplace.[1]

Identifying Company Weaknesses and Resource Deficiencies

A *weakness* is something a company lacks or does poorly (in comparison to others) or a condition that puts it at a disadvantage. A company's internal weaknesses can relate to (a) deficiencies in competitively important skills or expertise, (b) a lack of competitively important physical, human, organizational, or intangible assets, or (c) missing or weak competitive capabilities in key areas. *Internal weaknesses are thus shortcomings in a company's complement of resources.* A weakness may or may not make a company competitively vulnerable, depending on how much the weakness matters in the market-

---

[1]In the past decade, there's been considerable research into the role a company's resources and competitive capabilities play in crafting strategy and in determining company profitability. The findings and conclusions have coalesced into what is called the resource-based view of the firm. Among the most insightful articles are Birger Wernerfelt, "A Resource-Based View of the Firm," *Strategic Management Journal*, September–October 1984, pp. 171–80; Jay Barney, "Firm Resources and Sustained Competitive Advantage," *Journal of Management*, 17, no. 1, 1991, pp. 99–120; Margaret A. Peteraf, "The Cornerstones of Competitive Advantage: A Resource-Based View," *Strategic Management Journal*, March 1993, pp. 179–91; Birger Wernerfelt, "The Resource-Based View of the Firm: Ten Years After," *Strategic Management Journal*, 16 (1995), pp. 171–74 and Jay B. Barney, "Looking Inside for Competitive Advantage," *Academy of Management Executive* 9, no. 4 (November 1995), pp. 49–61.

TABLE 4.1 SWOT Analysis—What to Look for in Sizing Up a Company's Strengths, Weaknesses, Opportunities, and Threats

Potential Resource Strengths and Competitive Capabilities

- A powerful strategy supported by good skills and expertise in key areas
- A strong financial condition; ample financial resources to grow the business
- Strong brand-name image/company reputation
- A widely recognized market leader and an attractive customer base
- Ability to take advantage of economies of scale and/or learning and experience curve effects
- Proprietary technology/superior technological skills/important patents
- Cost advantages
- Strong advertising and promotion
- Product innovation skills
- Proven skills in improving production processes
- A reputation for good customer service
- Better product quality relative to rivals
- Wide geographic coverage and distribution capability
- Alliances/joint ventures with other firms

Potential Company Opportunities

- Serving additional customer groups or expanding into new geographic markets or product segments
- Expanding the company's product line to meet a broader range of customer needs
- Transferring company skills or technological know-how to new products or businesses
- Integrating forward or backward
- Falling trade barriers in attractive foreign markets
- Openings to take market share away from rival firms
- Ability to grow rapidly because of strong increases in market demand
- Acquisition of rival firms
- Alliances or joint ventures that expand the firm's market coverage and competitive capability
- Openings to exploit emerging new technologies
- Market openings to extend the company's brand name or reputation to new geographic areas

Potential Resource Weaknesses and Competitive Deficiencies

- No clear strategic direction
- Obsolete facilities
- A weak balance sheet; burdened with too much debt
- Higher overall unit costs relative to key competitors
- Missing some key skills or competencies/lack of management depth
- Subpar profitability because . . .
- Plagued with internal operating problems
- Falling behind in R&D
- Too narrow a product line relative to rivals
- Weak brand image or reputation
- Weaker dealer or distribution network than key rivals
- Subpar marketing skills relative to rivals
- Short on financial resources to fund promising strategic initiatives
- Lots of underutilized plant capacity
- Behind on product quality

Potential External Threats to a Company's Well-Being

- Likely entry of potent new competitors
- Loss of sales to substitute products
- Slowdowns in market growth
- Adverse shifts in foreign exchange rates and trade policies of foreign governments
- Costly new regulatory requirements
- Vulnerability to recession and business cycle
- Growing bargaining power of customers or suppliers
- A shift in buyer needs and tastes away from the industry's product
- Adverse demographic changes
- Vulnerability to industry driving forces

---

place and whether it can be overcome by the resources and strengths in the company's possession.

Table 4.1 indicates the kinds of factors to be considered in determining a company's resource strengths and weaknesses. Sizing up a company's resource capabilities and deficiencies is akin to constructing *a strategic balance sheet* where resource strengths represent *competitive assets* and resource weaknesses represent *competitive liabilities*. Obviously, the ideal condition is for the company's strengths/competitive assets to outweigh its weaknesses/competitive liabilities by an ample margin—50-50 balance is definitely not the desired condition!

Basic Concept

A company's resource strengths represent competitive assets; its resource weaknesses represent competitive liabilities.

Once managers identify a company's resource strengths and weaknesses, the two compilations need to be carefully evaluated for their competitive and strategy-making implications. Some strengths are more *competitively important* than others because they matter more in forming a powerful strategy, in contributing to a strong market position, and in determining profitability. Likewise, some weaknesses can prove fatal if not remedied, while others are inconsequential, easily corrected, or offset by company strengths. A company's resource weaknesses suggest a need to review its resource base: What existing resource deficiencies need to be remedied? Does the company have important resource gaps that need to be filled? What needs to be done to augment the company's future resource base?

Identifying Company Competencies and Capabilities

Core Competencies: A Valuable Company Resource   One of the most valuable resources a company has is the ability to perform a competitively relevant activity very well. A competitively important internal activity that a company performs better than other competitively important internal activities is termed a *core competence*.

Basic Concept

A core competence is something a company does well relative to other internal activities; a distinctive competence is something a company does well relative to competitors.

What distinguishes a *core* competence from a competence is that a *core* competence is *central* to a company's competitiveness and profitability rather than peripheral. A core competence can relate to demonstrated expertise in performing an activity, to a company's scope and depth of technological know-how, or to a *combination* of specific skills that result in a competitively valuable capability. Frequently, a core competence is the product of effective collaboration among different parts of the organization, of individual resources teaming together. Typically, *core competencies reside in a company's people, not in its assets on the balance sheet.* They tend to be grounded in skills, knowledge, and capabilities.

In practice, companies exhibit many different types of core competencies: skills in manufacturing a high-quality product, know-how in creating and operating a system for filling customer orders accurately and swiftly, fast development of new products, the capability to provide good after-sale service, skills in selecting good retail locations, innovativeness in developing popular product features, skills in merchandising and product display, expertise in an important technology, a well-conceived methodology for researching customer needs and tastes and spotting new market trends, skills in working with customers on new applications and uses of the product, and expertise in integrating multiple technologies to create whole families of new products.

Plainly, *a core competence gives a company competitive capability* and thus qualifies as a genuine company strength and resource. A company may have more than one core competence, but rare is the company that can legitimately claim more than several.

Strategic Management Principle

A distinctive competence empowers a company to build competitive advantage.

Distinctive Competencies: A Competitively Superior Company Resource   Whether a company's core competence represents a *distinctive* competence depends on how good the competence is relative to what competitors are capable of—is it a competitively superior competence or just an internal company competence? *A distinctive competence is a competitively important activity that a company performs well in comparison to its competitors.*[2] Most every com-

---

[2]For a fuller discussion of the core competence concept, see C. K. Prahalad and Gary Hamel, "The Core Competence of the Corporation," *Harvard Business Review* 68, no. 3 (May–June 1990), pp. 79–93.

pany does one competitively important activity *enough better than other activities* that it can claim its best-performed activity as a core competence. But an internal assessment of what a company does best doesn't translate into a distinctive competence unless the company performs that activity in a *competitively superior* fashion. For instance, most all retailers believe they have core competencies in product selection and in-store merchandising, but many retailers who build strategies on these competencies run into trouble because they encounter rivals whose competencies in these areas are better. Consequently, *a core competence becomes a basis for competitive advantage only when it is a distinctive competence.*

Sharp Corporation's distinctive competence in flat-panel display technology has enabled it to dominate the worldwide market for liquid-crystal-displays (LCDs). The distinctive competencies of Toyota, Honda, and Nissan in low-cost, high-quality manufacturing and in short design-to-market cycles for new models have proven to be considerable competitive advantages in the global market for motor vehicles. Intel's distinctive competence in rapidly developing new generations of ever more powerful semiconductor chips for personal computers has given the company a dominating position in the personal computer industry. Motorola's distinctive competence in virtually defect-free manufacture (six-sigma quality—an error rate of about one per million) has contributed significantly to the company's world leadership in cellular telephone equipment. Rubbermaid's distinctive competence in developing innovative rubber and plastics products for household and commercial use has made it the clear leader in its industry.

The importance of a distinctive competence to strategy making rests with (1) the competitively valuable capability it gives a company, (2) its potential for being a cornerstone of strategy, and (3) the competitive edge it can potentially produce in the marketplace. It is always easier to build competitive advantage when a firm has a distinctive competence in performing activities important to market success, when rival companies do not have offsetting competencies, and when it is costly and time-consuming for rivals to imitate the competence. A distinctive competence is thus an especially valuable competitive asset, with potential to be the mainspring of a company's success—unless it is trumped by more powerful resources of rivals.

Determining the Competitive Value of a Company Resource   No two companies are alike in their resources. They don't have the same skill sets, assets (physical, human, organizational, and intangible), competitive capabilities, and market achievements— a condition that results in different companies having different resource strengths and weaknesses. *Differences in company resources are an important reason why some companies are more profitable and more competitively successful than others.* A company's success is more certain when it has appropriate and ample resources with which to compete, and especially when it has a valuable strength, asset, capability, or achievement with the potential to produce competitive advantage.

For a particular company resource—whether it be a distinctive competence, an asset (physical, human, organizational, or intangible), an achievement, or a competitive capability—to qualify as the basis for sustainable competitive advantage, it must pass four tests of competitive value:[3]

---

[3]See David J. Collis and Cynthia A. Montgomery, "Competing on Resources: Strategy in the 1990s," *Harvard Business Review* 73, no. 4 (July–August 1995), pp. 120–23.

1. *Is the resource hard to copy?* The more difficult and more expensive it is to imitate a resource, the greater its potential competitive value. Hard-to-copy resources limit competition, making any profit stream they are able to generate more sustainable. Resources can be difficult to copy because of their uniqueness (a fantastic real estate location, patent protection), because they must be built over time in ways that are difficult to accelerate (a brand name, mastery of a technology), and because they carry big capital requirements (a new cost-effective plant to manufacture semiconductor chips can cost $1 to $2 billion).

2. *How long does the resource last?* The longer a resource lasts, the greater its value. Some resources lose their value quickly because of the rapid speeds with which technologies or industry conditions are moving. The value of FedEx's resources to provide overnight package delivery is rapidly being undercut by fax machines and electronic mail. The value of the programming know-how underlying Netscape's software for browsing the Internet is a rapidly depreciating asset because of the lightning speed with which Internet technology is advancing.

3. *Is the resource really competitively superior?* Companies have to guard against pridefully believing that their core competences are distinctive competences or that their brand name is more powerful than those of rivals. Who can really say whether Coca-Cola's consumer marketing skills are better than Pepsi-Cola's or whether Mercedes-Benz's brand name is more powerful than BMW's or Lexus's?

4. *Can the resource be trumped by the different resources/capabilities of rivals?* Many commercial airlines (American Airlines, Delta Airlines, United Airlines, Singapore Airlines) have succeeded because of their resources and capabilities in offering safe, convenient, reliable air transportation services and in providing an array of amenities to passengers. However, Southwest Airlines has been more consistently profitable by building the capabilities to provide safe, reliable, fewer frills services at radically lower fares. Intel's and Microsoft's resources have trumped those of IBM in personal computers—IBM's long-standing industry experience and prestigious brand name has faded as a dominating factor in choosing what PC to buy; whether a PC has the "Intel inside" sticker and the ability to run the latest Windows programs have become bigger buying considerations than the brand name on the PC.

The vast majority of companies are not well endowed with competitively valuable resources, much less with competitively superior resources capable of passing the above four tests with flying colors. Most businesses have a mixed bag of strengths/assets/competencies/capabilities—one or two quite valuable, some good, many satisfactory to mediocre. Only a few companies, usually industry leaders or future leaders, possess a superior resource of great competitive value. Furthermore, nearly all companies have competitive liabilities: internal weaknesses, a lack of assets, missing expertise or capabilities, or resource deficiencies.

Strategic Management Principle

Successful strategists seek to capitalize on what a company does best—its expertise, resource strengths, and strongest competitive capabilities.

Even if a company doesn't possess a competitively superior resource, the potential for competitive advantage is not lost. *Sometimes a company derives significant competitive vitality, even competitive advantage, from a collection of good to adequate resources that, in combination, have competitive power.* Toshiba's laptop computers are the market share leader—an indicator that Toshiba is good at something. Yet, Toshiba's laptops are not demonstrably faster than rivals' laptops, nor do they have superior performance features than rival brands (bigger screens, more memory, longer battery power, a better pointing device, and so on), nor does Toshiba provide clearly superior technical support services. And Toshiba laptops are definitely not cheaper, model for model, than comparable brands. But while Toshiba laptops do not consistently rank first in performance ratings or have low-price appeal, Toshiba's competitive superiority springs from a *combination* of "good" resource strengths and capabilities—its strategic partnerships with suppliers of laptop components, its efficient assembly capability, its design expertise, its skills in choosing quality components, its creation of a wide selection of models, the attractive mix of built-in performance features found in each model when balanced against price, the much-better-than-average reliability of its laptops (based on buyer ratings), and its very good technical support services (based on buyer ratings). The verdict from the marketplace is that Toshiba laptops are better, *all things considered*, than rival brands.

From a strategy-making perspective, a company's resource strengths are significant because they can form the cornerstones of strategy and the basis for creating competitive advantage. If a company doesn't have ample resources and competitive capabilities around which to craft an attractive strategy, managers need to take decisive remedial action to upgrade existing organizational resources and capabilities and add others. At the same time, managers have to look toward correcting competitive weaknesses that make the company vulnerable, hold down profitability, or disqualify it from pursuing an attractive opportunity. The strategy-making principle here is simple: *A company's strategy should be tailored to fit its resource capabilities—taking both strengths and weaknesses into account*. It is foolhardy to pursue a strategic plan that can be undermined by company weaknesses or that cannot be competently executed. As a rule, managers should build their strategies around exploiting and leveraging company capabilities—*its most valuable resources*—and avoid strategies that place heavy demands on areas where the company is weakest or has unproven ability. Companies fortunate enough to have a distinctive competence or other competitively superior resource must be wise in realizing that its value will be eroded by time and competition.[4] So attention to building a strong resource base for the future and to maintaining the competitive superiority of an existing distinctive competence are ever-present requirements.

Selecting the Competencies and Capabilities to Concentrate On   Enterprises succeed over time because they can do certain things that their customers value better than their rivals. The essence of astute strategy making is selecting the competencies and capabilities to concentrate on and to underpin the strategy. Sometimes the company already has competitively valuable competencies and capabilities in place and sometimes it has to be proactive in developing and building new competencies and capabilities to complement and strengthen its existing resource base. Sometimes the desired competencies and capabilities need to be developed internally, and sometimes it is best to outsource them by working with key suppliers and forming strategic alliances.

Identifying a Company's Market Opportunities

Market opportunity is a big factor in shaping a company's strategy. Indeed, managers can't properly tailor strategy to the company's situation without first identifying each company opportunity, appraising the growth and profit potential each one holds, and

---

[4]Collis and Montgomery, "Competing on Resources: Strategy in the 1990s," p. 124.

ILLUSTRATION CAPSULE 10   TCI's Retreat to a Vision and Strategy in Line with Its Resources and Market Opportunities

In early 1997, Tele-Communications Inc., the biggest cable TV provider in the United States with 14 million subscribers, announced that its much heralded vision of transforming itself into an information superhighway and multimedia powerhouse providing cable television, telephone, Internet access, and an array of futuristic data and telecommunications services to all customers in its cable franchise territories was too sweeping, overhyped, and infeasible for the company to pursue profitably within the announced time frame. John Malone, the company's CEO and widely regarded as one of the most astute and influential visionaries of how new information superhighway technologies could transform the world of media and communications, said:

> We were just chasing too many rabbits at the same time. The company got overly ambitious about the things it could do simultaneously.
>
> If you read our annual report last year, you'd think we're one-third data, one-third telephone and one-third video entertainment, instead of 100 percent video entertainment and two experiments. Right now, we've got zero revenue from residential telephone service, diminishing revenue from high-speed Internet, and $6 billion in revenue from video entertainment.
>
> My job is to prick the bubble. Let's get real.

For years, Malone and TCI had been touting the potential of deploying newly discovered telecommunications technologies over the company's existing cable connections to deliver a dazzling array of information and telecommunications products and services in head-on competition against the telephone companies. The first generation of expanded services was to be rolled out in 1996 and 1997 via a new digital-cable box installed on residential TVs that would access 500 channels, provide on-screen viewer guides, and deliver better sound and picture quality. However, the manufacturer of the boxes encountered problems and was able to produce only small quantities. Meanwhile, aggressive investment in new technological infrastructure ($1.6 billion in 1996) to deliver the expanded array of products/services put a strain on TCI's cash flow and prompted bond-rating agencies to put the company on their watch lists for possible credit rating downgrade. TCI's stock price went nowhere in a strong stock market. Plus the new Telecommunications Act enacted into law in 1996 created a swirl of strategic maneuvers by local and long-distance telephone companies to position themselves to compete nationwide in both the telephone business and in information superhighway products and services, a development that meant cable operators suddenly confronted a whole new set of larger, resource-rich competitors.

TCI's new, narrower vision was to focus more on the cable TV business (under attack from alternative providers utilizing satellite dish technology as well as from the fiber optic wire capability being installed by telephone companies) and to push the vision of information superhighway and multimedia provider farther out into the future, conditional upon clearer technological opportunities to profit from investments to modify the existing cable system and provide a wider array of products and services. The retrenched strategy involved slower rollout of the new digital cable box (to give the supplier time to ramp up production and work out quality bugs), continued market testing of telephone service, curtailed investment in two-way communications capabilities until the company's debt levels were reduced and cash flows were stronger, and until it was clear that the new technologies would be both cost-effective and competitive against the fiberoptic and wireless technologies being installed by rivals. TCI also decided to spin off some of the company's businesses into independent companies (Liberty Media's programming assets, a satellite operation, international operations, and telephone operations) and put some life back into the company's languishing stock price.

Source: Based on information in "Malone Says TCI Push Into Phones, Internet Isn't Working for Now," *The Wall Street Journal*, January 2, 1997, pp. A1 and A3.

crafting strategic initiatives to capture the most promising of the company's market opportunities. Depending on industry conditions, a company's opportunities can be plentiful or scarce and can range from wildly attractive (an absolute "must" to pursue) to marginally interesting (low on the company's list of strategic priorities). Table 4.1 presents a checklist of things to be alert for in identifying a company's market opportunities.

In appraising a company's market opportunities and ranking their attractiveness, managers have to guard against viewing every *industry* opportunity as a *company* opportunity. Not every company in an industry is equipped with the resources to pursue each opportunity that exists—some companies have more capabilities to go after particular opportunities than others, and a few companies may be hopelessly outclassed in trying to contend for a piece of the action. Wise strategists are alert to when a company's resource strengths and weaknesses make it better suited to pursuing some market opportunities than others. Wise strategists are also alert to opportunities that don't match especially well with existing resources, but still offer attractive growth potential if the company aggressively moves to develop or acquire the missing resource capabilities. *The market opportunities most relevant to a company are those that offer important avenues for profitable growth, those where a company has the most potential for competitive advantage, and those that match up well with the financial and organizational resource capabilities which the company already possesses or can acquire.*

> **Strategic Management Principle**
>
> *A company is well-advised to pass on a particular market opportunity unless it has or can build the resource capabilities to capture it.*

Identifying the Threats to a Company's Future Profitability

Often, certain factors in a company's external environment pose *threats* to its profitability and market standing: the emergence of cheaper technologies, rivals' introduction of new or better products, the entry of lower-cost foreign competitors into a company's market stronghold, new regulations that are more burdensome to a company than to its competitors, vulnerability to a rise in interest rates, the potential of a hostile takeover, unfavorable demographic shifts, adverse changes in foreign exchange rates, political upheaval in a foreign country where the company has facilities, and the like. External threats may pose no more than a moderate degree of adversity (all companies confront some threatening elements in the course of doing business) or they may be so imposing as to make a company's situation and outlook quite tenuous. Management's job is to identify the threats to the company's future well-being and evaluate what strategic actions can be taken to neutralize or lessen their impact.

Table 4.1 presents a list of potential threats to a company's future profitability and market position. Opportunities and threats point to the need for strategic action. Tailoring strategy to a company's situation entails (1) pursuing market opportunities well suited to the company's resource capabilities and (2) building a resource base that helps defend against external threats to the company's business.

> **Strategic Management Principle**
>
> *Successful strategists aim at capturing a company's best growth opportunities and creating defenses against external threats to its competitive position and future performance.*

SWOT analysis is therefore more than an exercise in making four lists. The important part of SWOT analysis involves *evaluating* a company's strengths, weaknesses, opportunities, and threats and *drawing conclusions* about (1) how best to deploy the company's resources in light of the company's internal and external situation and (2) how to build the company's future resource base. SWOT analysis isn't complete until several questions about the company's resource base are answered: What adjustments in the company's resource base are needed to respond to emerging industry and competitive conditions? Are there resource gaps that need to be filled? In what ways does the company need to strengthen its resource base? What actions are needed to build the company's future resource base? Which opportunities should be given top priority in allocating resources?

QUESTION 3: ARE THE COMPANY'S PRICES AND COSTS COMPETITIVE?

Company managers are often stunned when a competitor cuts price to "unbelievably low" levels or when a new market entrant comes on strong with a very low price. The competitor may not, however, be "dumping," buying market share, or waging a desperate move to gain sales; it may simply have substantially lower costs. *One of the most telling signs of whether a company's business position is strong or precarious is whether its prices and costs are competitive with industry rivals.* Price-cost comparisons are especially critical in a commodity-product industry where the value provided to buyers is the same from seller to seller, price competition is typically the ruling market force, and lower-cost companies have the upper hand. But even in industries where products are differentiated and competition centers around the different attributes of competing brands as much as around price, rival companies have to keep their costs *in line* and make sure that any added costs they incur create added buyer value and don't result in prices that customers consider "out-of-line."

Assessing whether a company's costs are competitive with those of its close rivals is a necessary and crucial part of company situation analysis.

Competitors usually don't incur the same costs in supplying their products to end users. The cost disparities can range from tiny to competitively significant and can stem from any of several factors:

- Differences in the prices paid for raw materials, components parts, energy, and other items purchased from suppliers.

- Differences in basic technology and the age of plants and equipment. (Because rival companies usually invest in plants and key pieces of equipment at different times, their facilities have somewhat different technological efficiencies and different fixed costs (depreciation, maintenance, property taxes, and insurance. Older facilities are typically less efficient, but if they were less expensive to construct or were acquired at bargain prices, they *may* still be reasonably cost competitive with modern facilities.)

- Differences in production costs from rival to rival due to different plant efficiencies, different learning and experience curve effects, different wage rates, different productivity levels, and the like.

- Differences in marketing costs, sales and promotion expenditures, advertising expenses, warehouse distribution costs, and administrative costs.

- Differences in inbound transportation costs and outbound shipping costs.

- Differences in forward channel distribution costs (the costs and markups of distributors, wholesalers, and retailers associated with getting the product from the point of manufacture into the hands of end users).

Principle of Competitive Markets

The higher a company's costs are above those of close rivals, the more competitively vulnerable it becomes.

- Differences in rival firms' exposure to the effects of inflation, changes in foreign exchange rates, and tax rates (a frequent occurrence in global industries where competitors have operations in different nations with different economic conditions and governmental taxation policies).

For a company to be competitively successful, its costs must be in line with those of close rivals. While some cost disparity is justified so long as the products or services of closely competing companies are sufficiently differentiated, a high-cost firm's market position becomes increasingly vulnerable the more its costs exceed those of close rivals.

Strategic Cost Analysis and Value Chains

Competitors must be ever alert to how their costs compare with rivals'. While every firm engages in *internal* cost analysis to stay on top of what its own costs are and how they might be changing, *strategic* cost analysis goes a step further to explore how costs compare against rivals. *Strategic cost analysis focuses on a firm's cost position relative to its rivals'.*

Every company's business consists of a *collection of activities* undertaken in the course of designing, producing, marketing, delivering, and supporting its product or service. Each of these activities give rise to costs. The combined costs of all these various activities define the company's internal cost structure. Further, the cost of each activity contributes to whether the company's overall cost position relative to rivals is favorable or unfavorable. The task of strategic cost analysis is to compare a company's costs *activity by activity* against the costs of key rivals and to learn which internal activities are a source of cost advantage or disadvantage. A company's relative cost position is a function of how the overall costs of the activities it performs in conducting its business compare to the overall costs of the activities performed by rivals.

> **Basic Concept**
>
> *Strategic cost analysis involves comparing how a company's unit costs stack up against the unit costs of key competitors activity by activity, thereby pinpointing which internal activities are a source of cost advantage or disadvantage.*

The Concept of a Company Value Chain   The primary analytical tool of strategic cost analysis is a *value chain* identifying the separate activities, functions, and business processes performed in designing, producing, marketing, delivering, and supporting a product or service.[5] The chain starts with raw materials supply and continues on through parts and components production, manufacturing and assembly, wholesale distribution, and retailing to the ultimate end user of the product or service.

A *company's value chain* shows the linked set of activities and functions it performs internally (see Figure 4.1). The value chain includes a profit margin because a markup over the cost of performing the firm's value-creating activities is customarily part of the price (or total cost) borne by buyers—creating value that exceeds the cost of doing so is a fundamental objective of business. Disaggregating a company's operations into strategically relevant activities and business processes exposes the major elements of the company's cost structure. Each activity in the value chain incurs costs and ties up assets; assigning the company's operating costs and assets to each individual activity in the chain provides cost estimates for each activity. Quite often, there are linkages between activities such that the way one activity is performed can spill over to affect the costs of performing other activities (for instance, Japanese VCR producers were able to reduce prices from $1,300 in 1977 to under $300 in 1984 by spotting the impact of an early step in the value chain, product design, on a later step, production, and deciding to drastically reduce the number of parts).[6]

> **Basic Concept**
>
> *A company's value chain identifies the primary activities that create value for customers and the related support activities.*

Why the Value Chains of Rival Companies Often Differ   A company's value chain and the manner in which it performs each activity reflect the evolution of its own

---

[5]Value chains and strategic cost analysis are described at greater length in Michael E. Porter, *Competitive Advantage* (New York: Free Press, 1985), chapters 2 and 3; Robin Cooper and Robert S. Kaplan, "Measure Costs Right: Make the Right Decisions," *Harvard Business Review* 66, no. 5 (September–October, 1988), pp. 96–103; and John K. Shank and Vijay Govindarajan, *Strategic Cost Management* (New York: Free Press, 1993), especially chapters 2–6 and 10.

[6]M. Hegert and D. Morris, "Accounting Data for Value Chain Analysis," *Strategic Management Journal* 10 (1989), p. 183.

FIGURE 4.1   Representative Company Value Chain

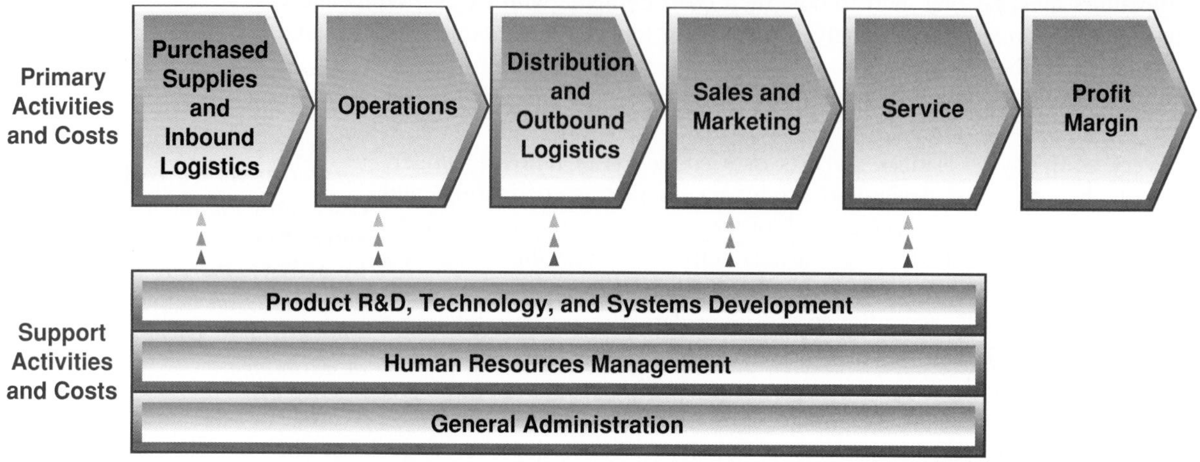

Primary Activities and Costs

Purchased Supplies and Inbound Logistics → Operations → Distribution and Outbound Logistics → Sales and Marketing → Service → Profit Margin

Support Activities and Costs

Product R&D, Technology, and Systems Development

Human Resources Management

General Administration

Primary Activities

- **Purchased Supplies and Inbound Logistics**—Activities, costs, and assets associated with purchasing fuel, energy, raw materials, parts components, merchandise, and consumable items from vendors; receiving, storing, and disseminating inputs from suppliers; inspection; and inventory management.
- **Operations**—Activities, costs, and assets associated with converting inputs into final product form (production, assembly, packaging, equipment maintenance, facilities, operations, quality assurance, environmental protection).
- **Distribution and Outbound Logistics**—Activities, costs, and assets dealing with physically distributing the product to buyers (finished goods warehousing, order processing, order picking and packing, shipping, delivery vehicle operations, establishing and maintaining a network of dealers and distributors).
- **Sales and Marketing**—Activities, costs, and assets related to sales force efforts, advertising and promotion, market research and planning, and dealer/distributor support.
- **Service**—Activities, costs, and assets associated with providing assistance to buyers, such as installation, spare parts delivery, maintenance and repair, technical assistance, buyer inquiries, and complaints.

Support Activities

- **Research, Technology, and Systems Development**—Activities, costs, and assets relating to product R&D, process R&D, process design improvement, equipment design, computer software development, telecommunications systems, computer-assisted design and engineering, new database capabilities, and development of computerized support systems.
- **Human Resources Management**—Activities, costs, and assets associated with the recruitment, hiring, training, development, and compensation of all types of personnel; labor relations activities; development of knowledge-based skills and core competencies.
- **General Administration**—Activities, costs, and assets relating to general management, accounting and finance, legal and regulatory affairs, safety and security, management information systems, forming strategic alliances and collaborating with strategic partners, and other "overhead" functions.

Source: Adapted from Michael E. Porter, *Competitive Advantage* (New York: The Free Press, 1985), pp. 37–43.

business and internal operations, its strategy, the approaches it is using to execute its strategy, and the underlying economics of the activities themselves.[7] Consequently, it is normal for the value chains of rival companies to differ, perhaps substantially—a

---

[7]Porter, *Competitive Advantage*, p. 36.

condition that complicates the task of assessing rivals' relative cost positions. For instance, competing companies may differ in their degrees of vertical integration. Comparing the value chain for a fully integrated rival against a partially integrated rival requires adjusting for differences in scope of activities performed—clearly the *internal* costs for a manufacturer that makes all of its own parts and components will be greater than the *internal* costs of a producer that buys the needed parts and components from outside suppliers and only performs assembly operations.

Likewise, there is legitimate reason to expect value chain and cost differences between a company that is pursuing a low-cost/low-price strategy and a rival positioned at the high-end of the market with a prestige quality product that possesses a wealth of features. In the case of the low-cost firm, the costs of certain activities along the company's value chain should indeed be relatively low whereas the high-end firm may understandably be spending relatively more to perform those activities that create the added quality and extra features.

Moreover, cost and price differences among rival companies can have their origins in activities performed by suppliers or by forward channel allies involved in getting the product to end users. Suppliers or forward channel allies may have excessively high cost structures or profit margins that jeopardize a company's cost competitiveness even though its costs for internally performed activities are competitive. For example, when determining Michelin's cost competitiveness vis-à-vis Goodyear and Bridgestone in supplying replacement tires to vehicle owners, one has to look at more than whether Michelin's tire manufacturing costs are above or below Goodyear's and Bridgestone's. If a buyer has to pay $400 for a set of Michelin tires and only $350 for comparable sets of Goodyear or Bridgestone tires, Michelin's $50 price disadvantage in the replacement tire marketplace can stem not only from higher manufacturing costs (reflecting, *perhaps*, the added costs of Michelin's strategic efforts to build a better quality tire with more performance features) but also from (1) differences in what the three tire makers pay their suppliers for materials and tire-making components and (2) differences in the operating efficiencies, costs, and markups of Michelin's wholesale distributors and retail dealers versus those of Goodyear and Bridgestone. Thus, determining whether a company's prices and costs are competitive from an end user's standpoint requires looking at the activities and costs of competitively relevant suppliers and forward allies, as well as the costs of internally performed activities.

A company's cost competitiveness depends not only on the costs of internally performed activities (its own value chain) but also on costs in the value chains of its suppliers and forward channel allies.

The Value Chain System for an Entire Industry As the tire industry example makes clear, a company's value chain is embedded in a larger system of activities that includes the value chains of its upstream suppliers and downstream customers or allies engaged in getting its product/service to end users.[8] Accurately assessing a company's competitiveness in end-use markets requires that company managers understand the entire value chain system for delivering a product or service to end-users, not just the company's own value chain. At the very least, this means considering the value chains of suppliers and forward channel allies (if any)—as shown in Figure 4.2. Suppliers' value chains are relevant because suppliers perform activities and incur costs in creating and delivering the purchased inputs used in a company's own value chain; the cost and quality of these inputs influence a company's own cost and/or differentiation capabilities. Anything a company can do to reduce its suppliers' costs or improve suppliers'

[8]Porter, *Competitive Advantage*, p. 34.

FIGURE 4.2   The Value Chain System

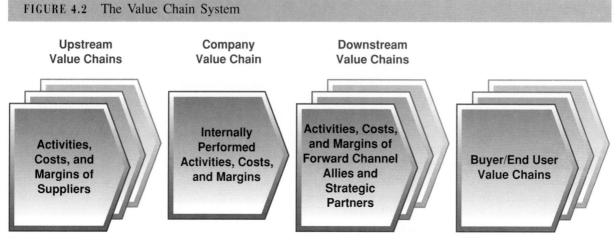

Source: Adapted from Michael E. Porter, *Competitive Advantage* (New York: The Free Press, 1985), p. 35.

effectiveness can enhance its own competitiveness—a powerful reason for working collaboratively or partnering with suppliers. Forward channel value chains are relevant because (1) the costs and margins of downstream companies are part of the price the ultimate end user pays and (2) the activities performed by forward channel allies affect the end user's satisfaction. There are powerful reasons for a company to work closely with forward channel allies to revise or reinvent their value chains in ways that enhance their mutual competitiveness. Furthermore, a company may be able to improve its competitiveness by undertaking activities that beneficially impact *both* its own value chain and its customers' value chains. For instance, some aluminum can producers constructed plants next to beer breweries and delivered cans on overhead conveyors directly to brewers' can-filling lines. This resulted in significant savings in production scheduling, shipping, and inventory costs for both container producers and breweries.[9] The lesson here is that a company's relative cost position and overall competitiveness is linked to the entire industry value chain system and to customers' value chains as well.

Although the value chains in Figures 4.1 and 4.2 are representative, the activity makeup of the chains and the relative importance of the activities within them vary by industry and by company position. Value chains for products differ from value chains for services. The major value chain elements for the pulp and paper industry (timber farming, logging, pulp mills, papermaking, printing, and publishing) differ from the major chain elements for the home appliance industry (parts and components manufacture, assembly, wholesale distribution, retail sales). The value chain for the soft-drink industry (processing of basic ingredients, syrup manufacture, bottling and can filling, wholesale distribution, retailing) differs from the makeup of the chain for the computer software industry (programming, disk loading, marketing, distribution). A producer of bathroom and kitchen faucets depends heavily on the activities of wholesale distributors and building supply retailers in winning sales to homebuilders and do-it-yourselfers. A wholesaler's most important activities and costs deal with purchased goods, inbound logistics, and outbound logistics. A hotel's most important activities and costs are in operations—check-in and check-out, maintenance and housekeeping, dining and room service, conventions and meetings, and

[9]Hegert and Morris, "Accounting Data for Value Chain Analysis," p. 180.

accounting. A global public accounting firm's most important activities and costs revolve around customer service and human resources management (recruiting and training a highly competent professional staff). Outbound logistics is a crucial activity at Domino's Pizza but comparatively insignificant at Blockbuster. Sales and marketing are dominant activities at Nike but only minor activities at electric and gas utilities. Consequently, generic value chains like those in Figures 4.1 and 4.2 are illustrative, not absolute, and may have to be adapted to fit a particular company's circumstances.

Developing the Data for Strategic Cost Analysis   Once the major value chain elements are identified, the next step in strategic cost analysis involves breaking down a firm's departmental cost accounting data into the costs of performing specific activities.[10] The appropriate degree of disaggregation depends on the economics of the activities and how valuable it is to develop cross-company cost comparisons for narrowly defined activities as opposed to broadly defined activities. A good guideline is to develop separate cost estimates for activities having different economics and for activities representing a significant or growing proportion of cost.[11]

Traditional accounting identifies costs according to broad categories of expenses—wages and salaries, employee benefits, supplies, travel, depreciation, R&D, and other fixed charges. *Activity-based costing* entails defining expense categories based on the specific activities being performed and then assigning costs to the appropriate activity responsible for creating the cost. An example is shown in Table 4.2.[12] Perhaps 10 percent of the companies that have explored the feasibility of activity-based costing have adopted this accounting approach. To fully understand the costs of activities all along the industry value chain, cost estimates for activities performed in suppliers' and customers' value chains also have to be developed.

To benchmark the firm's cost position against rivals, costs for the same activities for each rival must be estimated—an advanced art in competitive intelligence. But despite the tediousness of developing cost estimates activity by activity and the imprecision of some of the estimates for rivals, the payoff in exposing the costs of particular internal tasks and functions and the company's cost competitiveness makes activity-based costing a valuable strategic analysis tool.[13] Illustration Capsule 11 shows a simplified value chain comparison for two prominent brewers of beer—Anheuser-Busch (the U.S. industry leader) and Adolph Coors (the third-ranking U.S. brewer).

The most important application of value chain analysis is to expose how a particular firm's cost position compares with its rivals'. What is needed is competitor versus competitor cost estimates for supplying a product or service to a well-defined customer group or market segment. The size of a company's cost advantage/disadvantage can vary from item to item in the product line, from customer group to customer group (if different distribution channels are used), and from geographic market to geographic market (if cost factors vary across geographic regions).

---

[10]For discussions of the accounting challenges in calculating the costs of value chain activities, see Shank and Govindarajan, *Strategic Cost Management*, pp. 62–72 and chapter 5, and Hegert and Morris, "Accounting Data for Value Chain Analysis," pp. 175–88.

[11]Porter, *Competitive Advantage*, p. 45.

[12]For a discussion of activity-based cost accounting, see Cooper and Kaplan, "Measure Costs Right: Make the Right Decisions," pp. 96–103; Shank and Govindarajan, *Strategic Cost Management*, Chapter 11; and Joseph A. Ness and Thomas G. Cucuzza, "Tapping the Full Potential of ABC," *Harvard Business Review* 73 no. 4 (July–August 1995), pp. 130–38.

[13]Shank and Govindarajan, *Strategic Cost Management*, p. 62.

TABLE 4.2   The Difference between Traditional Cost Accounting and Activity-Based Cost Accounting

Traditional Cost Accounting Categories in Departmental Budget		Cost of Performing Specific Departmental Activities Using Activity-Based Cost Accounting	
Wages and salaries	$350,000	Evaluate supplier capabilities	$135,750
Employee benefits	115,000	Process purchase orders	82,100
Supplies	6,500	Expedite supplier deliveries	23,500
Travel	2,400	Expedite internal processing	15,840
Depreciation	17,000	Check quality of items purchased	94,300
Other fixed charges	124,000	Check incoming deliveries against purchase orders	48,450
Miscellaneous operating expenses	25,250	Resolve problems	110,000
		Internal administration	130,210
	$640,150		$640,150

Source: Adapted from information in Terence P. Paré, "A New Tool for Managing Costs," *Fortune*, June 14, 1993, pp. 124–29.

Benchmarking the Costs of Key Activities

Benchmarking the performance of company activities against rivals and other best-practice companies provides hard evidence of a company's cost competitiveness.

Many companies today are benchmarking the costs of performing a given activity against competitors' costs (and/or against the costs of a noncompetitor in another industry that efficiently and effectively performs much the same activity or business process). Benchmarking focuses on cross-company comparisons of how well basic functions and processes in the value chain are performed—how materials are purchased, how suppliers are paid, how inventories are managed, how employees are trained, how payrolls are processed, how fast the company can get new products to market, how the quality control function is performed, how customer orders are filled and shipped, and how maintenance is performed.[14] *The objectives of benchmarking are to understand the best practices in performing an activity, to learn how lower costs are actually achieved, and to take action to improve a company's cost competitiveness whenever benchmarking reveals that the costs of performing an activity are out of line with those of other companies.*

In 1979, Xerox became an early pioneer in the use of benchmarking when Japanese manufacturers began selling midsize copiers in the United States for $9,600 each—less than Xerox's production costs.[15] Although Xerox management suspected its Japanese competitors were dumping, it sent a team of line managers to Japan, including the head of manufacturing, to study competitors' business processes and costs. Fortunately, Xerox's joint venture partner in Japan, Fuji-Xerox, knew the competitors well. The team found that Xerox's costs were excessive due to gross

[14]For more details, see Gregory H. Watson, *Strategic Benchmarking: How to Rate Your Company's Performance Against the World's Best* (New York: John Wiley, 1993) and Robert C. Camp, *Benchmarking: The Search for Industry Best Practices That Lead to Superior Performance* (Milwaukee: ASQC Quality Press, 1989). See also Alexandra Biesada, "Strategic Benchmarking," *Financial World*, September 29, 1992, pp. 30–38.

[15]Jeremy Main, "How to Steal the Best Ideas Around," *Fortune*, October 19, 1992, pp. 102–3.

ILLUSTRATION CAPSULE 11 Value Chains for Anheuser-Busch and Adolph Coors Beers

In the table below are average cost estimates for the combined brands of beer produced by Anheuser-Busch and Coors. The example shows raw material costs, other manufacturing costs, and forward channel distribution costs. The data are for 1982.

Value Chain Activities and Costs	Estimated Average Cost Breakdown for Combined Anheuser-Busch Brands		Estimated Average Cost Breakdown for Combined Adolph Coors Brands	
	Per 6-Pack of 12-oz. Cans	Per Barrel Equivalent	Per 6-Pack of 12-oz Cans	Per Barrel Equivalent
1. Manufacturing costs:				
Direct production costs:				
Raw material ingredients	$0.1384	$ 7.63	$0.1082	$ 5.96
Direct labor	0.1557	8.58	0.1257	6.93
Salaries for nonunionized personnel	0.0800	4.41	0.0568	3.13
Packaging	0.5055	27.86	0.4663	25.70
Depreciation on plant and equipment	0.0410	2.26	0.0826	4.55
Subtotal	0.9206	50.74	0.8396	46.27
Other expenses:				
Advertising	0.0477	2.63	0.0338	1.86
Other marketing costs and general administrative expenses	0.1096	6.04	0.1989	10.96
Interest	0.0147	0.81	0.0033	0.18
Research and development	0.0277	1.53	0.0195	1.07
Total manufacturing costs	$1.1203	$ 61.75	$1.0951	$ 60.34
2. Manufacturer's operating profit	0.1424	7.85	0.0709	3.91
3. Net selling price	1.2627	69.60	1.1660	64.25
4. Plus federal and state excise taxes paid by brewer	0.1873	10.32	0.1782	9.82
5. Gross manufacturer's selling price to distributor/wholesaler	1.4500	79.92	1.3442	74.07
6. Average margin over manufacturer's cost	0.5500	30.31	0.5158	28.43
7. Average wholesale price charged to retailer (inclusive of taxes in item 4 above but exclusive of other taxes)	$ 2.00	$110.23	$ 1.86	$102.50
8. Plus other assorted state and local taxes levied on wholesale and retail sales (this varies from locality to locality)	0.60		0.60	
9. Average 20% retail markup over wholesale cost	0.40		0.38	
10. Average price to consumer at retail	$ 3.00		$ 2.84	

Note: The difference in the average cost structures for Anheuser-Busch and Adolph Coors is, to a substantial extent, due to A-B's higher proportion of super-premium beer sales. A-B's super-premium brand, Michelob, was the best-seller in its category and somewhat more costly to brew than premium and popular-priced beers.

Source: Compiled by Tom McLean, Elsa Wischkaemper, and Arthur A. Thompson, Jr., from a wide variety of documents and field interviews.

ILLUSTRATION CAPSULE 12   Ford Motor Company's Benchmarking of Its Accounts
                            Payable Activity

In the 1980s Ford's North American accounts payable department employed more than 500 people. Clerks spent the majority of their time straightening out the relatively few situations where three documents—the purchase order issued by the purchasing department, the receiving document prepared by clerks at the receiving dock, and the invoice sent by the vendor/supplier to accounts payable—did not match. Sometimes resolving the discrepancies took weeks of time and the efforts of many people. Ford managers believed that by using computers to automate some functions performed manually, head count could be reduced to 400. Before proceeding, Ford managers decided to visit Mazda—a company in which Ford had recently acquired a 25 percent ownership interest. To their astonishment, Mazda handled its accounts payable function with only five people. Following Mazda's lead, Ford benchmarkers created an invoiceless system where payments to suppliers were triggered automatically when the goods were received. The reengineered system allowed Ford to reduce its accounts payable staff to under 200, a lot more than Mazda but much better than would have resulted without benchmarking the accounts payable activity.

Sources: Michael Hammer and James Champy, *Reengineering the Corporation* (New York: HarperBusiness, 1993), pp. 39–43, and Jeremy Main, "How to Steal the Best Ideas Around," *Fortune*, October 19, 1992, p. 106.

inefficiencies in its manufacturing processes and business practices; the study proved instrumental in Xerox's efforts to become cost competitive and prompted Xerox to embark on a long-term program to benchmark 67 of its key work processes against companies identified as having the "best practices" in performing these processes. Xerox quickly decided not to restrict its benchmarking efforts to its office equipment rivals but to extend them to any company regarded as "world class" in performing an activity relevant to Xerox's business. Illustration Capsule 12 describes one of Ford Motor's benchmarking experiences.

Sometimes cost benchmarking can be accomplished by collecting information from published reports, trade groups, and industry research firms and by talking to knowledgeable industry analysts, customers, and suppliers (customers, suppliers, and joint-venture partners often make willing benchmarking allies). Usually, though, benchmarking requires field trips to the facilities of competing or noncompeting companies to observe how things are done, ask questions, compare practices and processes, and perhaps exchange data on productivity, staffing levels, time requirements, and other cost components. However, benchmarking involves competitively sensitive information about how lower costs are achieved, and close rivals can't be expected to be completely open, even if they agree to host facilities tours and answer questions. But the explosive interest of companies in benchmarking costs and identifying best practices has prompted consulting organizations (for example, Andersen Consulting, A. T. Kearney, Best Practices Benchmarking & Consulting, and Towers Perrin) and several newly formed councils and associations (the International Benchmarking Clearinghouse and the Strategic Planning Institute's Council on Benchmarking) to gather benchmarking data, do benchmarking studies, and distribute information about best practices and the costs of performing activities to clients/ members without identifying the sources. The ethical dimension of benchmarking is discussed in Illustration Capsule 13. Over 80 percent of *Fortune* 500 companies now engage in some form of benchmarking.

Benchmarking is a manager's best tool for determining whether the company is performing particular functions and activities efficiently, whether its costs are in line with competitors, and which activities and processes need to be improved. It is a way

---

ILLUSTRATION CAPSULE 13   Benchmarking and Ethical Conduct

Because actions between benchmarking partners can involve competitively sensitive data and discussions, conceivably raising questions about possible restraint of trade or improper business conduct, the SPI Council on Benchmarking and The International Benchmarking Clearinghouse urge all individuals and organizations involved in benchmarking to abide by a code of conduct grounded in ethical business behavior. The code is based on the following principles and guidelines:

- In benchmarking with competitors, establish specific ground rules up front, e.g., "We don't want to talk about those things that will give either of us a competitive advantage; rather, we want to see where we both can mutually improve or gain benefit." Do not discuss costs with competitors if costs are an element of pricing.

- Do not ask competitors for sensitive data or cause the benchmarking partner to feel that sensitive data must be provided to keep the process going. Be prepared to provide the same level of information that you request. Do not share proprietary information without prior approval from the proper authorities of both parties.

- Use an ethical third party to assemble and blind competitive data, with inputs from legal counsel, for direct competitor comparisons.

- Consult with legal counsel if any information gathering procedure is in doubt, e.g., before contacting a direct competitor.

- Any information obtained from a benchmarking partner should be treated as internal, privileged information. Any external use must have the partner's permission.

- Do not:
  - Disparage a competitor's business or operations to a third party.
  - Attempt to limit competition or gain business through the benchmarking relationship.
  - Misrepresent oneself as working for another employer.

- Demonstrate commitment to the efficiency and effectiveness of the process by being adequately prepared at each step, particularly at initial contact. Be professional, honest, and courteous. Adhere to the agenda—maintain focus on benchmarking issues.

Sources: The SPI Council on Benchmarking, The International Benchmarking Clearinghouse, and conference presentation of AT&T Benchmarking Group, Des Moines, Iowa, October 1993.

---

of learning which companies are best at performing certain activities and functions and then imitating—or, better still, improving on—their techniques. Toyota managers got their idea for just-in-time inventory deliveries by studying how U.S. supermarkets replenished their shelves. Southwest Airlines reduced the turnaround time of its aircraft at each scheduled stop by studying pit crews on the auto racing circuit.

Strategic Options for Achieving Cost Competitiveness

Value chain analysis and benchmarking can reveal a great deal about a firm's cost competitiveness. One of the fundamental insights of strategic cost analysis is that a company's competitiveness depends on how well it manages its value chain relative to how well competitors manage theirs.[16] Examining the makeup of a company's own value chain and comparing it to rivals' indicates who has how much of a cost advantage/disadvantage and which cost components are responsible. Such information is vital in crafting strategies to eliminate a cost disadvantage or create a cost advantage.

---

[16]Shank and Govindarajan, *Strategic Cost Management*, p. 50.

Looking again at Figure 4.2, observe that important differences in the costs of competing firms can occur in three main areas: in the suppliers' part of the industry value chain, in a company's own activity segments, or in the forward channel portion of the industry chain. If a firm's lack of cost competitiveness lies either in the backward (upstream) or forward (downstream) sections of the value chain, then reestablishing cost competitiveness may have to extend beyond the firm's own in-house operations. When a firm's cost disadvantage stems from the costs of items purchased from suppliers (the upstream end of the industry chain), company managers can take any of several strategic steps:[17]

Strategic actions to eliminate a cost disadvantage need to be linked to the location in the value chain where the cost differences originate.

- Negotiate more favorable prices with suppliers.
- Work with suppliers to help them achieve lower costs.
- Integrate backward to gain control over the costs of purchased items.
- Try to use lower-priced substitute inputs.
- Do a better job of managing the linkages between suppliers' value chains and the company's own chain; for example, close coordination between a company and its suppliers can permit just-in-time deliveries that lower a company's inventory and internal logistics costs and that may also allow its suppliers to economize on their warehousing, shipping, and production scheduling costs—a win-win outcome for both (instead of a zero-sum game where a company's gains match supplier concessions).[18]
- Try to make up the difference by cutting costs elsewhere in the chain.

A company's strategic options for eliminating cost disadvantages in the forward end of the value chain system include:[19]

- Pushing distributors and other forward channel allies to reduce their markups.
- Working closely with forward channel allies/customers to identify win-win opportunities to reduce costs. A chocolate manufacturer learned that by shipping its bulk chocolate in liquid form in tank cars instead of 10-pound molded bars, it saved its candy bar manufacturing customers the cost of unpacking and melting, and it eliminated its own costs of molding bars and packing them.
- Changing to a more economical distribution strategy, including forward integration.
- Trying to make up the difference by cutting costs earlier in the cost chain.

When the source of a firm's cost disadvantage is internal, managers can use any of nine strategic approaches to restore cost parity:[20]

---

[17]Porter, *Competitive Advantage*, chapter 3.

[18]In recent years, most companies have moved aggressively to collaborate with and partner with key suppliers to implement better supply chain management, often achieving cost savings of 5 to 25 percent. For a discussion of how to develop a cost-saving supply chain strategy, see Shashank Kulkarni, "Purchasing: A Supply-side Strategy," *Journal of Business Strategy* 17, no. 5 (September–October 1996), pp. 17–20.

[19]Porter, *Competitive Advantage*, Chapter 3.

[20]Ibid.

1. Streamline the operation of high-cost activities.

2. Reengineer business processes and work practices (to boost employee productivity, improve the efficiency of key activities, increase the utilization of company assets, and otherwise do a better job of managing the cost drivers).

3. Eliminate some cost-producing activities altogether by revamping the value chain system (for example, shifting to a radically different technological approach or maybe bypassing the value chains of forward channel allies and marketing directly to end users).

4. Relocate high-cost activities to geographic areas where they can be performed more cheaply.

5. See if certain activities can be outsourced from vendors or performed by contractors more cheaply than they can be done internally.

6. Invest in cost-saving technological improvements (automation, robotics, flexible manufacturing techniques, computerized controls).

7. Innovate around the troublesome cost components as new investments are made in plant and equipment.

8. Simplify the product design so that it can be manufactured more economically.

9. Make up the internal cost disadvantage through savings in the backward and forward portions of the value chain system.

From Value Chain Activities to Competitive Capabilities to Competitive Advantage

How well a company manages its value chain activities is a key to building valuable competencies and capabilities and leveraging them into sustainable competitive advantage. With rare exceptions, a firm's products or services are not a basis for sustainable competitive advantage—it is too easy for a resourceful company to clone, improve on, or find a substitute for them.[21] Rather, a company's competitive edge is usually grounded in its skills, know-how, and capabilities relative to those of its rivals and, more specifically, in the scope and depth of its ability to perform competitively crucial activities along the value chain better than rivals.

Developing the capability to perform competitively crucial value chain activities better than rivals is a dependable source of competitive advantage.

Competitively valuable competencies and capabilities emerge from a company's experience, learned skills, organizational routines and operating practices, and focused efforts in performing one or more related value chain components—they are not simply a consequence of the company's collection of resources. FedEx has purposefully built and integrated its resources to create the internal capabilities for providing customers with guaranteed overnight delivery services. McDonald's ability to turn out virtually identical-quality hamburgers at some 20,000-plus outlets around the world reflects impressive capability to replicate its operating systems at many locations through detailed rules and procedures and intensive training of franchise operators and outlet managers. Merck and Glaxo, two of the world's most competitively capable pharmaceutical companies, built their strategic

---

[21]James Brian Quinn, *Intelligent Enterprise* (New York: Free Press, 1993), p. 54.

positions around expert performance of a few key activities: extensive R&D to achieve first discovery of new drugs, a carefully constructed approach to patenting, skill in gaining rapid and thorough clinical clearance from regulatory bodies, and unusually strong distribution and sales force capabilities.[22]

Creating valuable competitive capabilities typically involves integrating the knowledge and skills of individual employees, leveraging the economies of learning and experience, effectively coordinating related value chain activities, making trade-offs between efficiency and flexibility, and exerting efforts to gain dominating expertise over rivals in one or more value chain activities critical to customer satisfaction and market success. Valuable capabilities enhance a company's competitiveness. The strategy-making lesson here is that sustainable competitive advantage can flow from concentrating company resources and talent on one or more competitively sensitive value chain activities; competitive advantage results from developing distinctive capabilities to serve customers—capabilities that buyers value highly and that company rivals don't have and are unable or unwilling to match.

QUESTION 4: HOW STRONG IS THE COMPANY'S COMPETITIVE POSITION?

Using the tools of value chains, strategic cost analysis, and benchmarking to determine a company's cost competitiveness is necessary but not sufficient. A broader assessment needs to be made of a company's competitive position and competitive strength. Particular issues that merit examination include (1) whether the firm's market position can be expected to improve or deteriorate if the present strategy is continued (allowing for fine-tuning), (2) how the firm ranks *relative to key rivals* on each industry key success factor and each relevant measure of competitive strength and resource capability, (3) whether the firm enjoys a competitive advantage over key rivals or is currently at a disadvantage, and (4) the firm's ability to defend its market position in light of industry driving forces, competitive pressures, and the anticipated moves of rivals.

Systematic assessment of whether a company's overall competitive position is strong or weak relative to close rivals is an essential step in company situation analysis.

Table 4.3 lists some indicators of whether a firm's competitive position is improving or slipping. But company managers need to do more than just identify the areas of competitive improvement or slippage. They have to judge whether the company has a net competitive advantage or disadvantage vis-á-vis key competitors and whether the company's market position and performance can be expected to improve or deteriorate under the current strategy.

Managers can begin the task of evaluating the company's competitive strength by using benchmarking techniques to compare the company against industry rivals not just on cost but also on such important measures as product quality, customer service, customer satisfaction, financial strength, technological skills, product cycle time (how quickly new products can be taken from idea to design to market), and the possession of competitively important resources and capabilities. It is not enough to benchmark the costs of activities and identify best practices; a company should benchmark itself against competitors on all strategically and competitively important aspects of its business.

---

[22]Quinn, *Intelligent Enterprise*, p. 34.

TABLE 4.3   The Signs of Strength and Weakness in a Company's Competitive Position

Signs of Competitive Strength	Signs of Competitive Weakness
• Important resource strengths, core competencies, and competitive capabilities • A distinctive competence in a competitively important value chain activity • Strong market share (or a leading market share) • A pace-setting or distinctive strategy • Growing customer base and customer loyalty • Above-average market visibility • In a favorably situated strategic group • Well positioned in attractive market segments • Strongly differentiated products • Cost advantages • Above-average profit margins • Above-average technological and innovational capability • A creative, entrepreneurially alert management • In position to capitalize on emerging market opportunities	• Confronted with competitive disadvantages • Losing ground to rival firms • Below-average growth in revenues • Short on financial resources • A slipping reputation with customers • Trailing in product development and product innovation capability • In a strategic group destined to lose ground • Weak in areas where there is the most market potential • A higher-cost producer • Too small to be a major factor in the marketplace • Not in good position to deal with emerging threats • Weak product quality • Lacking skills, resources, and competitive capabilities in key area • Weaker distribution capability than rivals

Competitive Strength Assessments

The most telling way to determine how strongly a company holds its competitive position is to quantitatively assess whether the company is stronger or weaker than close rivals on each of the industry's key success factors and on each pertinent indicator of competitive capability and potential competitive advantage. Much of the information for competitive strength assessment comes from prior analytical steps. Industry and competitive analysis reveals the key success factors and competitive determinants that separate industry winners from losers. Competitor analysis and benchmarking data provide information for judging the strengths and capabilities of key rivals.

Step one is to make a list of the industry's key success factors and most telling determinants of competitive advantage or disadvantage (6 to 10 measures usually suffice). Step two is to rate the firm and its key rivals on each strength indicator. Rating scales from 1 to 10 are best to use, although ratings of stronger (+), weaker (−), and about equal (=) may be appropriate when information is scanty and assigning numerical scores conveys false precision. Step three is to sum the individual strength overall ratings to get an measure of competitive strength for each competitor. Step four is to draw conclusions about the size and extent of the company's net competitive advantage or disadvantage and to take specific note of those strength measures where the company is strongest and weakest.

High competitive strength ratings signal a strong competitive position and possession of competitive advantage; low ratings signal a weak position and competitive disadvantage.

Table 4.4 provides two examples of competitive strength assessment. The first one employs an *unweighted rating scale*. With unweighted ratings each key success factor/competitive strength measure is assumed to be *equally important* (a rather dubious assumption). Whichever company has the highest strength rating on a given measure has an implied edge on that factor; the size of its edge is mirrored in the margin of difference between its rating and the ratings assigned to rivals. Summing a company's strength ratings on all the

TABLE 4.4   Illustrations of Unweighted and Weighted Competitive Strength Assessments

A. Sample of an Unweighted Competitive Strength Assessment

Rating scale: 1 = Very weak; 10 = Very strong

Key Success Factor/Strength Measure	ABC Co.	Rival 1	Rival 2	Rival 3	Rival 4
Quality/product performance	8	5	10	1	6
Reputation/image	8	7	10	1	6
Manufacturing capability	2	10	4	5	1
Technological skills	10	1	7	3	8
Dealer network/distribution capability	9	4	10	5	1
New product innovation capability	9	4	10	5	1
Financial resources	5	10	7	3	1
Relative cost position	5	10	3	1	4
Customer service capabilities	5	7	10	1	4
Unweighted overall strength rating	61	58	71	25	32

B. Sample of a Weighted Competitive Strength Assessment

Rating scale: 1 = Very weak; 10 = Very strong

Key Success Factor/Strength Measure	Weight	ABC Co.	Rival 1	Rival 2	Rival 3	Rival 4
Quality/product performance	0.10	8/0.80	5/0.50	10/1.00	1/0.10	6/0.60
Reputation/image	0.10	8/0.80	7/0.70	10/1.00	1/0.10	6/0.60
Manufacturing capability	0.10	2/0.20	10/1.00	4/0.40	5/0.50	1/0.10
Technological skills	0.05	10/0.50	1/0.05	7/0.35	3/0.15	8/0.40
Dealer network/distribution capability	0.05	9/0.45	4/0.20	10/0.50	5/0.25	1/0.05
New product innovation capability	0.05	9/0.45	4/0.20	10/0.50	5/0.25	1/0.05
Financial resources	0.10	5/0.50	10/1.00	7/0.70	3/0.30	1/0.10
Relative cost position	0.35	5/1.75	10/3.50	3/1.05	1/0.35	4/1.40
Customer service capabilities	0.15	5/0.75	7/1.05	10/1.50	1/0.15	4/1.60
Sum of weights	1.00					
Weighted overall strength rating		6.20	8.20	7.00	2.15	4.90

A weighted competitive strength analysis is conceptually stronger than an unweighted analysis because of the inherent weakness in assuming that all the strength measures are equally important.

measures produces an overall strength rating. The higher a company's overall strength rating, the stronger its competitive position. The bigger the margin of difference between a company's overall rating and the scores of lower-rated rivals, the greater its implied net competitive advantage. Thus, ABC's total score of 61 (see the top half of Table 4.4) signals a greater net competitive advantage over Rival 4 (with a score of 32) than over Rival 1 (with a score of 58).

However, it is better methodology to use a weighted rating system because the different measures of competitive strength are unlikely to be equally important. In a commodity-product industry, for instance, having low unit costs relative to rivals is nearly always the most important determinant of competitive strength. But in an industry with strong product differentiation the most significant measures of competitive strength may be brand awareness, amount of advertising, reputation for quality, and distribution capability. In a *weighted rating system* each measure of competitive strength is assigned a weight based on its perceived importance in shaping competitive success. The largest weight could be as high as .75 (maybe even higher) when one particular competitive variable is overwhelmingly decisive or as low as .20 when two or three strength measures are more important than the rest. Lesser competitive strength indicators can carry weights of .05 or .10. No matter whether the differences between the weights are big or little, *the sum of the weights must add up to 1.0.*

Weighted strength ratings are calculated by deciding how a company stacks up on each strength measure (using the 1 to 10 rating scale) and multiplying the assigned rating by the assigned weight (a rating score of 4 times a weight of .20 gives a weighted rating of .80). Again, the company with the highest rating on a given measure has an implied competitive edge on that measure, with the size of its edge reflected in the difference between its rating and rivals' ratings. The weight attached to the measure indicates how important the edge is. Summing a company's weighted strength ratings for all the measures yields an overall strength rating. Comparisons of the weighted overall strength scores indicate which competitors are in the strongest and weakest competitive positions and who has how big a net competitive advantage over whom.

The bottom half of Table 4.4 shows a sample competitive strength assessment for ABC Company using a weighted rating system. Note that the unweighted and weighted rating schemes produce a different ordering of the companies. In the weighted system, ABC Company dropped from second to third in strength, and Rival 1 jumped from third into first because of its high strength ratings on the two most important factors. Weighting the importance of the strength measures can thus make a significant difference in the outcome of the assessment.

Competitive strength assessments provide useful conclusions about a company's competitive situation. The ratings show how a company compares against rivals, factor by factor or capability by capability. Moreover, the overall competitive strength scores indicate whether the company is at a net competitive advantage or disadvantage against each rival. The firm with the largest overall competitive strength rating can be said to have a net competitive advantage over each rival.

Knowing where a company is competitively strong and where it is weak is essential in crafting a strategy to strengthen its long-term competitive position. As a general rule, a company should try to convert its competitive strengths into sustainable competitive advantage and take strategic actions to protect against its competitive weaknesses. At the same time, competitive strength ratings point to which rival companies may be vulnerable to competitive attack and the areas where they are weakest. When a company has important competitive strengths in areas where one or more rivals are weak, it makes sense to consider offensive moves to exploit their competitive weaknesses.

Competitive strengths and competitive advantages enable a company to improve its long-term market position.

QUESTION 5: WHAT STRATEGIC ISSUES DOES THE COMPANY FACE?

The final analytical task is to zero in on the issues management needs to address in forming an effective strategic action plan. Here, managers need to draw upon

Identifying and thoroughly understanding the strategic issues a company faces is a prerequisite to effective strategy-making.

all the prior analysis, put the company's overall situation into perspective, and get a lock on exactly where they need to focus their strategic attention. This step should not be taken lightly. Without a precise fix on what the issues are, managers are not prepared to start crafting a strategy—a good strategy must offer a plan for dealing with all the strategic issues that need to be addressed.

To pinpoint issues for the company's strategic action agenda, managers ought to consider the following:

- Does the present strategy offer attractive defenses against the five competitive forces—particularly those that are expected to intensify in strength?
- Should the present strategy be adjusted to better respond to the driving forces at work in the industry?
- Is the present strategy closely matched to the industry's *future* key success factors?
- Does the present strategy adequately capitalize on the company's resource strengths?
- Which of the company's opportunities merit top priority? Which should be given lowest priority? Which are best suited to the company's resource strengths and capabilities?
- What does the company need to do to correct its resource weaknesses and to protect against external threats?
- To what extent is the company vulnerable to the competitive efforts of one or more rivals and what can be done to reduce this vulnerability?
- Does the company possess competitive advantage or must it work to offset competitive disadvantage?
- Where are the strong spots and weak spots in the present strategy?
- Are additional actions needed to improve the company's cost position, capitalize on emerging opportunities, and strengthen the company's competitive position?

The answers to these questions point to whether the company can continue the same basic strategy with minor adjustments or whether major overhaul is called for.

The better matched a company's strategy is to its external environment and to its resource strengths and capabilities, the less need there is to contemplate big shifts in strategy. On the other hand, when the present strategy is not well-suited for the road ahead, managers need to give top priority to the task of crafting a better strategy.

Table 4.5 provides a format for doing company situation analysis. It incorporates the concepts and analytical techniques discussed in this chapter and provides a way of reporting the results of company situation analysis in a systematic, concise manner.

KEY POINTS

There are five key questions to consider in performing company situation analysis:

1. *How well is the present strategy working?* This involves evaluating the strategy from both a qualitative standpoint (completeness, internal consistency, rationale, and suitability to the situation) and a quantitative standpoint (the strategic and financial

TABLE 4.5 Company Situation Analysis

1. Strategic Performance Indicators

Performance Indicator	19__	19__	20__	20__	20__
Market share	___	___	___	___	___
Sales growth	___	___	___	___	___
Net profit margin	___	___	___	___	___
Return on equity investment	___	___	___	___	___
Other?	___	___	___	___	___

2. Internal Resource Strengths and Competitive Capabilities

Internal Weaknesses and Resource Deficiencies

External Opportunities

External Threats to the Company's Well-Being

3. Competitive Strength Assessment

Rating scale: 1 = Very weak; 10 = Very strong

Key Success Factor/Competitive Strength Measure	Weight	Firm A	Firm B	Firm C	Firm D	Firm E
Quality/product performance	___	___	___	___	___	___
Reputation/image	___	___	___	___	___	___
Manufacturing capability	___	___	___	___	___	___
Technological skills and know-how	___	___	___	___	___	___
Dealer network/distribution capability	___	___	___	___	___	___
New product innovation capability	___	___	___	___	___	___
Financial resources	___	___	___	___	___	___
Relative cost position	___	___	___	___	___	___
Customer service capability	___	___	___	___	___	___
Other?	___	___	___	___	___	___
Overall strength rating	___	___	___	___	___	___

4. Conclusions Concerning Competitive Position

(Improving/slipping? Competitive advantages/disadvantages?)

5. Major Strategic Issues the Company Must Address

results the strategy is producing). The stronger a company's current overall performance, the less likely the need for radical strategy changes. The weaker a company's performance and/or the faster the changes in its external situation (which can be gleaned from industry and competitive analysis), the more its current strategy must be questioned.

2. *What are the company's resource strengths and weaknesses and its external opportunities and threats?* A SWOT analysis provides an overview of a firm's situation and is an essential component of crafting a strategy tightly matched to the company's situation. A company's resource strengths, competencies, and competitive capabilities are important because they are the most logical and appealing building blocks for strategy; resource weaknesses are important because they may represent vulnerabilities that need correction. External opportunities and threats come into play because a good strategy necessarily aims at capturing a company's most attractive opportunities and at defending against threats to its well-being.

3. *Are the company's prices and costs competitive?* One telling sign of whether a company's situation is strong or precarious is whether its prices and costs are competitive with industry rivals. Strategic cost analysis and value chain analysis are essential tools in benchmarking a company's prices and costs against rivals, determining whether the company is performing particular functions and activities cost effectively, learning whether its costs are in line with competitors, and deciding which internal activities and business processes need to be scrutinized for improvement. Value chain analysis teaches that how competently a company manages its value chain activities relative to rivals is a key to building valuable competencies and competitive capabilities and then leveraging them into sustainable competitive advantage.

4. *How strong is the company's competitive position?* The key appraisals here involve whether the company's position is likely to improve or deteriorate if the present strategy is continued, how the company matches up against key rivals on industry KSFs and other chief determinants of competitive success, and whether and why the company has a competitive advantage or disadvantage. Quantitative competitive strength assessments, using the methodology presented in Table 4.4, indicate where a company is competitively strong and weak and provide insight into the company's ability to defend or enhance its market position. As a rule a company's competitive strategy should be built around its competitive strengths and should aim at shoring up areas where it is competitively vulnerable. Also, the areas where company strengths match up against competitor weaknesses represent the best potential for new offensive initiatives.

5. *What strategic issues does the company face?* The purpose of this analytical step is to develop a complete strategy-making agenda using the results of both company situation analysis and industry and competitive analysis. The emphasis here is on drawing conclusions about the strengths and weaknesses of a company's strategy and framing the issues that strategy makers need to consider.

Good company situation analysis, like good industry and competitive analysis, is crucial to good strategy making. A competently done evaluation of a company's resources and competencies exposes strong and weak elements in the present strategy, points to important company capabilities and vulnerabilities, and indicates the company's ability to protect or improve its competitive position in light of driving forces, competitive pressures, and the competitive strength of rivals. Managers need such understanding to craft a strategy that fits the company's situation well.

Collis, David J., and Cynthia A. Montgomery. "Competing on Resources: Strategy in the 1990s." *Harvard Business Review* 73 no. 4 (July–August 1995), pp. 118–28.

Fahey, Liam, and H. Kurt Christensen. "Building Distinctive Competencies into Competitive Advantages." Reprinted in Liam Fahey, *The Strategic Planning Management Reader*. Englewood Cliffs, N.J.: Prentice-Hall, 1989, pp. 113–18.

Prahalad, C. K., and Gary Hamel. "The Core Competence of the Corporation." *Harvard Business Review* 90, no. 3 (May–June 1990), pp. 79–93.

Shank, John K., and Vijay Govindarajan. *Strategic Cost Management: The New Tool for Competitive Advantage.* New York: Free Press, 1993.

Stalk, George, Philip Evans, and Lawrence E. Shulman. "Competing on Capabilities: The New Rules of Corporate Strategy." *Harvard Business Review* 70, no. 2 (March–April 1992), pp. 57–69.

Watson, Gregory H. *Strategic Benchmarking: How to Rate Your Company's Performance Against the World's Best.* New York: John Wiley & Sons, 1993.

SUGGESTED READINGS

5 STRATEGY AND COMPETITIVE ADVANTAGE

Successful business strategy is about actively shaping the game you play, not just playing the game you find.

Adam M. Brandenburger and Barry J. Nalebuff

The essence of strategy lies in creating tomorrow's competitive advantages faster than competitors mimic the ones you possess today.

Gary Hamel and C. K. Prahalad

Competitive strategy is about being different. It means deliberately choosing to perform activities differently or to perform different activities than rivals to deliver a unique mix of value.

Michael E. Porter

Strategies for taking the hill won't necessarily hold it.

Amar Bhide

Winning business strategies are grounded in sustainable competitive advantage. A company has *competitive advantage* whenever it has an edge over rivals in attracting customers and defending against competitive forces. There are many routes to competitive advantage: developing a product that becomes the industry standard, manufacturing the best-made product on the market, delivering superior customer service, achieving lower costs than rivals, having a more convenient geographic location, developing proprietary technology, incorporating features and styling with more buyer appeal, having the capability to bring new products to market faster than rivals, having greater technological expertise than rivals, developing unique competencies in customized mass production techniques, doing a better job of supply chain management than rivals, building a better-known brand name and reputation, and providing buyers more value for the money (a combination of good quality, good service, and acceptable price). *Investing aggressively in creating sustainable competitive advantage is a company's single most dependable contributor to above-average profitability.*

To succeed in building a competitive advantage, a company's strategy must aim at providing buyers with what they perceive as superior value—a good product at a lower price or a better product that is worth paying more for. This translates into performing value chain activities differently than rivals and building competencies and resource capabilities that are not readily matched.

This chapter focuses on how a company can achieve or defend a competitive advantage.[1] We begin by describing the basic types of competitive strategies in some depth. Next are sections examining the pros and cons of a vertical integration strategy and the merits of cooperative strategies. There are also major sections surveying the use of offensive moves to build competitive advantage and the use of defensive moves to protect it. In the concluding section we look at the competitive importance of timing strategic moves—when it is advantageous to be a first-mover and when it is better to be a fast-follower or late-mover.

---

[1]The definitive work on this subject is Michael E. Porter, *Competitive Advantage* (New York: Free Press, 1985). The treatment in this chapter draws heavily on Porter's pioneering contribution.

THE FIVE GENERIC COMPETITIVE STRATEGIES

A company's competitive strategy consists of its business approaches and initiatives to attract customers and fulfill their expectations, to withstand competitive pressures, and to strengthen its market position.[2] The competitive aim, quite simply, is to do a significantly better job of providing what buyers are looking for, enabling the company to earn a competitive advantage and outcompete rivals. The core of a company's competitive strategy consists of its internal initiatives to deliver superior value to customers. But it also includes offensive and defensive moves to counter the maneuvering of key rivals, actions to shift resources around to improve the firm's long-term competitive capabilities and market position, and tactical efforts to respond to whatever market conditions prevail at the moment.

The objective of competitive strategy is to knock the socks off rival companies by doing a significantly better job of providing what buyers are looking for.

Companies the world over are imaginative in conceiving strategies to win customer favor, outcompete rivals, and secure a market edge. Because a company's strategic initiatives and market maneuvers are usually tailor-made to fit its specific situation and industry environment, there are countless variations in the strategies that companies employ—strictly speaking, there are as many competitive strategies as there are competitors. However, when one strips away the details to get at the real substance the biggest and most important differences among competitive strategies boil down to (1) whether a company's market target is broad or narrow and (2) whether it is pursuing a competitive advantage linked to low costs or product differentiation. Five distinct approaches stand out:[3]

1. *A low-cost leadership strategy*—Appealing to a broad spectrum of customers based on being the overall low-cost provider of a product or service.

2. *A broad differentiation strategy*—Seeking to differentiate the company's product offering from rivals' in ways that will appeal to a broad spectrum of buyers.

3. *A best-cost provider strategy*—Giving customers more value for the money by combining an emphasis on low cost with an emphasis on upscale differentiation; the target is to have the best (lowest) costs and prices relative to producers of products with comparable quality and features.

4. *A focused or market niche strategy based on lower cost*—Concentrating on a narrow buyer segment and outcompeting rivals by serving niche members at a lower cost than rivals.

5. *A focused or market niche strategy based on differentiation*—Concentrating on a narrow buyer segment and outcompeting rivals by offering niche members a customized product or service that meets their tastes and requirements better than rivals' offerings.

Each of these five generic competitive approaches stakes out a different market position—as shown in Figure 5–1. Each involves distinctively different approaches to competing and operating the business. The listing in Table 5–1 highlights the

---

[2]Competitive strategy has a narrower scope than business strategy. Competitive strategy deals exclusively with management's action plan for competing successfully and providing superior value to customers. Business strategy not only concerns how to compete but also how management intends to address the full range of strategic issues confronting the business.

[3]The classification scheme is an adaptation of one presented in Michael E. Porter, *Competitive Strategy: Techniques for Analyzing Industries and Competitors* (New York: Free Press, 1980), chapter 2 and especially pp. 35–39 and 44–46.

FIGURE 5-1 The Five Generic Competitive Strategies

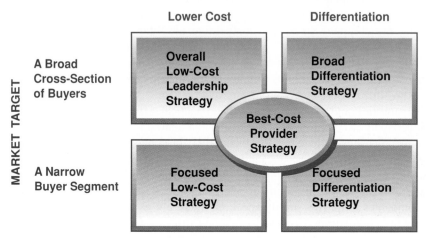

Source: Adapted from Michael E. Porter, *Competitive Strategy* (New York: Free Press, 1980), pp. 35–40.

contrasting features of these generic competitive strategies (for simplicity, the two strains of focused strategies are combined under one heading since they differ fundamentally on only one feature—the basis of competitive advantage).

Low-Cost Provider Strategies

Striving to be the industry's overall low-cost provider is a powerful competitive approach in markets where many buyers are price sensitive. The aim is to operate the business in a highly cost-effective manner and open up a sustainable cost advantage over rivals. A low-cost provider's strategic target is *low cost relative to competitors*, not the absolutely lowest possible cost. In pursuing low-cost leadership, managers must take care to include features and services that buyers consider essential—a product that is too spartan and frills-free weakens rather than strengthens competitiveness. Furthermore, it matters greatly whether the company achieves its cost advantage in ways difficult for rivals to copy or match. The value of a cost advantage depends on its sustainability. If rivals find it relatively easy and/or inexpensive to imitate the leader's low-cost methods, then the low-cost leader's advantage is too short-lived to yield a valuable edge.

A low-cost leader's basis for competitive advantage is lower overall costs than competitors. Successful low-cost leaders are exceptionally good at finding ways to drive costs out of their businesses.

A low-cost leader has two options for achieving superior profit performance. Option one is to use the lower-cost edge to underprice competitors and attract price-sensitive buyers in great enough numbers to increase total profits.[4] Option two is to

---

[4]The trick to profitably underpricing rivals is either to keep the size of the price cut smaller than the size of the firm's cost advantage (thus reaping the benefits of both a bigger profit margin per unit sold and the added profits on incremental sales) or to generate enough added volume to increase total profits despite thinner profit margins (larger volume can make up for smaller margins provided the price reductions bring in enough extra sales).

TABLE 5-1 Distinctive Features of the Generic Competitive Strategies

Type of Feature	Low-Cost Leadership	Broad Differentiation	Best-Cost Provider	Focused Low-Cost and Focused Differentiation
Strategic target	• A broad cross-section of the market.	• A broad cross-section of the market.	• Value-conscious buyers.	• A narrow market niche where buyer needs and preferences are distinctively different from the rest of the market.
Basis of competitive advantage	• Lower costs than competitors	• An ability to offer buyers something different from competitors.	• Give customers more value for the money	• Lower cost in serving the niche (focused low cost) *or* an ability to offer niche buyers something customized to their requirements and tastes (focused differentiation).
Product line	• A good basic product with few frills (acceptable quality and limited selection).	• Many product variations, wide selection, strong emphasis on the chosen differentiating features.	• Good-to-excellent attributes, several-to-many upscale features.	• Customized to fit the specialized needs of the target segment
Production emphasis	• A continuous search for cost reduction without sacrificing acceptable quality and essential features.	• Invent ways to create value for buyers; strive for product superiority.	• Incorporate upscale features and attributes at low cost.	• Tailor-made for the niche.
Marketing emphasis	• Try to make a virtue out of product features that lead to low cost.	• Build in whatever features buyers are willing to pay for. • Charge a premium price to cover the extra costs of differentiating features.	• Underprice rival brands with comparable features	• Communicate the focuser's unique ability to satisfy the buyer's specialized requirements
Sustaining the strategy	• Economical prices/ good value. • All elements of strategy aim at contributing to a sustainable cost advantage—the key is to manage costs down, year after year, in every area of the business.	• Communicate the points of difference in credible ways. • Stress constant improvement and innovation to stay ahead of imitative competitors. • Concentrate on a few key differentiating features; tout them to create a reputation and brand image.	• Unique expertise in managing costs down and product/ service caliber up simultaneously.	• Remain totally dedicated to serving the niche better than other competitors; don't blunt the firm's image and efforts by entering segments with substantially different buyer requirements or adding other product categories to widen market appeal.

refrain from price-cutting altogether, be content with the present market share, and use the lower-cost edge to earn a higher profit margin on each unit sold, thereby raising the firm's total profits and overall return on investment.

Illustration Capsule 14 describes ACX Technologies' strategy for gaining low-cost leadership in aluminum cans.

Opening Up a Cost Advantage   To achieve a cost advantage, a firm's cumulative costs across its value chain must be lower than competitors' cumulative costs. There are two ways to accomplish this:[5]

- Do a better job than rivals of performing internal value chain activities efficiently and of managing the factors that drive the costs of value chain activities.
- Revamp the firm's value chain to permit some cost-producing activities to be bypassed altogether.

Let's look at each of the two avenues.

Controlling the Cost Drivers   A firm's cost position is the result of the behavior of costs in each activity in its total value chain. Any of nine different cost drivers can come into play in determining a company's costs in a particular value chain activity:[6]

1. *Economies or diseconomies of scale.* The costs of a particular value chain activity are often subject to economies or diseconomies of scale. Economies of scale arise whenever activities can be performed more cheaply at larger volumes than smaller volumes and from the ability to spread out certain costs like R & D and advertising over a greater sales volume. Astute management of those activities subject to scale economies or diseconomies can be a major source of cost savings. For example, manufacturing economies can usually be achieved by simplifying the product line, by scheduling longer production runs for fewer models, and by using common parts and components in different models. In global industries, making separate products for each country market instead of selling a standard product worldwide tends to boost unit costs because of lost time in model changeover, shorter production runs, and inability to reach the most economic scale of production for each country model. Scale economies or diseconomies also arise in how a company manages its sales and marketing activities. A geographically organized sales force can realize economies as regional sales volume grows because a salesperson can write larger orders at each sales call and/or because of reduced travel time between calls; on the other hand, a sales force organized by product line can encounter travel-related diseconomies if salespersons have to spend travel time calling on distantly spaced customers. Boosting local or regional market share can lower sales and marketing costs per unit, whereas opting for a bigger national share by entering new regions can create scale diseconomies unless and until market penetration reaches efficient proportions.

2. *Learning and experience curve effects.* The cost of performing an activity can decline over time due to economies of experience and learning. Experience-based cost savings can come from much more than just personnel learning how to perform their tasks more efficiently and the debugging of new technologies. Other valuable

[5]Michael E. Porter, *Competitive Advantage* (New York: Free Press, 1985), p. 97.
[6]The list and explanations are condensed from Porter, *Competitive Advantage*, pp. 70–107.

ILLUSTRATION CAPSULE 14   ACX Technologies' Strategy to Become a Low-Cost Producer of Aluminum Cans

ACX Technologies began as an idea of William Coors, CEO of Adolph Coors beer company, to recycle more used aluminum cans back into new cans. Typical aluminum can-making operations involved producing thick aluminum slabs from a smelter using bauxite ore combined with as much as 50 percent scrap aluminum, including used aluminum beverage cans; the slabs of aluminum ingot were fed into a rolling mill to achieve the required thickness. Cans were then formed by stamping pieces of thin aluminum sheet into a seamless can with the top open for filling.

Coors's idea was to produce aluminum-can sheet from 95 percent recycled cans. He began by purchasing rights to technology that his company had helped develop in Europe; the technology used lower-cost electric arc furnaces to melt aluminum scrap directly, short-cutting the smelter process, which required heavy capital investment and big production volumes to be competitive. Coors then built a plant in Colorado that could grind and melt used cans and pour hot aluminum through a continuous caster to make aluminum sheet suitable for the tops and tabs of beverage cans. It took seven years to develop alloys with the desired attributes and to fine-tune the process—Coors originally believed it could be done in less than two years.

In mid-1991 Coors announced it would build a new $200 million mill in Texas to make sheet aluminum for the body of the can—the product with the most exacting specifications but also the number one end use for aluminum in the United States. Production was expected to begin by mid-1992, but problems and delays soon pushed the start-up date into fall 1993. The new plant's low-cost advantages stemmed from several factors:

- Lower capital investment.
- Use of 95 percent recycled aluminum cans as feedstock—reducing raw material costs in producing aluminum sheet by 10 to 15.
- Lower electricity requirements—electric arc technology used only about one-fifth of the electricity of bauxite-smelter technology.
- Comparatively low electric rates at the Texas location.

- Reduced labor costs as compared to bauxite-smelter technology.

Overall, production costs were expected to be anywhere from 20 to 35 percent below the costs of aluminum can producers using traditionally produced aluminum sheet, depending on the prevailing market prices for aluminum ingot and scrap aluminum. In addition, the mill had greater flexibility than traditional producers to vary its alloy mixes to meet different customer specifications.

Meanwhile, in December 1992 during construction of the Texas plant, Coors decided to spin off all aluminum can operations (along with a paper-packaging operation making patented polyethylene cartons with high-quality metallic graphics—packaging for Cascade boxes and Lever 2000 soapbars are examples; a ceramics unit making materials for high-tech applications; and several developmental businesses) into a new publicly owned company called ACX Technologies. The new company had 1992 revenues of $570 million, about 28 percent of which were sales to Coors. The breakdown of revenues in 1992 was aluminum for cans 17 percent, graphics packaging 37 percent, ceramics materials 32 percent, and developmental businesses 14 percent (including corn wet milling, biotechnology, defense electronics, and biodegradable polymers).

In summer 1993, the Texas plant was in start-up and can makers began testing the quality of its aluminum sheet. Coors was the first to qualify ACX's output for use; at year-end 1993 four other can users were testing the suitability of the plant's output for their products. ACX expected the plant to ship close to 50 million pounds of aluminum by year-end 1993 and 100 million pounds or more in 1994 as new customers placed orders. Analysts believed that ACX, given its cost advantage, could grow its annual volume to 1.0 to 1.5 billion pounds in 10 years as it perfected the process and gained acceptance for the quality of its output.

The company's new shares were issued at $10.75 in December 1992 when it went public. In the first 20 days of trading the price climbed to $21.75. Later in 1993, shares traded as high as $46. In May 1994 they were trading in the mid-$30s.

Sources: Based on information published by The Robinson-Humphrey Company and on Marc Charlier, "ACX Strives to Become Aluminum's Low-Cost Producer," *The Wall Street Journal*, September 29, 1993, p. B2.

sources of learning/experience economies include seeing ways to improve plant layout and work flows, to modify product designs to enhance manufacturing efficiency, to redesign machinery and equipment to gain increased operating speed, and to tailor parts and components in ways that streamline assembly. Learning can also reduce the cost of constructing and operating new retail outlets, new plants, or new distribution facilities. Plus there are learning benefits from getting samples of a rival's products and having design engineers study how they are made, benchmarking company activities against the performance of similar activities in other companies, and interviewing suppliers, consultants, and ex-employees of rival firms to tap into their wisdom. Learning tends to vary with the amount of management attention devoted to capturing the benefits of experience of both the firm and outsiders. Astute managers make a conscious effort not only to capture learning benefits but also to keep the benefits proprietary by building or modifying production equipment in-house, endeavoring to retain knowledgeable employees (to reduce the risk of them going to work for rivals firms), limiting the dissemination of cost-saving information through employee publications that can fall into rivals' hands, and enforcing strict nondisclosure provisions in employment contracts.

3. *The cost of key resource inputs.* The cost of performing value chain activities depends in part on what a firm has to pay for key resource inputs. All competitors do not incur the same costs for items purchased from suppliers or for resources used in performing value chain activities. How well a company manages the costs of acquiring inputs is often a big driver of costs. Input costs are a function of three factors:

- *Union versus nonunion labor*—Avoiding the use of union labor is often a key to low-cost manufacturing, not just to escape paying high wages (because such prominent low-cost manufacturers as Nucor and Cooper Tire are noted for their incentive compensation systems that allow their nonunion workforces to earn more than their unionized counterparts at rival companies) but rather to escape union work rules that stifle productivity.
- *Bargaining power vis-à-vis suppliers*—Many large enterprises (Wal-Mart, Home Depot, the world's major motor vehicle producers) have used their bargaining clout in purchasing large volumes to wrangle good prices on their purchases from suppliers. Differences in buying power among industry rivals can be an important source of cost advantage or disadvantage.
- *Locational variables*—Locations differ in their prevailing wage levels, tax rates, energy costs, inbound and outbound shipping and freight costs, and so on. Opportunities may exist for reducing costs by relocating plants, field offices, warehousing, or headquarters operations.

4. *Linkages with other activities in the company or industry value chain.* When the cost of one activity is affected by how other activities are performed, costs can be reduced by making sure that linked activities are performed in cooperative and coordinated fashion. For example, when a company's quality control costs or materials inventory costs are linked to the activities of suppliers, costs can be saved by working cooperatively with key suppliers on the design of parts and components, quality-assurance procedures, just-in-time delivery, and integrated materials supply. The costs of new product development can often be reduced by having cross-functional task forces (perhaps including representatives of suppliers and key customers) jointly work on R&D, product design, manufacturing plans, and market launch. Linkages with forward channels tend to center on location of warehouses,

materials handling, outbound shipping, and packaging (nail manufacturers, for example, learned that nails delivered in prepackaged 1-pound, 5-pound, and 10-pound assortments instead of 100-pound bulk cartons could reduce a hardware dealer's labor costs in filling individual customer orders). The lesson here is that effective coordination of linked activities holds potential for cost reduction.

5. *Sharing opportunities with other organizational or business units within the enterprise.* Different product lines or business units within an enterprise can often share the same order processing and customer billing systems, use a common sales force to call on customers, share the same warehouse and distribution facilities, or rely upon a common customer service and technical support team. Such combining of like activities and the sharing of resources across sister units can create significant cost savings. Cost sharing can help achieve scale economies, shorten the learning curve in mastering a new technology, and/or promote fuller capacity utilization. Furthermore, the know-how gained in one division or geographic unit can be used to help lower costs in another; sharing know-how across organizational lines has significant cost-saving potential when the activities are similar and know-how is readily transferred from one unit to another.

6. *The benefits of vertical integration versus outsourcing.* Partially or fully integrating into the activities of either suppliers or forward channel allies can allow an enterprise to detour suppliers or buyers with bargaining power. Vertical integration forward or backward also has potential if merging or tightly coordinating adjacent activities in the industry value chain offers significant cost savings. On the other hand, it is sometimes cheaper to outsource certain functions and activities to outside specialists who by virtue of their expertise and volume, can perform the activity/function more cheaply.

7. *Timing considerations associated with first-mover advantages and disadvantages.* Sometimes the first major brand in the market is able to establish and maintain its brand name at a lower cost than later brand arrivals—being a first-mover turns out to be cheaper than being a late-mover. On other occasions, such as when technology is developing fast, late purchasers can benefit from waiting to install second- or third-generation equipment that is both cheaper and more efficient; first-generation users often incur added costs associated with debugging and learning how to use an immature and unperfected technology. Likewise, companies that follow rather than lead new product development efforts sometimes avoid many of the costs that pioneers incur in performing pathbreaking R&D and opening up new markets.

8. *The percentage of capacity utilization.* Capacity utilization is a big cost driver for value chain activities that have substantial fixed costs associated with them. Higher rates of capacity utilization allow depreciation and other fixed costs to be spread over a larger unit volume, thereby lowering fixed costs per unit. The more capital-intensive the business and/or the higher the percentage of fixed costs as a percentage of total costs, the more important this cost driver becomes because there's such a stiff unit-cost penalty for underutilizing existing capacity. In such cases, finding ways to operate close to full capacity on a year-round basis can be an important source of cost advantage.[7]

---

[7]A firm can improve its capacity utilization by *(a)* serving a mix of accounts with peak volumes spread throughout the year, *(b)* finding off-season uses for its products, *(c)* serving private-label customers that can intermittently use the excess capacity, *(d)* selecting buyers with stable demands or demands that are counter to the normal peak/valley cycle, *(e)* letting competitors serve the buyer segments whose demands fluctuate the most, and *(f)* sharing capacity with sister units having a different seasonal production pattern (producing snowmobiles for the winter season and jet skis for summer water sports).

9. *Strategic choices and operating decisions.* A company's costs can be driven up or down by a fairly wide assortment of managerial decisions:

- Increasing/decreasing the number of products or varieties offered.
- Adding/cutting the services provided to buyers.
- Incorporating more/fewer performance and quality features into the product.
- Paying higher/lower wages and fringes to employees relative to rivals and firms in other industries.
- Increasing/decreasing the number of different forward channels used in distributing the firm's product.
- Lengthening/shortening delivery times to customers.
- Putting more/less emphasis than rivals on the use of incentive compensation to motivate employees and boost worker productivity.
- Raising/lowering the specifications for purchased materials.

Managers intent on achieving low-cost leader status have to develop sophisticated understanding of how the above nine factors drive the costs of each activity in the value chain. Then they not only have to use their knowledge to reduce costs for every activity where cost savings can be identified but they have to do so with enough ingenuity and commitment that the company ends up with a sustainable cost advantage over rivals.

Outperforming rivals in controlling the factors that drive costs is a very demanding managerial exercise.

Revamping the Makeup of the Value Chain   Dramatic cost advantages can emerge from finding innovative ways to restructure processes and tasks, cut out frills, and provide the basics more economically. The primary ways companies can achieve a cost advantage by reconfiguring their value chains include:

- Simplifying product design (utilizing computer-assisted design techniques, reducing the number of parts, standardizing parts and components across models and styles, shifting to an easy-to-manufacture product design).
- Stripping away the extras and offering only a basic, no-frills product or service, thereby cutting out activities and costs of multiple features and options.
- Shifting to a simpler, less capital-intensive, or more streamlined or flexible technological process (computer-assisted design and manufacture, flexible manufacturing systems that accommodate both low-cost efficiency and product customization).
- Finding ways to bypass the use of high-cost raw materials or component parts.
- Using direct-to-end-user sales and marketing approaches that cut out the often large costs and margins of wholesalers and retailers (costs and margins in the wholesale-retail portions of the value chain often represent 50 percent of the price paid by final consumers).
- Relocating facilities closer to suppliers, customers, or both to curtail inbound and outbound costs.
- Dropping the "something-for-everyone" approach and focusing on a limited product/service to meet a special, but important, need of the target buyer, thereby eliminating activities and costs of numerous product versions.

- Reengineering core business processes to consolidate work steps and cut out low-value-added activities (many low-cost providers are adept at learning how to operate with exceptionally small corporate staffs and corporate overheads).

- Using electronic communications technologies to eliminate paperwork (paperless invoice systems and electronic funds transfer), reduce printing and copying costs, speed communications via e-mail, curtail travel costs via teleconferencing, distribute information via company intranets, and establish relationships with customers using Websites and Web pages—companies the world over are using such technologies to restructure how they do business. Ford Motor has aggressively adopted videoconferencing and computer-assisted design and manufacturing technologies—its new "global car" (marketed as the Contour in North America) was developed by a team of designers at Ford locations around the world who used an on-line computer network to share ideas, create the actual designs, integrate the designs for the various parts and components (the chassis, engine, transmission, body. and instrumentation), and build and test prototypes via computer simulations. The Internet is fast becoming an attractive channel for retailing new software products (downloading new software directly from the Internet eliminates the costs of producing and packaging disks, then shipping and distributing them through wholesale and retail channels).

Companies can sometimes achieve dramatic cost advantages from creating altogether new value chain systems or from restructuring existing value chains and slicing out cost-producing activities that produce little customer value. For example, both Hallmark and American Greetings are marketing CD-ROM software that allows customers to select or design a card electronically, type in the recipient's name and address, and click on an "order" icon; computer technicians at the company take over from there—printing and mailing the card to arrive via regular mail or e-mail on the appropriate date. Card senders can pick out all the cards they want to send for an entire year at a single time if they wish and get a confirmation from the company that the appropriate card has been sent on its way. Such electronic value chains can radically alter how greeting cards are designed, produced, distributed, sold, and delivered.

Dell Computer has proved a pioneer in revamping the value chain in manufacturing and marketing PCs. Whereas most PC makers produce their models in volume and sell them through independent dealers and distributors, Dell markets directly to consumers, building its PCs as customers order them and shipping them to customers within a few days of receiving the order. Dell's value chain approach has proved cost effective in coping with the PC industry's blink-of-an-eye product life cycle (new models equipped with faster chips and new features appear every few months). Dell's build-to-order strategy enables it to avoid misjudging buyer demand for its various models and being saddled with fast-obsoleting components and finished goods inventories; its sell-direct strategy slices dealer/distributor costs and margins out of the value chain (although some of these savings are offset by the cost of Dell's direct marketing and customer support activities—functions that would otherwise be performed by dealers and distributors). In 1996, Dell's shipments of PCs grew 58 percent compared to growth of 30 percent for industry leader Compaq Computer and of 15 percent for the industry as a whole. In a number of industries, efforts are under way to restructure the value chain to remove the inefficiencies and costs of getting goods and services from the producer to the end users. Illustration Capsule 15 provides additional examples of the cost advantages of value chain restructuring.

Iowa Beef Packers, FedEx, and Southwest Airlines have been able to win strong competitive positions by restructuring the traditional value chains in their industries.

In beef packing, the traditional cost chain involved raising cattle on scattered farms and ranches, shipping them live to labor-intensive, unionized slaughtering plants, and then transporting whole sides of beef to grocery retailers whose butcher departments cut them into smaller pieces and packaged them for sale to grocery shoppers. Iowa Beef Packers revamped the traditional chain with a radically different strategy—large automated plants employing nonunion labor were built near economically transportable supplies of cattle, and the meat was partially butchered at the processing plant into smaller high-yield cuts (sometimes sealed in plastic casing ready for purchase), boxed, and shipped to retailers. IBP's inbound cattle transportation expenses, traditionally a major cost item, were cut significantly by avoiding the weight losses that occurred when live animals were shipped long distances; major outbound shipping cost savings were achieved by not having to ship whole sides of beef with their high waste factor. Iowa Beef's strategy was so successful that it became the largest U.S. meatpacker, surpassing the former industry leaders, Swift, Wilson, and Armour.

FedEx innovatively redefined the value chain for rapid delivery of small parcels. Traditional firms like Emery and Airborne Express operated by collecting freight packages of varying sizes, shipping them to their destination points via air freight and commercial airlines, and then delivering them to the addressee. Federal Express opted to focus only on the market for overnight delivery of small packages and documents. These were collected at local drop points during the late afternoon hours and flown on company-owned planes during early evening hours to a central hub in Memphis where from 11 P.M. to 3 A.M. each night all parcels were sorted, then reloaded on company planes, and flown during the early morning hours to their destination points, where they were delivered the next morning by company personnel using company trucks. The cost structure achieved by FedEx is low enough to permit it to guarantee overnight delivery of a small parcel anywhere in the United States for a price as low as $13.

Southwest Airlines has tailored its value chain to deliver low-cost, convenient service to passengers. It has mastered fast turnarounds at the gates (about 15 minutes versus 45 minutes for rivals); because the short turnarounds allow the planes to fly more hours per day, Southwest can schedule more flights per day with fewer aircraft. Southwest does not offer inflight meals, assigned seating, baggage transfer to connecting airlines, or first-class seating and service, thereby eliminating all the cost-producing activities associated with these features. Automated ticketing at its airport ticket counters and gates encourages customers to bypass travel agents (allowing Southwest to avoid paying commissions and to avoid the costs of maintaining an elaborate on-line computerized reservation system readily available to every travel agent) and also reduces the need for so many agents. Southwest's full-service rivals have higher costs because they must perform all the activities associated with providing meal service, assigned seating, premium classes of service, interline baggage checking, and computerized reservation systems.

Internet entrepreneurs are currently leading a revolution to revamp the value chains for providing traditional mail services, for providing all sorts of information to businesses and households, for conducting meetings via cameras and computers while the attendees sit at their desks in their offices, for providing long-distance telephone services via the Internet, for shopping for goods and services, for trading stocks, and on and on. They are employing "virtual value chains" and exploiting the new economics of doing business in the market*space* of the World Wide Web and commercial on-line services. Web pages are fast becoming retail showrooms and a new retail channel where business can sometimes be transacted faster, better, and less expensively than in the physical world of the marketplace. The shift to E-mail, faxing, and electronic funds transfer (which utilize digital or virtual value chains) is undermining the business of the U.S. Postal Service (which estimates that 25 percent of its revenues are at risk).

Source: Based in part on information in Michael E. Porter, *Competitive Advantage* (New York: Free Press, 1985), p. 109 and Jeffrey F. Rayport and John J. Sviokla, "Exploiting the Virtual Value Chain," *Harvard Business Review* 73, no. 6 (November–December 1995), pp. 75–85.

The Keys to Success in Achieving Low-Cost Leadership   Managers intent on pursuing a low-cost-provider strategy have to scrutinize each cost-creating activity and determine what drives its cost. Then they have to use their knowledge about the cost drivers to manage the costs of each activity downward. They have to be proactive in restructuring the value chain, reengineering business processes, and eliminating non-essential work steps—some companies have been able to reduce the costs of reengineered activities by 30 to 70 percent, compared to the 5 to 10 percent possible with creative tinkering and adjusting.

Successful low-cost providers usually achieve their cost advantages by exhaustively pursuing cost savings throughout the value chain. All avenues for reducing costs are explored and no area of potential is overlooked—the success of Japanese manufacturers is largely due to their persistent search for continuous cost reductions across all aspects of their operations. Normally, low-cost producers have cost-conscious corporate cultures featuring broad employee participation in cost-control efforts, ongoing efforts to benchmark costs against best-in-class performers of an activity, intensive scrutiny of operating expenses and budget requests, programs to promote continuous cost improvement, limited perks and frills for executives, and adequate, but not lavish, facilities.

But while low-cost providers are champions of frugality, they are usually aggressive in investing in resources and capabilities that promise to drive costs out of the business. Wal-Mart, for example, employs state-of-the-art technology throughout its operations—its distribution facilities are an automated showcase, it uses on-line computer systems to order goods from suppliers and manage inventories, its stores are equipped with cutting-edge sales-tracking and check-out systems, and it operates a private satellite-communications system that daily sends point-of-sale data to 4,000 vendors.

Companies that employ low-cost leadership strategies include Lincoln Electric in arc-welding equipment, Briggs and Stratton in small gasoline engines, BIC in ball-point pens, Black & Decker in power tools, Stride Rite in footwear, Beaird-Poulan in chain saws, Ford in heavy-duty trucks, General Electric in major home appliances, Toys-R-Us in discount retailing, and Southwest Airlines in commercial airline travel.

The Competitive Defenses of Low-Cost Leadership   Being the low-cost provider in an industry provides some attractive defenses against the five competitive forces.

- In meeting the challenges of *rival competitors*, the low-cost company is in the best position to compete on the basis of price, to use the appeal of lower price to grab sales (and market share) from rivals, to remain profitable in the face of strong price competition, and to survive price wars and earn above-average profits (based on bigger profit margins or greater sales volume). Low cost is a powerful defense in markets where many buyers are price sensitive and price competition thrives.

- In defending against the power of *buyers*, low costs provide a company with partial profit-margin protection, since powerful customers are rarely able to bargain price down past the survival level of the next most cost-efficient seller.

- In countering the bargaining leverage of *suppliers*, the low-cost producer is more insulated than competitors from powerful suppliers if the primary source of its cost advantage is greater internal efficiency. (A low-cost provider whose cost advantage stems from being able to buy components at favorable prices from outside suppliers could be vulnerable to the actions of powerful suppliers.)

- As concerns *potential entrants*, the low-cost leader can use price-cutting to make it harder for a new rival to win customers; the pricing power of the low-cost provider acts as a barrier for new entrants.
- In competing against *substitutes*, a low-cost leader is better positioned to use low price as a defense against companies trying to gain market inroads with a substitute product or service.

A low-cost leader is in the strongest position to win the business of price-sensitive buyers, set the floor on market price, and still earn a profit.

A low-cost company's ability to set the industry's price floor and still earn a profit erects protective barriers around its market position. Anytime price competition becomes a major market force, less efficient rivals get squeezed the most. Firms in a low-cost position relative to rivals have a competitive edge in profitably selling to price-sensitive buyers.

When a Low-Cost Provider Strategy Works Best   A competitive strategy predicated on low-cost leadership is particularly powerful when

1. Price competition among rival sellers is especially vigorous.
2. The industry's product is essentially standardized or a commodity readily available from a host of sellers (a condition that allows buyers to shop for the best price).
3. There are few ways to achieve product differentiation that have value to buyers (put another way, the differences between brands do not matter much to buyers), thereby making buyers very sensitive to price differences.

In markets where rivals compete mainly on price, low cost relative to competitors is the only competitive advantage that matters.

4. Most buyers use the product in the same ways—with common user requirements, a standardized product can satisfy the needs of buyers. In this case low selling price, not features or quality, becomes the dominant factor in causing buyers to choose one seller's product over another's.
5. Buyers incur low switching costs in changing from one seller to another, thus giving them the flexibility to switch readily to lower-priced sellers having equally good products.
6. Buyers are large and have significant power to bargain down prices.

As a rule, the more price sensitive buyers are and the more inclined they are to base their purchasing decisions on which seller offers the best price, the more appealing a low-cost strategy becomes.

The Pitfalls of a Low-Cost Provider Strategy   Perhaps the biggest pitfall of a low-cost provider strategy, however, is getting carried away with overly aggressively price-cutting and ending up with lower, rather than higher, profitability. A low-cost/low-price advantage results in superior profitability only if (1) prices are cut by less than the size of the cost advantage or (2) the added gains in unit sales are large enough to bring in a bigger total profit despite lower margins per unit sold—a company with a 5 percent cost advantage cannot cut prices 20 percent, end up with a volume gain of only 10 percent, and still expect to earn higher profits!

A second big pitfall is not emphasizing avenues of cost advantage that can be kept proprietary or that relegate rivals to playing catch-up. The value of a cost advantage depends on its sustainability. Sustainability, in turn, hinges on whether the company achieves its cost advantage in ways difficult for rivals to copy or match.

A third pitfall is becoming too fixated on cost reduction. Low cost cannot be pursued so zealously that a firm's offering ends up being too spartan and frills-free to generate buyer appeal. Furthermore, a company driving zealously to push its costs down has to guard against misreading or ignoring subtle but significant market swings—like growing buyer interest in added features or service, declining buyer sensitivity to price, or new developments that start to alter how buyers use the product. A low-cost zealot risks getting left behind if buyers begin to opt for enhanced quality, innovative performance features, faster service, and other differentiating features.

A low-cost provider's product offering must always contain enough attributes to be attractive to prospective buyers.

Even if these mistakes are avoided, a low-cost competitive approach still carries risk. Technological breakthroughs can open up cost reductions for rivals that nullify a low-cost leader's past investments and hard-won gains in efficiency. Heavy investments in cost reduction can lock a firm into both its present technology and present strategy, leaving it vulnerable to new technologies and to growing customer interest in something other than a cheaper price.

Differentiation Strategies

Differentiation strategies are an attractive competitive approach when buyer preferences are too diverse to be fully satisfied by a standardized product or when buyer requirements are too diverse to be fully satisfied by sellers with identical capabilities. To be successful with a differentiation strategy, a company has to study buyers' needs and behavior carefully to learn what they consider important, what they think has value, and what they are willing to pay for. Then the company has to either incorporate selected buyer-desired attributes that set its offering visibly and distinctively apart from rivals or else develop *unique* capabilities to serve buyer requirements. Competitive advantage results once a sufficient number of buyers become strongly attached to the differentiated attributes, features, or capabilities. The stronger the buyer appeal of the differentiated offering, the more that customers *bond* with the company and the stronger the resulting competitive advantage.

The essence of a differentiation strategy is to be unique in ways that are valuable to customers and that can be sustained.

Successful differentiation allows a firm to

- Command a premium price for its product, and/or
- Increase unit sales (because additional buyers are won over by the differentiating features), and/or
- Gain buyer loyalty to its brand (because some buyers are strongly attracted to the differentiating features and bond with the company and its products).

Differentiation enhances profitability whenever the extra price the product commands outweighs the added costs of achieving the differentiation. Company differentiation strategies fail when buyers don't value the brand's uniqueness enough to buy it instead of rivals' brands and/or when a company's approach to differentiation is easily copied or matched by its rivals.

Types of Differentiation Themes   Companies can pursue differentiation from many angles: a unique taste (Dr Pepper and Listerine), a host of features (America Online), reliable service (FedEx in overnight package delivery), spare parts availability (Caterpillar guarantees 48-hour spare parts delivery to any customer anywhere in the world or else the part is furnished free), more for the money (McDonald's and Wal-Mart), engineering design and performance (Mercedes in automobiles), prestige and distinctiveness (Rolex in watches), product reliability (Johnson & Johnson in baby products), quality manufacture (Karastan in carpets and Honda in automobiles), technological leadership (3M Corporation in bonding and coating products), a full range of services (Merrill Lynch), a complete line of products (Campbell's soups), and top-of-the-line image and reputation (Gucci, Ralph Lauren, and Chanel in fashions and accessories, Ritz-Carlton in hotels, and Mont Blanc and Cross in writing instruments).

Easy-to-copy differentiating features cannot produce sustainable competitive advantage.

The most appealing approaches to differentiation are those that are hard or expensive for rivals to duplicate. Indeed, resourceful competitors can, in time, clone almost any product or feature or attribute—if American Airlines creates a program for frequent fliers, so can Delta; if Ford offers a 30,000-mile bumper-to-bumper warranty on its new cars, so can Chrysler and Nissan. This is why *sustainable* differentiation usually has to be linked to unique internal skills, core competencies, and capabilities. When a company has competencies and capabilities that competitors cannot readily match and when its expertise can be used to perform activities in the value chain where differentiation potential exists, then it has a strong basis for sustainable differentiation. As a rule, differentiation yields a longer-lasting and more profitable competitive edge when it is based on new product innovation, technical superiority, product quality and reliability, and comprehensive customer service. Such attributes are widely perceived by buyers as having value; moreover, the competencies and competitive capabilities required to produce them tend to be tougher for rivals to copy or overcome profitably.

Where Along the Value Chain to Create the Differentiating Attributes Differentiation is not something hatched in marketing and advertising departments, nor is it limited to the catchalls of quality and service. Differentiation is about understanding what the customer values, about where along the value chain to create the differentiating attributes, and about what resources and capabilities are needed to produce brand uniqueness. Differentiation possibilities exist in virtually every activity along an industry's value chain, most commonly in:

1. *Purchasing and procurement activities* that ultimately spill over to affect the performance or quality of the company's end product. (McDonald's gets high ratings on its french fries partly because it has very strict specifications on the potatoes purchased from suppliers.)

2. *Product R&D activities* that aim at improved product designs and performance features, expanded end uses and applications, shorter lead times in developing new models, more frequent first-on-the-market victories, wider product variety, added user safety, greater recycling capability, or enhanced environmental protection.

3. *Production R&D and technology-related activities* that permit custom-order manufacture at an efficient cost, make production methods more environmentally safe, or improve product quality, reliability, and appearance. (Vehicle manufacturers have developed flexible manufacturing systems that allow different models to be made on the same assembly line and to equip models with different options as they come down the assembly line.)

4. *Manufacturing activities* that reduce product defects, prevent premature product failure, extend product life, allow better warranty coverages, improve

economy of use, result in more end-user convenience, or enhance product appearance. (The quality edge enjoyed by Japanese automakers stems partly from their distinctive competence in performing assembly-line activities.)

5. *Outbound logistics and distribution activities* that allow for faster delivery, more accurate order filling, and fewer warehouse and on-the-shelf stockouts.

6. *Marketing, sales, and customer service activities* that can result in superior technical assistance to buyers, faster maintenance and repair services, more and better product information, more and better training materials for end users, better credit terms, quicker order processing, more frequent sales calls, or greater customer convenience.

Managers need to fully understand the value-creating differentiation options and the activities that drive uniqueness to devise a sound differentiation strategy and evaluate various differentiation approaches.[8]

Achieving a Differentiation-Based Competitive Advantage   The cornerstone of a successful differentiation strategy is creating buyer value in ways unmatched by rivals. There are four differentiation-based approaches to creating buyer value. One is to incorporate product attributes and user features that lower the buyer's overall costs of using the company's product—Illustration Capsule 16 lists options for making a company's product more economical. A second approach is to incorporate features that raise the performance a buyer gets out of the product—Illustration Capsule 17 contains differentiation avenues that enhance product performance and buyer value.

A differentiator's basis for competitive advantage is either a product/service offering whose attributes differ significantly from the offerings of rivals or a set of capabilities for delivering customer value that are unmatched by rivals.

A third approach is to incorporate features that enhance buyer satisfaction in noneconomic or intangible ways. Goodyear's new Aquatread tire design appeals to safety-conscious motorists wary of slick roads in rainy weather. Wal-Mart's campaign to feature products "Made in America" appeals to customers concerned about the loss of American jobs to foreign manufacturers. Rolls-Royce, Tiffany's, and Gucci have competitive advantages linked to buyer desires for status, image, prestige, upscale fashion, superior craftsmanship, and the finer things in life. L. L. Bean makes its mail-order customers feel secure in their purchases by providing an unconditional guarantee with no time limit: "All of our products are guaranteed to give 100 percent satisfaction in every way. Return anything purchased from us at anytime if it proves otherwise. We will replace it, refund your purchase price, or credit your credit card, as you wish."

A fourth approach is to compete on the basis of capabilities—to deliver value to customers via competitive capabilities that rivals don't have or can't afford to match.[9] *The strategy-making challenge is selecting which differentiating capabilities to develop.* Successful capabilities-driven differentiation begins with a deep understanding of what customers need and ends with building organizational capabilities to satisfy these needs better than rivals. The Japanese auto manufacturers have the capability to bring new models to market faster than American and European automakers, thereby allowing them to satisfy changing consumer preferences for one

---

[8]Porter, *Competitive Advantage*, p. 124.

[9]For a more detailed discussion, see George Stalk, Philip Evans, and Lawrence E. Schulman, "Competing on Capabilities: The New Rules of Corporate Strategy," *Harvard Business Review* 70, no.2 (March–April 1992), pp. 57–69.

ILLUSTRATION CAPSULE 16   Differentiating Features That Lower Buyer Costs

A company doesn't have to resort to price cuts to make it cheaper for a buyer to use its product. An alternative is to incorporate features and attributes into the company's product/service package that

- Reduce the buyer's scrap and raw materials waste. Example of differentiating feature: cut-to-size components.
- Lower the buyer's labor costs (less time, less training, lower skill requirements). Examples of differentiating features: snap-on assembly features, modular replacement of worn-out components.
- Cut the buyer's downtime or idle time. Examples of differentiating features: greater product reliability, ready spare parts availability, or less frequent maintenance requirements.
- Reduce the buyer's inventory costs. Example of differentiating feature: just-in-time delivery.
- Reduce the buyer's pollution control costs or waste disposal costs. Example of differentiating feature: scrap pickup for use in recycling.
- Reduce the buyer's procurement and order-processing costs. Example of differentiating feature: computerized on-line ordering and billing procedures.

- Lower the buyer's maintenance and repair costs. Example of differentiating feature: superior product reliability.
- Lower the buyer's installation, delivery, or financing costs. Example of differentiating feature: 90-day payment same as cash.
- Reduce the buyer's need for other inputs (energy, safety equipment, security personnel, inspection personnel, other tools and machinery). Example of differentiating feature: fuel-efficient power equipment.
- Raise the trade-in value of used models.
- Lower the buyer's replacement or repair costs if the product unexpectedly fails later. Example of differentiating feature: longer warranty coverage.
- Lower the buyer's need for technical personnel. Example of differentiating feature: free technical support and assistance.
- Boost the efficiency of the buyer's production process. Examples of differentiating features: faster processing speeds, better interface with ancillary equipment.

Source: Adapted from Michael E. Porter, *Competitive Advantage* (New York: Free Press, 1985), pp. 135–37.

vehicle style versus another. CNN has the capability to cover breaking news stories faster and more completely than the major networks. Microsoft, with its three PC operating systems (DOS, Windows 95, and Windows NT), its large project teams of highly talented and antibureaucratic programmers who thrive on developing complex products and systems, and its marketing savvy and know-how, has greater capabilities to design, create, distribute, advertise, and sell an array of software products for PC applications than any of its rivals. Microsoft's capabilities are especially suited to fast-paced markets with short product life cycles and competition centered around evolving product features.

Real Value, Perceived Value, and Signals of Value   Buyers seldom pay for value they don't perceive, no matter how real the unique extras may be.[10] Thus the price premium that a differentiation strategy commands reflects *the value actually delivered* to the buyer and *the value perceived* by the buyer (even if not actually delivered). Actual and perceived value can differ whenever buyers have trouble assessing what their experience with the product will be. Incomplete knowledge on the part of buyers often causes them to judge value based on such *signals* as price (where price

---

[10]This discussion draws from Porter, *Competitive Advantage*, pp. 138–42. Porter's insights here are particularly important to formulating differentiating strategies because they highlight the relevance of "intangibles" and "signals."

ILLUSTRATION CAPSULE 17   Differentiating Features That Raise the Performance a User Gets

To enhance the performance a buyer gets from using its product/service, a company can incorporate features and attributes that

- Provide buyers greater reliability, durability, convenience, or ease of use.
- Make the company's product/service cleaner, safer, quieter, or more maintenance-free than rival brands.
- Exceed environmental or regulatory standards.

- Meet the buyer's needs and requirements more completely, compared to competitors' offerings.
- Give buyers the option to add on or to upgrade later as new product versions come on the market.
- Give buyers more flexibility to tailor their own products to the needs of their customers.
- Do a better job of meeting the buyer's future growth and expansion requirements.

Source: Adapted from Michael E. Porter, *Competitive Advantage* (New York: Free Press, 1985), pp. 135–38.

connotes quality), attractive packaging, extensive ad campaigns (i.e., how well known the product is), ad content and image, the quality of brochures and sales presentations, the seller's facilities, the seller's list of customers, the firm's market share, length of time the firm has been in business, and the professionalism, appearance, and personality of the seller's employees. Such signals of value may be as important as actual value (1) when the nature of differentiation is subjective or hard to quantify, (2) when buyers are making a first-time purchase, (3) when repurchase is infrequent, and (4) when buyers are unsophisticated.

A firm whose differentiation strategy delivers only modest extra value but clearly signals that extra value may command a higher price than a firm that actually delivers higher value but signals it poorly.

Keeping the Cost of Differentiation in Line   Once a company's managers identify what approach to creating buyer value and establishing a differentiation-based competitive advantage makes the most sense, given the company's situation and what rivals are doing, they must develop the capabilities and build in the value-creating attributes at an acceptable cost. Differentiation usually raises costs. The trick to profitable differentiation is either to keep the costs of achieving differentiation below the price premium the differentiating attributes can command in the market-place (thus increasing the profit margin per unit sold) or to offset thinner profit margins with enough added volume to increase total profits (larger volume can make up for smaller margins provided differentiation adds enough extra sales). It usually makes sense to incorporate extra differentiating features that are not costly but add to buyer satisfaction—FedEx installed systems that allowed customers to track packages in transit by connecting to FedEx's World Wide Web site and entering the airbill number; some hotels and motels provide in-room coffeemaking amenities for the convenience of guests or early-morning complimentary coffee-to-go in their lobbies; many McDonald's outlets have play areas for small children.

What Makes a Differentiation Strategy Attractive   Differentiation offers a buffer against the strategies of rivals when it results in enhanced buyer loyalty to a company's brand or model and greater willingness to pay a little (perhaps a lot!) more for it. In addition, successful differentiation (1) erects entry barriers in the form of customer loyalty and uniqueness that newcomers find hard to hurdle, (2) lessens buyers' bargaining power since the products of alternative sellers are less attractive to them, and (3) helps a firm fend off threats from substitutes not having comparable features or attributes. If differentiation allows a company to charge a higher price and have bigger profit margins, it is in a stronger position to withstand the efforts of powerful vendors to get a higher price for the items they supply. Thus, as with cost leadership, successful differentiation creates lines of defense for dealing with the five competitive forces.

For the most part, differentiation strategies work best in markets where (1) there are many ways to differentiate the company's offering from that of rivals and many buyers perceive these differences as having value, (2) buyer needs and uses of the item or service are diverse, (3) few rival firms are following a similar differentiation approach, and (4) technological change is fast-paced and competition revolves around evolving product features.

The Pitfalls of a Differentiation Strategy There are, of course, no guarantees that differentiation will produce a meaningful competitive advantage. If buyers see little value in the unique attributes or capabilities a company stresses, then its differentiation strategy will get a "ho-hum" reception in the marketplace. In addition, attempts at differentiation are doomed to fail if competitors can quickly copy most or all of the appealing product attributes a company comes up with. Rapid imitation means that a firm never achieves real differentiation, since competing brands keep changing in like ways each time a company makes a new move to set its offering apart from rivals'. Thus, to build competitive advantage through differentiation a firm must search out lasting sources of uniqueness that are burdensome for rivals to overcome. Other common pitfalls and mistakes in pursuing differentiation include:[11]

Any differentiating element that works well tends to draw imitators.

- Trying to differentiate on the basis of something that does not lower a buyer's cost or enhance a buyer's well-being, as perceived by the buyer.
- Overdifferentiating so that price is too high relative to competitors or that the array of differentiating attributes exceeds buyers' needs.
- Trying to charge too high a price premium (the bigger the price differential the harder it is to keep buyers from switching to lower-priced competitors).
- Ignoring the need to signal value and depending only on intrinsic product attributes to achieve differentiation.
- Not understanding or identifying what buyers consider as value.

A low-cost producer strategy can defeat a differentiation strategy when buyers are satisfied with a basic product and don't think "extra" attributes are worth a higher price.

The Strategy of Being a Best-Cost Provider

This strategy aims at giving customers *more value for the money*. It combines a strategic emphasis on low cost with a strategic emphasis on *more than minimally acceptable* quality, service, features, and performance. The idea is to create superior value by meeting or exceeding buyers' expectations on key quality-service-features-performance attributes and by beating their expectations on price. The aim is to become the low-cost provider of a product or service with *good-to-excellent* attributes, then use the cost advantage to underprice brands with comparable attributes. Such a competitive approach is termed a *best-cost provider strategy* because the producer has the best (lowest) cost relative to producers whose brands have comparable quality-service-features-performance attributes.

---

[11]Porter, *Competitive Advantage*, pp. 160–62.

ILLUSTRATION CAPSULE 18   Toyota's Best-Cost Producer Strategy for Its Lexus Line

Toyota Motor Co. is widely regarded as a low-cost producer among the world's motor vehicle manufacturers. Despite its emphasis on product quality, Toyota has achieved absolute low-cost leadership because of its considerable skills in efficient manufacturing techniques and because its models are positioned in the low-to-medium end of the price spectrum where high production volumes are conducive to low unit costs. But when Toyota decided to introduce its new Lexus models to compete in the luxury-car market, it employed a classic best-cost producer strategy. Toyota's Lexus strategy had three features:

- Transferring its expertise in making high-quality Toyota models at low cost to making premium quality luxury cars at costs below other luxury-car makers, especially Mercedes and BMW. Toyota executives reasoned that Toyota's manufacturing skills should allow it to incorporate high-tech performance features and upscale quality into Lexus models at less cost than other luxury-car manufacturers.

- Using its relatively lower manufacturing costs to underprice Mercedes and BMW, both of which had models selling in the $40,000 to $75,000 range (and some even higher). Toyota believed that with its cost advantage it could price

attractively equipped Lexus models in the $38,000 to $42,000 range, drawing price-conscious buyers away from Mercedes and BMW and perhaps inducing quality-conscious Lincoln and Cadillac owners to trade up to a Lexus.

- Establishing a new network of Lexus dealers, separate from Toyota dealers, dedicated to providing a level of personalized, attentive customer service unmatched in the industry.

The Lexus 400 series models were priced in the $48,000 to $55,000 range and competed against Mercedes's 300/400E series, BMW's 535i/740 series, Nissan's Infiniti Q45, Cadillac Seville, Jaguar, and Lincoln Continental. The lower-priced Lexus 300 series, priced in the $30,000 to $38,000 range, competed against Cadillac Eldorado, Acura Legend, Infiniti J30, Buick Park Avenue, Mercedes's C-Class series, BMW's 315 series, and Oldsmobile's Aurora line.

Lexus's best-cost producer strategy was so successful that Mercedes introduced a new C-Class series, priced in the $30,000 to $35,000 range, to become more competitive. The Lexus LS 400 models and the Lexus SC 300/400 models ranked first and second, respectively, in the widely watched J. D. Power & Associates quality survey for 1993 cars; the entry-level Lexus ES 300 model ranked eighth.

The competitive advantage of a best-cost provider comes from matching close rivals on quality-service-features-performance and beating them on cost. To become a best-cost provider, a company must match quality at a lower cost than rivals, match features at a lower cost than rivals, match product performance at a lower cost than rivals, and so on. What distinguishes a successful best-cost provider is having the resources, know-how, and capabilities to incorporate upscale product or service attributes at a low cost. The most successful best-cost producers have competencies and capabilities to simultaneously drive unit costs down and product caliber up—see Illustration Capsule 18.

A best-cost provider strategy has great appeal from the standpoint of competitive positioning. It produces superior customer value by balancing a strategic emphasis on low cost against a strategic emphasis on differentiation. In effect, it is a *hybrid* strategy that allows a company to combine the competitive advantage of both low cost and differentiation to deliver superior buyer value. In markets where buyer diversity makes product differentiation the norm and many buyers are price and value sensitive, a best-cost producer strategy can be more advantageous than either a pure low-cost producer strategy or a pure differentiation strategy keyed to product superiority. This is because a best-cost provider can position itself near the middle of the market with either a medium-quality product at a below-average price or a very good product at a medium price. Often the

The most powerful competitive approach a company can pursue is to strive relentlessly to become a lower-and-lower-cost producer of a higher-and-higher-caliber product, aiming at eventually becoming the industry's absolute lowest-cost producer and, simultaneously, the producer of the industry's overall best product.

majority of buyers prefer a midrange product rather than the cheap, basic product of a low-cost producer or the expensive product of a top-of-the-line differentiator.

Focused or Market Niche Strategies

What sets focused strategies apart from low-cost or differentiation strategies is concentrated attention on a narrow piece of the total market. The target segment or niche can be defined by geographic uniqueness, by specialized requirements in using the product, or by special product attributes that appeal only to niche members. The aim of a focus strategy is to do a better job of serving buyers in the target market niche than rival competitors. *A focuser's basis for competitive advantage is either (1) lower costs than competitors in serving the market niche or (2) an ability to offer niche members something they perceive is better.* A focused strategy based on low cost depends on there being a buyer segment whose requirements are less costly to satisfy compared to the rest of the market. A focused strategy based on differentiation depends on there being a buyer segment that wants or needs special product attributes or company capabilities.

Examples of firms employing some version of a focused strategy include Netscape (a specialist in software for browsing the World Wide Web), Porsche (in sports cars), Cannondale (in top-of-the-line mountain bikes), commuter airlines like Horizon, Comair, and Atlantic Southeast (specializing in low-traffic, short-haul flights linking major airports with smaller cities 100 to 250 miles away), Jiffy Lube International (a specialist in quick oil changes, lubrication, and simple maintenance for motor vehicles), and Bandag (a specialist in truck tire recapping that promotes its recaps aggressively at over 1,000 truck stops). Microbreweries, local bakeries, bed-and-breakfast inns, and local owner-managed retail boutiques are all good examples of enterprises that have scaled their operations to serve narrow or local customer segments. Illustration Capsule 19 describes Motel 6's focused low-cost strategy and Ritz-Carlton's focused differentiation strategy.

Focused low-cost strategies are fairly common. Producers of private-label goods are able to lower product development, marketing, distribution, and advertising costs by concentrating on making generic items imitative of name-brand merchandise and selling directly to retail chains wanting a basic house brand to sell at a discount to price-sensitive shoppers. Discount stock brokerage houses have lowered costs by focusing on customers who are willing to forgo the investment research, advice, and financial services offered by full-service firms like Merrill Lynch in return for 30 percent or more commission savings on their buy-sell transactions. Pursuing a cost advantage via focusing works well when a firm can lower costs significantly by concentrating its energies and resources on a well-defined market segment.

At the other end of the market spectrum, focusers like Godiva Chocolates, Chanel, Rolls-Royce, Häagen-Dazs, and W. L. Gore (the maker of Gore-Tex) employ successful differentiation strategies targeted at upscale buyers. Indeed, most markets contain a buyer segment willing to pay a big price premium for the very finest items available, thus opening the window for some competitors to pursue differentiation-based focus strategies aimed at the very top of the market. Another successful focused differentiator is a "fashion food retailer" called Trader Joe's, a 74-store chain that is a combination gourmet deli and food warehouse.[12] Customers shop Trader Joe's as much for entertainment as for conventional grocery items—the store stocks all kinds of out-of-the-ordinary culinary treats like raspberry salsa, salmon burgers, and jasmine fried rice, as well as the standard goods normally found in

---

[12]Gary Hamel, "Strategy as Revolution," *Harvard Business Review* 74, no. 4 (July–August 1996), p. 72.

ILLUSTRATION CAPSULE 19   Focused Strategies in the Lodging Industry: Motel 6 and Ritz-Carlton

Motel 6 and Ritz-Carlton compete at opposite ends of the lodging industry. Motel 6 employs a focused strategy keyed to low cost; Ritz-Carlton employs a focused strategy based on differentiation.

Motel 6 caters to price-conscious travelers who want a clean, no-frills place to spend the night. To be a low-cost provider of overnight lodging, Motel 6 (1) selects relatively inexpensive sites on which to construct its units—usually near interstate exits and high traffic locations but far enough away to avoid paying prime site prices; (2) builds only basic facilities—no restaurant or bar and only rarely a swimming pool; (3) relies on standard architectural designs that incorporate inexpensive materials and low-cost construction techniques; and (4) has simple room furnishings and decorations. These approaches lower both investment costs and operating costs. Without restaurants, bars, and all kinds of guest services, a Motel 6 unit can be operated with just front desk personnel, room cleanup crews, and skeleton building-and-grounds maintenance. To promote the Motel 6 concept with travelers who have simple overnight requirements, the chain uses unique, recognizable radio ads done by nationally syndicated radio personality Tom Bodett; the ads describe Motel 6's clean rooms, no-frills facilities, friendly atmosphere, and dependably low rates (usually under $30 per night).

In contrast, the Ritz-Carlton caters to discriminating travelers and vacationers willing and able to pay for top-of-the-line accommodations and world-class personal service. Ritz-Carlton hotels feature (1) prime locations and scenic views from many rooms, (2) custom architectural designs, (3) fine dining restaurants with gourmet menus prepared by accomplished chefs, (4) elegantly appointed lobbies and bar lounges, (5) swimming pools, exercise facilities, and leisure-time options, (6) upscale room accommodations, (7) an array of guest services and recreation opportunities appropriate to the location, and (8) large, well-trained professional staffs who do their utmost to make each guest's stay an enjoyable experience.

Both companies concentrate their attention on a narrow piece of the total market. Motel 6's basis for competitive advantage is lower costs than competitors in providing basic, economical overnight accommodations to price-constrained travelers. Ritz-Carlton's advantage is its capability to provide superior accommodations and unmatched personal service for a well-to-do clientele. Each is able to succeed, despite polar opposite strategies, because the market for lodging consists of diverse buyer segments with diverse preferences and abilities to pay.

supermarkets. What sets Trader Joe's apart is not just its unique combination of food novelties and competitively priced grocery items but the opportunity it provides to turn an otherwise mundane shopping trip into a whimsical treasure hunt.

When Focusing Is Attractive   A focused strategy based either on low cost or differentiation becomes increasingly attractive as more of the following conditions are met:

- The target market niche is big enough to be profitable.
- The niche has good growth potential.
- The niche is not crucial to the success of major competitors.
- The focusing firm has the capabilities and resources to serve the targeted niche effectively.
- The focuser can defend itself against challengers based on the customer goodwill it has built up and its superior ability to serve buyers comprising the niche.

A focuser's specialized competencies and capabilities in serving the target market niche provide a basis for defending against the five competitive forces. Multisegment rivals may not have the capability to truly meet the expectations of the focused firm's target clientele. Entry into a focuser's target segment is made harder by the focused firm's unique capabilities in serving the market niche—the barrier of trying to match the focuser's capabilities deters potential newcomers. A focuser's capabilities in serving the niche also present a hurdle that makers of substitute products must overcome. The bargaining leverage of powerful customers is blunted somewhat by their own unwillingness to shift their business to rival companies less capable of meeting their expectations.

Focusing works best (1) when it is costly or difficult for multisegment competitors to meet the specialized needs of the target market niche, (2) when no other rival is attempting to specialize in the same target segment, (3) when a firm doesn't have the resources or capabilities to go after a bigger piece of the total market, and (4) when the industry has many different niches and segments, allowing a focuser to pick an attractive niche suited to its resource strengths and capabilities.

The Risks of a Focused Strategy   Focusing carries several risks. One is the chance that competitors will find effective ways to match the focused firm in serving the target niche. A second is that the niche buyer's preferences and needs might shift toward the product attributes desired by the majority of buyers. An erosion of the differences across buyer segments lowers entry barriers into a focuser's market niche and provides an open invitation for rivals to compete for the focuser's customers. A third risk is that the segment becomes so attractive it is soon inundated with competitors, splintering segment profits.

VERTICAL INTEGRATION STRATEGIES AND COMPETITIVE ADVANTAGE

Vertical integration extends a firm's competitive scope within the same industry. It involves expanding the firm's range of activities backward into sources of supply and/or forward toward end users of the final product. Thus, if a manufacturer invests in facilities to produce certain component parts rather than purchase them from outside suppliers, it remains in essentially the same industry as before. The only change is that it has business units in two production stages in the industry's value chain system. Similarly, if a paint manufacturer elects to integrate forward by opening 100 retail stores to market its products directly to consumers, it remains in the paint business even though its competitive scope extends further forward in the industry chain.

Vertical integration strategies can aim at *full integration* (participating in all stages of the industry value chain) or *partial integration* (building positions in just some stages of the industry's total value chain). A firm can accomplish vertical integration by starting its own operations in other stages in the industry's activity chain or by acquiring a company already performing the activities it wants to bring in-house.

The Strategic Advantages of Vertical Integration

The only good reason for investing company resources in vertical integration is to strengthen the firm's competitive position.[13] Unless vertical integration produces sufficient cost savings to justify the extra investment or yields a differentiation-based competitive advantage, it has no real payoff profitwise or strategywise.

---

[13]See Kathryn R. Harrigan, "Matching Vertical Integration Strategies to Competitive Conditions," *Strategic Management Journal* 7, no. 6 (November–December 1986), pp. 535–56; for a discussion of the advan-

Backward Integration   Integrating backward generates cost savings only when the volume needed is big enough to capture the same scale economies suppliers have and when suppliers' production efficiency can be matched or exceeded with no drop-off in quality. The best potential for being able to reduce costs via backward integration exists when suppliers have sizable profit margins, when the item being supplied is a major cost component, and when the needed technological skills are easily mastered. Backward vertical integration can produce a differentiation-based competitive advantage when a company, by performing activities in-house that were previously outsourced, ends up with a better-quality product/service offering, improves the caliber of its customer service, or in other ways enhances the performance of its final product. On occasion, integrating into more stages along the value chain can add to a company's differentiation capabilities by allowing it to build or strengthen its core competencies, better master key skills or strategy-critical technologies, or add features that deliver greater customer value.

A vertical integration strategy has appeal only if it significantly strengthens a firm's competitive position.

Backward integration can also spare a company the uncertainty of depending on suppliers of crucial components or support services, and it can lessen a company's vulnerability to powerful suppliers that raise prices at every opportunity. Stockpiling, fixed-price contracts, multiple-sourcing, long-term cooperative partnerships, or the use of substitute inputs are not always attractive ways for dealing with uncertain supply conditions or with economically powerful suppliers. Companies that are low on a key supplier's priority list can find themselves waiting on shipments every time supplies get tight. If this occurs often and wreaks havoc in a company's own production and customer relations activities, backward integration may be an advantageous strategic solution.

Forward Integration   The strategic impetus for forward integration has much the same roots. In many industries, independent sales agents, wholesalers, and retailers handle competing brands of the same product; they have no allegiance to any one company's brand and tend to push "what sells" or earns them the biggest profits. Undependable sales and distribution channels can give rise to costly inventory pile-ups and frequent underutilization of capacity, undermining the economies of a steady, near-capacity production operation. In such cases, a manufacturer may find it competitively advantageous to integrate forward into wholesaling and/or retailing in order to have outlets fully committed to representing its products. A manufacturer can sometimes profit from investing in company-owned distributorships, franchised dealer networks, and/or a chain of retail stores if it is able to realize higher rates of capacity utilization or build a stronger brand image. There are also occasions when integrating forward into the activity of selling directly to end users can produce important cost savings and permit lower selling prices by eliminating many of the costs of using wholesale-retail channels.

For a raw materials producer, integrating forward into manufacturing may permit greater product differentiation and provide an avenue of escape from the price-oriented competition of a commodity business. Often, in the early phases of an industry's value chain, intermediate goods are commodities in the sense that they have essentially identical technical specifications irrespective of producer (as is the case with crude oil, poultry, sheet steel, cement, and textile fibers). Competition in

tages and disadvantages of vertical integration, see John Stuckey and David White, "When and When *Not* to Vertically Integrate," *Sloan Management Review* (Spring 1993), pp. 71–83.

the markets for commodity products is usually fiercely price competitive, with the shifting balance between supply and demand giving rise to volatile profits. However, the closer the activities in the chain get to the ultimate consumer, the greater the opportunities for a firm to break out of a commodity-like competitive environment and differentiate its end product through design, service, quality features, packaging, promotion, and so on. Product differentiation often reduces the importance of price compared to other value-creating activities and improves profit margins.

The Strategic Disadvantages of Vertical Integration

Vertical integration has some substantial drawbacks, however. It boosts a firm's capital investment in the industry, increasing business risk (what if the industry goes sour?) and perhaps denying financial resources to more worthwhile pursuits. A vertically integrated firm has vested interests in protecting its present investments in technology and production facilities. Because of the high costs of abandoning such investments before they are worn out, fully integrated firms tend to adopt new technologies slower than partially integrated or nonintegrated firms. Second, integrating forward or backward locks a firm into relying on its own in-house activities and sources of supply (that later may prove more costly than outsourcing) and may result in less flexibility in accommodating buyer demand for greater product variety.

The big disadvantage of vertical integration is that it locks a firm deeper into the industry; unless operating across more stages in the industry's value chain builds competitive advantage, it is a questionable strategic move.

Third, vertical integration can pose problems of balancing capacity at each stage in the value chain. The most efficient scale of operation at each activity link in the value chain can vary substantially. Exact self-sufficiency at each interface is the exception not the rule. Where internal capacity is insufficient to supply the next stage, the difference has to be bought externally. Where internal capacity is excessive, customers need to be found for the surplus. And if by-products are generated, they have to be disposed of.

Fourth, integration forward or backward often calls for radically different skills and business capabilities. Parts and components manufacturing, assembly operations, wholesale distribution, and retailing are different businesses with different key success factors. Managers of a manufacturing company should consider carefully whether it makes good business sense to invest time and money in developing the expertise and merchandising skills to integrate forward into wholesaling or retailing. Many manufacturers learn the hard way that owning and operating wholesale-retail networks present many headaches, fit poorly with what they do best, and don't always add the kind of value to their core business they thought they would. Integrating backward into parts and components manufacture isn't as simple or profitable as it sometimes sounds either. Personal computer makers, for example, frequently have trouble getting timely deliveries of the latest semiconductor chips at favorable prices. Most, though, don't come close to having the resources or capabilities to integrate backward into chip manufacture; the semiconductor business is technologically sophisticated and entails heavy capital requirements and ongoing R&D effort, and mastering the manufacturing process takes a long time.

Fifth, backward vertical integration into the production of parts and components can reduce a company's manufacturing flexibility, lengthening the time it takes to make design and model changes and to bring new products to market. Companies that alter designs and models frequently in response to shifting buyer preferences often find vertical integration into parts and components burdensome because of constant retooling and redesign costs and the time it takes to implement coordinated changes. Outsourcing parts and components is often cheaper and less complicated than making them in-house, allowing a company to be more nimble in adapting its product offering to buyer preferences. Most of the world's automakers, despite their expertise in automotive technology and manufacturing, have concluded that they are better off from the standpoints of quality, cost, and design flexibility purchasing many of their parts and components from manufacturing specialists rather than trying to supply their own needs.

Unbundling and Outsourcing Strategies   In recent years, some vertically integrated companies have found operating in many stages of the industry value chain to be so competitively burdensome that they have adopted *vertical deintegration* (or unbundling) strategies. Deintegration involves withdrawing from certain stages/activities in the value chain system and relying on outside vendors to supply the needed products, support services, or functional activities. Outsourcing pieces of the value chain formerly performed in-house makes strategic sense whenever:

- An activity can be performed better or more cheaply by outside specialists.
- The activity is not crucial to the firm's ability to achieve sustainable competitive advantage and won't hollow out its core competencies, capabilities, or technical know-how. (Outsourcing of maintenance services, data processing, accounting, and other administrative support activities to companies specializing in these services has become commonplace.)
- It reduces the company's risk exposure to changing technology and/or changing buyer preferences.
- It streamlines company operations in ways that improve organizational flexibility, cut cycle time, speed decision making, and reduce coordination costs.
- It allows a company to concentrate on its core business.

Often, many of the advantages of vertical integration can be captured and many of the disadvantages avoided by forging close, long-term cooperative partnerships with key suppliers and tapping into the capabilities that able suppliers have developed. In years past, many companies' relationships with suppliers were of an arms-length nature where the nature of the items supplied were specified in detailed, short-term contracts.[14] Although a company might engage the same supplier repeatedly, there was no expectation that this would be the case; price was usually the determining factor for awarding contracts to suppliers, and companies maneuvered for leverage over suppliers to get the lowest possible prices. The threat of switching suppliers was the primary weapon. To make this threat credible, short-term contracts with multiple suppliers were preferred to long-term ones with single suppliers in order to promote lively competition among suppliers. Today, such approaches are being abandoned in favor of dealing with fewer, highly capable suppliers that are treated as long-term *strategic partners*. Cooperative relationships and alliances with key suppliers are replacing contractual, purely price-oriented relationships. There's more of a concerted effort to coordinate related value chain activities and to build important capabilities by working closely with suppliers.

---

[14]Robert H. Hayes, Gary P. Pisano, and David M. Upton, *Strategic Operations: Competing Through Capabilities* (New York: Free Press, 1996), pp. 419–22.

Weighing the Pros and Cons of Vertical Integration

All in all, then, a strategy of vertical integration can have both important strengths and weaknesses. Which direction the scales tip on vertical integration depends on (1) whether it can enhance the performance of strategy-critical activities in ways that lower cost or increase differentiation, (2) its impact on investment costs, flexibility and response times, and administrative overheads associated with coordinating operations across more stages, and (3) whether it creates competitive advantage. The issue of vertical integration hinges on which capabilities and value-chain activities need to be performed in-house in order for a company to be successful and which can be safely delegated to outside suppliers. Absent solid benefits, vertical integration is not likely to be an attractive competitive strategy option.

COOPERATIVE STRATEGIES AND COMPETITIVE ADVANTAGE

Many companies have begun forming strategic alliances and cooperative relationships with other companies to complement their own strategic initiatives and strengthen their competitiveness in domestic and international markets. Strategic alliances are cooperative agreements between firms that go beyond normal company-to-company dealings but that fall short of merger or full partnership and ownership ties.[15] Alliances and/or cooperative agreements can involve joint research efforts, technology sharing, joint use of production facilities, marketing one another's products, or joining forces to manufacture components or assemble finished products.

Companies enter into alliances or establish cooperative agreements for several strategically beneficial reasons.[16] The five most important are to collaborate on technology or the development of promising new products, to improve supply chain efficiency, to gain economies of scale in production and/or marketing, to fill gaps in their technical and manufacturing expertise, and to acquire or improve market access. Allies learn much from one another in performing joint research, sharing technological know-how, and collaborating on complementary new technologies and products. Manufacturers pursue alliances with parts and components suppliers to gain the efficiencies of better supply chain management and to speed new products to market. By joining forces in producing components, assembling models, or marketing their products, companies can realize cost savings not achievable with their own small volumes; they can also learn how to improve their quality control and production procedures by studying one another's manufacturing methods. Often alliances are formed to share distribution facilities and dealer networks or to jointly promote complementary products, thereby mutually strengthening their access to buyers.

While a few firms can pursue their strategies alone, it is becoming increasingly common for companies to pursue their strategies in collaboration with suppliers, distributors, makers of complementary products, and sometimes even select competitors.

Not only can alliances offset competitive disadvantages but they also can result in the allied companies' directing their competitive energies more toward mutual rivals and less toward one another. Who partners with whom affects the pattern of industry rivalry. Many runner-up companies, wanting to preserve their independence, resort to

[15]A number of strategic alliances do involve minority ownership by one, occasionally both, alliance members however. See C. A. Bartlett and S. Ghoshal, *Managing Across Borders: The Transnational Solution* (Boston: Harvard Business School Press, 1989), p. 65 and Kenichi Ohmae, "The Global Logic of Strategic Alliances," *Harvard Business Review* 89, no. 2 (March–April 1989), pp. 143–54.
[16]Porter, *The Competitive Advantage of Nations*, p. 66; see also Jeremy Main, "Making Global Alliances Work," *Fortune*, December 17, 1990, pp. 121–26.

alliances rather than merger to try to close the competitive gap on leading companies—*they rely on collaboration with others to enhance their own capabilities,
develop valuable new strategic resources, and compete effectively.* Industry leaders
pursue cooperative alliances in order to better fend off ambitious rivals and to open
up new opportunities.

Strategic cooperation is a much-favored, indeed necessary, approach in industries
like electronics, semiconductors, computer hardware and software, and telecommunications where technological developments are occurring at a furious pace along
many different paths and advances in one technology spill over to affect others (often
blurring industry boundaries). Whenever industries are experiencing high-
velocity technological change in many areas simultaneously, firms find it
essential to have cooperative relationships with other enterprises to stay on
the leading edge of technology and product performance even in their own
area of specialization. They cooperate in technology development, in sharing R&D information of mutual interest, in developing new products that
complement each other, and in building networks of dealers and distributors to handle their products. Competitive advantage emerges when a
company acquires valuable resources and capabilities through alliances and cooperative agreements that it could not otherwise obtain on its own—this requires real in-
the-trenches collaboration between the partners to create new value together, not
merely an arm's-length exchange of ideas and information. Unless partners value the
skills, resources, and contributions each brings to the alliance and the cooperative
arrangement results in win-win outcomes, it is doomed.

> *Alliances and cooperative agreements between companies can lead to competitive advantage in ways that otherwise are beyond a company's reach.*

Cooperative strategies and alliances to penetrate international markets are also
common between domestic and foreign firms. Such partnerships are useful in putting
together the resources and capabilities to do business over more country markets. For
example, U.S., European, and Japanese companies wanting to build market footholds
in the fast-growing China market have all pursued partnership arrangements with
Chinese companies to help in dealing with governmental regulations, to supply
knowledge of local markets, to provide guidance on adapting their products to
Chinese consumers, to set up local manufacturing capabilities, and to assist in
distribution, marketing, and promotional activities.

General Electric has formed over 100 cooperative partnerships in a wide range of
areas; IBM has joined in over 400 strategic alliances.[17] Alliances are so central to
Corning's strategy that the company describes itself as a "network of
organizations." Microsoft and Netscape have both been aggressive users of
cooperative strategies, forming scores of alliances with the providers of
complementary technologies and products to build and strengthen their
competitive positions. In the PC industry cooperative alliances are pervasive because the different components of PCs and the software to run them
is supplied by so many different companies—one set of companies provide
the microprocessors, another group makes the motherboards, another the
monitors, another the keyboards, another the printers, and so on. Moreover,
their facilities are scattered across the United States, Japan, Taiwan, Singapore, and Malaysia. Close collaboration on product development, logistics, production, and the timing of new product releases works to the advantage of nearly all PC
industry members.

> *Alliances and cooperative arrangements, whether they bring together companies from different parts of the industry value chain or different parts of the world, are a fact of life in business today.*

---

[17]Michael A. Hitt, Beverly B. Tyler, Camilla Hardee, and Daewoo Park, "Understanding Strategic Intent in
the Global Marketplace," *Academy of Management Executive*, 9, no. 2 (May 1995), p. 13.

The Achilles' heel of alliances and cooperative strategies is the danger of becoming dependent on other companies for *essential* expertise and capabilities over the long term. To be a market leader (and perhaps even a serious market contender), a company must develop its own capabilities in areas where internal strategic control is pivotal to protecting its competitiveness and building competitive advantage. Moreover, acquiring essential know-how and capabilities from one's allies sometimes holds only limited potential (because one's partners guard their most valuable skills and expertise); in such instances, acquiring or merging with a company possessing the desired know-how and resources is a better solution.

USING OFFENSIVE STRATEGIES TO SECURE COMPETITIVE ADVANTAGE

Competitive advantage is nearly always achieved by successful offensive strategic moves—moves calculated to yield a cost advantage, a differentiation advantage, or a resource or capabilities advantage. Defensive strategies can protect competitive advantage but rarely are the basis for creating the advantage. How long it takes for a successful offensive to create an edge varies with the competitive circumstances.[18] The

Competitive advantage is usually acquired by employing a creative offensive strategy that isn't easily thwarted by rivals.

buildup period, shown in Figure 5–2, can be short, if the requisite resources and capabilities are already in place or if the offensive produces immediate buyer response (as can occur with a dramatic price cut, an imaginative ad campaign, or a new product that proves to be a smash hit). Or the buildup can take much longer, if winning consumer acceptance of an innovative product will take some time or if the firm may need several years to debug a new technology and bring new capacity on-line. Ideally, an offensive move builds competitive advantage quickly; the longer it takes, the more likely rivals will spot the move, see its potential, and begin a counterresponse. The size of the advantage (indicated on the vertical scale in Figure 5–2) can be large (as in pharmaceuticals where patents on an important new drug produce a substantial advantage) or small (as in apparel where popular new designs can be imitated quickly).

Following a successful competitive offensive is a *benefit period* during which the fruits of competitive advantage can be enjoyed. The length of the benefit period depends on how much time it takes rivals to launch counteroffensives and begin closing the gap. A lengthy benefit period gives a firm valuable time to earn above-average profits and recoup the investment made in creating the advantage. The best strategic offensives produce big competitive advantages and long benefit periods.

As rivals respond with counteroffensives to close the competitive gap, the *erosion period* begins. Competent, resourceful competitors can be counted on to counterattack with initiatives to overcome any market disadvantage they face—they are not going to stand idly by and passively accept being outcompeted without a fight.[19] Thus, to sustain an initially won competitive advantage, a firm must come up with follow-on offensive and defensive moves. Preparations for the next round of strategic moves ought to be made during the benefit period so that the needed resources are in place when competitors mount efforts to cut into the leader's advantage. Unless the firm stays a step ahead of rivals by initiating one series of offensive and defensive

---

[18] Ian C. MacMillan, "How Long Can You Sustain a Competitive Advantage?" reprinted in Liam Fahey, *The Strategic Planning Management Reader* (Englewood Cliffs, N.J.: Prentice-Hall, 1989), pp. 23–24.

[19] Ian C. MacMillan, "Controlling Competitive Dynamics by Taking Strategic Initiative," *The Academy of Management Executive* 2, no. 2 (May 1988), p. 111.

FIGURE 5-2 The Building and Eroding of Competitive Advantage

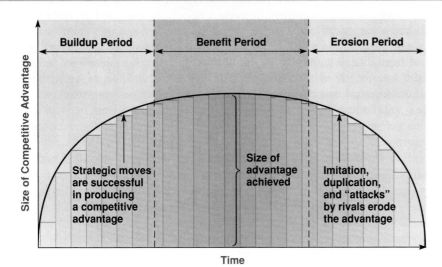

moves after another to protect its market position and retain customer favor, its market advantage will erode.

There are six basic types of strategic offensives:[20]

- Initiatives to match or exceed competitor strengths.
- Initiatives to capitalize on competitor weaknesses.
- Simultaneous initiatives on many fronts.
- End-run offensives.
- Guerrilla offensives.
- Preemptive strikes.

Initiatives to Match or Exceed Competitor Strengths

There are two instances in which it makes sense to mount offensives aimed at neutralizing or overcoming the strengths and capabilities of rival companies. The first is when a company has no choice but to try to whittle away at a strong rival's competitive advantage. The second is when it is possible to gain profitable market share at the expense of rivals despite whatever resource strengths and capabilities they have. Attacking the strengths of rivals is most likely to meet with success when a firm has either a *superior* product offering or *superior* organizational resources and capabilities. The merit of challenging a rival's strengths head-on depends on the trade-off between the costs of the offensive and its competitive benefits. Absent good prospects for added profitability and a more solidified competitive position, such an offensive is ill advised.

One of the most powerful offensive strategies is to challenge rivals with an equally good or better product at a lower price.

---

[20]Philip Kotler and Ravi Singh, "Marketing Warfare in the 1980s," *The Journal of Business Strategy* 1, no. 3 (Winter 1981), pp. 30–41; Philip Kotler, *Marketing Management*, 5th ed. (Englewood Cliffs, N.J.: Prentice-Hall, 1984), pp. 401–6; and Ian MacMillan, "Preemptive Strategies," *Journal of Business Strategy* 14, no. 2 (Fall 1983), pp. 16–26.

The classic avenue for attacking a strong rival is with an equally good offering at a lower price.[21] This can produce market share gains if the targeted competitor has strong reasons for not resorting to price cuts of its own and if the challenger convinces buyers that its product is just as good. However, such a strategy increases total profits only if the gains in unit sales are enough to offset the impact of lower prices and thinner margins per unit sold. A more potent and sustainable basis for mounting a price-aggressive challenge is to *first* achieve a cost advantage and then hit competitors with a lower price.[22] Price-cutting supported by a cost advantage can be continued indefinitely. Without a cost advantage, price-cutting works only if the aggressor has more financial resources and can outlast its rivals in a war of attrition.

Challenging larger, entrenched competitors with aggressive price-cutting is foolhardy unless the aggressor has either a cost advantage or greater financial strength.

Other strategic options for attacking a competitor's strengths include leapfrogging into next-generation technologies to make the rival's products and/or production processes obsolete, adding new features that appeal to the rival's customers, running comparison ads, constructing major new plant capacity in the rival's backyard, expanding the product line to match the rival model for model, and developing customer service capabilities that the rival doesn't have. As a rule, challenging a rival on competitive factors where it is strong is an uphill struggle. Success can be long in coming and usually hinges on developing a cost advantage, a service advantage, a product with attractive differentiating features, or unique competitive capabilities (fast design-to-market times, greater technical know-how, or agility in responding to shifting customer requirements).

Initiatives to Capitalize on Competitor Weaknesses

In this offensive approach, a company tries to gain market inroads by directing its competitive attention to the weaknesses of rivals. There are a number of ways to achieve competitive gains at the expense of rivals' weaknesses:

- Concentrate on geographic regions where a rival has a weak market share or is exerting less competitive effort.

- Pay special attention to buyer segments that a rival is neglecting or is weakly equipped to serve.

- Go after the customers of rivals whose products lag on quality, features, or product performance; in such cases, a challenger with a better product can often convince the most performance-conscious customers to switch to its brand.

- Make special sales pitches to the customers of rivals who provide subpar customer service—it may be relatively easy for a service-oriented challenger to win a rival's disenchanted customers.

- Try to move in on rivals that have weak advertising and weak brand recognition—a challenger with strong marketing skills and a recognized brand name can often win customers away from lesser-known rivals.

- Introduce new models or product versions that exploit gaps in the product lines of key rivals; sometimes "gap fillers" turn out to be a market hit and develop into new growth segments—witness Chrysler's success in minivans. This initiative works well when new product versions satisfy neglected buyer needs.

---

[21]Kotler, *Marketing Management*, p. 402.
[22]Ibid., p. 403.

As a rule, initiatives that exploit competitor weaknesses stand a better chance of succeeding than do those that challenge competitor strengths, especially if the weaknesses represent important vulnerabilities and the rival is caught by surprise with no ready defense.[23]

Simultaneous Initiatives on Many Fronts

On occasion a company may see merit in launching a grand competitive offensive involving multiple initiatives (price cuts, increased advertising, new product introductions, free samples, coupons, in-store promotions, rebates) across a wide geographic front. Such all-out campaigns can throw a rival off-balance, diverting its attention in many directions and forcing it to protect many pieces of its customer base simultaneously. Microsoft is employing a grand offensive to outmaneuver rivals in securing a prominent role on the Internet for its software products.[24] It allocated $160 million and 500 of its most talented programmers to the task of rapidly introducing upgraded versions of Internet Explorer (to overtake Netscape's Navigator Web browser), incorporated Explorer in the Windows 95 package and allowed Internet users to download Explorer free, negotiated deals with America Online and CompuServe to utilize Internet Explorer, put several thousand programmers to work on a variety of Internet-related projects (with R&D budgets of over $500 million), assigned another large group of programmers the task of retrofitting Microsoft's product line to better mesh with the Internet, entered into a joint venture with NBC to form a new cable channel called MSNBC, invested $1 billion in the common stock of Comcast (the second largest U.S. cable provider) to give it leverage in pushing for faster advances in Internet-related cable technologies to speed data transfer, and formed alliances with NBC, ESPN, Disney, Dreamworks, and others to provide content for Microsoft Network and MSNBC. Multifaceted offensives have their best chance of success when a challenger not only comes up with an especially attractive product or service but also has a brand name and reputation to secure broad distribution and retail exposure. Then it can blitz the market with advertising and promotional offers and perhaps entice significant numbers of buyers to switch their brand allegiance.

End-Run Offensives

End-run offensives seek to avoid head-on challenges tied to aggressive price-cutting, escalated advertising, or costly efforts to outdifferentiate rivals. Instead the idea is to maneuver *around* competitors, capture unoccupied or less contested market territory, and change the rules of the competitive game in the aggressor's favor. Examples of end-run offensives include launching initiatives to build strong positions in geographic areas where close rivals have little or no market presence, trying to create new segments by introducing products with different attributes and performance features to better meet the needs of selected buyers, and leapfrogging into next-generation technologies. A successful end-run offensive allows a company to gain a significant first-mover advantage in a new arena and force competitors to play catch-up.

---

[23]For a discussion of the use of surprise, see William E. Rothschild, "Surprise and the Competitive Advantage," *Journal of Business Strategy* 4, no. 3 (Winter 1984), pp. 10–18.

[24]A more detailed account of Microsoft's grand offensive is presented in Brent Schendler, "Software Hardball," *Fortune*, September 30, 1996, pp.106–16.

Guerrilla Offensives

Guerrilla offensives are particularly well-suited to small challengers who have neither the resources nor the market visibility to mount a full-fledged attack on industry leaders.[25] A guerrilla offensive uses the hit-and-run principle, selectively trying to grab sales and market share wherever and whenever an underdog catches rivals napping or spots an opening to lure their customers away. There are several ways to wage a guerrilla offensive:[26]

1. Go after buyer groups that are not important to major rivals.

2. Go after buyers whose loyalty to rival brands is weakest.

3. Focus on areas where rivals are overextended and have spread their resources most thinly (possibilities include going after selected customers located in isolated geographic areas, enhancing delivery schedules at times when competitors' deliveries are running behind, adding to quality when rivals have quality control problems, and boosting technical services when buyers are confused by competitors' proliferation of models and optional features).

4. Make small, scattered, random raids on the leaders' customers with such tactics as occasional lowballing on price (to win a big order or steal a key account).

5. Surprise key rivals with sporadic but intense bursts of promotional activity to pick off buyers who might otherwise have selected rival brands.

6. If rivals employ unfair or unethical competitive tactics and the situation merits it, file legal actions charging antitrust violations, patent infringement, or unfair advertising.

Preemptive Strikes

Preemptive strategies involve moving first to secure an advantageous position that rivals are foreclosed or discouraged from duplicating. What makes a move "preemptive" is its one-of-a-kind nature—whoever strikes first stands to acquire competitive assets that rivals can't readily match. A firm can bolster its competitive capabilities with several preemptive moves:[27]

• Expand production capacity well ahead of market demand in hopes of discouraging rivals from following with expansions of their own. When rivals are "bluffed" out of adding capacity for fear of creating long-term excess supply and having to struggle with the bad economics of underutilized plants, the preemptor stands to win a bigger market share as market demand grows and it has the production capacity to take on new orders.

---

[25]For an interesting study of how small firms can successfully employ guerrilla-style tactics, see Ming-Jer Chen and Donald C. Hambrick, "Speed, Stealth, and Selective Attack: How Small Firms Differ from Large Firms in Competitive Behavior," *Academy of Management Journal* 38, no. 2 (April 1995), pp. 453–82.

[26]For more details, see Ian MacMillan "How Business Strategists Can Use Guerrilla Warfare Tactics," *Journal of Business Strategy* 1, no. 2 (Fall 1980), pp. 63–65; Kathryn R. Harrigan, *Strategic Flexibility* (Lexington, Mass.: Lexington Books, 1985), pp. 30–45; and Liam Fahey, "Guerrilla Strategy: The Hit-and-Run Attack," in Fahey, *The Strategic Management Planning Reader*, pp. 194–97.

[27]The use of preemptive moves is treated comprehensively in Ian MacMillan, "Preemptive Strategies," *Journal of Business Strategy* 14, no. 2 (Fall 1983), pp. 16–26. What follows in this section is based on MacMillan's article.

- Tie up the best (or the most) raw material sources and/or the most reliable, high-quality suppliers with long-term contracts or backward vertical integration. This move can relegate rivals to struggling for second-best supply positions.

- Secure the best geographic locations. An attractive first-mover advantage can often be locked up by moving to obtain the most favorable site along a heavily traveled thoroughfare, at a new interchange or intersection, in a new shopping mall, in a natural beauty spot, close to cheap transportation or raw material supplies or market outlets, and so on.

- Obtain the business of prestigious customers.

- Build a "psychological" image in the minds of consumers that is unique and hard to copy and that establishes a compelling appeal and rallying cry. Examples include Nike's "Just do it" tag line, Avis's well-known "We try harder" theme; Frito-Lay's guarantee to retailers of "99.5% service"; and Prudential's "piece of the rock" image of safety and permanence.

- Secure exclusive or dominant access to the best distributors in an area.

To be successful, a preemptive move doesn't have to totally block rivals from following or copying; it merely needs to give a firm a "prime" position that is not easily circumvented. Fox's stunning four-year, $6.2 billion contract to televise NFL football (a preemptive strike that ousted CBS) represented a bold strategic move to transform Fox into a major TV network alongside ABC, CBS, and NBC. DeBeers became the dominant world distributor of diamonds by buying up the production of most of the important diamond mines. Du Pont's aggressive capacity expansions in titanium dioxide, while not blocking all competitors from expanding, did discourage enough to give it a leadership position in the industry.

Choosing Whom to Attack

Aggressor firms need to analyze which of their rivals to challenge as well as how to outcompete them. Any of four types of firms can make good targets:[28]

1. *Market leaders.* Offensive attacks on a market leader make the best sense when the leader in terms of size and market share is not a "true leader" in serving the market well. Signs of leader vulnerability include unhappy buyers, a product line that is inferior to what several rivals have, a competitive strategy that lacks real strength based on low-cost leadership or differentiation, strong emotional commitment to an aging technology the leader has pioneered, outdated plants and equipment, a preoccupation with diversification into other industries, and mediocre or declining profitability. Offensives to erode the positions of market leaders have real promise when the challenger is able to revamp its value chain or innovate to gain a fresh cost-based or differentiation-based advantage.[29] Attacks on leaders don't have to result in making the aggressor the new leader to be judged successful; a challenger may "win" by simply wresting enough sales from the leader to become a stronger runner-up. Caution is well advised in challenging strong market leaders—there's a significant risk of squandering valuable resources in

---

[28]Kotler, *Marketing Management*, p. 400.
[29]Porter, *Competitive Advantage*, p. 518.

a futile effort or starting a fierce and profitless industrywide battle for market share.

2. *Runner-up firms*. Runner-up firms are an especially attractive target when a challenger's resource strengths and competitive capabilities are well suited to exploiting their weaknesses.

3. *Struggling enterprises that are on the verge of going under*. Challenging a hard-pressed rival in ways that further sap its financial strength and competitive position can weaken its resolve and hasten its exit from the market.

4. *Small local and regional firms*. Because these firms typically have limited expertise and resources, a challenger with broader capabilities is well positioned to raid their biggest and best customers—particularly those who are growing rapidly, have increasingly sophisticated requirements, and may already be thinking about switching to a full-service supplier.

Choosing the Basis for Attack   A firm's strategic offensive should, at a minimum, be tied to its most potent competitive assets—its core competencies, resource strengths, and competitive capabilities. Otherwise the prospects for success are indeed dim. The centerpiece of the offensive can be a new-generation technology, a newly developed competitive capability, an innovative new product, introduction of attractive new performance features, a cost advantage in manufacturing or distribution, or some kind of differentiation advantage. If the challenger's resources and competitive strengths amount to a competitive advantage over the targeted rivals, so much the better.

> *At the very least, an offensive must be tied to a firm's resource strengths; more optimally, it is grounded in competitive advantage.*

USING DEFENSIVE STRATEGIES TO PROTECT COMPETITIVE ADVANTAGE

In a competitive market, all firms are subject to challenges from rivals. Market offensives can come both from new entrants in the industry and from established firms seeking to improve their market positions. The purpose of defensive strategy is to lower the risk of being attacked, weaken the impact of any attack that occurs, and influence challengers to aim their efforts at other rivals. While defensive strategy usually doesn't enhance a firm's competitive advantage, it helps fortify a firm's competitive position, protect its most valuable resources and capabilities from imitation, and sustain whatever competitive advantage it does have.

> *The foremost purpose of defensive strategy is to protect competitive advantage and fortify the firm's competitive position.*

A company can protect its competitive position in several ways. One is trying to block the avenues challengers can take in mounting an offensive. The options include:[30]

- Hiring additional employees to broaden or deepen the company's core competencies or capabilities in key areas (so as to be able to overpower rivals who attempt to imitate its skills and resources).

- Enhancing the flexibility of resource assets and competencies (so that they can be quickly redeployed or adapted to meet changing market conditions),

---

[30]Porter, *Competitive Advantage*, pp. 489–94.

thereby being in a greater state of readiness for new developments than rivals.

- Broadening the firm's product line to close off vacant niches and gaps to would-be challengers.
- Introducing models or brands that match the characteristics challengers' models already have or might have.
- Keeping prices low on models that most closely match competitors' offerings.
- Signing exclusive agreements with dealers and distributors to keep competitors from using the same ones.
- Granting dealers and distributors volume discounts to discourage them from experimenting with other suppliers.
- Offering free or low-cost training to product users.
- Endeavoring to discourage buyers from trying competitors' brands by (1) providing coupons and sample giveaways to buyers most prone to experiment and (2) making early announcements about impending new products or price changes to induce potential buyers to postpone switching.
- Raising the amount of financing provided to dealers and buyers.
- Reducing delivery times for spare parts.
- Lengthening warranty coverages.
- Participating in alternative technologies.
- Protecting proprietary know-how in product design, production technologies, and other value chain activities.
- Contracting for all or most of the output of the best suppliers to make it harder for rivals to obtain parts and components of equal quality.
- Avoiding suppliers that also serve competitors.
- Purchasing natural resource reserves ahead of present needs to keep them from competitors.
- Challenging rivals' products or practices in regulatory proceedings.

Moves such as these not only buttress a firm's present position, they also present competitors with a moving target. Protecting the status quo isn't enough. A good defense entails adjusting quickly to changing industry conditions and, on occasion, being a first-mover to block or preempt moves by would-be aggressors. A mobile defense is preferable to a stationary defense.

A second approach to defensive strategy entails signaling challengers that there is a real threat of strong retaliation if a challenger attacks. The goal is to dissuade challengers from attacking at all or at least divert them to options that are less threatening to the defender. Would-be challengers can be signaled by:[31]

- Publicly announcing management's commitment to maintain the firm's present market share.
- Publicly announcing plans to construct adequate production capacity to meet and possibly surpass the forecasted growth in industry volume.

---

[31]Ibid., pp. 495–97. The listing here is selective; Porter offers a greater number of options.

- Giving out advance information about a new product, technology breakthrough, or the planned introduction of important new brands or models in hopes that challengers will delay moves of their own until they see if the announced actions actually happen.

- Publicly committing the company to a policy of matching competitors' terms or prices.

- Maintaining a war chest of cash and marketable securities.

- Making an occasional strong counterresponse to the moves of weak competitors to enhance the firm's image as a tough defender.

Another way to dissuade rivals is to try to lower the profit inducement for challengers to launch an offensive. When a firm's or industry's profitability is enticingly high, challengers are more willing to tackle high defensive barriers and combat strong retaliation. A defender can deflect attacks, especially from new entrants, by deliberately forgoing some short-run profits and using accounting methods that obscure profitability.

FIRST-MOVER ADVANTAGES AND DISADVANTAGES

When to make a strategic move is often as crucial as *what* move to make. Timing is especially important when *first-mover advantages* or *disadvantages* exist.[32] Being first to initiate a strategic move can have a high payoff when (1) pioneering helps build a firm's image and reputation with buyers, (2) early commitments to supplies of raw materials, new technologies, distribution channels, and so on can produce an absolute cost advantage over rivals, (3) first-time customers remain strongly loyal to pioneering firms in making repeat purchases, and (4) moving first constitutes a preemptive strike, making imitation extra hard or unlikely. The bigger the first-mover advantages, the more attractive that making the first move becomes.

Because of first-mover advantages and disadvantages, competitive advantage is often attached to when *a move is made as well as to* what *move is made.*

However, a wait-and-see approach doesn't always carry a competitive penalty. Being a first-mover may entail greater risks than being a late-mover. First-mover disadvantages (or late-mover advantages) arise when (1) pioneering leadership is much more costly than followership and the leader gains negligible experience curve effects, (2) technological change is so rapid that early investments are soon obsolete (thus allowing following firms to gain the advantages of next-generation products and more efficient processes), (3) it is easy for latecomers to crack the market because customer loyalty to pioneering firms is weak, and (4) the hard-earned skills and know-how developed by the market leaders during the early competitive phase are easily copied or even surpassed by late-movers. Good timing, therefore, is important in deciding whether to be a first-mover, a fast-follower, or a cautious late-mover.

KEY POINTS

The challenge of competitive strategy—whether it be overall low-cost, broad differentiation, best-cost, focused low-cost, or focused differentiation—is to create a competitive advantage for the firm. Competitive advantage comes from positioning a

---

[32]Porter, *Competitive Strategy*, pp. 232–33.

firm in the marketplace so it has an edge in coping with competitive forces and in attracting buyers.

A strategy of trying to be the low-cost provider works well in situations where:

- The industry's product is essentially the same from seller to seller (brand differences are minor).
- Many buyers are price-sensitive and shop for the lowest price.
- There are only a few ways to achieve product differentiation that have much value to buyers.
- Most buyers use the product in the same ways and thus have common user requirements.
- Buyers' costs in switching from one seller or brand to another are low (or even zero).
- Buyers are large and have significant power to negotiate pricing terms.

To achieve a low-cost advantage, a company must become more skilled than rivals in managing the cost drivers and/or it must find innovative cost-saving ways to revamp its value chain. Successful low-cost providers usually achieve their cost advantages by imaginatively and persistently ferreting out cost savings throughout the value chain. They are good at finding ways to drive costs out of their businesses.

Differentiation strategies seek to produce a competitive edge by incorporating attributes and features into a company's product/service offering that rivals don't have or by developing competencies and capabilities that buyers value and that rivals don't have. Anything a firm can do to create buyer value represents a potential basis for differentiation. Successful differentiation is usually keyed to lowering the buyer's cost of using the item, raising the performance the buyer gets, or boosting a buyer's psychological satisfaction. To be sustainable, differentiation usually has to be linked to unique internal expertise, core competencies, and resources that give a company capabilities its rivals can't easily match. Differentiation tied just to unique physical features seldom is lasting because resourceful competitors are adept at cloning, improving on, or finding substitutes for almost any feature or trait that appeals to buyers.

Best-cost provider strategies combine a strategic emphasis on low cost with a strategic emphasis on more than minimal quality, service, features, or performance. The aim is to create competitive advantage by giving buyers more value for the money; this is done by matching close rivals on key quality-service-features-performance attributes and beating them on the costs of incorporating such attributes into the product or service. To be successful with a best-cost provider strategy, a company must have unique expertise in incorporating upscale product or service attributes at a lower cost than rivals; it must have the capability to manage unit costs down and product/service caliber up simultaneously.

The competitive advantage of focusing is earned either by achieving lower costs in serving the target market niche or by developing an ability to offer niche buyers something appealingly different from rival competitors—in other words, it is either *cost-based* or *differentiation-based*. Focusing works best when:

- Buyer needs or uses of the item are diverse.
- No other rival is attempting to specialize in the same target segment.
- A firm lacks the capability to go after a wider part of the total market.

- Buyer segments differ widely in size, growth rate, profitability, and intensity in the five competitive forces, making some segments more attractive than others.

Vertically integrating forward or backward makes strategic sense only if it strengthens a company's position via either cost reduction or creation of a differentiation-based advantage. Otherwise, the drawbacks of vertical integration (increased investment, greater business risk, increased vulnerability to technological changes, and less flexibility in making product changes) outweigh the advantages (better coordination of production flows and technological know-how from stage to stage, more specialized use of technology, greater internal control over operations, greater scale economies, and matching production with sales and marketing). There are ways to achieve the advantages of vertical integration without encountering the drawbacks.

A variety of offensive strategic moves can be used to secure a competitive advantage. Strategic offensives can be aimed either at competitors' strengths or at their weaknesses; they can involve end-runs or simultaneously launched initiatives on many fronts; they can be designed as guerrilla actions or as preemptive strikes; and the target of the offensive can be a market leader, a runner-up firm, or the smallest and/or weakest firms in the industry.

The strategic approaches to defending a company's position usually include (1) making moves that fortify the company's present position, (2) presenting competitors with a moving target to avoid "out of date" vulnerability, and (3) dissuading rivals from even trying to attack.

The timing of strategic moves is important. First-movers sometimes gain strategic advantage; at other times, such as when technology is developing fast, it is cheaper and easier to be a follower than a leader.

SUGGESTED READINGS

Aaker, David A. "Managing Assets and Skills: The Key to a Sustainable Competitive Advantage." *California Management Review* 31, no. 2 (Winter 1989), pp. 91–106.

Barney, Jay B. *Gaining and Sustaining Competitive Advantage*. Reading, Mass.: Addison-Wesley, 1997, especially chapters 6, 7, 9, 10, and 14.

Cohen, William A. "War in the Marketplace." *Business Horizons* 29, no. 2 (March–April 1986), pp. 10–20.

Coyne, Kevin P. "Sustainable Competitive Advantage—What It Is, What It Isn't." *Business Horizons* 29, no. 1 (January–February 1986), pp. 54–61.

D'Aveni, Richard A. *Hypercompetition: The Dynamics of Strategic Maneuvering* (New York: Free Press, 1994), chaps. 1, 2, 3, and 4.

Hamel, Gary, "Strategy as Revolution." *Harvard Business Review* 74, no. 4 (July–August 1996), pp. 69–82.

Harrigan, Kathryn R. "Guerrilla Strategies of Underdog Competitors." *Planning Review* 14, no. 16 (November 1986), pp. 4–11.

———. "Formulating Vertical Integration Strategies." *Academy of Management Review* 9, no. 4 (October 1984), pp. 638–52.

———. "Matching Vertical Integration Strategies to Competitive Conditions." *Strategic Management Journal* 7, no. 6 (November–December 1986), pp. 535–56.

Hout, Thomas, Michael E. Porter, and Eileen Rudden. "How Global Companies Win Out." *Harvard Business Review* 60, no. 5 (September–October 1982), pp. 98–108.

MacMillan, Ian C. "Preemptive Strategies." *Journal of Business Strategy* 14, no. 2 (Fall 1983), pp. 16–26.

————. "Controlling Competitive Dynamics by Taking Strategic Initiative." *The Academy of Management Executive* 2, no. 2 (May 1988), pp. 111–18.

Porter, Michael E. *Competitive Advantage* (New York: Free Press, 1985), chaps. 3, 4, 5, 7, 14, and 15.

————. "What Is Strategy." *Harvard Business Review* 74, no. 6 (November–December 1996), pp. 61–78.

Rothschild, William E. "Surprise and the Competitive Advantage." *Journal of Business Strategy* 4, no. 3 (Winter 1984), pp. 10–18.

Schnarrs, Steven P. *Managing Imitation Strategies: How Later Entrants Seize Markets from Pioneers.* New York: Free Press, 1994.

Stuckey, John and David White, "When and When *Not* to Vertically Integrate." *Sloan Management Review* (Spring 1993), pp. 71–83.

Venkatesan, Ravi. "Strategic Outsourcing: To Make or Not to Make." *Harvard Business Review* 70, no. 6 (November–December 1992), pp. 98–107.

6 MATCHING STRATEGY TO A COMPANY'S SITUATION

The task of matching strategy to a company's situation is complicated because of the many external and internal factors managers have to weigh. However, while the number and variety of considerations is necessarily lengthy, the most important drivers shaping a company's best strategic options fall into two broad categories:

- The nature of industry and competitive conditions.
- The firm's own resources and competitive capabilities, market position, and best opportunities.

The dominant *strategy-shaping industry and competitive conditions* revolve around what stage in the life cycle the industry is in (emerging, rapid growth, mature, declining), the industry's structure (fragmented versus concentrated), the relative strength of the five competitive forces, the impact of industry driving forces, and the scope of competitive rivalry (particularly whether the company's market is globally competitive). The pivotal *company-specific considerations* are (1) whether the company is an industry leader, an up-and-coming challenger, a content runner-up, or an also-ran struggling to survive, and (2) the company's set of resource strengths and weaknesses, competitive capabilities, and market opportunities and threats. But even these few categories occur in too many combinations to cover here. However, we can demonstrate what the task of matching strategy to the situation involves by considering the strategy-making challenges that exist in six classic types of industry environments:

1. Competing in emerging and rapidly growing industries.
2. Competing in high-velocity markets.
3. Competing in maturing industries.
4. Competing in stagnant or declining industries.
5. Competing in fragmented industries.
6. Competing in international markets.

and in three classic types of company situations:

1. Firms in industry leadership positions.
2. Firms in runner-up positions.
3. Firms that are competitively weak or crisis-ridden.

STRATEGIES FOR COMPETING IN EMERGING INDUSTRIES

An emerging industry is one in the early, formative stage. Most companies in an emerging industry are in a start-up mode, adding people, acquiring or constructing facilities, gearing up production, trying to broaden distribution and gain buyer acceptance. Often, there are important product design and technological problems to be worked out as well. Emerging industries present managers with some unique strategy-making challenges:[1]

- Because the market is new and unproven, there are many uncertainties about how it will function, how fast it will grow, and how big it will get. Firms have to scramble to get hard information about competitors, how fast products are gaining buyer acceptance, and users' experiences with the product; because of the industry's newness, there are no organizations or trade associations gathering and distributing information to industry members. The little historical data available is virtually useless in making sales and profit projections because the past is an unreliable guide to the future.

- Much of the technological know-how tends to be proprietary and closely guarded, having been developed in-house by pioneering firms; some firms may file patents to secure competitive advantage.

- Often, there are conflicting judgments about which of several competing technologies will win out or which product attributes will gain the most buyer favor. Until market forces sort these things out, wide differences in product quality and performance are typical and rivalry centers around each firm's efforts to get the market to ratify its own strategic approach to technology, product design, marketing, and distribution.

- Entry barriers tend to be relatively low, even for entrepreneurial start-up companies; well-financed, opportunity-seeking outsiders are likely to enter if the industry has promise for explosive growth.

- Strong experience curve effects often result in significant cost reductions as volume builds.

- Since all buyers are first-time users, the marketing task is to induce initial purchase and to overcome customer concerns about product features, performance reliability, and conflicting claims of rival firms.

- Many potential buyers expect first-generation products to be rapidly improved, so they delay purchase until technology and product design mature.

- Sometimes, firms have trouble securing ample supplies of raw materials and components (until suppliers gear up to meet the industry's needs).

- Many companies, finding themselves short of funds to support needed R&D and get through several lean years until the product catches on, end up merging with competitors or being acquired by financially strong outsiders looking to invest in a growth market.

The two critical strategic issues confronting firms in an emerging industry are (1) how to finance start-up and initial operations until sales take off and (2) what

---

[1]Michael E. Porter, *Competitive Strategy* (New York: Free Press, 1980), pp. 216–23.

market segments and competitive advantages to go after in trying to secure a leading position.[2] Competitive strategies keyed either to low cost or differentiation are usually viable. Focusing should be considered when financial resources are limited and the industry has too many technological frontiers to pursue at once. Because an emerging industry has no established "rules of the game" and industry participants employ widely varying strategic approaches, a well-financed firm with a powerful strategy can shape the rules and become the recognized industry leader.

Strategic success in an emerging industry calls for bold entrepreneurship, a willingness to pioneer and take risks, an intuitive feel for what buyers will like, quick response to new developments, and opportunistic strategy making.

Dealing with all the risks and opportunities of an emerging industry is one of the most challenging business strategy problems. To be successful, companies usually have to pursue one or more of the following avenues:[3]

1. Try to win the early race for industry leadership with bold entrepreneurship and a creative strategy. Broad or focused differentiation strategies keyed to product superiority typically offer the best chance for early competitive advantage.

2. Push to perfect the technology, to improve product quality, and to develop attractive performance features.

3. As technological uncertainty clears and a dominant technology emerges, adopt it quickly. (However, while there's merit in trying to be the industry standard bearer on technology and to pioneer the "dominant product design," firms have to beware of betting too heavily on their own preferred technological approach or product design—especially when there are many competing technologies, R&D is costly, and technological developments can quickly move in surprising new directions.)

4. Form strategic alliances with key suppliers to gain access to specialized skills, technological capabilities, and critical materials or components.

5. Try to capture any first-mover advantages by commiting early to promising technologies, allying with the most capable suppliers, expanding product selection, improving styling, capturing experience curve effects, and getting well-positioned in new distribution channels.

6. Pursue new customer groups, new user applications, and entry into new geographical areas (perhaps utilizing joint ventures if financial resources are constrained).

7. Make it easier and cheaper for first-time buyers to try the industry's first-generation product. Then as the product becomes familiar to a wide portion of the market, begin to shift the advertising emphasis from creating product awareness to increasing frequency of use and building brand loyalty.

8. Use price cuts to attract the next layer of price-sensitive buyers.

9. Expect well-financed outsiders to move in with aggressive strategies as industry sales start to take off and the perceived risk of investing in the industry lessens. Try to prepare for the entry of powerful competitors by forecasting *(a)* who the probable entrants will be (based on present and future entry barriers) and *(b)* the types of strategies they are likely to employ.

---

[2]Charles W. Hofer and Dan Schendel, *Strategy Formulation: Analytical Concepts* (St. Paul, Minn.: West Publishing, 1978), pp. 164–65.

[3]Phillip Kotler, *Marketing Management*, 5th ed. (Englewood Cliffs, N.J.: Prentice-Hall, 1984), p. 366, and Porter, *Competitive Strategy*, chapter 10.

The short-term value of winning the early race for growth and market share leadership has to be balanced against the longer-range need to build a durable competitive edge and a defendable market position.[4] New entrants, attracted by the growth and profit potential, may crowd the market. Aggressive newcomers, aspiring to industry leadership, can quickly become major players by acquiring and merging the operations of weaker competitors. Young companies in fast-growing markets face three strategic hurdles: (1) managing their own rapid expansion, (2) defending against competitors trying to horn in on their success, and (3) building a competitive position extending beyond their initial product or market. Up-and-coming companies can help their cause by selecting knowledgeable members for their boards of directors, by hiring entrepreneurial managers with experience in guiding young businesses through the start-up and takeoff stages, by concentrating on outinnovating the competition, and perhaps by merging with or acquiring another firm to gain added expertise and a stronger resource base.

STRATEGIES FOR COMPETING IN HIGH VELOCITY MARKETS

Some companies find themselves in markets characterized by rapid-fire technological change, short product life cycles (because of the pace with which next-generation products are being introduced) entry of important new rivals, frequent launches of new competitive moves by rivals (including mergers and acquisitions to build a stronger, if not dominant, market position), and rapidly evolving customer requirements and expectations—all occurring at once. High-velocity change is the prevailing condition in microelectronics, in personal computer hardware and software, in telecommunications, in the whole cyberspace arena of the Internet and company intranets, and in health care.

High-velocity market environments pose a big strategy-making challenge.[5] Since news of this or that important competitive development is a daily happening, it is an imposing task just to monitor, assess, and react to unfolding events. Competitive success in fast-changing markets tends to hinge on building the following elements into company strategies:

1. *Invest aggressively in R&D to stay on the leading edge of technological know-how.* Having the expertise and capability to advance the state of technological know-how and translate the advances into innovative new products (and to remain close on the heels of whatever advances and features are pioneered by rivals) is a necessity in high-tech markets. But it is often important to focus the R&D effort in a few critical areas not only to avoid stretching the company's resources too thinly but also to deepen the firm's expertise, master the technology, fully capture experience curve effects, and become the dominant leader in a particular technology or product category.[6]

---

[4]Hofer and Schendel, *Strategy Formulation*, pp. 164–65.

[5]The strategic issues companies must address in fast-changing market environments are thoroughly explored in Richard A. D'Aveni, *Hyper-Competition: Managing the Dynamics of Strategic Manuevering* (New York: Free Press, 1994). See, also, Richard A. D'Aveni, "Coping with Hypercompetition: Utilizing the New 7S's Framework," *Academy of Management Executive,* 9, no. 3 (August 1995), pp. 45–56 and Bala Chakravarthy, "A New Strategy Framework for Coping with Turbulence," *Sloan Management Review* (Winter 1997), pp. 69–82.

[6]For insight into building competitive advantage through R&D and technological innovation, see Shaker A. Zahra, Sarah Nash, and Deborah J. Bickford, "Transforming Technological Pioneering into Competitive Advantage," *Academy of Management Executive,* 9, no. 1 (February 1995), pp. 32–41.

2. *Develop the organizational capability to respond quickly to important new events.* Quick reaction times are essential because it is impossible to predict or foresee all of the changes that will occur. Moreover, a competitor has to alertly and swiftly shift resources to respond to the actions of rivals or new technological developments or evolving customer needs or opportunities to move against slower competitiors. Resource flexibility tends to be a key success factor, as does the ability to *adapt* existing competencies and capabilities, to *create new competencies and capabilities*, and to *match rivals* on whatever technological approaches and product features they are able to pioneer successfully. Absent such organizational capabilities as speed, agility, flexibility, and innovativeness in finding new and better ways to please customers, a company soon loses its competitiveness. Being a fast follower, if not the first mover, is critical.

3. *Rely on strategic partnerships with outside suppliers and with companies making tie-in products to perform those activities in the total industry value chain where they have specialized expertise and capabilities.* In many high-velocity industries, technology is branching off to create so many new paths and product categories that no company has the resources and competencies to pursue them all. Specialization (to promote the necessary technical depth) and focus strategies (to preserve organizational agility and leverage the firm's expertise) are essential. Companies build their competitive position not just by strengthening their own resource base but also by partnering with suppliers making state-of-the-art parts and components and by collaborating with the leading makers of tie-in products. For example, the makers of personal computers rely heavily on the makers of faster chips, the makers of monitors and screens, the makers of hard disks and disk drives, and software developers to be the source of most of the innovative advances in PCs. The makers of PCs concentrate on *assembly*—none have integrated backward into parts and components, because the most effective way to provide a state-of-the-art product is to outsource the latest, most advanced components from technologically sophisticated suppliers. An outsourcing strategy also allows a company the flexibility to replace suppliers that fall behind on technology or product features or that cease to be competitive on price. Moreover, computer software developers collaborate with the various hardware manufacturers to have cutting-edge software products ready for the market when next-generation hardware products are introduced.

In fast-paced markets, in-depth expertise, speed, agility, innovativeness, opportunism, and resource flexibility are critical organizational capabilities.

When a fast-evolving market environment entails many technological areas and product categories, competitors have little choice but to employ some type of focus strategy and concentrate on being the leader in a particular category. Cutting-edge know-how and first-to-market capabilities are very valuable competitive assets. Moreover, the pace of competition demands that a company have quick reaction times and flexible, adaptable resources—organizational agility is a huge asset. So is the ability to collaborate with suppliers, effectively combining and meshing their resources with the firm's own resources. The challenge is to strike a good balance between building a rich internal resource base that, on the one hand, keeps the firm from being at the mercy of its suppliers and allies and, on the other hand, maintains organizational agility by relying on the resources and expertise of outsiders.

STRATEGIES FOR COMPETING IN MATURING INDUSTRIES

Rapid growth or fast-paced market change doesn't go on forever. However, the transition to a slower-growth, maturing industry environment does not begin on an easily predicted schedule, and the transition can be forestalled by further technological advances, product innovations, or other driving forces that keep rejuvenating market demand. Nonetheless, when growth rates do slacken, the transition to market maturity usually produces fundamental changes in the industry's competitive environment:[7]

1. *Slowing growth in buyer demand generates more head-to-head competition for market share.* Firms that want to continue on a rapid-growth track start looking for ways to take customers away from competitors. Outbreaks of price-cutting, increased advertising, and other aggressive tactics to gain market share are common.

2. *Buyers become more sophisticated, often driving a harder bargain on repeat purchases.* Since buyers have experience with the product and are familiar with competing brands, they are better able to evaluate different brands and can use their knowledge to negotiate a better deal with sellers.

3. *Competition often produces a greater emphasis on cost and service.* As sellers all begin to offer the product attributes buyers prefer, buyer choices increasingly depend on which seller offers the best combination of price and service.

4. *Firms have a "topping out" problem in adding production capacity.* Slower rates of industry growth mean slowdowns in capacity expansion. Each firm has to monitor rivals' expansion plans and time its own capacity additions to minimize industry oversupply. With slower industry growth, the mistake of adding too much capacity too soon can adversely affect company profits well into the future.

5. *Product innovation and new end-use applications are harder to come by.* Producers find it increasingly difficult to create appealing new performance features, find further uses for the product, and sustain buyer excitement.

6. *International competition increases.* Growth-minded domestic firms start to seek out sales opportunities in foreign markets. Some companies, looking for ways to cut costs, relocate plants to countries with lower wage rates. Greater product standardization and diffusion of technology reduce entry barriers and make it possible for enterprising foreign companies to become serious market contenders in more countries. Industry leadership passes to companies that build strong competitive positions in most of the world's major geographic markets and win the biggest global market shares.

7. *Industry profitability falls temporarily or permanently.* Slower growth, increased competition, more sophisticated buyers, and occasional periods of overcapacity put pressure on industry profit margins. Weaker, less-efficient firms are usually the hardest hit.

8. *Stiffening competition leads to mergers and acquisitions among former competitors, drives the weakest firms out of the industry, and, in general, produces industry consolidation.* Inefficient firms and firms with weak competitive strategies can achieve respectable results in a fast-growing industry with booming sales. But the intensifying competition that accompanies industry maturity exposes competitive weakness and throws second- and third-tier competitors into a survival-of-the-fittest contest.

---

[7]Porter, *Competitive Strategy*, pp. 238–40.

As the new competitive character of industry maturity begins to hit full force, there are several strategic moves that firms can initiate to strengthen their positions.[8]

Pruning the Product Line   A wide selection of models, features, and product options has competitive value during the growth stage when buyers' needs are still evolving. But such variety can become too costly as price competition stiffens and profit margins are squeezed. Maintaining too many product versions prevents firms from achieving the economies of long production runs. In addition, the prices of slow-selling versions may not cover their true costs. Pruning marginal products from the line lowers costs and permits more concentration on items whose margins are highest and/or where the firm has a competitive advantage.

In a maturing industry, strategic emphasis needs to be on efficiency-increasing, profit-preserving measures: pruning the product line, improving production methods, reducing costs, accelerating sales promotion efforts, expanding internationally, and acquiring distressed competitors.

More Emphasis on Process Innovations   Efforts to "reinvent" the manufacturing process can have a fourfold payoff: lower costs, better production quality, greater capability to turn out multiple or customized product versions, and shorter design-to-market cycles. Process innovation can involve mechanizing high-cost activities, revamping production lines to improve labor efficiency, building flexibility into the assembly process so that customized product versions can be easily produced, creating self-directed work teams, reengineering the manufacturing portion of the value chain, and increasing use of advanced technology (robotics, computerized controls, and automatic guided vehicles). Japanese firms have become remarkably adept at using manufacturing process innovation to become lower-cost producers of higher-quality products.

A Stronger Focus on Cost Reduction   Stiffening price competition gives firms extra incentive to reduce unit costs. Such efforts can cover a broad front: Companies can push suppliers for better prices, switch to lower-priced components, develop more economical product designs, cut low-value activities out of the value chain, streamline distribution channels, and reengineer internal processes.

Increasing Sales to Present Customers   In a mature market, growing by taking customers away from rivals may not be as appealing as expanding sales to existing customers. Strategies to increase purchases by existing customers can involve providing complementary items and ancillary services, and finding more ways for customers to use the product. Convenience food stores, for example, have boosted average sales per customer by adding video rentals, automatic bank tellers, and deli counters.

Purchasing Rival Firms at Bargain Prices   Sometimes the facilities and assets of distressed rivals can be acquired cheaply. Bargain-priced acquisitions can help create a low-cost position if they also present opportunities for greater operating efficiency. In addition, an acquired firm's customer base can provide expanded market coverage. The most desirable acquisitions are those that enhance the acquiring firm's competitive strength.

Expanding Internationally   As its domestic market matures, a firm may seek to enter foreign markets where attractive growth potential exists and where competitive

---

[8]The following discussion draws on Porter, *Competitive Strategy* pp. 241–46.

pressures are not especially strong. Several manufacturers in highly industrialized nations found international expansion attractive because equipment no longer suitable for domestic operations could be used in plants in less-developed foreign markets (a condition that lowered entry costs). Such possibilities arise when (1) foreign buyers have less sophisticated needs and have simpler, old-fashioned, end-use applications, and (2) foreign competitors are smaller, less formidable, and do not employ the latest production technology. Strategies to expand internationally also make sense when a domestic firm's skills, reputation, and product are readily transferable to foreign markets. Even though the U.S. market for soft drinks is mature, Coca-Cola has remained a growth company by upping its efforts to penetrate foreign markets where soft-drink sales are expanding rapidly.

Building New or More Flexible Capabilities   The stiffening pressures of competition in a maturing or already mature market can often be combatted by strengthening the company's resource base and competitive capabilities. This can mean adding new competencies or capabilities, deepening existing competencies to make them harder to imitate, or striving to make core competencies more flexible and adaptable to changing customer requirements and expectations. Microsoft has responded to competitors' challenges by expanding its already large cadre of talented programmers. Chevron has developed a best-practices discovery team and a best-practices resource map to enhance its speed and effectiveness in transferring efficiency improvements in one oil refinery to its other refineries.

Strategic Pitfalls

Perhaps the greatest strategic mistake a company can make as an industry matures is steering a middle course between low cost, differentiation, and focusing—blending efforts to achieve low cost with efforts to incorporate differentiating features and efforts to focus on a limited target market. Such strategic compromises typically result in a firm ending up "stuck in the middle" with a fuzzy strategy, too little commitment to winning a competitive advantage based on either low cost or differentiation, an average image with buyers, and little chance of springing into the ranks of the industry leaders. Other strategic pitfalls include being slow to adapt existing competencies and capabilities to changing customer expectations, concentrating more on short-term profitability than on building or maintaining long-term competitive position, waiting too long to respond to price-cutting, getting caught with too much capacity as growth slows, overspending on marketing efforts to boost sales growth, and failing to pursue cost reduction soon enough and aggressively enough.

One of the biggest mistakes a firm can make in a maturing industry is pursuing a compromise between low-cost, differentiation, and focusing such that it ends up with a fuzzy strategy, an ill-defined market identity, no competitive advantage, and little prospect of becoming an industry leader.

STRATEGIES FOR FIRMS IN STAGNANT OR DECLINING INDUSTRIES

Many firms operate in industries where demand is barely growing, flat, or even declining. Although harvesting the business to obtain the greatest cash flow, selling out, or preparing for close-down are obvious end-game strategies for uncommitted competitors with dim long-term prospects, strong competitors may be able to achieve good performance in a stagnant market environment.[9] Stagnant demand by itself is not enough to make an industry unattractive. Selling out may or may not be practical, and closing operations is always a last resort. Businesses competing in slow-growth/declining industries have to accept the difficult realities of a stagnating market environment and resign themselves to performance targets consistent with available market opportunities. Cash flow and return-on-investment criteria are more appropriate than growth-oriented performance measures, but sales and market share growth are by no means ruled out. Strong competitors may be able to take sales from weaker rivals, and the acquisition or exit of weaker firms creates opportunities for the remaining companies to capture greater market share.

Achieving competitive advantage in stagnant or declining industries usually requires pursuing one of three competitive approaches: focusing on growing market segments within the industry, differentiating on the basis of better quality and frequent product innovation, or becoming a lower cost producer.

In general, companies that succeed in stagnant industries employ one of three strategic themes:[10]

1. *Pursue a focused strategy by identifying, creating, and exploiting the growth segments within the industry.* Stagnant or declining markets, like other markets, are composed of numerous segments or niches. Frequently, one or more of these segments is growing rapidly, despite stagnation in the industry as a whole. An astute competitor who is first to concentrate on the attractive growth segments can escape stagnating sales and profits and possibly achieve competitive advantage in the target segments.

2. *Stress differentiation based on quality improvement and product innovation.* Either enhanced quality or innovation can rejuvenate demand by creating important new growth segments or inducing buyers to trade up. Successful product innovation opens up an avenue for competing besides meeting or beating rivals' prices. Such differentiation can have the additional advantage of being difficult and expensive for rival firms to imitate.

3. *Work diligently and persistently to drive costs down.* When increases in sales cannot be counted on to increase earnings, companies can improve profit margins and return on investment by stressing continuous productivity improvement and cost reduction year after year. Potential cost-saving actions include (a) outsourcing functions and activities that can be performed more cheaply by outsiders, (b) completely redesigning internal business processes, (c) consolidating underutilized production facilities, (d) adding more distribution channels to ensure the unit volume needed for low-cost production, (e) closing low-volume, high-cost distribution outlets, and (f) cutting marginally beneficial activities out of the value chain.

These three strategic themes are not mutually exclusive.[11] Introducing new, innovative versions of a product can *create* a fast-growing market segment. Similarly, relentless pursuit of greater operating efficiencies permits price reductions that can bring price-conscious buyers back into the market. Note that all three themes are spin-offs of the generic competitive strategies, adjusted to fit the circumstances of a tough industry environment.

The most attractive declining industries are those in which sales are eroding only slowly, there is large built-in demand, and some profitable niches remain. The most

---

[9]R. G. Hamermesh and S. B. Silk, "How to Compete in Stagnant Industries," *Harvard Business Review* 57, no. 5 (September–October 1979), p. 161.

[10]Ibid., p. 162.

[11]Ibid., p. 165.

ILLUSTRATION CAPSULE 20   Yamaha's Strategy in the Piano Industry

For some years now, worldwide demand for pianos has been declining—in the mid-1980s the decline was 10 percent annually. Modern-day parents have not put the same stress on music lessons for their children as prior generations of parents did. In an effort to see if it could revitalize its piano business, Yamaha conducted a market research survey to learn what use was being made of pianos in households that owned one. The survey revealed that the overwhelming majority of the 40 million pianos in American, European, and Japanese households were seldom used. In most cases, the reasons the piano had been purchased no longer applied. Children had either stopped taking piano lessons or were grown and had left the household; adult household members played their pianos sparingly, if at all—only a small percentage were accomplished piano players. Most pianos were serving as a piece of fine furniture and were in good condition despite not being tuned regularly. The survey also confirmed that the income levels of piano owners were well above average.

Yamaha's piano strategists saw the idle pianos in these upscale households as a potential market opportunity. The strategy that emerged entailed marketing an attachment that would convert the piano into an old-fashioned automatic player piano capable of playing a wide number of selections recorded on 3.5-inch floppy disks (the same kind used to store computer data). The player piano conversion attachment carried a $2,500 price tag. Concurrently, Yamaha introduced Disklavier, an upright acoustic player piano model that could play *and record* performances up to 90 minutes long; the Disklavier retailed for $8,000. At year-end 1988 Yamaha offered 30 prerecorded disks for $29.95 each and since then has released a continuing stream of new selections. Yamaha believed that these new high-tech products held potential to reverse the downtrend in piano sales.

common strategic mistakes companies make in stagnating or declining markets are (1) getting trapped in a profitless war of attrition, (2) diverting too much cash out of the business too quickly (thus further eroding performance), and (3) being overly optimistic about the industry's future and spending too much on improvements in anticipation that things will get better.

Illustration Capsule 20 describes the creative approach taken by Yamaha to reverse declining market demand for pianos.

STRATEGIES FOR COMPETING IN FRAGMENTED INDUSTRIES

A number of industries are populated by hundreds, even thousands, of small and medium-sized companies, many privately held and none with a substantial share of total industry sales.[12] The standout competitive feature of a fragmented industry is the absence of market leaders with king-sized market shares or widespread buyer recognition. Examples of fragmented industries include book publishing, landscaping and plant nurseries, real estate development, banking, mail-order catalog sales, computer software development, custom printing, kitchen cabinets, trucking, auto repair, restaurants and fast food, public accounting, apparel manufacture and apparel retailing, paperboard boxes, log homes, hotels and motels, and furniture.

Any of several reasons can account for why the supply side of an industry is fragmented:

- Low entry barriers allow small firms to enter quickly and cheaply.
- The technologies embodied in the industry's value chain are exploding into so many new areas and along so many different paths that specialization is essential just to keep abreast in any one area of expertise.

---

[12]This section is summarized from Porter, *Competitive Strategy*, chapter 9.

- An absence of large-scale production economies permits small companies to compete on an equal cost footing with larger firms.
- Buyers require relatively small quantities of customized products (as in business forms, interior design, and advertising); because demand for any particular product version is small, sales volumes are not adequate to support producing, distributing, or marketing on a scale that yields advantages to a large firm.
- The market for the industry's product/service is becoming more global, allowing competitors in more and more countries to be drawn into the same competitive market arena (as in apparel manufacture).
- Market demand is so large and so diverse that it takes very large numbers of firms to accommodate buyer requirements (restaurants, energy, apparel, computer products and computer software).
- The industry is so new that no firms have yet developed their resource base and competitive capabilities to command a significant market share.

Some fragmented industries consolidate naturally as they mature. The stiffer competition that accompanies slower growth shakes out weak, inefficient firms leading to a greater concentration of larger, more visible sellers. Others remain atomistically competitive because it is inherent in the nature of their businesses. And still others remain stuck in a fragmented state because existing firms lack the resources or ingenuity to employ a strategy powerful enough to drive industry consolidation.

Competitive rivalry in fragmented industries can vary from moderately strong to fierce. Low barriers make entry of new competitors an ongoing threat. Competition from substitutes may or may not be a major factor. The relatively small size of companies in fragmented industries puts them in a weak position to bargain with powerful suppliers and buyers, although sometimes they can become members of a cooperative, using their combined leverage to negotiate better sales and purchase terms. In such an environment, the best a firm can expect is to cultivate a loyal customer base and grow a bit faster than the industry average. Competitive strategies based either on low cost or product differentiation are viable unless the industry's product is highly standardized or a commodity (like sand, concrete blocks, paperboard boxes). Focusing on a well-defined market niche or buyer segment usually offers more competitive advantage potential than striving for broad market appeal. Suitable options in a fragmented industry include

- *Constructing and operating "formula" facilities*—This strategic approach is frequently employed in restaurant and retailing businesses operating at multiple locations. It involves constructing standardized outlets in favorable locations at minimum cost and then polishing to a science how to operate all outlets in a superefficient manner. McDonald's, Home Depot, and 7-Eleven have pursued this strategy to perfection, earning excellent profits in their respective industries.
- *Becoming a low-cost operator*—When price competition is intense and profit margins are under constant pressure, companies can stress no-frills operations featuring low overhead, high-productivity/low-cost labor, lean capital budgets, and dedicated pursuit of total operating efficiency. Successful low-cost producers in a fragmented industry can play the price-cutting game and still earn profits above the industry average.
- *Increasing customer value through integration*—Backward or forward integration into additional value chain activities may contain opportunities

to lower costs or enhance the value provided to customers. One example is a supplier taking on the manufacture of several related parts, assembling them into a modular component system, and providing the ultimate manufacturer with something that is readily inserted or attached to the final product. Another example is a manufacturer opening a series of regional distribution centers to provide overnight delivery to area retailers.

- *Specializing by product type*—When a fragmented industry's products include a range of styles or services, a strategy to focus on one product/service category can be very effective. Some firms in the furniture industry specialize in only one furniture type such as brass beds, rattan and wicker, lawn and garden, or early American. In auto repair, companies specialize in transmission repair, body work, or speedy oil changes.

> *In fragmented industries competitors usually have wide enough strategic latitude to (1) compete broadly or focus and (2) pursue either a low-cost or a differentiation-based competitive advantage.*

- *Specialization by customer type*—A firm can stake out a market niche in a fragmented industry by catering to those customers (1) who are interested in unique product attributes, customized features, carefree service, or other "extras," (2) who are the least price sensitive, or (3) who have the least bargaining leverage (because they are small in size or purchase small amounts).

- *Focusing on a limited geographic area*—Even though a firm in a fragmented industry can't win a big share of total industrywide sales, it can still try to dominate a local/regional area. Concentrating company efforts on a limited territory can produce greater operating efficiency, speed delivery and customer services, promote strong brand awareness, and permit saturation advertising, while avoiding the diseconomies of stretching operations out over a much wider area. Supermarkets, banks, and sporting goods retailers successfully operate multiple locations within a limited geographic area.

In fragmented industries, firms generally have the strategic freedom to pursue broad or narrow market targets and low-cost or differentiation-based competitive advantages. Many different strategic approaches can exist side by side.

STRATEGIES FOR COMPETING IN INTERNATIONAL MARKETS

Companies are motivated to expand into international markets for any of several reasons:

- *To seek new customers for their products or services*—Selling in additional country markets can propel higher revenues and profits and provide an avenue for sustaining attractively high rates of growth over the long-term.

- *A competitive need to achieve lower costs*—Many companies are driven to sell in more than one country because the sales volume in their own domestic markets is not large enough to fully capture manufacturing economies of scale; moreover, locating plants or other operations in countries where labor, materials, or technology costs are lower can often substantially improve a firm's cost competitiveness.

- *To capitalize on its competencies and resource strengths*—A company with valuable competencies and capabilities may be able to leverage them into a position of advantage in foreign markets as well as in its own domestic market.

- *To obtain valuable natural resource deposits in other countries*—In natural resource-based industries (like oil and gas, minerals, rubber, and lumber), companies often find it necessary to pursue access to attractive raw material supplies in foreign countries.

- *To spread its business risk across a wider market base*—A company spreads business risk by operating in a number of different foreign countries rather than depending entirely on operations in its own domestic market.

Whatever the motivation for foreign country operations, strategies for competing internationally have to be situation-driven. Special attention has to be paid to how national markets differ in buyer needs and habits, distribution channels, long-run growth potential, driving forces, and competitive pressures. Aside from the basic market differences from country to country, four other situational considerations are unique to international operations: cost variations among countries, fluctuating exchange rates, host government trade policies, and the pattern of international competition.

Competing in international markets poses a bigger strategy-making challenge than competing in only the company's home market.

Country-to-Country Cost Variations   Differences in wage rates, worker productivity, inflation rates, energy costs, tax rates, government regulations, and the like create sizable variations in manufacturing costs from country to country. Plants in some countries have major manufacturing cost advantages because of lower input costs (especially labor), relaxed government regulations, or unique natural resources. In such cases, the low-cost countries become principal production sites, with most of the output being exported to markets in other parts of the world. Companies with facilities in these locations (or that source their products from contract manufacturers in these countries) have a competitive advantage. The competitive role of low manufacturing costs is most evident in low-wage countries like Taiwan, South Korea, China, Singapore, Malaysia, Vietnam, Mexico, and Brazil, which have become production havens for goods with high labor content.

Another important manufacturing cost consideration in international competition is the concept of *manufacturing share* as distinct from brand share or market share. For example, although less than 40 percent of all the video recorders sold in the United States carry a Japanese brand, Japanese companies do 100 percent of the manufacturing—all sellers source their video recorders from Japanese manufacturers.[13] In microwave ovens, Japanese brands have less than a 50 percent share of the U.S. market, but the manufacturing share of Japanese companies is over 85 percent. *Manufacturing share is significant because it is a better indicator than market share of the industry's low-cost producer.* In a globally competitive industry where some competitors are intent on global dominance, being the worldwide low-cost producer is a powerful competitive advantage. Achieving low-cost producer status often requires a company to have the largest worldwide manufacturing share, with production centralized in one or a few superefficient plants. However, important marketing and distribution economies associated with multinational operations can also yield low-cost leadership.

---

[13]C. K. Prahalad and Yves L. Doz, *The Multinational Mission* (New York: Free Press, 1987), p. 60.

Fluctuating Exchange Rates   The volatility of exchange rates greatly complicates the issue of geographic cost advantages. Currency exchange rates often fluctuate as much as 20 to 40 percent annually. Changes of this magnitude can totally wipe out a country's low-cost advantage or transform a former high-cost location into a competitive-cost location. A strong U.S. dollar makes it more attractive for U.S. companies to manufacture in foreign countries. A falling dollar can eliminate much of the cost advantage that foreign manufacturers have over U.S. manufacturers and can even prompt foreign companies to establish production plants in the United States.

Host Government Trade Policies   National governments enact all kinds of measures affecting international trade and the operation of foreign companies in their markets. Host governments may impose import tariffs and quotas, set local content requirements on goods made inside their borders by foreign-based companies, and regulate the prices of imported goods. In addition, outsiders may face a web of regulations regarding technical standards, product certification, prior approval of capital spending projects, withdrawal of funds from the country, and minority (sometimes majority) ownership by local citizens. Some governments also provide subsidies and low-interest loans to domestic companies to help them compete against foreign-based companies. Other governments, anxious to obtain new plants and jobs, offer foreign companies a helping hand in the form of subsidies, privileged market access, and technical assistance.

Multicountry Competition versus Global Competition

There are important differences in the patterns of international competition from industry to industry.[14] At one extreme is *multicountry* or *multidomestic competition* where each country market is self-contained—buyers in different countries have different expectations and like different styling and features, competition in each national market is independent of competition in other national markets, and the set of rivals competing in each country differ from place to place. For example, there is a banking industry in France, one in Brazil, and one in Japan, but market conditions and buyer expectations in banking differ markedly among the three countries, the lead banking competitors in France differ from those in Brazil or in Japan, and the competitive battle going on among the leading banks in France is unrelated to the rivalry taking place in Brazil or Japan. Because each country market is self-contained in multicountry competition, a company's reputation, customer base, and competitive position in one nation have little or no bearing on its ability to compete successfully in another. As a consequence, the power of a company's strategy in any one nation and any competitive advantage it yields are largely confined to that nation and do not spill over to other countries where it operates. *With multicountry competition there is no "international market," just a collection of self-contained country markets.* Industries characterized by multicountry competition include beer, life insurance, apparel, metals fabrication, many types of food products (coffee, cereals, canned goods, frozen foods), and many types of retailing.

   At the other extreme is *global competition* where prices and competitive conditions across country markets are strongly linked together and the term international

> Multicountry *(or multidomestic) competition exists when competition in one national market is independent of competition in another national market—there is no "international market," just a collection of self-contained country markets.*

[14]Michael E. Porter, *The Competitive Advantage of Nations* (New York: Free Press, 1990), pp. 53–54.

or global market has true meaning. In a global industry, a company's competitive position in one country both affects and is affected by its position in other countries.

Global competition *exists when competitive conditions across national markets are linked strongly enough to form a true international market and when leading competitors compete head-to-head in many different countries.*

In multicountry competition, rival firms vie for national market leadership. In globally competitive industries, rival firms vie for worldwide leadership.

Rival companies compete against each other in many different countries, but especially so in countries where sales volumes are large and where having a competitive presence is strategically important to building a strong global position in the industry. In global competition, a firm's overall advantage grows out of its entire worldwide operations; the competitive advantage it enjoys at its home base are linked to advantages growing out of its operations in other countries (having plants in low-wage countries, a capability to serve corporate customers with multinational operations of their own, and a brand reputation that is transferable from country to country). *A global competitor's market strength is directly proportional to its portfolio of country-based competitive advantages.* Global competition exists in automobiles, television sets, tires, telecommunications equipment, copiers, watches, and commercial aircraft.

An industry can have segments that are globally competitive and segments where competition is country by country.[15] In the hotel-motel industry, for example, the low- and medium-priced segments are characterized by multicountry competition because competitors mainly serve travelers within the same country. In the business and luxury segments, however, competition is more globalized. Companies like Nikki, Marriott, Sheraton, and Hilton have hotels at many international locations and use worldwide reservation systems and common quality and service standards to gain marketing advantages with frequent travelers.

In lubricants, the marine engine segment is globally competitive because ships move from port to port and require the same oil everywhere they stop. Brand reputations have a global scope, and successful marine engine lubricant producers (Exxon, British Petroleum, and Shell) operate globally. In automotive motor oil, however, multicountry competition dominates. Countries have different weather conditions and driving patterns, production is subject to limited scale economies, shipping costs are high, and retail distribution channels differ markedly from country to country. Thus domestic firms, like Quaker State and Pennzoil in the United States and Castrol in Great Britain, can be leaders in their home markets without competing globally.

All these considerations, along with the obvious cultural and political differences between countries, shape a company's strategic approach in international markets.

Types of International Strategies

A company participating in international markets has seven strategic options:

1. *License foreign firms to use the company's technology or produce and distribute the company's products* (in which case international revenues will equal the royalty income from the licensing agreement).

2. *Maintain a national (one-country) production base and export goods to foreign markets* using either company-owned or foreign-controlled forward distribution channels.

---

[15]Ibid., p. 61.

3. *Follow a multicountry strategy,* varying the company's strategic approach (perhaps a little, perhaps a lot) from country to country in accordance with differing buyer needs and competitive conditions. While the company may use the same basic competitive theme (low cost, differentiation, best cost) in most or all country markets, product attributes are customized to fit local buyers' preferences and expectations and the target customer base may vary from broad in some countries to narrowly focused in others. Furthermore, strategic moves in one country are made independent of those in another country; cross-country strategy coordination is a lower priority than matching company strategy to host-country market and competitive conditions.

4. *Follow a global low-cost strategy* and strive to be a low-cost supplier to buyers in most or all strategically important markets of the world. The company's strategic efforts are coordinated worldwide to achieve a low-cost position relative to all competitors.

5. *Follow a global differentiation strategy* whereby the company's product is differentiated on the same attributes in all countries to create a globally consistent image and a consistent competitive theme. The firm's strategic moves are coordinated across countries to achieve consistent differentiation worldwide.

6. *Follow a global focus strategy,* serving the same identifiable niche in each of many strategically important country markets. Strategic actions are coordinated globally to achieve a consistent low-cost or differentiation-based competitive approach in the target niche worldwide.

7. *Follow a global best-cost provider strategy* and strive to match rivals on the same product attributes and beat them on cost and price *worldwide.* The firm's strategic moves in each country market are coordinated to achieve a consistent best-cost position worldwide.

Licensing makes sense when a firm with valuable technical know-how or a unique patented product has neither the internal capability nor the resources to compete effectively in foreign markets. By licensing the technology or the production rights to foreign-based firms, the firm at least realizes income from royalties.

Using domestic plants as a production base for exporting goods to foreign markets is an excellent initial strategy for pursuing international sales. It minimizes both risk and capital requirements, and it is a conservative way to test the international waters. With an export strategy, a manufacturer can limit its involvement in foreign markets by contracting with foreign wholesalers experienced in importing to handle the entire distribution and marketing function in their countries or regions. If it is better to maintain control over these functions, a manufacturer can establish its own distribution and sales organizations in some or all of the target foreign markets. Either way, a firm minimizes its direct investments in foreign countries because of its home-based production and export strategy. Such strategies are commonly favored by Korean and Italian companies—products are designed and manufactured at home and only marketing activities are performed abroad. Whether such a strategy can be pursued successfully over the long run hinges on the relative cost competitiveness of a home-country production base. In some industries, firms gain additional scale economies and experience curve benefits from centralizing production in one or several giant plants whose output capability exceeds demand in any one country market; obviously, to capture such economies a company must export to markets in other countries. However, this strategy is vulnerable when manufacturing costs in the home country are much higher than in foreign countries where rivals have plants. The pros and cons of a multicountry strategy versus a global strategy are a bit more complex.

A Multicountry Strategy or a Global Strategy?

The need for a multicountry strategy derives from the sometimes vast differences in cultural, economic, political, and competitive conditions in different countries. The more diverse national market conditions are, the stronger the case for a *multicountry strategy* where the company tailors its strategic approach to fit each host country's market situation. Usually, but not always, companies employing a multicountry strategy use the same basic competitive theme (low-cost, differentiation, or best-cost) in each country, making whatever country-specific variations are needed to best satisfy customers and to position itself against local rivals. They may aim at broad market targets in some countries and focus more narrowly on a particular niche in others. The bigger the country-to-country variations, the more that a company's overall international strategy becomes a collection of its individual country strategies.[16]

A multicountry strategy is appropriate for industries where multicountry competition dominates, but a global strategy works best in markets that are globally competitive or beginning to globalize.

While multicountry strategies are best suited for industries where multicountry competition dominates, global strategies are best suited for globally competitive industries. A *global strategy* is one where a company's approach to competing is mostly the same in all countries. Although *minor* country-to-country differences in strategy do exist to accommodate specific conditions in host countries, the company's fundamental approach (low-cost, differentiation, best-cost or focused) remains the same worldwide. Moreover, a global strategy involves (1) integrating and coordinating the company's strategic moves worldwide and (2) selling in many if not all nations where there is significant buyer demand. Table 6–1 provides a point-by-point comparison of multicountry versus global strategies. The question of which of these two strategies to pursue is the foremost strategic issue firms face when they compete in international markets.

The strength of a multicountry strategy is that it matches the company's competitive approach to host country circumstances. A multicountry strategy is essential when there are significant country-to-country differences in customers' needs and buying habits (see Illustration Capsule 21), when buyers in a country insist on special-order or highly customized products, when regulations require that products sold locally meet strict manufacturing specifications or performance standards, and when trade restrictions are so diverse and complicated they preclude a uniform, coordinated worldwide market approach. However, a multicountry strategy has two big drawbacks: It is very difficult to transfer and exploit a company's competencies and resources across country boundaries, and it does not promote building a single, unified competitive advantage. The primary orientation of a multicountry strategy is responsiveness to local country conditions, not building well-defined competencies and competitive capabilities that can ultimately produce a competitive advantage over other international competitors and the domestic companies of host countries.

A global strategy, because it is more uniform from country to country, can concentrate on building the resource strengths to secure a sustainable low-cost or

---

[16]It is, however, possible to connect the strategies in different countries by making an effort to transfer ideas, technologies, competencies, and capabilities that work successfully in one country market to another country market whenever such transfers appear advantageous. Operations in each country can be thought of as "experiments" that result in learning and in capabilities that merit transfer to other country markets. For more details on the usefulness of such a "transnational" strategy, see C. A. Bartlett and S. Ghoshal, *Managing Across Borders: The Transnational Solution* (Boston: Harvard Business School Press, 1989).

TABLE 6-1 Differences between Multicountry and Global Stategies

	Multicountry Strategy	Global Strategy
Strategic Arena	• Selected target countries and trading areas.	• Most countries which constitute critical markets for the product, at least North America, the European Community, and the Pacific Rim (Australia, Japan, South Korea, and Southeast Asia).
Business Strategy	• Custom strategies to fit the circumstances of each host country situation; little or no strategy coordination across countries.	• Same basic strategy worldwide; minor country-by-country variations where essential.
Product-line Strategy	• Adapted to local needs.	• Mostly the same attributes and variety of models/styles worldwide.
Production Strategy	• Plants scattered across many host countries.	• Plants located on the basis of maximum competitive advantage (in low-cost countries, close to major markets, geographically scattered to minimize shipping costs, or use of a few world-scale plants to maximize economies of scale—as most appropriate).
Source of Supply for Raw Materials and Components	• Suppliers in host country preferred (local facilities meeting local buyer needs; some local sourcing may be required by host government).	• Attractive suppliers located anywhere in the world.
Marketing and Distribution	• Adapted to practices and culture of each host country.	• Much more worldwide coordination; minor adaptation to host country situations if required.
Company Organization	• Form subsidiary companies to handle operations in each host country; each subsidiary operates more or less autonomously to fit host country conditions.	• All major strategic decisions are closely coordinated at global headquarters; a global organizational structure is used to unify the operations in each country.

differentiation-based advantage over both international and domestic rivals. Whenever country-to-country differences are small enough to be accommodated within the framework of a global strategy, a global strategy is preferable to a multicountry strategy because of the value of uniting a company's efforts worldwide to create strong, competitively valuable competencies and capabilities not readily matched by rivals.

Global Strategy and Competitive Advantage

A firm can gain competitive advantage (or offset domestic disadvantages) with a global strategy in two ways.[17] One way exploits a global competitor's ability to deploy R&D, parts manufacture, assembly, distribution centers, sales and marketing, customer service centers and other activities among nations in a manner that

---

[17]Ibid., p. 54.

ILLUSTRATION CAPSULE 21   Multicountry Strategies: Microsoft in PC Software and Nestlé in Instant Coffee

In order to best serve the needs of users in foreign countries, Microsoft localizes many of its software products to reflect local languages. In France, for example, all user messages and documentation are in French and all monetary references are in French francs. In the United Kingdom, monetary references are in British pounds and user messages and documentation reflect certain British conventions. Various Microsoft products have been localized into more than 30 languages.

Nestlé is the world's largest food company with over $50 billion in revenues, market penetration on all major continents, and plants in over 70 countries. A star performer in Nestlé's food products lineup is coffee, accounting for sales of over $5 billion and operating profits of $600 million. Nestlé is the world's largest producer of coffee. Nestlé produces 200 types of instant coffee, from lighter blends for the U.S. market to dark espressos for Latin America. To keep its instant coffees matched to consumer tastes in different countries (and

areas within some countries), Nestlé operates four coffee research labs to experiment with new blends in aroma, flavor, and color. The strategy is to match the blends marketed in each country to the tastes and preferences of coffee drinkers in that country, introducing new blends to develop new segments when opportunities appear, and altering blends as needed to respond to changing tastes and buyer habits.

In Britain, Nescafé was promoted extensively to build a wider base of instant coffee drinkers. In Japan, where Nescafé was considered a luxury item, the company made its Japanese blends available in fancy containers suitable for gift-giving. In 1993 Nestlé began introducing Nescafé instant coffee and Coffee-Mate creamer in several large cities in China. As of 1992 the company's Nescafé brand was the leader in the instant coffee segment in virtually every national market but the U.S., where it ranked number two behind Maxwell House.

Sources: Company annual reports and Shawn Tully, "Nestlé Shows How to Gobble Markets," *Fortune*, January 16, 1989, pp. 74–78 and "Nestlé: A Giant in a Hurry," *Business Week*, March 22, 1993, pp. 50–54.

lowers costs or achieves greater product differentiation. A second way draws on a global competitor's ability to deepen or broaden its resource strengths and capabilities and to coordinate its dispersed activities in ways that a domestic-only competitor cannot.

Locating Activities   To use location to build competitive advantage, a global firm must consider two issues: (1) whether to concentrate each activity it performs in one or two countries or to spread it across many nations and (2) in which countries to locate particular activities. Activities tend to be concentrated in one or two locations when there are significant economies of scale in performing them, when there are advantages in locating related activities in the same area to better coordinate them, and when a steep learning or experience curve is associated with performing an activity in a single location. Thus in some industries scale economies in parts manufacture or assembly are so great that a company establishes one large plant from which it serves the world market. Where just-in-time inventory practices yield big cost savings and/or where the assembly firm has long-term partnering arrangements with its key suppliers, parts manufacturing plants may be clustered around final assembly plants.

A global strategy enables a firm to pursue sustainable competitive advantage by locating activities in the most advantageous nations and coordinating its strategic actions worldwide; a domestic-only competitor forfeits such opportunities.

On the other hand, dispersing activities is more advantageous than concentrating them in several instances. Buyer-related activities—such as distribution to dealers, sales and advertising, and after-sale service—usually must take place close to buyers. This means physically locating the ability to perform such activities in every country market where a global firm has major customers (unless buyers in several adjoining countries can be served quickly from a nearby central location). For example, firms that make mining and oil-drilling equipment maintain operations in many international locations to support customers' needs for speedy equipment repair and technical assistance. Large public accounting firms have numerous international offices to service the foreign operations of their multinational corporate clients. A global competitor that effectively disperses its buyer-related activities can gain a service-based competitive edge in world markets over rivals whose buyer-related activities are more concentrated—this is one reason the Big Six public accounting firms have been so successful relative to second-tier firms. Dispersing activities to many locations is also advantageous when high transportation costs, diseconomies of large size, and trade barriers make it too expensive to operate from a central location. Many companies distribute their products from multiple locations to shorten delivery times to customers. In addition, dispersing activities to hedge against the risks of fluctuating exchange rates, supply interruptions (due to strikes, mechanical failures, and transportation delays), and adverse political developments has advantages. Such risks are greater when activities are concentrated in a single location.

The classic reason for locating an activity in a particular country is lower costs.[18] Even though a global firm has strong reason to disperse buyer-related activities to many locations, such activities as materials procurement, parts manufacture, finished goods assembly, technology research, and new-product development can frequently be performed wherever advantage lies. Components can be made in Mexico, technology research done in Frankfurt, new products developed and tested in Phoenix, and assembly plants located in Spain, Brazil, Taiwan, and South Carolina. Capital can be raised in whatever country it is available on the best terms.

Low cost is not the only locational consideration, however. A research unit may be situated in a particular nation because of its pool of technically trained personnel. A customer service center or sales office may be opened in a particular country to help develop strong relationships with pivotal customers. An assembly plant may be located in a country in return for the host government's allowing freer import of components from large-scale, centralized parts plants located elsewhere.

Strengthening the Resource Base and Coordinating Cross Border Activities   A global strategy allows a firm to leverage its core competencies and resource strengths to compete successfully in additional country markets. Relying upon use of the same types of competencies, capabilities, and resource strengths in country after country contributes to the development of broader/deeper competencies and capabilities—ideally helping a company achieve *dominating depth* in some valuable area (whether it be competent performance of certain value chain activities, superior technical expertise, marketing know-how, or some other competitive asset). Dominating depth in a valuable capability or resource or value chain activity is a strong basis for sustainable competitive advantage. A company may not be able to achieve dominating depth with a domestic-only strategy because a one-country customer base may simply be too small to support such a resource buildup.

Aligning and coordinating company activities located in different countries contributes to sustainable competitive advantage in several different ways. If a firm learns how to assemble its product more efficiently at its Brazilian plant, the accumulated knowledge and expertise can be transferred to its assembly plant in Spain. Knowledge gained in marketing a company's product in Great Britain can be used to

---

[18]Ibid., p. 57.

introduce the product in New Zealand and Australia. A company can shift production from one country to another to take advantage of exchange rate fluctuations, to enhance its leverage with host country governments, and to respond to changing wage rates, energy costs, or trade restrictions. A company can enhance its brand reputation by consistently incorporating the same differentiating attributes in its products in all worldwide markets where it competes. The reputation for quality that Honda established worldwide first in motorcycles and then in automobiles gave it competitive advantage in positioning its lawnmowers at the upper end of the market—the Honda name gave the company instant credibility with buyers.

A global competitor can choose where and how to challenge rivals. It may decide to retaliate against aggressive rivals in the country market where the rival has its biggest sales volume or its best profit margins in order to reduce the rival's financial resources for competing in other country markets. It may decide to wage a price-cutting offensive against weak rivals in their home markets, capturing greater market share and subsidizing any short-term losses with profits earned in other country markets.

A company operating only in its home country can't pursue the competitive advantage opportunities of locating activites in the lowest-cost countries, using the added sales in foreign markets to broaden/deepen company competencies and capabilities, and coordinating cross-border activities. When a domestic company finds itself at a competitive disadvantage against global companies, one option is shifting from a domestic strategy to a global strategy.

The Use of Strategic Alliances to Enhance Global Competitiveness

Strategic alliances and cooperative agreements are a potentially fruitful means for firms in the same industry to compete on a more global scale while still preserving their independence. Typically such arrangements involve joint research efforts, technology sharing, joint use of production facilities, marketing one another's products, or joining forces to manufacture components or assemble finished products. Historically, export-minded firms in industrialized nations sought alliances with firms in less-developed

Strategic alliances can help companies in globally competitive industries strengthen their competitive positions while still preserving their independence.

countries to import and market their products locally—such arrangements were often necessary to win local government approval to enter a less-developed country's market or to comply with governmental requirements for local ownership. More recently, companies from different parts of the world have formed strategic alliances and partnership arrangements to strengthen their mutual ability to serve whole continents and move toward more global market participation. Both Japanese and American companies are actively forming alliances with European companies to strengthen their ability to compete in the 12-nation European Community and to capitalize on the opening up of Eastern European markets. Many U.S. and European companies are allying with Asian companies in their efforts to enter markets in China, India, and other Asian countries. Illustration Capsule 22 describes Toshiba's successful use of strategic alliances and joint ventures to pursue related technologies and product markets.

Cooperative arrangements between domestic and foreign companies have strategic appeal for reasons besides market access.[19] One is to capture economies of scale in production and/or marketing—the cost reductions can be the difference that allows a

---

[19]Porter, *The Competitive Advantage of Nations*, p. 66; see also Jeremy Main, "Making Global Alliances Work," *Fortune*, December 17, 1990, pp. 121–26.

ILLUSTRATION CAPSULE 22 Toshiba's Use of Strategic Alliances and Joint Ventures

Toshiba, Japan's oldest and third largest electronics company (after Hitachi and Matsushita), over the years has made technology licensing agreements, joint ventures, and strategic alliances cornerstones of its corporate strategy. Using such partnerships to complement its own manufacturing and product innovation capabilities, it has become a $37 billion maker of electrical and electronics products—from home appliances to computer memory chips to telecommunications equipment to electric power generation equipment.

Fumio Sato, Toshiba's CEO, contends that joint ventures and strategic alliances are a necessary component of strategy for a high-tech electronics company with global ambitions:

> It is no longer an era in which a single company can dominate any technology or business by itself. The technology has become so advanced, and the markets so complex, that you simply can't expect to be the best at the whole process any longer.

Among Toshiba's two dozen major joint ventures and strategic alliances are

- A five-year-old joint venture with Motorola to design and make dynamic random access memory chips (DRAMs) for Toshiba and microprocessors for Motorola. Initially the two partners invested $125 million apiece in the venture and have since invested another $480 million each.
- A joint venture with IBM to make flat-panel liquid crystal displays in color for portable computers.
- Two other joint ventures with IBM to develop computer memory chips (one a "flash" memory chip that remembers data even after the power is turned off).
- An alliance with Sweden-based Ericsson, one of the world's biggest telecommunications manufacturers, to develop new mobile telecommunications equipment.
- A partnership with Sun Microsystems, the leading maker of microprocessor-based

workstations, to provide portable versions of the workstations to Sun and to incorporate Sun's equipment in Toshiba products to control power plants, route highway traffic, and monitor automated manufacturing processes.

- A $1 billion strategic alliance with IBM and Siemens to develop and produce the next-generation DRAM—a single chip capable of holding 256 million bits of information (approximately 8,000 typewritten pages).
- An alliance with Apple Computer to develop CD-ROM-based multimedia players that plug into a TV set.
- A joint project with the entertainment division of Time Warner to design advanced interactive cable television technology.

Other alliances and joint ventures with General Electric, United Technologies, National Semiconductor, Samsung (Korea), LSI Logic (Canada), and European companies like Olivetti, SCS-Thomson, Rhone-Poulenc, Thomson Consumer Electronics, and GEC Alstholm are turning out such products as fax machines, copiers, medical equipment, computers, rechargeable batteries, home appliances, and nuclear and steam power generating equipment.

So far, none of Toshiba's relationships with partners have gone sour despite potential conflicts among related projects with competitors (Toshiba has partnerships with nine other chip makers to develop or produce semiconductors). Toshiba attributes this to its approach to alliances: choosing partners carefully, being open about Toshiba's connections with other companies, carefully defining the role and rights of each partner in the original pact (including who gets what if the alliance doesn't work out), and cultivating easy relations and good friendships with each partner. Toshiba's management believes that strategic alliances and joint ventures are an effective way for the company to move into new businesses quickly, share the design and development costs of ambitious new products with competent partners, and achieve greater access to important geographic markets outside Japan.

Source: Based on Brenton R. Schlender, "How Toshiba Makes Alliances Work," *Fortune*, October 4, 1993, pp. 116–20.

company to be cost competitive. By joining forces in producing components, assembling models, and marketing their products, companies can realize cost savings not achievable with their own small volumes. A second reason is to fill gaps in technical expertise and/or knowledge of local markets (buying habits and product preferences of consumers, local customs, and so on). Allies learn much from one another in performing joint research, sharing technological know-how, and studying one another's manufacturing methods. A third reason is to share distribution facilities and dealer networks, thus mutually strengthening their access to buyers. And finally, allied companies can direct their competitive energies more toward mutual rivals and less toward one another; by teaming up, both may end up stronger and better able to close the gap on leading companies.

Alliances between domestic and foreign companies have their pitfalls, however. Collaboration between independent companies, each with different motives and perhaps conflicting objectives, is not easy.[20] It requires many meetings of many people working in good faith over a period of time to iron out what is to be shared, what is to remain proprietary, and how the cooperative arrangements will work. Cross-border allies typically have to overcome language and cultural barriers; the communication, trust-building, and coordination costs are high in terms of management time. Often, once the bloom is off the rose, partners discover they have deep differences of opinion about how to proceed and conflicting objectives and strategies. Tensions build up, working relationships cool, and the hoped-for benefits never materialize.[21] Many times, allies find it difficult to collaborate effectively in competitively sensitive areas, thus raising questions about mutual trust and forthright exchanges of information and expertise. There can also be clashes of egos and company cultures. The key people on whom success or failure depends may have little personal chemistry, be unable to work closely together or form a partnership, or be unable to come to consensus. For example, the alliance between Northwest Airlines and KLM Royal Dutch Airlines linking their hubs in Detroit and Amsterdam resulted in a bitter feud among the top officials of both companies (who, according to some reports, refuse to speak to each other) and precipitated a battle for control of Northwest Airlines engineered by KLM; the dispute was rooted in a clash of philosophies about how to run an airline business (the American way versus the European way), basic cultural differences between the two companies, and an executive power struggle over who should call the shots.[22]

Strategic alliances are more effective in combating competitive disadvantage than in gaining competitive advantage.

Most important, though, is the danger of depending on another company for essential expertise and capabilities over the long term. To be a serious market contender, a company must ultimately develop internal capabilities in most all areas instrumental in strengthening its competitive position and building a competitive advantage. When learning essential know-how and capabilities from one's allies holds only limited potential (because one's partners guard their most valuable skills and expertise), acquiring or merging with a company possessing the desired know-how and resources is a better solution. Strategic alliances are best used as a transitional way to combat competitive disadvantage in international markets; rarely can they be relied on as ways to create competitive

---

[20]For an excellent discussion of company experiences with alliances and partnerships, see Rosabeth Moss Kanter, "Collaborative Advantage: The Art of the Alliance," *Harvard Business Review* 72, no. 4 (July–August 1994), pp. 96–108.

[21]Jeremy Main, "Making Global Alliances Work," p. 125.

[22]Details of the disagreements are reported in Shawn Tully, "The Alliance from Hell," *Fortune*, June 24, 1996, pp. 64–72.

ILLUSTRATION CAPSULE 23   Company Experiences With Cross-Border Strategic Alliances

As the chairman of British Aerospace recently observed, a strategic alliance with a foreign company is "one of the quickest and cheapest ways to develop a global strategy." AT&T formed joint ventures with many of the world's largest telephone and electronics companies. Boeing, the world's premier manufacturer of commercial aircraft, partnered with Kawasaki, Mitsubishi, and Fuji to produce a long-range, wide-body jet for delivery in 1995. General Electric and Snecma, a French maker of jet engines, have a 50-50 partnership to make jet engines to power aircraft made by Boeing, McDonnell-Douglas, and Airbus Industrie (Airbus, the leading European maker of commercial aircraft, was formed by an alliance of aerospace companies from Britain, Spain, Germany, and France). The GE/Snecma alliance is regarded as a model because it existed for 17 years and it produced orders for 10,300 engines, totaling $38 billion.

Since the early 1980s, hundreds of strategic alliances have been formed in the motor vehicle industry as car and truck manufacturers and automotive parts suppliers moved aggressively to get in stronger position to compete globally. Not only have there been alliances between automakers strong in one region of the world and automakers strong in another region but there have also been strategic alliances between vehicle makers and key parts suppliers (especially those with high-quality parts and strong technological capabilities). General Motors and Toyota in 1984 formed a 50-50 partnership called New United Motor Manufacturing Inc. (NUMMI) to produce cars for both companies at an old GM plant in Fremont, California. The strategic value of the GM-Toyota alliance was that Toyota would learn how to deal with suppliers and workers in the United States (as a prelude to building its own plants in the United States) while GM would learn about Toyota's approaches to manufacturing and management. Each company sent managers to the NUMMI plant to work for two or three years to learn and absorb all they could, then transferred their NUMMI "graduates" to jobs where they could be instrumental in helping their companies apply what they learned. Toyota moved quickly to capitalize on its experiences at NUMMI. By 1991 Toyota had opened two plants on its own in North America, was constructing a third plant, and was producing 50 percent of the vehicles it sold in North America in its North American plants. While General Motors incorporated much of its NUMMI learning into the management practices and manufacturing methods it was using at its newly opened Saturn plant in Tennessee, it proceeded more slowly than Toyota. American and European companies are generally regarded as less skilled than the Japanese in transferring the learning from strategic alliances into their own operations.

Many alliances fail or are terminated when one partner ends up acquiring the other. A 1990 survey of 150 companies involved in terminated alliances found that three-fourths of the alliances had been taken over by Japanese partners. A nine-year alliance between Fujitsu and International Computers, Ltd., a British manufacturer, ended when Fujitsu acquired 80 percent of ICL. According to one observer, Fujitsu deliberately maneuvered ICL into a position of having no better choice than to sell out to its partner. Fujitsu began as a supplier of components for ICL's mainframe computers, then expanded its role over the next nine years to the point where it was ICL's only source of new technology. When ICL's parent, a large British electronics firm, saw the mainframe computer business starting to decline and decided to sell, Fujitsu was the only buyer it could find.

Source: Jeremy Main, "Making Global Alliances Work," *Fortune*, December 17, 1990, pp. 121–26.

advantage. Illustration Capsule 23 relates the experiences of companies with cross-border strategic alliances.

Companies can realize the most from a strategic alliance by observing five guidelines:[23]

1. Pick a compatible partner; take the time to build strong bridges of communication and trust, and don't expect immediate payoffs.

2. Choose an ally whose products and market strongholds *complement* rather than compete directly with the company's own products and customer base.

---

[23]Ibid.

3. Learn thoroughly and rapidly about a partner's technology and management; transfer valuable ideas and practices into one's own operations promptly.

4. Don't share competitively sensitive information with a partner.

5. View the alliance as temporary (5 to 10 years); continue longer if it's beneficial but don't hesitate to terminate the alliance and go it alone when the payoffs run out.

Strategic Intent, Profit Sanctuaries, and Cross-Subsidization

Competitors in international markets can be distinguished not only by their strategies but also by their long-term strategic objectives and strategic intent. Four types of competitors stand out:[24]

- Firms whose strategic intent is *global dominance* or, at least, a high ranking among the global market leaders (such firms typically have operations in most or all of the world's biggest and most important country markets and are pursuing global low-cost, best-cost or differentiation strategies).

- Firms whose primary strategic objective is *achieving or maintaining domestic dominance* in their home market, but who pursue international sales in several or many foreign markets as a "sideline" to bolster corporate growth; the international sales of such firms is usually under 20 percent of total corporate sales.

- *Multinational firms employing multicountry strategies* to build their international sales revenues; the strategic intent of such firms is usually to expand sales in foreign markets at a fast enough pace to produce respectable revenue and profit growth.

- *Domestic-only firms* whose strategic intent does not extend beyond building a strong competitive position in their home country market; such firms base their competitive strategies on domestic market conditions and watch events in the international market only for their impact on the domestic situation.

When all four types of firms find themseves competing head-on in the same market arena, the playing field is not necessarily level for all the players. Consider the case of a purely domestic U.S. company in competition with a Japanese company operating in many country markets and aspiring to global dominance. Because of its multicountry sales and profit base, the Japanese company has the option of lowballing its prices in the U.S. market to gain market share at the expense of the U.S. company, subsidizing any losses with profits earned in Japan and its other foreign markets. If the U.S. company, with all of its business being in the U.S. market, retaliates with matching price cuts, it exposes its entire revenue and profit base to erosion. Its profits can be squeezed and its competitive strength gradually sapped even if it is the U.S. market leader. However, if the U.S. company is a multinational competitor and operates in Japan as well as elsewhere, it can counter Japanese pricing in the United States with retaliatory price cuts in Japan (its competitor's main profit sanctuary) and in other countries where it competes against the same Japanese company.

The point here is that a domestic-only company can have a hard time competing on an equal footing with either multinational or global rivals that can rely on profits earned in other country markets to support a price-cutting offensive. When aggressive

---

[24]Prahalad and Doz, *The Multinational Mission*, p. 52.

global or multinational competitors enter a domestic-only company's market, one of the domestic-only competitor's best defenses is to switch to a multinational or global strategy to give it the same cross-subsidizing capabilities the aggressors have.

Profit Sanctuaries and Critical Markets   *Profit sanctuaries* are country markets where a company derives substantial profits because of its strong or protected market position. Japan, for example, is a profit sanctuary for most Japanese companies because trade barriers erected around Japanese industries by the Japanese government effectively block foreign companies from competing for a large share of Japanese sales. Protected from the threat of foreign competition in their home market, Japanese companies can safely charge higher prices to their Japanese customers and thus earn attractively large profits on sales made in Japan. In most cases, a company's biggest and most strategically crucial profit sanctuary is its home market, but multinational companies also have profit sanctuaries in those country markets where they enjoy strong competitive positions, big sales volumes, and attractive profit margins.

Profit sanctuaries are valuable competitive assets in global industries. Companies with large, protected profit sanctuaries have competitive advantage over companies that don't have a dependable sanctuary. Companies with multiple profit sanctuaries have a competitive advantage over companies with a single sanctuary—not only do they have a broader and more diverse market base, but their multiple profit sanctuaries give them multiple financial pockets and the flexibility to redeploy profits and cash flows generated in their market strongholds to support new strategic offensives to gain market share in additional country markets. The resource advantage of multiple profit sanctuaries gives a global or multinational competitor the ability to wage a market offensive against a domestic competitor whose only profit sanctuary is its home market.

> *A particular nation is a company's* **profit sanctuary** *when the company, either because of its strong competitive position or protective governmental trade policies, derives a substantial part of its total profits from sales in that nation.*

To defend against competitive strength of global competitors with multiple profit sanctuaries, companies don't have to compete in all or even most foreign markets, but they do have to compete in all critical markets. *Critical markets* are markets in countries

- That are the profit sanctuaries of key competitors.
- That have big sales volumes.
- That contain prestigious customers whose business it is strategically important to have.
- That offer exceptionally good profit margins due to weak competitive pressures.[25]

The more critical markets a company participates in, the greater its ability to draw upon its resources and competitive strength in these markets to cross-subsidize its efforts to defend against offensives waged by competitors intent on global dominance.

The Competitive Power of Cross-Subsidization   Cross-subsidization—supporting competitive efforts in one market with resources and profits diverted from operations in other markets—is a powerful competitive weapon. Take the case of an aggressive

---

[25]Ibid., p. 61.

global firm with multiple profit sanctuaries that is intent on achieving global market dominance over the long-term and that seeks to improve its market share at the expense of a domestic-only competitor and a multicountry competitor. The global competitor can charge a low enough price to draw customers away from a domestic-only competitor, all the while gaining market share, building name recognition, and *covering any losses with profits earned in its other critical markets*. It can adjust the depth of its price-cutting to move in and capture market share quickly, or it can shave prices slightly to make gradual market inroads over a decade or more so as not to threaten domestic firms precipitously and perhaps trigger protectionist government actions. When attacked in this manner, a domestic company's best short-term hope is to pursue immediate and perhaps dramatic cost reduction and, if the situation warrants, to seek government protection in the form of tariff barriers, import quotas, and antidumping penalties. In the long term, the domestic company has to find ways to compete on a more equal footing—a difficult task when it must charge a price to cover full unit costs plus a margin for profit while the global competitor can charge a price only high enough to cover the incremental costs of selling in the domestic company's profit sanctuary. The best long-term defenses for a domestic company are to enter into strategic alliances with foreign firms or to compete on an international scale, although sometimes it is possible to drive enough costs out of the business over the long term to survive with a domestic-only strategy. As a rule, however, competing only domestically is a perilous strategy in an industry populated with global competitors who engage in cross-subsidization tactics.

A competent global competitor with multiple profit sanctuaries can wage and generally win a competitive offensive against a domestic competitor whose only profit sanctuary is its home market.

To defend against aggressive international competitors intent on global dominance, a domestic-only competitor usually has to abandon its domestic focus, become a multinational competitor, and craft a multinational competitive strategy.

While a company with a multicountry strategy has some cross-subsidy defense against a company with a global strategy, its vulnerability comes from a probable cost disadvantage and more limited competitive advantage opportunities. A global competitor with a big manufacturing share and world-scale state-of-the-art plants is almost certain to be a lower-cost producer than a multicountry strategist with many small plants and short production runs turning out specialized products country by country. Companies pursuing a multicountry strategy thus need differentiation and focus-based advantages keyed to local responsiveness in order to defend against a global competitor. Such a defense is adequate in industries with significant enough national differences to impede use of a global strategy. But if an international rival can accommodate necessary local needs within a global strategy and still retain a cost edge, then a global strategy can defeat a multicountry strategy.[26]

STRATEGIES FOR INDUSTRY LEADERS

The competitive positions of industry leaders normally range from stronger-than-average to powerful. Leaders typically are well-known, and strongly entrenched leaders have proven strategies (keyed either to low-cost leadership or to differentiation). Some of the best-known industry leaders are Anheuser-Busch (beer), Intel (microprocessors), McDonald's (fast food), Gillette (razor blades), Campbell Soup

---

[26]One way a global competitor can attack a multicountry competitor is by developing the capability to manufacture products customized for each country market at its world-scale plants; many manufacturers have become expert at designing assembly lines with the flexibility to turn out customized versions of a mass-produced product—so-called flexible mass production techniques. The advantage of flexible mass production is that it permits product customization and low-cost mass production *at the same time*.

(canned soups), Gerber (baby food), AT&T (long-distance telephone service), East-man Kodak (camera film), and Levi Strauss (jeans). The main strategic concern for a leader revolves around how to sustain a leadership position, perhaps becoming the *dominant* leader as opposed to *a* leader. However, the pursuit of industry leadership and large market share per se is primarily important because of the competitive advantage and profitability that accrue to being the industry's biggest company.

Three contrasting strategic postures are open to industry leaders and dominant firms:[27]

1. **Stay-on-the-offensive strategy**—This strategy rests on the principle that the best defense is a good offense. Offensive-minded leaders stress being first-movers to sustain their competitive advantage (lower cost or differentiation) and to reinforce their reputation as *the* leader. A low-cost provider aggressively pursues cost reduction, and a differentiator constantly tries new ways to set its product apart from rivals' brands and become the standard against which rivals' products are judged. The theme of a stay-on-the-offensive strategy is relentless pursuit of continuous improvement and innovation. Striving to be first with new products, better performance features, quality enhancements, improved customer services, or ways to cut production costs not only helps a leader avoid complacency but it also keeps rivals on the defensive scrambling to keep up. Offensive options can also include initiatives to expand overall industry demand—discovering new uses for the product, attracting new users of the product, and promoting more frequent use. In addition, a clever offensive leader stays alert for ways to make it easier and less costly for potential customers to switch their purchases from runner-up firms to its own products. Unless a leader's market share is already so dominant that it presents a threat of antitrust action (a market share under 60 percent is usually "safe"), a stay-on-the-offensive strategy means trying to grow *faster* than the industry as a whole and wrest market share from rivals. A leader whose growth does not equal or outpace the industry average is losing ground to competitors.

Industry leaders can strengthen their long-term competitive positions with strategies keyed to aggressive offense, aggressive defense, or muscling smaller rivals into a follow-the-leader role.

2. **Fortify-and-defend strategy**—The essence of "fortify and defend" is to make it harder for new firms to enter and for challengers to gain ground. The goals of a strong defense are to hold on to the present market share, strengthen current market position, and protect whatever competitive advantage the firm has. Specific defensive actions can include:

- Attempting to raise the competitive ante for challengers and new entrants by increased spending for advertising, higher levels of customer service, and bigger R&D outlays.

- Introducing more product versions or brands to match the product attributes of challengers' brands or to fill vacant niches that competitors could slip into.

- Adding personalized services and other "extras" that boost customer loyalty and make it harder or more costly for customers to switch to rival products.

- Keeping prices reasonable and quality attractive.

- Building new capacity ahead of market demand to discourage smaller competitors from adding capacity of their own.

[27]Kotler, *Marketing Management*, chapter 23; Michael E. Porter, *Competitive Advantage* (New York: Free Press, 1985), chapter 14; and Ian C. MacMillan, "Seizing Competitive Initiative," *The Journal of Business Strategy* 2, no. 4 (Spring 1982), pp. 43–57.

- Investing enough to remain cost competitive and technologically progressive.
- Patenting the feasible alternative technologies.
- Signing exclusive contracts with the best suppliers, distributors, and dealers.

A fortify-and-defend strategy best suits firms that have already achieved industry dominance and don't wish to risk antitrust action. It also works when a firm wishes to milk its present position for profits and cash flow because the industry's prospects for growth are low or because further gains in market share do not appear profitable enough to go after. But a fortify-and-defend strategy always entails trying to grow as fast as the market as a whole (to stave off market share slippage) and requires reinvesting enough capital in the business to protect the leader's ability to compete.

3. **Follow-the-leader strategy**—With this strategy the leader uses its competitive muscle (ethically and fairly!) to encourage runner-up firms to be content followers rather than aggressive challengers. The leader plays competitive hardball when smaller rivals rock the boat with price cuts or mount new market offensives that threaten its position. Specific responses can include quickly matching and perhaps exceeding challengers' price cuts, using large promotional campaigns to counter challengers' moves to gain market share, and offering better deals to the major customers of maverick firms. Leaders can also court distributors to dissuade them from carrying rivals' products, provide salespersons with documented information about the weaknesses of an aggressor's products, or try to fill any vacant positions in their own firms by making attractive offers to the better executives of rivals that "get out of line." When a leader consistently meets any moves to cut into its business with strong retaliatory tactics, it sends clear signals that offensive attacks on the leader's position will be met head-on and probably won't pay off. However, leaders pursuing this strategic approach should choose their battles. For instance, it makes sense to assume a hands-off posture and not respond in hardball fashion when smaller rivals attack each other's customer base in ways that don't affect the leader.

STRATEGIES FOR RUNNER-UP FIRMS

Runner-up firms have smaller market shares than the industry leader(s). Some runner-up firms are up-and-coming *market challengers*, using offensive strategies to gain market share and build a stronger market position. Others behave as *content followers*, willing to coast along in their current positions because profits are adequate. Follower firms have no urgent strategic issue to confront beyond "What kinds of strategic changes are the leaders initiating and what do we need to do to follow along?"

Rarely can a runner-up firm successfully challenge an industry leader with a copycat strategy.

A challenger firm interested in improving its market standing needs a strategy aimed at building a competitive advantage of its own. *Rarely can a runner-up firm improve its competitive position by imitating the strategies of leading firms. A cardinal rule in offensive strategy is to avoid attacking a leader head-on with an imitative strategy, regardless of the resources and staying power an underdog may have.*[28] Moreover, if a challenger has a 5 percent market share and needs a 20 percent share to earn attractive returns, it needs a more creative approach to competing than just "try harder."

---

[28]Porter, *Competitive Advantage*, p. 514.

In industries where large size yields *significantly* lower unit costs and gives large-share competitors an *important* cost advantage, small-share firms have only two viable strategic options: initiate offensive moves to gain sales and market share (so as to build the production volumes needed to approach the scale economies enjoyed by larger rivals) or withdraw from the business (gradually or quickly). The competitive strategies most underdogs use to build market share are based on (1) a combination of actions to drive down costs and to lower prices to win customers from weak, higher-cost rivals and (2) using differentiation strategies based on quality, technological superiority, better customer service, best cost, or innovation. Achieving low-cost leadership is usually open to an underdog only when one of the market leaders is not already solidly positioned as the industry's low-cost producer. But a small-share firm may still be able to narrow any cost disadvantage by eliminating marginal activities from the value chain, finding ways to better manage cost drivers and improve operating efficiency, or merging with or acquiring rival firms (the combined production volumes may provide the scale needed to achieve size-related economies).

When scale economies or experience curve effects are small and a large market share produces no cost advantage, runner-up companies have more strategic flexibility and can consider any of the following six approaches:[29]

1. **Vacant-niche strategy**—This version of a focused strategy involves concentrating on customer or end-use applications that market leaders have bypassed or neglected. An ideal vacant niche is of sufficient size and scope to be profitable, has some growth potential, is well-suited to a firm's own capabilities and resources, and is not interesting to leading firms. Two examples where vacant-niche strategies worked successfully are regional commuter airlines serving cities with too few passengers to attract the interest of major airlines and health foods producers (like Health Valley, Hain, and Tree of Life) that cater to local health food stores—a market segment traditionally ignored by Pillsbury, Kraft General Foods, Heinz, Nabisco, Campbell Soup, and other leading food products firms.

2. **Specialist strategy**—A specialist firm trains its competitive effort on one market segment: a single product, a particular end use, or buyers with special needs. The aim is to build competitive advantage through product uniqueness, expertise in special-purpose products, or specialized customer services. Smaller companies that successfully use a specialist focused strategy include Formby's (a specialist in stains and finishes for wood furniture, especially refinishing), Liquid Paper Co. (a leader in correction fluid for writers and typists), Canada Dry (known for its ginger ale, tonic water, and carbonated soda water), and American Tobacco (a leader in chewing tobacco and snuff).

3. **Ours-is-better-than-theirs strategy**—The approach here is to use a differentiation-based focus strategy keyed to superior product quality or unique attributes. Sales and marketing efforts are aimed directly at quality-conscious and performance-oriented buyers. Fine craftsmanship, prestige quality, frequent product innovations, and/or close contact with customers to solicit their input in developing a better product usually undergird this "superior product" approach. Some examples include Beefeater and Tanqueray in gin, Tiffany in diamonds and jewelry, Chicago

---

[29]For more details, see Kotler, *Marketing Management*, pp. 397–412; R. G. Hamermesh, M. J. Anderson, Jr., and J. E. Harris, "Strategies for Low Market Share Businesses," *Harvard Business Review* 56, no. 3 (May–June 1978), pp. 95–102; and Porter, *Competitive Advantage*, chapter 15.

Cutlery in premium-quality kitchen knives, Baccarat in fine crystal, Cannondale in mountain bikes, Bally in shoes, and Patagonia in apparel for outdoor recreation enthusiasts.

4. Content-follower strategy—Follower firms deliberately refrain from initiating trendsetting strategic moves and from aggressive attempts to steal customers away from the leaders. Followers prefer approaches that will not provoke competitive retaliation, often opting for focus and differentiation strategies that keep them out of the leaders' paths. They react and respond rather than initiate and challenge. They prefer defense to offense. And they rarely get out of line with the leaders on price. Union Camp (in paper products) has been a successful market follower by consciously concentrating on selected product uses and applications for specific customer groups, focused R&D, profits rather than market share, and cautious but efficient management.

5. Growth-via-acquisition strategy—One way to strengthen a company's position is to merge with or acquire weaker rivals to form an enterprise that has more competitive strength and a larger share of the market. Commercial airline companies such as Northwest, US Airways, and Delta owe their market share growth during the past decade to acquisition of smaller, regional airlines. Likewise, the Big Six public accounting firms extended their national and international coverage by merging or forming alliances with smaller CPA firms at home and abroad.

6. Distinctive-image strategy—Some runner-up companies build their strategies around ways to make themselves stand out from competitors. A variety of strategic approaches can be used: creating a reputation for charging the lowest prices, providing prestige quality at a good price, going all-out to give superior customer service, designing unique product attributes, being a leader in new product introduction, or devising unusually creative advertising. Examples include Dr Pepper's strategy in calling attention to its distinctive taste and Mary Kay Cosmetics' distinctive use of the color pink.

In industries where big size is definitely a key success factor, firms with low market shares have some obstacles to overcome: (1) less access to economies of scale in manufacturing, distribution, or sales promotion; (2) difficulty in gaining customer recognition; (3) an inability to afford mass media advertising on a grand scale; and (4) difficulty in funding capital requirements.[30] But *it is erroneous to view runner-up firms as inherently less profitable or unable to hold their own against the biggest firms.* Many firms with small market shares earn healthy profits and enjoy good reputations with customers. Often, the handicaps of smaller size can be surmounted and a profitable competitive position established by (1) focusing on a few market segments where the company's resource strengths and capabilities can yield a competitive edge; (2) developing technical expertise that will be highly valued by customers; (3) getting new or better products into the market ahead of rivals and building a reputation for product leadership; and (4) being more agile and innovative in adapting to evolving market conditions and customer expectations than stodgy, slow-to-change market leaders. Runner-up companies have a golden opportunity to make big market share gains if they pioneer a leapfrog technological breakthrough, if they are first to market with a new or dramatically improved product, or if the leaders stumble or become complacent.

---

[30]Hamermesh, Anderson, and Harris, "Strategies for Low Market Share Businesses," p. 102.

Otherwise, runner-up companies have to patiently nibble away at the leaders and build sales at a more moderate pace over time.

STRATEGIES FOR WEAK BUSINESSES

A firm in an also-ran or declining competitive position has four basic strategic options. If it can come up with the financial resources, it can launch an *offensive* turnaround strategy keyed either to low-cost or "new" differentiation themes, pouring enough money and talent into the effort to move up a notch or two in the industry rankings and become a respectable market contender within five years or so. It can employ a *fortify-and-defend* strategy, using variations of its present strategy and fighting hard to keep sales, market share, profitability, and competitive position at current levels. It can opt for an *immediate abandonment strategy* and get out of the business, either by selling out to another firm or by closing down operations if a buyer cannot be found. Or it can employ a *harvest strategy*, keeping reinvestment to a bare-bones minimum and taking actions to maximize short-term cash flows in preparation for an orderly market exit. The gist of the first three options is self-explanatory. The fourth merits more discussion.

The strategic options for a competitively weak company include waging a modest offensive to improve its position, defending its present position, being acquired by another company, or employing a harvest strategy.

A *harvest strategy* steers a middle course between preserving the status quo and exiting as soon as possible. Harvesting is a phasing down or endgame strategy that involves sacrificing market position in return for bigger near-term cash flows or profits. The overriding financial objective is to reap the greatest possible harvest of cash to use in other business endeavors. The operating budget is chopped to a rock-bottom level; reinvestment in the business is held to a bare minimum. Capital expenditures for new equipment are put on hold or given low priority (unless replacement needs are unusually urgent); instead, efforts are made to stretch the life of existing equipment and make do with present facilities as long as possible. Price may be raised gradually, promotional expenses slowly cut, quality reduced in not-so-visible ways, nonessential customer services curtailed, and the like. Although such actions may result in shrinking sales and market share, if cash expenses can be cut even faster, then after-tax profits and cash flows are bigger (at least temporarily). The business gradually declines, but not before a sizable cash harvest is realized.

Harvesting is a reasonable strategic option for a weak business in the following circumstances:[31]

1. When the industry's long-term prospects are unattractive.

2. When rejuvenating the business would be too costly or at best marginally profitable.

3. When the firm's market share is becoming more costly to maintain or defend.

4. When reduced competitive effort will not trigger an immediate or rapid fall-off in sales.

5. When the enterprise can redeploy the freed resources in higher opportunity areas.

---

[31]Phillip Kotler, "Harvesting Strategies for Weak Products," *Business Horizons* 21, no. 5 (August 1978), pp. 17–18.

6. When the business is *not* a crucial or core component of a diversified company's overall lineup of businesses (harvesting a sideline business is strategically preferable to harvesting a mainline or core business).

7. When the business does not contribute other desired features (sales stability, prestige, a product that complements others in the company's lineup of offerings) to a diversified company's overall business portfolio.

The more of these seven conditions present, the more ideal the business is for harvesting.

Turnaround Strategies for Businesses in Crisis

Turnaround strategies are needed when a business worth rescuing goes into crisis; the objective is to arrest and reverse the sources of competitive and financial weakness as quickly as possible. Management's first task is to diagnose what lies at the root of poor performance. Is it an unexpected downturn in sales brought on by a weak economy? An ill-chosen competitive strategy? Poor execution of an otherwise workable strategy? High operating costs? Important resource deficiencies? An overload of debt? Can the business be saved, or is the situation hopeless? Understanding what is wrong with the business and how serious its problems are is essential because different diagnoses lead to different turnaround strategies.

Some of the most common causes of business trouble include: taking on too much debt, overestimating the potential for sales growth, ignoring the profit-depressing effects of an overly aggressive effort to "buy" market share with deep price cuts, being burdened with heavy fixed costs because of an inability to utilize plant capacity, betting on R&D efforts to boost competitive position and profitability and failing to come up with effective innovations, betting on technological long shots, being too optimistic about the ability to penetrate new markets, making frequent changes in strategy (because the previous strategy didn't work out), and being overpowered by the competitive advantages enjoyed by more successful rivals. Curing these kinds of problems and turning the firm around can involve any of the following actions:

- Selling off assets to raise cash to save the remaining part of the business.
- Revising the existing strategy.
- Launching efforts to boost revenues.
- Pursuing cost reduction.
- Using a combination of these efforts.

Selling Off Assets   Assets reduction/retrenchment strategies are essential when cash flow is critical and when the most practical ways to generate cash are (1) through sale of some of the firm's assets and (2) through retrenchment (pruning of marginal products from the product line, closing or selling older plants, reducing the workforce, withdrawing from outlying markets, cutting back customer service, and the like). Sometimes crisis-ridden companies sell off assets not so much to unload losing operations and to stem cash drains as to raise funds to save and strengthen the remaining business activities.

Strategy Revision   When weak performance is caused by bad strategy, the task of strategy overhaul can proceed along any of several paths: (1) shifting to a new competitive approach to rebuild the firm's market position; (2) overhauling internal operations, resource capabilities, and functional strategies to better support the same overall business strategy; (3) merging with another firm in the industry and forging a new strategy keyed to the newly merged firm's strengths; and (4) retrenching into a reduced core of products and customers more closely matched to the firm's resource capabilities. The most appealing path depends on prevailing industry conditions, the firm's resource strengths and weaknesses, its competitive capabilities, and the severity of the crisis. Situation analysis of the industry, major competitors, and the firm's own competitive position and its competencies and resources are prerequisites for action. As a rule, successful strategy revision must be tied to the ailing firm's strengths and near-term competitive capabilities and directed at its best market opportunities.

Boosting Revenues   Revenue-increasing turnaround efforts aim at generating increased sales volume. There are a number of options: price cuts, increased promotion, a bigger sales force, added customer services, and quickly achieved product improvements. Attempts to increase revenues and sales volumes are necessary (1) when there is little or no room in the operating budget to cut expenses and still break even and (2) when the key to restoring profitability is increased use of existing capacity. If buyer demand is not especially price sensitive because of differentiating features, the quickest way to boost short-term revenues may be to raise prices rather than opt for volume-building price cuts.

Cutting Costs   Cost-reducing turnaround strategies work best when an ailing firm's value chain and cost structure are flexible enough to permit radical surgery, when it can identify and correct operating inefficiencies, when the firm's costs are obviously bloated and there are many places where savings can be quickly achieved, and when the firm is relatively close to its break-even point. Accompanying a general belt-tightening can be an increased emphasis on paring administrative overheads, elimination of nonessential and low-value-added activities, modernization of existing plant and equipment to gain greater productivity, delay of nonessential capital expenditures, and debt restructuring to reduce interest costs and stretch out repayments.

Combination Efforts   Combination turnaround strategies are usually essential in grim situations that require fast action on a broad front. Likewise, combination actions frequently come into play when new managers are brought in and given a free hand to make whatever changes they see fit. The tougher the problems, the more likely the solutions will involve multiple strategic initiatives.

Turnaround efforts tend to be high-risk undertakings, and they often fail. A landmark study of 64 companies found no successful turnarounds among the most troubled companies in eight basic industries.[32] Many of the troubled businesses waited too long to begin a turnaround. Others found themselves short of both the cash and entrepreneurial talent needed to compete in a slow-growth industry. Better-positioned rivals simply proved too strong to defeat in a long, head-to-head contest. Even when successful, many troubled companies go through a series of turnaround

---

[32]William K. Hall, "Survival Strategies in a Hostile Environment," *Harvard Business Review* 58, no. 5 (September–October 1980), pp. 75–85. See also Frederick M. Zimmerman, *The Turnaround Experience: Real-World Lessons in Revitalizing Corporations* (New York: McGraw-Hill, 1991), and Gary J. Castrogiovanni, B. R. Baliga, and Roland E. Kidwell, "Curing Sick Businesses: Changing CEOs in Turnaround Efforts," *Academy of Management Executive* 6, no. 3 (August 1992), pp. 26–41.

attempts and management changes before long-term competitive viability and profitability are finally restored.

THIRTEEN COMMANDMENTS FOR CRAFTING SUCCESSFUL BUSINESS STRATEGIES

Business experiences over the years prove again and again that disastrous courses of action can be avoided by adhering to good strategy-making principles. The wisdom gained from these past experiences can be distilled into 13 commandments that, if faithfully observed, can help strategists craft better strategic action plans.

1. *Place top priority on crafting and executing strategic moves that enhance the company's competitive position for the long term.* An ever-stronger competitive position pays off year after year, but the glory of meeting one quarter's and one year's financial performance targets quickly fades. Shareholders are never well served by managers who let short-term financial performance rule out strategic initiatives that will bolster the company's long-term position and strength. The best way to protect a company's long-term profitability is to strengthen the company's long-term competitiveness.

2. *Understand that a clear, consistent competitive strategy, when well crafted and well executed, builds reputation and recognizable industry position; a frequently changed strategy aimed at capturing momentary market opportunities yields fleeting benefits.* Short-run financial opportunism, absent any long-term strategic consistency, tends to produce the worst kind of profits: one-shot rewards that are unrepeatable. Over the long haul, a company that has a well-conceived, consistent competitive strategy aimed at securing an ever-stronger market position will outperform and defeat a rival whose strategic decisions are driven by a desire to meet Wall Street's short-term expectations. In an ongoing enterprise, the game of competition ought to be played for the long term, not the short term.

3. *Avoid "stuck in the middle" strategies that represent compromises between lower costs and greater differentiation and between broad and narrow market appeal.* Middle-of-the-road strategies rarely produce sustainable competitive advantage or a distinctive competitive position—well-executed best-cost producer strategies are the only exception where a compromise between low cost and differentiation succeeds. Usually, companies with compromise or middle-of-the-road strategies end up with average costs, average features, average quality, average appeal, an average image and reputation, a middle-of-the-pack industry ranking, and little prospect of climbing into the ranks of the industry leaders.

4. *Invest in creating a sustainable competitive advantage.* It is the single most dependable contributor to above-average profitability.

5. *Play aggressive offense to build competitive advantage and aggressive defense to protect it.*

6. *Avoid strategies capable of succeeding only in the most optimistic circumstances.* Expect competitors to employ countermeasures and expect times of unfavorable market conditions.

7. *Be cautious in pursuing a rigid or inflexible strategy that locks the company in for the long term with little room to maneuver—inflexible strategies can*

BUILDING SHAREHOLDER VALUE: THE ULTIMATE JUSTIFICATION FOR DIVERSIFYING

Diversifying into new businesses is justifiable only if it builds shareholder value. To enhance shareholder value, more must be accomplished than simply spreading the company's business risk across more than one industry. Shareholders can easily diversify risk on their own by purchasing stock in companies in different industries. Strictly speaking, *diversification does not create shareholder value unless a diversified group of businesses perform better under a single corporate umbrella than they would operating as independent, stand-alone businesses.* For example, if company A diversifies by purchasing company B and if A and B's consolidated profits in the years to come prove no greater than what each would have earned on its own, then A's diversification into business B won't provide its shareholders with added value. Company A's shareholders could have achieved the same 2 + 2 = 4 result by merely purchasing stock in company B. Shareholder value is not *created* by diversification unless it produces a 2 + 2 = 5 effect where sister businesses perform better together as part of the same firm than they could have performed as independent companies.

> *To create shareholder value, a diversifying company must get into businesses that can perform better under common management than they could perform as standalone enterprises.*

Three Tests for Judging a Diversification Move

The problem with such a strict benchmark of whether diversification has enhanced shareholder value is that it requires speculation about how well a diversified company's businesses would have performed on their own. Comparisons of actual performance against the hypothetical of what performance might have been under other circumstances are never very satisfactory and, besides, they represent after-the-fact assessments. Strategists have to base diversification decisions on *future* expectations. Attempts to gauge the impact of particular diversification moves on shareholder value do not have to be abandoned, however. Corporate strategists can make before-the-fact assessments of whether a particular diversification move can increase shareholder value by using three tests:[1]

1. **The attractiveness test:** The industry chosen for diversification must be attractive enough to yield consistently good returns on investment. Whether an industry is attractive depends chiefly on the presence of favorable competitive conditions and a market environment conducive to long-term profitability. Such indicators as rapid growth or a sexy product are unreliable proxies of attractiveness.

2. **The cost-of-entry test:** The cost to enter the target industry must not be so high as to erode the potential for good profitability. A catch-22 can prevail here, however. The more attractive the industry, the more expensive it can be to get into. Entry barriers for start-up companies are nearly always high— were barriers low, a rush of new entrants would soon erode the potential for high profits. And buying a company already in the business often entails a high acquisition cost because of the industry's strong appeal.

3. **The better-off test:** The diversifying company must bring some potential for competitive advantage to the new business it enters, or the new business

---

[1]Michael E. Porter, "From Competitive Advantage to Corporate Strategy," *Harvard Business Review* 45, no. 3 (May–June 1987), pp. 46–49.

must offer added competitive advantage potential to the company's present businesses. The opportunity to create sustainable competitive advantage where none existed before means there is also opportunity for added profitability and shareholder value. The better-off test entails examining potential new businesses to determine if they have competitively valuable value chain matchups with the company's existing businesses—matchups that offer opportunities to reduce costs, to transfer skills or technology from one business to another, to create valuable new capabilities, or to leverage existing resources. Without such matchups, one has to be skeptical about the potential for the businesses to perform better together than apart.

Diversification moves that satisfy all three tests have the greatest potential to build shareholder value over the long term. Diversification moves that can pass only one or two tests are suspect.

DIVERSIFICATION STRATEGIES

Once the decision is made to diversify, a choice must be made whether to diversify into *related* businesses or *unrelated* businesses or some mix of both. Businesses are related when there are competitively valuable relationships among their value chains activities. Businesses are unrelated when there are no common similarities or matchups in their respective value chains. Figure 7–1 shows the paths a company can take in moving from a single-business enterprise to a diversified enterprise. Vertical integration strategies may or may not enter the picture depending on whether forward or backward integration strengthens a firm's competitive position. Once diversification is accomplished, management's task is to figure out how to manage the collection of businesses the company has invested in—the six fundamental strategic options are shown in the last box of Figure 7–1.

We can better understand the strategic issues corporate managers face in creating and managing a diversified group of businesses by looking at six diversification-related strategies:

1. Strategies for entering new industries—acquisition, start-up, and joint ventures.
2. Related diversification strategies.
3. Unrelated diversification strategies.
4. Divestiture and liquidation strategies.
5. Corporate turnaround, retrenchment, and restructuring strategies.
6. Multinational diversification strategies.

The first three are ways to diversify; the last three are strategies to strengthen the positions and performance of companies that have already diversified.

Strategies for Entering New Businesses

Entry into new businesses can take any of three forms: acquisition, internal start-up, and joint ventures.

Acquisition of an Existing Business   Acquisition is the most popular way to diversify into another industry. Not only is it a quicker way to enter the target market than trying to launch a brand-new operation from the ground up but it offers an effective way to hurdle such entry barriers as acquiring technological experience, establishing

FIGURE 7-1   Corporate Strategy Alternatives

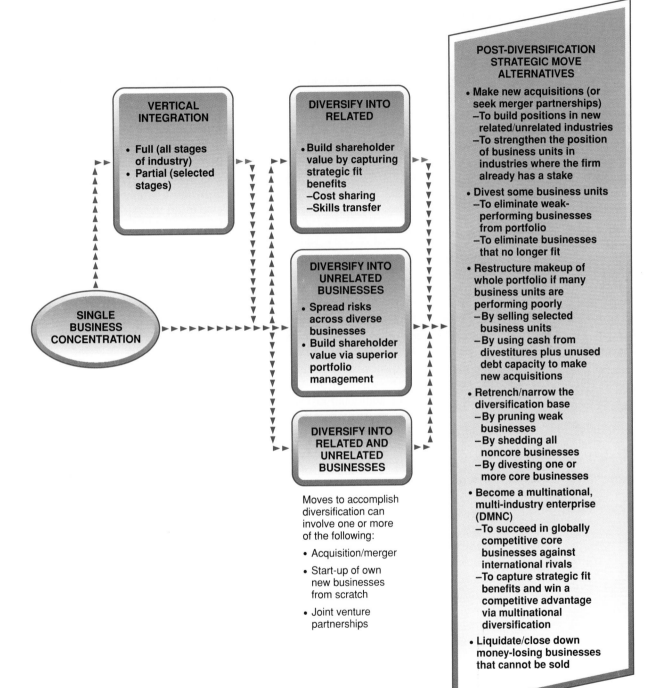

supplier relationships, becoming big enough to match rivals' efficiency and unit costs, having to spend large sums on introductory advertising and promotions to gain market visibility and brand recognition, and securing adequate distribution.[2] In many industries, going the internal start-up route and trying to develop the knowledge, resources, scale of operation, and market reputation necessary to become an effective competitor can take years. Acquiring an already established concern allows the entrant to move directly to the task of building a strong market position in the target industry.

However, finding the right kind of company to acquire sometimes presents a challenge.[3] The big dilemma an acquisition-minded firm faces is whether to pay a premium price for a successful company or to buy a struggling company at a bargain price. If the buying firm has little knowledge of the industry but ample capital, it is often better off purchasing a capable, strongly positioned firm—unless the price of such an acquisition is prohibitive and flunks the cost-of-entry test. On the other hand, when the acquirer sees promising ways to transform a weak firm into a strong one and has the resources, the know-how, and the patience to do it, a struggling company can be the better long-term investment.

One of the big stumbling blocks to entering attractive industries by acquisition is the difficulty of finding a suitable company at a price that satisfies the cost-of-entry test.

The cost-of-entry test requires that the expected profit stream of an acquired business provide an attractive return on the total acquisition cost and on any new capital investment needed to sustain or expand its operations. A high acquisition price can make meeting that test improbable or difficult. For instance, suppose that the price to purchase a company is $3 million and that the business is earning after-tax profits of $200,000 on an equity investment of $1 million (a 20 percent annual return). Simple arithmetic requires that the acquired business's profits be tripled for the purchaser to earn the same 20 percent return on the $3 million acquisition price that the previous owners were getting on their $1 million equity investment. Building the acquired firm's earnings from $200,000 to $600,000 annually could take several years—and require additional investment on which the purchaser would also have to earn a 20 percent return. Since the owners of a successful and growing company usually demand a price that reflects their business's future profit prospects, it's easy for such an acquisition to fail the cost-of-entry test. A would-be diversifier can't count on being able to acquire a desirable company in an appealing industry at a price that still permits attractive returns on investment.

Internal Start-Up　　Achieving diversification through *internal start-up* involves creating a new company under the corporate umbrella to compete in the desired industry. A newly formed organization not only has to overcome entry barriers, it also has to invest in new production capacity, develop sources of supply, hire and train employees, build channels of distribution, grow a customer base, and so on. Generally, forming a start-up company to enter a new industry is more attractive when (1) there is ample time to launch the business from the ground up, (2) incumbent firms are likely to be slow or ineffective in responding to a new entrant's efforts to crack the market, (3) internal entry has lower costs than entry via acquisition, (4) the company already has in-house most or

---

[2]In recent years, hostile takeovers have become a hotly debated and sometimes abused approach to acquisition. The term *takeover* refers to the attempt (often sprung as a surprise) of one firm to acquire ownership or control over another firm against the wishes of the latter's management (and perhaps some of its stockholders).

[3]Michael E. Porter, *Competitive Strategy: Techniques for Analyzing Industries and Competitors* (New York: Free Press, 1980), p. 354–55.

all of the skills it needs to compete effectively, (5) adding new production capacity will not adversely impact the supply-demand balance in the industry, and (6) the targeted industry is populated with many relatively small firms so the new start-up does not have to compete head-to-head against larger, more powerful rivals.[4]

Joint Ventures   Joint ventures are a useful way to gain access to a new business in at least three types of situations.[5] First, a joint venture is a good way to do something that is uneconomical or risky for an organization to do alone. Second, joint ventures make sense when pooling the resources and competencies of two or more organizations produces an organization with more resources and competitive assets to be a strong market contender. In such cases, each partner brings special talents or resources that the other doesn't have and that are important for success. Third, joint ventures with foreign partners are sometimes the only or best way to surmount import quotas, tariffs, nationalistic political interests, and cultural roadblocks. The economic, competitive, and political realities of nationalism often require a foreign company to team up with a domestic partner to gain access to the national market in which the domestic partner is located. Domestic partners offer outside companies the benefits of local knowledge, managerial and marketing personnel, and access to distribution channels. However, such joint ventures often pose complicated questions about how to divide efforts among the partners and about who has effective control.[6] Conflicts between foreign and domestic partners can arise over whether to use local sourcing of components, how much production to export, whether operating procedures should conform to the foreign company's standards or to local preferences, who has control of cash flows, and how to distribute profits.

The biggest drawbacks to entering an industry by forming a start-up company internally are the costs of overcoming entry barriers and the extra time it takes to build a strong and profitable competitive position.

RELATED DIVERSIFICATION STRATEGIES

A related diversification strategy involves diversifying into businesses whose value chains possess competitively valuable "strategic fits" with those of the company's present business(es). *Strategic fit* exists between different businesses whenever their value chains are similiar enough to present opportunities for technology sharing, for exercising more bargaining leverage with common suppliers, for joint manufacture of parts and components, for sharing a common sales force, for using the same distribution facilities, for using the same wholesale distributors or retail dealers, for combining after-sale service activities, for exploiting common use of a well-known brand name, for transferring competitively valuable know-how or capabilities from one business to another, or for combining similar value chain activites to achieve lower costs. Strategic fits can exist anywhere along the businesses' respective value chains—in the relationships with suppliers, in R&D and technology activiities, in manufacturing, in sales and marketing, or in distribution activities.

Related diversification involves diversifying into businesses with competitively valuable strategic fits and matchups in their value chains.

What makes related diversification an attractive strategy is the opportunity to convert the strategic fit relationships between the value chains of different businesses

---

[4]Ibid., pp. 344–45.

[5]Peter Drucker, *Management: Tasks, Responsibilities, Practices* (New York: Harper & Row, 1974), pp. 720–24. Strategic alliances offer much the same benefits as joint ventures, but represent a weaker commitment to entering a new business.

[6]Porter, *Competitive Strategy*, p. 340.

ILLUSTRATION CAPSULE 24   Koch Industries' Efforts to Link Its Diversification Strategy to Core Competencies and Capabilities

At Koch Industries, one of the five largest privately held companies in America, development of a company vision and strategy involved an analysis of the company's competencies and capabilities and deciding how to match these competencies and capabilities with perceived market opportunities. One executive observed, "We thought we were in the oil business, but we found out our real expertise is in the gathering, transportation, processing, and trading business." While the company developed these competencies in gathering, refining, transporting, and trading crude oil, management realiza-

tion of what the company's capabilities were led to expansion into gas liquids, and then into gas gathering, transportation, processing, and trading. Involvement in gas operations led Koch into ammonia transportation and trading, operations more closely related to Koch's oil business than service station operations. More recent acquisitions have involved transferring Koch's core capabilities to grain gathering and cattle feedlots, business activities which draw on the company's expertise in gathering, transportation, processing, and trading.

Source: Tyler Cowen and Jerry Ellig, "Market-Based Management at Koch Industries: Discovery, Dissemination, and Integration of Knowledge," *Competitive Intelligence Review* 6, no. 4 (Winter 1995), p. 7.

What makes related diversification attractive is the opportunity to turn strategic fits into competitive advantage.

into competitive advantage. When a company diversifies into businesses that present opportunities to (1) transfer expertise or capabilities or technology from one business to another, (2) combine the related activities of separate businesses into a single operation and reduce costs, (3) leverage a company's brand-name reputation in new businesses, and/or (4) conduct the related value chain activities in such collaborative fashion as to create valuable competitive capabilities, it gains competitive advantage over rivals that have not diversified or that have diversified in ways that don't give them access to such strategic-fit benefits.[7] The greater the relatedness among the businesses of a diversified company, the greater the opportunities for skills transfer and/or combining value chain activities to lower costs and/or collaborating to create new resource strengths and capabilities and/or using a common brand name and the bigger the window for creating competitive advantage.[8]

Moreover, *a diversified firm that exploits these value-chain matchups and captures the benefits of strategic fit can achieve a consolidated performance greater than the sum of what the businesses can earn pursuing independent strategies.* Competitively valuable strategic fits (assuming corporate management is able to effectively capture the benefits of the value chain matchups) make related diversification a 2 + 2 = 5 phenomenon. The competitive edge flowing from strategic fits along the value chains of related businesses provides a basis for them performing better together than as stand-alone enterprises. The bigger the strategic-fit benefits, the more that related diversification is capable of 2 + 2 = 5 performance—thereby satisfying the better-off test for building shareholder value.

[7]Michael E. Porter, *Competitive Advantage* (New York: Free Press, 1985), pp. 318–19 and pp. 337–53; Kenichi Ohmae, *The Mind of the Strategist* (New York: Penguin Books, 1983), pp. 121–24; and Porter, "From Competitive Advantage to Corporate Strategy," pp. 53–57. For an empirical study confirming that strategic fits are capable of enhancing performance (provided the resulting resource strengths are competitively valuable and difficult to duplicate by rivals), see Constantinos C. Markides and Peter J. Williamson, "Corporate Diversification and Organization Structure: A Resource-Based View," *Academy of Management Journal*, 39, no. 2 (April 1996), pp. 340–67.

[8]For a discussion of the strategic significance of cross-business coordination and insight into how it works, see Jeanne M. Liedtka, "Collaboration across Lines of Business for Competitive Advantage," *Academy of Management Executive* 10, no. 2 (May 1996), pp. 20–34.

Related Diversification in Actual Practice Some of the most commonly used approaches to related diversification are

- Entering businesses where sales force, advertising, brand name, and distribution facilities can be shared (a maker of cookies and crackers diversifying into salty snack foods).

- Exploiting closely related technologies and technical expertise (a creator of software for mainframe computers diversifying into software for networking of PCs, for company intranets, and for stand-alone PCs).

- Transferring know-how and expertise from one business to another (a successful operator of Italian restaurants acquiring a chain specializing in Mexican food).

- Transferring the organization's brand name and reputation with consumers to a new product/service (a tire manufacturer acquiring a chain of car care centers specializing in brake repair and muffler and shock-absorber replacement).

- Acquiring new businesses that will uniquely help the firm's position in its existing businesses (a cable TV broadcaster purchasing a sports team or a movie production company to provide original programming).

Examples of related diversification abound. BIC Pen, which pioneered inexpensive disposable ballpoint pens, used its core competencies in low-cost manufacturing and mass merchandising as its basis for diversifying into disposable cigarette lighters and disposable razors—both of which required low-cost production know-how and skilled consumer marketing for success. Sony, a leading consumer electronics company, employed a technology-related and marketing-related diversification strategy when it decided to enter the videogame industry and to transfer its competencies and capabilities in electronics technology, its marketing know-how, and its brand name credibility to the manufacture and sale of videogame players and the marketing of videogames. Procter & Gamble's lineup of products includes Jif peanut butter, Duncan Hines cake mixes, Folger's coffee, Tide laundry detergent, Crisco vegetable oil, Crest toothpaste, Ivory soap, Charmin toilet tissue, and Head and Shoulders shampoo—all different businesses with different competitors and different production requirements. But P&G's products still represent related diversification because they all move through the same wholesale distribution systems, are sold in common retail settings to the same shoppers, are advertised and promoted in the same ways, and use the same marketing and merchandising skills. Illustration Capsule 25 shows the business portfolios of several companies that have pursued a strategy of related diversification.

Strategic Fit, Economies of Scope, and Competitive Advantage

A related diversification strategy is appealing from several angles. It allows a firm to preserve a degree of unity in its business activities, reap the benefits of skills transfer and/or lower costs and/or common brand-name usage and/or stronger competitive capabilities, and still spread investor risks over a broader business base.

Diversifying into businesses where technology, facilities, functional activities, or distribution channels can be shared can lead to lower costs because of economies of scope. *Economies of scope* exist whenever it is less costly for two or more businesses to be operated under centralized management than to function as independent businesses. These economies can arise from

Strategic fits among related businesses offer the competitive advantage potential of (a) lower costs, (b) efficient transfer of key skills, technological expertise, or managerial know-how from one business to another, (c) ability to share a common brand name, and/or (d) enhanced resource strengths and competitive capabilities.

ILLUSTRATION CAPSULE 25   Examples of Companies with Related Business Portfolios

Presented below are the business portfolios of three companies that have pursued some form of related diversification. Can you identify the strategic fits and value chain relationships that exist among their businesses?

Gillette

- Blades and razors
- Toiletries (Right Guard, Foamy, Dry Idea, Soft & Dry, White Rain)
- Jafra skin care products
- Oral-B toothbrushes and dental care products
- Writing instruments and stationery products (Paper Mate pens, Parker pens, Waterman pens, Liquid Paper correction fluids)
- Braun shavers, coffeemakers, alarm clocks, mixers, hair dryers, and electric toothbrushes

Philip Morris Companies

- Cigarettes (Marlboro, Virginia Slims, Benson & Hedges, Merit, and numerous other brands)

- Miller Brewing Company (Miller Genuine Draft, Miller Lite, Icehouse, Red Dog)
- Kraft General Foods (Maxwell House, Sanka, Oscar Mayer, Kool-Aid, Jell-O, Post cereals, Birds-Eye frozen foods, Kraft cheeses, Crystal Light, Tombstone pizza)
- Mission Viejo Realty

Johnson & Johnson

- Baby products (powder, shampoo, oil, lotion)
- Band-Aids and wound care products
- Stayfree, Carefree, and Sure & Natural, feminine hygiene products
- Nonprescription drugs (Tylenol, Pepcid AC, Mylanta, Motrin, Monistat-7)
- Prescription drugs
- Surgical and hospital products
- Reach dental products
- Accuvue contact lenses
- Skin care products

Source: Company annual reports

Economies of scope *arise from the ability to eliminate costs by operating two or more businesses under the same corporate umbrella; the cost-saving opportunities can stem from interrelationships anywhere along the businesses' value chains.*

cost-saving opportunities to share resources or combine activities anywhere along the respective value chains of the businesses and from shared use of an established brand name. The greater the economies of scope, the greater the potential for creating a competitive advantage based on lower costs.

Both skills transfer and combining the performance of closely related value chain activies enable the diversifier to earn greater profits from joint operation of different businesses than the businesses could earn as independent, stand-alone enterprises. The key to skills transfer opportunities and to cost saving economies of scope is diversification into businesses with strategic fit. While strategic-fit relationships can occur throughout the value chain, most fall into one of four categories.

Technology Fits   Different businesses have *technology fit* when there is potential for sharing common technology, exploiting the full range of business opportunities associated with a particular technology, or transferring technological know-how from one business to another. Businesses with technology-sharing benefits can perform better together than apart because of potential cost-savings in technology development and new product R&D, because of shorter times in getting new products to market, important complementarity or interdependence between the resulting products that leads to increased sales of both, and/or the technology transfer potential between businesses allows more effective or efficient performance of technology-related activities.

Operating Fits   Different businesses have *operating fit* when there are opportunities to combine activities or transfer skills/capabilities in procuring materials, conducting

R&D, improving production processes, manufacturing components, assembling finished goods, or performing administrative support functions. Sharing-related operating fits usually present cost-saving opportunities; some derive from the economies of combining activities into a larger-scale operation *(economies of scale)*, and some derive from the ability to eliminate costs by performing activities together rather than independently *(economies of scope)*. The bigger the proportion of cost that a shared activity represents, the more significant the shared cost savings become and the bigger the cost advantage that can result. With operating fit, the most important skills transfer opportunities usually relate to situations where supply chain management or manufacturing expertise in one business has beneficial applications in another.

Distribution and Customer-Related Fits   When the value chains of different businesses overlap such that the products are used by the same customers, distributed through common dealers and retailers, or marketed and promoted in similar ways, then the businesses enjoy *market-related strategic fit*. A variety of cost-saving opportunities (or economies of scope) spring from market-related strategic fit: using a single sales force for all related products rather than having separate sales forces for each business, advertising the related products in the same ads and brochures, using a common brand name, coordinating delivery and shipping, combining after-sale service and repair organizations, coordinating order processing and billing, using common promotional tie-ins (cents-off couponing, free samples and trial offers, seasonal specials, and the like), and combining dealer networks. Such value-chain matchups usually allow a firm to economize on its marketing, selling, and distribution costs.

In addition to economies of scope, market-related fit can involve opportunities to transfer selling skills, promotional skills, advertising skills, or product differentiation skills from one business to another. Moreover, a company's brand name and reputation in one product can often be transferred to other products. Honda's name in motorcycles and automobiles gave it instant credibility and recognition in entering the lawnmower business without spending large sums on advertising. Canon's reputation in photographic equipment was a competitive asset that aided the company's diversification into copying equipment. Panasonic's name in consumer electronics (radios, TVs) was readily transferred to microwave ovens, making it easier and cheaper for Panasonic to diversify into the microwave oven market.

Managerial Fits   This type of fit emerges when different business units have comparable types of entrepreneurial, administrative, or operating problems, thereby allowing managerial know-how in one line of business to be transferred to another. Transfers of managerial expertise can occur anywhere in the value chain. Ford transferred its automobile financing and credit management know-how to the savings and loan industry when it acquired some failing savings and loan associations during the 1989 bailout of the crisis-ridden S&L industry. Wal-Mart transferred its managerial know-how in discount merchandising to its newly created Sam's Wholesale Club division and thereby successfully entered the wholesale discounting business.

Capturing Strategic-Fit Benefits

It is one thing to diversify into industries with strategic fit and another to actually realize the benefits of doing so. To capture economies of scope, related activities must be merged into a single operating unit and coordinated; then the cost savings must be squeezed out. Merged functions and coordination can entail reorganization costs, and management must determine that the benefit of *some* centralized strategic control is great enough to warrant sacrifice of business-unit autonomy. Likewise, where skills or technology transfer is the cornerstone of strategic fit, managers must find a way to make the transfer effective without stripping too many skilled personnel from the business with the expertise. The more a company's diversification strategy is tied to skills or technology transfer, the more it has to develop a big enough and talented enough pool of specialized personnel not only to supply new businesses with the skill or technology but also to master the skill/technology enough to create competitive advantage.

A company with the know-how to expand its stock of strategic assets faster and at lower cost than rivals obtains sustainable competitive advantage.

One additional benefit flows from companies becoming adept at capturing strategic fits across businesses: the potential for the firm to expand its pool of resources and strategic assets and to create new ones *faster and more cheaply* than rivals who are not diversified across related businesses.[9] One reason some firms pursuing related diversification perform better over the long-term than others is that they are better at exploiting the linkages between their related businesses; such know-how over the long term translates into an ability to *accelerate* the creation of valuable new core competencies and competitive capabilities. In a competitively dynamic world, the ability to accumulate strategic assets faster than rivals is a potent and dependable way for a diversified company to earn superior returns over the long term.

UNRELATED DIVERSIFICATION STRATEGIES

Despite the strategic-fit benefits associated with related diversification, a number of companies opt for unrelated diversification strategies—diversifying into *any industry* with a good profit opportunity. *In unrelated diversification there is no deliberate effort to seek out businesses having strategic fit with the firm's other businesses.* While companies pursuing unrelated diversification may try to make certain their diversification targets meet the industry-attractiveness and cost-of-entry tests, the conditions needed for the better-off test are either disregarded or relegated to secondary status. Decisions to diversify into one industry versus another are the product of a search for "good" companies to acquire—*the basic premise of unrelated diversification is that any company that can be acquired on good financial terms and that has satisfactory profit prospects represents a good business to diversify into.* Much time and effort goes into finding and screening acquisition candidates using such criteria as:

A strategy of unrelated diversification involves diversifying into whatever industries and businesses hold promise for attractive financial gain; exploiting strategic-fit relationships is secondary.

- Whether the business can meet corporate targets for profitability and return on investment.
- Whether the new business will require infusions of capital to replace fixed assets, fund expansion, and provide working capital.
- Whether the business is in an industry with significant growth potential.
- Whether the business is big enough to contribute significantly to the parent firm's bottom line.

---

[9]Constantinos C. Markides and Peter J. Williamson, "Related Diversification, Core Competences and Corporate Performance," *Strategic Management Journal* 15 (Summer 1994), pp. 149–65.

- Whether there is a potential for union difficulties or adverse government regulations concerning product safety or the environment.

- Whether the industry is unusually vulnerable to recession, inflation, high interest rates, or shifts in government policy.

Sometimes, companies with unrelated diversification strategies concentrate on identifying acquisition candidates that offer quick opportunities for financial gain because of their "special situation." Three types of businesses may hold such attraction:

- *Companies whose assets are undervalued*—opportunities may exist to acquire such companies for less than full market value and make substantial capital gains by reselling their assets and businesses for more than the purchase price.

- *Companies that are financially distressed*—such businesses can often be purchased at a bargain price, their operations turned around with the aid of the parent companies' financial resources and managerial know-how, and then either held as long-term investments (because of their strong earnings or cash flow potential) or sold at a profit, whichever is more attractive.

- *Companies that have bright growth prospects but are short on investment capital*—capital poor, opportunity-rich companies are usually coveted diversification candidates for a financially strong, opportunity-seeking firm.

Companies that pursue unrelated diversification nearly always enter new businesses by acquiring an established company rather than by forming a start-up subsidiary within their own corporate structures. Their premise is that growth by acquisition translates into enhanced shareholder value. Suspending application of the better-off test is seen as justifiable so long as unrelated diversification results in sustained growth in corporate revenues and earnings and so long as none of the acquired businesses end up performing badly.

Illustration Capsule 26 shows the business portfolios of several companies that have pursued unrelated diversification. Such companies are frequently labeled *conglomerates* because there is no strategic theme in their diversification makeup and because their business interests range broadly across diverse industries.

The Pros and Cons of Unrelated Diversification

Unrelated or conglomerate diversification has appeal from several financial angles:

1. Business risk is scattered over a set of *diverse* industries—a superior way to diversify financial risk as compared to related diversification because the company's investments can be spread over businesses with totally different technologies, competitive forces, market features, and customer bases.[10]

2. The company's financial resources can be employed to maximum advantage by investing in *whatever industries* offer the best profit prospects (as opposed

---

[10]While such arguments have logical appeal, there is research showing that related diversification is less risky from a financial perspective than is unrelated diversification; see, Michael Lubatkin and Sayan Chatterjee, "Extending Modern Portfolio Theory into the Domain of Corporate Diversification: Does It Apply?" *Academy of Management Journal* 37, no. 1 (February 1994), pp. 109–36.

ILLUSTRATION CAPSULE 26   Diversified Companies with Unrelated Business Portfolios

Union Pacific Corporation
- Railroad operations (Union Pacific Railroad Company)
- Oil and gas exploration
- Mining
- Microwave and fiber optic transportation information and control systems
- Hazardous waste management disposal
- Trucking (Overnite Transportation Company)
- Oil refining
- Real estate

Rockwell International
- Industrial automation products (Reliance electric, Allen-Bradley, Sprecher & Schuh, Datamyte, Rockwell, Dodge, Electro Craft)
- Commercial aviation electronics systems
- Semiconductors
- PC modems
- Defense electronics systems
- Aerospace (Rocketdyne reusable Space Shuttle Main Engines, codeveloper of the X-33 and X-34 reusable launcher for satellites and heavy payloads)
- Heavy-duty automotive systems (axles, brakes, clutches, transmissions)
- Light automobile systems (sunroofs, doors, access controls, seat adjustment controls, suspension systems, electric motors, wheels)
- Newspaper printing press systems

Cooper Industries
- Crescent wrenches and Nicholson files
- Champion spark plugs
- Gardner-Denver mining equipment

United Technologies, Inc.
- Pratt & Whitney aircraft engines
- Carrier heating and air-conditioning equipment
- Otis elevators
- Norden defense systems
- Hamilton Standard controls
- Automotive components

Textron, Inc.
- Bell helicopters
- Paul Revere Insurance
- Cessna Aircraft
- E-Z-Go golf carts
- Missile reentry systems
- Textron automotive interior and exterior parts
- Specialty fasteners
- Avco Financial Services
- Jacobsen turf care equipment
- Tanks and armored vehicles,

The Walt Disney Company
- Theme parks
- Movie production (for both children and adults)
- Videos
- Children's apparel
- Toys and stuffed animals
- Television broadcasting (ABC network and The Disney Channel)

American Standard
- Air-conditioning products (Trane, American Standard)
- Plumbing products (American Standard, Ideal Standard, Standard, Porcher)
- Automotive Products (commercial and utility vehicle braking and control systems)

Source: Company annual reports.

to considering only opportunities in related industries). Specifically, cash flows from company businesses with lower growth and profit prospects can be diverted to acquiring and expanding businesses with higher growth and profit potentials.

3. Company profitability may prove somewhat more stable because hard times in one industry may be partially offset by good times in another—ideally, cyclical downswings in some of the company's businesses are counterbalanced by cyclical upswings in other businesses the company has diversified into.

4. To the extent that corporate-level managers are exceptionally astute at spotting bargain-priced companies with big upside profit potential, shareholder wealth can be enhanced.

While entry into an unrelated business can often pass the attractiveness and the cost-of-entry tests (and sometimes even the better-off test), a strategy of unrelated diversification has drawbacks. One Achilles' heel of conglomerate diversification is the big demand it places on corporate-level management to make sound decisions regarding fundamentally different businesses operating in fundamentally different industry and competitive environments. The greater the number of businesses a company is in and the more diverse they are, the harder it is for corporate-level executives to oversee each subsidiary and spot problems early, to have real expertise in evaluating the attractiveness of each business's industry and competitive environment, and to judge the caliber of strategic actions and plans proposed by business-level managers. As one president of a diversified firm expressed it:

> *The two biggest drawbacks to unrelated diversification are the difficulties of competently managing many different businesses and being without the added source of competitive advantage that strategic fit provides.*

> . . . we've got to make sure that our core businesses are properly managed for solid, long-term earnings. We can't just sit back and watch the numbers. We've got to know what the real issues are out there in the profit centers. Otherwise, we're not even in a position to check out our managers on the big decisions.[11]

With broad diversification, corporate managers have to be shrewd and talented enough to (1) tell a good acquisition from a bad acquisition, (2) select capable managers to run each of many different businesses, (3) discern when the major strategic proposals of business-unit managers are sound, and (4) know what to do if a business unit stumbles.[12] Because every business tends to encounter rough sledding, a good way to gauge the risk of diversifying into new unrelated areas is to ask, "If the new business got into trouble, would we know how to bail it out?" When the answer is no, unrelated diversification can pose significant financial risk and the business's profit prospects are more chancy.[13] As the former chairman of a *Fortune* 500 company advised, "Never acquire a business you don't know how to run." It takes only one or two big strategic mistakes (misjudging industry attractiveness, encountering unexpected problems in a newly acquired business, or being too optimistic about how hard it will be to turn a struggling subsidiary around) to cause corporate earnings to plunge and crash the parent company's stock price.

Second, without the competitive advantage potential of strategic fit, consolidated performance of an unrelated multibusiness portfolio tends to be no better than the sum of what the individual business units could achieve if they were independent, and it may be worse to the extent that corporate managers meddle unwisely in business-unit operations or hamstring them with corporate policies. Except, perhaps, for the added financial backing that a cash-rich corporate parent can provide, a strategy of unrelated diversification does nothing for the competitive strength of the individual business units. Each business is on its own in trying to build a competitive edge—the unrelated nature of sister businesses offers no common ground for cost reduction, skills transfer, or technology sharing. In a widely diversified firm, the value added by corporate managers depends primarily on how good they are at deciding what new businesses to add, which ones to get rid of, how best to deploy available financial resources to build

---

[11]Carter F. Bales, "Strategic Control: The President's Paradox," *Business Horizons* 20, no. 4 (August 1977), p. 17.

[12]For a review of the experiences of companies that have pursued unrelated diversification successfully, see Patricia L. Anslinger and Thomas E. Copeland, "Growth through Acquisitions: A Fresh Look," *Harvard Business Review* 74, no. 1 (January–February 1996), pp. 126–35.

[13]Of course, management may be willing to assume the risk that trouble will not strike before it has had time to learn the business well enough to bail it out of almost any difficulty. But there is research that shows this is very risky from a financial perspective; see, for example, Lubatkin and Chatterjee, "Extending Modern Portfolio Theory into the Domain of Corporate Diversification: Does It Apply?" pp. 132–33.

a higher-performing collection of businesses, and the quality of the guidance they give to the managers of their business subsidiaries.

Third, although in theory unrelated diversification offers the potential for greater sales-profit stability over the course of the business cycle, in practice attempts at countercyclical diversification fall short of the mark. Few attractive businesses have opposite up-and-down cycles; the great majority of businesses are similarly affected by economic good times and hard times. There's no convincing evidence that the consolidated profits of broadly diversified firms are more stable or less subject to reversal in periods of recession and economic stress than the profits of less diversified firms.

Despite these drawbacks, unrelated diversification can sometimes be a desirable corporate strategy. It certainly merits consideration when a firm needs to diversify away from an endangered or unattractive industry and has no distinctive competencies or capabilities it can transfer to an adjacent industry. There's also a rationale for pure diversification to the extent owners have a strong preference for investing in several unrelated businesses instead of a family of related ones. Otherwise, the argument for unrelated diversification hinges on the case-by-case prospects for financial gain.

A key issue in unrelated diversification is how wide a net to cast in building the business portfolio. In other words, should a company invest in few or many unrelated businesses? How much business diversity can corporate executives successfully manage? A reasonable way to resolve the issue of how much diversification is to ask "What is the least diversification it will take to achieve acceptable growth and profitability?" and "What is the most diversification that can be managed given the complexity it adds?"[14] The optimal amount of diversification usually lies between these two extremes.

Unrelated Diversification and Shareholder Value

Unrelated diversification is fundamentally a finance-driven approach to creating shareholder value whereas related diversification is fundamentally strategy-driven.

Unrelated diversification is a financial approach to creating shareholder value; related diversification, in contrast, represents a strategic approach.

Related diversification represents a strategic approach to building shareholder value because it is predicated on exploiting the linkages between the value chains of different businesses to lower costs, transfer skills and technological expertise across businesses, and gain other strategic-fit benefits. The objective is to convert the strategic fits among the firm's businesses into an extra measure of competitive advantage that goes beyond what business subsidiaries are able to achieve on their own. The added competitive advantage a firm achieves through related diversification is the driver for building greater shareholder value.

In contrast, *unrelated diversification is principally a financial approach to creating shareholder value* because it is predicated on astute deployment of corporate financial resources and executive skill in spotting financially attractive business opportunities. Since unrelated diversification produces no strategic-fit opportunities of consequence, corporate strategists can't build shareholder value by acquiring companies that create or compound competitive advantage for its business subsidiaries—in a conglomerate, competitive advantage doesn't go beyond what each business subsidiary can achieve independently through its own competitive strategy. Consequently, for unrelated diversification to result in enhanced shareholder

---

[14]Drucker, *Management: Tasks, Responsibilities, Practices,* pp. 692–93.

value (above the 2 + 2 = 4 effect that the subsidiary businesses could produce operating independently), corporate strategists must exhibit *superior skills* in creating and managing a portfolio of diversified business interests. This specifically means:

- Doing a superior job of diversifying into new businesses that can produce consistently good returns on investment (satisfying the attractiveness test).
- Doing a superior job of negotiating favorable acquisition prices (satisfying the cost-of-entry test).
- Being shrewd enough to sell previously acquired business subsidiaries at their peak and getting premium prices (this requires skills in discerning when a business subsidiary is on the verge of confronting adverse industry and competitive conditions and probable declines in long-term profitability).
- Wisely and aggressively shifting corporate financial resources out of businesses where profit opportunities are dim and into businesses where rapid earnings growth and high returns on investment are occurring.
- Doing such a good job overseeing the firm's business subsidiaries and contributing to how they are managed (by providing expert problem-solving skills, creative strategy suggestions, and decision-making guidance to business-level managers) that the businesses perform at a higher level than they would otherwise be able to do (a possible way to satisfy the better-off test).

For corporate strategists to build shareholder value in some way other than through strategic fits and competitive advantage, they must be smart enough to produce financial results from a group of businesses that exceed what business-level managers can produce.

To the extent that corporate executives are able to craft and execute a strategy of unrelated diversification that produces enough of the above outcomes for an enterprise to consistently outperform other firms in generating dividends and capital gains for stockholders, then a case can be made that shareholder value has truly been enhanced. Achieving such results consistently requires supertalented corporate executives, however. Without them, unrelated diversification is a very dubious and unreliable way to try to build shareholder value—there are far more who have tried and failed than who have tried and succeeded.

DIVESTITURE AND LIQUIDATION STRATEGIES

Even a shrewd corporate diversification strategy can result in the acquisition of business units that, down the road, just do not work out. Misfits cannot be completely avoided because it is difficult to foresee how getting into a new line of business will actually work out. In addition, long-term industry attractiveness changes with the times; what was once a good diversification move into an attractive industry may later turn sour. Subpar performance by some business units is bound to occur, thereby raising questions of whether to keep them or divest them. Other business units, despite adequate financial performance, may not mesh as well with the rest of the firm as was originally thought.

A business needs to be considered for divestiture when corporate strategists conclude it no longer fits or is an attractive investment.

Sometimes, a diversification move that seems sensible from a strategic-fit standpoint turns out to lack *cultural fit*.[15] Several pharmaceutical companies had just this experience. When they diversified into cosmetics and perfume, they discov-

---

[15]Ibid., p. 709.

ered their personnel had little respect for the "frivolous" nature of such products compared to the far nobler task of developing miracle drugs to cure the ill. The absence of shared values and cultural compatibility between the medical research and chemical-compounding expertise of the pharmaceutical companies and the fashion-marketing orientation of the cosmetics business was the undoing of what otherwise was diversification into businesses with technology-sharing potential, product-development fit, and some overlap in distribution channels.

When a particular line of business loses its appeal, the most attractive solution usually is to sell it. Normally such businesses should be divested as fast as is practical. To drag things out serves no purpose unless time is needed to get it into better shape to sell. The more business units in a diversified firm's portfolio, the more likely that it will have occasion to divest poor performers, "dogs," and misfits. A useful guide to determine if and when to divest a business subsidiary is to ask the question, "If we were not in this business today, would we want to get into it now?"[16] When the answer is no or probably not, divestiture should be considered.

Divestiture can take either of two forms. The parent can spin off a business as a financially and managerially independent company in which the parent company may or may not retain partial ownership. Or the parent may sell the unit outright, in which case a buyer needs to be found. As a rule, divestiture should not be approached from the angle of "Who can we pawn this business off on and what is the most we can get for it?"[17] Instead, it is wiser to ask "For what sort of organization would this business be a good fit, and under what conditions would it be viewed as a good deal?" Organizations for which the business is a good fit are likely to pay the highest price.

Of all the strategic alternatives, liquidation is the most unpleasant and painful, especially for a single-business enterprise where it means the organization ceases to exist. For a multi-industry, multibusiness firm to liquidate one of its lines of business is less traumatic. The hardships of job eliminations, plant closings, and so on, while not to be minimized, still leave an ongoing organization, perhaps one that is healthier after its pruning. In hopeless situations, an early liquidation effort usually serves owner-stockholder interests better than an inevitable bankruptcy. Prolonging the pursuit of a lost cause exhausts an organization's resources and leaves less to liquidate; it can also mar reputations and ruin management careers. The problem, of course, is differentiating between when a turnaround is achievable and when it isn't. It is easy for managers to let their emotions and pride overcome sound judgment when a business gets in such deep trouble that a successful turnaround is remote.

CORPORATE TURNAROUND, RETRENCHMENT, AND PORTFOLIO RESTRUCTURING STRATEGIES

Turnaround, retrenchment, and portfolio restructuring strategies come into play when a diversified company's management has to restore an ailing business portfolio to good health. Poor performance can be caused by large losses in one or more business units that pull the corporation's overall financial performance down, a disproportion-

---

[16]Ibid., p. 94.
[17]Ibid., p. 719.

ate number of businesses in unattractive industries, a bad economy adversely impacting many of the firm's business units, an excessive debt burden, or ill-chosen acquisitions that haven't lived up to expectations.

Corporate turnaround strategies focus on efforts to restore a diversified company's money-losing businesses to profitability instead of divesting them. The intent is to get the whole company back in the black by curing the problems of those businesses that are most responsible for pulling overall performance down. Turnaround strategies are most appropriate when the reasons for poor performance are short-term, the ailing businesses are in attractive industries, and divesting the money losers does not make long-term strategic sense.

Corporate retrenchment strategies involve reducing the scope of diversification to a smaller number of businesses. Retrenchment is usually undertaken when corporate management concludes that the company is in too many businesses and needs to narrow its business base. Sometimes diversified firms retrench because they can't make certain businesses profitable after several frustrating years of trying or because they lack funds to support the investment needs of all of their business subsidiaries. More commonly, however, corporate executives conclude that the firm's diversification efforts have ranged too far afield and that the key to improved long-term performance lies in concentrating on building strong positions in a smaller number of businesses. Retrenchment is usually accomplished by divesting businesses that are too small to make a sizable contribution to earnings or that have little or no strategic fit with the businesses that management wants to concentrate on. Divesting such businesses frees resources that can be used to reduce debt, to support expansion of the remaining businesses, or to make acquisitions that strengthen the company's competitive position in one or more of the remaining businesses.

Portfolio restructuring strategies involve radical surgery on the mix and percentage makeup of the types of businesses in the portfolio. For instance, one company over a two-year period divested 4 business units, closed down the operations of 4 others, and added 25 new lines of business to its portfolio, 16 through acquisition and 9 through internal start-up. Other companies have elected to demerge their businesses and split into two or more independent companies—AT&T, for instance, has divided into three companies (one for long distance and other telecommunications services that will retain the AT&T name, one for manufacturing telephone equipment callent Lucent Technologies, and one for computer systems, called NCR, that essentially represents the divestiture of AT&T's earlier acquisition of NCR). Restructuring can be prompted by any of several conditions:

1. When a strategy review reveals that the firm's long-term performance prospects have become unattractive because the portfolio contains too many slow-growth, declining, or competitively weak business units.

2. When one or more of the firm's principal businesses fall prey to hard times.

3. When a new CEO takes over and decides to redirect where the company is headed.

4. When "wave of the future" technologies or products emerge and a major shakeup of the portfolio is needed to build a position in a potentially big new industry.

5. When the firm has a unique opportunity to make an acquisition so big that it has to sell several existing business units to finance the new acquisition.

6. When major businesses in the portfolio have become more and more unattractive, forcing a shakeup in the portfolio in order to produce satisfactory long-term corporate performance.

7. When changes in markets and technologies of certain businesses proceed in such different directions that it is better to split the company into separate pieces rather than remain together under the same corporate umbrella.

Portfolio restructuring involves revamping a diversified company's business makeup through a series of divestitures and new acquisitions.

Candidates for divestiture typically include not only weak or up-and-down performers or those in unattractive industries, but also those that no longer fit (even though they may be profitable and in attractive-enough industries).

Many broadly diversified companies, disenchanted with the performance of some acquisitions and having only mixed success in overseeing so many unrelated business units, restructure to enable concentration on a smaller core of at least partially related businesses. Business units incompatible with newly established related diversification criteria are divested, the remaining units regrouped and aligned to capture more strategic fit benefits, and new acquisitions made to strengthen the parent company's position in the industries it has chosen to emphasize.[18]

Most recently, portfolio restructuring has centered on demerging—splitting a broadly diversified company into several independent companies. Notable examples of companies pursuing demerger include ITT, Westinghouse, and Britian's Imperial Chemical and Hanson, plc. Before beginning to divest and demerge in 1995, Hanson owned companies with more than $20 billion in revenues in businesses as diverse as beer, exercise equipment, tools, construction cranes, tobacco, cement, chemicals, coal mining, electricity, hot tubs and whirlpools, cookware, rock and gravel, bricks, and asphalt; understandably, investors and analysts had a hard time understanding the company and its strategies. By early 1997, Hanson had demerged into a $3.8 billion enterprise focused more narrowly on gravel, crushed rock, cement, asphalt, bricks, and construction cranes; the remaining businesses were divided into four groups and divested. Another example of portfolio restructuring is presented in Illustration Capsule 26 (see p. 226).

The strategies of broadly diversified companies to demerge and deconglomerate have been driven by a growing preference among company executives and investors for building diversification around the creation of strong competitive positions in a few, well-selected industries. Indeed, investor disenchantment with the conglomerate approach to diversification has been so pronounced (evident in the fact that conglomerates often have *lower* price-earnings ratios than companies with related diversification strategies) that some broadly diversified companies have restructured their portfolios and retrenched to escape being regarded as a conglomerate.

MULTINATIONAL DIVERSIFICATION STRATEGIES

The distinguishing characteristics of a multinational diversification strategy are a *diversity of businesses* and a *diversity of national markets*.[19] Not only do the managers of a diversified multinational corporation (DMNC) have to conceive and execute

---

[18]Evidence that corporate restructuring and pruning down to a narrower business base produces improved corporate performance is contained in Constantinos C. Markides, "Diversification, Restructuring and Economic Performance," *Strategic Management Journal* 16 (February 1995), pp. 101–18.

[19]C. K. Prahalad and Yves L. Doz, *The Multinational Mission* (New York: Free Press, 1987), p. 2.

a substantial number of strategies—at least one for each industry, with as many multinational variations as conditions in each country market dictate—but they also have the added challenge of conceiving good ways to coordinate the firm's strategic actions across industries and countries. This effort can do more than just bring the full force of corporate resources and capabilities to the task of building a strong competitive position in each business and national market. *Capitalizing on opportunities for strategic coordination across businesses and countries provides an avenue for sustainable competitive advantage not open to a company that competes in only one country or one business.*[20]

The Emergence of Multinational Diversification

Until the 1960s, multinational companies (MNCs) operated fairly autonomous subsidiaries in each host country, each catering to the special requirements of its own national market.[21] Management tasks at company headquarters primarily involved finance functions, technology transfer, and export coordination. Even though their products and competitive strategies were tailored to market conditions in each country, a multinational company could still realize competitive advantage by learning to transfer technology, manufacturing know-how, brand-name identification, and marketing and management skills from country to country quite efficiently, giving them an edge over smaller host country competitors. Standardized administrative procedures helped minimize overhead costs, and once an initial organization for managing foreign subsidiaries was put in place, entry into additional national markets could be accomplished at low incremental costs.

During the 1970s, however, buyer preferences for some products converged enough that it became feasible to market common product versions across different country markets. No longer was it essential or even desirable to have strategies and products custom-tailored to customer preferences and competitive conditions prevailing in specific country markets. Moreover, as Japanese, European, and U.S. companies pursued international expansion in the wake of trade liberalization and the opening up of market opportunities in both industrialized and less-developed countries, they found themselves in head-to-head competition in country after country.[22] *Global competition*—where the leading companies in an industry competed head to head in most of the world's major country markets—began to emerge.

As the relevant market arena in more and more industries shifted from national to international to global, traditional MNCs were driven to integrate their operations across national borders in a quest for better efficiencies and lower manufacturing costs. Instead of separately manufacturing a complete product range in each country, plants became more specialized in their production operations to gain the economies of longer production runs, to permit use of faster automated equipment, and to capture experience curve effects. Country subsidiaries obtained the rest of the product range they needed from sister plants in other countries. Gains in manufacturing efficiencies from converting to state-of-the-art, world-scale manufacturing plants more than offset increased international shipping costs, especially in light of the other advantages globalized strategies offered. With a global strategy, an MNC could

[20]Ibid., p. 15.

[21]Yves L. Doz, *Strategic Management in Multinational Companies* (New York: Pergamon Press, 1985), p. 1.

[22]Ibid., pp. 2–3.

locate plants in countries with low labor costs—a key consideration in industries whose products have high labor content. With a global strategy, an MNC could also exploit differences in tax rates, setting transfer prices in its integrated operations to produce higher profits in low-tax countries and lower profits in high-tax countries. Global strategic coordination also increased MNC's ability to take advantage of country-to-country differences in interest rates, exchange rates, credit terms, government subsidies, and export guarantees. These advantages made it increasingly difficult for a company that produced and sold its product in only one country to succeed in an industry populated with multinational competitors intent on achieving global dominance.

During the 1980s another source of competitive advantage began to emerge: using the strategic fit advantages of related diversification to build stronger competitive positions in several related global industries simultaneously. Being a diversified MNC (DMNC) became competitively superior to being a single-business MNC in cases where strategic fits existed across globally competitive industries. Related diversification proved most capable of producing competitive advantage when a multinational company's expertise in a core technology could be applied in different industries (at least one of which was global) and where there were important economies of scope and brand name advantages to being in a family of related businesses.[23] Illustration Capsule 27 describes how Honda has exploited gasoline engine technology and its well-known name by diversifying into a variety of products powered by gasoline engines.

A multinational corporation can gain competitive advantage by diversifying into global industries having related technologies or possessing value chain relationships that yield economies of scope.

Sources of Competitive Advantage for a DMNC

A strategy of related diversification into industries where global competition prevails opens several avenues of competitive advantage not available to a domestic-only competitor or a single-business competitor:

1. A diversified multinational company can realize competitive advantage by transferring its expertise in a core technology to other lines of business able to benefit from its technical know-how and capabilities.

2. A diversified multinational company with expertise in a core technology and a family of businesses using this technology can capture competitive advantage through a collaborative and strategically coordinated R&D effort on behalf of all the related businesses as a group.

3. A diversified multinational company with businesses that use the same distributors and retail dealers worldwide can (a) diversify into new businesses using the same worldwide distribution capabilities at relatively little expense and use the distribution-related economies of scope as a source of cost advantage over less diversified rivals, (b) can exploit its worldwide distribution capability by diversifying into businesses having attractive sales growth opportunites in the very country markets where its distribution capability is already established, and (c) can gain added bargaining leverage with retailers in securing attractive shelf space for any new products and businesses as its family of businesses grows in number and sales importance to the retailer. Sony, for example, has attractive competitive advantage potential in diversifying into the videogame industry to take on giants like

---

[23]Pralahad and Doz, *The Multinational Mission*, pp. 62–63.

ILLUSTRATION CAPSULE 27   Honda's Competitive Advantage

Expertise in the Technology of Gasoline Engines

At first blush anyone looking at Honda's lineup of products—cars, motorcycles, lawn mowers, power generators, outboard motors, snowmobiles, snowblowers, and garden tillers—might conclude that Honda has pursued unrelated diversification. But underlying the obvious product diversity is a common core: the technology of gasoline engines.

Honda's strategy involves transferring the company's expertise in gasoline engine technology to additional products, exploiting its capabilities in low-cost/high-quality manufacturing, using the widely known and respected Honda brand name on all the products, and promoting several products in the same ad (one Honda ad teased consumers with the question, "How do you put six Hondas in a two-car garage?" and then showed a garage containing a Honda car, a Honda motorcycle, a Honda snowmobile, a Honda lawnmower, a Honda power generator, and a Honda outboard motor). The relatedness in the value chains for the products in Honda's business lineup produces competitive advantage for Honda in the form of economies of scope, beneficial opportunities to transfer technology and capabilities from one business to another, and economical use of a common brand name.

Honda's Competitive Advantage

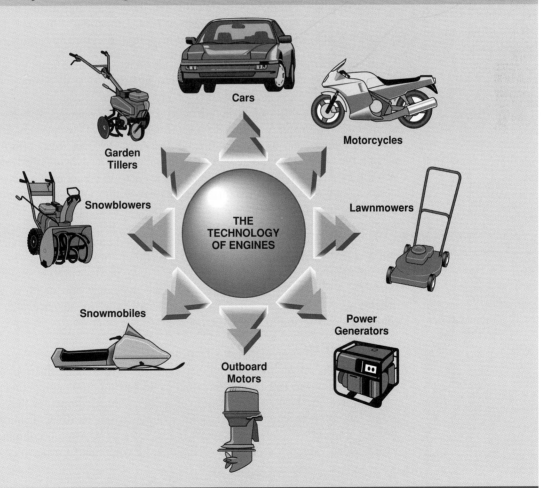

Source: Adapted from C. K. Prahalad and Yves L. Doz, *The Multinational Mission* (New York: Free Press, 1987), p. 62.

Nintendo and SEGA because (a) it has well-established distribution capabilities in consumer electronics worldwide that can be used for videogame game products, (b) it has the capability to go after videogame sales in all country markets where it presently does business, and (c) it has the marketing clout to persuade retailers to give Sony videogame products good visibility in retail stores.

4. A diversified multinational company can leverage its brand name by diversifying into additional businesses able to use its already established brand, thereby capturing economies of scope and marketing benefits. Sony, for example, doesn't have to spend nearly as much advertising and promoting its new videogame products against the offerings of Nintendo and Sega because the Sony brand name already has a strong reputation in consumer electronics worldwide.

5. A diversified multinational company can use the financial and organizational resources it has from operations in other countries to cross-subsidize a competitive assault on the market position of a one-country competitor.

6. A diversified multinational company can draw upon the financial resources in other lines of business to cross-subsidize a competitive offensive against a one-business multinational company or domestic company.

There's a growing evidence that all these advantages are significant enough to result in DMNCs' achieving high returns and having lower overall business risk.[24]

The Competitive Power of a Collaborative R&D Effort and Technology Transfer   By channeling corporate resources directly into a *combined* R&D/technology effort, as opposed to letting each business unit fund and direct its own R&D effort however it sees fit, the DMNC can merge its expertise and efforts *worldwide* to advance the core technology, pursue promising technological avenues to create new businesses, generate technology-based manufacturing economies within and across product/business lines, expedite across-the-board product improvements in existing businesses, and develop new products that complement and enhance the sales of existing products. If, on the other hand, R&D activities are decentralized and put totally under the direction of each existing business unit, R&D/technology investments are more prone to end up narrowly aimed at each business's own product-market opportunities. A splintered R&D effort is unlikely to produce the range and depth of strategic fit benefits as a broad, coordinated companywide effort to advance and exploit the company's full technological expertise.[25]

The Competitive Power of Related Distribution and Common Brand Name Usage   A DMNC that has diversified into global industries with related distribution channels and opportunities to use a common brand name has important competitive advantage potential a single-business competitor or a one-country competitor lacks. Consider, again, the competitive strength that Sony derives from its diversification into such globally competitive consumer goods industries as TVs, stereo equipment, radios, VCRs, video cameras, monitors and multimedia equipment for personal computers,

---

[24]See, for example, W. Chan Kim, Peter Hwang, and Willem P. Burgers, "Multinational's Diversification and the Risk-Return Tradeoff," *Strategic Management Journal* 14 (May 1993) pp. 275–86.
[25]Ibid.

CDs, and videogames—all distributed and marketed through the same types of distributors and retail dealers worldwide and all able to capitalize on use of the Sony brand name. Sony's approach to diversification has allowed it to build worldwide distribution capabilities in consumer electronics products, capture logistical and distribution-related economies of scope, and establish high levels of brand awareness for its products in countries all across the world.[26] A single-business competitor is disadvantaged in competing against Sony because it lacks access to distribution-related economies of scope, it doesn't have Sony's ability to transfer its brand reputation in one line of business to another and achieve advertising economies, and it can't match Sony's clout in bargaining for favorable shelf space in retail stores. A domestic-only compet-itor is at a disadvantage on costs if its national sales volume is too small to achieve the scale economies afforded by Sony's global-sized sales volume. Moreover, Sony's already-established *global* distribution capabilities and *global* brand-name recognition give it an important cost advantage over a one-country competitor looking at the costs of trying to expand into foreign country markets for the first time and better position itself as a global competitor against Sony. Similarly, Sony's econo-mies of scope (both distribution-related and brand name-related) give it a cost advan-tage over a one-business competitor (with no existing economies of scope) that might be looking to diversify into a business that Sony is already in.

A multinational corporation can also gain competitive advantage by diversifying into global industries with related distribution channels and opportunities for common use of a well-known brand.

The Competitive Power of Using Cross-Subsidization to Outcompete a One-Business Com-pany Both a one-business domestic company and a one-business multinational company are weakly positioned to defend their market positions against a DMNC determined to establish a solid long-term competitive position in their market and willing to accept lower short-term profits in order to do so. A one-business domestic company has only one profit sanctuary—its home market. A one-business multinational company may have profit sanctuaries in several country markets but all are in the same business. Each is vulnerable to a DMNC that launches a major strategic offensive in their profit sanctuaries and lowballs its prices and/or spends extravagantly on advertising to win market share at their expense. A DMNC's ability to keep hammering away at competitors with lowball prices year after year may reflect either a cost advantage growing out of its related diversification strategy or a willing-ness to cross-subsidize low profits or even losses with earnings from its profit sanctuaries in other country markets and/or its earnings from other businesses. Sony, for example, by pursuing related diversification keyed to product-distribution-technology strategic fit and managing its product fam-ilies on a global scale, has the ability to put strong competitive pressure on domestic companies like Zenith (which manufactures TVs and small computer sys-tems) and Magnavox (which manufactures TVs, VCRs, stereo equipment, and moni-tors for personal computers). Sony can lowball its prices on TVs or fund special promotions for its TVs, using earnings from its other country markets and lines of business to help support its assault. If Sony chooses, it can keep its prices low or spend lavishly on advertising for several years, persistently pecking away at Zenith's and Magnavox's market shares in TVs over time. At the same time, it can draw upon its considerable resources in R&D, its ability to transfer technology from one product

A well-diversified family of businesses and a multinational market base give a DMNC the power and resource strength to subsidize a long-term market offensive against one-market or one-business competitors with earnings from one or more of its country market profit sanctuaries and/or earnings in other businesses.

---

[26]Ibid., p. 64.

ILLUSTRATION CAPSULE 28   Mitsubishi: The Competitive Power of a Japanese Keiretsu

Mitsubishi is Japan's largest *keiretsu*—a family of affiliated companies. With combined 1995 sales of $184 billion, the Mitsubishi keiretsu consists of 28 core companies: Mitsubishi Corp. (the trading company), Mitsubishi Heavy Industries (the group's biggest manufacturer—shipbuilding, air conditioners, forklifts, robots, gas turbines), Mitsubishi Motors, Mitsubishi Steel, Mitsubishi Aluminum, Mitsubishi Oil, Mitsubishi Petrochemical, Mitsubishi Gas Chemical, Mitsubishi Plastics, Mitsubishi Cable, Mitsubishi Electric, Mitsubishi Construction, Mitsubishi Paper Mills, Mitsubishi Mining and Cement, Mitsubishi Rayon, Nikon, Asahi Glass, Kirin Brewery, Mitsubishi Bank (the world's fifth largest bank and the lead bank for family companies), Tokio Marine and Fire Insurance (one of the world's largest insurance companies), and eight others. Beyond this core group are hundreds of other Mitsubishi-related subsidiaries and affiliates.

The 28 core companies of the Mitsubishi *keiretsu* are bound together by cross-ownership of each other's stock (the percentage of shares of each core company owned by other members ranges from 17 percent to 100 percent, with an average of 27 percent), by interlocking directorships (it is standard for officers of one company to sit on the boards of other *keiretsu* members), joint ventures, and long-term business relationships. They use each other's products and services in many instances—among the suppliers to Mitsubishi Motor's Diamond

Star plant in Bloomington, Illinois, are 25 Mitsubishi and Mitsubishi-related suppliers. It is common for them to join forces to make acquisitions—five Mitsubishi companies teamed to buy a cement plant in California; Mitsubishi Corp. bought an $880 million chemical company in Pittsburgh with financial assistance from Mitsubishi Bank and Mitsubishi Trust, then sold pieces to Mitsubishi Gas Chemical, Mitsubishi Rayon, Mitsubishi Petrochemical, and Mitsubishi Kasei. Mitsubishi Bank and occasionally other Mitsubishi financial enterprises serve as a primary financing source for new ventures and as a financial safety net if *keiretsu* members encounter tough market conditions or have financial problems.

Despite these links, there's no grand Mitsubishi strategy. Each company operates independently, pursuing its own strategy and markets. On occasion, group members find themselves going after the same markets competing with each other. Nor do member companies usually get sweetheart deals from other members; for example, Mitsubishi Heavy Industries lost out to Siemens in competing to supply gas turbines to a new power plant that Mitsubishi Corp.'s wholly owned Diamond Energy subsidiary constructed in Virginia. But operating independence does not prevent them from recognizing their mutual interests, cooperating voluntarily without formal controls, or turning inward to *keiretsu* members for business partnerships on ventures perceived as strategically important.

---

family to another, and its expertise in product innovation to introduce appealing new features and better picture quality. Such competitive actions not only enhance Sony's own brand image but they make it very tough for Zenith and Magnavox to match its prices, advertising, and product development efforts and still earn acceptable profits. Sony can turn its attention to becoming attractively profitable once the battle for market share and competitive position is won.[27] Some additional aspects of the competitive power of broadly diversified enterprises is described in Illustration Capsule 28.

Although cross-subsidization is a potent competitive weapon, it can only be used sparingly because of its adverse impact on overall corporate profitability.

The Combined Effects of These Advantages Is Potent   Companies with a strategy of (1) diversifying into *related* industries and (2) competing *globally* in each of these industries thus can draw upon any of several competitive advantage opportunities to overcome a domestic-only rival or a single business rival. A DMNC's biggest competitive advantage potential comes from concentrating its diversification efforts in industries where there are technology-sharing and technology-transfer opportunities and where there are important economies of scope and brand-name benefits. The more a company's diversification

---

[27]Ibid.

A President's Council, consisting of 49 chairmen and presidents, meets monthly, usually the second Friday of the month. While the formal agenda typically includes a discussion of joint philanthropical and public relations projects and a lecture by an expert on some current topic, participants report instances where strategic problems or opportunities affecting several group members are discussed and major decisions made. It is common for a Mitsubishi company involved in a major undertaking (initiating its first foray into the U.S. or European markets or developing a new technology) to ask for support from other members. In such cases, group members who can take business actions that contribute to solutions are expected to do so. The President's Council meetings also serve to cement personal ties, exchange information, identify mutual interests, and set up follow-on actions by subordinates. Other ways that Mitsubishi uses to foster an active informal network of contacts, information sharing, cooperation, and business relationships among member companies include regular get-togethers of Mitsubishi-America and Mitsubishi-Europe executives and even a matchmaking club where member company employees can meet prospective spouses.

In recent years, Mitsubishi companies introduced a number of consumer products in the United States and elsewhere, all branded with a three-diamond logo de-rived from the crest of the founding samurai family—cars and trucks made by Mitsubishi Motors, big-screen TVs and mobile phones made by Mitsubishi Electric, and air conditioners produced by Mitsubishi Heavy Industries. Mitsubishi executives believe common logo usage has produced added brand awareness; for example, in the United States Mitsubishi Motors' efforts to advertise and market its cars and trucks helped boost brand awareness of Mitsubishi TVs. In several product categories one or more Mitsubishi companies operate in stages all along the industry value chain—from components production to assembly to shipping, warehousing, and distribution.

Similar practices exist in the other five of the six largest Japanese *keiretsu*: Dai-Ichi Kangin with 47 core companies, Mitsui Group with 24 core companies (including Toyota and Toshiba), Sanwa with 44 core companies, Sumitomo with 20 core companies (including NEC, a maker of telecommunications equipment and personal computers), and Fuyo with 29 core companies (including Nissan and Canon). Most observers agree that Japan's keiretsu model gives Japanese companies major competitive advantages in international markets. According to a Japanese economics professor at Osaka University, "Using group power, they can engage in cutthroat competition."

Source: Based on information in "Mighty Mitsubishi Is on the Move" and "Hands across America: The Rise of Mitsubishi," *Business Week*, September 24, 1990, pp. 98–107.

strategy yields these kinds of strategic fit benefits, the more powerful a competitor it becomes and the better its profit and growth performance is likely to be. Relying on strategic fit advantages to outcompete rivals is inherently more attractive than resorting to cross-subsidization.

While a DMNC can employ cross-subsidization tactics to muscle its way into attractive new markets or outcompete a particular rival, its ability to use cross-subsidization is limited by the need to maintain respectable levels of overall profitability. It is one thing to *occasionally* use a *portion* of the profits and cash flows from existing businesses to cover *reasonable* short-term losses to gain entry to a new business or a new country market or wage a competitive offensive against certain rivals. It is quite another thing to *regularly* use cross-subsidization tactics to fund competitive inroads in new areas and *weaken overall company performance* on an *ongoing* basis. A DMNC is under the same pressures as any other company to earn consistently acceptable profits across its whole business portfolio. At some juncture, every business and every market entered needs to make a profit contribution or become a candidate for abandonment. As a general rule, *cross-subsidization is justified only if there is a good prospect that the short-term impairment to corporate profitability will be offset by stronger competitiveness and better overall profitability over the long term.*

COMBINATION RELATED-UNRELATED DIVERSIFICATION STRATEGIES

Nothing prevents a company from diversifying into both related and unrelated businesses. Indeed, in actual practice the business makeup of diversified companies varies considerably. Some diversified companies are really *dominant-business enterprises*—one major "core" business accounts for 50 to 80 percent of total revenues and a collection of small related or unrelated businesses account for the remainder. Some diversified companies are *narrowly diversified* around a few (two to five) *related* or *unrelated* businesses. Some diversified companies are *broadly diversified* and have a wide ranging collection of either *related* businesses or *unrelated* businesses. And a few multibusiness enterprises have diversified into unrelated areas but have a collection of related businesses within each area—thus giving them a business portfolio consisting of *several unrelated groups of related businesses*. Companies have ample room to customize their diversification strategies to suit their own risk preferences and to fit most any strategic vision.

Moreover, the geographic markets of individual businesses within a diversified company can range from local to regional to national to multinational to global. Thus, a diversified company can be competing locally in some businesses, nationally in others, and globally in still others.

KEY POINTS

Most companies have their business roots in a single industry. Even though they may have since diversified into other industries, a substantial part of their revenues and profits still usually comes from the original or "core" business. Diversification becomes an attractive strategy when a company runs out of profitable growth opportunities in its core business (including any opportunities to integrate backward or forward to strengthen its competitive position). The purpose of diversification is to build shareholder value. Diversification builds shareholder value when a diversified group of businesses can perform better under the auspices of a single corporate parent than they would as independent, stand-alone businesses. Whether a particular diversification move is capable of increasing shareholder value hinges on the attractiveness test, the cost-of-entry test, and the better-off test.

There are two fundamental approaches to diversification—into related businesses and into unrelated businesses. The rationale for related diversification is *strategic:* diversify into businesses with strategic fit, capitalize on strategic-fit relationships to gain competitive advantage, then use competitive advantage to achieve the desired 2 + 2 = 5 impact on shareholder value. Businesses have strategic fit when their value chains offer potential (1) for realizing economies of scope or cost-saving efficiencies associated with sharing technology, facilities, distribution outlets, or combining related value chain activities; (2) for efficient transfer of key skills, technological expertise, or managerial know-how, (3) for using a common brand name, and/or (4) for strengthening a firm's resources and competitive capabilities.

The basic premise of unrelated diversification is that any business that has good profit prospects and can be acquired on good financial terms is a good business to diversify into. Unrelated diversification is basically a *financial* approach to diversification; strategic fit is a secondary consideration compared to the expectation of financial gain. Unrelated diversification surrenders the competitive advantage potential of strategic fit in return for such advantages as (1) spreading business risk over a variety of industries and (2) gaining opportunities for quick financial gain (if candidate acquisitions have undervalued assets, are bargain-priced and have good upside potential given the right management, or need the backing of a financially strong parent to capitalize on attractive opportunities). In theory, unrelated diversification also offers greater earnings stability over the business cycle, a third advantage. However, achieving these three outcomes consistently requires corporate executives who are smart enough to avoid the considerable disadvantages of unrelated diversification. The greater the number of businesses a conglomerate company is in and the more diverse these businesses are, the more that corporate executives are stretched to know enough about each business to distinguish a good acquisition from a risky one, select capable managers to run each business, know when the major strategic proposals of business units are sound, or wisely decide what to do when a business unit stumbles. Unless corporate managers are exceptionally shrewd and talented, unrelated diversification is a dubious and unreliable approach to building shareholder value when compared to related diversification.

Once diversification is accomplished, corporate management's task is to manage the firm's business portfolio for maximum long-term performance. Six options for improving a diversified company's performance include: (1) make new acquisitions, (2) divest weak-performing business units or those that no longer fit, (3) restructure the makeup of the portfolio when overall performance is poor and future prospects are bleak, (4) retrench to a narrower diversification base, (5) pursue multinational diversification, and (6) liquidate money-losing businesses with poor turnaround potential.

The most popular option for getting out of a business that is unattractive or doesn't fit is to sell it—ideally to a buyer for whom the business has attractive fit. Sometimes a business can be divested by spinning it off as a financially and managerially independent enterprise in which the parent company may or may not retain an ownership interest.

Corporate turnaround, retrenchment, and restructuring strategies are used when corporate management has to restore an ailing business portfolio to good health. Poor performance can be caused by large losses in one or more businesses that pull overall corporate performance down, by too many business units in unattractive industries, by an excessive debt burden, or by ill-chosen acquisitions that haven't lived up to expectations. Corporate turnaround strategies aim at restoring money-losing businesses to profitability instead of divesting them. Retrenchment involves reducing the scope of diversification to a smaller number of businesses by divesting those that are too small to make a sizable contribution to corporate earnings or those that don't fit with the narrower business base on which corporate management wants to concentrate company resources and energies. Restructuring strategies involve radical portfolio shakeups, divestiture of some businesses and acquisition of others to create a group of businesses with much improved performance potential.

Multinational diversification strategies feature a diversity of businesses and a diversity of national markets. Despite the complexity of having to devise and manage so many strategies (at least one for each industry, with as many variations for country markets as may be needed), multinational diversification can be a competitively advantageous strategy. DMNCs can use the strategic-fit advantages of related diversification (economies of scope, technology and skills transfer, and shared brand names) to build competitively strong positions in several related global industries simultaneously. Such advantages, if competently exploited, can allow a DMNC to outcompete a one-business domestic rival or a one-business multinational rival over time. A one-business domestic company has only one profit sanctuary—its home market. A single-business multinational company may have profit sanctuaries in several countries, but all are in the same business. Both are vulnerable to a DMNC that launches offensive campaigns in their profit sanctuaries. A DMNC can use a lower-cost advantage growing out of its economies of scope to underprice rivals and gain market share at their expense. Even without a cost advantage, the DMNC can decide to underprice such rivals and subsidize its lower profit margins (or even losses) with the profits earned in its other businesses. A well-financed and competently managed DMNC can sap the financial and competitive strength of one-business domestic-only and multinational rivals. A DMNC gains the biggest competitive advantage potential by diversifying into *related* industries where it can capture significant economies of scope, share technology and expertise, and leverage use of a well-known brand name.

SUGGESTED READINGS

Barney, Jay B. *Gaining and Sustaining Competitive Advantage*. Reading, Mass.: Addison-Wesley, 1997, chaps. 11 and 13.

Campbell, Andrew, Michael Goold, and Marcus Alexander. "Corporate Strategy: The Quest for Parenting Advantage." *Harvard Business Review* 73, no. 2 (March–April 1995), pp. 120–32.

———. "The Value of the Parent Company." *California Management Review* 38, no. 1 (Fall 1995), pp. 79–97.

Goold, Michael, and Kathleen Luchs. "Why Diversify? Four Decades of Management Thinking." *Academy of Management Executive* 7, no. 3 (August 1993), pp. 7–25.

Hoffman, Richard C. "Strategies for Corporate Turnarounds: What Do We Know about Them?" *Journal of General Management* 14, no. 3 (Spring 1989), pp. 46–66.

Liedtka, Jeanne M. "Collaboration across Lines of Business for Competitive Advantage." *Academy of Management Executive* 10, no.2 (May 1996), pp. 20–34.

Prahalad, C. K., and Yves L. Doz. *The Multinational Mission*. New York: Free Press, 1987, chaps. 1 and 2.

EVALUATING THE STRATEGIES OF DIVERSIFIED COMPANIES

8

O nce a company diversifies and has operations in a number of different industries, three issues dominate the agenda of the company's top strategy makers:

- How attractive is the group of businesses the company is in?
- Assuming the company sticks with its present lineup of businesses, how good is its performance outlook in the years ahead?
- If the previous two answers are not satisfactory: (*a*) should the company divest itself of low-performing or unattractive businesses, (*b*) what actions should the company take to strengthen the growth and profit potential of the businesses it intends to remain in, and (*c*) should the company move into additional businesses to boost its long-term performance prospects?

Crafting and implementing action plans to improve the overall attractiveness and competitive strength of a company's business lineup is the central strategic task of corporate-level managers.

Strategic analysis of diversified companies builds on the concepts and methods used for single-business companies. But there are also new aspects to consider and additional analytical approaches to master. The procedure for critiquing a diversified company's strategy, evaluating the attractiveness of the industries it diversified into, assessing the competitive strength and performance potential of its businesses, and deciding on what strategic actions to take next involves the following steps:

> If we can know where we are and something about how we got there, we might see where we are trending—and if the outcomes which lie naturally in our course are unacceptable, to make timely change.
>
> **Abraham Lincoln**
>
> The corporate strategies of most companies have dissipated instead of created shareholder value.
>
> **Michael Porter**
>
> Achieving superior performance through diversification is largely based on relatedness.
>
> **Philippe Very**

1. *Identifying the present corporate strategy*—whether the company is pursuing related or unrelated diversification (or a mixture of both), the nature and purpose of any recent acquisitions and divestitures, and the kind of diversified company that corporate management is trying to create.

2. *Applying the industry attractiveness test*—evaluating the long-term attractiveness of each industry the company is in.

3. *Applying the competitive strength test*—evaluating the competitive strength of the company's business units to see which ones are strong contenders in their respective industries.

4. *Applying the strategic fit test*—determining the competitive advantage potential of any value chain relationships and strategic fits among existing business units.

5. *Applying the resource fit test*—determining whether the firm's resource strengths match the resource requirements of its present business lineup.

6. *Ranking the businesses from highest to lowest on the basis of both historical performance and future prospects.*

7. *Ranking the business units in terms of priority for resource allocation* and deciding whether the strategic posture for each business unit should be aggressive expansion, fortify and defend, overhaul and reposition, or harvest/divest. (The task of initiating *specific* business-unit strategies to improve the business unit's competitive position is usually delegated to business-level managers, with corporate-level managers offering suggestions and having authority for final approval.)

8. *Crafting new strategic moves to improve overall corporate performance*—changing the makeup of the portfolio via acquisitions and divestitures, improving coordination among the activities of related business units to achieve greater cost-sharing and skills-transfer benefits, and steering corporate resources into the areas of greatest opportunity.

The rest of this chapter describes this eight-step process and introduces analytical techniques needed to arrive at sound corporate strategy appraisals.

IDENTIFYING THE PRESENT CORPORATE STRATEGY

Analysis of a diversified company's situation and prospects needs to begin with an understanding of its present strategy and business makeup. Recall from Figure 2–2 in Chapter 2 that one can get a good handle on a diversified company's corporate strategy by looking at:

Evaluating a diversified firm's business portfolio needs to begin with a clear identification of the firm's diversification strategy.

- The extent to which the firm is diversified (as measured by the proportion of total sales and operating profits contributed by each business unit and by whether the diversification base is broad or narrow).

- Whether the firm is pursuing related or unrelated diversification, or a mixture of both.

- Whether the scope of company operations is mostly domestic, increasingly multinational, or global.

- Any moves to add new businesses to the portfolio and build positions in new industries.

- Any moves to divest weak or unattractive business units.

- Recent moves to boost performance of key business units and/or strengthen existing business positions.

- Management efforts to capture strategic-fit benefits and use value-chain relationships among its businesses to create competitive advantage.

- The percentage of total capital expenditures allocated to each business unit in prior years (a strong indicator of the company's resource allocation priorities).

Getting a clear fix on the current corporate strategy and its rationale sets the stage for probing the strengths and weaknesses in its business portfolio and drawing conclusions about whatever refinements or major alterations in strategy are appropriate.

EVALUATING INDUSTRY ATTRACTIVENESS: THREE TESTS

A principal consideration in evaluating a diversified company's business makeup and the caliber of its strategy is the attractiveness of the industries it has diversified into. The more attractive these industries, the better the company's long-term profit prospects. Industry attractiveness needs to be evaluated from three angles:

The more attractive the industries that a company has diversified into, the better its performance prospects.

1. *The attractiveness of each industry represented in the business portfolio.* Management must examine each industry the firm has diversified into to determine whether it represents a good business for the company to be in. What are the industry's prospects for long-term growth? Do competitive conditions and emerging market opportunities offer good prospects for long-term profitability? Are the industry's capital, technology, and other resource requirements well-matched to company capabilities?

2. *Each industry's attractiveness relative to the others.* The issue here is "Which industries in the portfolio are the most attractive and which are the least attractive?" Comparing the attractiveness of the industries and ranking them from most attractive to least attractive is a prerequisite for deciding how best to allocate corporate resources.

3. *The attractiveness of all the industries as a group.* The question here is "How appealing is the mix of industries?" A company whose revenues and profits come chiefly from businesses in unattractive industries probably needs to consider restructuring its portfolio.

Evaluating the Attractiveness of Each Industry the Company Has Diversified Into

All the industry attractiveness considerations discussed in Chapter 3 come into play in assessing the long-term appeal of the industries a company has diversified into:

- *Market size and projected growth rate*—big industries are more attractive than small industries, and fast-growing industries tend to be more attractive than slow-growing industries, other things being equal.

- *The intensity of competition*—industries where competitive pressures are relatively weak are more attractive than industries where competitive pressures are strong.

- *Emerging opportunities and threats*—industries with promising opportunities and minimal threats on the near horizon are more attractive than industries with modest opportunities and imposing threats.

- *Seasonal and cyclical factors*—industries where demand is relatively steady year-round and not unduly vulnerable to economic ups and downs are more attractive than industries where there are wide swings in buyer demand within or across years.

- *Capital requirements and other special resource requirements*—industries with low capital requirements (or amounts within the company's reach) are relatively more attractive than industries where investment requirements could strain corporate financial resources. Likewise, industries which do *not* require specialized technology, hard-to-develop competencies, or unique capabilities (unless such requirements match well with a diversifier's own capabilities) are more attractive than industries where the resource requirements outstrip a firm's resources and capabilities.
- *Strategic fits and resource fits with the firm's present businesses*—an industry is more attractive to a particular firm if its value chain and resource requirements match up well with the value chain activities of other industries the company has diversified into and with the company's resource capabilities.
- *Industry profitability*—industries with healthy profit margins and high rates of return on investment are generally more attractive than industries where profits have historically been low or where the business risks are high.
- *Social, political, regulatory, and environmental factors*—industries with significant problems in such areas as consumer health, safety, or environmental pollution or that are subject to intense regulation are less attractive than industries where such problems are no worse than most businesses encounter.
- *Degree of risk and uncertainty*—industries with less uncertainty and business risk are more attractive than industries where the future is uncertain and business failure is common.

How well each industry stacks up on these factors determines how many are able to satisfy the *attractiveness test*. The ideal situation is for all of the industries represented in the company's portfolio to be attractive.

Measuring Each Industry's Attractiveness Relative to the Others

It is not enough, however, that an industry be attractive. Corporate resources need to be allocated to those industries of *greatest* long-term opportunity. Shrewd resource allocation is aided by ranking the industries in the company's business portfolio from most attractive to least attractive—a process that calls for quantitative measures of industry attractiveness.

The first step in developing a quantitative measure of long-term industry attractiveness is to select a set of industry attractiveness measures (such as those listed above). Next, weights are assigned to each attractiveness measure—it is weak methodology to assume that the various measures are equally important. While judgment is obviously involved in deciding how much weight to put on each attractiveness measure, it makes sense to place the highest weights on those important to achieving the company's vision or objective and that match up well with the company's needs and capabilities. The sum of the weights must add up to 1.0. Each industry is then rated on each of the chosen industry attractivenesss measures, using a 1 to 5 or 1 to 10 rating scale (where *a high rating signifies high attractiveness and a low rating signifies low attractiveness or unattractiveness*). Weighted attractiveness ratings are calculated by multiplying the industry's rating on each factor by the factor's weight. For example, a rating score of 8 times a weight of .30 gives a weighted rating of 2.40. The sum of weighted ratings for all the attractiveness factors provides a quantitative measure of the industry's long-term attractiveness. The procedure is shown below:

Industry Attractiveness Factor	Weight	Rating	Weighted Industry Attractiveness Rating
Market size and projected growth	.15	5	0.75
Intensity of competition	.30	8	2.40
Emerging industry opportunities and threats	.05	2	0.10
Resource requirements	.10	6	0.60
Strategic fit with other company businesses	.15	4	0.60
Social, political, regulatory, and environmental factors	.05	7	0.35
Industry profitability	.10	4	0.40
Degree of risk	.10	5	0.50
Sum of the assigned weights	1.00		
Industry Attractiveness Rating			5.70

Once industry attractiveness ratings are calculated for each industry in the corporate portfolio, it is a simple task to rank the industries from most to least attractive.

Calculating industry attractiveness scores presents two difficulties. One is deciding on appropriate weights for the industry attractiveness measures. The other is getting reliable data on which to assign accurate and objective ratings. Without good information, the ratings necessarily become subjective, and their validity hinges on whether management has probed industry conditions sufficiently to make dependable judgments. Generally, a company can come up with the statistical data needed to compare its industries on such factors as market size, growth rate, seasonal and cyclical influences, and industry profitability. The attractiveness measure where judgment weighs most heavily is in comparing the industries on intensity of competition, resource requirements, strategic fits, degree of risk, and social, regulatory, and environmental considerations. It is not always easy to conclude whether competition in one industry is stronger or weaker than in another industry because of the different types of competitive influences and the differences in their relative importance. Nonetheless, industry attractiveness ratings are a reasonably reliable method for ranking a diversified company's industries from most attractive to least attractive—they tell a valuable story about just how and why some of the industries a company has diversified into are more attractive than others.

The Attractiveness of the Mix of Industries as a Whole

For a diversified company to be a strong performer, a substantial portion of its revenues and profits must come from business units judged to be in attractive industries—those with relatively high attractiveness scores. It is particularly important that the company's principal businesses be in industries with a good outlook for growth and above-average profitability. Having a big fraction of the company's revenues and profits come from industries that are growing slowly or have low returns on investment tends to drag overall company performance down. Business units in the least attractive industries are potential candidates for divestiture, unless they are positioned strongly enough to overcome the unattractive aspects of their industry environments or they are a strategically important component of the portfolio.

EVALUATING THE COMPETITIVE STRENGTH OF EACH OF THE COMPANY'S BUSINESS UNITS

The task here is to evaluate whether each business unit in the corporate portfolio is well-positioned in its industry and whether it already is or can become a strong market contender. Appraising each business unit's strength and competitive position in its industry not only reveals its chances for success but also provides a basis for comparing the relative competitive strength of the different business units to determine which ones are strongest and which are weakest. Quantitative measures of each business unit's competitive strength and market position can be calculated using a procedure similar to that for measuring industry attractiveness.[1] Assessing the competitive strength of a diversified company's business subsidiaries should be based on such factors as;

- *Relative market share*—business units with higher *relative* market shares normally have greater competitive strength than those with lower shares. A business unit's *relative market share* is defined as the ratio of its market share to the market share of the largest rival firm in the industry, with market share measured in unit volume, not dollars. For instance, if business A has a 15 percent share of its industry's total volume and A's largest rival has 30 percent, A's relative market share is 0.5. If business B has a market-leading share of 40 percent and its largest rival has 30 percent, B's relative market share is 1.33.[2] Using *relative* market share instead of *actual* or *absolute* market share to measure competitive strength is analytically superior because a 10 percent market share is much stronger if the leader's share is 12 percent than if it is 50 percent; the use of relative market share captures this difference.[3]

- *Ability to compete on cost*—business units that are very cost competitive tend to be more strongly positioned in their industries than business units struggling to achieve cost parity with major rivals.

- *Ability to match industry rivals on quality and/or service*—a company's competitiveness depends in part on being able to satisfy buyer expectations with regard to features, product performance, reliability, service, and other important attributes.

- *Ability to exercise bargaining leverage with key suppliers or customers*—having bargaining leverage is a source of competitive advantage.

---

[1] The procedure also parallels the methodology for doing competitive strength assessments presented in Chapter 4 (see Table 4-4).

[2] Given this definition, only business units that are market share leaders in their respective industries will have relative market shares greater than 1.0. Business units that trail rivals in market share will have ratios below 1.0. The further below 1.0 a business unit's relative market share, the weaker is its competitive strengh and market position relative to the industry's market share leader.

[3] Equally important, relative market share is likely to reflect relative cost based on experience in producing the product and economies of large-scale production. Businesses with large reative market shares may be able to operate at lower unit costs than low-share firms because of technological and efficiency gains that attach to larger production and sales volume. As was discussed in Chapter 3, the phenomenon of lower unit costs can go beyond just the effects of scale economies; as the cumulative volume of production increases, the knowledge gained from the firm's growing production experience can lead to the discovery of additional efficiencies and ways to reduce costs even further. For more details on how the relationship between experience and cumulative production volume results in lower unit costs, see Figure 3–1 in Chapter 3. A sizable experience curve effect in an industry's value chain places a strategic premium on market share: the competitor that gains the largest market share tends to realize important cost advantages which, in turn, can be used to lower prices and gain still additional customers, sales, market share, and profit. Such conditions are an important contributor to the competitive strength that a company has in that business.

- *Technology and innovation capabilities*—business units recognized for their technological leadership and track record in innovation are usually strong competitors in their industry.
- *How well the business unit's competitive assets and competencies match industry key success factors*—the more a business unit's strengths match the industry's key success factors, the stronger its competitive position tends to be.
- *Brand-name recognition and reputation*—a strong brand name is nearly always a valuable competitive asset.
- *Profitability relative to competitors*—business units that consistently earn above-average returns on investment and have bigger profit margins than their rivals usually have stronger competitive positions than those with below-average profitability for their industry.

Other competitive strength indicators include knowledge of customers and markets, production capabilities, skills in supply chain management, marketing skills, ample financial resources, and proven know-how in managing the business. Analysts have a choice between rating each business unit on the same generic factors or rating each business unit's strength on those strength measures most pertinent to its industry. Either approach can be defended, although using strength measures specific to each industry is conceptually stronger because the relevant measures of competitive strength, along with their relative importance, vary from industry to industry.

As was done in evaluating industry attractiveness, weights need to be assigned to each of the strength measures to indicate their relative importance (using different weights for different business units is conceptually stronger when the importance of the strength measures differs significantly from business to business). As before, the sum of the weights must add up to 1.0. Each business unit is then rated on each of the chosen strength measures, using a 1 to 5 or 1 to 10 rating scale (where *a high rating signifies high competitive strength and a low rating signifies low strength*). Weighted strength ratings are calculated by multiplying the business unit's rating on each strength measure by the assigned weight. For example, a strength score of 6 times a weight of .25 gives a weighted strength rating of 1.50. The sum of weighted ratings across all the strength measures provides a quantitative measure of a business unit's overall competitive strength. The procedure is shown below:

Competitive Strength Measure	Weight	Strength Rating	Weighted Strength Rating
Relative market share	.20	5	1.00
Costs relative to competitors	.25	8	2.00
Ability to match or beat rivals on key product attributes	.10	2	0.20
Bargaining leverage with buyers/suppliers	.10	6	0.60
Technology and innovation capabilities	.05	4	0.20
How well resources are matched to industry key success factors	.15	7	1.05
Brand name reputation/image	.05	4	0.20
Profitability relative to competitors	.10	5	0.50
Sum of the assigned weights	1.00		
Competitive Strength Rating			5.75

Business units with relatively high overall competitive strength ratings (above 6.7 on a rating scale of 1 to 10) are strong market contenders in their industries. Businesses with relatively low overall ratings (below 3.3 on a 1 to 10 rating scale) are in competitively weak market positions.[4] Managerial evaluations of which businesses in the portfolio are strong and weak market contenders are a valuable consideration in deciding where to steer resources. *Shareholder interests are generally best served by concentrating corporate resources on businesses that can contend for market leadership in their industries.*

Using a Nine-Cell Matrix to Simultaneously Portray Industry Attractiveness and Competitive Strength

The industry attractiveness and business strength scores can be used to graphically portray the strategic positions of each business a diversified company is in. Long-term industry attractiveness is plotted on the vertical axis and competititive strength on the horizontal axis. A nine-cell grid emerges from dividing the vertical axis into three regions (high, medium, and low attractiveness) and the horizontal axis into three regions (strong, average, and weak competitive strength). High attractiveness is associated with scores of 6.7 or greater on a rating scale of 1 to 10, medium attractiveness is assigned to scores of 3.3 to 6.7, and so on; likewise, strong competitive strength is defined as a strength score greater than 6.7, average strength entails scores of 3.3 to 6.7, and so on—as shown in Figure 8-1. Each business unit in the corporate portfolio is plotted on the resulting nine-cell grid based on its overall attractiveness score and strength score and then shown as a "bubble," with the size of each bubble or circle scaled to what percent of revenues it generates relative to total corporate revenues.

In the attractiveness-strength matrix, each business's location is plotted using quantitative measures of long-term industry attractiveness and business strength/competitive position.

The attractiveness-strength matrix helps assign investment priorities to each of the company's business units. Businesses in the three cells at the upper left, where long-term industry attractiveness and business strength/competitive position are favorable, have top investment priority. The strategic prescription for businesses falling in these three cells is "grow and build," with businesses in the high-strong cell having the highest claim on investment funds. Next in priority come businesses positioned in the three diagonal cells stretching from the lower left to the upper right. These businesses are usually given medium priority. They merit steady reinvestment to maintain and protect their industry positions; however, if such a business has an unusually attractive opportunity, it can win a higher investment priority and be given the go-ahead to employ a more aggressive strategic approach. The strategy prescription for businesses in the three cells in the lower right corner of the matrix is typically harvest or divest (in exceptional cases where good turnaround potential exists, it can be "overhaul and reposition" using some type of turnaround approach).[5]

---

[4]If analysts lack sufficient data to do detailed strength ratings, they can rely on their knowledge of each business unit's competitive situation to classify it as being in a "strong," "average," or "weak" competitive position. If trustworthy, such subjective assessments of business-unit strength can substitute for quantitative measures.

[5]At General Electric, each business actually ended up in one of five types of categories: (1) *high-growth potential* businesses deserving top investment priority, (2) *stable base* businesses deserving steady reinvestment to maintain position, (3) *support* businesses deserving periodic investment funding, (4) *selective pruning or rejuvenation* businesses deserving reduced investment funding, and (5) *venture* businesses deserving heavy R&D investment.

FIGURE 8-1   A Representative Nine-Cell Industry Attractiveness-Competitive Strength Matrix

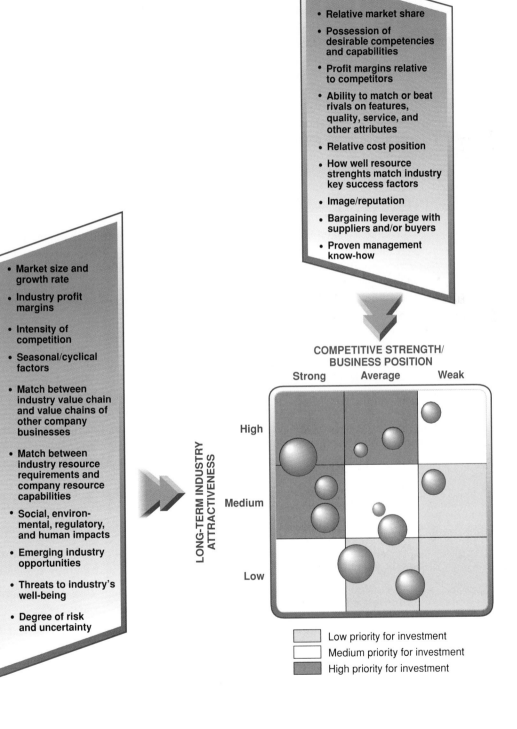

The nine-cell attractiveness-strength grid provides strong logic for concentrating resources in those businesses that enjoy a higher degree of attractiveness and competitive strength, being very selective in making investments in businesses with intermediate positions, and with drawing resources from businesses that are lower in attractiveness and strength unless they offer exceptional turnaround potential. This is why a diversified company needs to consider *both* industry attractiveness and business strength in allocating resources and investment capital to its different businesses.

A company may earn larger profits over the long term by investing in a business with a competitively strong position in a moderately attractive industry than by investing in a weak business in a glamour industry.

More and more diversified companies are concentrating their resources on industries where they can be strong market contenders and divesting businesses that are not good candidates for becoming market leaders. At General Electric, the whole thrust of corporate strategy and corporate resource allocation is to put GE's businesses into a number one or two position in both the United States and globally—see Illustration Capsule 29.

STRATEGIC-FIT ANALYSIS: CHECKING FOR COMPETITIVE ADVANTAGE POTENTIAL

The next analytical step is to determine the competitive advantage potential of any value chain relationships and strategic fits among the company's existing businesses. Fit needs to be looked at from two angles: (1) whether one or more business units have valuable strategic fit with other businesses the firm has diversified into and (2) whether each business unit meshes well with the firm's long-term strategic direction.

When a company's business portfolio includes subsidiaries with related technologies, similar value chain activities, overlapping distribution channels, common customers, or some other competitively valuable relationship, it gains competitive advantage potential not open to a company that diversifies into totally unrelated businesses. The more businesses it has with competitively valuable strategic fits, the greater a diversified company's potential for realizing economies of scope, enhancing the competitive capabilities of particular business units, strengthening the competitiveness of its product and business lineup, and leveraging its resources into a combined performance greater than the units could achieve operating independently.

Consequently, one essential part of evaluating a diversified company's strategy is to check its business portfolio for competitively valuable value chain matchups among the company's existing businesses:

- Which business units have value chain matchups that offer opportunities to combine the performance of related activities and thereby reduce costs?

- Which business units have value chain matchups that offer opportunities to transfer skills or technology from one business to another?

- Which business units offer opportunities to use a common brand name? to gain greater leverage with distributors/dealers in winning more favorable shelf space for the company's products?

- Which business units have value chain matchups that offer opportunities to create valuable new competitive capabilities or to leverage existing resources?

ILLUSTRATION CAPSULE 29   General Electric's Approach to Managing Diversification

When Jack Welch became CEO of General Electric in 1981, he launched a corporate strategy effort to reshape the company's diversified business portfolio. Early on he issued a challenge to GE's business-unit managers to become number one or number two in their industry; failing that, the business units either had to capture a decided technological advantage translatable into a competitive edge or face possible divestiture.

By 1990, GE was a different company. Under Welch's prodding, GE divested operations worth $9 billion—TV operations, small appliances, a mining business, and computer chips. It spent a total of $24 billion acquiring new businesses, most notably RCA, Roper (a maker of major appliances whose biggest customer was Sears), and Kidder Peabody (a Wall Street investment banking firm). Internally, many of the company's smaller business operations were put under the direction of larger "strategic business units." But, most significantly, in 1989, 12 of GE's 14 strategic business units were market leaders in the United States and globally (the company's financial services and communications units served markets too fragmented to rank).

During the 1990s, having divested most of the weak businesses and having built existing businesses into leading contenders, Welch launched initiatives to dramatically boost productivity and reduce the size of GE's bureaucracy. Welch argued that for GE to continue to be successful in a global marketplace, the company had to press hard for continuous cost reduction in each of its businesses, cut through bureaucratic procedures to shorten response times to changing market conditions, and dramatically improve its profit margins. In 1997, GE had the highest market capitalization of any company in the world.

GE Strategic Business Units	Market Standing in the United States	Market Standing in the World
Aircraft engines	First	First
Broadcasting (NBC)	First	Not applicable
Circuit breakers	Tied for first with two others	Tied for first with three others
Defense electronics	Second	Second
Electric motors	First	First
Engineering plastics	First	First
Factory automation	Second	Third
Industrial and power systems	First	First
Lighting	First	Second
Locomotives	First	Tied for first
Major home apliances	First	Tied for second
Medical diagnostic imaging	First	First

Source: Developed from information in Stratford P. Sherman, "Inside the Mind of Jack Welch," *Fortune*, March 27, 1989, pp. 39–50.

Figure 8-2 illustrates the process of identifying the value chains of each of the businesses, then searching for competitively valuable value chain matchups. Without a number of such matchups, one has to be skeptical about the potential for the company's businesses to perform better together than apart and whether its diversification approach is truly capable of enhancing shareholder value.

A second aspect of strategic fit that bears checking out is whether any businesses in the portfolio do not fit in well with the company's overall long-term direction and strategic vision. Sometimes a business, despite having certain value chain matchups, doesn't mesh well with the strategic markets or customer groups or product categories that corporate mangement is concentrating on—in other words, it doesn't fit strategically into the company's overall business picture. In such instances, the business probably needs to be considered for divestiture even though it may be making a positive contribution to company profits and cash flows. Businesses with no real

FIGURE 8-2   Comparing Value Chains to Identify Strategic Fits Among a Diversified Company's Business Units

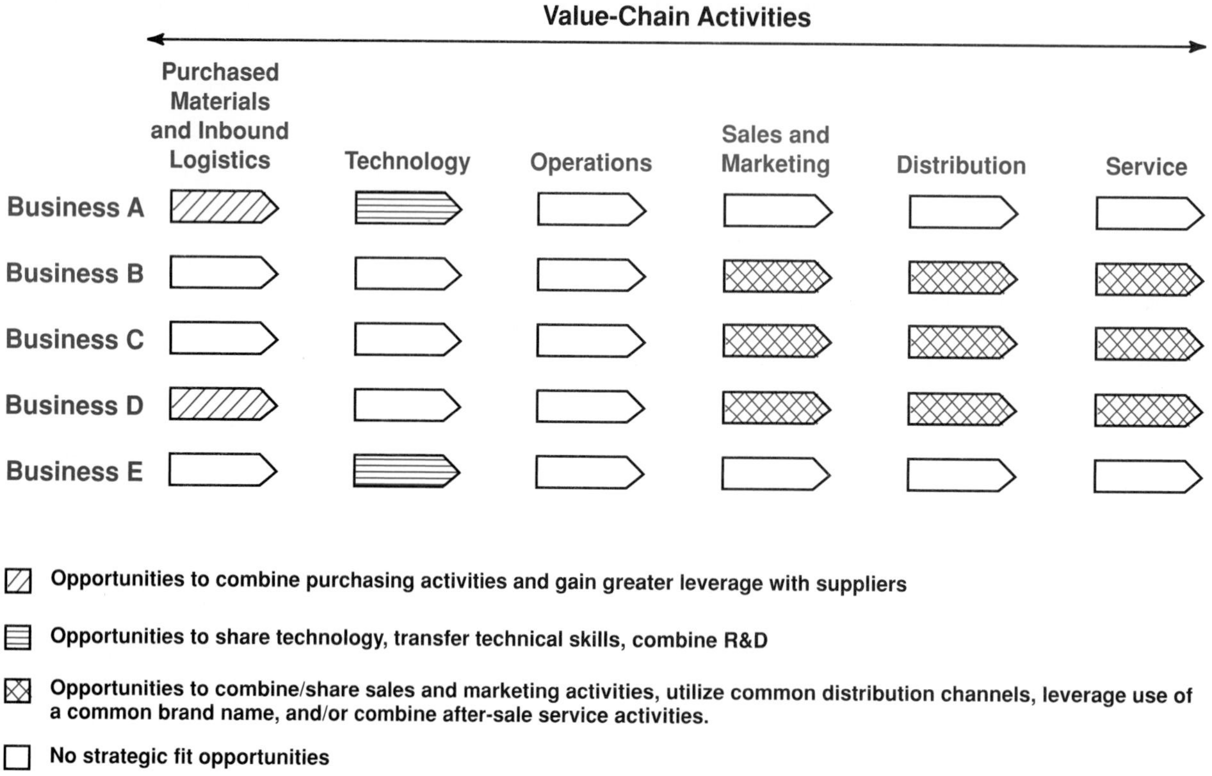

Value-Chain Activities

	Purchased Materials and Inbound Logistics	Technology	Operations	Sales and Marketing	Distribution	Service
Business A	▨	▤	▭	▭	▭	▭
Business B	▭	▭	▭	▨	▨	▨
Business C	▭	▭	▭	▨	▨	▨
Business D	▨	▭	▭	▨	▨	▨
Business E	▭	▤	▭	▭	▭	▭

▨ **Opportunities to combine purchasing activities and gain greater leverage with suppliers**

▤ **Opportunities to share technology, transfer technical skills, combine R&D**

▨ **Opportunities to combine/share sales and marketing activities, utilize common distribution channels, leverage use of a common brand name, and/or combine after-sale service activities.**

▭ **No strategic fit opportunities**

strategic value often end up being treated like an unwanted stepchild and are a distraction to top management. The only reasons to retain such businesses are if they are unusually good financial performers or offer superior growth opportunities—that is to say, if they are valuable *financially* even though they are not valuable strategically.

RESOURCE FIT ANALYSIS: DETERMINING HOW WELL THE FIRM'S RESOURCES MATCH BUSINESS UNIT REQUIREMENTS

The businesses in a diversified company's lineup need to exhibit good *resource fit* as well as good strategic fit. Resource fit exists when (1) businesses add to a company's resource strengths, either financially or strategically and (2) a company has the resources to adequately support the resource requirements of its businesses as a group without spreading itself too thinly. One important dimension of resource fit concerns whether the company's business lineup is well-matched to its financial resources.

Checking Financial Resource Fit: Cash Hog and Cash Cow Businesses

Different businesses have different cash flow and investment characteristics. For example, business units in rapidly growing industries are often "cash hogs"—so labeled because their annual cash flows aren't big enough to cover their annual capital requirements. To keep pace with rising demand, rapid-growth businesses frequently are looking at sizable annual capital investments for some years to come—for new facilities and equipment, for new product development or technology improvements, and for additional working capital to support inventory expansion and a larger base of operations. A business in a fast-growing industry becomes an even bigger cash hog when it has a relatively low market share and is pursuing a strategy to outgrow the market and gain enough market share to become an industry leader. When a rapid-growth business cannot generate a big enough cash flow from operations to finance its capital requirements internally, the needed financial resources must be provided by the corporate parent. Corporate management has to decide whether it is strategically and financially worthwhile to fund the perhaps considerable investment requirements of a cash hog business.

> *A "cash hog" business is one whose internal cash flows are inadequate to fully fund its needs for working capital and new capital investment.*

Business units with leadership positions in slow-growing industries with modest capital requirements may, however, be "cash cows," in the sense that they generate substantial cash surpluses over what is needed for capital reinvestment and other initiatives to sustain their leadership position. It is not unusual for businesses that are market leaders in industries where capital requirements are modest to generate sizable positive cash flows *over and above what is needed for reinvestment in operations*. Cash cow businesses, though often less attractive from a growth standpoint, are valuable businesses from a financial resources perspectives. The surplus cash flows they generate can be used to pay corporate dividends, finance acquisitions, and provide funds for investing in the company's promising cash hog businesses. It makes good financial and strategic sense for diversified companies to keep cash cow businesses in healthy condition, fortifying and defending their market position to preserve their cash-generating capability over the long term and thereby maintain an ongoing source of positive cash flows to redeploy elsewhere.

> *A "cash cow" business is a valuable part of a diversified company's business portfolio because it generates cash for financing new acquisitions, funding the capital requirements of cash hog businesses, and paying dividends.*

Viewing a diversified group of businesses as a collection of cash flows and cash requirements (present and future) is a major step forward in understanding the financial aspects of corporate strategy. Assessing the cash requirements of different businesses in a company's portfolio and determining which are cash hogs and which are cash cows highlights opportunities for shifting corporate financial resources between business subsidiaries to optimize the performance of the whole corporate portfolio, explains why priorities for corporate resource allocation can differ from business to business, and provides good rationalizations for both invest-and-expand strategies and divestiture. For instance, a diversified company can use the excess cash generated by cash cow business units to fund the investment requirements of *promising* cash hog businesses, eventually growing the hogs into self-supporting "stars" having strong competitive positions in attractive, high-growth markets.[6] Star businesses are the cash cows of the future—when the markets of star businesses begin to mature and their growth slows, their competitive strength should produce self-

---

[6]A star business, as the name implies, is one with a leading market share, a widely respected reputation, a solid track record of profitability, and excellent future growth and profit opportunities. Star businesses vary as to their cash hog status. Some can cover their investment needs with self-generated cash flows; others require capital infusions from their corporate parents to stay abreast of rapid industry growth. Normally, strongly positioned star businesses in industries where growth is beginning to slow tend to be self-sustaining in terms of cash flow and make little claim on the corporate parent's treasury. Young stars, however, may require substantial investment capital *beyond what they can generate on their own* and still be cash hogs.

generated cash flows more than sufficient to cover their investment needs. The "success sequence" is thus cash hog to young star (but perhaps still a cash hog) to self-supporting star to cash cow.

On the other hand, if a cash hog business has questionable promise (either because of low industry attractiveness or a weak competitive position), then it becomes a logical candidate for divestiture. Pursuing an aggressive invest-and-expand strategy for a competitively weak cash hog business seldom makes sense if the company has other attractive opportunities and if it will strain the corporate parent's financial resources to keep pumping more capital into the business to keep abreast of fast-paced market growth *and* to build an attractively strong competitive position. Such businesses are a financial drain and lack good financial resource fit. Divesting a less attractive cash hog business is usually the best alternative *unless* (1) it has valuable strategic fits with other business units or (2) the capital infusions needed from the corporate parent are modest relative to the funds available and there's a decent chance of growing the business into a solid bottom-line contributor.

Aside from cash flow considerations, a business has good financial fit when it contributes to the achievement of corporate performance objectives (profit growth, above-average return on investment, recognition as an industry leader, and so on) and when it enhances shareholder value. A business exhibits poor financial fit if it soaks up a disproportionate share of the company's financial resources, if it is a subpar or inconsistent bottom-line contributor, if it is unduly risky and failure would jeopardize the entire enterprise, or if it is too small to make a material earnings contribution even though it performs well. In addition, a diversified company's business portfolio lacks financial fit if its financial resources are stretched thinly across too many businesses. Severe financial strain can occur if a company borrows so heavily to finance new acquisitions that it has to trim way back on new capital expenditures for existing businesses and use the big majority of its financial resources to meet interest obligations and to pay down debt. Some diversified companies have found themselves in such an overextended or overleveraged financial situation that they have had to sell off some businesses to raise the money to meet existing debt obligations and fund essential capital expenditures for the remaining businesses.

> *Business subsidiaries that don't exhibit good strategic fit and good resource fit should be considered for divestiture unless their financial performance is outstanding.*

Checking Competitive and Managerial Resource Fits

A diversified company's strategy must aim at producing a good fit between its resource capability and the competitive and managerial requirements of its businesses.[7] Diversification is most likely to result in added shareholder value when the company has or can develop the competitive and managerial capabilities to be successful in each of the businesses/industries it has diversified into. The absence of good resource fit with one or more business units is serious enough to make such businesses prime divestiture candidates. Likewise, when a company's resources and capabilities are well suited to competing in new industries, it makes sense to take a hard look at acquiring companies in these industries and expanding the company's business lineup.

---

[7]For an excellent discussion of how to assess these fits, see Andrew Campbell, Michael Goold, and Marcus Alexander, "Corporate Strategy: The Quest for Parenting Advantage," *Harvard Business Review* 73, no. 2 (March–April 1995), pp. 120–32.

Checking a diversified company's business portfolio for competitive and managerial resource fits involves the following:

- Determining whether the company's resource strengths (skills, technological expertise, competitive capabilities) are well matched to the key success factors of the businesses it has diversified into.

- Determining whether the company has adequate managerial depth and expertise to cope with the assortment of managerial and operating problems posed by its present lineup of businesses (plus those it may be contemplating getting into).

- Determining whether competitive capabilities in one or more businesses can be transferred them to other businesses (capabilities that are often good candidates for transfer include short development times in bringing new products to market, strong partnerships with key suppliers, an R&D organization capable of generating technological and product opportunites in several different industry arenas simultaneously, a high degree of organizational agility in responding to shifting market conditions and emerging opportunities, or state-of-the-art systems for doing business via the Internet).

- Determining whether the company needs to invest in upgrading its resources or capabilities to stay ahead of (or at least abreast of) the efforts of rivals to upgrade their resource base. In a world of fast-paced change and competition, managers have to be alert to the need to continually invest in and upgrade the company's resources, however potent its current resources are. All resources depreciate in value as competitors mimic them or retaliate with a different (and perhaps more attractive) resource combination.[8] Upgrading resources and competencies often means going beyond just strengthening what the company already is capable of doing— it may involve adding new resource capabilities (like the ability to manage a group of diverse international manufacturing plants or developing technological expertise in related or complementary disciplines or a state-of-the-art-company intranet or an innovative Web page that draws many visits and gives all of its business units greater market exposure), building competencies that allow the company to enter another attractive industry, or widening the company's range of capabilities to match certain competitively valuable capabilities of rivals.

The complement of resources and capabilities at a firm's command determine its competitive strengths. The more a company's diversification strategy is tied to leveraging its resources and capabilities in new businesses, the more it has to develop a big enough and deep enough resource pool to supply these businesses with enough capability to create competitive advantage. Otherwise its strengths end up being stretched too thinly across too many businesses and the opportunity for competitive advantage lost.

Some Notes of Caution   Many diversification strategies built around transferring resource capabilities to new businesses never live up to their promise because the transfer process is not as easy as it might seem. Developing a resource capability in

---

[8]David J. Collis and Cynthia A. Montgomery, "Competing on Resources: Strategy in the 90s," *Harvard Business Review* 73, no. 4 (July–August 1995), p. 124.

one business nearly always involves much trial and error and much organizational learning, and is usually the product of close collaboration of many people working together over a period of time. The first step in transferring a resource capability developed in this manner to another business involves moving people with much of the know-how to the new business. Then these people not only have to learn the ins and outs of the new business well enough to see how best to integrate the capability into the operation of the receiving business but they also have to be adept in implanting all the needed organizational learning from the donor business. As a practical matter, transferring a resource capability in one business to another business can't be done without the receiving business undergoing significant organizational learning and team-building on its own to get up to speed in executing the transferred capability. It takes time, money, and patience for the transferred capability to be implanted and made fully operational. Sometimes unforeseen problems occur, resulting in debilitating delays or prohibitive expenses or inability on the part of the receiving business to execute the capability proficiently. As a consequence, the new business never performs up to expectations.

A second reason for the failure of a diversification move into a new business with seemingly good resource fit is that the causes of a firm's success in one business are sometimes quite entangled and the means of re-creating them hard to replicate.[9] It is easy to be overly optimistic about the ease with which a company that has hit a home run in one business can enter a new business with similar resource requirements and hit a second home run. Noted British retailer Marks & Spencer, despite its impressive resource capabilities (ability to choose excellent store locations, having a supplier chain that gives it both low costs and high merchandise quality, loyal employees, an excellent reputation with consumers, and strong management expertise) that have made it one of Britain's premier retailers for 100 years, has failed repeatedly in its efforts to diversify into department store retailing in the United States.

Diversifying into businesses with seemingly good resource fit is, by itself, not sufficient to produce success.

A third reason for diversification failure, despite apparent resource fit, is misjudging the difficulty of overcoming the resource strengths and capabilities of the rivals it will have to face in a new business. For example, Philip Morris, even though it had built powerful consumer marketing capabilities in its cigarette and beer businesses, floundered in soft drinks and ended up divesting its acquisition of 7UP after several frustrating years because of difficulties in competing against strongly entrenched and resource-capable rivals like Coca-Cola and PepsiCo.

RANKING THE BUSINESS UNITS ON THE BASIS OF PAST PERFORMANCE AND FUTURE PROSPECTS

Once a diversified company's businesses have been rated on the basis of industry attractiveness, competitive strength, strategic fit, and resource fit, the next step is to evaluate which businesses have the best performance prospects and which the worst. The most important considerations are sales growth, profit growth, contribution to company earnings, and the return on capital invested in the business (more and more companies are evaluating business performance on the basis of economic value added—the return on invested capital over and above the firm's cost of capital). Sometimes, cash flow generation is a big consideration, especially for cash cow businesses and businesses with potential for harvesting.

---

[9]Collis and Montgomery, "Competing on Resources: Strategy in the 90s," pp.121–22.

Information on each business's past performance can be gleaned from financial records.[10] While past performance is not necessarily a good predictor of future performance, it does signal which businesses have been strong performers and which have been weak performers. The industry attractiveness–competitive strength evaluations should provide a solid basis for judging future prospects. Normally, strong business units in attractive industries have better prospects than weak businesses in unattractive industries.

The growth and profit outlooks for a diversified company's principal or core businesses generally determine whether its portfolio as a whole is capable of strong, mediocre, or weak performance. Noncore businesses with subpar track records and long-term prospects are logical candidates for divestiture. Business subsidiaries with the brightest profit and growth prospects generally should head the list for corporate resource support.

DECIDING ON RESOURCE ALLOCATION PRIORITIES AND A GENERAL STRATEGIC DIRECTION FOR EACH BUSINESS UNIT

Using the information and results of the preceding evaluation steps, corporate strategists can decide what the priorities should be for allocating resources to the various business units and settle on a general strategic direction for each business unit. The task here is to draw some conclusions about which business units should have top priority for corporate resource support and new capital investment and which should carry the lowest priority. In doing the ranking, special attention needs to be given to whether and how *corporate* resources and capabilities can be used to enhance the competitiveness of particular business units.[11] Opportunities for capabilities/technology transfer or for combining activities to reduce costs or for infusions of new financial capital become especially important when a diversified firm has business units in less than desirable competitive positions, when improvement in some key success area could make a big difference to a particular business unit's performance, and when a cash hog business needs financial support to grow into a star performer.

Improving a diversified company's long-term financial performance entails concentrating company resources on businesses with good to excellent prospects and allocating only minimal resources to businesses with subpar prospects.

Ranking the businesses from highest to lowest priority process should also clarify management thinking about what the basic strategic approach for each business unit should be—*invest-and-grow* (aggressive expansion), *fortify-and-defend* (protect current position by strengthening and adding resource capabilities in needed areas), *overhaul-and-reposition* (make major competitive strategy changes to move the business into a different and ultimately stronger industry position), or *harvest-divest*. In deciding whether to divest a business unit, corporate managers should rely on a number of evaluating criteria: industry attractiveness, competitive strength, strategic fit with other businesses, resource fit, performance potential (profit, return on capital employed, economic value added, contribution to cash flow), compatibility with the

---

[10]Financial performance by line of business is typically contained in a company's annual report, usually in the notes to corporate financial statements. Line of business performance can also be found in a publicly owned firm's 10-K report filed annually with the Securities and Exchange Commission.

[11]Collis and Montgomery, "Competing on Resources: Strategy in the 90s," pp.126–28; Hofer and Schendel, *Strategy Formulation: Analytical Concepts*, p. 80; and Michael E. Porter, *Competitive Advantage* (New York: Free Press, 1985), chapter 9.

companies strategic vision and long-term direction, and ability to contribute to enhanced shareholder value.

To get ever-higher levels of performance out of a diversified company's business portfolio, corporate managers have to do an effective job of steering resources out of low-opportunity areas into high-opportunity areas. Divesting marginal businesses is one of the best ways of freeing unproductive assets for redeployment. Surplus funds from cash cow businesses and businesses being harvested also add to the corporate treasury. Options for allocating a diversified company's financial resources include (1) investing in ways to strengthen or expand existing businesses, (2) making acquisitions to establish positions in new industries, (3) funding long-range R&D ventures, (4) paying off existing long-term debt, (5) increasing dividends, and (6) repurchasing the company's stock. The first three are *strategic* actions to add shareholder value; the last three are *financial* moves to enhance shareholder value. Ideally, a company will have enough funds to do what is needed, both strategically and financially. If not, strategic uses of corporate resources should usually take precedence unless there is a compelling reason to strengthen the firm's balance sheet or divert financial resources to pacify shareholders.

CRAFTING A CORPORATE STRATEGY

The preceding analytical steps set the stage for crafting strategic moves to improve a diversified company's overall performance. The basic issue of "what to do" hinges on the conclusions drawn about the strategic and financial attractiveness of the group of businesses the company has diversified into.[12] Key considerations here are:

- Does the company have enough businesses in very attractive industries?
- Is the proportion of mature or declining businesses so great that corporate growth will be sluggish?
- Are the company's businesses overly vulnerable to seasonal or recessionary influences?
- Is the firm burdened with too many businesses in average to weak competitive positions?
- Is there ample strategic fit among the company's different businesses?
- Does the portfolio contain businesses that the company really doesn't need to be in?
- Is there ample resource fit among the company's business units?
- Does the firm have enough cash cows to finance the cash hog businesses with potential to be star performers?
- Can the company's principal or core businesses be counted on to generate dependable profits and/or cash flow?
- Does the makeup of the business portfolio put the company in good position for the future?

Answers to these questions indicate whether corporate strategists should consider divesting certain businesses, making new acquisitions, restructuring the makeup of the portfolio, altering the pattern of corporate resource allocation, or sticking with the existing business lineup and pursuing the opportunities they present.

---

[12]Barry Hedley, "Strategy and the Business Portfolio," *Long Range Planning* 10, no. 1 (February 1977), p. 13; and Hofer and Schendel, *Strategy Formulation*, pp. 82–86.

The Performance Test

A good test of the strategic and financial attractiveness of a diversified firm's business portfolio is whether the company can attain its performance objectives with its current lineup of businesses and resource capabilities. If so, no major corporate strategy changes are indicated. However, if a performance shortfall is probable, corporate strategists can take any of several actions to close the gap:[13]

1. *Alter the strategic plans for some (or all) of the businesses in the portfolio.* This option involves renewed corporate efforts to get better performance out of its present business units. Corporate managers can push business-level managers for strategy changes that yield better business-unit performance and, perhaps, provide higher-than-planned corporate resource support for these efforts. However, pursuing better short-term performance by zealously trimming resource initiatives aimed at bolstering a business's long-term competitive position has dubious value—it merely trades off better long-term performance for better short-term financial performance. In any case there are limits on how much extra near-term performance can be squeezed out.

2. *Add new business units to the corporate portfolio.* Boosting overall performance by making new acquisitions and/or starting new businesses internally raises some new strategy issues. Expanding the corporate portfolio means taking a close look at (*a*) whether to acquire related or unrelated businesses, (*b*) what size acquisition(s) to make, (*c*) how the new unit(s) will fit into the present corporate structure, (*d*) what specific features to look for in an acquisition candidate, and (*e*) whether acquisitions can be financed without shortchanging present business units on their new investment requirements. Nonetheless, adding new businesses is a major strategic option, one frequently used by diversified companies to escape sluggish earnings performance.

3. *Divest weak-performing or money-losing businesses.* The most likely candidates for divestiture are businesses in a weak competitive position, in a relatively unattractive industry, or in an industry that does not "fit." Funds from divestitures can, of course, be used to finance new acquisitions, pay down corporate debt, or fund new strategic thrusts in the remaining businesses.

4. *Form strategic alliances and collaborative partnerships to try to alter conditions responsible for subpar performance potentials.* In some situations, cooperative alliances with domestic or foreign firms, suppliers, customers, or special interest groups may help ameliorate adverse performance prospects.[14] Instituting resource sharing agreements with suppliers, select competitors, or firms with complementary products and collaborating closely on mutually advantageous initiatives are becoming increasingly used avenues for improving the competitiveness and performance potential of a company's businesses. Forming or supporting a political action group may be an

---

[13]Hofer and Schendel, *Strategy Formulation: Analytical Concepts*, pp. 93–100.

[14]For an excellent discussion of the benefits of alliances among competitors in global industries, see Kenichi Ohmae, "The Global Logic of Strategic Alliances," *Harvard Business Review* 67, no. 2 (March–April 1989), pp. 143–54.

effective way of lobbying for solutions to import-export problems, tax disincentives, and onerous regulatory requirements.

5. *Upgrade the company's resource base.* Achieving better performance may well hinge on corporate efforts to develop new resource strengths that will help select business units match the competitively valuable capabilities of their rivals or, better still, allow them to secure competitive advantage. One of the biggest ways that corporate-level managers of diversified companies can contribute to added shareholder value is to lead the development of cutting-edge capabilities and to marshal new kinds of corporate resources for deployment in a number of the company's businesses.

6. *Lower corporate performance objectives.* Adverse market circumstances or declining fortunes in one or more core business units can render companywide performance targets unreachable. So can overly ambitious objective setting. Closing the gap between actual and desired performance may then require downward revision of corporate objectives to bring them more in line with reality. Lowering performance objectives is usually a "last resort" option.

Identifying Additional Diversification Opportunities

One of the major corporate strategy-making concerns in a diversified company is whether to diversify further and, if so, how to identify the "right" kinds of industries and businesses to get into. For firms pursuing unrelated diversification, the issue of where to diversify next is based more on spotting a good financial opportunity and having the financial resources to pursue it than on industry or strategic criteria. Decisions to diversify into additional unrelated businesses are usually based on such considerations as whether the firm has the financial ability to make another acquisition, whether new acquisitions are badly needed to boost overall corporate performance, whether one or more acquisition opportunities have to be acted on before they are purchased by other firms, whether the timing is right for another acquisition (corporate management may have its hands full dealing with the current portfolio of businesses), and whether corporate management believes it possesses the range and depth of expertise to supervise an additional business.

Firms with unrelated diversification strategies hunt for businesses that offer attractive financial returns—regardless of what industry they're in.

Further diversification in firms with related diversification strategies involves identifying attractive industries having good strategic or resource fit with one or more existing businesses.

With a related diversification strategy, however, the search for new industries to diversify into is aimed at identifying other businesses (1) whose value chains have fits with the value chains of one or more businesses in the company's business portfolio and (2) whose resource requirements are well-matched to the firm's corporate resource capabilities.[15] Once strategic-fit and resource-fit opportunities in *attractive* new industries are identified, corporate strategists have to distinguish between opportunities where important competitive advantage potential exists (through cost savings, technology or capabilities transfer, leveraging a well-known brand name, and so on) and those where the strategic-fit and resource-fit benefits are marginally valuable. The size of the competitive advantage potential depends on whether the fits are competitively significant and on the costs and difficulties of merging or coordinating the business unit interrelationships to capture the fits.[16] Often, careful analysis reveals

---

[15]Porter, *Competitive Advantage*, pp. 370–71.
[16]Ibid., pp. 371–72.

that while there are many actual and potential business unit interrelationships and linkages, only a few have enough strategic importance to generate meaningful competitive advantage.

GUIDELINES FOR MANAGING THE PROCESS OF CRAFTING CORPORATE STRATEGY

Although formal analysis and entrepreneurial brainstorming normally undergird the corporate strategy-making process, there is more to where corporate strategy comes from and how it evolves. Rarely is there an all-inclusive grand formulation of the total corporate strategy. Instead, corporate strategy in major enterprises emerges incrementally from the unfolding of many different internal and external events, the result of probing the future, experimenting, gathering more information, sensing problems, building awareness of the various options, spotting new opportunities, developing responses to unexpected crises, communicating consensus as it emerges, and acquiring a feel for all the strategically relevant factors, their importance, and their interrelationships.[17]

Strategic analysis is not something that the executives of diversified companies do all at once. Such big reviews are sometimes scheduled, but research indicates that major strategic decisions emerge gradually rather than from periodic, full-scale analysis followed by prompt decision. Typically, top executives approach major strategic decisions a step at a time, often starting from broad, intuitive conceptions and then embellishing, fine-tuning, and modifying their original thinking as more information is gathered, as formal analysis confirms or modifies their judgments about the situation, and as confidence and consensus build for what strategic moves need to be made. Often attention and resources are concentrated on a few critical strategic thrusts that illuminate and integrate corporate direction, objectives, and strategies.

Strategic analysis in diversified companies is an eight-step process:

KEY POINTS

Step 1: *Get a clear fix on the present strategy.* Determine whether the company's strategic emphasis is on related or unrelated diversification; whether the scope of company operations is mostly domestic or increasingly multinational, what moves have been made recently to add new businesses and build positions in new industries, the rationale underlying recent divestitures, the nature of any efforts to capture strategic fits and create competitive advantage based on economies of scope and/or resource transfer, and the pattern of resource allocation to the various business units. This step sets the stage for thorough evaluation of the need for strategy changes.

Step 2: *Evaluate the long-term attractiveness of each industry the company is in.* Industry attractiveness needs to be evaluated from three angles: the attractiveness of each industry on its own, the attractiveness of each industry relative to the others, and the attractiveness of all the industries as a group. Quantitative measures of industry attractiveness, using the methodology presented, are a reasonably reliable method for ranking a diversified company's industries from most attractive to least attractive—they tell a

---

[17]Ibid., pp. 58 and 196.

valuable story about just how and why some of the industries a company has diversified into are more attractive than others. The two hardest parts of calculating industry attractiveness scores are deciding on appropriate weights for the industry attractiveness measures and knowing enough about each industry to assign accurate and objective ratings.

Step 3: Evaluate the relative competitive positions and business strength of each of the company's business units. Again, quantitative ratings of competitive strength are preferable to subjective judgments. The purpose of rating the competitive strength of each business is to gain clear understanding of which businesses are strong contenders in their industries, which are weak contenders, and the underlying reasons for their strength or weakness. One of the most effective ways to join the conclusions about industry attractiveness with the conclusions about competitive strength is to draw an industry attractiveness/competitive strength matrix displaying the positions of each business on a nine-cell grid.

Step 4: Determine the competitive advantage potential of any value chain relationships and strategic fits among existing business units. A business is more attractive *strategically* when it has value chain relationships with other business units that present opportunities to transfer skills or technology, reduce overall costs, share facilities, or share a common brand name—any of which can represent a significant avenue for producing competitive advantage beyond what any one business can achieve on its own. The more businesses with competitively valuable strategic fits, the greater a diversified company's potential for achieving economies of scope, enhancing the competitive capabilities of particular business units, and/or strengthening the competitiveness of its product and business lineup, thereby leveraging its resources into a combined performance greater than the units could achieve operating independently.

Step 5: Determine whether the firm's resource strengths match the resource requirements of its present business lineup. The businesses in a diversified company's lineup need to exhibit good *resource fit* as well as good strategic fit. Resource fit exists when (1) businesses add to a company's resource strengths, either financially or strategically and (2) a company has the resources to adequately support the resource requirements of its businesses as a group without spreading itself too thinly. One important dimension of resource fit concerns whether the company's business lineup is well-matched to its financial resources. Assessing the cash requirements of different businesses in a diversified company's portfolio and determining which are cash hogs and which are cash cows highlights opportunities for shifting corporate financial resources between business subsidiaries to optimize the performance of the whole corporate portfolio, explains why priorities for corporate resource allocation can differ from business to business, and provides good rationalizations for both invest-and-expand strategies and divestiture.

Step 6: Rank the past performance of different business units from best to worst and rank their future performance prospects from best to worst. The most important considerations in judging business-unit performance are sales growth, profit growth, contribution to company earnings, and the return on capital invested in the business. Sometimes, cash flow generation is a big consideration. Normally, strong business units in attractive industries have significantly better performance prospects than weak businesses or businesses in unattractive industries.

Step 7: *Rank the business units in terms of priority for resource allocation and decide whether the strategic posture for each business unit should be aggressive expansion, fortify and defend, overhaul and reposition, or harvest/ divest.* In doing the ranking, special attention needs to be given to whether and how *corporate* resources and capabilities can be used to enhance the competitiveness of particular business units. Options for allocating a diversified company's financial resources include (1) investing in ways to strengthen or expand existing businesses, (2) making acquisitions to establish positions in new industries, (3) funding long-range R&D ventures, (4) paying off existing long-term debt, (5) increasing dividends, and (6) repurchasing the company's stock. Ideally, a company will have the financial strength to accomplish what is needed strategically and financially; if not, strategic uses of corporate resources should usually take precedence.

Step 8: *Use the preceding analysis to craft a series of moves to improve overall corporate performance.* Typical actions include (1) making acquisitions, starting new businesses from within, and divesting marginal businesses or businesses that no longer match the company's long-term direction and strategy, (2) devising moves to strengthen the long-term competitive positions of the company's businesses, (3) capitalizing on strategic-fit and resource-fit opportunities and turning them into long-term competitive advantage, and (4) steering corporate resources out of low-opportunity areas into high-opportunity areas.

SUGGESTED READINGS

Campbell, Andrew, Michael Goold, and Marcus Alexander. "Corporate Strategy: The Quest for Parenting Advantage." *Harvard Business Review* 73, no. 2 (March–April 1995), pp. 120–32.

Haspeslagh, Phillippe C., and David B. Jamison. *Managing Acquisitions: Creating Value through Corporate Renewal.* New York: Free Press, 1991.

Naugle, David G., and Garret A. Davies. "Strategic-Skill Pools and Competitive Advantage." *Business Horizons* 30, no. 6 (November–December 1987), pp. 35–42.

Porter, Michael E. "From Competitive Advantage to Corporate Strategy." *Harvard Business Review* 65, no. 3 (May–June 1987), pp. 43–59.

9 IMPLEMENTING STRATEGY: BUILDING RESOURCE CAPABILITIES AND STRUCTURING THE ORGANIZATION

We strategize beautifully, we implement pathetically.

An auto-parts firm executive

Strategies are intellectually simple; their execution is not.

Lawrence A. Bossidy
CEO, Allied-Signal

Just being able to conceive bold new strategies is not enough. The general manager must also be able to translate his or her strategic vision into concrete steps that "get things done."

Richard G. Hamermesh

O nce managers have decided on a strategy, the emphasis turns to converting it into actions and good results. Putting a strategy into place and getting the organization to execute it well call for a different set of managerial tasks and skills. While crafting strategy is largely a market-driven entrepreneurial activity, implementing strategy is primarily an operations-driven activity revolving around the management of people and business processes. While successful strategy making depends on business vision, shrewd industry and competitive analysis, and good resource fit, successful strategy implementation depends on doing a good job of leading, working with and through others, allocating resources, building and strengthening competitive capabilities, installing strategy-supportive policies, and matching how the organization performs its core business activities to the requirements for good strategy execution. Implementing strategy is an action-oriented, make-things-happen task that tests a manager's ability to direct organizational change, motivate people, develop core competencies, build valuable organizational capabilities, achieve continuous improvement in business processes, create a strategy-supportive corporate culture, and meet or beat performance targets.

Experienced managers are emphatic in declaring that it is a whole lot easier to develop a sound strategic plan than it is to make it happen. According to one executive, "It's been rather easy for us to decide where we wanted to go. The hard part is to get the organization to act on the new priorities."[1] What makes strategy

---

[1]As quoted in Steven W. Floyd and Bill Wooldridge, "Managing Strategic Consensus: The Foundation of Effective Implementation," *Academy of Management Executive* 6, no. 4 (November 1992), p. 27.

implementation a tougher, more time-consuming management challenge than crafting strategy is the wide array of managerial activities that have to be attended to, the many ways managers can proceed, the demanding people-management skills required, the perseverance it takes to get a variety of initiatives launched and moving, the number of bedeviling issues that must be worked out, the resistance to change that must be overcome, and the difficulties of integrating the efforts of many different work groups into a smoothly functioning whole. *Just because managers announce a new strategy doesn't mean that subordinates will agree with it or cooperate in implementing it.* Some may be skeptical about the merits of the strategy, seeing it as contrary to the organization's best interests, unlikely to succeed, or threatening to their own careers. Moreover, company personnel may interpret the new strategy differently, be uncertain about how their departments will fare, and have different ideas about what internal changes are needed to execute the new strategy. Long-standing attitudes, vested interests, inertia, and ingrained organizational practices don't melt away when managers decide on a new strategy and start to implement it—especially when only a handful of people have been involved in crafting the strategy and the rationale for strategic change has to be sold to enough organization members to root out the status quo. It takes adept managerial leadership to overcome pockets of doubt and disagreement, build consensus for how to proceed, secure commitment and cooperation, and get all the implementation pieces into place and integrated. Depending on how much consensus building and organizational change is involved, the implementation process can take several months to several years.

> *The strategy-implementer's task is to convert the strategic plan into action and get on with what needs to be done to achieve the vision and targeted objectives.*

> *Companies don't implement strategies, people do.*

A FRAMEWORK FOR IMPLEMENTING STRATEGY

Implementing strategy entails converting the organization's strategic plan into action and then into results. Like crafting strategy, it's a job for the whole management team, not a few senior managers. While an organization's chief executive officer and the heads of business divisions, departments, and key operating units are ultimately responsible for seeing that strategy is implemented successfully, the implementation process typically impacts every part of the organizational structure, from the biggest organizational unit to the smallest frontline work group. Every manager has to think through the answer to "What has to be done in my area to implement our part of the strategic plan, and what should I do to get these things accomplished?" In this sense, *all managers become strategy implementers in their areas of authority and responsibility, and all employees are participants.*

> *Every manager has an active role in the process of implementing and executing the firm's strategic plan.*

One of the keys to successful implementation is for management to communicate the case for organizational change so clearly and persuasively that there is determined commitment throughout the ranks to carry out the strategy and meet performance targets. The ideal condition is for managers to arouse enough enthusiasm for the strategy to turn the implementation process into a companywide crusade. Management's handling of strategy implementation is successful when the company achieves the targeted strategic and financial performance and shows good progress in realizing its long-range strategic vision.

Unfortunately, there are no 10-step checklists, no proven paths, and few concrete guidelines for tackling the job—strategy implementation is the least charted, most open-ended part of strategic management. The best evidence on dos and don'ts comes from the reported experiences and "lessons learned" of managers and companies—and the wisdom they yield is inconsistent. What's worked well for some managers has been tried by others and found lacking. The reasons are understandable. Not only are some managers more effective than others in employing this or that recommended approach to organizational change, but each instance of strategy implementation takes place in a different organizational context. Different business practices and competitive circumstances, work environments and cultures, policies, compensation incentives, and mixes of personalities and organizational histories require a customized approach to strategy implementation—one based on individual company situations and circumstances and on the strategy implementer's best judgment and ability to use particular change techniques adeptly.

Implementing strategy is more art than science.

THE PRINCIPAL STRATEGY-IMPLEMENTING TASKS

While managers' approaches should be tailor-made for the situation, certain bases have to be covered no matter what the organization's circumstances; these include

- Building an organization with the competencies, capabilities, and resource strengths to carry out the strategy successfully.
- Developing budgets to steer ample resources into those value chain activities critical to strategic success.
- Establishing strategy-supportive policies and procedures.
- Instituting best practices and pushing for continuous improvement in how value chain activities are performed.
- Installing information, communication, and operating systems that enable company personnel to carry out their strategic roles successfully day in and day out.
- Tying rewards and incentives to the achievement of performance objectives and good strategy execution.
- Creating a strategy-supportive work environment and corporate culture.
- Exerting the internal leadership needed to drive implementation forward and to keep improving on how the strategy is being executed.

These managerial tasks, depicted in Figure 9–1, crop up repeatedly in the strategy implementation process, no matter what the specifics of the situation. One or two of these tasks usually end up being more crucial or time-consuming than others, depending on how radically different the strategy changes are that have to be implemented, the organization's financial condition and competitive capabilities, whether there are important resource weaknesses to correct or new competencies to develop, the extent to which the company is already able to meet the resource requirements for creating sustainable competitive advantage, the strength of ingrained behavior patterns that have to be changed, the personal and organizational relationships in the firm's history, any pressures for quick results and near-term financial improvements, and perhaps other important factors.

In devising an action agenda, *strategy implementers should begin with a probing assessment of what the organization must do differently and better to carry out the strategy successfully*, then consider how to make the necessary internal changes as rapidly as practical. The strategy implementer's actions should center on fitting how the organization performs its value chain activities and conducts its internal business to what it takes for first-rate strategy execution. A series of "fits" are needed. Organiza-

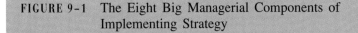

tional capabilities and resources must be carefully matched to the requirements of strategy—especially if the chosen strategy is based on a competence-based or resource-based competitive advantage. Financial resources must be allocated to provide departments with the people and operating budgets needed to execute their strategic roles effectively. The company's reward structure, policies, information systems, and operating practices need to push for strategy execution, rather than playing a merely passive role or, even worse, acting as obstacles. Equally important is the need for managers to do things in a manner and style that create and nurture a strategy-supportive work environment and corporate culture. The stronger such fits, the better the chances for successful strategy implementation. Systematic management efforts to match how the organization goes about its business with the needs of good strategy execution help unite the organization and produce a team effort to meet or beat performance targets. Successful strategy implementers have a knack for diagnosing what their organizations need to do to execute the chosen strategy well, and they are creative in finding ways to perform key value chain activities effectively.

LEADING THE IMPLEMENTATION PROCESS

One make-or-break determinant of successful strategy implementation is how well management leads the process. Managers can employ any of several leadership styles in pushing the implementation process along. They can play an active, visible, take-charge role or a quiet, low-key, behind-the-scenes one. They can make decisions authoritatively or on the basis of consensus; delegate much or little; be personally involved in the details of implementation or stand on the sidelines and coach others; proceed swiftly (launching implementation initiatives on many fronts) or deliberately (remaining content with gradual progress over a long time frame). How managers lead the implementation task tends to be a function of (1) their experience and knowledge about the business; (2) whether they are new to the job or veterans; (3) their network of personal relationships with others in the organization; (4) their own diagnostic, administrative, interpersonal, and problem-solving skills; (5) the authority they've been given; (6) the leadership style they're comfortable with; and (7) their view of the role they need to play to get things done.

Although major initiatives usually have to be led by the CEO and other senior officers, top-level managers still have to rely on the active support and cooperation of middle and lower managers to push strategy changes and see that key activities are performed well on a daily basis. Middle- and lower-level managers not only are responsible for initiating and supervising the implementation process in their areas of authority but they also are instrumental in getting subordinates to continuously improve on how strategy-critical value chain activities are performed and produce the frontline results that allow company performance targets to be met. How successful middle and lower managers are determines how proficiently the company executes its strategy on a daily basis—their role on the company's strategy implementation team is by no means minimal.

It is the job of middle and lower-level managers to push needed implementation actions on the front lines and to see that the strategy is well-executed on a daily basis.

The action agenda of senior-level strategy implementers, especially in big organizations with geographically scattered operating units, mostly involves communicating the case for change to others, building consensus for how to proceed, installing strong allies in positions where they can push implementation along in key organizational units, urging and empowering subordinates to get the process moving, establishing measures of progress and deadlines, recognizing and rewarding those who reach implementation milestones, reallocating resources, and personally presiding over the strategic change process. Thus, the bigger the organization, the more the success of the chief strategy implementer depends on the cooperation and implementing skills of operating managers who can push needed changes at the lowest organizational levels. In small organizations, the chief strategy implementer doesn't have to work through middle managers and can deal directly with frontline managers and employees. They can personally orchestrate the action steps and implementation sequence, observe firsthand how implementation is progressing, and decide how hard and how fast to push the process along. Either way, *the most important leadership trait is a strong, confident sense of "what to do" to achieve the desired results.* Knowing "what to do" comes from a savvy understanding of the business and the organization's circumstances.

The real strategy-implementing skill is being good at figuring out what it will take to execute the strategy proficiently.

In the remainder of this chapter and the next two chapters, we survey the ins and outs of the manager's role as chief strategy implementer. The discussion is framed around the eight managerial components of the strategy-implementation process. This chapter explores the management tasks of building a capable organization. Chapter 10 looks at budget allocations, policies, best practices, internal support systems, and strategically appropriate reward structures. Chapter 11 deals with creating a strategy-supportive corporate culture and exercising strategic leadership.

BUILDING A CAPABLE ORGANIZATION

Proficient strategy execution depends heavily on competent personnel, better-than-adequate competencies and competitive capabilities, and effective organization. Building a capable organization is thus always a top strategy-implementing priority. Three types of organization-building actions are paramount:

- Selecting able people for key positions.
- Making certain that the organization has the skills, core competencies, managerial talents, technical know-how, competitive capabilities, and resource strengths it needs.
- Organizing business processes, value chain activities, and decision making in a manner that is conducive to successful strategy execution.

Selecting People for Key Positions

Assembling a capable management team is one of the first cornerstones of the organization-building task. Strategy implementers must determine the kind of core management team they need to execute the strategy and then find the right people to fill each slot. Sometimes the existing management team is suitable; sometimes it needs to be strengthened or expanded by promoting qualified people from within or by bringing in outsiders whose experience, skills, and leadership styles suit the situation. In turnaround and rapid-growth situations, and in instances when a company doesn't have insiders with the needed experience and management know-how, filling key management slots from the outside is a fairly standard approach.

Putting together a strong management team with the right personal chemistry and mix of skills is one of the first strategy-implementing steps.

Putting together a core executive group starts with deciding what mix of backgrounds, experiences, know-how, values, beliefs, management styles, and personalities are needed to reinforce and contribute to successful strategy execution. As with any kind of team-building exercise, it is important to put together a compatible group of managers who possess the full set of skills to get things done. The personal chemistry needs to be right, and the talent base needs to be appropriate for the chosen strategy. Picking a solid management team is an essential organization-building function—often the first strategy implementation step to take.[2] Until key slots are filled with able people, it is hard for strategy implementation to proceed at full speed.

But a good management team is not enough. The task of staffing the organization with talented people must go much deeper into the organizational ranks. Companies like Electronic Data Systems (EDS), Microsoft, and McKinsey & Co. (one of the world's premier management consulting companies) make a concerted effort to recruit and retain the best and brightest talent they can find—having a cadre of people with strong technical skills is essential to their business. EDS requires college graduates to have at least a 3.5 grade-point average (on a 4.0 scale) just to qualify for an interview; Microsoft seeks out the world's most talented programmers to write code for its programs; McKinsey recruits MBAs only at the top ten business schools. The Big Six accounting firms screen candidates not only on the basis of their accounting expertise but also on whether they possess the people skills to relate well

---

[2]For an analytical framework in top-management team analysis, see Donald C. Hambrick, "The Top Management Team: Key to Strategic Success," *California Management Review* 30, no. 1 (Fall 1987), pp. 88–108.

with clients and colleagues. Southwest Airlines goes to considerable lengths to hire people who can have fun and be fun on the job; Southwest uses specially developed methods, including interviews with customers, to determine whether applicants for customer-contact jobs have outgoing personality traits that match its strategy of creating a high-spirited, fun-loving, in-flight atmosphere for passengers and going all-out to make flying Southwest a pleasant experience. The company is so selective that only about 3 percent of the candidates interviewed are offered jobs.

Building Core Competencies and Competitive Capabilities

<table>
<tr><td>

Strategic Management Principle

Building core competencies, resource strengths, and organizational capabilities that rivals can't match is a sound foundation for sustainable competitive advantage.

</td><td>

Two of the most important organization-building concerns are that of (1) staffing operating units with the specialized talents, skills, and technical expertise needed to give the firm a competitive edge over rivals in performing one or more critical value chain activities and (2) building competitively valuable organizational capabilities. When ease of imitation makes it difficult or impossible to beat rivals on the basis of a superior strategy, the other main avenue to industry leadership is to outexecute them (beat them with superior strategy implementation—more resources, superior talent, stronger or better capabilities, more attention to detail). Superior strategy execution is essential in situations where rival firms have very similar strategies and can readily duplicate one another's strategic maneuvers. Building core competencies, resource strengths, and organizational capabilities that rivals can't

</td></tr>
</table>

match is one of the best ways to outexecute them. This is why one of management's most important strategy-implementing tasks is to build competitively advantageous competencies and organizational capabilities.

Developing and Strengthening Core Competencies   Core competencies can relate to any strategically relevant factor. Honda's core competence is its depth of expertise in gasoline engine technology and small engine design. Intel's is in the design of complex chips for personal computers. Procter & Gamble's core competencies reside in its superb marketing-distribution skills and its R&D capabilities in five core technologies—fats, oils, skin chemistry, surfactants, and emulsifiers.[3] Sony's core competencies are its expertise in electronic technology and its ability to translate that expertise into innovative products (miniaturized radios and video cameras, TVs and VCRs with unique features, attractively designed PCs). Most often, a company's core competencies emerge incrementally as it moves either to bolster skills that contributed to earlier successes or to respond to customer problems, new technological and market opportunities, and the moves of rivals.[4] Wise company managers try to foresee coming changes in customer-market requirements and proactively build new competencies and capabilities that offer a competitive edge.

Four traits concerning core competencies and competitive capabilities are important to a strategy implementer's organization-building task:[5]

- Core competencies rarely consist of narrow skills or the work efforts of a single department. Rather, they are composites of skills and activities

---

[3]James Brian Quinn, *Intelligent Enterprise* (New York: Free Press, 1992), p. 76.
[4]Ibid.
[5]Quinn, *Intelligent Enterprise*, pp. 52–53, 55, 73, and 76.

performed at different locations in the firm's value chain that, when linked, create unique organizational capability.

- Because core competencies typically reside in the combined efforts of different work groups and departments, individual supervisors and department heads can't be expected to see building the overall corporation's core competencies as their responsibility.

- The key to leveraging a company's core competencies into long-term competitive advantage is concentrating more effort and more talent than rivals on deepening and strengthening these competencies.

- Because customers' needs change in often unpredictable ways and the know-how and capabilities needed for competitive success cannot always be accurately forecasted, a company's selected bases of competence need to be broad enough and flexible enough to respond to an unknown future.

The multiskill, multiactivity character of core competencies makes building and strengthening them an exercise in (1) managing human skills, knowledge bases, and intellect and (2) coordinating and networking the efforts of different work groups and departments at every related place in the value chain. It's an exercise best orchestrated by senior managers who appreciate the strategy-implementing significance of creating valuable competencies/capabilities and who have the clout to enforce the necessary cooperation among individuals, groups, departments, and external allies. Moreover, organization builders have to concentrate enough resources and management attention on core competence-related activities to achieve the *dominating depth* needed for competitive advantage.[6] This does not necessarily mean spending more money on competence-related activities than present or potential competitors. It does mean consciously focusing more talent on them and making appropriate internal and external benchmarking comparisons to move toward best-in-industry, if not best-in-world, status. To achieve dominance on lean financial resources, companies like Cray in large computers, Lotus in software, and Honda in small engines leveraged the expertise of their talent pool by frequently re-forming high-intensity teams and reusing key people on special projects.[7] In leveraging internal knowledge and skills rather than physical assets or market position, it is superior selection, training, powerful cultural influences, cooperative networking, motivation, empowerment, attractive incentives, organizational flexibility, short deadlines, and good databases—not big operating budgets—that are the usual keys to success.[8] One of Microsoft's keys to success in computer software is hiring the very brightest and most talented programmers it can find and motivating them with both good monetary incentives and the challenge of working on cutting-edge software design projects (although Microsoft also assigns small armies of these programmers to work on projects with high-priority or short deadlines).

Core competencies don't come into being or reach strategic fruition without conscious management attention.

Strategy implementers can't afford to become complacent once core competencies are in place and functioning. It's a constant organization-building challenge to broaden, deepen, or modify them in response to ongoing customer-market changes. But it's a task worth pursuing. Core competencies that are

[6]Ibid., p. 73.

[7]Ibid.

[8]Ibid., pp. 73–74.

finely honed and kept current with shifting circumstances can provide a big executional advantage. Distinctive core competencies and organizational capabilities are not easily duplicated by rival firms; thus any competitive advantage that results from them is likely to be durable. Dedicated management attention to the task of building strategically relevant internal skills and capabilities is always one of the keys to effective strategy implementation.

Developing and Strengthening Organizational Capabilities   Whereas the essence of astute strategy-making is *selecting* the competencies and capabilities to underpin the strategy, the essence of good strategy implementation is *building and strengthening* the competencies and capabilities to execute the chosen strategy proficiently. Sometimes a company already has the needed competencies and capabilities in place, in which case the strategy implementation task only involves efforts to strengthen and nurture them so as to promote better execution. Sometimes, however, management has be be proactive in developing *new* competencies and capabilities to complement the company's existing resource base and promote more proficient strategy execution. It is useful here to think of companies as a bundle of evolving competencies and capabilities, with the challenge being one of developing new capabilities and strengthening existing ones to achieve competitive advantage through superior strategy execution.

Organization-building that succeeds in developing valuable new competitive capabilities and strengthening existing ones can enable an enterprise to outcompete rivals on the basis of superior resources.

One issue is whether to develop the desired competencies and capabilities internally or whether it makes more sense to outsource them by partnering with key suppliers or forming strategic alliances. Decisions about whether to outsource or develop in-house capability often turn on the issue of what can be safely delegated to outside suppliers versus what internal capabilities are key to the company's long-term success. Either way, though, implementation actions are called for. Outsourcing involves identifying the most attractive providers and establishing collaborative relationships. Developing the capabilities in-house means hiring new personnel with skills and experience relevant to the desired capability, linking the individual skills/know-how to form organizational capability (a group's capabilities are partly a function of the working relationships among its members), building the desired levels of proficiency through repetition ("practice makes perfect"), and linking all the capability-related value chain activities.[9] Strong linkages with related activities are important. The capability to do something really complex (like design and manufacture a sports utility vehicle or create software that allows secure credit card transactions over the Internet) usually involves a number of skills, technological disciplines, competencies, and capabilities—some performed in-house and some provided by suppliers/allies. An important part of organization building is to think about which skills and activities need to be linked and made mutually reinforcing and then to forge the necessary collaboration and cooperation both internally and with outside resource providers.

Managers create organizational capabilities by integrating the skills and know-how of different people and groups in competitively valuable ways, and continuously tuning and recalibrating the components to match new strategic requirements over time.

All this should reemphasize that capability building is a time-consuming, hard-to-replicate exercise. Capabilities are difficult to purchase (except through outsiders who already have them and will agree to supply them) and difficult to imitate just by

---

[9]Robert H. Hayes, Gary P. Pisano, and David M. Upton, *Strategic Operations: Competing through Capabilities* (New York: Free Press, 1996), pp. 503–07.

watching others (just as one cannot become a good golfer by watching Tiger Woods play golf, a company cannot put a new capability in place by creating a new department and assigning it the task of emulating a capability rivals have). Capability building requires a series of organizational steps:

- First, the organization must develop the *ability* to do something, however imperfectly or inefficiently. This means selecting people with the needed skills and experience, upgrading or expanding individual abilities as needed, and then molding the efforts and work products of individuals into a cooperative group effort to create organizational *ability*.

- Then as experience builds, such that the organization can accomplish the activity consistently well and at an acceptable cost, the ability begins to translate into a *competence* and/or a *capability*.

- Should the organization get so good (by continuing to polish and refine and deepen its skills and know-how) that it is better than rivals at the activity, the capability becomes a *distinctive competence* with potential for competitive advantage.

Building capabilities either internally or in collaboration with others takes time and considerable organizing skill.

Sometimes these steps can be short-circuited by acquiring the desired capability through collaborative efforts with external allies or by buying a company that has the needed capability. Indeed, a pressing need to acquire certain capabilities quickly is one reason to acquire another company—an acquisition aimed at building greater capability can be every bit as competitively valuable as an acquisition aimed at adding the acquired company's products/services to the acquirer's business lineup. Capabilities-motivated acquisitions are essential (1) when an opportunity can disappear faster than a needed capability can be created internally and (2) when industry conditions, technology, or competitors are moving at such a rapid clip that time is of the essence.

Organizational competencies and capabilities emerge from establishing and nurturing collaborative working relationships between individuals and groups in different departments and between a company and its external allies.

The Strategic Role of Employee Training Training and retraining are important parts of the strategy implementation process when a company shifts to a strategy requiring different skills, managerial approaches, and operating methods. Training is also strategically important in organizational efforts to build skills-based competencies. And it is a key activity in businesses where technical know-how is changing so rapidly that a company loses its ability to compete unless its skilled people have cutting-edge knowledge and expertise. Successful strategy implementers see that the training function is adequately funded and that effective training programs are in place. If the chosen strategy calls for new skills, deeper technological capability, or building and using new capabilities, training should be placed near the top of the action agenda because it needs to be done early in the strategy implementation process.

Matching Organization Structure to Strategy

There are few hard-and-fast rules for organizing the work effort in a strategy-supportive fashion. Every firm's organization chart is idiosyncratic, reflecting prior organizational patterns, executive judgments about how best to arrange reporting relationships, the politics of who to give which assignments, and varying internal circumstances. Moreover, every strategy is grounded in its own set of key success factors and value chain activities. So a customized organization structure is appropriate. The following are helpful guidelines in fitting structure to strategy:

- Pinpoint the primary value chain activities, competencies, and competitive capabilities that are important in successfully executing the strategy.
- Determine whether some value chain activities (especially noncritical support activities, but perhaps selected primary activities) can be outsourced more efficiently or effectively than they can be performed internally.
- Determine which of the strategy-critical activities/capabilities require close collaboration with suppliers, forward channel allies (distributors or dealers or franchisees), makers of complementary products, or even competitors.
- Make those primary value chain activities and capabilities to be performed/developed internally and strategy-critical organizational units the main building blocks in the organization structure.
- Determine the degrees of authority needed to manage each organizational unit, striking a balance between centralizing decision making under the coordinating authority of a single manager and pushing decision making down to the lowest organizational level capable of making timely, informed, competent decisions.
- If all facets of an internal strategy-critical activity/capability cannot be placed under the authority of a single manager, establish ways to bridge departmental lines and achieve the necessary coordination.
- Determine how the relationships with outsiders are to be managed and assign responsibility for building the necessary organizational bridges.

Pinpointing Strategy-Critical Activities and Competitive Capabilities   In any business, some activities in the value chain are always more critical to success than others. From a strategy perspective, a certain portion of an organization's work involves routine administrative housekeeping (doing the payroll, administering employee benefit programs, handling grievances, providing corporate security, maintaining fleet vehicles). Others are support functions (data processing, accounting, training, public relations, market research, purchasing). Among the primary value chain activities are certain crucial business processes that have to be performed either exceedingly well or in closely coordinated fashion for the organization to develop the capabilities needed for strategic success. For instance, hotel/motel enterprises have to be good at fast check-in/check-out, room maintenance, food service, and creating a pleasant ambiance. A manufacturer of chocolate bars must be skilled in purchasing quality cocoa beans at low prices, efficient production (a fraction of a cent in cost savings per bar can mean seven-figure improvement in the bottom line), merchandising, and promotional activities. In discount stock brokerage, the strategy-critical activities are fast access to information, accurate order execution, efficient record-keeping and transactions processing, and good customer service. In specialty chemicals, the critical activities are R&D, product innovation, getting new products onto the market quickly, effective marketing, and expertise in assisting customers. In the electronics industry, where technology is racing along, a company's cycle time in getting new, cutting-edge products to market is the critical organizational capability. Strategy-critical activities and capabilities vary according to the particulars of a firm's strategy, value chain makeup, and competitive requirements.

Two questions help identify what an organization's strategy-critical activities are: "What functions have to be performed extra well or in timely fashion to achieve sustainable competitive advantage?" and "In what value chain activities would malperformance seriously endanger strategic success?"[10] The answers generally point to the crucial activities and organizational capabilities where organization-building efforts must be concentrated.

Reasons to Consider Outsourcing Certain Value Chain Activities   Managers too often spend inordinate amounts of time, psychic energy, and resources wrestling with functional support groups and other internal bureaucracies, diverting attention from the company's strategy-critical activities. One way to detour such distractions is to cut the number of internal staff support activities and, instead, source more of what is needed from outside vendors.

Each supporting activity in a firm's value chain and within its traditional staff groups can be considered a "service."[11] Indeed, most overheads are just services the company chooses to produce internally. However, many such services can typically be purchased from outside vendors. What makes outsourcing attractive is that an outsider, by concentrating specialists and technology in its area of expertise, can frequently perform these services *as well or better and usually more cheaply* than a company that performs the activities only for itself. But there are other reasons to consider outsourcing. From a strategic point of view, outsourcing non-crucial support activities (and maybe selected primary activities in the value chain) can decrease internal bureaucracies, flatten the organization structure, heighten the company's strategic focus, and increase competitive responsiveness.[12] The experiences of companies that obtain many support services from outside vendors indicate that *outsourcing activities not crucial to building those organizational capabilities needed for long-term competitive success allows a company to concentrate its own energies and resources on those value chain activities where it can create unique value, where it can be best in the industry (or, better still, best in the world), and where it needs strategic control to build core competencies, achieve competitive advantage, and manage key customer-supplier-distributor relationships.*

Outsourcing noncritical value chain activities and even select primary activities has many advantages.

Critics contend that extensive outsourcing can hollow out a company, leaving it at the mercy of outside suppliers and barren of the competencies and organizational capabilities needed to be master of its own destiny.[13] However, a number of companies have successfully relied on outside components suppliers, product designers, distribution channels, advertising agencies, and financial services firms to perform significant value chain activities. For years Polaroid Corporation bought its film medium from Eastman Kodak, its electronics from Texas Instruments, and its cameras from Timex and others, while it concentrated on producing its unique self-developing film packets and designing its next generation of cameras and films. Nike concentrates on design, marketing, and distribution to retailers, while outsourcing virtually all production of its shoes and sporting apparel. Many mining companies outsource geological work, assaying, and drilling. Ernest and Julio Gallo Winery outsources 95 percent of its grape production, letting farmers take on the weather and

---

[10]Peter F. Drucker, *Management: Tasks, Responsibilities, Practices* (New York: Harper & Row, 1974), pp. 530, 535.

[11]Quinn, *Intelligent Enterprise*, p. 32.

[12]Ibid., pp. 33 and 89. See, also, James Brian Quinn and Frederick G. Hilmer, "Strategic Outsourcing," *Sloan Management Review* (Summer 1994), pp. 43–55.

[13]Ibid., pp. 39–40.

other grape-growing risks while it concentrates on wine production and the marketing-sales function.[14] The major airlines outsource their in-flight meals even though food quality is important to travelers' perception of overall service quality. Eastman Kodak, Ford, Exxon, Merrill Lynch, and Chevron have outsourced their data-processing activities to computer service firms, believing that outside specialists can perform the needed services at lower costs and equal or better quality. Chrysler has transformed itself from a high-cost producer into a low-cost producer by abandoning internal production of many parts and components and instead outsourcing them from more efficient suppliers; greater reliance on outsourcing has also enabled Chrysler to shorten the time it takes to bring new models to market. *Outsourcing certain value chain activities makes strategic sense whenever outsiders can perform them at lower cost and/or with higher value-added than the buyer company can perform them internally.*[15]

Reasons to Consider Partnering with Others to Gain Competitively Valuable Capabilities
But there is another equally important reason to look outside for help. *Strategic partnerships, alliances, and close collaboration with select suppliers, distributors, the makers of complementary products and services, and even competitors can add to a company's arsenal of capabilities and contribute to better strategy execution.* Partnering with outsiders can result in bringing new technology on-line quicker, in quicker delivery and/or lower inventories of parts and components, in providing better or faster technical assistance to customers, in geographically wider distribution capability, in the development of multiple distribution outlets, in deeper technological know-how, in economical custom manufacture, in more extensive after-sale support services, and so on. By building, continually improving, and then leveraging these kinds of organizational capabilities, a company develops the resource strengths needed for competitive success—it puts in place enhanced ability to do things for its customers that deliver value to customers and that rivals can't quite match.

Microsoft's Bill Gates and Intel's Andrew Grove meet periodically to explore how their organizations can share information, work in parallel, and team together to sustain the "Wintel" standard that pervades the PC industry. The automobile manufacturers work closely with their suppliers to advance the design and functioning of parts and components, to incorporate new technology, to better integrate individual parts and components to form engine cooling systems, transmission systems, electrical systems, and so on—all of which helps shorten the cycle time for new models, improve the quality and performance of their vehicles, and boost overall production efficiency. The soft-drink producers (Coca-Cola and PepsiCo) and the beer producers (Anheuser-Busch and Miller Brewing) all cultivate their relationships with their bottlers/distributors to strengthen access to local markets and build the loyalty, support, and commitment for corporate marketing programs, without which their own sales and growth are weakened. Similarly, the fast-food enterprises like McDonald's and Taco Bell find it essential to work hand-in-hand with franchisees on outlet cleanliness, consistency of product quality, in-store ambience, courtesy and friendliness of store personnel, and other aspects of store operations—unless franchisees

---

[14]Ibid., p. 43.

[15]Ibid., p. 47. The growing tendency of companies to outsource important activities and the many reasons for building cooperative, collaborative alliances and partnerships with other companies is detailed in James F. Moore, *The Death of Competition* (New York: HarperBusiness, 1996), especially Chapter 3.

deliver sufficient customer satisfaction to attract repeat business on an ongoing basis, a fast-food chain's sales and competitive standing suffer quickly. *Strategic partnerships, alliances, and close collaboration with suppliers, distributors, the makers of complementary products/services and competitors make good strategic sense whenever the result is to enhance organizational resources and capabilities.*

Making Strategy-Critical Activities/Capabilities the Main Building Blocks of the Internal Organization   The rationale for making strategy-critical activities and capabilities the main building blocks in structuring a business is compelling: If activities/capabilities crucial to strategic success are to have the resources, decision-making influence, and organizational impact needed, they have to be centerpieces in the organizational scheme. Plainly, a new or changed strategy is likely to lead to new or different key activities, competencies, or capabilities and, therefore, require new or different organizational arrangements; without them, the resulting mismatch between strategy and structure can open the door to implementation and performance problems.[16]

> **Strategic Management Principle**
>
> *Attempting to carry out a new strategy with an old organizational structure is usually unwise.*

Senior executives seldom send a stronger signal about what is strategically important than by making key business units and critical activities prominent organizational building blocks and, further, giving the managers of these units a visible, influential position in the organizational pecking order. When key business units are put down on a level with or, worse, superseded by less important divisions or departments, they usually end up with fewer resources and less clout than they deserve in the organization's power structure. When top management fails to devote attention to organizing in a way that produces effective performance of strategy-critical activities and processes and develops needed capabilities, the whole strategy implementation effort is weakened. It is thus essential that the primary value-creating, success-causing activities and business processes be prominent in the company's organization structure and deeply ingrained in how the organization does its work. Anything else risks a serious mismatch between structure and strategy.

> **Strategic Management Principle**
>
> *Matching structure to strategy requires making strategy-critical activities and strategy-critical organizational units the main building blocks in the organization structure.*

---

[16]The importance of matching organization design and structure to the particular needs of strategy was first brought to the forefront in a landmark study of 70 large corporations conducted by Professor Alfred Chandler of Harvard University. Chandler's research revealed that changes in an organization's strategy bring about new administrative problems which, in turn, require a new or refashioned structure for the new strategy to be successfully implemented. He found that structure tends to follow the growth strategy of the firm—but often not until inefficiency and internal operating problems provoke a structural adjustment. The experiences of these firms followed a consistent sequential pattern: new strategy creation, emergence of new administrative problems, a decline in profitability and performance, a shift to a more appropriate organizational structure, and then recovery to more profitable levels and improved strategy execution. That managers should reassess their company's internal organization whenever strategy changes is pretty much common sense. A new or different strategy is likely to entail new or different key activities, competencies, or capabilities and, therefore, require new or different internal organizational arrangements; if workable organizational adjustments are not forthcoming, the resulting mismatch between strategy and structure can open the door to implementation and performance problems. For more details, see Alfred Chandler, *Strategy and Structure* (Cambridge, Mass.: MIT Press, 1962).

Although the stress here is on designing the organization structure around the needs of effective strategy execution, it is worth noting that structure can and does influence the choice of strategy. A good strategy must be doable. When an organization's present structure is so far out of line with the requirements of a particular strategy that the organization would have to be turned upside down to implement it, the strategy may not be doable and should not be given further consideration. In such cases, structure shapes the choice of strategy. The point here, however, is that once strategy is chosen, structure must be modified to fit the strategy if, in fact, an approximate fit does not already exist. Any influences of structure on strategy should, logically, come before the point of strategy selection rather than after it.

In grafting routine and staff support activities onto the basic structure, company managers should be guided by the strategic relationships among the primary and support functions comprising the value chain. Activities can be related by the flow of work along the value chain, the type of customer served, the distribution channels used, the technical skills and know-how needed to perform them, their contribution to building a core competence or competitive capability, their role in a work process that spans traditional departmental lines, their role in how customer value is created, their sequence in the value chain, the skills or technology transfer opportunities they present, and the potential for combining or coordinating them in a manner that will reduce total costs, to mention some of the most obvious. If the needs of successful strategy execution are to drive organization design, then the relationships to look for are those that (1) link one work unit's performance to another and (2) can be melded into a competitively valuable competence or capability.

Managers need to be particularly alert to the fact that *in traditional functionally organized structures, pieces of strategically relevant activities and capabilities often end up scattered across many departments.* The process of filling customer orders accurately and promptly is a case in point. The order fulfillment process begins when a customer places an order, ends when the goods are delivered, and typically includes a dozen or so steps performed by different people in different departments.[17] Someone in customer service receives the order, logs it in, and checks it for accuracy and completeness. It may then go to the finance department, where someone runs a credit check on the customer. Another person may be needed to approve credit terms or

Functional specialization can result in the pieces of strategically relevant activities and capabilities being scattered across many different departments.

special financing. Someone in sales calculates or verifies the correct pricing. When the order gets to inventory control, someone has to determine if the goods are in stock. If not, a back order may be issued or the order routed to production planning so that it can be factored into the production schedule. When the goods are ready, warehouse operations prepares a shipment schedule. Personnel in the traffic department determine the shipment method (rail, truck, air, water) and choose the route and carrier. Product handling picks the product from the warehouse, verifies the picking against the order, and packages the goods for shipment. Traffic releases the goods to the carrier, which takes responsibility for delivery to the customer. Each handoff from one department to the next entails queues and wait times. Although such organization incorporates Adam Smith's division of labor principle (every person involved has specific responsibility for performing one simple task) and allows for tight management control (everyone in the process is accountable to a manager for efficiency and adherence to procedures), *no one oversees the whole process and its result.*[18] Accurate, timely order fulfillment, despite its relevance to effective strategy execution, ends up being neither a single person's job nor the job of any one functional department—it is a capability that grows out of the combined pieces of many people's jobs in different units.[19] Other strategy-critical activities that are often fragmented include obtaining feedback from customers and making product modifications to meet their needs, speeding new products to market (a task that is often fragmented among R&D, engineering, purchasing, manufacturing, and market-

---

[17]Michael Hammer and James Champy, *Reengineering the Corporation* (New York: HarperBusiness, 1993), pp. 26–27.
[18]Ibid.
[19]Ibid., pp. 27–28.

ILLUSTRATION CAPSULE 30   Process Organization at Lee Memorial Hospital and St. Vincent's Hospital

At acute care hospitals such as Lee Memorial in Fort Myers, Florida, and St. Vincent's in Melbourne, Australia, medical care is delivered by interdisciplinary teams of doctors, nurses, laboratory technicians, and so on that are organized around the needs of the patients and their families rather than around functional departments within the hospital; these hospitals have created focused care or treatment-specific wards within the hospital to treat most of a patient's needs, from admission to discharge. Patients are no longer wheeled from department to department for procedures and tests; instead, teams have the equipment and resources within each focused care unit to provide total care for the patient. While the hospitals had some concern about functional inefficiency in the use of some facilities, process organization has resulted in substantially lower operating cost, faster patient recovery, and greater satisfaction on the part of patients and caregivers.

Source: Iain Somerville and John Edward Mroz, "New Competencies for a New World," in *The Organization of the Future*, edited by Frances Hesselbein, Marshall Goldsmith, and Richard Beckard, (San Francisco: Jossey-Bass, 1997), p.71.

ing), improving product quality, managing relationships with key suppliers, and building the capability to conduct business via the Internet.

Managers have to guard against organization designs that unduly fragment strategically relevant activities. Parceling strategy-critical work efforts across many specialized departments contributes to an obsession with activity (performing the assigned tasks in the prescribed manner) rather than result (lower costs, short product development times, higher product quality, customer satisfaction, competitive advantage). So many handoffs lengthen completion time and frequently drive up overhead costs since coordinating the fragmented pieces can soak up hours of effort on the parts of many people. *One obvious solution is to pull the pieces of strategy-critical processes out of the functional silos and create process-complete departments able to perform all the cross-functional steps needed to produce a strategy-critical result—* see Illustration Capsule 30 for an example of process organization. In recent years, many companies have reengineered their work flows, moving from functional structures to process structures pursued this solution where it was feasible to do so.[20] Nonetheless, some fragmentation is necessary, even desirable. Traditional functional centralization works to good advantage in support activities like finance and accounting, human resource management, and engineering, and in such primary activities as R&D, manufacturing, and marketing.

Thus the primary organizational building blocks within a business are usually a combination of traditional functional departments and process-complete departments. In enterprises with operations in various countries around the world, the basic building blocks may also include geographic organizational units, each of which has profit-loss responsibility for its area. In vertically integrated firms, the major building blocks are divisional units, each of which performs one (or more) of the major processing steps along the value chain (raw materials production, components manufacture, assembly, wholesale distribution, retail store operations); each division in the value chain sequence may operate as a profit center for performance measurement purposes. The typical building blocks of a diversified company are its individual

---

[20]For a detailed review of one company's experiences with reengineering, see Donna B. Stoddard, Sirkka L. Jarvenpaa, and Michael Littlejohn, "The Reality of Business Reengineering: Pacific Bell's Centrex Provisioning Process," *California Management Review* 38, no. 3 (Spring 1996), pp. 57–76.

businesses, with each business unit usually operating as an independent profit center and with corporate headquarters performing support functions for all the businesses.

Determining the Degree of Authority and Independence to Give Each Unit and Each Employee
Companies must decide how much authority to give managers of each organization unit (especially the heads of business subsidiaries, functional departments, and process departments) and how much decision-making latitude to give individual employees in performing their jobs. In a highly centralized organization, top executives retain authority for most strategic and operating decisions and keep a tight rein on business-unit heads and department heads; comparatively little discretionary authority is granted to subordinate managers and individual employees. One weakness of centralized organization is that its vertical, hierarchical character tends to stall decision making until the review-approval process runs its course through the layers of the management bureaucracy. Furthermore, to work well, centralized decision making requires top-level managers to gather and process whatever knowledge is relevant to the decision. When the relevant knowledge resides at lower organizational levels or is technical or detailed or hard to express in words, it is difficult and time-consuming to get all of the facts and nuances in front of the decision maker—knowledge cannot be "copied" from one mind to another. In many cases, it is better to put decision-making authority in the hands of the people most familiar with the situation and train them to exercise good judgment, rather than trying to convey the knowledge and information up the line to the person with the decision-making authority.

There are serious disadvantages to having a small number of all-knowing, top-level managers micromanage the business.

In a highly decentralized organization, managers (and, increasingly, many nonmanagerial employees) are empowered to act on their own in their areas of responsibility—plant managers are empowered to order new equipment as needed and make arrangements with suppliers for parts and components; process managers (or teams) are empowered to manage and improve their assigned process; and employees with customer contact are empowered to do what it takes to please customers. At Starbucks, for example, employees are empowered to exercise initiative in promoting customer satisfaction—there's the story of a store employee, who when the computerized cash register system went off-line, enthusiastically told waiting customers "free coffee."[21] In a diversified company operating on the principle of decentralized decision making, business unit heads have broad authority to run the subsidiary with comparatively little interference from corporate headquarters; moreover, the business head gives functional and process department heads considerable decision-making latitude.

The purpose of decentralization is not to push decisions down to lower levels but to lodge decision-making authority in those persons or teams closest to and most knowledgeable about the situation.

Delegating greater authority to subordinate managers and employees creates a more horizontal organization structure with fewer layers. Whereas in a centralized vertical structure managers and workers have to go up the ladder of authority for an answer, in a decentralized horizontal structure they develop their own answers and action plans—making decisions and being accountable for results is part of their job. Decentralized decision making usually shortens organizational response times, plus it spurs new ideas, creative thinking, innovation, and greater involvement on the part of subordinate managers and employees.

---

[21]Iain Somerville and John Edward Mroz, "New Competencies for a New World," in *The Organization of the Future*, ed. Frances Hesselbein, Marshall Goldsmith, and Richard Beckard, (San Francisco: Jossey-Bass, 1997), p.70.

In recent years, there's been a decided shift from authoritarian, hierarchical structures to flatter, more decentralized structures that stress employee empowerment. The new preference for leaner management structures and empowered employees is grounded in three tenets.

1. *With the world economy moving swiftly from the Industrial Age to the Knowledge/Information/Systems Age, traditional hierarchical structures built around functional specialization have to undergo radical surgery to accommodate greater emphasis on building competitively valuable cross-functional capabilities*; the best companies have to be able to act and react quickly and to create, package, and rapidly move information to the point of need—in short, companies have to reinvent their organizational arrangements.

2. *Decision-making authority should be pushed down to the lowest organizational level capable of making timely, informed, competent decisions*—to those people (managers or nonmanagers) nearest the scene who are knowledgeable about the issues and trained to weigh all the factors. Insofar as strategic management is concerned, decentralization means that the managers of each organizational unit should not only lead the crafting of their unit's strategy but also lead the decision making on how to implement it. Decentralization thus requires selecting strong managers to head each organizational unit and holding them accountable for crafting and executing appropriate strategies for their units. Managers who consistently produce unsatisfactory results and have poor track records in strategy making and strategy implementing have to be weeded out.

3. *Employees below the management ranks should be empowered to exercise judgment on matters pertaining to their jobs.* The case for empowering employees to make decisions and be accountable for their performance is based on the belief that a company that draws on the combined brainpower of all its employees can outperform a company where people management means transferring executives' decisions about what to do and how to do it into the actions of workers-doers. To ensure that the decisions of empowered people are as well-informed as possible, great pains have to be taken to put accurate, timely data into everyone's hands and make sure they understand the links between their performance and company performance. Delayered corporate hierarchies coupled with today's electronic communication systems make greater empowerment feasible. It's possible now to create "a wired company" where people at all organizational levels have direct electronic access to data, other employees, managers, suppliers, and customers; they can access information quickly (via the Internet or company intranet), check with superiors or whoever else as needed, and take responsible action. Typically, there are genuine morale gains when people are well-informed and allowed to operate in a self-directed way. But there is an organizing challenge as well: how to exercise adequate control over the actions of empowered employes so that the business is not put at risk at the same time that the benefits of empowerment are realized.[22]

> *Successful strategy inplementation involves empowering others to act on doing all the things needed to put the strategy into place and execute it proficiently.*

---

[22]Exercising adequate control in businesses that demand short response times, innovation, and creativity is a serious requirement. For example, Kidder, Peabody & Co. lost $350 million when a trader allegedly booked fictitious profits; Sears took a $60 million write-off after admitting that employees in its automobile service departments recommended unnecessary repairs to customers. For a discussion of the problems

One of the biggest exceptions to decentralizing strategy-related decisions and giving lower-level managers more operating rein arises in diversified companies with related businesses. In such cases, strategic-fit benefits are often best captured by either centralizing decision-making authority or enforcing close cooperation and shared decision making.[23] For example, if businesses with overlapping process and product technologies have their own independent R&D departments, each pursuing their own priorities, projects, and strategic agendas, it's hard for the corporate parent to prevent duplication of effort, capture either economies of scale or economies of scope, or broaden the vision of the company's R&D efforts to embrace new technological paths, product families, end-use applications, and customer groups. Likewise, centralizing control over the related activities of separate businesses makes sense when there are opportunities to share a common sales force, use common distribution channels, rely upon a common field service organization to handle customer requests for technical assistance or provide maintenance and repair services, and so on. And for reasons previously discussed, limits also have to be placed on the independence of functional managers when pieces of strategy-critical processes are located in different organizational units and require close coordination for maximum effectiveness.

> *Centralizing strategy-implementing authority at the corporate level has merit when the related activities of related businesses need to be tightly coordinated.*

Reporting Relationships and Cross-Unit Coordination   The classic way to coordinate the activities of organizational units is to position them so that those most closely related report to a single person (a functional department head, a process manager, a geographic area head). Managers higher up in the pecking order generally have authority over more organizational units and thus the clout to coordinate and unify the activities of units under their supervision. In such structures, the chief executive officer, chief operating officer, and business-level managers end up as central points of coordination. When a firm is pursuing a related diversification strategy, coordinating the related activities of independent business units often requires the centralizing authority of a single corporate-level officer. Also, companies with either related or unrelated diversification strategies commonly centralize such staff support functions as public relations, finance and accounting, employee benefits, and information systems at the corporate level.

But, as the customer order fulfillment example illustrates, it isn't always feasible to position all the pieces of a strategy-critical process and/or all interrelated organizational units vertically under the coordinating authority of a single executive. Formal reporting relationships have to be supplemented. Options for unifying the strategic efforts of interrelated organizational units include the use of coordinating teams, cross-functional task forces, dual reporting relationships, informal organizational networking, voluntary cooperation, incentive compensation tied to group performance measures, and strong executive-level insistence on teamwork and interdepartmental cooperation (including removal of recalcitrant managers who stonewall collaborative efforts).[24] See Illustration

---

and possible solutions, see Robert Simons, "Control in an Age of Empowerment," *Harvard Business Review* 73 (March–April 1995), pp. 80–88.

[23]For a discussion of the importance of cross-business coordination, see Jeanne M. Liedtka, "Collaboration across Lines of Business for Competitive Advantage," *Academy of Management Executive* 10, no. 2 (May 1996), pp. 20–34.

[24]At ABB, a $30 billion European-based company that makes power generation and electrical equipment and offers a wide range of engineering services, a top executive promptly replaced the managers of several plants who were not fully committed to collaborating closely on eliminating duplication in product development and production efforts among plants in several different countries. Earlier, the executive, noting that negotiations among the managers had stalled on which labs and plants to close, had met with all

ILLUSTRATION CAPSULE 31   Cross-Unit Coordination on Technology at 3M Corp.

At 3M, technology experts in more than 100 3M labs around the world have come to work openly and cooperatively without resorting to turf protection tactics or not-invented-here mind-sets. 3M management has been successful in creating a collegial working environment that results in the scientists calling upon one another for assistance and advice and in rapid technology transfer.

Mangement formed a Technical Council, composed of the heads of the major labs; the Council meets monthly and has a three-day annual retreat to discuss ways to improve cross-unit transfer of technology and other issues of common interest. In addition, management created a broader-based Technical Forum, composed of scientists and technical experts chosen as representatives, to facilitate grassroots communication among employees in all the labs. One of the Forum's responsibilities is to organize employees with similar technical interests from all the labs into chapters; chapter members attend regular seminars with experts from outside the company. There's also an annual three-day technology fair at which 3M scientists showcase their latest findings for colleagues and expand their network of acquaintances.

As a result of these collaborative efforts, 3M has developed a portfolio of more than 100 technologies and it has created the capability to routinely utilize these technologies in product applications in three different divisions that each serve multiple markets.

Source: Adapted from Sumantra Ghoshal and Christopher A. Bartlett, "Changing the Role of Top Management: Beyond Structure to Process," *Harvard Business Review* 73, no. 1 (January–February 1995), pp. 93–94.

Capsule 31 for a more detailed example of putting the necessary organizational arrangements into place and creating the desired results.

The key in weaving support activities into the organization design is to establish reporting and coordinating arrangements that:

- Maximize how support activities contribute to enhanced performance of the primary activities in the firm's value chain.
- Contain the costs of support activities and minimize the time and energy internal units have to spend doing business with each other.

Without such arrangements, the cost of transacting business internally becomes excessive, and the managers of individual organizational units, forever diligent in guarding their turf, can weaken the strategy execution effort and become part of the strategy-implementing problem rather than part of the solution.

Assigning Responsibility for Collaboration with Outsiders   Someone or some group must be given authority and responsibility for collaborating with each major outside constituency involved in strategy execution. This means having managers with responsibility for making particular strategic partnerships or alliances generate the intended benefits. If close working relationships with suppliers are crucial, then authority and responsibility for supply chain management must be given formal status on the company's organization chart and a significant position in the pecking order. If distributor/dealer/franchisee relationships are important, someone must be assigned the task of building the bridges of cooperation and nurturing the relationships. If working in parallel with providers of complementary products and services contributes to enhanced organizational capability, then cooperative organizational arrangements of some kind have to be put in place and managed to good effect. Just appointing and empowering relationship managers is not enough; there have to be

---

the managers, asked them to cooperate to find a solution, discussed with them which options were unacceptable, and given them a deadline to find a solution. When the asked-for teamwork wasn't forthcoming from several managers attending the meeting, they were replaced.

multiple ties at multiple levels to ensure proper communication, coordination, and control.[25]

The key to cooperative alliances and partnerships is effectively managing the relationship and capturing the potential gain in resource capability, not in doing the deal.

The organizing challenge is to find ways to span the boundaries of independent organizations and produce the collaborative efforts needed to enhance a company's own competitive capabilites and resource strengths.[26] *Forming alliances and cooperative relationships presents immediate opportunities and opens the door to future possibilities, but nothing valuable is realized until the relationship grows, develops, and blossoms.* Unless top management sees that such bridge building occurs and that ample effort goes into creating productive working relationships, the company's power to execute its strategy is weakened.

The Strategic Advantages And Disadvantages Of Different Organizational Structures

There are five basic building block schemes for matching structure to strategy: (1) functional and/or process specialization, (2) geographic organization, (3) decentralized business divisions, (4) strategic business units, and (5) matrix structures featuring dual lines of authority and strategic priority. Each has strategic advantages and disadvantages, and each has to be supplemented with formal and informal organizational arrangements to fully coordinate the work effort, develop core competencies, and build competitive capabilities.

Functional and Process Organization Structures Organizational structures anchored around functionally specialized departments and strategy-critical processes are far and away the most popular way to match structure to strategy in single-business enterprises. However, just what form the functional and process specialization takes varies according to the nature of the value chain. For instance, a technical instruments manufacturer may be organized around research and development, engineering, production, technical services, quality control, marketing, personnel, and finance and accounting. A hotel may have an organization based on front-desk operations, housekeeping, building maintenance, food service, convention services and special events, guest services, personnel and training, and accounting. A discount retailer may divide its organizational units into purchasing, warehousing and distribution, store operations, advertising, merchandising and promotion, customer service, and corporate administrative services. Functional and process organizational approaches are diagrammed in Figure 9–2.

Making specialized functions or processes the main organizational building blocks works well so long as strategy-critical activities closely match functional specialties and/or business processes, there's minimal need for interdepartmental coordination, and top-level management is able to short-circuit departmental rivalries and create a spirit of teamwork, trust, and internal cooperation. Departmental units having expertise in performing every facet of the activity is an attractive way (1) to exploit any learning/experience curve benefits or economy-of-scale opportunities of division of

---

[25]Rosabeth Moss Kanter, "Collaborative Advantage: The Art of the Alliance," *Harvard Business Review* 72, no. 4 (July–August 1994), pp. 105–06.

[26]For an excellent review of ways to effectively manage the relationship between alliance partners, see Kanter, *op. cit.*, pp. 96–108.

FIGURE 9-2 Functional and Process Organizational Structures

A. The Building Blocks of a "Typical" Functional Organizational Structure

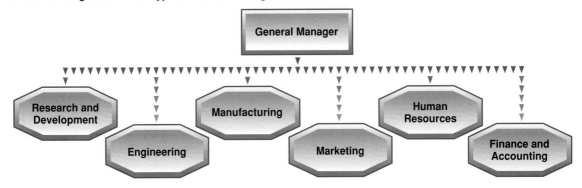

B. The Building Blocks of a Process-Oriented Structure

STRATEGIC ADVANTAGES	STRATEGIC DISADVANTAGES
• Centralized control of strategic results.	• Functional specialization is conducive to fragmentation of strategy-critical processes.
• Best suited for structuring a single business.	• Emphasis on functional specialization poses organizational barriers to creating cross-functional core competencies and to close collaboration across departmental lines.
• Well-suited to businesses where the strategy-critical value chain components consist of discipline-specific or process-oriented activities.	
• Promotes in-depth functional expertise.	• Can lead to interfunctional rivalry and conflict, rather than team-play and cooperation.
• Well suited to developing functional and/or process related skills and competencies.	• Multilayered management bureaucracies and centralized decision-making slow response times.
• Conducive to exploiting learning/experience curve effects associated with functional specialization or process specialization.	• Organizing around functional departments development of managers with cross-functional experience because the ladder of advancement is up the ranks within the same functional area.
• Enhances operating efficiency where tasks are routine and repetitive.	• Forces profit responsibility to the top.
• Can be a basis for competitive advantage when dominating depth in a function or process is a key success factor.	• Functional specialists often attach more importance to what's best for the functional area than to what's best for the whole business.
• Process organization provides a way to avoid fragmentation of strategy-critical activities across functional departments.	• Functional myopia often works against creative entrepreneurship and rapid adaptation to changing market circumstances.
	• Functional specialization poses barriers to creating cross-functional competencies and close departmental collaboration.

labor and the use of specialized technology and equipment and (2) to develop deep expertise in an important business function or process. When dominating depth in one or more functional specialties or business processes enhances operating efficiency and/or creates a competitively valuable competence, it becomes a basis for competitive advantage (lower cost or greater organizational capability).

The traditional functional structures that used to dominate single-business enterprises have three big shortcomings: excessive functional myopia, the potential for fragmentation of strategy-critical business processes across functional lines, and the difficulty of building cross-functional competencies and capabilities. Functional specialists are prone to focus inward on departmental matters and upward at their boss's priorities but not outward on the business, the customer, or the industry.[27] Members of functional departments usually have strong departmental loyalties and are protective of departmental interests. There's a natural tendency for each functional department to push for solutions and decisions that advance its well-being and influence. All this creates an organizational environment where functional departments operate as vertical silos or stovepipes and become a breeding ground for bureaucracies, empire building, authoritarian decision making, and narrow perspectives. In addition, the preoccupation of functional departments with developing deeper expertise and improving functional performance works against devising creative responses to major customer-market-technological changes; functional heads are often quick to oppose ideas or alternatives that aren't compatible with functional interests. Classical functional structures also worsen the problems of process fragmentation whenever a firm's value chain includes strategy-critical activities that, by their very nature, are cross-functional rather than discipline specific. Likewise, it's tough to develop cross-functional core competencies and capabilities in an environment dominated by strongly entrenched functional empires that don't "talk the same language" and that prefer to do their own thing without outside interference.

A big weakness of functional departments is that they are prone to develop strong functional mind-sets and approach strategic issues more from a functional than a business perspective.

Interdepartmental politics, functional empire building, functional myopia, process fragmentation, and a need to build cross-functional competencies and capabilities can impose a time-consuming administrative burden on the general manager, who is the only person on a functionally dominated organization chart with authority to contain rivalries and to enforce interdepartmental cooperation. In a functionally dominated structure, much of a GM's time and energy is spent keeping lines of communication open across departments, tempering departmental rivalries, convincing stovepipe thinkers of the merits of broader solutions, devising ways to secure cooperation, and working to mold desirable cross-functional core competencies and capabilities. To achieve the cross-functional coordination necessary for strategic success, a GM either has to (1) supplement the functional organization structure by creating process-complete departments to handle strategy-critical activities that cross functional lines or (2) be tough and uncompromising in insisting that functional department heads be team players and that functional specialists collaborate and cooperate.

Increasingly during the last decade, companies have found that rather than continuing to scatter related pieces of a business process across several functional departments and scrambling to integrate their efforts, it is better to reengineer the work effort and create process departments by pulling the people who performed the pieces in functional departments into a group that works together to perform the whole

---

[27]Hammer and Champy, *Reengineering the Corporation*, p. 28.

process.[28] This is what Bell Atlantic did in cutting through its bureaucratic procedures for connecting a telephone customer to its long-distance carrier.[29] In Bell Atlantic's functional structure, when a business customer requested a connection between its telephone system and a long-distance carrier for data services, the request traveled from department to department, taking two to four weeks to complete all the internal processing steps. In reengineering that process, Bell Atlantic pulled workers doing the pieces of the process from the many functional departments and put them on teams that, working together, could handle most customer requests in a matter of days and sometimes hours. Because the work was recurring—similar customer requests had to be processed daily—the teams were permanently grouped into a process department. In the electronics industry where product life cycles are often less than a year, companies have formed process departments charged with cutting the time it takes to develop new technologies and get new products to market. Some companies, however, have stopped short of creating process departments and, instead, either appointed process managers or interdisciplinary teams to oversee coordination of fragmented processes and strategy-critical activities. While the means of unifying the performance of strategy-critical processes and activities has varied, many companies have now incorporated some form of process organization to counteract the weaknesses of a purely functional structure. The methods of reengineering fragmented processes and creating more process-complete work flows, as well as the results that reengineering can produce, are presented in Illustration Capsule 32.

Geographic Forms of Organization   Organizing on the basis of geographic areas or territories is a common structural form for enterprises operating in diverse geographic markets or serving an expansive geographic area. As Figure 9–3 indicates, geographic organization has advantages and disadvantages, but the chief reason for its popularity is that it promotes improved performance.

In the private sector, a territorial structure is typically used by discount retailers, power companies, cement firms, restaurant chains, and dairy products enterprises. In the public sector, such organizations as the Internal Revenue Service, the Social Security Administration, the federal courts, the U.S. Postal Service, state troopers, and the Red Cross have adopted territorial structures in order to be directly accessible to geographically dispersed clienteles. Multinational enterprises use geographic structures to manage the diversity they encounter operating across national boundaries, often dividing into a domestic division and an international division or, when international operations are quite large, dividing into divisions for each continent or major country.

A geographic organization structure is well-suited to firms pursuing different strategies in different geographic regions.

Raymond Corey and Steven Star cite Pfizer International as a good example of a company whose strategic requirements made geographic decentralization advantageous:

> Pfizer International operated plants in 27 countries and marketed in more than 100 countries. Its product lines included pharmaceuticals (antibiotics and other ethical prescription drugs), agricultural and veterinary products (such as animal feed supplements and vaccines and pesticides), chemicals (fine chemicals, bulk pharmaceuticals, petrochemicals, and plastics), and consumer products (cosmetics and toiletries).

[28]Ibid., p. 66.
[29]Ibid., pp. 66–67.

ILLUSTRATION CAPSULE 32   Reengineering: How Companies Do It and the Results They Have Gotten

Reengineering strategy-critical business processes to reduce fragmentation across traditional departmental lines and cut bureaucratic overheads has proven to be a legitimate organization design tool. It's not a passing fad or another management program of the month. Process organization is every bit as valid an organizing principle as functional specialization. Strategy execution is improved when the pieces of strategy-critical activities and core business processes performed by different departments are properly integrated and coordinated.

Companies that have reengineered some of their business processes have ended up compressing formerly separate steps and tasks into jobs performed by a single person and integrating jobs into team activities. Reorganization then follows, a natural consequence of task synthesis and job redesign. The experiences of companies that have successfully reengineered and restructured their operations in strategy-supportive ways suggest attacking process fragmentation and overhead reduction in the following fashion:

- Develop a flow chart of the total business process, including its interfaces with other value-chain activities.

- Try to simplify the process first, eliminating tasks and steps where possible and analyzing how to streamline the performance of what remains.

- Determine which parts of the process can be automated (usually those that are repetitive, time-consuming, and require little thought or decision); consider introducing advanced technologies that can be upgraded to achieve next-generation capability and provide a basis for further productivity gains down the road.

- Reengineer, then reorganize.

- Evaluate each activity in the process to determine whether it is strategy-critical or not. Strategy-critical activities are candidates for benchmarking to achieve best-in-industry or best-in-world performance status.

- Weigh the pros and cons of outsourcing activities that are noncritical or that contribute little to organizational capabilities and core competencies.

- Design a structure for performing the activities that remain; reorganize the personnel and groups who perform these activities into the new structure.

Reengineering can produce dramatic gains in productivity and organizational capability when done properly. In the order-processing section of General Electric's circuit breaker division, elapsed time from order receipt to delivery was cut from three weeks to three days by consolidating six production units into one, reducing a variety of former inventory and handling steps, automating the design system to replace a human custom-design process, and cutting the organizational layers between managers and workers from three to one. Productivity rose 20 percent in one year, and unit manufacturing costs dropped 30 percent.

Northwest Water, a British utility, used reengineering to eliminate 45 work depots that served as home base to crews who installed and repaired water and sewage lines and equipment. Now crews work directly from their vehicles, receiving assignments and reporting work completion from computer terminals in their trucks. Crew members are no longer employees but contractors to Northwest Water. These reengineering efforts not only eliminated the need for the work depots but also allowed Northwest Water to eliminate a big percentage of the bureaucratic personnel and supervisory organization that managed the crews.

There's no escaping the conclusion that reengineering, in concert with electronic communication systems, empowerment, and the use of self-directed work teams, provides company managers with important new organization design options. Organizational hierarchies can be flattened and middle-management layers removed. Responsibility and decision-making authority can be pushed downward and outward to those places in the organization where customer contacts are made. Strategy-critical processes can be unified, performed more quickly and at lower cost, and made more responsive to changing customer preferences and expectations. Used properly, these new design approaches can trigger big gains in organizational creativity and employee productivity.

Sources: Based on information in James Brian Quinn, *Intelligent Enterprise* (New York: Free Press, 1992), p. 162; T. Stuart, "GE Keeps Those Ideas Coming," *Fortune*, August 12, 1991; Gene Hall, Jim Rosenthal, and Judy Wade, "How to Make Reengineering Really Work," *Harvard Business Review* 71, no. 6 (November–December 1993), pp. 119–31; and Ann Majchrzak and Qianwei Wang, "Breaking the Functional Mind-Set in Process Organizations," *Harvard Business Review* 74, no. 5 (September–October 1996), pp. 93–99.

FIGURE 9-3   A Representative Geographic Organizational Structure

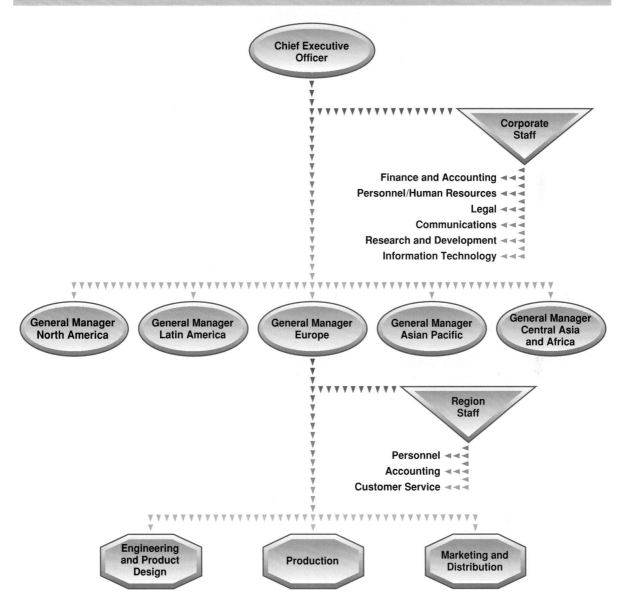

STRATEGIC ADVANTAGES

• Allows tailoring of strategy to needs of each geographical market.
• Delegates profit/loss responsibility to lowest strategic level.
• Improves functional coordination within the target market.
• Takes advantage of economies of local operations.
• Regional units make an excellent training ground for higher-level general managers.

STRATEGIC DISADVANTAGES

• Poses a problem of how much geographic uniformity headquarters should impose versus how much geographic diversity should be allowed.
• Greater difficulty in maintaining consistent company image/reputation from area to area when geographic managers exercise much strategic freedom.
• Adds another layer of management to run the geographic units.
• Can result in duplication of staff services at headquarters and geographic levels, creating a cost disadvantage.

Ten geographic Area Managers reported directly to the President of Pfizer International and exercised line supervision over Country Managers. According to a company position description, it was "the responsibility of each Area Manager to plan, develop, and carry out Pfizer International's business in the assigned foreign area in keeping with company policies and goals."

Country Managers had profit responsibility. In most cases a single Country Manager managed all Pfizer activities in his country. In some of the larger, well-developed countries of Europe there were separate Country Managers for pharmaceutical and agricultural products and for consumer lines.

Except for the fact that New York headquarters exercised control over the to-the-market prices of certain products, especially prices of widely used pharmaceuticals, Area and Country Managers had considerable autonomy in planning and managing the Pfizer International business in their respective geographic areas. This was appropriate because each area, and some countries within areas, provided unique market and regulatory environments. In the case of pharmaceuticals and agricultural and veterinary products (Pfizer International's most important lines), national laws affected formulations, dosages, labeling, distribution, and often price. Trade restrictions affected the flow of bulk pharmaceuticals and chemicals and packaged products, and might in effect require the establishment of manufacturing plants to supply local markets. Competition, too, varied significantly from area to area.[30]

At Andersen Consulting, the basic organizational building blocks are the individual practice groups making up the geographic offices scattered across the world.

Decentralized Business Units   Grouping activities along business and product lines has been a favored organizing device among diversified enterprises for the past 75 years, beginning with the pioneering efforts of Du Pont and General Motors in the 1920s. Separate business/product divisions emerged because diversification made a functionally specialized manager's job incredibly complex. Imagine the problems a manufacturing executive and his/her staff would have if put in charge of, say, 50 different plants using 20 different technologies to produce 30 different products in eight different businesses/industries. In a multibusiness enterprise, the practical organizational sequence is corporate to business to functional area within a business rather than corporate to functional area (aggregated for all businesses).

Thus while functional departments, process departments, and geographic divisions are the standard organizational building blocks in a single-business enterprise, in a

In a diversified firm, the basic organizational building blocks are its business units; each business is operated as a stand-alone profit center.

multibusiness corporation the basic building blocks are the individual businesses.[31] Authority over each business unit is typically delegated to a business-level manager. The approach is to put entrepreneurial general managers in charge of each business unit, give them authority to formulate and implement a business strategy, motivate them with performance-based incentives, and hold them accountable for results. Each business unit then operates as a stand-alone profit center and is organized around whatever functional/process departments and geographic units suit the business's strategy, key activities, and operating requirements.

Fully independent business units, however, pose an obstacle to companies pursuing related diversification: *There is no mechanism for coordinating related activities across business units or for sharing/tranferring/developing mutually beneficial resource*

---

[30]Raymond Corey and Steven H. Star, *Organization Strategy: A Marketing Approach* (Boston: Harvard Business School, 1971), pp. 23–24.

[31]Over 90 percent of the *Fortune* 500 firms employ a business unit or divisional organizational structure.

strengths. As the label implies, divisions divide, creating potentially insulated units with barriers that inhibit sharing or building mutually beneficial resource strengths. It can be tough to get independent business units and autonomy-conscious business-unit managers to coordinate related activities and collaborate in ways that leverage resource strengths and enhance organizational capabilities. They are prone to argue about turf and resist being held accountable for activities outside their control.

To capture strategic-fit and resource-fit benefits in a diversified company, corporate headquarters must superimpose some internal organizational means of cutting across boundaries and coordinating related business-unit activities. One option is to centralize related functions at the corporate level—for example, set up a corporate R&D department (if there are technology and product development fits), create a special corporate sales force to call on customers who purchase from several of the company's business units, combine the dealer networks and sales force organizations of closely related businesses, merge the order processing and shipping functions of businesses with common customers, or consolidate the production of related components and products into fewer, more efficient plants. In addition, corporate officers can develop bonus arrangements that give business-unit managers strong incentives to work together. If the strategic-fit relationships involve skills or technology transfers across businesses, corporate headquarters can mandate the transfer of people with the requisite experience and know-how from one business to another or form interbusiness teams to open the flow of proprietary technology, managerial know-how, and related skills between businesses.

> **Strategic Management Principle**
>
> *A decentralized business-unit structure can block success of a related diversification strategy unless specific organizational arrangements are devised to coordinate the related activities of related businesses.*

A typical line-of-business organization structure is shown in Figure 9–4, along with the strategy-related pros and cons of this organizational form.

Strategic Business Units In broadly diversified companies, the number of decentralized business units can be so great that the span of control is too much for a single chief executive. Then it may be useful to group related businesses and to delegate authority over them to a senior executive who reports directly to the chief executive officer. While this imposes a layer of management between business-level managers and the chief executive, it may nonetheless improve strategic planning and top-management coordination of diverse business interests. This explains both the popularity of the group vice president concept among multibusiness companies and the creation of strategic business units.

A *strategic business unit* (SBU) is a grouping of business subsidiaries based on important strategic elements common to all. The elements can be an overlapping set of competitors, closely related value chain activities, a common need to compete globally, emphasis on the same kind of competitive advantage (low cost or differentiation), common key success factors, or technologically related growth opportunities. At General Electric, a pioneer in the concept of SBUs, 190 businesses were grouped into 43 SBUs and then aggregated further into six "sectors."[32] At Union Carbide, 15 groups and divisions were decomposed into 150 "strategic planning units" and then regrouped and combined into 9 new "aggregate planning units." At General Foods, SBUs were

> **Basic Concept**
>
> *A strategic business unit (SBU) is a grouping of related businesses under the supervision of a senior executive.*

[32]William K. Hall, "SBUs: Hot, New Topic in the Management of Diversification," *Business Horizons* 21, no. 1 (February 1978), p. 19. For an excellent discussion of the problems of implementing the SBU concept at 13 companies, see Richard A. Bettis and William K. Hall, "The Business Portfolio Approach—Where It Falls Down in Practice," *Long Range Planning* 16, no. 2 (April 1983), pp. 95–104.

FIGURE 9–4   A Decentralized Line-of-Business Organization Structure

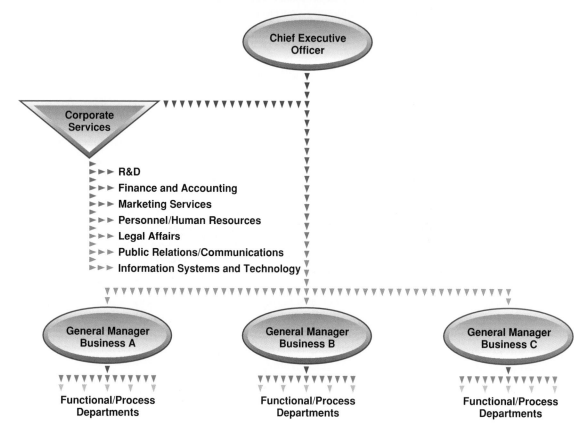

STRATEGIC ADVANTAGES

- Offers a logical and workable means of decentralizing responsibility and delegating authority in diversified organizations.
- Puts responsibility for crafting and implementing business strategy in closer proximity to each business's unique environment.
- Allows each business unit to organize around its own key value chain activities, business processes, and functional requirements.
- Frees CEO to handle corporate strategy issues.
- Puts clear profit/loss accountability on shoulders of business-unit managers.

STRATEGIC DISADVANTAGES

- May lead to costly duplication of staff functions at corporate and business-unit levels, thus raising administrative overhead costs.
- Poses a problem of what decisions to centralize and what decisions to decentralize (business managers need enough authority to get the job done, but not so much that corporate management loses control of key business-level decisions).
- May lead to excessive division rivalry for corporate resources and attention.
- Business/division autonomy works against achieving coordination of related activities in different business units, thus blocking to some extent the capture of strategic-fit and resource-fit benefits.
- Corporate management becomes heavily dependent on business-unit managers.
- Corporate managers can lose touch with business-unit situations, end up surprised when problems arise, and not know much about how to fix such problems.

originally defined on a product-line basis but were later redefined according to menu segments (breakfast foods, beverages, main meal products, desserts, and pet foods). SBUs make headquarters' reviews of the strategies of lower-level units less imposing (there is no practical way for a CEO to conduct in-depth reviews of a hundred or more different businesses). A CEO can, however, effectively review the strategic plans of a lesser number of SBUs, leaving detailed business strategy reviews and direct supervision of individual businesses to the SBU heads. Figure 9–5 illustrates the SBU form of organization, along with its strategy-related pros and cons.

The SBU concept provides broadly diversified companies with a way to rationalize the organization of many different businesses and a management arrangement for capturing strategic-fit benefits and streamlining strategic planning and budgeting processes. The strategic function of the group vice president is to provide the SBU with some cohesive direction, enforce coordination across related businesses, and keep an eye out for trouble at the business-unit level, providing counsel and support as needed. The group vice president, as coordinator for all businesses in the SBU, can promote resource sharing and skills/technology transfers where appropriate and unify the decisions and actions of businesses in the SBU. The SBU, in effect, becomes a strategy-making, strategy-implementing unit with a wider field of vision and operations than a single business unit. It serves as a broadly diversified company's mechanism for capturing strategic-fit benefits across businesses and adding to the competitive advantage that each business in the SBU is able to build on its own. Moreover, it affords opportunity to "cross-pollinate" the activities of separate businesses, ideally creating enough new capability to stretch a company's strategic reach into adjacent products, technologies, and markets.

SBU structures are a means for managing broad diversification and enforcing strategic coordination across related businesses.

Matrix Forms of Organization   A matrix organization is a structure with two (or more) channels of command, two lines of budget authority, and two sources of performance and reward. The key feature of the matrix is that authority for a business/product/project/venture and authority for a function or business process are overlaid (to form a matrix or grid), and decision-making responsibility in each unit/cell of the matrix is shared between the business/project/venture team manager and the functional/process manager—as shown in Figure 9–6. In a matrix structure, subordinates have a *continuing dual assignment*: to the product line/project/business/venture and to their home-base function/process. The resulting structure is a compromise between organizing solely around functional/process specialization or around product line, project, line-of-business, or special venture divisions.

Matrix structures, although complex to manage and sometimes unwieldy, allow a firm to be organized in two different strategy-supportive ways at the same time.

A matrix-type organization is a genuinely different structural form and represents a "new way of life." It breaks the unity-of-command principle; two reporting channels, two bosses, and shared authority create a new kind of climate. In essence, the matrix is a conflict-resolution system through which strategic and operating priorities are negotiated, power is shared, and resources are allocated on the basis of "strongest case" for what is best overall for the unit.[33]

---

[33]For two excellent critiques of matrix organizations, see Stanley M. Davis and Paul R. Lawrence, "Problems of Matrix Organizations," *Harvard Business Review* 56, no. 3 (May–June 1978), pp. 131–42, and Erik W. Larson and David H. Gobeli, "Matrix Management: Contradictions and Insights," *California Management Review* 29, no. 4 (Summer 1987), pp. 126–38.

FIGURE 9-5   An SBU Organization Structure

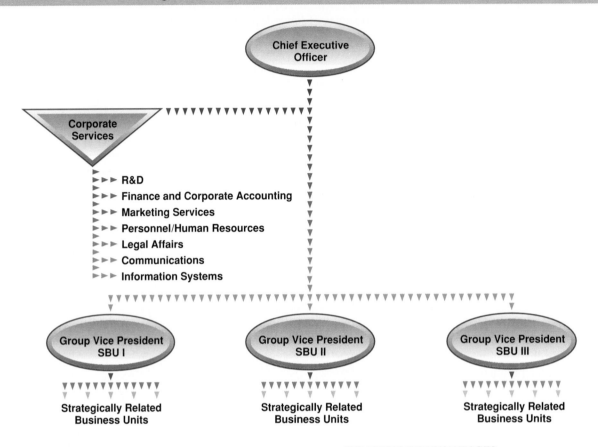

STRATEGIC ADVANTAGES

- Provides a strategically relevant way to organize the business-unit portfolio of a broadly diversified company.

- Facilitates the coordination of related activities within an SBU, thus helping to capture the benefits of strategic fits and resource fits among related businesses.

- Promotes more cohesiveness and collaboration among separate but related businesses.

- Allows strategic planning to be done at the most relevant level within the total enterprise.

- Makes the task of strategic review by top executives more objective and more effective.

- Helps allocate corporate resources to areas with greatest growth and profit opportunities.

- Group VP position is a good training ground for future CEOs.

STRATEGIC DISADVANTAGES

- It is easy for the definition and grouping of businesses into SBUs to be so arbitrary that the SBU serves no other purpose than administrative convenience. If the criteria for defining SBUs are rationalizations and have little to do with the nitty-gritty of strategy coordination, then the groupings lose real strategic significance.

- The SBUs can still be myopic in charting their future direction.

- Adds another layer to top management.

- The roles and authority of the CEO, the group vice president, and the business-unit manager have to be carefully worked out or the group vice president gets trapped in the middle with ill-defined authority.

- Unless the SBU head is strong willed, very little strategy coordination or collaboration is likely to occur across business units in the SBU.

- Performance recognition gets blurred; credit for successful business units tends to go to corporate CEO, then to business-unit head, last to group vice president.

FIGURE 9-6   A Matrix Organization Structure

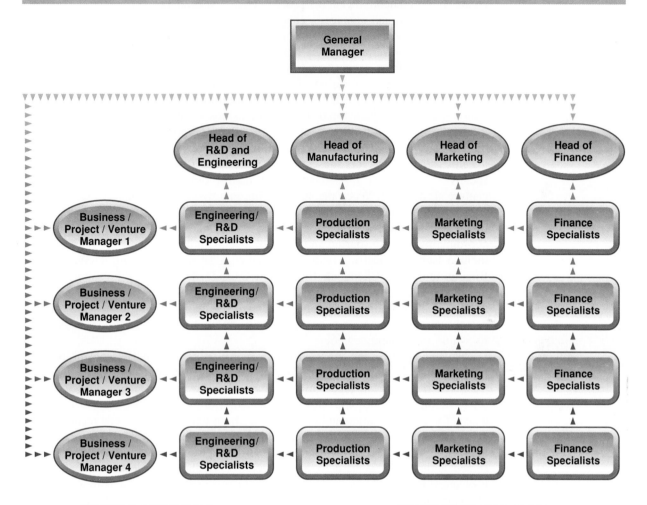

STRATEGIC ADVANTAGES

- Gives formal attention to each dimension of strategic priority.
- Creates checks and balances among competing viewpoints.
- Facilitates capture of functionally based strategic fits in diversified companies.
- Promotes making trade-off decisions on the basis of "what's best for the organization as a whole."
- Encourages cooperation, consensus-building, conflict resolution, and coordination of related activities.

STRATEGIC DISADVANTAGES

- Very complex to manage.
- Hard to maintain "balance" between the two lines of authority.
- So much shared authority can result in a transactions logjam and disproportionate amounts of time being spent on communications, consensus building, and collaboration.
- It is hard to move quickly and decisively without checking with or getting clearance from many other people.
- Promotes organizational bureaucracy and hamstrings creative entrepreneurship and initiative.
- Works at cross purposes with efforts to empower down-the-line managers and employees.

The impetus for matrix organizations stems from growing use of strategies that create a simultaneous need for process teams, special project managers, product managers, functional managers, geographic area managers, new-venture managers, and business-level managers—all of whom have important responsibilities. When at least two of several variables (product, customer, technology, geography, functional area, business process, and market segment) have roughly equal priorities, a matrix organization can be an effective structural form. A matrix structure promotes internal checks and balances among competing viewpoints and perspectives, with separate managers for different dimensions of strategic initiative. A matrix arrangement thus allows each of several strategic considerations to be managed directly and to be formally represented in the organization structure. In this sense, it helps middle managers make trade-off decisions from an organizationwide perspective.[34] The other big advantage of matrix organization is that it can help capture strategic fit. When the strategic fits in a diversified company are related to a specific functional area (R&D, technology, marketing), or cross traditional functional lines, matrix organization can be a reasonable structural arrangement for coordinating activity sharing and skills transfer. Companies using matrix structures include General Electric, Texas Instruments, Citibank, Shell Oil, TRW, Bechtel, Boeing, and Dow Chemical. Illustration Capsule 33 describes how one broadly diversified company with global strategies in each of its businesses developed a matrix structure to manage its operations worldwide. However, in most companies, use of matrix organization is confined to a *portion* of what the firm does rather than its whole organizing scheme.

Many companies and managers shun matrix organization because of its chief weaknesses.[35] It is a complex structure to manage; people end up confused or frustrated over who to report to for what. Working relationships among different organizational units become more complicated. Moreover, because the matrix signals a need for communication and consensus, a "transactions logjam" can result. People in one area are pushed into transacting business with people in another area and networking their way through bureaucracies. Action turns into paralysis since, with shared authority, it is hard to move decisively without first checking with other people and getting clearance. Much time and psychic energy get eaten up in meetings and communicating back and forth. Sizable transactions costs and longer decision times can result with little value-added work accomplished. Even so, in some situations the benefits of conflict resolution, consensus building, and coordination outweigh these weaknesses, as the ABB example in Illustration Capsule 33 indicates.

Supplementing the Basic Organization Structure   None of the basic structural designs is wholly adequate for organizing the total work effort in strategy-supportive ways. Some weaknesses can be corrected by using two or more of the structural designs simultaneously—many companies are large enough and diverse enough to have SBUs, business units with functional and/or process departments, geographic organizational structures in one or more businesses, and units employing matrix principles. But in many companies strategy-supportive organization requires supplementing the formal structure with special coordinating mechanisms and efforts to build

---

[34]Davis and Lawrence, "Problems of Matrix Organizations," p. 132.

[35]Thomas J. Peters and Robert H. Waterman, Jr., *In Search of Excellence* (New York: Harper & Row, 1982), pp. 306–7.

ILLUSTRATION CAPSULE 33   Matrix Organization in a Diversified Global Company: The Case of Asea Brown Boveri

Asea Brown Boveri (ABB) is a diversified multinational corporation headquartered in Zurich, Switzerland. ABB was formed in 1987 through the merger of Asea, one of Sweden's largest industrial enterprises, and Brown Boveri, a major Swiss company. Both companies manufactured electrical products and equipment. Following the merger, ABB acquired or took minority positions in 60 companies, mostly outside Europe. In 1996 ABB had annual revenues of $34 billion and employed 210,000 people around the world, including 130,000 in Western Europe, 30,000 in North America, 10,000 in South America, and 10,000 in India. The company was a world leader in the global markets for electrical products, electrical installations and service, and power-generation equipment and was the dominant European producer. European sales accounted for 60 percent of revenues, while North America accounted for 30 percent and Asia 15 percent.

To manage its global operations, ABB had devised a matrix organization that leveraged its core competencies in electrical-power technologies and its ability to achieve global economies of scale while, at the same time, maximizing its national market visibility and responsiveness. At the top of ABB's corporate organization structure was an executive committee composed of the CEO and 12 colleagues; the committee consisted of Swedes, Swiss, Germans, and Americans, several of whom were based outside Switzerland. The group, which met every three weeks at various locations around the world, was responsible for ABB's corporate strategy and performance.

Along one dimension of ABB's global matrix were 50 or so business areas (BAs), each representing a closely related set of products and services. The BAs were grouped into eight "business segments"; each segment was supervised by a different member of the executive committee. Each BA had a leader charged with responsibility for (1) devising and championing a global strategy, (2) setting quality and cost standards for the BA's factories worldwide, (3) deciding which factories would export to which country markets, (4) rotating people across borders to share technical expertise, create mixed-nationality teams to solve BA problems, and build a culture of trust and communication, and (5) pooling expertise and research funds for the benefit of the BA worldwide. BA leaders worked out of whatever world location made the most sense for their BA.

Along the other dimension of the matrix was a group of national enterprises with presidents, boards of directors, financial statements, and career ladders. The presidents of ABB's national enterprises had responsibility for maximizing the performance and effectiveness of all ABB activities within their country's borders. Country presidents worked closely with the BA leaders to evaluate and improve what was happening in ABB's business areas in their countries.

Inside the matrix were 1,300 "local" ABB companies with an average of 200 employees, each headed by a president. The local company president reported both to the national president in whose country the local company operated and to the leader of the BA to which its products/services were assigned. Each local company was a subsidiary of the ABB national enterprise where it was located. Thus, all of ABB's local companies in Norway were subsidiaries of ABB Norway, the national company for Norway; all ABB operations in Portugal were subsidiaries of ABB Portugal, and so on. The 1,300 presidents of ABB's local companies were expected to be excellent profit center managers, able to answer to two bosses effectively. The local president's global boss was the BA manager who established the local company's role in ABB's global strategy and, also, the rules a local company had to observe in supporting this strategy. The local president's country boss was the national CEO, with whom it was necessary to cooperate on local issues.

ABB believed that its matrix structure allowed it to optimize its pursuit of global business strategies and, at the same time, maximize its performance in every country market where it operated. The matrix was a way of being global and big strategically, yet small and local operationally. Decision making was decentralized (to BA leaders, country presidents, and local company presidents), but reporting and control was centralized (through the BA leaders, the country presidents, and the executive committee). ABB saw itself as a federation of national companies with a global coordination center.

Only about 100 professionals were located in ABB's corporate headquarters in Zurich. A management information system collected data on all profit centers monthly, comparing actual performance against budgets and forecasts. Data was collected in local currencies but translated into U.S. dollars to allow for cross-border analysis. ABB's corporate financial statements were reported in U.S. dollars, and English was ABB's official language. All high-level meetings were conducted in English.

Source: Compiled from information in William Taylor, "The Logic of Global Business: An Interview with ABB's Percy Barnevik," *Harvard Business Review* 69, no. 2 (March–April 1991), pp. 90–105 and company annual reports.

organizational capabilities. Seven of the most frequently used devices for supplementing the basic building block structure are:

- *Special project teams*—creating a separate, largely self-sufficient work group to oversee the completion of a special activity (setting up a new technological process, bringing out a new product, starting up a new venture, merging with another company, seeing through the completion of a government contract, supervising the construction and opening of a new plant). Project teams are especially suitable for short-term, one-of-a-kind situations when the normal organization is not equipped to achieve the same results in addition to regular duties. (At 3M Corp. project teams are the basic organizational building blocks for the company's 3,900 profit centers.)

- *Cross-functional task forces*—bringing a number of top-level executives and/or specialists together to solve problems requiring specialized expertise from several parts of the organization, coordinating strategy-related activities that span departmental boundaries, or exploring ways to leverage the skills of different functional specialists into broader core competencies. Task forces seem to be most effective when they have fewer than 10 members, membership is voluntary, the seniority of the members is proportional to the importance of the problem, the task force moves swiftly to deal with its assignment, they are used sparingly, no staff is assigned, and documentation is scant.[36] Companies that have used task forces successfully form them to solve pressing problems, produce some solutions efficiently, and then disband them.

- *Venture teams*—forming a group of individuals to manage the launch of a new product, entry into a new geographic market, or creation of a specific new business. Dow, General Mills, Westinghouse, General Electric, and Monsanto used the venture-team approach to renew an entrepreneurial spirit. The difficulties with venture teams include deciding who the venture manager should report to; whether funding for ventures should come from corporate, business, or departmental budgets; how to keep the venture clear of bureaucratic and vested interests; and how to coordinate large numbers of different ventures.

- *Self-contained work teams*—forming a group of people drawn from different disciplines who work together on a semipermanent basis to continuously improve organizational performance in such strategy-related areas as shortening the lab-to-market cycle time, boosting product quality, improving customer service, cutting delivery times, eliminating stockouts, reducing the costs of purchased materials and components, increasing assembly-line productivity, trimming equipment downtime and maintenance expenses, or designing new models. American Express cut out three layers of hierarchy when it developed self-managed teams to handle all types of customer inquiries in a single-call, quick-resolution manner.[37]

- *Process teams*—putting functional specialists who perform pieces of a business process together on a team instead of assigning them to their home-base functional department. Such teams can be empowered to reengineer the process, held accountable for results, and rewarded on the

---

[36]Ibid., pp. 127–32.
[37]Quinn, *Intelligent Enterprise*, p. 163.

basis of how well the process is performed. Much of Chrysler's revitalization is due to dramatically revamping its new-model development process using "platform teams."[38] Each platform team consists of members from engineering, design, finance, purchasing, and marketing. The team is responsible for the car's design from beginning to end, has broad decision-making power, and is held accountable for the success or failure of their design. Teams coordinate their designs with manufacturing so that the models will be easier to build and consult regularly with purchasing agents about parts quality. In one case Chrysler purchasing agents elected to pay 30 percent more for a better part because the engineer on the platform team believed the added cost would be offset by the time saved during assembly.

- *Contact managers*—appointing someone to serve as a single point of contact for customers when customer-related activities are so multi-faceted that integrating them for a single person or team to perform is impractical.[39] Acting as a buffer between internal processes and the customer, the contact person answers customer questions and coordinates the solutions to customer problems as if he or she were responsible for performing the called-for activities. To perform this role, contact persons need access to all the information that the persons actually performing the activities use and the ability to contact those people with questions and requests for further assistance when necessary. The best results are achieved when contact persons are empowered to use their own judgment to get things done in a manner that will please customers. Duke Power, a Charlotte-based electric utility, uses empowered customer service representatives to resolve the problems of residential customers while shielding them from whatever goes on "behind the scenes" to produce solutions.

- *Relationship managers*—appointing people who have responsibility for orchestrating and integrating company efforts to build strong working relationships with allies and strategic partners. Relationship managers have many roles and functions: getting the right people together, promoting good rapport, seeing that plans for specific activities are developed and carried out, helping adjust procedures to link the partners better and iron out operating dissimilarities, and nurturing interpersonal ties. Lines of communication have to be established and kept open, with enough information sharing to make the relationship work and frank discussion of conflicts, trouble spots, and changing situations.

Organizational capabilities emerge from effectively coordinating and networking the efforts of different work groups, departments, and external allies, not from how the boxes on the organization chart are arranged.

The ways of developing stronger core competencies and organizational capabilities (or creating altogether new ones) are much more idiosyncratic. Not only do different companies and executives tackle the challenge in different ways but different capabilities require different organizing techniques. Thus generalizing about *how* to build capabilities is misleading. Suffice it to say here that it entails *a process of consciously knitting the efforts of individuals and groups together* and that it is a task senior management must lead and be deeply involved in. Effectively managing both internal processes and external bridge-building with partners to create and develop valuable

---

[38]"Can Jack Smith Fix GM?" *Business Week*, November 1, 1993, pp. 130–31.
[39]Hammer and Champy, *Reengineering the Corporation*, pp. 62–63.

competencies and capabilities ranks very high on the "things to do" list of senior executives in today's companies.

Perspectives on Organizing the Work Effort and Building Capabilities   All the basic building block designs have their strengths and weaknesses. To do a good job of matching structure to strategy, strategy implementers have to pick a basic design, modify it as needed to fit the company's business makeup, and then supplement it

There's no perfect or ideal organization structure.

with coordinating mechanisms and communication arrangements to support execution of the firm's strategy. Building core competencies and competitive capabilities is a *process* that nearly always involves close collaboration between individuals and groups in different departments and between a company and its external allies—they emerge from establishing and nurturing cooperative working relationships among people and groups to perform activities in a more customer-satisfying fashion, not from rearranging boxes on an organization chart. While companies may not set up "ideal" organizational arrangements in order to avoid disturbing certain existing reporting relationships or to accommodate the personalities of certain individuals involved, internal politics, and other idiosyncracies, the goal of building a competitively capable organization usually is predominant in considering how to set up the organization chart.

ORGANIZATIONAL STRUCTURES OF THE FUTURE

Many of today's companies are winding up the task of remodeling their traditional hierarchical structures once built around functional specialization and centralized authority. Such structures still make good strategic and organizational sense so long as (1) activities can be divided into simple, repeatable tasks that can be mastered quickly and then efficiently performed in mass quantity, (2) there are important benefits to deep functional expertise in each managerial discipline, and (3) customer needs are sufficiently standardized that it is easy to prescribe procedures for satisfy-

During the past decade, new strategic priorities and rapidly shifting competitive conditions have triggered revolutionary changes in how companies are organizing the work effort.

ing them. But traditional hierarchies are a liability in businesses where customer preferences are shifting from standardized products to custom orders and special features, product life cycles are growing shorter, custom mass-production methods are replacing standardized mass production techniques, customers want to be treated as individuals, the pace of technological change is accelerating, and market conditions are fluid. Multilayered management hierarchies and functionalized bureaucracies that require people to look upward in the organizational structure for answers tend to bog down in such environments. They can't deliver responsive customer ser-

vice or adapt fast enough to changing conditions. Functional silos, task-oriented work, process fragmentation, layered management hierarchies, centralized decision making, big functional and middle-management bureaucracies, lots of checks and controls, and long response times undermine competitive success in fluid or volatile environments. Success in fast-changing markets depends on strategies built around such valuable competencies and organizational capabilities as quick response to shifting customer preferences, short design-to-market cycles, make-it-right-the-first-time quality, custom-order and multiversion production, expedited delivery, personalized customer service, accurate order filling, rapid assimilation of new technologies, creativity and innovativeness, and speedy reactions to external competitive developments.

These new components of business strategy have been driving a revolution in corporate organization for the past decade.[40] Much of the corporate downsizing movement was and is aimed at busting up functional and middle-management bureaucracies and recasting authoritarian pyramidal organizational structures into flatter, decentralized structures. The latest organizational designs for matching structure to strategy feature fewer layers of management authority, small-scale business units, reengineered work processes to cut back on fragmentation across functional department lines,[41] the development of stronger competencies and organizational capabilities and the creation of new ones as needed, collaborative partnerships with outsiders, empowerment of firstline supervisors and nonmanagement employees, lean staffing of corporate support functions, open communications vertically and laterally (via e-mail), computers and telecommunications technologies to provide fast access to and dissemination of information, and accountability for results rather than emphasis on activity. The new organizational themes are lean, flat, agile, responsive, and innovative. The new tools of organizational design are managers and workers empowered to act on their own judgments, reengineered work processes, self-directed work teams, and networking with outsiders to improve existing organizational capabilities and create new ones. The new organization-building challenge is to outcompete rivals on the basis of superior organizational capabilities and resource strengths.

The command-and-control paradigm of vertically layered structures assumes that the people actually performing work have neither the time nor the inclination to monitor and control it and that they lack the knowledge to make informed decisions about how best to do it; hence, the need for prescribed procedures, close supervision, and managerial control of decision making. In flat, decentralized structures, the assumptions are that people closest to the scene are capable of making timely, responsible decisions when properly trained and when provided with access to the needed information. There is a strong belief that decentralized decision making shortens response times and spurs new ideas, creative thinking, innovation, and greater involvement on the part of subordinate managers and employees. Hence, jobs are defined more broadly; several tasks are integrated into a single job where possible. People operate in a more self-directed fashion. Decision-making authority is pushed down to the lowest level capable of taking competent, responsible action in a timely fashion. Fewer managers are needed because deciding how to do things becomes part of each person's or team's job and because electronic technology makes information readily available and communications instantaneous.

The organizations of the future will have several new characteristics:

- Fewer boundaries between different vertical ranks, between functions and disciplines, between units in different geographic locations, and between the company and its suppliers, distributors/dealers, strategic allies, and customers.

---

[40]Evidence to this effect is contained in the scores of examples reported in Tom Peters, *Liberation Management* (New York: Alfred A. Knopf, 1992); Quinn, *Intelligent Enterprise;* and Hammer and Champy, *Reengineering the Corporation.*

[41]However, it sometimes takes more than reengineering and process organization structures to eliminate the old functional mind-sets of employees; in particular, managers also have to work at instilling a collaborative culture and fostering a collective sense of responsibility among the members of the process team. Collective responsibility can be ingrained by basing rewards on group performance, rotating assignments among the process team members, holding periodic unitwide meetings to discuss process improvements, and designing process procedures that promote a high degree of collaboration among employees doing different pieces of the process. See Ann Majchrzak and Qianwei Wang, "Breaking the Functional Mind-set in Process Organizations," *Harvard Business Review* 74, no. 5 (September–October 1996), pp. 93–99.

ILLUSTRATION CAPSULE 34   Organizational Approaches for International and Global Markets

A 1993 study of 43 large U.S.-based consumer products companies conducted by McKinsey & Co., a leading management consulting firm, identified internal organizational actions with the strongest and weakest links to rapidly growing sales and profits in international and global markets.

Organizational Actions Strongly Linked to International Success

- Centralizing international decision making in every area except new product development.

- Having a worldwide management development program and more foreigners in senior management posts.

- Requiring international experience for advancement into top management.

- Linking global managers with videoconferencing and electronic mail.

- Having product managers of foreign subsidiaries report to a country general manager.

- Using local executives to head operations in foreign countries (however, this is rapidly ceasing to distinguish successful companies

because nearly everyone has implemented such a practice).

Organizational Actions Weakly Linked to International Success

- Creating global divisions.

- Forming international strategic business units.

- Establishing centers of excellence (where a single company facility takes global responsibility for a key product or emerging technology (too new to evaluate pro or con).

- Using cross-border task forces to resolve problems and issues.

- Creating globally-integrated management information systems.

However, the lists of organizational dos and don'ts are far from decisive. In general, the study found that internal organizational structure "doesn't matter that much" as compared to having products with attractive prices and features. It is wrong to expect good results just because of good organization. Moreover, certain organizational arrangements, such as centers of excellence, are too new to determine whether they positively affect sales and profit growth.

Source: Based on information reported by Joann S. Lublin, "Study Sees U.S. Businesses Stumbling on the Road to Globalization," *The Wall Street Journal*, March 22, 1993, p. B4B.

- A capacity for change and rapid learning.
- Collaborative efforts among people in different functional specialities and geographic locations—essential to create organization competencies and capabilities.
- Extensive use of digital technology—personal computers, wireless telephones, videoconferencing, and other state-of-the-art electronic products.

Illustration Capsule 34 reports the results of a study of trends in organizational arrangements in multinational and global companies.

KEY POINTS

The job of strategy implementation is to convert strategic plans into actions and good results. The test of successful strategy implementation is whether actual organization performance matches or exceeds the targets spelled out in the strategic plan. Shortfalls in performance signal weak strategy, weak implementation, or both.

In deciding how to implement strategy, managers have to determine what internal conditions are needed to execute the strategic plan successfully. Then they must create these conditions as rapidly as practical. The process of implementing and executing strategy involves

- Building an organization with the competencies, capabilities, and resource strengths to carry out the strategy successfully.

- Developing budgets to steer ample resources into those value chain activities critical to strategic success.

- Establishing strategy-supportive policies and procedures.

- Instituting best practices and pushing for continuous improvement in how value chain activities are performed.

- Installing information, communication, and operating systems that enable company personnel to carry out their strategic roles successfully day in and day out.

- Tying rewards and incentives to the achievement of performance objectives and good strategy execution.

- Creating a strategy-supportive work environment and corporate culture.

- Exerting the internal leadership needed to drive implementation forward and to keep improving on how the strategy is being executed.

The strategy-implementing challenge is to create a series of tight fits (1) between strategy and the organization's competencies, capabilities, and structure, (2) between strategy and budgetary allocations, (3) between strategy and policy, (4) between strategy and internal support systems, (5) between strategy and the reward structure, and (6) between strategy and the corporate culture. The tighter the fits, the more powerful strategy execution becomes and the more likely targeted performance can actually be achieved.

Implementing strategy is not just a top-management function; it is a job for the whole management team. *All managers function as strategy implementers* in their respective areas of authority and responsibility. *All managers* have to consider what actions to take in their areas to achieve the intended results—they each need an action agenda.

The three major organization-building actions are (1) filling key positions with able people, (2) building the core competencies, resource strengths, and organizational capabilities needed to perform its value chain activities proficiently, and (3) structuring the internal work effort and melding it with the collaborative efforts of strategic allies. Selecting able people for key positions tends to be one of the earliest strategy implementation steps because it takes a full complement of capable managers to get changes in place and functioning smoothly.

Building strategy-critical core competencies and competitive capabilities not easily imitated by rivals is one of the best ways to outexecute rivals with similar strategies and gain a competitive advantage. Core competencies emerge from skills and activities performed at different points in the value chain that, when linked, create unique organizational capability. The key to leveraging a company's core competencies into long-term competitive advantage is to concentrate more effort and more talent than rivals do on strengthening and deepening organizational competencies and capabilities. The multiskill, multiactivity character of core competencies and capabilities makes achieving dominating depth an exercise in (1) managing human skills, knowledge bases, and intellect and (2) coordinating and networking the efforts of different work groups, departments, and collaborative allies. It is a task that senior management must lead and be deeply involved in chiefly because it is senior managers who are in the best position to guide and enforce the necessary networking and cooperation among individuals, groups, departments, and external allies.

Building organizational capabilities is more than just an effort to strengthen what a company already does, however. There are times when management has to be *proactive* in developing *new* competencies and capabilities to complement the company's existing resource base and promote more proficient strategy execution. It is useful here to think of companies as a bundle of evolving competencies and capabilities, with the organization-building challenge being one of developing new capabilities and strengthening existing ones in a fashion calculated to achieve competitive advantage through superior strategy execution.

One capability-building issue is whether to develop the desired competencies and capabilities internally or whether it makes more sense to outsource them by partnering with key suppliers or forming strategic alliances. Decisions about whether to outsource or develop in-house capability often turn on the issues of (1) what can be safely delegated to outside suppliers versus what internal capabilities are key to the company's long-term success and (2) whether noncritical activities can be outsourced more effectively or efficiently than they can be performed internally. Either way, though, implementation actions are called for. Outsourcing means launching initiatives to identify the most attractive providers and to establish collaborative relationships. Developing the capabilities in-house means hiring new personnel with skills and experience relevant to the desired organizational competence/capability, then linking the individual skills/know-how to form organizational capability.

Matching structure to strategy centers around making strategy-critical activities the main organizational building blocks, finding effective ways to bridge organizational lines of authority and coordinate the related efforts of separate internal units and individuals, and effectively networking the efforts of internal units and external collaborative partners. Other big considerations include what decisions to centralize and what decisions to decentralize.

All organization structures have strategic advantages and disadvantages; *there is no one best way to organize*. Functionally specialized organization structures have *traditionally* been the most popular way to organize single-business companies. Functional organization works well where strategy-critical activities closely match discipline-specific activities and minimal interdepartmental cooperation is needed. But it has significant drawbacks: functional myopia and empire building, interdepartmental rivalries, excessive process fragmentation, and vertically layered management hierarchies. In recent years, process organization has been used to circumvent many of the disadvantages of functional organization.

Geographic organization structures are favored by enterprises operating in diverse geographic markets or across expansive geographic areas. SBU structures are well-suited to companies pursuing related diversification. Decentralized business-unit structures are well-suited to companies pursuing unrelated diversification. Matrix structures work well for companies that need separate lines of authority and managers for each of several strategic dimensions (products, buyer segments, functional departments, projects or ventures, technologies, core business processes, geographic areas) yet also need close cooperation between these managers to coordinate related value chain activities, share or transfer skills, and perform certain related activities jointly.

Whatever formal organization structure is chosen, it usually has to be supplemented with interdisciplinary task forces, incentive compensation schemes tied to measures of joint performance, empowerment of cross-functional teams to perform and unify fragmented processes and strategy-critical activities, special project and venture teams, self-contained work teams, contact managers, relationship managers, and special efforts to knit the work of different individuals and groups into valuable competitive capabilities. Building core competencies and competitive capabilities emerge from establishing and nurturing collaborative working relationships between individuals and groups in different departments and between a company and its external allies, not from how the boxes are arranged on an organization chart.

New strategic priorities like short design-to-market cycles, multiversion production, and personalized customer service are promoting a revolution in organization building featuring lean, flat, horizontal structures that are responsive and innovative. Such designs for matching structure to strategy involve fewer layers of management authority, small-scale business units, reengineering work processes to reduce fragmentation across departmental lines, the creation of process departments and cross-functional work groups, managers and workers empowered to act on their own judgments, collaborative partnerships with outsiders (suppliers, distributors/dealers, companies with complementary products/services, and even select competitors), increased outsourcing of noncritical activities, lean staffing of internal support functions, and use of computers and telecommunications technologies to provide fast access to information.

Aaker, David A. "Managing Assets and Skills: The Key to a Sustainable Competitive Advantage." *California Management Review* 31 (Winter 1989), pp. 91–106.

Bartlett, Christopher A., and Sumantra Ghoshal. "Matrix Management: Not a Structure, a Frame of Mind." *Harvard Business Review* 68, no. 4 (July–August 1990), pp. 138–45.

Hall, Gene, Jim Rosenthal, and Judy Wade. "How to Make Reengineering Really Work." *Harvard Business Review* 71, no. 6 (November–December 1993), pp. 119–31.

Hambrick, Donald C. "The Top Management Team: Key to Strategic Success." *California Management Review* 30, no. 1 (Fall 1987), pp. 88–108.

Hammer, Michael, and James Champy. *Reengineering the Corporation.* New York: HarperBusiness, 1993, chaps. 2 and 3.

Howard, Robert. "The CEO as Organizational Architect: An Interview with Xerox's Paul Allaire." *Harvard Business Review* 70, no. 5 (September–October 1992), pp. 107–19.

Kanter, Rosabeth Moss. "Collaborative Advantage: The Art of the Alliance." *Harvard Business Review* 72, no. 4 (July–August 1994), pp. 96–108.

Katzenbach, Jon R., and Douglas K. Smith. "The Discipline of Teams." *Harvard Business Review* 71, no. 2 (March–April 1993), pp. 111–24.

Larson, Erik W., and David H. Gobeli. "Matrix Management: Contradictions and Insights." *California Management Review* 29, no. 4 (Summer 1987), pp. 126–27.

Markides, Constantinos C. and Peter J. Williamson. "Corporate Diversification and Organizational Structure: A Resource-Based View." *Academy of Management Journal* 39, no. 2 (April 1996), pp. 340–67.

Pfeffer, Jeffrey. "Producing Sustainable Competitive Advantage through the Effective Management of People." *Academy of Management Executive* 9, no. 1 (February 1995), pp. 55–69.

Powell, Walter W. "Hybrid Organizational Arrangements: New Form or Transitional Development?" *California Management Review* 30, no. 1 (Fall 1987), pp. 67–87.

Prahalad, C. K., and Gary Hamel. "The Core Competence of the Corporation." *Harvard Business Review* 68 (May–June 1990), pp. 79–93.

Rackham, Neil, Lawrence Friedman, and Richard Ruff. *Getting Partnering Right: How Market Leaders Are Creating Long-Term Competitive Advantage.* New York: McGraw-Hill, 1996.

Quinn, James Brian. *Intelligent Enterprise.* New York: Free Press, 1992, chaps. 2 and 3.

Stalk, George, Philip Evans, and Lawrence E. Shulman. "Competing on Capabilities: The New Rules of Corporate Strategy." *Harvard Business Review* 70, no. 2 (March–April 1992), pp. 57–69.

Yip, George S. *Total Global Strategy: Managing for Worldwide Competitive Advantage.* Englewood Cliffs, N.J.: Prentice-Hall, 1992, chap. 8.

SUGGESTED READINGS

10 IMPLEMENTING STRATEGY: BUDGETS, POLICIES, BEST PRACTICES, SUPPORT SYSTEMS, AND REWARDS

I n the previous chapter we emphasized the importance of building organization capabilities and structuring the work effort so as to perform strategy-critical activities in a coordinated and competent manner. In this chapter we discuss five additional strategy-implementing tasks:

... Winning companies know how to do their work better.

Michael Hammer and James Champy

If you talk about change but don't change the reward and recognition system, nothing changes.

Paul Allaire
CEO, Xerox Corporation

If you want people motivated to do a good job, give them a good job to do.

Frederick Herzberg

... You ought to pay big bonuses for premier performance ... be a top payer, not in the middle or low end of the pack.

Lawrence Bossidy
CEO, AlliedSignal

1. Reallocating resources to match the budgetary and staffing requirements of the new strategy.
2. Establishing strategy-supportive policies and procedures.
3. Instituting best practices and mechanisms for continuous improvement.
4. Installing support systems that enable company personnel to carry out their strategic roles day in and day out.
5. Employing motivational practices and incentive compensation methods that enhance commitment to good strategy execution.

LINKING BUDGETS TO STRATEGY

Implementing strategy forces a manager into the budget-making process. Organizational units need big enough budgets to carry out their parts of the strategic plan. There has to be ample funding of efforts to strengthen existing competencies and capabilities and/or to develop new ones. Organizational units, especially those charged with performing strategy-critical activities, have to be staffed with enough of the right kinds of people, be given enough operating funds to do their work proficiently, and have the funds to invest in needed operating systems, equipment, and facilities. Strategy implementers must screen subordinates' requests for new capital projects and bigger operating budgets, distinguishing between what would be nice and what can make a cost-effective contribution to strategy execution and enhanced competitive capabilities. Moreover, implementers have to make a persuasive, documented case to superiors on what additional resources and competitive assets, if any, it will take to execute their assigned pieces of company strategy.

How well a strategy implementer links budget allocations to the needs of strategy can either promote or impede the implementation process. Too little funding slows progress and impedes the ability of organizational units to execute their pieces of the strategic plan. Too much funding wastes organizational resources and reduces financial performance. Both outcomes argue for the strategy implementer to be deeply involved in the budgeting process, closely reviewing the programs and budget proposals of strategy-critical organization units.

Implementers must also be willing to shift resources from one area to another to support new strategic initiatives and priorities. A change in strategy nearly always calls for budget reallocations. Units important in the old strategy may now be oversized and overfunded. Units that now have a bigger and more critical role may need more people, different support systems, new equipment, additional facilities, and above-average increases in their operating budgets. Strategy implementers need to be active and forceful in shifting resources, downsizing some areas, upsizing others, and amply funding activities with a critical role in the new strategy. They have to exercise their power to allocate resources to make things happen and make the tough decisions to kill projects and activities that are no longer justified. The funding requirements of the new strategy *must* drive how capital allocations are made and the size of each unit's operating budgets. Underfunding units and activities pivotal to strategic success can defeat the whole implementation process.

Aggressive resource reallocation can have a positive strategic payoff. For example, at Harris Corporation, where the strategy was to quickly transfer new research results to organizational units that could turn them into areas commercially viable products, top management regularly shifted groups of engineers out of research projects and moved them (as a group) into new commercial venture divisions. Boeing used a similar approach to reallocating ideas and talent; according to one Boeing officer, "We can do it (create a big new unit) in two weeks. We couldn't do it in two years at International Harvester."[1] Forceful actions to reallocate funds and move people into new units signal a strong commitment to implementing strategic change and are frequently needed to catalyze the implementation process and give it credibility.

Fine-tuning the implementation of a company's existing strategy seldom requires big movements of people and money. The needed adjustments can usually be accomplished through above-average budget increases to units where new initiatives are contemplated and below-average increases (or even small cuts) for the remaining units. The chief exception occurs where a prime ingredient of corporate/business strategy is to create altogether new competencies/capabilities or to generate fresh, new products and business opportunities within the existing budget. Then, as propos-

> **Strategic Management Principle**
>
> *Depriving strategy-critical groups of the funds needed to execute their pieces of the strategy can undermine the implementation process.*
>
> *New strategies usually call for significant budget reallocations.*

---

[1]Thomas J. Peters and Robert H. Waterman, Jr., *In Search of Excellence* (New York: Harper & Row, 1980), p. 125.

als and business plans worth pursuing bubble up from below, decisions have to be made about where the needed capital expenditures, operating budgets, and personnel will come from. Companies like 3M, GE, and Boeing shift resources and people from area to area on an as-needed basis to support the launch of new products and new business ventures. They empower "product champions" and small bands of would-be entrepreneurs by giving them financial and technical support and by setting up organizational units and programs to help new ventures blossom more quickly. Microsoft is quick to disband some project teams and create others to pursue fresh software projects or new ventures like MSN.

CREATING STRATEGY-SUPPORTIVE POLICIES AND PROCEDURES

Changes in strategy generally call for some changes in work practices and how operations are conducted. Asking people to alter established procedures and behavior always upsets the internal order of things. It is normal for pockets of resistance to develop and for people to exhibit some degree of stress and anxiety about how the changes will affect them, especially when the changes may eliminate jobs. Questions are also likely to arise over what activities need to be done in rigidly prescribed fashion and where there ought to be leeway for independent action.

Prescribing policies and operating procedures aids the task of implementing strategy in several ways:

1. New or freshly revised policies and procedures provide top-down guidance to operating managers, supervisory personnel, and employees about how certain things now need to be done and what behavior is expected, thus establishing some degree of regularity, stability, and dependability in how management has decided to try to execute the strategy and operate the business on a daily basis.

2. Policies and procedures help align actions and behavior with strategy throughout the organization, placing limits on independent action and channeling individual and group efforts along the intended path. Policies and procedures counteract tendencies for some people to resist or reject common approaches—most people refrain from violating company policy or ignoring established practices without first gaining clearance or having strong justification.

3. Policies and standardized operating procedures help enforce needed consistency in how particular strategy-critical activities are performed in geographically scattered operating units. Eliminating significant differences in the operating practices and procedures of units performing common functions is necessary to avoid sending mixed messages to internal personnel and to customers who do business with the company at multiple locations.

4. Because dismantling old policies and procedures and instituting new ones alter the character of the internal work climate, strategy implementers can use the policy-changing process as a powerful lever for changing the corporate culture in ways that produce a stronger fit with the new strategy.

Company managers, therefore, need to be inventive in devising policies and practices that can provide vital support to effective strategy implementation. McDonald's policy manual, in an attempt to steer "crew members" into stronger quality and service behavior patterns, spells out such detailed procedures as "Cooks must turn, never flip, hamburgers. If they haven't been purchased, Big Macs must be discarded

ILLUSTRATION CAPSULE 35 Nike's Manufacturing Policies and Procedures

When Nike decided on a strategy of outsourcing 100 percent of its athletic footwear from independent manufacturers (that, for reasons of low cost, all turned out to be located in Taiwan, South Korea, Thailand, Indonesia, and China), it developed a series of policies and production practices to govern its working relationships with its "production partners" (a term Nike carefully nurtured because it implied joint responsibilities):

- Nike personnel were stationed on-site at all key manufacturing facilities; each Nike representative tended to stay at the same factory site for several years to get to know the partner's people and processes in detail. They functioned as liaisons with Nike headquarters, working to match Nike's R&D and new product design efforts with factory capabilities and to keep monthly orders for new production in line with the latest sales forecasts.
- Nike instituted a quality assurance program at each factory site to enforce up-to-date and effective quality management practices.

- Nike endeavored to minimize ups and downs in monthly production orders at factory sites making Nike's premium-priced top-of-the-line models (volumes typically ran 20,000 to 25,000 pairs daily); the policy was to keep month-to-month variations in order quantity under 20 percent. These factories made Nike footwear exclusively and were expected to co-develop new models and to co-invest in new technologies.
- Factory sites that made mid-to-low-end Nike products in large quantities (usually 70,000 to 85,000 pairs per day), known as "volume producers," were expected to handle most ups and downs in monthly orders themselves; these factories usually produced shoes for five to eight other buyers, giving them the flexibility to juggle orders and stabilize their production.
- It was strict Nike policy to pay its bills from production partners on time, providing them with predictable cash flows.

Source: Based on information in James Brian Quinn, *Intelligent Enterprise* (New York: Free Press, 1992), pp. 60–64.

in 10 minutes after being cooked and french fries in 7 minutes. Cashiers must make eye contact with and smile at every customer." Caterpillar Tractor has a policy of guaranteeing its customers 24-hour parts delivery anywhere in the world; if it fails to fulfill the promise, it supplies the part free. Hewlett-Packard requires R&D people to make regular visits to customers to learn about their problems, talk about new product applications, and, in general, keep the company's R&D programs customer-oriented. Mrs. Fields' Cookies has a policy of establishing *hourly* sales quotas for each store outlet; furthermore, it is company policy for cookies not sold within two hours after being baked to be removed from the case and given to charitable organizations. Illustration Capsule 35 describes Nike's manufacturing policies in some detail.

Well-conceived policies and procedures aid implementation; out-of-sync policies are barriers.

Thus there is a definite role for new and revised policies and procedures in the strategy implementation process. Wisely constructed policies and procedures help enforce strategy implementation by channeling actions, behavior, decisions, and practices in directions that improve strategy execution. When policies and procedures aren't strategy-supportive, they become a barrier to the kinds of changes in attitude and behavior strategy implementers are trying to promote. Often, people opposed to certain elements of the strategy or certain implementation approaches will hide behind or vigorously defend long-standing policies and operating procedures in an effort to stall implementation or divert the approach to implementation along a different route. Anytime a company alters its strategy, managers should review existing policies and operating procedures, revise or discard those that are out of sync, and formulate new ones.

None of this implies that companies need thick policy manuals to guide strategy implementation and daily operations. Too much policy can be as stifling as wrong policy or as chaotic as no policy. There is wisdom in a middle approach: prescribe enough policies to give organizational members clear direction and to place desirable boundaries on their actions, then empower them to do act within these boundaries however they think makes sense. Such latitude is especially appropriate when individual creativity and initiative are more essential to good strategy execution than standardization and strict conformity.[2] Creating a strong, supportive fit between strategy and policy can therefore mean more policies, fewer policies, or different policies. It can mean policies that require things to be done a certain way or policies that give employees leeway to do activities the way they think best.

INSTITUTING BEST PRACTICES AND A COMMITMENT TO CONTINUOUS IMPROVEMENT

Identifying and implementing best practices is a journey, not a destination.

If value-chain activities are to be performed as effectively and efficiently as possible, each department and unit needs to benchmark how it performs specific tasks and activities against best-in-industry or best-in-world performers. A strong commitment to searching out and adopting best practices is integral to effective strategy implementation—especially for strategy-critical and big-dollar activities where better quality or lower costs impact bottom-line performance.[3]

The benchmarking movement to search out, study, and implement best practices has stimulated greater management awareness of the strategy-implementing importance of reengineering (the redesign of business processes), total quality management (TQM), and other continuous improvement programs. TQM is a philosophy of managing and set of business practices that emphasizes continuous improvement in all phases of operations, 100 percent accuracy in performing activities, involvement and empowerment of employees at all levels, team-based work design, benchmarking, and fully satisfying customer expectations. A 1991 survey by The Conference Board showed 93 percent of manufacturing companies and 69 percent of service companies had implemented some form of quality improvement program.[4] Another survey found that 55 percent of American executives and 70 percent of Japanese executives used quality improvement information at least monthly as part of their assessment of overall performance.[5] An Arthur D. Little study reported that 93 percent of the 500 largest U.S. firms had adopted TQM in some form as of 1992. Analysts have attributed the quality of many Japanese products to dedicated application of TQM principles. Indeed, *quality improvement processes have now become a globally pervasive part of the fabric of implementing strategies keyed to defect-free manufacture, superior product quality, superior customer service, and total customer satisfaction.*

Management interest in quality improvement programs typically originates in a company's production areas—fabrication and assembly in manufacturing enterprises, teller transactions in banks, order picking and shipping at catalog firms, or customer-contact interfaces in service organizations. Other times, interest begins with executives who hear TQM presentations, read about TQM, or talk to people in other companies that have benefited from total quality programs. Usually, interested man-

---

[2]Ibid., p. 65.

[3]For a discussion of the value of benchmarking in implementing strategy, see Yoshinobu Ohinata, "Benchmarking: The Japanese Experience," *Long Range Planning* 27, no. 4 (August 1994), pp. 48–53.

[4]Judy D. Olian and Sara L. Rynes, "Making Total Quality Work: Aligning Organizational Processes, Performance Measures, and Stakeholders," *Human Resource Management* 30, no. 3 (Fall 1991), p. 303.

[5]Ibid.

TABLE 10-1 Components of Popular TQM Approaches and 1992 Baldridge Award Criteria

DEMING'S 14 POINTS

1. Constancy of purpose
2. Adopt the philosophy
3. Don't rely on mass inspection
4. Don't award business on price
5. Constant improvement
6. Training
7. Leadership
8. Drive out fear
9. Break down barriers
10. Eliminate slogans and exhortations
11. Eliminate quotas
12. Pride of workmanship
13. Education and retraining
14. Plan of action

THE JURAN TRILOGY

1. *Quality Planning*
   • Set goals
   • Identify customers and their needs
   • Develop products and processes
2. *Quality control*
   • Evaluate performance
   • Compare to goals and adapt
3. *Quality improvement*
   • Establish infrastructure
   • Identify projects and teams
   • Provide resources and training
   • Establish controls

CROSBY'S 14 QUALITY STEPS

1. Management commitment
2. Quality improvement teams
3. Quality measurement
4. Cost of quality evaluation
5. Quality awareness
6. Corrective action
7. Zero-defects committee
8. Supervisor training
9. Zero-defects day
10. Goal-setting
11. Error cause removal
12. Recognition
13. Quality councils
14. Do it over again

THE 1992 BALDRIDGE AWARD CRITERIA (1000 points total)

1. *Leadership* (90 points)
   • Senior executive
   • Management for quality
   • Public responsibility
2. *Information and analysis* (80 points)
   • Scope and management of quality and performance data
   • Competitive comparisons and benchmarks
3. *Strategic quality planning* (60 points)
   • Strategic quality and planning process
   • Quality and performance plans
4. *Human resource development and management* (150 points)
   • Human resource management
   • Employee involvement
   • Employee education and training
   • Employee performance and recognition
   • Employee well-being and morale

5. *Management of process quality* (140 points)
   • Design and introduction of products and services
   • Process management—production and delivery
   • Process management—business and support
   • Supplier quality
   • Quality assessment
6. *Quality and operational results* (180 points)
   • Product and service quality
   • Company operations
   • Business process and support services
   • Supplier quality
7. *Customer focus and satisfaction* (300 points)
   • Customer relationships
   • Commitment to customers
   • Customer satisfaction determination
   • Customer satisfaction results
   • Customer satisfaction comparisons
   • Future requirements and expectations

Source: As presented in Thomas C. Powell, "Total Quality Management as Competitive Advantage," *Strategic Management Journal* 16, no. 1 (January 1995) p. 18 and based on M. Walton, *The Deming Management Method* (New York: Pedigree, 1986); J. Juran, *Juran on Quality by Design* (New York: Free Press, 1992); Philip Crosby, *Quality Is Free: The Act of Making Quality Certain* (New York: McGraw-Hill, 1979); and S. George, *The Baldridge Quality System* (New York: Wiley, 1992).

agers have quality and customer-satisfaction problems they are struggling to solve. See Table 10-1 for the different kinds of features emphasized by the leading proponents of TQM and for the criteria employed in selected winners of the Malcolm Baldridge Award for Quality.

While TQM concentrates on the production of quality goods and the delivery of excellent customer service, to succeed it must extend organizationwide to employee efforts in all departments—HR, billing, R&D, engineering, accounting and records, and information systems—that may lack less-pressing customer-driven incentives to

TABLE 10-2   Twelve Aspects Common to TQM and Continuous Improvement Programs

1. Committed leadership: a near-evangelical, unwavering, long-term commitment by top managers to the philosophy, usually under a name something like Total Quality Management, Continuous Improvement (CI), or Quality Improvement (QI).

2. Adoption and communication of TQM: using tools like the mission statement, and themes or slogans.

3. Closer customer relationships: determining customers' (both inside and outside the firm) requirements, then meeting those requirements no matter what it takes.

4. Closer supplier relationships: working closely and cooperatively with suppliers (often sole-sourcing key components), ensuring they provide inputs that conform to customers' end-use requirements.

5. Benchmarking: researching and observing operating competitive practices.

6. Increased training: usually includes TQM principles, team skills, and problem-solving.

7. Open organization: lean staff, empowered work teams, open horizontal communications, and a relaxation of traditional hierarchy.

8. Employee empowerment: increased employee involvement in design and planning, and greater autonomy in decision-making.

9. Zero-defects mentality: a system in place to spot defects as they occur, rather than through inspection and rework.

10. Flexible manufacturing: (applicable only to manufacturers) can include just-in-time inventory, cellular manufacturing, design for manufacturability (DFM), statistical process control (SPC), and design of experiments (DOE).

11. Process improvement: reduced waste and cycle times in all areas through cross-departmental process analysis.

12. Measurement: goal-orientation and zeal for data, with constant performance measurement, often using statistical methods.

Source: Thomas C. Powell, "Total Quality Management as Competitive Advantage," *Strategic Management Journal* 16, no. 1 (January 1995) p. 19.

TQM entails creating a total quality culture bent on continuously improving the performance of every task and value-chain activity.

improve. This is because the institution of best practices and continuous improvement programs involves reforming the corporate culture and shifting to a total quality/continuous improvement philosophy that permeates the organization—see Table 10-2 for the features common to most TQM programs.[6] TQM aims at instilling enthusiasm and commitment to doing things right from top to bottom of the organization. It entails a restless search for continuing improvement, the little steps forward each day that the Japanese call *kaizen*. TQM is a race without a finish. The managerial objective is to kindle a burning desire in people to use their ingenuity and initiative to progressively improve on how tasks are performed. TQM preaches that there's no such thing as good enough and that everyone has a responsibility to

[6]For a discussion of the shift in work environment and culture that TQM entails, see Robert T. Amsden, Thomas W. Ferratt, and Davida M. Amsden, "TQM: Core Paradigm Changes," *Business Horizons* 39, no. 6 (November–December 1996), pp. 6–14.

ILLUSTRATION CAPSULE 36 Motorola's Approach to TQM and Teamwork

Motorola is rated as one of the best companies in measuring performance against its strategic targets and in promoting total quality practices that lead to continuous improvement. Motorola was selected in 1988 as one of the first winners of the Malcolm Baldrige Quality Award and has since improved on its own award-winning efforts. In 1993, the company estimated it was saving about $2.2 billion annually from its team-oriented approach to TQM and continuous improvement.

A central feature of Motorola's approach is a year-long contest highlighting the successes of employee teams from around the world in improving internal company practices, making better products, saving money, pleasing customers, and sharing best practices with other Motorola groups. The contest, known as the Total Customer Satisfaction Team Competition, in 1992 attracted entries from nearly 4,000 teams involving nearly 40,000 of Motorola's 107,000 employees. Preliminary judging eventually reduced the 1992 finalists to 24 teams from around the world, all of which were invited to Chicago in January 1993 to make a 12–minute presentation to a panel of 15 senior executives, including the CEO. Twelve teams were awarded gold medals and 12 silver medals. The gold medalists are listed below.

Motorola does not track the costs of the contest because "the benefits are so overwhelming." It has sent hundreds of videos about the contests to other companies wanting details. However, TQM consultants are skeptical whether other companies have progressed far enough in establishing a team-based quality culture to benefit from a companywide contest. The downsides to such elaborate contests, they say, are the added costs (preparation, travel, presentation, and judging) and the risks to the morale of those who don't win.

Gold Medal Teams	Work Location	Achievement
B.E.A.P. Goes On	Florida	Removed bottleneck in testing pagers by using robots.
The Expedition	Malaysia	Designed and delivered a new chip for Apple Computer in six months.
Operation Paging Storm	Singapore	
ET/EV=1	Illinois	Eliminated component alignment defect in papers.
The Mission	Arizona	Streamlined order process for auto electronics.
Class Act	Illinois	Developed quality system for design of iridium satellites.
Dyna-Attackers	Dublin	Cut training program from five years to two with better results.
Orient Express	Malaysia	Cut production time and defect rate on new battery part.
The Dandles	Japan	Cut response time on tooling orders from 23 days to 4.
Cool Blue Racers	Arizona	Improved efficiency of boiler operations.
IO Plastics Misload	Manila	Cut product development time in half to win IBM contract.
		Eliminated resin seepage in modulator assembly.

Source: Based on information reported in Barnaby J. Feder, "At Motorola, Quality Is a Team Sport," *New York Times*, January 21, 1993, pp. C1 and C6.

participate in continuous improvement—see Illustration Capsule 36 describing Motorola's approach to involving employees in the TQM effort.

Effective use of TQM/continuous improvement techniques is a valuable competitive asset—one that can produce important competitive capabilities (in product design, cost reduction, product quality, and customer service) and be a source of competitive advantage.[7] Not only do ongoing incremental improvements add up over time and strengthen organizational capabilities but TQM/continuous improvement

---

[7]Thomas C. Powell, "Total Quality Management as Competitive Advantage," *Strategic Management Journal* 16 (1995), pp. 15–37. See, also, Richard M. Hodgetts, "Quality Lessons from America's Baldrige Winners," *Business Horizons* 37, no. 4 (July–August 1994), pp. 74–79 and Richard Reed, David J. Lemak, and Joseph C. Montgomery, "Beyond Process: TQM Content and Firm Performance," *Academy of Management Review* 21, no. 1 (January 1996), pp. 173–202.

programs have hard-to-imitate aspects. While it is relatively easy for rivals to under-take benchmarking, process improvement, and quality training, it is much more difficult for them to implant a total quality culture, empower employees, and generate deep and genuine management commitment to TQM philosophy and practices. TQM requires a substantial investment of management time and effort; some managers and employees resist TQM, viewing it as ideological or faddish. It is expensive (in terms of training and meetings) and it seldom produces short-term results. The longer term payoff depends heavily on management's success in instilling a culture within which TQM philosophies and practices can thrive.

Having the capability to generate continuous improvements in important value-chain activities is a valuable competitive asset.

The Difference between TQM and Process Reengineering   Best practices, process reengineering, and continuous improvement efforts like TQM all aim at improved efficiency and reduced costs, better product quality, and greater customer satisfaction. *The essential difference between process reengineering and TQM is that reengineering aims at quantum gains on the order of 30 to 50 percent or more, whereas total quality programs stress incremental progress, striving for inch-by-inch gains again and again.* The two approaches to improved performance of value-chain activities are not mutually exclusive; it makes sense to use them in tandem. Reengineering can be used first to produce a good basic design that dramatically improves a business process. Total quality programs can then be used to work out bugs, perfect the process, and gradually improve both efficiency and effectiveness. Such a two-pronged approach to implementing organizational and strategic change is like a marathon race where you run the first four laps as fast as you can, then gradually pick up speed the remainder of the way.

Reengineering seeks one-time quantum improvement; TQM seeks ongoing incremental improvement.

Capturing the Potential Benefits   Research indicates that some companies benefit from reengineering and TQM and some do not.[8] Usually, the biggest beneficiaries are companies that view such programs not as ends in themselves but as tools for implementing and executing company strategy more effectively. The skimpiest payoffs from best practices, TQM, and reengineering occur when company managers seize them as something worth trying, novel ideas that could improve things; in most such instances, they result in strategy-blind efforts to simply manage better. There's an important lesson here. Best practices, TQM, and reengineering all need to be seen and used as part of a bigger-picture effort to execute strategy proficiently. Only strategy can point to which activities matter and what performance targets make the most sense. Absent a strategic framework, managers lack the context in which to fix things that really matter to business-unit performance and competitive success.

When best practices, reengineering, and TQM are not part of a wider-scale effort to improve strategy execution and business performance, they deteriorate into strategy-blind efforts to manage better.

To get the most from benchmarking, best practices, reengineering, TQM, and related tools for enhancing organizational competence in executing strategy, managers have to start with a clear fix on the indicators of successful strategy execution—defect-free manufacture, on-time delivery, low overall costs, exceeding customers' expectations, faster cycle time, increased product innovation, or some other specific performance measure. Benchmarking most or all value-chain activities against best-

---

[8] See, for example, Gene Hall, Jim Rosenthal, and Judy Wade, "How to Make Reengineering Really Work," *Harvard Business Review* 71, no. 6 (November–December 1993), pp. 119–31.

in-industry and best-in-world performance provides a basis for setting internal performance milestones and longer-range targets.

Then comes the managerial task of building a total quality culture and instilling the necessary commitment to achieving the targets and performance measures that the strategy requires. The action steps managers can take include:[9]

1. Visible, unequivocal, and unyielding commitment to total quality and continuous improvement, including a quality vision and specific, measurable quality goals.

2. Nudging people toward TQ-supportive behaviors by initiating such organizational programs as
   - Screening job applicants rigorously and hiring only those with attitudes and aptitudes right for quality-based performance.
   - Quality training for most employees.
   - Using teams and team-building exercises to reinforce and nurture individual effort (expansion of a TQ culture is facilitated when teams become more cross-functional, multitask, and increasingly self-managed).
   - Recognizing and rewarding individual and team efforts regularly and systematically.
   - Stressing prevention (doing it right the first time) not inspection (instituting ways to correct mistakes).

3. Empowering employees so that authority for delivering great service or improving products is in the hands of the doers rather than the overseers.

4. Using on-line information systems to provide all parties with the latest best practices and actual experiences with them, thereby speeding the diffusion and adoption of best practices throughout the organization and also allowing them to exchange data and opinions about how to improve/upgrade the best practices.

5. Preaching that performance can, and must, be improved because competitors are not resting on past laurels and customers are always looking for something better.

If the targeted performance measures are appropriate to the strategy and if top executives, middle managers, professional staff, and line employees buy into the process of continuous improvement, then the work climate will promote proficient strategy execution and good bottom-line business performance.

INSTALLING SUPPORT SYSTEMS

Company strategies can't be implemented or executed well without a number of support systems for business operations. American, United, Delta, and other major airlines cannot hope to provide world-class service without a computerized reservation system, an accurate and fast baggage handling system, and a strong aircraft maintenance program. FedEx has a computerized parcel-tracking system that can instantly report the location of any given package in its transit-delivery process; it

---

[9]Olian and Rynes, "Making Total Quality Work," pp. 305–6 and 310–11 and Paul S. Goodman and Eric D. Darr, "Exchanging Best Practices Information through Computer-Aided Systems," *Academy of Management Executive* 10, no. 2 (May 1996), p. 7.

has communication systems that allow it to coordinate its 21,000 vans nationwide to make an average of 720,000 stops per day to pick up customer packages; and it has leading-edge flight operations systems that allow a single controller to direct as many as 200 FedEx aircraft simultaneously, overriding their flight plans should weather or special emergencies arise—all these operations essential to FedEx's strategy of next-day delivery of a package that "absolutely, positively has to be there."[10]

Otis Elevator has a sophisticated support system called OtisLine to coordinate maintenance nationwide.[11] Trained operators take all trouble calls, input critical information on a computer screen, and dispatch people directly via a beeper system to the local trouble spot. From the trouble-call inputs, problem patterns can be identified nationally and the information communicated to design and manufacturing personnel, allowing them to quickly alter design specifications or manufacturing procedures to correct recurring problems. Also, much of the information needed for repairs is provided directly from faulty elevators through internally installed microcomputer monitors, further lowering outage time.

Strategic Management Principle

Innovative, state-of-the-art support systems can be a basis for competitive advantage if they give a firm capabilities that rivals can't match.

Procter & Gamble codes the more than 900,000 call-in inquiries it receives annually on its toll-free 800 number to obtain early warning signals of product problems and changing tastes.[12] Arthur Andersen Worldwide has an electronic system linking more than 82,000 people in 360 offices in 76 countries; the system has data, voice, and video capabilities and includes an electronic bulletin board for posting customer problems, for organizing around a customer's problem using people from all over the world, as well as the capability to collect, index, and distribute files containing information on particular subjects, customers, solutions, and company resources.[13] Andersen's Knowledge Xchange system captures the lessons learned in the company's daily work and research and makes it available to Andersen personnel 24 hours a day. Wal-Mart's computers transmit daily sales data to Wrangler, a supplier of blue jeans; using a model that interprets the data and software applications that act on these interpretations, specific quantities of specific sizes and colors are then shipped to specific stores from specific warehouses—the system lowers logistics and inventory costs and leads to fewer stockouts.[14] Domino's Pizza has computerized systems at each outlet to help with ordering, inventory, payroll, cash flow, and work control functions, freeing managers to spend more time on supervision, customer service, and business development.[15] Most telephone companies, electric utilities, and TV broadcasting systems have on-line monitoring systems to spot transmission problems within seconds and increase the reliability of their services. Software companies need systems that allow them to distribute their products on the Internet. At Mrs. Fields' Cookies, computer systems monitor hourly sales and suggest product mix changes, promotional tactics, or operating adjustments to improve customer response—see Illustration Capsule 37. Many companies have installed software systems on their company intranets to catalog best practices

---

[10]James Brian Quinn, *Intelligent Enterprise* (New York: Free Press, 1992) pp. 114–15.

[11]Ibid., p. 186.

[12]Ibid., p. 111.

[13]James Brian Quinn, Philip Anderson, and Sydney Finkelstein, "Leveraging Intellect," *Academy of Management Executive* 10, no. 3 (November 1996), p. 9.

[14]Stephan H. Haeckel and Richard L. Nolan. "Managing by Wire," *Harvard Business Review* 75, no. 5 (September–October 1993), p. 129.

[15]Quinn, *Intelligent Enterprise,* p. 181.

ILLUSTRATION CAPSULE 37   Management Information and Control Systems at Mrs. Fields' Cookies, Inc.

Mrs. Fields' Cookies is one of the best known specialty foods companies with over 800 outlets in operation in malls, airports, and other high pedestrian-traffic locations around the world. The business concept for Mrs. Fields' Cookies, as articulated by Debbi Fields, the company's founder and CEO, is "to serve absolutely fresh, warm cookies as though you'd stopped by my house and caught me just taking a batch from the oven." The company promotes its products mainly by sampling; store employees walk around giving away cookie samples. Another is for Fields to make unannounced visits to her stores, where she masquerades as a casual shopper to test the enthusiasm and sales techniques of store crews, sample the quality of the cookies they are baking, and observe customer reactions.

In 1978 when Debbi Fields opened her second store in San Francisco, 45 miles away from the first store in Palo Alto, she confronted the logistical problems of maintaining hands-on management and control at remote locations. Debbi's husband Randy developed a software program to issue instructions and advice to store managers and to provide a way of exercising control over store operations. Each morning local managers enter information on their store PCs—the day of the week, the month (to pick up seasonal shopping patterns), special mall activities or local events expected to influence traffic patterns, and the weather forecast. Randy's software program analyzes this information, together with the store's recent performance history, and prints out a daily sales goal (broken down by the hour). With the hourly sales quotas also comes an hourly schedule of how many batches of cookies to mix and bake and when to offer free samples.

As the day progresses, store managers type in actual hourly sales figures and customer counts. If customer counts are up but sales are lagging, the computerized software system recommends more aggressive sampling or more suggestive selling. If it becomes obvious the day is going to be a bust for the store, the computer automatically revises the sales projections for the day, reducing hourly quotas and instructing how much to cut back cookie baking. To facilitate crew scheduling by the store manager, sales projections are also provided for two weeks in advance. If a store manager has a specific problem, it can be entered on the system and routed to the appropriate person. The system gives store managers more time to work with their crews and achieve sales quotas, as opposed to handling administrative chores.

When Mrs. Fields' Cookies began to expand into Europe and Asia, the company's information technology department modified the software to take into account the different shopping patterns, buyer preferences, labor laws, languages, and supplier arrangements being encountered in foreign countries. A second generation of software, called the Retail Operations Intelligence system, was also developed; ROI has modules for inventory control, interviewing and hiring, repair and maintenance, lease management, and e-mail. All job applicants must sit at the store's terminal and answer a computerized set of questions as part of the interview process; the questions help store managers identify candidates with aptitudes for warmth, friendliness, and the ability to have a good time giving away samples, baking fresh batches, and talking to customers during the course of a sale.

Because the day-to-day variations in the cookie business are fairly easy to model and employee turnover in retail outlets like Mrs. Fields' is high, having the capability to "manage-by-wire" and run basic store operations on autopilot much of the time is a valuable strategy-implementing, strategy-executing assist. Debbi Fields also uses the electronic system as a means of projecting her influence and enthusiasm into stores far more frequently than she can reach through personal visits.

Source: Developed from information in Mike Korologos, "Debbi Fields," *Sky Magazine*, July 1988, pp. 42–50 and Stephan H. Haeckel and Richard L. Nolan, "Managing by Wire," *Harvard Business Review* 75, no. 5 (September–October 1993), pp. 123–24.

information and promote faster best practices transfer and implementation organizationwide.[16] Companies everywhere are rushing to create on-line data systems, connect more employees to the Internet and company intranets, use electronic mail as a

---

[16]Such systems speed organizational learning by providing fast, efficient communication, creating an organizational memory for collecting and retaining best practice information, and permitting people all across the organization to exchange information and updated solutions. See Goodman and Darr, "Exchanging Best Practices Information through Computer-Aided Systems," pp. 7–17.

major means of internal and external communication, and build Web pages to participate in the rapidly expanding world of electronic commerce.

Well-conceived, state-of-the art support systems not only facilitate better strategy execution, they also can strengthen organizational capabilities enough to provide a competitive edge over rivals. For example, a company with a differentiation strategy based on superior quality has added capability if it has systems for training personnel in quality techniques, tracking product quality at each production step, and ensuring that all goods shipped meet quality standards. A company striving to be a low-cost provider is competitively stronger if it has a benchmarking system that identifies opportunities to drive costs out of the business. Fast-growing companies get an important assist from recruiting systems that help attract and hire qualified employees in large numbers. In businesses such as public accounting and management consulting where large numbers of professional staffers need cutting-edge technical know-how, companies can gain a competitive edge if they have superior systems for training and retraining employees regularly and keeping them supplied with up-to-date information. Companies that rely on empowered customer service employees to act promptly and creatively in pleasing customers have to have state-of-the-art information systems that put essential data at employees' fingertips and give them instantaneous communications capabilities. Young companies wanting to build a business spanning a wide geographic area, grow rapidly, go public, and achieve a prominent industry standing have to invest more in organizational systems and infrastructure than small companies content to build a single-location business at a cautious pace. In today's business environment, competitive advantage goes to those firms most able to mobilize information and create systems to use knowledge effectively.

Companies that have learned how to use e-mail and word-processing systems proficiently and pervasively are much less hierarchical and tend to respond much faster to developing events than companies relying on traditional communication methods. Avid users of e-mail become available to anybody and everybody, resulting in a more open and democratic way of operating; moreover, information doesn't get screened and filtered. Because information is quickly broadcast and many people in different geographical areas can communicate readily, companies can conduct debates and develop solutions more rapidly. Microsoft makes exceptionally strong use of e-mail to distribute information, debate issues, mobilize its responses to developing events, speedily put people to work on emerging issues, and redeploy its resources. Intel is another company that uses e-mail to boost its agility. Price Waterhouse utilizes an on-line word-processing system to create client proposals that can be enriched by contributions from personnel in any of its offices around the world.

Installing Adequate Information Systems, Performance Tracking, and Controls

Accurate information is an essential guide to action. Every organization needs systems for gathering and storing data, tracking key performance indicators, identifying and diagnosing problems, and reporting strategy-critical information. Telephone companies have elaborate information systems to measure signal quality, connection times, interrupts, wrong connections, billing errors, and other measures of reliability. To track and manage the quality of passenger service, airlines have information systems to monitor gate delays, on-time departures and arrivals, baggage-handling times, lost baggage complaints, stockouts on meals and drinks, overbookings, and maintenance delays and failures. Many companies have provided customer-contact personnel with instant electronic access to customer databases so that they can respond effectively to customer inquiries and personalize customer services. Companies that rely on empowered employees need measurement and feedback systems to monitor the performance of workers and guide them to act within specified limits so that unwelcome surprises are avoided.[17]

Accurate, timely information allows organizational members to monitor progress and take corrective action promptly.

Electronic information systems allow managers to monitor implementation initiatives and daily operations, steering them to a successful conclusion in case early steps don't produce the expected progress or things seem to be drifting off course. Information systems need to cover five broad areas: (1) customer data, (2) operations data, (3) employee data, (4) supplier/partner/collaborative ally data, and (5) financial performance data. All key strategic performance indicators have to be measured as often as practical. Many retail companies generate daily sales reports for each store and maintain up-to-the-minute inventory and sales records on each item. Manufacturing plants typically generate daily production reports and track labor productivity on every shift. Many retailers and manufacturers have on-line data systems connecting them with their suppliers that monitor inventories, process orders and invoices, and track shipments. Monthly profit-and-loss statements and statistical summaries, long the norm, are fast being replaced by daily statistical updates and even up-to-the-minute performance monitoring that electronic technology makes possible. Such diagnostic control systems allow managers to detect problems early, intervene when needed, and adjust either the strategy or how it is being implemented. Early experiences are sometimes difficult to assess, but they yield the first hard data and should be closely scrutinized as a basis for corrective action. Ideally, statistical reports should flag big or unusual variances from preset performance standards.

Effective companies use computer-aided electronic systems to share data and information at lightning speed.

Statistical information gives the strategy implementer a feel for the numbers; reports and meetings provide a feel for new developments and problems; and personal contacts add a feel for the people dimension. All are good barometers of overall performance and good indicators of which things are on and off track.

Exercising Adequate Controls over Empowered Employees   A major problem facing today's managers is how to ensure that the actions of empowered subordinates stay within acceptable bounds and don't expose the organization to excessive risk.[18] There are dangers to leaving employees to their own devices in meeting performance standards. The media is full of reports of employees whose decisions or behavior went awry, either costing the company huge sums in losses or causing embarrassing lawsuits. Managers can't spend all their time making sure that everyone's decisions and behavior are between the white lines, yet they have a clear responsibility to institute adequate checks and balances and protect against unwelcome surprises. One of the main purposes of diagnostic control systems to track performance is to relieve managers of the burden of constant monitoring and give them time for other issues. But diagnostic controls are only part of the answer. Another valuable lever of control

---

[17]For a discussion of the need for putting appropriate boundaries on the actions of empowered employees and possible control and monitoring systems that can be used, see Robert Simons, "Control in an Age of Empowerment," *Harvard Business Review* 73 (March–April 1995), pp. 80–88.

[18]Ibid. See, also, David C. Band and Gerald Scanlan, "Strategic Control through Core Competencies," *Long Range Planning* 28, no. 2 (April 1995), pp. 102–14.

is establishing clear boundaries on behavior without telling employees what to do. Strictly prescribed rules and procedures discourage initiative and creativity. It is better to set forth what *not* to do, allowing freedom of action within specified limits. Another control device is face-to-face meetings to review information, assess progress and performance, reiterate expectations, and discuss the next action steps.

DESIGNING STRATEGY-SUPPORTIVE REWARD SYSTEMS

Strategies can't be implemented and executed with real proficiency unless organizational units and individuals are committed to the task. Company managers typically try to enlist organizationwide commitment to carrying out the strategic plan by motivating people and rewarding them for good performance. A manager has to do more than just talk to everyone about how important new strategic practices and performance targets are to the organization's future well-being. No matter how inspiring, talk seldom commands people's best efforts for long. *To get employees' sustained, energetic commitment, management has to be resourceful in designing and using motivational incentives—both monetary and nonmonetary.* The more a manager understands what motivates subordinates and the more he or she relies on motivational incentives as a tool for implementing strategy, the greater will be employees' commitment to good day in, day out execution of their roles in the company's strategic plan.

The role of the reward system is to make it personally satisfying and economically beneficial for organizational members to help the company execute its strategy competently, please customers, and realize the company's vision.

While financial incentives (salary increases, performance bonuses, stock options, and retirement packages) are the core component of most companies' reward systems, managers normally make extensive use of such nonmonetary incentives as frequent words of praise (or constructive criticism), special recognition at company gatherings or in the company newsletter, more (or less) job security, interesting assignments, opportunities to transfer to attractive locations, increased (or decreased) job control and decision-making autonomy, and the carrot of promotion and the stick of being "sidelined" in a routine or dead-end job. Effective managers are further alert to the motivating power of giving people a chance to be part of something exciting, giving them an opportunity for greater personal satisfaction, challenging them with ambitious performance targets, and the intangible bonds of group acceptance. But the motivation and reward structure has to be used *creatively* and tied directly to achieving the performance outcomes necessary for good strategy execution.

One of the biggest strategy-implementing challenges is to employ motivational techniques that build wholehearted commitment and winning attitudes among employees.

Strategy-Supportive Motivational Practices

Successful strategy implementers inspire and challenge employees to do their best. They get employees to buy into the strategy and commit to making it work. They structure individual efforts into teams and work groups in order to facilitate an exchange of ideas and a climate of support. They allow employees to participate in making decisions about how to perform their jobs, and they try to make jobs interesting and satisfying. They devise strategy-supportive motivational approaches and use them effectively. Consider some actual examples:

- At Mars Inc. (best known for its candy bars), every employee, including the president, gets a weekly 10 percent bonus by coming to work on time each day that week. This on-time incentive is designed to minimize absenteeism and tardiness and maximize the amount of labor time available for operating high-speed candy-making equipment (utilizing each available minute of machine time to produce the greatest number of candy bars reduces costs significantly).[19]

- In a number of Japanese companies, employees meet regularly to hear inspirational speeches, sing company songs, and chant the corporate litany. In the United States, Tupperware conducts a weekly Monday night rally to honor, applaud, and fire up its salespeople who conduct Tupperware parties. Amway and Mary Kay Cosmetics hold similar inspirational get-togethers for their sales forces.[20]

- Nordstrom typically pays its retail salespeople an hourly wage higher than the prevailing rates paid by other department store chains, plus it pays them a commission on each sale. Spurred by a culture that encourages salespeople to go all out to satisfy customers, to exercise their own best judgment, and to seek out and promote new fashion ideas, Nordstrom salespeople often earn twice the average incomes of sales employees at competing stores.[21] Nordstrom's rules for employees are simple: "Rule #1: Use your good judgment in all situations. There will be no additional rules."

- Microsoft, realizing that software creation is a highly individualistic effort, interviews hundreds of propective programmers to find the few most suited to write code for its programs. It places new recruits onto three-to seven-person teams under experienced mentors to work on the next generation of software programs. While project team members can expect to put in 60-to 80-hour workweeks to meet deadlines for getting new programs to market, the best programmers seek out and stay with Microsoft largely because they believe that Microsoft will determine where the industry moves in the future and working for Microsoft will allow them to share in the excitement, challenge, and rewards of working on this frontier (and only partly because of Microsoft's very attractive pay scales and lucrative stock option program).[22]

- Lincoln Electric, a company deservedly famous for its piecework pay scheme and incentive bonus plan, rewards individual productivity by paying workers for each nondefective piece produced (workers have to correct quality problems on their own time—defects can be traced to the worker who caused them). The piecework plan motivates workers to pay attention to both quality and volume produced. In addition, the company sets aside a substantial portion of its profits above a specified base for worker bonuses. To determine the size of each worker's bonus Lincoln Electric rates each worker on four equally important performance measures: dependability, quality, output, and ideas and cooperation. The higher a worker's merit rating, the higher the incentive bonus earned; the highest rated workers in good profit years receive bonuses of as much as 110 percent of their piecework compensation.[23]

---

[19]Peters and Waterman, *In Search of Excellence*, p. 269.

[20]Ibid., p. xx.

[21]Jeffrey Pheffer, "Producing Sustainable Competitive Advantage through the Effective Management of People," *Academy of Management Executive* 9, no. 1 (February 1995), pp. 59–60.

[22]Quinn, Anderson, and Finkelstein, "Leveraging Intellect," p. 8.

[23]Pheffer, "Producing Sustainable Competitive Advantage through the Effective Management of People," p. 59.

- A California automobile assembly plant run by Toyota emphasizes symbolic egalitarianism. All employees (managers and workers alike) wear blue smocks, there are no reserved spaces in the employee parking lot, there's no executive dining room—everyone eats in the same plant cafeteria, and there are only two job classifications for skilled trades and only one job classification for all other workers.[24]

- Monsanto, FedEx, AT&T, Advanced Micro Devices, and many other companies have tapped into the motivational power of self-managed teams and achieved very good results. Teams work because of the peer monitoring and expectations of coworkers that are brought to bear on each team member.

- Several Japanese automobile producers, believing that providing employment security is a valuable contributor to worker productivity and company loyalty, elect not to lay off factory workers but instead put them out in the field to sell vehicles when business slacks off for a period. Mazda, for example, during a sales downturn in Japan in the 1980s, shifted factory workers to selling its models door-to-door, a common practice in Japan. At the end of the year, when awards were given out to the best salespeople, Mazda found its top ten salespeople were all factory workers, partly because they were able to explain the product effectively. When business picked up and the factory workers returned to the plant, their experiences in talking to customers yielded useful ideas in improving the features and styling of Mazda's product line.[25]

- At GE Medical Systems, a program called Quick Thanks! allows an employee to nominate any colleague to receive a $25 gift certificate redeemable at certain stores and restaurants in appreciation of a job well done. Employees often hand out the award personally to deserving coworkers (in a recent 12-month period over 10,000 Quick Thanks! awards were presented). Peers prove to be tougher than executives in praising colleagues; for the recipient, the approving acknowledgment of coworkers matters more than the $25.[26]

These motivational approaches accentuate the positive; others blend positive and negative features. Consider the way Harold Geneen, former president and chief executive officer of ITT, allegedly combined the use of money, tension, and fear:

> Geneen provides his managers with enough incentives to make them tolerate the system. Salaries all the way through ITT are higher than average—Geneen reckons 10 percent higher—so that few people can leave without taking a drop. As one employee put it: "We're all paid just a bit more than we think we're worth." At the very top, where the demands are greatest, the salaries and stock options are sufficient to compensate for the rigors. As someone said, "He's got them by their limousines."
>
> Having bound his [managers] to him with chains of gold, Geneen can induce the tension that drives the machine. "The key to the system," one of his [managers] explains, "is the profit forecast. Once the forecast has been gone over, revised, and agreed on, the managing director has a personal commitment to Geneen to carry it out. That's how he produces the tension on which the success depends." The tension goes through the company, inducing ambition, perhaps exhilaration, but always with some sense of fear: what happens if the target is missed?[27]

---

[24]Ibid., p. 63.

[25]Ibid., p. 62.

[26]Steven Kerr, "Risky Business: The New Pay Game," *Fortune*, July 22, 1996, p. 95.

[27]Anthony Sampson, *The Sovereign State of ITT* (New York: Stein and Day, 1973), p. 132.

Balancing Positive and Negative Motivational Considerations   If a strategy implementer's motivational approach and reward structure induces too much stress, internal competitiveness, and job insecurity, the results can be counterproductive. The
prevailing view is that a manager's push for strategy implementation should be more
positive than negative because when cooperation is positively enlisted and rewarded,
rather than strong-armed by a boss's orders, people tend to respond with
more enthusiasm, effort, creativity, and initiative. Yet it is unwise to com-   *Positive motivational approaches*
pletely eliminate pressure for performance and the anxiety it evokes. There   *generally work better than*
is no evidence that a no-pressure work environment leads to superior   *negative ones.*
strategy execution or sustained high performance. As the CEO of a major
bank put it, "There's a deliberate policy here to create a level of anxiety.
Winners usually play like they're one touchdown behind."[28] High-performing organizations need ambitious people who relish the opportunity to climb the ladder of
success, love a challenge, thrive in a performance-oriented environment, and find
some competition and pressure useful to satisfy their own drives for personal recognition, accomplishment, and self-satisfaction. Unless compensation, career, and job
satisfaction consequences are tied to successfully implementing strategic initiatives
and hitting strategic performance targets, few people will attach much significance to
the company's vision, objectives, and strategy.

Linking the Reward System to Strategically Relevant Performance Outcomes

The most dependable way to keep people focused on competent strategy execution
and achieving company performance targets is to *generously* reward individuals and
groups who achieve their assigned performance targets and deny rewards
to those who don't. *The use of incentives and rewards is the single most*   **Strategic Management Principle**
powerful tool management has to win strong employee commitment to
diligent, competent strategy execution. Failure to use this tool wisely and   *A properly designed reward*
powerfully weakens the entire implementation/execution process. Deci-   *structure is management's*
sions on salary increases, incentive compensation, promotions, who gets   *most powerful strategy-*
which key assignments, and the ways and means of awarding praise and   *implementing tool.*
recognition are the strategy implementer's foremost devices to get attention
and build commitment. Such decisions seldom escape the closest employee scrutiny,
saying more about what is expected and who is considered to be doing a good job
than any other factor. A company's system of incentives and rewards thus ends up
being the way its strategy is emotionally ratified in the form of real commitment.
Performance-based incentives make it in employees' self-interest to exert their best
efforts to achieve performance targets and to execute the strategy competently[29]

The key to creating a reward system that promotes good strategy execution is to
make strategically relevant measures of performance *the dominating basis* for
designing incentives, evaluating individual and group efforts, and handing out rewards. Performance targets have to be established for every unit, every manager,
every team or work group, and perhaps every employee—targets that measure
whether implementation is on track. If the company's strategy is to be a low-cost
provider, the incentive system must reward actions and achievements that result in

---

[28]As quoted in John P. Kotter and James L. Heskett, *Corporate Culture and Performance* (New York: Free
Press, 1992), p. 91.
[29]For a countervailing view on the merits of incentives, see Alfie Kohn, "Why Incentive Plans Cannot
Work," *Harvard Business Review* 71, no. 6 (November–December 1993), pp. 54–63.

lower costs. If the company has a differentiation strategy predicated on superior quality and service, the incentive system must reward such outcomes as zero defects, infrequent need for product repair, low numbers of customer complaints, and speedy order processing and delivery. If a company's growth requires new product innovation, incentives should be tied to factors such as the percentages of revenues and profits coming from newly introduced products.

Some of the best performing companies—Banc One, Nucor Steel, Lincoln Electric, Electronic Data Systems, Wal-Mart, Remington Products, and Mary Kay Cosmetics—owe much of their success to incentives and rewards that induce people to do the things critical to good strategy execution and competing effectively. At Banc One (one of the 10 largest U.S. banks and also one of the most profitable banks in the world based on return on assets), producing consistently high levels of customer satisfaction makes a big difference in how well it fares against rivals; customer satisfaction ranks high on Banc One's list of strategic priorities. To enhance employee commitment to the task of pleasing customers, Banc One ties the pay scales in each branch office to that branch's customer satisfaction rating—the higher the branch's ratings, the higher that branch's pay scales. By shifting from a theme of equal pay for equal work to one of equal pay for equal performance, Banc One has focused the attention of branch employees on the task of pleasing, even delighting, their customers.

Nucor's strategy was (and is) to be *the* low-cost producer of steel products. Because labor costs are a significant fraction of total cost in the steel business, Nucor's low-cost strategy entails achieving lower labor costs per ton of steel than competitors'. Nucor management designed an incentive system to promote high worker productivity and drive labor costs per ton below rivals'. Management has organized each plant's workforce into production teams (each assigned to perform particular functions) and, working with the teams, has established weekly production targets for each team. Base pay scales are set at levels comparable to wages for similar manufacturing jobs in the areas where Nucor has plants, but workers can earn a 1 percent bonus for each 1 percent that their output exceeds target levels. If a production team exceeds its weekly production target by 10 percent, team members receive a 10 percent bonus in their next paycheck; if a team exceeds its quota by 20 percent, team members earn a 20 percent bonus. Bonuses are paid every two weeks based on the prior two weeks' actual production levels. The results of Nucor's piece-rate incentive plan are impressive. Nucor's labor productivity (in tons produced per worker) runs over 20 percent above the average of the unionized workforces of the industry's large, integrated steel producers like U.S. Steel and Bethlehem Steel. Nucor enjoys about a $30 to $60 per ton cost advantage (a substantial part of which comes from its lower labor costs), and Nucor workers are the highest-paid workers in the steel industry.

As the example in Illustration Capsule 38 demonstrates, compensating and rewarding organization members on criteria not directly related to successful strategy execution undermines organization performance and condones the diversion of time and energy in less strategically relevant directions.

The Importance of Basing Incentives on Achieving Results, Not on Performing Assigned Functions To create a system of rewards and incentives that support strategy, emphasis has to be put on rewarding people for accomplishing results, not for dutifully performing assigned functions. Focusing jobholders' attention and energy on "what to achieve" as opposed to "what to do" makes the work environment *results-oriented*. It is flawed management to tie incentives and rewards to satisfactory performance of duties and

ILLUSTRATION CAPSULE 38   The Folly of the Reward System in the Claims Division of a Large Insurance Company

The past reward practices of the health care claims division of a large insurance company demonstrate the folly of hoping for one behavior but rewarding another behavior. Seeking to encourage employees to be accurate in paying surgical claims, the company tracked the number of returned checks and letters of complaint filed by policyholders. However, employees in the claims department frequently found it hard to tell from physician filings which of two surgical procedures, with different allowable benefits, was performed, and writing for clarification greatly reduced the number of claims paid within two days of receipt (a performance standard the company stressed). Consequently, the workers' norm quickly became "when in doubt, pay it out."

This practice was made worse by the firm's reward system which called for merit increases of 5 percent for "outstanding" employees, 4 percent for "above average" employees (most employees not rated as outstanding were designated as above average), and 3 percent for all other employees. Many employees were indifferent to the potential of an extra 1 percent reward for avoiding overpayment errors and working hard enough to be rated as outstanding.

However, employees were not indifferent to a rule which stated that employees forfeited their entire merit raise at the next six-month merit review if they were absent or late for work three or more times in any six-month period. The company, while hoping for performance, was rewarding attendance. But the absent-lateness rule was not as stringent as it might seem because the company counted the number of "times" rather than the number of "days"—a one-week absence counted the same as a one-day absence. A worker in danger of getting a third absence within a six-month period could sometimes stay away from work during the second absence until the first absence was over six months old; the limiting factor was that after a certain number of days the worker was paid sickness benefits instead of his or her regular pay (for workers with 20 or more years of service, the company provided sickness benefits of 90 percent of normal salary tax-free!!!).

Source: Steven Kerr, "On the Folly of Rewarding A, While Hoping for B," *Academy of Management Executive* 9, no. 1 February 1995), p. 11.

activities in hopes that the by-products will be the desired business outcomes and achievements.[30] In any job, performing assigned tasks is not equivalent to achieving intended outcomes. Working hard, staying busy, and diligently attending to assigned duties do not guarantee results. (As any student knows, just because an instructor teaches doesn't mean students are learning. Teaching and learning are different things—the first is an activity and the second is a result. The enterprise of education would no doubt take on a different character if teachers were rewarded for the result of what is learned instead of the activity of teaching.)

Incentive compensation for top executives is typically tied to company profitability (earnings growth, return on equity investment, return on total assets, economic value added), the company's stock price performance, and perhaps such measures as market share, product quality, or customer satisfaction that indicate the company's market position, overall competitiveness, and future prospects have improved. However, incentives for department heads, teams, and individual workers are often tied to outcomes more closely related to their area of responsibility. In manufacturing, incentive compensation may be tied to unit manufacturing costs, on-time production and shipping, defect rates, the number and extent of work stoppages due to labor disagreements and equipment breakdowns, and so on. In marketing, there may be

> *It is folly to reward one outcome in hopes of getting another outcome.*

> *The whats to accomplish—the performance measures on which rewards and incentives are based—must be tightly connected to the requirements of successful strategy execution and good company performance.*

---

[30]See Steven Kerr, "On the Folly of Rewarding A While Hoping for B," *Academy of Management Executive* 9 no. 1 (February 1995), pp. 7–14; Kerr, "Risky Business: The New Pay Game," pp. 93–96; and Doran Twer, "Linking Pay to Business Objectives," *Journal of Business Strategy* 15, no. 4 (July–August 1994), pp. 15–18.

incentives for achieving dollar sales or unit volume targets, market share, sales penetration of each target customer group, the fate of newly introduced products, the frequency of customer complaints, the number of new accounts acquired, and customer satisfaction. Which performance measures to base incentive compensation on depends on the situation—the priority placed on various financial and strategic objectives, the requirements for strategic and competitive success, and what specific results are needed in different facets of the business to keep strategy execution on track.

Guidelines for Designing Incentive Compensation Systems   The concepts and company experiences discussed above yield the following guidelines for creating an incentive compensation system to help drive successful strategy execution:

1. *The performance payoff must be a major, not minor, piece of the total compensation package*—at least 10 to 12 percent of base salary. Incentives that amount to 20 percent or more of total compensation are big attention getters, likely to really drive individual effort; incentives amounting to less than 5 percent of total compensation have comparatively weak motivational impact. Moreover, the payoff for high performers must be substantially greater than the payoff for average performers and the payoff for average performers substantially bigger than for below average performers.

2. *The incentive plan should extend to all managers and all workers*, not just be restricted to top management. It is a gross miscalculation to expect that lower-level managers and employees will work their tails off to hit performance targets just so a few senior executives can get lucrative bonuses!

3. *The reward system must be administered with scrupulous care and fairness.* If performance standards are set too high or if individual/group performance evaluations are not accurate and well documented, dissatisfaction and disgruntlement with the system will overcome any positive benefits.

4. *The incentives must be tightly linked to achieving only those performance targets spelled out in the strategic plan* and not to any other factors that get thrown in because they are thought to be nice. Performance evaluation based on factors not tightly related to the strategy signal that either the strategic plan is incomplete (because important performance targets were left out) or management's real agenda is something other than what was stated in the strategic plan.

5. *The performance targets each individual is expected to achieve should involve outcomes that the individual can personally affect.* The role of incentives is to enhance individual commitment and channel behavior in beneficial directions. That won't happen when the performance measures an individual is judged by are outside his/her arena of influence.

6. *Keep the time between the performance review and payment of the reward short.* A lengthy interval between review and payment breeds discontent and works against reinforcing cause and effect.

7. *Make liberal use of nonmonetary rewards; don't rely solely on monetary rewards.* Money, when used properly, is a great motivator, but praise, special recognition, handing out plum assignments, and so on can be potent motivators as well.

8. *Skirting the system to find ways to reward nonperformers must be absolutely avoided.* It is debatable whether exceptions should be made for people who've tried hard, gone the extra mile, yet still come up short because of circumstances beyond their control—arguments can be made either way. The problem with making exceptions for unknowable, uncontrollable, or unforeseeable circumstances is that once "good" excuses start to creep into justifying rewards for nonperformers, the door is open for all kinds of "legitimate" reasons why actual performance failed to match targeted performance. In short, people at all levels have to be held accountable for carrying out their assigned parts of the strategic plan, and they have to know their rewards are based on their accomplishments.

Once the incentives are designed, they have to be communicated and explained. Everybody needs to understand how incentives are calculated and how individual/group performance targets contribute to organizationwide performance targets. Moreover, the reasons for anyone's failure or deviations from targets have to be explored fully to determine whether the causes are poor individual/group performance or circumstances beyond the control of those responsible. The pressure to achieve the targeted strategic and financial performance and continuously improve on strategy execution should be unrelenting. A "no excuses" standard has to prevail.[31] But with the pressure to perform must come deserving and meaningful rewards. Without an ample payoff, the system breaks down, and the strategy implementer is left with the unworkable option of barking orders and pleading for compliance.

A Few Cautions about Performance-Based Incentive Pay In some foreign countries, incentive pay runs counter to local customs and cultural norms. Professor Steven Kerr cites the time he lectured an executive education class on the need for more performance-based pay and a Japanese manager protested, "You shouldn't bribe your children to do their homework, you shouldn't bribe your wife to prepare dinner, and you shouldn't bribe your employees to work for the company."[32] Singling out individuals and commending them for unusually good effort can also be a problem; Japanese culture considers public praise of an individual an affront to the harmony of the group. In some countries, employees have a preference for nonmonetary rewards—more leisure time, important titles, access to vacation villages, and nontaxable perks.

A change in strategy nearly always calls for budget reallocations. Reworking the budget to make it more strategy-supportive is a crucial part of the implementation process because every organization unit needs to have the people, equipment, facilities, and other resources to carry out its part of the strategic plan (but no more than what it really needs!). Implementing a new strategy often entails shifting resources from one area to another—downsizing units that are overstaffed and overfunded, upsizing those more critical to strategic success, and killing projects and activities that are no longer justified.

KEY POINTS

---

[31]Tom Peters and Nancy Austin, *A Passion for Excellence* (New York: Random House, 1985), p. xix.
[32]Kerr, "Risky Business: The New Pay Game," p. 96. For a more general criticism of why performance incentives are a bad idea, see Kohn, "Why Incentive Plans Cannot Work," pp. 54–63.

Anytime a company alters its strategy, managers are well advised to review existing policies and operating procedures, deleting or revising those that are out of sync and deciding if additional ones are needed. Prescribing new or freshly revised policies and operating procedures aids the task of implementation (1) by providing top-down guidance to operating managers, supervisory personnel, and employees regarding how certain things need to be done; (2) by putting boundaries on independent actions and decisions; (3) by promoting consistency in how particular strategy-critical activities are performed in geographically scattered operating units; and (4) by helping to create a strategy-supportive work climate and corporate culture. Thick policy manuals are usually unnecessary. Indeed, when individual creativity and initiative are more essential to good execution than standardization and conformity, it is better to give people the freedom to do things however they see fit and hold them accountable for good results rather than try to control their behavior with policies and guidelines for every situation. Hence, creating a supportive fit between strategy and policy can mean many policies, few policies, or different policies.

Competent strategy execution entails visible, firm managerial commitment to best practices and continuous improvement. Benchmarking, instituting best practices, reengineering core business processes, and total quality management programs all aim at improved efficiency, lower costs, better product quality, and greater customer satisfaction. *All these techniques are important tools for learning how to execute a strategy more proficiently.* Benchmarking provides a realistic basis for setting performance targets. Instituting "best-in-industry" or "best-in-world" operating practices in most or all value-chain activities is essential to create a quality-oriented, high-performance work environment. Reengineering is a way to make quantum progress in being world class while TQM instills a commitment to continuous improvement. Effective use of TQM/continuous improvement techniques is a valuable competitive asset in a company's resource portfolio—one that can produce important competitive capabilities (in reducing costs, speeding new products to market, or improving product quality, service, or customer satisfaction) and be a source of competitive advantage.

Company strategies can't be implemented or executed well without a number of support systems to carry on business operations. Well-conceived, state-of-the-art support systems not only facilitate better strategy execution, they can also strengthen organizational capabilities enough to provide a competitive edge over rivals. In an age of computers, computerized monitoring and control systems, E-mail, the Internet, company intranets, and wireless communications capabilities, companies can't hope to outexecute their competitors without cutting-edge information systems and technologically sophisticated operating capabilities that enable fast, efficient, and effective organization action.

Strategy-supportive motivational practices and reward systems are powerful management tools for gaining employee buy-in and commitment. The key to creating a reward system that promotes good strategy execution is to make strategically relevant measures of performance *the dominating basis* for designing incentives, evaluating individual and group efforts, and handing out rewards. Positive motivational practices generally work better than negative ones, but there is a place for both. There's also a place for both monetary and nonmonetary incentives.

For an incentive compensation system to work well (1) the monetary payoff should be a major percentage of the compensation package, (2) the use of incentives should extend to all managers and workers, (3) the system should be administered with care and fairness, (4) the incentives should be linked to performance targets spelled out in the strategic plan, (5) each individual's performance targets should involve outcomes the person can personally affect, (6) rewards should promptly follow the determination of good performance, (7) monetary rewards should be supplemented with liberal use of nonmonetary rewards, and (8) skirting the system to reward nonperformers should be scrupulously avoided.

SUGGESTED READINGS

Denton, Keith D. "Creating a System for Continuous Improvement." *Business Horizons* 38, no. 1 (January–February 1995), pp. 16–21.

Grant, Robert M., Rami Shani, and R. Krishnan, "TQM's Challenge to Management Theory and Practice." *Sloan Management Review* (Winter 1994), pp. 25–35.

Haeckel, Stephan H. and Richard L. Nolan. "Managing by Wire." *Harvard Business Review* 75, no. 5 (September–October 1993), pp. 122–32.

Herzberg, Frederick. "One More Time: How Do You Motivate Employees?" *Harvard Business Review* 65, no. 4 (September–October 1987), pp. 109–20.

Kerr, Steven. "On the Folly of Rewarding A While Hoping for B." *Academy of Management Executive* 9 no. 1 (February 1995), pp. 7–14.

Kiernan, Matthew J. "The New Strategic Architecture: Learning to Compete in the Twenty-First Century." *Academy of Management Executive* 7, no. 1 (February 1993), pp. 7–21.

Kohn, Alfie. "Why Incentive Plans Cannot Work." *Harvard Business Review* 71, no. 5 (September–October 1993), pp. 54–63.

Olian, Judy D. and Sara L. Rynes, "Making Total Quality Work: Aligning Organizational Processes, Performance Measures, and Stakeholders," *Human Resource Management* 30, no. 3 (Fall 1991), pp. 303–33.

Ohinata, Yoshinobu. "Benchmarking: The Japanese Experience." *Long Range Planning* 27, no. 4 (August 1994), pp. 48–53.

Pfeffer, Jeffrey. "Producing Sustainable Competitive Advantage through the Effective Management of People." *Academy of Management Executive* 9, no. 1 (February 1995), pp. 55–69.

Quinn, James Brian. *Intelligent Enterprise*. New York: Free Press, 1992, chap. 4.

Shetty, Y. K. "Aiming High: Competitive Benchmarking for Superior Performance." *Long-Range Planning* 26, no. 1 (February 1993), pp. 39–44.

Simons, Robert. "Control in an Age of Empowerment." *Harvard Business Review* 73 (March–April 1995), pp. 80–88.

Wiley, Carolyn. "Incentive Plan Pushes Production." *Personnel Journal* (August 1993), pp. 86–91.

IMPLEMENTING STRATEGY: CULTURE AND LEADERSHIP

I n the previous two chapters we examined six of the strategy implementer's tasks—building a capable organization, steering ample resources into strategy-critical activities and operating units, establishing strategy-supportive policies, instituting best practices and programs for continuous improvement, creating internal support systems to enable better execution, and employing appropriate motivational practices and compensation incentives. In this chapter we explore the two remaining implementation tasks: creating a strategy-supportive corporate culture and exerting the internal leadership needed to drive implementation forward.

Weak leadership can wreck the soundest strategy; forceful execution of even a poor plan can often bring victory.

Sun Zi

An organization's capacity to execute its strategy depends on its "hard" infrastructure—its organizational structure and systems—and on its "soft" infrastructure—its culture and norms.

Amar Bhide

Ethics is the moral courage to do what we know is right, and not to do what we know is wrong.

C. J. Silas
CEO, Philips Petroleum

. . . A leader lives in the field with his troops.

H. Ross Perot

BUILDING A STRATEGY-SUPPORTIVE CORPORATE CULTURE

Every company has its own unique culture—one made distinctive by its own business philosophy and principles, its own ways of approaching problems and making decisions, its own embedded patterns of "how we do things around here," its own lore (stories told over and over to illustrate company values and what they mean to employees), its own taboos and political don'ts, its own organizational personality. The bedrock of Wal-Mart's culture is dedication to customer satisfaction, zealous pursuit of low costs, a strong work ethic, Sam Walton's legendary frugality, the ritualistic Saturday morning headquarters meetings to exchange ideas and review problems, and company executives' commitment to visiting stores, talking to customers, and soliciting suggestions from employees. At McDonald's the constant message from management is the overriding importance of quality, service, cleanliness, and value; employees are drilled over and over on the need for attention to detail and perfection in every fundamental of the business. At Microsoft, there are stories of the long hours programmers put in, the emotional peaks and valleys in encountering and overcoming coding problems, the exhilaration of completing a complex program on schedule, the satisfaction of working on cutting-edge projects, and the rewards of being part of a

---

ILLUSTRATION CAPSULE 39   The Culture at Nordstrom

The culture at Nordstrom, a department store retailer noted for exceptional commitment to its customers, revolves around the company's motto: "Respond to Unreasonable Customer Requests." Living up to the company's motto is so strongly ingrained in behavior that employees learn to relish the challenges that some customer requests pose. Usually, meeting customer demands in pleasing fashion entails little more than gracious compliance and a little extra personal attention. But occasionally it means paying a customer's parking ticket when in-store gift wrapping takes longer than normal or hand-delivering items purchased by phone to the airport for a customer with an emergency need.

At Nordstrom, each out-of-the-ordinary customer request is seen as an opportunity for a "heroic" act by an employee and a way to build the company's reputation for great service. Nordstrom encourages these acts by promoting employees noted for outstanding service, keeping scrapbooks of "heroic" acts, and basing the compensation of salespeople mainly on commission (it is not unusual for good salespeople at Nordstrom to earn double what they would at other department store retailers).

For go-getters who truly enjoy retail selling and pleasing customers, Nordstrom is a great company to work for. But the culture weeds out those who can't meet Nordstrom's demanding standards and rewards those who are prepared to be what Nordstrom stands for.

Nordstrom starts new employees, even those with advanced degrees, out on the sales floor. Promotion is strictly from within, and when a new store is opened, its key people are recruited from other stores around the country to help perpetuate Nordstrom's culture and values and to make sure the new store is run the Nordstrom way.

Source: Based on information in Tracy Goss, Richard Pascale, and Anthony Athos, "Risking the Present for a Powerful Future," *Harvard Business Review* 71, no. 6 (November–December 1993), pp. 101–2 and Jeffrey Pheffer, "Producing Sustainable Competitive Advantage through the Effective Management of People," *Academy of Management Executive* 9, no. 1 (February 1995), pp. 59–60 and 65.

team responsible for developing trailblazing software. Illustration Capsule 39 describes the culture at Nordstrom's.

Where Does Corporate Culture Come From?

Corporate culture refers to a company's values, beliefs, traditions, operating style, and internal work environment.

The taproot of corporate culture is the organization's beliefs and philosophy about how its affairs ought to be conducted—the reasons why it does things the way it does. A company's culture is manifested in the values and principles that management preaches and practices, in its ethical standards and official policies, in its stakeholder relationships (especially its dealings with employees, unions, stockholders, vendors, and the communities in which it operates), in its traditions, in its supervisory practices, in employees' attitudes and behavior, in the legends people repeat about happenings in the organization, in the peer pressures that exist, in the organization's politics, and in the "chemistry" and "vibrations" that permeate its work environment. All these forces, some of which operate quite subtly, combine to define an organization's culture.

Beliefs and practices that become embedded in a company's culture can originate anywhere: from one influential individual, work group, department, or division, from the bottom of the organizational hierarchy or the top.[1] Very often, many components of the culture are associated with a founder or other early leaders who articulated them as a company philosophy or as a set of principles the organization should rigidly adhere to or as company policies. Sometimes, elements of the culture spring from the company's vision, its strategic intent, and core components of its strategy (like obsessive emphasis on low cost or technological leadership or first-rate quality). Over time, these cultural underpinnings take root, become embedded in how the

---

[1]John P. Kotter and James L. Heskett, *Corporate Culture and Performance* (New York: Free Press, 1992), p. 7.

A company's culture is a product of internal social forces; it is manifested in the values, behavioral norms, and ways of operating that prevail across the organization.

company conducts its business, come to be shared by company managers and employees, and then persist as new employees are encouraged to embrace them. Fast-growing companies risk creating a culture by chance rather than by design if they rush to hire employees mainly for their technical skills and credentials and neglect to screen out candidates whose values, philosophies, and personalities aren't compatible with the organizational character, vision, and strategy that management is trying to cultivate.

Once established, company cultures can be perpetuated in many ways: continuity of leadership, screening and selecting new group members according to how well their values and personalities fit in (as well as on the basis of talents and credentials), systematic indoctrination of new members in the culture's fundamentals, the efforts of senior group members to reiterate core values in daily conversations and pronouncements, the telling and retelling of company legends, regular ceremonies honoring members who display cultural ideals, and visibly rewarding those who follow cultural norms and penalizing those who don't.[2] However, even stable cultures aren't static. Crises and new challenges evolve into new ways of doing things. Arrival of new leaders and turnover of key members often spawn new or different values and practices that alter the culture. Diversification into new businesses, expansion into different geographical areas, rapid growth that adds new employees, and the exploding use of the Internet, company intranets, and electronic mail can all cause a culture to evolve. Indeed, one of the most important business phenomena of the late 1990s is the historic impact that widespread use of PCs and information technology is having on corporate cultures and on how a company's internal and external business is conducted.

Although it is common to speak about corporate culture in the singular, companies typically have multiple cultures (or subcultures).[3] Values, beliefs, and practices can vary by department, geographic location, division, or business unit. Global companies are highly multicultural. A company's subcultures can clash, or at least not mesh well, if recently acquired business units have not yet been assimilated or if different units operate in different countries or have varying managerial styles, business philosophies, and operating approaches. The human resources manager of a global pharmaceutical company who took on an assignment in the Far East discovered, to his surprise, that one of his biggest challenges was to persuade his company's managers in China, Korea, Malaysia, and Taiwan to accept promotions—their cultural values were such that they did not believe in competing with their peers for career rewards or personal gain, nor did they relish breaking ties to their local communities to assume cross-national responsibilities.[4] Many companies that have merged with or acquired foreign companies have to deal with language and custom-based cultural differences.

The Power of Culture

The beliefs, vision, objectives, and business approaches and practices underpinning a company's strategy may be compatible with its culture or they may not. When they are, the culture becomes a valuable ally in strategy implementation and execution.

---

[2]Ibid., pp. 7–8.

[3]Ibid., p. 5.

[4]John Alexander and Meena S. Wilson, "Leading across Cultures: Five Vital Capabilities," in *The Organization of the Future,* Frances Hesselbein, Marshall Goldsmith, and Richard Beckard, (San Francisco: Jossey-Bass, 1997), pp. 291–92.

When they are not, a company usually finds it difficult to implement the strategy successfully.[5]

A culture grounded in values, practices, and behavioral norms that match what is needed for good strategy execution helps energize people to do their jobs in a strategy-supportive manner. For example, a culture where frugality and thrift are values widely shared by organizational members is very conducive to successful execution of a low-cost leadership strategy. A culture where creativity, embracing change, and challenging the status quo are pervasive themes is conducive to successful execution of a product innovation and technological leadership strategy. A culture built around such principles as listening to customers, encouraging employees to take pride in their work, and giving employees a high degree of decision-making responsibility is conducive to successful execution of a strategy of delivering superior customer service. When a company's culture is out of sync with what is needed for strategic success, the culture has to be changed as rapidly as can be managed; the more entrenched the culture, the greater the difficulty of implementing new or different strategies. A sizable and prolonged strategy-culture conflict weakens and may even defeat managerial efforts to make the strategy work.

An organization's culture is an important contributor (or obstacle) to successful strategy execution.

Strong cultures promote good strategy execution when there's fit with the strategy and hurt execution when there's little fit.

A tight culture-strategy alignment acts in two ways to channel behavior and influence employees do their jobs in a strategy-supportive fashion:[6]

1. *A work environment where the culture matches well with the conditions for good strategy execution provides a system of informal rules and peer pressures regarding how to conduct business and how to go about doing one's job.* Strategy-supportive cultures shape the mood, temperament, and motivation of the workforce, positively affecting organizational energy, work habits and operating practices, the degree to which organizational units cooperate, and how customers are treated. Culturally approved behavior thrives, while culturally disapproved behavior gets squashed and often penalized. In a company where strategy and culture are misaligned, ingrained values and operating philosophies don't cultivate strategy-supportive ways of operating; often, the very kinds of behavior needed to execute strategy successfully run afoul of the culture and attract criticism rather than praise and reward.

A deeply rooted culture well matched to strategy is a powerful lever for successful strategy execution.

2. *A strong strategy-supportive culture nurtures and motivates people to do their jobs in ways conducive to effective strategy execution; it provides structure, standards, and a value system in which to operate; and it promotes strong employee identification with the company's vision, performance targets, and strategy.* All this makes employees feel genuinely better about their jobs and work environment and the merits of what the company is trying to accomplish. Employees are stimulated to take on the challenge of realizing the company's vision, do their jobs competently and with enthusiasm, and collaborate with others to execute the strategy.

This says something important about the task of leading strategy implementation: *Anything so fundamental as implementing a strategic plan involves moving the organization's culture into close alignment with the requirements for proficient strategy execution.* The optimal condition is a work environment that energizes the organization in a strategy-supportive fashion, promoting "can-do" attitudes and

[5]Ibid.
[6]Ibid., pp. 15–16.

acceptance of change where needed, enlisting and encouraging people to perform strategy-critical activities in superior fashion, and breeding needed organizational competencies and capabilities. As one observer noted:

> It has not been just strategy that led to big Japanese wins in the American auto market. It is a culture that enspirits workers to excel at fits and finishes, to produce moldings that match and doors that don't sag. It is a culture in which Toyota can use that most sophisticated of management tools, the suggestion box, and in two years increase the number of worker suggestions from under 10,000 to over 1 million with resultant savings of $250 million.[7]

Strong versus Weak Cultures

Company cultures vary widely in the degree to which they are embedded in company practices and behavioral norms. A company's culture can be weak and fragmented in the sense that many subcultures exist, few values and behavioral norms are widely shared, and there are few traditions. In weak or fragmented culture companies, there's little cohesion and glue across units from a business principles and work climate perspective—top executives don't espouse any business philosophy or extol use of particular operating practices. Because of a lack of common values and ingrained business approaches, organizational members typically have no deeply felt sense of identity with the company's vision and strategy; instead, many employees view the company as a place to work and their job as a way to make a living. While they may have some bonds with and loyalty toward their department, their colleagues, their union, or their boss, the weak company culture breeds no strong employee allegiance to what the company stands for and no sense of urgency about pushing strategy execution along. As a consequence, weak cultures provide no strategy-implementing assistance.

Strong Culture Companies   On the other hand, a company's culture can be strong and cohesive in the sense that the company conducts its business according to a clear and explicit set of principles and values, that management devotes considerable time to communicating these principles and values and explaining how they relate to its business environment, and that the values are shared widely across the company—by senior executives and rank-and-file employees alike.[8] Strong culture companies typically have creeds or values statements, and executives regularly stress the importance of using these values and principles as the basis for decisions and actions taken throughout the organization. In strong culture companies values and behavioral norms are so deeply rooted that they don't change much when a new CEO takes over—although they can erode over time if the CEO ceases to nurture them.

In a strong culture company, values and behavioral norms are like crabgrass: deeply rooted and difficult to weed out.

Three factors contribute to the development of strong cultures: (1) a founder or strong leader who establishes values, principles, and practices that are consistent and sensible in light of customer needs, competitive conditions, and strategic requirements; (2) a sincere, long-standing company commitment to operating the business according to these established traditions; and (3) a genuine concern for the well-being of the organization's three biggest constituencies—customers, employees, and shareholders. Continuity of leadership, small group size, stable group membership,

---

[7]Robert H. Waterman, Jr., "The Seven Elements of Strategic Fit," *Journal of Business Strategy* 2, no. 3 (Winter 1982), p. 70.

[8]Terrence E. Deal and Allen A. Kennedy, *Corporate Cultures* (Reading, Mass.: Addison-Wesley, 1982), p. 22.

geographic concentration, and considerable organizational success all contribute to the emergence of a strong culture.[9]

During the time a strong culture is being implanted, there's nearly always a good strategy-culture fit (which partially accounts for the organization's success). Mismatches between strategy and culture in a strong culture company tend to occur when a company's environment undergoes rapid-fire change, prompting a drastic strategy revision that clashes with the entrenched culture. In such cases, a major culture-changing effort has to be launched. Both IBM and Apple Computer have been going through wrenching culture changes to adapt to the new computer industry environment now driven by the so-called Wintel standard—Microsoft (with its Windows operating systems for PCs and its Windows-based PC software programs) and Intel (with its successive generations of faster microprocessors for PCs). IBM's bureaucracy and mainframe culture clashed with the shift to a PC-dominated world. Apple's culture clash stemmed from strong company sentiment to continue on with internally developed Macintosh technology (incompatible with all other brands of computers) despite growing preferences for Wintel-compatible equipment and software.

A strong culture is a valuable asset when it matches the requirements for good strategy execution and a dreaded liability when it doesn't.

Low-Performance or Unhealthy Cultures

A number of unhealthy cultural characteristics can undermine a company's business performance.[10] One is a politicized internal environment that allows influential managers to operate their fiefdoms autonomously and resist needed change. In politically dominated cultures, many issues get resolved on the basis of turf, vocal support or opposition by powerful executives, personal lobbying by a key executive, and coalitions among individuals or departments with vested interests in a particular outcome. What's best for the company plays second fiddle to personal aggrandizement.

A second unhealthy cultural trait, one that can plague companies suddenly confronted with fast-changing business conditions, is hostility to change and to people who champion new ways of doing things. Executives who don't value managers or employees with initiative or new ideas dampen experimentation and efforts to improve the status quo. Avoiding risks and not screwing up become more important to a person's career advancement than entrepreneurial successes and innovative accomplishments. This trait is most often found in companies with multilayered management bureaucracies that have enjoyed considerable market success in years past but whose business environments have been hit with accelerating change. General Motors, IBM, Sears, and Eastman Kodak are classic examples; all four gradually became burdened by a stifling bureaucracy that rejected innovation. Now, they are struggling to reinvent the cultural approaches that caused them to succeed in the first place.

A third unhealthy characteristic is promoting managers who understand complex organization structures, problem solving, budgets, controls, and how to handle administrative detail better than they understand vision, strategies, competitive capabilities, inspiration, and culture building. While the former are adept at organizational maneuvering, if they ascend to senior executive positions, the company can find itself short of the entrepreneurial skills and leadership needed to introduce new strategies, reallocate resources, build new competitive capabilities, and fashion a new culture—a condition that ultimately erodes long-term performance.

---

[9]Vijay Sathe, *Culture and Related Corporate Realities* (Homewood, Ill.: Richard D. Irwin, 1985).

[10]Kotter and Heskett, *Corporate Culture and Performance*, chapter 6.

A fourth characteristic of low-performance cultures is an aversion to looking outside the company for superior practices and approaches. Sometimes a company enjoys such great market success and reigns as an industry leader for so long that its management becomes inbred and arrogant. It believes it has all the answers or can develop them on its own. Insular thinking, inward-looking solutions, and a must-be-invented-here syndrome often precede a decline in company performance. Kotter and Heskett cite Avon, BankAmerica, Citicorp, Coors, Ford, General Motors, Kmart, Kroger, Sears, Texaco, and Xerox as examples of companies that had low-performance cultures during the late 1970s and early 1980s.[11]

Changing problem cultures is very difficult because of the heavy anchor of deeply held values, habits, and the emotional clinging of people to the old and familiar. Sometimes executives succeed in changing the values and behaviors of small groups

Once a culture is established, it is difficult to change.

of managers and even whole departments or divisions, only to find the changes eroded over time by the actions of the rest of the organization. What is communicated, praised, supported, and penalized by the entrenched majority undermines the new emergent culture and halts its progress. Executives can revamp formal organization charts, announce new strategies, bring in managers from the outside, introduce new technologies, and open new plants, yet fail to change embedded cultural traits and behaviors because of skepticism about the new directions and covert resistance to them.

Adaptive Cultures

In fast-changing business environments, the capacity to introduce new strategies and organizational practices is a necessity if a company is to perform well over long periods of time.[12] Strategic agility and fast organizational response to new conditions require a culture that quickly accepts and supports company efforts to adapt to environmental change rather than a culture that has to be coaxed and cajoled to change.

In adaptive cultures, members share a feeling of confidence that the organization can deal with whatever threats and opportunities come down the pike; they are receptive to risk-taking, experimentation, innovation, and changing strategies and practices whenever necessary to satisfy the legitimate interests of stakeholders—

Adaptive cultures are a strategy implementer's best ally.

customers, employees, shareowners, suppliers, and the communities where the company operates. Hence, members willingly embrace a proactive approach to identifying issues, evaluating the implications and options, and implementing workable solutions—there's a spirit of doing what's necessary to ensure long-term organizational success *provided core values and business principles are upheld in the process.* Entrepreneurship is encouraged and rewarded. Managers habitually fund product development, evaluate new ideas openly, and take prudent risks to create new business positions. Strategies and traditional operating practices are modified as needed to adjust to or take advantage of changes in the business environment. The leaders of adaptive cultures are adept at changing the right things in the right ways, not changing for the sake of change and not compromising core values or business principles. Adaptive cultures are supportive of managers and employees at all ranks who propose or help initiate useful change; indeed, executives consciously seek, train, and promote individuals who display these leadership traits.

One outstanding trait of adaptive cultures is that top management, while orchestrating responses to changing conditions, demonstrates genuine care for the well-being of

---

[11]Ibid., p. 68.

[12]This section draws heavily from Kotter and Heskett, *Corporate Culture and Performance*, chapter 4.

all key constituencies—customers, employees, stockholders, major suppliers, and the communities where the company operates—and tries to satisfy all their legitimate interests simultaneously. No group is ignored, and fairness to all constituencies is a decision-making principle—a commitment often described as "doing the right thing."[13] Pleasing customers and protecting, if not enhancing, the company's long-term well-being is seen as the best way of looking out for the interests of employees, stockholders, suppliers, and communities where the company operates. Management concern for the well-being of employees is a big factor in gaining employee support for change—employees understand that changes in their job assignments are part of the process of adapting to new conditions and that their job security will not be threatened in the process of adapting to change, unless the company's business unexpectedly reverses direction. In cases where workforce downsizing becomes necessary, management concern for employees dictates that separation be handled in a humane fashion. Management efforts to make the process of adapting to change fair, keeping adverse impacts to a minimum, breeds acceptance of and support for change among all stakeholders.

In less-adaptive cultures where resistance to change is the norm, managers avoid risk-taking and prefer following to leading when it comes to technological change and new product innovation.[14] They believe in moving cautiously and conservatively, endeavoring not to make "mistakes" and making sure they protect or advance their own careers, the interests of their immediate work groups, or their pet projects.

Creating the Fit between Strategy and Culture

It is the *strategy maker's* responsibility to select a strategy compatible with the "sacred" or unchangeable parts of prevailing corporate culture. It is the *strategy implementer's* task, once strategy is chosen, to change whatever facets of the corporate culture hinder effective execution.

Changing a company's culture and aligning it with strategy are among the toughest management tasks—easier to talk about than do. The first step is to diagnose which facets of the present culture are strategy-supportive and which are not. Then, managers have to talk openly and forthrightly to all concerned about those aspects of the culture that have to be changed. The talk has to be followed swiftly by visible actions to modify the culture—actions that everyone will understand are intended to establish a new culture more in tune with the strategy.

Symbolic Actions and Substantive Actions   Managerial actions to tighten the culture-strategy fit need to be both symbolic and substantive. Symbolic actions are valuable for the signals they send about the kinds of behavior and performance strategy implementers wish to encourage. The most important symbolic actions are those that top executives take to serve as role models—leading cost reduction efforts by curtailing executive perks; emphasizing the importance of responding to customers' needs by requiring all officers and executives to spend a significant portion of each week talking with customers and understanding their requirements; and assuming a high profile in altering policies and practices that hinder the new strategy. Another category of symbolic actions includes the events to designate and honor people whose actions and performance exemplify what is called for in the new culture. Many universities give outstanding teacher awards each year to symbolize their esteem for instructors with exceptional classroom talents. Numerous businesses have

[13]Ibid., p. 52.
[14]Ibid., p. 50.

employee-of-the-month awards. The military has a long-standing custom of awarding ribbons and medals for exemplary actions. Mary Kay Cosmetics awards an array of prizes—from ribbons to pink automobiles—to its beauty consultants for reaching various sales plateaus.

The best companies and the best executives expertly use symbols, role models, ceremonial occasions, and group gatherings to tighten the strategy-culture fit. Low-cost leaders like Wal-Mart and Nucor are renowned for their spartan facilities, executive frugality, intolerance of waste, and zealous control of costs.

Awards ceremonies, role models, and symbols are a fundamental part of a strategy implementer's culture-shaping effort.

Executives sensitive to their role in promoting strategy-culture fits make a habit of appearing at ceremonial functions to praise individuals and groups that "get with the program." They honor individuals who exhibit cultural norms and reward those who achieve strategic milestones. They participate in employee training programs to stress strategic priorities, values, ethical principles, and cultural norms. Every group gathering is seen as an opportunity to implant values, praise good deeds, reinforce cultural norms, and promote changes that assist strategy implementation. Sensitive executives make sure that organizational members will construe current decisions and policy changes as consistent with and supportive of the company's new strategic direction.[15]

In addition to being out front personally and symbolically, leading the push for new behaviors and communicating the reasons for new approaches, strategy-implementers have to convince all those concerned that the effort is more than cosmetic. Talk and plans have to be complemented by substantive actions and real movement. The actions taken have to be credible, highly visible, and indicative of management's commitment to new strategic initiatives and the associated cultural changes. There are several ways to accomplish this. One is to engineer some quick successes that highlight the benefits of strategy-culture changes, thus making enthusiasm for the changes contagious. However, instant results are usually not as important as having the will and patience to create a solid, competent team committed to pursuing the strategy. The strongest signs that management is truly committed to creating a new culture include: replacing old-culture managers with "new breed" managers, changing long-standing policies and operating practices that are dysfunctional or that impede new initiatives, undertaking major reorganizational moves that bring structure into better alignment with strategy, tying compensation incentives directly to the new measures of strategic performance, and shifting substantial resources from old-strategy projects and programs to new-strategy projects and programs.

At the same time, chief strategy-implementers must be careful to *lead by example*. For instance, if the organization's strategy involves a drive to become the industry's

Senior executives must personally lead efforts to align culture with strategy.

low-cost producer, senior managers must display frugality in their own actions and decisions: Inexpensive decorations in the executive suite, conservative expense accounts and entertainment allowances, a lean staff in the corporate office, scrutiny of budget requests, and so on. The CEO of SAS Airlines, Jan Carlzon, symbolically reinforced the primacy of quality service for business customers by flying coach instead of first class and by giving up his seat to waitlisted travelers.[16]

---

[15]Judy D. Olian and Sara L. Rynes, "Making Total Quality Work: Aligning Organizational Processes, Performance Measures, and Stakeholders," *Human Resource Management* 30, no. 3 (Fall 1991), p. 324.

[16]Ibid.

Implanting the needed culture-building values and behavior depends on a sincere, sustained commitment by the chief executive coupled with persistence in reinforcing the culture at every opportunity through both word and deed. Neither charisma nor personal magnetism are essential. However, personally talking to many groups about the reasons for change *is* essential; cultural changes are seldom accomplished successfully from an office. Moreover, creating and sustaining a strategy-supportive culture is a job for the whole management team. Major cultural change requires many initiatives from many people. Senior officers, department heads, and middle managers have to reiterate values, "walk the talk," and translate the desired cultural norms and behavior into everyday practice. In addition, strategy implementers must enlist the support of firstline supervisors and employee opinion leaders, convincing them of the merits of practicing and enforcing cultural norms at the lowest levels in the organization. Until a big majority of employees joins the new culture and shares a commitment to its basic values and norms, there's considerably more work to be done in both instilling the culture and tightening the culture-strategy fit.

The task of making culture supportive of strategy is not a short-term exercise. It takes time for a new culture to emerge and prevail; it's unrealistic to expect an overnight transformation. The bigger the organization and the greater the cultural shift needed to produce a culture-strategy fit, the longer it takes. In large companies, changing the corporate culture in significant ways can take three to five years at minimum. In fact, it is usually tougher to reshape a deeply ingrained culture that is not strategy-supportive than it is to instill a strategy-supportive culture from scratch in a brand-new organization.

Building Ethical Standards and Values into the Culture

A strong corporate culture founded on ethical business principles and moral values is a vital force behind continued strategic success. Many executives are convinced that a company must care about how it does business; otherwise a company's reputation, and ultimately its performance, is put at risk. Corporate ethics and values programs are not window dressing; they are undertaken to create an environment of strongly held values and convictions and to make ethical conduct a way of life. Morally upstanding values and high ethical standards nurture the corporate culture in a very positive way—they connote integrity, "doing the right thing," and genuine concern for stakeholders.

An ethical corporate culture has a positive impact on a company's long-term strategic success; an unethical culture can undermine it.

Companies establish values and ethical standards in a number of ways.[17] Companies steeped in tradition with a rich folklore to draw on rely on word-of-mouth indoctrination and the power of tradition to instill values and enforce ethical conduct. But many companies today set forth their values and codes of ethics in written documents. Table 11–1 indicates the kinds of topics such statements cover. Written statements have the advantage of explicitly stating what the company intends and expects, and they serve as benchmarks for judging both company policies and actions and individual conduct. They put a stake in the ground and define the company's position. Value statements serve as a cornerstone for culture building; a code of ethics serves as a cornerstone for developing a corporate conscience.[18] Illustration Capsule 40

---

[17]The Business Roundtable, *Corporate Ethics: A Prime Asset*, February 1988, pp. 4–10.

[18]For a discussion of the strategic benefits of formal statements of corporate values, see John Humble, David Jackson, and Alan Thomson, "The Strategic Power of Corporate Values," *Long Range Planning* 27, no. 6 (December 1994), pp. 28–42. For a study of the status of formal codes of ethics in large U. S. corporations,

TABLE 11-1　Topics Generally Covered in Value Statements and Codes of Ethics

Topics Covered in Values Statements	Topics Covered in Codes of Ethics
• Importance of customers and customer service • Commitment to quality • Commitment to innovation • Respect for the individual employee and the duty the company has to employees • Importance of honesty, integrity, and ethical standards • Duty to stockholders • Duty to suppliers • Corporate citizenship • Importance of protecting the environment	• Honesty and observance of the law • Conflicts of interest • Fairness in selling and marketing practices • Using inside information and securities trading • Supplier relationships and purchasing practices • Payments to obtain business/Foreign Corrupt Practices Act • Acquiring and using information about others • Political activities • Use of company assets, resources, and property • Protection of proprietary information • Pricing, contracting, and billing

presents the Johnson & Johnson Credo, the most publicized and celebrated code of ethics and values among U.S. companies. J&J's CEO calls the credo "the unifying force for our corporation." Illustration Capsule 41 presents the pledge that Bristol-Myers Squibb makes to all of its stakeholders.

Values and ethical standards must not only be explicitly stated but they must also be ingrained into the corporate culture.

Once values and ethical standards have been formally set forth, they must be ingrained in the company's policies, practices, and actual conduct. Implementing the values and code of ethics entails several actions:

- Incorporating the statement of values and the code of ethics into employee training and educational programs.
- Explicit attention to values and ethics in recruiting and hiring to screen out applicants who lack compatible character traits.
- Communication of the values and ethics code to all employees and explaining compliance procedures.
- Management involvement and oversight, from the CEO down to firstline supervisors.
- Strong endorsements by the CEO.
- Word-of-mouth indoctrination.

In the case of codes of ethics, special attention must be given to sections of the company that are particularly sensitive and vulnerable—purchasing, sales, and political lobbying.[19] Employees who deal with external parties are in ethically sensitive positions and often are drawn into compromising situations. Procedures for enforcing ethical standards and handling potential violations have to be developed.

---

see Patrick E. Murphy, "Corporate Ethics Statements: Current Status and Future Prospects," *Journal of Business Ethics* 14 (1995), pp. 727–40.

[19]Ibid., p. 7.

ILLUSTRATION CAPSULE 40   The Johnson & Johnson Credo

- We believe our first responsibility is to the doctors, nurses, and patients, to mothers and all others who use our products and services.
- In meeting their needs everything we do must be of high quality.
- We must constantly strive to reduce our costs in order to maintain reasonable prices.
- Customers' orders must be serviced promptly and accurately.
- Our suppliers and distributors must have an opportunity to make a fair profit.
- We are responsible to our employees, the men and women who work with us throughout the world.
- Everyone must be considered as an individual.
- We must respect their dignity and recognize their merit.
- They must have a sense of security in their jobs.
- Compensation must be fair and adequate, and working conditions clean, orderly, and safe.
- Employees must feel free to make suggestions and complaints.
- There must be equal opportunity for employment, development, and advancement for those qualified.

- We must provide competent management, and their actions must be just and ethical.
- We are responsible to the communities in which we live and work and to the world community as well.
- We must be good citizens—support good works and charities and bear our fair share of taxes.
- We must encourage civic improvements and better health and education.
- We must maintain in good order the property we are privileged to use, protecting the environment and natural resources.
- Our final responsibility is to our stockholders.
- Business must make a sound profit.
- We must experiment with new ideas.
- Research must be carried on, innovative programs developed, and mistakes paid for.
- New equipment must be purchased, new facilities provided, and new products launched.
- Reserves must be created to provide for adverse times.
- When we operate according to these principles, the stockholders should realize a fair return.

Source: 1982 Annual Report.

The compliance effort must permeate the company, extending into every organizational unit. The attitudes, character, and work history of prospective employees must be combined. Every employee must receive adequate training. Line managers at all levels must give serious and continuous attention to the task of explaining how the values and ethical code apply in their areas. In addition, they must insist that company values and ethical standards become a way of life. In general, instilling values and insisting on ethical conduct must be looked on as a continuous culture-building, culture-nurturing exercise. Whether the effort succeeds or fails depends largely on how well corporate values and ethical standards are visibly integrated into company policies, managerial practices, and actions at all levels.

A results-oriented culture that inspires people to do their best is conducive to superior strategy execution.

Building a Spirit of High Performance into the Culture

An ability to instill strong individual commitment to strategic success and to create an atmosphere in which there is constructive pressure to perform is one of the most valuable strategy-implementing skills. When an organization performs consistently at or near peak capability, the outcome is not only more success but also a culture permeated with a spirit of high performance. Such a spirit of performance should not be confused with whether employees are "happy" or "satisfied" or whether they "get along well together." An organization with a spirit of high performance emphasizes achievement and excellence. Its culture is results-

---

ILLUSTRATION CAPSULE 41   The Bristol-Myers Squibb Pledge

To those who use our products . . .
We affirm Bristol-Myers Squibb's commitment to the highest standards of excellence, safety, and reliability in everything we make. We pledge to offer products of the highest quality and to work diligently to keep improving them.

To our employees and those who may join us . . .
We pledge personal respect, fair compensation, and equal treatment. We acknowledge our obligation to provide able and humane leadership throughout the organization, within a clean and safe working environment. To all who qualify for advancement, we will make every effort to provide opportunity.

To our suppliers and customers . . .
We pledge an open door, courteous, efficient, and ethical dealing, and appreciation for their right to a fair profit.

To our shareholders . . .
We pledge a companywide dedication to continued profitable growth, sustained by strong finances, a high level of research and development, and facilities second to none.

To the communities where we have plants and offices . . .
We pledge conscientious citizenship, a helping hand for worthwhile causes, and constructive action in support of civic and environmental progress.

To the countries where we do business . . .
We pledge ourselves to be a good citizen and to show full consideration for the rights of others while reserving the right to stand up for our own.

Above all, to the world we live in . . .
We pledge Bristol-Myers Squibb to policies and practices which fully embody the responsibility, integrity, and decency required of free enterprise if it is to merit and maintain the confidence of our society.

Source: 1990 Annual Report.

---

oriented, and its management pursues policies and practices that inspire people to do their best.[20]

Companies with a spirit of high performance typically are intensely people-oriented, and they reinforce their concern for individual employees on every conceivable occasion in every conceivable way. They treat employees with dignity and respect, train each employee thoroughly, encourage employees to use their own initiative and creativity in performing their work, set reasonable and clear performance expectations, use the full range of rewards and punishment to enforce high-performance standards, hold managers at every level responsible for developing the people who report to them, and grant employees enough autonomy to stand out, excel, and contribute. To create a results-oriented culture, a company must make champions out of the people who turn in winning performances:[21]

- At Boeing, General Electric, and 3M Corporation, top executives make a point of honoring individuals who believe so strongly in their ideas that they take it on themselves to hurdle the bureaucracy, maneuver their projects through the system, and turn them into improved services, new products, or even new businesses. In these companies, "product champions" are given high visibility, room to push their ideas, and strong executive support.

---

[20]For a more in-depth discussion of what it takes to create a climate and culture that nurtures success, see Benjamin Schneider, Sarah K. Gunnarson, and Kathryn Niles-Jolly, "Creating the Climate and Culture of Success," *Organizational Dynamics* (Summer 1994), pp. 17–29.

[21]Thomas J. Peters and Robert H. Waterman, Jr., *In Search of Excellence* (New York: Harper & Row, 1982), pp. xviii, 240, and 269, and Thomas J. Peters and Nancy Austin, *A Passion for Excellence* (New York: Random House, 1985), pp. 304–7.

Champions whose ideas prove out are usually handsomely rewarded; those whose ideas don't pan out still have secure jobs and are given chances to try again.

- Some companies upgrade the importance and status of individual employees by referring to them as Cast Members (Disney), crew members (McDonald's), or associates (Wal-Mart and J. C. Penney). Companies like Mary Kay Cosmetics, Tupperware, and McDonald's actively seek out reasons and opportunities to give pins, buttons, badges, and medals for good showings by average performers—the idea being to express appreciation and give a motivational boost to people who stand out doing "ordinary" jobs.

- McDonald's has a contest to determine the best hamburger cooker in its entire chain. It begins with a competition to determine the best hamburger cooker in each store. Store winners go on to compete in regional championships, and regional winners go on to the "All-American" contest. The winners get trophies and an All-American patch to wear on their shirts.

- Milliken & Co. holds Corporate Sharing Rallies once every three months; teams come from all over the company to swap success stories and ideas. A hundred or more teams make five-minute presentations over a two-day period. Each rally has a major theme—quality, cost reduction, and so on. No criticisms and negatives are allowed, and there is no such thing as a big idea or a small one. Quantitative measures of success are used to gauge improvement. All those present vote on the best presentation and several ascending grades of awards are handed out. Everyone, however, receives a framed certificate for participating.

What makes a spirit of high performance come alive is a complex network of practices, words, symbols, styles, values, and policies pulling together that produces extraordinary results with ordinary people. The drivers of the system are a belief in the worth of the individual, strong company commitment to job security and promotion from within, managerial practices that encourage employees to exercise individual initiative and creativity in doing their jobs, and pride in doing the "itty-bitty, teeny-tiny things" right.[22] A company that treats its employees well generally benefits from increased teamwork, higher morale, and greater employee loyalty.

While emphasizing a spirit of high performance nearly always accentuates the positive, there are negative reinforcers too. Managers whose units consistently perform poorly have to be removed. Aside from the organizational benefits, weak-performing managers should be reassigned for their own good—people who find themselves in a job they cannot handle are usually frustrated, anxiety-ridden, harassed, and unhappy.[23] Moreover, subordinates have a right to be managed with competence, dedication, and achievement. Unless their boss performs well, they themselves cannot perform well. In addition, weak-performing workers and people who reject the cultural emphasis on dedication and high performance have to be weeded out. Recruitment practices need to aim at hiring only motivated, ambitious applicants whose attitudes and work habits mesh well with a results-oriented corporate culture.

---

[22]Jeffrey Pheffer, "Producing Sustainable Competitive Advantage through the Effective Management of People," *Academy of Management Executive* 9, no.1 (February 1995), pp. 55–69.

[23]Peter Drucker, *Management: Tasks, Responsibilities, Practices* (New York: Harper & Row, 1974), p. 457.

EXERTING STRATEGIC LEADERSHIP

The litany of good strategic management is simple enough: formulate a sound strategic plan, implement it, execute it to the fullest, win! But it's easier said than done. Exerting take-charge leadership, being a "spark plug," ramrodding things through, and getting things done by coaching others to do them are difficult tasks.[24] Moreover, a strategy manager has many different leadership roles to play: visionary, chief entrepreneur and strategist, chief administrator and strategy implementer, culture builder, resource acquirer and allocator, capabilities builder, process integrator, coach, crisis solver, taskmaster, spokesperson, negotiator, motivator, arbitrator, consensus builder, policy maker, policy enforcer, mentor, and head cheerleader.[25] Sometimes it is useful to be authoritarian and hard-nosed; sometimes it is best to be a perceptive listener and a compromising decision maker; sometimes a strongly participative, collegial approach works best; and sometimes being a coach and advisor is the proper role. Many occasions call for a highly visible role and extensive time commitments, while others entail a brief ceremonial performance with the details delegated to subordinates.

For the most part, major change efforts have to be vision driven and led from the top. Leading change has to start with diagnosing the situation and then deciding which way to handle it. Six leadership roles dominate the strategy implementer's action agenda:

1. Staying on top of what is happening and how well things are going.

2. Promoting a culture in which the organization is "energized" to accomplish strategy and perform at a high level.

3. Keeping the organization responsive to changing conditions, alert for new opportunities, bubbling with innovative ideas, and ahead of rivals in developing competitively valuable competencies and capabilities.

4. Building consensus, containing "power struggles," and dealing with the politics of crafting and implementing strategy.

5. Enforcing ethical standards.

6. Pushing corrective actions to improve strategy execution and overall organization performance.

Staying on Top of How Well Things Are Going

To stay on top of how well the implementation process is going, a manager needs to develop a broad network of contacts and sources of information, both formal and informal. The regular channels include talking with key subordinates, presentations and meetings, reviews of the latest operating results, talking to customers, watching the competitive reactions of rival firms, tapping into the grapevine, listening to rank-

---

[24]For an excellent survey of the problems and pitfalls in making the tranisition to a new strategy and to fundamentally new ways of doing business, see John P. Kotter, "Leading Change: Why Transformation Efforts Fail," *Harvard Business Review* 73, no. 2 (March–April 1995), pp. 59–67. See, also, Thomas M. Hout and John C. Carter, "Getting It Done: New Roles for Senior Executives," *Harvard Business Review* 73 no. 6 (November–December 1995), pp. 133–45 and Sumantra Ghoshal and Christopher A. Bartlett, "Changing the Role of Top Management: Beyond Structure to Processes," *Harvard Business Review* 73 no. 1 (January–February 1995), pp. 86–96.

[25]For a very insightful and revealing report on how one CEO leads the organizational change process, see Noel Tichy and Ram Charan, "The CEO as Coach: An Interview with Allied Signal's Lawrence A. Bossidy," *Harvard Business Review* 73, no. 2 (March–April 1995), pp. 68–78.

and-file employees, and observing the situation firsthand. However, some information is more trustworthy than the rest, and the views and perspectives offered by different people can vary widely. Presentations and briefings by subordinates may represent "the truth but not the whole truth." Bad news or problems may be minimized or in some cases not reported at all as subordinates delay conveying failures and problems in hopes that more time will give them room to turn things around. Hence, strategy managers have to make sure that they have accurate information and a "feel" for the existing situation. One way this is done is by regular visits "to the field" and talking with many different people at many different levels. The technique of "managing by walking around" (MBWA) is practiced in a variety of styles:[26]

> *MBWA is one of the techniques effective leaders use to stay informed on how well strategy implementation and execution is proceeding.*

- At Hewlett-Packard, there are weekly beer busts in each division, attended by both executives and employees, to create a regular opportunity to keep in touch. Tidbits of information flow freely between down-the-line employees and executives—facilitated in part because "the HP Way" is for people at all ranks to be addressed by their first names. Bill Hewlett, one of HP's cofounders, had a companywide reputation for getting out of his office and "wandering around" the plant greeting people, listening to what was on their minds, and asking questions. He found this so valuable that he made MBWA a standard practice for all HP managers.

- McDonald's founder Ray Kroc regularly visited store units and did his own personal inspection on Q.S.C.&V. (Quality, Service, Cleanliness, and Value)—the themes he preached regularly. There are stories of his pulling into a unit's parking lot, seeing litter lying on the pavement, getting out of his limousine to pick it up himself, and then lecturing the store staff at length on the subject of cleanliness.

- The CEO of a small manufacturing company spends much of his time riding around the factory in a golf cart, waving to and joking with workers, listening to them, and calling all 2,000 employees by their first names. In addition, he spends a lot of time with union officials, inviting them to meetings and keeping them well informed about what is going on.

- Wal-Mart executives have had a long-standing practice of spending two to three days every week visiting Wal-Mart's stores and talking with store managers and employees. Sam Walton, Wal-Mart's founder, insisted, "The key is to get out into the store and listen to what the associates have to say. Our best ideas come from clerks and stockboys."

- Jack Welch, CEO of General Electric, not only spends several days each month personally visiting GE operations and talking with major customers but also arranges his schedule so that he can spend time talking with virtually every class of GE managers participating in courses at the company's famed leadership development center at GE's Crotonville, New York, headquarters. As Welch put it, "I'm here every day, or out into a factory, smelling it, feeling it, touching it, challenging the people."[27]

---

[26]Peters and Waterman, *In Search of Excellence,* pp. xx, 15, 120–23, 191, 242–43, 246–47, 287–90. For an extensive discussion of the benefits of MBWA, see Peters and Austin, *A Passion for Excellence,* chapters 2, 3, and 19.

[27]As quoted in Ann M. Morrison, "Trying to Bring GE to Life," *Fortune,* January 25, 1982, p. 52.

- Some activist CEOs make a point of holding key meetings out in the field—at the premises of a major customer or at the facility of a business unit with a troublesome problem—to get their managers out of their comfort zones and create enough of a shared framework for constructive dialogue, disagreement and open debate, and collective solution.

Most managers attach great importance to spending time in the field, observing the situation firsthand and talking informally to many different people at different organizational levels. They believe it is essential to have a "feel" for situations, gathering their own firsthand information and not just relying on information gathered or reported by others. Successful executives are aware of the isolation of spending too much time in their offices or in meetings, the dangers of surrounding themselves with people who are not likely to offer criticism and different perspectives, and the risk of getting too much of their information secondhand, screened and filtered, and sometimes dated. As a Hewlett-Packard official expresses it in the company publication *The HP Way*:

> Once a division or department has developed a plan of its own—a set of working objectives—it's important for managers and supervisors to keep it in operating condition. This is where observation, measurement, feedback, and guidance come in. It's our "management by wandering around." That's how you find out whether you're on track and heading at the right speed and in the right direction. If you don't constantly monitor how people are operating, not only will they tend to wander off track but also they will begin to believe you weren't serious about the plan in the first place. It has the extra benefit of getting you off your chair and moving around your area. By wandering around, I literally mean moving around and talking to people. It's all done on a very informal and spontaneous basis, but it's important in the course of time to cover the whole territory. You start out by being accessible and approachable, but the main thing is to realize you're there to listen. The second reason for MBWA is that it is vital to keep people informed about what's going on in the company, especially those things that are important to them. The third reason for doing this is because it is just plain fun.

Such contacts give the manager a feel for how things are progressing, and they provide opportunity to speak with encouragement, lift spirits, shift attention from the old to the new priorities, create some excitement, and project an atmosphere of informality and fun—all of which drive implementation forward in positive fashion and intensify the organizational energy behind strategy execution.

Fostering a Strategy-Supportive Climate and Culture

Strategy-implementers have to be out front in promoting a strategy-supportive organizational climate and culture. When major strategic changes are being implemented, a manager's time is best spent *personally leading the changes* and promoting needed cultural adjustments. Gradual progress is often not enough. Conservative incrementalism seldom leads to major cultural adaptations; more usually, gradualism is defeated by the stubbornness of entrenched cultures and the ability of vested interests to thwart or minimize the impact of piecemeal change. Only with bold leadership and concerted action on many fronts can a company succeed in tackling so large and difficult a task as major cultural change. When only strategic fine-tuning is being implemented, it takes less time and effort to bring values and culture into alignment with strategy, but there is still a lead role for the manager to play in pushing ahead and prodding for continuous improvements.

Successful culture changes have to be personally led by top management; it's a task that can't be delegated to others.

The single most visible factor that distinguishes successful culture-change efforts from failed attempts is competent leadership at the top. Effective management action to match culture and strategy has several attributes:[28]

- A stakeholders-are-king philosophy that links the need to change to the need to serve the long-term best interests of all key constituencies.

- An openness to new ideas.

- Challenging the status quo with very basic questions: Are we giving customers what they really need and want? How can we be more competitive on cost? Why can't design-to-market cycle time be halved? What new competitive capabilities and resource strengths do we need? How can we grow the company instead of downsizing it? Where will the company be five years from now if it sticks with just its present business?

- Creating events where everyone in management is forced to listen to angry customers, dissatisfied stockholders, and alienated employees to keep management informed and to help them realistically assess the organization's strengths and weaknesses.

- Persuading individuals and groups to commit themselves to the new direction and energizing them to make it happen despite the obstacles.

- Repeating the new messages again and again, explaining the rationale for change, and convincing skeptics that all is not well and that fundamental changes in culture and operating practices are essential to the organization's long term well-being.

- Recognizing and generously rewarding those who exhibit new cultural norms and who lead successful change efforts—this helps expand the coalition for change.

Great power is needed to force major cultural change—to overcome the springback resistance of entrenched cultures—and great power normally resides only at the top. Moreover, the interdependence of values, strategies, practices, and behaviors inside organizations makes it difficult to change anything fundamental without simultaneous wider-scale changes. Usually the people with the power to effect change of that scope are those at the top.

Only top management has the power and organizational influence to bring about major cultural change.

Both words and deeds play a part in leading cultural change. Words inspire people, infuse spirit and drive, define strategy-supportive cultural norms and values, make clear the reasons for strategic and organizational change, legitimize new viewpoints and new priorities, urge and reinforce commitment, and arouse confidence in the new strategy. Deeds add credibility to the words, create strategy-supportive symbols, set examples, give meaning and content to the language, and teach the organization what sort of behavior is needed and expected.

Highly visible symbols and imagery are needed to complement actions. One General Motors manager explained how symbolism and managerial style accounted for the striking difference in performance between two large plants:[29]

At the poorly performing plant, the plant manager probably ventured out on the floor once a week, always in a suit. His comments were distant and perfunctory. At South Gate, the better plant, the plant manager was on the floor all the time. He wore a baseball cap and a UAW jacket. By the way, whose plant do you think was spotless? Whose looked like a junkyard?

[28]Ibid., pp. 84, 144, and 148.

[29]As quoted in Peters and Waterman, *In Search of Excellence*, p. 262.

As a rule, the greater the degree of strategic change being implemented and the greater the shift in cultural norms needed to accommodate a new strategy, the more visible and clear the strategy implementer's words and deeds need to be. Moreover, the actions and images, both substantive and symbolic, have to be hammered out regularly, not just restricted to ceremonial speeches and special occasions. In such instances maintaining a high profile and "managing by walking around" are especially useful.

What the strategy leader says and does plants the seeds of cultural change and has a significant bearing on down-the-line strategy implementation and execution.

In global companies, leaders have to learn how to function effectively with diversity in cultures and behavioral norms and with the expectations of people who sometimes fervently insist on being treated as distinctive individuals or groups—a one-size-fits-all leadership approach won't work. Effective cross-cultural leadership requires sensitivity to cultural differences, discerning when diversity has to be accommodated and when differences can be and should be narrowed.[30]

Keeping the Internal Organization Responsive and Innovative

While formulating and implementing strategy is a manager's responsibility, the task of generating fresh ideas, identifying new opportunities, and responding to changing conditions cannot be accomplished by a single person. It is an organizationwide task, particularly in large corporations. One of the toughest parts of strategic leadership is generating fresh ideas from the rank and file, managers and employees alike, and promoting an entrepreneurial, opportunistic spirit that permits continuous adaptation to changing conditions. A flexible, responsive, innovative internal environment is critical in fast-moving high-technology industries, in businesses where products have short life cycles and growth depends on new product innovation, in companies with widely diversified business portfolios (where opportunities are varied and scattered), in markets where successful product differentiation depends on outinnovating the competition, and in situations where low-cost leadership hinges on continuous improvement and new ways to drive costs out of the business. Managers cannot mandate such an internal work climate by simply exhorting people to "be creative."

The faster a company's business environment changes, the more attention managers must pay to keeping the organization innovative and responsive.

Empowering Champions   One useful leadership approach is to take special pains to foster, nourish, and support people who are willing to champion new technologies, new operating practices, better services, new products, and new product applications and are eager to try carrying out their ideas. One year after taking charge at Siemens-Nixdorf Information Systems, Gerhard Schulmeyer produced the merged company's first profit after losing hundreds of millions of dollars annually since 1991; he credited the turnaround to the creation of 5,000 "change agents," almost 15 percent of the workforce, who volunteered for active roles in the company's change agenda while continuing to perform their regular jobs. As a rule, the best champions are persistent, competitive, tenacious, committed, and fanatic about the idea and seeing it through to success.

Identifying and empowering champions helps promote an environment of innovation and experimentation.

To promote a climate where champion innovators can blossom and thrive, strategy managers need to do several things. First, individuals and groups have to be encouraged to be creative, hold informal brainstorming sessions, let their imaginations fly in all

---

[30]For a discussion of this dimension of leadership, see Alexander and Wilson, "Leading across Cultures: Five Vital Capabilities," pp. 287–94.

directions, and come up with proposals. The culture has to nurture, even celebrate, experimentation and innovation. Everybody must be expected to contribute ideas, show initiative, and pursue continuous improvement. The trick is to keep a sense of urgency alive in the business so that people see change and innovation as a necessity. Second, people with maverick ideas or out-of-the-ordinary proposals have to be tolerated and given room to operate. Above all, would-be champions who advocate radical or different ideas must not be looked on as disruptive or troublesome. Third, managers have to promote lots of "tries" and be willing to tolerate mistakes and failures. Most ideas don't pan out, but the organization learns from a good attempt even when it fails. Fourth, strategy managers should be willing to use all kinds of organizational forms to support ideas and experimentation—venture teams, task forces, "performance shootouts" among different groups working on competing approaches, informal "boot-legged" projects composed of volunteers, and so on. Fifth, strategy managers have to see that the rewards for successful champions are large and visible and that people who champion an unsuccessful idea are encouraged to try again rather than be punished or sidelined. In effect, the leadership task is to create an adaptive, innovative culture that responds to changing conditions rather than fearing the new conditions or seeking to minimize them. Companies with innovative cultures include Sony, 3M, Motorola, and Levi Strauss. All four inspire their employees with strategic visions to excel and be world-class at what they do.

Leading the Process of Developing New Capabilities Often, effectively responding to changing customer preferences and competitive conditions requires top management intervention to establish new capabilities and resource strengths. Senior management usually has to lead the effort because core competencies and competitive capabilities typically come from the combined efforts of different work groups, departments, and collaborative allies. The tasks of managing human skills, knowledge bases, and intellect and then integrating them to forge competitively advantageous competencies and capabilities is best orchestrated by senior managers who appreciate their strategy-implementing significance and who have the clout to enforce the necessary networking and cooperation among individuals, groups, departments, and external allies.

> *It's a constant organization-building challenge to broaden, deepen, or modify organization capabilities and resource strengths in response to ongoing customer-market changes.*

> *The ideal leadership outcome is for senior management to proactively develop new competencies and capabilities to complement the company's existing resource base and promote more proficient strategy execution.*

Effective company managers try to anticipate changes in customer-market requirements and proactively build new competencies and capabilities that offer a competitive edge over rivals. Senior managers are in the best position to see the need and potential of new capabilities and then to play a lead role in building capabilities and strengthening company resources. Building new competencies and capabilities ahead of rivals to gain a competitive edge is strategic leadership of the best kind, but strengthening the company's resource base in reaction to the newly developed capabilities of pioneering rivals is the most frequent occurrence.

Dealing with Company Politics

A manager can't effectively formulate and implement strategy without being perceptive about company politics and being adept at political maneuvering.[31] Politics virtually always comes into play in formulating the strategic plan. Inevitably, key

---

[31]For further discussion of this point see Abraham Zaleznik, "Power and Politics in Organizational Life," *Harvard Business Review* 48, no. 3 (May–June 1970), pp. 47–60; R. M. Cyert, H. A. Simon, and D. B.

individuals and groups form coalitions, and each group presses the benefits and potential of its own ideas and vested interests. Political considerations enter into decisions about which objectives take precedence and which lines of business have top priority in resource allocation. Internal politics is a factor in building a consensus for one strategic option over another.

As a rule, there is even more politics in implementing strategy than in formulating it. Typically, internal political considerations affect whose areas of responsibility get reorganized, who reports to whom, who has how much authority over subunits, what individuals should fill key positions and head strategy-critical activities, and which units will get the biggest budget increases. As a case in point, Quinn cites a situation where three strong managers who fought each other constantly formed a potent coalition to resist a reorganization scheme that would have coordinated the very things that caused their friction.[32]

Company politics presents strategy leaders with the challenge of building consensus for the strategy and how to implement it.

A strategy manager must therefore understand how an organization's power structure works, who wields influence in the executive ranks, which groups and individuals are "activists" and which are defenders of the status quo, who can be helpful and who may not be in a showdown on key decisions, and which direction the political winds are blowing on a given issue. When major decisions have to be made, strategy managers need to be especially sensitive to the politics of managing coalitions and reaching consensus. As the chairman of a major British corporation expressed it:

> I've never taken a major decision without consulting my colleagues. It would be unimaginable to me, unimaginable. First, they help me make a better decision in most cases. Second, if they know about it and agree with it, they'll back it. Otherwise, they might challenge it, not openly, but subconsciously.[33]

The politics of strategy centers chiefly around stimulating options, nurturing support for strong proposals and killing weak ones, guiding the formation of coalitions on particular issues, and achieving consensus and commitment. Successful executives rely upon the following political tactics:[34]

- Letting weakly supported ideas and proposals die through inaction.
- Establishing additional hurdles or tests for strongly supported ideas that the manager views as unacceptable but that are best not opposed openly.
- Keeping a low political profile on unacceptable proposals by getting subordinate managers to say no.
- Letting most negative decisions come from a group consensus that the manager merely confirms, thereby reserving personal veto for big issues and crucial moments.
- Leading the strategy but not dictating it—giving few orders, announcing few decisions, depending heavily on informal questioning, and seeking to probe and clarify until a consensus emerges.

Trow, "Observation of a Business Decision," *Journal of Business*, October 1956, pp. 237–48; and James Brian Quinn, *Strategies for Change: Logical Incrementalism* (Homewood, Ill.: Richard D. Irwin, 1980).

[32]Quinn, *Strategies for Change*, p. 68.

[33]Ibid., p. 65. This statement was made by Sir Alastair Pilkington, Chairman, Pilkington Brothers, Ltd.

[34]Ibid., pp. 128–45.

- Staying alert to the symbolic impact of one's actions and statements lest a false signal stimulate proposals and movements in unwanted directions.

- Ensuring that all major power bases within the organization have representation in or access to top management.

- Injecting new faces and new views into considerations of major changes to prevent those involved from coming to see the world the same way and then acting as systematic screens against other views.

- Minimizing political exposure on issues that are highly controversial and in circumstances where opposition from major power centers can trigger a "shootout."

The politics of strategy implementation is especially critical when it comes to introducing a new strategy against the resistance of those who support the old one. Except for crisis situations where the old strategy is plainly revealed as out-of-date, it is usually bad politics to push the new strategy by attacks on the old one.[35] Bad-mouthing old strategy can easily be interpreted as an attack on those who formulated it and those who supported it. The old strategy and the judgments behind it may have been well-suited to the organization's earlier circumstances, and the people who made these judgments may still be influential. In addition, the new strategy and/or the plans for implementing it may not have been the first choices of others, and lingering doubts may remain. Good arguments may exist for pursuing other actions. Consequently, in trying to surmount resistance, nothing is gained by knocking the arguments for alternative approaches. Such attacks often produce alienation instead of cooperation.

In short, to bring the full force of an organization behind a strategic plan, the strategy manager must assess and deal with the most important centers of potential support for and opposition to new strategic thrusts.[36] He or she needs to secure the support of key people, co-opt or neutralize serious opposition and resistance when and where necessary, learn where the zones of indifference are, and build as much consensus as possible. Political skills are a definite, maybe even necessary, managerial asset.

Enforcing Ethical Behavior

For an organization to display consistently high ethical standards, the CEO and those around the CEO must be openly and clearly committed to ethical and moral conduct.[37] In companies that strive hard to make high ethical standards a reality, top management communicates its commitment in a code of ethics, in speeches and company publications, in policies on the consequences of unethical behavior, in the deeds of senior executives, and in the actions taken to ensure compliance. Senior management repeatedly tells employees that it is not only their duty to observe ethical codes but also to report ethical violations. While such companies have provisions for disciplining violators, the main purpose of enforcement is to encourage compliance rather than administer punishment. Although the CEO leads the

---

[35]Ibid., pp. 118–19.
[36]Ibid., p. 205.
[37]The Business Roundtable, *Corporate Ethics*, pp. 4–10.

High ethical standards cannot be enforced without the open and unequivocal commitment of the chief executive.

enforcement process, all managers are expected to make a personal contribution by stressing ethical conduct with their subordinates and monitoring compliance with the code of ethics. "Gray areas" must be identified and openly discussed with employees, and procedures created for offering guidance when issues arise, for investigating possible violations, and for resolving individual cases. The lesson from these companies is that it is never enough to assume activities are being conducted ethically, nor can it be assumed that employees understand they are expected to act with integrity.

Managers can do several concrete things to exercise ethics leadership.[38] First and foremost, they must set an excellent ethical example in their own behavior and establish a tradition of integrity. Company decisions have to be seen as ethical—"actions speak louder than words." Second, managers and employees have to be educated about what is ethical and what is not; ethics training programs may have to be established and gray areas pointed out and discussed. Everyone must be encouraged to raise issues with ethical dimensions, and such discussions should be treated as a legitimate topic. Third, top management should regularly restate its clear support of the company's ethical code and take a strong stand on ethical issues. Fourth, top management must be prepared to act as the final arbiter on hard calls; this means removing people from a key position or terminating them when they are guilty of a violation. It also means reprimanding those who have been lax in monitoring and enforcing ethical compliance. Failure to act swiftly and decisively in punishing ethical misconduct is interpreted as a lack of real commitment.

A well-developed program to ensure compliance with ethical standards typically includes (1) an oversight committee of the board of directors, usually made up of outside directors; (2) a committee of senior managers to direct ongoing training, implementation, and compliance; (3) an annual audit of each manager's efforts to uphold ethical standards and formal reports on the actions taken by managers to remedy deficient conduct; and (4) periodically requiring people to sign documents certifying compliance with ethical standards.[39]

Leading the Process of Making Corrective Adjustments

No strategic plan and no scheme for strategy implementation can foresee all the events and problems that will arise. Making adjustments and midcourse corrections, as well as pushing for ever better execution is a normal and necessary part of leading the process of implementing and executing strategy. The *process* of deciding when to make adjustments and what adjustments to make varies according to the situation. In a crisis, the typical leadership approach is to have key subordinates gather information, identify options, and make recommendations, then personally preside over extended discussions of the proposed responses and try to build a quick consensus among members of the executive inner circle. If no consensus emerges and action is required immediately, the burden falls on the strategy manager to choose the response and urge its support.

Corrective adjustments in the company's approach to strategy implementation are normal and have to be made as needed.

When the situation allows managers to proceed more deliberately in deciding when to make changes and what changes to make, strategy managers seem to prefer

---

[38]Ibid.
[39]Ibid.

a process of gradually solidifying commitment to a particular course of action.[40] The process that managers go through in deciding on corrective adjustments is essentially the same for both proactive and reactive changes: They sense needs, gather information, broaden and deepen their understanding of the situation, develop options and explore their pros and cons, put forth action proposals, generate partial (comfort-level) solutions, build consensus, and finally formally adopt an agreed-on course of action.[41] The ultimate managerial prescription may have been given by Rene Mc-Pherson, former CEO at Dana Corporation. Speaking to a class of students at Stanford University, he said, "You just keep pushing. You just keep pushing. I made every mistake that could be made. But I just kept pushing."[42]

All this, once again, highlights the fundamental nature of strategic management: The job of formulating and implementing strategy is not one of steering a clear-cut course while carrying out the original strategy intact according to some preconceived plan. Rather, it is one of creatively (1) adapting and reshaping strategy to unfolding events and (2) drawing upon whatever managerial techniques are needed to align internal activities and behaviors with strategy. The process is interactive, with much looping and recycling to fine-tune and adjust visions, objectives, strategies, resources, capabilities, implementation approaches, and cultures to one another in a continuously evolving process. The best tests of good strategic leadership are improving business performance and a company that is agile, that is capable of adapting to multiple changes, and that is a good place to work.

KEY POINTS

Building a strategy-supportive corporate culture is important to successful implementation because it produces a work climate and organizational esprit de corps that thrive on meeting performance targets and being part of a winning effort. An organization's culture emerges from why and how it does things the way it does, the values and beliefs that senior managers espouse, the ethical standards expected of all, the tone and philosophy underlying key policies, and the traditions the organization maintains. Culture thus concerns the atmosphere and "feeling" a company has and the style in which it gets things done.

Very often, the elements of company culture originate with a founder or other early influential leaders who articulate certain values, beliefs, and principles the company should adhere to, which then get incorporated into company policies, a creed or values statement, strategies, and operating practices. Over time, these values and practices become shared by company employees and managers. Cultures are perpetuated as new leaders act to reinforce them, as new employees are encouraged to adopt and follow them, as legendary stories that exemplify them are told and retold, and as organizational members are honored and rewarded for displaying the cultural norms.

Company cultures vary widely in strength and in makeup. Some cultures are strongly embedded, while others are weak and fragmented in the sense that many subcultures exist, few values and behavioral norms are shared companywide, and there are few strong traditions. Some cultures are unhealthy, dominated by self-serving politics, resistant to change, and too inwardly focused; such cultural traits are

---

[40]Quinn, *Strategies for Change*, pp. 20–22.
[41]Ibid., p. 146.
[42]As quoted in Peters and Waterman, *In Search of Excellence*, p. 319.

often precursors to declining company performance. In fast-changing business environments, adaptive cultures are best because the internal environment is receptive to change, experimentation, innovation, new strategies, and new operating practices needed to respond to changing stakeholder requirements. One significant defining trait of adaptive cultures is that top management genuinely cares about the well-being of all key constituencies—customers, employees, stockholders, major suppliers, and the communities where it operates—and tries to satisfy all their legitimate interests simultaneously.

The philosophy, goals, and practices implicit or explicit in a new strategy may or may not be compatible with a firm's culture. A close strategy-culture alignment promotes implementation and good execution; a mismatch poses real obstacles. Changing a company's culture, especially a strong one with traits that don't fit a new strategy's requirements, is one of the toughest management challenges. Changing a culture requires competent leadership at the top. It requires symbolic actions (leading by example) and substantive actions that unmistakably indicate top management is seriously committed. The stronger the fit between culture and strategy, the less managers have to depend on policies, rules, procedures, and supervision to enforce what people should and should not do; rather, cultural norms are so well observed that they automatically guide behavior.

Healthy corporate cultures are also grounded in ethical business principles and moral values. Such standards connote integrity, "doing the right thing," and genuine concern for stakeholders and for how the company does business. To be effective, corporate ethics and values programs have to become a way of life through training, strict compliance and enforcement procedures, and reiterated management endorsements.

Successful strategy implementers exercise an important leadership role. They stay on top of how well things are going by spending considerable time outside their offices, wandering around the organization, listening, coaching, cheerleading, picking up important information, and keeping their fingers on the organization's pulse. They take pains to reinforce the corporate culture through the things they say and do. They encourage people to be creative and innovative in order to keep the organization responsive to changing conditions, alert to new opportunities, and anxious to pursue fresh initiatives. They support "champions" of new approaches or ideas who are willing to stick their necks out and try something innovative. They work hard at building consensus on how to proceed, on what to change and what not to change. They enforce high ethical standards. And they push corrective action to improve strategy execution and overall strategic performance.

A manager's action agenda for implementing and executing strategy is thus expansive and creative. As we indicated at the beginning of our discussion of strategy implementation (Chapter 9), eight bases need to be covered:

1. Building an organization capable of carrying out the strategy successfully.

2. Developing budgets to steer ample resources into those value-chain activities critical to strategic success.

3. Establishing strategically appropriate policies and procedures.

4. Instituting best practices and mechanisms for continuous improvement.

5. Installing support systems that enable company personnel to carry out their strategic roles successfully day in and day out.

6. Tying rewards and incentives tightly to the achievement of performance objectives and good strategy execution.

7. Creating a strategy-supportive work environment and corporate culture.

8. Leading and monitoring the process of driving implementation forward and improving on how the strategy is being executed.

Making progress on these eight tasks sweeps broadly across virtually every aspect of administrative and managerial work.

Because each instance of strategy implementation occurs under different organizational circumstances, a strategy implementer's action agenda always needs to be situation specific—there's no neat generic procedure to follow. And, as we said at the beginning, implementing strategy is an action-oriented, make-the-right-things-happen task that challenges a manager's ability to lead and direct organizational change, create or reinvent business processes, manage and motivate people, and achieve performance targets. If you now better understand the nature of the challenge, the range of available approaches, and the issues that need to be considered, we will look upon our discussion in these last three chapters as a success.

SUGGESTED READINGS

Badaracco, Joe and Allen P. Webb. "Business Ethics: A View from the Trenches." *California Management Review* 37, no. 2 (Winter 1995), pp. 8–28.

Clement, Ronald W. "Culture, Leadership, and Power: The Keys to Organizational Change." *Business Horizons* 37, no. 1 (January–February 1994), pp. 33–39.

Deal, Terrence E., and Allen A. Kennedy. *Corporate Cultures*. Reading, Mass.: Addison-Wesley, 1982, especially chaps. 1 and 2.

Eccles, Robert G. "The Performance Measurement Manifesto." *Harvard Business Review* 69 (January–February 1991), pp. 131–37.

Farkas, Charles M. and Suzy Wetlaufer, "The Ways Chief Executive Officers Lead," *Harvard Business Review* 74 no. 3 (May–June 1996), pp. 110–122.

Floyd, Steven W., and Bill Wooldridge. "Managing Strategic Consensus: The Foundation of Effective Implementation." *Academy of Management Executive* 6, no. 4 (November 1992), pp. 27–39.

Gabarro, J. J. "When a New Manager Takes Charge." *Harvard Business Review* 64, no. 3 (May–June 1985), pp. 110–23.

Ghoshal, Sumantra and Christopher A. Bartlett. "Changing the Role of Top Management: Beyond Structure to Processes." *Harvard Business Review* 73 no. 1 (January–February 1995), pp. 86–96.

Ginsburg, Lee and Neil Miller, "Value-Driven Management," *Business Horizons* (May–June 1992), pp. 25–27.

Green, Sebastian. "Strategy, Organizational Culture, and Symbolism." *Long Range Planning* 21, no. 4 (August 1988), pp. 121–29.

Heifetz, Ronald A. and Donald L. Laurie. "The Work of Leadership." *Harvard Business Review* 75, no. 1 (January–February 1997), pp. 124–34.

Humble, John, David Jackson, and Alan Thomson. "The Strategic Power of Corporate Values." *Long Range Planning* 27, no. 6 (December 1994), pp. 28–42.

Kirkpatrick, Shelley A., and Edwin A. Locke. "Leadership: Do Traits Matter?" *Academy of Management Executive* 5, no. 2 (May 1991), pp. 48–60.

Kotter, John P. "What Leaders Really Do." *Harvard Business Review* 68 no. 3 (May–June 1990), pp. 103–11.

———. "Leading Change: Why Transformation Efforts Fail." *Harvard Business Review* 73, no. 2 (March–April 1995), pp. 59–67.

————, and James L. Heskett. *Corporate Culture and Performance*. New York: Free Press, 1992.

Miles, Robert H. *Corporate Comeback: The Story of Renewal and Transformation at National Semiconductor*. San Francisco: Jossey-Bass, 1997.

Murphy, Patrick E. "Corporate Ethics Statements: Current Status and Future Prospects." *Journal of Business Ethics* 14 (1995), pp. 727–40.

O'Toole, James. "Employee Practices at the Best-Managed Companies." *California Management Review* 28, no. 1 (Fall 1985), pp. 35–66.

Paine, Lynn Sharp. "Managing for Organizational Integrity." *Harvard Business Review* 72, no. 2 (March–April 1994), pp. 106–17.

Reimann, Bernard C., and Yoash Wiener. "Corporate Culture: Avoiding the Elitist Trap." *Business Horizons* 31, no. 2 (March–April 1988), pp. 36–44.

Schneider, Benjamin, Sarah K. Gunnarson, and Kathryn Niles-Jolly. "Creating the Climate and Culture of Success." *Organizational Dynamics* (Summer 1994), pp.17–29.

Scholz, Christian. "Corporate Culture and Strategy—The Problem of Strategic Fit." *Long Range Planning* 20 (August 1987), pp. 78–87.

II

CASES IN STRATEGIC MANAGEMENT

PART

A GUIDE TO CASE ANALYSIS

I n most courses in strategic management, students use cases about actual companies to practice strategic analysis and to gain some experience in the tasks of crafting and implementing strategy. A case sets forth, in a factual manner, the events and organizational circumstances surrounding a particular managerial situation. It puts readers at the scene of the action and familiarizes them with all the relevant circumstances. A case on strategic management can concern a whole industry, a single organization, or some part of an organization; the organization involved can be either profit seeking or not-for-profit. The essence of the student's role in case analysis is to *diagnose* and *size up* the situation described in the case and then to *recommend* appropriate action steps.

> I keep six honest serving men
> (They taught me all I knew);
> Their names are What and Why and When;
> And How and Where and Who.
>
> **Rudyard Kipling**

WHY USE CASES TO PRACTICE STRATEGIC MANAGEMENT?

> A student of business with tact
> Absorbed many answers he lacked.
> But acquiring a job,
> He said with a sob,
> "How does one fit answer to fact?"

The foregoing limerick was used some years ago by Professor Charles Gragg to characterize the plight of business students who had no exposure to cases.[1] The facts are that the mere act of listening to lectures and sound advice about managing does little for anyone's management skills and that the accumulated managerial wisdom cannot effectively be passed on by lectures and assigned readings alone. If anything had been learned about the practice of management, it is that a storehouse of ready-made textbook answers does not exist. Each managerial situation has unique aspects, requiring its own diagnosis, judgment, and tailor-made actions. Cases provide would-be managers with a valuable way to practice wrestling with the actual problems of actual managers in actual companies.

The case approach to strategic analysis is, first and foremost, an exercise in learning by doing. Because cases provide you with detailed information about conditions and problems of different industries and companies, your task of analyz-

---

[1]Charles I. Gragg, "Because Wisdom Can't Be Told," in *The Case Method at the Harvard Business School*, ed. M. P. McNair (New York: McGraw-Hill, 1954), p. 11.

ing company after company and situation after situation has the twin benefit of boosting your analytical skills and exposing you to the ways companies and managers actually do things. Most college students have limited managerial backgrounds and only fragmented knowledge about companies and real-life strategic situations. Cases help substitute for on-the-job experience by (1) giving you broader exposure to a variety of industries, organizations, and strategic problems; (2) forcing you to assume a managerial role (as opposed to that of just an onlooker); (3) providing a test of how to apply the tools and techniques of strategic management; and (4) asking you to come up with pragmatic managerial action plans to deal with the issues at hand.

OBJECTIVES OF CASE ANALYSIS

Using cases to learn about the practice of strategic management is a powerful way for you to accomplish five things:[2]

1. Increase your understanding of what managers should and should not do in guiding a business to success.

2. Build your skills in sizing up company resource strengths and weaknesses and in conducting strategic analysis in a variety of industries and competitive situations.

3. Get valuable practice in identifying strategic issues that need to be addressed, evaluating strategic alternatives, and formulating workable plans of action.

4. Enhance your sense of business judgment, as opposed to uncritically accepting the authoritative crutch of the professor or "back-of-the-book" answers.

5. Gaining in-depth exposure to different industries and companies, thereby acquiring something close to actual business experience.

If you understand that these are the objectives of case analysis, you are less likely to be consumed with curiosity about "the answer to the case." Students who have grown comfortable with and accustomed to textbook statements of fact and definitive lecture notes are often frustrated when discussions about a case do not produce concrete answers. Usually, case discussions produce good arguments for more than one course of action. Differences of opinion nearly always exist. Thus, should a class discussion conclude without a strong, unambiguous consensus on what do to, don't grumble too much when you are *not* told what the answer is or what the company actually did. Just remember that in the business world answers don't come in conclusive black-and-white terms. There are nearly always several feasible courses of action and approaches, each of which may work out satisfactorily. Moreover, in the business world, when one elects a particular course of action, there is no peeking at the back of a book to see if you have chosen the best thing to do and no one to turn to for a provably correct answer. The only valid test of management action is *results*. If the results of an action turn out to be "good," the decision to take it may be presumed "right." If not, then the action chosen was "wrong" in the sense that it didn't work out.

Hence, the important thing for a student to understand in case analysis is that the managerial exercise of identifying, diagnosing, and recommending builds your skills;

[2]Ibid., pp. 12–14; and D. R. Schoen and Philip A. Sprague, "What Is the Case Method?" in *The Case Method at the Harvard Business School*, ed. M. P. McNair, pp. 78–79.

discovering the right answer or finding out what actually happened is no more than frosting on the cake. Even if you learn what the company did, you can't conclude that it was necessarily right or best. All that can be said is "here is what they did . . ."

The point is this: *The purpose of giving you a case assignment is not to cause you to run to the library or surf the Internet to discover what the company actually did but, rather, to enhance your skills in sizing up situations and developing your managerial judgment about what needs to be done and how to do it.* The aim of case analysis is for *you* to bear the strains of thinking actively, of offering your analysis, of proposing action plans, and of explaining and defending your assessments—this is how cases provide you with meaningful practice at being a manager.

PREPARING A CASE FOR CLASS DISCUSSION

If this is your first experience with the case method, you may have to reorient your study habits. Unlike lecture courses where you can get by without preparing intensively for each class and where you have latitude to work assigned readings and reviews of lecture notes into your schedule, a case assignment requires conscientious preparation before class. You will not get much out of hearing the class discuss a case you haven't read, and you certainly won't be able to contribute anything yourself to the discussion. What you have got to do to get ready for class discussion of a case is to study the case, reflect carefully on the situation presented, and develop some reasoned thoughts. Your goal in preparing the case should be to end up with what you think is a sound, well-supported analysis of the situation and a sound, defensible set of recommendations about which managerial actions need to be taken. The Strat-Tutor software package that accompanies this edition will assist you in preparing the cases—it contains a set of study questions for each case and step-by-step tutorials to walk you through the process of analyzing and developing reasonable recommendations.

To prepare a case for class discussion, we suggest the following approach:

1. *Read the case through rather quickly for familiarity.* The initial reading should give you the general flavor of the situation and indicate which issue or issues are involved. If your instructor has provided you with study questions for the case, now is the time to read them carefully.

2. *Read the case a second time.* On this reading, try to gain full command of the facts. Begin to develop some tentative answers to the study questions your instructor has provided or that are provided on the Strat-Tutor software package. If your instructor has elected not to give you assignment questions or has elected not to use Strat-Tutor, then start forming your own picture of the overall situation being described.

3. *Study all the exhibits carefully.* Often, there is an important story in the numbers contained in the exhibits. Expect the information in the case exhibits to be crucial enough to materially affect your diagnosis of the situation.

4. *Decide what the strategic issues are.* Until you have identified the strategic issues and problems in the case, you don't know what to analyze, which tools and analytical techniques are called for, or otherwise how to proceed. At times the strategic issues are clear—either being stated in the case or else obvious from reading the case. At other times you will have to dig them out from all the information given; if so, the study questions and the case preparation exercises on Strat-Tutor will guide you.

5. *Start your analysis of the issues with some number crunching.* A big majority of strategy cases call for some kind of number crunching—calculating assorted financial ratios to check out the company's financial condition and recent performance, calculating growth rates of sales or profits or unit volume, checking out profit margins and the makeup of the cost structure, and understanding whatever revenue-cost-profit relationships are present. See Table 1 for a summary of key financial ratios, how they are calculated, and what they show. If you are using Strat-TUTOR, much of the number-crunching has been computerized and you'll spend most of your time interpreting the growth rates, financial ratios, and other calculations provided.

6. *Use whichever tools and techniques of strategic analysis are called for.* Strategic analysis is not just a collection of opinions; rather, it entails application of a growing number of powerful tools and techniques that cut beneath the surface and produce important insight and understanding of strategic situations. Every case assigned is strategy related and contains an opportunity to usefully apply the weapons of strategic analysis. Your instructor is looking for you to demonstrate that you know *how* and *when* to use the strategic management concepts presented in the text chapters. The case preparation guides on Strat-TUTOR will point you toward the proper analytical tools needed to analyze the case situation.

7. *Check out conflicting opinions and make some judgments about the validity of all the data and information provided.* Many times cases report views and contradictory opinions (after all, people don't always agree on things, and different people see the same things in different ways). Forcing you to evaluate the data and information presented in the case helps you develop your powers of inference and judgment. Asking you to resolve conflicting information "comes with the territory" because a great many managerial situations entail opposing points of view, conflicting trends, and sketchy information.

8. *Support your diagnosis and opinions with reasons and evidence.* The most important things to prepare for are your answers to the question "Why?" For instance, if after studying the case you are of the opinion that the company's managers are doing a poor job, then it is your answer to "Why?" that establishes just how good your analysis of the situation is. If your instructor has provided you with specific study questions for the case or if you are using the case preparation guides on Strat-TUTOR, by all means prepare answers that include all the reasons and number-crunching evidence you can muster to support your diagnosis. Work through the case preparation exercises on Strat-TUTOR *conscientiously* or, if you are using study questions provided by the instructor, *generate at least two pages of notes!*

9. *Develop an appropriate action plan and set of recommendations.* Diagnosis divorced from corrective action is sterile. The test of a manager is always to convert sound analysis into sound actions—actions that will produce the desired results. Hence, the final and most telling step in preparing a case is to develop an action agenda for management that lays out a set of specific recommendations on what to do. Bear in mind that proposing realistic, workable solutions is far preferable to casually tossing out off-the-top-of-your-head suggestions. Be prepared to argue why your recommendations are more attractive than other courses of action that are open. You'll find Strat-TUTOR's case preparation guides helpful in performing this step, too.

TABLE 1   A Summary of Key Financial Ratios, How They Are Calculated, and What They Show

Ratio	How Calculated	What It Shows
Profitability Ratios		
1. Gross profit margin	$\dfrac{\text{Sales} - \text{Cost of goods sold}}{\text{Sales}}$	An indication of the total margin available to cover operating expenses and yield a profit.
2. Operating profit margin (or return on sales)	$\dfrac{\text{Profits before taxes and before interest}}{\text{Sales}}$	An indication of the firm's profitability from current operations without regard to the interest charges accruing from the capital structure.
3. Net profit margin (or net return on sales)	$\dfrac{\text{Profits after taxes}}{\text{Sales}}$	Shows after tax profits per dollar of sales. Subpar profit margins indicate that the firm's sales prices are relatively low or that costs are relatively high, or both.
4. Return on total assets	$\dfrac{\text{Profits after taxes}}{\text{Total assets}}$ or $\dfrac{\text{Profits after taxes} + \text{interest}}{\text{Total assets}}$	A measure of the return on total investment in the enterprise. It is sometimes desirable to add interest to aftertax profits to form the numerator of the ratio since total assets are financed by creditors as well as by stockholders; hence, it is accurate to measure the productivity of assets by the returns provided to both classes of investors.
5. Return on stockholder's equity (or return on net worth)	$\dfrac{\text{Profits after taxes}}{\text{Total stockholders' equity}}$	A measure of the rate of return on stockholders' investment in the enterprise.
6. Return on common equity	$\dfrac{\text{Profits after taxes} - \text{Preferred stock dividends}}{\text{Total stockholders' equity} - \text{Par value of preferred stock}}$	A measure of the rate of return on the investment the owners of the common stock have made in the enterprise.
7. Earnings per share	$\dfrac{\text{Profits after taxes} - \text{Preferred stock dividends}}{\text{Number of shares of common stock outstanding}}$	Shows the earnings available to the owners of each share of common stock.
Liquidity Ratios		
1. Current ratio	$\dfrac{\text{Current assets}}{\text{Current liabilities}}$	Indicates the extent to which the claims of short-term creditors are covered by assets that are expected to be converted to cash in a period roughly corresponding to the maturity of the liabilities.
2. Quick ratio (or acid-test ratio)	$\dfrac{\text{Current assets} - \text{Inventory}}{\text{Current liabilities}}$	A measure of the firm's ability to pay off short-term obligations without relying on the sale of its inventories.
3. Inventory to net working capital	$\dfrac{\text{Inventory}}{\text{Current assets} - \text{Current liabilities}}$	A measure of the extent to which the firm's working capital is tied up in inventory.
Leverage Ratios		
1. Debt-to-assets ratio	$\dfrac{\text{Total debt}}{\text{Total assets}}$	Measures the extent to which borrowed funds have been used to finance the firm's operations.
2. Debt-to-equity ratio	$\dfrac{\text{Total debt}}{\text{Total stockholders' equity}}$	Provides another measure of the funds provided by creditors versus the funds provided by owners.

TABLE 1   Ratios, How They Are Calculated, and What They Show (*cont.*)

Ratio	How Calculated	What It Shows
Leverage Ratios (*cont.*)		
3. Long-term debt-to-equity ratio	$\dfrac{\text{Long-term debt}}{\text{Total stockholders' equity}}$	A widely used measure of the balance between debt and equity in the firm's long-term capital structure.
4. Times-interest-earned (or coverage) ratio	$\dfrac{\text{Profits before interest and taxes}}{\text{Total interest charges}}$	Measures the extent to which earnings can decline without the firm becoming unable to meet its annual interest costs.
5. Fixed-charge coverage	$\dfrac{\text{Profits before taxes and interest} + \text{Lease obligations}}{\text{Total interest charges} + \text{Lease obligations}}$	A more inclusive indication of the firm's ability to meet all of its fixed-charge obligations.
Activity Ratios		
1. Inventory turnover	$\dfrac{\text{Sales}}{\text{Inventory of finished goods}}$	When compared to industry averages, it provides an indication of whether a company has excessive or perhaps inadequate finished goods inventory.
2. Fixed assets turnover	$\dfrac{\text{Sales}}{\text{Fixed assets}}$	A measure of the sales productivity and utilization of plant and equipment.
3. Total assets turnover	$\dfrac{\text{Sales}}{\text{Total assets}}$	A measure of the utilization of all the firm's assets; a ratio below the industry average indicates the company is not generating a sufficient volume of business, given the size of its asset investment.
4. Accounts receivable turnover	$\dfrac{\text{Annual credit sales}}{\text{Accounts receivable}}$	A measure of the average length of time it takes the firm to collect the sales made on credit.
5. Average collection period	$\dfrac{\text{Accounts receivable}}{\text{Total sales} \div 365}$ or $\dfrac{\text{Accounts receivable}}{\text{Average daily sales}}$	Indicates the average length of time the firm must wait after making a sale before it receives payment.
Other Ratios		
1. Dividend yield on common stock	$\dfrac{\text{Annual dividends per share}}{\text{Current market price per share}}$	A measure of the return to owners received in the form of dividends.
2. Price-earnings ratio	$\dfrac{\text{Current market price per share}}{\text{After tax earnings per share}}$	Faster-growing or less-risky firms tend to have higher price-earnings ratios than slower-growing or more-risky firms.
3. Dividend payout ratio	$\dfrac{\text{Annual dividends per share}}{\text{After tax earnings per share}}$	Indicates the percentage of profits paid out as dividends.
4. Cash flow per share	$\dfrac{\text{After tax profits} + \text{Depreciation}}{\text{Number of common shares outstanding}}$	A measure of the discretionary funds over and above expenses that are available for use by the firm.

Note: Industry-average ratios against which a particular company's ratios may be judged are available in *Modern Industry* and *Dun's Reviews* published by Dun & Bradstreet (14 ratios for 125 lines of business activities), Robert Morris Associates' *Annual Statement Studies* (11 ratios for 156 lines of business), and the FTC-SEC's *Quarterly Financial Report* for manufacturing corporations.

As long as you are conscientious in preparing your analysis and recommendations, and have ample reasons, evidence, and arguments to support your views, you shouldn't fret unduly about whether what you've prepared is the right answer to the case. In case analysis there is rarely just one right approach or set of recommendations. Managing companies and devising and implementing strategies are not such exact sciences that there exists a single provably correct analysis and action plan for each strategic situation. Of course, some analyses and action plans are better than others; but, in truth, there's nearly always more than one good way to analyze a situation and more than one good plan of action. So, if you have carefully prepared the case using either the Strat-Tutor case preparation guides or your instructor's assignment questions, don't lose confidence in the correctness of your work and judgment.

PARTICIPATING IN CLASS DISCUSSION OF A CASE

Classroom discussions of cases are sharply different from attending a lecture class. In a case class students do most of the talking. The instructor's role is to solicit student participation, keep the discussion on track, ask "Why?" often, offer alternative views, play the devil's advocate (if no students jump in to offer opposing views), and otherwise lead the discussion. The students in the class carry the burden for analyzing the situation and for being prepared to present and defend their diagnoses and recommendations. Expect a classroom environment, therefore, that calls for *your* size-up of the situation, *your* analysis, what actions *you* would take, and why *you* would take them. Do not be dismayed if, as the class discussion unfolds, some insightful things are said by your fellow classmates that you did not think of. It is normal for views and analyses to differ and for the comments of others in the class to expand your own thinking about the case. As the old adage goes, "Two heads are better than one." So it is to be expected that the class as a whole will do a more penetrating and searching job of case analysis than will any one person working alone. This is the power of group effort, and its virtues are that it will help you see more analytical applications, let you test your analyses and judgments against those of your peers, and force you to wrestle with differences of opinion and approaches.

To orient you to the classroom environment on the days a case discussion is scheduled, we compiled the following list of things to expect:

1. Expect students to dominate the discussion and do most of the talking. The case method enlists a maximum of individual participation in class discussion. It is not enough to be present as a silent observer; if every student took this approach, there would be no discussion. (Thus, expect a portion of your grade to be based on your participation in case discussions.)

2. Expect the instructor to assume the role of extensive questioner and listener.

3. Be prepared for the instructor to probe for reasons and supporting analysis.

4. Expect and tolerate challenges to the views expressed. All students have to be willing to submit their conclusions for scrutiny and rebuttal. Each student needs to learn to state his or her views without fear of disapproval and to overcome the hesitation of speaking out. Learning respect for the views and approaches of others is an integral part of case analysis exercises. But there are times when it is OK to swim against the tide of majority opinion. In the practice of management, there is always room for originality and unorthodox

approaches. So while discussion of a case is a group process, there is no compulsion for you or anyone else to cave in and conform to group opinions and group consensus.

5. Don't be surprised if you change your mind about some things as the discussion unfolds. Be alert to how these changes affect your analysis and recommendations (in the event you get called on).

6. Expect to learn a lot from each case discussion; use what you learned to be better prepared for the next case discussion.

There are several things you can do on your own to be good and look good as a participant in class discussions:

- Although you should do your own independent work and independent thinking, don't hesitate before (and after) class to discuss the case with other students. In real life, managers often discuss the company's problems and situation with other people to refine their own thinking.

- In participating in the discussion, make a conscious effort to contribute, rather than just talk. There is a big difference between saying something that builds the discussion and offering a long-winded, off-the-cuff remark that leaves the class wondering what the point was.

- Avoid the use of "I think," "I believe," and "I feel"; instead, say, "My analysis shows —" and "The company should do . . . because —" Always give supporting reasons and evidence for your views; then your instructor won't have to ask you "Why?" every time you make a comment.

- In making your points, assume that everyone has read the case and knows what it says; avoid reciting and rehashing information in the case—instead, use the data and information to explain your assessment of the situation and to support your position.

- Bring the printouts of the work you've done on Strat-TUTOR or the notes you've prepared (usually two or three pages' worth) to class and rely on them extensively when you speak. There's no way you can remember everything off the top of your head—especially the results of your number crunching. To reel off the numbers or to present all five reasons why, instead of one, you will need good notes. When you have prepared thoughtful answers to the study questions and use them as the basis for your comments, *everybody* in the room will know you are well prepared, and your contribution to the case discussion will stand out.

PREPARING A WRITTEN CASE ANALYSIS

Preparing a written case analysis is much like preparing a case for class discussion, except that your analysis must be more complete and put in report form. Unfortunately, though, there is no ironclad procedure for doing a written case analysis. All we can offer are some general guidelines and words of wisdom—this is because company situations and management problems are so diverse that no one mechanical way to approach a written case assignment always works.

Your instructor may assign you a specific topic around which to prepare your written report. Or, alternatively, you may be asked to do a comprehensive written case analysis, where the expectation is that you will (1) *identify* all the pertinent issues that management needs to address, (2) perform whatever *analysis* and *evaluation* is appropriate, and (3) propose an *action plan* and *set of recommendations* addressing the issues you have identified. In going through the exercise of identify, evaluate, and recommend, keep the following pointers in mind.[3]

Identification   It is essential early on in your paper that you provide a sharply focused diagnosis of strategic issues and key problems and that you demonstrate a good grasp of the company's present situation. Make sure you can identify the firm's strategy (use the concepts and tools in Chapters 1–8 as diagnostic aids) and that you can pinpoint whatever strategy implementation issues may exist (again, consult the material in Chapters 9–11 for diagnostic help). Consult the key points we have provided at the end of each chapter for further diagnostic suggestions. Review the study questions for the case on Strat-TUTOR. Consider beginning your paper with an overview of the company's situation, its strategy, and the significant problems and issues that confront management. State problems/issues as clearly and precisely as you can. Unless it is necessary to do so for emphasis, avoid recounting facts and history about the company (assume your professor has read the case and is familiar with the organization).

Analysis and Evaluation   This is usually the hardest part of the report. Analysis is hard work! Check out the firm's financial ratios, its profit margins and rates of return, and its capital structure, and decide how strong the firm is financially. Table 1 contains a summary of various financial ratios and how they are calculated. Use it to assist in your financial diagnosis. Similarly, look at marketing, production, managerial competence, and other factors underlying the organization's strategic successes and failures. Decide whether the firm has valuable resource strengths and competencies and, if so, whether it is capitalizing on them.

Check to see if the firm's strategy is producing satisfactory results and determine the reasons why or why not. Probe the nature and strength of the competitive forces confronting the company. Decide whether and why the firm's competitive position is getting stronger or weaker. Use the tools and concepts you have learned about to perform whatever analysis and evaluation is appropriate. Work through the case preparation exercise on Strat-TUTOR if one is available for the case you've been assigned.

In writing your analysis and evaluation, bear in mind four things:

1. You are obliged to offer analysis and evidence to back up your conclusions. Do not rely on unsupported opinions, over-generalizations, and platitudes as a substitute for tight, logical argument backed up with facts and figures.

2. If your analysis involves some important quantitative calculations, use tables and charts to present the calculations clearly and efficiently. Don't just tack the exhibits on at the end of your report and let the reader figure out what they mean and why they were included. Instead, in the body of your report cite some of the key numbers, highlight the conclusions to be

---

[3]For some additional ideas and viewpoints, you may wish to consult Thomas J. Raymond, "Written Analysis of Cases," in *The Case Method at the Harvard Business School*, ed. M. P. McNair, pp. 139–63. Raymond's article includes an actual case, a sample analysis of the case, and a sample of a student's written report on the case.

drawn from the exhibits, and refer the reader to your charts and exhibits for more details.

3. Demonstrate that you have command of the strategic concepts and analytical tools to which you have been exposed. Use them in your report.

4. Your interpretation of the evidence should be reasonable and objective. Be wary of preparing a one-sided argument that omits all aspects not favorable to your conclusions. Likewise, try not to exaggerate or overdramatize. Endeavor to inject balance into your analysis and to avoid emotional rhetoric. Strike phrases such as "I think," "I feel," and "I believe" when you edit your first draft and write in "My analysis shows," instead.

Recommendations   The final section of the written case analysis should consist of a set of definite recommendations and a plan of action. Your set of recommendations should address all of the problems/issues you identified and analyzed. If the recommendations come as a surprise or do not follow logically from the analysis, the effect is to weaken greatly your suggestions of what to do. Obviously, your recommendations for actions should offer a reasonable prospect of success. High-risk, bet-the-company recommendations should be made with caution. State how your recommendations will solve the problems you identified. Be sure the company is financially able to carry out what you recommend; also check to see if your recommendations are workable in terms of acceptance by the persons involved, the organization's competence to implement them, and prevailing market and environmental constraints. Try not to hedge or weasel on the actions you believe should be taken.

By all means state your recommendations in sufficient detail to be meaningful—get down to some definite nitty-gritty specifics. Avoid such unhelpful statements as "the organization should do more planning" or "the company should be more aggressive in marketing its product." For instance, do not simply say "the firm should improve its market position" but state exactly how you think this should be done. Offer a definite agenda for action, stipulating a timetable and sequence for initiating actions, indicating priorities, and suggesting who should be responsible for doing what.

In proposing an action plan, remember there is a great deal of difference between, on the one hand, being responsible for a decision that may be costly if it proves in error and, on the other hand, casually suggesting courses of action that might be taken when you do not have to bear the responsibility for any of the consequences. A good rule to follow in making your recommendations is: *Avoid recommending anything you would not yourself be willing to do if you were in management's shoes.* The importance of learning to develop good judgment in a managerial situation is indicated by the fact that, even though the same information and operating data may be available to every manager or executive in an organization, the quality of the judgments about what the information means and which actions need to be taken does vary from person to person.[4]

It goes without saying that your report should be well organized and well written. Great ideas amount to little unless others can be convinced of their merit—this takes tight logic, the presentation of convincing evidence, and persuasively written arguments.

---

[4]Gragg, "Because Wisdom Can't Be Told," p. 10.

RESEARCHING COMPANIES AND INDUSTRIES VIA THE INTERNET AND ON-LINE DATA SERVICES

Very likely, there will be occasions when you need to get additional information about some of the assigned cases, perhaps because your instructor has asked you to do further research on the industry or because you are simply curious about what has happened to the company since the case was written. These days it is relatively easy to run down recent industry developments and to find out whether a company's strategic and financial situation has improved, deteriorated, or changed little since the conclusion of the case. The amount of information about companies and industries available on the Internet and through on-line data services is formidable and expanding rapidly.

On-Line Data Services   Lexis/Nexis, Bloomberg Financial News Services, and other on-line subscription services available in many university libraries provide access to a wide array of business reference material. For example, the Lexis/Nexis COMPANY library contains full-text 10-Ks, 10-Qs, annual reports, company profiles for more than 11,000 U.S. and international companies, and a variety of other valuable data files. The Lexis/Nexis files listed below are particularly useful in researching companies and industries:

Publication/subject	Lexis/Nexis file name
Market Share Reporter (an excellent source of market share statistics)	MKTSHR
Hoover company profiles	HOOVER
Hoover profiles of international companies	HVRWLD
Standard & Poor's Register	SPCORP
Securities and Exchange Commission	SEC
Company annual reports	ARS
Company annual 10-K filings	10-K
Company quarterly 10-Q filings	10-Q
Company newswire stories	CONEWS
Business wire	BWIRE
Public relations newswire	PRNEWS
S&P Daily News	SPNEWS

Company Web Pages and Other Websites Containing Business Information   Many companies (and the number increases daily) have Websites with information about products, financial performance, recent accomplishments, late-breaking company developments, and rundowns on company objectives, strategy, and future plans. Some company Web pages include links to the home pages of industry trade associations where you can find information about industry size, growth, recent industry news, statistical trends, and future outlook. A number of business periodicals like *Business Week, The Wall Street Journal,* and *Fortune* have Internet editions that contain the full text of many of the articles that appear in their paper editions. You can access these sites by typing in the proper Internet address for the company, trade association, or publication. The following Websites are particularly good locations for company and industry information:

- Securities and Exchange Commission EDGAR database (contains company 10-Ks, 10-Qs, etc.) *http://www.sec.gov/cgi-bin/srch-edgar/*
- NASDAQ *http://www.nasdaq.com/*
- CNNfn: The Financial Network *http://cnnfn.com/*
- Hoover's Online *http://hoovers.com/*
- *American Demographics*/Marketing Tools *http://www.marketingtools.com/*
- Industry Net *http://www.industry.net/*
- *Wall Street Journal*—Interactive edition *http://update.wsj.com/*
- *Business Week http://www.businessweek.com/*
- *Fortune http://www.pathfinder/com/@@cUyeVQQAtmYhdMyb/fortune/*
- MSNBC Commerce News *http://www.msnbc.com/news/COM__front.asp/*
- *Los Angeles Times http://www.latimes.com/*
- *New York Times http://www.nytimes.com/*
- News Page *http://www.newspage.com/*
- Electric Library *http://www.elibrary/com/*
- International Business Resources on the WWW *http://ciber.bus.msu.edu/busref.htm/*

Some of these Internet sources require subscriptions in order to access their entire databases.

Using a Search Engine   Alternatively, or in addition, you can quickly locate and retrieve information on companies, industries, products, individuals, or other subjects of interest using such Internet search engines as Lycos, Alta Vista, Infoseek, Excite, Yahoo!, and Magellan. Search engines find articles and other information sources that relate to a particular industry, company name, topic, phrase, or "keyword" of interest. Some search engines contain bigger indexes of submitted Uniform Resource Locator addresses than others, so it is essential to be alert to the coverage of each search engine—*the information sources covered by each search engine are specified on the search engine's Website.* Each of the search engines also provide guidelines for how to formulate your query for information sources. You may find the following brief descriptions of frequently-used search engines helpful in selecting which one to try:

- Alta Vista (*http://www.altavista.digital.com/*)—Digital Equipment claims that Alta Vista searches the largest index and database on the Web of any engine: over 30 million Web pages on over 475,000 servers plus 14,000 articles posted in various news groups as of early 1997. For the latest information on what you can find using the Alta Vista search engine, visit the Website. Alta Vista searches the full text of all documents in its database. The search results give a higher score to documents where the keywords are in the first few words of the document or title; higher scores are also given to documents containing multiple use of the keywords.
- Infoseek Net Search (*http://www.infoseek.com/*)—Infoseek lets you use natural language phrases like "find information on discounted Caribbean cruises" as well as traditional keyword searches. It is good for searching

popular Web pages but is considered less efficient than Alta Vista in finding obscure names and keywords. Infoseek looks for keywords in the title of a document or at the beginning of a document page. It is more likely to return Internet addresses to a query where the keyword(s) appear frequently in the document.

- Yahoo (*http://www.yahoo.com*)—Yahoo is not actually a search engine, but a catalog of Websites that have been submitted to Yahoo by Webpage authors. Yahoo identifies the Internet addresses for a query that contain the specified keywords in the title of the document or in the description of the document.
- Lycos (*http://www.lycos.com*)—An up-to-date list of the sources that Lycos searches can be found on its Webpage. Lycos searches abstracts based on titles and the first few words of key paragraphs for the keywords listed in a query. It does not search the full text of a document.
- Excite (*http://www.excite.com*)—Excite is a full-text search engine that scans Websites, Usenet news, and other sources as described on its opening Web pages. Like Alta Vista, it gives a higher score to documents that contain the keyword in the title or is repeated frequently in the full text of the document. Excite is unusual in that it understands synonyms. Not only does it return documents that match keywords in a query, but it also returns documents that contain synonyms of keywords listed in a query.

Our tips for making the quickest and most effective use of search engines are listed below:

- Make your search as specific as possible. Search engines are very efficient and may retrieve thousands of matches to a very general request.
- Use Boolean operators like AND, AND NOT, OR, and parentheses to narrow the scope of your search. These operators help zero in on those items of greatest relevance to what you are looking for.
- Each search engine will have specific commands that will further limit the search results. Make sure that you inspect the search engine's advanced search tips to determine how to use those capabilities.
- Some search engines are upper- and lower-case sensitive. As a rule, your query should be entered with the correct upper-case and lower-case letters because of the capitalization-sensitive nature of certain search engines.

Keep in mind that the information retrieved by a search engine is "unfiltered" and may include sources that are not reliable or that contain inaccurate or misleading information. Be wary of information provided by authors who are unaffiliated with reputable organizations or publications or which doesn't come from the company or a credible trade association—be especially careful in relying on the accuracy of information you find posted on various bulletin boards. Articles covering a company or issue should be copyrighted or published by a reputable source. If you are turning in a paper containing information gathered from the Internet, you should cite your sources (providing the Internet address and date visited); it is also wise to print Web pages for your research file (some Web pages are updated frequently).

The Learning Curve Is Steep   With a modest investment of time, you will learn how to use Internet sources and search engines to run down information on companies and industries quickly and efficiently. And it is a skill that will serve you well into the

---

TABLE 2 The Ten Commandments of Case Analysis

To be observed in written reports and oral presentations, and while participating in class discussions.

1. Read the case twice, once for an overview and once to gain full command of the facts; then take care to explore every one of the exhibits.

2. Make a list of the problems and issues that have to be confronted.

3. Do enough number crunching to discover the story told by the data presented in the case. (To help you comply with this commandment, consult Table 1 to guide your probing of a company's financial condition and financial performance.)

4. Look for opportunities to apply the concepts and analytical tools in the text chapters.

5. Be thorough in your diagnosis of the situation (either make a one- or two-page outline of your assessment or work through the exercises on Strat-Tutor).

6. Support any and all opinions with well-reasoned arguments and numerical evidence; don't stop until you can purge "I think" and "I feel" from your assessment and, instead, are able to rely completely on "My analysis shows."

7. Develop charts, tables, and graphs to expose more clearly the main points of your analysis.

8. Prioritize your recommendations and make sure they can be carried out in an acceptable time frame with the available skills and financial resources.

9. Review your recommended action plan to see if it addresses all of the problems and issues you identified.

10. Avoid recommending any course of action that could have disastrous consequences if it doesn't work out as planned; therefore, be as alert to the downside risks of your recommendations as you are to their upside potential and appeal.

---

future. Once you become familiar with the data available at the different Websites mentioned above and with using a search engine, you will know where to go to look for the particular information that you want. Search engines nearly always turn up too many information sources that match your request rather than two few; the trick is to learn to zero in on those most relevant to what you are looking for. Like most things, once you get a little experience under your belt on how to do company and industry research on the Internet, you will find that you can readily find the information you need.

THE TEN COMMANDMENTS OF CASE ANALYSIS

As a way of summarizing our suggestions about how to approach the task of case analysis, we have compiled what we like to call "The Ten Commandments of Case Analysis." They are shown in Table 2. If you observe all or even most of these commandments faithfully as you prepare a case either for class discussion or for a written report, your chances of doing a good job on the assigned cases will be much improved. Hang in there, give it your best shot, and have some fun exploring what the real world of strategic management is all about.

AMERICA ONLINE, INC.

Arthur A. Thompson, *The University of Alabama*

John E. Gamble, *University of South Alabama*

America Online was founded in the early 1980s as Control Video Corp. with the business purpose of creating an on-line service that specialized in video games for Atari computer-game machine users. At the time, two brands of PCs, the Apple II and the Commodore 64, dominated the market for play-ing on-line computer games. But because of painfully slow modems and modest PC processing power, playing video games on-line was not popular and Control Video soon failed. The company was reorganized by James Kimsey and Stephen Case as Quantum Computer Services and focused its energies on developing customized on-line services for other companies. Quantum created a service for Commodore computers, then a leading brand, called Q-Link; Commodore ended up selling millions of its PCs and Q-Link was a hit with Commodore users. Quantum generated enough revenues to keep the company going. During the next several years, Quantum expanded to serve other computer users. Steve Case made a deal with Apple Computer in 1987 to create software packages for its Apple II and Macintosh models, and he convinced Tandy Corp. to support a new on-line service for purchasers of its DOS-based Radio Shack computers. Then in 1989 Apple withdrew from its deal at the last minute. Frustrated by the turn of events with Apple, Quantum decided to introduce the software service it designed for Apple under the name America Online.

Quantum's strategy to promote use of its on-line service was to blanket PC users with diskettes containing the America Online software. It gave the disks away at trade shows, got them included in magazine subscription mail-outs, had them at-tached to magazine covers at newsstands, and mailed them to selected households. By 1990, management decided to bring all of its segmented on-line services together under one overall service. Quantum changed its name to America Online in 1991 and went public in 1992, raising $66 million to fund its expansion. Steve Case was named CEO shortly thereafter.

When he took over as CEO, America Online, with only 200,000 subscribers and 250 employees, was well behind CompuServe and Prodigy, the two leading on-line services. In early 1993, AOL cut its monthly fee well below what CompuServe and Prodigy were charging and began mailing out massive numbers of diskettes with free trial offers. AOL's membership growth accelerated to the point where it had trouble handling the influx of new subscribers. Users would get abruptly disconnected, and logging on in peak periods sometimes took over an hour. Numerous complaints led Steve Case to issue a letter of apology and to promise network improvements. Case proceeded to initiate agreements with NBC, the *New York Times,* CNN, *Time,* and others to provide AOL with content for its service. Investments were made to handle a bigger volume of users, AOL made acquisitions to boost its network and multimedia expertise and its software development capabilities, and the company continued to solicit new members with aggressive marketing.

By early 1995, America Online had 1 million subscribers, but still trailed Prodigy (which had 1.5 million subscribers), and industry leader CompuServe (which had over 2 million subscribers). The company then began offering members Internet and World Wide Web access and kept flooding the market with diskettes, running arresting ads and come-ons, and offering consumers first 10 then 15 free hours to try the service, all the while improving the breadth and quality of the content of its services. By 1997, America Online was the undisputed market leader with 8 million subscribers and the on-line industry's most extensive array of custom features. Revenues in fiscal year 1996 were $1.1 billion and were projected to reach $1.5 billion at the end of fiscal year 1997 (June 30)—see Exhibit 1. Headquartered in Dulles, Virginia, and with over 6,000 employees, the company had operations in the United States, Canada, Great Britain, France, and Germany, and was the acknowledged global leader in interactive services. According to one survey in early 1996, AOL generated 30 percent of all traffic on the World Wide Web.

Going into 1997, Prodigy, co-owned by IBM and Sears, had become largely irrelevant in the on-line market and its owners were trying to figure out how to dispose of their ownership interest. CompuServe, majority-owned by H&R Block, was in disarray and its management was examining alternative strategies to rejuvenate its competitiveness and restore profitability—according to media reports, the decision had already been made to abandon the mass consumer market for on-line services and retrench to the business of being an Internet access provider. AOL's principal competitor in 1997 was the World Wide Web and the exploding diversity of content that was available on the Internet; its biggest rivals were Internet access providers, not on-line services like Prodigy and CompuServe. During the past 12 months, Internet access providers had been luring customers away from America Online, CompuServe, and Prodigy by offering faster and cheaper connections to the Internet. Exhibit 2 shows the number of subscribers of AOL's largest rivals as of early 1997.

STEPHEN M. CASE: CHAIRMAN, PRESIDENT, AND CEO OF AMERICA ONLINE

Steve Case became a cofounder of Quantum Computer Services at the age of 27. Prior to that he had held marketing positions at Pizza Hut and Procter & Gamble. He

EXHIBIT 1   Selected Financial and Operating Highlights, America Online, Inc., 1992–1996
(Amounts in thousands, except per share data)

	Year ended June 30,				
	1996	**1995**	**1994**	**1993**	**1992**
Statement of Operations Data:					
On-line service revenues	$ 991,656	$ 344,309	$ 98,497	$37,648	$26,095
Other revenues	102,198	49,981	17,225	14,336	12,658
Total revenues	1,093,854	394,290	115,722	51,984	38,753
Income (loss) from operations	65,243	(21,449)	4,176	1,702	3,685
Income (loss) before extraordinary item	29,816	(35,751)	2,154	246	2,344
Net income (loss)[1]	29,816	(35,751)	2,154	1,379	3,768
Income (loss) per common share:					
Income (loss) before extraordinary item	$ 0.28	$ (0.51)	$ 0.03	$ –	$ 0.05
Net income (loss)	$ 0.28	$ (0.51)	$ 0.03	$ 0.02	$ 0.08
Weighted average shares outstanding	108,097	69,550	69,035	58,572	45,656
	As of June 30,				
	1996	**1995**	**1994**	**1993**	**1992**
Balance Sheet Data:					
Working capital (deficiency)	$ (19,328)	$ 271	$ 38,679	$10,498	$12,363
Total assets	958,754	405,413	155,178	39,279	31,144
Total debt	22,519	21,856	9,341	2,959	2,672
Stockholders' equity	512,502	216,812	98,802	23,785	21,611
Other Data (at fiscal year end):					
Worldwide subscribers	6,198	3,005	903	303	182

[1]Net income in the fiscal year ended June 30, 1996, includes charges of approximately $17.0 million for acquired research and development, $8.0 million for the settlement of a class action lawsuit, and $0.8 million for merger expenses. Net loss in the fiscal year ended June 30, 1995, includes charges of approximately $50.3 million for acquired research and development and $2.2 million for merger expenses.

Source: 1996 Annual Report.

was born and raised in Honolulu, where his father was a lawyer and his mother a teacher. Case's entrepreneurial spirit surfaced at an early age. When he was six, Case and his brother opened a juice stand and charged two cents a cup, but many of their customers gave them a nickel and let them keep the change—an experience which taught the boys the value of high margins. A few years later, the two brothers started a business selling a variety of products door-to-door and by mail. Then they began selling ad circulars and, in addition, shared a newspaper route.

Case attended Williams College where he majored in political science and was the lead singer in two rock groups. After graduating in 1980, he accepted a marketing position at Procter & Gamble and worked on Lilt, a home permanent kit. Unhappy with managing a mature business, Case left after two years to join Pizza Hut as manager of pizza development. The job involved a lot of travel and he often spent evenings exploring his new laptop PC. He joined an early on-line service called The Source and became fascinated with the possibilities. In 1983, his brother, then an

EXHIBIT 2   America Online's Major U.S. Rivals, 1997

Competitor	Number of Subscribers	Comments
CompuServe	3,300,000	No flat-rate monthly fee. Sluggish software. Specializes in business and technical content.
Microsoft Network	2,000,000	Flat-rate monthly fee. Available only to Windows95 users. Advertising supported. Cutting-edge software. Beginning to assemble proprietary content.
Prodigy	1,000,000	Offers proprietary content. No proprietary software required.
AT&T WorldNet	850,000	Largest Internet service provider. Flat-fee access. Has overcome early start-up problems.
Netcom	590,000	Has decided to cut flat-rate consumer service and focus on higher-paying business users. Not the place for home users anymore.
MCI Internet	325,000	Sells Internet access to long distance customers as part of its MCI One package.
Earthlink	257,000	Charges a $25 setup fee; offers inexpensive 800-number access.
IBM	200,000	Has ultrareliable network and offers international dial-up access. Good for "experts."
Mindspring	122,000	Charges a $25 setup fee; responsive customer service; 24-hour toll-free support. Popular in New York City area.
Sprint Internet Passport	60,000	Provides Internet access as part of its long-distance offering; wants customers to obtain Internet access from long-distance provider.

Source: Based in large part on information in *Fortune,* April 14, 1997, p. 174.

investment banker, introduced him to the founders of Control Video; they offered him a job as a marketing assistant on the spot and he accepted. When the company's video game business soured, the board of directors brought in entrepreneur Jim Kimsey as CEO, who proceeded to groom Case to take over the top spot; Kimsey and Case convinced venture capitalists to put up $5 million to back their idea of forming an on-line service for users of Commodore computers, and Control Video became Quantum Computer Services. It was Case who engineered Quantum's deals with Apple Computer and Tandy (although he used up much of the $5 million in capital in the process and had some of the venture capital board members calling on Kimsey to fire him).

When he was made CEO in 1992, Case quickly fashioned a growth-at-any-cost strategy and charged ahead. Despite numerous doom-and-gloom predictions over the years by industry observers that AOL would stumble or that its membership growth would soon slow to a crawl, Steve Case kept making new acquisitions, forging new alliances, adjusting the company's marketing strategies, and adapting AOL's services and content to fast-paced changes in the marketplace. Between August 1994 and February 1996, America Online purchased nine Internet-related companies in an effort to strengthen its competitive capabilities (see Exhibit 3); Case financed all the acquisitions by giving the owners of the acquired companies shares of America Online stock. He had pushed AOL to add business-oriented services to generate off-peak, daytime traffic using a high-speed TCP/IP data connections technology

EXHIBIT 3   America Online's Acquisitions, August 1994–February 1996

Date	Price in Stock	Company Acquired
Aug. 1994	$34 million	Redgate Communications. Ted Leonsis' company, which made multimedia CD-ROMs with on-line links
Nov. 1994	$35 million	ANS, creator of the Internet network. Provided much-needed, high-speed network capacity
Nov. 1994	$6 million	Navisoft, a maker of software for creating Web sites
Dec. 1994	$41 million	Booklink Technologies, provided AOL's initial Web browser, which it has subsequently dropped for browsers from Netscape and Microsoft
May 1995	$30 million	Medior, interactive media developer
May 1995	$15 million	WAIS, developer of Web server software, which aids users in creating their own Web pages
June 1995	$11 million	Global Network Navigator, provided the foundation for AOL's new Internet-only service
Sept. 1995	$15 million	Ubique, makes software for building 3-D worlds, which will be used to enhance AOL's chat forums
Feb. 1996	$59 million	Johnson-Grace, data compression. Provided expertise and capability for speeding transmission of text and images

Source: America Online and *Business Week,* April 15, 1996, p. 82.

network in the U.S. to serve business users. During the course of a major internal reorganization, he had recruited Robert Pittman, a cofounder of MTV, to head the AOL Networks division that was responsible for consumer Internet services and also formed the AOL Studios division to orchestrate new on-line content and the ANS Communications division to oversee high-speed networking for AOL and for business customers.

When Microsoft announced that it would bundle the software to access its new Microsoft Network in with its Windows 95 operating system software, Steve Case was a leader in urging the Justice Department to block the move as an "unfair advantage." Microsoft, however, was allowed to proceed. Later, in March 1996, Case negotiated a head-turning pact with Microsoft whereby AOL would integrate Microsoft's Internet Explorer (a Web browser) into its on-line software; Microsoft, in return, would include AOL software in every copy of its Windows 95 operating system. He explained the reasons for choosing Microsoft's Internet Explorer over Netscape's Navigator, the market share leader in Web browsers:[1]

> . . . there were a number of reasons we went with Microsoft. We think the Internet Explorer technology is evolving at a rapid rate and its modular design will enable us to plug it in to AOL quickly. Strategically, we thought it would be smart for us to make sure there were two strong providers of Web technology in the marketplace. We didn't want

[1]As quoted in "AOL CEO Steve Case," *Forbes,* October 7, 1996, p. 95.

anyone, whether Microsoft or Netscape, to have the kind of monopoly in Web technology that Microsoft has in operating systems.

But we also wanted to have a relationship with Netscape. So we made them the primary browser for Global Network Navigator (GNN), our second brand, an on-line service for sophisticated users.

Shortly after the deal with Microsoft, Netscape agreed to design future versions of Navigator to work seamlessly with AOL's software. Case also negotiated an agreement with AT&T whereby AOL would give AT&T's WorldNet customers access to AOL at a discount if AT&T would install a link to AOL from its new WorldNet service that provided unlimited Internet access for a flat $19.95 per month. Less than 12 months after announcing its new service, AT&T had attracted 850,000 WorldNet subscribers; Case believed that AT&T's customers would like the option to cruise AOL from the Net—and not incidentally, such an entry allowed AOL members to detour use of a local AOL access number that might be busy. Case anticipated that as the Web took on a bigger and bigger cyberspace role, it would become increasingly common for customers to cruise AOL from the Net and vice versa. CompuServe, following AOL's lead, signed a similar deal with AT&T for a WorldNet link a few months later. Another of Case's moves was to engineer a partnership with Intuit (the developer of Quicken financial software) to offer AOL members electronic banking services. Case had also been instrumental in helping AOL form partnerships with media giants Time Warner, Viacom, Disney/ABC, the *New York Times,* and others to bolster its content offerings. Case believed that it was critical for AOL to move quickly in forming alliances and negotiating deals that would keep AOL racing ahead of the competition, noting, "This is a momentum game."

Because of his success in transforming AOL into one of the most potent forces in cyberspace, Steve Case was often asked to speak at PC-related conventions, usually drawing packed audiences. His views were widely sought by business reporters, industry analysts, and executives from Internet-related companies. One admiring venture capitalist observed, "He's done a masterful job. Steve Case walks on water as far as I am concerned."[2] General Alexander Haig, an AOL board member, said Case "borders on genius. If you look at how this young fella has positioned this company, he has ventures with every big player in the business. Instead of being beaten to death by Microsoft, as everyone predicted, they came courting him."[3] Another close observer of Case and AOL said, "Every time people ask 'How is he going to survive?' he makes the right moves."[4] Nonetheless, Steve Case had taken a number of potshots from critics—Ned Brainard of *HotWired,* for example, labeled Steve Case as a "shameless self-promoter." Disgruntled AOL members had, from time to time, posted messages on AOL bulletin boards "flaming" Steve Case and AOL for policies and practices they disagreed with, long wait times to get help from customer support representatives, excessive busy signals at peak hours (that spurred such labels as America On Hold), and assorted other grievances.

Although Steve Case functioned as an ardent and visible spokesman for AOL and had fashioned a hard-charging image for AOL, he displayed a low-key management style in his relationships with AOL executives and employees. His trademark attire was a pair of khakis and open-collar shirt, and he was a regular attendee at the company's weekly beer busts, mixing freely among those who showed up. But Case

---

[2]As quoted in "The Online World of Steve Case," *Business Week,* April 15, 1996, p. 79.

[3]Ibid., p. 80.

[4]Ibid.

was also a hands-on manager who was very much involved and stayed on top of how things were going. To help him keep AOL's daily operations under control (the company was adding about 200 new employees on average each month), he recruited an executive from FedEx, William Razzouk, to be the company's president and chief operating officer in April 1996. However Razzouk's command-and-control management style clashed with Case's and with AOL's laid-back, collegial culture, and he abruptly resigned after four months on the job. So far, Steve Case had decided to postpone recruiting a replacement because "at this time in our development it made more sense for me to be more involved in day-to-day decisions."[5]

AMERICA ONLINE IN MID-1996

When AOL's fiscal year ended on June 30, 1996, Steve Case could point with justifiable pride to some impressive accomplishments over the past 12 months: AOL had doubled the number of subscribing members from 3,005,000 to 6,198,000, boosted revenues from $394 million to $1.1 billion, and posted after-tax profits of $29.8 million (more than the company had earned in prior years combined). The company had successfully launched its new AOL 3.0 software that gave consumers a faster, more convenient on-line experience, a better Web browser, more powerful navigation, enhanced communication, and greater personalization capabilities (such as giving members Web publishing tools to create their own Web page and options that allowed them to track the performance of their stock portfolios). Several new original content channels had been created: the Style Channel, Thrive, The Hub, Digital City, International, Games, and Love@AOL. AOL had increased its call-in capability from 20,000 to 140,000 modems and had 650 phone numbers in 470 cities, giving it the largest private dial-up network in the world. It had launched AOL in France, Germany, Great Britain, and Canada and announced a joint venture with Mitsui and Nikkei to begin service in Japan in 1997. The company had built alliances with Apple Computer, Microsoft, Netscape, Sun Microsystems, Disney, and AT&T. The number of customer support representatives had been increased from 1,800 to 3,200. A new pricing plan (the "Value Plan") had been created for heavy users that provided 20 hours of service for $19.95 per month, with a $2.95 hourly fee for usage in excess of 20 hours per month. A new AOL Visa card had been introduced. Companies such as Eddie Bauer, Lands' End, L. L. Bean, and JC Penney were participating in on-line shopping programs on AOL, an area that was expected to grow rapidly in the months and years to come.

Steve Case, in his letter to shareholders, detailed the company's recent progress and set forth his vision of AOL's future business and long-term direction:

> What an incredible year. In a complex and dynamic market, we focused on what consumers wanted and it was a winning strategy.
>
> . . . Despite the investments we made to grow rapidly, we also grew profitably; in the most recent quarter, for example, we set new records for gross profit margins and earnings-per-share from operations. . . .
>
> We made significant strides in positioning the company to be the global leader in interactive services. We expanded globally, through a successful launch in Europe. We launched locally, through the creation of Digital Cities. We grew our portfolio of new content brands, partnering with small entrepreneurs and large media companies. We extended initiatives to build new sources of revenue streams from advertising, transactions,

---

[5]As quoted in "AOL CEO Steve Case," p. 96.

and new distribution channels—revenue streams that we expect will significantly drive future profitability. We beefed up our AOLnet data network to reduce costs and position us to grow rapidly and exploit new opportunities such as Internet telephony. We expanded our team and now have more than 5,300 people dedicated to bringing the magic of interactive services to tens of millions of people worldwide.

For more than a decade, we've led the industry—first as the tiny upstart with some better ideas, and more recently as the market leader with a passion about the possibilities of this new interactive medium and a conviction that tens of millions of people can benefit from what AOL has to offer. Over the past decade, we've seen considerable change, as many competitors and technologies have come and gone . . .

But now we enter a new phase for this industry, and for our company. The pace of innovation is quickening, as Internet technologies evolve and a flood of new companies attempt to get a piece of the action. We believe we are uniquely positioned to capitalize on this opportunity, but we recognize that we must constantly reshape our company to cement our position of global leadership.

We are making great strides in the area we care most about: providing consumers with a superior interactive experience that can enhance the way they get information, communicate with others, buy products, and learn new things. . . . But the "new AOL" is not just about new software . . . powerful new tools . . . plug-and-play architecture . . . members will soon benefit from new features such as real-time audio and video, as well as the much-awaited launch of "AOL Phone" which will enable members to talk to each other using their own voices.

We have taken steps to re-establish AOL as the value leader in the consumer market. Our low $9.95 monthly fee continues to be attractive to the mainstream consumer audience we're targeting, but we recently added a $19.95 "Value Plan" that has been well received by our heavier users as well as by families worried about running up big bills. Price will continue to be an important competitive factor, so we have been testing a wide variety of alternatives. . . .

We have embraced the Internet—and improved on it. There is no question about the importance of the Internet, and the role it will play in the future. Over the past year, we have emerged as the leading way people connect to the Internet. Nevertheless, we recognized that our Internet experience wasn't all that it could be, so we've focused on integrating "best of breed" technologies (from Microsoft, Netscape, Sun, Macromedia, and others) to make them really easy to use, and then adding to that mix our own unique technologies—such as compression that makes the Web much more usable for people with typical modems—to provide a differentiated experience. For example, given that people are often frustrated by the slowness of accessing pages on the World Wide Web, we bought the company with the industry's best compression technology, so we are uniquely positioned to provide consumers with a faster Web experience. Additionally, we have expanded the ability of our members to publish directly on the Web, added one-click hyperlink tools for e-mail and personal folders, and launched Virtual Places, which we consider to be the most sophisticated community-building tool on the Web.

. . . We have had great success with our marketing efforts centered around making it easy to try AOL by broadly distributing free AOL software. That effort will continue; indeed, it will be expanded, as we have signed agreements to get AOL software pre-installed with Windows95 and Macintosh computers. But as we reach out to the unserved 89% of U.S. households, we recognize we need to do more. Our new advertising campaign will focus on differentiation—explaining, for example, how AOL is "the Internet and a whole lot more."

. . . With 6 million members now and a goal to reach 10 million members in 1997, our size gives us a significant strategic advantage. As more Web sites recognize that they cannot be profitable without advertising, and can't generate significant advertising revenues without reaching a large audience, and cannot quickly and efficiently reach a large audience on their own, we expect a growing number of them to rush to align with AOL. These companies need our help in aggregating an audience, and we can leverage our distribution footprint to do that. . . . The media brands of the future are increasingly being nurtured on AOL, and we believe our mounting promotional power will enable us to build these brands into cyberspace hits.

. . . We believe the on-line business will evolve like other consumer media businesses, which means success will accrue to the companies with the largest audiences, as they will be able to leverage that audience reach to generate significant revenues and profits. Accordingly, we are rapidly growing revenues from advertising and transaction fees. Our advertising sales are now exceeding those of our on-line competitors combined. Our new Interactive Marketing division is already the industry leader in transactional revenues. We are also expanding our enterprise initiatives, to resell daytime network capacity and to build "private AOLs" for corporations. . . . Together, the development of these alternative sources of revenues (advertising, transactions, and business-to-business services) will enable us to improve the AOL value proposition, while also enhancing shareholder returns.

We are establishing the best-known brand in cyberspace, in the United States and throughout the world. AOL is far and away the leader in terms of consumer recognition. . . .

. . . A superior interactive experience will continue to be our "raison d'etre." For more than a decade we've assembled capabilities, features and content that we believe no one else can match, and as we roll out the "new AOL" this Fall, it will be quickly apparent that we have improved on that score.

. . . Despite the progress our industry has made in recent years, only 1 out of 10 U.S. households subscribes to any on-line service. As we reach out to the unserved market, we recognize that we must constantly raise the bar so we can provide an ever-widening audience with an engaging interactive experience that greatly changes and enhances the lives of millions of people.

With a renewed sense of focus and passion, AOL is well positioned to lead the charge towards embracing a mainstream audience—and that's precisely what we intend to do.

AMERICA ONLINE'S STRATEGY TO FINANCE ITS GROWTH

The company's rapid growth had been financed largely through new issues of common stock. The company had issued new shares in fiscal years 1993, 1994, and 1996, raising a total of nearly $320 million. The sale of preferred stock in 1996 yielded another $28 million. The capital raised from the sale of stock was used to pay for the costs of attracting new subscribers, new product development, and investments in modems, servers, and other equipment needed to operate and expand its on-line network capability. Management did not expect the company's cash flows from operations to move from negative to positive until sometime in 1997. The company had no long-term debt and, because of the negative cash flows, paid no dividends.

Exhibits 4, 5, and 6 show America Online's income statements, balance sheets, and cash flow statements for the past three years.

THE COSTS OF MARKETING, ACQUIRING NEW SUBSCRIBERS, AND DEVELOPING NEW PRODUCTS

Acquiring new subscribers represented a major drain on America Online's financial resources. In 1996 AOL's current marketing expenses were $213 million, up from $77 million in 1995; in both years, marketing expenditures amounted to about 20 percent of revenues. But these expenses did not include all that the company actually spent in soliciting new members.

EXHIBIT 4	Consolidated Statements of Operations, America Online, Inc., 1994–1996 (Amounts in thousands, except per share data)		

| | Year ended June 30, | | |
	1996	1995	1994
Revenues:			
On-line service revenues	$ 991,656	$ 344,309	$ 98,497
Other revenues	102,198	49,981	17,225
Total revenues	1,093,854	394,290	115,722
Costs and expenses:			
Cost of revenues	627,372	229,724	69,043
Marketing	212,710	77,064	23,548
Product development	53,817	14,263	5,288
General and administrative	110,653	42,700	13,667
Acquired research and development	16,981	50,335	–
Amortization of goodwill	7,078	1,653	–
Total costs and expenses	1,028,611	415,739	111,546
Income (loss) from operations	65,243	(21,449)	4,176
Other income (expense), net	(2,056)	3,074	1,810
Merger expenses	(848)	(2,207)	–
Income (loss) before provision for income taxes	62,339	(20,582)	5,986
Provision for income taxes	(32,523)	(15,169)	(3,832)
Net income (loss)	$ 29,816	$ (35,751)	$ 2,154
Earnings (loss) per share:			
Net income (loss)	$ 0.28	$ (0.51)	$ 0.03
Weighted average shares outstanding	108,097	69,550	69,035

Source: 1996 Annual Report.

AOL employed an accounting practice whereby it treated a large portion of the solicitation costs of new subscribers (including the costs of printing, producing, and shipping starter kits; the costs of obtaining mailing lists of qualified prospects; and the costs of those media ads classified as "direct response advertising") as a capital investment rather than as a current expense; it then depreciated these "capital investments" over the next 12 to 18 months. In 1996, AOL spent approximately $275 million on subscriber acquisition efforts that it classified as capital investment. Moreover, company accountants opted in 1996 to increase the time frame over which AOL amortized subscriber acquisition costs from 12 and 18 months to 24 months, a change that had the effect of increasing the company's reported 1996 earnings by $48 million (actions and outcomes that were described in the notes to the company's financial statements in its 1996 annual report). This change came on the heels of having agreed a few months earlier, following a review by the Securities and Exchange Commission, to reduce the portion of member-acquisition expenses it capitalized. An article in *Business Week* indicated that the company's practice of

EXHIBIT 5 Consolidated Balance Sheets, America Online, Inc., 1995–1996 (Amounts in thousands, except share data)

	June 30, 1996	June 30, 1995
Assets		
Current assets:		
Cash and cash equivalents	$ 118,421	$ 45,877
Short-term investments	10,712	18,672
Trade accounts receivable	42,939	32,176
Other receivables	29,674	11,381
Prepaid expenses and other current assets	68,832	25,527
Total current assets	270,578	133,633
Property and equipment at cost, net	101,277	70,919
Other assets:		
Product development costs, net	44,330	18,949
Deferred subscriber acquisition costs, net	314,181	77,229
License rights, net	4,947	5,579
Other assets	35,878	9,121
Deferred income taxes	135,872	35,627
Goodwill, net	51,691	54,356
	$ 958,754	$ 405,413
Liabilities and Stockholders' Equity		
Current liabilities:		
Trade accounts payable	$ 105,904	$ 84,640
Other accrued expenses and liabilities	127,898	23,509
Deferred revenue	37,950	20,021
Accrued personnel costs	15,719	2,863
Current portion of long-term debt	2,435	2,329
Total current liabilities	289,906	133,362
Long-term liabilities:		
Notes payable	19,306	17,369
Deferred income taxes	135,872	35,627
Other liabilities	1,168	2,243
Total liabilities	446,252	188,601
Stockholders' equity:		
Preferred stock, $.01 par value: 5,000,000 shares authorized, 1,000 shares issued and outstanding at June 30, 1996	1	–
Common stock, $.01 par value: 300,000,000 and 100,000,000 shares authorized, 92,626,000 and 76,728,268 shares issued and outstanding at June 30, 1996 and 1995, respectively	926	767
Additional paid-in capital	519,342	252,668
Accumulated deficit	(7,767)	(36,623)
Total stockholders' equity	512,502	216,812
	$ 958,754	$ 405,413

Source: 1996 Annual Report.

EXHIBIT 6 Consolidated Statements of Cash Flows, America Online, Inc., 1994–1996 (Amounts in thousands)

	Year ended June 30,		
	1996	**1995**	**1994**
Cash flows from operating activities:			
Net income (loss)	$ 29,816	$ (35,751)	$ 2,154
Adjustments to reconcile net income to net cash (used in) provided by operating activities:			
Depreciation and amortization	33,366	12,266	2,822
Amortization of subscriber acquisition costs	126,072	60,924	17,922
Loss on sale of property and equipment	44	37	5
Charge for acquired research and development	16,981	50,335	–
Changes in assets and liabilities:			
Trade accounts receivable	(10,435)	(14,373)	(4,266)
Other receivables	(18,293)	(9,086)	(626)
Prepaid expenses and other current assets	(43,305)	(19,635)	(2,873)
Deferred subscriber acquisition costs	(363,024)	(111,761)	(37,424)
Other assets	(26,938)	(6,051)	(2,542)
Trade accounts payable	21,150	60,805	10,224
Accrued personnel costs	12,856	1,850	397
Other accrued expenses and liabilities	104,531	5,747	9,474
Deferred revenue	17,929	7,190	2,322
Deferred income taxes	32,523	14,763	3,832
Total adjustments	(96,543)	53,011	(733)
Net cash (used in) provided by operating activities	(66,727)	17,260	1,421
Cash flows from investing activities:			
Short-term investments	7,960	5,380	(18,947)
Purchase of property and equipment	(50,262)	(59,255)	(18,010)
Product development costs	(32,631)	(13,054)	(5,131)
Sale of property and equipment	–	180	95
Purchase costs of acquired businesses	(4,133)	(20,523)	–
Net cash used in investing activities	(79,066)	(87,272)	(41,993)
Cash flows from financing activities:			
Proceeds from issuance of common stock, net	189,359	61,721	68,120
Proceeds from issuance of preferred stock, net	28,315	–	–
Principal and accrued interest payments on line of credit and long-term debt	(935)	(3,045)	(7,795)
Proceeds from line of credit and issuance of long-term debt	3,000	13,488	14,260
Principal payments under capital lease obligations	(1,402)	(368)	(83)
Net cash provided by financing activities	218,337	71,796	74,502
Net increase in cash and cash equivalents	72,544	1,784	33,930
Cash and cash equivalents at beginning of period	45,877	44,093	10,163
Cash and cash equivalents at end of period	$ 118,421	$ 45,877	$ 44,093
Supplemental cash flow information			
Cash paid during the period for:			
Interest	$ 1,659	$ 1,076	$ 577
Income taxes	–	–	–

Source: 1996 Annual Report.

treating subscriber acquisition expenses as a capital investment instead of as a current expense allowed the company to report a loss of only $35.8 million in 1995 instead of a loss of $84.5 million.[6]

In 1996, America Online's product development expenses were nearly $54 million, up from $14.3 million in 1995. These costs included amortization charges for software development (such as the new version of AOL 3.0), new content features, and other R&D activities relating to improving the content and functionality of the company's on-line services. AOL was endeavoring to position itself as a catalyst of innovation, not only investing in original content but also promoting new kinds of interactive programming and building previously unimagined services. The head of the AOL division responsible for content, Ted Leonsis, saw the company's programming challenge one of coming up with a content lineup that would outdraw Jerry Seinfeld (*Seinfeld*'s typical audience was 20 million people, whereas AOL's nightly audience was under 1 million); Leonsis said, "We have to be prime time."

THE EVENTS OF FALL 1996 AND EARLY 1997

The next nine months at AOL were eventful. In July 1996 AOL, pressured by inquiries from the Federal Trade Commission and several state attorneys general, settled a class-action lawsuit concerning its billing practices by agreeing to give members free time on-line. The agreement cost AOL about $8 million. On August 7, AOL's system crashed during an equipment upgrade and the network went dead for 19 hours; the failure made headlines in newspapers and on TV and users complained about being deprived of e-mail and their connections to the World Wide Web. In an apology to subscribers, Steve Case wrote, "I would like to be able to tell you this sort of thing will never happen again, but frankly, I can't make that commitment."

On August 28, the National Basketball Association sued AOL in federal court, charging it with misappropriating proprietary data and violating intellectual property laws by providing real-time updates on NBA games in progress, not only giving the scores as each point was made but also providing summaries of player performance. The NBA claimed that it had a clear legal right to charge TV networks, cable channels, radio stations, and phone services for real-time game information and that there was no basis for AOL being able to broadcast it for free. AOL claimed that it was exercising its constitutional right to free speech and that the NBA didn't own the underlying facts about its basketball games. The three other major professional sports leagues (for baseball, football, and ice hockey) filed briefs supporting the NBA's lawsuit. AOL subsequently altered its practice of reporting on games in progress by delaying its updates (in much the same way that ESPN SportsZone delayed its coverage and financial service organizations delayed their transmission of stock quotes).

In October, shares of AOL stock fell 10 percent the day following its 10-K filing with the Securities and Exchange Commission that noted its difficulties in retaining subscribers. AOL management attributed its problems with customer retention (referred to as customer "churn" because members joined for a few months and then canceled their service) to an increased number of lower-priced competitors and to the flat-rate monthly service pricing of many Internet service providers. In the October–December 1995 quarter AOL signed up 1.8 million new subscribers but 950,000

---

[6]Ibid., p. 81.

members canceled, for a net gain of 880,000. Analysts estimated that in the January–March 1996 quarter AOL signed up 2.3 million new users and 1.4 million quit. One analyst estimated that up to 45 percent of AOL's subscriber base canceled service each year; the same analyst observed that AOL spent more than $300 million in marketing in 1996 to add a net of 3.2 million subscribers to its membership base.[7] Steve Case indicated in fall 1996 that AOL's cost to acquire a subscriber averaged about $45 and that the company's churn in customers was running under 40 percent. It was not unusual for AOL to sign up 20,000 to 25,000 new trial users per day. As part of its efforts to improve subscriber retention, in mid-October AOL kicked off a new multimillion-dollar marketing campaign with TV ads featuring its new AOL 3.0 software and new content offerings.

Later in October, reacting to mounting criticism that the manner in which it accounted for its marketing expenses resulted in greatly overstated profits, America Online announced that it was changing its accounting practice of amortizing its marketing expenditures for acquiring new subscribers. Whereas the typical company charged marketing expenses against earnings as the expenses were incurred, it was AOL's practice to spread those marketing costs attributed to acquiring new subscribers over a 24-month period; AOL's accounting methodology (agreed to by its auditors, Ernst & Young) had the effect of increasing the company's reported short-term profits—an outcome that critics said was misleading to investors. AOL's decision to switch to a practice of charging subscriber acquisition costs as a current operating expense resulted in an immediate charge against prior earnings of $350 million—an amount over 50 times greater than the company's total profits in the five preceding years *combined* (see Exhibit 1).

The New Flat-Rate Pricing Option   In November 1996, AOL announced that starting in December it would give members the option to switch to unlimited usage for $19.95 per month instead of paying $9.95 for basic service of five hours per month and $2.95 for each additional on-line hour. It also offered several other pricing plans, including advance renewal rates of $14.95 per month for customers paying two years in advance, advance renewal rates of $17.95 for customers paying one year in advance, and a light usage program of three hours per month for $4.95 (with additional time at $2.95 per hour). At first, AOL indicated it would automatically switch members over to the $19.95 flat-rate plan unless they notified AOL that they preferred one of the other plans, but complaints from users and the potential of legal action in 20 states or more prompted the company to abandon this approach. In December, the company signed an agreement with 20 states allowing members to select which pricing plan they preferred. In addition to its new pricing options, America Online sought to further spur new subscriber sign-ups in November by boosting its trial offer from 15 free hours to 50 free hours.

The response to these marketing initiatives was overwhelming, greatly exceeding what AOL had expected and prepared for. Over 1.2 million new members signed on in the last quarter of 1996, and an estimated 75 percent of existing members switched to the new flat-rate, unlimited use pricing plan. Virtually overnight, usage of AOL's service jumped dramatically (especially during the peak hours of 8 P.M. until midnight), straining existing capacity and causing members to get busy signals when they dialed in and tried to sign on. In November 1996, the month before the

---

[7]*The Wall Street Journal*, October 2, 1996, p. B5.

unlimited use pricing plan went into effect, AOL members spent 66 million hours on-line, more than double the 30 million hours they averaged during the summer months of 1996 and 50 percent more than the 44 million hours logged in September. In December 1996, the total soared to more than 100 million hours and rose further to about 125 million hours in January 1997. The number of daily sessions rose from 6.2 million in October to more than 10 million in January 1997 and over 11 million in February. AOL users averaged more than 32 minutes per day in January compared to 14 minutes per day in September. And the number of simultaneous users increased from 185,000 in November to more than 260,000 in January. Member complaints about busy signals and congested network traffic escalated, even though AOL added about 20,000 modems to its network to accommodate increased call-ins and was adding thousands more weekly. One member's experience was typical: "It's literally impossible to get on AOL at night. I do business on the Internet and this has really hurt me."

AOL's Crash Program to Expand Its Network Capability   In January 1997, five AOL members filed a class-action in a state court in Los Angeles, alleging they were not getting the promised services due to repeated busy signals; class-action lawsuits were filed in three other states as well. State attorneys general from a number of states quickly joined in, reacting to a chorus of customer complaints. AOL responded by announcing it would spend $350 million to upgrade its network over the next five months; Steve Case indicated that the company would

- Add 150,000 modems by June 1997, bringing the total to 350,000 and providing the capability to handle 16 million member sessions a day.
- Break ground on a new 180,000-square-foot facility that would double the amount of data center space for AOL host computer systems.
- Add 600 more customer support representatives by June, bringing the total to 4,500.
- Add an 800 number dedicated to providing members with alternative access numbers.
- Offer credits or refunds on request to members who felt they had not gotten sufficient value from AOL due to its undercapacity problems.
- Cut back on recruitment of new members and hold its membership to the current 8 million level until the overcrowded conditions abated.
- Communicate frequently with members about the steps being taken to improve AOL's service.

In an open letter to members, Steve Case said:

Last Fall, you told us you wanted an unlimited use plan, and we delivered. Naturally, we anticipated more usage, and prepared for it, but we seriously underestimated the surge in demand that actually occurred.

We know that you are having problems getting on-line and we are working day and night to improve the situation. . . .

The events of the past few weeks have vividly reminded us of the responsibilities we have, as the service that 8 million members rely on each day. We take these responsibilities seriously, and I can assure you we will do everything in our power to meet them.

As January came to a close, America Online, under mounting pressure of legal action by state attorneys general in 36 states (several of whom took the position that

AOL's aggressive marketing practices, combined with the failure to supply the advertised services, constituted a deceptive business practice), reached a settlement and formally agreed to issue refunds or credit toward future service to cover network problems during December and January. Under terms of the agreement, customers could choose whether to receive credit for a free month of service or qualify for cash rebates up to $39.90. The pact also required America Online to temporarily curb its advertising and to make any ads "clearly and conspicuously" state that customers may encounter delays when trying to sign on. The financial impact on America Online was uncertain because it remained to be seen how many members would take advantage of the agreement; most analysts believed the total cost would be under $25 million. One legal issue still remained in several states, however: whether America Online and others made it easy enough for members to cancel their service. AOL members could not cancel on-line, and some members reported they could not reach customer service to cancel over the telephone.

By March 1997, AOL had a total of 250,000 modems in place, was handling more than 11 million connections per day, and distributing 10.5 million e-mail messages daily. On an average day, AOL members were spending just over 4 million hours on-line and accounting for 225 million Web hits daily. During January and February, extra modem capacity was added in 242 cities and new access numbers were added in 21 cities. To improve prime-time access, AOL contracted to obtain additional modem capacity from outside suppliers. These suppliers typically used their modem networks during the day to support business customers but agreed to rent AOL their networks between 7 P.M. and 2 A.M.; the temporary rental capacity was available in over 100 cities and efforts were under way to increase that number. Since January, AOL had added 650 customer support representatives, exceeding its target of 600 new hires by June. To try to maintain the loyalty of its members, AOL announced that it would give members who believed they had not gotten their money's worth because of busy signals a credit for one free month of service, no questions asked. It also agreed to consider cash refunds based on how much time a member was actually able to use; cash refunds had to be requested by telephone. Also the company made new redialer software available free to members who wished to switch from manually retyping their password after trying a pair of access numbers; the new auto-dialer software would try the same pair of access numbers from five to nine times without requiring any further entries on the member's part. In his monthly letter to subscribers, Steve Case said,

> . . . Nothing is more important to AOL's success than nurturing the sense that we are all part of a single community. We have all experienced a lot of anxiety in recent months, due to our problems with busy signals and the resulting firestorm of frustration that was created within the AOL community, in the media, and in the public at large. . . . We will keep working around the clock to better serve your needs, rebuild your confidence in us, and keep that sense of community strong.

Other AOL Developments in March–April 1997   Several other developments of significance transpired in March–April 1997:

- In an effort to begin boosting its revenues from advertising, AOL announced that it was opening up its popular chat rooms (known as "People Connection") to advertisers. The ads were to be placed in a corner of the screen in all public areas, but not the private chat rooms, and refreshed and rotated every 60 seconds using AOL's new ad server technology. Advertisers could create up to four different visuals for each ad space they bought. Members could click the ads to go to the advertiser's Website, its AOL content area, or a custom-created application. Over 70 percent of AOL's members used the chat areas, logging 1,000,000 hours of chat daily. America Online marketing executives believed that its 14,000 chat rooms accommodating up to 23 persons apiece gave advertisers a unique opportunity to reach upscale, well-educated consumers—a group that watched less television than average according to a recent Nielsen survey. AOL's member profile indicated that 63 percent were college graduates, compared to just 23 percent for the population as a whole. AOL was tracking the number of entries to AOL screens, the number of visits to each content area, and the time spent in each area so that it could document the amount of exposure that advertisers and merchandisers could expect.

• AOL launched use of AOL NetFind, an Internet navigation aid that featured use of a popular search engine called Excite. (AOL owned a 20 percent stake in Excite, the result of Excite's having purchased AOL's WebCrawler search and directory service in November 1996 in exchange for 1,950,000 shares of Excite's common stock.) The Excite search engine was used by about 50 percent of all on-line households at least once a month, according to a January 1997 survey. AOL NetFind allowed members to jump quickly from AOL's opening screen to the World Wide Web and have a simple, helpful, and intuitive way to find, not search for, the exact information they wanted concerning people, businesses, Web sites, newsgroups, reviews, and other matters. In addition to Excite, AOL's other NetFind partners included Switchboard, PLS, DejaNews, and Cyberpatrol; Cyberpatrol provided the technology for an "AOL NetFind preselected for Kids" feature that included Web sites for "suitable viewing." NetFind also included space for advertisers.

• AOL announced it had chosen VDOnet to supply software that would upgrade members' multimedia experience. The new software permitted users to see near TV-quality "streamed" video in real time without first having to download a file and wait for the file to be decompressed so it could be viewed. More than 700 Web sites were using VDOnet's software technology to broadcast programs to viewers, including CBS, MTV, Sportsline, and Tagesschau (Germany's most watched television news program).

• AOL demonstrated the next version of its software, 4.0, that was faster, more responsive, and more interactive. The new version, scheduled for introduction around mid-1997, allowed members to send other members e-mail with embedded color photographs, custom backgrounds, multiple attachments, and different fonts. On the chat side, members could display a photograph, graphic image, or live video camera footage while they were chatting. Users could also click on a button and request an AOL phone conversation with the person they were chatting with. Another new feature was Driveway, an off-line information option that could be customized by members to retrieve particular content from e-mail, newsgroups, the Web, and other places in an automated fashion. Other new features included e-mail spelling and grammar checking, greeting card creation, address book enhancements, 16-character screen names, additional security and control, and streaming video and multimedia enhancements for the World Wide Web.

- Ben Ezra Weinstein & Co. sued America Online for reporting wrong quotations of its stock price and incorrect trading volume for two days in early March; the company claimed that the misinformation led to confusion in the marketplace and precipitous drops in the actual price if its stock, causing damage to the company's shareholders and to the company. In its lawsuit, Ben Ezra Weinstein claimed that AOL was negligent because, based on the content of a recorded message from an AOL executive left on the answering machine of Michael Weinstein, acknowledging AOL knew about the software problem that caused the misquotes for "a few weeks" before it was corrected. Responding to an AOL press release saying that the lawsuit was a publicity stunt, Jack Ben Ezra, President of Ben Ezra Weinstein, said, "It's bad enough that AOL failed to correct a mistake it knew about; what's worse is that, unlike the traditional media, it does not appear to understand that as a conveyor of information, it can cause serious damage and it must correct misinformation immediately. . . . The issue here is not publicity, it is accountability."

In mid-March, attorneys for four California customers of AOL filed suit in U.S. District Court accusing America Online executives of wire fraud and racketeering and claiming that the company was party to offenses ranging from recklessly endangering customers' privacy rights to plundering their intellectual property.[8] The suit asserted that AOL committed mail fraud by mailing free software promising unlimited Internet access, and committed wire fraud with its advertising campaign touting unlimited access for $19.95. The complaint also contended that AOL's claim on the rights to materials posted in public areas of the service was a misappropriation of intellectual property rights because the company had not negotiated or paid for such material. Plaintiffs asked the court to appoint a receiver to take over the service and "operate AOL in a lawful manner." The plaintiffs alleged that the company should be defined as a public trust, be subject to federal communications legislation, and fall under regulatory scrutiny of the Federal Communications Commission. The plaintiffs further charged that AOL executives portrayed the company as vibrant, growing, and profitable, while selling large blocks of their own shares at enormous personal gain.

In early April, America Online agreed, as part of the terms of settling the earlier class-action lawsuits, to extend its offer of refunds to subscribers who had trouble getting on-line because of busy signals. The agreement called for customers who used AOL in February and March for 2 to 15 hours and had trouble logging on to receive refunds and credits. Those who used the service more than 15 hours were to receive a free month of service. Meanwhile, there were rumors in the media that America Online was considering purchasing CompuServe.

AOL's Progress in Europe

AOL's European expansion efforts were proceeding at a rapid pace. Going into 1997, the company had 325,000 members in Europe—some 200,000 in Germany, 100,000 in Great Britain, and 25,000 in France. Service had been initiated in Austria, Sweden, and Switzerland. In Germany, AOL had formed strategic partnerships with Axel Springer Verlag (which published Germany's largest newspaper,

[8]As reported by Dennis Anderson of the Associated Press and published in the *Tuscaloosa News* on March 15, 1997.

EXHIBIT 7	High–Low Prices of America Online's Common Stock, by Quarter, September 1994–March 1997		
For the quarter ended		**High**	**Low**
September 30, 1994		$10.28	$ 6.88
December 31, 1994		14.63	7.47
March 31, 1995		23.69	12.31
June 30, 1995		24.06	16.75
September 30, 1995		37.25	21.38
December 31, 1995		46.25	28.25
March 31, 1996		60.00	32.75
June 30, 1996		71.00	36.63
September 30, 1996		46.50	24.50
December 31, 1996		44.25	22.38
March 31, 1997		48.25	31.12

39 other magazines and newspapers, and had several radio and television stations) and with Bertelsmann AG, also a German publisher. Axel Springer Verlag had a 10 percent ownership stake in AOL Germany; AOL and Bertelsmann were joint venture partners in AOL Europe. America Online was endeavoring to partner with the best media and content companies in each distinct country market whenever it made good sense for an AOL international service to offer localized content tailored to a country's on-line community.

The number of European computers hooked to the Internet had grown from 4.2 million in 1995 to 10 million in early 1997, and was expected to grow rapidly over the upcoming years as European businesses and households awakened to the Internet's potential. European on-line services, such as Europe Online, Germany's Deutsche Telecom, and Italy's Video Online, were rushing to expand; Deutsche Telecom had 1.2 million members, more than AOL and CompuServe (which had an estimated 750,000 European members in mid-1996). So far, most of the PCs with Internet connections in Europe were high-speed connections for businesses rather than PCs in households.

Questions about America Online's Future Business Prospects

Despite the company's recent ascent as the global leader in on-line services, America Online faced formidable business obstacles and strategic challenges. During early 1997, there was much speculation about America Online's future as a viable business. After trading as high as $71 in May 1996, the stock was trading down in the $35–$45 range in the first quarter of 1997—see Exhibit 7. There were legitimate questions about (1) how much America Online would have to spend on marketing to continue to recruit millions of new subscribers and maintain its aggressive rate of growth, (2) whether it could marshal the financial resources to simultaneously fund the expansion of its network, upgrade its content, and spend the marketing dollars needed to add millions of new subscribers, (3) whether "alternative revenue sources" from advertising and transactions fees realized from the on-line shopping purchases of members would materialize to the degree management expected, and (4) whether AOL would or could ever earn respectable profits as on-line service.

The Bulls and the Bears   Bullish analysts believed AOL would recover from its change in accounting practices and the fallout over its flat-rate pricing, and that by the year 2000 AOL shareholders would be well pleased with how the company's stock price had performed since 1997. Pessimistic analysts said subscriber acquisition costs would eat into AOL's financial results each quarter, making it difficult for the company to ever earn decent profits or have positive cash flows. They were nervous about whether AOL could maintain its subscriber base, given members' irritation with busy signals and the competition from Internet access providers. They were concerned that since the busy signal debacle began in December 1996 AOL management had been forced to devote much of its energies to damage control rather than to strategy and growth. The pessimists were also skeptical about how much potential there was for America Online to grow its revenues from advertising and merchandise transactions.

Many industry observers believed both AOL and Internet access providers had to rethink their flat-rate pricing plans. There was speculation that AOL would soon announce premium services for which it would charge members additional fees. So far, AOL management had steadfastly maintained that the new features incorporated on AOL 4.0 would be standard for all members.

Why AOL Management Was Optimistic about the Company's Prospects   Company officials were confident that advertising revenues and fees derived from the on-line shopping purchases of members would become very important for AOL and play a large role in the company's future profitability. These "alternative revenue streams" had produced $40 million in the first three months of fiscal year 1997 versus $10.5 million for all of fiscal year 1996. Management expected that advertising revenues and transactions fees would reach 20 to 25 percent of total revenues before the 1997 fiscal year ended. AOL's margins on advertising revenues were huge—an estimated 60 to 70 percent—because there were very little incremental costs associated with providing advertising space and merchandising services as compared to investing in the network hardware and content needed to connect and satisfy new subscribers. This meant that it took smaller increases in advertising and transactions revenues to realize a boost in company earnings.

America Online management was confident that there was still a large untapped pool of potential subscribers in the United States—less than 40 percent of U.S. households had a PC as of early 1997 (and the percentage was expected to rise substantially in the years to come) and only 30 percent of the U.S. households with a PC subscribed to an on-line service. Furthermore, there were important developments on the near horizon that were expected to draw in new subscribers. Management expected that new software and multimedia capabilities being developed by Microsoft, Netscape, Pointcast, Marimba, VDOnet, Intel, BackWeb Technologies, and others, elements of which would be incorporated in its new 4.0 software, would have a dramatic effect in transforming how the Internet and the World Wide Web were used and in providing much richer multimedia experiences. Already many Web sites were broadcasting streaming video programs with near-TV quality and the number was expected to grow rapidly. Internet telephony was on the verge of becoming a market reality, making AOL Phone a feature that could soon be offered. New teleconferencing software, involving the use of small video cameras mounted on PC monitors, would make video phone calls on the Internet possible in upcoming months, and the cost of the needed software and equipment was expected to decline far enough and fast enough to make videophone communication widely used and affordable within several years. Moreover, software entrepreneurs were scheduled to introduce new products in 1997 that would help PC users cope with the information overload on the World Wide Web and the frustration of congestion and slow response times; the new software enabled users to specify the news, entertainment, information, and other Web fare they were interested in and have it automatically transmitted to their desktop—much like tuning in one's favorite TV channels and having a personalized broadcasting system. The new "Webcasting" software could retrieve the asked-for information at specified intervals for updates and had the capability to deliver rich visual images and animation approaching TV quality. Industry observers predicted that Webcasting software, because it "pushed" the desired information to the PC user's computer rather than requiring users to engage in time-consuming and sometimes frustrating searches of many Websites, offered the best avenue yet to build a business on the Internet through advertising and delivering customized content that people would be willing to pay for.

AOL management saw all these developments as boding well for its ability to attract millions of new subscribers. Steve Case offered his view about the market potential:[9]

> This is going to be a mass market. It is going to embrace tens of millions of consumers. The question is, What is it going to take to reach them? We think what it takes is an overall offering that is really, really easy to use. That is truly useful. That is fun. And affordable. And you leverage technology to enable that experience. And you partner with a wide variety of companies to contribute to that. . . . But the center of gravity has to be the consumer—what consumers want and how they want it.
>
> . . . If you want to reach a more mainstream audience, you have to make it more plug and play. One stop shopping. One disk to install. One price to pay. One customer service number to call. Building Web sites and hoping people will find them is a significant leap of faith.

AOL's Future Business: Content Provider, Connecting People to the Internet, or Something Else? More fundamentally, there were signs that the on-line industry was evolving into two businesses—content and connecting people to the Internet. Microsoft had recently altered its long-term strategy for the Microsoft Network (MSN), electing to unbundle the business of providing content and the business of connecting people to the Internet. Microsoft was making MSN content available free via the Internet and was supporting this content with revenues derived from advertising. Microsoft separately offered Microsoft Internet access and e-mail.

The multibillion-dollar question confronting AOL stockholders and Steve Case was "How do you make money on the World Wide Web and in on-line services?" Did AOL have a good business model and strategy or not? What business course should AOL pursue and what strategic position should it try to stake out? When would it start to be a moneymaking enterprise and would its profits ever justify what some considered as a lofty stock price (albeit less lofty than months earlier)? Did it still make sense, as Steve Case had professed on prior occasions, for America Online to sacrifice short-term profitability to achieve long-term global leadership?

(AOL's Web site address is *www.aol.com.*)

---

[9]As quoted in "AOL CEO Steve Case," pp. 94–95.

BEN & JERRY'S HOMEMADE, INC.

Arthur A. Thompson, *The University of Alabama*

In 1963, Bennett Cohen and Jerry Greenfield, the two slowest, chubbiest kids in their seventh-grade gym class, started to hang out together. They had just gone through the common experience of being chewed out for not being able to run a mile around their Long Island, New York, junior high school track in less than seven minutes. Three years later, as high school classmates, their friendship truly began. Jerry, a self-described social nerd, was academically bright, graduating 3rd in a class of over 600.[1] Ben was an independent spirit who was motivated to do things he initiated or was interested in and who was turned off by required assignments, prescribed conduct, and parental authority.

After high school, Jerry enrolled at Oberlin College and graduated in premed; Ben decided to go to Colgate University, but he rebelled against the structured collegiate atmosphere, had little interest in the courses he took, and made poor grades. During the summer between his freshman and sophomore year, Ben worked for an ice cream distributor in his hometown, driving through neighborhoods selling ice cream out of a truck. When he drew a high enough number in the draft lottery to be safe from having to serve in the Vietnam War, Ben dropped out of Colgate and started through a progression of menial jobs to cover living expenses, including jobs in an ice cream parlor and an ice cream plant. Jerry, who was never really committed to becoming a doctor, worked in several jobs as a hospital lab technician. Both qualified as hippies,

---

[1]Fred "Chico" Lager, *Ben & Jerry's: The Inside Scoop* (New York: Crown Publishers, 1994), p. 3.

in their personal appearance (beards, long hair, jeans, T-shirts) and in their counter-culture beliefs and lifestyle.

By 1977, both Ben and Jerry were anxious for a change in careers and began to discuss starting their own business. Their first choice, a bagel delivery service, didn't pan out. Their second choice was an ice cream shop. Cohen and Greenfield re-searched the business by visiting scoop shops and split the tuition on a $5 correspon-dence course in ice cream making offered by Penn State. They began looking for suitable communities and for used equipment in mid-1977. Both wanted to live in rural New England surroundings compatible with their 1960s counterculture lifestyle and perspective. By late 1977, they settled on Burlington, Vermont. In December, they formed a corporation and opened the first Ben & Jerry's scoop shop in a renovated gas station in downtown Burlington on May 5, 1978. Their $12,000 investment was financed in part by a loan from Cohen's father who, according to Ben, "saw this as a transition from my being a hippie to becoming a businessman." The two cofounders decided Jerry should assume the title of company president since Ben's name came first in the company's name. According to Greenfield:

> We didn't have a whole lot going for us. We had no assets or collateral to speak of. We were new to the area. We were young. We weren't married. And we had no business experience.[2]

Because of his biochemistry background, Jerry took on the task of figuring out the formula for their ice cream mix. With the aid of a calculator and an industry guide on making ice cream, Jerry started making test batches using cream, milk, cane sugar, egg yolks, and natural stabilizers. The cofounders' business concept was to make the best ice cream available (using only the highest-quality ingredients they could find) and to sell it at a price that everyone could afford. The shop attracted an ample clientele from the start, but slow wintertime sales prompted Cohen and Greenfield in 1979 to begin wholesaling their ice cream brand in 2½-gallon tubs to area restaurants. Jerry supervised production and Ben spent most of his time on the road making deliveries and selling new accounts; a manager was hired to run the scoop shop.

After a few months, it became apparent that restaurant sales alone wouldn't be enough to make the truck routes Ben was driving profitable. Then Ben hit on an idea that ultimately would transform the business: They would package the ice cream in pint cartons and wholesale them to area groceries and mom-and-pop stores along his truck route. Jerry was skeptical but Ben prevailed. A friend worked on the design for the pint carton; the end result was an oval logo featuring a man making ice cream, a slogan "Vermont's Finest All Natural Ice Cream" below the logo, a picture of the cofounders on the lid, and a sales pitch signed by Ben and Jerry to persuade consumers to buy the ice cream:

> This carton contains some of the finest ice cream available anywhere. We know because we're the guys who make it. We start with lots of fresh Vermont cream and the finest flavorings available. We never use any fillers or artificial ingredients of any kind. With our specially modified equipment, we stir less air into the ice cream creating a denser, richer, creamier product of uncompromisingly high quality. It costs more and it's worth it.[3]

Underneath was an offer to refund the purchase price to any unsatisfied customer. A big contributor to the company's image was the decision to use mostly hand-lettering and draw lines with just enough of a wiggle to look hand-drawn; the visual impact fit

---

[2]Ibid., p. 15.
[3]Ibid., p. 41.

nicely with the "homemade" impression that Ben and Jerry wanted the company's products to project.

Ben found that the best way to get small grocery stores to put Ben & Jerry's pint cartons in their freezer cases was to let them taste the product and then offer to refund the store's money if the stock didn't sell.[4] Within a few months Ben was able to increase distribution from 35 accounts to more than 200 accounts. Next, Ben approached several supermarket chains and eventually persuaded Grand Union to test-market Ben & Jerry's in nine stores. To promote the product, Jerry and Ben set up a dip case and scooped free samples for store shoppers. Sales proved brisk, and soon other supermarket chains elected to stock the Ben & Jerry's line.

Sales had grown enough by 1981 to require expanding production into a second building. Then *Time* magazine ran an August 1981 cover story on infatuation with superpremium ice cream; the article started off with the statement, "What you must understand is that Ben & Jerry's in Burlington, Vermont, makes the best ice cream in the world." Even though the article went on to state that other brands were equally great-tasting, sales of Ben & Jerry's pint cartons and customer counts at the scoop shop immediately took off. Cohen and Greenfield viewed the company's growth as both a lucky fluke and an adventure into the future.

Company revenues climbed from under $300,000 in 1980 to almost $10 million in 1985 to $78 million in 1990 and to nearly $150 million in 1994 (Exhibit 1). Growth came from expanding distribution into more metropolitan areas and states, stimulating buyer interest with an ongoing stream of exotic flavors (Chocolate Chip Cookie Dough, Cherry Garcia, Chunky Monkey), opening additional scoop shops (reaching a total of 100 in 1994), and adding a frozen yogurt line. To help raise additional capital to finance growth, the company went public in 1985. The Small Business Administration named cofounders Cohen and Greenfield as Small Business Persons of the Year in 1988. Going into the 1990s, the Ben & Jerry's brand was available in most major U.S. markets and was stocked in a sizable fraction of the supermarkets and retail outlets that sold ice cream in take-home cartons. By 1994, Ben & Jerry's products were distributed in all 50 states and the company was marketing 29 flavors in pint cartons and over 45 flavors in bulk. The company's 100 scoop shops were located in New England, New York, the mid-Atlantic region, Georgia, Florida, Ohio, Indiana, Illinois, and California. It also had 4 licensed shops in Canada, 3 in Russia, and 10 in Israel. In mid-1994, Ben & Jerry's became the market leader in the luxury/gourmet or superpremium ice cream segment, surpassing Häagen-Dazs.

Along the way, the company became something of a business phenomenon—partly because of its ice cream, partly because of the two cofounders' hippie backgrounds and iconoclastic business approaches, and partly because the company gained a reputation for social responsibility virtually unmatched in American business circles.

THE ICE CREAM AND FROZEN YOGURT INDUSTRY IN 1995

Ice cream, frozen yogurt, and related frozen dessert novelties constituted a $10 billion retail market going into 1995. With the exception of frozen yogurt, new low-fat ice creams, and certain novelty items, industry growth was sluggish if not stagnant. Per capita consumption had been stuck in the 13 to 15 quarts per year range for four decades. Although over 90 percent of U.S. households purchased ice cream

---

[4]Ibid., p. 42.

EXHIBIT 1   Financial Summary, Ben & Jerry's Homemade, Inc., 1987–1994 (in millions of dollars, except for per share data)

	1987	1988	1989	1990	1991	1992	1993	1994
Income Statement Data								
Net sales	$31.8	$47.6	$58.5	$77.0	$97.0	$132.0	$140.3	$148.8
Cost of sales	22.7	33.9	41.7	54.2	68.5	94.4	100.2	109.8
Gross profit	9.2	13.6	16.8	22.8	28.5	37.6	40.1	39.0
Selling, delivery and administrative expense	6.8	10.7	13.0	17.6	21.3	26.2	28.3	36.3
Operating income	2.4	3.0	3.8	5.2	7.2	11.3	11.9	2.7
Interest income	0.2	0.4	0.2	0.3	0.1	0.4	0.8	1.0
Interest expense	0.1	0.8	0.8	0.9	0.7	0.2	0.1	0.3
Other income (expense)	0.2	0.1	0.2	(0.1)	(0.1)	(0.2)	(0.5)	(7.2)†
Income before taxes	2.7	2.7	3.4	4.5	6.5	11.3	12.0	(3.8)
Income taxes	1.3	1.1	1.4	1.9	2.8	4.6	4.8	(1.9)
Net income	$ 1.4	$ 1.6	$ 2.1	$ 2.6	$ 3.7	$ 6.7	$ 7.2	(1.9)
Earnings per share	$ 0.28	$ 0.32	$ 0.40	$ 0.50	$ 0.67	$ 1.07	$ 1.01	$ (0.26)
Balance Sheet Data								
Current assets		$10.3	$10.5	$16.4	$23.7	$ 35.5	$ 42.4	$ 51.9
Current liabilities		4.7	4.7	8.2	12.7	17.5	13.1	14.5
Net property, plant, equipment		15.3	17.0	17.3	19.3	26.7	40.3	58.0
Total assets		26.3	28.1	34.3	43.1	88.2	106.4	120.3
Long-term debt		9.7	9.3	8.9	2.8	2.6	18.0	32.4
Stockholders' equity*		11.2	13.4	16.1	26.3	66.8	74.3	72.5

* No cash dividends have been paid since the company's founding. The company has stated it intends to reinvest earnings for use in its business and to finance future growth. The company's board of directors does not anticipate declaring any cash dividends in the foreseeable future.

† Includes a writedown of $6.8 million to replace certain of the software and equipment installed at the company's newly opened St. Albans, Vermont, plant.

Source: Company annual reports.

and frozen yogurt products, consumption was highest among families with young children and persons over 55 years old. Consumption patterns were only somewhat seasonal: about 30 percent of annual sales occurred during the summer months.

Market Trends and Consumer Preferences

The market for frozen dairy desserts consisted of many segments and product categories: superpremium (or luxury/gourmet) ice creams and frozen yogurt brands; premium ice cream, ice milk, and frozen yogurt products; economy and private-label ice cream, ice milk, and frozen yogurt products; low-fat ice cream products of a superpremium, premium, economy, or private-label nature; fruit sherbets and sorbets; and a growing array of bars and sandwich-type products containing ice cream, ice milk, frozen yogurt, and perhaps chocolate, fruits, cookies, nuts, and other mix-in items (generally lumped together in a category called frozen novelties). Superpremium ice creams traditionally were distinguished from premium ice creams by their higher butterfat content, the use of all-natural and other more expensive ingredients, and a lower level of "overrun" or air content. Superpremium brands, like Ben & Jerry's Homemade and Häagen-Dazs, tended to be more expensively packaged and usually carried prices double those of premium brands and triple those of economy and private-label brands. However, high butterfat content was becoming a questionable attribute on which to hang the superpremium designation, since a growing number of low-fat ice creams (like ConAgra's new Healthy Choice brand) were trying to win a "superpremium" image and "light" and low-fat varieties of high-end name brands were becoming common. For the most part, consumers were only dimly aware of the butterfat and overrun specifications that technically separated superpremium from premium and premium from economy/private-label designations. Instead, consumer opinions about where different brands ranked on the quality scale related chiefly to price, taste, flavors, selection, and brand image rather than to butterfat content and overrun.

Starting in the late 1980s, consumer concerns about fat, cholesterol, and artificial additives spawned a wave of new low-fat and nonfat frozen yogurt products and light and fat-free ice creams. At the same time, though, demand for rich superpremium brands like Häagen-Dazs, Ben & Jerry's, and Frusen Glädje continued to mushroom on into the early 1990s, as consumers looked for "the very best" or gave into desires for a special treat. By the second half of 1992, however, growth in the sales of high-fat, high-calorie frozen dairy products started tapering off. Then, when new government-mandated nutritional labels appeared on food products in mid-1994, consumers found it easier to compare the calories, fat, and cholesterol content of brands and flavors. Sales of rich ice cream and frozen novelties plateaued over the next six months, even declining in several instances, as some label-reading consumers switched to low-fat or nonfat ice cream and frozen yogurt products.

Historically, consumers tended to be more loyal to their favorite flavors than to any particular brand. If they were not committed to a particular flavor, buyers were likely to peruse several brands, check out the flavors available in the freezer case, and choose an appealing flavor at an acceptable price. Most ice cream purchasers were willing to try new brands and new flavors. The best way for ice cream producers to cultivate brand loyalty was to maintain a broad selection of flavors in the freezer case and introduce new flavors frequently.

Competition

The supply side of the U.S. frozen dairy dessert market was fragmented, consisting of several hundred local and regional companies plus a few competitors whose brands were available in most major markets nationally. In 1995, the major players included:

Brand	Marketer
Ben & Jerry's	Ben & Jerry's Homemade, Inc.
Häagen-Dazs	Pillsbury/Grand Metropolitan
Healthy Choice	ConAgra
TCBY	TCBY Enterprises, Inc.
Baskin-Robbins	Allied-Lyons North America
Breyers	Unilever
Colombo	General Mills
Dreyer's/Edy's	Dreyer's Grand Ice Cream
Kemps	BolsWessanen

Some ice cream/frozen yogurt marketers competed only in the on-premise retail scoop shop market segment (the most notable was Baskin-Robbins); some competed in both the on-premise and take-home segments (Ben & Jerry's, Häagen-Dazs, and TCBY operated a chain of scoop shops and had supermarket distribution as well); and the remainder—a big majority—competed exclusively in the take-home segment, selling through supermarkets, convenience stores, health-food stores, and assorted other retailers. A growing number of ice cream marketers were introducing frozen yogurt lines to stake out a position in the flourishing frozen yogurt segment and to avoid being totally dependent on the ice cream segment where the signs of long-term sales erosion and intensifying competition were much in evidence.

Marketers of ice creams were scrambling to introduce light/low-fat ice creams, frozen yogurt, and frozen novelties that had lower fat, lower cholesterol, and lower calories, yet tasted as good as the traditional products with rich ingredients. These new products vied with existing products for shelf space and had triggered a competitive shakeout among brands and flavors in freezer cases as retailers made room for increasingly popular products that appealed to health-conscious buyers.

Production   Manufacturing involved ingredients preparation, mixing, packaging, and freezing—about a six-hour process. Superpremium brands and brands with mix-ins cost the most to produce. Mix-in flavors usually consisted of a vanilla or chocolate base to which fruits, nuts, fudge or caramel syrups, or chunks of cookies or candy bars were added. The cost of mix-ins could range up to a third of cost of goods sold for some varieties. A brand's selling prices, however, were usually the same for all flavors, resulting in higher profit margins for traditional plain flavors than mix-in flavors. Superpremium brands were usually packaged in more expensive round pint containers with decorative colors and graphics; premium and economy brands were typically sold in half-gallon round or rectangular cartons. Manufacturing cost differences between brands were chiefly a function of the kinds of basic ingredients used, type and percentage of mix-ins used, packaging, labor costs, and depreciation. Some manufacturers had recently invested in large, automated plants (which increased depreciation costs but which trimmed labor costs and permitted greater output of a wider flavor variety.)

A number of marketers owned no manufacturing facilities, opting instead to have local or regional producers with excess capacity handle production on a contract basis. Such marketers also usually relied on the contract producer, often a dairy products company, to handle distribution to local retailers.

Distribution   Due to the importance of convincing retailers to stock a company's brand and of gaining favorable shelf locations in the freezer case, distribution capability was one of the keys to market and competitive success. Retailers preferred to allocate their limited freezer space to the best-selling brands and flavors. Large retailers stocked one or two superpremium brands, two (maybe three) premium brands, and one or two local brands; smaller retailers usually stocked just one superpremium brand, a local premium or economy brand, and perhaps one other brand. Supermarket chains almost always supplemented their name brand offerings with a selection of private-label or economy ice cream, ice milk, and frozen yogurt products. Both large and small retailers stocked an assortment of frozen novelties, with the range of selection depending on store size and customer mix.

The preferred method of distribution was to have an area distributor representative deliver supplies by truck to each retail location and stock the retailer's shelves. It was the distributor's job to sell retailers on a brand, help the retailer determine the number of shelf facings each brand should be allocated based on sales turnover and profit margins, and choose how many units of which flavors should be stocked. Häagen-Dazs had created a national network of distributors at considerable cost, getting about 50 percent of its products into stores with company-owned distributors and 50 percent with independent distributors. Ben & Jerry's utilized two primary distributors, Sut's Premium Ice Cream for much of New England and Dreyer's Grand Ice Cream for states in the Midwest and West; the company had a number of other local distributors that serviced limited market areas to round out its coverage of most geographic areas nationwide. Dreyer's accounted for 52 percent ($77.6 million) of Ben & Jerry's net sales in 1994, up from 49 percent ($65 million) in 1992.

Competitive Rivalry In the 1990s, rivalry among competing ice cream and frozen yogurt brands centered around ingredients (all-natural versus artificial, high-fat versus low-fat and fat-free, cholesterol levels), taste, flavor selection and variety, distribution capability, retail price, and brand image/reputation. Price competition was more a factor across categories (superpremium versus premium versus regular/economy versus private-label) than within categories. Market share gains were being made primarily by brands that (1) had succeeded in making their product offerings healthier without sacrificing taste, and/or (2) had captured buyer interest with a stream of new flavors, and/or (3) were adding new distributors to gain wider geographic coverage. Competition for shelf space was so intense that retailers were able to raise "slotting fees" (cash payments or off-price allowances that manufacturers customarily paid chain retailers, ostensibly to offset retailers' costs of slotting the product into their warehouses and getting it into their pricing, inventory, and ordering systems). Nor was it unusual for manufacturers and distributors to make payments (referred to as "grease") to individual buyers and purchasers to ensure that the people making decisions on which brands to stock were predisposed to their brands.

By 1994, supermarket sales of frozen yogurt had become a $600 million category. Market shares based on supermarket sales during the 52 weeks ended April 24, 1994, were as follows:[5]

Brand	Dollar Sales (in millions)	Percentage Share
Dreyer's/Edy's	$ 74.5	12.5%
Kemps	61.7	10.4
Ben & Jerry's	44.1	7.4
Breyers	36.3	6.1
Colombo	27.4	4.6
Häagen-Dazs	27.0	4.6
All private-label brands	94.0	15.8
All others	229.0	38.6
	$594.0	100.0%

[5]Compiled by Information Resources Inc., a market research company, and reported in *The Wall Street Journal.*

In 1994, Dannon Co., a unit of BSN Groupe, began introducing two frozen yogurt versions: Dannon Light and Dannon Pure Indulgence. Häagen-Dazs was placing more marketing emphasis on its lower-fat offerings such as Strawberry Duet and Orange Tango. TCBY Enterprises' new supermarket line of frozen yogurt included Honey Almond Vanilla and Brazil & Cashew Nut Crunch. ConAgra's Healthy Choice line included Peanut Butter Fudge and Caramel Pecan Crisp.

BEN & JERRY'S MARKET POSITION AND STRATEGY

During 1994, Ben & Jerry's overtook Häagen-Dazs as the market leader of the superpremium ice cream market nationwide. The company ranked among the top five marketers of ice cream and frozen yogurt. The Ben & Jerry's brand was sold in bulk to the Ben & Jerry's chain of retail scoop shops and to food-service enterprises, but the big majority of its sales were pint containers sold through supermarkets, convenience stores, delicatessens, and related food outlets. In 1988, the company introduced Peace Pops and Brownie Bars to supplement its product line and to gain more freezer case exposure. In 1989, it introduced Ben & Jerry's Light, with one-third less fat and 40 percent less cholesterol than its regular superpremium line, but Light was soon dropped due to poor sales. The frozen yogurt line was introduced in 1991. In early 1994, Ben & Jerry's introduced a "Smooth, No Chunks" line consisting of eight flavors of regular superpremium ice cream without mix-ins.

Competitive Strategy

The company competed on the basis of its product quality (chatty messages on the pint container boasted of great taste, delectable ingredients, and generous amounts of mix-ins), its ability to sustain buyer interest by creating innovative flavors, the product's Vermont-made character and the use of dairy ingredients coming only from Vermont family farms (which the company believed conveyed an image of quality and purity), its nationwide distribution capability, and its reputation for being an offbeat, funky, antiestablishment company. Customers were guaranteed satisfaction or their money back. Ben & Jerry's claimed its products contained 1½ to 2½ times more flavorings and chunks of mix-ins than rival brands (this was an outgrowth of Ben's insistence on personally approving all flavors and varieties—his sinus problems prevented him from distinguishing subtle flavors, plus he wanted different products to vary in texture and "mouth feel").[6] Also, the company's ice cream contained no preservatives or artificial ingredients except for those in some of the mix-in cookies and candies. Even though the company produced 30 flavors in packaged pints, it was the company's policy to distribute only about 12 to 18 flavors at any one time in any one area because of limited retailer shelf space; when a new flavor was introduced in an area, one of the less popular flavors was dropped. However, the company's product line for its scoop shops included an array of over 40 flavors.

Ben & Jerry's operated three plants in Vermont. Ben Cohen was passionate about the importance of making a high-quality product and was largely successful in instilling a strong commitment to quality throughout the production process. The company's most bedeviling production problem was getting the right amount of chunks into every pint. From the company's earliest days, Cohen insisted on adding

---

[6]Lager, *Ben & Jerry's: The Inside Scoop*, p. 22.

generous proportions of mix-ins and using big chunks instead of small pieces. but the available ice cream-making equipment did not accommodate large chunks easily; spouts on the pint-filling machines jammed frequently and it was virtually impossible to ensure that each pint contained the same number of chunks. The company's most frequent customer complaint was that a particular pint didn't have enough chunks in it. The company had received an average of about 11.75 complaints per 80,000 pints since 1991. In 1993, the company received a batch of bad chocolate from one of its vendors that unknowingly was used in two flavors; rather than totally recalling the product, the company did a partial recall—retrieving unsold pints from distributors but not from retail stores. Responsibility for quality assurance was divided among four departments; quality managers reported to plant and production managers.

Conventional approaches to marketing and promotion were not employed. The company did no formal market research and no test-marketing; only a minimal amount of media advertising was done to promote the company's product line—a reflection of the cofounders' disapproval of commercialism and Madison Avenue glitz. The big majority of the company's media expenditures were for ads to introduce Ben & Jerry's products in new markets; otherwise, the company relied primarily on giving away free samples and word-of-mouth advertising by satisfied customers. Where needed, the company paid slotting fees to gain shelf space and wider market exposure.

Ben Cohen, who took a personal interest in and, in effect, dominated the company's approach to marketing, decided that the company's selling and promotional activities should revolve mainly around distributing free samples, hosting fun-oriented special attractions and educational events, and participating in or sponsoring campaigns that drew attention to social issues. A converted bus with solar-powered systems, known as the Cowmobile, carried traveling vaudeville acts around the country and served free scoops of ice cream. Labeling on the company's pint containers promoted campaigns to ban Bovine Growth Hormone and to promote support for the family farm (over 500 farms in Vermont supplied the company's dairy ingredients). Summer music festivals were sponsored at locations around the country. On one occasion Cohen and another company officer drove a truck containing Peace Pops and ice cream to a rally in Concord, New Hampshire, protesting the licensing of the Seabrook nuclear plant; Ben spoke at the rally and, afterward, passed out free Peace Pops and ice cream to the protesters. The company's annual shareholder meetings (which lasted several days) and factory tours at the Waterbury plant (the second most popular tourist attraction in Vermont) were utilized as promotional vehicles. Publicity surrounding these events broadened consumer awareness of the company's products and gave the company a certain mystique. Where Häagen-Dazs presented itself as a worldly, elegant, sophisticated, and snobbish product, Ben & Jerry's endeavored to be unpretentious, genuine, and down-home. Ben Cohen wanted consumers' image of the company to be one of "two real guys, Ben and Jerry, who live in Vermont, the land of green grass, blue sky, and black-and-white cows and who make world class ice cream in some really unusual flavors."[7]

In 1984, a few years after Pillsbury purchased Häagen-Dazs from Reuben Mattus (the New York City entrepreneur who in 1960 created the brand and spawned the birth of the superpremium segment), Pillsbury brought pressure on Häagen-Dazs's distributors in New England that also carried Ben & Jerry's to either drop Ben & Jerry's or risk losing their distribution rights for Häagen-Dazs. Ben & Jerry's filed for

---

[7]Lager, *Ben & Jerry's: The Inside Scoop*, pp. 81–82.

a restraining order in federal court and fashioned a PR campaign against Pillsbury using the slogan "What's the Doughboy Afraid of?" Jerry Greenfield picketed Pillsbury's Minneapolis headquarters and handed out leaflets describing Pillsbury's attempt to keep Ben & Jerry's off supermarket shelves:

> They are not content to compete with us based on product, price, or marketing . . . Do you think that maybe the Doughboy is afraid of the American Dream? We only want to make our ice cream in Vermont and let the people of Boston and New England make their choice in the supermarket . . . Next time you're in your local market, pick up a pint of Ben & Jerry's and give it a taste. Because to tell you the truth, *that's* what the Doughboy is really afraid of.

Ben & Jerry's also developed a kit that supporters could use to write protest letters, printed T-shirts with the Doughboy slogan, affixed labels with the Doughboy slogan on pint containers, set up an 800 phone number for callers wanting information, ran an ad in *Rolling Stone* magazine to sell Doughboy bumper stickers for $1, and rented a billboard on a busy Boston route that headlined, "Don't Let Pillsbury Put the Squeeze on Ben & Jerry's." The campaign was cast as Pillsbury, a $4 billion *Fortune* 500 company, against two hippies. The media picked up the story, and after a few months Pillsbury signed a legal agreement to cease its loyalty program.

In late 1992, Häagen-Dazs introduced a line of chunky flavors designed to compete against the chunky flavors that were so much a part of Ben & Jerry's success. During the first half of 1993, Häagen-Dazs promoted these flavors with heavy media advertising and deep price discounting. In several key markets, Häagen-Dazs pints were retailing for half the regular price. Ben & Jerry's chose not to match the discounted prices, although it did offer distributors and retailers more promotional deals. While the company lost some market share during the discounting period, Ben & Jerry's market share was four points higher at the end of 1993 than at the beginning of the year.

Starting in March 1994, Ben & Jerry's introduced a new eight-flavor "Smooth, No Chunks" line to broaden its ability to satisfy consumer tastes for ice cream. Prior to the Smooth line (which included vanilla, vanilla bean, deep dark chocolate, and mocha fudge), the company had not competed in the traditional flavor area, preferring to set itself apart with its trendsetting chunky flavors. Management considered the Smooth, No Chunks line to be the company's most significant new product launch since the 1991 introduction of the frozen yogurt line. Launch of the new line was supported with national TV and print advertising, outdoor billboards in selected regions, and cents-off coupons. The Smooth, No Chunks line captured an estimated 6 percent national market share in 1994. Also in 1994, the company began marketing Ben & Jerry's pints and Peace Pops in gourmet stores and selected supermarkets in and around London, England.

Pint sales represented 84 percent of total revenues in 1993. Sales of 2½-gallon bulk containers to scoop shops accounted for 8 percent of revenues. Novelty products generated 5 percent of revenues, and sales of company-owned scoop shops represented 3 percent of revenues. Franchised scoop shops averaged $300,000 in sales annually, well above the industry average of $200,000.

One of the company's competitive strengths—product quality and creamy taste—turned out to be a source of competitive weakness starting in 1994. Its superpremium ice cream products contained comparatively high amounts of calories, saturated fat, and cholesterol. Exhibits 2 and 3 provide comparative nutrition statistics on selected brands of ice creams and frozen yogurts. Many consumers who bought upscale products like Ben & Jerry's were exactly the type likely to read the newly instituted nutritional labels. The new federal labeling requirements were said to be at the root

EXHIBIT 2 Comparative Nutrition Statistics of Selected Ice Cream Brands, January 1995

Nutritional Attribute	Ben & Jerry's Peanut Butter Cup	Ben & Jerry's Chocolate Chip Cookie Dough	Ben & Jerry's Rain Forest Crunch	Ben & Jerry's Cherry Garcia	Ben & Jerry's Wavy Gravy	Häagen-Dazs Macadamia Brittle	Häagen-Dazs Vanilla	Dreyer's Grand Rocky Road	Dreyer's Grand Light, Vanilla	Dreyer's Grand No Sugar Added Chocolate Chip	Barber's Best Rum Raisin
Calories (½-cup serving)	340	280	300	250	310	300	270	170	110	100	190
Calories from fat	220	150	200	140	200	180	160	90	35	40	90
Total fat (grams)	24	17	22	16	22	20	18	10	4	5	10
Percent of daily value	37	26	34	25	34	31	28	16	6	7	16
Saturated fat (grams)	11	9	11	10	9	11	11	5	2.5	2.5	7
Percent of daily value	55	45	55	50	45	56	54	27	12	13	33
Cholesterol (milligrams)	70	80	85	75	75	110	120	25	25	15	40
Percent of daily value	23	27	28	25	25	36	40	9	8	5	14

Nutritional Attribute	Edy's Grand Cherry Chocolate Chip	Edy's Grand Light Rocky Road	Four Winds Fudge Royale	Breyers Deluxe Rocky Road	Breyers Cookies in Cream	Breyers Reduced Fat Praline Almond Crunch	Kemps Kids Ice Cream, Dinosaur Egg Crunch	City Market Vanilla	Healthy Choice Rocky Road	Healthy Choice Black Forest	Meadow Gold Low Fat Cherry Vanilla
Calories (½-cup serving)	150	120	130	190	170	140	140	140	140	120	110
Calories from fat	80	40	60	80	80	45	60	70	20	20	20
Total fat (grams)	8	5	6	9	9	5	7	7	2	2	2
Percent of daily value	13	7	10	14	14	8	11	11	3	3	3
Saturated fat (grams)	5	25	4	5	6	3	4.5	4.5	1	1	1
Percent of daily value	23	12	20	25	30	15	23	23	5	5	5
Cholesterol (milligrams)	25	25	25	25	30	35	25	30	<5	5	10
Percent of daily value	8	8	8	8	10	12	8	10	1	3	3

Source: Compiled by the case author from nutritional labels of respective products.

of the company's January 1995 announcement that fourth-quarter 1994 sales had declined and that the company expected to post its first quarterly loss since it went public in 1985. Until recently, company management had expressed doubts about medical research linking excessive cholesterol and fat intake to a variety of heart, circulation, and other health-related problems. A 1989 *Washington Post* story quoted Ben Cohen as stating that cholesterol concerns were a fad; he went on to say:

> Ice cream in moderation is an incredibly healthy thing. We are not recommending that people eat a pint a day . . . Some people do, and I appreciate it.[8]

---

[8]From Daniel Seligman, "Ben & Jerry Save the World," *Fortune*, June 1, 1991, p. 248.

EXHIBIT 3 Comparative Nutrition Statistics of Selected Frozen Yogurt Brands, January 1995

Nutritional Attribute	Ben & Jerry's Toffee Crunch	Ben & Jerry's Coffee Almond Fudge	Häagen-Dazs Exträas Strawberry Cheesecake Craze	Häagen-Dazs Chocolate	Dreyer's Marble Fudge	Dreyer's Raspberry Vanilla Swirl	Dreyer's Fat Free Vanilla Chocolate Swirl	I Can't Believe It's Yogurt Nonfat Not Just Plain Vanilla
Calories ($\frac{1}{2}$-cup serving)	190	200	220	160	110	100	90	90
Calories from fat	50	60	70	25	25	25	0	0
Total fat (grams)	6	7	8	2.5	3	2.5	0	0
Percent of daily value	9	11	12	4	4	4	0	0
Saturated fat (grams)	2.5	2	4	1.5	1.5	1.5	0	0
Percent of daily value	13	11	19	7	8	8	0	0
Cholesterol (milligrams)	10	15	65	30	10	10	0	0
Percent of daily value	4	4	22	11	3	3	0	0

Nutritional Attribute	Kemps M&M's Brownie Fudge	Kemps Nonfat Chocolate Toffee Sundae	Edy's Chocolate	Edy's Fat Free Chocolate	Edy's Heath Toffee Crunch	Breyers Natural Black Cherry	Breyers Chocolate	TCBY Classic Vanilla	TCBY Dutch Chocolate
Calories ($\frac{1}{2}$-cup serving)	150	120	100	90	120	140	150	110	100
Calories from fat	35	0	25	0	35	30	25	10	10
Total fat (grams)	4	0	3	0	4	3	3	1.5	1.5
Percent of daily value	6	0	4	0	6	5	5	2	2
Saturated fat (grams)	2	0	15	0	2	2.5	2	1	1
Percent of daily value	10	0	8	0	10	13	10	6	6
Cholesterol (milligrams)	10	0	10	0	10	15	15	5	5
Percent of daily value	3	0	3	0	3	5	5	1	1

Source: Compiled by the case author from nutritional labels of respective products.

A section in the company's 1994 annual report took issue with critics who insisted that selling a high-fat, high-sugar product was inherently irresponsible:

The criticism that a company which makes full-fat ice cream is socially irresponsible seems a bit sanctimonious. Each person must decide whether to eat some foods for pleasure, foods that do not pretend to be nutritionally balanced staples. It is no secret that ice cream, if eaten excessively or obsessively, can cause nutritional problems. But to maintain that foods that give us cheap thrills and are fun to eat should not be sold by "responsible" companies is more puritanical than progressive. Ben & Jerry's is founded on fun, even mischief, and most people hope it doesn't stray far from the frivolous, the inane, the hilarious, and the quixotic. Providing healthy alternatives to its original super premium ice cream will go a long way toward satisfying customers' various needs.

BEN & JERRY'S STATEMENT OF MISSION

Growing Ben & Jerry's ice cream business in Burlington into a $100 million–plus public corporation had never been an objective or even a dim hope in the minds of the two cofounders. All Cohen and Greenfield were looking to do originally was create a business that would provide them a living wage. Their antiwar, antibusiness convictions, ingrained during the Vietnam protest era, made both cofounders uncomfortable managing a multimillion-dollar company with well-known products and a built-in profit orientation. As sales headed toward $1 million in 1982 and with managerial responsibilities escalating, Jerry announced his intention to leave the company at year-end, partly because of burnout from working 12- to 16-hour days, seven days a week, partly because he wanted to be with his girlfriend who was moving to Arizona, partly because he disliked the problems that came with supervising 20 employees, and partly because he wanted to get away from the growing pressures to think and act like a businessperson. During 1982, Ben also struggled with his future role, concerned that his socially activist beliefs and laidback approach to life clashed with how businesses were normally run.

For a while in 1982, the two cofounders flirted with selling the company, even going so far as to list the company with a Vermont broker that specialized in selling rural businesses. Ben was seriously ambivalent about selling out, however. When a friend convinced him that a large company could indeed be run in a compassionate and socially progressive manner, Ben canceled the planned sale and decided to hold onto his 50 percent ownership in the company. Jerry ended up keeping a 10 percent stake; the remainder of his share was later sold in small-share lots to 1,800 Vermont investors. When Jerry left at the end of 1982, Ben took over as CEO, becoming the dominant influence on the company's culture, leading its marketing and promotion efforts, and orchestrating company undertakings to enrich the quality of life for suppliers, employees, the communities where the company operated, and society at large. After living in Arizona for a little over two years, Jerry returned to Vermont in 1985. For a time thereafter, he served as a paid consultant to the company on a variety of issues, and then rejoined the company full time in 1987 as director of promotions.

Company policies and programs to promote the cofounders' sense of social mission were collectively referred to internally as "caring capitalism." Fervent in his conviction that business had a responsibility to give back to the community, Cohen diligently ferreted out ways for the company to pursue a social mission and a business mission simultaneously. Cohen described the kind of joint commitment he wanted the company to display:

> It's not a question of making great ice cream, making some money, and then going and doing socially responsible things. Caring about the community has to be imbued throughout the organization so that it impacts every decision we make.[9]

With Cohen's prodding (and sometimes authoritarian insistence), Ben & Jerry's instituted an assortment of practices and actions that were deemed worthy:

---

[9]Lager, *Ben & Jerry's: The Inside Scoop*, p. 181.

- Ingredients were sourced to serve social purposes. A Yonkers, New York, bakery that provided jobs for the homeless, the former homeless, and the hard-core unemployed was chosen to supply the brownies used as a mix-in for the company's Chocolate Fudge Brownie flavor; a portion of the bakery's profits were used for transitional housing, counseling, and training its employees. The blueberries for a flavor called Wild Maine Blueberry were all purchased from a Passamaquoddy Indian farming group in Maine. Cashew and Brazil nuts for the Rain Forest Crunch flavor were sourced in part from native forest people in Brazil, allowing them to earn 3 to 10 times their previous income and helping encourage preservation of the Brazilian rain forest. The apple pie mix-in for Apple Pie frozen yogurt was baked by recovering addicts and alcoholics who worked at a New Jersey bakery that donated 10 percent of profits to Operation Mustard Seed—a community-based ministry for people in recovery. The company's pint labels for these flavors carried messages to consumers telling them about the sources of such ingredients.

- When federal subsidies to dairy farmers were trimmed back, resulting in declining milk prices, Ben & Jerry's continued to pay its Vermont milk suppliers above-market rates that added about $500,000 annually to the company's cost. Ben Cohen explained, "We refuse to profit off the misfortune of our dairy suppliers due to some antiquated, misguided, convoluted federal system."[10]

- The company was actively committed to working with farmers to produce milk without the use of rBGH (recombinant Bovine Growth Hormone), a synthetic hormone developed by Monsanto that could increase milk production by as much as 20 percent when injected into cows. The company's opposition to rBGH was based on concerns about its effect on the health of dairy cows and an expected adverse impact on the economic viability of small family farms if rBGH came into widespread use. Ben Cohen testified at Federal Drug Administration hearings in May 1993 against FDA approval of rBGH and, assuming FDA approval, for full disclosure to consumers. The company agreed to pay a premium of about $500,000 to its Vermont dairy suppliers in exchange for their pledge not to use rBGH.

- The company's newest 17 million-gallon per year ice cream plant was deliberately located in an economically distressed area of Vermont.

- When a production line had to be closed for three and a half months, the affected employees (roughly 35) were not laid off but instead were kept on the payroll to do odd jobs around the plant and in the community.[11] Their assignments included painting all the fire hydrants in North Springfield, doing yard work, winterizing homes for the elderly and disabled, and putting on a Halloween benefit for local children's causes.

- In 1985, the company established the Ben & Jerry's Foundation to fund community-oriented projects that were models for social change and that approached societal problems in nontraditional ways, incorporated a

[10]Ibid.

[11]Jennifer J. Laabs, "Ben & Jerry's Caring Capitalism," *Personnel Journal,* November 1992, p. 55.

spirit of hope and generosity, or enhanced people's quality of life. The activities of the Foundation were funded by annual contributions from the company equal to 7.5 percent of the company's pretax profits; Ben Cohen gave the foundation 50,000 shares of his Ben & Jerry's stock as an initial endowment. In 1993, the Foundation distributed $808,000 to 142 projects. The Foundation had a policy of granting no more than $15,000 to any one project.

- In 1988, the two cofounders organized 400 companies into a group called "1% for Peace," which sought to redirect 1 percent of the national defense budget into activities promoting peace through understanding. The Ben & Jerry's Foundation agreed to donate the equivalent of 1 percent of the company's pretax profits to support the organization's cause. To promote the effort, Ben decided to name one of the company's frozen novelties "Peace Pops."

- Admissions proceeds from factory tours at the Waterbury plant were allocated 50 percent to the Employee Community Fund, which supported local causes, and 50 percent to the company's Entrepreneurial Fund, which awarded low-interest loans to people starting new businesses, including employees.[12]

- Believing that environmental issues had to be taken seriously, the company appointed an environmental affairs director and invested in state-of-the-art greenhouse technology for treating wastewater at its plants. Ice cream waste was donated to a pig farm in Stowe, Vermont. Five-gallon white plastic buckets containing ingredients from suppliers were shredded into "regrind," which was recycled into other plastic products; starting in 1994, the company switched to returnable containers to eliminate the need to grind and recycle 1 million bulk containers annually. The company used office supplies made from recycled materials where possible. In 1994, two environmental consultants were brought in to evaluate how the company could improve on the adverse impacts its operations had as concerned waste, energy use, packaging, transportation, and chemical use.

- A Ben & Jerry's scoop shop in Harlem, New York, employed 12 homeless workers; 75 percent of the store's profits were donated to a Harlem shelter and drug-crisis center. A Baltimore scoop shop employed people in a rehabilitation program for the psychiatrically disabled. An Ithaca, New York, scoop shop was partnered with a youth services organization to provide job experience and business training for disadvantaged teenagers. In all three cases, Ben & Jerry's waived its usual franchise fee and provided extra management assistance to get the businesses up and running.[13]

- The company supported the Burlington Peace & Justice Coalition, which opposed the Gulf War and joined with 18 other companies in sponsoring a full-page ad in the *New York Times* urging President Bush and Congress to give economic sanctions against Iraq more time to work.

- The company took a public stand against a large Canadian hydroelectric project that would flood lands on which Cree Indians resided.

[12]Ibid., p. 55.
[13]Lager, *Ben & Jerry's: The Inside Scoop*, p. 188.

- Truckloads of ice cream seconds were sent to flood victims along the Mississippi River in 1993.
- In 1992 and 1993, the company focused most of its social mission efforts and resources on supporting the Children's Defense Fund's "Leave No Child Behind" campaign.
- Ben & Jerry's annual shareholder meetings included promotions for world peace, environmental causes, and efforts to solve social ills.
- Management believed that efforts to create a richer quality of life for society began with employees. The company provided a comprehensive employee benefits package, offered a minimum wage of $8 an hour, and went to great lengths to provide a progressive, caring work environment.
- The company donated $1,240,000 to help renovate a 652-unit apartment complex in Times Square in New York City that provided housing for low-income and homeless single adults, including people who were AIDS patients or had a history of mental illness.
- In 1994, grants were made to the Boreal Forest Advocacy Project in Alaska to help halt efforts to open up the pristine interior region of Alaska to timber operations and to the Farm Labor Research Project to improve the working conditions and wages for farm workers in North Carolina's pickle industry.

As the company developed and its involvement in political and social causes became integral to the company's culture and policies, the need to formalize the role of social activism in the company became a concern to the cofounders, other senior managers, and outside board members. A series of discussions to develop a mission statement was initiated in 1988. A three-part mission statement emerged (see Exhibit 4), but a heated debate ensued over what weight was to be given each part.[14] Some argued for greater weight being given to the economic mission on grounds that rewards for shareholders and employees were integral to the company's long-term success and its ability to give something back to the community and society at large. Others, led by Ben Cohen, argued for the greatest weight being placed on the social mission. In the end, the company's board of directors agreed to equal weighting for the three mission elements and to recognize that the elements were interdependent. Following adoption of the mission statement in 1988, a review of the company's social performance, compiled and/or verified by an independent auditor, was included in the annual report to shareholders. The auditor's first report commended the company on its charitable contributions and societal improvement efforts but criticized the company's nutritional labels, the high-fat and high-cholesterol content of its products, and its failure to offer products for health-conscious consumers. In the company's 1992 annual report to shareholders, Ben Cohen wrote:

> The most amazing thing is that our social values—that part of our company mission statement that calls us to use our power as a business to improve the quality of life in our local, national and international communities—have actually helped us to become a stable, profitable, high-growth company. This is especially interesting because it flies in the face of those business theorists who state that publicly held corporations cannot make a profit and help the community at the same time, and moreover that such companies have no business trying to do so. The issues here are heart, soul, love and spirituality. Corporations

---

[14]Ibid., pp. 183–84.

EXHIBIT 4   Ben & Jerry's Statement of Mission

Ben & Jerry's is dedicated to the creation and demonstration of a new corporate concept of linked prosperity. Our mission consists of three interrelated parts:

Product Mission
To make, distribute and sell the finest-quality all-natural ice cream and related products in a wide variety of innovative flavors made from Vermont dairy products.

Social Mission
To operate the company in a way that actively recognizes the central role that business plays in the structure of society by initiating innovative ways to improve the quality of life of a broad community: local, national and international.

Economic Mission
To operate the company on a sound financial basis of profitable growth, increasing value for our shareholders and creating career opportunities and financial rewards for our employees.

Underlying the mission of Ben & Jerry's is the determination to seek new and creative ways of addressing all three parts, while holding a deep respect for individuals, inside and outside the company, and for the communities of which they are a part.

Source: Company annual report.

---

which exist solely to maximize profit become disconnected from their soul—the spiritual interconnectedness of humanity. Like individuals, businesses can conduct themselves with the knowledge that the hearts, souls and spirits of all people are interconnected; so that as we help others, we cannot help helping ourselves.

The unusually prominent role of the social mission resulted in considerable free publicity for the company and its products, as interested reporters regularly developed stories on the company's latest social program and demonstrations of "caring capitalism." Moreover, the company's strong social component was a source of pride and motivation for those employees who were of liberal political and social persuasion. Liberal elements within the general population were likewise attracted by Ben & Jerry's attempt to balance financial and market success against the need to contribute meaningfully to society's overall well-being; management believed many of the company's customers patronized the Ben & Jerry's brand because they knew about and approved of the company's record of social responsibility.

HUMAN RESOURCE PRACTICES

Ben & Jerry's compensation philosophy was based on the concept of linked prosperity—every employee was seen as a contributor to the company's success; thus, if the company prospered, so should employees.

The Salary Ratio Policy

Until 1992, the company's policy was that the salary of the company's highest-paid executive could not be more than five times what the lowest-paid employee could earn annually; the ratio was adjusted to 7:1 in 1992, after heated debate and much reluctance on Ben Cohen's part, because the company's salary cap was making it difficult to attract and retain capable executives. Ben & Jerry's policy of tying top management compen-

EXHIBIT 5   Compensation of Executive Officers and Directors of Ben & Jerry's Homemade, Inc., 1993

Name and Principal Position	Year	Annual Compensation			Long-Term Compensation	All Other Compensation§
		Salary	Bonus†	Other Annual Compensation‡	Restricted Stock Awards	
Ben Cohen, chairperson and CEO	1993	$133,212	—			$2,664
	1992	123,173	$600			2,469
	1991	100,000	300			2,006
Jerry Greenfield, vice chairperson	1993	132,517	—			2,650
	1992	123,173	600			2,469
	1991	95,567	300			1,911
Charles Lacy, president and COO	1993	150,262	1,970			3,045
	1992	131,346	2,714	$20,498		2,635
	1991	98,462	1,529		$96,250	1,998
Frances Rathke, CFO, treasurer, and secretary	1993	110,000	1,581			2,232
	1992	97,557	2,206	8,078		1,959
	1991	75,000	1,155		19,250	1,523
Elizabeth Bankowski,* director of social mission development	1993	105,000	694			2,114
	1992	87,691	1,041			—
	1991	3,077	—			—

Note: Directors who are not employees of the company receive $9,000 per year plus expenses.

* Bankowski's 1991 compensation is exclusive of $36,000 paid by the company for consulting services prior to her becoming a full-time employee.

† "Bonus" includes the $600 bonus paid to all employees in 1992 ($300 in 1991) and also includes discretionary distributions under the Company's profit-sharing plan pursuant to which a cash bonus was awarded to all employees (other than cofounders Ben Cohen and Jerry Greenfield) in 1993 based on a percentage of the profits of the company and the employee's length of service.

‡ "Other Annual Compensation" includes tax reimbursement on stock awards and gross up.

§ "All Other Compensation" includes company contributions to 401(K) plans.

Source: 1993 10-K Report.

sation to the pay scale for entry-level jobs had drawn more attention, internally and externally, than any other company practice. The policy was a source of great pride to the cofounders and many employees because it made a strong philosophical statement that corporate America tended to overcompensate top executives relative to the earnings and contribution of entry-level employees and that salary ranges from top to bottom should be reduced (the ratio in the largest corporations typically exceeded 50 to 1). Cohen, several board members, and numerous employees believed the policy symbolized values that were the soul of the company's culture.

Yet, the policy, even after the 7:1 adjustment, was a source of problems and continuing controversy. The 7:1 salary cap meant that the top salary was always tied to the pay scale for entry-level jobs. Raising either the top salary or the entry-level salary had repercussions throughout the company's salary structure, as well as having significant bottom-line impact. The company raised its minimum wage for entry-level jobs to $8 an hour in 1992. In 1994, the lowest salary plus benefits equaled about $23,000 a year. Still, the highest executive salary in 1994 was under $160,000, quite low for a $150 million company. Salary compression generated a morale problem among middle and upper-level managers; the small salary differences dampened individual incentives to excel and produce superior results. Furthermore, many employees did not agree that tying compensation levels to an arbitrary ratio was inherently more equitable or fair than paying market rates for jobs performed. Exhibit 5 shows compensation for the company's senior executives as of early 1994. The average salary of the top 10 percent of the company's best-paid employees in 1994 was $83,617, including benefits; the pay of the lowest-paid 10 percent averaged $25,472. Also in 1994, the average pay of the company's 299 male employees was $33,392; pay for the 215 female employees averaged $32,128.

Profit Sharing

Ben & Jerry's concept of linked prosperity also included a stock purchase plan and a profit-sharing plan. Five percent of the company's pretax profits were set aside for profit sharing. The size of each employee's profit-sharing bonus was a function of length of service. The formula was straightforward: The dollars in the profit-sharing pool (equal to 5 percent of pretax profits) were divided by the combined number of months everybody employed had worked for the company; this yielded the bonus amount per month employed. That number was multiplied by the number of months each individual had been employed at Ben & Jerry's to get the size of the individual's bonus. Profit-sharing payouts to the company's 500 employees totaled $1,148,839 in 1992, $671,675 in 1993, and $247,000 in 1994. Going into 1994, employees (excluding founders and top management) owned only 0.04 percent of the company's stock. In 1994, the company began to grant stock options to employees at all levels.

The Employee Benefits Package

All full-time employees received the same basic benefit package, regardless of salary or wage level—see Exhibit 6. When looking at changes in the employee benefits program, the company *first* considered the impact they would have on workers and *then* the impact on the budget.[15] All changes were examined by an advisory group of employees; advisory group members were allotted ample time to discuss proposals with fellow workers. Some special benefits, such as stock options or stock grants, were based on salary level; for example, it was normal for stock options to be granted in proportion to an employee's annual salary or wage.

The Work Environment

The work environment at Ben & Jerry's was characterized by casual dress, informality, attempts to make the atmosphere fun and pleasurable, and frequent communication between employees and top management. There was no dress code—T-shirts and jeans were a wardrobe must. Ben Cohen was noted for not owning a suit. Managers believed that dressing casually made it easier to communicate with and relate to workers (70 percent of Ben & Jerry's employees worked in the company's three manufacturing plants). Top management believed it was important to recognize and celebrate achievements throughout the organization and for managers to coach employees and listen to their views and criticisms without getting defensive. Ben Cohen had some definite views about what the company's culture should be like.[16]

> I want our people to love their work and have positive feelings about the company. Everyone should feel taken care of and listened to. This should be a company that gives generously, and where people feel joy, warmth, support, and accomplishment.

---

[15]Laabs, "Ben & Jerry's Caring Capitalism," p. 54.

[16]Lager, *Ben & Jerry's: The Inside Scoop,* p. 166.

EXHIBIT 6   Summary of Ben & Jerry's Employee Benefits Package

- Short-term disability plan pays 60% of salary for six months.
- Long-term disability plan pays 60% of salary after 6 months for duration of disability.
- Women who have new babies receive six weeks' full pay after delivery and 60% of salary for the next six weeks.
- Fathers may take a 12-week paternity leave; the first two weeks are paid in full; the remaining 10 are unpaid.
- A parent who adopts a child may take four weeks off with full pay if he or she is the primary caregiver, or take two weeks off with pay if he or she is the secondary caregiver.
- Children's center.
- Health and dental insurance for hourly and salaried workers (health coverage includes mammograms and well-baby care); coverage begins on the first day of employment. Dependent coverage for children, spouses, or gay or lesbian partners was available for $2.10 per week, or $4.93 per family. Employees could contribute up to $5,000 per year pretax to an account that would pay for noncovered medical expenses.
- The company contributes $1,500 toward adoption costs.
- Financial counseling, including home ownership workshops.
- Cholesterol and blood pressure screening on-site.
- Smoking cessation classes.
- Life insurance (two times salary); additional coverage up to five times annual pay could be obtained at low rates.
- Tuition reimbursement (three classes a year).
- Profit-sharing plan.
- Free health club access.
- 401(k) plan (the company matched employee contributions up to 2% of salary).
- Employee stock purchase plan.
- A housing loan program where employees with three or more years of service could borrow up to $6,000 for down payments on new home purchases (the company established a loan pool of $250,000 to fund the program).
- Sabbatical leave program.
- Employee assistance program to help workers with drug, alcohol, marital, and other family problems (106 employees had used this program as of 1993).
- Free ice cream.

Sources: Jennifer J. Laabs, "Ben & Jerry's Caring Capitalism," *Personnel Journal*, November 1991, p. 57; 1994 company annual report, pp. 13–14.

People were treated with fairness and respect. Employee opinions were sought out and given serious consideration, and employees were expected to take responsibility for doing their jobs well. No organization chart existed, yet people generally understood the division of responsibilities. Rank and hierarchy were viewed with distaste; people preferred to get things done cooperatively rather than by authoritarian means.

Staff meetings were held every six weeks to two months; the two cofounders frequently attended, listening to employees, relating plans and the latest information, and telling jokes. The meetings were also a forum for discussing issues raised by employees (topics included plant safety, burnout from long work schedules, or whether to have Coca-Cola or Pepsi in the lunchroom vending machines). To foster more two-way communication at the staff meetings, the attendees would sometimes be divided into representative groups of five to eight people to discuss specific issues intensively and then present their conclusions to the whole group; typical topics for such discussions included cutting expenses, enhancing factory tours, and which fringe benefits ought to be added. The staff meetings were used not only to involve employees in the decision-making process but also to articulate the company's operating philosophy, expound on core values and beliefs, and build commitment to the culture.

Starting in 1990, a 10-page employee-opinion survey was conducted every two years; results indicated that roughly 60 percent believed the company's social mission was in tune with their own values (12 percent believed the social mission was too conservative and 27 percent saw it as too radical).[17] The 1992 survey revealed that 93 percent of the employees liked working at Ben & Jerry's; 84 percent thought the social mission was important to the company's success.[18] To ensure that no employee was offended by the language used in company communication, the vocabulary in all company memos, handbooks, and other literature was gender- and sexual-orientation neutral. For example, the company used the term partner instead of spouse. According to one employee:

> It wasn't until I actually got into the company that I really came to appreciate it, but this is a very, very open company, where you can work and be yourself. No one here is in the closet—and I mean that in the literal sense. I'm an openly gay person, and my partner works in the marketing department. This is a company that's very open and accepting; there aren't any lines drawn. I can't imagine any typical company making me feel this comfortable.[19]

Personnel Journal gave Ben & Jerry's its 1992 Optimas Award in the Quality of Life category for creating a supportive environment for employees.[20]

There were indications that the cultures at the company's three plants, distribution center, and central administrative office were becoming more distinct as opposed to growing more homogenous. Morale at the Waterbury plant was lowest, partly because of a series of managers with less than exemplary leadership and delegation skills. Workers at the Springfield plant were quite active in supporting the company's social mission in their community. At the newly opened St. Albans plant, morale was high; a strong team approach to problem solving made people feel involved and respected. The company's distribution center, with 19 employees and 8 truck drivers engaged in shipping 40 truckloads per week, was the first to implement team organization and a total quality management process. Following criticism from the social auditor in 1993 that safety needed more attention, company managers undertook initiatives to address safety issues. A companywide committee had been formed to oversee implementation of safety policies, and on-site committees were formed to recommend actions to improve and monitor safety procedures.

The 1994 employee survey revealed a somewhat surprising amount of employee dissatisfaction and concerns. Satisfaction with pay was down; only 49 percent of

[17]Ibid., p. 214.

[18]Ibid., p. 228.

[19]Laab, "Ben & Jerry's Caring Capitalism," p. 52.

[20]Ibid., p. 50.

salaried employees felt pay levels were fair, compared to 69 percent for hourly employees. There were concerns about job classifications, the job review process, a lack of training opportunities, a lack of enough promotion opportunities, the influx of professional managers, and expanded use of part-time and temporary employees. Performance appraisals, working conditions, job safety, responsiveness to complaints or suggestions, and training and development received overall negative ratings from employees. Many people working in administration expressed concern that decisions were ill-founded or badly communicated, that top management was remote and overworked, and that the company was drifting. People felt that executives had not formed a strong strategic vision, not created a workable growth strategy, and not made timely decisions.

The Joy Gang   In 1988, Jerry Greenfield created the Joy Gang, a roving band of six employees from different departments whose sole mission was to promote fun and enjoyment in the workplace. Greenfield, the company's self-proclaimed minister of joy, often remarked, "If it's not fun, why do it."[21] The Joy Gang sponsored company celebrations of lesser holidays, like national clash-dressing day that provided workers a chance to dress in outrageous outfits and compete for prizes, and put on monthly events for either the entire company or a department. On one occasion, the Joy Gang cooked an Italian meal for third shift (11:30 PM to 8:00 AM) production workers and brought in a DJ to play songs on request.[22] On another occasion, the Joy Gang purchased a stereo and, using speakers mounted on the ceiling, arranged for music from local radio stations to be heard daily throughout a plant's production area. When company parties were held, arrangements were made for child care on-site so that parents who wished could attend.

BEN & JERRY'S MANAGEMENT TEAM

Jerry Greenfield served as company president from 1977 until January 1983, when he elected to withdraw from company operations and temporarily moved to Arizona.[23] Ben Cohen succeeded Greenfield as president and CEO. Cohen emerged as the company's spiritual leader, espousing the values he believed the company should champion, leading efforts to support the social mission, and directing marketing and promotion. But the administrative tedium of overseeing daily operations never appealed to him.

Fred "Chico" Lager was brought in as treasurer, general manager, and member of the board of directors in November 1982; previously, he had been owner/operator of a Burlington restaurant and nightclub. Lager, age 28 at the time, had an MBA, a talent for professional management, and philosophically believed in the merits of the company's social mission; as general manager, he assumed primary responsibility for day-to-day operations and functioned as unofficial leader of the company's economic mission. Over the next several years, Ben Cohen's presence diminished from a daily operations standpoint; a marketing director was hired in 1986 to assume duties

---

[21]Ibid., p. 51.

[22]Ibid., p. 52.

[23]Greenfield moved back to Vermont in 1985 and through 1986 was a consultant to the company on promotional activities, special projects, and various policy decisions. In January 1987 he rejoined the company full-time as director of promotions.

Cohen had always taken responsibility for. In February 1989, Chico Lager was named president and CEO; Cohen retained the title of chairperson of the board and, as the company's spiritual leader and biggest stockholder, continued to wield a heavy hand in major decisions and policies.

Without Cohen's on-the-scene daily involvement, the company's focus under Lager drifted more to developing and strengthening the company's market position. Concerned about reduced attention to the social mission, Cohen applied increasing pressure on Lager and the company's other board members, eventually winning the board's approval of the mission statement (Exhibit 4). Lager never was given the leeway as CEO to run the company as he saw fit. Ben quickly intervened whenever he believed company managers were not running the business in accordance with his values and vision for the company.

In January 1991, Chico Lager relinquished the title of president and CEO. Charles "Chuck" Lacy was named president and chief operating officer; Lacy had joined the company in 1988 as director of special projects, moving up to general manager when Chico Lager became president. Lacy had a background as a social activist, once being arrested for civil disobedience at a rally protesting construction of the Seabrook nuclear plant in New Hampshire. Ben Cohen reassumed the title of CEO in January 1991, involving himself in projects and issues that interested him. Jerry Greenfield took on the title of vice chairperson, soon becoming as much of a presence and a force in the business as Cohen and Lacy. In early 1992, Ben was so pleased with how well things were going, he decided to take a six-month sabbatical leave; a *Forbes* article attributed his leave to "a bad case of the guilties" over his and the company's financial success.

Ironically, Ben Cohen's management style frequently clashed with his beliefs about the merits of participatory decision making and how subordinates should be treated. He exercised personal authority over virtually all major decisions, was a taskmaster and perfectionist who held everyone to very high standards, rarely praised the work and efforts of others, and was quick to stress what was wrong or had fallen through the cracks. While Ben believed in soliciting employees' input, it was more a matter of getting their ideas on how to achieve certain objectives rather than on what the company's objectives, strategies, and policies should be. According to Chico Lager:[24]

> Ben was usually so single-mindedly convinced that he was right about something that he often didn't even acknowledge the legitimacy of alternative points of view . . . criticism from Ben, particularly given his role in the company, was powerful and demoralizing.
>
> Once Ben made a decision, it was usually only a matter of time until he changed his mind . . . Operating in a last-minute crisis mode was the norm if it was something in which Ben was involved, and as a result, the organization was in a constant state of turmoil . . . In his mind, he was just improving on whatever decision he'd made, all for the greater good of the business, and in fact, more often than not, he was.
>
> "Ben is Ben," was the saying most managers used to explain the phenomena, which essentially meant that you should just expect him to change his mind or come up with some seemingly whacked-out idea, and not be surprised when he did. Of course, a lot of Ben's seemingly whacked-out ideas weren't so wacky, once they were implemented.
>
> A large part of my job was insulating the rest of the organization from Ben, a role I'd inherited from Jerry. People who couldn't challenge Ben face to face would come into my

---

[24]Lager, *Ben & Jerry's: The Inside Scoop,* pp. 150–151, 163.

office, leaving it to me to take their case to Ben. It was also my job to soften what Ben said to people, taking out the bite and getting them focused on the message.

As a result of being second-guessed all the time, people were reluctant to proceed with anything until they had Ben's input . . .

Ben was always trying to convince people that when things didn't get fixed, it only meant they had to shout louder or in a different direction, but that under no circumstances should they give up and accept things that weren't right.

When Ben told the staff to shout louder, he was mostly referring to people who didn't report to him. As in other companies led by strong-willed visionary entrepreneurs, there were no areas that had been managed more from the top down than those Ben had direct responsibility for.

The Search for a New CEO.   In June 1994, Ben Cohen announced he was stepping down as Ben & Jerry's chief executive officer and that the company was launching a six-month search for a replacement (see Exhibit 7 for a description of the company's top-management team at the time of Cohen's announcement). Chuck Lacy was to retain his title of president and COO. Ben Cohen, 43 years old, while resigning as CEO, planned to remain chairperson of the board and concentrate on "the fun stuff—product development and promotion." Cohen indicated that the company was looking for candidates with "gentleness of spirit" who had the experience in international marketing to launch the Ben & Jerry's brand in overseas markets or experience in franchising to expand its chain of 100 scoop shops. Cohen said:

> This is a great opportunity for someone who cares about people, has the skills and vision to see around the corners of our future business development, and has always wanted to wear jeans to work.
>
> There's a tremendous amount of potential in ice cream novelty and single-portion servings. There's growth by expanding franchised scoop shops and other food-service venues. The potential internationally is quite large.[25]

As part of its wide-ranging search for a new CEO, the company conducted an essay contest in which aspirants were asked to state in 100 words or less "why I would be a great CEO for Ben & Jerry's." All interested persons were invited to enter the essay contest. If the essay contest failed to turn up attractive candidates, the board of directors planned to retain an executive search firm. To attract top corporate talent, the company said it was abandoning its policy of limiting the salary of the highest paid officer to seven times that of the lowest paid full-time worker, instead placing no cap on executive pay.

(The company's Web site address is *www.benjerry.com.*)

---

[25]As quoted in *The Wall Street Journal,* June 14, 1994, p. B1, and January 10, 1995, p. B1.

EXHIBIT 7　Profile of Key Executives of Ben & Jerry's Homemade, Inc., 1994

Ben Cohen, age 42, a founder of the company, was president and chief executive officer from January 1983 until February 1989, when he became chairperson. He resumed the position of chief executive officer of the company as of January 1, 1991, and spent the principal portion of his time on new product development and marketing strategy, in addition to those matters considered by the board of directors at its monthly meetings.

Cohen first became involved with ice cream in 1968 as an independent mobile ice cream retailer with Pied Piper Distributors, Inc., Hempstead, New York, during three summers. He was promoted within the Pied Piper organization, and his responsibilities were broadened to include warehousing, inventory control, and driver training. He spent three years, from 1974 to 1977, as a crafts teacher at Highland Community, Paradox, New York, a residential school for disturbed adolescents, before moving to Vermont to form the company with Jerry Greenfield. Cohen had been a director of the company since 1977. Cohen was a director of Community Products, Inc., manufacturer of Rain Forest Crunch candy, a director of Oxfam America, and a trustee of Hampshire College.

Jerry Greenfield, age 42, became a director and vice chairperson on the board in 1990 and spent the principal portion of his time on sales, promotion, and distribution. Greenfield was a founder of the company and was president from 1977 until January 1983. After graduating from Oberlin College in 1973 with a BA in biology, Greenfield engaged in biochemical research at the Public Health Research Institute in New York City and then at the University of North Carolina, Chapel Hill. Greenfield moved to Vermont to establish the company with Cohen in 1977. Effective in January 1983, Greenfield elected to withdraw from the daily operations of the company and moved to Arizona. Greenfield moved back to Vermont in 1985 and through 1986 was a consultant to the company, participating in promotional activities, special projects, and certain major policy decisions. Effective January 1, 1987, Greenfield became a full-time employee of the company.

Charles Lacy, age 37, had been president and chief operating officer of the company since January 1, 1991. He became a director in 1991. He first joined the company in 1988 as director of Special Projects and became general manager in February 1989. Lacy was responsible for the day-to-day operations and for long-term strategic planning of the company. From 1984 until joining Ben & Jerry's, Lacy was a finance and business development executive with United Health Services, a chain of nonprofit hospitals and clinics in upstate New York. He has a BA from Amherst College and an MBA from Cornell University.

Elizabeth Bankowski, age 46, became a director of the company in 1990, having served as a consultant to the company since earlier that year. She joined the company as an employee and director of Social Mission Development in December 1991. Bankowski was chief of staff to the governor of Vermont from 1985 through 1989. She held the office of secretary of Civil and Military Affairs.

Fred "Chico" Lager, age 39, had been a director and consultant to or officer of the company since 1982. He joined the company as treasurer and general manager in November 1982. From February 1989 until his resignation in early 1991, he was president and chief executive officer of the company. Lager was a director of Seventh Generation, Inc., a mail-order marketer, and Working Assets. Lager served as chairperson of the Compensation Committee of the board of directors and as a member of the Audit Committee of the board of directors.

EXHIBIT 7   Profile of Key Executives of Ben & Jerry's Homemade, Inc., 1994 (*continued*)

Frances Rathke was named chief financial officer and chief accounting officer of the company in April 1990, and secretary and treasurer effective January 1, 1991. Rathke joined the company in April 1989 as its controller. From September 1982 to March 1989, she was a manager at Coopers & Lybrand, independent public accountants, in Boston, Massachusetts. Rathke was a certified public accountant.

Holly Alves, age 38, joined the company as director of marketing in April 1990. From 1986 to 1990, she was the marketing director of ESPRIT, Inc., a worldwide manufacturer and retailer of clothing. Prior to that, Alves worked for Hannaford Brothers, Inc., a food distributor and supermarket company, as the director of advertising.

Bruce Dillingham, age 50, joined the company as director of manufacturing in January 1993. He had been with Digital Equipment Corporation since 1966. Dillingham has held many manufacturing management positions, including production manager, manufacturing business manager for Industrial Products, plant manager in Kanata, Canada, and startup plant manager in Enfield, Connecticut. Dillingham introduced the High Performance Work System concept to Digital. Digital's Enfield plant had been recognized for its pioneering efforts in the integration of people and technology.

Keith Hunt, age 43, joined the company as director of Human Resources in February 1993. From 1982 to 1993 Hunt was with Scott Paper Company. His most recent position was manager, Human Resources. He also held positions as manager, Manufacturing, and as manager of Organizational Effectiveness, providing leadership in a large system change. From 1975 to 1982, Hunt worked for Procter & Gamble as senior consultant/Organizational Development for Research and Development, Manufacturing, and engineering organizations.

John Stigmon, age 45, joined the company in July 1991 as director of Retail Operations. From 1989 until 1991 he was employed by Circle K, a convenience store chain, as national product manager of Food Service. From 1987 until 1989 Stigmon was self-employed, assisting entrepreneurial companies in the development of franchise programs. From 1976 until 1987 Stigmon was employed by Swensen's Ice Cream Co. in various management positions, including group vice president of Franchise Operations from 1984 to 1987.

Rei Tanaka, age 50, joined the company in late March 1994 as director of sales. From 1991 to March 1994, Tanaka was a marketing and sales consultant to Meteor Publishing Corporation, a division of Hosiery Corporation of America. From 1990 until 1991 Tanaka was senior vice president, Marketing and Sales/Circulation, for Marvel Entertainment Group, Inc. From 1978 until 1989 Tanaka was employed by Harlequin Enterprises Ltd., a division of Torstar Corporation, in various management positions in North America and international sales and distribution divisions, including executive vice president, North American Retail Division.

Source: 1993 10-K Report.

ANDREW S. GROVE: CEO OF INTEL CORPORATION

Arthur A. Thompson, *University of Alabama*

John E. Gamble, *University of South Alabama*

In February 1997, Dr. Andrew S. Grove, Intel's Chairman and CEO, could look back with satisfaction on the company's last decade. In 1986, with its memory chip business under fierce competitive assault, Intel had reported a loss of $205 million on sales of $1.3 billion and was beginning the process of fashioning a new vision and long-term direction for the company and launching a radically different strategy. Ten years later, under Grove's leadership, things could scarcely have turned out better. Intel reported 1996 earnings of $5.2 billion on sales of nearly $20.8 billion—a performance good enough to make Intel the sixth most profitable company in the world (trailing only General Electric, Royal Dutch Shell, Exxon, Philip Morris, and IBM). Analysts were predicting that Intel would earn the most profits of any company in the world before the year 2000. Intel's stock closed on January 31, 1997, at an all-time record high. Intel's Pentium microprocessors and Microsoft's Windows operating systems and software ruled the PC industry worldwide—creating what many referred to as the "Wintel standard" and prompting *Fortune* to label Andy Grove and Bill Gates (Microsoft's CEO and the wealthiest person in the world) as "the Lords of Wintel." No technology had done more to spur the Information Revolution than the microprocessor—the "brain" that controlled the central processing of data in PCs and other computers, computer-related equipment, and electronics products. And no company had done more to make the microprocessor the dominant technology of the times than Intel.

EXHIBIT 1   Actual and Projected Advances in Intel's Microprocessors, 1971–2011

Chip	Public Debut	Intel's Initial Price	Number of Transistors	Initial Mips*
4004	11/71	$ 200	2,300	0.06
8008	4/72	$ 300	3,500	0.06
8080	4/74	$ 300	6,000	0.6
8086	6/78	$ 360	29,000	0.3
8088	6/79	$ 360	29,000	0.3
i286	2/82	$ 360	134,000	0.9
i386	10/85	$ 299	275,000	5
i486	4/89	$ 950	1.2 million	20
PENTIUM	3/93	$ 878	3.1 million	100
PENTIUM PRO	3/95	$ 974	5.5 million	300
Projections				
786	1997	$1,000	8 million	500
886	2000	$1,000	15 million	1,000
1286	2011	N/A	1 billion	100,000

*Millions of instructions per second.

Source: Intel Corp., Dataquest Inc., as reported in *Business Week,* December 9, 1996, p. 150.

Nonetheless, Andy Grove remained restless and uneasy about Intel's competitive success, seeing no reason to be complacent that over 80 percent of the world's 250 million personal computers were powered by Intel microprocessors and over 90 percent of all new PCs were currently being assembled with "Intel Inside." Always acting on his personal motto "only the paranoid survive" (a reflection of his conviction that some fear was a healthy antidote for the complacency that organizational success tended to breed), Grove was worrisomely pondering Intel's future direction and strategy, convinced that the biggest and best of the microprocessor revolution was yet to come. In his keynote speech exploring the past, present, and future of the microprocessor and the computing industry at the November 1996 Comdex Convention (the PC industry's major showplace for new products), Dr. Grove predicted stunning improvements in microprocessor performance over the next 15 years. The first Intel microprocessor (the Intel 4004) contained 2,300 transistors when it was introduced in 1971. The Pentium Pro processors Intel was producing in 1997 contained 5.5 million transistors. Grove predicted that microprocessors in 2011 would have about 1 billion transistors (see Exhibit 1). He also predicted that microprocessor computational speeds would likely rise from the current Pentium Pro frequency of 300 million instructions per second to 100,000 million instructions per second by 2011 (speeds that would outcompute a dozen of 1996's fastest supercomputers). Grove believed the forthcoming technological advances would give personal computers dramatically greater capabilities and further revolutionize their role in business, education, and household life. Grove concluded that the forthcoming advances in microprocessors would require Intel and the PC industry to pursue continuously evolving business directions and strategies:

> To move on to another 25 years that are as productive, exciting, and rewarding as the first 25, we must redefine our business. We must look at it as more than just building and selling PCs—but as delivering information and interactive experiences.

PROJECTED GROWTH IN THE USE OF MICROPROCESSORS

The world's chip population was an estimated 350 billion as of early 1997, including 15 billion microprocessors of all types and sizes—equal to more than 2 microprocessors for every person on earth. Most homes in the United States and other industrial nations contained products, aside from personal computers, with microprocessors: TV sets, VCRs, cameras, wristwatches, kitchen appliances, mobile phones, and stereo equipment (although the microprocessors in such products were much smaller than those in PCs). Cars typically had 10 microprocessors and some fully equipped luxury models had as many as 50. Future microprocessors for computers were expected to have the power of 250 Pentium Pros. The projected growth in the number of microprocessor chips, coupled with the advances in processing speeds, meant that the world's computing power would double every two years or so.

The growing capability of chipmakers to put more and more transistors on a single silicon chip meant that more and more functions and "products" could be incorporated onto a single chip. One sliver of silicon would be able to hold all the circuitry presently scattered among the multiple chips (products) of various suppliers. The chips of the future would, in effect, be "systems-on-a-chip," making the technology race among chipmakers a contest of who would be among the few survivors making system-chips.

Even though Intel's microprocessor output accounted for less than 2 percent of the total number of microprocessors produced annually, its chips were among the most powerful of any chipmaker and commanded far greater prices than the relatively unsophisticated microprocessors in watches and TVs. In 1997 Intel was the world's biggest and most powerful chip maker (see Exhibit 2). Andy Grove, of course, intended for Intel to be not just one of the survivors making system-chips but rather to continue on as the unquestioned industry leader, setting the pace and creating the standards for the microprocessor revolution yet to come.

COMPANY BACKGROUND

In 1968 three Ph.D. engineers (Gordon Moore, Robert Noyce, and Andrew Grove) left their jobs at Fairchild Semiconductor to join Arthur Rock, a San Francisco venture capitalist who had raised $2.5 million in start-up capital, in forming Intel Corporation. The purpose of the new company was to design and manufacture very complex silicon chips using large-scale integration (LSI) technology. Rock became chairman, Moore was president, and Noyce (co-inventor of the integrated circuit in 1957) was executive vice-president in charge of product development and worked with Moore on long-range planning. Grove headed manufacturing. Early on, Intel adopted what Gordon

EXHIBIT 2   The World's Ten Largest Makers of Chips (All Types), 1982, 1987, 1992, and 1996

1982	1987	1992	1996
Texas Instruments	NEC	INTEL	INTEL
Motorola	Toshiba	NEC	NEC
NEC	Hitachi	Toshiba	Motorola
Hitachi	Motorola	Motorola	Hitachi
Philips	Texas Instruments	Hitachi	Toshiba
Toshiba	Fujitsu	Texas Instruments	Texas Instruments
National	Philips	Fujitsu	Samsung
INTEL	National	Mitsubishi	Fujitsu
Fujitsu	Mitsubishi	Philips	Mitsubishi
Matsushita	INTEL	Matsushita	SGS-Thomson

Source: Intel's 1992 Annual Report and Dataquest.

Moore called the "Goldilocks strategy."[1] Noyce and Moore saw that Intel had a choice of three technologies: an easy one that could quickly be copied by Texas Instruments and Fairchild; a complicated one that might bankrupt the company before an acceptable product could be marketed, and a moderately complicated one. They decided, like Goldilocks in the fairy tale, on the middle course because, as Moore explained, "The key was the right degree of difficulty. Too easy, you get competition too soon. Too hard, you run out of money before you get it done."

In 1968, Intel began semiconductor production in a one-room lab that Andy Grove said looked "like Willy Wonka's factory, with hoses and wires and contraptions chugging along." First year sales were under $3,000, but then grew rapidly as sales of Intel's first semiconductor memory chips took off. The company became profitable in 1971. The company's success in memory chips provided resources for working on a project to design and develop a microprocessor or computer-on-a-chip. Intel's first microprocessor, the 4004, was introduced in 1971; more advanced designs (the 8008, 8080, and 8088) followed. Intel turned down a chance to introduce what amounted to the first PC in the mid-1970s, believing its chances for long-term success lay more in producing memory chips for mainframe computers. But when IBM chose the 8088 chip for its PC in 1981, Intel began putting more emphasis on developing microprocessors for PCs.

A New Vision and Strategy

While Intel's sales of microprocessors grew steadily following IBM's decision to use Intel chips, memory chips remained Intel's primary business into the mid-1980s, accounting for about 70 percent of revenues. But Japanese producers of memory chips, intent on dominating the world market, began a campaign of aggressive price cutting in 1985. Their strategy was to underprice U.S. producers by 10 percent; each time Intel and other U.S. memory chip manufacturers matched the Japanese price

[1]Robert Lenzner, "The Reluctant Entrepreneur," *Forbes*, September 11, 1995, p. 165.

cuts, the Japanese producers responded with another 10 percent price cut. Their lower costs enabled them to underprice Intel and other U.S. producers. Gordon Moore, Intel's chairman and CEO, and Andy Grove, promoted to president and COO when Robert Noyce stepped down from his top management role in 1979, were forced to reevaluate Intel's strategy and long-term direction. The determined efforts of the Japanese memory chip producers (led by Hitachi, NEC, Mitsubishi, and Fujitsu) to take market share away from Intel and other U.S. producers raised serious questions in the minds of both Moore and Grove about whether Intel could lower its costs enough to be profitable in memory chips. Together, they initiated a thorough review of Intel's options to compete successfully against the Japanese. Three options emerged—build a giant memory chip factory with scale economies sufficient to overcome the cost advantage of Intel's Japanese rivals, accelerate the company's R&D effort to come up with a more advanced memory chip that would justify a higher price, and retreat to market niches for memory chips not of interest to the Japanese. After a year of frustrating debates and much soul-searching, Grove and Moore gradually came to realize none of these options had long-term appeal— indeed, they saw no attractive solution anywhere in the memory chip business. One day in 1985, pondering the actions they needed to take, Grove posed a hypothetical question to Gordon Moore, "If we got kicked out and the board brought in a new CEO, what do you think he would do?" Moore answered without hesitation, "He would get us out of memories." Grove then responded with, "Why shouldn't you and I walk out the door, come back and do it ourselves?"[2]

That pivotal conversation set Intel on a new course. Grove and Moore convinced Intel's board of directors that Intel needed to abandon the memory chip business where it had gotten its start and quickly set in motion a series of initiatives for Intel to begin concentrating its full energies on its secondary microprocessor business. In 1985 and 1986, Moore and Grove closed eight Intel memory chip plants, cut the workforce by 30 percent, reduced salaries, insisted some workers take time off without pay, and refocused the company on advancing the technology of microprocessors. Their vision was to make Intel the leader in developing ever more powerful microprocessors and to make Intel-designed chips the industry standard in powering personal computers. By the early 1990s, Intel's business strategy was squarely aimed at becoming the world's preeminent supplier of building blocks to create advanced computing and communications systems for PC users.

Exhibit 3 presents highlights of Intel's performance since 1983.

GORDON MOORE: COFOUNDER OF INTEL

Gordon Moore and Robert Noyce were among the eight persons who led the launch of Fairchild Semiconductor in the late 1950s and helped build it into the world's largest producer of integrated circuits. Moore and Noyce resigned from Fairchild to found Intel because they wanted to regain the satisfaction of research and development in a small, growing company.

Born in a small town 50 miles south of San Francisco in 1928, Gordon Moore graduated from California Institute of Technology with a Ph.D. in physics and chemistry at age 26. After working a few years in the Applied Physics lab at John

---

[2]As related in Adam M. Brandenberger and Barry J. Nalebuff, "Inside Intel," *Harvard Business Review* 74, no. 6 (November–December 1996), p. 172.

EXHIBIT 3   Highlights of Intel's Performance, 1983–1996

	Employees	Net investment in property, plant & equip.	Total assets	Long-term debt & put warrants	Stockholders' equity	Additions to property, plant & equipment
1996	48,500	$8,487	$23,735	$1,003	$16,872	$3,024
1995	41,600	7,471	17,504	1,125	12,140	3,550
1994	32,600	5,367	13,816	1,136	9,267	2,441
1993	29,500	3,996	11,344	1,114	7,500	1,933
1992	25,800	2,816	8,089	622	5,445	1,228
1991	24,600	2,163	6,292	503	4,418	948
1990	23,900	1,658	5,376	345	3,592	680
1989	21,700	1,284	3,994	412	2,549	422
1988	20,800	1,122	3,550	479	2,080	477
1987	19,200	891	2,499	298	1,276	302
1986	18,200	779	1,977	287	1,245	155
1985	21,300	848	2,153	271	1,421	236
1984	25,400	778	2,029	146	1,360	388
1983	21,500	504	1,680	128	1,122	145

	Net revenues	Cost of sales	Research & development	Operating income (loss)	Net income (loss)	Earnings (loss) per share	Dividends declared per share
1996	$20,847	$9,164	$1,808	$7,553	$5,157	$ 5.81	$0.19
1995	16,202	7,811	1,296	5,252	3,566	4.03	0.15
1994	11,521	5,576	1,111	3,387	2,288	2.62	$0.115
1993	8,782	3,252	970	3,392	2,295	2.60	0.10
1992	5,844	2,557	780	1,490	1,067	1.24	0.05
1991	4,779	2,316	618	1,080	819	0.98	—
1990	3,921	1,930	517	858	650	0.80	—
1989	3,127	1,721	365	557	391	0.52	—
1988	2,875	1,506	318	594	453	0.63	—
1987	1,907	1,044	260	246	248	0.34	—
1986	1,265	861	228	(195)	(203)	(0.29)	—
1985	1,364	943	195	(60)	2	0.01	—
1984	1,629	883	180	250	198	1.13	—
1983	1,122	624	142	139	116	.70	—

Hopkins University, Moore returned to California in 1956 when William Shockley, the Nobel Prize-winning co-inventor of the transistor, invited Moore to join Shockley Semiconductor as a research chemist. Shockley's company failed less than two years later despite the efforts of Moore, Robert Noyce (also a Shockley employee), and several others to overcome the founder's erratic management style. Moore, Noyce, and six others—the so-called Fairchild eight—invested $500 each, and with the backing of aircraft pioneer Sherman Fairchild, started Fairchild Semiconductor. Moore started as manager of engineering, then became director of research. Ten years later, Moore and Noyce were ready to strike out on their own and resigned their positions at Fairchild to form Intel. Although the production of memory chips was starting to become a commodity business in the late 1960s, Moore and Noyce believed they could produce chip versions of their own design that would perform more functions at less cost for the customer and thus command a premium price. As Moore recalled,

> We thought we saw in semiconductor memory an opportunity to make a product of almost arbitrary complexity that could be used in all digital systems and that would change the leverage from low-cost assembly back to cleverness in processing silicon.[3]

The founders' vision proved accurate until 1985 when the low-price appeal of Japanese-made memory chips overwhelmed the proprietary design advantages of Intel's memory chips.

Gordon Moore served as Intel's president between 1975 and 1979, as CEO from 1975 until 1987, and as chairman of the Intel's board from 1979 until he opted for semiretirement (a three-day workweek) in 1995. His office at Intel was a nondescript cubicle facing the headquarters' driveway that belied any of the trappings of his influence and wealth (he owned approximately 46 million shares of Intel stock, worth over $700 million in early 1997). During his years at the helm, Moore's approach to running Intel was governed largely by the mistakes he observed at Shockley and Fairchild. He believed in minimizing bureaucracy, eliminating bottlenecks between Intel's research labs and manufacturing operations so that Intel could speed the transfer of new products from lab to factory to market, and holding regular one-on-one meetings with subordinates to facilitate the transfer of information in both directions.

Moore's Law

In a little noticed article in a 1965 issue of *Electronics* magazine, Gordon Moore said the power and complexity of silicon chips would double every year with proportionate decreases in cost. Moore later adjusted the time frame to doubling every 18 months or so. His predictions have been largely confirmed. In 1982, for example, Intel's 286 was rated at 1 million instructions per second (mips) and cost $360; the Pentium Pro launched in March 1995 processed 300 mips at a cost of $974, a per mips cost of $3.24—a stunning 99 percent plunge over 13 years—see Exhibit 4. The axiom positing that the performance of chip technology, as measured against price, doubles roughly every 18 months has since become widely known as Moore's Law. Moore's Law is the main reason that new computer hardware is outdated within months and that chip technology is being incorporated into more and more products to perform more and more functions.

While Gordon Moore thought Andy Grove's projections for the computing power of microprocessors in 2011 (a 10-gigahertz chip with a billion transistors on a 0.08-micron process) were aggressive due to the number of technological problems that yet had to be hurdled, he had no doubt that in another 15 years PCs would be equipped with far more powerful chips—the only question in his mind was how much more powerful. Moore saw the big upcoming breakthrough in PC technology as good voice recognition:

---

[3]As quoted in Lenzner, "The Reluctant Entrepreneur," p. 165.

EXHIBIT 4 The Evidence for Moore's Law: Increases in Transistors per Chip and Declines in Memory Cost per Bit

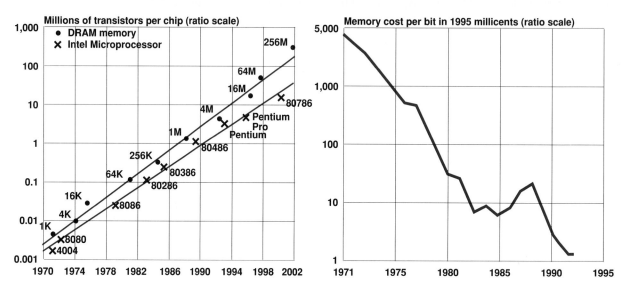

Source: VLSI Research, Inc., as published in *Forbes,* March 25, 1995, p. 116.

I really think a computer you can talk to—one that can understand your speech, not only the words but also the meaning—is going to change the way computing is done, and I think that is a role that is well worth shooting for.

That's the kind of thing that is going to open up computing to the 85 percent of the people who are nonparticipants today. That requires a lot of processing and a lot of memory, but I really think it's going to be an attractive deal. You can ask your computer to go out on the Net and get you some information. Like I would ask my technical assistant to go out and get me data on such-and-such and have the computer come back with it. I think that's fantastic, and I think it's doable.[4]

ANDREW S. GROVE: INTEL'S CHAIRMAN AND CEO

Born András Gróf in Budapest in 1936, he was the son of a Jewish dairyman and grew up surrounded by the anti-Semitic politics of the Nazis during World War II and the oppressive Soviet policies during Josef Stalin's domination of Eastern Europe. Young Gróf liked to sing opera and, for a time, considered becoming a journalist until some of his writing was rejected because of a relative's arrest. Science became his career pursuit, partly because it wasn't easily colored by politics.

Grove left Hungary for the United States a year after the 1956 Soviet invasion, arriving at the Brooklyn Navy Yard aboard a ship filled with refugees. He moved in with an uncle in the Bronx, enrolled at City College of New York, worked in the summer as a busboy at a resort in the Catskills, and graduated with a bachelor's degree in chemical engineering in 1960, finishing first in his class. Grove's professors urged him to pursue a graduate degree; he moved west, enrolled at the University of

---

[4]As quoted in *PC Magazine*, March 25, 1997, p. 239.

California, Berkley, and received his Ph.D. in chemical engineering in 1963. At a professor's urging, Grove interviewed for jobs at Bell Laboratories (one of the best places for a scientist to begin a research career in those days) and at Silicon Valley's Fairchild Semiconductor. His interview with Gordon Moore at Fairchild went so well, Grove decided he wanted to work for him and turned down the attractive job offer from Bell Laboratories. Grove started as Gordon Moore's assistant, then became Fairchild Semiconductor's director of research.

When Moore and Noyce left Fairchild to form Intel, they invited Andy Grove to come along as a researcher. But Grove was soon given responsibility for Intel's manufacturing operations, an assignment that sparked his interest in management techniques. While Intel's technological prowess was rooted in the brilliance of Moore and Noyce, it was Andy Grove's growing management skills and relentless production discipline that resulted in their ideas being rapidly transformed into market-ready products. Grove rose quickly to executive vice-president and was promoted to president and COO in 1979. When Gordon Moore decided to relinquish active management responsibility and serve only as Intel's chairman in 1987, Grove was named president and chief executive officer.

Grove's Management Style

Grove wasted no time in defining his management style and articulating a philosophy of how to manage. In 1971, he started a late list to identify employees arriving after 8 A.M. He became noted for having regular one-on-one sessions with subordinates. Soon after becoming president and COO in 1979, Grove launched Operation Crush, an all-out campaign to wrest 2,000 customers away from Motorola within a year; Intel beat the goal by 500. His 1983 book, *High-Output Management,* sold 70,000 copies and advanced the thesis that a manager's job should be controlled with the same precision as a factory. Grove insisted that the executive staff at Intel take an active role in monitoring operations. Widely regarded for his managerial acumen, he had taught management classes at nearby Stanford University and authored a newspaper column giving advice on business and management problems. His 1996 book, *Only the Paranoid Survive: How to Exploit the Crisis Points That Challenge Every Company and Career*, was a best-seller also.

Under Grove, Intel was very aggressive in protecting its technology. The company put much energy and resources into suing Advanced Micro Devices, Cyrix Corp., and others for alleged patent and copyright violations. Grove once sent a violin to former White house budget director Richard Darman to protest the government's "fiddling" with the trade policies of Japan while the U.S. chip industry burned.

Grove was aggressively outspoken, feisty, coldly analytical, a natural whip cracker, and a hands-on manager whose high level of involvement and relentless attention to detail could both inspire and intimidate subordinates. According to one Intel executive, "Andy is so incredibly articulate and so powerful that he can tear somebody apart. Those close to him know he is very sensitive to people, but he won't let friendship get in the way of demanding peak performance."[5] Grove was an ardent believer in "constructive confrontation" where any Intel employee could (and should) challenge anyone else, including Grove, without regard for bureaucratic protocol and managerial rank—no one had any fear of getting fired for disagreeing with a decision or for

---

[5]As quoted in *Business Week*, March 16, 1987, p. 68.

offering an unpopular opinion. Grove and Intel personnel waged frequent, and sometimes heated debates, via e-mail to flesh out issues and expose differing viewpoints; the correspondence back and forth was usually widely distributed across the company, with all interested parties invited to participate. In this regard, Intel's culture, shaped personally by Andy Grove, was very egalitarian. Like Gordon Moore, Grove's office consisted of a cubicle in an open space surrounded by similar cubicles, a symbol of Intel's open, egalitarian, proactive culture. Grove's cubicle was crowded with management and technical books and festooned with Post-it notes.[6] Grove deliberately made himself highly accessible, making it clear that people should stop by whenever he was around and discuss whatever was on their mind. Grove saw fast, open communications as one of the keys to preventing creeping bureaucracy, to keeping Intel agile and responsive, and to winning the world race to put more transistors on ever-smaller slivers of silicon. One of his pet projects was exhorting Intel employees to make powerful, proficient use of e-mail; he believed companies that used e-mail effectively moved faster and were much less hierarchical (interestingly enough, Grove was not a personal fan of PCs until 1989 when Intel adopted e-mail companywide and he was forced to deal with his PC everyday—using e-mail taught him the virtue of the PC as a communications device; prior to Intel's conversion to e-mail and Microsoft's introduction of Windows 3.0 in 1990, he found using PCs a cumbersome and tedious ordeal).

Grove relished immersing himself in issues, exploring all the data and angles, and analyzing things from every perspective. He regularly tried to prove his own thinking and conclusions wrong by running experiments, reexamining theories that pointed to a different conclusion than the one he had reached, and looking for examples that ran counter to his thinking.[7]

Grove's Law

Grove's motto, "Only the paranoid survive"—commonly referred to at Intel as Grove's Law—permeated Intel's culture, creating an environment that was always forward looking and driving to advance the technology, lest the company be overtaken and outmaneuvered by rivals or lose ground to alternative technologies. Mirroring his motto perfectly, Andy Grove exhibited a restless, hard-charging spirit, forever fretting about the different ways Intel's fortunes could be altered by fast-paced market changes, weighing the implications of new industry developments, and pondering Intel's next moves.

Grove's paranoia about staying ahead of competitors, his constant worrying about the future role of the PC and the directions in which the industry could move, his insistence that Intel move rapidly and aggressively across a number of fronts to sustain its leadership position, and his forcefully articulated views about how to manage (as revealed in interviews with the media and in his books on management)—all considered pluses, resulted in Grove being widely acknowledged as one of the world's foremost management gurus. In its January 13, 1997 issue, *Business Week* named Andrew Grove as one of the top 25 managers of the year, stating:

> Intel CEO Andrew S. Grove just won't slow down. He led the world's largest chipmaker to another super year, shrugging off such rivals as Motorola and Cyrix. Revenues for 1996 should climb 24 percent, topping $20 billion. Grove, 60, also fought off prostate cancer,

---

[6]So described in "The Education of Andrew Grove," *Business Week*, January 16, 1995, p. 60.

[7]Brandenberger and Nalebuff, "Inside Intel," pp. 169–70.

penned a best-seller, and helped defeat California's Proposition 211, which would have made it easier for investors to file securities-litigation suits.

INTEL'S STRATEGY

With Grove at the helm, Intel's senior management going into 1997 had fashioned a strategy anchored around several elements:

- Advancing microprocessor technology in a manner calculated to sustain Intel's position as the global leader of the microprocessor revolution.
- Continuing to build Intel's brand-name recognition and reputation via the Intel Inside campaign.
- Leading an industrywide effort to transform PCs into the data processing-information-communications-multimedia appliance of the future.
- Expanding Intel's product line to include innovative products (besides microprocessors) that would grow the role of and importance of PCs in both the home and the workplace.
- Collaborating with PC component makers, the makers of PCs (its biggest customers), Microsoft and other software developers, Hollywood's movie studios and creative artists, Sony, cable companies, Sematech (the chip industry consortium), and assorted other companies having complementary technologies and products so as to advance the performance capabilities of PCs and further Intel's objective of making the PC an indispensable and pervasive appliance.

Intel's strategy reflected Grove's vision of the potential of personal computers:

> The PC is it. We can make it so superb as an entertainment machine, and so vital as a communications medium for both the home and the workplace, that it will battle with TV for people's disposable time.[8]

Intel's Strategy in Microprocessors

Andy Grove, Gordon Moore, and other senior Intel executives envisioned that the PCs-of-the-future would incorporate, as standard features and at much lower cost, such capabilities as crisp digital video, excellent stereo sound, advanced and easily manipulated 3-D graphics, and rich voice, fax, and data communications (including videoconferencing and electronic meeting capability). Intel intended to incorporate such capabilities into the design architecture of its next-generation microprocessors, thereby eliminating the need to rely on hardware add-ons for such features. As of the mid-1990s, many of the multimedia and communications features of PCs were provided by manufacturers of special purpose chips that surrounded the microprocessor on the PC's motherboard—where the key circuitry of the PC was located. Motherboards combined the microprocessor and the ancillary chips performing various logic functions (referred to as chipsets) to form the basic subsystem of a PC.

Intel entered the business of making motherboards in 1993, electing to compete head-on against Taiwan's computer industry which then made 80 percent of the motherboards worldwide for companies not making their own. The decision to

---

[8]As quoted in Brent Schendler, "Why Andy Grove Can't Stop," *Fortune*, July 10, 1995, p. 90.

produce motherboards was driven by two considerations: (1) Intel believed that Taiwan motherboard producers were too slow to adapt their products to the latest Intel innovations and (2) producing motherboards would better enable Intel engineers to smoothly integrate new functions (such as sound, high-tech graphics, fax, modem, and videoconferencing capabilities). Intel produced an estimated 10 million motherboards containing Pentium chips in 1995 (versus 20 million for the Taiwanese producers) and 15 million Pentium-based motherboards in 1996 at plants in Oregon, Ireland, Puerto Rico, and Malaysia.

In 1996, Intel began shipping the successor to its highly-successful Pentium chip, designated as the Pentium Pro. Running at initial speeds of 166 to 200MHz, the Pentium Pro was ideal for demanding 32-bit software applications; it delivered workstation performance at PC prices and could also be used to drive network servers. In 1997 Intel began shipping 200-megahertz Pentium and all Pentium Pro chips with its new MMX (multimedia extension) technology, Intel's first step to significantly enhance the functionality of PCs (aside from just greater computing power). Intel's MMX technology speeded up such multimedia features as audio, TV-quality video, and 3-D graphics and made interactive video games much more realistic.

The Cannibal Principle

Intel's strategy to annex the functions of chips produced by others was a natural outgrowth of technological advances in electronic circuitry, rather than an aggressive invasion of the market territories of makers of other types of chips. Having ancillary chips to perform specialized functions slowed computer speeds and required complex software for smooth integration. The more functions combined on a microprocessor, the faster the computer runs, the cheaper PCs are to make (because the costs of the ancillary chips and software are eliminated), and the more reliable they are. As Gordon Moore explained:

> The whole point of integrated circuits is to absorb the functions of what previously were discrete electronic components, to incorporate them in a single new chip, and then to give them back for free, or at least for a lot less money than what they cost as individual parts. Thus, semiconductor technology eats everything, people who oppose it get trampled. I can't think of another technology or industry quite like it.[9]

The incorporation of more and more functions on a single chip, known across the industry as the Cannibal Principle, put the world's chipmakers in a technological race to make "system-chips" and to survive the inevitable shakeout among chip producers.

Intel's annexation strategy was a product of Grove's growing frustration with the slow evolution of the IBM-compatible PC platform, which in 1991 was not much advanced beyond the basic design IBM had introduced in 1984.[10] Grove worried about Intel's losing ground to competing platforms—Apple Computer's Macintosh, Motorola's Power PC, and Sun Microsystems's SPARC designs. Sluggish advances were making it possible for AMD, Cyrix, and others to clone Intel's chips and erode Intel's market share within 6 to 12 months of each new chip Intel introduced. Grove was concerned that Intel's $5 billion investment in R&D and plants to introduce the

---

[9]As quoted in Schendler, "Why Andy Grove Can't Stop," p. 91.
[10]"Intel Unbound," *Business Week*, October 9, 1995, p. 148.

Pentium generation wouldn't pay off unless the Pentium incorporated more proprietary technology and functions to make it harder for rival chipmakers to clone the Pentium. Consequently, in the early stages of the Pentium's development, Grove decided to assign Intel engineers the task of designing a bigger piece of the PC platform—not only incorporating more logic functions into the Pentium but also building chip sets (the collection of logic semiconductor chips that surround the microprocessor and synchronize the actions of various components) and building motherboards. When the Pentium was introduced in 1995, Intel started selling chip sets and motherboards directly to PC manufacturers, allowing them to speed new Pentium-equipped PCs to market without having to wait on other chipmakers and Taiwanese motherboard producers to incorporate the Pentium and otherwise advance the performance capabilities of PCs. And it put Intel in a commanding position to advance the technology of PC platforms and market a host of PC improvements that would transform the PC into an all-purpose, multimedia, videoconferencing information appliance.

Intel's strategy of annexation and vertical integration into motherboards was, in 1997, having a big effect on the industry and on PC customers. Because of the way advances in the technology of microcircuitry worked, Intel could literally obliterate the markets for specialized chips by unilaterally deciding to design their functions into its own new and more powerful chips; at the same time, though, PC users came out winners because Intel's new chips, priced at the same level as its prior generation chips, delivered faster, easier, cheaper computation and performance. The losers, of course, were the companies whose chips were no longer needed as PC add-ons.[11] For example, Cirrus Logic, which made graphics accelerator chips, was laying staff off because its chip's function was incorporated on Intel's new MMX microprocessors (Cirrus Logic's stock price dropped from the mid-50s in 1995 to $14.50 per share in early 1997). Creative Labs, which made its name by expanding the PC's audio capability with its Sound Blaster card, was expecting a big sales drop-off since Intel's newest microprocessors would enable full stereo sound as a standard feature. C-Cube Microsystems made a chip that compressed and decompressed video on PCs; this function was also standard on Intel's latest microprocessors. U.S. Robotics, one of the leading makers of modems, was predicting a sales slowdown because in 1997 every Intel-based PC could come with a fast, cheap modem chip that used the microprocessor. All told, 57 new instructions were included in the first MMX processors that Intel began marketing in mass quantities in 1997. Grove commented:

> You can't stand still. These guys have got to find new ways to add value.[12]

> We either deliver something that's going to appeal to the next 100 million people who want computers, and to the next 50 million who want to replace their computers with something else, or we won't grow.[13]

Thus, Grove's strategy was for Intel Architecture Laboratories (IAL) in Hillsboro, Oregon, to proceed full steam to design additional functions and instructions into forthcoming generations of Intel chips. When Grove established IAL in 1991, its mission and strategic role was to look for basic improvements in design that Intel

[11]"Digital Octopus," *Forbes*, June 17, 1996, p. 106.
[12]Ibid.
[13]As quoted in *Business Week*, October 9, 1995, p. 152.

EXHIBIT 5   Intel's Increasing Share of PC Revenues, 1985 versus 1995

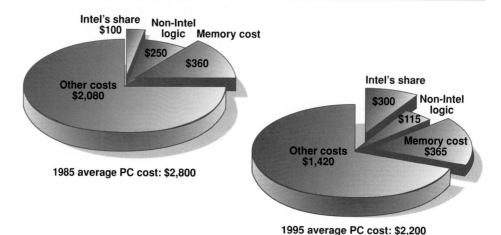

Source: InStat, as reported in *Forbes,* June 17, 1996, p. 106.

could share with PC manufacturers to advance PC capabilities. At the time, Grove saw a need for increased R&D effort on Intel's part to fill the void created when PC manufacturers, struggling to cope with price wars in the PC market, trimmed their R&D budgets significantly as a cost-containing, profit-preserving measure. Intel spent about $1 billion on R&D to develop the Pentium; future chip generations were expected to cost at least that much, if not more. But, increasingly, Intel was allocating more R&D dollars to projects other than just advancing the technology of microprocessors.

Intel's Growing Share of the PC Business

In 1985 major PC makers designed and assembled much of what was inside PCs.[14] They purchased disk drives, monitors, power supplies, and chips from outside suppliers. Usually, they designed their own motherboards, graphic chip sets, disk-drive controllers, and software that made the PC IBM-compatible. Intel's contribution was chips, mainly the microprocessor. But, a decade later in 1995 the process of making PCs was much different. Only a few PC makers still produced motherboards, notably IBM and Compaq, but even they couldn't produce a motherboard design as quickly as Intel and were initially sourcing their Pentium Pro–based motherboards from Intel until they could get their own designs ready. Intel's contribution to PC manufacture included microprocessors, motherboards, chip sets, and integrating software. Exhibit 5 shows Intel's shifting share of the revenues from the sale of a typical PC. Some observers speculated that Intel's strategy of grafting more functions onto its microprocessors would allow the average price of mainstream PCs to be brought down to the $1,000–$1,500 range, and perhaps even below, thereby opening the PC market to new groups of buyers. In 1997, a number of PC makers were offering low-end models in the $900–$1,200 range.

---

[14]Ibid.

Intel's Pricing Strategy

It was Intel's practice to introduce a new generation of microprocessors at a fairly high price (about $975 for the Pentium and Pentium Pro), then cut prices periodically as Intel plants increased production and as rival chipmakers introduced Intel clones. It was not unusual for Intel to cut prices as much as 30 percent within less than a year of initial introduction, depending on production capability and Intel's desire to stimulate additional sales or stave off market share erosion to lower-priced clones. Typically, Intel cut prices drastically on older chip generations as volume and demand built for its newer generations of microprocessors. In recent years, Intel's prices for mass-market Pentium chips had bottomed out in the $200–$250 range—a price low enough to generate multimillion-dollar sales volumes, but still yield good profit margins for Intel. The goal Grove set for Intel was to peg the price and power of its microprocessor at levels that would enable PC makers to double the performance of their models at every price point every year.

The Challenge of Rising Capital Costs

Intel's strategy of introducing ever more powerful and feature-laden microprocessors had a downside: Aside from incurring R&D costs of about $1 billion for each new chip generation, Intel had to gut and refurbish its existing fabrication plants every three years to produce the new chips and sometimes build a new plant to accommodate the expected demand. Intel's capital expenditures to re-equip existing semiconductor factories and build new ones had escalated rapidly with each new, more sophisticated generation of microprocessors. Industrywide, the capital costs to build a top-of-the-line chip fabrication plant had risen from $14 million in 1966 to $100 million in 1983 to $1 billion in 1995, and was expected to rise to $2.5 billion around the year 2000. If the trend continued, the cost of future plants would approach $10 billion before 2010. The reason for the sharp escalation in capital costs was that it took increasingly exotic tools and equipment to etch finer and finer lines on a silicon chip—the width of the thinnest circuit line or transistor element had dropped from 0.5 microns to 0.35 microns in 1996 and was projected to decline steadily to 0.08 microns by 2011 (see Exhibit 6). Finer etching also required more labor and production time. Intel estimated that each succeeding generation of microprocessors required more than twice the capital and manufacturing capacity for production. The air in chipmaking plants had to be virtually dust free; workers entered through airlocks, wore special head-to-toe clothing, and exhaled into filtered tubes. The company's production executives tended to describe chipmaking as part chemistry, part physics, and part manufacturing management magic. The escalating cost of chip fabrication was dubbed Moore's Second Law in a 1995 *Forbes* article. Intel, of course, intended to be among the handful of chip producers that could afford to build top-of-the-line chip fabrication plants.

In 1995, 209 new chip fabrication plants had been announced worldwide; many were expected to cost about $1.5 billion on completion. The huge investment was causing many producers to enter into joint ventures to build new fabrication plants, including Motorola and Toshiba, Hitachi and Texas Instruments, and AMD and Fujitsu. So far, Intel had opted to go it alone. In 1997 Intel had 12 plants worldwide involved in various aspects of chip fabrication; in recent years, Intel had built a new fabrication plant about every nine months and had recently announced its intent to build a new plant every six months. Every Intel site around the world underwent

EXHIBIT 6   Actual and Projected Features of Microprocessors, 1993–2011

Year	DRAM Capacity	Microprocessor Speed	Width of Thinnest Circuit Line
1993 actual	16 megabits	150 megahertz	0.50 micron
1996 projected	64 megabits	350 megahertz	0.35 micron
1999 projected	256 megabits	400 megahertz	0.25 micron
2002 projected	1,024 megabits	500 megahertz	0.18 micron
2005 projected	4 gigabits	600 megahertz	0.12 micron
2008 projected	16 gigabits	700 megahertz	0.10 micron
2011 projected	64 gigabits	800 megahertz	0.08 micron

Note: One micron is about 1/100th the width of a human hair.

Source: *Business Week,* July 4, 1994, pp. 86–87.

some kind of renovation and/or construction in 1995 and 1996. Going into 1997, Intel's plants were producing about 50 million Pentium and Pentium Pro microprocessors annually.

So far, Intel's high degree of profitability, cash flows from depreciation, and low dividend payout had provided sufficient financial resources and financial strength for Intel to fund the capital requirements associated with refurbishing its existing "fab" plants and building new plants—see the statistics in Exhibit 3. Intel's earnings in 1996 were greater than the combined profits of the top ten PC manufacturers. Intel had led the semiconductor industry in new capital investment for the last six years. It was Intel's practice to build its new fabrication plants about two years in advance of needing them, before it had finished developing the forthcoming new chip generation and before it could be certain that the PC industry would grow fast enough to absorb the added capacity. As Grove put it, "Our fabs are fields of dreams. We build them and hope people will come."[15] Intel management believed that continued growth in company earnings would be necessary for Intel to finance the projected costs of new equipment and facilities and still realize good returns on investment.

THE "INTEL INSIDE" CAMPAIGN

To dampen the sales of clones of Intel microprocessors marketed by AMD, Cyrix, and others, Intel initiated a marketing program in 1990 to build the Intel brand and make PC users aware of the benefits of genuine Intel technology and products. As part of the campaign, Intel asked PC makers to put a distinctive "Intel Inside" sticker on their machines; most of Intel's top microprocessor customers participated. Manufacturers who used Intel microprocessors in their PCs could not only mark their PCs with the Intel Inside logo but could also use the logo on their packaging and in their ads and brochures. The company also sponsored television and print advertising campaigns stressing that by choosing an Intel-based PC, users got the ultimate in quality, reliability, software compatibility, and value. The marketing program was a

[15]As quoted in David Kirkpatrick, "Intel's Amazing Profit Machine," *Fortune,* February 17, 1997, p. 64.

huge success and had become a prominent element in Intel's strategy ever since. Not only did Intel continue to sustain its dominant market share but customer feedback revealed that PC buyers, not just computer techies, really cared about their computer's chip and its performance capabilities.

Intel sought to leverage its brand reputation with PC buyers by giving the names Pentium and Pentium Pro to its two most recent chip generations instead of assigning them numbers like it did with its 286, 386, and 486 chip generations. The Pentium name was extremely familiar to PC buyers, not just because of Intel's own promotional efforts but also because of scores of media stories about the Pentium and Pentium Pro and because both the Pentium/Pentium Pro names and Intel Inside logos were used in most all ads run by the PC manufacturers touting their models. PC industry experts believed that in 1996 Intel was spending over $100 million annually to boost its name recognition among consumers, including ads on MTV, CNN, and various Internet services.

PC users who bought Intel brand products were backed up by the company's extensive customer support organization. Intel had multilingual customer support centers in Swindon, U.K.; Provo, Utah; Beaverton, Oregon; and Tsukuba, Japan. Technicians stood by to answer customer questions over the phone or else through Intel's FaxBack service that included troubleshooting tips.

The Pentium Flaw Embarrassment

In October 1994, Thomas Nicely, a mathematics professor at Lynchburg College in Virginia, posted a notice on an Internet bulletin board detailing the presence of a minor calculation flaw in how Intel's new Pentium chip did division in certain situations. CNN picked up the story and a wave of negative publicity followed. Intel responded that the chances of anyone encountering the flaw were virtually minute (company engineers had discovered the problem months earlier and were practically finished with their fix). Then, in early December, IBM announced that the chances of encountering the flaw were much greater than Intel was acknowledging and that, to protect consumers, IBM was halting shipment of Pentium-based computers (a move that some analysts said was made to deliberately make Intel look bad and make IBM look good). Within days, Intel offered all owners of a Pentium-based computer a free, no-questions-asked replacement of their Pentium chip and took a $475 million write-off to cover the costs. While the episode was described in the media as a public relations disaster for Intel and as evidence of a lack of consumer marketing savvy on Intel's part, only a small number of PC owners asked for a replacement. Looking back, Andy Grove blamed himself for the miscue, indicating that he analyzed the issue from the perspective of a scientist and engineer (according to Intel's calculations, the problem occurred too rarely to concern anyone but the most demanding scientists) instead of stepping outside Intel and looking at the issue from the perspective of a buyer wanting to be confident about the integrity of Intel's products and expecting the company to stand behind them.

INTEL'S MOVE FROM INDUSTRY FOLLOWER TO INDUSTRY LEADER

Andy Grove began to see the need for Intel to take more of an industry leadership role in the early 1990s when it became apparent that the speed of Intel's processors was starting to outpace the performance of other PC components. The existing "bus"—the internal network that directed electrons—delivered data to the microprocessor at speeds far slower than the upcoming Pentium generation would be able to handle. Bus designs were, at the time, the province of IBM and other PC makers, but Grove knew of no sufficiently fast designs in development. An Intel division had proposed a new bus design called PCI, yet Grove was skeptical about Intel's getting involved in PC architecture. Intel executives persisted and, after several heated discussions, Grove came to the conclusion that if Intel didn't initiate a new bus design, it wouldn't happen in time to make the Pentium the big success that Intel was counting on. At the 1991 Comdex convention, Grove delivered the keynote speech and demonstrated how a laptop PC equipped with Intel's new PCI and some special chips could receive e-mail messages and graphics delivered over a wireless network—a real breakthrough at the time that proved to be a smashing hit at the convention. Dell, IBM, and several other computer companies endorsed Intel's PCI and sent representatives to appear on stage with Grove at the convention. Impressed by the stir his demo created and the willingness of the PC makers to follow Intel's lead, Grove saw that Intel could gain considerable competitive strength if it could achieve the same kind of leadership on other fronts. As he put it, "That was the 'Aha!' for me."[16]

Around the same time, Grove paid a visit on Steve Jobs, who had left Apple Computer and had subsequently founded Next (which Apple purchased in late 1996 and brought Jobs back into the Apple fold). Job's was leading an effort at Next to develop a high-end, easy-to-use PC specially designed for high-performance multimedia applications. Jobs did a demo of the new PC for Grove. Inspired by the capabilities he had seen, Grove returned to Intel, called a meeting of some key executives, and announced that he wanted Intel to initiate development of the same kinds of features for the entire PC industry and to make PCs as good as the Next computer that Steve Jobs was developing. Thus began Intel's foray into areas outside microprocessors and Intel's efforts to become the PC industry's technological leader across a wide front.

INTEL'S STRATEGY TO INTRODUCE INNOVATIVE PRODUCTS

Andy Grove's blossoming vision of the PC as tomorrow's information appliance—one destined to push TVs, VCRs, game players, cable boxes, and telephones into the background—required Intel to do more than just lead the advance of the microprocessor. As he began to see in the early 1990s and reiterated again in mid-1995, "The typical PC doesn't push the limits of our microprocessors. It's simply not as good as it should be, and that's not good for our customers."[17] To enhance the versatility of PCs and more fully utilize the capabilities of Intel's microprocessors, Intel had introduced a number of PC-based business and personal communications products:

- Intel produced and marketed chip products (microprocessors, microcontrollers and memory components) used in keyboards, printers, copiers, and fax machines, which enhanced the PC's capabilities and made PCs easier to use. In addition, these products were being used to enhance

---

[16]As quoted in Kirkpatrick, "Intel's Amazing Profit Machine," p. 63.
[17]As quoted in Brent Schendler, "Why Andy Grove Can't Stop," *Fortune*, July 10, 1995, p. 91.

the functionality of cellular phones, pagers, digital cameras, and personal digital assistants (pocket-size electronic organizers).

- The ProShare line of conferencing products was introduced in 1994. In 1995 the ProShare Conferencing Video System 200, which offered file and document-sharing capabilities, became one of the industry's leading desktop conferencing products. It was certified in over 25 countries and won several industry awards. Also in 1995, Intel introduced a group videoconferencing system for meeting rooms. (Flagstar Bank was using Intel's conferencing system to link its mortgage loan officers and home loan applicants with Flagstar's mortgage underwriters and to conduct mortgage application interviews. Customers using the interactive sessions got loans approved in as little as 15 minutes, compared to days or even weeks using the traditional approval system. Flagstar credited the ProShare system with making Flagstar the fourth largest wholesale mortgage lender in the United States.) Videoconferencing software was projected to be a $1 billion market in 1997.

- Intel's new Universal Serial Bus, introduced in 1996, used a single type of connector to attach printers, modems, CD-ROM drives, and other peripherals, making connections a simple step and speeding the flow of data into and out of the computer a hundredfold. The new USB addressed the often painful experience of attaching peripherals having different, incompatible connectors.

- Intel's "Intercast" plug-in cards simultaneously allow PCs to receive TV pictures from broadcast or cable and, in the blank spaces of TV signals, Web pages, and text. The technology allowed PC screens to be divided into four quadrants, with broadcast signals appearing in one and text and other information appearing in the others. MTV, CNN, and NBC were early users of Intel's intercast technology.

- Intel's new i960 RP processor, a single-chip intelligent input/output subsystem for servers, reduced data bottlenecks and enhanced server performance.

- During the last four years, Intel had introduced a number of hardware and software products aimed at making PC networks easier to install and manage.

- Intel had a 70-person software lab in Shanghai developing multimedia and 3-D content in Chinese.

- Intel programmers had developed a software product called Streaming Media Viewer that software developers could incorporate into their products and allow users to view video as it arrived from the World Wide Web. Intel and Sony Music in mid-1996 began testing the performance of the technology at their respective Web sites; the technology eliminated the need to download large video files and store them on the receiving PC before they could be played back. Sony saw the technology as a new way to present and market the work of its music artists, to provide viewers with new multimedia and digital programming, and to hold on-line interviews and backstage sessions with their artists and bands. In early 1997, Sony, along with several cable channels, began broadcasting video programs at their Internet sites that PC users could view directly on their monitors. Numerous other Web sites were rapidly installing the capability to deliver "streaming video" programs and content.

- Intel Architecture Laboratories (IAL) had created an add-in circuit card for PCs that enabled a site's computer to broadcast video on a Pentium Pro microprocessor (slower, earlier-generation microprocessors didn't have the power to perform this function).

- IAL had also created software to help popularize long-distance telephone calls on the Internet. While several small software companies such as VocalTec and Quarterdeck sold software programs that allowed PC users to make long-distance calls via the Internet, their products were incompatible with each other and PC users were only able to contact persons using the same brand of software. IAL had worked with the Internet industry to get Intel's software adopted as the industry standard (over 120 companies had embraced Intel's standard as of mid-1996) and was making the software available free on its Web site. Intel had licensed the software to Microsoft, which was also giving the software away free on its Web site. IAL's director, Craig Kinnie, observed, "Until we took a role in driving the standards, Internet telephones were largely toys."[18] One analyst predicted that by late 1997 over 30 million Web browsers would be equipped with Intel's software standard for using Internet phones (only an estimated 30,000 people were making Internet calls using software technology introduced by other companies in 1995). In late 1996, Intel and Microsoft introduced software enabling video phone calls and videoconferencing over the Internet.

- Intel had developed hardware-based cryptographic technology that provided increased levels of security for data communicated over the Internet. Ron Smith, vice-president and general manager of Intel's Semiconductor Product Group, indicated that it was Intel's strategy to "provide the hardware technologies that are the backbone to strengthen the protection of Internet communications."

- In December 1996 Intel introduced its CablePort family of hardware and software products for cable operators that integrated all the functions required to deliver Internet communications to PCs. These products made it possible for cable operators to begin offering subscribers with PCs a variety of media-rich interactive services; the capability could be installed in subscribers' homes in as little as 15 minutes.

Intel had additional products in various stages of development and was announcing the introduction of new products and the availability of new Intel technologies on a weekly, sometimes daily, basis—the company's latest product and technology offerings were posted on its Web site (http://www.intel.com). The company was steadily increasing its R&D budget (see Exhibit 2) and was looking for strategically valuable ways to broaden its product line; approximately 8,000 Intel employees were engaged in the company's R&D efforts. In 1996, Intel spent approximately $500 million on R&D projects to develop products that were not directly involved with new generations of microprocessors; in 1990, R&D expenditures in these areas were virtually zero.[19] Intel's reputation for innovation was among the best of any U.S. company—it was ranked third on innovativeness among all U.S. companies in a 1997 *Fortune* survey.[20]

---

[18]As quoted in Kirkpatrick, "Intel's Amazing Profit Machine," p. 64.
[19]Kirkpatrick, "Intel's Amazing Profit Machine," p. 63.
[20]See "The Most Admired Companies," *Fortune*, March 3, 1997, p. 74.

INTEL'S STRATEGY OF COLLABORATING WITH OTHERS

An important element of Intel's strategy was to work closely with other PC component producers, PC manufacturers, software developers, cable TV companies, media and telecommunications companies, and entertainment companies to make the PC a superb entertainment machine and a vital all-purpose, information-communications appliance for both the home and the workplace. Andy Grove explained that structural changes in the PC industry since the mid-1980s made collaborative alliances and partnering with others a strategic necessity for Intel:[21]

> The breakup of the old computer industry is what gave Intel its chance and made the mass-produced computer possible. The old computer industry was vertically aligned: Each company sold a completely integrated product based on its own proprietary technology. Companies like IBM and Digital Equipment designed and built their computers from the bottom up—silicon chips, software, disk drives, everything. These vertically integrated companies would compete against other vertically integrated companies, and buyers had to commit to the whole package of one manufacturer or another.
>
> . . . a new horizontal industry model is replacing the old vertical one. In the PC age, everybody's products have to work with everybody else's products . . .
>
> Businesses compete for market share within each horizontal specialty. Intel is up against companies like Motorola in the basic silicon architecture. In operating systems it's Microsoft vs. Apple vs. IBM vs. Novell. Borland competes with Lotus and scores of other companies in all the varieties of applications software, like spreadsheets and word processors. And then you've got the Compaqs and Dells and many others making and selling the PCs. . . .
>
> The new computing industry resists central guidance. Nobody can tell anyone else what to do. Your PC might have a processor from Intel, a display from Sharp, a hard disk from Conner, memory from Toshiba, a modem from U.S. Robotics, an operating system from Microsoft, applications from four different vendors, and yet it all works together. If it didn't, none of these products would sell.

Because PCs contained components from so many different vendors, Andy Grove believed industry participants in different horizontal specialties had to develop new products in parallel—for example, it was important for the product development efforts of monitor, keyboard, printer, disk drive, hard drive, memory chip, fax, modem, CD-ROM, and printer manufacturers, as well as the PC makers, to keep pace with Intel's introductions of a new generation of microprocessors; uneven advances in the technology of various PC components made it hard for PC buyers to realize the maximum benefit from improved performance capabilities of any one PC component. Likewise, as Intel introduced new generations of microprocessors, it was beneficial for Microsoft and other developers of operating systems and software to be ready to go to market with new software systems and products that capitalized on the speed of Intel's new processors.

Andy Grove and Bill Gates, recognizing the strategic interdependence of Intel and Microsoft, began meeting intermittently in the 1980s to share ideas and discuss mutually beneficial avenues of cooperating; in the 1990s, their meetings increased to two or three items annually. Grove explained:[22]

---

[21]As quoted in *Fortune*, February 22, 1993, p. 57.

[22]As quoted in Brent Schendler, "A Conversation With the Lords of Wintel," *Fortune*, July 8, 1996, p. 44.

1986 is when IBM began to lose it. For reasons of their own, they were reluctant to get involved with our 386 microprocessor. That's when Compaq got into the act. Then in 1990, Microsoft split with IBM and introduced Windows 3.0. As these things happened, instead of being two junior partners of a senior partner, we became equal players without that senior partner being present. If you look at this as a molecule, a lot of the bonds to that third atom in the molecule faded and were rebuilt between our two companies.

Bill Gates elaborated:

Both our companies really encouraged Compaq to not just be the leader in portables, which is what they were at that point, but to be the performance leader too. After that, there was a bit of a vacuum in PC leadership and both of our organizations recognized the need and opportunity to step in and fill it. But one key thing to know about the chronology of our relationship is that there's been more time spent on Intel/Microsoft collaboration in the last couple of years than in all the preceding decade put together.

The meetings between Grove and Gates alternated between Intel and Microsoft sites, with lower-level personnel from both companies who were in almost daily communication doing the preliminary spadework and shaping the agenda. As PC technology branched out to involve graphics, audio, video, networks, e-mail, and the Internet, each new technological branch spawned its own nucleus of collaborations between Intel and Microsoft, expanding the number of areas of cooperation and coordination and sometimes blurring their dividing lines due to the growing technology interfaces between one technology or product and another. Both Grove and Gates believed the existing technological constraints to burgeoning use of the Internet could best be overcome by a combination of Intel chips and Microsoft software. Both agreed that the PC of the future would be more versatile and engaging, having the capabilities of a TV, a video game machine, and a VCR, offering videophone and videoconferencing capabilities, and being a true multimedia appliance. Both saw the Internet as the place where the most exciting new technological developments were happening; according to Grove:[23]

No question—the Internet is the best thing that could happen to our industry. Basically, every computer in the world is going to be connected to every other computer in the world, and the PC will be the canvas that creative people make their stuff on.

Both agreed that the shift to digital TV, combined with the move to digitally create and store music, film, and print content would make it possible for faster microprocessors and better software to transform PCs from an information appliance into a combination information-communication-multimedia appliance capable of delivering laser-disk-quality video and sound. Gates saw more breakthroughs further down the road: the ability to talk to PCs, the ability of PCs to respond to gestures, and perhaps more.

The Intel-Microsoft alliance was not without friction and discord, however. Andy Grove and Bill Gates were both high-tempered and opinionated, had occasional shouting matches and vigorous disagreements, and were not afraid to point out shortcomings or mistakes of the other's companies. One of their most recent conflicts was over native signal processing (NSP), a pet initiative of Grove to write software to help new Intel microprocessors deliver better, livelier multimedia performance

---

[23]As quoted in Brent Schendler, "Riding the Real Trends in Technology," *Fortune*, February 19, 1996, p. 60.

(Intel had over 2,000 programmers writing software programs to help Intel products perform better). The NSP project involved writing code that would control the way the Pentium processors would allocate their time, giving top priority to multimedia tasks that enhanced what viewers saw and heard and delaying tasks involving routine data handling and other Windows functions. An Intel executive explained what Intel was trying to achieve with its NSP initiative:[24]

> What we are doing is putting rabbits out there to run ahead of the hounds like Microsoft to make them run faster. Sometimes the hounds might catch the rabbit—Microsoft could well provide its own alternative to our NSP software that ultimately wins. But to do that they have to run faster, and that's what we really care about.

Microsoft, preoccupied with its launch and promotion of Windows 95 up until fall 1995, didn't share the same sense of urgency as Intel about enhanced multimedia performance. So Intel proceeded on its own. But Intel programmers happened to select a method for handling 3-D graphics and audio that wouldn't run on Windows 95, greatly limiting its utility for buyers of new PCs, almost all of which were equipped with Windows 95. In abandoning the NSP initiative, Grove confessed that in retrospect it was dumb for Intel to develop software that was contrary to the features of Windows 95.

Still, there was a big strategic conflict between Intel and Microsoft. Intel's long-term strategic interest was in driving the advance of the PC platform and creating demand for new, more powerful, and more feature-rich PC capabilities. While enhancing the performance of new computers mattered to Microsoft, it also had to be concerned with supplying software for the 250 million PCs sold earlier and still in use and in making its new software products mostly compatible with its earlier program versions. Moreover, while quick to acknowledge their companies' interdependence and the need to work in parallel on new chips and software, Grove and Gates publicly acknowledged in a *Fortune* interview that there was nothing exclusive or permanent about the Intel-Microsoft alliance:[25]

Gates: . . . there's no exclusive tie going in either direction. If somebody walked into Microsoft tomorrow and said they had a microprocessor that's cheaper and faster. . . .

Grove: Well, you've done it. You've tried it. You didn't succeed, either. . . .

Gates: And vice versa. Intel aids and abets non-Microsoft operating systems.

Grove: Still, we have our biggest successes when we apply our muscle and their muscle to the same problem.

Intel's Other Alliances

While Intel's greatest collaborative effort was with Microsoft, Grove and Intel had forged dozens of strategic alliances and cooperative ventures covering a wide variety of strategic arenas. On Internet software, Intel worked as closely with Netscape, which dominated the market for browser software, as it did with Microsoft. Intel was allied with Microsoft, Pointcast, America Online, IBM, Cisco Systems, and others to develop and promote Internet software that would allow PC users to specify the content they wanted delivered from the Internet to their desktop without having to

---

[24]As quoted in Schendler, "Why Andy Grove Can't Stop," p. 94.
[25]Ibid., p. 58.

browse the Internet to find what they wanted and that would also allow (*a*) Web site owners to "push" their content to interested PC users and (*b*) companies to push industry news, company announcements, and data to employees' desktops. The staggering amount of information on the Web was making manual searches of the Internet an unsustainable approach, both from a time standpoint and a line-jamming standpoint. Software that allowed PC users to tune in to Internet broadcasts or "Webcasts," receive automatic updates (for weather, stock quotes, sports scores, and news of interest), and receive visual images and animation approaching TV quality was expected to greatly broaden and heighten consumer and business interest in using PCs to access the Internet. Such "Webcasting" capability was integrated into the new 4.0 version of Microsoft's Internet Explorer introduced in mid-1997; other Intel allies, including Netscape and Pointcast, were introducing Webcasting products as well.

Intel was working with the makers of regular modems and cable modems to speed communications and data transfer capabilities via the Internet; its collaboration with cable modem manufacturers extended to ways of merging PCs, TVs, and telephones into a single device. Andy Grove believed cable modems were a promising way to unclog the Internet and to turn the PC into a multimedia appliance in the home. Intel was also working with local and long-distance companies on using telephone lines and fiberoptic cable to create an information superhighway to businesses, government organizations, and households. More and more companies either had or were installing network capabilities that allowed employees with desktops to have a constant Internet connection.

Intel had recently entered into cooperative arrangements with Sony Music, various movie studios (Universal Studios, DreamWorks SKG, and MCA), and assorted Hollywood entertainment groups to accelerate development of PC multimedia products with innovative content that would potentially appeal to mass audiences. Intel and Creative Artists Agency (one of Hollywood's most powerful talent agencies) had opened a center to promote faster development of PC-based entertainment software, including videogames. Intel was in discussions with Walt Disney about new ways of distributing Disney's media products electronically. One of Intel's most talented senior executives, Avram Miller, was assigned the task of figuring out ways to persuade creative Hollywood minds to develop innovative PC content. While Andy Grove was intrigued with prospect of creating computer entertainment products with broad consumer appeal, he was unsure what form it would take:[26]

> It's like a soapy elephant—slippery and big. The problem is that neither we nor the people in Hollywood seem to know what to do with digital media. Whoever figures it out will have the key to pulling people away from their television sets.

Intel had invested over $500 million in 50-plus companies that were pursuing ways to make the PC a media-rich appliance and was actively collaborating with them to develop new products in parallel. Among others, Intel had an ownership stake in such companies as Palace, which created virtual communities on the Internet; Digital Planet, which developed episodic, interactive stories for the World Wide Web; Willisville, which was trying to combine shopping, chat, and storytelling on-line; CNET, which ran Internet sites and produced broadcast shows devoted to technology; and OZ Interactive, which specialized in 3-D Internet software. The objective of

---

[26]As quoted in Schendler, "Why Andy Grove Can't Stop," p. 98.

Intel's Internet media strategy was to bring PC users the best possible multimedia experience on the Internet and to make the PC a life tool as well as a work tool.

Intel was working with Starbucks to link selected Starbucks' cafés and allow patrons to send and receive video e-mail. Andy Grove was especially interested in Intel's cooperative efforts with Eastman Kodak, Sony, Konica, Hewlett-Packard, and others to make digital cameras easier and cheaper to use.

Intel, Macromedia, and Marimba were working jointly on an "Infinite CD" for the Public Broadcasting Service (PBS) that would allow PBS to broadcast video footage of its programs on PBS Online on the Internet and provide a wide variety of customized programs to schools, families, and individuals; the new technology would also allow users to request information of interest that could be downloaded on their PCs. The Infinite CD technology incorporated use of an Intel Pentium processor with MMX technology.

Intel was collaborating closely with dozens of software developers and PC components manufacturers to upgrade sound and video quality and capability on PCs. These alliances were integral to Intel's larger strategic objective of bringing PC users the best possible multimedia experience on the Internet. Microsoft had joined forces with Intel in leading this effort.

Intel and Microsoft, in close conjunction with leading PC makers and other hardware and software vendors, were leading an industry initiative to develop industry standards for a network PC platform, called NetPC, that would be cheaper to buy and less expensive to operate than standard PCs. The Intel-Microsoft NetPC would incorporate a Pentium 100 MHz or greater microprocessor, run on Microsoft operating systems, and have other specifications aimed at maximizing user flexibility and minimizing user costs. Many PC manufacturers, including Hewlett-Packard, Compaq, Dell Computer, Digital Equipment, Gateway 2000, Packard Bell NEC, and Texas Instruments, supported the Intel-Microsoft initiative to establish open industry-wide standards, as opposed to the proprietary designs of a single company, so that customers would not have to incur the costs and complexity associated with multiple and perhaps incompatible computing systems. However, neither Andy Grove or Bill Gates believed that so-called $500 network computers or Internet terminals that provided the requisite software and computing power (when connected to network servers or to the Internet) would greatly erode high-performance PC sales and usage; they did not believe PC users would be attracted to a device that put them at the mercy of Internet service providers or network servers and the rules and controls imposed by network czars. With a stand-alone PC, users had their own independent software and computing power, not only giving them greater control of what they wanted to do and when they wanted to do it but also giving them a device with far greater performance capability on the Internet or connected to a network. Bill Gates had written an essay posted on the Internet explaining why he saw limited value in a cheap, diskless PC (Gates's critics said, however, that his judgment was colored by the fact that the very purpose of such devices was to eliminate the need for Microsoft operating systems and software). Grove was more open than Gates to the idea of developing low-cost devices to plug into the Internet or networks and indicated that Intel would be a leading player in NetPCs if demand for them really took off.

Intel had launched cooperative efforts with motor vehicle and motor vehicle parts producers to develop Pentium processor–based computing applications for cars and trucks. Intel believed that PC technology was a versatile platform for a wide variety of in-vehicle applications—driver information displays, the ability to access real-time traffic information and weather forecasts, placing and receiving telephone calls, sending and receiving e-mail and faxes, speech recognition/synthesis (for hands-free interaction with the in-vehicle computing system), and using Intel's MMX technology to facilitate in-vehicle playing of full-length movies, videogames, and stereo selections. Intel had information on its Connected Car PC technology posted on its Web site (http://developer.intel.com/).

Intel and the U.S. Department of Energy were collaborating on a project to build the world's fastest supercomputers using Pentium Pro processors and off-the-shelf products and technologies. In December 1996, a supercomputer that utilized 7,264 Pentium Pro processors and that could perform 1 trillion operations per second was functioning, a computing achievement equivalent to breaking the sound barrier—the previous performance record was 368 billion operations per second. At completion, the project was expected to result in a supercomputer that used 9,200 Pentium Pro processors and that could perform 1.4 trillion operations per second.

INTEL'S PRINCIPAL COMPETITORS

In 1997, Intel's two biggest competitors were Advanced Micro Devices (AMD) and Cyrix, both of which made "Intel-clone" microprocessors and marketed them at prices below those charged by Intel. A partnership among Motorola, IBM, and Apple Computer to produce and market Power PC chips for Apple's line of PCs and for certain IBM PCs represented a third competitor. Sun Microsystems was a fourth competitor, producing and marketing a microprocessor line that competed against Intel chips in a limited number of computing applications.

Advanced Micro Devices

Since making its first Intel 8088 clone in the early 1980s, AMD had carved out a niche providing less expensive microprocessors than Intel's mainstream offerings. During the 1992–1996 period, AMD had supplied 40 million microprocessors for PCs, mostly 486 clones that went into the low-end PC models and brands. AMD's intended competitor for Intel's Pentium, the K5, was conceived as a high-end chip, but design flaws and defects delayed production over six months, cost the company sales with a number of PC vendors (including industry leader, Compaq Computer), and resulted in significant financial losses—AMD lost $69 million on sales of nearly $2 billion in 1996. AMD only sold 2 million K5 chips in 1996, mostly overseas. AMD introduced a redesigned 117 MHz K5 chip in spring 1997 that performed at speeds comparable to a 200 MHz Pentium and a Cyrix 6x86-166+. Acer had announced plans to use the new K5 chip in its low-end computers; Polywell was also marketing PCs with the K5. Expectations were that AMD would sell about 3 million K5 chips in 1997.

To bolster its competitive strength, AMD in early 1996 acquired NexGen for $630 million in stock (a price many Wall Street analysts viewed as exorbitant for a company with only $21 million in revenues). AMD, confident that NexGen had strong technology despite its low sales, promptly scrapped its own design for a chip to compete with Intel's Pentium Pro in favor of a design (subsequently named the K6) that NexGen had under development. Whereas previous generations of AMD chips had been clones of Intel's designs, AMD and NexGen engineers had designed the K5 and K6 from scratch. A licensing agreement with Intel gave AMD the right to see and use Intel's MMX technology to develop microprocessors with MMX-compatible features. However, because the K6's circuitry was different from the

Pentium Pro's, AMD had to implement its own version of MMX in its central processing unit. AMD also had to pay Intel a royalty for every MMX-compatible microprocessor it sold. AMD hoped that its K6 chip would be an attractive alternative to Intel's higher-priced Pentium Pro chip. AMD was planning to introduce 180, 200, and 233 MHz versions of its K6 chip during 1997 and a 300 MHz version was in the works for 1998.

AMD expected that 5 of the top 10 PC manufacturers would be using the K6 in some of their models during 1997; analysts projected that AMD could sell up to 5 million K6 chips in 1997. The K6 was expected to sell for about 25 percent less than Intel's Pentium Pro chips. As of 1997, AMD had two state-of-the-art chip fabrication plants. AMD's other lines of business, which accounted for 70 percent of revenues in 1996, were expected to do well in 1997; AMD was second to Intel in the market for flash memory.

Cyrix Corp

In early 1996, Cyrix introduced its 6x86 design—a 133 MHz chip—that outperformed Intel's Pentium 166 MHz chip. Later in 1996, Cyrix began marketing a 150 MHz version of its 6x86 design that matched the performance of Intel's 200 MHz Pentium chip. The superior performance of Cyrix's 6x86 designs was widely reported in PC industry publications. Cyrix expected the reported high performance of its 6x86 chips in laboratory tests to capture the attention of PC makers and draw sales away from Intel Pentiums, but as of early 1997 orders had been disappointingly low. Cyrix had a new M2 microprocessor which it planned to introduce in the second half of 1997 to compete against Intel's MMX Pentium Pro line. The M2 was expected to debut in 180 and 200 MHz versions, graduating to a 225 MHz version shortly thereafter. Rather than licensing MMX technology from Intel, Cyrix had equipped the M2 with its own version of the instruction set. Prior litigation between Cyrix and Intel had resulted in court decisions that gave Cyrix the right to clone MMX technology from public documentation and to use the MMX tag in marketing its own chips. Industry analysts expected Cyrix to be more successful in marketing its M2 against Intel's MMX Pentiums in the price-sensitive home computer and notebook segments; the stigma of a non-Intel chip posed a high barrier for Cyrix to hurdle in penetrating the high-end desktop and notebook segments, especially as concerned corporate PC buyers.

In 1995 Cyrix reported earnings of $15.6 million on revenues of $228 million; in 1996, the company lost $26 million on revenues of $184 million. Cyrix did not manufacture its own microprocessors, preferring instead to source them from IBM Microelectronics and SGS-Thomson Microelectronics.

Motorola, IBM, Apple Computer, and the Power PC

Motorola, Apple, and IBM initiated a partnership in 1991 to develop the Power PC chip as an alternative to Intel chips. After production delays and disagreements over design, IBM and Apple finally agreed to a common design in 1995. The Power PC (along with Sun Microsystems' UltraSPARC chip) was a reduced instruction-set computing (RISC) processor whereas Intel, AMD, and Cyrix chips were complex instruction-set computing (CISC) processors. Chips incorporating RISC designs used simpler instruction sets to achieve higher computing speeds than CISC processors. Historically, RISC designs also delivered better floating point performance (important to workstation users running computer-assisted design, imaging, and 3-D modeling applications), currently making them the leading option for professionals having calculation-intensive computing tasks. RISC chips had two big liabilities: they didn't have the widespread compatibility of CISC processors (they were backward incompatible) and there were substantially fewer software programs written for RISC processors.[27]

Motorola was the principal producer of Power PC chips for Apple's line of Macintosh PCs; Motorola supplied Power PCs for about 4 million Macintosh computers in 1995. Apple's market share of PC sales had eroded from 8 percent in 1995 to only about 5 percent in early 1997. Many corporate purchasers of PCs were concerned about Apple Computer's deteriorating financial condition (the company had lost $936 million in the last five quarters) and were skeptical about the ability of RISC-based chip producers and software developers to keep pace with the rapid technology advances being engineered by Intel and Microsoft. Apple had announced sharp cutbacks in R&D expenditures in an attempt to narrow its losses. However, Apple introduced a number of new, more powerful Macintosh models in February 1997 that management believed would help rejuvenate sales; Apple was also said to be considering a major push to promote wider use of lower-priced network PCs as a way to boost its sagging market share. IBM produced Power PCs for use in certain of its PC models, in workstations, and in servers; in 1996 IBM was the world's second largest PC vendor, with a market share of nearly 9 percent.

In 1996, Motorola earned $1.15 billion on sales of $28 billion; the company's 1996 earnings were well below the record of $1.8 billion set in 1995. IBM had 1996 earnings of $5.4 billion on sales of $76 billion. Apple Computer lost $867 million on sales of $8.8 billion in 1996.

INTEL'S FUTURE PROSPECTS

In 1997, Intel was expected to ship 80 million Pentium and Pentium Pro microprocessors for use in PCs and network servers. Worldwide sales of PCs were forecast to grow 15.5 percent in 1997 to $182.5 billion, an increase below the 20 percent growth in 1996. Worldwide spending on all computer products and services was expected to surpass $700 billion in 1997, equal to a growth rate of 12.3 percent (versus 14.1 percent in 1996 and 14.5 percent in 1995). The fastest growth was expected to occur in Asia outside Japan, where use of PCs was still relatively limited and where the market potential was largely untapped. The Chinese market was the largest in the Asia-Pacific region (with projected growth of 25–35 percent annually over the next several years), followed in order by Korea and Japan. PC sales in Europe were forecast to grow only 8 percent annually during the rest of the century because European companies were incorporating information technology into their operations at a slower pace. Both Andy Grove and Bill Gates in their recent trips to Europe had warned of a growing technology deficit between U.S. and European companies and the competitive danger to European companies of lagging behind in the use of PCs, e-mail, the Internet, company intranets, and company extranets (the term given to on-line links with suppliers and customers).

---

[27]Intel had developed its own RISC chip in the late 1980s because Andy Grove thought it would serve as a valuable insurance policy in case RISC technology won out over CISC technology (as many industry pundits were then predicting). At the time, Grove saw RISC technology as unlikely to replace CISC technology in PCs, despite its advantages, owing to the significant backward incompatibility problems.

Intel had 1,000 chip designers working on future chip generations; each generation under development was said by industry trade sources to be code-named for a Pacific Northwest river (Intel did not publicly comment on as yet unannounced chip generations). The *Klamath*, allegedly scheduled for introduction in mid-1997 according to industry reports, was said to be a smaller, less complex MMX version of the Pentium Pro; it supposedly would (1) have initial speeds of 233 MHz, graduating to 266 MHz soon thereafter, (2) have lower power consumption, (3) be more adept at running 16-bit code than the Pentium Pro, and (4) match the Pentium Pro's performance for 32-bit code.

Intel's subsequent chip generation, code-named the *Deschutes*, was said to be scheduled for market introduction in early 1998 and by year-end was expected to become Intel's Pentium Pro equivalent for portable or laptop PCs—Pentium Pro chips consumed too much power and generated too much heat to be used successfully in mobile PCs. Until then, high-end laptop PCs were expected to be equipped with 166- and possibly 200 MHz Pentium processors.

The *Katmai*, rumored to debut in mid-1998, was expected to advance MMX technology a notch (and to be known as MMX 2) by incorporating more 32-bit instructions than the original MMX (which consisted largely of 16-bit instructions). Industry sources believed that in late 1998, Intel would introduce its *Willamette* generation having the capabilities to outperform Klamath and Deschutes by close to 50 percent. Willamette chips were expected to be the chip of choice for desktop PCs in 1999 and most of 2000.

Late in 1999 or early in 2000, industry sources expected Intel to start shipping a radically more potent chip, code-named the *Merced,* that would incorporate a new chip architecture called *IA-64.* The Merced reportedly would have the capability to run 16-bit and 32-bit tasks without software assistance and would possess many of the advantages of RISC technology. However, for PC users to realize the Merced's full computing potential, a new 64-bit operating system (presumably from Microsoft) would be required.

Meanwhile, announcements of technology advances and new products were appearing daily to enhance the functionality of PCs at home and at work, use of the Internet, and use of company intranets and extranets. U.S. companies were leading the parade of hardware and software innovation worldwide; Asian companies were next in line and European companies trailed in developing infotech products. New developments were occurring at such a fast and furious pace that the end result was unpredictable. The Internet was central to most of the forthcoming developments in information technology. As Andy Grove put it, "The Internet is like a 20-foot tidal wave coming thousands of miles across the Pacific, and we are in kayaks. Its . . . gaining momentum, and its going to lift you and drop you. It affects everybody—the computer industry, telecommunications, the media, chipmakers, and the software world."[28]

TOP MANAGEMENT CHANGES AT INTEL

On May 21, 1997, Andy Grove relinquished the title of CEO, turning the reins over to Craig Barrett, who took on the title of president and CEO. Grove assumed the title of chairman of the board of directors, replacing Gordon Moore. Moore indicated that

---

[28]As quoted in Schendler, "A Conversation With the Lords of Wintel," p. 46.

as chairman emeritus he would continue to work three days a week at Intel. Grove's change in title signaled a likely cutback in the amount of time he would devote to daily operating issues, but he was expected to continue to exert strong influence over the company's strategy and long-term direction. Grove, who underwent a much-publicized series of treatments for prostate cancer in 1996, was said to be healthy and was expected to remain Intel's chairman for as much as five years, maybe more.

Barrett, 57, was a former Stanford University management professor prior to joining Intel in 1974. He became head of manufacturing in 1990 and had been Intel's chief operating officer since 1993, with responsibility for running most of Intel's day-to-day operations. He was regarded as a no-nonsense manager who had been instrumental, along with Grove, in making Intel's manufacturing operations a strategic asset. Barrett had coordinated the company's aggressive expansion of chipmaking capacity during the 1990s and led Intel's effort to incorporate the latest chip-processing technologies.

Barrett was an avid outdoorsman who spent much of his leisure time fishing at his Montana ranch; he lived in Phoenix because of its proximity to mountains where he liked to hike, commuting to Intel headquarters in Santa Clara three days a week and working from an Intel office in Phoenix the other two days. Barrett's management style differed from Andy Grove's; according to Barrett:[29]

> I don't run Intel. I delegate, and Intel runs itself. I try to rally the people around a goal and get them all aimed at achieving it.

Asked about the pace of change and technology advance that Intel was pioneering, Barrett replied:[30]

> We picture ourselves going down the road at 120 miles an hour. Somewhere there's going to be a brick wall to cross, but our view is it's better to run into the wall than to anticipate it and stop short.

(For those who might be interested, there's a wealth of information available at the company's Web site—*www.intel.com.*)

---

[29]As quoted in the *The Wall Street Journal*, January 14, 1997, p. B1.
[30]As quoted in Kirkpatrick, "Intel's Amazing Profit Machine," p. 72.

THE FUDGE COTTAGE*

Deborah R. Ettington, *Eastern Michigan University*

Shalini Venkateswaran, *Eastern Michigan University*

Christine Overhiser North would soon become sole owner of The Fudge Cottage, though she had been functioning as the primary decision maker for several years. She had helped her parents with their business since it was started in Ridgefield, Michigan, in 1981. Her involvement grew as her parents aged and began to have health problems. They planned to transfer their shares of the business to her within the next couple of years. In the past few years, Christine had been so occupied with the daily operations, she had given little thought to the future. She was spending too much time at the store, yet did not seem to be making enough profit to support her family. This had become a bigger concern since she was going through a divorce and could not depend on her husband's financial contributions. Sales had been flat at around $200,000 for five years, down from their highest level of $250,000 in 1987. Christine wanted to spend more time with her daughter, and she was concerned about future medical expenses for her parents. Should she sell the business and look for other employment? She had to decide on a plan of action.

> Our family has been in business twelve years here. We've been working hard doing what we thought was a good job but we don't seem to be getting anywhere. For the amount of stress and work, we need to figure out if we can do better. It has felt like I was helping

*Serpil Bayraktar participated in the field research. This case was originally presented at the 1995 annual meeting of the North American Case Research Association. The authors gratefully acknowledge the generosity of the people of The Fudge Cottage. All events and individuals are real, but names of the company, people, and locations have been disguised at the business owner's request.

Mom and Dad out. I didn't feel like it was a real job. Now I have this big baby and I'm not sure what to do with it. I'm almost 40, and now that I need to support myself and my daughter, I need to start thinking about what's good for us. Is it worth my investing more time in the business?

HISTORY OF THE FUDGE COTTAGE

Mr. and Mrs. Fred Overhiser started The Fudge Cottage on October 1, 1981, in Ridgefield, a small city north of Detroit, Michigan. Mr. Overhiser learned how to make fudge from one of the best fudge makers on Mackinac Island and then improved the recipe. (Mackinac Island was a well-known Northern Michigan tourist destination with fudge made and sold in a number of stores.) Mrs. Overhiser described how the business started.

In 1981 there was a bad recession. Fred's company went bankrupt and my job moved to St. Louis, but I wanted to be where my kids were. Fred wasn't very employable, but he knew how to make fudge. The more he made it, the more he understood the nature of it and experimented to make it the best.

We started out doing wholesale from the back of a deli. Fred and I worked seven days and nights a week. He would make it; I would cut and package it. We'd go out together to drugstores and small supermarkets and party stores and sell them our fudge. We got into the Quick Pic stores at the end of the year. On Christmas Day, my son Carl, Christine, Fred and I were making these hangers to hang poles from the ceiling near the cash register. Big companies could spend money to get close to the register, but we couldn't get shelf space.

It got to be too much. We tried a delivery service owned by a woman we knew. That got us 7-Eleven and another big account, but her ladies didn't want to carry fudge. They set it where the hot air register would blow on it. At first the money was coming in, then it was going down, but we were working so hard we didn't have time to notice we were on the verge of bankruptcy. We decided we needed to have our own retail operation, so no one could do that to us again.

In May 1982 the Overhisers began their first retail operation on the opening day of a weekend flea market. On the day after Thanksgiving 1982, they opened their second retail store in downtown Ridgefield, about 20 miles from the flea market. After moving production to this new location, the Overhisers concentrated more on retail sales and gradually phased out of the wholesale market, so that by 1984 The Fudge Cottage had very few wholesale accounts. The Overhisers also started carrying other lines of products made outside of their establishment, including handmade chocolates.

In 1983 The Fudge Cottage had sales revenues of $94,000, and net income was over $8,000. By 1986 sales had increased to $225,000, but the business was losing money. Over the years as the opportunities arose, they supplied fudge to the Detroit Zoo and tour boats serving Boblo Island, a Canadian amusement park on the Detroit River. From August through October 1986, the Overhisers sold over 3,000 pounds of fudge during the "Yes! Michigan" campaign at Chuck Muer Restaurants, a very successful group of seafood restaurants. An opportunity arose to open a kiosk in a food court in an upscale suburban mall. Christine described how the opportunity turned sour.

We were convinced we needed to add more stores. What a mistake—just a nightmare. Costs kept escalating, the opening kept being delayed. Finally, we had to pull out. They sued us to recover their costs in preparing the site, and we settled out of court for around $8,000. After that, we lost confidence; we didn't trust our judgment anymore.

Sales peaked in 1987 at $250,000. By 1989 sales had declined to $197,000, so in 1990 the Overhisers added a third retail site, a space in another weekend-only flea market, about 50 miles from Ridgefield. Mrs. Overhiser described the rise and fall of this location.

> The place was so huge, twice the size of the other market. They wanted us to come in, thought it was big enough to handle two fudge stores, so they put us on the far side from each other. It started out terrific, but there wasn't enough demand for two stores.
>
> We decided to close after two years—it was a relief to not have to bother with it.

By 1993 sales at the original two locations had returned to $211,000, but the company was losing money. (See Exhibits 1 and 2 for financial statements from 1989 to 1993.) Christine cut her own salary.

> We had to cut back, things weren't working. If I had to go without a salary in the summer I'd do it to get things back on track.

CHRISTINE'S BACKGROUND

As Christine considered what other career options she might pursue, she recalled that she had always been involved with food and that she enjoyed working with people and applying her artistic abilities.

> In high school I worked at a cider mill, I really enjoyed it. It was hustle bustle, really busy. The owners were good people. They treated me like a day manager. I was self-motivated. I always looked for things to do.
>
> After that I worked in a new health food store started by a friend's mom. Everyone left but me, so I ended up being the manager. I was good at organizing; it was all common sense, although I didn't really have any training for what I was doing.
>
> Then I went to work at Charlie's, a Chuck Muer restaurant. It was a good corporation—they had procedures, manuals, tests for everything. I waitressed, hostessed, cashiered, bartended. Sometimes I'd help the managers. It was good training on salesmanship and how to relate to people. I was there a total of 6½ years, then there was a lot of stress for me associated with bartending and I developed a back problem. It was time for me to go.

Christine had helped her parents with bookkeeping from the beginning, but in the spring of 1983 she began to work in the store full-time to help them out.

> Based on my restaurant experience, I saw what needed to be done and I developed procedures, opening and closing checklists, a manual for the cash register. If anyone had any problems they would know what to do.
>
> We had an employee who was a fudge maker; she wasn't used to reporting to anyone. Dad didn't like to confront her; he would just let her show up when she could. I was used to working with people who were responsible. Jackie sometimes wouldn't show up or would be hours late. We bucked heads so she didn't stay too much longer.
>
> It used to be play, using my artistic ability. I was doing what I loved, having flexibility, having Mom and Dad there to help with my daughter. I still really enjoy designing the store displays, gift baskets, tins and trays, making sure everything is attractive, so that the patterns and colors have a flow and balance.

EXHIBIT 1   The Fudge Cottage's Income Statements, 1989–1993

	1989	1990	1991	1992	1993
Sales	$ 197,284	$ 209,910	$219,908	$ 216,440	$ 210,919
Purchases	83,756	92,888	85,679	93,200	90,001
Gross profit	$ 113,528	$ 117,022	$134,229	$ 123,240	$ 120,918
Operating expenses:					
Rent*	$ 28,335	$ 28,830	$ 36,918	$ 33,283	$ 29,262
Vehicle expenses	1,844	402	1,205	1,883	3,337
Depreciation	3,982	3,705	3,608	2,610	1,355
Insurance†	924	1,891	6,993	11,090	10,168
Utilities	2,149	2,477	2,677	2,767	2,775
Maintenance	1,418	1,200	1,169	1,887	1,437
Officers salaries‡	25,850	29,140	25,341	21,420	9,800
Interest	2,641	1,537	1,725	1,831	2,973
Total fixed expenses	$ 67,143	$ 69,182	$ 79,636	$ 76,771	$ 61,107
Telephone	1,665	1,692	2,044	2,073	1,819
Advertising and promotion	4,671	4,600	3,135	3,615	5,985
Delivery	0	0	0	0	40
Store supplies	7,152	7,860	8,541	10,022	9,887
Wages	21,988	25,886	23,275	22,779	29,748
Office expenses	1,844	1,895	2,262	3,294	2,643
Legal and accounting	3,416	2,483	2,058	1.188	2,587
Payroll taxes	4,358	4,950	4,459	4,600	3,666
Other taxes	1,163	991	1,034	599	907
Outside services	0	204	759	207	20
Total selling & admin expenses	$ 46,257	$ 50,561	$ 47,567	$ 48,377	$ 57,702
Miscellaneous costs§	939	1,149	1,549	1,801	2,805
Total operating expenses	$ 114,339	$ 120,892	$128,752	$ 126,949	$ 121,614
Operating income (loss)	$ (811)	$ (3,870)	$ 5,477	$ (3,709)	$ (696)
Other income (Exp.)					
Misc. income	$ 236	$ 15	$ 0	$ 0	$ 0
Sale of equipment	1,303	0	0	207	759
Total other income	$ 1,539	$ 15	$ 0	$ 207	$ 759
Net income before taxes	$ 728	$ (3,855)	$ 5,477	$ (3,502)	$ 63

*Rent includes $15,000 per year for Ridgefield and 23% of sales at the flea market stores.
†Includes business insurance and health insurance for Christine, her parents, her daughter, Stacy and Mike.
‡This is the annual amount that Christine takes out of the business as a salary.
§Includes dues and subscriptions, travel and entertainment, educational expense, and donations.

Source: Company Records.

EXHIBIT 2   The Fudge Cottage's Balance Sheets, Years Ending September 30, 1989–1993

	1989	1990	1991	1992	1993
Assets					
Current assets					
Cash	$ 1,813	$ (1,273)	$ (969)	$ (1,701)	$ 2,061
Inventory	12,777	10,759	9,434	7,436	11,441
Employee advances	200	200	200	200	200
Prepaid tax	. . .	. . .	. . .	249	. . .
Total current assets	$ 14,790	$ 9,686	$ 8,665	$ 6,184	$ 13,701
Fixed assets					
Equipment	$ 18,776	$ 19,076	$ 22,192	$ 22,192	$ 19,635
Vehicles	11,076	11,076	11,076	. . .	. . .
Leasehold improvements	17,125	17,313	21,629	22,379	22,379
Total fixed assets	$ 46,977	$ 47,465	$ 54,897	$ 44,571	$ 42,014
Less: Accumulated depreciation	(35,117)	(38,822)	(42,430)	(38,150)	(37,446)
Net fixed assets	$ 11,860	$ 8,643	$ 12,467	$ 6,421	$ 4,569
Other assets:					
Deposits	1,300	1,300	1,300	1,300	1,300
Total assets	$ 27,950	$ 19,629	$ 22,432	$ 13,905	$ 19,570
Liabilities and Shareholders' Equity					
Current liabilities					
Installment payable—auto	$ 2,292	$ 2,641	$ 2,641	. . .	. . .
Installment payable—bank	250	. . .	878	. . .	. . .
Notes payable	5,000	4,000	4,000	4,000	. . .
Income tax payable	. . .	. . .	. . .	. . .	869
Accrued taxes	347	348	325	295	(121)
Total current liabilities	$ 7,889	$ 6,989	$ 7,844	$ 4,295	$ 748
Long-term liabilities					
Installment payable	. . .	. . .	. . .	. . .	$ 902
Installment payable—auto	7,427	4,786	2,144	. . .	. . .
Loans from shareholders	6,796	5,871	4,984	5,625	9,035
Total long-term liabilities	$ 14,233	$ 10,657	$ 7,128	$ 5,625	$ 9,937
Shareholder's equity					
Common stock	$ 300	$ 300	$ 300	$ 300	$ 300
Retained earnings	5,538	1,683	7,160	3,658	8,584
Total shareholder's equity	$ 5,838	$ 1,983	$ 7,460	$ 3,958	$ 8,884
Total liability and shareholder's equity	$ 27,950	$ 19,629	$ 22,432	$ 13,905	$ 19,570

Source: Company Records.

EXHIBIT 3   U.S. Manufacturers' Shipments of Confectionery Products: 1981 to 1992

Year	Quantity (millions of pounds)	Value (millions of dollars)	Per Capita Consumption (pounds)*	Per Capita Consumption (dollars)*
1992	5,314	$10,265	21.2	$40.40
1991	4,989	9,710	20.3	38.90
1990	4,840	9,004	20.1	36.70
1989	4,852	8,682	20.4	35.80
1988	4,570	8,278	19.2	34.40
1987	4,231	7,678	18.3	32.30
1986	4,201	7,280	18.4	31.30
1985	4,326	7,092	19.1	30.70
1984	4,265	6,610	18.9	28.90
1983	4,064	5,983	17.9	26.70
1982	3,798	5,650	16.7	24.80
1981	3,630	5,171	16.1	22.90

*Production plus imports minus exports divided by population, including armed forces abroad, as of July 1, 1992 of 257,919,000.

Source: U.S. Department of Commerce, Bureau of the Census, *Current Industrial Reports* and *Current Population Reports.*

When the Overhisers began to experience health problems that kept them from working regularly, Christine took over more and more responsibility and began to wonder if it was worth it.

I'm pulled in so many directions. I try not to be here when I don't have to, but I work twelve to fifteen hours a day, seven days a week during the holidays. I'm the last one to leave town. After the store closes, I'm packing orders, then I go upstairs and do book work. By 1:00 in the morning my legs feel like rubber. Then I have to do it all over again the next day.

Christine's attorney suggested that she try looking for assistance at a local college. As a result, she began working with two MBA students who gathered information for her about the competition and the market. The students used the Internet and library databases to locate information about candy demand and supply.

CONFECTIONERY CONSUMPTION IN THE UNITED STATES

The confectionery industry consisted of chocolate and nonchocolate candies. Exhibits 3 and 4 show trends in U.S. manufacturers' shipments of confectionery products. According to some industry observers, chocolates were declining in popularity relative to nonchocolate candies due to the higher fat content of chocolate (see excerpts from articles in Exhibit 5). Yet, other observers noted that the healthy food craze seemed to have peaked in 1990, and consumers were only interested in healthier

EXHIBIT 4 Quantity and Value of Shipments of Confectionery by Type of Product, 1992 and 1991 (Quantity in Millions of Pounds; Value in Millions of Dollars)

	1992		1991	
	Quantity	**Value**	**Quantity**	**Value**
Total shipments	5,314	$10,265	4,989	$9,710
Chocolate	2,657	6,565	2,615	6,452
Solid	356	774	337	688
Solid with inclusions	71	759	239	650
Enrobed or molded				
Candy, fruit, or nut center	1,261	2,986	1,265	3,015
Bakery product center	176	410	164	383
Panned	383	989	439	1,139
Assortments and other	210	646	172	578
Nonchocolate type	2,461	3,323	2,200	2,926
Hard candy	698	1,089	657	1,003
Chewy candy	408	670	397	664
Soft candy	644	611	588	548
Iced coated	28	45	29	53
Panned	507	702	369	471
Licorice	176	206	160	187
Confectionery not specified by kind	195	377	174	332

Source: U.S. Department of Commerce, Bureau of the Census, *Current Industrial Reports.*

products if they tasted good (*Advertising Age,* May 2, 1994, p. S-6). Candy consumption was also believed to be somewhat countercyclical: "When people can't afford big luxuries, they downscale a bit. A video rental and a box of candy replaces dinner and a movie" (*DM,* February 1994, p. 56). Christine wasn't sure to what extent these observations were relevant for a specialty store such as The Fudge Cottage which focused on premium quality sweets.

FUDGE AND CHOCOLATE RETAILERS IN MICHIGAN

According to the American Business Directories, in Michigan in 1993 sixteen retailers, including The Fudge Cottage, specialized in fudge. Of the 16 businesses, only 7 could be reached by telephone to respond to a survey developed by the MBA students. The remaining businesses were closed for the winter. Exhibit 6 gives survey questions and results.

The variety of products sold in seven retail businesses surveyed were very similar, ranging from fudge, brittle, taffy, chocolate, candy, and ice cream to gift baskets and other confectionery items. Most of the 16 fudge stores in Michigan were located in recreational areas and catered to vacationers and water sports enthusiasts. Therefore, summer was their busiest season. This was contrary to The Fudge Cottage's busy season, which ran from August to April. (See Exhibit 7 for sales by month in 1988.)

EXHIBIT 5   Excerpts from Four Published Reports Concerning U.S.
Confectionery Consumption, 1994–1995

- A West Coast merchant notes that "right now, for example, the nonchocolate items are really heating up. For a while chocolate was the market heavy, now the chewy and hard candy items are making headway." The reason for the shift? Some say chocolate was indeed "heavy," with a higher fat content than sugar-based candy items. . . . A healthy serving of savory new entries in the nonchocolate segment of the candy market has others speculating that the new products are also driving the market shift. "People, especially kids, are always looking for something new," says a West Coast buyer. "Five years ago new items in the chocolate category were boosting sales in that area; today, it's new items in nonchocolate." (*DM,* February 1994, p. 56)

- Research by NPD Group, a market researcher, shows consumers' concerns about serving food with fat are stabilizing, with 49% saying they're very cautious about serving such foods, compared with 51% in 1990. It's not that Americans are kicking the health habit. They're tired of compromising on taste. (*Advertising Age,* May 1994, p. S-6.)

- The entire nonchocolate segment of the candy market, while still dwarfed by chocolate, has grown significantly over the past year, primarily because of its lack of fat. Sales of nonchocolate candy for 1994 amounted to $143.7 million, compared to $765.2 million for chocolate. However, shipments of nonchocolate candy grew 4.8% during that same period, compared to 0.8% for chocolate. . . . Some makers of chocolate candy are coming out with new, lower-fat products, hoping to pre-empt a shift away from chocolate. (*Brandweek,* September 1995, pp. 39–40)

- According to the 1993 Consumer Survey of Lite Confections, Americans will buy a greater quantity and variety of lite candies if they taste good. The study discovered that: 1. Interest in both lower fat and lower calorie confections is strong. 2. Taste is a key ingredient to gain trial and repeat sales. 3. Lower fat and lower calorie together may be better received than either claim alone. 4. Many consumers expect to pay more for lite confections. 5. Teens are more favorably disposed to lite confections. (*Candy Industry,* January 1995, pp. 48–50)

Respondents agreed that sales in the last five years were either the same or worse compared to previous years, but that sales had started increasing again in 1993.

Five of the seven companies had two branches in Michigan, both located in tourist areas. Only two firms, the national retail chain Fannie May, and a company based in the tourist town of Frankenmuth, had more than five stores around Michigan. All but Fannie May were family-run small businesses with 3 to 10 employees, depending on the time of the year. Their experience in the market ranged from 6 to 107 years.

In specialty chocolates, there were two nationwide chains, Godiva and Fannie May, with stores located in shopping malls near Ridgefield. Major department stores in the malls also carried different lines of hand-made chocolates. The Godiva chocolates were priced around $28 per pound.

RIDGEFIELD, MICHIGAN

The Fudge Cottage's principal market was Ridgefield, Michigan. Downtown Ridgefield was considered quaint and attracted visitors from other Detroit suburbs, especially during several seasonal festivals. The Downtown Development Authority was planning a $2.8 million renovation of the two intersecting downtown streets, Main

---

EXHIBIT 6   Results of Telephone Survey of 7 Michigan Fudge Shops

1. What are your main products?

Fudge	7	Brittle	1
Chocolate	5	Taffy	2
Ice Cream	2	Candy	4

2. Do you do wholesale and mail order or only retail? Who are your customers?

Occasional mail order	5	All	2
Mostly retail (customers are tourists)	7		

3. Total number of branches you have open in the United States.

2 branches	5	Many branches around U.S.	1
5 to 6 branches	1		

4. How long have you been in business?

6 years	4	30 years	1
Up to 13 years	1	107 years	1

5. How many employees do you have (full time and part time)?

2 FT, 3 PT	1	10 FT	1
3 FT	3	35 to 100 PT and FT total,	
4 FT, 1 district manager	1	depending on the season	1

6. How much fudge do you make in a day (average)?

30–50 lb/day	2	Hard to say	4
Make fudge once a week (undecided about exact quantity)	1		

7. What form of advertising do you use?

Brochures	2	Only newspapers	1
Local newspapers and coupons	3	Very little	1

8. What is your busiest season?

Summer	4	Thanksgiving to New Year's	1
October	1	No peak season	1

9. How do you evaluate sales during the last five years?

1993 has been good	2	Has varied, 1993 good	1
Same the last five years	3	Slow because of recession	1

10. How much do you charge per pound of fudge?

$6.95	3	$8.95	1
$7.50	1	Would not	
$8.80	1	tell surveyor	1

---

and Church, and the sidewalks. The Fudge Cottage was located in a small section of stores just off Main Street. Neighboring stores sold gifts and specialty crafts. Other downtown stores specialized in bridal needs, products made in Michigan, greeting cards, and fine art. The historic district on the other side of town was known for its antique stores, which attracted out-of-town shoppers. There were also many gift and flower shops in the surrounding community outside the downtown. (See Exhibit 8 for occupancy rates and demographics for the area.)

The one other candy store in downtown Ridgefield, Martin's Candy, was also family-owned. Christine believed its service was probably about the same as at The Fudge Cottage, but it had a more old-fashioned look. The product line was also different; Martin's chocolate offerings tended to be lower-priced (around $12 per

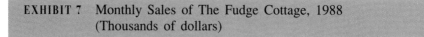

EXHIBIT 7   Monthly Sales of The Fudge Cottage, 1988
(Thousands of dollars)

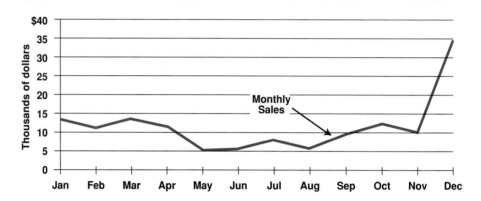

pound), mostly molded chocolates they made themselves off the premises. Martin's also carried bagged hard candy and frozen yogurt. Christine knew that store personnel at Martin's sometimes referred customers looking for fudge, truffles, or European chocolates to The Fudge Cottage. Martin's Candy was located on Main Street, which Christine considered a much better location than the location for The Fudge Cottage because of more visibility from the street and the greater volume of foot traffic, especially during festivals. On the other hand, The Fudge Cottage had a small parking lot in front which was much more convenient than parallel parking on Main Street.

THE FUDGE COTTAGE STAFF

The Fudge Cottage employed two regular nonfamily members. Stacy, who worked at the counter full-time, had been employed at the Ridgefield store since 1985 and was viewed almost as a member of the family. Christine felt they had a very good working relationship and made a good team at work. Stacy had recently been voted "best sales clerk" in a "best in town" contest sponsored by the local newspaper. Christine was proud of this recognition of Stacy's rapport with customers. She recognized that Stacy's sincere approach to working with customers to find the right gift or product to serve for a special event was invaluable to The Fudge Cottage's reputation for service. In addition to working on the counter, Stacy helped Christine in almost every aspect of the business including public relations, promotions, advertising, packaging, and preparing gift baskets.

Mike had been working part-time for about 2 years, learning to make fudge and brittle from Mr. Overhiser, who continued to work 20 hours a week when his health permitted. Mike appeared to enjoy his job.

> Fred can be a pain to work for, but he took me in when I needed a job and taught me how to make fudge. I'm going to make it the best I can for as long as I can.

Friends and other family members helped out weekends at the flea market. Additional minimum wage earners were hired for the retail counter during peak sales seasons. Christine reported that Stacy and Mike knew the business and customers well enough to provide excellent customer service, but she had a difficult time hiring additional helpers with the needed interpersonal skills and dependable work habits. Many businesses in the area had "help wanted" signs posted.

EXHIBIT 8   Demographics of Ridgefield, Michigan

Population	
1990 Census:	35,476
2000 Projected:	40,953
Average household income:	$46,000
Employment, by occupation	
Professional	2,889
Clerical	2,865
Management	2,326
Craftsmen	2,065
Operators	1,881
Technical	572
Other	4,265
Total	16,863
Years of schooling	
High school	35%
College 1–3 years	19%
College 4+ years	27%
Unemployment rate:	2.4%
Largest taxpayers	
Utility companies	2
Manufacturing companies	6
Real estate firms	3
Packaging company	1
Research & development firms	8
Grocery chain	1
Service firms	3

Downtown businesses: 130 stores; 75% retail and 25% services, including real estate, law, and insurance.

Occupancy rate of downtown storefronts	
1992:	90%
1993:	98%

Business changes in 1993:
  19 stores closed
  28 stores opened
  8 expansions
  4 changes of ownership

Source: Chamber of Commerce; Downtown Development Authority.

An outside accounting service helped The Fudge Cottage file its tax returns and prepared its financial statements. Christine had completed courses on small business management and accounting and had recently purchased a personal computer. She wondered if she should do more of the bookkeeping herself. She was also contemplating taking some classes on Windows and DOS applications.

Christine found herself working 80 or more hours during the busiest weeks, and knew she was not as efficient as she would like to be. She had to help Stacy and Mike selling on the counter or making fudge during store hours and very little time was available to complete all the paperwork and other things associated with the business. This led to Stacy working overtime to complete all necessary tasks, a condition that had in the past proved expensive.

Christine made all business decisions herself, after extensive discussions with her staff, especially Stacy. In recent months her father had been mainly interested in the fudge making, but she did sometimes clash with him when she wanted to do something different from what had been done before.

> I guess I'm too much like Dad sometimes; we're both stubborn. Mom serves as a good sounding board for both of us, but because her health prevents her from being at the store, she's not usually around when a conflict comes up. Sometimes I back off when Dad disagrees, but other times I don't. He has a big heart, but not always a good business sense.

"EVERYONE WILL EAT CHOCOLATE . . . SELECT PEOPLE LOVE FUDGE"

Stacy described the Ridgefield customers:

> Most customers are women between 25 and 55. Women buy a piece or two at a time. Men are honest about how much they'll eat, and buy more. We have a lot of repeat customers. I bet we have a couple hundred regular customers that I know kind of what they like. A lot of people from businesses around here.
>
> Everyone will eat chocolate. People buy chocolates because they have a sweet tooth. Fudge is different; select people love fudge. I think fudge is associated with Mackinac, a Michigan-made thing. I remember when I was a little girl we used to go up to Mackinac in the summer, and we always bought fudge.

Christine and Stacy felt that the Ridgefield customers were price-sensitive, and followed discount offerings and coupons very carefully.

Mrs. Overhiser observed that customers at the flea market location had changed over time:

> Originally, the flea market had traders dealing in antiques and hand-crafted items, and shoppers were mostly working class. Over the past two years, the merchandise has changed to factory closeouts and low-priced items, and shoppers are mostly bargain hunters.
>
> Income is down considerably from what it used to be. It isn't just us. A lot of people who've been there a long time are considering pulling out, although there is always someone to take their place.

In addition to retail sales, the Fudge Cottage had some corporate accounts including accounting firms, law firms, a telephone company, and a dental office. The firms ordered fudge for Christmas and other holidays and accounted for 4 to 5 percent of total sales in 1993. Christine believed corporate clients were less price-sensitive, but she also thought that if The Fudge Cottage attempted a large price increase, they might choose to buy other gift items.

WOULD YOU LIKE A SAMPLE?

The Fudge Cottage produced a large variety of fudge flavors, hand-made chocolates, and peanut and cashew brittle. It also carried such specialty candy as Jelly Belly's, and decorative gift tins. Purchases were gift-wrapped at no additional charge. Chris-

EXHIBIT 9   Fudge Cottage Products

Fudge Flavors
    Chocolate
    Vanilla
    German chocolate
    Chocolate pecan
    Chocolate walnut
    Oreo
    Michigan cherry
    Pumpkin
    Maple walnut
    Peanut butter
    Raspberry

Brittle Flavors
    Peanut
    Cashew

Hand-Made Chocolates
    Potato chips dipped in milk, dark, and white chocolate
    Graham crackers dipped in milk or dark chocolate
    Miniature truffles
    Chocolate-covered pretzels
    Macadamia snappers
    Cashew snappers
    Almond snappers
    Chocolate-covered oreos
    Chocolate creams
    Sugar-free chocolates
    Sugar-free truffles
    Sugar-free snappers

Source: Observation of case writer.

tine enjoyed choosing the gift wrap, and received many compliments on the quality of its wrapping and other packaging. At the Ridgefield store only, The Fudge Cottage retailed a unique line of handmade chocolates, including a dietetic version, that was obtained from a supplier. (See Exhibit 9 for a sample of products sold.) At the flea market, The Fudge Cottage primarily sold fudge and caramel apples.

The Fudge Cottage had always followed a markup system for pricing its products. A 100 percent markup was added to the purchase price of chocolates and candies to determine the retail price. A 200 percent markup was added to the cost of ingredients for pricing fudge and brittle. (See Exhibit 10 for sales breakdowns and prices.)

Christine was proud that The Fudge Cottage was well-known in the Ridgefield area and received a lot of support from the local churches and Chamber of Commerce. Mrs. Overhiser believed that the store owed much of its reputation to her husband's fondness for passing out samples of his fudge in the early days.

Every afternoon Fred wouldn't say anything but he'd bag up some fudge or brittle and take off for a walk. He'd visit different merchants and they'd give samples to their customers.

EXHIBIT 10 Store Data

Dimensions of Stores
Ridgefield
  Total   1450 square feet: 1/3 retail; 1/3 production; 1/3 office
                           and storage
  Flea Market   196 square feet

Revenue Mix
  Ridgefield   25% fudge; 40% chocolates; 35% other candy
  Flea Market   75% fudge; 25% caramel apples and bulk candy

Product Prices—1993
  Fudge $6.50/pound
  Hand-made chocolates   15.95/pound
  Other candies   5.50/pound average

Source: Interviews with management

He liked being generous to people, liked extra advertising. He basked in the glory of people raving about his wonderful fudge and brittle at events. We'd cut up pounds and pounds of fudge, walking around offering samples during events.

The Fudge Cottage had experimented with different promotions. In 1991 and 1992 it tried advertising on cable TV in response to a promotional price from the local cable company. As the promotional price was effective only for two years, the Overhiser's decided not to pursue it further. The Fudge Cottage had used coupons extensively in the past. It was also involved in a "Ridgefield Shopper" discount card program that was a joint effort by downtown businesses to respond to competition from shopping malls. Christine and her parents had not formally evaluated the effects of these promotions. However, they felt that the cable TV advertising had been successful, but that response to the Ridgefield Shopper card had not been positive due to inconsistency in how different merchants implemented the program.

THE PASSION OF FUDGE MAKING

Mr. Overhiser learned the recipe for fudge from a Mackinac Island fudge maker and modified it by using only natural ingredients and eliminating the use of preservatives. His secret recipe fudge could be refrigerated and frozen without spoiling the taste or developing the granular texture common to Mackinac fudge. However, as the product was made with no preservatives, the shelf life was one to two weeks unless it was frozen. Because of the short shelf life, The Fudge Cottage product was less attractive to corporate and wholesale accounts than mass-manufactured fudge. Mr. Overhiser believed that if the recipe was changed to incorporate preservatives, he would probably need outside expertise.

Due to limited facilities and staff, The Fudge Cottage could only make either fudge or brittle at any one time. There was no formal production schedule, but different flavors of fudge or brittle were produced when inventory appeared low. There was a window between the production and retail areas so that customers could observe fudge or brittle being made. Mr. Overhiser controlled the quality of the fudge making personally.

I teach these young people how to make it. Once they learn it, they go off on their own and do it their way and they get soft batches and then we have to throw it away.

His wife believed fudge making was the "passion of his life."

It fills a need for him. When people make comments about the candy, when things are going well at the store, he is happy, and he hums while he works.

In fact, Christine found that sometimes it was difficult to prevent her father from making fudge, even if it wasn't needed.

Fudge and brittle were made of sugar, cocoa, butter, and nuts. The major ingredient for making fudge was sugar, which was obtained from a dealer who had agreed to supply sugar to The Fudge Cottage at a price based on the price of sugar quoted on the commodities exchange. Christine had been investigating nut suppliers in the area and believed that the nuts were being purchased at a fair price for nuts.

FILLING OUT THE PRODUCT LINE

Nonchocolate candies sold at The Fudge Cottage were purchased from 10 to 15 large suppliers and regional candy distributors. The other materials that The Fudge Cottage bought were packing and gift wrapping materials. Christine continually investigated sources of supply to obtain the lowest price and highest quality possible.

Christine was concerned about The Fudge Cottage's dependence on a single supplier for the fine hand-made chocolates sold in the Ridgefield store. The supplier, a small business located 50 miles away, was owned by a man about her parents' age, and Christine wondered if he might be planning to retire soon. If he sold the business, would the quality remain the same? If he closed the business, Christine would need to locate another supplier. She had tried other suppliers in the past and found their quality lacking. Another problem was that the chocolate supplier had increased his prices annually. Christine was reluctant to raise retail prices frequently because her customers were so price-sensitive.

SOURCES OF FUNDS

The Fudge Cottage had relied on family in the past for funds to expand the business, which limited the level of investment they had been able to undertake. At the end of 1993, The Fudge Cottage had $3700 in loans outstanding from Christine and her parents. (See the balance sheet in Exhibit 2.)

Christine had found that over the years the business generated positive cash flow from September to May. But The Fudge Cottage had to draw from a bank line of credit from May through August at interest rates Christine considered high. Varying monthly sales between May and August made it hard to predict the amount of borrowing. Every year, so far, the business had managed to repay its seasonal borrowings from cash inflows received between September and April.

OPPORTUNITIES FOR THE BUSINESS

Stacy was encouraging Christine to consider an opportunity to relocate to a larger retail space on Main Street. Christine had heard that other businesses had grown significantly after moving onto Main or Church, but she was concerned about the added expense of the higher rent and the risk of lost sales because some current customers would fail to follow the business to a new location. Opening a store in a

EXHIBIT 11 Cost of Leasing Pushcart at Fairlane Mall	
Security deposit (refundable when merchant leaves)	$150.00
New merchant fee (one-time fee for startup costs, first six halogen bulbs, and use of signs, employee aprons, and market stool)	$375.00
Monthly cleaning/marketing fee (includes merchant association fee, common area cleaning, electricity, trash collection)	$110.00
Monthly rent, plus 12% of sales over $1250 per week	
January–October	$ 1,000
November and December	$ 2,000

Source: Mall St. Journal, Fairlane Mall, Dearborn, MI, Fall 1994.

local mall was another possibility, but Christine believed the mall rental rates were much higher than she was paying currently. (See Exhibit 11 for information gathered by the MBA students about the cost of renting a pushcart in one mall.) Christine was also afraid of repeating previous bad experiences with new areas.

> I'm afraid to leave this place and go somewhere else. It all fits and works well here. Yet I'm also afraid of someone coming in and doing it bigger and better.

Christine was aware that if preservatives could be added to the fudge, The Fudge Cottage could pursue wholesale and corporate accounts further away from Ridgefield. Were there other things she should consider? How could she find the time to investigate new ideas, while still running the store and caring for her family? Should she try to sell the store and move on to something else?

THE FUTURE FOR CHRISTINE AND THE FUDGE COTTAGE

Christine commented on her experiences at The Fudge Cottage and the satisfaction she got out of her management roles:

> I guess I'm really a pretty simple person. I just want to be happy at what I'm doing, knowing that I can do it with integrity and honesty. The store fulfills a lot of things for me. I feel natural, comfortable, in a business setting. There's a lot of fulfillment here. It feels really good when the store is busy and a lot of people are complimenting us on what we have and the job we do. I enjoy pulling things together visually. When I'm on the counter, I'm into the flow of it. I even like the organizational part, learning how to do more on the computer, and starting to develop budgets and understanding my costs better after the MBA students got me started. I like the variety. If I had to do just one aspect all the time, it would be grueling.
>
> The only task I really dislike is working with employees who don't have their hearts in the business the way Stacy and I do. To some of them, it's just a job and their attitude seems to be "what can you do for me." I try to be flexible, hoping that if I'm loyal to them, they'll be there for us, but while some are very good, others just don't seem to care.

Christine wasn't sure what she might like to do if she wasn't running the store. She recalled that her "what I want to be when I grow up" dreams as a child were similar to many girls—teacher, mom, nurse. She was interested in interior design in high school, and had thought at one time about studying gerontology because she enjoyed working with older people. She had taken a variety of courses through the community college and adult education, but had not focused on any other career paths. As Christine contemplated what strategy she should follow, she knew she couldn't continue at The Fudge Cottage without improving the profitability of the business.

> We're still around and a lot of places aren't. We're doing something right, but I can't afford to make $9,000 or $10,000 a year anymore. I didn't used to have to think about goals, now I do.

CINEPLEX ODEON CORP. (B)

Joseph Lampel, *New York University*

Jamal Shamsie, *New York University*

As the summer of 1995 drew to a close, there seemed to be no relief in sight for Cineplex Odeon Corporation. The company reported a loss of over $30 million for the first six months of the year, up significantly from the $12 million loss it had sustained during the comparable period in 1994. These results suggested a sharp reversal for Cineplex Odeon in its attempts to gradually return to profitability (see Exhibit 1). The bleak figures also raised serious concerns about the ability of Alan Karp, president and CEO of the company, to turn things around.

Just a few months earlier, Karp's plan to reverse the fortunes of his fledgling company by merging with Cinemark USA had fallen apart. The merger would have created Cineplex International and made the new company the largest theater chain in North America. With more than 2,800 screens, or about 11 percent of the total screens in North America, Cineplex International would have controlled 800 more screens than its nearest competitor. Allen Karp would have remained as president and CEO of the merged company, but the position of chairman would have gone to Lee Roy Mitchell, the founder and majority owner of Cinemark.

This case is drawn entirely from published sources and is the most recent of the case series on Cineplex Odeon prepared by the case researchers. The case authors wish to thank Xavier Gonzalez-Sanfeliu and Katherine White for their assistance. Copyright © 1995 by Joseph Lampel and Jamal Shamsie.

EXHIBIT 1   Cineplex Odeon's Income Statements, 1990–1994 (in millions of U.S. dollars)

	1994	1993	1992	1991	1990
Revenues					
Admissions	$ 384.0	$ 388.9	$ 373.3	$ 386.2	$ 439.0
Concessions	133.7	138.4	125.4	124.0	134.3
Other	21.7	18.9	20.1	28.1	41.5
	$ 539.4	$ 546.2	$ 518.7	$ 538.3	$ 614.8
Expenses					
Theater operations	$ 458.2	$ 459.7	$ 463.5	$ 481.7	$ 552.5
General & administrative	15.9	15.5	17.5	20.1	24.6
Depreciation & amortization	40.7	41.6	42.3	43.3	53.5
	$ 514.8	$ 516.8	$ 523.3	$ 545.1	$ 630.6
Interest expense	$ 33.4	$ 28.0	$ 34.4	$ 52.9	$ 60.6
Other income or (expenses)	(2.9)	1.3	0.6	(5.3)	(77.7)*
Income taxes	2.4	1.7	1.3	(1.2)	2.0
Income or (loss) from discontinued operations	—	(8.3)	(1.6)	(13.3)	20.2
Net income	$ (14.2)	$ (7.4)	$ (41.3)	$ (77.2)	$(135.9)

*Reflects charges for restructuring program, including sale of noncore assets and write-down of assets and losses on investments.

Source: Cineplex Odeon Annual Reports.

The proposed merger did have the support of Cineplex Odeon's two largest shareholders: entertainment conglomerate MCA and the Bronfman family, which controlled the Seagram liquor business. However, even as the details of the merger were still being worked out, Edgar Bronfman Jr., CEO of Seagram, announced his intention to acquire 80 percent of MCA. The proposed acquisition disrupted the delicate balance of power in the yet to be established Cineplex International. Bronfman's purchase would have given him effective control of the new company, through a combination of the shares held by MCA and his trust company.

Although the merger was called off, Allen Karp remained quite enthusiastic about Cineplex Odeon's future prospects, despite five straight years of losses totaling $276 million. Nevertheless, when asked what impact a Seagram-MCA combination might have on Cineplex Odeon, he conceded that he had not even begun to consider what strategic benefits Seagram might bring to Cineplex. "We don't know where it's going to end up," he said.[1]

---

[1]*Financial Post.* "Taking a front row seat," April 15, 1995.

THE EARLY YEARS ⸻

An Opportunity for Multiplex Theaters

The origins of Cineplex Odeon date back to 1979 when Garth Drabinsky, a young filmmaker, joined forces with Nathan Taylor, an industry veteran. Taylor had long championed the concept of theaters with multiple screens. Drabinsky found the idea appealing, and together the two formed Cineplex. Their first multiplex theater was located in Toronto's Eaton Center, a newly developed shopping center. It contained as many as 18 separate theaters, each with a seating capacity ranging from 60 to 150 people.[2]

Cineplex saw itself as a niche player. It countered the trend in the industry that saw exhibitors using their large theaters to get the potentially lucrative releases from the Hollywood distributors. Instead, the newly developed multiplex chain used its small screens to show specialty movies, in particular foreign art films that could not be shown profitably in large theaters. As Taylor put it, Cineplex was not out to challenge the major chains, but to complement them:

> We are seeking to develop a market that to some extent doesn't exist. We are taking specialized markets and filling their needs. It's a latent market and a different niche than the major chains go after.[3]

In addition, Cineplex sought to obtain successful U.S. films after they had completed their run with the larger theater chains. It was commonly known that the share of the box office receipts accruing to the distributor decreased with the run of the movie. Although this allowed exhibitors to keep more of the revenues, the inevitable decline in attendance ordinarily forced large theaters to discontinue exhibition once the number of empty seats exceeded a certain level. It was at this point that Cineplex could pick up the films and, by virtue of its small theaters, keep most of the seats full.

The advantages of the multiplex concept were primarily due to a carefully planned use of shared facilities. All the theaters in a location were served by a single box office and a single concession stand. The use of advanced projection technology made it possible for one or two projectionists, in a centralized projection booth, to handle the showing of the films in all of the theaters different auditoriums. Show times were staggered to avoid congestion at the ticket office and the concession counter. Even advertising costs were lowered by using a single ad for all the films playing at a particular location.

The success of the multiplex concept spurred Cineplex to expand its operations across Canada. The company also entered the large U.S. market with the development of a 14-screen theater complex in the Beverly Hills section of Los Angeles. By the end of 1982, the company was operating almost 150 screens in about 20 different locations.

A Close Brush with Bankruptcy

The rapid rate of expansion brought Cineplex face-to-face with financial and market realities which its owners had not anticipated. During its expansion, the firm had amassed $21 million in debt, mostly in high and floating interest rates. The debt and associated interest payments became a bigger-than-expected burden when an eco-

---

[2]*Financial Post.* "Cineplex getting in the big picture," June 14, 1980.
[3]Report on *Business Magazine.* "Upwardly mogul." December 1985.

nomic recession hit that cut deeply into the company's earnings. To make matters worse, U.S. distributors were increasingly reluctant to supply Cineplex with hit films for fear of alienating the two large Canadian exhibition chains, Famous Players and Canadian Odeon. Without the revenues of major U.S. releases, the firm's future showing specialty films and second-run movies looked increasingly bleak.

To avert bankruptcy, Cineplex took steps throughout 1983 to reduce its debt and improve its cash flow. The actions included selling off some of the company's assets, raising funds through the public offering of more shares, and persuading the banks to extend further credit. However, these measures did not address the company's blocked access to major releases. To break through this barrier, Garth Drabinsky sought government intervention. Using his legal training, Drabinsky marshaled the evidence and managed to convince the Canadian government that strong grounds existed for launching an investigation into the existence of a conspiracy aimed at depriving Cineplex of access to major releases.

In the face of a government investigation, and possible sanctions, the U.S. distributors modified their stance and agreed to a system of competitive bidding that would ensure that all exhibitors had equal access to their films. With this hurdle surmounted, Drabinsky was able to secure greater financial backing, particularly from institutional investors. A large investment came from a trust company representing the Bronfmans, a powerful business family associated with the Seagram liquor business.

To Drabinsky, the close brush with bankruptcy also had revealed a basic flaw in his company's position. He became acutely aware that his small theaters generated insufficient revenues to bid for early runs of the most lucrative U.S. films. So when the principal owner of Canadian Odeon passed away, Drabinsky saw an opportunity that was not to be missed. Canadian Odeon had been greatly weakened by the new bidding system that Drabinsky had helped to bring about. Alarmed by Odeon's poor performance, the heirs finally accepted Drabinsky's offer of a little over $22 million for the entire chain.

The acquisition of Canadian Odeon in the spring of 1984, at what many viewed as a bargain basement price, began a remarkable turnaround for a company that just two years earlier had faced bankruptcy. Now, with over 450 screens in as many as 170 different locations, Cineplex Odeon was a major player in the industry. Drabinsky relished his comeback and was not above taking a passing shot at his detractors: "A lot of people who were waiting for me to go under were disappointed. Well they didn't get their jollies."[4]

A BLOCKBUSTER STRATEGY

Making Movie-Going a Larger-than-Life Experience

The formation of Cineplex Odeon crowned Drabinsky's comeback from the verge of bankruptcy, but he was not content to rest on his laurels. Now that he controlled one of North America's major theater chains, he set out to transform the moviegoing experience itself. The popularity of pay-television channels and movie rentals was making it increasingly difficult to lure movie fans and moviewatchers from the comfort of their homes.

To try to boost attendance at Cineplex Odeon's theaters, Drabinsky sought to change the public's perceptions of the moviegoing experience by renovating the

---

[4]*Macleans.* "King of the silver screen." September 28, 1987.

theaters, beginning with the physical layout. Cineplex Odeon abandoned the uniformly drab design, common in most theater chains, in favor of artwork in the lobbies, lush woolen carpets spread over marble floors, and coral-and-peach color-coordinated walls. The screening auditoriums featured scientifically contoured seats, digital background music, and state-of-the-art projection systems. As a final touch, the firm reintroduced real buttered popcorn in the concession stands and cafés that offered freshly brewed cappuccino.

Cineplex Odeon's metamorphosis was completed with the unveiling of a new company logo in the form of a curved bowl that was reminiscent of a Greek amphitheater. Furthermore, in choosing colors for the logo, Drabinsky decided on a combination of imperial purple and fuschia. For him, the logo was not mere representation; it was intended to make people sit up and take notice. As Drabinsky put it, "I felt that this would be more of a bravado kind of statement. I don't think anyone was ready for that."[5]

Cineplex Odeon's new format differed sharply from the prevailing industry response to the threats posed by pay television and take-home videocassettes. Most theater chains sought to cut their fixed costs by slicing old movie palaces into tiny cinemas, and by eliminating many services that were deemed inessential. Drabinsky, on the other hand, believed that the moviegoing experience extended beyond what was shown on the screen. As the customer entered the theater, he or she was meant to leave behind mundane existence and gradually move into a different reality. In the words of Drabinsky:

> We are determined to give back to our patrons the rush and excitement and anticipation and curiosity that should be theirs when they leave the techno-regimented world of their daily lives for the fantasy world of escape that is the movies.[6]

A Costly Operation

Drabinsky's push for glamour and glitz was very costly. Cineplex Odeon typically spent almost $3 million on a typical six-screen multiplex, a third more than the average for the industry. However, Drabinsky was convinced that the additional investment would bear fruit not only at the box office but at the concession counter as well. The classier upscale atmosphere was meant to entice customers into spending more time in the theaters before and after the movie, resulting in higher sales at the concession counter. Indeed, the concessions at Cineplex Odeon's theaters usually generated approximately $2 per moviegoer, which was close to twice the industry average.

Despite the higher concession sales, Drabinsky was forced to search for other sources of revenues to cover all of the fixed costs of a typical Cineplex Odeon theater. He raised admission fees well above the competition in most markets and began to show commercials before the screening of the main feature. Both moves were highly unpopular. Irate patrons expressed their anger in a number of cities, sometimes by protesting outside Cineplex Odeon's theaters. The most publicized of these protests occurred in New York City where Mayor Ed Koch joined picketers in a call for a boycott of the chain because of its price increase.

Drabinsky countered these criticisms with a series of promotional gimmicks. Most significant among these were the lower admission prices that were offered on Tuesdays.

---

[5]*Macleans.* "Big money at the movies." July 28, 1986.
[6]*Business Journal.* "Movie mogul." October 1982.

This pricing strategy was designed to make movies more accessible to the general public. Attendance at Cineplex theaters climbed substantially on these Tuesdays, generating additional revenues as well as much-needed goodwill among customers.

Drabinsky also made an effort to reduce costs wherever possible. Earlier, Canadian Odeon's management was a target. Upon acquisition, Drabinsky dismissed about two-thirds of Canadian Odeon's head-office staff and cut the pay of the remaining personnel by 10 percent. But the expense of Drabinsky's strategy to turn moviegoing into a luxury experience forced another round of stringent cost-cutting. Drabinsky's latest cost-cutting campaign did not leave any facet of the firm's operations untouched. Even the traditional cardboard containers used to sell popcorn were replaced with bags, a move that saved Cineplex Odeon close to $1 million per year.

A Powerful Competitor

Drabinsky's tough, uncompromising management style made Cineplex Odeon a formidable market foe. In every market that Cineplex Odeon entered, Drabinsky used all the means at his disposal to gain market share and to keep rivals on the defensive. He pursued Famous Players, his long-standing rival in Canada, with special vengeance. In 1986, for example, Drabinsky seized an opportunity to lease part of a building in Toronto that housed the Imperial Theater, a six-theater complex operated by Famous Players. Since the part of the building leased by Cineplex Odeon contained the main entrance to all of Famous Players' theaters in the complex, Drabinsky decided to deny Famous Players any public access, ultimately forcing it to close down and sell all of its theaters in this key location to Cineplex Odeon.

Such hardball tactics reflected the adverserial approach to business that had earned Drabinsky the nickname "Darth," after the supervillain Darth Vader. In an industry known for tough negotiators and agile deal makers, Drabinsky gained a reputation as a tenacious and abrasive businessman. He used his astute bargaining skills to make a series of acquisitions across Canada and the United States (see Exhibit 3). His biggest acquisition involved the Plitt theater chain, which had almost 600 screens in over 200 locations.

By January 1, 1989, Cineplex Odeon was the second largest motion picture exhibitor in North America with just over 1,800 screens in 500 different locations (see Exhibits 4 and 5). Almost two-thirds of the company's screens were located in the United States and were scattered over 20 different states. The remaining one-third of these screens were situated in six different Canadian provinces. Cineplex Odeon theaters could be found in virtually all major population centers, from New York to Los Angeles in the United States, and from Toronto to Vancouver in Canada.

Drabinsky endeavored to use the size of his chain to obtain added clout with film studios and distributors. He consistently used Cineplex Odeon's strong presence in major metropolitan locations and its large number of screens as leverage to obtain potential hits on more favorable terms, but his insistence on having his way often created tensions in his relationships with suppliers. For example, Columbia Pictures did not yield to Drabinsky's demand that Bernardo Bertolucci's oriental epic *The Last Emperor* be made available for wide release during the Christmas period. In retaliation, Drabinsky refused to exhibit another film produced by the studio that was slated for release during the same holiday season. This episode created additional tension in Drabinsky's relationship with Columbia, resulting in the diversion of more of the studio's films to other chains, such as Famous Players, Drabinsky's major Canadian competitor.

EXHIBIT 2   Cineplex Odeon's Balance Sheets, 1990–1994 (in millions of U.S. dollars)

| | | | Years ending December 31 | | |
Assets	1994	1993	1992	1991	1990
Current assets					
Cash	$ 1.2	$ 1.3	$ 1.4	$ 1.1	—
Accounts receivable	10.4	15.8	15.3	21.5	$ 37.4
Inventories	5.9	6.4	5.2	5.3	5.6
Prepaid expenses	2.0	1.9	2.6	2.4	2.3
Advances to distributors	1.4	3.9	5.0	7.5	14.4
Distribution costs	—	—	1.2	2.2	3.9
Fixed assets					
Properties, equipment leaseholds, net	606.9	619.3	658.6	710.7	743.9
Other assets					
Long-term investments	10.8	3.8	5.6	6.7	4.7
Goodwill	37.5	38.7	40.1	41.7	42.9
Deferred charges	9.7	6.1	6.8	6.0	1.2
Total assets	$ 685.7	$ 697.1	$ 741.6	$ 805.1	$ 856.3
Liabilities and Shareholders' Equity					
Current liabilities					
Bank loans	—	—	—	—	$ 27.0
Accounts payable	$ 68.7	$ 73.8	$ 77.2	$ 89.7	95.5
Income taxes payable	0.6	0.9	1.0	2.3	4.1
Current portion of long-term debt	7.3	51.1	31.0	62.4	4.6
Deferred income	14.7	13.9	10.9	14.5	18.3
Long-term debt & capitalized leases	386.7	343.5	420.3	419.8	534.6
Other liabilities					
Pension obligations	1.4	1.5	2.3	2.6	4.0
Deferred income	10.3	12.1	—	—	—
Shareholders' equity					
Capital stock	472.4	457.8	445.1	408.5	285.1
Foreign exchange adjustment	0.6	5.3	9.1	19.2	19.8
Retained earnings (deficit)	(276.8)	(262.6)	(255.3)	(213.9)	(136.7)
Total liabilities and shareholders' equity	$ 685.7	$ 697.1	$ 741.6	$ 805.1	$ 856.3

Source: Cineplex Odeon Annual Reports.

Moving beyond Theaters

In 1982, at a time when Cineplex was still a small company screening foreign and art films, Drabinsky moved to consolidate and expand the company's other film-related activities. These ventures consisted mainly of a filmmaking subsidiary originally started by Nathan Taylor, and a film distribution arm, launched by Drabinsky in 1979.

The filmmaking subsidiary was one of Canada's largest and was located just north of Toronto. Its facilities were rented out to various groups for film and television production, and included two sound stages, dressing and wardrobe rooms, a carpen-

EXHIBIT 3   U.S. Theater Chains Acquired by Cineplex Odeon, 1985–1987

1985   Plitt Theaters
        Los Angeles, California
        574 screens/209 locations

1986   Septum Cinemas
        Atlanta, Georgia
        48 screens/12 locations

1986   Essaness Theaters
        Chicago, Illinois
        41 screens/13 locations

1986   RKO Century Warner Theaters
        New York, New York
        97 screens/42 locations

1986   Neighbourhood Theaters
        Richmond, Virginia
        76 screens/25 locations

1986   SRO Theaters
        Seattle, Washington
        99 screens/33 locations

1987   Walter Reade Organization
        New York, New York
        11 screens/8 locations

1987   Circle Theaters
        Washington, D.C.
        80 screens/22 locations

Source: Cineplex Odeon.

try mill, a plaster shop, and editing and screening rooms. Drabinsky had originally created the distribution arm to provide foreign and art films to the newly developed Cineplex chain. It quickly developed into one of the largest distribution companies in Canada, acquiring the right to distribute films to theaters and on videocassettes, as well as for use on network and pay television.

In 1986, Drabinsky increased his company's involvement in filmmaking through the acquisition of the Film House. The Toronto-based facility consisted of a large film processing laboratory and a fully equipped postproduction sound studio. Following its purchase of the Film House, Cineplex Odeon increased the capacity of its film laboratory and constructed new upgraded sound facilities.

In addition, Drabinsky expanded the film production and distribution activities of his firm into the United States. With this move into a larger market, Cineplex Odeon was able to step up its level of participation in filmmaking. It began to contribute towards the production of small-budget films such as Paul Newman's *The Glass Menagerie* and Prince's rock concert film *Sign 'O' the Times*.

Finally, Drabinsky entered into a collaborative venture with MCA, a large U.S. entertainment conglomerate. The two companies agreed to jointly develop and operate

EXHIBIT 4   Cineplex Odeon's Theater Locations, 1995

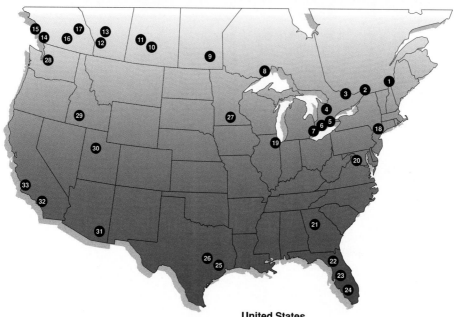

Canada

Province	Locations	Screens
Quebec		
1. Quebec City	9	30
2. Montreal	23	97
Ontario		
3. Ottawa	9	38
4. Toronto	24	141
5. Niagara Peninsula	10	41
6. London	11	34
7. Windsor	3	8
8. Thunder Bay	3	15
Manitoba		
9. Winnipeg	3	9
Saskatchewan		
10. Regina	1	6
11. Saskatoon	2	6

	Locations	Screens
Alberta		
12. Calgary	11	48
13. Edmonton	7	47
British Columbia		
14. Vancouver	9	40
15. Victoria	1	3
16. Kamloops	1	4
17. Prince George	1	3
	128	570

United States

State	Locations	Screens
New York / New Jersey		
18. New York & Metropolitan Area	50	190
Illinois		
19. Chicago	46	214
District of Columbia / Maryland / Virginia		
20. Washington DC & Metropolitan Area	30	133
Georgia		
21. Atlanta	22	102
Florida		
22. Jacksonville	3	17
23. Orlando	3	21
24. Tampa	7	38
Texas		
25. Houston	9	63
26. Temple	2	11

	Locations	Screens
Minnesota		
27. Minneapolis	7	31
Washington		
28. Seattle/Tacoma	17	75
Idaho		
29. Boise	5	21
Utah		
30. Salt Lake City	12	54
Arizona		
31. Tucson	4	25
California		
32. Los Angeles	7	49
33. San Francisco	4	11
	228	1,055

Source: Cineplex Odeon Annual Reports.

a large film studio and theme park in Orlando, Florida that would compete with Disney World. At the same time, Drabinsky persuaded MCA to purchase a large block of shares in Cineplex Odeon, making it a significant partner in his growing company.

All of these moves reflected Drabinsky's determination to transform Cineplex Odeon into a corporation that would straddle every part of the movie industry. As he put it:

EXHIBIT 5   Number of Screens of Leading Theater Chains, United States and Canada, 1988–1994

Theater Chains	Number of Screens						
	1994	1993	1992	1991	1990	1989	1988
United Artists*	2,204	2,250	2,378	2,398	2,560	2,699	2,677
Carmike Cinemas	2,035	1,732	1,570	1,387	975	813	701
Cineplex Odeon	1,643	1,609	1,619	1,700	1,700	1,940	1,832
American Multi-Cinema	1,636	1,614	1,585	1,629	1,606	1,649	1,614
General Cinema	1,221	1,351	1,396	1,466	1,502	1,453	1,400
Cinemark*	1,214	1,059	996	939	856	645	401
Sony	912	869	868	890	857	837	822
National Amusements*	848	845	725	725	670	625	552
Regal Cinemas	722	n.a.	n.a.	n.a.	n.a.	n.a.	n.a.
Act III Theatres	568	535	533	500	486	486	404
Hoyts	519	521	460	444	430	610	550
Famous Players	441	441	474	481	484	472	448
Cinamerica	341	341	382	464	496	444	456

*Includes some screens outside United States and Canada.
n.a. — not available

Source: Standard & Poors.

It's an amalgamated company with revenue from theaters, distribution, production, the studio, and, down the road, live theater. People aren't buying a share in this company just to have a share in a motion picture. They're getting a share in a vertically integrated entertainment corporation.[7]

A PERFORMANCE UNDER SCRUTINY

Relentless Expansion

Although Cineplex Odeon had already grown to a size beyond that of most of its competitors, Drabinsky had no plans to slow his company's rapid pace of expansion. The firm continued to construct new theaters, and to refurbish existing ones. For Drabinsky, the expansion had a dual purpose. First, he wanted to surge past all of his competitors and capture a leading share of the North American market. Second, Drabinsky believed that only a larger Cineplex Odeon could force the major distributors to give the chain the big-budget movies at more favorable terms.

Plans for theater expansion were not confined to the North American continent. Drabinsky had also unveiled plans to spend around $100 million to develop over 100 screens in the United Kingdom by the end of 1990. He believed that better theaters and faster release of major U.S. films would reverse the decline in attendance and reinvigorate the British market.

---

[7]*Financial Times.* " 'Darth' plays movie hardball—and wins." December 28, 1987.

In addition to theater expansion, Drabinsky was increasingly involving his company in film production since it had the capacity to both distribute and exhibit movies. During 1988, Cineplex Odeon helped to finance and distribute movies by such noted directors as John Schlesinger and Oliver Stone. The firm also negotiated a joint production agreement with small production companies headed by Robert Redford and Taylor Hackford. But Drabinsky had frequently stated that Cineplex Odeon would limit its involvement to a few low-budget films and would not venture into the risky business of producing big-budget movies.

Drabinsky also extended Cineplex Odeon's production activities to other entertainment areas. During 1988, Cineplex Odeon financed the run of several lavish Broadway musicals in Toronto. Drabinsky then decided to convert the Toronto theater Cineplex had wrested from the Famous Players chain into a 2,100-seat center for the performing arts. The theater, a vaudeville palace in a previous incarnation, was restored to its former glory, and then used to stage the Canadian production of Andrew Lloyd Webber's *The Phantom of the Opera*. The musical opened in the fall of 1989 with an initial production cost in excess of $6.5 million.

Drabinsky's unrelenting drive for growth placed tremendous strain on the company's finances. In 1987, Cineplex Odeon consummated its first initial public offering of common stock in the United States and was listed on the New York Stock Exchange. Despite this substantial enlargement of the company's equity base, most of the financing during 1987 and 1988 was through the use of debt. During 1988, Cineplex Odeon asked the banks to boost its line of credit by another $175 million to $750 million. Subsequently, the company sold off 50 percent of the Film House, its film production operation in Toronto, and most of its share in the Florida theme park to a British entertainment firm. Drabinsky also raised additional capital by selling off some theaters, and then leasing them back.

The financial uncertainty created apprehension among the company's stockholders, who could still recall his narrow escape from bankruptcy six years earlier. Drabinsky, however, denied that he was undermining Cineplex Odeon by involving the company in activities it could ill afford. He was determined to keep Cineplex Odeon ready to take advantage of emerging opportunities. When asked to predict the company's future development, he had this to say:

> If you asked me five years ago what Cineplex would look like today, I wouldn't have predicted what we have today. So when you ask me today what Cineplex will look like in five years, I can't tell you exactly.[8]

Grab for Control

Since its inception, Cineplex Odeon had remained firmly under the control of Drabinsky, who continuously sought to find ways to increase his power. He became president of the company in 1980, added the title of chief executive officer in 1982, and was finally confirmed as chairman of the board in 1986. The titles reflected Drabinsky's total domination of the company. It was well known that no one was allowed to speak on behalf of the company except Drabinsky.

Drabinsky's consolidation of power was accompanied by significant turnover among the firm's top executives. Those who survived were, for the most part, people with close personal ties to Drabinsky. One of the most important loyalists was Myron Gottlieb, who had also been one of Drabinsky's early financial backers. Gottlieb's

---

[8]*Financial Post.* "Clash of the movie titans." April 22–24, 1989.

career in Cineplex Odeon closely dovetailed that of Drabinsky. He became the vice-chairman of the board in 1982, and was appointed chief administrative officer in 1985.

As long as Drabinsky continued to pile success upon success, his aggressive style and disregard for conventions had been tolerated. His dominance over all aspects of Cineplex Odeon had been deemed necessary for the pursuit of his unique and ambitious vision. But as doubts grew about the financial health of Cineplex Odeon in 1988 and 1989 Drabinsky's reputation as a brilliant strategist was gradually subjected to increased scrutiny. In particular, Drabinsky began to feel some heat from the largest shareholders. Both MCA and the Bronfmans were concerned about the amount of debt that the company was accumulating with his aggressive expansion, particularly into areas outside of film exhibition.

By the beginning of 1989, Drabinsky recognized that he no longer enjoyed the full support of Cineplex Odeon's two major shareholders. Consequently, he and Gottlieb, his longtime associate, sought to gain control of Cineplex Odeon by making an offer to buy the 30 percent stake held by the Bronfman Trust. Taken together with the 8 percent stake that was already owned by Drabinsky and Gottlieb, they would have had enough shares to outvote and outflank MCA, which was restricted to a 33 percent limit on voting rights.

But the management of MCA felt betrayed by the deal Drabinsky had struck with the Bronfman Trust behind their backs. MCA moved swiftly to obtain an injunction preventing the deal from going through, even as Drabinsky and Gottlieb were in the process of putting on the finishing touches. A financial analyst attempted to explain the reasons for MCA's reaction:

> No one understands what Drabinsky and Gottlieb are up to. They pulled out of the Florida deal, they sold off Film House, they are taking bigger risks in film production, and now the Bronfmans are getting out. From MCA's point of view there are probably lots of reasons to stop Garth from getting control.[9]

MCA eventually managed to get the court to rule that the offer that had been made by Drabinsky and his associates should be extended to all of Cineplex Odeon's outstanding shareholders. This forced Drabinsky and Gottlieb to scramble for over $1 billion of financing to back such an offer. But with Cineplex's deteriorating financial situation, the two men could not put together the needed financial backing. The resulting fallout created so much shareholder turmoil that the company's board of directors decided to oust Drabinsky and Gottlieb from their management positions and gave them $8 million golden parachutes. The directors also agreed to sell the Live Theater division to the two ousted executives, including the renovated 2,100-seat Pantages theater and the rights to the Canadian production of *The Phantom of the Opera*.

A BALANCING ACT

A Show of Restraint

When Drabinsky was pushed out, he left behind a company carrying a massive $655 million debt load, a number of holdings unrelated to the core film exhibition business, and a pack of hungry stock speculators nipping at its heels. Cineplex Odeon reported a loss of almost $79 million in 1989, the first since its acquisition of Odeon theaters had transformed it into a major exhibitor. Analysts believed that the com-

---

[9]*Enroute.* "The world according to Garp." November 1991.

pany was losing money at the rate of $4 million to $5 million each month, partly as a result of its heavy interest payments.

The task of turning around Cineplex Odeon fell to Allan Karp, a mild-mannered individual who had been hired by Drabinsky as senior executive vice-president just three years earlier. Karp moved quickly to reassure nervous investors and bankers that Cineplex was prepared to scale back on its earlier ambitions and concentrate on paying down its massive debt. He moved quickly to rid the company of a small exhibition chain in Great Britain, divested Cineplex Odeon's residual interest in the Universal Studio amusement park in Florida, and sold off interests in the film lab and postproduction facility in Toronto. Cineplex realized gross proceeds of $154 million on the sale of these and other noncore assets, most of which was used to pay down the long-term debt.

At the same time, Karp began to cut operating and overhead costs. The company's corporate jet, limousines, and personal bodyguards, which were reflective of Drabinsky's imperial style, were the first to go. By 1991, a series of layoffs also saw head-office staff cut in half from 375 to 190. "We've got a lot fewer chiefs," said Karp, adding with a wry smile. "Hell, we've got a lot fewer Indians."[10] The firm even sold off several theaters, reducing its holdings by almost 200 screens, in order to concentrate more heavily on its theater operations in large metropolitan centers.

Karp also took the battle to cut costs down to the theater level. He worked closely with management teams, including theater managers, to review every aspect of the costs of a theater operation—supplies, advertising, insurance, and even energy costs. The company boasted of annual savings of $3 million in its electricity bill after implementing a program for switching all of its theaters in North America to super-efficient lightbulbs. Karp commented on the results that he was able to achieve through his team approach:

> We want to make local management feel like they're involved in the company's strategic direction rather than the top-down dictatorial approach preferred by my predecessor. We want to be able to make incremental improvements to our operations across the board.[11]

Finally, Karp initiated efforts to increase the concession revenues from each of the theaters. With the implementation of Project Popcorn in 1993, the company expanded its line of concession offerings to include bulk candy, fruit juices, and bottled waters. In 1994, Cineplex also introduced mobile hawking carts that would allow it to sell coffee and popcorn to people standing in the ticket line, as well as those already seated in the theaters. Bulk candy sales may have added $10 million to $20 million to the firm's sales in 1994; and the introduction of hawking carts may have added another $5 to $10 million.

New Avenues for Growth

By 1994, Cineplex had refocused its efforts on the core exhibition business. It had gotten out of the money-losing ancillary businesses, reduced its overhead from $35 million in 1989 to $15 million, and cut its debt from $695 million in 1989 to $370 million (see Exhibit 2). As a result of the steps taken by Karp to steer the firm onto a more stable financial path, Cineplex appeared poised to remain a key player in the

---

[10]Ibid.
[11]*Variety.* "Exhibber back from the brink." July 25–31, 1994.

exhibition business. Almost 85 percent of the company's U.S. screens were in the top 15 U.S. markets, while 75 percent of its Canadian screens were in the top ten Canadian markets (see Exhibit 4).

The improvements that Karp made to Cineplex's bottom line were sufficient to help secure more financing. He had been able to convince the company's two major shareholders, entertainment conglomerate MCA and the Bronfman family controlled trust, to convert most of their loans into equity. Furthermore, Cineplex had managed to extend the maturity date for its bank debts and to raise another $380 million through a bond offering and through additional bank credit lines.

The relief from financial pressures allowed Karp to switch the strategic focus back to a relatively modest expansion program. Cineplex announced plans to spend $57.5 million on refurbishment and construction of new theaters, which would add up to 254 new screens to the circuit. As part of this effort, the company has been introducing DTS sound systems in many of its theaters. The system creates a powerful audiovisual experience by using a separate CD-ROM disk to project sound into the audience.

In 1993, Cineplex acquired distribution rights in Canada for films that owned by Gramercy Pictures. Gramercy was a recently formed joint marketing venture of MCA's Universal Films and Polygram's Filmed Entertainment Unit. In spite of this move back into distribution, Cineplex's senior executives were aware that they had to avoid a repeat of the overaggressive expansion that was undertaken by Drabinsky. The company's chief financial officer, Ellis Jacob, strongly supported such a strategy of cautious growth: "Our focus now is to be much more cautious about what we do. We're looking at all opportunities and seeing what makes sense for Cineplex."[12]

Allan Karp also began to show keen interest in the possibility of further growth opportunities through mergers or acquisitions with other exhibition chains. "I don't think there's a major chain that hasn't come to us. There's opportunity out there given the right chemistry.[13] Karp believed that Cineplex was capable of running a theater chain twice as big. He was convinced that if a suitable partner could be found for a merger, his company could eliminate the other company's overhead with the resulting cost savings flowing directly to the bottom line. But Karp also understood that any merger or acquisition would not be easy to push through, noting, "We've got substantial hurdles before we're prepared to go to our shareholders and bankers to say we want to fund acquisitions."[14]

CINEPLEX ODEON'S SEARCH FOR A FUTURE

In early 1995, Karp felt he had found an ideal partner with which to return to more ambitious plans for the future of Cineplex Odeon. Like Karp, Cinemark founder Lee Roy Mitchell believed that only a large chain could develop the resources to exhibit movies in state-of-the-art theaters with digital sound, cushy seating, clean floors, and smiling service. Karp and Mitchell also agreed that revolutionizing the international exhibition business was the next frontier. The prospects of international expansion had drawn the two men together two years earlier, and led to the conversations that culminated in plans for the merger. Mitchell's company had already been expanding

---

[12]Ibid.

[13]Ibid.

[14]*Financial Post.* "Taking a front row seat."

outside the U.S., opening multiplexes in Latin American countries ranging from Mexico to Chile, and even in Asian countries as far afield as China.

With the collapse of the attempted merger, Cineplex Odeon had to face the future alone again. But Karp was enthusiastic about the control that the Bronfman family had acquired through Seagram's purchase of MCA. At the same time, it was not clear what benefits Karp might be able to gain from this merging of its two largest shareholders. There was widespread speculation that Edgar Bronfman Jr., CEO of Seagram, was interested in expanding within the entertainment industry. Karp hoped that Cineplex Odeon would be an essential component of this expansion.

Meanwhile, as losses continued to mount, analysts were still waiting for Karp's next move. While Karp had managed to pull the company back from the imminent danger of bankruptcy, he had yet to provide the shareholders with any cause for celebration. The latest results indicated that Cineplex Odeon was still searching for a return to profitability. Karp attributed his company's recent jump in losses to an industrywide decline in theater attendance, due to a shortage of good films. But industry watchers noted that Cineplex was more hard hit than its competitors by sluggish attendance. Said one analyst: "They said they've done this great restructuring, then the question to ask is, why are they still losing money?"[15]

BACKGROUND INFORMATION ON THE MOVIE INDUSTRY

The number of movies available for exhibition had grown significantly over the past decade, although there had been a recent decrease in films released by the smaller independent distribution companies. The number of feature-length films released over the last five years were as follows:

	1994	1993	1992	1991	1990
Major Distributors	198	195	175	176	166
Smaller Distributors	184	149	256	248	221
Total Releases	382	344	431	424	387

In spite of the growth of many smaller suppliers, the bulk of the revenues still came from films distributed by the eight major companies, most of which had dominated the industry for more than 50 years. Based in Hollywood, these companies included Warner Brothers, Disney, Paramount, 20th Century Fox, Universal, and Columbia. In 1994, the 198 films that were released by these six firms accounted for almost 90 percent of the box office dollars in the U.S. and Canada.

The relative success of the major distributors stemmed in large part from their greater financial resources. The typical Hollywood studio spent, on the average, almost $34 million for each of the films produced during 1994, up from $16 million only five years earlier. Another $8 to $10 million was usually spent to market or

---

[15]*Financial Post.* "$15M loss at Cineplex." May 6, 1995.

advertise the movie and up to $5 million could be spent on making sufficient copies of the film so that it could be released to a wide number of theaters.

The movies of smaller distributors usually had budgets under $10 million and frequently lacked the major stars or production values that could increase their chances of striking it rich at the box office. In fact, an industry publication recently reported that more than half of the movies offered by smaller distributors did not ever play in theaters, but were released directly into the movie rental market.

Although the major distributors dominated the industry, they had long since abandoned their practice of binding the most attractive movie directors and stars to long term employment contracts. Most of the Hollywood movies were being made by contracting with small production outfits to handle particular aspects of a film. The major distributor might either fund a movie from start to finish or provide a portion of the financing in return for a share of the subsequent box office receipts.

As a result of lackluster financial results, some of the smaller distributors had either folded their operations or merged with other distributors. Even some of the major distributors had resorted to merger, the most notable being MGM with United Artists. These trends indicated that in the future fewer major distributors would control the total number of movies available to theaters for exhibition.

Exhibition of Movies

Since 1980, the number of U.S. movie screens had risen approximately 57 percent to about 26,600 as of the end of 1994. About 45 percent of these were collectively held by the top 10 exhibition chains. During the 1990s, the number of screens had grown about 13 percent:

1994	26,586
1993	25,737
1992	25,105
1991	24,570
1990	23,689

However, movie theater attendance had increased less than 30 percent since 1980. There had been a growing emphasis on improving the quality of theaters in order to entice more people into visiting them. This had resulted in large-scale renovations of existing theaters as well as the construction of new ones. During this process, hundreds of smaller independent theaters were forced to sell out to the larger chains that could more easily raise the capital to make the necessary investments.

During the 1980s, some of the major movie distributors also began to buy up theater chains. MCA, the parent of Universal Studios, owned more than 40 percent of Cineplex Odeon Theaters. Sony, the parent of Columbia and Tri-Star Pictures, operated the former Loews Theaters. Paramount's parent company, Viacom, and Warner's parent company, Time Warner, were partners in Cinamerica Theaters. Distribution companies said that by owning theaters, they could better guarantee the public a higher quality presentation of their movies.

In the late 1940s, the U.S. Justice Department had ruled that the same companies could not make as well as show movies. The legislation was a result of allegations that the major Hollywood movie studios that owned theaters were restricting their movies to their own theaters and engaging in fixing prices. However, the attitudes towards restrictions on the ownership of movie theaters had become more relaxed in recent years, in part because of clearer and more stringent regulations that mandated fair access to movies by all exhibitors.

Revenues from Theaters

There was a widespread debate about the effects of recessions on movie attendance. Some financial analysts had recently shown that box office receipts decreased during the recessionary periods of the early 1930s and the early 1970s. For the most part, however, annual ticket sales had been relatively stable at around one billion admissions per year for almost 30 years. Total theater admissions in 1994 were about 1.29 billion, up from 1.19 billion admissions recorded five years earlier.

The audience for movies in theaters was heavily dominated by younger individuals, particularly below 40 years of age. But recent evidence suggested that the traditional drop in attendance after the age of 40 was lessening. The recent breakdown for attendance by age groups had been as follows:

	1994	1992	1990	1988	1986
20 years and under	27%	28%	31%	32%	35%
21–39 years	37	41	45	45	51
40 years and over	36	30	24	23	14

Box office receipts had risen considerably over the years, largely as a result of increases in the prices of tickets. There was considerable seasonal variation in ticket sales, with almost half of the sales coming between late May and early September and between late November and early January. The box office receipts for U.S. theaters for the years 1990–1994 is presented below:

1994	$5.40 billion
1993	$5.15
1992	$4.87
1991	$4.80
1990	$5.02

The average ticket price rose to $4.18 in 1994, up from $3.36 in 1984. Theater owners were generally reluctant to raise ticket prices more rapidly than inflation for fear of losing viewers. Increasingly, however, they relied upon the lobby concession stand to make their profits. Once inside the theaters, moviegoers were a captive market for popcorn, soft drinks, and candy that could be sold at inflated prices. Recent surveys indicated that exhibition chains derived as much as 30 percent of their revenues from high-margin items sold at their concession stands.

Splitting of Revenues

There had been considerable wrangling between the distributors and exhibitors over the distribution of box office revenues. Exhibitors licensed films through either direct negotiation or by submitting bids to distributors. Rental fees—which averaged out to about 50 percent of ticket sales—were largely based on a revenue-sharing formula.

There were different kinds of revenue sharing agreements. Under a gross receipts allocation, a distributor received a percentage of box office sales, with the percentage declining over the period during which the movie was shown at the theater. With a first-run film, the distributor generally received 70 percent of the ticket sales initially, with its share gradually declining to as little as 30 percent. When a theater showed a movie that had already been out for a while, the rental fee typically started at a much lower 35 percent of ticket sales, and then often declined to 30 percent.

Distributors could sometimes insist on a different type of revenue sharing formula. The most common of these was known as the 90/10 clause. When such a clause applied, a theater operator received a negotiated allowance from ticket sales for theater expenses, while the distributor received 90 percent of all box office receipts above this amount.

In recent years, exhibitors had been able to use the increased supply of movies to negotiate a larger share of the box office receipts. But the increase in the total number of screens was working to help distributors regain the upper hand. Several growing exhibition chains had to compete with each other to get the potential hit movies because they had theater screens in many of the same geographic locations.

Movie distributors were using their revenues from videocassettes and pay TV to reduce their dependence on the theaters. Still, distribution companies reached more people through exhibiting their movies in theaters. More significantly, the values of their movies on videocassettes and pay TV were heavily dependent upon a respectable theatrical run. A movie that was successful at the box office was far more likely to be shown on pay TV and generate more videocassette rentals. The sources of revenues for a movie released by a major film distributor had changed significantly over the years:

	1994	1990	1985	1980
Theaters	44%	38%	48%	76%
Videocassettes	38	45	32	2
Pay television	12	13	10	6
Network television	6	7	9	15

Note: Information for the section on "Background Information on the Movie Industry" was obtained from Standard & Poors, *The International Motion Pictures Almanac* and *Variety*.

(Cineplex Odeon's Web site address is *www.investlink.com/cineplex.*)

CANNONDALE CORPORATION AND THE MOUNTAIN BIKE INDUSTRY

Romuald A. Stone, *Keller Graduate School of Management*

It was mid-June 1995 and Joseph Montgomery, the president and chief executive officer of Cannondale, had just received the 1995 Southern New England Entrepreneur of the Year Award. As he sat in his office in a renovated red barn at the company's headquarters in Georgetown, Connecticut, he was contemplating the future for Cannondale Corporation, a manufacturer of high-performance aluminum bicycles and accessories. Fiscal 1995, marked by record sales and profits and the successful completion of its initial public offering, was an important year in the company's history. Cannondale's sales for 1995 totaled $122.1 million, a 20 percent increase over the previous year. Net income was $7.5 million as compared to losses posted the previous three years. As he reflected on his achievements over the 25-year history of the company and in particular the past year, Montgomery recognized that he had some important decisions to make if Cannondale was to continue to grow and be a major player in the specialty mountain bicycle market. Crafting an attractive strategic plan to carry Cannondale into the next century was one of Joe Montgomery's top priorities.

EXHIBIT 1   Bicycles and Automobiles in Use in Selected Countries, 1985–1988

Country	Bicycles (millions)	Autos (millions)	Bikes per Auto	Bikes per Person
China	300.0	1.2	250.0	0.27
United States	103.0	139.0	0.7	0.42
Japan	60.0	30.7	2.0	0.49
India	45.0	1.5	30.0	0.06
West Germany	45.0	26.0	1.7	0.74
Mexico	12.0	4.8	2.5	0.16
Holland	11.0	4.9	2.2	0.79
Australia	6.8	7.1	0.9	0.42
South Korea	6.0	0.3	20.0	0.15
Argentina	4.5	3.4	1.3	0.16
Egypt	1.5	0.5	3.0	0.03
Tanzania	0.5	0.5	1.0	0.02

Source: Perry, *Bike Cult,* p. 237.

THE GLOBAL BICYCLE MARKET[1]

In 1994 there were about one billion bicycles in the world, twice the number of cars. More than 100 million bicycles were produced that year, outnumbering car production by three to one. Exhibit 1 shows the number of bicycles and automobiles in selected countries. With about 5.6 billion people in the world, there was one bicycle for every six persons.

Bicycles were used throughout the world for transport (70 percent), recreation (29 percent), and competition (1 percent). Bicycling was the primary means of land transport, other than walking. For example, traffic controllers in China saw an average of 10,000 cyclists per hour pass the busiest urban intersections. In the city of Tianjin, with more than four million people, there were up to 50,000 cyclists per hour passing through high-traffic intersections. In general, adult cyclists outnumbered children (under 16) by about two to one, and while estimates varied, women rode bicycles as often as men.

Western Europeans were the biggest users of bicycles among the world's industrial nations (an estimated 115 million Western Europeans owned bicycles). Communities in the Netherlands, Denmark, and Germany were called "bicycle friendly" because of their balanced use of bicycles for transport, recreation, and sport. Cycling facilities such as bike lanes and parking sites, along with traffic calming and intermodal transit links, encouraged people to use bicycles for 20 to 50 percent of all urban trips.

In the United States, bicycles were used mainly for recreation. There were about 100 million bicycle owners with more females (55 percent) cycling than males, and

[1]Extracted from David B. Perry, *Bike Cult: The Ultimate Guide to Human-Powered Vehicles* (New York: Four Walls Eight Windows 1995), pp. 234–39.

more adults (55 percent) cycling than children (45 percent). According to the National Sporting Goods Association, about 57 million individuals rode a bicycle at least six times in a year. There were about 4.9 million bicycle commuters, 250,000 bicycle racers, 25 million mountain bike/hybrid riders, 1.7 million bicycle tourers, and 3.8 million participants in recreational bicycle events.

In some regions of Africa and Latin America, bicycle use was heavy. But in general, African and Latin American governments tended to stigmatize bicycles as an underdeveloped "Third World" means of mobility. While many leaders in these countries enjoyed the prestige of cars and new highways, their people often relied on walking instead of cycling for essential transport; bicycles were the second most common source of individual transportation, and motor vehicles and public transportation systems ranked third in importance.

In cities such as Moscow in the former Soviet Union, where public mass transit was widely used, bicycles were rare. In the countries of Eastern Europe, such as in Hungary, bicycles were used for roughly half of all trips to work. It remained to be seen whether Eurasian countries would deal with rising economic and environmental problems by encouraging the use of bicycles.

The majority of the world's bicycles were made and used in Asia. Seventy-five percent of the world's bicycles were produced in China, India, Taiwan, Japan, and Thailand. In 1987 China, known as the "Kingdom of the Bicycle," produced more bicycles than the number of passenger cars made by all of the world's automobile manufacturers combined. China had produced over 40 million units per year since 1987 (see Exhibit 2). Domestic demand in China was estimated at 30 million units per year, with the remaining production destined for export. The China Bicycle Company (CBC) of Guangzhou was one of the dominant Chinese bike manufacturers. The company was founded by Jerome Sze, a Hong Kong businessman, and began making bicycles for Western firms such as Schwinn in the 1970s. In 1992, CBC was rated as one of the top 10 foreign investment enterprises in China.[2]

Taiwan was the world's second largest producer, making almost 10 million bicycles in 1987 and about 7 million in 1993. Taiwan producers made over 70 percent of the bikes sold in the United States. The biggest Taiwanese bike makers were Giant Manufacturing Company and Merida Industry Co.

THE UNITED STATES BICYCLE INDUSTRY

The U.S. bicycle industry was approximately a $3.5 billion per year industry, counting the retail value of bicycles, related parts, and accessories through all channels of distribution.[3] Bicycle sales for the United States over a 15-year period, including both dealer and mass merchant channels are shown in Exhibit 3.[4]

The number of bicycle riders in the United States was expected to grow in coming years as provisions of the 1990 Clean Air Act and the 1991 Intermodal Surface Transportation Efficiency Act gave local communities a mandate to build bicycling into their future transit plans. Interest in physical fitness, new on-and-off-road pathways for bicycle use, and the introduction of the mountain bike had already expanded

---

[2]Ibid.

[3]Taken from Cannondale's prospectus, September 21, 1995, unless otherwise noted.

[4]National Bicycle Dealers Association 1994–95 Statpak.

EXHIBIT 2   Bicycle and Automobile Production in Selected Countries in Millions, 1986–87 versus 1991

| Country | 1986–87 | | 1991 |
	Bicycles	Autos	Bicycles
China	41.0	0.004	36.0
Taiwan	9.9	0.20	7.7
Japan	7.8	7.89	7.8
United States	5.8	7.10	7.6
Soviet Union	5.4	1.33	
India	5.4	0.15	7.7
France	4.5		
West Germany	2.9	4.37	4.9
South Korea	2.6	0.79	1.5
Brazil	2.5	0.68	2.3
Indonesia	1.0		2.0
Italy	1.6	1.71	
Poland	1.3	0.30	
United Kingdom	1.2	1.14	1.1
Canada	1.2	0.81	
Thailand	0.7		1.0
Others	10.5	6.54	
World Total	99.0	33.01	100.5

Source: Perry, *Bike Cult*, p. 237.

the number of adult cyclists. Some experts suggested the industry could grow even faster by shifting its focus away from individual sales and toward promoting bicycling as a sport and transportation alternative.[5]

Approximately 12.5 million bicycles were sold in the United States during calendar 1994. About 24 percent of the domestic unit sales, representing 48 percent of retail dollar sales, were through specialty bicycle retailers, with the balance through mass-merchandise retailers. Other major markets included Europe and Japan, where approximately 16 million and 8.5 million bicycles respectively were sold in 1994.

There were an estimated 31 million active adult cyclists in the United States in 1992 who used their bicycles at least once weekly. Adult bicycles fell into five broad categories: mountain, racing, hybrid, touring, and specialty. Mountain bikes combined elements from classic balloon-tire bikes, known in the 1970s as "klunkers," with the lightweight alloy components of quality touring and racing bikes. Mountain bikes featured suspension systems, low gears, beefed-up frames, and straight handlebars (allowing a more upright cycling position than racing or touring bikes) and were designed for heavy-duty touring over rugged terrain as well as reliable on-road

---

[5]J. Larson, "The Bicycle Market," *American Demographics* (March 1995), pp. 42–50.

EXHIBIT 3   Unit Sales of Bicycles in the United States, 1980–1994 (in millions)

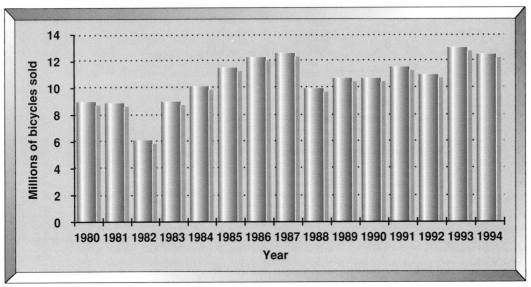

Source: Bicycle Manufacturers Association (includes bicycle wheel sizes 20 inches and over).

transportation.[6] Mountain bikes were the fastest growing segment of the adult market, accounting for 64 percent of all bicycles sold in the United States in 1994.

Road racing bikes were lightweight with thin tires and drop (curved) handlebars. Hybrid bikes had straight handlebars and a more upright riding position like mountain bikes, but used thinner tires; they were suited for both on- and off-road use. In Europe, hybrid bicycles were often called commuter bicycles and were widely used for general transportation.

Touring bikes were similar to road racing bikes in appearance, but the frames were designed to carry packs and other touring supplies. Ten-speed bikes, a popular American variation of the touring bike first marketed in the 1960s, were superseded by mountain bikes and hybrid bikes in the 1990s.[7]

The specialty bicycle market encompassed various niche products, including multisport, tandem, and Bicycle Moto-Cross (BMX) bikes. BMX bikes, which featured small 20-inch wheels, a relatively short but very strong and light frame, and no gears, were originally designed for short races over dirt tracks but were more commonly used by children and adolescents for everyday recreational use.[8]

The adult bicycle market had grown more rapidly than the market as a whole in recent years, largely due to such innovations as lighter weight frames and suspension systems that not only had attracted first-time buyers but also had induced many bike owners to replace their first-generation (1980s) mountain bikes. It appeared that aluminum frames, which were generally lighter than steel frames, and suspension bikes, which offered greater comfort and control than nonsuspended bikes, were becoming increasingly significant in the high-performance segment of the bicycle

[6]Perry, *Bike Cult.*

[7]Ibid.

[8]GT Bicycles prospectus, 1995.

market. High-performance bicycles were sold primarily through specialty bicycle retailers who could provide skilled service.

The Growth in Mountain Biking

The growth in mountain biking had been a major factor in the overall growth of the U.S. bicycle market. The number of mountain bikers in the United States grew from 200,000 in 1983 to approximately 25 million in 1992, and mountain bike sales grew from 54 percent of domestic unit sales in 1992 to 64 percent in 1994. Three factors contributed to the popularity of mountain bikes: (1) they were more comfortable to ride than typical touring or racing models; (2) they could be ridden over much wider types of terrain than other bicycles; and (3) more adults were turning toward outdoor activities in their leisure time. Recent developments were also adding to the growth in the mountain bike category. Cross-country mountain bike racing was an Olympic sport for the first time in 1996, reflecting the growth of mountain bike racing as both a participant and spectator sport. Downhill racing was proving to be increasingly popular with spectators, combining high speed and technically advanced equipment with the excitement of professional athletes and emerging personalities in the sport. The ski resort industry was also promoting summer use of ski mountains for biking, with many ski resorts equipping ski lifts to carry bikes and riders uphill.

Distribution

In the U.S. bicycle industry, two primary distribution systems existed. Mass merchandisers such as Kmart, Sears, Wal-Mart, and toy stores accounted for about 76 percent of all bikes sold and about one-half of the dollars spent on bikes in 1994. Most of the bikes sold by mass merchandisers were at price points below $200, and tended to be heavy, without the precision machining or reliable components demanded by fitness riders. These bikes were fine for cycling around the neighborhood, but not for serious biking. The mass merchant's advantages were price and the convenience of shopping at multipurpose mass merchant outlets.[9]

Specialty bicycle shops, which numbered approximately 6,800 in the United States in 1994, accounted for 24 percent of unit sales and about one-half of dollar sales. Bicycle dealer brands generally started at price points above $200, though some dealers were moving down to meet mass merchant competition. The average price of a bicycle sold at a bicycle shop was about $300, though prices for the best models could range into the thousands. The independent bicycle dealer's ability to offer bicycles that were lighter, more durable, assembled properly, and matched to the individual rider's needs, worked to the dealer's advantage. In addition, specialty bike dealers commanded a vast majority of parts and accessories sales, and virtually 100 percent of the service market. Dealers dominated the market in bicycles selling for $250 and higher. The growing interest in a total fitness lifestyle had also caught the attention of specialty bicycle dealers. Roughly one-half of the bicycle stores in the United States sold some kind of indoor exercise equipment (exercise bikes, weight machines, and all associated accessories). A small but growing fraction of the market included bikes sold through catalog marketers (e.g., L. L. Bean), outdoor shops, and warehouse clubs.

---

[9]The National Bicycle Dealers Association 1994–95, Statpak.

EXHIBIT 4	1995 Share of U.S. Bicycle Market

Manufacturer	Market Share
Trek	24%
Cannondale	12
Specialized	12
Schwinn	7
Giant	6
Diamond Back	6
GT	6
Mongoose	3

Note: Adult bikes priced $400 and up.

Source: *USA Today.*

Mountain bikes (26-inch wheel size) represented 63 percent of the bikes sold through the specialty channel in 1995. Traditional road bikes (27-inch wheels) made up less than 1 percent of the market, with children's bikes (20-inch wheels) comprising 20 percent of specialty dealer unit sales. The midsize 24-inch wheel bicycle category comprised 4 percent of dealer bike sales.[10]

A strong accessories segment was also a key part of the sales mix. Helmets (there were at least 20 brands) provided a high level of protection and fashion. Bicycle-specific clothing, water bottles, bottle holders, seat covers, and luggage packs and carriers were other popular accessories.

The Independent Dealer

According to the National Bicycle Dealers Association figures for 1994–95, the vast majority of the 6,800 bicycle dealerships in the United States were single-location/one owner enterprises (about 85 percent), though there was a trend toward more multiple-store ownership (about 13 percent of stores reported having at least two locations). About 70 percent were so-called "family" bike shops that offered a range of products. About 25 percent concentrated on the high end, referred to as "pro shops." California had the largest number of dealers, with more than 1,000, followed by New York and Florida. The average bicycle retailer had annual sales of about $400,000 per store per year and carried four brands. Gross margins on bicycles averaged about 34 percent. Margins on parts, accessories, and service were generally higher than those for bicycles. Bicycles comprised about one-half of the gross sales dollars of the typical bicycle dealer, the other half going to sales of parts, accessories, and service.

Efforts to Promote Bicycling[11]

Federal transportation policy promoted increased use of bicycling and encouraged engineers to accommodate bicycle and pedestrian needs in designing transportation

---

[10]Ibid.

[11]Extracted from U.S. Department of Transportation, *The National Bicycling and Walking Study* (FHWA Publication No. 94-023). Washington, DC: Government Printing Office, 1993.

facilities for urban and suburban areas. Government support for bicycling was contained in the Intermodal Surface Transportation Efficiency Act (ISTEA) of 1991. This federal legislation recognized the transportation value of bicycling and walking and offered mechanisms to increase consideration of bicyclists' and pedestrians' needs within the nation's intermodal transportation system. Federal funding was available from a number of programs, and planning requirements for bicycling were established for states and metropolitan planning organizations. Other provisions included the requirement that states establish and fund a bicycle and pedestrian coordinator in their departments of transportation, and that bicyclist and pedestrian safety continue to be priority areas for highway safety program funding. In addition, Congress directed the secretary of transportation to develop an action plan for enhancing the use of bicycles as a mode of transportation.

The 1990 Clean Air Act set standards for air quality and required some metropolitan areas to develop methods to reach compliance. One of the approaches involved taking steps to make bicycling a more viable transportation alternative.

OVERVIEW OF DOMESTIC AND FOREIGN COMPETITORS[12]

Three large American manufacturers dominated the unit sales statistics: Huffy Corp., Murray Ohio Mfg., and Roadmaster. Most of their bicycles were sold through department stores and chain retailers. Companies specializing in bicycles for the independent bicycle dealer channel were frequently based in the United States. However, many had much of their manufacturing done overseas, primarily in Taiwan and China for frames and in Japan for components. The major dealer-channel brands that did a significant portion of their manufacturing in the United States were Trek, Raleigh, and Cannondale. There were dozens of small United States bike makers (approximately 100 brands in all). Other major dealer brands included Giant, Schwinn, Diamond Back, GT, Mongoose, and Specialized. In 1994–95, imports accounted for about 44 percent of the total U.S. bicycle market (including mass merchants), with 53 percent from Taiwan, 43 percent from China, and the rest from other sources, such as Korea and Hong Kong. Many quality bicycles sold through the independent bicycle dealer channel were imported, and the U.S. bicycle dealer network, as well as consumers, relied heavily on free global trade for merchandise.

Cannondale's Rivals in the Mountain Bike Segment

The high-performance segment of the bicycle industry was quite competitive in the United States and many other countries. Competition was based primarily on perceived value, brand image, performance features, product innovation, and price. Competition in foreign markets was affected by duties, tariffs, foreign exchange fluctuations, taxes and the effect of various trade agreements and import restrictions. By the mid-1990s, there were several key competitors in the industry. Exhibit 4 depicts the approximate percentage shares of the U.S. market held by manufacturers of adult bikes priced at $400 and up.[13] Below is a brief profile of each of Cannondale's major competitors.

---

[12]Extracted from The National Bicycle Dealers Association 1994–95 Statpak.

[13]P. McGeehan, "Schwinn Pedals Back: Biking Icon Wants to Lose Training Wheels," *USA Today* (August 8, 1995), p. 01B.

Trek Bicycle Corporation   Trek, a privately held company, was the industry leader and a pioneer in carbon fiber frames. The Waterloo, Wisconsin, firm had about $300 million in revenue on sales of more than 900,000 bikes in 1995. Approximately 35 percent of its total revenue came from international sales. The company employed 800 people in the United States and 75 people overseas to build and distribute its bicycle line that included over 65 mountain, road, multitrack, touring, tandem, and children's models.

Trek began in 1976 by hand-building steel frames in a rented facility in Waterloo, Wisconsin. Pursuing high-quality workmanship, the firm expanded quickly, generating $750,000 in sales after just three years. It quickly gained a reputation for quality American-made bicycles. In 1986, sales reached $16 million. But the company then hit hard times. The company sustained losses, accumulated unsold inventory, and employee morale was low. In stepped the founder of Trek, Dick Burke, who quickly took charge and articulated a back-to-basics philosophy that rallied employees and reenergized the company with a new mission statement: "Build a quality product; offer a competitive value; deliver it on time; and create a positive work environment."[14] In addition, Burke revised Trek's marketing strategy, developed new and innovative road bikes, and introduced a new line of mountain bikes. Burke emphasized quality and efficiency in Trek's plant operations and pushed service excellence as the cornerstone of the sales department. As a result of these initiatives, Trek's sales took off, reaching $250 million in 1994.

Specialized Bicycle Components   Specialized was a private firm founded by Mike Sinyard in 1974 in Morgan Hill, California, that got its start importing Italian-made bicycle components. In 1981 the company launched the first mass-produced mountain bike—the Stumpjumper (the original model is at the Smithsonian Institution in Washington, D.C.). This was followed by a host of derivative products for both off-road and city cycling. Schwinn's failure to recognize the growing mountain bike market gave Specialized the edge it needed to carve out a place for itself, and the company became noted for its innovation and marketing skills. Products tested by its professional racing team were typically on the market within a year.[15] A 1992 article in *Nation's Business* reported that Specialized had enjoyed average compound sales growth of 30 percent per year, with sales reaching about $130 million in 1992. The firm had about 250 employees.

In 1995, Specialized introduced a second brand, Full Force, for sale through mass merchants and general sporting-goods stores. This distribution channel strategy was designed to access the large number of bicycle buyers who never went to an independent shop. According to Christopher Murphy, director of marketing, a new line of bikes under a separate name would permit Specialized to go after the mass market consumer without damaging its independent dealer base.[16] To pull customers into specialty shops, Specialized also set up several hundred company dealers to service Full Force bikes.

Schwinn Cycling and Fitness   Schwinn was founded in 1895 in Chicago by German bikemaker Ignaz Schwinn. At one time, Schwinn was the most prestigious bicycle company in the industry with as much as 25 percent of the market, selling 1.6 million

---

[14]Taken from "Reinventing the Wheel (A Brief History of the Trek Bicycle Corporation)," company document.

[15]"Reinventing the Wheel," *The Economist* (August 1, 1992), pp. 61–62.

[16]M. Barrier, "Wheels of Change in Bicycle Retailing," *Nation's Business* (February 1996), pp. 40–42.

units a year. During its 100-year history, Schwinn had sold more than 40 million bicycles.[17] Changing consumer tastes and tough new competitors with lighter, high-tech products began to slowly erode Schwinn's dominant position in the 1970s.

Rather than innovate, Schwinn became obsessed with cutting costs by moving production overseas in the 1970s. However, a series of management blunders eventually contributed to Schwinn's demise. Initially, it outsourced its bicycles from Japan. But by 1978 Taiwanese manufacturers were beating the Japanese on price. Schwinn shifted gears and began importing Taiwanese-made Giant bikes, on which Schwinn put its nameplate. When Giant became a competitor, Schwinn formed an alliance with China Bicycle Company, but after a few years CBC also used the knowledge gained in collaborating with Schwinn to launch its own brand in the U.S and compete against Schwinn.

To make matters worse, Schwinn made the strategic mistake of ignoring the mountain bike craze for most of the 1980s. By 1992, two-thirds of all bikes sold were mountain bikes. The proverbial writing was on the wall, and Schwinn filed for Chapter 11 bankruptcy protection in 1992.[18]

In January 1993, what was left of Schwinn was purchased by an investor group and sport accessory manufacturer Scott Sports Group for $43 million (Scott was a maker of ski equipment and Scott bikes). Scott moved Schwinn to Boulder, home of the University of Colorado and thousands of outdoor enthusiasts.[19] The new owners redesigned all 48 Schwinn models from juvenile bikes to $3,000 racing bikes. Management projected selling about 400,000 redesigned bikes—mostly Asian-made models that retailed for $200–$400—the lower end of the adult bike market.

One of the major challenges Schwinn's management faced was changing the company's image. Historically, Schwinn was viewed as a maker of sturdy, low-cost bikes, which ran counter to the 1990s consumer preference for trendier, high-performance mountain bikes. "They want to position this company as high-end, high-tech," observed Cannondale CEO Montgomery. "And what they've got is this traditional, old-fashioned Harley-Davidson type of product. That's their greatest marketing challenge."[20]

Schwinn's director of marketing, Greg Bagni, commented on a fundamental shift in strategy. "We've evolved from a marketing-driven company to a market-driven company. A marketing-driven company will try to sell a warehouse full of yellow bikes . . . a market-driven company will determine what the consumer wants first."[21]

Schwinn bicycle sales peaked in 1988 at $212 million. In 1995, the bike division was expected to generate revenue of about $120 million. Schwinn was unprofitable in 1995, with management hopeful that the company would turn a profit in 1996.

Giant Global Group   Giant, which began as a small Taiwanese exporter of bicycles, in 1995 was the world's largest bicycle exporter as measured by value. It had achieved its growth from an early alliance with Schwinn, which effectively gave Giant the market savvy and production know-how it needed to be a major competitive force in the industry.

[17]E. Eckstein, "100 years—Schwinntennial: The Company Celebrates a Century of Building and Memories," *The Dallas Morning News* (August 30, 1995), p. 1C.

[18]L. Loro, "Schwinn Aims to Be a Big Wheel Again," *Advertising Age* (January 1995).

[19]McGeehan, "Schwinn Pedals Back."

[20]Ibid.

[21]Loro, "Schwinn Aims to Be a Big Wheel Again."

When Schwinn began looking for a source of low-cost bicycles in 1978, it began importing a small quantity of bikes from Giant. When Schwinn's Chicago plant went on strike in 1981, Schwinn management decided against negotiating a settlement. The company closed its plant and moved all its engineers and equipment to the Giant factory in Taiwan in order to ensure adequate inventory for its dealers. As part of the deal, Schwinn handed over everything—technology, engineering, volume—that Giant needed to become a dominant bikemaker. In return, Schwinn imported Giant's bikes and marketed them under the Schwinn name. By 1984, Giant was shipping 700,000 bicycles to Schwinn, representing 70 percent of Schwinn's and Giant's sales. By 1987, Giant was selling its own brand-name bikes in Europe and the United States. To gain market share, Giant told dealers its bikes were Schwinn clones and 10–15 percent cheaper. To help build up its U.S. distribution, it hired several Schwinn executives.

By 1995, Giant was producing about 2 million bicycles per year, about 1.5 million in Taiwan and about half a million in China. Revenues for 1995 were expected to reach $485 million. Giant projected U.S. sales of over 250,000 units in 1995 and more than 300,000 units in 1996. Giant was also reported to be considering building a U.S. plant before the end of the century.[22]

Diamond Back   Schwinn continued aggressive moves to market its own bicycle by forging a new alliance with China Bicycle Company (CBC). As with Giant, Schwinn began importing CBC bikes and selling them under the Schwinn name. Schwinn taught CBC about the U.S. specialty dealer market, raised the Chinese factory's quality standards and lent it credibility. Using its newly gained knowledge and technological advances, CBC increased its sales of bicycles to Europe. In 1990, CBC acquired a medium-size U.S. bicycle importer and distributor, which owned the Diamond Back name. This move opened the door for CBC to enter the U.S. market. Diamond Back had a 5 to 10 percent share of the U.S. market in 1995.

GT Bicycles, Inc.   GT Bicycle management described the company as a leading designer, manufacturer, and marketer of mid- to premium-priced mountain and juvenile BMX bicycles sold under the company's GT, Powerlite, Robinson, and Dyno brand names. The company differentiated itself by providing bicycles with the latest technology, innovative designs, and advanced components and accessories. The firm distributed its bicycles, parts, and accessories as well as parts and accessories of more than 140 other manufacturers to more than 4,000 independent dealers through its own Riteway Products distribution network. Bicycle sales accounted for 76 percent of the company's net sales in 1995. The remainder was from the sale of bike parts and accessories. International markets accounted for 24 percent of total revenue. The company had about 500 full-time and part-time employees in 1995.

GT Bicycles was founded in 1979 in a garage by cycling enthusiasts Gary Turner and Richard Long. In the following decade, the company expanded from making bikes mostly for youngsters into a full-line producer, with special emphasis on mountain bikes. The company was headquartered in Santa Ana, California, and had approximately 350 employees.

---

[22]"Executive Interview: Giant Bicycle's Tony Lo," *Bicycle Business Journal* 49 no. 10 (October 1, 1995), pp. 34–35.

In 1995, GT Bicycles posted net sales of $168.9 million, up 16 percent from $145.7 million the previous year. The company recorded a net loss in 1995 of $284,000, which included a nonrecurring charge of $6.8 million in the fourth quarter. For 1994, GT posted a profit of $882,000. GT went public on October 18, 1995. It issued 3.15 million new shares and received net proceeds of approximately $40.2 million, of which approximately $37.1 million was used to repay debt.

GT Bicycles sold more than 100 bike models, including juvenile BMX bikes and 37 "All Terra" models for the burgeoning mountain bike market. GT mountain bikes were considered one of the top brands in the market. According to industry analysts, GT Bicycles had positioned itself to move into the top five bike makers based on its strength in the youth market. One analyst noted that "They have an extremely strong position with young people . . . . They have a virtual lock on the Generation X market, and they're attuned to the tastes of these young consumers."[23] Industry observers also noted GT exploited its target niche with aggressive marketing and a high profile. Like other manufacturers, GT promoted and maintained its four branded lines of bicycles with focused promotional efforts such as sponsorship of professional juvenile BMX and mountain bicycle racing teams and national, regional, and local bicycle races, as well as cooperative advertising programs with independent bicycle dealers.

In recognition of its marketing capabilities and commitment to product innovation, GT Bicycle was selected by the United States Cycling Federation (now known as USA Cycling, Inc.) as the exclusive "Official Bicycle Manufacturer" of road and track bicycles for the United States Cycling Team for four years, which included the 1995 World Championships and the 1996 Olympic Games.[24] GT had helped develop the fastest bike in the world, the Superbike 2, which was made from composite plastics and weighed only 15 pounds. The bike was used by members of the U.S. Olympic team in the 1996 games. The company's touring freestyle team displayed the firm's triple triangle logo at exhibitions across the country. GT was also the largest exhibitor (of over 900 exhibitors) at the Interbike International Bicycle Expo in Anaheim, California.

Mongoose Bicycles   In July 1995, Bell Sports Corporation completed its merger with American Recreation Company Holdings, which formerly marketed and distributed the Mongoose mountain, BMX, and juvenile bikes. Bell Sports was a leading designer, manufacturer, and marketer of bicycle helmets and bicycle accessories. Bell expected the merger to double its revenues ($103 million in 1995), extend its product offerings, and strengthen its distribution with many of the nation's top mass merchant retailers.

In his letter to shareholders, Bell's CEO noted that Mongoose was one of the fastest growing bicycle lines in North America. Net sales totaled $41.5 million for fiscal 1995 and the compound annual growth rate for the three-year period 1993 to 1995 was 30 percent.[25] In 1995 there were 20 different models of Mongoose mountain bicycles, ranging from full-suspension bikes to basic all-terrain machines.

---

[23]G. Boucher, "O.C. Mountain Bike Maker to Sell Stock," *Los Angeles Times* (August 16, 1995), p. 1, Pt. D.

[24]GT Bicycles prospectus, October 12, 1995.

[25]Bell Sports 1995 Performance Report.

Bell's strategic intent was to lead the global bicycle helmet market and select categories of the bicycle accessory market. Bell had plans to build the Mongoose line into a formidable competitor in the mountain bike segment.

CANNONDALE COMPANY BACKGROUND

The birth and early history of Cannondale was aptly captured in a 1986 article in *New England Business*:[26]

"I always wanted to start my own business," says the 46-year-old [Joe] Montgomery; he began the search for opportunities when he started working on Wall Street as an analyst in the 1960s for companies such as Prudential-Bache. His employers were looking for fast-track companies in leisure-time industries such as snowmobiles, but he was looking for less obvious opportunities.

"The bike industry was a sleepy industry," Montgomery said. "The industry had old ideas and designs. Anyone who was really aggressive and designed a functional, quality product could make a go. It was a field ripe for new ideas."

In 1972 he had one—a mini-trailer that bike campers could use to tow their gear. He quit his job and on the strength of a contract with a distributor, got a $60,000 loan to finance production.

Sales for the trailer started soft and, working in improvised company offices above a pickle store in Cannondale, Conn., he developed bicycle accessories to expand the line. The timing was good. The 1973 Arab fuel embargo hit, sparking a two-year bike boom, and his sales leapt ahead to $2.3 million by 1974. Then, in 1975, recession hit and the boom ended. The speed and degree of the drop in bike sales was terrifying. In 1974, 14.1 million units sold. In 1975, 7 million sold. Bike shops all over America closed.

"It was a big washout. A lot of people who were tired of some rat race and figured they'd open a bike shop went under. Our sales were cut in half, and we were stuck with $250,000 in bad debts." Having just gotten started, he wasn't about to file for bankruptcy protection.

"The worse thing you can do in this situation is put your head in the sand. You've got to call the guy and say, 'Look, I know what I owe. Here's my business plan, my cash flow analysis. Not only will I pay you what I owe you, I'll continue to buy from you.'"

His creditors liked his approach, and their cooperation helped the company out of trouble. But Montgomery acknowledges it was a sweat. "Very scary," he said. "Very scary."

Through the 1970s and early '80s, Cannondale quietly achieved steady annual sales of around $8 million and became known for an expanding line of quality bike camping equipment. Montgomery wanted to make a bicycle, though. In 1982, he got a letter from a 25-year-old engineer named David Graham, who felt he was stagnating in the Electric Boat facility in Groton, Conn.

"David wrote, 'I'm an engineer and I want to build an aluminum bike.'" Montgomery remembered. "We'd been working on bikes way back in the '70s, and I was pretty sure I wanted to make an aluminum one. Graham took a 50 percent pay cut to come here."

The first Cannondale aluminum bike came out in 1983. It hadn't been easy. There had been production problems: All the fabrication equipment for the aluminum frame had to be custom designed, and they had trouble getting components that would fit the unusually fat tubing. (Like almost all bike manufacturers, Cannondale makes practically nothing on their own bike except the frame. Gears, shifters, and other components are obtained from outside suppliers. Most of these are from the Far East, which somewhat dilutes current company efforts to position itself as an "American-made" bike.)

---

[26]R. E. Charm, "Like the Company's Sales, Aluminum Bike of Cannondale Stands out from the Pack," *New England Business* 8 (November 3, 1986), p. 41 (3).

Finally, the bike hit dealers' floors. It was weird-looking, expensive at $600, and had a number of bugs still to be worked out. But the equipment nuts, the "spoke sniffers" who permeate the bicycling world and are ever on the lookout for something new, embraced it.

For them, the prime attractions were the technical advantages of aluminum. Aluminum, of course, is light, and in premium bikes, light weight is a vital sales point. Yet Cannondale bikes are not appreciably lighter than comparable steel frame bikes, because Graham took advantage of aluminum and used more of it, making the frame tubing thicker and making the bike structurally stiffer.

Ted Constantino, editor of *Bicycle Guide,* a Boston-based consumer specialty magazine, explains that a stiff frame without any "give" makes for a more efficient bike. "There's a feeling you get on a Cannondale that every kilowatt of energy you put into the pedal comes out the rear wheel."

As important to sales as what the frame does is its distinctive look. "It doesn't hurt," Montgomery ingenuously acknowledges. "If I'm a spoke sniffer, I am proud you can see that I ride something different."

. . . Cannondale as an American company is bucking prevailing trends in the bike industry. The majority of premium bikes sold in the United States are made in the Far East. European and American companies used to dominate until the mid-'70s, when the now familiar one-two punch of high quality and low price from Japan hit the market. During the next ten years, old names such as Raleigh, Motobecane, and Puch ran into deep trouble.

But Cannondale saw sales explode right out of the gate; from 1983 to 1985 it grew at a 30 percent annual rate. They expanded their line from one model to 15. In 1984, Cannondale netted a lucrative contract making private-label bikes for L.L. Bean. Market demand and publicity within the industry helped it to expand its dealer network through North America, and then to Europe. It found itself continually expanding its headquarters in Georgetown, which now employs 80, and its production facility in Bedford, Penn., which now employs 175.

. . . If not the largest, it certainly may be the most talked about bike company. In that great consumer undercurrent of hearsay that can make or break a product, Cannondale has been designated as the "best" bike around. That means it's trendy. Trendy is transitory, and Montgomery knows he'll have to work hard to get beyond it. For now, though, trendy is OK. Trendy is something Joe Montgomery can take to the bank.

CANNONDALE CORP. IN 1995

Cannondale's main business was high-performance bicycles (85 percent of revenue). It was a leader in the use of lightweight aluminum as a material for bicycle frames. Although other manufacturers had recently increased their effort in aluminum, only a few of their models had aluminum frames (for example, seven of Specialized 35 models had aluminum frames, as did seven of Trek's 50 models). All 53 of Cannondale's bicycle models offered for the 1996 model year were constructed with hand-welded aluminum frames and were hand-assembled. The company's bicycles, marketed under the Cannondale brand name and carrying a "Handmade in USA" logo, were sold through specialty bicycle retailers in the United States and in more than 60 foreign countries. Cannondale also manufactured and sold bicycle accessories, including clothing, packs, bags, bike trailers, and components (15 percent of revenue). Industry analysts estimated that Cannondale had a 12 percent share of the over-$400 segment of bicycles sold through independent bicycle dealers in the U.S., equal to Specialized's share of 12 percent and less than Trek's 24 percent (see Exhibit 4).[27]

---

[27]Montgomery Securities, *Basic Report: Consumer Products: Cannondale Corporation* July 11, 1995.

Corporate headquarters and all support elements were located in Georgetown, Connecticut. Manufacturing facilities for bicycles and clothing were located in Bedford, Pennsylvania, with accessories, some clothing, and bike subassemblies produced in its Phillipsburg, Pennsylvania, plant. At the end of July 1995, Cannondale employed a total of 715 full time employees in the United States, 104 in its European subsidiary, and 17 in its Japanese subsidiary. The company's employees were not represented by a union.

Cannondale's product line covered all segments of the market, from high-performance racers to novice mountain bikers. In the past, the company had targeted only the high end of the market—the 11 million racers and cycling enthusiasts. However, in the past three years, Cannondale had broadened its product line to accommodate the growth in the mountain bike segments. In 1995, Cannondale generated 51 percent of its revenues from mountain bikes; 44 percent of the product styles Cannondale offered were mountain bikes. Road bikes accounted for 8 percent of sales and 34 percent of the styles offered, while hybrids accounted for 8 percent of sales and 16 percent of the styles.[28] Exhibit 5 shows a time line of Cannondale's growth and key innovations since 1971.

Cannondale's Business Strategy[29]

Cannondale's overall business strategy had a growing vertical integration component. The company manufactured its own frames in the United States whereas most of its competitors imported their frames from the Far East. Cannondale was one of the first companies to concentrate on aluminum frames and enjoyed the premier position in this category, as bicyclists continued to gravitate toward lighter weight, sturdier, high-performance bicycles. In addition, Cannondale was developing a proprietary line of components under the CODA (Cannondale Original Design Application) brand that was used in a growing portion of its product mix and was becoming more important in the aftermarket.[30] With components such as handlebars, brakes, cranks, and derailleurs comprising a significant portion of a bike's value, Cannondale hoped to gain a competitive advantage over other manufacturers who relied on outside component suppliers such as Shimano, SunTour, and Campionolo. As Cannondale became more vertically integrated in producing bicycle components and relied less on outside component suppliers, its operating margins were expected to improve because of the associated cost savings.

Product Innovation   Cannondale's products were designed for cyclists who wanted high-performance, high-quality bicycles. It differentiated its bicycles through technological innovations that made its bicycles lighter, stronger, faster, and more comfortable. The company had an ongoing commitment to research and development and had continued to expand and develop its aluminum bicycle line with a series of innovations, focusing on proprietary frame designs, suspension systems and components. The company's bicycle line had grown from 21 models in 1992 to 53 models in 1996.

---

[28]Ibid.

[29]Extracted from Cannondale's Prospectus, September 21, 1995, unless otherwise noted.

[30]Montgomery, *Basic Report.*

EXHIBIT 5   25 Years of Cannondale Innovations

1971
Joe Montgomery starts Cannondale at the Cannondale train station in Wilton, Connecticut. Cannondale gets its name when employee Peter Meyers, ordering the company's first telephone from a pay phone at the station, is asked how the new company should be listed. Unsure of what to say, Peter notices the train station's sign and says, "Cannondale."

1972
The Bugger, the world's first bicycle-towed trailer, is introduced by Cannondale.

1974
The Toot seat bag, with a revolutionary flexible internal liner, helps Cannondale on its way to becoming the industry's leading bag manufacturer.

1977
Cannondale's Bedford, Pennsylvania, factory opens in a refurbished truck terminal. Total work force: seven.

1983
The ST500 — Cannondale's first bicycle, and the world's first affordable aluminum bike with large-diameter tubes — is introduced. Despite widespread industry skepticism, sales are strong.

1984
Cannondale produces its first mountain bike, the SM500, and its first road racing bike, the SR900.

1988
Cannondale bicycles make their Olympic debut at the Summer Games in Seoul, South Korea.

1989
Cannondale Europe is established in the Netherlands, European response to American-made Cannondales is enthusiastic, and sales quickly grow to 35% of total revenues.

1990
Patented Seat Cleat seat bag attachment system is introduced, immediately obsoleting all other mounting systems.

1991
Cannondale begins operations in Japan. The company ignores conventional wisdom by establishing a subsidiary and bypassing Japanese trading companies, despite widespread industry skepticism, sales are strong.

EXHIBIT 5 (concluded)

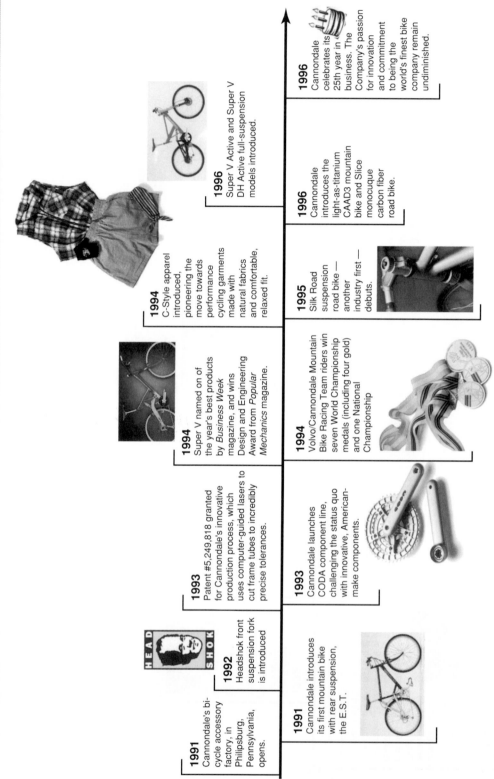

1991
Cannondale's bi-cycle accessory factory, in Philipsburg, Pennsylvania, opens.

1992
Headshok front suspension fork is introduced

1993
Patent #5,249,818 granted for Cannondale's innovative production process, which uses computer-guided lasers to cut frame tubes to incredibly precise tolerances.

1994
Super V named on of the year's best products by *Business Week* magazine, and wins Design and Engineering Award from *Popular Mechanics* magazine.

1994
C-Style apparel introduced, pioneering the move towards performance cycling garments made with natural fabrics and comfortable, relaxed fit.

1996
Super V Active and Super V DH Active full-suspension models introduced.

1996
Cannondale celebrates its 25th year in business. The Company's passion for innovation and commitment to being the world's finest bike company remain undiminished.

1991
Cannondale introduces its first mountain bike with rear suspension, the E.S.T.

1993
Cannondale launches CODA component line, challenging the status quo with innovative, American-make components.

1994
Volvo/Cannondale Mountain Bike Racing Team riders win seven World Championship medals (including four gold) and one National Championship

1995
Silk Road suspension road bike — another industry first — debuts.

1996
Cannondale introduces the light-as-titanium CAAD3 mountain bike and Slice monocuque carbon fiber road bike.

Source: Cannondale 1996 product catalog.

Cannondale's know-how and manufacturing skills enabled the company to be a first mover and a trendsetter in introducing innovative products. Its first product, the Bugger bicycle trailer, was an industry first that pioneered an entire product category. It was the first to produce large-diameter aluminum-tubed bicycles in 1983. It introduced its first mountain bike in 1984. In 1990, the company led the industry in introducing suspension systems in bicycles and in 1996 was setting the industry standard for full-suspension bicycles. Joe Montgomery described his philosophy toward innovation: "We approach everything we do—and I mean everything—with an eye toward innovation. And to a large extent, it's the innovations we've developed on the design and manufacturing side that allow us to continually bring these exciting new products to market."[31]

Manufacturing   The centerpiece of Cannondale's manufacturing strategy was its flexible manufacturing system. The strengths of the system included reduced production time, simultaneous production of various models, and small batch sizes without high tooling changeover costs. A patented process employed lasers and other devices to cut the uniquely configured joints of various bicycle models without individual setup or changeover. Patented self-fixturing joint designs and hold devices allowed the parts to interlock without special tools as they were readied for welding. The manufacturing system enabled the cost effective production of a wide product line and a broad range of models in a single day in order to respond to consumer demands. Where it once took 17 days to complete a bike, it currently took only three. Further efficiencies in the development process for other parts were realized through a new prototyping and tooling center with CAD/CAM technology. The company was committed to maintaining its competitive position by supporting research into further improvements in its manufacturing process and drastically reducing the time required to design and produce new bike models.

Cannondale considered its domestic manufacturing base a key competitive advantage. Whereas the majority of bike companies bought most if not all of their models from Far Eastern manufacturers, Cannondale made its own bikes at its plant in Pennsylvania. As Montgomery explained, "When you go to Asia to get a new frame design manufactured, the manufacturer makes three bikes for each one you order; one for you, one to sell to another bike company, and one to sell under their own brand name. By the time your new bike finally makes it into bike shops, the market is flooded with similar designs." He went on to describe the advantage of operating his own factories:

> First off, our factories don't have other customers ahead of us in line. When we make an improvement, or add a model, the reaction is instantaneous. Also, our proprietary designs remain proprietary. And of course, our product doesn't spend an extra six months on the water or stuck in customs, before finally becoming available to customers.[32]

Purchasing   Aluminum tubing was the primary material used to manufacture bicycles. In return for favorable pricing and delivery terms and certain technical assistance, Cannondale entered into an agreement with Alcoa and certain other suppliers. Most of its bicycle components were purchased from Japanese, Taiwanese, and United States OEM suppliers. Its largest component supplier was Shimano, which

[31]M. Sloane, Cannondale: A Company Built on Innovation.
[32]Ibid.

was the source of approximately 23 percent of total inventory purchases in fiscal 1995. Cannondale recently shifted its strategy to use more domestic suppliers in order to reduce lead times and lower inventory levels on hand. In addition, the firm was concentrating buying power among fewer suppliers, which allowed the company to secure higher-volume purchase discounts.[33]

In fiscal 1993, Cannondale revised its purchasing practices in an effort to reduce costs. Its goals included: (1) reducing inventory replenishment time through increased use of domestic suppliers; (2) obtaining price reduction in return for larger purchase commitments; (3) reducing inventory costs for new products by involving the purchasing department early in the design and development process; and (4) reducing inventory costs by reducing the variety of similar components in the full product line.

Marketing   The goal of Cannondale's sales and marketing program was to establish the company as the leading high-performance bicycle brand in the specialty bicycle retail channel. The marketing effort centered around promoting Cannondale's product innovation, performance, and quality leadership, generating publicity from the Volvo/Cannondale mountain bike racing team, and designing a media campaign designed to attract consumers to specialty bicycle retailers.

Promotion   In 1994, Cannondale formed the Volvo/Cannondale bike racing team. The team proved to be an early success, winning two gold medals at the September 1994 World Championships at Vail, Colorado. The team had generated considerable publicity in both the cycling and general press and through television coverage. Cannondale leveraged the success of its racing team by using photo images of the athletes in print media, on point-of-sale literature, banners, product packaging, and product catalogs. Volvo was committed as a sponsor of the team through December 1997. In addition, Cannondale supported racing teams in other cycling areas, such as the New Balance/Cannondale triathlon racing team and the Timex/Cannondale road racing team, as well as a number of individual sponsorships. Cannondale also sponsored six athletes at the 1996 Summer Olympic Games in Atlanta. These efforts built brand awareness and aided product innovation.

The public relations effort had been supplemented by a series of ads placed in magazines for cycling enthusiasts. However, the company's advertising effort had recently been expanded to include ads in general lifestyle magazines so as to reach upscale adults with interests in outdoor and leisure activities.

Sales and Distribution   Cannondale's distribution strategy was to sell its bicycles through specialty bicycle retailers who it believed could provide knowledgeable sales assistance regarding the technical and performance characteristics of its products and offer an ongoing commitment to service. Cannondale bicycles were not available through mass merchandisers, who generally carried lower priced products and who typically did not have the expertise to sell and support high-performance bikes. The company had not awarded exclusive rights to retailers in any territory.

Cannondale had historically utilized a small network of dealers to sell and service its brand of bicycles. One key component of its strategy involved adding significant numbers of new retailers to its existing network. The company was committed to broadening its domestic dealer base by 10–15 percent per year, with a goal of

---

[33]Montgomery, *Basic Report.*

expanding it from 1,000 to 1,500 locations. When considering a new retailer, several factors were considered: market density in terms of competition, population and demographics; ability of the retailer to optimize market penetration; commitment to service and the high performance segment of the market; and dealer creditworthiness.

Additionally, Cannondale had moved to broaden its product line to incorporate the under-$400 segment of the market (the price range that accounted for 65 percent of the bikes sold in the independent bike dealer channel). In 1995, the company had introduced a $400 mountain bike and a $400 hybrid bike that both sold in greater volume in the retail market than expected. With these new retail price points, the company had a product line that covered almost 100 percent of price ranges of bikes normally stocked by independent bike dealers, up from approximately 30 percent previously. Of the 3 million units sold through the independent bike dealer market, 1 million were priced above $500, while the remaining 2 million were priced below $500.[34] Industry analysts did not expect Cannondale to suffer brand-name degradation as a result of its move to lower price points. Most observers believed Cannondale would not introduce new models at price points below $300, but rather would continue its practice of introducing innovative products at the high end to help maintain the brand's image as upscale and elite.[35]

Cannondale's average selling price was not expected to decline significantly because of lower price points. The company's average wholesale selling price was $500 in 1995, roughly equivalent to an average retail price of about $800, essentially unchanged from 1994. Cannondale's margins on lower-priced bikes in 1995 were below average and management was looking at ways to increase margins on lower-priced products.[36]

Research and Development   Cannondale's product development strategy was directed at making its bicycles lighter, stronger, faster, and more comfortable. Its Volvo/Cannondale mountain bike racing team was closely tied into the company's research and development (R&D) process, thus allowing regular testing of both prototypes and finished production models. This collaboration, combined with the racing experience of its engineering staff, produced revisions, new designs, and new product ideas. In fiscal 1995, Cannondale spent $1.8 million or 1.5 percent of revenue on R&D.

The company's research and development efforts had, over the years, produced significant innovations in products and components (it had 48 current patents). One of the most significant recent innovations in the bicycle industry had been the introduction of suspension. Cannondale had developed several proprietary suspension systems and enhancements. Its Headshok incorporated the suspension and steering mechanisms into one unit built into the head tube of the bicycle. This design provided more accurate steering control than other front suspension models and also allowed easy adjustability while riding.

To ensure structural integrity of its designs, an experimental stress and analysis laboratory was used to collect data on stresses placed on products during actual riding conditions. This information was analyzed and incorporated into the design of new products utilizing Cannondale's computer aided design system. In addition,

---

[34]Ibid.
[35]Ibid.
[36]Ibid.

EXHIBIT 6   Adult Bicycle Unit Sales by Retail Price

Retail Price Distribution	U.S. Specialty Bicycle Retailer Market[1]	Cannondale 1995 Models	Cannondale 1996 Models
$600 and over	7%	38	39
$500–599	5%	2	2
$400–499	8%	7	3
$300–399	24%	3	9
TOTAL	44%	50	53

[1]Percent of total unit sales by specialty bicycle retailers for calendar 1994.

Source: Company prospectus.

stress analysis testing was conducted during production to verify conformance to design specifications.

International Operations[37]   Cannondale entered the international market in 1989 when it established a European subsidiary, Cannondale Europe, in the Netherlands. Although Cannondale Europe imported parts and frames made in Cannondale's U.S. facility and assembled them, it was primarily a selling and distribution organization that reached all of Western Europe directly and served Eastern Europe through distributors. Sales in Europe had grown at a compound rate of 28 percent since 1993, above the U.S. growth rate of 19 percent for the same period (see Exhibit 9). Sales trends were stronger in Europe than for the company's other global regions. The weak dollar had contributed greatly to the price/value of Cannondale's products in most of Europe.

Cannondale Japan was established in 1992. This subsidiary imported fully assembled bikes and was primarily a selling organization. Since 1993, sales had grown at a compound rate of 37 percent. Although the growth rate was impressive, penetration of the market was still under 1 percent.

Cannondale's Product Line

Bicycles   In 1996 Cannondale offered 53 models of bicycles, all of which featured aluminum frames. Exhibit 6 depicts Cannondale's unit sales of adult models by price point (i.e., retail price range) and the number of Cannondale models offered in each price range. Exhibit 7 lists the company's product offerings by category of bicycle, number of models, and suggested retail price range. Cannondale's full suspension mountain bikes (Super V DH Active, Super V Active, and Super V Carbon) featured front and rear suspension to allow for greater control and comfort at high speeds without sacrificing light frame weight. In December 1995, the Super V DH Active model was the recipient of *VeloNews* magazine's Technical Development of the Year award. Presented by one of the sport's most influential publications, the recognition strengthened Cannondale's reputation as the cycling industry's leading innovator. To

---

[37]Ibid.

EXHIBIT 7	Cannondale's Product Lineup for 1996	
Category	Number of Models	Suggested Retail Price Range
Mountain bikes (full suspension)	6	$1,099–$4,876
Mountain bikes (front suspension)	7	499–2,600
Mountain bikes (non-suspended)	10	399–1,246
Road bikes (front suspension)	2	1,249–2,167
Road bikes (non-suspended)	9	649–3,251
Multisport bikes	2	1,349–2,926
Hybrid bikes	7	399–1,246
Touring bikes	3	649–1,300
Tandem bikes	3	2,199–2,599
BMX framesets	4	329–429

Source: Company records.

meet various rider performance criteria, Cannondale offered frames in various tube configurations made possible by its proprietary Cannondale Advanced Aluminum Design (CAAD). The CAAD frames, as well as many of its bikes, were designed by the firm's research and development staff with input from the Volvo/Cannondale mountain bike racing team.

Cannondale's touring bikes included many of the performance features of its other models, but with a longer wheelbase that provided stability when riders were carrying additional gear for camping and touring. The company's flexible manufacturing techniques allowed for small production runs of specialty bicycles such as tandem bikes, which were produced in both mountain bike and road racing models. Finally, the company offered four models of BMX framesets. These were frames without components, which allowed riders to adapt the bike for their particular needs. All of the BMX models featured oversized aluminum tubes and were designed for high performance off-road use.

Bicycle Accessories   The accessory line helped the company to more fully capitalize on its distribution channel capability and, at the same time, build brand-name recognition. As with bicycles, Cannondale sought to differentiate its accessories through innovation.

Packs and Bags   Cannondale offered a variety of bags and panniers (bags mounted on the sides of the wheels for touring): mountain bike bags, lightweight, moderate-capacity road bike bags, and large capacity touring bags. The company also made fanny packs, duffels, and a backpack designed specifically for cyclists. The patented Seat Cleat bag attachment was honored by *Industrial Design* magazine for its design innovation.

Apparel   The apparel line was divided into three general categories. Spring/summer apparel included shorts, jerseys, and skinsuits, designed with performance characteristics such as aerodynamic cut, articulated sleeves that "reached" toward the handlebars, and patented BioSuede chamois liners. The fall/winter apparel line included jackets, jerseys, vests, tights, and accessories, designed to be layered in different combinations for a wide variety of conditions. C-style apparel was designed for rugged mountain biking activities, and featured a looser fit for unrestricted movement and the use of weather resistant fabrics; the category included fleece jerseys, shorts, T-shirts, Lycra jerseys and jackets.

Components   In 1994, Cannondale began sales of CODA components, featuring brakes, handlebars, bar-ends, seat binders, grips, cranksets and hubs, and began using these components on certain of its bikes. The company focused its R&D efforts on developing components superior to or more cost effective than those available from other parts manufacturers. In 1992, almost all of the non-frame components on Cannondale bikes were supplied by third parties; in 1996 20 percent were Cannondale components.

Other Accessories   Cannondale's other accessories included tools, pumps, water bottles, and bicycle trailers. In 1994, it began selling Cannondale brand helmets manufactured by a third party.

CANNONDALE'S FINANCIAL PERFORMANCE

Exhibit 8 presents selected consolidated financial data for the five-year period ended July 1, 1995. Management attributed the increase in net sales over this period to expansion of its specialty bicycle dealer network in the United States and abroad, more bicycle models, and marketing and sales efforts to strengthen the company's brand name. Over the previous two years, the firm's worldwide retailer network had increased to more than 3,400 from approximately 1,800 at the end of 1993.

Gross profit margins improved significantly from 26.5 percent in fiscal 1993 to 34.6 percent in 1995. The improvement was attributed to increasing economies of scale, favorable product mix, cost savings in its activity cost chain, and by the strengthening Japanese yen relative to the dollar.

Although the company experienced some difficulty in fiscal 1992 and 1993 as a result of low gross margins that stemmed from ineffective financial and operating controls and foreign currency losses, the company had since developed a more efficient manufacturing strategy and a more comprehensive currency hedging strategy that positioned it for margin improvement and more consistency. After posting three successive years of losses, net income rebounded to $7.6 million in 1995.

Because of foreign currency gains (losses) over the last three fiscal periods totaling ($271,000), ($111,000), and $249,000 respectively, Cannondale had entered into forward foreign currency contracts to purchase and sell European and Japanese currencies to reduce exposure to foreign currency risk.

Exhibit 9 presents net sales, operating income, and identifiable assets summarized by geographic area.

EXHIBIT 8 Consolidated Financial Data for Cannondale Corp., 1991–95 (in thousands of dollars, except per share data)

	Twelve Months Ended July 1, 1995	Twelve Months Ended July 2, 1994	Ten Months Ended July 3, 1993	Twelve Months Ended September 4, 1992	Twelve Months Ended August 31, 1991
Statement of Operations Data:					
Net sales	$ 122,081	$ 102,084	$ 80,835	$ 76,911	$ 54,544
Cost of sales	79,816	72,083	59,429	58,927	37,623
Gross profit	42,265	30.001	21,406	17,984	16,921
Expenses:					
Selling, general and administrative	27,023	22,290	19,615	18,527	11,993
Research and development	1,751	1,317	1,105	1,314	907
Stock option compensation	—	2,046	—	—	—
Agent and distributor termination costs	—	—	271	1,196	—
Total operating expenses	28,774	25,653	20,991	21,037	12,900
Operating income (loss)	13,491	4,348	415	(3,053)	4,021
Other income (expense):					
Interest expense	(3,929)	(4,460)	(4,177)	(2,990)	(1,976)
Foreign exchange and other	24	324	828	(868)	419
Total other income (expense)	(3,905)	(4,136)	(3,349)	(3,858)	(1,557)
Income (loss) before income taxes, minority interest and extraordinary item	9,586	212	(2,934)	(6,911)	2,464
Income tax benefit (expense)	(1,353)	(791)	(179)	1,422	(959)
Minority interest in net loss (income) of consolidated subsidiary	—	—	—	850	(343)
Income (loss) before extraordinary item	8,233	(579)	(3,113)	(4,639)	1,162
Extraordinary item, net of income taxes(1)	(685)	—	(464)	—	—
Net income (loss)	7,548	(579)	(3,577)	(4,639)	1,162
Accumulated preferred stock dividends(2)	(400)	(1,008)	—	—	—
Income (loss) applicable to common shares and equivalents	$ 7,148	$ (1,587)	$ (3,577)	$ (4,639)	$ 1,162

Cannondale's primary sources of working capital over the previous three years had been borrowings under its revolving credit agreements, proceeds from the issuance of $10 million of subordinated notes in 1992, $6.7 million of short-term borrowings in 1993 (exchanged for preferred stock), and proceeds of approximately $8.3 million that remained from its initial public offering of common stock in November 1994.

Initial Public Offering In November 1994, Cannondale went public, offering 2.3 million shares of common stock at a price of $13 per share. The net proceeds of

EXHIBIT 8   (concluded)

	Twelve Months Ended July 1, 1995	Twelve Months Ended July 2, 1994	Ten Months Ended July 3, 1993	Twelve Months Ended September 4, 1992	Twelve Months Ended August 31, 1991
Per Common Share:					
Income (loss) before extraordinary item(3)	$ 1.18	$ (.37)	$ (.73)	$ (1.08)	$ .28
Income (loss)	$ 1.08	$ (.37)	$ (.83)	$ (1.08)	$ .28
Weighted average common and common equivalent shares outstanding (4)	6,606	4,246	4,291	4,296	4,179
Balance Sheet Data:					
Working capital	$ 22,313	$ 6,366	$ 6,107	$ 3,615	$ 1,903
Total assets	84,008	67,870	65,245	57,877	35,617
Subordinated debt	—	9,179	9,323	8,692	383
Total long-term and subordinated debt, excluding current portion	5,602	16,174	17,195	16,176	6,566
Preferred stock	—	6,718	6,718	—	—
Total stockholders' equity, including preferred stock	36,088	9,640	8,220	4,525	6,893

1. Extraordinary items consist of the costs relating to early extinguishment of debt, net of applicable tax benefit, if any.
2. Reflects preferred stock dividends accumulated during the fiscal period. All cumulative preferred stock dividends were paid in 1995 at the time of the redemption of the preferred stock in connection with the Company's initial public offering.
3. No cash dividends were declared or paid on the common stock during any of these periods.
4. Shares underlying options granted during fiscal 1994 are treated as outstanding for fiscal 1994 and all prior periods, using the treasury stock method. Weighted average number of shares outstanding in 1995 reflects the issuance of 2,300,000 shares of Common Stock in connection with the Company's initial public offering.

Source: Annual report.

approximately $26.8 million were used to retire high-cost debt, pay accrued interest, and redeem all its outstanding shares of redeemable convertible preferred stock. Joe Montgomery owned 30.2 percent of the company stock; company employees owned another 15 percent.

THE CANNONDALE PHILOSOPHY

Cannondale's strategy and operating philosophy was based on its mission to be the best cycling company in the world. To this end, the company had formulated six operating principles:

1. We care about our customers, suppliers and each other.
2. We design and deliver a stream of innovative products.
3. We continuously improve.
4. We concentrate on detail.
5. We limit our distribution to the best bicycle retailers in the world.
6. We govern our every deed by what is just and right.

EXHIBIT 9   Selected Financial Data for Cannondale Corp., By Geographic Area, 1993–1995

	Year Ended July 1, 1995	Year Ended July 2, 1994	Ten-Month Period Ended July 3, 1993
Net sales:			
United States	$ 88,888	$ 79,207	$ 60,964
Foreign	64,791	54,280	42,519
Intercompany	(31,598)	(31,403)	(22,648)
	$ 122,081	$ 102,084	$ 80,835
Operating earnings:			
United States	$ 6,830	$ 2,391	$ 452
Foreign	6,421	2,229	(32)
Intercompany	240	(272)	(5)
	$ 13,491	$ 4,348	$ 415
Identifiable assets:			
United States	$ 70,918	$ 61,230	$ 55,334
Foreign	21,760	20,952	18,658
Intercompany	(8,670)	(14,312)	(8,747)
	$ 84,008	$ 67,870	$ 65,245

Source: Annual report.

APPENDIX: A SHORT HISTORY OF THE BICYCLE[38]

The exact origins of the bicycle are unknown. Some researchers have suggested that an early prototype can be found in the ancient tombs of Egypt and among the frescoes of Pompeii. The oldest known depiction of a machine similar to a modern bicycle was discovered in 1966 when Italian monks restoring the manuscripts of Leonardo da Vinci discovered a drawing from about 1490 that closely resembled a bicycle with pedals, a chain drive, and crude handlebars.[39] However, as with da Vinci's ideas for a helicopter and other visionary machines, the bicycle probably never was made into a prototype.

It was almost three centuries later when a Frenchman, M. de Sivrac, invented the Celerifere. The basic design consisted of two wheels joined by a wooden frame resembling the body of a horse. This 18th-century contraption included a saddle for the rider and required foot power for motion. Obviously, this early model never made it into production. At the beginning of the 19th century another Frenchman, Nicéphore

---

[38]This section extracted from R. A. Smith, *A Social History of the Bicycle: Its Early Life and Times in America.* New York: American Heritage Press, 1972.

[39]R. Ballantine, and R. Grant, *Richard's Ultimate Bicycle Book.* New York: Dorling Kindersley, Inc., 1992.

Niepce, came out with a design that consisted of two wheels held together by a beam (called the celeripede). The rider basically straddled the beam while holding onto a crossbar and running to propel the bicycle forward. Major shortcomings of Niepce's bicycle were that it had no pedals or brakes and poor steering capability.

The next big improvement in basic mechanics and design was made by Baron Karl von Drais of Karlsruhe, Germany, who added a fork for the front wheel, which permitted the device to be steered by handlebars. His 1815 bicycle had a wooden beam with triangulated legs, wooden wheels with leather-covered tires and iron rims, an armrest to go with the steering mechanism, an upholstered seat, a spoon brake operated by hand, a kickstand, and a luggage rack. Von Drais is considered the "father of the bicycle" because he was the first to patent and popularize his invention, the Laufmaschine.[40]

Over the next several years many individuals copied the Baron's basic model, making minor improvements such as adding an adjustable saddle. In 1821 Louis Gompertz developed a machine that could be propelled by working both one's feet and arms (something akin to the exercise machines found in gyms and fitness centers today). Again, several inventors tinkered with the Gompertz design over the years, but none really advanced the state of mechanics until 1836 when Kirkpatrick McMillian, a Scottish blacksmith, came up with a model where the real wheel was rotated by a system of cranks and levers. Now for the fist time, a rider could lift his feet entirely off the ground and still propel the bicycle forward. These machines weighed about 150 pounds and had no brakes. The cost to purchase a celeripede was high and out of the reach of ordinary citizens; thus it became known as the dandy-horse, available only to those with resources to purchase one.

Up to this point in the bicycle's development, the biggest problem centered on how to get the rider's feet completely off the ground and use them more efficiently. The answer finally came in 1863 when French carriage maker Pierre Lallement and Ernest Michaux put cranks with pedals on the front wheel. The steering column was straight, while the main tube, holding the seat, was curved, resembling an animal's spine.[41] The 60-pound machine was called the velocipede:

> It consisted of two iron-tired wooden wheels mounted one behind the other, a front fork and handle-bars to permit steering, pedals on the axle of the front wheel, and a saddle fastened to the wooden frame with a steel spring. The spring was not very effective in absorbing bumps, and the machine deserved its popular name of boneshaker. Although not yet called a bicycle, to all intents and purposes it was one.[42]

In 1866 Lallement traveled to the United States settling in Ansonia, Connecticut, and formed a partnership for the purpose of manufacturing the velocipede. However, the venture folded for lack of adequate capital and failure to interest prospective manufacturers. To his credit, Lallement succeeded in raising enough consumer interest in the machine to create a "velocipede craze." The craze did not last. There were just too many design shortcomings in this early version of the bicycle to stimulate the demand necessary to make the product a viable consumer good. The heavy weight, lack of brakes, and weak structural integrity of the wooden wheels motivated inventors to go back to the drawing boards.

---

[40]Perry, *Bike Cult.*

[41]D. V. Herlihy, "The Bicycle Story," *Invention & Technology,* 7 no. 4 (spring 1992), pp. 48–59.

[42]Ibid., p. 6.

Finally, in May 1869 the English firm of Reynolds and May introduced the first machine designated as a bicycle. The "ordinary" or "high wheeler" as it was called was made of iron instead of wood and had solid rubber tires. The front wheel was extremely large, almost as tall as a man. The idea was that the larger the wheel, the faster the speed. Riders were perched almost directly above the front wheel for pedaling efficiency. One problem riders faced, however, was that if the front wheel struck a rut, the bike would cartwheel, arcing the rider head-first into the ground.[43] Despite this safety shortcoming, the ordinary was a marked improvement over the earlier Lallement machine. Other inventors contributed subsequent refinements that included rubber-covered pedals and improved steel rims, and Parisian designers increased the size of the front wheel and reduced the diameter of the rear wheel.

In the summer of 1876 the United States celebrated its first centennial in Philadelphia with an exposition that displayed many of the latest products and technological wonders in the world. On display was the very first "ordinary" bicycle. This was the exposure the early bicycle needed. The enthusiastic response by attendees at the exhibition prompted a Baltimore firm to begin importing the English bicycle.

Also attending the exposition in Philadelphia was Albert A. Pope, a former Civil War officer from Boston. Pope fell in love with the "ordinary" and sensed the moneymaking potential of the invention. The next year he made a field trip to England to inspect cycle factories. In 1877 he began importing bicycles in Boston and opened a school to teach individuals how to ride. The following year he contracted with a mechanic named Atwell to build the first American-made bicycle (the "Columbia" model ordinary) based on the English design (it weighed 70 pounds). This event launched Pope's career as the father of the American bicycle industry and the beginning of the bicycle age in the United States.

However, before the bicycle became a popular item with the public, Pope had to overcome numerous legal, marketing, and technological obstacles. On the legal side, he was successful in fighting the parade of holders of ancient bicycle patents who wanted royalties on every bicycle produced. The most serious of his legal battles involved the horse carriage traffic, which until then had no real competition in the use of highways and streets. It seemed that the bicycles were foreign to the horses, which often bolted whenever they saw one approaching. Citizens were furious and fought back by having ordinances passed that restricted cyclists near horses. Pope fought a long campaign against these laws without much success. Pope also funded much of the legal expense involved in fighting anticycling regulations that had been enacted during the boneshaker era. One of the greatest contributions made by Pope and the cycle industry at this time was the effort to upgrade both city streets and country highways. Pope lobbied heavily for better roads and donated money to MIT to subsidize the teaching of road construction.

On the marketing side, Pope was confronted with the challenge of stimulating consumer demand for bicycles. He promoted the bicycle as a device to improve one's health, fitness, and happiness and even argued that it would help improve humanity. To counter the many physicians who disparaged cycling as a health hazard, Pope offered prizes to doctors who published the best articles defending cycling as a positive step toward enhancing health and fitness. In addition, Pope and other bicycle manufacturers underwrote distribution of the first publications directed toward bicycling (*Bicycle World* and *The Wheel*). They also underwrote publication of a monthly

[43]Ballantine and Grant.

magazine, *Wheelman* (later changed to *Outing*), one of the most important sporting publications ever published in the United States. He played a key role in founding one of the many cycling clubs that sprang up throughout the United States. Pope also recognized the importance of distribution, reasoning that it would do manufacturers no good to stimulate consumer interest if the bicycles could not be delivered efficiently to the consumer. To this end, he proposed a national network of dealers who would retail the bicycle at a set price, whether the sale was made in Maine or California. He was one of the first to offer guarantees for products. In addition, cycle makers created the system of planned obsolescence to stimulate sales by concealing models until they could be unveiled at the cycle shows. Pope's innovative marketing ideas were later embraced by the automobile industry.

Technologically, Pope's bicycle had some drawbacks. The "ordinary" had to be fitted to the buyer since the diameter of the front wheel had to conform to the length of the cyclist's legs. Moreover, the wheels of the "ordinary" had steel rims and solid rubber tires. The tires were either shrunk on the rims or held on by a wire or rope through the center. The larger the diameter of the tire, the more comfortable the ride. However, the bigger tires had a nasty side effect: The tires would twist off the rims when rounding corners, causing the rider to crash and destroy a machine that cost more than $100.

It was not until the early 1880s that the world's love affair with the bicycle began to take off. The catalyst was a technological advancement referred to as the "safety bicycle." This version reduced the diameter of the front wheel and slanted the fork forward slightly. This modification allowed manufacturers to move the saddle farther back, thus moving the rider's center of gravity aft and reducing the propensity to sail over the handlebars when encountering a bump, rut, or obstacle along the rider's path. Then in 1884, an Englishman, J. K. Starley, made the "Rover" that provided the booster shot needed to get the Western world hooked on the bicycle. His vehicle had two wheels of approximately the same size and was propelled by an endless chain running over the pedal-driven sprocket and then over the gears at the axle of the rear wheel. The saddle was mounted near the center of a triangular frame with the steering mechanism connected to the front fork. By 1886, successive frame modifications (specifically the diamond pattern) had transformed the "Rover" into the basic bicycle design in use today.

In the United States the turning point came when A. H. Overman of Chicopee, Massachusetts, patented the Victor Bicycle in 1887, the first of a long series of models to roll off his assembly line. The Victor had two wheels of equal size connected to a frame built on the system of the triangular truss, the so-called diamond frame, and propelled by an endless chain. The bicycle weighed 50 pounds.

Over the next 10 years several additional changes to the bicycle were made. By early 1890 the pneumatic tire had been invented by an Irish veterinary surgeon named John B. Dunlop. The introduction of ball bearings and lighter steel tubing led the way to a better machine and the addition of the coaster brake perfected it. The net result of these improvements was a decade when Americans went crazy over a fast machine (this same love affair with machines and speed resurfaced with the automobile and airplane in the early 1900s). By 1900, 300 firms were producing one million bicycles per year. Robert Smith aptly describes the impact the bicycle craze had on the American public and economy:

> This delirium was directly translated into an industrial boom during the otherwise chronic depression that began in 1891 and lasted until after 1898. While farm prices fell and

unemployment grew, the bicycle firms of Pope, Overman, Spaulding, and others were booming to the accompanying "ding-a-ling" of bicycle bells and the shouted curses of wagonmen. While William Jennings Bryan threatened the cities of the land in his "Cross of Gold" speech, Americans took to the Bicycle with such abandon and in such numbers as to force the police of New York City to put their patrolmen on wheels just to give them an even chance at the apprehension of criminals. The getaway car had yet to chug on the scene, but the getaway bicycle was already present. It turned out to be a grand and glorious debauch in speed and freedom, the likes of which Americans had never seen.[44]

By the early 1900s, the introduction of the automobile, an expanding interurban railway system, and consumer interests in other sports effectively ended the bicycle boom. As America's love affair with the automobile intensified, the bicycle rapidly was reduced to the level of a child's toy. By 1941, 85 percent of all bicycles produced were for children.

Not until the Great Depression did the bicycle industry experience a rebirth. As unemployment grew, few people could afford automobiles or public transportation. In 1936 alone over one million bicycles were sold.

After the United States entered the war in 1941, the federal government encouraged bicycle makers to increase production as a partial solution to gas rationing. After the war ended, bicycle production gradually increased as more young people took to the bicycle.

By the 1960s, cities began to be congested and polluted by the increasing number of cars. In 1966, the federal government responded to calls from ecologically oriented cyclists and joined other interest groups and awarded grants to cities to develop bicycle paths. By the early 1970s, cycling was experiencing a comeback in the United States. In 1973, more than 15 million bikes were sold, more than any year before or after.

From about 1893 to 1962, bicycle designs remained relatively unchanged. The diamond frame, which consisted of three triangles and a pair of forks, was the dominant design. In 1962 Alexander Moulton, an English engineer, developed the first really new bicycle design since the safety bicycle: the cross frame. The cross frame consisted of a large horizontal oval tube from which projected two parallel tubes: one supported the seat and the other held the bearings for the steering mechanism. Besides its unique design, what set the Moulton bicycle apart from earlier designs was the incorporation of a suspension system. More recent advances in gears, brakes, tires, and most significantly, in lightweight materials have had a profound impact on diversity in bicycle use: sport, touring, transport, a way back to nature, and a fitness activity.[45]

It was in the late 1970s in northern California's Garian County, when co-inventor Joe Breeze, Gary Fisher, Tom Richey, and many others invented the mountain bike, now the affluent world's most popular bicycle.[46] Although the most popular bikes back then were road bikes, Joe and his buddies discovered cyclocross, a European version of off-road racing that used skinny-tire bikes. They began training with one-speed bikes on the local mountain, Mount Tamalpais. Gradually they experimented with using classic fat tires and adding racing and touring components, plus the off-road features of motocross bikes. The first mass-produced mountain bike hit the market in 1981; and as they say, the rest is history.

---

[44]Ibid., pp. 14–15.

[45]Ballantine and Grant.

[46]J. Breeze, "Who Really Invented the Mountain Bike?" *Bicycling* (March 1996), pp. 60–68.

EXHIBIT 10   American Bicycle Industry Technological Contributions
to Transportation

1. Introduced use of assembly-line techniques to mass produced vehicles.
2. Made revolutionary advances in metallurgy.
3. Pioneered product testing.
4. Developed machines to carry out small operations.
5. Experimented successfully with variable-speed gears, the shaft-driven wheel, improved ball bearings, and the extensive use of lightweight steel tubing.
6. Pioneered development of brakes for moving vehicles.
7. Invented and perfected the tubeless pneumatic tire.
8. Spearheaded establishment of an extensive sales force.
9. Guaranteed products for the first time.
10. Created the system of planned obsolescence to stimulate sales.
11. Developed the idea of concealing models until they could be unveiled at cycle shows.
12. Created the ballyhoo and the hard sell that were later a part of the automobile business.
13. Upgraded city and country roads.
14. Developed concept and use of road maps.
15. Inaugurated regular reports on road conditions.
16. Listed approved hotels and taverns for travelers.
17. Developed traffic control systems and signs.

By the 1990s, the manufacture of bicycles was no longer dominated by low-cost mass-producers but increasingly by trendsetting innovators. Driving this change has been new technology and the transformation of bicycling from a transport industry to a popular sport and hobby.[47]

The bicycle has taken its proper place in history as one of the forerunners of our modern system of transportation. As noted in the case, the bicycle continues to be an important mode of transportation in many countries, with systems of bicycle paths that rival highways. Despite its short history the American bicycle industry has made significant pioneering contributions to manufacturing and the transportation industry (see Exhibit 10).

(Cannondale's Web site address is *www.cannondale.com.*)

---

[47]"Reinventing the Wheel," *The Economist* (August 1, 1992), pp. 61–62.

CUCHARA VALLEY SKI RESORT

Gary Bridges, *University of Southern Colorado*

"This is not going to be an easy job," Gary White muttered to himself as he began to spread out worksheets, financial statements, snowfall reports, and other data. He had been associated with the ski area in a variety of capacities for about 10 years and had witnessed all of its ups and downs. Gary was currently a professor at the business school of a nearby university. His roles at the ski resort had included two stints as controller, informal consultant, ski instructor, member of the ski patrol, owner and operator of three base area shops, and a home owner in the ski area's residential neighborhood. Now, as a consultant for another prospective buyer, he was being asked to give an opinion on whether the resort could ever be financially viable; and if so, to recommend specific actions.

Gary had made some hard decisions in his life—as an Air Force pilot and in his prior corporate position as an auditor. He had moved his family to this rural, mountain area 10 years ago in the hope that this lifestyle would be better for raising a family. They had become involved in community, church, and school activities and become as much "locals" as "outsiders" could become. He had watched the valley residents band together and provide the support services that the ski area needed. But more times than anyone was willing to admit, the result had been disappointment and even financial ruin for some of the residents. Yet, every year carried a new hope that the ski area would open and provide much-needed jobs to the valley.

Gary thought back to when the resort first opened. Located in the southern part of Colorado, Cuchara Valley Ski Resort (CVSR) was a small ski area tucked away in the Sangre de Cristo mountain range in the shadows of the towering Huajatallos

EXHIBIT 1   CVSR Distances to Major Cities

Denver	186 miles
Colorado Springs	114 miles
Amarillo	281 miles
Albuquerque	297 miles
Dallas / Fort Worth	640 miles
Oklahoma City	540 miles
Wichita	507 miles

(known locally as the Spanish Peaks). Two miles away was the unincorporated village of Cuchara, Colorado. The resort was developed and opened in December 1981 by local entrepreneurs and Texas developers under the name Panadero Ski Resort. The name had been changed as the result of a dispute between one of the original developers and a new owner.

The resort property covered 335 acres. The ski trails and terrain covered about 50 acres, 90 percent of which was public land for which the resort had acquired a use permit from the U.S. Forest Service. Because of the resort's distance from major lodging facilities five different sets of condominiums had been built early in the ski area's history. In addition, approximately 37 acres of the original land had been sold as individual ½-acre lots at an average price of $30,000. Twenty homes had been built; the average value of these homes was $500,000. Except for the ten acres that had been designated as green space, the remaining land was available for further development as single- or multi-family dwellings.

Because of its Southern Colorado location, Cuchara Valley Ski Resort had always been attractive to skiers from Texas, Oklahoma and Kansas, especially those who drove. It was so much closer than other Colorado ski areas and didn't require crossing any mountain passes.

Even before the ski resort was built, the area had attracted visitors at other times of the year. The Cuchara area had been a popular summer resort for many years, with many of its summer residents being from this same market. Summer visitors enjoyed fishing, camping, horseback riding, and hiking. In the fall, visitors would come to see the brilliant color changes of the valley's spectacular aspen forests. Hunters from many states also came in search of the area's wildlife—bear, mule deer, elk, and mountain lion.

An additional draw to the area was an 18-hole, championship golf course, Grandote, which was located approximately 14 miles from the ski resort in the community of La Veta. The golf course normally operated from May through September and had been recognized as one of the 10 best golf courses in Colorado by a national golf publication. Despite its excellent design, the golf course seemed to constantly flirt with financial disaster; it was currently plagued by litigation, IRS liens, and a duel between past and present owners.

Until 1986, the CVSR partnership/management group had stayed basically intact, but, as Gary was fond of saying, the owners now changed as often as the fall leaves. The itinerant ownership was partly the result of considerable uncertainty in the Texas investment community brought about by the Arab oil embargo in the 1970s and the resulting volatility of oil prices. Collectively, the owners' lack of experience in ski resort management resulted in well-intentioned but often inappropriate expectations. During the 1985–1986 ski season, the resort's Texas lender (Summit Savings) balked at advancing more money for operations. In a fit of brinkmanship, the resort's owners closed the resort in mid-February, a full six weeks ahead of schedule. The early closure left area businesses struggling to dispose of excess inventory. The resort's early and sudden closure badly damaged its reputation as several out-of-state church groups and other guests with confirmed reservations for Spring Break had to scramble to make last-minute arrangements.

The lender began foreclosure proceedings and the owners sued. Gary, along with the resort's mountain manager, was asked to work with a court-appointed receiver who supervised the 1986 summer maintenance operations. Eventually, the parties reached a settlement whereby the partners escaped financial liability and the lender took possession of the resort in the fall of 1986.

The loan to develop and open the ski resort amounted to approximately $22 million. Appraisals done shortly after foreclosure estimated a total value of between $8 million and $10 million. The lender/owner, Summit Savings, realized that the value of a ski resort resided in a business that was operating and generating revenue rather than in the assets themselves, so it agreed to provide operating funds for the 1986–87 ski season while it tried to sell the resort.

The 1986–87 ski season saw the most snowfall in the resort's history but because of the prior year's early closure, the slow start in advertising, and a general uncertainty about the resort's future, the skier count was disappointing.

Not long after the 1986–87 season ended, Summit Savings merged with seven other marginal S&Ls in Texas, as part of a restructuring effort known as the Southwest Plan. The newly formed S&L was called Sunbelt Savings. From Gary's perspective, this turned out to be an "unholy alliance" as it resulted in yet another top management group: Soon after Sunbelt Savings was formed, a different group of S&L executives in Texas assumed responsibility for the Cuchara Valley Ski Resort. Their first action was to hire a management company called Club Corporation of America (CCA) from Dallas, Texas to operate the ski area for the 1987–88 ski season. Gary remembered the local residents questioning the reasons for hiring an out-of-state management group. Their fears were confirmed when they learned that CCA's expertise was managing golf courses.

The organization chart of CVSR's ownership/management became even more complicated when the Resolution Trust Company (RTC) assumed control of Sunbelt Savings. All decisions then had to be cleared through RTC officials. After dismissing CCA in 1988, the new and improved RTC-managed Sunbelt Savings agreed to fund Cuchara's operations for the 1988–89 ski season, during which the resort attracted the third highest skier count (25,055) in Cuchara's operating history. Despite this relatively successful season, Sunbelt Savings decided that it would not provide operating funds for the 1989–90 season nor for the foreseeable future. They made this announcement three weeks before the scheduled opening. Sunbelt retained a skeleton crew to answer telephones and to show the property to prospective buyers.

The resort remained closed for three seasons (1989–90, 1990–91, and 1991–92). During this time, there were an array of "lookers" professing their desire to buy the ski resort. Finally, in 1991, a Texas businessman who owned a summer home in Cuchara began serious negotiations with the RTC. The sale was finalized in 1992 with the RTC financing a little over half of the purchase price.

Gary had liked the new owner and felt that he started his ownership with the best interests of the resort and the surrounding area in mind. The new owner believed that with the relatively low cash investment, CVSR could generate positive cash flow in the short term and eventually become profitable.

After two seasons (1992–93 and 1993–94), it was clear that the owner's expectations were overly optimistic. At the end of a lower-than-expected 1993–94 season, during which the owner had to provide additional cash for operations, he accepted a new investor's offer to assume financial and operating responsibility for the ski operations for the 1994–95 ski season.

Had someone been telling this story to Gary, he knew he would have laughed out loud and said "preposterous" to what happened next. But he had been there and he knew it was all true: The investor ran out of money before the first snowfall and never opened the resort. He not only failed to open the resort for business, but he also made off with the funds from preseason ticket sales and left many employees and local merchants unpaid for their services. With legal help, the Texas owner regained full control; but doing so took several months, and the (1994–95) ski season was over by then. It was safe to say that it had not been a good winter for the valley.

SNOW AND WATER

Cuchara's southern location had to be considered a mixed blessing in that its snowfall was always consistently inconsistent. The original developers realized this and constructed a snow-making system which, in theory, could cover 75 percent of the skiable terrain with man-made snow. But because of faulty installation, occasional unseasonably warm temperatures during the ski season, and technological advances, the snow-making system was, although operable, inefficient and bordering on obsolete. Nevertheless, man-made snow had been what kept the resort open during its frequent dry periods.

Snow-making was almost always done at night when the temperatures were colder; effective snow-making required temperatures below 28 degrees Fahrenheit. Snow-making systems rely on a system of pumps and compressors to move the water great distances up very steep terrain and then spray it through guns (actually high-pressure nozzles with fan blades) under pressure. Cuchara's system was all electrical and operated off of a separate electric meter. Each night (eight to ten hours) of snow-making operation cost approximately $1,500 in electricity usage.

Management usually started making snow in November, well before the resort opened, so as to have a sufficient base for the resort's traditional mid-December opening. December's natural snowfall alone usually was not sufficient to accommodate skiing. It was extremely important to have good snow (a 30″ to 45″ base was considered adequate) at Christmas because December and March were always the biggest months of the season.

Temperature and utility costs were critical determinants of the resort's snow-making strategy, but the most limiting constraint to short-term snow-making ability and long-term planning had always been the availability of water. Baker Creek flowed from a source high in the peaks of the Sangre de Cristo range and was the resort's only source of water for snow-making and domestic use (homes, condos, and restaurants). The resort owned water rights under Colorado water law allowing it to divert a specified volume (measured by cubic feet per second) out of Baker Creek. Water for domestic use was pumped to a 100,000-gallon storage tank. In addition, the resort stored approximately one-and-a-half acre-feet (1 million gallons) of water in a small pond.

Without this pond as a storage facility, it would have been impossible to make snow. Heavy snow-making would empty the pond in about eight hours, and it took twelve hours to refill under most conditions. The County Water Commissioner would constantly monitor the metered usage of snow-making water to ensure that the resort did not use more than its legal entitlement.

Gary felt that additional water (and storage) was a must. Snow-making needed expanding and, eventually, additional housing would be required if CVSR were to become a true destination resort. He knew that water rights could be bought and sold on an open market basis, with higher priority rights (lower numbers) costing more than lower priority rights (higher numbers). Each residential unit required the water right for one Equal Quantity Ratio (EQR), or enough water to supply the annual needs of a typical family of four (estimated at about 88,000 gallons). This arbitrary unit of water right sold for between $1200 and $2000. Since CVSR already used its entire allotment of 347 EQRs, the resort would need to buy additional EQRs (which it then would make available to homeowners or hotel developers) if it hoped to develop additional lots. EQRs for another 50 units could cost as much as $100,000.

"Of course," Gary thought, "owning the rights and actually getting the water could be two different things." He knew that owning the water rights to a stream such as Baker Creek would not guarantee that the actual volume of water in that stream (determined by snowfall) would be enough to fulfill an owner's legal water rights, especially the demand a fully developed resort might create. Could Mother Nature be counted on to ensure that Baker Creek would always have enough water to meet the resort's growing needs? Gary had never seen Baker Creek dry, but beyond that, he didn't have an answer. He made a note to recommend a water resource expert.

EXHIBIT 2   Comparative Data on Skiing Characteristics at Selected Ski Resorts

Ski Resort	Elevation Top	Elevation Base	Number of Lifts	Vertical Drop	Number of Trails
Cuchara	10,801 ft	9,248 ft	4	1,562 ft	24
Monarch	11,900 ft	10,790 ft	4	1,160 ft	54
Taos, N.M.	11,819 ft	9,207 ft	11	2,612 ft	72
Wolf Creek	11,775 ft	10,350 ft	6	1,425 ft	50

RESORT SERVICES

Next Gary took a look at the resort's services. He wanted to present a clear picture of what the resort had to offer skiers. "Good people" was the first item he wrote down. Most of the employees were year-round valley residents, and they had always done their best to be friendly and helpful to resort visitors. The resort's wages had always been below the Colorado ski industry's averages, though, and it was getting harder and harder to lure quality, skilled employees back for the see-saw ride.

SKIING TERRAIN

The skiing terrain at CVSR was considered moderate, with 40 percent beginner, 40 percent intermediate, and 20 percent expert runs. The U.S. Forest Service had recently allowed Cuchara to open an additional 45 acres of expert terrain called The Burn, but it was ungroomed and was not served by a lift (see Exhibit 2 for comparative data on ski lifts).

Lift Tickets, Ski Rental, and Ski School

The resort's moderate ticket prices that ranged from $15 to $25 placed Cuchara near the lowest of Colorado's and New Mexico's lift ticket prices (see Exhibit 3). Ski rentals were available at the base area and in the village of Cuchara. The equipment was acceptable, although not in top notch shape. Prices were standard for the industry.

The ski school offered basic group and private lessons. As with rentals, ski school prices were competitive. Ski instructors were typically local residents who knew the mountain well.

FOOD AND LODGING

At the base area, CVSR had available a snack bar, the Warming Hut, where skiers could purchase food and drinks from morning until late afternoon. A full service dining facility, Baker Creek Restaurant, was also located in the base area and served lunch and dinner. A limited number of other restaurants and bars were located in the village of Cuchara and in La Veta.

Although cabins and condos were located within the resort's "borders," none were currently owned by CVSR. Consequently, resort employees reserved lodging for all overnight skiers through local property managers who had contracted with the owners of condos and cabins to provide reservation and cleaning services. When the

EXHIBIT 3	Lift Ticket Prices at Selected Ski Resorts, 1994–1995 Season		
Resort	**Adult Full Day**	**Child Full Day**	**Adult Half Day**
Cuchara	$25	$15	$18
Monarch	$27	$16	$22
Taos, NM	$37	$22	$24
Wolf Creek	$31	$19	$22

resort was busy, especially during Christmas vacation and Spring Break, the housing on the resort property would be filled; the resort would then direct overnight guests to the limited local hotels in Cuchara and La Veta. Almost all of the ownership groups had recognized the need for more beds in the resorts, but no one had had enough money to build additional facilities.

CVSR did not provide transportation to and from Cuchara or La Veta. Gary knew that the larger ski areas in the state had ski-in/ski-out lodging adjacent to their slopes. At CVSR, skiers could drive from the condos to the base area in a matter of minutes, although slippery, steep roads and limited base area parking might be considered by some to be problematic. Other resorts had solved such problems by providing bus service from the lodging facilities to the base area; Cuchara had no transportation services within the resort property. Was lodging a problem for CVSR? Gary wondered if the lack of rooms near the base area should be considered a major constraint on the resort's long term viability.

Other Services

CVSR tried to behave as much like a larger resort as it could. A few times during the season there would be a dance band or a concert at the restaurant or the warming hut. Outside of these typically peak periods, the base area was closed down at night except for the restaurant.

The base area had a small shopping area with six retail spaces open during the day that sold t-shirts, sweatshirts, and ski-related gear such as goggles, gloves, etc. Child care could also be arranged for either the day or night.

MARKET DATA

Target Customers

Cuchara's management had consistently marketed the resort to families and groups (mostly church groups) who were beginner and intermediate skiers and who typically drove to Colorado. Gary remembered meeting a chaperone for a group from Texas who told him that somewhat isolated places were, in her mind, a great destination for middle school and high school kids. She had said that it was much easier to "chaperone" when you didn't have to worry about the kids out walking up and down the streets of an unfamiliar ski town. Gary was not sure that was the "marketing theme" the resort wanted to use.

In fact, Gary's years of watching the numbers had led him to the conclusion that church groups were usually break-even business at best and were often loss leaders, at least where lift tickets, ski rentals, and ski lessons were concerned because of the sizable discounts given. However, management generally felt that at least during slower periods (January and February), groups helped pay the bills until March. (Because Spring Break schedules were not as standardized as Christmas vacation dates, the resort was generally busy throughout the month of March.) There was also a glimmer of long-term strategic thinking that members of these groups would return with their families or in smaller groups and pay the regular prices.

CVSR did not totally ignore the southeastern Colorado market. The resort focused on the same beginner/intermediate skier, especially those who might want to "try out" skiing but didn't necessarily have the money or want to spend the money to go to the larger ski areas (destination resorts). In fact, it was typical of skiers in this market to arrive in the morning and drive home after a day's skiing, thereby avoiding the cost of lodging.

Location

Gary got out a map and began to look at various distances. CVSR was 114 miles south of Colorado Springs, the closest airport with substantial commercial air service. Pueblo was 35 miles closer but it was served only by commuter service that connected in Denver. La Veta, located 15 miles from CVSR, had an unattended runway that could accommodate small jets but had no scheduled air service and had no instrument landing capability.

The resort was 31 miles west of Interstate Highway 25, Colorado's only north-south interstate. Residents of large cities in Texas, Kansas, and Oklahoma could drive to Cuchara in eight to ten hours (see Exhibit 1).

Competition

The nearest competitors to Cuchara were Wolf Creek Ski Area (a Colorado ski area approximately three hours' driving time west), Monarch Ski Area (a Colorado ski area approximately three hours driving time north and west) and Taos Ski Area (a New Mexico ski area approximately two hours driving time west and south). Getting to any of these three ski areas from any eastern or southeastern destination required not only additional hours on the road but also substantial mountain driving over high mountain passes. For someone who was not used to this kind of driving, snow packed or icy mountain roads could be most unnerving.

As Gary sifted through the industry data and brochures he had on these competitors, he noted that ticket prices were anywhere from $1 to $12 higher than those at Cuchara (see Exhibit 3). But if a group were coming from outside the state, would a few dollars a day per person really matter? Gary wasn't sure. Ski rental and ski school prices weren't an issue: Unless you went to Aspen or one of the other destination resorts, prices for rentals and ski lessons were about the same everywhere.

Next he took a look at the terrain and snowfall. All of the competitors had more skiable terrain than did Cuchara. Each also had considerably more expert runs. Since Gary and his family had been skiing for years, that was especially appealing to him. Then he looked at the snowfall charts. "No comparison," he thought. All three competitors had more snowfall than Cuchara had. In fact, Wolf Creek typically received more snowfall than any ski area in Colorado.

And what about the night life, the restaurants, and all those other things skiers liked to do when they weren't skiing. Gary thought that, in general, the competing ski areas were as isolated as Cuchara. None had significant development surrounding the base area as some of the destination resorts did. But Gary had to admit that each of the competitors had larger towns and more entertainment within 20 to 30 miles.

The last thing that Gary considered was off-season activity. Most large ski areas in the state had found ways to use the slopes or other facilities during the summer. Some resorts had installed alpine slides. An alpine slide was a concrete bobsled-like path that was placed on the slopes; visitors rode to the top on the ski lifts and then came down the concrete slide on a cart with wheels that had limited steering and braking capability. Some resorts groomed their trails for mountain biking and let biker and bike ride the ski lifts up the mountain. Concerts, fairs, and other types of gatherings were also typical. These types of activities were supported, of course, by the resorts' abundance of lodging and shopping.

CVSR and its competitors did not typically have summer activities. Summer activity in Taos was certainly big because of its Native American influence and its artist community. But most of this activity occurred in the city of Taos, not at the ski area. Gary thought that CVSR probably had the most potential of the four ski areas because of the lodging that was reasonably close to the base area and because of the well-established summer resident/visitor clientele that had been coming to the Cuchara Valley annually for many years. Throughout the changing ownership of CVSR, Gary had seen various events organized such as classical and popular music concerts, art shows, etc. Attendance had been acceptable for first-time events, but none had been continued from year to year so as to build a reputation.

MARKETING ACTIVITIES

Gary knew that Cuchara primarily used direct mail to reach previous guests and group leaders. In addition, management had occasionally put employees on the road to make direct contact with church groups in Texas, Oklahoma, and Kansas.

For the southeastern Colorado market, CVSR usually bought TV and radio spots in Pueblo and Colorado Springs that emphasized low prices and no lift lines. The resort would also sell discount tickets to the military and through various retail outlets such as convenience stores and supermarkets.

Gary had learned from resort employees who had worked at other ski areas that ski shows were generally an important marketing tool in that travel agents attended them and could provide important group business. He knew that shows were held in Wichita, Kansas; in Dallas and Amarillo, Texas; and, of course, in Denver. Typically, two or three attractive and enthusiastic marketing representatives from each ski resort would attend these shows and set up attractive booths highlighting their resorts' strengths. CVSR's attention to ski shows had been spotty at best.

From what Gary knew, it only cost between $125 and $200 to set up a booth at one of these shows, and it seemed to him that traveling to regional shows would be cheaper than visiting individual groups and would result in far more contacts. But what about personal service? Gary knew that the friendliness of the valley people was an appealing feature of Cuchara. Traveling to cities and making personal visits with church groups was a nice touch. Unfortunately, no data had been kept on these issues. So Gary could not determine if direct mail, personal visits, or ski shows resulted in the most "bang for your buck."

COLORADO SKI INDUSTRY

Gary thought he had better have a look at the big picture also. He found that data from Colorado Ski Country USA showed the Colorado ski industry to be maturing; it had increased its skier visits only ½ percent in the 1993–94 season and then had suffered a similar percentage decline in the 1994–95 season (see Exhibit 4). (A skier visit or skier day represented one skier buying one lift ticket on a given day; if a particular skier skied more than one day, the skier was counted each of these days.)

The larger Colorado ski resorts had been attacking the stagnant growth by expanding their skiable terrain and adding high speed lifts and other amenities. In fact, Colorado ski resorts had spent $44.5 million on capital improvements during 1992–93 and $43.5 million during 1993–94.

While the statewide skier visit count was holding its own, summer and winter vacation air travel into Denver International Airport (DIA) had declined. In addition, winter overnight lodging figures in the ski areas were down. Industry experts had interpreted this to mean that many of the skiers were coming from Colorado's Front Range (Boulder, Denver, Colorado Springs, and other cities along the eastern edge of the Rockies). Gary knew that for several years these Front Range cities had been experiencing a significant population migration from other states. Perhaps that increase had created a set of new Colorado residents who were interested in skiing.

Other data showed that tourism (winter and summer visitors) in Colorado was becoming more of a regional activity. The number of visitors statewide who arrived by car had increased significantly.

EXHIBIT 4   Trend in Number of Skier Days at Cuchara Valley Ski Resort versus All Colorado Ski Resorts, 1981–82 to 1994–95

Season	All Colorado Ski Resorts*	Cuchara Valley Ski Resort
1981–82	7,616,699	12,567
1982–83	8,200,442	22,263
1983–84	8,617,318	35,337
1984–85	9,052,345	31,232
1985–86	9,110,597	12,998
1986–87	8,453,359	16,495
1987–88	9,557,002	16,383
1988–89	9,981,916	25,055
1989–90	9,703,927	CLOSED
1990–91	9,788,487	CLOSED
1991–92	10,427,994	CLOSED
1992–93	11,111,290	22,775
1993–94	11,011,290	17,203
1994–95	11,105,106	CLOSED

*Colorado Ski Country, USA

FINANCIAL DATA

The final item on Gary's list was the financial data he had assembled (Exhibits 5–7). He knew that Cuchara earned revenue from lift ticket sales, ski equipment rentals, ski lessons, child care, and food service. First he looked at the revenue and expense data for the two seasons (1992–93 and 1993–94) the resort had been operating under the current owner. The owner had given the ski shop to a local resident rent free. In return, the shopkeeper had stocked a small amount of CVSR merchandise as well as the merchandise she sold. The shopkeeper's only obligation was to remit sales dollars from the resort's merchandise to the resort.

Gary also noted that during the first season (1992–93), the restaurant had been closed and the Warming Hut had been leased out. Only a rent amount was collected. In the following season, both food establishments had been operated by the resort.

Overall, the report showed a small profit in the neighborhood of $36,000 over the two-season period. At least that's what it said on paper. But Gary knew that the spreadsheet only covered the two seasons, the four months each year during which skiers could use the mountain. It didn't reflect the expenses of the other eight months of each year. Summer maintenance on the equipment and lifts was required, and someone had to be around to answer the phones. In addition, the fall months (usually beginning in October) always saw a flurry of activity as the resort geared up for the coming season. Marketing activities increased, equipment was readied, and employees were hired and trained.

Next he looked at the list of assets (Exhibit 7). Some of these assets were "the originals"—Sno-Cats, chair lift motors and assemblies, etc. Some major replacements were due. While depreciation amounts had always been included in expense records, he knew no real cash existed to make the kind of capital improvements that were going to be necessary in the near future.

EXHIBIT 5 Cuchara Valley Ski Resort Financial Summary, 1981–82 Season through 1993–94 Season

Revenue

Season	Skier Count	Lift Tickets	Ski School	Ski Rental	Baker Creek	Warming Hut	Totals
1981–82	12,567	Unknown	Unknown	Unknown	Unknown	Unknown	
1982–83	22,263	Unknown	Unknown	Unknown	Unknown	Unknown	
1983–84	35,337	$312,696	$ 32,679	$ 0	$ 85,304	$ 73,921	$504,600
1984–85	31,232	315,264	34,666	65,880	139,035	96,397	651,242
1985–86	12,998	113,946	21,771	62,766	53,239	59,589	311,311
1986–87	16,495	145,442	17,918	52,727	29,783	52,704	298,574
1987–88	16,383	114,848	17,689	50,031	35,162	48,247	265,977
1988–89	25,055	260,660	52,960	106,696	0	76,178	496,494
1989–90	CLOSED	0	0	0	0	0	0
1990–91	CLOSED	0	0	0	0	0	0
1991–92	CLOSED	0	0	0	0	0	0
1992–93	22,775	323,053	41,140	97,646	CLOSED	LEASED	461,839
1993–94	17,300	195,305	54,898	94,397	67,528	57,998	470,126

EXHIBIT 6 Monthly Departmental Revenue, Expense, and Profit Statistics for Cuchara Valley Ski Resort, 1992–93 and 1993–94 Seasons

	1992–93 Season				1993–94 Season				
	Dec 92	Jan 93	Feb 93	Mar 93	Dec 93	Jan 94	Feb 94	Mar 94	TOTAL
Ski Operations									
Revenue	$ 58,649	$102,397	$ 3,328	$ 96,578	$ 78,555	$ 21,479	$ 49,695	$ 54,478	$ 465,159
Expenses	61,603	76,731	37,157	37,157	70,494	69,414	45,184	32,267	430,006
Profit (Loss)	(2,954)	25,666	(33,829)	59,421	8,061	(47,935)	4,511	22,210	35,153
Ski School									
Revenue	6,907	18,108	544	18,405	25,197	4,981	13,239	12,034	99,415
Expenses	13,467	23,099	1,332	1,332	9,082	14,128	9,448	17,412	89,300
Profit (Loss)	(6,560)	(4,991)	(788)	17,073	16,114	(9,146)	3,791	(5,378)	10,115
Ski Rental									
Revenue	18,756	37,417	1,068	36,758	33,433	10,672	23,179	28,904	190,187
Cost of Sales	0	0	0	0	658	0	0	0	658
Gross Margin	18,756	37,417	1,068	36,758	32,775	10,672	23,179	28,904	189,530
Expenses	9,006	14,606	4,406	4,406	18,720	10,767	6,148	8,964	77,024
Profit (Loss)	9,750	22,811	(3,338)	32,352	14,055	(95)	17,031	19,940	112,506
Ski Merchandise									
Revenue	3,245	3,805	249	0	3,898	1,628	2,362	4,516	19,703
Cost of Sales	3,630	3,492	149	0	1,652	6,996	1,777	886	18,583
Gross Margin	(385)	314	100	0	2,245	(5,368)	584	3,630	1,120
Expenses	0	0	0	0	326	0	0	0	326
Profit (Loss)	(385)	314	100	0	1,919	(5,368)	584	3,630	794
Food & Beverages									
Revenue	2,151	2,448	2,134	0	41,746	22,087	30,711	27,642	128,917
Cost of Sales	0	0	0	0	24,953	12,049	13,006	5,561	55,570
Gross Margin	2,151	2,448	2,134	0	16,793	10,037	17,705	22,080	73,347
Expenses	1,249	2,296	2,121	2,121	40,750	23,356	12,345	12,777	97,016
Profit (Loss)	902	151	12	(2,121)	(23,957)	(13,319)	5,360	9,303	(23,670)
Property Management									
Revenue	3,945	12,422	(6)	1,224	9,340	54,342	28,701	22,447	132,415
Cost of Sales	0	0	0	0	325	44,276	15,157	36,841	96,598
Gross Margin	3,945	12,422	(6)	1,224	9,015	10,067	13,544	(14,394)	35,817
Expenses	0	(0)	0	(15,500)	9,394	3,819	3,243	4,099	5,056
Profit (Loss)	3,945	12,422	(6)	16,724	(378)	6,248	10,301	(18,494)	3,0761
General & Administrative									
Expenses	6,988	10,038	6,134	322	12,214	15,233	7,443	6,390	64,762
Marketing									
Expenses	9,692	15,576	3,087	583	11,929	8,766	8,041	6,237	63,912
TOTAL REVENUE	93,653	176,597	7,317	152,965	192,168	115,190	147,886	150,021	1,035,796
TOTAL COST OF SALES	3,630	3,492	149	0	27,588	63,321	29,940	43,288	171,409
TOTAL GROSS MARGIN	90,022	173,105	7,167	152,965	164,580	51,869	117,946	106,732	864,387
TOTAL EXPENSES	102,005	142,346	54,237	30,421	172,910	145,483	91,853	88,147	827,403
TOTAL PROFIT (LOSS)	$ (11,983)	$ 30,759	$(47,070)	$122,544	$ (8,330)	$(93,615)	$ 26,093	$ 18,585	$ 36,984

EXHIBIT 7   List of Cuchara Valley Ski Resort's Assets as of August 1, 1994

ASSETS	COST
Warming Hut	
Equipment	$ 55,574
Improvements	10,193
Total	$ 65,767
VEHICLES	$ 9,428
Operations Equipment	$207,761
Snow-Making Equipment	
Compressor Line	$172,903
Improvements	2,267
Total	$175,170
LIFTS	$212,766
Rental Equipment	
Skis, Boots & Poles	$ 10,294
Bindings	24,964
Skis	31,168
Total	$ 66,426
Baker Creek	
Kitchen Equipment	$ 13,582
Cooler	6,150
Improvements	2,050
Cash Registers	5,114
Total	$ 26,896
Office Equipment	$ 20,216
GRAND TOTAL	$784,430

CUCHARA VALLEY SKI RESORT'S PROSPECTS

Gary decided that the key to preparing a financial proforma was a good estimate of skier visits. Unfortunately, the frequent closures and erratic marketing efforts and inconsistent snow (Exhibit 8) made this a daunting task. He had already reviewed the ticket sales breakdown (Exhibit 9). He had data on skier visits to other Colorado resorts (Exhibit 10) and he was confident that the large corporate-owned ski areas would continue to spend heavily on expansion plans to increase market share. There were rumors that some of the major Colorado resorts were considering mergers or acquisitions that would result in consolidation of ownership. Gary also remembered the fate of a small ski area called Conquistador, located at Westcliffe, Colorado, about 60 miles from Cuchara. Conquistador had almost mirrored Cuchara's experi-

EXHIBIT 8   Snowfall at Cuchara Valley Ski Resort, by Month, 1985–1996 (in inches)

Season	Sept	Oct	Nov	Dec	Jan	Feb	Mar	Apr	May	Total
1985–86	2.50	10.00	25.00	10.00	18.00	21.00	41.50	47.00	15.00	190.00
1986–87	1.50	16.75	33.74	21.00	39.50	74.75	126.10	30.50	21.25	365.09
1987–88	0.00	0.00	50.00	36.00	29.50	19.00	83.25	25.00	18.00	260.75
1988–89	1.00	0.00	33.75	32.50	35.75	52.75	12.00	14.75	0.00	182.50
1989–90	3.00	20.00	7.00	39.50	30.25	43.00	33.00	35.75	22.25	233.75
1990–91	0.00	25.25	36.00	30.25	17.75	32.25	70.00	37.00	2.50	251.00
1991–92	0.00	15.50	74.50	7.00	27.75	59.50	40.75	3.50	0.00	228.50
1992–93	0.00	5.75	85.50	39.75	13.00	47.50	55.25	56.00	19.00	321.75
1993–94	6.75	19.88	31.75	31.25	28.00	22.00	66.00	70.50	5.00	281.13
1994–95	0.25	14.5	27.25	10.5	21.25	16.5	47.5	113	10.75	261.50
1995–96	16.00	1.00	14.25	24.75	24.25	22.25	58.25	10.00	0.00	170.75
AVG	2.82	11.69	38.07	25.68	25.91	37.32	57.60	40.27	10.34	249.70
MIN	0.00	0.00	7.00	7.00	13.00	16.50	12.00	3.50	0.00	170.75
MAX	16.00	25.25	85.50	39.75	39.50	74.75	126.10	113.00	22.25	365.09

EXHIBIT 9   Breakdown of CVSR Ticket Sales, By Type, 1993–94 Season

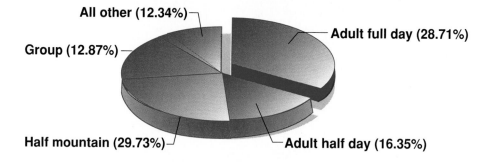

All other (12.34%)
Group (12.87%)
Adult full day (28.71%)
Half mountain (29.73%)
Adult half day (16.35%)

ence, and its most recent owners had decided to sell off all of its assets and abandon efforts to operate a ski area. Was Cuchara doomed to this fate? On the other hand, Wolf Creek and Monarch ski areas had experienced growth in their skier visits during 1994–95, 3 percent and 12 percent, respectively. Gary felt that an increase in lift ticket prices was certainly appropriate, and he realized that promotional discounts and the variety of less-than-full price tickets sold reduced the average revenue per lift ticket to something less than the price charged for an adult, full-day ticket. He believed that an increase to $28 for an adult, full-day ticket was warranted. Using historical data (Exhibit 5), he could determine an average revenue-per-skier for each of the departments including lift tickets. This would be a starting point for estimating future revenues.

EXHIBIT 10   Colorado Skier Visits, 1993–94 and 1994–95 Seasons

Destination Resorts	1993–94	1994–95
Aspen Highlands	106,197	159,288
Aspen Mountain	359,848	329,535
Buttermilk	172,948	168,439
Crested Butte	530,088	485,840
Cuchara Valley	17,300	Closed
Howelson Hill	16,171	14,095
Monarch	158,148	162,982
Powderhorn	61,202	80,241
Purgatory	302,103	382,839
Ski Sunlight	88,251	93,952
Snowmass	814,852	767,509
Steamboat	1,021,149	1,013,606
Telluride	300,388	301,748
Wolf Creek	140,456	157,995
Total	4,089,099	4,118,069
FRONT RANGE DESTINATION RESORTS		
Arapahoe Basin	257,358	262,240
Arrowhead	23,721	28,641
Beaver Creek	504,516	538,897
Breckenridge	1,215,013	1,227,357
Copper Mountain	842,210	770,973
Keystone	1,095,857	1,042,171
Silver Creek	93,516	92,547
Vail	1,527,698	1,568,360
Winter Park	1,008,040	986,077
Total	6,567,929	6,517,263
FRONT RANGE RESORTS		
Eldora	145,011	145,370
Loveland Basin	295,000	258,000
Ski Cooper	67,193	66,404
Totals	507,204	469,774
GRAND TOTALS	11,164,232	11,105,106
Number Increase (decrease)	52,942	(59,126)
Percent Increase (decrease)	0.48	(0.53)

Source: Colorado Ski Country USA

CALLAWAY GOLF COMPANY

John E. Gamble, *University of South Alabama*

The important thing in the golf swing is getting the body to control the motion of the arms, the hands and the club. You know, if you think in terms of your body being the engine—and all of the power generating from this engine through your arms and hands and into the golf club— you're going to be a lot more consistent as far as being able to square the club face off and also creating a lot more power in your golf swing. The hands and arms have to complement the motion of the body. As I term it—it is the dog wagging the tail, rather than the tail wagging the dog.[1]

These comments were made in a golf instruction video by David Leadbetter, a native of England and former player on the European and South African professional golf tours. Leadbetter was one of the world's most sought-after golf instructors, teaching thousands of amateurs and coaching professionals such as Nick Faldo and Nick Price at his clinic in Orlando, Florida. His techniques were based on a keen understanding of the physics of a golf swing. During a golf swing, the club head traveled in an arc around the golfer's body, making contact with the ball for a period of 300 to 500 milliseconds. During this very brief period of contact, inertia was transferred from the club head to the ball and the ball was propelled forward at a speed of up to 150 miles per hour. There were an infinite number of variations in a golfer's swing that could alter the swing path, causing the club head to strike the ball not squarely, but somewhat off-center and at an angle—either open or closed to the target. The more that a golfer's

---

[1] *A Lesson with Leadbetter: The Full Golf Swing,* Telstar Video Entertainment, 1990.

swing path deviated from square contact with the ball, the greater the loss of accuracy and distance. A golfer lost approximately 12.5 yards of distance for every millimeter that the ball was struck off the club head's center. Leadbetter's teaching techniques endeavored to minimize the effects of a golfer's swing path deviations.

Ely Callaway, the founder of Callaway Golf Company, also understood the importance of the physics of golf, so much so that he made the phrase "you can't argue with physics" the company's slogan. Callaway Golf revolutionized the golf industry in 1991 by introducing an oversized club head that was more forgiving of golfers' imperfect swing characteristics. A Callaway senior vice president stated in a 1995 *Fortune* interview that the company's objective was to design a club that would allow you to "miss (the center of the club head) by an inch" and still achieve distance and accuracy. The company designed and manufactured technologically advanced clubs that were "demonstrably superior to, and pleasingly different from," competitors' golf clubs.[2] In late-1996 David Leadbetter signed a five-year contract to endorse Callaway products because, "After testing Callaway Golf clubs, then visiting the Test Center and the factory and seeing the investment they have made in technology and the attention to quality, I realized that Callaway and I have the same objectives. We both are committed to helping golfers enjoy the game and play the best they possibly can."[3]

The company's high-tech golf clubs became so popular with golfers in the 1990s that Callaway Golf's sales revenues in 1996 were more than 65 times above the 1989 level of $10 million. Going into 1997, Callaway Golf Company was the most successful company in the golf equipment industry; in 1996, it earned net profits of $122 million on sales of $678 million. The company had sold over $1.6 billion of its golf equipment to golfing retailers since its founding in 1981 and Callaway's stock had split three times and appreciated 1,000 percent since its initial public offering in November 1992. Exhibits 1, 2, and 3 present Callaway Golf's recent financial performance.

Nonetheless, in 1997 Callaway Golf was being challenged in the marketplace by a number of aggressive rivals touting clubs with various differentiating designs and features, each claiming that its club design was superior and would help golfers hit better shots.

COMPANY HISTORY

When Ely (rhymes with *feely*) Reeves Callaway, Jr. graduated from Emory University in Atlanta, his father said, "Don't go to work for the family."[4] Ely Callaway, Sr. and almost everyone else in La Grange, Georgia, worked for the younger Callaway's uncle, Fuller Callaway. Fuller Callaway owned farms, 23 cotton mills, the local bank, and the local department store. Heeding his father's advice, Ely Callaway, Jr. decided to join the army just prior to World War II. By the age of 24, the younger Callaway had achieved the rank of major and was responsible for purchasing all of the cotton clothing for the U.S. armed forces. At the peak of World War II, Callaway's apparel procurement division of the U.S. Army purchased 70 percent of all cotton clothing manufactured by the U.S. apparel industry.

After the war, Callaway was hired as a sales representative with textile manufacturer, Deering, Millikin & Company. Ely Callaway rose quickly through the company's

---

[2]*Business Week,* September 16, 1991, p. 71.
[3]"Callaway Golf News Release," *Callaway Golf Company,* 1996.
[4]*Inc.,* December 1994, p. 62.

EXHIBIT 1   Callaway Golf Company, Financial Summary, 1989–96 (in thousands, except per share amounts)

	1996	1995	1994	1993	1992	1991	1990	1989
Net sales	$ 678,512	$ 553,287	$ 448,729	$254,645	$132,058	$54,753	$21,518	$10,380
Pretax income	195,595	158,401	129,405	69,600	33,175	10,771	2,185	329
Estimated ranking within industry—sales***	1st	1st	1st	1st	2nd	6th	14th	23rd
Pretax income as a percent of sales	29%	29%	29%	27%	25%	20%	10%	3%
Net income	$ 122,337	$ 97,736	$ 78,022	$ 42,862*	$ 19,280	$ 6,416	$ 1,842	$ 329
Net income as a percent of sales	18%	18%	17%	17%*	15%	12%	9%	3%
Fully diluted earnings per share****	$1.73	$1.40	$1.07	$0.61	$0.28	$0.11	$0.04	$0.01
Shareholders' equity	$ 362,267	$ 224,934	$ 186,414	$116,577	$ 49,750	$15,227	$ 8,718	$ 6,424
Market capitalization at Dec. 31	$2,261,152	$1,604,741	$1,127,823	$901,910	$245,254	**	**	**

Notes: * Includes cumulative effect of an accounting change of $1,658,000
         ** The company was not public until November 1992
        *** Estimated by Golf Pro Magazine
       **** Adjusted for all stock splits through February 10, 1995 not adjusted for February 10, 1995 stock split

Source: Callaway Golf Company.

EXHIBIT 2   Callaway Golf Company, Income Statements, 1993–96
(in thousands, except per share amounts)

	1996	1995	1994	1993
Net sales	$678,512	$553,287	$448,729	$254,645
Cost of goods sold	317,353	270,125	208,906	115,458
Gross profit	361,159	283,162	239,823	139,187
Selling expenses	80,701	64,310	59,065	38,485
General & administrative expenses	74,476	55,891	47,848	28,633
Research & development costs	16,154	8,577	6,380	3,653
Income from operations	189,828	154,384	126,530	68,416
Other income	5,767	4,017	2,875	1,184
Income before income taxes and cumulative effect of accounting change	195,595	158,401	129,405	69,600
Provision for income taxes	73,258	60,665	51,383	28,396
Cumulative effect of accounting change	n/a	n/a	n/a	(1,658)
Net income	$122,337	$ 97,736	$ 78,022	$ 42,862
Primary earnings per share	$ 1.73	$ 1.40	$ 1.07	$ 0.62
Fully diluted earnings per share	$ 1.73	$ 1.40	$ 1.07	$ 0.60
Common equivalent shares	70,661	69,855	73,104	68,964

Source: Callaway Golf Company.

ranks by selling textiles to the manufacturers that he had purchased apparel from while in the Army. Callaway was later hired away from Deering, Millikin by Textron, which subsequently sold its textile business to Burlington Industries—the largest textile manufacturer in the world at the time. Ely Callaway was promoted to president and chief operating officer of Burlington Industries, but he left the company in 1973 after losing a bid to become its chief executive officer.

Callaway had long believed that Burlington Industries' success was a result of its ability to provide customers with unique and superior quality products. When Callaway left Burlington and the textile industry, he decided to launch his own business founded on that same philosophy. In 1974 Ely Callaway, Jr. established Callaway Vineyard and Winery outside of San Diego. The established California vineyards scoffed at Callaway's entry into the industry and predicted a rapid failure of the venture. Not only did Callaway have no experience running a winery, but additionally, no vineyard had ever been successful in the San Diego area. Ely Callaway understood the risks involved, and was much better prepared to run a start-up vineyard than skeptics believed. He began by transplanting the very best grape vines from Italy to California and hired wine-making experts to manage the day-to-day operations of the vineyard. Callaway's strategy was to focus on a narrow segment of the wine market where competition with the established wineries was not as strong and barriers to entry were relatively low. Callaway Vineyard and Winery limited distribution of its products to exclusive restaurants that chose to stock only the highest quality wines. The company made no attempt to distribute its high quality wine through traditional retail channels. In 1981, Ely sold the company to Hiram Walker & Sons, Inc. for a $14 million profit.

EXHIBIT 3   Callaway Golf Company, Balance Sheets, 1993–96 (in thousands)

Assets	1996	1995	1994	1993
Current Assets:				
Cash and cash equivalents	$108,457	$ 59,157	$ 54,356	$ 48,996
Accounts receivable, net	74,477	73,906	30,052	17,546
Inventories, net	98,333	51,584	74,151	29,029
Deferred taxes	25,948	22,688	25,596	13,859
Other current assets	4,298	2,370	3,235	2,036
Total current assets	311,513	209,705	187,390	111,466
Property, plant & equipment, net	91,346	69,034	50,619	30,661
Other assets	25,569	11,236	5,613	2,233
Total assets	$428,428	$ 289,975	$243,622	$144,360
Liabilities & Shareholders' Equity				
Current liabilities:				
Accounts payable and accrued expenses	$ 14,996	$ 26,894	$ 17,678	$ 11,949
Accrued employee compensation & benefits	16,195	10,680	9,364	6,104
Accrued warranty expense	27,303	23,769	18,182	9,730
Income taxes payable	2,558	1,491	11,374	n/a
Total current liabilities	61,052	62,834	56,598	27,783
Long-term liabilities		2,207	610	n/a
Shareholders' equity:				
Common stock		709	680	676
Paid-in-capital		214,846	75,022	60,398
Unearned compensation		(2,420)	(3,670)	(2,591)
Retained earnings		131,712	114,402	58,094
Less Grantor stock trust*		(119,913)		
Total shareholders' equity	362,267	224,934	186,414	116,577
Total liabilities and shareholders' equity	$428,428	$ 289,975	$243,622	$144,360

* The sale of 5,300,000 shares to the Grantor stock trust had no net impact to shareholders' equity. The shares in the trust may be used to fund the Company's obligations with respect to one or more of the Company's non-qualified employee benefit plans.

Source: Callaway Golf Company.

Later that same year, Ely Callaway decided to enter the golf club industry and, once again, apply his concept of "providing a product that is demonstrably superior to what's available in significant ways and, most importantly, pleasingly different."[5] Callaway purchased Hickory Stick, USA, a manufacturer and marketer of replicas of old-fashioned hickory-shafted clubs, for $400,000. From the outset, Callaway grasped the limitations of the company's hickory-shafted product line and realized that the company would have to extend its product line beyond replicas of antique golf clubs to provide an acceptable return on his investment.

Callaway noticed that most golf equipment had changed very little since the 1920s and believed that many golfers would purchase technologically advanced golf equipment

[5]*Business Week*, September 16, 1991, p. 71.

if it would improve their game. Ely Callaway and Richard Helmstetter—Callaway Golf's senior executive vice president and chief designer—put together a team of five aerospace and metallurgical engineers to develop the S_2H_2 (short straight hollow hosel) line of irons. The S_2H_2 line was introduced in 1989 and was well-received by golfers. Two years later the company introduced the Big Bertha driver—named after the World War I German long distance cannon. The Big Bertha was revolutionary in that it was much larger than conventional woods and lacked a hosel so that the weight could be better distributed throughout the club head. This innovative design gave the club head a larger sweet spot, which allowed a player to mishit or strike the golf ball off-center of the club head and not suffer much loss of distance or accuracy.

THE GOLF EQUIPMENT INDUSTRY

In 1995, 25 million Americans played golf and it was expected that an additional 2 million more Americans would pick up the sport by the end of the decade. The typical golfer was a 40-year old white-collar male with a household income of $57,000 who played golf about twice a month. Many women, juniors, and senior citizens also enjoyed the sport. In 1995 there were 5.4 million women and 2 million teenage golfers in the United States. Avid golfers—those who played more than 61 rounds of golf annually—were on average 50 years old and had an annual household income of $59,000. In 1995, 490 million rounds of golf were played in the U.S., and a record 468 new and expanded golf courses were added in the United States during the year. It was expected that another 450 courses would be added in 1996 to the 15,390 U.S. private and public golf courses. Exhibit 4 provides the number of golfers in the U.S. during 1986, 1991–1994, and the forecasted number of golfers for the years 1995–1999.

Golf was popular in developed countries, worldwide—especially so in Asia where there were over 16.5 million golfers. Most of Europe's 2.3 million golfers resided in England, France, Germany, Scotland, Ireland, and Sweden, but the sport was becoming popular in former Soviet-bloc countries like Croatia, Estonia, the Czech Republic, Poland, and Russia. Before the fall of the Soviet Union, previous communist leaders had denounced the sport as the epitome of capitalist excesses, but Western influences and new-found individual freedom were fueling a desire to play golf in Russia and other new democracies. Russia's first country club opened in Moscow in 1993 and Russian golfers expected to see over 100 golf courses and 100,000 golfers in the country within the next 25 years. In 1993, Metal-Park, Ltd., a joint venture between a private interest and the Russian government, introduced the first Russian-made golf equipment. The company's Czar brand included 15 drivers, two lines of irons, and four different putters. The company's drivers were over 95 percent titanium and were produced in the same factory that produced Russian naval cruise missiles, air-to-surface missiles, and the titanium fins of the MiG-29 jet aircraft. A company vice president commented, "We make the MiGs in one room, the five irons in another."[6]

The wholesale value of golf equipment sales in the U.S. had increased from $740 million in 1986 to over $2.4 billion in 1996. The wholesale value of golf equipment imported into the U.S. during 1996 was $521 million. Almost all of the imported equipment was golf club components and golf accessories such as bags, grips, and head covers. Exhibit 5 provides wholesale sporting goods equipment sales for selected years during the 1986–1997 period. The growth in golf equipment sales was

---

[6]*Wall Street Journal*, August 8, 1995, p. A1.

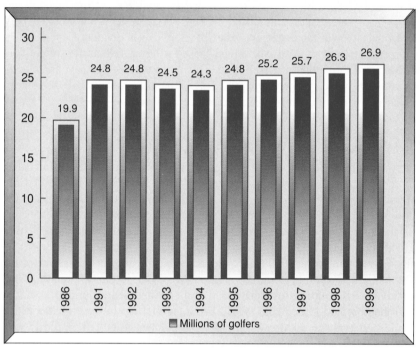

EXHIBIT 4   Number of U.S. Golfers, 1986, 1991–1994, Forecasts for 1995–1999

Source: *Golf Shop Operations,* July 1995.

attributed not so much to an increase in the number of golfers, but to the introduction of technologically advanced equipment offered by Callaway Golf and other manufacturers like Karsten Manufacturing (Ping), Cobra, and Taylor Made. Many of these technological advances made the game much easier for beginners to learn than was possible with older equipment. Additionally, experienced players frequently looked for equipment that could help them improve their game.

Key Technological Innovations

The golfing industry had come up with four major innovations that made it easier for golfers to hit better shots and improve their scores: (1) perimeter-weighting in the late-1960s; (2) metal woods in the early-1980s, (3) graphite shafts in the late-1980s, and (4) oversized club heads in the early-1990s. Perimeter-weighting came about due to the poor putting of Karsten Solheim, a General Electric mechanical engineer, who took up golf at the age of 47 in 1954. Solheim designed a putter for himself that he found provided more "feel" when he struck the ball. Solheim moved much of the club head weight to the heel and toe, leaving a cavity at the rear and center of the club. Solheim made his putters by hand until 1967 when he left GE and founded Karsten Manufacturing. Karsten Manufacturing's Ping line of putters and irons were thought to be among the most technologically advanced throughout the 1980s and reigned as the market leaders.

Perimeter-weighted or cavity-back clubs had a larger "sweet spot" because of a higher moment of inertia or resistance to twisting. The resistance to twisting reduced the gear effect of the club head and resulted in straighter, longer shots with irons. In addition to perimeter-weighting, Karsten Solheim also developed the investment-casting manufacturing process. This process allowed club heads to be formed from

EXHIBIT 5	Wholesale Sales of Sporting Goods Equipment, 1986, 1993–1997 (in millions of dollars)					
	1997E	**1996**	**1995**	**1994**	**1993**	**1986**
Exercise	$ 2,215	$ 2,070	$ 1,935	$ 1,825	$ 1,755	$ 680
Golf Equipment	2,410	2,295	2,130	1,793	1,490	740
Camping	1,530	1,500	1,508	1,275	1,225	580
Baseball/Softball	365	350	349	348	328	240
Tennis	258	245	235	259	380	255
Soccer	215	200	185	175	155	90
Total Sports Equipment	$15,866	$15,181	$14,804	$13,877	$12,433	$8,250

Source: *1997 State of the Industry Report,* Sporting Goods Manufacturers Association.

molds, rather than forged from steel—the traditional manufacturing process. By the 1970s, Karsten manufactured a full line of perimeter-weighted putters and irons that carried the Ping brand. Solheim named the brand Ping because of the sound the cavity-back club head made when it struck the ball. In 1996, over 90 percent of all irons sold worldwide were perimeter-weighted. Exhibit 6 depicts Karsten's Ping ISI perimeter-weighted irons and nickel putters that were introduced in 1996.

Karsten Manufacturing's investment-casting manufacturing process made the manufacture of perimeter-weighted metal "woods" possible. Taylor Made, a division of French ski manufacturer, Salomon, designed the first metal "wood" which, like the perimeter-weighted irons, had the advantage of a larger "sweet spot" than traditional clubs. Metal "woods" actually had no wood components, but were called woods because for decades it had been traditional to use wooden clubs for driving from the tee and for long fairway shots. The hollow metal head made it possible to move the weight to the heel and toe of the club head, as was done with perimeter-weighted irons. Conventional wood heads were solid persimmon and had a uniform weight distribution.

The characteristics of the golf club shaft impacted a club's performance almost as much as the club head. Distance and accuracy were largely a function of shaft characteristics. Weak or overly flexible shafts could torque as a result of the swinging action and the weight of the club head. The torquing of the shaft created a gear effect that resulted in a mishit golf ball. Additionally, the flex of the shaft had the ability to increase club head speed and improve accuracy. Shafts with greater flex at the tip or club head end of the shaft were advantageous to high handicappers because they helped produce greater club head speed at the point of contact with the golf ball, caused the ball to have a higher trajectory, and promoted greater distance. Professional golfers preferred shafts that flexed a few inches higher or nearer the grip of the shaft because a higher flex point produced added control of the shot.

Graphite shafts were introduced in 1969 by Shakespeare, but were not accepted by golfers because they flexed too much and overly dampened the "feel" of the club striking the ball. By the early 1990s, technological advances in graphite materials, shaft design, and production had eliminated the previous torsion problems, and graphite shafts quickly gained acceptance by both amateur and professional golfers. Shaft manufacturers were using aerospace technology to improve graphite shafts that had as many as 14 to 16 layers of composite materials (carbon fibers, Kevlar, boron, glass fiber-reinforced epoxy resins, and synthetic fibers). In 1995, graphite accounted for 35 percent of all golf club shafts, with steel alloy accounting for the other 65 percent of the

EXHIBIT 6   Sample Ad for Ping Clubs

market. Because of the higher prices commanded by graphite, the dollar volume of graphite shafts actually exceeded that of steel alloy shafts. Industry analysts expected graphite to overtake steel alloy in both dollar volume and unit volume by 2000.

Callaway Golf was the first golf club manufacturer to actually increase the size of the hollow metal wood and make the size of the "sweet spot" bigger. The larger the club head, the bigger the "sweet spot," but weight was the primary constraint in increasing club head size. If oversized club heads were too heavy, golfers could not achieve as great a swing speed or club head speed as they could with lighter club heads. Slower swing and club head speeds resulted in shorter flight distances. The vice president of research and development for Head Golf described the challenge of trying to increase the size of metal "wood" club heads:[7]

> The problem with a big driver is that you have to keep the total weight about the same as a normal-sized driver in order to give the same feel to the golfer. You can't build an overweight club or one that you can't swing at the same speed. A slightly bigger head pulls a little more drag through the air, but it's negligible. Making a bigger head is like blowing

[7]*Machine Design,* April 23, 1992, p. 32.

bubble gum. You have the same amount of gum but you've got to make a bigger bubble, so the metal walls will be thinner.

A number of materials, including stainless steel, titanium, silicon aluminum carbide, and thermoplastics, were experimented with to find a way of increasing club head size without adding weight to the club head or diminishing the structural integrity of the club head. By 1992, most manufacturers had discovered that titanium was the best material for oversized drivers because the material was 20 percent lighter and 40 percent stronger than stainless steel. By using titanium, club manufacturers were able to increase the size of oversized drivers by about 30 percent. A design engineer for Ram Golf explained why material selection was vital to the structural integrity of the club head.[8]

> Keeping weight to a minimum is the single biggest aggravation. Once you have a shape you're comfortable with, the challenge is to design a driver that will meet your weight standards. Everybody wants to go bigger, bigger, and bigger in drivers, but as you go bigger, your wall gets thinner. You could make a driver three times the normal size, but it would be like tinfoil. It would fold up and crush on impact.

By 1995, most golf club manufacturers had at least one titanium driver with a graphite shaft in its product line. Callaway introduced its titanium Great Big Bertha, Taylor Made had a line of titanium Burner Bubble drivers, Titleist introduced titanium Supersize Howitzers, and MacGregor Golf had introduced its T920 titanium metal "wood" that had been designed on Cray Research's $20-million supercomputer. The investment-casting process had made metal "wood" club manufacturing easy enough that new start-up companies could easily join the 350-plus manufacturers in 1997 and increase the already large selection of clubs available to golfers.

Competitive Rivalry in the Golf Equipment Industry

For decades, the golf equipment industry had been dominated by Wilson Sporting Goods, MacGregor Golf, Inc., and Spalding Sporting Goods. All three companies were very conservative in their approach to new product development—sticking to lines of the standard steel-shafted, forged steel clubs that had been popular since the 1920s. They were caught completely off-guard by the success of companies like Karsten Manufacturing and Callaway Golf. The technological advances offered by the new golf companies were readily accepted by amateur golfers, and the market shares of the established brands of the three traditional industry leaders quickly eroded. An executive for one of the new manufacturers stated that Wilson's inability to introduce new innovative products of its own had resulted in the company's market share diminishing to a "rounding error."[9]

In the late 1980s, as many as 20 manufacturers accounted for about 80 percent of all golf equipment sales. But by 1997, the industry had already consolidated to the point where six companies commanded over 80 percent of the market for golf equipment. It was estimated that only those six of the more than 350 manufacturers were profitable. Even though long-time industry participants like Wilson, MacGregor, and Spalding had recently introduced technologically advanced lines of clubs, they were all experiencing difficulty regaining any lost market share.

Manufacturing.   Most club makers produced only the club head and purchased shafts and grips from suppliers. Grip manufacturers such as Eaton/Golf Pride and Lamkin

---

[8]Ibid.
[9]*Fortune*, June 12, 1995, p. 110.

offered a number of models, but club manufacturers usually chose to purchase a limited variety of grips from a single source, since most golfers did not have strong preferences for one brand of grip over another. According to a marketing manufacturer for Golf Pride, "Sizes, designs, and cosmetics are more for golf manufacturers than golfers. I honestly don't think golfers give a darn."[10]

Golf club shafts did make a difference to golfers. Most golfers felt strongly about what type of shaft should accompany their set of clubs. True Temper had the best reputation in steel shafts and had dominated the steel shaft segment of the industry since it introduced the steel shaft in 1924. As the 1990s progressed, a larger and larger percentage of golfers shifted to graphite shafts for both drivers and irons. Graphite shaft manufacturers could easily produce a broad line of shafts with varying degrees of flex at a number of flexpoints. Many golfers were persuaded that the unique characteristics of graphite contributed to game improvement.

Few companies other than True Temper and Brunswick had the financial resources to compete in the steel shaft segment of the industry—a typical steel shaft manufacturing facility required a $40-$50 million capital investment. A graphite shaft manufacturing facility involved a much lower capital investment, making it feasible for a number of manufacturers to compete for market share in supplying graphite shafts. Companies such as Aldila, United Sports Technologies, HST, SpryoTech, Unifiber, and Graman USA were competent manufacturers of high-quality graphite shafts and had made it difficult for True Temper to build a dominant market share in the graphite segment as it had done in steel.

Unifiber offered high-quality graphite shafts designed for distance and accuracy, Graman USA had a line of graphite shafts utilizing its Triple Flexpoint System that the company claimed offered greater acceleration and stability, and HST designed and manufactured Taylor Made's innovative Bubble Shaft. Cobra Golf and Callaway Golf were the only club manufacturers who had integrated backward into the design and manufacture of graphite shafts. Cobra Golf produced 100 percent of its graphite shafts in-house, and management believed that this capability provided the company with a significant cost advantage relative to other club makers. Cobra Golf was acquired in 1996 by Fortune Brands (formerly American Brands), which also owned Foot-Joy (a leading maker of golf shoes) and Titleist (the maker of the most popular brand of golf balls and also a producer of golf clubs and other golf equipment). Fortune Brands management had stated that it intended to utilize Cobra's golf club shaft facilities to produce shafts for its Cobra and Titleist brands of golf clubs.

Marketing.   As television networks aired more professional golf tournaments, endorsements by professional golfers started to play a major role in the marketing of golf equipment. The dollar volume of player endorsements was estimated to be three times greater than the projected total 1997 Professional Golfers Association (PGA) prize money payout of $75 million.

Professional golfer endorsements had been instrumental in the success of some fledgling companies. In 1990, Cobra Golf offered Greg Norman shares of stock and Australian distribution rights to the new company's products in return for the golfer's use and endorsement of Cobra equipment. Norman accepted the offer and, after the company went public, sold 450,000 Cobra shares for $12 million. Norman received an additional $30 million from the sale of his remaining Cobra Golf shares when Fortune Brands acquired Cobra in early 1996. Norman's endorsement of Cobra golf

----

[10]*Golf Shop Operations,* October 1995, p. 35.

EXHIBIT 7   Top 10 1996 PGA Tournament Money Winners (through the MCI Heritage Classic) and Endorsed Golf Equipment

Rank	Player	Irons	Driver	Putter
1	Fred Couples	Lynx	Callaway	Ping
2	Phil Mickelson	Yonex	Yonex	Yonex
3	Greg Norman	Cobra	Cobra	Ping
4	Nick Faldo	Mizuno	Mizuno	Odyssey
5	Mark O'Meara	Taylor Made	Taylor Made	Ping
6	Davis Love III	Mizuno	Cleveland	Ping
7	Tommy Tolles	Ping	Callaway	Ping
8	Vijay Singh	Wilson	Cobra	Ping
9	Scott Hoch	Yonex	Yonex	Maxfli
10	Tom Lehman	Cobra	Taylor Made	Taylor Made

Source: *Golf Pro*, May 1996.

clubs helped make Cobra Golf a strong rival to Callaway and provided Norman with lucrative stock options, a $750,000 per year retainer, and $800,000 in bonuses for tournament performance.

Fred Couples' three-year service agreement with Ashworth to wear the company's apparel led to Couples' ownership of 533,000 shares of the company's stock (4.6 percent of common shares) valued at approximately $3 million in early 1997. Tiger Woods's entry into the PGA set a new standard for endorsement contracts—Woods got $10 million for endorsing Titleist golf clubs and $40 million for endorsing Nike apparel and footwear. Most professional golfers were attempting to negotiate larger contract amounts after Tiger Woods's agreements were announced. Exhibit 7 lists the top 10 money winners for the 1996 PGA Tour and the equipment that each professional endorsed and used in competiton.

Most pro-line or high-quality golf equipment manufacturers distributed their products through on-course pro shops and a select number of off-course golf equipment retailers, such as Edwin Watts and Nevada Bob's. The off-course pro shops were quickly accounting for the largest portion of retail golf club sales because they carried a wider variety of brands and marketed more aggressively than on-course shops. Most on-course pro shops sold only to members or carried few clubs since their members purchased golf clubs less frequently than apparel and footwear. In 1995 on-course pro shops carried, on average, five brands of drivers, six brands of irons, and six brands of putters, while off-course golf equipment specialists carried, on average, 12 brands of drivers, 23 brands of irons, and 18 brands of putters.

Pro-line manufacturers chose to limit their channels of distribution to on-course and off-course pro shops because they believed that PGA professionals had the training necessary to properly match equipment to the customer. Manufacturers, such as Cobra, Callaway, and Karsten, all provided the pro shops with inexpensive devices that gave an estimate of the golfer's swing characteristics. The pro could take the readings from these devices and then "custom fit" the golfer with the proper clubs. "Custom fitting" could be done more precisely with more expensive, specialized computer equipment, but most pro shops had not invested in the new technology. The Sportech Swing Analyzer aided in custom fitting by recording 12 swing variables, such as club head speed and path, club face angle at impact, ball position, the golfer's weight distribution, ball flight pattern, and ball flight distance. The pro could use the fit data provided by the Swing Analyzer to select the appropriate club for the customer. Golf equipment manufacturers expected a larger percentage of golfers to demand more precise custom fitting from retailers in the future.

Pro shops generally chose to stock only pro-line equipment and did not carry less expensive, less technologically advanced equipment. Low-end manufacturers such as Spalding, MacGregor, and Dunlop sold their products mainly through discounters, mass merchandisers, and large sporting goods stores. These retailers had no custom fitting capabilities and rarely had sales personnel knowledgeable about the performance features of the different brands and models of golf equipment carried in the store. The appeal of such retail outlets was low price, and they mainly attracted beginning golfers and occasional golfers who were unwilling to invest in more expensive equipment.

CALLAWAY GOLF COMPANY

Callaway Golf Company's competitive strategy was rooted in Ely Callaway's philosophy that true long-term success comes from innovative products with "demonstrably superior and pleasingly different" features compared to products offered by competitors. Since the introduction of Callaway's S_2H_2 line of irons in 1989, the company had sought to develop, manufacture, and market the most technologically advanced golf clubs available. Richard Helmstetter and his team of engineers attempted to make quantum leaps in club performance with each new line of clubs introduced by the company.

Callaway Golf's Product Line

Callaway Golf's Big Bertha driver was the most innovative club in the industry when it was introduced in 1991—its key features were a bigger club head, a bigger "sweet spot," and a longer shaft, all of which helped to improve the consistency with which a golfer could drive the ball off the tee. Callaway wasted no time in capitalizing on the explosive popularity of its new driver; company managers understood that once a driver developed a following among golfers, these golfers usually wanted other woods to match their driver. The company subsequently introduced a series of fairway woods—a two wood, a three wood, a five wood, two styles of seven woods, and a nine wood—to complement the Big Bertha driver. Many golfers rushed to buy not only the Big Bertha driver but also the company's other Big Bertha metal woods; it was common for Big Bertha enthusiasts to have three or four of the Big Bertha fairway woods in their bag.

Four years later, the company again moved to set itself from rival equipment makers (most of whom had by then come out with imitative versions of the Big Bertha line) by introducing the Great Big Bertha driver made out of strong, lightweight titanium. The driver had a club head 30 percent larger than the original Big Bertha driver but was still just as light because of the substitution of titanium for stainless steel in the club head; the Great Big Bertha was the industry's most technologically advanced golf club and retailed for $500 (a heretofore unheard of price for a single golf club). The titanium Great Big Bertha was the best selling driver in the world in 1996.

To capitalize on the reputation and popularity of the Big Bertha metal woods, Callaway Golf introduced lines of stainless steel and graphite-shafted Big Bertha irons in 1994. The irons, while not as popular as the Big Bertha driver and metal woods, were nonetheless among the world's top three best-selling brands (the other two were Cobra and Ping) in 1996. The Big Bertha irons retailed for about $850 for a set of eight steel-shafted clubs and about $1100 for a set of eight graphite shafted clubs in 1997. As part of its ongoing product improvement efforts and to maintain product line freshness, Callaway came out with a "completely redesigned" second-generation version of its stainless steel Big Bertha irons in 1996; the enhancements involved redistributing the club head weight, improving the sole of the club head, adding an improved graphite shaft, and improving the club's sweet spot.

Callaway had been quite successful in building a strong-selling line of fairway woods around the Big Bertha and Great Big Bertha drivers. In 1997 Callaway offered seven different fairway woods based on the Big Bertha and Great Big Bertha designs. The company did not intend to offer a line of fairway woods based on the Biggest Big Bertha because of its extra-large size. Testing of the new driver indicated that the increased size was a disadvantage when shots were not hit off of a golf tee.

New Products for 1997. In May 1997, Callaway began selling another generation of technologically advanced irons—the Great Big Bertha Tungsten-Titanium irons. Company engineers had planned to develop a 100 percent titanium iron (improving on the Tommy Armour brand of titanium irons—the first titanium irons to appear on the market) but concluded after extensive testing that titanium's light weight made a 100 percent-titanium iron too large to perform well. Callaway's tungsten-titanium irons were slightly larger than prior-generation stainless steel Big Bertha irons and were 85 percent titanium. Callaway placed tungsten directly at the sweet spot to add mass to the 15 percent of the club head that should actually strike the ball. The addition of tungsten to the club head concentrated 40 percent of the club head weight directly at the sweet spot, creating the longest hitting iron Callaway had ever developed. The suggested retail price of the new titanium-tungsten irons was $210 per club for steel shafts and $250 per club for graphite shafts. Exhibit 8 presents Callaway's ads for its new titanium-tungsten irons and its new Biggest Big Bertha driver (which had a suggested retail price of $600).

In 1997 the company also began marketing a limited edition of Big Bertha Gold Irons that incorporated all of the design changes made in 1996, but the club was cast from an aluminum bronze alloy rather than stainless steel. The company said that the new Big Bertha Gold irons offered a softer "feel" and a richer look that came from natural tarnishing that occurs in aluminum bronze.

Ely Callaway believed that due to the difficulty of the game of golf (there was so much room for variation in *each* swing of the club and for off-center contact with the ball), serious golfers would be willing to invest in high-quality, premium-priced equipment, like the titanium Great Big Bertha or the Biggest Big Bertha, if such clubs could improve their game by being more forgiving on a less-than-optimum club swing:

> The game is the most complicated, most difficult known to man. It's one of the most frustrating. Therefore, it's not very rewarding. It's addictive! . . . Five-hundred dollars a club, the regular Big Bertha is $250 retail. And that was unheard of when we brought it out. 'You can't sell it.' That's what they all said. 'It's ugly, No. 1. And, No. 2, it's too high-priced.'[11]

Callaway Golf invested over $36.3 million in research and development between 1992 and 1996 to try to keep the company on the cutting edge of technology and to discover innovative, differentiating club designs that were more forgiving on mishits

---

[11]*Golf Digest,* November 1995, p.

EXHIBIT 8   Sample Ads for Callaway Golf's New Titanium-Tungsten Irons and Biggest Big Bertha Driver

A High Score Is Sometimes Good In Golf.

Brands Used as a Percentage of Total Drivers Chosen by All Professionals in All Tournaments on 5 Tours*
(PGA, Senior PGA, LPGA, NIKE and PGA European tours)

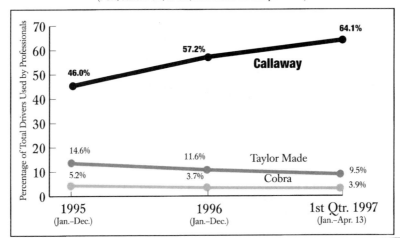

In the past two and a half years, our scores have gone higher and higher at Callaway Golf. And our driver lead among touring professionals competing on the five major tours has gotten bigger and bigger. That's a fact.

At the 1997 Masters, five of the top 10 finishers used Callaway Drivers. And on the five professional tours combined, the pros choose our drivers by almost a 7 to 1 margin over our nearest competitor – another new high – as of April 13, 1997.

Now that's what we call a scoring record. We've expanded our lead every year – from big to great big to biggest – while our competitors' numbers have shrunk from small to smaller. You can't fool the pros. That's why 64% of them are choosing Big Bertha®, Great Big Bertha® and Biggest Big Bertha™ Drivers when the money is on the line.

Big Bertha, How Golf Should Feel™

2285 Rutherford Road, Carlsbad, CA 92008 • (800) 228-2767
In California, call: (760) 931-1771 • In Canada, call toll-free: (800) 361-5678
Call us. We'll tell you who carries Callaway golf clubs in your area.
www.callawaygolf.com

*Source: The PGA, SPGA, LPGA & NIKE tours are surveyed by the Darrell Survey Co. The Eur. PGA is surveyed by Sports Marketing Surveys, LTD. Surveys are statements of fact and not meant as endorsements. Callaway®, Big Bertha®, Great Big Bertha®, Biggest Big Bertha™ and How Golf Should Feel™ are trademarks of Callaway Golf Company.

EXHIBIT 8 (concluded)

What's behind our new titanium irons?

In a word, tungsten.

Actually, there's a whole world of thinking behind our new Great Big Bertha® Tungsten•Titanium™ Irons.

We started with the same design principles as our No. 1 selling Big Bertha® Irons. Features like the S2H2® (Short Straight Hollow Hosel) club design, our trademark bore-through shaft and our patented 360° undercut channel.

Then we added an ultra-light titanium clubhead, weighted with a super-heavy tungsten inset. Why? Our testing revealed that an all-titanium clubhead was too big and unwieldy. The tungsten inset, on the other hand, keeps the center of gravity low and deep, and the size of the club manageable.

The results? A dramatically superior iron that gets the ball airborne more easily, especially with your long irons. The club is equally impressive in the rough, where you'll hit smoothly, without drag, for more accurate shots.

The new Great Big Bertha Tungsten•Titanium Irons deliver a more solid, pure feel than any irons you've ever swung. So try them today. They are, in a word, remarkable.

Callaway GOLF®

Big Bertha, How Golf Should Feel™
Distributed by:
BARRENECHEA GOLF EQUIPMENT
Av Rafael Nunez 5115, Cordoba, Argentina
54-543-21906 • Fax: 54-543-21747

www.callawaygolf.com

Callaway®, Great Big Bertha™, S2H2®, Big Bertha®, Tungsten•Titanium™ and How Golf Should Feel™ are trademarks of Callaway Golf Company.

and "poor" swings. So far, no other company in the industry had matched Callaway's commitment to R&D and product innovation.

The Helmstetter Test Center

In January 1994, Callaway Golf opened the Richard C. Helmstetter Test Center. The test center included a laboratory and a golfing area. The test center's destructive and durability laboratory utilized robots and air cannons to establish minimum thresholds of strength and durability for club heads and shafts. The club fitting and club specifications area of the test center allowed the company to match equipment to a golfer's swing characteristics. The Sir Isaac Analysis System utilized high-speed video equipment to accurately measure club head and ball velocity, side spin, back spin, side angle and launch angle. The system could record and playback a player swinging the club and striking the ball at 5 million frames per second. The equipment allowed the company to build a set of clubs for the touring professional that had the perfect swing weight, frequency, loft, lie, and length. Callaway had entered into an agreement with Disney to make the Sir Isaac system available at two of Disney's award winning courses, Osprey Ridge and Eagle Pines. The equipment was to be featured as part of the Callaway Golf Experience attraction at Walt Disney World Resort in Orlando, Florida.

The Helmstetter Test Center golfing area was an 8.1 acre outdoor testing facility that included three "putting" and "chipping" greens, a deep pot bunker, a shallow fairway bunker, and a 310-yard fairway that was 80 yards wide at its narrowest point. Sensors were located along the fairway that recorded the distance and dispersion (deviation from a straight path) of any ball landing in the test area. Atmospheric conditions, such as wind speed, direction, temperature, barometric pressure, humidity, and dewpoint were recorded by three weather stations located around the test site. The facility also included an artificial tee box and green that accurately simulated a real green. Ball reaction on the simulated green was almost identical to the other three greens and allowed the company to continue testing while the natural test site was being irrigated or mowed. The Helmstetter Test Center had two primary uses: it provided an ideal place to custom-fit clubs for the touring pros that used Callaway equipment and it allowed Calloway engineers to test new products during their developmental stage.

All of Callaway Golf's innovative clubs introduced in early 1997 had proven themselves at the test center. The titanium Biggest Big Bertha was 15 percent larger than the titanium Great Big Bertha and was equipped with a 46″ lightweight shaft. The total weight of the Biggest Big Bertha was less than the total weight of the titanium Great Big Bertha and the stainless steel Big Bertha drivers, which had 45″ and 44″ shafts, respectively.

Callaway's Backward Vertical Integration Strategy

Callaway Golf began to increase its scope of vertical integration as it grew and increased market share. In 1995, Callaway Golf entered into a 50–50 joint venture with Sturm, Ruger & Company that would include the construction of a foundry to produce the company's Ruger Titanium Great Big Bertha and Biggest Big Bertha club heads. Prior to the formation of the joint venture, Callaway had sourced all of its oversize titanium heads from Sturm, Ruger & Company. Callaway had agreed to purchase a minimum of $150 million worth of the joint venture's club heads between 1996 and 1998.

Callaway's management had also decided to produce up to 50 percent of its own shafts rather than source them from other companies. The company had made an offer to purchase its primary supplier of golf club shafts, Aldila, but Aldila management was not receptive to the offer. Callaway hired Aldila's senior vice president of marketing and sales to head up its move into shaft design, development, and manufacturing. Aldila's stock dropped from $8 to $4 per share after Callaway's orders began to decrease. Callaway had also entered into a licensing agreement with Nordstrom for the 1996 introduction of Callaway Golf apparel and shoes.

CALLAWAY GOLF'S MAJOR COMPETITORS

Callaway management viewed its strongest competitive rivals to be Karsten Manufacturing and Taylor Made, because of those companies' track record in product innovation and their strong brand recognition. Karsten's line of perimeter-weighted Ping irons had dominated the industry until the early 1990s (the perimeter-weighting feature pioneered by Karsten was a major technological breakthrough and had since become the industry standard in designing irons); Taylor Made's recently-introduced woods with a distinctive "bubble" shaft were also considered to be a high-tech innovation. Another industry leader was Cobra Golf Company.

Karsten Manufacturing

Karsten Manufacturing was not well known for its drivers, but had been the industry's premier manufacturer of irons since its Ping Eye 2 irons were introduced in the early 1980s. Its latest generation Ping irons, the ISI models introduced in 1996, were the most widely used iron on the PGA tour and the world's third best-selling brand of irons in 1996. The ISI line was available in three different metals—stainless steel, nickel, and copper. The nickel and copper versions of the irons were said to provide more "feel" and offer a better appearance than stainless steel. Ping putters were used by professional golfers more than any other brand and were the best selling putter in U.S. and international markets. Karsten had elected not to introduce a titanium driver, because its engineers believed that the material provided no advantage over stainless steel.

Taylor Made

Taylor's Made's Burner Bubble drivers were the industry's second best selling driver and the second most frequently used driver on professional tours—primarily because of the popularity of its Bubble shaft. The Bubble shaft design allowed some of the shaft weight to be moved from underneath the grip to just below the grip. Taylor Made management claimed that this weight relocation decreased the club's inertia, which resulted in faster club acceleration. The Bubble shaft also featured a reinforced midsection which was said to minimize any twisting of the club head during the swing. Taylor Made, following Callaway, had come out with a titanium driver that had its differentiating bubble shaft and copper-colored club head design. It also produced and marketed a line of irons with its patented Bubble shafts and introduced a line of bubble-shafted titanium irons and a new Titanium II bubble-shafted driver in Spring 1997.

Cobra Golf

Ely Callaway did not consider Cobra Golf—the industry's number two company in sales—to be a direct rival of Callaway Golf, since, in Callaway's opinion, Cobra's products did not match the quality and technological superiority of the Callaway product line or have any pioneering features that set its clubs apart from other brands:

"We respect Cobra. Good company with a good product. And they're just as different as night and day from us . . . because they are not in the business of creating radical new products."[12]

Cobra Golf had been acquired by Fortune Brands for $175 million in January 1996. Fortune Brands was a diversified company (much of its revenues came from tobacco products) that was also the parent owner of two other golf equipment companies, Titleist and Foot-Joy. Foot-Joy held number one positions in golf gloves and shoes—selling three times as many golf shoes as its nearest competitor. Titleist was the leading golf ball company with 34 percent of the U.S. market and a 28 percent market share worldwide. Fortune Brands management boasted that the company had the number one position in irons and was number two in clubs overall when the market shares of its Cobra and Titleist brands were combined. The company's golf and leisure products division had an operating profit of $125.3 million on sales of $811.4 million in 1996. Fortune Brands management had stated that it intended to gain cost sharing synergies between its Titleist and Cobra brands.

Cobra Golf held the industry's number one or two spot in irons (both Callaway and Cobra claimed their irons were the best-selling brand) and was number three in drivers and fairway woods (behind Callaway and Taylor Made) in 1996. Its King Cobra irons were completely redesigned and renamed King Cobra II in early 1997. The recently introduced King Cobra II irons had four enhancements—its new shafts were engineered to maximize control and resist twisting, and the club head was improved with a heel-side weight, an improved sole, and reconfigured perimeter weighting. The company also introduced a new Offset Titanium Driver that was designed to prevent a golfer from slicing or mishitting the ball. In addition, Cobra golf offered King Cobra Norman Grind irons for low-handicap golfers who wanted a more traditional club that did not have an offset club face and lacked the heel-side weighting. Exhibit 9 provides a price comparison of popular Callaway, Ping, Taylor Made, and Cobra clubs.

Competition from Makers of Knockoff Imitations

Ever since the Big Bertha driver had gained mass acceptance by professional and amateur golfers, Callaway Golf had been attacked by small golf companies offering clubs that were so similar in design and appearance that they infringed on Callaway's patents and trademarks. Knockoff clubs, although very similar in appearance to the branded clubs, were of inferior quality and typically sold for as much as 75 percent less than name-brand clubs. Some knockoff brands like the King Snake (a knockoff of Cobra Golf's King Cobra irons) were so successful that they outsold the models and brands offered by such well-known makers as Cleveland, Hogan, MacGregor, Ram, and Taylor Made. Callaway Golf, along with rivals Cobra Golf and Taylor Made, were all extremely committed to battling the makers of knockoff and counterfeit clubs. Callaway had success in battling knockoff brands like Canterbury Big Bursar irons in 1995 when it was awarded over $5 million in judgments and fines for imitative infringement. Callaway also worked with private investigators, U.S. Customs, and U.S. marshals to combat counterfeit clubs with the Big Bertha name on them. However, even when patent infringement imitators and counterfeiters were caught and convicted, it was difficult to collect damages because such companies usually had minimal assets to seize.

---

[12]Ibid.

EXHIBIT 9 Price Comparisons Between Selected Irons and Drivers Offered By Leading Golf Club Manufacturers, 1997

Graphite shafted irons			
Callaway	**Ping**	**Taylor Made**	**Cobra**
Big Bertha Stainless Steel	ISI-K Stainless Steel	Burner Bubble Irons	King Cobra II
$900	$1000	$1000	$850
Big Bertha Gold	ISI Copper		
$1300	$1300		
Great Big Bertha Tungsten-Titanium	ISI Nickel		
$1700	$1800		

Graphite shafted titanium drivers			
Callaway	**Ping**	**Taylor Made**	**Cobra**
Great Big Bertha	n/a	Burner Bubble	King Cobra Ti
$400		$300	$275
Biggest Big Bertha		Ti 2 Bubble	
$500		$500	

Source: Edwin Watts Golf Shops, February 18, 1997.

ENDORSEMENTS AND USE OF CALLAWAY PRODUCTS BY GOLF PROFESSIONALS

Callaway golf clubs were popular with both professionals and amateurs alike. Callaway drivers were endorsed by the professional golfers shown in Exhibit 10. However, many professional golfers used Callaway equipment even though they were not paid to endorse the company's products. In 1996, 57 percent of all drivers and 75 percent of all titanium drivers used in professional golf tournaments were made by Callaway Golf. During the year, the Great Big Bertha driver was used in 73 tournament wins, the Big Bertha driver was used in 38 wins, and Big Bertha irons were used in 34 professional golf tournament wins.

MANAGEMENT CHANGES AND THE FORMATION OF CALLAWAY GOLF BALL COMPANY

In May 1996 Ely Callaway announced that he was transferring his position as chief executive officer of Callaway Golf Company to Callaway president, Donald Dye. Dye had been a business associate of Ely Callaway since 1974 when Callaway owned Callaway Vineyard and Winery. Ely Callaway simultaneously announced that he and Taylor Made Golf Company CEO and President, Charles Yash, would launch

EXHIBIT 10	Callaway Golf Company Professional Staff Players, 1997
Tour	**Staff Players**
Professional Golfers Association	Paul Azinger, Mark Brooks, Olin Brown, Michael Christie, Jim Furyk, John Daly
Senior Professional Golfers Association	Jim Colbert, Bob Charles, Jim Dent, Dave Eichelberger, Walter Morgan, Bob Murphy, Chi Chi Rodriquez
Ladies Professional Golfers Association	Jane Geddes, Emilee Klein, Liselotte Neumann, Patty Sheehan, Annika Sorenstam, Wendy Ward
European Golfers Association	Stephen Ames, Colin Montgomerie
Nike	Tim Loustalot

Source: "Callaway Golf Staff Players." *Callaway Golf Company*, 1997.

Callaway Golf Ball Company—a subsidiary of Callaway Golf Company. "We believe that there is a good and reasonable opportunity for Callaway Golf Ball Company, in due time, to create, produce and merchandise a golf ball that will be demonstrably superior to, and pleasingly different from, any other golf ball we know of," said Callaway.[13] Yash, who turned around Taylor Made with the introduction of the Burner Bubble driver, resigned from the company to become President and CEO of Callaway Golf Ball Company. Upon announcing his decision to work with Callaway on the new venture, Yash commented, "This is an exciting and most unusual opportunity to develop a new and important golf ball franchise with Ely Callaway for Callaway Golf Company. As a competitor, I have been in awe of Callaway's accomplishments. As his partner, I look forward to the exciting opportunities and challenges Ely and I are sure to find in this new venture."[14]

The new company expected to begin offering golf balls in 1999. Investors believed that the company would prove to be a formidable rival to existing golf ball companies, Titleist, Spalding, Wilson, Maxfli, and Slazenger. A principal of an equity fund suggested that Callaway's entry into golf balls should be taken seriously by competitors. "Don't ever, I mean ever, bet against Ely Callaway."[15]

The company's Web site address is *www.callawaygolf.com*.

---

[13]"Donald H. Dye Given CEO Duties at Callaway Golf Company." *Two-Ten Communications, Ltd.*, 1996. http://www.twoten.press.net:80/stories/96/05/13/headlines/appointments\callaway.html (2/6/97).

[14]"Keeping His Eye On the Ball." *ParValu Stock Update*, 1996.

[15]Ibid.

RYKÄ, INC.: LIGHTWEIGHT ATHLETIC SHOES FOR WOMEN

Valerie J. Porciello, *Bentley College*

Alan N. Hoffman, *Bentley College*

Barbara Gottfried, *Bentley College*

On the day after Christmas 1990, Sheri Poe, president and chief executive officer of Rykä, Inc., knew she was on the verge of the marketing break she'd been waiting for. During the past year, Poe had sent several free pairs of Rykä athletic shoes to Oprah Winfrey, and today Poe was featured as a successful female entrepreneur on Winfrey's popular talk show with a television viewing audience numbering in the tens of millions—almost entirely women. Rykä's new line of Ultra-Lite aerobic shoes (see Exhibit 1) had just begun to penetrate the retail market. Poe could not have planned a better advertising spot than Winfrey tossing pairs of Rykä shoes into the studio audience exclaiming, "Can you believe how light these are?"

> Rykä has a great story to tell. We are the only athletic footwear company that is exclusively for women, by women, and now supporting women.
>
> **Sheri Poe**

Indeed, after the Oprah broadcast, the Ultra-Lite line became an overnight success. Lady Footlocker immediately put the Ultra-Lite shoe line in 200 stores, up from the 50 that had been carrying Rykä's regular line of athletic

The authors would like to thank Jeffrey Shuman, Holly Fowler, Maura Riley, Liliana Prado, Christine Forkus, and Mary Fandel for their valuable contributions to this case.

EXHIBIT 1   Literature Describing Rykä's Shoes

THE ULTIMATE LIGHTWEIGHT SHOE FOR THE ACTIVE WOMAN

Rykä shoes are made for top performance. You'll find that Rykä shoes will help you look good and feel great, no matter how demanding your fitness program.

Rykä shoes are designed, engineered, and manufactured by women for women. Because a woman's needs in a comfortable, attractive, high performance athletic shoe are different from a man's.

As you lace up for your first workout in your new Rykä shoes, you'll feel the difference. With every pair of Rykä shoes goes the positive energy of women who believe in other women.

Step forward with confidence, and be your best.

Sheri Poe

Sheri Poe
Founder and President

RYKÄ®

Specially designed for stepping, the RYKA STEP shoe has special flex channels placed in the forefoot providing the flexibility necessary for stepping while still maintaining excellent forefoot cushioning for aerobics.

Whether it's high impact, low impact, or step aerobics, RYKA's STEP shoes are superior in cushioning, shock absorption, stability and performance.

RYKA's STEP shoes are made with the highest performance midsole and outsole materials available - Nitrogen Ultra-Lite.

© 1994 RYKA, INC.

shoes. Retailers received thousands of requests for Rykä products from consumers, and the sharp upturn in demand quickly exhausted the company's inventories. It took Rykä over three months to catch up with the orders. Industry analysts believed that the shot in the arm provided by the Ultra-Lite sales literally saved the company.

Rykä, Inc., designed, developed, and marketed athletic footwear for women, including aerobic, aerobic/step, cross-training, walk-run, and walking shoes. The company's products were sold all over the world in sporting goods stores, athletic-footwear specialty stores, and department stores.

As a new entrant into the highly competitive athletic-footwear industry, an industry dominated by well-known giants with sales in the billions, the fledgling Rykä Corporation had had no choice but to rely on low-budget, guerrilla-marketing tactics such as the Oprah show appearance. After that time, however, Rykä marketing turned to radio and glossy magazine advertising. Rykä print ads appeared regularly in *City Sports, Shape, American Fitness, Elle,* and *IDEA Today,* magazines that particularly targeted women 21 to 35, who cared seriously not just about how they looked, but about physical fitness.

COMPANY BACKGROUND

Rykä was first organized in 1986 as ABE Corporation, but changed its name to Rykä in February 1987 when it commenced operations. The company was cofounded by Martin P. Birrittella and his wife, Sheri Poe. Prior to founding Rykä, Birrittella had worked at Matrix International Industries as a vice president of sales and marketing from 1980 to 1986. At Matrix he was responsible for developing and marketing footwear and health and fitness products, and had two patents pending for shoe designs that were assigned to Matrix. From 1982 to 1985, Sheri Poe was national sales manager for Matrix. She then moved to TMC Group, a $15-million giftware maker based in New Hampshire, where she was national accounts manager from May 1986 to June 1987.

Sheri Poe, Rykä's current president and chief executive officer, was one of only two female corporate CEOs in the state of Massachusetts. Poe, an exercise fanatic, admitted to really knowing nothing about making athletic shoes when she cofounded Rykä. In 1986 Poe had injured her back in an aerobics class and was convinced that the injury had been caused by her shoes, which had never fit properly. After an exhaustive search for footwear that would not cause her body stress, it occurred to Poe that many other women were probably having the same trouble she was finding a shoe that really fit, and she decided to start her own women's athletic-footwear company. As she conceived it, what would make Rykä distinctive was that rather than adapting men's athletic shoes for women, Rykä would design athletic shoes especially suited for women's feet and bodies. Rykä introduced its first two styles of athletic shoes in September 1987 and began shipping the shoes in March 1988.

Poe overcame considerable difficulty obtaining venture capital to finance Rykä's start-up. Potential investors questioned her ability to compete with industry leaders such as Nike and Reebok, given that she had no money and no retail experience. They turned down her requests for loans. Some of these same venture capitalists later called Poe to ask how they could get in on her $8 million business.

Since she couldn't get financing from venture capitalists, Poe mortgaged her own house and turned to family and friends to help finance the company. She also continued to search for willing investors and eventually discovered a Denver investment banker who agreed to do an initial public offering of common stock. Poe got a $250,000 bridge loan before the initial public offering—which happened to be about the time the stock market crashed in October 1987. Nevertheless, Rykä went public on April 15, 1988, and despite the unstable market, 4,000,000 shares in the company were sold at $1 per share in less than a week. The Denver firm completed a second offering before going out of business. Poe then turned to Paulson Capital Corporation in Oregon for a third offering in mid-1990.

SHERI POE

Sheri Poe believed that her status as Rykä's president inspired other women to buy the company's products. As she pointed out, "We're the only company that can tell women that the person running the company is a woman who works out every day." Poe's image and profile were the most critical components in Rykä's marketing strategy. Rather than using professional models, Rykä's print advertisements featured Poe working out; and in the company's recent venture into television advertising spots, Poe was the company spokesperson. The caption on a 1992 ad for Rykä's Series 900 aerobic shoe read, "Our president knows that if you huff and puff, jump up and down, and throw your weight around, you eventually get what you want." The ad evoked images of Poe's own determination to succeed, and endeavored to include her audience as co-conspirators who knew how hard it was for a woman to make it in the business world because they had "been there" themselves.

As part of Rykä's unique marketing strategy, Poe appeared on regional television and radio shows throughout the country and had been interviewed by numerous magazines and newspapers. Feature articles on Poe and Rykä had appeared in *Entrepreneurial Woman, Executive Female*, and *Working Woman*. Poe had successfully worked the female angle: she appealed to contemporary working women because, while being something of a celebrity, she came across as a down-to-earth woman who just happened to be a successful executive, and was a [divorced and now remarried] mother too. A *Boston Business Journal* article described her as a CEO whose title "does not cramp [her] style . . . she eschews power suits for miniskirts and jeans, drives herself to work, and lets calls from her kids interrupt her meetings."

THE ATHLETIC FOOTWEAR INDUSTRY

The $11-billion athletic-footwear industry was highly competitive. Three major firms dominated the market: Nike, Reebok, and L.A. Gear. Second-tier competitors included Adidas, Avia, Asics, and Converse. All these companies had greater financial strength and more resources than Rykä. While Rykä's sales were $12.1 million in 1992, Nike's were $3.4 billion, Reebok's $3.0 billion, and L.A. Gear's $430 million.

In 1987, the industry as a whole grew at a rate of 20 percent, but by 1991 the annual growth rate in sales had shrunk to approximately 4 percent. The athletic-footwear market was considered a mature market in 1993. Despite the subdued growth characteristics of the overall industry, however, a number of segments were rapidly expanding because of high specialization, technological innovation, and image and fashion appeal.

Product Specialization

The athletic footwear industry was divided into various submarkets by end-use specialization: basketball, tennis, running, aerobic, cross-training, walking, and so on. Rykä competed in only three segments: aerobic, walking, and cross-training shoes.

Aerobic Segment The aerobic segment of the athletic-shoe industry accounted for approximately $500 million in annual sales. Reebok pioneered the segment and continued to be the industry leader. The market was primarily made up of women and had grown rapidly in recent years. Rykä's number one market was aerobics; in 1991, 80 percent of Rykä's sales came from the Ultra-Lite and step aerobic lines.

Walking Segment The second major market Rykä competed in was the walking segment. This high-growth market was the fourth largest product category in the athletic shoe industry. In 1991, 70 million people walked for exercise, and sales reached $1.7 billion. Reebok led this segment and was concentrating its marketing efforts on young women. Nevertheless, while the male and younger female walking markets had experienced some growth, the walking segment was primarily focused on women 45 to 55 years old. Ten percent of Rykä's sales came from its Series 500 walking shoe, and the company expected the walking shoe segment to be its greatest growth category.

Cross-Training Segment Rykä also competed in the cross-training segment of the athletic-shoe market. Cross-training shoes were popular because they could be used for a variety of activities. Nike created this segment, and maintained the lead in market share. Overall sales for the segment were currently at $1.2 billion and growth was strong. Rykä derived 10 percent of its revenues from cross-training shoes.

Technological Innovation

Reebok and Nike were fast moving toward the goal of being identified as the most technologically advanced producers of performance shoes. Rykä understood that it had to keep up with research and development to survive. In October 1988, Rykä introduced its nitrogen footwear system, Nitrogen/ES (the ES stood for Energy Spheres). The system was developed over a two-year period by a design team with over 35 patents in shoe design and state-of-the-art composite plastics. The ES ambient air compression spheres contained nitrogen microballoons that provided significantly more energy return than the systems of any of Rykä's major competitors. Consumer response to the Nitrogen/ES shoe was excellent, and in 1989 Rykä discontinued sales of a number of models that did not include this special feature. Two patents were filed for the Nitrogen/ES System. One had been granted; the other was pending. Rykä was concerned that it would be easy for Reebok or Nike to adopt Rykä's technology with little risk of an infringement suit. Rykä's limited financial resources would make it burdensome to enforce its rights in a lengthy court battle.

Fashion

Rykä had focused on performance rather than fashion because Poe believed that fashion-athletic footwear was susceptible to faddish trends and to ups and downs in the economy, whereas the demand for performance shoes was based on the ongoing need of women to protect their physical well-being. Nevertheless, a large segment of athletic-footwear consumers purchased footwear products based on looks rather than function. In fact, fashion and styling trends were a mainstay among Rykä's major competitors, especially Reebok, the originator of the fashion aerobic-shoe market; 80 to 90 percent of fashion aerobic-shoe buyers did not participate in aerobics but wore the shoes for casual use and other recreational purposes.

Although Rykä's shoes were as technologically advanced as Reebok, Nike, or L.A. Gear's, they were often overlooked by fashion-conscious footwear shoppers unfamiliar with the Rykä name. Despite the fact that Rykä's sales had grown even during the most recent economic downturn, many retail shoe dealers didn't carry Rykä shoes, opting instead to stock brands that were well known and widely advertised. The lack of a nationally recognized name was a serious market obstacle for any footwear company. All manufacturers of branded footwear products, including Rykä, spent a substantial fraction of their revenues for advertising campaigns and marketing initiatives to expand their dealer networks and get their names before prospective buyers.

A ROCKY START AND A NEW DIRECTION

Given the saturation of the athletic-footwear market, athletic-shoe companies had to have more than a good product to stay alive; they needed to pull customers to their products with advertising and celebrity endorsements and to push their brands through retail outlets, most of which stocked several brands. Rykä concentrated much of its energies on marketing. As a new manufacturer in an already crowded industry, Poe understood the possibility of being marketed right out of business by big competitors like Nike and Reebok with hundreds of millions to spend on advertising and marketing. Rykä's approach was to offer similar products, but focus on the most cost-effective ways to reach its narrow target market, thus carving out a niche that the industry leaders wouldn't see as worth their time and attention.

Sheri Poe had learned the importance of focusing on a vacant market niche the hard way. When the company was first founded, it tried unsuccessfully to challenge the brand name manufacturers in all product categories, including running, tennis, aerobics, walking, and cross-training shoes. However, given its limited capital and the huge advertising budgets of Reebok, Nike, and L.A. Gear, Rykä quickly learned it could not compete in all these different markets at once. Rykä cut back on its product line and began to focus primarily on aerobic shoes and secondarily on walking shoes. Equally important, it decided to design shoes especially for women who wanted a lightweight, high-performance shoe that was attractive, comfortable, and well suited for exercise and physical fitness programs. Poe did not believe that Rykä had to become an industry giant to succeed.

In the already crowded athletic-footwear industry, the various competitors were continually jockeying for a better market position and a competitive edge. Currently, athletic footwear for women was the fastest growing segment of the athletic-footwear market. Women's athletic footwear accounted for 55 percent of Reebok's sales, 60 percent of Avia's sales, 45 percent of L.A. Gear's sales, and 17 percent of Nike's $2.2 billion in domestic sales. In recent years, Reebok and Nike had fought for the number one spot in the women's market; so far, Reebok had prevailed, but in each of the past two years, Nike had posted 30 percent growth in its sales of women's shoes. Continued growth in the women's athletic-footwear market was the most important trend in the sporting goods industry in 1993 and it was on this segment that Rykä had staked its future. Rykä believed it was taking the product in a truly new direction.

Rykä strategy was to design and manufacture shoes specifically for women, while the women's shoe lines of the big-name shoe companies were typically smaller sizes of men's shoes made on men's lasts. Rykä had developed a fitness shoe crafted specifically for women's feet that incorporated a patented design for better shock absorption and durability. None of the other companies in the athletic-shoe industry could boast of having designed their shoes exclusively for the physical characteristics and needs of women; all other contenders had broader lines or different target markets. However, it was the Ultra-Lite mid-sole, Rykä's most significant and successful product advancement, that put Rykä on a par with or perhaps ahead of competitors in terms of product attributes. The Rykä Ultra-Lite aerobics shoe weighed 7.7 ounces, roughly 30 percent of the weight of a regular aerobic shoe. Within two months of its introduction in December 1990 (and Poe's appearance on Oprah), the company had sold all its Ultra-Lites (the suggested retail price was $70 a pair). It took Rykä three months to begin filling additional shoe orders from retailers; this created concerns that Rykä might not be able to capitalize on the success of its new line. Both Nike and Reebok quickly came out with a line of lightweight aerobic shoes. Despite the competition, however, Rykä's Ultra-Lite line continued to attract buyers, accounting for close to 90 percent of its $8.8 million in gross sales for 1991.

Having established a sales base and clientele in the aerobics category, Rykä sought to further differentiate its products from competitors. Its current product line included a Series 900 aerobic/step shoe, a Series 700 aerobic shoe, a Series 800 cross-training shoe, and a Series 500 walking shoe. To make sure its shoe designs were not perceived as too specialized, Rykä had developed the Aerobic Step 50/50 model and a lightweight version of it, the Step-Lite 50/50 model; these two product versions could be worn for both high-impact and step aerobics. Included in the Series 500 walking shoe line was a dual purpose walk/run shoe, the 570, for women who complemented their walking routine with running, but didn't want to buy different shoes for each separate activity. Rykä was considering a special new series for people with foot problems or back problems because an increasing number of podiatrists and chiropractors were recommending Rykä walking shoes to their patients.

THE RYKÄ ROSE FOUNDATION

The Rykä ROSE (Regaining One's Self-Esteem) Foundation was a not-for-profit organization created by Sheri Poe to help women who had been victims of violent crimes. The foundation was launched in September 1992, and Poe herself personally pledged $250,000. Poe founded the ROSE Foundation because she was raped at age 19. The trauma resulting from the rape led to further suffering from bulimia. She saw herself as a survivor who needed to do something to help fellow victims. "For me, having a company that just made a product was not enough. I wanted to do something more."

Rykä had made a commitment to donate 7 percent of its pretax profits to the foundation and to sponsor special fundraising events to help strengthen community prevention and treatment programs for women who were victims of violent crimes. Rykä included information on the foundation in brochures that were packaged with each box of shoes. For Poe, this was more than a marketing ploy to win customers' approval of the company's social conscience and boost their loyalty to the company's products. She considered Rykä's financial commitment to the ROSE Foundation a natural extension of the company's commitment to women.

The foundation had created alliances with health clubs, nonprofit organizations, and corporations in an effort to reach women directly with educational materials and programs. In addition, the ROSE Foundation funded a $25,000 grants program to encourage organizations to develop creative solutions to the widespread problem of violence against women. One of the foundation's beneficiaries, the National Victim Center, received an award of $10,000 to set up a toll-free telephone number for victims and their families through which they could obtain immediate information, referrals, and other types of assistance.

Poe hoped that the foundation would act as a catalyst for coalition-building to help stop violence against women. But she also saw the foundation as a means of involving retailers in marketing socially responsible programs directly to women. Lady Foot Locker was the first retailer to join forces with the ROSE Foundation. In October 1993, Lady Foot Locker conducted a two-week promotional campaign in its 550 U.S. stores, distributing free education brochures and holding a special sweepstakes contest to raise awareness about violence against women. Customer response was overwhelmingly positive, and Lady Foot Locker was considering a future partnership with the ROSE Foundation. Foot Locker, Champs, and Athletic X-press had also expressed interest in the foundation. MVP Sports, a New England retailer that operated eight stores in the New England area, had recently sponsored a two-week information-based campaign featuring Sheri Poe in radio, TV, and newspaper advertisements. Doug Barron, president of MVP Sports, was so impressed with the concept and progressive thinking of the Rykä ROSE Foundation that he decided his company would donate $2 to the foundation for each pair of Rykä athletic shoes sold during the 1992 holiday season.

Poe considered Rykä and its foundation unique. As she saw it, the company had a great story to tell. Not only was it the only athletic-footwear company that was exclusively for women, it supported women. It was "the first athletic shoe with a soul." She believed that the foundation would appeal to Rykä customers who appreciated the idea that their buying power was helping less fortunate women. But Poe's choice to make Rykä a socially responsible company right from the beginning did not enjoy unanimous approval. Critics had suggested that Rykä would be better off funneling any extra cash back into the company until it was financially strong and well established in the marketplace. Supporters, however, claimed that the reputation Rykä had garnered as an ethical company, one as concerned about social issues as about the bottom line, effectively appealed to socially concerned women consumers; they argued that the ROSE Foundation was worth in good press whatever it cost the company in actual dollars, because the company had effectively carved out a niche that spoke on many different levels to both women's societal concerns and their lifestyles.

MARKETING

Rykä's promotional strategy was aimed at creating both brand awareness and sales at the retail level. In 1988, Rykä entered into a six-figure, eight-year licensing agreement with the U.S. Ski Team that permitted Rykä to market its products as the team's official training shoes. Also in 1988, the American Aerobics Association International boosted Rykä's brand name recognition when it chose Rykä to replace Avia as the association's preferred brand of aerobics shoes. In 1989 *Shape* magazine named Rykä number one in its aerobic shoe category.

Most recently, Rykä had begun sponsoring aerobics teams and aerobics championships in Las Vegas, Nevada; the Canadian team was sponsored by Rykä Athletic Footwear. In September 1992, Rykä was the premier sponsor and the official shoe of the Canadian National Aerobic championship held in Vancouver, B.C. To ensure the success of the event and build awareness for the sport of competitive aerobics, Rykä successfully promoted the Canadian Nationals through retailers, athletic clubs, and individuals. Given that virtually every previous aerobics competition worldwide had been sponsored by Reebok, Canada's selection of Rykä as official sponsor was a significant milestone for Rykä, as well as marking Rykä's international recognition as a core brand in the women's athletic market.

The Rykä Training Body

Early on, Sheri Poe determined that the most effective way to reach the female aerobics niche was by promoting Rykä shoes to aerobics instructors. Rykä spent almost as much as the industry leaders on print advertisements in aerobics instructors' magazines, and very little on print advertising elsewhere. Unlike its big competitors, Rykä did not use celebrity endorsements to sell its products; the company's marketing theory was that women cared more about what felt good on their feet than about what any particular celebrity had to say.

Beyond advertising in aerobics magazines, Rykä had successfully used direct-mail marketing techniques to convince aerobics instructors to become participants in the Rykä Training Body. In 1993 this group consisted of more than 40,000 women employed as fitness instructors and personal trainers throughout the country. They were sent Rykä product information four to six times per year and given discounts on Rykä shoes. Rykä also had a group of these instructors tied in with designated local retailers; the role of these instructors was to direct students to those retailers, who then offered discounts on Rykä shoes to the students. From time to time, Rykä-affiliated instructors put on demonstrations to educate consumers about what to look for in an aerobics shoe.

In addition to increasing sales and promoting the Rykä name, the relationship between Rykä and the aerobics profession had led to significant product design innovations. Aerobic instructors' suggestions, based on their own experience as well as on feedback from students in their classes, had led to such improvements as more effective cushioning and better arch support. Also, instructor feedback helped Rykä become the first manufacturer to respond to the new step-aerobics trend by developing and marketing lightweight shoes specifically designed to support up-and-down step motions.

Dealer Relations, Promotions, and Advertising

Rykä's marketing efforts were also aimed at the retail dealers who sold Rykä products. In Rykä's early days, Poe and her advertising manager, Laurie Ruddy, personally visited retail stores to meet salespeople and sell them on Rykä products. In 1993, the vice president of sales and marketing had responsibility for maintaining contact with retailers and developing incentive programs, giveaways, and small monetary bonuses to keep salespeople excited. The company also provided premiums, such as fanny packs or water bottles, for customers.

Given the highly competitive nature of the athletic footwear industry, Rykä management believed effective advertising was crucial in promoting the features of Rykä shoes and creating buyer preference for the Rykä brand. As a two-year old company in 1989, Rykä had found itself strapped for cash to invest in promotional efforts to penetrate the athletic-shoe market; its $3.5 million loss that year was largely attributable to advertising expenditures of approximately $2.5 million—an amount that was huge for Rykä but small compared to the more than $100 million combined spending for advertising by Nike, Reebok, and L.A. Gear.

Recently, Rykä had begun to advertise beyond trade publications. Because of ads appearing in *Shape, City Sports, American Fitness, ELLE,* and *Idea Today* magazines in 1993, Rykä's brand recognition was considerably higher, even though Rykä's advertising and marketing budget was only about nine percent of sales. However, Poe attributed Rykä's marketing success primarily to its direct marketing techniques, especially its targeting of certified aerobic instructors to wear Rykä shoes. In October 1992, after three successive quarters of record sales and little profitability, Poe announced that Rykä was going to expand its direct marketing to consumers, even if it required increased spending to penetrate the marketplace beyond aerobics instructors. At the time, Rykä's total advertising budget was approximately $1.5 million. By way of comparison, Nike had spent $20 million on a 1991 pan-European campaign to launch a single new model, and Reebok was in the midst of a $28 million ad campaign that specifically targeted women.

OPERATIONS

As was common in the athletic-footwear industry, Rykä shoes were made by independent manufacturers in Europe and the Far East, including South Korea and Taiwan, according to Rykä product specifications. Rykä's troubles in its first three years were made worse by the poor quality of products provided by its manufacturer in Taiwan. By 1992–93, however, the shoes were being sourced from Korean manufacturers and strict quality-control measures were in effect. The company relied on a Far Eastern buying agent, under Rykä's direction, for the selection of suppliers, inspection of goods prior to shipment, and shipment of finished goods.

Rykä's management believed that outsourcing its footwear products minimized company investment in fixed assets and lowered costs and business risk. Because there was underutilized factory manufacturing capacity in countries outside South Korea and Taiwan, Rykä's management believed that alternative sources of product manufacturing were readily available should the company need them. Because of volatile exchange rates, the potential for trade disputes and tariff adjustments, the risks of foreign political upheaval, and a strong desire to avoid heavy dependence on one supplier, Rykä preferred to remain free of any long-term contract with manufacturers, relying instead on short-term purchases. Orders were placed on a volume basis through its agent and Rykä received finished products within 120 days of an order. When necessary, Rykä paid a premium to reduce the time required to deliver finished goods from the factory to meet customer demand.

The principal raw materials in Rykä shoes were leather, rubber, ethylvinyl acetate, polyurethane, cambrelle, and pigskin, all of which were readily obtainable from numerous suppliers in the United States and abroad. Nevertheless, even though Rykä or its contract manufacturers could locate new sources of raw materials within a relatively short period of time if needed, Rykä's outsourcing strategy of placing orders as needed with whichever contract manufacturers had the best price made it vulnerable to any unexpected difficulties in manufacturing or shipment. Rykä did not maintain large stockpiles of inventory to buffer any delays in deliveries from producers.

Distribution

Rykä products were sold in sporting goods stores, athletic footwear stores, selected high-end department stores (Nordstrom's), and sport-specialty retailers including Foot Locker, Lady Foot Locker, Athlete's Foot Store, FOOTACTION, U.S. Athletics, and Oshman's.

Rykä's biggest retail dealer was Lady Foot Locker, which had 476 stores in the United States and 250 stores in Canada. In November 1992, Rykä announced that starting in early 1993, 400 Lady Foot Locker stores would display permanent Rykä signage, identifying Rykä as a brand especially promoted by Foot Locker. During the spring of 1992, FOOTACTION USA, a division of the Melville Corporation, and the second largest specialty-footwear retailer in the country, began selling Rykä athletic shoes on a trial basis in 40 stores. The trial was so successful that FOOTACTION agreed to purchase five styles of Rykä shoes for its stores; in September 1992, Rykä announced that 150 FOOTACTION stores would begin to carry its products nationally.

In late 1992, Rykä received orders from three large retail sporting goods chains, adding well over 200 store outlets to its distribution network. The 12th largest sporting goods retailer in the country, MC Sporting Goods, based in Grand Rapids, Michigan, decided to carry five styles of Rykä athletic shoes in each of its 73 stores. Tampa-based Sports and Recreation started selling four styles of Rykä athletic shoes in its 23 sporting goods stores; Charlie Burks, head footwear buyer for Sports and Recreation, based his decision to stock Rykä shoes on his belief that the chain's customers were looking for new, exciting styles of athletic shoes at affordable prices and that Rykä delivered on performance, fashion, and value. Athletic Express, with 135 stores, was Rykä's third new account.

In 1989, Lady Foot Locker and Foot Locker retailers accounted for 13 percent of Rykä's net sales. As of 1993, Rykä had expanded its dealer base to the point where no single retail chain or group under common control accounted for more than 10 percent of its total revenue.

Key Personnel

When Rykä was in its initial start-up mode, Sheri Poe used industry-standard salaries, stock options, and the opportunity for significant input into the day-to-day operations of the company to attract four top executives from Reebok for positions in sales, advertising, and public relations. Even though the new executive team was able to double sales between Rykä's first and second years, the compensation burden for four high-powered executives was too much for the young company. Three of the four Reebok veterans had since left the company. In 1988, Rykä had only 4 employees. In 1993, Rykä employed 22 people at its Norwood headquarters and 35 sales representatives across the country. Rykä's small size permitted agility and flexibility, enabling the company to implement changes quickly. The company's outsourcing strategy allowed it to get new designs into stores fast, sometimes within 120 days, and to respond promptly to increases or decreases in the sales of particular models.

In November 1992, Rykä appointed Roy S. Kelvin, a former New York investment banker, to be vice president and chief financial officer. Poe expected Kelvin's background would be valuable in helping Rykä raise capital to finance the company's growing operating requirements. Some people also believed Kelvin's appointment was an acknowledgment on Poe's part that Rykä was competing for funds in an old boys' network and that it was extremely valuable to have a former member of the network to make contacts with the investment community and give the company financial credibility. Kelvin's other priorities were to find ways to trim operating expenses and improve profit margins.

FINANCIAL INFORMATION

So far Rykä had financed its operations principally through public stock offerings, warrants to purchase additional common shares, and private sales of its common stock; the company had netted approximately $7.2 million from stock sales. As of

EXHIBIT 2   Rykä's Stock Price Performance, 1991–92

	1992		1991	
Calendar Period	**High**	**Low**	**High**	**Low**
First quarter	$2.31	$0.53	$1.06	$0.22
Second quarter	2.44	1.19	0.87	0.50
Third quarter	1.69	1.19	0.90	0.56
Fourth quarter	1.89	0.97	0.78	0.56

Note: Rykä's common stock was traded on NASDAQ. The company did not pay dividends to its stockholders and did not plan to pay dividends in the foreseeable future.

Source: 1992 annual report.

EXHIBIT 3   Financial Summary for Rykä, Inc., 1991–92

	Year Ended December 31		Percent Change
	1992	**1991 (1)**	
Gross sales	$ 13,329,777	$ 8,838,911	50.8%
Discounts, returns, and allowances	1,136,134	860,986	32.0
Net sales	12,193,643	7,977,925	52.8
Cost of goods sold	8,867,375	5,231,346	69.5
Gross profit	3,326,268	2,746,579	21.1
Operating expenses			
General and administrative	1,239,245(2)	1,287,925	–3.8
Marketing	1,722,618	1,396,769	23.3
Research and development	148,958	155,576	–4.3
Total operating expenses	3,110,821	2,840,270	9.5
Operating income (loss)	215,447	(93,691)	
Other (income) expense:			
Interest expense	516,455	418,469	23.4
Interest income	(4,196)	(12,648)	–66.8
Total other (income) expense	512,259	405,821	26.2
Net loss	$ (296,812)	$ (499,512)	–40.6
Net loss per share	$ (0.01)	$ (0.03)	
Weighted average shares outstanding	19,847,283	18,110,923	
Cash and cash equivalents	$ 1,029,161	$ 166,030	519.9%
Current assets	8,199,411	4,367,255	87.7
Total assets	8,306,262	4,498,021	84.7
Current liabilities	4,134,974	3,623,668	14.1
Stockholders' equity	4,153,410	834,902	397.5

Note 1: To provide comparability with the current year presentation, $410,000 of 1991 product financing expenses has been reclassified from cost of goods sold to interest expense.
Note 2: General and administrative expense includes a charge of $138,000 for reserves against a receivable relating to the liquidation of the company's licensed distributor in the U.K.

Source: Company annual report.

EXHIBIT 4 Rykä's Financial Performance, 1988–92

	Year Ended December 31				
	1992	**1991**	**1990**	**1989**	**1988**
Statement of Operations Data					
Net sales	$12,193,643	$ 7,977,925	$ 4,701,538	$ 4,916,542	$ 991,684
Gross profit before inventory write-down	3,326,268	2,746,579	1,013,445	1,364,340	308,901
Inventory write-down to lower of cost or market			906,557		
Gross profit	3,326,288	2,746,579	106,888	1,364,340	308,901
Costs and expenses	3,110,821	2,840,270	3,598,728	4,368,774	1,687,806
Operating income (loss)	215,447	(93,691)	(3,491,840)	(3,004,434)	(1,378,905)
Interest expense, net	512,260	405,821	218,817	548,149	148,485
Expenses incurred in connection with termination of merger agreement			377,855		
Net loss	$ (296,813)	$ (499,512)	$(4,088,512)	$(3,522,583)	$(1,527,390)
Net loss per share	$ (0.01)	$ (0.03)	$ (0.27)	$ (0.31)	$ (0.16)
Weighted average shares outstanding	19,847,283	18,110,923	15,336,074	11,616,088	9,397,360
Number of common shares outstanding	23,101,948	18,136,142	18,005,142	13,242,500	10,252,500
Balance Sheet Data					
Total assets	$ 8,319,229	$ 4,498,021	$ 2,711,713	$ 3,553,000	$ 2,073,058
Total debt	410,673	68,258	88,149	974,521	247,340
Net working capital	4,077,404	743,587	1,097,827	1,643,352	1,140,173
Stockholders' equity	4,166,377	834,902	1,299,264	1,848,059	1,341,858

Source: Company annual report.

mid-1992, private investors owned 65 percent of Rykä's common stock and Sheri Poe controlled most of the remaining 35 percent. In September 1992, the company was engaged in raising additional financial capital. Rykä had extended the date for redemption of its outstanding common stock purchase warrants issued in the company's 1990 public offering another two weeks. Poe was very pleased with the response to the warrant solicitation and agreed to the extension to allow the maximum number of shareholders to exercise their warrants. If all public and underwriter warrants were exercised, the company expected to receive approximately $6.3 million in gross proceeds. Stock price data is shown in Exhibit 2. Exhibits 3 and 4 present recent financial data.

In 1991, Rykä had negotiated an agreement with its Korean trading company to increase its line of credit from $2.5 million to $3.5 million. Additional working capital was available from a letter of credit financing agreement and an accounts receivable line of credit.

Rykä's product costs were higher than those of larger companies for several reasons. Rykä's small sales volumes (under 500,000 pairs annually) made it difficult to take advantage of volume production discounts offered by contract manufacturers. Moreover, the company had opted to pay somewhat higher prices for its products in order to achieve and maintain higher quality. Also, Rykä's inventory financing arrangement with its Korean trading company included financing costs, commissions, and fees, adding further to Rykä's overall cost per pair.

The Future

While Sheri Poe was proud of what Rykä had accomplished over the past six years, she knew the company's market position was far from secure. Competition in athletic footwear was fierce. Nike and Reebok were formidable rivals. For Rykä to be successful over the long term, the company would need both a sound strategy and ample capital.

(For information on how well Rykä has fared, you can do an Internet search using one of the Web's search engines or you can visit the company's Web site at *www.ryka.com.*)

REFERENCES

Colter, Gene. "On Target: Athletics Shoes Just for Women; Women's Awareness of Athletic Shoes; Special Super Show Athletics Issue." *Footwear News*, Feb 18, 1991.

Dutter, Greg. "Making Strides." *Sporting Goods Business*, March 1992, p. 34.

Fucini, Suzy. "A Women's Game: Women Have Become the Hottest Focus of Today's Marketing." *Sporting Goods Dealer*, Aug. 1992, p. 34.

Goodman, Doug. "Reebok Chief Looks Beyond Nike." *Advertising Age*, January 29, 1990, p. 57.

Grimm, Matthew, "Nike Targets Women with Print Campaign." *Adweek's Marketing Week*, Dec. 10, 1990, p. 12.

Hower, Wendy. "Gender Gap: The Executive Suite is Still Wilderness for Women." *Boston Business Journal*, July 27, 1992, sec 2 p. 5.

Kelly, Craig T. "Fashion Sells Aerobics Shoes." January 1990, p. 39.

Lee, Sharon; McAllister, Robert; Rooney, Ellen; Tedeschi, Mark. "Community Ties Nourish Growth of Aerobic Sales; Aerobic Programs Boost Sales of Aerobic Shoes." *Footwear News*, Oct. 7, 1991, p. 17.

Magiera, Marcy. "Nike Again Registers No. 1 Performance." *Advertising Age*, May 7, 1990, p. 4.

Magiera, Marcy. "Nike Again Registers No. 1 Performance." *Advertising Age*, January 29, 1990, p. 16.

New England Retailer Joins Rykä in Fight Against Domestic Violence." *Business Wire.* Nov 13, 1990.

"Nike Takes Reebok's Edge; Advertising Expenditures of Top Sports Shoes Manufacturers." Nexis "mrktng," April 16, 1992, p. 10.

Poe, Sheri. "To Compete with Giants, Choose Your Niche." *Nation's Business*, July 1992, p. 6.

Powell, Robert J. "Rykä Is Off and Running." *Boston Business Journal*, Feb. 29, 1988, p. 3.

"Rykä Adds 100 Stores to Distribution Network." *Business Wire*, Nov. 3, 1992.

"Rykä Announces Extension for Warrant Redemption." *Business Wire*, Sept. 11, 1992.

"Rykä Announces Record First Quarter 1991 Results." *Business Wire*, April 24, 1991.

"Rykä Completes $4.7 Million Offering." *Business Wire*, July 24, 1990.

"Rykä Introduces New Nitrogen System." *Business Wire*, Oct. 20, 1988.

"Rykä Launches ROSE Foundation to Help Stop Violence Against Women." Rykä, Inc., News Release, Sept. 28, 1992.

Rykä 1991 in Review, Annual Report, Rykä, Inc.

"A Rykä Rose: Sheri Poe on Career, Family, and Purpose." *Sporting Goods Dealer*, Sept. 1992.

"Rykä to expand its presence in Foot Locker Stores," *Business Wire*, June 4, 1992.

"Rykä Vaults to $8M in Its Lightweight Sneaks." *Boston Business Journal*, March 30, 1992, p. 9.

Simon, Ruth. "The No-P/E stocks." *Forbes*, Oct. 2, 1989, p. 40.

Touby, Laurel Allison. "Creativity vs. Cash." *Working Woman*, Nov. 1991, p. 73.

Witt, Louise. "Rykä Turns to Aerobics for Toehold in Market," *Boston Business Journal*, April 1, 1991, p. 6.

Wolfensberger, Beth. "Shoe Marketers Have Itch to Enter Niche Markets." *Boston Business Journal*, March 19, 1990, p. 7.

VIDEO CONCEPTS, INC.

John Dunkelberg, *Wake Forest University*

Tom Goho, *Wake Forest University*

As Chad Rowan, the owner of Video Concepts, looked over his monthly income statement, he could only shake his head about how everything might have been so much different. In many ways he was a successful entrepreneur, having started and grown a profitable business. In other ways, he felt trapped in a long-term, no-win situation. The question now was what actions to take given the business predicament he faced. Basically, Chad had a profitable business. But the profits were relatively small, and had stopped growing since a strong competitor, Blockbuster Video, had moved into town. They were not enough to pay off his long-term debts and provide him with any more than a subsistence living. In addition, the chances of selling his business for enough to pay off his debts, and then start another business, were not good.

In reflecting on what might have been, Chad commented:

I had really hoped to expand Video Concepts into several similar-sized towns within a couple of hours driving distance from here. The financial projections, which had been fairly accurate until Blockbuster arrived, indicated expansion was possible. I thought I was growing fast and had put about as much capital into the business as I could afford. I had even hoped to get a partner to go into this business with me, and one was very interested. Right now, however, I do not feel that I'm getting a very good return on my time and capital.

I guess I'm getting a taste of my own medicine. As I grew, several local businesses went out of business, but the good news is that the total market has grown since Blockbuster opened its store. Their marketing clout has brought more people into the market.

[To compete with Blockbuster] I've tried everything I can think of to get market share. The only way to increase revenues seems to be to raise the rental price, but my lower price is the best marketing strategy I have. If I raise the price, I'm afraid I will lose a lot of market share.

CHAD ROWAN'S BUSINESS BACKGROUND

Chad Rowan had been interested in having his own business since he had started and operated a lawn service business in high school. Chad had started in the ninth grade mowing lawns for his neighbors using his family's lawn mower. By the time he had graduated from high school, his lawn service clientele was big enough to support the purchase of a riding mower, two smaller mowers, two blowers, a lawn aerator, an edger, and a trimmer; he also had to employ three of his high school friends to keep abreast of demand for his services. The profits from the lawn service business were enough to pay Chad's tuition to college, and he continued to operate the business throughout his four college years.

Chad majored in business and took the only two courses that were available in entrepreneurship and small business management. During his senior year he began to look into the video rental business, which at that time was a relatively new industry. His investigation resulted in a research paper on the video rental business. The paper included a business plan for the start-up of a small video rental store with an inventory of about 500 videotapes. By the middle of his senior year, Chad knew he wanted to start a video rental business and had identified a site, a vacant retail store in the downtown business district of his hometown.

VIDEO CONCEPTS: THE FIRST THREE YEARS

After graduation in 1987, Chad opened Video Concepts, a video rental store with 200 square feet of retail space and a 500-tape rental library in Lexington, North Carolina, a town of about 28,000 people. Video Concepts started slowly but was profitable within six months. Chad tried several innovative marketing techniques including home delivery, a free rental after ten rentals, and selling soft drinks and popcorn both at the store and with the delivered videos. To help reduce the expense of the start-up business, Chad lived at home with his parents and took only $500 a month for his own wages. Revenues that first year were $64,000 with all surplus cash flows being used to buy additional videotapes. At the end of the first year's operation, Chad decided to expand and open a second, larger store.

A one-thousand-square-foot retail store was available in a small shopping center that served a major neighborhood area. Chad borrowed $80,000 from his banker to open the second store, using the value of some corporate stocks that he owned as collateral. The loan was a seven-year note with only interest due during the term of the loan and the entire principal due in seven years. The new store had 3,000 video tapes. Chad purchased all his new releases through Major Video, one of the top three wholesale distributors in the United States. To increase the size of his video library, he purchased over 2,000 used tapes from a firm that bought up tapes from bankrupt firms for resale. Over the next two years, Video Concepts' revenues continued to grow rapidly and operations remained profitable. Chad, however, continued to reinvest all profits in purchasing additional tapes. Revenues during the second year increased to $173,000, and then in the third year to $278,000.

GROWTH CONTINUES

The chance to open a third store became a reality when a furniture retail store located in Lexington's busiest shopping district decided to move to its own, larger building on the outskirts of town. The store contained 3,000 square feet of space, enough to hold over 12,000 tapes on display. Chad obtained a three-year lease on the store and opened his third video rental store in the fall of 1990. Video Concepts now had stores in the three main shopping areas of Lexington.

The new Video Concepts store used open display racks for the videotapes, and customers could quickly and easily locate the type of movies they wanted by going to the appropriate section (marked new releases, horror, science fiction, action, classical, and so on) and walking down the aisle. Checking out was quick and easy, thanks to a new computer software program that reduced checkout time to less than 30 seconds per customer. In addition, the software program provided a management information capability that allowed Chad to keep track of the number of times each tape was rented, how many tapes each customer rented, and who had past-due tapes. The system also allowed Chad to easily track sales on a daily, weekly, or monthly basis. The third store and the more efficient operating practices enabled Video Concepts to become a growing and fairly profitable business.

During the next year, growth in rental volume at the three Video Concept stores continued, with the majority of the gains coming from the new store. Chad continued the policy of a free rental after ten rentals, reduced the price per rental to $1.99 per night, and introduced some advertising centered primarily on local high school promotional events. The original two stores experienced little revenue growth but remained profitable.

Video Concepts' aggressive expansion and rising market share forced weaker video rental outlets in Lexington to go out of business. By the summer of 1991, only 6 of Chad's original 17 competitors were still operating. Chad thought his aggressive pricing strategy, high quality service, and good selection of new releases were factors in the demise of some of his smaller competitors. The six remaining competitors had an average inventory of less than 1,000 videotapes and none had more than 1,600 tapes. Chad estimated that combined annual revenues from video rentals in all stores in Lexington was about $600,000 in early 1991.

The increase in video rental chain stores nationally had not gone unnoticed by Chad, and he had visited several competitors' stores in nearby cities. During his visits, Chad had primarily tried to see what other video rental businesses were doing and learn what he could do to be more efficient and stay competitive. Although he had visited Blockbuster Video stores in several nearby cities, Chad estimated that Blockbuster outlets would require annual revenues of at least $600,000 to be profitable. For this reason Chad believed that Lexington was too small to attract a major video rental chain store. He also believed that his three-store Video Concepts operation was as well stocked and efficiently operated as any of the national chains, including Blockbuster.

Believing that Video Concepts' market position in Lexington was secure, he began paying himself a modest annual salary of $15,000. In addition, he decided to start paying off the second loan of $200,000 that he had taken out to open the third store. To obtain this last loan, Chad had used all the assets that he owned as collateral because he believed that these stores were an excellent investment. In the summer of 1991, with sales increasing every month, Chad had reason to think that Video Concepts represented a very good investment.

SERIOUS COMPETITION ARRIVES

In August, Blockbuster Entertainment announced that it would open a store in Lexington. Blockbuster, although a very young corporation, was the largest video rental chain store in the United States. Blockbuster had grown from 19 stores in 1986 to 2,829 stores (1,805 company-owned and 1,024 franchises) in 1991 and had total revenues of about $1.2 billion. The typical Blockbuster store carried 8,000 to 14,000 tapes and the stores ranged in size from 4,000 to 10,000 square feet. In 1991 the 1,248 company-owned Blockbuster stores that had been in operation for more than a year were averaging monthly revenues of $75,000.

Although the growth in the United States in consumer spending on video rentals seemed to have slowed, Blockbuster Video believed it had the opportunity to take market share away from the smaller competitors through its strategy of building large stores with a greater selection of tapes than most of its competitors. As the largest video rental chain in the United States, Blockbuster also had advantages in marketing and in the purchase of inventory. Blockbuster Video's standard pricing was $3.50 per tape for two nights, but local stores had some pricing discretion.

In the fall of 1991, Blockbuster built a new store almost across the street from Chad's main Video Concepts store. It purchased a vacant lot for $310,000 and then leased a 6,400-square-foot building, which was built to its specifications, under a long-term lease agreement for $8.50 per square foot for the first three years. The cost of completely furnishing the building, including the videotapes, was about $375,000, and Blockbuster spent over $150,000 on the grand opening promotions. Altogether, Blockbuster spent about $835,000 to open its Lexington store compared to the just over $200,000 that Video Concepts had spent to open its similar-sized store. Blockbuster's operating costs were comparable to Video Concepts' since the computer checkout equipment was similar and both firms had approximately the same personnel costs. Both firms depreciated their tapes over 12 months.

BLOCKBUSTER'S IMPACT ON VIDEO CONCEPTS

Chad decided not to try to meet the grand opening blitz by Blockbuster with an advertising promotion of his own, but he did start including brochures on Video Concepts with each rental. The brochure noted that the rental fee at Video Concepts was lower than Blockbuster's, that Video Concepts had a new game section where Nintendo games were available, that Video Concepts was a family entertainment store (no X-rated videos), and that Video Concepts was a locally owned store that supported local school events. Chad felt his past reputation for low prices ($1.99 versus $3.50 at Blockbuster), his hometown ownership, and courteous service were the appropriate strategic response to a well-financed competitor. He did not believe that he should even attempt to match Blockbuster's advertising budget and that he should not try to beat Blockbuster at its game. Chad felt the best approach was continue to do what he did best and not try to match Blockbuster's marketing strategy. He did, however, increase the number of tapes purchased for each new release.

With the opening of the new Blockbuster store and its attendant grand opening marketing campaign, Video Concept's revenues dropped about 25 percent for two months and then started slowly climbing back to prior levels. During this two-month period, Chad had worked even harder to provide excellent customer service through brief training sessions for his employees. He had always had employee training sessions, but these emphasized the competitive threat from Blockbuster and the need to provide the best customer service possible. The primary points of these sessions were directed toward informing customers, as they checked out, of how many rentals they had to go before they would obtain a free rental, the customers' ability to reserve videos, and Video Concepts' willingness to deliver videos to customers' homes at no extra charge. (These were all services that Blockbuster did not offer.)

Nonetheless, Video Concepts' revenues hit a plateau of just under $40,000 per month and stayed there, with the normal minor seasonal variations, for the next 12 months. During this time, Chad attempted several marketing promotions including rent-one-get-one-free on the normally slow nights (Mondays, Tuesdays, and Wednesdays), and he mailed brochures to all of Video Concepts customers that included a brief highlighting of the advantages of shopping Video Concepts over Blockbuster (lower price and the extra services), and a free rental coupon.

The promotions seemed to help Video Concepts maintain its current revenue level, but they were costly and resulted in lower profitability for the three-store operation. To try to improve Video Concepts' profitability, Chad examined his operation for ways of further improving efficiency. By studying the hour-by-hour sales patterns, he was able to more efficiently schedule his employees. He also used the information provided by the software program to determine when the rentals of "hit" and/or new releases had peaked.

Hit videos presented two big problems. One concerned how many tapes to purchase. There seemed to be little correlation between a hit at the box office and a hit from rentals. When a movie was first released for video rental, Chad would buy 40 to 50 videotapes at a cost of about $60 each. The demand for these videos would be very high for about six weeks to three months, after which the demand would drop significantly. The second problem was to determine when and how many of the tapes to sell before the demand dropped to the level of non-hit videos. Once a hit video rental had peaked, Chad had learned that there was a fairly good market for used tapes for a short period of time and, if the tape was not sold during this time, he would end up with a tape that had very little rental demand and little resell value. Chad believed that he had solved the second problem by carefully watching the sales figures for the tapes. Analysis of this information helped to minimize his investment in tape inventory and marginally improved cash flow.

THE DILEMMA

Two years after Blockbuster had opened its store, Chad carefully analyzed the financial statements for Video Concepts—see Exhibits 1 and 2. The company was profitable and had been able to maintain revenues. Chad estimated that the arrival of Blockbuster had increased the demand for video rentals in Lexington to about $1,300,000 a year. He believed Blockbuster's share was about $700,000 a year and that the few remaining independents had around $100,000 a year in revenues.

Chad saw the current competitive situation as being fairly straightforward. Video Concepts had a store that was comparable to Blockbuster's in tape selection, personnel costs, and efficiency of operation. Video Concepts had a cost advantage in having lower store leasing costs ($3.50 per square foot versus $8.50), but Blockbuster had a bigger advantage in being able to use its purchasing power to purchase videotapes at a much lower cost. Video Concepts' major marketing strength was its lower rental price ($1.99 versus $3.50) but Blockbuster utilized a much larger advertising budget to attract customers. (All the Blockbuster stores in that region of North Carolina charged $3.50 rental except the one in Lexington.)

As had happened nationwide, the growth of video rental revenue leveled off in the Lexington area starting in 1992. Nationwide in 1992, sales increased only 4.7 percent for Blockbuster stores that had been in operation more than one year. Future industry growth did not look bright, as there were signs of market

EXHIBIT 1   Video Concepts' Income Statement, 12 Months Ending
June 30, 1993

Revenues	$465,958
Cost of goods*	192,204
Gross profit	273,754
Expenses	
Salaries**	108,532
Payroll taxes	11,544
Utilities	20,443
Rent	23,028
Office expenses	26,717
Maintenance	6,205
Advertising expenses	4,290
Interest expenses	27,395
Total expenses	228,154
Income before taxes	45,600
Taxes	10,944
Net income	$ 34,656

*Cost of goods = purchase price minus
market value of tapes. This method is used
because most of the tapes purchased are
depreciated over a 12-month period.
**Salaries include Chad's salary of $15,000.

maturity and, more importantly, telecommunications companies were accelerating efforts to create an information superhighway to households using fiber optics technology that permitted in-home viewing of movies on a pay-per-view basis. This technology, however, was still in developmental stages and its spread to small towns was years away. Nonetheless, it was becoming more apparent every day that the long-term threat of fiber optics technology to render video rentals obsolete was real.

Looking to the future, Chad felt that for all his efforts, the net income from the Video Concepts operation would not provide him as high a return on his time and his capital as he had expected. He was still paying only the interest on his long-term loans, and current cash flows were not big enough to pay down his bank loans very quickly. Chad was considering several options. One alternative was to raise the price of an overnight rental to $2.49 to make the business more profitable; but Chad was afraid of what the consequences of such a move might be. He also was thinking about hiring someone to manage the business so that he could find another job for himself. He had had offers of corporate jobs in the past and was considering exploring this option again. Another alternative was to try to sell the business. As Chad pondered these alternatives, he tried to think of a solution that he might have overlooked. What he was sure of, however, was that he did not wish to keep working 12-hour days at a business that did not seem to have a bright future.

EXHIBIT 2 Video Concepts' Balance Sheet, 12 Months Ending
June 30, 1993

Assets	
Cash	$ 15,274
Inventory	4,162
Prepaid expenses	1,390
Total current assets	20,826
Office equipment	48,409
Furniture and fixtures	53,400
Videocassette tapes	303,131
Leasehold improvements	39,800
Accumulated depreciation*	(151,981)
Total assets	$ 313,585
Liabilities and Stockholders' Equity	
Accounts payable	$ 15,429
Sales taxes payable	2,415
Payroll taxes payable	3,270
Total current liabilities	21,114
Bank term loan	247,518
Common stock	20,800
Retained earnings	24,153
Total liabilities and equity	$ 313,585

*Includes the depreciation of tapes.

REFERENCES

"Blockbuster Idea Might Work for Computer Industry," *MacWeek,* May 24, 1993, p. 62.

"Blockbuster, IBM Plans Set Retailers Spinning," *Variety,* May 17, 1993, p. 117.

"Blockbuster Sizes Up PPV Potential: Talks Home Delivery with Bell Atlantic," *Billboard,* January 30, 1993, p. 11.

"Blockbuster Goes After a Bigger, Tougher Rep," *Variety,* January 25, 1993, p. 151.

"Changes in Distribution Landscape Have Players Scouting Claims," *Billboard,* May 16, 1993, p. 52.

"Oscar Noms Mean Gold for Video Industry," *Variety,* February 24, 1992, p. 79.

"Play It Again and Again Sam," *Newsweek,* December 16, 1991, p. 57.

"Recording Industry Hits Blockbuster," *Advertising Age,* May 17, 1993, p. 46.

"Record Store of Near Future: Computers Replace the Racks", *The New York Times,* May 12, 1993, p. A1.

"Stretching the Tape," *The New York Times,* April 22, 1993, p. B5.

"Video and Laser Hot Sheet," *Rolling Stone,* March 4, 1993, p. 72.

"VSDA Regaining Its Sense of Direction", *Variety,* June 8, 1992, p. 19.

NINTENDO VERSUS SEGA (A): THE VIDEOGAME INDUSTRY[1]

Romuald A. Stone, *Keller Graduate School of Management*

Video and computer games emerged as a great unforeseen by-product of the electronic age. As technological advances made simulation increasingly more realistic, videogames allowed the player to set sail for the New World with a boatload of colonists, to take command of a WWII German U-boat, to fly air-to-air and ground strike missions as a pilot on board the *USS Eisenhower,* to enter several mystical worlds to untangle an ancient web of treachery and deceit, or to match wits with seven PGA golfers on tour. Half the top 100 games of 1994 (categories included party, family, trivia, word, puzzles, arcade, real-life strategy, abstract strategy, adventure, and war games) were for computers or videogames, up from 37 percent in 1993. For the first time ever, an electronic game ("Myst" by Broderbund) was named 1994 Game of the Year by *Games* magazine.[2]

In 1994, videogames were a $5 billion a year business in the United States (a $4 billion market in Japan, $15 billion worldwide). Nine years earlier, the industry appeared dead; retail videogame sales were less than $100 million in 1985, down from

[1]The generous cooperation of David Cole, president, DFC Intelligence Research, in providing information on the U.S. videogame industry is greatly appreciated. Used with permission.
[2]B. Hochberg, ed., "Games 100," *Games* (December 1994), pp. 67–76.

EXHIBIT 1   Size of the U.S. Market for Videogames: Hardware and Software, 1977–1994

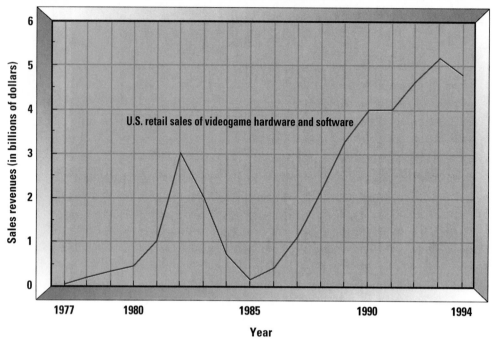

Sources: Nintendo of America and Gerard Klauer Mattison & Co.

$3 billion in 1982 (see Exhibit 1). The rebirth of the industry exceeded everyone's expectations. Since 1985, Nintendo and SEGA had dominated the industry with over 150 million of their game machines sold worldwide (over 50 million were in U.S. households). Nearly two-thirds of the children in North America between the ages of 6 and 14 played videogames. Worldwide, Nintendo generated net sales of $4.7 billion and SEGA $4 billion in their 1994 fiscal years ending March 31, 1994.

After years of steady growth, videogame industry revenues were expected to decline slightly in 1994 and 1995. Industry analysts attributed the decline to a maturing market, although new game systems were expected to offset some of the decline.

INDUSTRY BACKGROUND[3]

The first home videogame system was the Odyssey, released by Magnavox in 1972. The Odyssey required that plastic overlays be attached to the television set. Despite an extensive marketing campaign by Magnavox, the Odyssey never caught on and it died after a year on the market.

It took a successful arcade game to build demand for the first home videogame systems. In 1972, Nolan Bushnell created the first electronic arcade videogame, "Pong." Pong was a simple coin-operated table-tennis game that caught on in bars and arcades. With $500, Bushnell and a buddy formed Atari in 1972 to manufacture

---

[3]Extracted from Standard & Poor's *Industry Surveys* (Toys), 1991, pp. L46–47; and DFC Intelligence Research, *The U.S. Market for Video Games and Interactive Electronic Entertainment* (San Diego, 1995).

Pong machines. The success of Pong did not go unnoticed and brought numerous imitators to the newly emerging industry; by 1973, 90 percent of all Pong machines in arcades were clones manufactured by 25 competitors of Atari. Home versions quickly followed. In the years since, rapid imitation has continued to characterize the industry.

In 1976, Fairfield Camera & Instrument released the "Channel F," the first home system to accept interchangeable cartridges. Previously, home videogame systems played only a limited number of preprogrammed games. Once a player tired of those games the systems were relegated to a back closet and forgotten. With interchangeable cartridges, the software became separated from the hardware. By buying a new cartridge, a system played entirely new games.

Nolan Bushnell realized that interchangeable cartridges were the wave of the future. Two months after the release of Channel F, he sold Atari to Warner Communications for $27 million for the purpose of raising capital to release a new game system. Warner's Chairman and CEO Steven Ross saw the revolutionary potential of videogames. The company's 1976 annual report observed:

> Toys and games of skill go back to the early history of human life. Stones, bones, and wood were early materials for games, and many of those are still highly salable product today. As technology advanced, games were spring driven, later battery powered, and now they have begun to incorporate electronics. Each new development somewhat eclipsed the past, but virtually every game that was ever enjoyed by a lot of people is still made and sold. Electronic games are a logical step in this historic process.

In 1977, Atari released its "video computer system" (VCS) or 2600 home system. Over the next few years, Atari established the 2600 as the dominant videogame system. Industry growth got a booster shot with the introduction in arcades of "Space Invaders" in 1979 and "Pac-Man" in 1981. Atari was the first company to license an arcade game for a home system when it licensed "Space Invaders" for the 2600. The 1980s release of "Space Invaders" on the 2600 was a smash hit and Atari's sales doubled. Atari followed with the equally successful home version of "Pac-Man" in 1982. Atari remained the undisputed industry leader through 1982, consistently maintaining a 70 to 80 percent share of the home videogame market.

But Atari faced intensifying competitive rivalry starting in the early 1980s. In 1982, 350 new game titles were released by a growing number of competitors. Mattel had joined the fray with Intellivision in late 1979, and Coleco made a splash in early 1983 by introducing ColecoVision (both second-generation systems with improved graphics). Other entrants included Milton Bradley (its Vectrex system flopped) and the toy subsidiaries of Quaker Oats and General Mills.[4]

By the mid-1980s, the market had turned down sharply. According to Warner Communications' 1983 annual report, in December 1981 there was only one other manufacturer of Atari-compatible cartridges; a year later, there were more than 20. The report observed, "Throughout 1983 and into 1984, unsuccessful software manufacturers liquidated their factory inventories at close-out prices, causing damaging price competition and compounding retailers' inventory problems at a time when demand fell from the peak of 1982." Warner Communications ultimately buried truckloads of unsellable videogame cartridges in the Arizona desert. Warner reported a $539 million loss on its consumer electronics business in 1983.

---

[4]S. P. Schnaars, *Managing Imitation Strategies* (New York: Simon & Schuster, 1994).

In 1984, Warner Communications and Mattel were nearly driven to bankruptcy by the losses of their videogame subsidiaries. Warner sold its Atari division that year, and Mattel and Coleco announced they were leaving the videogame business in 1985. When U.S. sales collapsed to only $100 million in 1985, it seemed that the videogame business was dying a rapid death.

Enter Nintendo and SEGA

Nintendo proved predictions of the industry's imminent demise wrong when it introduced its Nintendo Entertainment System (NES) in 1985. Encouraged by earlier success with its Famicom game system in Japan, Nintendo ignored analysts who felt that the videogame business was a fad whose time had passed and began selling its NES in New York in the fall of 1985. In 1986, the company sold 1.1 million NES units, largely on the strength of "Super Mario Brothers," a game that eventually sold 40 million copies. Sales of game systems and game cartridges took off. By 1988, Nintendo had captured an 80 percent share of a much rejuvenated $2.3 billion U.S. videogame market.

In reviewing the recent ups and downs in the videogame industry, Steven Schnaars described how American market analysts and competitors regarded Nintendo's entry and early success:

> Domestic observers were skeptical of the market's staying power, and the American sellers were reluctant to commit heavily for fear of being burned again. *Business Week* echoed the timidity of the industry in 1988: The "current video game revival may already be past its prime." An Atari executive acknowledged that "we're not overextending ourselves on a category that might go south again." Nintendo, some seemed to think, was repeating past mistakes. It simply did not know the risks inherent in the American market.[5]

However, Nintendo learned a valuable lesson from Warner's failure: it was important to control the supply of game cartridges to ensure quality and prevent fierce price competition. To this end, Nintendo required game developers to follow strict rules. Prior to release, Nintendo had to approve the content of the games. In addition, the agreement required licensees to order games from Nintendo. The licensee developed a game and then placed an order with Nintendo who became the sole manufacturer of cartridges. The minimum order was for 10,000 cartridges, paid in advance. Licensees were charged about twice the cost of manufacturing. This included a royalty to Nintendo, but did not include distribution and marketing costs. Nintendo made money whether or not the game sold. Licensees were also limited to developing five NES games a year, and they could not release an NES game on a competing system for a period of two years.[6]

But Nintendo did more than just manage the supply side of the market successfully. The company also succeeded in establishing one of the strongest brand names in the industry. The "Official Nintendo Seal of Quality," familiar to children throughout America, was prominently displayed on all of its products. Nintendo also provided "game counselors"—videogame experts available to players by phone, which helped maintain customer loyalty. In 1993, Nintendo's game counselors handled 8 million phone calls and letters, with cumulative contacts surpassing the 30 million mark.[7]

---

[5]Ibid., p. 178.

[6]DFC Intelligence Research.

[7]Extracted from Standard & Poor's *Industry Surveys* (Toys), 1993, pp. L46–47.

SEGA first entered the American videogame market in 1986 with its 8-bit Master System. Although the system was generally considered to have better graphics than Nintendo, it achieved only a 15 percent market share. Nintendo's early lead had allowed it to develop a high level of brand awareness and a more extensive library of games. In addition, Nintendo's success gave it the financial resources to support an aggressive program of game introductions and advertising that SEGA couldn't match with its limited sales. SEGA, however, remained committed to the U.S. market and, in late 1989, introduced its 16-bit Genesis system. While 1989 sales of Genesis were respectable, Nintendo remained dominant with a market share of approximately 85 percent, despite the fact that it was competing with the older technology contained in its 8-bit system.[8]

Videogames in the 1990s

In the early 1990s, Nintendo lost its grip on the videogame market due to complacency and slow reaction to SEGA's competitive moves. Nintendo waited 18 months before coming out with its 16-bit system to compete with Genesis.[9] The NES was doing so well that Nintendo did not want to cannibalize sales by introducing a more advanced system. By the time Nintendo did release its Super NES (16-bit), SEGA had even more games available, including the popular "Sonic the Hedgehog." In addition, Nintendo's high fees alienated retailers and software developers; SEGA's license fees were lower. Nintendo's effort to maintain enthusiasm for its games by limiting supply backfired when retailers repeatedly stocked out of Nintendo games and began looking for other videogame suppliers. SEGA also targeted a broader market than Nintendo, focusing on adults as well as teenagers. Its marketing included TV ads that disparaged Nintendo as a system for ninnies.[10]

Helping SEGA's sales was the explosive popularity of its uncensored version of the explicitly violent game, "Mortal Kombat," which Nintendo also released but without the explicit violence.[11] Howard Lincoln, Nintendo's then senior vice president, acknowledged losing tens of thousands of "Mortal Kombat" sales by not releasing the violent version. But he supported the decision by reiterating Nintendo's commitment to being socially responsible in the types of games it offered for children and adolescents.

By the early 1990s, SEGA's Genesis held a competitive, if not commanding, market share for 16-bit systems, a small but growing segment of the overall market. SEGA's mid-1992 decision to offer its lightning fast "Sonic the Hedgehog" game with the customer's purchase of the company's 16-bit Genesis system further eroded Nintendo's position. When SEGA introduced a CD-ROM attachment for its Genesis machine in November 1992, it gained further momentum. SEGA's strength in the 16-bit market continued to grow throughout 1993, ending with a 51 percent share and the segment leadership (see Exhibit 2). By the end of fiscal year 1994, SEGA had sold over 17 million Genesis players since its debut in 1989; Nintendo had sold over 18 million Super NES system players. SEGA was projected to be the videogame leader in the 16-bit segment in 1995 with about 52 percent of overall sales.

---

[8]Ibid.

[9]J. Carlton, "Video Games Sell in Record Numbers This Christmas," *The Wall Street Journal*, December 20, 1993, p. B3.

[10]Ibid.

[11]The potential for licensing titles increased significantly in 1991 after Nintendo ceased requiring its software developers to license titles exclusively to Nintendo.

EXHIBIT 2	Estimated Sales and Market Share Summary Data: 16-Bit Hardware, Software, and Add-Ons, 1992–1996 (in millions)				
	1992	1993	1994	1995	1996
Nintendo Super NES	$1,733	$1,890	$1,728	$1,000	$ 720
SEGA Genesis and CD	1,151	1,938	1,710	1,073	719
Total 16-bit	$2,884	$3,828	$3,438	$2,073	$1,439
Percent change		33%	–10%	–40%	–31%
Market Share					
Nintendo Super NES	60%	49%	50%	48%	50%
SEGA Genesis and CD	40	51	50	52	50
Total 16-bit	100%	100%	100%	100%	100%

Source: Gerard Klauer Mattison & Co.

According to one observer, "SEGA has succeeded in positioning itself as the cooler machine. . . . The MTV generation plays SEGA and your little brother plays Nintendo."[12]

Beyond 2000[13]

Observers believed the outcome of the current videogame wars would determine the future for the next generation of videogames. The long-term outlook for videogame systems was unclear. There was no way to predict how long the next generation game systems would last before they were replaced with still another wave of new products.

Trying to forecast video gaming beyond the next generation was viewed as pure speculation; however, analysts offered several observations. The ideal videogame system should have the power of a computer at an inexpensive price. Most importantly, it should be "plug and play," not only from the standpoint of installing software easily but also from the standpoint that a consumer did not have to worry about whether a given piece of software would play on his or her system. Analysts believed that in the future a given title would need to play on any brand of machine, whether it was manufactured by SEGA, Nintendo, 3DO, Sony, or another company. Future advances in technology were expected to facilitate releasing games that could be played on multiple platforms.

However, the idea of having one common platform excited everyone except the hardware manufacturers. It would make life easier on developers, retailers, and consumers. Despite this, there seemed to be little chance of that happening within the next five years. So far, no platform had emerged as dominant. Some experts expected the next generation of games to involve three or four relatively popular platforms, none of which would be compatible.

It was also difficult to speculate about the type of machine that would dominate in the future. Would it be a system dedicated solely to entertainment, or would the

---

[12]A. Pollack, "Sega Takes Aim at Disney World," *New York Times*, July 4, 1993, pp. 1, 6.
[13]Extracted largely from DFC Intelligence Research report.

videogame machine of the future be multipurpose, more like today's computers? Some saw videogame machines being replaced by an all-purpose electronic device that could deliver not only games but television programs, movies, and data. According to Nat Goldhaber, president of Kaleida Labs, "Once they no longer control the box, and once digital distribution of games becomes possible, how then will SEGA and Nintendo continue to be successful?"[14]

THE INTERACTIVE MULTIMEDIA MARKET[15]

Consumers were demonstrating a strong interest in interactive multimedia forms of entertainment. In 1991, for example, consumers spent approximately $7 billion on interactive coin-operated arcade games compared to $5.1 billion spent on tickets to movies. Although videogame players and typical personal computers offered only limited graphics performance, over 150 million households worldwide were consumers of interactive entertainment and education software. In 1991, U.S. consumers spent approximately $3 billion on interactive game software.

The potential customers for interactive multimedia systems formed a consumer pyramid roughly divided into four tiers, consisting of innovators, early adopters, other current interactive system users, and mass market consumers (see Exhibit 3).

Products that penetrated the first three tiers included both personal computers and SEGA and Nintendo videogame consoles. SEGA introduced its 16-bit Genesis system in the United States in 1989. This system offered a significant increase in performance and visual realism over existing 8-bit systems. (Think of the bits as the width of the highway along which game data travels; more bits allow better, faster, more dynamic games.)[16] Prior to Genesis, Nintendo had a dominant market share,

---

EXHIBIT 3 Multimedia Market Pyramid

Innovators have a history of buying new systems that offer significant technological improvements over existing alternatives and are generally insensitive to price, software availability, brand identification, breadth of distribution, and factory support. It is believed that the class of innovators for home interactive media products consists of approximately 500,000 consumers.

Early adopters are similar to innovators except that they consider price/performance and software availability more carefully. Like innovators, they are motivated consumers who learn about a product through word-of-mouth even if it is not advertised heavily. It is believed the class of early adopters consists of several million consumers.

Interactive system users are consumers who currently own at least one interactive system such as a videogame console or a personal computer. These consumers base their purchase decisions on value, software availability, and price. It is believed that there are approximately 50 million households worldwide who are consumers of interactive entertainment and education software.

Mass market consumers are those who have televisions but are not current users of interactive multimedia products.

Source: 3DO 10-K.

---

[14]Pollack, "Sega Takes Aim," p. 6.
[15]Extracted from The 3DO Company 10-K, 1993.
[16]M. Snider, "Video Market No Longer a 2-Player Game," *USA Today*, November 4, 1993, p. 1D.

strong brand recognition, broad distribution, and over 60 independent software companies supplying software exclusively for its 8-bit format, while SEGA had limited market share, distribution, or independent software support. Moreover, the price of SEGA's new 16-bit system was approximately twice that of Nintendo's 8-bit system. Despite these considerable obstacles, the superior characteristics of the Genesis system enabled SEGA to rapidly penetrate the first tier, selling an estimated 400,000 systems in the first year alone. By 1992, Genesis had entered the third tier, with an estimated worldwide base of approximately 9 million systems, and captured 40 percent of the U.S. 16-bit market.

Although some videogame consoles and personal computers penetrated the third tier of interactive customers, no interactive multimedia system gained acceptance as a mass market standard equivalent to that of the VCR and audio CD player in the consumer electronics market. To be successful in reaching the mass market, any new interactive platform had to provide several enhancements over existing systems: (1) a dramatic increase in audiovisual realism to appeal to innovators, (2) the broad-based support of hardware system manufacturers and software developers required to reach early adopters and achieve acceptance as a standard platform, and (3) sufficient value and affordability to reach current interactive system users and address the mass market. Existing interactive multimedia devices had not achieved full mass market penetration because they had not satisfied all of these criteria.

Advances in digital processing, storage, graphics, compression, and communication technologies enabled a new generation of devices to address the home interactive multimedia market. Initial attempts focused on adding CD-ROM drives to existing videogames and PC-like architectures. Several large Japanese companies developed interactive video devices that utilized a CD-ROM drive. Some of the major computer product manufacturers, including Apple Computer, Microsoft, Silicon Graphics, IBM, and Sony were believed to be developing interactive video products.

Several major companies in the cable and telecommunications industry were developing methods to deliver interactive multimedia products and services through existing or planned cable and telephone networks. Additional strategic alliances and partnerships were expected to emerge as this information superhighway technology developed further.

VIDEOGAME TECHNOLOGY[17]

There were seven principal types of hardware platforms for playing videogames: 8-bit, 16-bit, 32-bit, and 64-bit consoles, portable (handheld) systems, CD-based systems, and personal computers. Videogame machines were actually small computers. For example, the 16-bit chip that powered the SEGA Genesis also ran Apple's first Macintosh. The most popular 8-bit, 16-bit, and portable hardware systems were manufactured and marketed by Nintendo and SEGA. While videogame software was marketed primarily in cartridge form for 8-, 16-, and 32-bit types of videogame systems, software products in the CD form were expected to replace cartridge-based products as the primary format during the next several years. Companies such as 3DO Company, SEGA, and Atari had developed and were marketing CD-based delivery systems. In addition, a number of companies had announced the develop-

---

[17]Extracted from Activision, Inc., 10-K, March 31, 1994.

EXHIBIT 4 Estimated Sales and Market Share Summary by Segment, 1992–1996 (in millions)

	1992	1993	1994	1995	1996
8-bit	$ 720	$ 370	$ 124	$ 62	$ 30
16-bit	2,884	3,828	3,438	2,073	1,439
Portables	967	795	805	645	389
Next generation	49	115	658	2,030	4,014
Total industry	$4,620	$5,108	$5,025	$4,810	$5,872
Market Share					
8-bit	16%	7%	2%	1%	1%
16-bit	62	75	68	43	25
Portables	21	16	16	13	7
Next generation	1	2	13	42	68
Total industry	100%	100%	100%*	100%*	100%*

* Does not equal 100% due to rounding.

Source: Gerard Klauer Mattison & Co.

ment of 32-bit or 64-bit game systems, collectively referred to as "next generation" players. Currently, there were more than 20 consumer computing and gaming formats available in the United States, all of which were incompatible. Exhibit 4 shows estimated sales and market shares for the 8-bit, 16-bit, portable, and next generation segments.

8-Bit Videogame Systems Home entertainment systems based on 8-bit microprocessors were introduced in the early 1980s. Nintendo introduced the NES in the United States in 1985. It was estimated that at the end of 1993, the installed base of 8-bit videogame systems in the United States was approximately 35 million units, with approximately 700-plus software titles available for use with such videogame systems. Software cartridges available for use on NES were developed by Nintendo as well as approximately 65 authorized Nintendo licensees worldwide.

Sales of 8-bit videogame systems and software cartridges for such systems had declined significantly in recent years because of the advanced capabilities of newer platforms. It was not expected that significant growth opportunities remained in this segment (see Exhibit 4). Nintendo announced it would discontinue manufacture of its NES.

16-Bit Videogame Systems In 1989, SEGA introduced the 16-bit Genesis videogame system in the United States. The Genesis featured a more powerful microprocessor, more colors, and superior graphics, animation, and sound relative to the NES. Nintendo introduced its 16-bit Super NES, with similar capabilities to Genesis, in the United States in September 1991. The 16-bit systems, because of their larger memories and more advanced hardware, offered more realistic video images, natural sounds, and synthesized music. The challenge for software developers and publishers was to produce compelling products that took advantage of the game-playing capacity of the 16-bit systems. Suggested U.S. retail prices for SEGA's and Nintendo's 16-bit consoles started at less than $100, and prices for the software products to be used on such consoles ranged from $19.95 to $79.95. It has been estimated that the installed base of 16-bit game systems in the United States was approximately 35 million (SEGA had 17 million) and the number of software titles available for use with the Genesis and the Super NES exceeded 500 and 350, respectively.

Opportunities for 16-bit cartridge-based software were declining, as sales of both 16-bit hardware and software continued to weaken in the United States (see Exhibit 4). Declining 8-bit and 16-bit sales in Japan—which historically was an early indicator of market changes in the interactive entertainment software industry—led analysts to predict that strong sales of 16-bit software in the United States would not continue beyond calendar year 1995. It was anticipated that 32-bit and 64-bit hardware and CD-based systems would displace 16-bit hardware.

32-Bit Videogame Systems   In November 1994, SEGA launched its Genesis 32-X adapter, which converted 16-bit Genesis videogame players into a more powerful 32-bit machine. The upgrade was designed to provide the more than 17 million Genesis owners a way to move to the next level in videogames (arcade-quality graphics and speed) at a reasonable cost. Other 32-bit systems included SEGA's Saturn and Sony's PlayStation, both released in Japan in 1994 and expected to be released sometime in 1995 in the United States. Nintendo's portable Virtual Boy player was also introduced in the United States in early 1995. Combined sales for the three nonportable 32-bit players (SEGA 32-X, Saturn, and PlayStation) were expected to reach $664 million in 1995, or about 33 percent of the market (see Exhibit 5). Both Nintendo and SEGA and their competitors had announced plans to introduce 64-bit machines sometime in 1995 that would eclipse the 32-bit players.

64-Bit Videogame Systems   In November 1993, Atari introduced the Atari Jaguar, a 64-bit multimedia entertainment system at a suggested retail price of $249.95. The Jaguar featured two proprietary chips (named "Tom" and "Jerry") developed in its own facilities, video with 24-bit graphics with up to 16 million colors, and a 3-D engine that could render 3-D shaded or texture map polygons in real time. The system also supported real-time texture mapping that allowed for realistic surfaces to be applied over the 3-D polygons. Atari believed the graphics of the Jaguar video were equal to or superior to any other system currently available. Jaguar incorporated a 16-bit CD quality sound system, which provided realistic sounds in the software and included human voices. The Jaguar also had a high-speed serial port that would allow for future connection into telephone networks as well as modem-based, two-player games over telephone lines.

Both Nintendo and SEGA were expected to introduce 64-bit players for home use in 1995, the Ultra 64 and Saturn. Nintendo's Ultra 64 was being designed by Silicon Graphics Inc., whose computer workstations had been used to design the 3-D special effects in such movies as *Jurassic Park, Terminator 2*, and *The Abyss*.[18] Estimated sales and market share positions for each of the major next generation machines are shown in Exhibit 5.

---

[18]Snider, "Video Market."

EXHIBIT 5 Estimated Sales and Market Share Summary: "Next Generation" Hardware and Software, 1993–1996 (in millions)

	1993	1994	1995	1996
3DO-based	$ 29	$370	$ 680	$1,260
Atari Jaguar	7	66	157	118
SEGA 32-X	—	158	218	133
Philips CD-I	78	64	54	171
SEGA Saturn	—	—	230	570
Sony PlayStation	—	—	216	570
Nintendo Ultra-64	—	—	475	1,193
Total next generation	$114	$658	$2,030	$4,015
Market Share				
3DO-based	25%	56%	34%	31%
Atari-Jaguar	6%	10%	8%	3%
SEGA 32-X	—	24%	11%	3%
Philips CD-I	68%	10%	3%	4%
SEGA Saturn	—	—	11%	14%
Sony PlayStation	—	—	11%	14%
Nintendo Ultra-64	—	—	23%	30%
Total next generation	100%	100%	100%*	100%*

* Does not equal 100% due to rounding.

Source: Gerard Klauer Mattison & Co.

Handheld (Portable) Game Systems   Nintendo's release in 1989 of the Game Boy, a battery-operated, handheld interactive entertainment system incorporating an 8-bit microprocessor, revolutionized the handheld game machine market. Previously, the only handheld games available were dedicated to a single game. Game Boy offered a portable gaming system—a take-along Nintendo that allowed players to insert any number of different game cartridges. SEGA's color Game Gear handheld system, released in 1991, competed directly with the Nintendo Game Boy. Atari offered a color portable handheld game system called the Atari Lynx, released in 1992. The Lynx provided 16-bit color graphics, stereo sound, fast action, and depth of game play, and came complete with a built-in, eight-directional joypad and a 3.5-inch full color LCD offering up to 16 colors at one time from a palette of over 4,000 colors. At the end of 1993, the purchased base of handheld game systems was approximately 13 million and the numbers of software titles available for use with the Game Boy, the Game Gear, and the Atari Lynx were over 320, 100, and 65, respectively. In 1994, sales of handheld systems were expected to reach $806 million (see Exhibit 6), representing a 16 percent share of the market (see Exhibit 4).

CD-Based Systems[19]   With the introduction in recent years of computer disk drives that read optical laser disks, or "CDs," the ability to deliver complex entertainment

---

[19]Extracted from Activision Form 10-K, p. 8.

EXHIBIT 6 Estimated Sales and Market Share Summary: Portable Game Players, 1992–1996 (in millions)

	1992	1993	1994	1995	1996
Nintendo Game Boy	$770	$563	$415	$298	$220
SEGA Game Gear	162	219	388	348	169
Atari Lynx	35	13	3	—	—
Total portables	$967	$795	$806	$646	$389
Percent change		–18%	1%	–20%	–40%
Market Share					
Nintendo Game Boy	80%	71%	52%	46%	57%
SEGA Game Gear	17	28	48	54	43
Atari Lynx	4	2	0	—	—
Total portables	100%*	100%*	100%	100%	100%

* Does not equal 100% due to rounding.

Source: Gerard Klauer Mattison & Co.

software made significant technological advances. A CD had over 600 times more memory capacity than an 8-bit standard cartridge, enabling CD systems to incorporate large amounts of data, full motion video, and high-quality sound, thus creating vivid multimedia experiences.

In addition to personal computer disk drives that read CDs, known as CD-ROM drives, several CD-based videogame systems had been introduced by videogame hardware manufacturers: SEGA introduced its SEGA CD in 1992; 3DO released the 3DO Multiplayer in 1993; and Sony Corporation had a CD-based game system under development. Nintendo's Ultra 64 did not employ CD capability. As the installed base of CD-ROM drives for personal computers increased and as the videogame industry moved more toward CD-based delivery systems, it was believed that the differences between videogame hardware and personal computers would narrow.

The market for entertainment software in a CD format was at an early stage of development. As industry standards were developed and prices for CD-based hardware declined, analysts estimated that the 1.4 million CD-ROM-equipped videogame machines in play at the close of 1993 could more than triple to 4.9 million units by the end of 1995. However, the CD-based market presented particular challenges for software developers and publishers. Entertainment software would have to incorporate increasingly sophisticated graphics (video and animation), data, and interactive capabilities, resulting in higher development costs and requiring successful software developers to coordinate talent from a variety of programming and technology disciplines in the development process.

CD-based delivery systems did, however, present advantages to software publishers. CDs could be manufactured for $1 to $2 apiece (about 75 percent or more below the cost of traditional videogame cartridges) and, unlike floppy disks, could not yet be readily copied. Publishers could therefore expect to achieve higher profit margins from the sale of CDs than were the norm in the cartridge-based videogame or floppy disk–based computer software market. In addition, once a master copy was made, extra copies could be produced in small batch lots as needed. With a cartridge game, the manufacturing process took about two months at a cost per cartridge of $10 to $20 (not including licensing fees).

Despite all the advantages, CD-ROM technology was far from ideal. The biggest problem related to playing videogames was speed. Compared to a cartridge system, it took longer to access data on a compact disk. Access times were important, as most videogames required fast-paced action. Any slowdown in the access and processing of data negatively affected game play. However, as the technology advanced and game developers became more experienced with CD-ROM, speed was expected to become less of a concern. Another related problem with CD-ROM technology was that the hardware was more expensive to manufacture. There was no standalone CD player under $200. Interviews of consumers revealed that CDs were easily damaged by users. A single scratch could make a CD unreadable. Finally, there were a number of CD-ROM formats; a title written for one format would not necessarily work on another system.[20]

Exhibit 7 compares the major cartridge and CD-based systems.

Personal Computers Approximately 36 percent of U.S. households had personal computers and the number was growing rapidly. In 1994 alone, American consumers spent $9 billion to buy nearly 7 million personal computers. This presented a new threat for videogame marketers. Industry analysts estimated that the home computer market was already siphoning off nearly 15 percent of videogame sales.

Although millions of Americans used home computers for spreadsheets and word processing, home computers were also taking on a different role. Most PCs sold featured multimedia packages that included faster processors, more memory and storage capacity, CD-ROM drives, and sound cards, all of which served to make personal computers a complete family entertainment center and all-purpose appliance for the Information Age.[21] The number of home computers with multimedia CD-ROMs was predicted to be more than 17 million by the end of 1995. It was expected that over half the households in the United States would have PCs by the end of the century.

COIN-OPERATED ARCADE GAMES/THEME PARKS

Americans were spending approximately $7 billion on arcade games as of 1994. With the $5 billion spent on home videogame hardware and software, the $12 billion total was nearly two and one-half times the size of the $5 billion movie box office. Arcades had experienced a resurgence in interest in recent years, partly because arcades were becoming more "family-friendly." Although many arcades were still dark, smoky, scary dens located in shopping malls, a newer breed of family entertainment centers offered batting cages, bumper cars, fast food, and so on to draw the whole family rather than just teen-aged boys.[22] The video arcade was traditionally the launching ground for games designed for home use and videogame buyers also liked to sharpen their game-playing skills in arcades before buying home versions of the game.

---

[20]DFC Intelligence Research.

[21]L. Armstrong et al., "Home Computers," *Business Week*, November 28, 1994, pp. 89–94.

[22]Gerard Klauer Mattison & Co., Inc., *Interactive Electronic Industry: Entertainment Industry Overview* (New York, 1993), p. 9.

EXHIBIT 7   Comparative Data for Selected Video Game Systems, 1994

	Nintendo NES	SEGA Genesis	Nintendo SNES	Philips CD-I	SEGA CD	3DO	Atari Jaguar	SEGA Genesis 32-X
Release date	10/85	1/90	9/91	1991	10/92	10/93	11/93	11/94
U.S. installed base	35 million	17 million	18 million	250,000	1.5 million	200,000	125,000	500,000
Retail price	No longer manufactured	$90 to $120 (depending on bundled software)	$90 to $120 (depending on bundled software)	$300 (basic system); $500 (full system)	$220	$400	$250	$160
Available titles 1/95	700+	500+	350+	150+	50+	100+	<20	<10
Software unit sales (1994)	4 million (estimated)	23 million (estimated)	22 million (estimated)	<2 million	5 million (estimated)	<2 million	<1 million	NA
System type	Cartridge	Cartridge	Cartridge	Compact disc	CD	CD	Cartridge	Cartridge
System capabilities	8-bit processor, 1.79 MHz, 16 colors, Resolution 256 × 240	16-bit processor, 7.6 MHz, 64 colors, Resolution 320 × 224	16-bit processor, 3.58 MHz, 256 colors, Resolution 512 × 418	16-bit processor, 15.5 MHz, 16.7 million colors	16-bit processor, Genesis processor, 12.7 MHz	32-bit RISC processor, 12.5 MHz, 16.7 million colors, Resolution 640 × 480	64-bit RISC processor, 16.7 million colors, Resolution 720 × 480	32-bit RISC processor, 23 MHz, 50,000 polygons/ second, 32,768 colors

Sources: DFC Intelligence estimates based on company reports and various industry sources. 1994 software sales are preliminary estimates and intended to be ballpark figures only.

SEGA operated two miniature theme parks in Japan, featuring both traditional videogames and larger virtual-reality and interactive rides that took players on adventures such as space battles or ghost hunts.[23] The company planned to open as many as 50 high-tech theme parks in the United States by the end of the century and was aggressively looking for partners to help. The first U.S. park was scheduled to be built in Los Angeles at an estimated cost of $25 million.

SOFTWARE

Since 1988, the number of available videogame titles had increased substantially, primarily because of the large number of SEGA and Nintendo licensees. At the end of 1994, for example, Nintendo had a library of 466 titles; SEGA had more than 500 titles for Genesis, 175 CD titles, and more than 200 titles for the Game Gear player.

Competitive forces in the entertainment software and videogame marketplace had increased the need for higher quality, distinctive entertainment software concepts. Competition for titles, themes, and characters from television, motion picture, and other media to create "hits" was increasing development costs for software producers. Substantial nonrefundable advance licensing fees and significant advertising expenses added to the financial risk. Moreover, the ability to incorporate compelling story lines or game experiences with full motion video, digital sound, other lifelike technology, and ease of use presented artistic as well as technical challenges that added to the cost equation.[24]

Software was priced to generate most of the profit; the hardware typically sold for less than $200. Game software for most machines ran between $40 and $60. Software developer costs to create a new videogame ranged from $75,000 to $300,000, with some CD titles costing $1 million to develop.[25] The cost to manufacture an interactive CD selling for $40 was approximately $1 to $2. A software publisher could produce a videogame cartridge (excluding royalties) for between $10 to $20 per unit.[26] To compensate for games that turned out to be duds, companies needed some megahits.[27] In 1992, SEGA had worldwide revenues of $450 million sales of one game, "Sonic 2." In August 1993, the top five videogames accounted for 27 percent of industry sales, with the next five games accounting for about 8.3 percent. Sales were even more concentrated among the top titles during the holiday season.

Both SEGA and Nintendo each had more than 65 companies licensed to develop software for use with their respective systems. Typically, the software developer submitted a prototype for evaluation and approval from Nintendo or SEGA, including all artwork to be used in packaging and marketing the product. With several kinds of CD players, all incompatible, software developers trying to penetrate the entire market had to incur additional expense to re-create their games for each different system.[28]

Several motion picture companies had recently entered the interactive entertainment software segment. Paramount created Paramount Interactive in 1993 to develop

---

[23]D. P. Hamilton, "SEGA Looks Abroad for Partners to Open Theme Parks in U.S.," *The Wall Street Journal*, August 16, 1994, p. B6.

[24]Ibid.

[25]T. Abate, "Atari Wants Back in the Game," *San Francisco Examiner*, February 13, 1994, p. E5.

[26]3DO Company 10-K, 1993, p. 6.

[27]N. Hutheesing, "Platform Battle," *Forbes*, May 9, 1994, pp. 168–170.

[28]Ibid.

products based on Paramount's motion pictures, television, and sports properties. Early game titles included "*Viper: Assault on the Outfit*," a futuristic car adventure based on the television series, and "*Star Trek: Deep Space Nine—The Hunt*," a role-playing adventure. In an exclusive agreement with Paramount, software publishers Spectrum HoloByte released several titles based on *Star Trek: The Next Generation.* Warner Bros. teamed up with game publisher Konami to release *Batman—The Animated Series* for Super NES. Warner also worked with Konami and Virgin Interactive Entertainment (VIE) to feature over 1,500 original animations within game play. According to Martin Alper, CEO of VIE, "This level of collaboration between a major studio and a game company is unique and, no doubt, will become a benchmark for future products of this nature."[29]

Capital Cities/ABC Inc. formed a joint venture in December 1994 with Electronic Arts, a pioneer in interactive software, to develop software and videogames based on ABC's children and news TV shows. The new venture was expected to produce about 12 titles a year, starting in December 1995, mostly on CD-ROM, and expand eventually to about 25 titles a year.[30] In December 1994, the Walt Disney Co. also announced formation of a new computer software unit that would produce educational programs and videogames inspired by its movies. The division intended to focus initially on SEGA and Nintendo videogames and CD-ROM educational software linked to its animated musicals, including *Pocahontas.*[31]

Earlier attempts to link movies and games had failed, most notably Walt Disney's film based on "Super Mario Bros.," the best-selling videogame series ever. However, more efforts to create movies bringing the best-selling arcade games to the silver screen were under way. *Double Dragon* was released in November 1994; *Street Fighter* (at a cost of $40 million) was released in December 1994;[32] *Mortal Kombat* ($36 million) was released in April 1995. Also on the horizon were movies based on "Doom," "Myst," "King's Quest," and "Leisure Suit Larry."

VIDEOGAME DEVELOPMENT ISSUES

Firms had to resolve four key considerations in developing a videogame: (1) what development and distribution agreement to arrange, (2) whether to acquire content or create original content, (3) which platform to develop for, and (4) future employment concerns.[33]

Development and Distribution Agreements   The distribution channels for videogames and other multimedia were constantly evolving. The common method was for a publisher to hire a developer to create a title. The developer was responsible for ensuring the quality of the product. The publisher handled manufacturing, packaging, marketing, and distribution issues. The publisher bore the risk if the product failed.

---

[29]Much of this section is extracted from J. Abrams, "Hollywood Comes to Las Vegas," *Dealerscope*, February 1994, pp. 24, 26.

[30]E. Jensen, "Capital Cities and Electronic Arts Plan Venture in Software and Video Games," *The Wall Street Journal*, December 6, 1994, p. B4.

[31]J. Horn, "Disney Forms Interactive Unit Division to Create Computer Software Linked to Its Movies," *San Francisco Chronicle*, December 6, 1994, p. D3.

[32]J. Carlton, "Capcom Bets That Stars and a Story Can Turn a Hot Game into a Hit Film," *The Wall Street Journal*, October 6, 1994, pp. B1, B6.

[33]This section extracted from DFC Intelligence Research.

Generally, developers were paid a royalty based on wholesale revenues. This royalty varied greatly, but typically ranged from 5 to 15 percent.

Many developers attempted to publish their own titles. Affiliated label and copublishing programs became a popular means for small companies to publish their own titles and maintain their independence. Under an affiliated label program, a developer handled marketing and publishing, while a copublisher dealt with distribution. In return, the developer received a royalty of up to 75 percent of wholesale revenue. A variation on the affiliated label program was expected to become the distribution method of choice.

Acquiring Content   In the past, companies that owned popular intellectual property would license that property for use in videogames in return for a modest royalty. But the vast market potential for games had made content-owners reluctant to license their properties, and acquiring high-potential creative content was becoming difficult and time-consuming. Many large entertainment conglomerates had set up interactive divisions to create titles based on their own intellectual creations and titles. In the future, it was expected that more publishers would be forced to base their games on original content or else rely on works in the public domain.

Platform Considerations   The videogame market was fast reaching the point where it was essential that a software title be released for a number of different hardware platforms. However, the number of hardware platforms was growing. Each platform was incompatible and required a different set of development tools. The personal computer was the easiest platform to develop for, but personal computer titles had limited revenue potential. Creating titles for different platform systems was time-consuming and difficult. As a general rule, it took 12 to 18 months to develop a software title for the first platform, and 3 to 6 months for each additional platform.

The manufacturers of platforms systems controlled who could develop for their system. A license from the platform provider was required to develop a videogame for the platform provider's system. Licensees paid the platform provider royalty fees based on sales volume. Platform providers often regulated content and limit the number of titles that could be released. Nintendo and SEGA had high licensing fees and were strict about what titles could be released for their systems. 3DO had lower licensing fees and was not as strict about regulating content.

Publishers had to carefully consider which platforms to develop for. No CD-ROM platform had a large enough installed base to make it feasible to publish a title for just that one platform. In deciding which platform to develop for, game creators considered development costs, installed base figures, licensing fees, and player demographics.

Employment Concerns   Top development talent was a rare commodity. In the future, talented developers were expected to have significant bargaining power. Hollywood guilds and agents were beginning to organize multimedia developers. As this trend continued, development costs were projected to rise.

THE VIDEOGAME DEVELOPMENT PROCESS[34] ───────

The development of videogames required a blend of technology and creative talent. Typically, a development team was formed that included a producer, designers, pro-

---

[34]Extracted from DFC Intelligence Research.

grammers, musicians, and graphic artists. The average cartridge game involved the efforts of 10 to 15 individuals, although it was not unusual for game development teams to be larger.

The producer oversaw the project and was responsible for coordinating the efforts of the development team. Designers came up with the basic concepts for the game, drafted the script, and were responsible for the characters, plot, and overall objectives of the game. Graphic artists drew the characters and objects in the game. Programmers wrote the computer code that incorporated all the various elements into a form that worked on the appropriate hardware platform.

Once a workable version of the game had been created, preliminary testing was done to evaluate the computer code and to ensure all the game elements were in place. If all went well, the game was play-tested to find any hidden bugs. The next level involved bringing in a group of outside players to gauge the game's reception with the general public. After the completion of all testing, a product was sent off for manufacturing and packaging.

Because it took 10 to 15 months to complete an original game and then another 3 to 6 months to port that game to another platform, development risks were quite high. A lot could change between the time a design was started and the time it was launched in the marketplace. A platform that was popular last year could be out of fashion 12 months later.

DEMOGRAPHICS

Videogames were in 69 percent of homes with adolescents, 12 to 17; computers were in 18 percent of homes with children under 18.[35] Not all videogame customers were adolescents, however. Adults—mostly men—rented sports games like "Bill Walsh College Football" and "NBA Jam." Men in their 20s and 30s represented a growing portion of the videogame market.[36] Nintendo's U.S. player demographics are shown in Exhibit 8. The U.S. population of 10- to 20-year-olds and 30- to 50-year-olds is shown in Exhibit 9.

EXHIBIT 8   Nintendo SNES U.S. Player Demographics

Age	Percent of Players	
Under 6	2%	
6–14	48	
15–17	11	
18+	39	

Gender	Percent of SNES Players	Percent of Game Boy Players
Male	82%	59%
Female	18%	41%

Source: Nintendo.

---

[35]"Electronic Games Look to Untapped Girls' Market," *San Jose Mercury News,* November 11, 1994, p. 2D.

[36]D. Wharton, "Video Legions," *Los Angeles Times* (Valley Edition), November 18, 1994, p. 10.

EXHIBIT 9   U.S. Population Data, Actual and Projected, 1984–2000

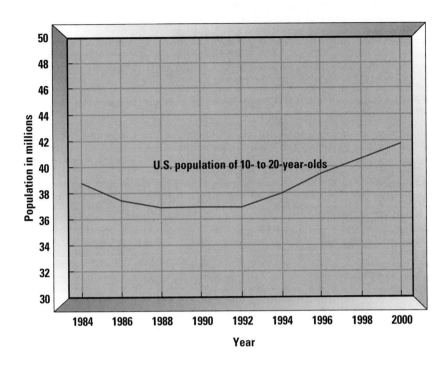

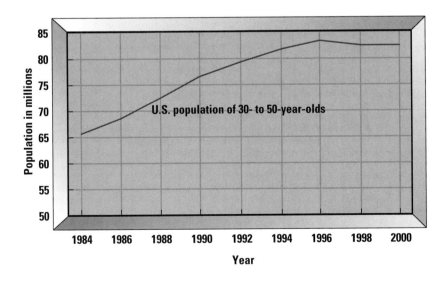

Source: Gerard Klauer Mattison & Co.

Studies indicated that many children who grew up playing videogames continued to do so as adults. There were several key differences between adult and younger players. Adolescents were more concerned with what is "in" and "hot." The adult market was composed of numerous niches, each with an interest in a different type of game. Adults liked titles that fit in with their lifestyles and interests. It was difficult to create one title that appealed to the entire adult market. In addition, the biggest complaint among adults was that most games took too much time to play. Adults preferred to play games in short bursts during free moments.[37]

Generally, videogames were not popular with women. Many of the most popular games dealt with such activities as street fighting, car racing, and football. According to the Software Publishers Association, about 28 percent of computer game and 21 percent of videogame players were female. Only one top videogame, Nintendo's "Super Metroid," had a female lead character. Software developers were slowly responding to this untapped market and rolling out games for girls. SEGA, for example, had formed a task force composed of the top female marketers and game developers in the company to develop software products that appealed to female tastes.

A clue to what videogames appealed to women came from Nintendo's experience with its Game Boy handheld players. The company found that women accounted for 40 percent of the 27 million worldwide buyers of Game Boy, a figure double the percentage of women buying its other games. Women also liked "Tetris," a geometric videogame that was packaged with Game Boy. One 14-year-old boy wrote Nintendo about his mother, saying, "Almost 24 hours a day she plays Tetris . . . I can't hardly play more than one game a day."[38] Nintendo had hired experts to study adult Game Boy habits.

In another study of 10,000 children playing video and computer games over two years, Electronic Arts found that girls (1) identified with characters in videogames, (2) liked fast action and competitive games less than boys, (3) preferred something they can learn from, and (4) really enjoyed puzzle solving and cooperative games that allowed them to create and design.

The biggest challenge in the videogame industry was to get more adults and females to play videogames. Although numerous studies were underway, no successful approaches had yet emerged.

MARKETING[39]

In years past, the marketing of videogames was unsophisticated. Demand was stimulated by the advertising campaigns of platform providers such as Nintendo and SEGA. Demand was so strong for "hit" games that publishers merely had to get them into stores. Advertising led to word-of-mouth publicity and sometimes only consisted of ads in leading videogame consumer magazines and a booth at the Consumer Electronics Show.

As of 1994, videogame marketing was becoming a more significant competitive factor. As retail shelf space became more crowded with videogame platforms and game software, companies initiated a marked shift in marketing strategy. The major videogame releases started to be promoted much like a release from a major movie

---

[37]DFC Intelligence Research.

[38]J. Carlton, "Game Makers Study How Tetris Hooks Women," *The Wall Street Journal*, May 10, 1994, p. B1.

[39]Extracted from DFC Intelligence Report.

EXHIBIT 10   Estimated U.S. Retail Outlet Market Shares for
Videogames, 1994

Toys "Я" Us	20%
Other toy stores (e.g., Kay Bee Toys)	10
Computer software (e.g., Babbages)	15
Video and music stores (e.g., Blockbuster)	15
Consumer electronics (e.g., Best Buy)	5
Mass merchants (e.g., Wal-Mart)	35
	100%

Source: DFC Intelligence estimates based on various
industry sources.

studio. Television advertising, promotional tie-ins, merchandising, direct mail, and special launch parties became commonplace.

Many industry observers saw the videogame industry becoming a "hits"-driven business as marketing costs escalated and access to retail space became tighter. Small game publishers without the resources of the big players in the industry faced an uphill battle. Retailers only took their product if they had a strong brand name, backed with advertising dollars. But without shelf space, it was hard for small publishers to build a brand image and start generating the revenue necessary to fund large-scale marketing campaigns.

Toy stores and computer software stores were the traditional retailers of videogames. However, as the videogame business grew, other retailers began carrying videogame software because of the high margins. In 1994, over 20,000 stores in the United States carried videogames. Toys "Я" Us was the leading retailer with an estimated 20 percent of the U.S. market; mass merchandisers (e.g., Wal-Mart and Kmart) captured about 35 percent of all videogame sales. Exhibit 10 shows estimated market share by retail outlet.

Shifting consumer interest in videogames created challenges for retailers. Only a few years ago, demand for games was so high that a retailer could sell whatever was put on the shelf—even the bad games sold. The major complaint of retailers was not having enough products. Nintendo went so far as to ration games in 1988 and 1989. All this changed as the market became flooded with new products in the 1990s and Nintendo began to face increased competition from SEGA. In 1994, retailers found many of the 16-bit cartridges sitting unsold on the shelf; sales seemed to be concentrated in a handful of hit titles. Moreover, it was the practice of many retailers to sell newly stocked games at full list price for 30 to 60 days, after which they were sold at a discount. With retailers holding excess inventory, it was not uncommon to see games that originally listed for $60 discounted to the $15 to $20 range. DFC Intelligence Research identified that retailers were most concerned about the difficulty of deciding what to buy, the lack of a return policy, and heavy price discounting due to increased competition. In 1994, retailers had become very careful about what they would stock. Retail buyers looked at three things when deciding which brands and titles to stock: the quality of the game, the amount of advertising the publisher planned to do, and the reputation of the publisher.

Despite overcrowding of traditional distribution channels, analysts expected new channels of distribution to emerge. Technology was making new forms of distribution possible. Several companies were experimenting with direct marketing, the use of cable television, and on-line distribution via the Internet. There was also the potential that the increased bandwidth of phone and cable systems could make multiplayer networked gaming possible.

SEASONALITY[40]

Retail sales of videogames were quite slow between May and August. Analysts attribute the seasonal sales slowdown to several factors. First, teenagers spent more time outside in warmer weather and less time indoors playing videogames. They also watched less TV during these months, thus making them less reachable via advertising. In addition, because they were out of school, there was less "I got to level 10, how far did you get?" to spur sales. Finally, sales were slower because the publishers put out fewer games. Two-thirds of the videogame sales occurred during the year-end holiday season.

THE INFORMATION SUPERHIGHWAY[41]

According to best estimates, there were approximately 25 million people on the Internet, with the number of users growing by about 2.5 million each month. While most media companies were scrambling to develop strategies to put themselves on the Internet, both Nintendo and SEGA nixed any plan to put their games on-line even though on-line services were one of the fastest-growing segments in the global media market. Companies like America Online, CompuServe, Delphi, and Prodigy had recently enjoyed double-digit growth. Microsoft planned to introduce an on-line service in 1995. On-line services had also taken off in Japan. Most observers believed that games would become an important ingredient in all these services. In fact, one observer predicted that in the not-too-distant future, people miles apart would play tennis, golf, and perhaps Virtuality Boxing together on global information highways.[42] George Lucas, creator of the *Star Wars* and *Indiana Jones* film trilogies, in an interview in *The Wall Street Journal*, commented on the future interaction of entertainment and technology:

> "Well, I have a game company, and I think view-on-demand games will take off pretty quickly. It's a little bit problematical about how it's going to work, but it seems obvious that home delivery of games is a natural . . . Interactive games that involve more than one player . . . will be popular. You're playing with two or three other people at the same time at various places over the phone . . ."[43]

Nintendo and SEGA pursued radically different strategies for bringing telecommunications to their game machines, neither of which included the telephone. Nintendo elected to go the satellite route. In 1993, Nintendo paid $8 million for a 20 percent stake in St. Giga, a troubled Japanese satellite broadcaster, for the purpose of

---

[40]This section was extracted from Gerard Klauer Mattison Industry Overview, 1993.

[41]This section was extracted from M. Schrage, "Why Sonic the Hedgehog Needs to Jump onto the Info Highway," *Los Angeles Times* (Business Section), November 3, 1994, p. 1.

[42]J. Guyon, "Virtual Center," *The Wall Street Journal* (Entertainment & Technology), March 21, 1994, p. R18.

[43]T. R. King, "Lucasvision," *The Wall Street Journal* (Entertainment & Technology), March 21, 1994, p. R20.

downloading games by satellite to Japan's 14 million Nintendo game players. Although considered a novel distribution concept, this approach did not support any opportunity for networked games that people could play with or against each other.

SEGA began test-marketing its SEGA Channel in the United States in early 1994, and formed SEGA Digital Communications Ltd. in July 1994 to put videogames on cable in Japan. However, the technology was such that the system did not allow for networked game-playing.

New services were springing up to deliver games over phone lines. Catapult Entertainment, Inc., was selling Xband Videogame Network, which matched players of similar skill levels to play SEGA with people around the country. The service required use of a $70 Xband modem available in toy and computer stores. A similar on-line service was available for computer games users from ImagiNation that connected evenly matched players who paid a base fee of $9.95 for five hours of play. Microsoft planned to offer PlayersNet, a software package that allowed PC users to compete against each other over computer networks or telephone lines using a modem.

Some industry analysts predicted that videogame companies were well positioned to take advantage of future opportunities related to the "information superhighway." They argued that a videogame machine could evolve into a set-top box that connected to fiber-optic cable networks and delivers interactive services into the home. Companies with the skills to develop and market such hardware at prices well below the cost of home computers could then offer interactive products with the potential to capture a sizable share of the game-playing market.[44]

PROFILES OF SELECTED VIDEOGAME COMPETITORS

Nintendo and SEGA's key competitors in the videogame industry included Sony, 3DO, Atari, and Philips Electronics NV. Commodore reentered the videogame industry with a CDTV system in 1991, and more recently with the Amiga CD32; however, sales were less than expected, and the company was not considered a significant player. In late 1994, Apple Computer, Inc., formed an alliance with Japan's largest toy maker (Bandai Co., Ltd.) to build a low-cost CD-ROM videogame player, which was expected to be available worldwide for the 1995 holiday season. Exhibit 11 summarizes estimated U.S. videogame industry retail sales and market share statistics for each of the key competitors.

Nintendo Company, Ltd.[45]

Nintendo began as a playing card manufacturer in 1889 in Kyoto, Japan. In 1994, the company was headed by the great grandson of Nintendo's founder, Hiroshi Yamauchi. Yamauchi had been in charge since becoming the company's president in 1922 at the age of 22.

Under Yamauchi's leadership the company began to expand into the toy business. Nintendo became NCL, Nintendo Company, Ltd., and went public in the early 1960s. In 1975, Nintendo made its first venture into videogames when it got a license to sell Magnavox's videogame system in Japan. Nintendo released its own home videogame system in 1977 and soon began to develop arcade games.

---

[44]DFC Intelligence Research.

[45]Nintendo's company background provided by DFC Intelligence Research.

EXHIBIT 11 Estimated U.S. Videogame Industry Sales and Market Share Data: Retail Sales of Hardware and Software, 1992–1996 (in millions)

	1992	Share	1993	Share	1994	Share	1995	Share	1996	Share
Nintendo										
NES Hardware	$ 180	4%	$ 120	2%	$ 49	1%	$ 25	1%	$ 10	0%
NES Software	540	12	250	5	75	1	38	1	20	0
Game Boy Hardware	320	7	263	5	165	3	138	3	100	2
Game Boy Software	450	10	300	6	250	5	160	3	120	2
Super NES Hardware	743	16	625	12	518	10	250	5	180	3
Super NES Software	990	21	1,265	25	1,210	24	750	16	540	9
Ultra 64 Hardware	—	—	—	—	—	—	125	3	563	10
Ultra 64 Software	—	—	—	—	—	—	350	7	630	11
Total Nintendo	$3,223	70%	$2,823	55%	$2,267	45%	$1,835	38%	$2,162	37%
SEGA										
Genesis Hardware	$ 440	$ 10	$ 550	$ 11	$ 400	$ 8	$ 223	$ 5	$ 170	$ 3
Genesis Software	650	14	1,156	23	1,000	20	675	14	480	8
Game Gear Hardware	72	2	99	2	223	4	223	5	89	2
Game Gear Software	90	2	120	2	165	3	125	3	80	1
SEGA CD Hardware	45	1	150	3	173	3	100	2	36	1
SEGA CD Software	17	0	83	2	138	3	75	2	33	1
32-X Hardware	—	—	—	—	75	1	94	2	50	1
32-X Software	—	—	—	—	83	2	124	3	83	1
Saturn Hardware	—	—	—	—	—	—	164	—	350	6
Saturn Software	—	—	—	—	—	—	66	—	220	4
Total SEGA	$1,313	$ 28	$2,157	$ 42	$2,255	$ 45	$1,868	$ 39	$1,591	$ 27
Atari										
Jaguar Hardware	—	—	$ 5	$ 0.1	$ 42	$ 1	$ 80	$ 2	$ 48	$ 1
Jaguar Software	—	—	2	0.0	24	0	60	1	38	1
Lynx Hardware	$ 20	$ 0	9	0.2	2	0	—	—	—	—
Lynx Software	15	0	4	0.1	1	0	—	—	—	—
Jaguar CD Hardware	—	—	—	—	—	—	10	0	18	0
Jaguar CD Software	—	—	—	—	—	—	8	0	15	0
Total Atari	$ 35	$ 1	$ 20	$ 0.4	$ 69	$ 1	$ 157	$ 3	$ 118	$ 2
3DO-based										
Hardware	—	—	$ 21	$ 0	$ 167	$ 3	$ 350	$ 7	$ 600	$ 10
Software	—	—	8	0	204	4	330	7	660	11
Total 3DO-based	—	—	$ 29	$ 1	$ 370	$ 7	$ 680	$ 14	$1,260	$ 21
Sony										
PlayStation Hardware	—	—	—	—	—	—	$ 150	$ 3	$ 350	$ 6
PlayStation Software	—	—	—	—	—	—	66	1	220	4
Total Sony	—	—	—	—	—	—	$ 216	$ 4	$ 570	$ 10
Philips CD-I										
CD-I Hardware	$ 35	$ 1	$ 50	$ 1	$ 40	$ 1	$ 39	$ 1	$ 105	$ 2
CD-I Software	14	0	28	1	24	0	15	0	66	1
Total CD-I	$ 49	$ 1	$ 78	$ 2	$ 64	$ 1	$ 54	$ 1	$ 171	$ 3
Total Industry	$4,619	100%	$5,107	100%	$5,024	100%	$4,809	100%	$5,872	100%
Percent change from prior year			10.6%		–1.6%		–4.3%		22.1%	

Nintendo eventually designed a game system that could use interchangeable cartridges. The machine, called the Famicom (short for Family Computer), was released in Japan in 1983. The 8-bit Famicom sold for about $100, considerably less than the $250 to $300 most game systems cost at that time. Nintendo sold 500,000 units in the Famicom's first two months. The 14 competing systems soon withdrew from the market and Nintendo became the home videogame leader in Japan.

In 1980, Nintendo decided to enter the U.S. market and Nintendo of America (NOA) was established as an independent subsidiary. The first president of NOA was Minoru Arakawa, Hiroshi Yamauchi's son-in-law. The original goal of NOA was to break into the $7 billion a year arcade business. Arcade games from Japan were shipped to the United States and distributed by NOA.

At first, business for NOA was slow, mainly because Nintendo did not have a hit game. That changed in 1981 with the release of "Donkey Kong," created by legendary Nintendo game developer, Sigeru Miyamota. Donkey Kong was such a success in the United States that NOA ended its second year in business with over $100 million in sales.

In 1984, Nintendo began to think about bringing the Famicom to the United States. But, because the U.S. home videogame market had crashed in 1983, no manufacturers, distributors, or retailers would have anything to do with videogames. Nintendo decided to proceed cautiously and began to test the Famicom in New York in 1985. For the U.S. release, the Famicom was renamed the Nintendo Entertainment System (NES). Slowly orders began to come in, and over Christmas 1985, 50,000 units were sold.

The NES went on sale nationwide in 1986. By the end of its first year more than 1 million units were sold in the United States. Three million units had been sold by the end of 1987, and "The Legend of Zelda" became the first game to sell over a million copies. Nintendo mania had begun.

As the NES gained momentum, sales increased from $1 billion in 1987 to over $5 billion in 1992. Game Boy, a portable videogame system released in 1989, sold 40,000 units the first day it was available in the United States. The Super Nintendo Entertainment System (SNES) was released in the United States in 1991. Sales of the SNES took off in 1992, fueled by Nintendo's marketing expertise and the release of Capcom's "Street Fighter II." The SNES then became Nintendo's top-selling system.

As of 1994, Nintendo was contending with some significant changes in its business. Nintendo faced mounting competition and a declining 16-bit market. Nintendo received a wake-up call in 1993 when SEGA passed Nintendo in sales of 16-bit systems. Nintendo suddenly realized it no longer had the monopoly it once enjoyed. Unhappy with the performance of his U.S. subsidiary, Yamauchi replaced his son-in-law as the leader of NOA and installed Howard Lincoln, a senior vice president, as chairman.

Exhibit 12 presents summary financial data on Nintendo. During fiscal year 1994, Nintendo sold more videogame cartridges than in any previous year. However, consolidated net sales fell to $4.714 billion, a 23.5 percent decline from the previous year, and the company's consolidated net income of $511 million decreased by 40 percent from 1993. This represented Nintendo's first decline in sales and net income since it introduced the Famicom in Japan in 1983. Nintendo's stock fell from a high of ¥17,500 ($150.86) in 1992 to a low of ¥6,140 ($59.61) in 1994.

Sales in Nintendo's home sanctuary were healthy in fiscal 1994, but the strong yen seriously affected the company's performance around the globe. A weak economy in Europe and a soft market in the United States, coupled with increased competition,

EXHIBIT 12	Consolidated Financial Summary for Nintendo Co., Ltd., 1992–1994 (in thousands of $)		

	Year Ended March 31		
	1994	**1993**	**1992**
Statement of Operations Data			
Net sales	$4,714,675	$6,161,840	$4,843,475
Cost of goods sold	2,887,106	3,758,376	2,926,885
Gross profit	$1,827,569	$2,403,464	$1,916,590
Selling, general, and administrative expenses	693,507	650,360	483,115
Operating income	$1,134,062	$1,753,104	$1,433,475
Other income/(expenses):			
Interest income	110,392	175,380	206,823
Other	(230,727)	(104,973)	(81,971)
Total	(120,335)	70,407	124,852
Income before income taxes	$1,013,727	$1,823,511	$1,558,327
Income taxes	576,497	967,261	807,653
Foreign currency translation adjustments	73,968	4,031	224
Net income	$ 511,198	$ 860,281	$ 750,898
Net income per share	$3.61	$6.08	$5.30
Cash dividend	0.68	0.68	0.52
Balance Sheet Data			
Cash and cash equivalents	$3,334,679	$3,425,000	$2,549,144
Current assets	5,037,417	4,638,570	3,968,830
Total assets	5,740,070	5,248,012	4,458,664
Current liabilities	1,355,426	1,693,274	1,587,965
Total liabilities	1,427,515	1,762,738	1,626,353
Stockholders' equity	4,312,555	3,485,274	2,832,311

Source: Company annual reports.

further hurt export sales. The fact that Nintendo did not introduce any new product categories in 1994 did not help its performance. However, Nintendo's overall financial position remained quite strong. The company had cash and cash equivalents of over $3.334 billion, no debt, and total liabilities of only $1.427 billion. Nintendo's liabilities-to-equity ratio was 0.33 at the end of fiscal year 1994, down from 0.51 the previous year.

For the six-month period ending September 30, 1994 (fiscal year 1995), Nintendo reported that earnings slipped 17 percent to $520 million from $623 million in the same period the previous year. Weak demand for its old games coupled with a strong yen against the dollar hurt sales revenue. Nintendo projected selling 6.5 million units of software worldwide in 1995, but later revised its estimate to a more realistic 2.5 million. Nintendo counted on Virtual Boy and Ultra 64 to reverse declining profits and help fuel sales growth in 1995.[46]

---

[46]"Tough Year Crimps Nintendo Earnings," *USA Today*, November 22, 1994, p. 08B.

SEGA Enterprises, Ltd.[47]

SEGA Enterprises, Ltd. (SEGA) was one of the few Japanese companies started by Americans. In 1951, two Americans in Tokyo, Raymond Lemaire and Richard Stewart, began importing jukeboxes to supply American military bases in Japan. Their company eventually expanded into amusement game imports and adopted the slogan "service and games."[48] The modern SEGA began to take shape in 1956 when a Brooklyn-born entrepreneur named David Rosen, who had been stationed in Japan with the Air Force, returned to Japan and began importing mechanical coin-operated amusement machines as Rosen Enterprises. In 1965, the "service and games" company merged with Rosen Enterprises. Not happy with the game machines available from U.S. manufacturers, Rosen decided to make his own and acquired a Japanese factory that made jukeboxes and slot machines. The company stamped SEGA on its games—short for service games—and Rosen adopted the brand name that persists today.[49] The next year it began its transformation from importer to manufacturer, producing a submarine warfare arcade game called "Periscope," which became a worldwide hit.

SEGA was acquired by Gulf & Western (G&W) in 1969 and went public in 1974. Hayao Nakayama, a Japanese entrepreneur and former SEGA distributor, was recruited to head SEGA's Japanese operation; Rosen headed the U.S. operation. Through the 1970s and early 1980s, the videogame industry went through a boom period. SEGA's revenues reached $214 million in 1982. The overall game industry hit $3 billion in 1982, but collapsed three years later with sales of $100 million. G&W became anxious to divest SEGA. Nakayama and Rosen organized a buyout of SEGA's assets for $38 million in 1984 and SEGA Enterprises, Ltd., was formed. The deal was backed by CSK, a large Japanese software company that currently owned 20 percent of SEGA. Nakayama became the chief executive and Rosen headed the U.S. subsidiary. SEGA went public in 1986. Rosen was later made a director of SEGA and cochairman of its American subsidiary.

SEGA of America was formed in 1986. Its first task was to market SEGA's first home videogame system, the 8-bit Master System. SEGA had been beaten to the punch in Japan by Nintendo, which got a jump on the market with its 1983 release of the 8-bit Famicom. Unfortunately for SEGA, Nintendo also won the 8-bit war in the United States and the Master System slowly died out. Meanwhile, Nintendo essentially grabbed the entire home videogame market share in the United States and Japan.

Europe was a different story. SEGA systems achieved success in Europe, while Nintendo sales were slow. SEGA of Europe accounted for a large share of SEGA's revenues, and some of SEGA's recent sales declines were due to the slumping European market.

SEGA did not begin to see mass-scale success until the release of its 16-bit Genesis system in 1989. The Genesis system was not an immediate hit. It took the release of "Sonic the Hedgehog" in 1991 for sales to take off. In 1994, the Genesis was challenging Nintendo's SNES as the leading 16-bit system in the United States, and SEGA was considered Nintendo's equal in the videogame industry.

Fiscal 1994 was a lackluster year for SEGA as well as Nintendo. A weak Japanese economy and a dismal consumer market in Europe coupled with an unexpectedly

---

[47]Portions of SEGA's company history extracted from DFC Intelligence Research.

[48]"Sega's American Roots," *The New York Times*, July 4, 1993, p. 6.

[49]R. Brandt, R. D. Hof, and P. Coy, "SEGA!" *Business Week*, February 21, 1994, pp. 66–74.

EXHIBIT 13 Consolidated Financial Summary for SEGA Enterprises, Ltd., 1993–1994 (in thousands of $)

	Year Ended March 31	
	1994	**1993**
Net sales	$4,038,197	$3,578,968
Cost of goods sold	2,916,161	2,301,496
Gross profit	$1,122,036	$1,277,472
Selling, general and administrative expenses	831,837	697,988
Operating income	$ 290,199	$ 579,484
Other income/(expenses):		
Interest income	47,561	33,353
Other	(78,865)	(104,024)
Total	(31,304)	(70,671)
Income before income taxes	$ 258,895	$ 508,813
Income taxes	249,259	267,102
Foreign currency statements translation	99,089	22,752
Net income	$ 108,725	$ 264,463
Net income per share	$ 1.09	$ 2.72
Cash dividend	0.37	0.21
Cash and cash equivalents	1,000,262	963,646
Current assets	2,398,652	2,185,073
Total assets	3,482,821	3,026,354
Current liabilities	1,261,454	1,084,437
Total liabilities	1,973,999	2,001,006
Stockholders' equity	1,508,822	1,025,348
Effective tax rate	0.52	0.52

Source: Company annual reports.

sharp appreciation of the yen against other major currencies resulted in a 12.8 percent increase in net consolidated sales from fiscal 1993 to $4 billion but a 58.9 percent decline in net income to $108.7 million (see Exhibit 13). The sharp decrease in net income was caused by a net loss from SEGA's European operations. From a high of ¥11,000 in 1992, SEGA's stock price declined to a low of ¥7,010 at the end of 1994.

Exhibit 14 depicts SEGA's sales by division (nonconsolidated). Sales of consumer products in 1994 reached $2.3 billion, a 16 percent increase, and accounted for 66.6 percent of net sales. Strong overseas demand for SEGA's products, particularly in the United States, offset the falloff in sales to Europe. Revenues from amusement center operations increased by 18.1 percent to $598.5 million, or about 17.4 percent of net sales. Revenue from amusement machine sales increased by 2.1 percent to $505.5 million, or 14.7 percent of net sales. Royalties on game software were up 302 percent to $41.4 million.

In the first six months of fiscal 1995 (ending September 1994), SEGA's unconsolidated pretax profit fell 43 percent to ¥16.33 billion ($166.97 million), down from

EXHIBIT 14   SEGA's Nonconsolidated Sales by Division (in millions of $)

	1994	1993
Net sales:	$3,432.2	$2,983.1
Consumer products	2,286.8	1,971.4
Domestic sales	249.7	166.2
Exports	2,037.1	1,805.2
Amusement center operations	598.5	506.6
Amusement machine sales:	505.5	494.9
Domestic sales	377.9	398.4
Exports	127.6	96.5
Royalties on game software	41.4	10.3

Source: Company annual reports.

¥28.58 billion the previous year. Sales fell 25 percent, to ¥151.07 billion, from ¥200.65 billion. Analysts said the declines were expected due to slumping global demand for videogames and the soaring yen, which made Japanese products less competitive abroad.[50]

In its home market of Japan, SEGA was being badly outcompeted by Nintendo (90 percent of all game sales in Japan went to Nintendo), in part because of distribution problems and in part because SEGA's sports-oriented games were not as popular in Japan. SEGA's market strength was in its American and European operations, which had some autonomy from Tokyo. It was reported (unconfirmed) in the press that SEGA of America contributed about 25 percent to the parent company's overall revenue.

Sony Corporation[51]

Sony Corporation was established in Japan in May 1946 as Tokyo Tsushin Kogyo Kabushiki Kaisha. In January 1958, it changed its name to Sony Kabushiki Kaisha (Sony Corporation in English). Sony Corporation of America was formed in 1960. Sony engaged in the development, manufacture, and sale of various kinds of electronic equipment, instruments, and devices. In addition, Sony had a strong presence in the entertainment industry. Its music group (Sony Music Entertainment, Inc.) included such companies as Columbia Records Group, Epic Records Group, TriStar Music Group, and others. Sony's Pictures Group included four motion picture companies: Columbia Pictures, TriStar Pictures, Sony Pictures Classics, and Triumph Releasing Corporation.

Eager to claim a stake in the fast-growing videogame business, Sony Corp. set up a new division in May 1994, Sony Computer Entertainment of America, to develop and market a next generation home videogame, called the Sony PlayStation (PSX). The PSX had been under development for more than four years and represented an

---

[50]"Video-Game Maker's Profit Plunged in Fiscal First Half," *The Wall Street Journal*, November 14, 1994, p. B5.

[51]Extracted largely from Sony Corporation *Annual Report*, 1993.

important element in Sony's strategy to dominate the entertainment markets for hardware and software.[52] According to Sony, the game player, powered by a 32-bit microprocessor, provided three-dimensional animated graphics, compact-disc quality sound, and digital full-motion video. The system was released in Japan in December 1994; a U.S. and European release was scheduled for sometime in 1995.

As a new entrant in the stable of next generation systems, PSX faced heavy competition from 3DO, the Atari Jaguar, systems planned by Nintendo and SEGA, as well as multimedia PCs. The PSX was not compatible with any existing hardware standard. Sony reported that more than 160 videogame developers and publishers in Japan had agreed to support the PlayStation.[53]

Despite Sony's lack of history in videogame hardware, and no particular success in software, the company was considered a formidable competitor in both videogame hardware and software because of its well-known brand name and image with U.S. consumers and its access to Columbia and TriStar film libraries.

Sony's entrance did not go unnoticed by SEGA Enterprises Ltd. President Hayao Nakayama who candidly expressed his view that Sony Corp. was likely to become SEGA's biggest adversary in home videogames in the coming year. "Sony is a much stronger company than another company I cannot name [Nintendo] . . . [Sony] has much more experience in the consumer market."[54] It was also rumored that SEGA delayed introducing Saturn from 1994 to 1995 in order to reengineer its system to compete better against Sony's new PSX system.

Exhibit 15 presents selected financial data for Sony Corp. For the fiscal year ended March 31, 1994, Sony reported consolidated net income of $148.5 million on total sales of $36.25 billion. Although sales increased by 5.3 percent over the previous year, net income was down by 52.5 percent due to factors including the appreciation of the yen (approximately 16 percent, 24 percent, and 31 percent against the U.S. dollar, the German mark, and the pound sterling, respectively), intensified price competition, and disappointing performance of a number of Sony Pictures Entertainment's motion pictures. Sony estimated that if the value of the yen had remained the same as in the previous fiscal year, corporate sales would have been $4.8 billion over the reported figure.

Sony did not anticipate a better year in 1995. The company expected a continued unfavorable operating environment due to uncertainty in the foreign currency market, delayed economic recovery in Japan and Europe, and intensifying price competition in audiovisual equipment markets in Japan and overseas. For the nine months ending December 31, 1994, Sony reported a net loss of $2.8 billion on net sales of $29.8 billion.

To counter the unfavorable forces in its environment, Sony's strategy called for aggressively moving forward to develop appealing electronics products and to promote its activities in the entertainment business. Sony also planned to reshape its corporate structure by eliminating product groups and establishing eight new companies within its organization. Finally, the company planned to make every effort to enhance overall performance by reviewing every activity in an effort to reduce costs and streamline company operations.

---

[52]McGowan and S. Ciccarelli, *Interactive Entertainment Industry Overview* (New York: Gerard Klauer Mattison & Co., 1994).

[53]DFC Intelligence Research.

[54]"SEGA Now Considers Sony, Not Nintendo, as Top Rival," *The Wall Street Journal*, September 15, 1994, p. B5.

EXHIBIT 15 Selected Financial Data for Sony Corp., 1993–1994 (in millions of $)

	1994	1993
Statement of Operations Data		
Total revenue	$36,250	$34,422
Cost and expenses:		
Cost of sales	26,756	25,249
Selling, general administrative expenses	8,526	8,082
Total expenses	35,282	33,331
Operating income	968	1,090
Other income:		
Interest and dividends	373	397
Foreign exchange gain, net	344	193
Other	450	376
Total	1,167	966
Other expenses:		
Interest	672	788
Other	470	472
Total	1,142	1,260
Income before taxes	993	796
Income taxes	763	718
Income before minority interest	229	369
Minority interest in consolidated subsidiaries	80	56
Net income	$ 149	$ 313
Net income per depositary share	$ 0.41	$ 0.79
Balance Sheet Data		
Cash and cash equivalents	$ 5,486	$ 4,970
Current assets	19,647	18,189
Working capital	5,982	3,164
Total assets	41,455	39,050
Current liabilities	13,366	15,025
Long-term obligations	13,947	10,974
Total stockholders' equity	12,908	12,312

Source: Annual reports and Form 20-F.

The 3DO Company[55]

3DO was a relatively new player in the videogame industry. The company was initially formed in 1989 when the principals of NTG Engineering, Inc., launched an effort to create a new home interactive multimedia platform by developing technology that

---

[55]Extracted from The 3DO Company's Form 10-K, 1993 and 1994.

achieved a breakthrough in audiovisual realism. In September 1991, the company was incorporated as SMSG, Inc., in California and changed its name to The 3DO Company in September 1992. In May 1993, 3DO had an initial public offering of $48.6 million. In June 1994, the company raised $37 million through a private placement.

The company's initial product design was the 3DO Interactive Multiplayer, which ran interactive entertainment, education, and information applications developed specifically for the 3DO format. It also played conventional CDs and displays photo CDs, but it was not compatible with other commercially available software formats.

3DO's goal was to license its technology to manufacturers of consumer electronics and personal computer systems. Six global electronics companies were licensed to manufacture the 3DO Interactive Multiplayer system. Panasonic Company, a division of Matsushita Electric Corporation of America, had marketed a version of the 3DO system in the United States since October 1993 and introduced a version in Japan in March 1994. More than 500,000 3DO systems had been sold worldwide through 1994. Other companies licensed to use 3DO's technology included AT&T, Sanyo Electric Co., Goldstar and Samsung Electronics Co., Ltd., Creative Technology, Ltd., and Toshiba Corporation. The Goldstar 3DO system was launched in November 1994. 3DO systems were available at over 6,500 retail locations.

While early reports indicated videogame sales were flat for other systems, retailers reported 3DO games were selling well during the 1994 holiday season. No doubt contributing to 3DO's success were several recent awards, which included "Best System of 1994" from *DieHard GameFan* magazine and best overall game system from the *Los Angeles Daily News* (December 11, 1994). The 3DO system was also recommended as the game system to buy for the holidays by the *Miami Herald* (December 2, 1994).

3DO and its licensees were expanding the available base of software titles (over 135 titles released through 1994) in a variety of application areas, including action/strategy, sports, simulations, interactive movies, information, education, and music/arts. However, 3DO's ability to offer more game titles was hampered by a fracas with software developers over licensing fees. 3DO required developers to pay a $3 surcharge on top of the current royalty of $3 a copy for every CD produced. According to Tom Zito, president of Digital Pictures Inc., a software developer that had created four games for 3DO, "This is going to make me seriously think about investing company resources in developing more titles for their platform."[56] 3DO systems retailed for approximately $399 and were bundled with two free titles through the 1994 holiday season.

In an effort to gain a performance edge over its competitors, 3DO planned to introduce in late 1995 a peripheral upgrade, the M2 Accelerator, which promised to introduce movielike graphics and sound to its videogame players. The add-on accessory utilized a new Motorola PowerPC microprocessor and was expected to hit the market just as Nintendo and SEGA introduced their new machines. The company had not announced the price.

Management expected to incur substantial operating losses as it continued to develop its product, promote growth, and develop and publish software titles. For fiscal years ended March 31, 1994 and 1993, 3DO incurred net losses of $51.4 million and $15.4 million, respectively. Revenue for 1994 totaled $10.3 million. There was no revenue for 1993. Exhibit 16 presents selected financial data for 3DO since start-up operations began.

---

[56]J. A. Trachtenberg, "Should Santa Bring a Nintendo, SEGA, Atari or What?" *The Wall Street Journal*, December 6, 1994, p. B1.

EXHIBIT 16 Selected Financial Data for 3DO, 1992–1993 (in thousands, except per share data)

	1994	1993	1992*
Statement of Operations Data			
Total revenue	$ 10,295	$ 0	$ 0
Cost of development systems	3,464	0	0
Gross profit	6,831	0	0
Operating expenses:			
Research and development	23,412	11,434	1,146
Sales and marketing	8,248	1,993	64
General and administrative expenses	6,175	2,008	552
Acquisitions of NTG royalty rights	21,353	0	0
Total operating expenses	59,188	15,435	2,762
Operating loss	(52,357)	(15,435)	(2,762)
Interest income	949	50	29
Other income	27	0	0
Loss before provision for income taxes	(51,381)	(15,385)	(2,733)
Provision for income taxes	50	1	1
Net loss	$(51,431)	$(15,386)	$(2,734)
Net loss per share	$ (2.60)	$ (1.02)	$ (0.18)
Shares used in per share calculations	19,747	15,018	15,014

	March 31	
	1994	**1993**
Balance Sheet Data		
Cash, cash equivalents, and short-term investments	$ 14,301	$ 2,827
Current assets	18,333	3,301
Working capital	9,960	(1,175)
Total assets	25,870	6,437
Current liabilities	8,373	4,476
Note payable to stockholder	474	474
Total liabilities	9,991	6,396
Total stockholders' equity (deficit)	15,879	(959)

* Period from October 1, 1991 (inception), to March 31, 1992.

Source: 3DO 10-K.

For the first nine months of fiscal year 1995 ended December 31, 1994, 3DO generated $22 million in total revenues, or a 262 percent increase over the same period in 1993. The company incurred a nine-month loss of $38.3 million as compared to a loss of $44 million for the same nine months of 1993.

In December 1994, the company announced a corporate restructuring. The company consolidated its technology, advanced development, product management, licensing, and business development groups into a new business operations department. Analysts said the move signaled the firm's desire to conserve cash and put off another public offering since its stock continued to drift downward.

Atari Corporation[57]

Atari Corporation (Atari) designed and marketed interactive multimedia entertainment systems and related software and peripheral products. Atari's principal products were Jaguar, a 64-bit interactive multimedia entertainment system, along with related game software and peripheral products; Lynx, a 16-bit portable color handheld videogame; and the Falcon 030 series of personal computers. Manufacture of these products was performed by subcontractors. The principal methods of distribution were through mass market retailers, consumer electronic specialty stores, and distributors of electronic products. Atari had approximately 117 employees worldwide.

Management recognized in the fall of 1991 that the computer and videogame products it was marketing were rapidly becoming technologically obsolete. Intense competitive rivalry from larger competitors and shrinking margins in computer products profits led Atari to exit this line of products and to refocus itself as an interactive media entertainment company. In an effort to ensure its competitive advantage in this new market, Atari developed a 64-bit videogame system called Jaguar, which it began shipping in the fourth quarter of 1993. Jaguar was assembled by IBM in the United States, and currently sold for $249.

The Atari Jaguar was named the industry's "Best New Game System" (*VideoGames Magazine*), "Best New Hardware System" (*Game Informer*), and "1993 Technical Achievement of the Year" (*DieHard GameFan*). In April 1994, the Jaguar was given the European Computer Trade Show Award for "Best Hardware of the Year."

With the hardware developed (Atari was already working on a second-generation Jaguar system), Atari was busy developing more software titles such as "Alien vs. Predator," "Kasumi Ninja," and "Star Raiders 2000." To ensure a good supply of software titles for Jaguar, Atari licensed more than 125 third-party publishers and developers. By early 1995, Atari was expected to have more than 50 software titles available to users.

Atari planned to introduce a peripheral unit in the fall of 1995 that would enable the Jaguar to play CD-ROM games and regular audio CDs. The expected retail price was $149. Also in development was a full motion video cartridge that would enable the CD-ROM to play movies. The company was also funding development of a virtual reality system for Jaguar. In addition, Atari had decided to produce and market videogame software for PCs, citing economy-of-scale benefits in developing a title for both the Jaguar and personal computer.

Atari's president, Sam Trmiel, was upbeat in his message to shareholders in the company's 1993 annual report: "We have completed our restructuring and consolidation around the world. As the business grows, we will reap the benefits of our streamlined central distribution in Europe and consolidation of U.S. operations." In his 1994 message he ended by saying: "The video game industry is now 20 years old and has provided millions of players with challenging and enjoyable experiences. We are well positioned for the next surge, the 32/64 bit generation."

Exhibit 17 presents selected financial data for Atari. In fiscal year 1994, Atari generated net sales of $38.4 million as compared to $28.8 million in 1993, an increase of 33 percent. The increased sales were primarily a result of Atari's national

---

[57]Extracted from Atari Corporation *Annual Report*, 1993 and 1994.

EXHIBIT 17   Selected Financial Data for Atari, 1992–1994 (in thousands, except per share data)

	1994	1993	1992
Statement of Operations Data			
Net sales	$ 38,444	$ 28,805	$127,340
Cost of sales	35,093	42,550	132,455
Gross profit	3,351	(13,745)	(5,115)
Operating expenses:			
Research and development	5,775	4,876	9,171
Sales and distribution	14,454	8,895	31,125
General and administrative expenses	7,169	7,558	16,544
Restructuring charges	0	12,425	17,053
Total operating expenses	27,398	33,754	73,893
Operating loss	(24,047)	(47,499)	(79,008)
Settlements of patent litigation	32,062	0	0
Exchange gain (loss)	1,184	(2,234)	(5,589)
Interest income	2,015	2,039	4,039
Other income	484	854	927
Interest expense	(2,304)	(2,290)	(3,522)
Loss before provision for income taxes	9,394	(49,130)	(83,153)
Income tax credit	0	264	434
Income (loss) before extraordinary credit	9,394	(48,866)	(82,719)
Discontinued operations	0	0	9,000
Income (loss) before extraordinary credit	$ 9,394	$(49,394)	$ (73,719)
Extraordinary credit	0	0	104
Income (loss)	$ 9,394	$(49,394)	$ (73,615)
Net profit (loss) per share	$ 0.16	$ (0.85)	$ (1.28)
Shares used in per share calculations	58,962	57,148	57,365

	December 31		
	1994	1993	1992
Balance Sheet Data			
Cash, cash equivalents, and short-term investments	$ 22,592	$ 23,059	$ 39,290
Current assets	113,188	50,599	109,551
Working capital	92,670	33,107	75,563
Total assets	131,042	74,833	138,508
Current liabilities	20,518	17,492	33,988
Total long-term obligations	43,454	52,987	53,937
Total stockholders' equity	67,070	4,354	50,583

Source: Atari Corporation 10-K.

rollout of its new 64-bit Jaguar entertainment system and related software. Sales of Jaguar represented 77 percent of total sales in 1994 as compared to 13 percent in 1993. The Jaguar was launched in two markets in the fall of 1993, and approximately 100,000 units were sold by the end of 1994. Jaguar game players were sold with little or no margin, but significantly higher margins were achieved on software sales. Sales of Lynx and Falcon 030 computers and other older products represented 23 percent of sales in 1994 as compared to 87 percent in 1993. Atari paid no income taxes in 1994 because of operating loss carryforwards. Overall, Atari reported net income for 1994 of $9.4 million as compared to a net loss of $48.9 million in 1993.

Atari's future financial performance hinged on how successful the company's management would be in implementing its turnaround strategy and adapting to future changes in the highly competitive market. Atari's net sales in 1994 were largely dependent on the success of the Jaguar system and related software. Management felt that until such time as Jaguar achieved broad market acceptance and hardware and related software products were sold in substantial volume, the company would not achieve profitability.

In November 1994, Atari announced it completed a deal with SEGA that included a licensing agreement and an equity investment in Atari. The company received $50 million from SEGA in exchange for a license covering the use of a library of patents. SEGA also made an equity investment in Atari of $40 million to acquire common stock equal to a 7 percent interest. Both companies entered into cross-licensing agreements through the year 2001, which allowed them to publish on each of their respective game platforms.

Philips Electronics NV

Founded in 1891, Philips Electronics NV (Philips) was Europe's largest consumer electronics company. The Dutch electronics giant also produced semiconductors and PCs and was a world leader in lightbulb manufacturing. Philips owned 79 percent of PolyGram (recordings), 35 percent of Matsushita Electronics (component venture with Matsushita), and 32 percent of Grundig (electronics, Germany). For inventing the digital audio technology used in CD players, Philips and Sony received royalties on each one sold.

The company was number 32 in *Fortune*'s 1994 Global 500 ranking of the world's largest industrial corporations and was listed among the top eight companies in the global electronics industry that included Hitachi, Matsushita Electric, GE, Samsung, Sony, and NEC. In fiscal 1994, Philips earned a net profit of $1.176 billion on total sales of $33.7 billion (see Exhibit 18). By the end of 1994, the company had several hundred subsidiaries in over 60 countries and employed 238,500 people worldwide.

Philips was organized into six product divisions, one of which included "Other Consumer Products." Within this division was Philips Media, which had operations in four key business areas: software development in entertainment and electronic publishing applications, systems development and hardware/software distribution, cable TV, and media-based services. Philips Media was responsible for the CD-I game platform and software.

Philips was one of the first companies in the world to market a CD-based interactive entertainment system (called CD-I). The basic machine looked like a simplified VCR; it could play interactive movies and encyclopedias, regular movie videos, videogames, and conventional music CDs.

By its own admission Philips's marketing of its CD-I was confused and unfocused before 1993. Until the company decided to stress the machine's ability to play games and movies, consumers didn't know whether it was a video player, a home computer, a game console, or a toy. Limited game titles left consumers unconvinced that the format would last. Sales were dismal. After several years on the market, the installed base of CD-I machines in the United States at the end of 1994 was estimated at 250,000.

EXHIBIT 18   Selected Financial Data for Philips Electronics N.V., 1993–
             1994 (in millions of $)

	1994	1993
Statement of Operations Data		
Net sales	$33,689	$31,626
Direct costs of sales	(24,461)	(23,154)
Gross income	9,228	8,472
Selling expenses	(6,484)	(6,438)
General and administrative expenses	(815)	(766)
Other business income	148	110
Income from operations	2,077	1,378
Financial income and expenses	(478)	(559)
Income before taxes	1,599	819
Income taxes	(330)	(185)
Income after taxes	1,269	634
Equity in income of unconsolidated companies	72	(24)
Group income	1,341	610
Share of other group equity in group income	(207)	(151)
Net income from normal business operations	1,134	459
Extraordinary items—net	42	596
Net income	$ 1,176	$ 1,055
Balance Sheet Data		
Cash and cash equivalents	$ 1,560	$ 1,248
Current assets	16,517	14,840
Working capital	6,348	5,987
Total assets	26,586	24,884
Current liabilities	10,169	8,853
Long-term obligations	3,316	2,898
Total stockholders' equity	7,007	6,155

Source: Annual reports.

Philips tried to build market visibility by improving its marketing effort. A lengthy, high-quality, soft-sell infomercial began running in 1994. Hardware prices were slashed, with some units selling below $300. The company beefed up its software library with top-shelf feature films, music titles (from its Polygram recordings subsidiary), and games; Philips also signed on several leading developers in PC-based CD-ROM games. In 1994, the company introduced over 100 new CD-I software titles; the software catalog included nearly 300 titles.

Analysts projected modest sales of CD-I hardware and software. The CD-I was simply another platform with a chance of carving out a small share of the market for compact disc game players. Moreover, because the CD-I used a 16-bit processor, some perceived the machine as being based on outdated technology. However, Philips seemed to recognize the problems with the CD-I and focused a lot of resources on software development for other platforms as well as the CD-I.

NINTENDO VERSUS SEGA (B): THE VIDEOGAME WARS

Romuald A. Stone, *Keller Graduate School of Management*

Nintendo and SEGA had been the giants in the videogame industry throughout the 1980s. During this period, the two competitors engaged in fierce rivalry that was labeled the "Videogame Wars." The fight was intensifying, with SEGA recently winning some crucial engagements in the battle for market share

Despite generally flat sales in 1994, the videogame wars were taking on a new dimension in 1995 as "next generation" game players were being released worldwide by Nintendo, SEGA, and new competitors. The entries included Nintendo's Ultra 64, SEGA's Saturn, and Sony Corp.'s Play-Station, joining 3DO's Interactive Multiplayer and Atari Corp.'s Jaguar already on the market. Not all of these game players were expected to win a big enough market following to survive. The challenge for competitors was getting limited shelf space and lining up software developers. One industry observer predicted that consumers would become "very, very confused about what videogame player to buy: Sony versus Atari versus 3DO versus Nintendo versus SEGA? Sixteen-bit versus 32-bit versus 64-bit?"[2] The rapidly growing base of home computers equipped with high-tech entertainment options and CD-ROMs further added to the confusion.

Once upon a time (1988, to be exact), Nintendo sat alone atop the mountain, master of its domain. Then came SEGA, scraping and clawing up the slope. The two stood precariously together—plumber vs. hedgehog—each trying to elbow the other off the peak. Later, when they paused and looked down, the two would see new videogame challengers approaching on all sides, each promising a higher level of technology . . . Suddenly, the game was wide open again. And Nintendo's—and SEGA's—grip could be slipping . . . This was all-out war.[1]

---

[1]M. Snider, "Video Market No Longer a 2-Player Game," *USA Today*, November 4, 1993, p. 1D.

[2]A. Harmon, "What's Coming, When, and Why It's a Big Deal," *Los Angeles Times*, December 18, 1994, p. 6.

Sales were expected to improve significantly once the next generation systems were fully on line in 1996, but profits were expected to be weak. Hardware margins were thin because low retail hardware prices were imperative for building a base to generate software demand. Software sales entailed much higher gross margins. But with the shift to newer game playing systems in 1995–96, margins were expected to be depressed by a rising percent of low-margin hardware sales. For software publishers and developers, increased competition had driven up the cost of securing licenses and developing games for an audience that sought out newer, more action-packed, or more interesting games with better visual graphics.[3] Moreover, software publishers and developers had to decide whether to incur the costs of programming their games to run on all or most of the different types/brands of game players or to gamble on developing software compatible with only one or two game platforms that might fail to win a significant share of the hardware systems purchased by consumers. Consumers, also, were in somewhat of a quandary because if they purchased a new game-playing hardware system that failed to attract many software developers, then the system wouldn't run many of the games on the market.[4]

NINTENDO AND SEGA PROFILES

Nintendo Company, Ltd.

Background[5]   Nintendo in 1994 was one of the world's largest hardware manufacturers and software developers for interactive entertainment. A profile of Nintendo's first 100 years is presented in Exhibit 1. Exhibit 2 shows a time line of Nintendo's milestones from 1983 to 1994.

Nintendo was credited with singlehandedly reviving the videogame industry after the industry collapsed in the early 1980s due to the weight of too many bad games (such as Atari's ET), poor marketing, and overproduction. In order to get a handle on what kids really wanted, Nintendo sent its representatives to video arcades around the country to learn firsthand why young people went to the arcades rather than playing at home for free. What they discovered set the stage for the eventual Nintendo-led recovery of the videogame industry.

> It wasn't the games themselves or a fickle market, but the arcade-quality, full-animation, imaginative play of the arcade games that the videogame providers—in their gold-rush, sucker-born-every-minute mentality—could not or would not provide for the home player. So Nintendo introduced a game system that was not simply a "player," but a sophisticated device with the power of a personal computer, able to reproduce near arcade-quality games on the home screen.[6]

Nintendo's arcade-quality machine was its Nintendo Entertainment System (NES). The NES was far superior to those of the Atari generation. In 1985, when the NES

---

[3]S. McGowan and S. Ciccarelli, Interactive Entertainment Industry Overview (New York: Gerard Klauer Mattison & Co., 1994).

[4]DFC Intelligence Research, *The U.S. Market for Video Games and Interactive Electronic Entertainment* (San Diego, 1995).

[5]Additional background information is contained in Case 11, Nintendo versus SEGA (A).

[6]S. Wolpin, "How Nintendo Revived a Dying Industry," *Marketing Communications* 14, no. 5, (1989), p. 38.

EXHIBIT 1   Nintendo's 100-Year History

1889 Fusajiro Yamauchi, great-grandfather of the present president, began manufacturing "Hanafuda," Japanese playing cards, in Kyoto.

1933 Established an unlimited partnership, Yamauchi Nintendo & Co.

1947 Began a distribution company, Marufuku Co. Ltd.

1950 Changed the company name from Marufuku Co. Ltd. to Nintendo Playing Card Co. Ltd. Hiroshi Yamauchi took office as president. Absorbed the manufacturing operation of Yamauchi Nintendo & Co.

1952 Consolidated factories were dispersed in Kyoto.

1953 Became the first to succeed in manufacturing mass-produced plastic playing cards in Japan.

1959 Started selling cards printed with Walt Disney characters, opening a new market in children's playing cards. The card department boomed!

1962 In January, listed stock on the second section of the Osaka Stock Exchange and on the Kyoto Stock Exchange.

1963 Changed company name to Nintendo Co. Ltd. and started manufacturing games in addition to playing cards.

1969 Expanded and reinforced the game department; built a production plant in Uji City, a suburb of Kyoto.

1970 Stock listing was changed to the first section of the Osaka Stock Exchange. Reconstruction and enlargement of corporate headquarters was completed. Started selling the Beam gun Series, employing opto-electronics. Introduced electronic technology into the toy industry for the first time in Japan.

1973 Developed laser clay shooting system to succeed bowling as a major pastime.

1974 Developed image projection system employing 16mm film projector for amusement arcades. Began exporting them to America and Europe.

1975 In cooperation with Mitsubishi Electric, developed videogame system using electronic video recording (EVR) player. Introduced the microprocessor into the videogame system the next year.

1977 Developed home-use videogames in cooperation with Mitsubishi Electric.

1978 Created and started selling coin-operated videogames using microcomputers.

1979 Started an operations division for coin-operated games.

1980 Announced a wholly owned subsidiary, Nintendo of America Inc. in New York. Started selling "GAME & WATCH" product line.

1981 Developed and began distribution of the coin-operated videogame "Donkey Kong." This videogame enjoyed great popularity.

1982 Merged New York subsidiary into Nintendo of America Inc., a wholly owned subsidiary headquartered in Seattle, Washington, with a capital investment of $600,000.

1983 Built a new plant in Uji City to increase production capacity and to allow for business expansion. Established Nintendo Entertainment Centers Ltd. In Vancouver, B.C., Canada, to operate a family entertainment center. Raised authorized capital of Nintendo of America Inc. to $10 million. In July, listed stock on the first section of the Tokyo Stock Exchange. Started selling the home videogame console "Family Computer" (Famicom), employing a custom CPU (custom processing unit) and PPU (picture processing unit).

1984 Developed and started selling the unique two-screen interactive coin-operated videogame "VS. System."

1985 Started to sell the U.S. version of Family Computer "Nintendo Entertainment System" in America. Developed and started selling game software "Super Mario Bros." for the family computer.

1986 Developed and started selling the "Family Computer Disk Drive System" to expand the functions of the Family Computer. Began installation of the "Disk Writer" to rewrite game software.

1987 Sponsored a Family Computer "Golf Tournament" as a communications test using the public telephone network and Disk Faxes to aid in building a Family Computer network.

1988 Nintendo of America Inc. published the first issue of *Nintendo Power* magazine in July. Researched and developed the Hands Free controller, making the Nintendo Entertainment System accessible to many more Nintendo fans.

1989 Released "The Adventure of Link," sequel to the top-selling game "The Legend of Zelda" in the United States. Started "World of Nintendo" displays in the United States to help market Nintendo products. Studies show that children are as familiar with "Mario" as they are with Mickey Mouse and Bugs Bunny!

1990 Introduced Game Boy, the first portable, handheld game system with interchangeable game paks. Nintendo Power Fest featuring the Nintendo World Championships tours the country. Japan enters the 16-bit market by releasing the Super Famicom in the fall.

1991 Nintendo introduces World Class Service Center locations across the United States. The 16-bit Super NES, along with "Super Mario World," is released in the United States.

1992 The Super NES Super Scope and Mario Paint with the Super NES Mouse Accessory were released. The long-awaited "Zelda" sequel, "The Legend of Zelda: A Link to the Past," arrived for the Super NES.

1993 Nintendo announces the advent of the Super FX Chip, breakthrough technology for home video systems. The first game using the Super FX Chip, "Star Fox," is released in April.

Source: Nintendo of America.

EXHIBIT 2   Nintendo Time Line of Significant Events, 1983–1994

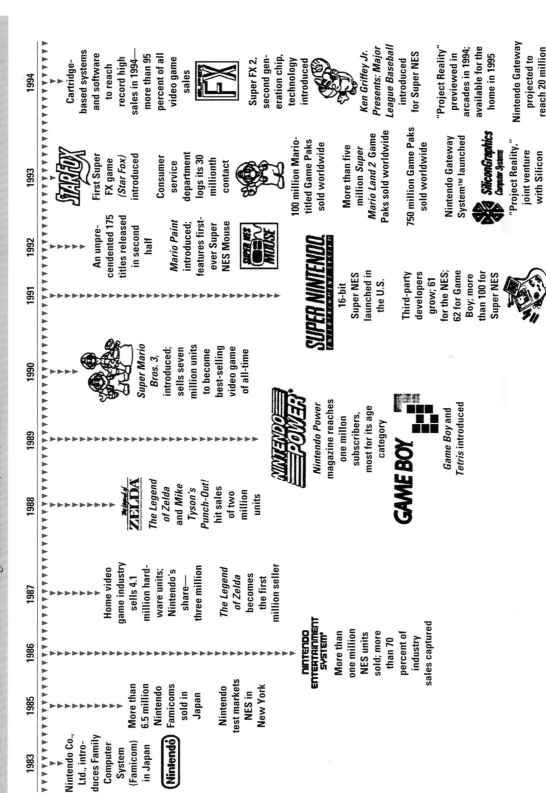

1983 — Nintendo Co., Ltd., introduces Family Computer System (Famicom) in Japan

1985 — More than 6.5 million Nintendo Famicoms sold in Japan; Nintendo test markets NES in New York

1986 — Nintendo Entertainment System; More than one million NES units sold; more than 70 percent of industry sales captured

1987 — Home video game industry sells 4.1 million hardware units; Nintendo's share—three million; The Legend of Zelda becomes the first million seller

1988 — The Legend of Zelda; The Legend of Zelda and Mike Tyson's Punch-Out! hit sales of two million units

1989 — Nintendo Power; Nintendo Power magazine reaches one million subscribers, most for its age category; Game Boy; Game Boy and Tetris introduced

1990 — Super Mario Bros. 3, introduced; sells seven million units to become best-selling video game of all-time

1991 — Super Nintendo Entertainment System; 16-bit Super NES launched in the U.S.; Third-party developers grow; 61 for the NES; 62 for Game Boy; more than 100 for Super NES

1992 — An unprecedented 175 titles released in second half; Mario Paint introduced; features first-ever Super NES Mouse; Super NES Mouse

1993 — Star Fox; First Super FX game (Star Fox) introduced; Consumer service department logs its 30 millionth contact; 100 million Mario-titled Game Paks sold worldwide; More than five million Super Mario Land 2 Game Paks sold worldwide; 750 million Game Paks sold worldwide; Nintendo Gateway System™ launched; Silicon Graphics Computer Systems; "Project Reality," joint venture with Silicon Graphics, Inc., announced

1994 — FX; Cartridge-based systems and software to reach record high sales in 1994—more than 95 percent of all video game sales; Super FX 2, second generation chip, technology introduced; Ken Griffey Jr. Presents: Major League Baseball introduced for Super NES; "Project Reality" previewed in arcades in 1994; available for the home in 1995; Nintendo Gateway projected to reach 20 million travelers

was introduced, 1.1 million units were sold. At the end of 1988, Nintendo accounted for $1.7 billion of the $2.3 billion videogame business. Nintendo sold its game players at cost and made money on the software. Through 1994, Nintendo had sold more than 100 million hardware systems and more than 750 million game packs worldwide. During most of the 1980s, Nintendo was the undisputed leader in the videogame industry, controlling 80 percent of the market at the end of the decade. By 1994, however, Nintendo's market share had declined to about 45 percent and was expected to decline further as SEGA continued its "take no prisoners" strategy.

Financial performance[7]   For the six-month period ending September 30, 1994 (fiscal year 1995), Nintendo's earnings slipped 17 percent to $520 million from $623 million in the same period the previous year. Weak demand for its old games coupled with a strong yen against the dollar hurt sales revenue. Nintendo projected selling 6.5 million units of software worldwide in 1995, but later revised its estimate down to 2.5 million. Nintendo was counting on Virtual Boy and Ultra 64 to reverse declining profits and help fuel sales growth in 1995.[8]

During fiscal year 1994 (April 1993–March 1994), Nintendo sold more videogame cartridges than in any previous year. However, consolidated net sales fell to $4.714 billion, a 23.5 percent decline from the previous year, and the company's consolidated net income of $511 million was 40 percent lower than in 1993 (see Exhibit 3). This represented Nintendo's first decline in sales and net income since it introduced the Famicom in Japan in 1983. Nintendo's stock fell from a high of ¥17,500 ($150.86) in 1992 to a low of ¥6,140 ($59.61) in 1994.

Sales in Nintendo's home Japanese market sanctuary were strong in fiscal 1994, but the rising value of the yen seriously affected the company's performance around the globe. A weak economy in Europe and a soft market in the United States, coupled with increased competition, eroded export sales. Moreover, Nintendo did not introduce any new product categories in 1994.

Nintendo's Strategy and Product Development

A New Strategy   Responding to SEGA's advances, Nintendo appointed Howard Lincoln as head of Nintendo of America and began to make changes in its strategy in 1994. Nintendo historically had demanded that third-party software developers sign exclusive deals and pay 30 percent royalties for the privilege of writing games for its systems. SEGA slowly began taking the top independent software developers away from Nintendo and into its own camp. To counter SEGA's moves, Nintendo started paying companies to write software exclusively for it. Sources reported that Nintendo paid a development fee plus royalties of 2 percent to 12 percent, worth millions of dollars for a hit game.[9] Nintendo also planned to increase the amount spent for in-house game development and production from its current 35 percent of software sales.

While other companies embraced CD-ROM technology, Nintendo elected to stay out of the multimedia end of the business. Its Ultra 64 player played only cartridges. According to Takashi Kawaguchi, assistant manager at Nintendo's public relations

---

[7]This section parallels the information in Nintendo versus SEGA (A) for readers of this case who may not have reviewed part (A).

[8]"Tough Year Crimps Nintendo Earnings," *USA Today*, November 22, 1994, p. O8B.

[9]R. Brandt, "Is Nintendo a Street Fighter Now?" *Business Week*, August 29, 1994, p. 35.

EXHIBIT 3 Consolidated Financial Summary for Nintendo Co., Ltd., 1992–1994 (in thousands of $)

	Year Ended March 31		
	1994	**1993**	**1992**
Statement of Operations Data			
Net sales	$4,714,675	$6,161,840	$4,843,475
Cost of goods sold	2,887,106	3,758,376	2,926,885
Gross profit	$1,827,569	$2,403,464	$1,916,590
Selling, general, and administrative expenses	693,507	650,360	483,115
Operating income	$1,134,062	$1,753,104	$1,433,475
Other income/(expenses):			
Interest income	110,392	175,380	206,823
Other	(230,727)	(104,973)	(81,971)
Total	(120,335)	70,407	124,852
Income before income taxes	$1,013,727	$1,823,511	$1,558,327
Income taxes	576,497	967,261	807,653
Foreign currency translation adjustments	73,968	4,031	224
Net income	$ 511,198	$ 860,281	$ 750,898
Net income per share	$3.61	$6.08	$5.30
Cash dividend per share	0.68	0.68	0.52
Balance Sheet Data			
Cash and cash equivalents	$3,334,679	$3,425,000	$2,549,144
Current assets	5,037,417	4,638,570	3,968,830
Total assets	5,740,070	5,248,012	4,458,664
Current liabilities	1,355,426	1,693,274	1,587,965
Total liabilities	1,427,515	1,762,738	1,626,353
Stockholders' equity	4,312,555	3,485,274	2,832,311

Source: Company annual reports.

department, "The video game market is a big market that already exists and is still growing, but the multimedia market still remains an illusion that so far has no substance, and we see no point in going into what does not exist."[10] Some observers believed that Nintendo had lost the technological edge to SEGA and the newer, smaller videogame makers offering CD-ROM, virtual reality, and multimedia options.

When Nintendo saw in early 1994 that it was losing market share to SEGA, the company quickly concluded it needed both a management and an image overhaul. Nintendo President Yamauchi laid part of the blame on his son-in-law, Nintendo of America Inc. President Minoru Arakawa (whose authority was reduced by the appointment of Howard Lincoln as chairman in early 1994). When SEGA ran compara-

---

[10]M. Nashima, "Next-Generation Machines Taking On Sega, Nintendo," *The Japan Times Weekly International Edition*, 34, no. 9 (1994), p. 13.

tive ads in 1990 disparaging Nintendo's software as "games for ninnies," Nintendo did not respond. According to Yamauchi, Arakawa "allowed SEGA to brand our games as children's toys. It was a serious mistake."[11] Arakawa subsequently issued a statement saying that 1994 would be the most aggressive marketing year Nintendo of America had ever seen. Leo Burnett USA, a Chicago ad agency, was selected to design Nintendo's first TV ad campaign. Previously, Nintendo had limited advertising to its own magazine, *Nintendo Power*, circulated to 1 million Nintendo owners. Sean McGowan, a toy analyst with Gerard Klauer Mattison, characterized Nintendo's situation:

> Nintendo has a lot of catching up to do, both in advertising and corporate strategy. The next generation of videogames is being decided now, and Nintendo has lost the edge. That will be hard to recapture with newcomers as powerful as Sony entering the game.[12]

Nintendo made another about-face in early 1994 when it reversed its strategy of not selling videogames directly to video rental dealers. With the videogame rental business representing more than $1 billion a year, Nintendo decided it needed to be a competitor in that segment as well. Nintendo had avoided the rental business in years past because it could not collect royalties on each rental transaction (its only profit came from the one-time sale of cartridges to video rental dealers). However, as the law prohibiting royalty arrangements was to expire in 1997, Nintendo hoped to have the law amended to allow the company to collect royalties on game rentals.[13]

Nintendo was closely watching development of SEGA's cable TV game channel in the United States and its recent efforts to provide the same service in Japan. In January 1995, Nintendo announced the formation of an alliance with GTE Interactive Media to develop, market, and distribute videogames over telephone lines into interactive television sets. Commenting on the venture, Nintendo's chairman noted, "I think we recognize the market is changing and I don't think it's wise to go it alone in circumstances like that."[14] For Nintendo, the alliance gave the company access to GTE's telephone customer network. For GTE, the alliance provided access to entertainment media that GTE felt would drive initial consumer interest in interactive TV. Initial games were to be developed for Nintendo's Super NES and then later for Ultra 64.

Other moves included introducing more (and better) software titles, including the much-anticipated "Donkey Kong Country." Nintendo also softened its opposition to the depiction of violence in Nintendo-licensed videogames. The company began manufacturing Game Boy systems in the People's Republic of China in order to gain access to that large and new market and opened two new subsidiaries in Spain and Australia. Overall, Nintendo had a substantial customer base, experience in the industry, and was dedicated to providing the consumer with a quality experience.[15]

[11]N. Gross and R. D. Hof, "Nintendo's Yamauchi: No More Playing Around," *Business Week*, February 21, 1994, p. 71.

[12]K. Fitzgerald, "Nintendo's Task for Burnett: Image Overhaul," *Advertising Age*, February 28, 1994, pp. 3, 45.

[13]J. Greenstein, "In About-Face, Nintendo Turns to Rental Stores," *Video Business*, April 29, 1994, pp. 1, 12.

[14]J. Carlton, "Nintendo, GTE Unit Offer Games for Interactive TV," *The Wall Street Journal*, January 4, 1995, p. B7.

[15]DFC Intelligence Research.

New Product Development   In August 1993, Nintendo introduced the Nintendo Gateway System, a sophisticated computer designed as an interactive, multimedia information and entertainment system for travelers in airplanes, cruise ships, and hotels. The system was powered by the 16-bit Super NES. At the end of 1994, Nintendo expected to have the systems installed on 170 planes belonging to Northwest Airlines, China Air, Virgin Atlantic, and several other airlines. Nintendo also expanded the system to selected hotels and Holland America cruise ships in 1994. Nintendo expected the Gateway System to ultimately provide a full spectrum of entertainment and information services to 20 million travelers worldwide. With 15 million Super NES units in American homes, Nintendo believed it would be doubling its reach and expanding its audience as well.[16]

In early 1994, Nintendo introduced an adapter that let users of its Game Boy machines play their games on Nintendo's 16-bit system. The company then took 16-bit game machines to a new level when it launched a turbo-charged chip, the Super FX 2, for its 16-bit NES system. The Super FX 2 was a proprietary custom chip, which Nintendo incorporated into its software game cartridges to enhance graphic and speed capabilities, essentially offering players realistic simulation experiences. The Super NES with the FX 2 chip was the most advanced cartridge-based 16-bit game machine in the industry.

Nintendo had recently teamed up with Silicon Graphics, Inc., to design a new game system called Ultra 64. Silicon Graphics had developed the special effects in *Jurassic Park* and *Aladdin*. The technology, called Reality Immersion Technology, allowed videogame players to interact with virtual game environments (a computer-generated 3-D world). This new generation of entertainment created infinitely evolving worlds that instantly and continuously reacted to the commands and whims of individual players. With Reality Immersion Technology, videogame players, for the first time ever, became part of the game itself. Nintendo's strategy was to skip the transition to 32-bit machines (nonportable) and go directly to 64-bit technology. Nintendo planned for the Ultra 64 to be on the market by the end of 1995.

In early 1995, Nintendo introduced a new low-priced virtual reality game system in the United States and Japan. The new game system, called "Virtual Boy," was a portable, table-top unit that did not connect to a TV. The game used 32-bit technology designed to produce a 3-D experience not possible on conventional television or LCD screens. The new system sold for under $200.[17]

Outlook[18]   Nintendo's strategy was characterized by industry observers as "slow and steady wins the race." Whereas SEGA was releasing products and expanding into new areas, Nintendo's strategy focused on making quality videogames. While industry observers suspected that Nintendo had ambitions of being a leading videogame provider for the upcoming interactive age, its present strategic posture was seen as "wait and see."

Until the release of Ultra 64, Nintendo was working hard to keep the 16-bit Super NES alive. Still, recent sales were slumping, in part because of slowing demand for

---

[16]Nintendo Press Release, "Nintendo Gateway System Takes Off," January 6, 1994.

[17]"Nintendo to Begin Selling 'Virtual Reality' System," *The Wall Street Journal*, November 15, 1994, p. B6.

[18]Extracted from DFC Intelligence Research report.

16-bit systems as consumers waited for the next generation systems to come on line in 1995.

SEGA Enterprises, Ltd.

SEGA considered itself a leader in interactive digital entertainment media, with operations on five continents competing in three core business segments: consumer products, amusement center operations, and amusement machines. SEGA produced both hardware and software in these areas. Since 1989, SEGA had quadrupled in size, from more than $800 million in annual sales to $4 billion in fiscal year 1994. SEGA, which once had only a 10 percent share of the U.S. videogame market, had emerged to contend for market leadership with Nintendo. The two companies in 1994 had approximately equal shares in the U.S. market. In Europe, SEGA had more than a 66 percent share but it trailed Nintendo by a 9 to 1 margin in Japan. More details on SEGA's company history are presented in Case 11, Nintendo versus SEGA (A).

Positioning for the 1990s   Some critics questioned whether Hayao Nakayama, SEGA's president and CEO, had the leadership and managerial skills to continue to strengthen SEGA's position in the industry. He had been characterized as an American-style decision-making manager with a good sense of humor. He spoke very rapidly, was opinionated, and impatiently ordered subordinates around. Some said he was obsessed with competing with Nintendo. Like his counterpart at Nintendo, Hiroshi Yamauchi, he did not play videogames.

In 1990, SEGA hired a new chief executive, Thomas Kalinske, to run its U.S. subsidiary, SEGA America Inc. Nakayama specifically hired Kalinske to beat Nintendo and gave Kalinske unprecedented autonomy to do just that. Kalinske was an experienced marketer, with stints as CEO of toymaker Matchbook International Inc. and 15 years with Mattel Inc. earlier in his career. To catch Nintendo, Kalinske took decisive and bold steps that included cutting the price of Genesis 25 percent to $149, recruiting software developers to create new games, and accepting lower royalties, sometimes 15 percent below Nintendo's.[19] The strategy worked. SEGA managed to cut Nintendo's 90 percent market share in 1990 to about 50 percent in 1993, increasing its own market position from a meager 7 percent to almost 50 percent in the process. SEGA's U.S. sales increased from an estimated $280 million in 1990 to more than $1 billion in 1994. Kalinske offered a hint of SEGA's future strategic direction when he said, "I see us as a new form of entertainment company . . . I don't think we should be happy until there are more people using our products than sitting down to watch "Melrose Place" or "Beverly Hills 90210.""[20]

Financial Performance[21]   Fiscal 1994 was a lackluster year for SEGA as well as Nintendo. A weak Japanese economy and a dismal consumer market in Europe, coupled with an unexpectedly sharp appreciation of the yen against other major currencies, resulted in a modest 12.8 percent increase in net consolidated sales from fiscal 1993 to $4 billion and a precipitous 58.9 percent decline in net income to $108.7 million (see Exhibit 4). From a high of ¥11,000 in 1992, SEGA's stock price declined to a low of ¥7,010 at the end of 1994. Exhibit 5 depicts SEGA's sales by division.

---

[19]N. Hutheesing, "How a Cool Sega Zapped Nintendo," *Forbes* 15, no. 42 (1993), pp. 72–73.

[20]Brandt, "Is Nintendo a Street Fighter Now?", p. 69.

[21]This section parallels information presented in Nintendo versus SEGA (A).

EXHIBIT 4   Consolidated Financial Summary for SEGA Enterprises,
Ltd., 1993–1994 (in thousands of $)

	Year Ended March 31	
	1994	**1993**
Statement of Operations Data		
Net sales	$4,038,197	$3,578,968
Cost of goods sold	2,916,161	2,301,496
Gross profit	$1,122,036	$1,277,472
Selling, general, and administrative expenses	831,837	697,988
Operating income	$ 290,199	$ 579,484
Other income/(expenses):		
Interest income	47,561	33,353
Other	(78,865)	(104,024)
Total	(31,304)	(70,671)
Income before income taxes	$ 258,895	$ 508,813
Income taxes	249,259	267,102
Foreign currency translation	99,089	22,752
Net income	$ 108,725	$ 264,463
Net income per share	$1.09	$2.72
Cash dividend per share	0.37	0.21
Balance Sheet Data		
Cash and cash equivalents	$1,000,262	$ 963,646
Current assets	2,398,652	2,185,073
Total assets	3,482,821	3,026,354
Current liabilities	1,261,454	1,084,437
Total liabilities	1,973,999	2,001,006
Stockholders' equity	1,508,822	1,025,348

Source: Company annual reports.

EXHIBIT 5   SEGA's Nonconsolidated Sales by Division, 1993–1994
(in millions of $)

	1994	**1993**
Net sales:	$3,432.2	$2,983.1
Consumer products	2,286.8	1,971.4
Domestic sales	249.7	166.2
Exports	2,037.1	1,805.2
Amusement center operations	598.5	506.6
Amusement machine sales:	505.5	494.9
Domestic sales	377.9	398.4
Exports	127.6	96.5
Royalties on game software	41.4	10.3

Source: Company annual reports.

In the first six months of fiscal 1995 (ending September 1994), SEGA's unconsolidated pretax profit fell 43 percent to ¥16.33 billion ($166.97 million), down from ¥28.58 billion the previous year. Sales fell 25 percent, to ¥151.07 billion, from ¥200.65 billion. Analysts said the declines were expected due to slumping global demand for videogames and the soaring yen, which made Japanese products less competitive abroad.[22]

In Japan, SEGA continued to trail far behind Nintendo's commanding 90 percent market share because of distribution problems and because its sports-oriented games were not as popular in Japan. SEGA's financial performance and competitive strength depended primarily on its American and European operations, which had some autonomy from Tokyo. SEGA of America accounted for about 25 percent to the parent company's overall revenue.

SEGA's Strategy and Product Development

Grand Strategy   SEGA's president had made no secret of his strategic intent: to build an entertainment empire. "We'd like to resemble a combination of Sony and Disneyland by the 21st century."[23] To achieve this goal, SEGA had adopted a technology-oriented strategic plan that focused on acquiring and maintaining competitive advantage in such fields as multimedia, computer graphics, virtual reality, and high-tech amusement theme parks. Anticipating the convergence of the worlds of computers, communications, and entertainment, SEGA had stepped up R&D spending in multimedia, "edutainment," and audiovisual products. The company had approximately 850 employees working on interactive amusements for homes, arcade, and theme parks, representing the highest investment in R&D in the industry. SEGA's drive to achieve of industry dominance led the company to make alliances with AT&T in communications, Hitachi in chips, Yamaha in sound, JVC in game machines, and potentially Microsoft in software.

In an effort to counter competition from inexpensive multimedia home computers, SEGA explored the possibility of making some of its popular videogame software available for PCs equipped with CD-ROM drives. According to *The Wall Street Journal:*

> If SEGA does decide to embrace the PC, the company will be making a major break with tradition. Up to now, SEGA has developed its own software mainly for use on its own proprietary game systems. Unlike its archrival Nintendo Co., which relies heavily on outside software developers, SEGA develops roughly 45 percent of the software for its game machines in-house.[24]

Since SEGA competed in both home and arcade games (Nintendo was only in home games), it was able to develop expensive technology for arcade machines as then transition the technology to home machines as the price of computer chips fell. Additionally, SEGA planned to move beyond auto racing and action games, at which it excelled, to more general multimedia entertainment featuring full motion video, drama, and characters besides Sonic that could be as popular as Mickey Mouse.[25]

[22]"Video-Game Maker's Profit Plunged in Fiscal First Half," *The Wall Street Journal*, November 14, 1994, p. B5.

[23]"The High-Tech Art of Having Fun," *Asia Week* 18, no. 36 (1992), p. 65.

[24]D. P. Hamilton, "SEGA May Make Some Video Games Available for PCs," *The Wall Street Journal*, May 16, 1994, p. B6.

[25]A. Pollack, "SEGA Takes Aim at Disney World," *New York Times*, July 4, 1993, p. 6.

One component of SEGA's strategic move into more general multimedia entertainment was its formation in 1994 of the SEGA Club, a vehicle for marketing its games to the nearly 32 million children aged 3 to 11. SEGA's objective was to be an industry leader in bringing good, clean videogame entertainment and educational products to the videogame market for teens and pre-teens.

Because SEGA's sales in Japan entailed bigger margins than its overseas sales, management wanted to increase the company's Japanese market share. The strategy involved efforts to boost sales through a combination of new products, increased advertising, and more extensive marketing.

The company planned a complete review of its operations in Europe in order to respond more effectively to consumer preferences and competitive conditions in particular local European markets and to improve sales and gross margins. To stimulate demand for its high-tech entertainment products, SEGA planned to release PICO, Saturn, and the 32-X adapter in Europe.

SEGA viewed Asia both as a high-potential market and as a center for manufacturing. The company produced all of its videogame players in Japan in cooperation with a subsidiary of Hitachi Ltd. Localizing production in Asia (but outside Japan) was expected to result in an increased ratio of non-Japan manufacturing, lower costs, and decreased risks associated with fluctuations in the value of the Japanese yen. To lower production costs in Japan, SEGA planned to increase imports of parts and components for its hardware and software products.

SEGA's future strategy aimed at capturing some of the $6 billion U.S. theme park market. Plans called for constructing small theme parks that combined high-tech amusement center machines using state-of-the-art computer graphics with virtual-reality technologies to fully engross players in the game's environment. SEGA's strategy was not to imitate Disney but to reinvent the amusement park:

> Whereas Disney built huge amusement parks with roller coasters and log flume rides, SEGA wants to build small theme parks that will provide the same thrills using computer simulations known as virtual reality—a Disneyland in a box.[26]

Whereas Disney had only three huge parks to attract patrons, SEGA said it would build 50 parks in Japan and another 50 in the United States over the next several years. Unlike the Disney attractions that remained fixed for decades, a virtual reality attraction could be changed just by changing the software. The same simulator could be used for a space battle or a police chase.[27] According to Tom Kalinske, "We want consumers to spend their time and money with SEGA entertainment when they're out of the home and when they're inside the home . . . we want to provide entertainment that you'd rather do with us than any of the alternative forms, whether TV, local TV, or whatever."[28]

By 1995, SEGA derived about one-sixth of its consolidated revenue from amusement center operations. One analyst predicted that SEGA would enjoy gross margins above 30 percent, compared to Disney's 25 percent for its theme parks in Florida and California. While SEGA had no experience running amusement parks, management believed the company knew how to provide "experiences" based on its experiences and know-how in operating more than 1,200 video arcades in Japan.

[26]Ibid.

[27]"Big Plans for Theme Parks," *New York Times*, July 4, 1993, p. 6.

[28]J. Battle and B. Johnstone, "Seizing the Next Level," *Wired*, December 1993, p. 126.

New Product Development   SEGA's newest product for the home market was its new $399 CDX player, introduced in April 1994. This player used Genesis cartridges and SEGA CD games in one portable module that also functioned as a compact disc player. American Telephone & Telegraph planned to introduce the Edge 16, an under-$150 modem, to permit two Genesis machines to communicate over phone lines.

In November 1994, SEGA introduced its newest multimedia product in Japan, the 32-bit Saturn console; the model was scheduled for release in the United States in the fall of 1995. This game unit had a built-in CD-ROM player (quadruple-speed) and enough processing power to reproduce movielike sound and visual effects.

To enhance demand for the firm's 16-bit game players, SEGA had developed a hardware booster (Super Genesis 32-X) that enabled 32-bit game cartridges to play on its 16-bit players. SEGA expected to have more than 120 games specifically designed for the 32-X by December 1995.

One problem SEGA faced, however, was the numerous game system formats it had on the market. The feeling among some observers was that SEGA was trying to cover too many bases at one time. Multiple systems not only confused some customers but also held potential for the various systems cannibalizing each other. SEGA management was aware of these problems but felt the pluses outweighed the minuses.

In 1994, SEGA test-marketed its SEGA Channel via cable TV in the United States. Genesis owners could pay $12 to $20 per month for unlimited playing time. Subscribers could choose from a wide selection of popular Genesis games, special versions of soon to be released titles, gameplay tips, news, contests, and promotions. The SEGA Channel was cited by the editors of *Science Magazine* as one of 1994's innovative products and achievements in science and technology in the magazine's seventh annual "Best of What's New" special awards section in its December issue. SEGA was also gearing up to introduce a similar game channel in Japan. However, the number of Japanese homes wired for cable was small at 1.6 million (a 5 percent penetration rate) compared to the United States with more than 60 percent of U.S. homes wired for cable. The diffusion of cable systems in Japan had been hurt by the widespread use of wireless satellite systems.

One of SEGA's most innovative new products was a children's book that interacted with a TV through an electronic pen. The booklike toy, called "PICO" (about $160), involved touching a pen to a picture in a book; the image of the picture, as modified by the electronic pen, appeared on the TV screen. This product, released in Japan in June 1993, represented SEGA's first entry into the emerging edutainment market.

Both Nintendo and SEGA started offering videogame systems that could be attached to exercise equipment in the fall of 1994. SEGA offered add-on units, while Nintendo's product was built into a Life Fitness exercise bike. The systems were designed so that videogame characters reported the user's speed and effort during the workout, offering entertainment and distraction while motivating exercise. Analysts believed these so-called exertainment systems could become a $2 billion business in a few years.[29]

Outlook[30]   Whereas Nintendo's strategy reflected a posture of "slow and steady wins the race," SEGA appeared to operate on the principle of "first at all costs." SEGA had been burned badly by entering the 8-bit market after Nintendo and seemed determined not to be a technology follower again.

---

[29]K. Fitzgerald, "It's Sonic vs. The Stairmaster," *Advertising Age*, June 13, 1994, p. 26.

[30]Extracted from DFC Intelligence Research report.

The SEGA Genesis was the first 16-bit system on the market, 18 months before Nintendo's 16-bit Super NES. The SEGA CD was released well before any competing systems. Recently, SEGA had introduced its 32-bit system, Genesis 32-X, a full year before similar systems from Nintendo and Sony.

So far, the strategy of being first had served SEGA well. Nintendo was forced into playing catch-up and SEGA was challenging Nintendo for the lead in the U.S. videogame market. Sales of the SEGA CD had been less than spectacular, but the system had gone a long way toward enhancing SEGA's reputation.

PRICING

Price was a key competitive weapon in the battle for market share among game players and, ultimately, videogame software. 3DO learned a hard lesson when it introduced its interactive player in the United States at an initial price of $699 with disappointing results. According to one Japanese consumer-electronics official, 3DO is "an object lesson in how not to approach the U.S. market . . . For our company we would only enter the U.S. market if we could price our machines at under $200."[31] 3DO eventually dropped the price of its system to $399, but many parents still considered that too expensive.

One pricing tactic that had proven successful in the past was getting consumers to buy a fully equipped system in installments. This had been SEGA's strategy and one that others appeared to be following. For example, a fully loaded Genesis system had three components, all of which could be purchased separately: a $100 game player, a $200 SEGA CD, and a $150 Genesis 32-X. The cost of such a system exceeded the $399 price tag of a 3DO player, even though a 3DO system had superior performance.[32]

The potential for rapid growth in the videogame cartridge rental market held the threat of cannibalizing retail sales of game cartridges and ultimately increasing competition for retail shelf space and pricing and margin pressures.[33] On the other hand, a growing preference for using a CD-ROM format for games held potential for significant reduction in production costs. A CD-ROM game could be pressed and packaged for less than $3, as compared to a cartridge-based system where chip costs and manufacturing expenses could push the cost to make a top-quality cartridge over $20. The cost advantage of the CD-ROM format, coupled with greater ability to match production with demand, offered game providers a significant improvement in the cost make-up of their value chain systems.

ADVERTISING AND MARKETING

Growing advertising budgets for new game titles signalled just how competitive the industry was becoming. Acclaim Entertainment spent $10 million in its marketing campaign to launch "Mortal Kombat II" in September 1994. The original version had sold more than 6 million games since it was introduced in September 1993. The game, in which players ripped out the hearts of their enemies, was manufactured for both Nintendo and SEGA home systems. SEGA reportedly spent $45 million on a world-

[31]S. Mansfield, "Sony, NEC Video Game Entries No Threat to Sega, Nintendo," *Electronic Business Buyer*, 1994, pp. 30, 32.

[32]DFC Intelligence Research.

[33]Activision's Form 10-K, 1994, p. 15.

wide marketing blitz to promote the game, "Sonic & Knuckles." Nintendo spent $17 million to promote its new game "Donkey Kong Country" for the 1994 holiday season. Good Times Entertainment undertook a $3 million to $5 million campaign for its October 1994 launch of "Doom II," a follow-up to "Doom," one of the industry's most successful computer software titles.[34] Videogame industry analysts predicted that advertising could be the deciding factor in the 1994 race between Nintendo and SEGA to keep their sales pumped up until their newer, more powerful videogame systems came on the market. In 1993 alone, Nintendo spent more than $165 million on marketing support. Despite the big dollars expended on advertising and marketing, word-of-mouth, rental, and borrowing games continued as powerful influences on unit sales volumes. Many game players preferred to try a game before they purchased it.

MOUNTING CONCERN ABOUT SEX AND VIOLENCE IN VIDEOGAMES

Violence in America was considered by many people to have reached epidemic proportions in 1994. All across the United States—in cities and towns large and small—citizens were increasingly fearful and concerned that violence was out of control. There was no one reason for the outgrowth of violence and violent behavior, but many experts said that the pervasive violence in television programming, films, and videogames was one seed that promoted physical aggression in some individuals and helped create a culture tolerant of violence.

Just as television emerged as a powerful social and cultural force in the early 1950s, videogames were said to be emerging as a potentially powerful influence on children's behavior in the 1990s. While the impact of the growing violence in videogames was debatable, the years of research on violence in television programming provided instructive warning. According to Parker Page, president of the Children's Television Resource and Education Center, "years of research indicate that children who watch a steady diet of violent programming increase their chances of becoming more aggressive towards other children, less cooperative and altruistic, more tolerant of real life violence and more afraid of the world outside their homes.[35] The advent of virtual reality technology in videogame programming led Page to express a special concern in his testimony before a joint Senate subcommittee hearing held in December 1993.

> Mortal Kombat is simply the first in a new generation of video games that allows software designers to combine high levels of violence with fully digitalized human images. No more cute hedge hogs or cartoonish Super Mario Brothers—increasingly, the characters that a young player beheads, disembowels or crushes will look more and more like the kids at school, the neighbor who lives down the street or the young woman heading for aerobics class.[36]

Alarmed by the violent content of many videogames, parents and concerned citizens started lobbying for a comprehensive, industrywide videogame rating system

---

[34]J. A. Trachtenberg, "Zap! Smash! Aggressive Ads Plug Game Sequels," *The Wall Street Journal*, August 24, 1994, p. B1.

[35]U.S. Senate, Violence in Videogames: Joint Hearing of the Judiciary Subcommittee on Juvenile Justice and Government Affairs Subcommittee on Regulation and Government Information (testimony of Parker Page, PhD). 103rd Cong., 1993.

[36]Ibid.

that would give parents the information they needed to make informed choices. To address these concerns, Senators Lieberman and Kohl sponsored legislation to establish the National Independent Council for Entertainment in Video Devices as an independent agency of the federal government to oversee the development of "voluntary" standards to alert parents to the content of videogames. In his testimony before the hearing, Robert Chase, vice president of the National Education Association, expressed the collective concern of educators, children's advocates, and parents:

> America's children are faced with a bewildering set of messages from television, movies, music, electronic games, and print media. Too often, the almost unrelenting assault on the senses encouraging aggression and irresponsibility are in direct opposition to the values families hope to instill and the mores our society struggles to preserve. Parents, social scientists, and the community at large share deep trepidation about the fruits of this ever widening dispersal of negative images. The explosion of media in the latter half of this century has made the problem all the more pervasive and the challenges for parents and community leaders all the more difficult.[37]

At the same hearing, the Software Publishers Association (SPA) provided a counter argument:

> In our attempt to protect our children from those relatively few video games which contain unacceptable violence, however, we must not lose sight of the fact that the vast majority of videogames are appropriate for children, and have the potential for developing many important and socially desirable skills. As stated so eloquently by Bob Keeshan, otherwise known as Captain Kangaroo, "Video games . . . provide the potential for heretofore unknown opportunities for information, education and delightful entertainment . . . The technology is to be encouraged because, used appropriately, such games can be a tool for education as well as entertainment."[38]

The SPA indicated in its testimony that the software entertainment industry was committed to moving quickly and decisively on the violence issue. The SPA was in the process of working with a coalition of concerned parties to establish a rating system that would be easy for consumers to understand and one that the industry could implement. Nintendo and SEGA had also initiated moves toward a rating system.

Nintendo's Position

When Nintendo entered the U.S. videogame industry in 1985, the company established written Game Content Guidelines requiring games marketed under the Nintendo Seal of Quality to meet the following standards:

- No sexually suggestive or explicit content.
- No sexist language or depictions.
- No random, gratuitous, or excessive violence.
- No graphic illustration of death.
- No domestic violence or abuse.
- No excessive force in sports games.
- No ethnic, racial, religious, or sexual stereotypes.

---

[37]Ibid. (testimony of Robert Chase).
[38]Ibid. (testimony of Ilene Rosenthal).

- No profanity or obscenity.
- No use of drugs, smoking materials, or alcohol.
- No subliminal political messages or overt political statements.

As an example of Nintendo's pledge to control and monitor its game content, the company insisted that one of its largest licensees, Acclaim Entertainment, remove objectionable material from the controversial arcade game, "Mortal Kombat." In its original form, the game included scenes in which characters' heads were ripped off, their spines were pulled out, they were impaled on spikes, and they spurted blood when hit. All of these graphics were deemed unacceptable and removed from the Nintendo version of the game. SEGA released the game in its entirety.

Some games had been simply rejected outright, since no amount of modification would make them acceptable to Nintendo. One such game was "Night Trap," which contained full motion videos of young, scantily-clad females being attacked by hooded men who drilled holes in their bodies to suck out blood.

Howard Lincoln, Nintendo's then senior vice-president (and later chairman), reiterated his company's continued commitment to wholesome family entertainment that was both challenging and exciting to youth while remaining nonoffensive to parents:

> This will remain our philosophy despite the fact we have been criticized by both video game players and others in our industry for taking what we feel is the only responsible approach . . . we believe our game guidelines have served us and our customers well for the past eight years. And we have no intention of abandoning this approach.[39]

However, Nintendo apparently decided to moderate its position following a raft of angry letters from users. Nintendo's 1994 holiday season new version of the "Mortal Kombat" game was just as gruesome as the arcade version.

SEGA's Position

In 1993, SEGA established a three-pronged approach designed to help parents determine the age-appropriateness of its stable of interactive video software.[40] It included a rating classification system, a toll-free hotline, and an informational brochure. Building on the motion picture industry model, the SEGA rating system applied one of three classifications to each interactive video program it released:

GAF   For general audiences.

MA-13 For mature audiences age 13 and over.

MA-17 Adult appropriate, not suitable for those under age 17.

SEGA's toll-free hotline was staffed by professionals who could supplement the rating classification by informing parents about the specific content of each SEGA product. SEGA also offered its "Everybody Wins" brochure that provided additional information to shoppers at more than 2,800 retail stores. In addition, SEGA formed an independent Videogame Rating Council consisting of experts in the areas of psychology, sociology, cinema, and education to evaluate games and assign appropriate rating classifications. By the end of 1993, 173 SEGA titles had been rated with the following distribution: 86 percent rated for general audiences (GA); 10 percent

---

[39]Ibid. (testimony of Howard C. Lincoln).

[40]Ibid. (testimony of William White, vice-president, SEGA of America Inc.).

EXHIBIT 6   Rating Guidelines of Two Organizations, 1994

Interactive Digital Software was using five categories by age to rate video game cartridges such as Nintendo, Sega, Atari. They were:

- Early childhood, ages 3 and up
- Kids to adult, ages 6 and up
- Teen, ages 13 and up
- Mature, ages 17 and up
- Adults only

The Software Publishers Association was using a label that showed the level of violence, sex, and strong language used in a computer software or CD-ROM game. Games with no offensive material received a "Suitable for all audiences" label.

Source: *The Washington Post.*

earned an MA-13 rating; and only 4 percent were targeted for exclusively adult (MA-17) audiences. To make SEGA's rating system work, the company decided that products bearing the MA-17 label should not be distributed to retail toy stores.

Progress Report

In July 1994, the U.S. Senate subcommittee endorsed rating guidelines issued by an industry trade group, the Interactive Digital Software Association (IDSA)—see Exhibit 6. The IDSA ratings provided age guidance with five categories similar to those used by the Motion Picture Association of America.[41] Retailers who rented games planned to adhere to the ratings guidelines. Some mass merchants (Sears, Wal-Mart, Toys "Я" Us) had vowed to carry only rated videogames. An informal survey of retailers, however, revealed that large numbers of unrated games were on retailers' shelves for the 1994 seasonal buying rush.[42] Although the IDSA had rated more than 280 titles, the ratings were apparently completed after game packages were printed.

The SPA encountered similar problems. At the end of 1994, only 40 CD-ROM and other software game titles had been rated. Exhibit 6 depicts SPA rating guide-

[41]M. Moran, "Retailers See Videogame Ratings as a Helpful Guide," *Video Business* 14, no. 32 (1994), pp. 12, 16.

[42]P. Farhi, "A Waiting Game for Rating Games," *The Washington Post*, December 24, 1994, p. D1.

lines. Ken Wasch, executive director of the SPA, commented: "I wish more had been rated, but it took longer than we expected to get products submitted, to get them rated, and to get them to the stores."[43]

There was no agreement among game producers on an industrywide rating system. Some observers believed the existence of several rating systems would confuse consumers. There also appeared to be a debate emerging whether widespread dissemination of rated products would ultimately hurt or help sales.

THE FUTURE

The intensifying rivalry between Nintendo and SEGA was heightening the need for each company to develop a viable long-term competitive strategy. While it seemed clear that videogames had staying power in the entertainment industry, neither company's future success was assured as computers, telecommunications technologies, and entertainment merged to create a vista of new multimedia options—some of which represented opportunities and some of which posed threats. The challenges for Nintendo and SEGA were how to capitalize on their prior successes and market reputations, what directions to pursue, and how to exploit the opportunities before them and win a sustainable competitive advantage. Where would Nintendo and SEGA be in the year 2000? Who would emerge as the dominant provider of videogames?

(For updated information on Nintendo and SEGA, you may wish to explore their Web sites: *www.nintendo.co.jp* and *www.sega.co.jp*. The Sony Web site at *www.sony.co.jp* has updates on its PlayStation offerings. You might also want to use one of the Web's search engines to research recent trends in the videogame industry.)

---

[43]Ibid.

PASTA PERFECT, INC.*

Joan Winn, *University of Denver*

John W. Mullins, *University of Denver*

"This is a tough call," said Jim Leonard, director of Pasta Perfect, Inc., to Tom Walker, the company's president, "Clearly, our results in the retail stores are not what we'd like them to be, and that concerns me a great deal. On the other hand, I'm not sure we have what it takes to succeed in supermarkets, and to put our funds there is not what we told the shareholders we would do with their money when we raised the last round of capital."

It was October 1988, and the Pasta Perfect board was discussing a change in strategy, from development of a chain of specialty retail shops, to selling fresh pasta and sauces through supermarkets. Pasta Perfect, headquartered in St. Louis, Missouri, operated 14 fresh pasta shops in the St. Louis and Chicago metropolitan areas. In spite of its rapid growth, however, the company had not reached profitability. While everyone in the small company was frustrated over the firm's poor performance, no one felt the frustration more acutely then did Tom Walker. It was he who had conceived the idea of a chain of fresh pasta stores. It was he who had put together a management team and recruited a board of directors, including Jim Leonard, a venture capitalist. And it was Tom Walker who had convinced investors to put up several rounds of capital to build the business. Now it appeared that these investors, who included friends and family as well as almost 7,000 shareholders in the now publicly held firm, were at risk of losing their entire investment in Pasta Perfect. To Tom, it was clear that something had to change. "I've tried everything

*All events and individuals in this case are real, but names and locations have been disguised.
Copyright © 1996 by Joan Winn and John W. Mullins and the North American Case Research Association

that my 15 years in retailing have taught me, and except for store #102, we just can't seem to turn the corner to positive contribution from the stores. I don't like to admit it, but I'm afraid we need to find another path.''

THE CHANGING PASTA MARKET

The first American pasta factory had opened in 1848 in Brooklyn, New York. By 1981, the average American consumed about 12 pounds of pasta per year, or about one serving a week. For years, pasta had been considered a starchy, inexpensive belly stuffer.[1] Spaghetti or macaroni and cheese made an economical dinner at the end of the week; canned ravioli was a quick, hot lunch.[2] But as people started paying closer attention to health, exercise, and nutrition in the early 1980s, pasta's image began to change to one of a healthy gourmet food.

Throughout the 1980s, pasta sales enjoyed a steady 5 percent per year growth as pasta became a featured item in gourmet restaurants and cookbooks. In 1982, Morisi & Sons in Brooklyn, New York, began manufacturing flavored dried pasta. That same year, fresh pasta appeared in supermarkets in New York City and Los Angeles. As the pasta market grew in sales and in its upscale appeal, these new developments created new market niches. The dried pasta category remained a hotly competitive one, with consumers choosing a brand mainly on the basis of price, and retailers demanding price promotions from manufacturers. The new specialty pastas, including flavored dried pastas and an expanding variety of fresh pastas were viewed differently, however, by both consumers and retailers. These specialty products appealed to upscale urban and suburban adults who sought convenient, yet nutritious and tasty meals. Specialty pastas were generally marketed in the higher-margin deli sections of supermarkets, instead of in the grocery aisle, partly to avert price comparisons with lower-cost dried pasta.[3] Such products were also found in small Italian food shops in urban neighborhoods having large Italian populations.

THE PASTA INDUSTRY IN THE LATE 1980s

By 1987, American pasta factories were producing nearly 3 billion pounds of pasta—$1.6 billion at wholesale prices—per year. Average per capita consumption had grown to more than 16 pounds per year. This was an increase of 6 percent from 1986, and an average increase of 4–5 percent per year since 1980. The National Pasta Association predicted consumption of 24 pounds per person or 192 servings annually by 1995. In 1988, more than 40 percent of sales came from the retail dry packaged pastas; 60 percent came from the prepared pasta market, which included frozen, canned, and jarred pasta products.[4]

In spite of this pattern of growth, dried pasta was viewed as a commodity business, with retail prices averaging less than one dollar per pound. No brand had achieved national distribution and even the big, market-savvy companies had been unable to successfully establish strong brand identities. "The game of price is really

---

[1]Brain Bagot, ''Mangia! Mangia!'' *Marketing & Media Decisions* (June 1989), pp. 83–93.

[2]Frances Huffman ''The Pasta Payoff,'' *Entrepreneur* (June 1990), pp. 72–78.

[3]Josh Eppinger, ''Pasta LaBella's Fight to Become a Major National Brand,'' *Adweek's Marketing Week* (February 5, 1990) p. 28.

[4]Marilyn Myers ''America's Pasta Passion,'' *Food Arts* (October 1991), p. 70.

the game of pasta," observed Hugh Peters, senior product manager for Mueller's Pasta Products. Timothy Dunn, senior investment officer with PNC Financial saw pasta as "a volume business. Name recognition is important, but I don't think people really see much difference between [brands] . . . they'll buy whatever they can get a deal on"[5]

In 1987, the top five leading brands were Mueller's, with sales of $154 million, Creamette with sales of $125 million, General Foods' Ronzoni with $92 million in sales, San Giorgio with $67 million in sales, and Prince with sales of $59 million. Together, however, these five brands accounted for only about one third of the pasta sold nationally, with the remaining share of market spread across a variety of regional brands.

Although the growth of the dry pasta market had been steady, the growth of refrigerated fresh pasta had been tremendous. Sales of refrigerated fresh pasta, which was soft and flexible, rather than dried into rigid sticks, had risen 30 percent per year since 1985, approaching $100 million in 1988. Sales were predicted to top $150 million by 1990 and $250 million by 1995. This rapid growth occurred in spite of retail prices averaging over three dollars per pound, more than three times the price of dried pasta.

In early 1987, the American Italian Pasta Company (AIPC), in Excelsior Springs, Missouri, began supplying Kroger supermarkets, a large midwestern chain, with private-label packages of refrigerated fresh pasta. AIPC provided merchandising support, including in-store product demonstrations and mobile pasta cart display units. AIPC founder Richard Thompson planned to launch his own brand, Pasta LaBella, by 1989. Also in 1987, Vivace, another small manufacturing newcomer, started marketing fresh pasta to Houston area supermarkets.[6]

By late 1987, there were over 50 manufacturers of refrigerated pasta who marketed their product outside their immediate neighborhood. Because fresh pasta was relatively new, these regional brands were not well entrenched. Carnation's Contadina Fresh, which went national after Nestlé (Carnation's corporate parent) acquired a small, New York-based fresh pasta producer in 1986 for $56 million, was the only brand that enjoyed more than a local following. Contadina's pasta sales were expected to exceed $60 million in 1988, serving 37 metropolitan markets nationally.

This rapid growth of refrigerated fresh pasta had been made possible by the recent development of gas-flushed packaging technology that extended the shelf life of the product. The soft fresh pasta was manufactured using new, high-tech equipment, which gently folded the pasta and placed it in an attractively labeled clear plastic container; the container was then filled with a mixture of nitrogen and other gases and sealed. This packaging prevented the growth of mold and kept the pasta fresh and appealing for 90 days.

MARKETING OF PASTA PRODUCTS

Pasta was advertised mainly through radio and newspaper ads, coupons and reduced prices, and in-store demonstrations and sampling. Most of the advertising dollars were spent on sauce, rather than pasta. National advertising for pastas was rare, since there were distinct regional differences in customer preferences. Most dry pasta

[5]Bagot, p. 83.
[6]Huffman, pp. 72–78.

brands did not advertise, since profit margins were thin and purchasing tended to be dictated by price. Creamette was projected to spend about $7 million in advertising in 1988, more than $5 million more than anticipated by second-place spender Prince.

Most media advertising was directed toward sauces, partly because sauces commanded a higher profit margin, but also because they could be differentiated from each other. Ragu, founded in 1937 in Rochester, New York, had gone national in 1969 when it was acquired by Chesebrough-Ponds. In 1982, Campbell's introduced Prego and the sauce wars had intensified. Unilever had acquired Chesebrough-Ponds in 1987, spending more than $20 million in advertising, $15 million on network TV alone. Ragu was the industry leader, having successfully captured more than half of the sauce market, with over $400 million in sales in 1987. Hunt's had introduced Prima Salsa in the mid-1970s, but had pulled it off the shelves in the early 1980s due to stiff competition from Ragu. Other sauce competitors included various regional brands such as Progresso, sold mostly in the Northeast, and Contadina, which was sold in the refrigerated section of the store next to its pastas.

THE ORIGINS OF PASTA PERFECT

In 1983, Tom Walker had seen the potential for growth and profitability in the fresh pasta market. Walker, who had recently left his vice-president's position with a major specialty apparel retailer and moved to St. Louis, had been looking for a niche in which to build a specialty retail business of his own. "When we lived on the east coast, there was a fresh pasta store that Jan and I frequented at least once a week. The pasta and sauces were wonderful. And since fresh pasta cooks in just two minutes, we could have a gourmet meal on the table in 10 minutes when we got home from work." With the growth he saw in the pasta market, combined with the burgeoning trends toward fitness and nutrition and his retailing background, Walker decided he had found his niche. "I knew that consumers were increasingly interested in freshness, whether in fresh-baked chocolate chip cookies in the shopping mall, freshly ground coffee from the grocery store, or other food products. I also saw that fresh products could command a price premium over conventional packaged products. And I knew from that little store back east just how good fresh pasta really is." Tom could barely contain his enthusiasm and excitement as he set to work planning a chain of retail stores that would sell fresh pasta and sauces to take home. He envisioned small, attractive shops in high-traffic areas, targeted at upscale consumers who wanted a convenient meal that they could quickly purchase and prepare at home. Italian cuisine was popular in St. Louis, so Tom was convinced that there was ample demand for his product. And, since pasta was made largely from inexpensive ingredients—semolina flour, eggs, and water—Tom felt that gross margins were likely to be attractive enough to cover the costs of operating small stores.

Confident in the future of fresh pasta, Tom decided to devote his full-time attention to his new venture. He wrote a business plan, found partners with time and money to invest (one of whom came from an Italian family), and set out to raise the additional money needed to get his business underway. He talked to family and friends and quickly sold several of them on his idea. With $35,000 raised and his partner's family sauce recipes adapted to large quantity production, he was ready to launch Pasta Perfect.

The first store opened in May 1984, in St. Louis, Missouri. By September 1985, there were five Pasta Perfect stores in the St. Louis area. By October 1988, there were 10 stores in St. Louis and four in Chicago, with the newest Chicago store having opened in June.

The company's plan was to cluster groups of stores in large metropolitan areas. This would provide economies of scale in preparation and delivery, as well as advertising and store supervision, and allow the company to maintain the high standards for product quality, freshness, and customer service for which it was increasingly well known. The young company's growth was helped along by favorable articles in the St. Louis newspapers, whose food writers sung the praises of Pasta Perfect's products.

As of late 1988, Pasta Perfect had encountered little direct competition in its offerings of fresh pasta products. Several stores specializing in fresh pasta products had emerged in New York and California, but Pasta Perfect was the only specialty retail chain in Missouri and Illinois. Packaged, refrigerated fresh pasta was just starting to appear in St. Louis and Chicago supermarkets.

THE PASTA PERFECT STORE CONCEPT

Pasta Perfect stores were designed with two-income families in mind, where time savings and quality were more important than price in home-food purchasing decisions. Pasta Perfect stores were located in high traffic urban locations or in strip shopping centers anchored by major supermarket chains for easy access. Since fresh pasta sold at a premium price over the conventional dried pasta products found on supermarket shelves, it was important that Pasta Perfect stores look attractive and inviting, with an atmosphere that conveyed quality, freshness, and convenience.

Each Pasta Perfect store featured green and white colors with natural wood furnishings and a prominently displayed Pasta Perfect logo. Displays of the products offered for sale were planned with eye appeal in mind. Seven of the stores featured limited seating for 8 to 15 people, and offered, in addition to Pasta Perfect's assortment of take-home products, a light lunch menu consisting of cold sandwiches, soups, pasta salads, desserts, and beverages. Seating had been planned into these stores because Pasta Perfect had found it difficult to lease locations as small as the 400 to 500 square feet needed. Thus, some stores were as large as 2,000 square feet.

Furniture and equipment in the stores consisted principally of a pasta cutting machine, refrigerators, display and storage cases, counters, display and storage shelving, and various smaller equipment such as a cash register, scale, bowls and jars for product display, and utensils. Stores that served prepared items also contained tables and chairs.

Pasta Perfect offered fresh pasta in five regular flavors—egg, herb, spinach, black pepper, egg-free—plus weekly specials such as lemon and tomato basil. Pasta was delivered to each store in whole sheets and then cut to order in front of the customer, wrapped in butcher paper, and sealed with a bright red and green label that gave cooking instructions, Pasta Perfect's best-selling pastas were fettucini (wide), linguine (narrow), tagliarini (thin), and angel hair (fine). Pasta Perfect also sold its own sauces for pasta, plus various fresh and frozen specialty products including salads and other Italian specialties such as ravioli, manicotti, and lasagna. The assortment of sauces for its fresh pasta included tomato, meat, white clam, alfredo (heavy cream with freshly grated cheese) and bolognese (tomatoes with Italian sausage, wine, and fresh vegatables). Pasta Perfect also offered other food and nonfood products, including fresh bread, various imported and domestic food products, Italian cookbooks, and utensils.

Operations

Stores were open from 11:00 A.M. to 7:00 P.M. six days a week, with most of the stores open from 11:00 to 5:00 on Sundays as well. For each store, the company employed a full-time manager who was responsible for two to four part-time employees. To assure that individual stores were operated at a high level of quality, Pasta Perfect took great care in its selection and training of managers and provided a detailed training and operations manual to each manager.

Most of the products sold in Pasta Perfect stores were prepared at Pasta Perfect's commissary, located in a St. Louis suburb. This central preparation center served all of the stores in the metropolitan area, in an effort to reduce the investment and space needed for each store, and to increase control over product quality, freshness, and costs.

Pasta was prepared daily and delivered to the St. Louis area stores in a refrigerated truck designed to hold the products at their desired refrigerated temperatures. Sauces were packaged in microwave-safe and freezer-safe containers. Fresh pasta for the Chicago stores was produced in a back kitchen area in one of those stores. Sauces and other refrigerated and frozen products were prepared in St. Louis and shipped to the Chicago stores via refrigerated common carrier. Because fresh pasta has a shorter shelf life than dried pasta, careful rotation of stock and effective management of inventory levels were necessary to maintain product freshness and control waste.

PASTA PERFECT'S FINANCIAL PERFORMANCE

Pasta Perfect had financed its operations and its growth by raising several rounds of capital. Its first five stores were funded by private investors, whom Tom Walker was able to interest in purchasing equity or providing convertible debt to his young company. Then in December 1985, Pasta Perfect raised $1.5 million in an initial public offering. In April 1988, another $800,000 was raised in a second public offering in which all shareholders were offered "rights" to purchase additional shares. This offering had been made possible by the relatively strong sales of the new Chicago stores, compared to the St. Louis stores, in spite of the fact that the company had yet to turn the corner toward profitability. Exhibit 1 shows balance sheet information as of April 1988 (adjusted to include the capital raised in April 1988). Exhibit 2 shows the company's profit and loss history. Individual store performance data is shown in Exhibit 3, and the planned operating performance of Pasta Perfect stores is shown in Exhibit 4.

In the fiscal year ended April 1, 1988, only two of the St. Louis stores and one of the Chicago stores were contributing positively to overhead and profit, but two of these three were barely profitable (see Exhibit 4). Results for the current fiscal year to date were similar to those in fiscal year 1988. Over the four years of the company's existence, a series of steps had been taken to address Pasta Perfect's poor performance.

In late 1986 and early 1987, a series of productivity enhancements and personnel changes at Pasta Perfect's St. Louis commissary had led to significant reductions in the labor portion of product costs as well as improved quality and consistency

EXHIBIT 1   Pasta Perfect's Balance Sheet, 1985–1988

	Fiscal years ending			
	March 29, 1985	March 28, 1986	April 3, 1987	April 1, 1988
Assets				
Current assets:				
Cash and temporary cash investments	$ 1,693	$1,115,647	$ 301,158	$ 701,195
Notes receivable	800			
Accounts receivable	516	1,936	14,461	2,758
Inventories	9,372	19,351	45,644	41,418
Prepaid expenses	706	7,411	1,056	2,838
Receivable on exercise of common stock purchase warrants			150,000	
Total current assets	$ 13,067	$1,144,345	$ 512,319	$ 749,199
Property and equipment				
Furniture and equipment, at cost	$ 47,195	$ 194,543	$ 389,780	$ 399,529
Leasehold improvements	17,978	106,571	291,586	261,769
Less accumulated depreciation	(6,079)	(24,417)	(81,419)	(155,362)
Net property and equipment	$ 59,094	$ 276,697	$ 599,947	$ 505,936
Other assets:				
Organizational expense	$ 2,643	$ 1,906	$ 1,168	—
Deposits	1,945	7,792	16,414	18,340
Total other assets	4.588	9,698	17,582	18,340
Total Assets	$ 76,749	$1,430,740	$1,129,848	$1,272,475
Liabilities and Stockholders' Equity				
Current liabilities:				
Notes payable	$ 25,672	$ 4,602	—	—
Accounts payable	10.257	37,624	130,856	66,459
Accrued liabilities	27,684	14,922	61,879	137,199
Long-term debt due within one year	2,470	8,963	32,370	47,352
Total current liabilities	$ 66,083	$ 66,111	$ 225,105	$ 251,010
Long-term debt due after one year	$ 4,269	$ 49,963	$ 151,260	$ 173,960
Subordinated debentures	60,000	—	—	—
Total liabilities	$130,352	$ 116,074	$ 376,365	$ 424,970
Stockholders' equity:				
Common stock	$ 6,286	$ 42,249	$ 43,788	$ 51,507
Capital in excess of par value	56,264	1,648,827	1,781,095	2,467,283
Accumulated deficit	(116,153)	(376,410)	(1,071,400)	(1,671,285)
Total equity (deficit)	(53,603)	1,314,666	753,483	847,505
Total liabilities and stockholders' equity	$ 76,749	$1,430,740	$1,129,848	$1,272,475

EXHIBIT 2   Pasta Perfect's Income Statement, 1985–1988

	March 29, 1985	March 28, 1986	April 3, 1987	April 1, 1988
Gross sales	$130,180	$303,458	$1,009,723	$1,289,037
Promotional discounts	(10,156)	(23,034)	(111,521)	(136,344)
Net sales	$120,024	$280,424	$ 898,202	$1,152,693
Operating costs and expenses:				
Cost of sales*	$ 86,938	$194,753	$ 440,195	$ 525,369
Selling, general, admin**	132,522	362,894	1,164,653	1,204,373
Total expenses	219.460	557,647	1,604,848	1,729,742
Operating loss	($ 99,436)	($277,223)	($ 706,646)	($ 577,049)
Other income (expense):				
Interest income	$ 447	$ 22,173	$ 39,266	$ 8,547
Interest expense	(6,967)	(8,543)	(29,440)	(33,250)
Miscellaneous income	7,270	3,336	1,830	1,867
Total other income (expense)	750	16,966	11,656	(22,836)
Net loss	($ 98,686)	($260,257)	($ 694,990)	($ 499,885)

* Full cost of products sold in Pasta Perfect stores, including both fixed and variable commissary costs associated with the manufacture of Pasta Perfect's pasta and sauce products.

** Includes all store level expenses other than cost of sales, and all regional and headquarters expenses.

of the company's pasta and sauce products. These changes resulted in a reported commissary contribution of $43,000 in FY 1987 (see Exhibit 3), compared to an expected break-even performance. Since products were passed from the commissary to the stores at transfer prices intended to recover the full variable and fixed costs to make them, these transfer prices were reduced at the beginning of FY 1988 so that the margin improvements (about 4 percent of retail sales) would be reflected in store operating performance figures.

More generally, new flavors of pasta and sauces were developed and offered on a rotating basis, in order to encourage more frequent customer visits to the stores. Lunch menus and espresso were added in the larger stores, and delivery and some catering were tested. Radio advertising and newspaper coupons were developed to expand consumer awareness and bring new customers into the stores, and sales contests and other employee incentives were put in place.

In 1987 and early 1988, approximately $200,000 was spent on a radio advertising campaign designed to stimulate lagging sales in the St. Louis stores (advertising expenses are reported in region overhead in Exhibit 3). While the campaign did increase awareness of Pasta Perfect in St. Louis and had a modestly positive impact on sales, the overall result was a significant increase in the size of St. Louis operating losses in the year ended April 1988 compared to the year ended April 1987 (see Exhibit 3). The lack of success of this effort, coupled with steadily worsening economic conditions in St. Louis led Walker to conclude that significant improvement in operating performance in St. Louis was extremely unlikely in the short run. While some St. Louis stores could be closed to mitigate theses losses, rent would still

EXHIBIT 3 Comparative Store Data for Pasta Perfect, 1987 versus 1988

	52 Week Year Ending April 1, 1988		52 Week Year Ending April 3, 1987		1987–1988 Increase (decrease)	
	Net Sales	Contribution	Net Sales	Contribution	Net Sales	Contribution
St. Louis stores						
#101	$ 55,881	($ 9,751)	$ 77,335	($ 6,636)	($ 21,454)	($ 3,116)
#102	158,655	33,611	165,597	21,451	(6,943)	(12,110)
#103	139,082	(11,074)	119,077	(22,518)	20,005	11,444
#104	closed	closed	27,725	(20,386)	(27,725)	20,386
#106	107,956	1,614	117,154	(2,890)	(9,199)	4,505
#107	59,345	(21,809)	56,703	(19,639)	2,643	(2,169)
#108	40,066	(10,965)	77,618	(12,420)	(37,551)	1,455
#109	105,825	(8,861)	91,748	(5,433)	14,077	(3,428)
#110	60,125	(19,478)	64,129	(6,385)	(4,004)	(13,092)
#111	64,546	(8,181)	24,232	43	40,315	(8,223)
	$ 791,481	($ 54,894)	$821,317	($ 74,815)	($ 29,836)	$ 19,921
Wholesale	13,336	4,059	12,387	3,237	2,649	821
St. Louis commissary*	–0–	11,475	–0–	43,227	(1,700)	(31,752)
St. Louis region overhead**		(95,901)		(209,322)		113,421
St. Louis totals	$ 804,817	($135,261)	$833,704	($237,673)	($ 28,887)	$102,411
Chicago stores						
#201***	$ 122,692	($ 14,276)	$ 30,989	($ 5,204)	$ 91,703	($ 9,072)
#202****	162,705	525	33,509	723	129,195	(198)
#203	62,480	(2,728)	–0–	–0–	62,480	(2,728)
	$ 347,876	($ 16,480)	$ 64,498	($ 4,381)	$283,378	($ 11,998)
Chicago commissary*	–0–	(6,325)	–0–	242		(6,567)
Chicago region overhead**		(50,749)		(29,122)		(21,627)
Chicago totals	$ 347,876	($ 73,554)	$ 64,498	($ 33,361)	$283,378	($ 40,193)
Administration*****		(245,237)		(395,523)		150,286
Store closing cost		(122,997)		(35,466)		(87,531)
Other		(22,837)		7,032		(29,869)
Total company	$1,152,693	($599,885)	$898,202	($694,990)	$254,491	$ 95,105

*   No sales are shown for the commissaries, since all their products are shipped to the stores and booked as intracompany transfers.
**   Region overhead consists of advertising and the salary and expenses of a regional manager.
***   Stores #201 and #202 opened in February 1987.
**** Store #203 opened in October 1987.
***** The decline of administrative expense from FY 1987 to FY 1988 is due largely to the elimination of a former vice president of marketing position and a store procedures and training position at headquarters, and a reduction in expense associated with new store openings, together with other administrative efficiencies. See Exhibit 5 for detail of administration expense.

be due unless landlords could find new tenants for the spaces, something Walker deemed unlikely in the deteriorating economic environment in St. Louis.

In Chicago, the picture was somewhat brighter, at least as to revenue. Given its sales problems in St. Louis (see Exhibit 3), Pasta Perfect had decided to secure the best possible locations for its stores in Chicago. All three Chicago stores were located in upscale neighborhoods with busy foot traffic passing the store, in contrast

EXHIBIT 4   Pasta Perfect's Target Performance for Each Store

Sales		$150,000
Cost of goods sold		60,000
Gross margin		90,000
Store operating expenses		
Payroll and benefits	33,000	
Store rent	12,000	
Equipment lease expense	7,000	
Occupancy costs*	3,000	
Other store operating	3,000	
Total store operating expenses		58,000
Store contribution to overhead and profit		32,000
Regional overhead per store**		10,000
Contribution to overhead and profit		$ 22,000

* Utilities and real estate taxes.
** Advertising and regional manager salary and expense.

to the strip shopping center approach which had been used in St. Louis. This decision had paid off in terms of sales, as Chicago store sales were 75 percent higher than St. Louis store sales, on an average per store basis. "Such locations do not come cheap, however," said Walker, and store rent averaged $35,000 per year in Chicago, compared to $13,000 in St. Louis. In addition, Walker found he had to pay $5,000 more in salary in Chicago to attract competent store managers. The additional rent and payroll costs, together with somewhat lower gross margins due to lower levels of production in Chicago and freight costs on goods shipped from St. Louis, consumed the lion's share of the extra revenues. Thus, the Chicago region was not profitable either.

While Walker held out hope that the Chicago market could be a profitable one for Pasta Perfect, his hopes were contingent on getting a few more stores opened to expand Pasta Perfect's market presence and permit economies of scale in pasta production and store supervision. Though he and his leasing agent had identified two promising locations, neither was currently vacant, although the leases of the current tenants were expiring within 90 to 120 days and would not be renewed. More importantly, however, his company was running out of time. "To open, say, three new stores will consume about $120,000 of our remaining capital, assuming equipment from underperforming stores in St. Louis is moved to Chicago. And by the time we get the new stores built our and open—six months or so from now—our current burn rate will leave us perilously low on cash.

In October 1988, Pasta Perfect's cash reserves stood at $450,000, and the company was losing $45,000 per month in cash, or $540,000 per year. Tom Walker had prepared a summary (see Exhibit 5) of the company's current cash flow performance, and he realized that the company's cash would not last long if things continued as they were. "At this point, it does not seem realistic to think we can turn our store operations around fast enough. Though our Chicago store sales are much better than our sales in St. Louis, our higher rent, payroll, and supervision costs eat up all the

EXHIBIT 5   Pasta Perfect's Sources of Annual Negative Cash Flow as of October 1988

St. Louis region operations	$135,000
Chicago region operations	80,000
Costs of being public company[1]	80,000
Store equipment lease payments	120,000
Other G & A[2]	175,000
Total	$590,000

[1]Includes cost of audited financial statements, legal fees, and expenses associated with reporting to Pasta Perfect's 7,000 public shareholders.
[2]Includes salaries of president, controller, two accounting clerks, secretary, office expenses.
Note: Store rent expenses, which are included in the operations figures above, totaled $130,000 per year for the St. Louis region (10 stores), and $140,000 per year for the Chicago region (4 stores). The leases were due to expire at various dates from 1989 through 1993.

extra revenues. We can't seem to make money in our stores, even in Chicago. And, while we sure wouldn't have come this far without the public offerings, it costs a lot of money to be publicly held (see Exhibit 5). I believe we have no choice but to consider alternatives to our present strategy. I'm really frustrated at our inability to make our stores economically viable!"

PASTA PERFECT'S FUTURE

Tom Walker had proposed two options for the board to consider. First, Pasta Perfect could continue to open additional stores in Chicago. Opening more stores in St. Louis was out of the question, since the St. Louis economy had soured in the last year. Many shopping centers in metropolitan St. Louis, including some where Pasta Perfect stores were located, were losing tenants; unemployment was rising, and other economic indicators pointed to a prolonged economic slump in the area. All of the St. Louis stores but two were losing money. Prospects in Chicago seemed brighter, since sales volumes in the new Chicago stores were so much higher than in the St. Louis stores. On the other hand, the higher operating costs in Chicago were troublesome and seemingly largely out of Tom's control, given the high levels of rent and manager salaries that prevailed in Chicago. "I must admit," said Walker, "that I am not at all confident that the Chicago stores as a group, much less the company as a whole, can be made profitable before we run out of cash."

Walker's second option was to change the direction of the company altogether, and shift from a specialty store retailing strategy to one of selling pasta and sauces in supermarkets. Contadina refrigerated fresh pasta had recently appeared in St. Louis supermarkets, but there were no well-established competitors. Individual supermarkets in Chicago had just begun experimenting with local pasta brands. Tom reasoned that, if the national fresh pasta market was projected to reach something like $125 million in 1991 (he had read this figure in a trade magazine), he could estimate the market potential in Pasta Perfect's markets by comparing their population to that of

EXHIBIT 6   Population Data for Pasta Perfect's Markets

Geographic Area	Population
Metropolitan St. Louis	2,493,000
Metropolitan Chicago	8,240,000
Missouri	5,117,000
Illinois	11,431,000
United States	248,710,000

Source: *Statistical Abstract of the United States,* U.S. Department of Commerce, 1994.

the United States in total (see Exhibit 6). It seemed likely that Contadina would secure the leading market share, given its head start, but Tom thought a 20 percent share for Pasta Perfect might be within reach by the end of calendar year 1989.

To enter the supermarket distribution channel would require that Pasta Perfect's products be packaged using the same gas-flushed technology employed by Contadina. The manufacturing and packaging line necessary would cost about $250,000 to install, and a small facility would have to be leased to accommodate it. No one in Pasta Perfect knew anything about this technology, and the company lacked sophisticated food manufacturing expertise. Alternatively, Walker could contract, at least at the outset, with either of two firms located in Alabama and Iowa which were already in gas-flushed pasta manufacturing and packaging. Doing so would save cash and perhaps mitigate the risks somewhat.

Walker reasoned that there would be room for the Pasta Perfect brand on the supermarket shelves, and that Pasta Perfect's good reputation might make it possible to secure shelf space. He had spoken to a merchandise manager at the leading supermarket chain in St. Louis, and she seemed open to the idea of carrying Pasta Perfect products in her chain's 60 stores. However, what kind of margins could be obtained was less certain. Heavy promotional costs and probable inefficiencies while Pasta Perfect installed and attempted to master the new technology (or lower margins if production were outsourced) could easily reduce margins (net of these costs) to as little as 20 percent of sales until all the kinks were worked out.

There were several additional risks and barriers to adopting the supermarket strategy, as well. The first was that Tom's skills and past experience were in retailing. He and others on the management team knew relatively little about selling *to* supermarket retailers. (Exhibit 7 shows profiles of the company's officers and directors.) Walker had managed groups of stores for a large apparel chain, so he knew how to set up store systems and attract and motivate store employees, skills which had enabled Pasta Perfect to grow quickly. But he had little experience on the buying side of the business, and his direct selling experience was limited to selling barbecue accessories to chain retailers in a previous entrepreneurial venture. No one on the board or the management team had any previous manufacturing experience, and Walker believed manufacturing expertise was among the critical success factors for a supermarket-driven strategy. Tom wondered whether he could attract a strong manufacturing person given the company's financial condition.

Additionally, many supermarket chains required substantial promotional allowances, including slotting allowances (fees paid to gain shelf space for new

---

EXHIBIT 7   Pasta Perfect's Officers and Board of Directors

Thomas L. Walker, President and Director, age 42, founded the Company in 1983. Mr. Walker has approximately 15 years experience in the retailing industry. From 1980–1983 Mr. Walker managed [. . .], a marketer of barbecue products and Walker Associates, a retail management consulting firm. From 1977–1980 he was employed by [a large apparel retailer] where he was responsible initially for implementing store systems, procedures and training programs for new stores organized by that corporation, and later for the general management of one division of stores. Mr. Walker received an MBA degree from the Stanford University Graduate School of Business.

Lloyd W. Anderson, age 39, has served as Controller of the Company since January 1986, and was elected Secretary and Treasurer in January 1988. Mr. Anderson has over 13 years of accounting and finance experience. From 1983 to 1985 he was a consultant for . . . a large residential land developer. From 1978 to 1983 he worked for . . . , last serving as vice president of finance. Mr. Anderson is a certified public accountant and member of the American Institute of Certified Public Accountants.

James P. Leonard, Director, age 35, has been a principal or general partner of [a venture capital firm] since 1983. From 1979 to 1983 he was President of [a medical equipment company]. Mr. Leonard is also secretary, treasurer and a director of [several companies]. Mr. Leonard is a graduate of Boston College.

William R. Patrick, Director, age 45, is a private investor and is president of . . . a consulting firm. Mr. Patrick was a founder, chief executive officer and chairman of the board of directors of . . . a publicly held company. Mr. Patrick received an MBA degree from the Harvard Business School.

Principal Shareholders

Name	Number of Shares
Thomas L. Walker	66,030,556[1]
James P. Leonard	33,159,518[2]
William R. Patrick	2,333,723
Venture Capital Company 1	36,459,794
Venture Capital Company 2	33,159,518
Total shares outstanding	525,456,630

---

[1]Does not include options to purchase up to an additional 22,500,000 shares contingent upon profits being achieved by the company. Mr. Walker's shares are held jointly with his wife Jan H. Walker.
[2]Mr. Leonard owns no shares of record personally, but may be considered the beneficial owner of the 33,159,505 shares owned by Venture Capital Company 2.

---

products, sometimes as high as $300 per item per store to introduce new items) and introductory deals, in order to place new products on their shelves. While Walker had heard that slotting allowances were sometimes waived for small local suppliers, the totality of these marketing costs could make it costly to change to a supermarket strategy. And even if the company were to close its retail stores to focus on supermarkets, the company remained liable for store rents and payments on equipment leases (see Exhibit 5). Walker did not know how quickly his company could get out from under these obligations.

A final concern was that, in the prospectus for the recent rights offering, the company had indicated that it would use the proceeds of the offering to expand its retail chain. Using the proceeds in another manner could prompt some shareholders to believe that the company had misled them in the rights offering prospects, and perhaps lead to shareholder lawsuits against the company and/or against its officers and directors personally. Tom knew his intentions were honorable in proposing the supermarket strategy, but he also knew that two of his directors served on the boards of other small firms, and they could not afford even the appearance of impropriety.

The board faced a difficult choice. The specialty stores were losing money. Unless these stores became profitable, the company's 7,000 shareholders would probably lose their entire investments. On the other hand, the supermarket channel, while potentially more attractive, carried substantial risks as well, and exposed the directors to possible personal liabilities if the new strategy failed and shareholders sued them based on the company's failure to disclose its planned use of funds from the rights offering.

Time was of the essence, since the company's cash reserves were dwindling. "I'm really troubled by our choices," said Jim Leonard. "I've lost some confidence in our retailing strategy, in spite of the fact that our products are head-and-shoulders better than anybody else's. I think supermarkets could sell our stuff, but I don't know that we can get it on the shelf, I don't know how long our learning curve might be with the new technology, and I'm concerned about doing something different with our shareholders' money than we said we would do. We're between a rock and a hard place, I'm afraid."

CORAL DIVERS RESORT*

CASE

14

Kent E. Neupert, *University of Houston*

Paul W. Beamish, *University of Western Ontario*

Jonathon Greywell locked the door on the equipment shed and began walking back along the boat dock to his office. He thought about the matters that had weighed heavily on his mind during the last few months. Over the years, Greywell had established a solid reputation for the Coral Divers Resort as a safe and knowledgeable scuba diving resort. It offered not only diving, but a beachfront location. As a small but well regarded all-around dive resort in the Bahamas, many divers had come to prefer his resort to other, crowded tourists resorts in the Caribbean.

However, over the last three years, revenues had declined and, for 1995, bookings were flat for the first half of the year. Greywell felt he needed to do something to increase business before things got worse. He wondered if he should add some specialized features to the resort that would distinguish it from others. One approach was to focus on family outings. Rascals in Paradise, a travel company that specialized in family diving vacations, had offered to help him convert his resort to one that specialized in family diving vacations. They had shown him the industry demographics that indicated that families were a growing market segment (see Exhibit 1) and made suggestions about what changes would need to be made at the resort. They had even offered to create menus for children and to show the cook how to prepare the meals.

*The research assistance of Tara Hanna is gratefully acknowledged. Certain names and other identifying information may have been disguised to protect confidentiality.

EXHIBIT 1   U.S. Population Demographics and Income Distribution: 1970, 1980, and 1990

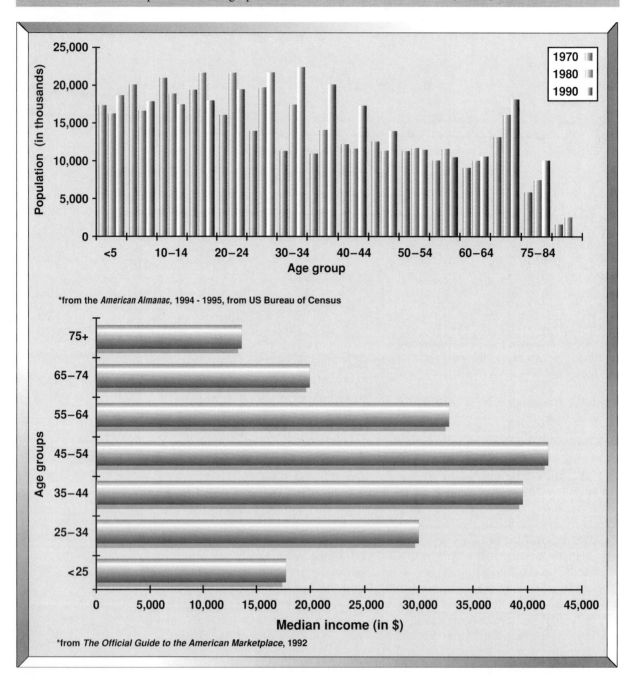

*from the *American Almanac*, 1994 - 1995, from US Bureau of Census

*from *The Official Guide to the American Marketplace*, 1992

    Another potential strategy for the Coral Divers Resort was adventure diving. Other resort operators in the Bahamas were offering adventure-oriented deep depth dives, shark dives, and night dives. The basic ingredients for adventure diving, reef sharks in the waters near New Providence and famous deep water coral walls, were already in place. However, either of these strategies, family or adventure, would require changes and additions to his current operations. He was not sure whether any of the changes was worth the time and investment or whether he should instead try to improve upon what he was already doing.

A final option, and one which he had only recently thought about, was to leave New Providence and try to relocate elsewhere. At issue here was how much he might be able to recover if he sold Coral Divers and whether better opportunities existed elsewhere in the Bahamas or around the Caribbean.

SCUBA DIVING INDUSTRY OVERVIEW

Skin diving is an underwater activity of ancient origin in which a diver swims freely, unencumbered by lines or air hoses. Modern skin divers use three pieces of basic equipment: a face mask for vision, webbed rubber fins for propulsion, and a snorkel tube for breathing just below the water's surface. The snorkel is a plastic tube shaped like a J and fitted with a mouthpiece. When the opening of the snorkel is above water, a diver is able to breathe. For diving to greater depths, the breath must be held; otherwise, water enters the mouth through the snorkel.

Scuba diving provides divers with the gift of time to relax and explore the underwater world without having to surface for their next breath. Scuba is an acronym for **S**elf **C**ontained **U**nderwater **B**reathing **A**pparatus. While attempts to perfect this type of apparatus date from the early 20th century, it was not until 1943 that the most famous scuba, or Aqualung, was invented by the Frenchmen Jacques-Yves Cousteau and Emil Gagnan. The Aqualung made recreational diving possible for millions of nonprofessional divers. Scuba diving is also called free diving, because the diver has no physical connection with the surface. Although some specially trained commercial scuba divers descend below 100 m (328 ft) for various kinds of work, recreational divers rarely go below a depth of 40 m (130 ft) because of increased risk of nitrogen narcosis, a type of intoxication similar to drunkenness, or oxygen toxicity, which causes blackouts or convulsions.

The scuba diver wears a tank that carries a supply of pressurized breathing gas, either air or a mixture of oxygen and other gases. The heart of the breathing apparatus is the breathing regulator and the pressure-reducing mechanisms that deliver gas to the diver on each inhalation. In the common scuba used in recreational diving, the breathing medium is air. As the diver inhales, a slight negative pressure occurs in the mouthpiece, which signals the valve that delivers the air to open. The valve closes when the diver stops inhaling, and a one-way valve allows the exhaled breath to escape as bubbles into the water. When using a tank and regulator, a diver can make longer and deeper dives and still breathe comfortably.

Along with scuba gear and its tanks of compressed breathing gases, the scuba diver's essential equipment include a soft rubber mask with a large faceplate; a soft rubber diving suit for protection from cold; long, flexible, swimming flippers for the feet; a buoyancy compensator device (known as a BC or BCD); weight belt; waterproof watch; wrist compass; and diver's knife. For protection from colder water, neoprene-coated foam rubber wet suits consisting of jacket, pants, hood, and gloves are worn.

Certification Organizations[1]

There are several international and domestic organizations that train and certify scuba divers. PADI (Professional Association of Diving Insructors), NAUI (National Asso-

---

[1]Information on certifying agencies drawn from materials published by the various organizations.

ciation of Underwater Instructors), SSI (Scuba Schools International), and NASDS (National Association of Scuba Diving Schools) are the most well known of these organizations. Of these, PADI is the largest certifying organization.

PADI (Professional Association of Diving Instructors) is the largest recreational scuba diver training organization in the world. Founded in 1967, PADI has issued more than 5.5 million certifications since it began operation. Since 1985, seven of every ten American divers and an estimated 55 percent of all divers around the world are trained by PADI instructors using PADI's instructional programs. At present PADI certifies well over half a million divers internationally each year and has averaged a 12 percent increase in certifications each year since 1985. In 1994, PADI International issued 625,000 certifications, more than in any other single year in company history.

PADI's main headquarters is in Santa Ana, California. Its distribution center is in the U.K., and it has seven local area offices in Australia, Canada, Japan, New Zealand, Norway, Sweden, and Switzerland with professionals and member groups in 175 countries and territories. PADI is made up of four groups: PADI Retail Association, PADI International Resort Association, Professional Members, and PADI Alumni Association. The three association groups emphasize the "Three E's" of recreational diving: Education, Equipment, and Experience. By supporting each facet, PADI provides holistic leadership to advance recreational scuba diving and snorkel swimming to equal status with other major leisure activities, while maintaining and improving the excellent safety record PADI has experienced. PADI offers seven levels of instruction and certification ranging from entry level to instructor.

NAUI (National Association of Underwater Instructors) first began operation in 1960. The organization was formed by a nationally recognized group of instructors known as the National Diving Patrol. Since its beginning, NAUI has been active worldwide, certifying sport divers in various levels of proficiency from basic skin diver to instructor. In addition, NAUI regularly conducts specialty courses for cave diving, ice diving, wreck diving, underwater navigation, and search and recovery.

Industry Demographics[2]

Scuba diving has grown steadily in popularity, especially in recent years. For the period 1989–1994, increases in the number of certifications averaged over 10 percent per year. The total number of certified divers worldwide is estimated to be over 10 million. Of these newly certified scuba divers, approximately 65 percent are male and 35 percent are female. Approximately half are married. Approximately 70 percent of them are between the ages of 18 and 34, while about 25 percent are between 35 and 49 (see Exhibit 2). They are generally well educated, with 80 percent having a college education. Overwhelmingly, they are employed in professional, managerial, and technical occupations. Their average annual household income is $75,000. Forty-five percent of divers travel most often with their families. Another 40 percent travel with friends or informal groups.

Divers are attracted to diving for various reasons: seeking adventure and being with nature are the most often cited reasons (over 75 percent for each). Socializing, stress relief, and travel also are common motivations. Two-thirds of divers travel overseas on diving trips once every three years, while 60 percent travel domestically on dive trips each year. On average, divers spend $2,816 on dive trips annually, with

---

[2]This section draws from results of surveys conducted by SCUBA diving organizations and publications for the years 1991–1993.

EXHIBIT 2 Diver Demographics: Age of Divers

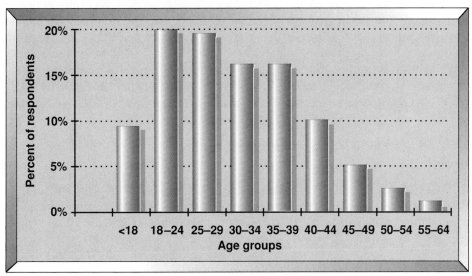

*Information taken from the PADI 1991 Diver Survey Results and Analysis, Premiminary Draft

an average equipment investment of $2,300. Aside from upgrades and replacements, the equipment purchase could be considered a one-time cost. Warm water diving locations are generally chosen 2 to 1 over cold water diving sites. Cozumel in Mexico, the Cayman Islands, and the Bahamas are the top three diving destinations outside the continental United States for Americans.

According to a consumer survey, the "strongest feelings" that divers associate with their scuba diving experiences are "excitement" and "peacefulness." In a recent survey, the two themes drew an equal number of responses. However, there seem to be very distinct differences in the two responses. One suggests a need for stimulation, while the other suggests relaxation and escape. Visual gratification ("beauty") is another strong motivation for divers. The feelings of "freedom, weightlessness, and flying" were also popular responses.

Under PADI regulations, 12 is the minimum age for certification by the majority of scuba training agencies. At age 12, a child can earn a Junior Diver certification. A Junior Diver meets the same standards as an Open Water diver but generally must be accompanied on dives by a parent or other certified adult. At age 15, the Junior Diver certification can be upgraded to Open Water status by an instructor. This upgrade may require a skills review and evaluation. Pre-dive waiver and release forms require the signature of a parent or guardian until the minor turns 18.

A cautious approach to young divers is based on the concept of readiness to dive. An individual's readiness to dive is determined by physical, mental, and emotional maturity. Physical readiness is easiest to access: Is the child large and strong enough to handle scuba equipment? An air tank and weight belt can weigh over 40 pounds, although most dive shops can provide equipment specially sized for smaller divers. Mental readiness refers to whether the child has the academic background and conceptual development to understand diving physics and perform the arithmetic required for certification. The arithmetic understanding focuses on allowable bottom time, which requires factoring in depth, number of dives, and length of dives.

Emotional readiness is the greatest concern. Will the junior diver accept the responsibility of being a dive buddy? Divers never dive alone and dive buddies are supposed to look out for and rely on each other. Do they comprehend the safety rules of diving and willingly follow them? Most dive centers accept students from age 12, but the final determination of readiness to dive rests with the scuba instructor. Instructors are trained to evaluate the readiness of all students prior to completion of the course work and will only award a certification to those who earn it, regardless of age.

DIVING IN THE BAHAMAS[3]

New Providence Island, the Bahamas

New Providence Island is best known for its major population center, Nassau. Nassau's early development was based on its superb natural harbor. As the capital of the Bahamas, it is the seat of government, also home to 400 banks, elegant homes, ancient forts, and a wide variety of duty-free shopping. It has the island's most developed tourist infrastructure with elegant resort hotels, casinos, cabaret shows, and cruise ship docks. More than two-thirds of the population of the Bahamas live on New Providence and most of these 150,000 people live in or near Nassau, on the northeast corner of the island.

With thousands of vacationers taking resort courses (introductory scuba courses taught in resort pools), Nassau has become known as a destination that is as good for an exploratory first dive as it is for more advanced diving. There are many professional dive operations in the Nassau/Paradise Island area. (See Exhibit 3.) While all offer resort courses, many also offer a full menu of dive activities designed for the more advanced and experienced diver. Within a 30-minute boat ride of most operations are shipwrecks, beautiful shallow reefs, and huge schools of fish.

In contrast to the bustle of Nassau, the south side of New Providence Island is quieter and more laid back. Large tracts of pine trees and rolling hills dominate the central regions, while miles of white sand beach surround the island. At the west end of the island is Lyford Cay, an exclusive residential area. Nearby, the winding canals of the Coral Harbour area offer easy access to the sea. While golf and tennis are available, the primary attraction is good scuba diving and top quality dive operators.

The southwest side of the island has been frequently used as an underwater movie/film set. The "Bond Wrecks" are popular diving destinations for divers and operators. The Vulcan Bomber used in *Thunderball* has aged into a framework draped with colorful gorgonians and sponges. The freighter Tears of Allah, where James Bond eluded the Tiger Shark in *Never Say Never Again,* remains a popular dive attraction in just 40 feet of water. The photogenic appeal of this wreck has improved with age as more and more marine life congregates on this artificial reef.

There are also natural underwater attractions. Shark Wall and Shark Buoy are popular dive spots. Drop-dives like Tunnel Wall feature a network of crevices and tunnels beginning in 30 feet of water and exiting along the vertical wall at 70 or 80 feet. Southwest Reef offers magnificent coral heads in only 15 to 30 feet of water, with schooling grunts, squirrelfish, and barracuda. A favorite of the shallow reef areas is Goulding Cay, where broad stands of Elkhorn coral reach nearly to the surface.

---

[3]Based on information drawn from *The Islands of the Bahamas; 1994 Dive Guide,* published by the Bahamas Ministry of Tourism, Commonwealth of the Bahamas, in conjunction with The Bahama Diving Association.

EXHIBIT 3   Names and Location of Diving Operators in the Bahamas (Based on The Bahamas Diving Association membership)

Abaco
Brendal's Dive Shop
Dive Abaco
Walker's Cay Undersea Adventures

Andros
Small Hope Bay Lodge

Bimini
Bimini Undersea Adventures

Cat Island
Cat Island Dive Center

Eleuthera/Habour Island
Romora Bay Club
Valentine's Dive Center

Exuma
Exuma Fantasea

Long Island
Stella Maris Resort

New Providence Island/Nassau
Bahama Divers
Coral Divers Resort
Custom Aquatics
Dive Dive Dive
Diver's Haven
Nassau Scuba Center
Stuart Cove's Dive South Ocean
Sun Divers
Sunskiff Divers

San Salvador
Riding Rock Inn

Live-Aboard Dive Boats
Blackbeard's Cruises
Bottom Time Adventures
Nekton Diving Cruises
Out Island Voyages
Sea Dragon
Sea Fever Diving Cruises

TYPES OF DIVING

A wide array of diving activities are available in the Bahamas. These include shark dives, wreck dives, wall dives, reef dives, drift dives, night dives, and so forth. Illustrative examples follow.

Shark Diving

The top three operators of shark dives in the Caribbean are in the Bahamas. While shark diving trips vary with the operators running them, there is at least one common factor in the Bahamas: the Caribbean reef shark (Carcharhinus perezi). When the dive boat reaches the site, the sound of the motor acts as a dinner bell. Even before the divers are in the water, the sharks gather for their handouts.

Long Island in the Bahamas was the first area to promote shark feed dives on a regular basis. This method began twenty years ago and has remained relatively unchanged. The feed is conducted as a feeding frenzy. Sharks circle as divers enter the water. After the divers position themselves with their backs to a coral wall, the feeder enters the water with a bucket of fish. This is placed in the sand in front of the divers and the action develops quickly. At Walker's Cay, in Abaco, the method is similar except for the number and variety of sharks in the feed. While Caribbean reef sharks make up the majority, lemon sharks, bull sharks, hammerhead sharks, and other species also appear.

The shark feed off Freeport, Grand Bahama, is a very organized event in which the sharks are fed either by hand or off the point of a polespear. The divers are arranged in a semi-circle with safety divers guarding the viewers as the feeder is positioned at the middle of the group. If the sharks become unruly, the food is withheld until they calm down. The sharks then go into a regular routine of circling, taking their place in line and advancing to receive the food. Although the sharks come within touching distance, most divers resist the temptation to reach out.

Shark Wall, on the southwest side of New Providence, is a pristine drop-off decorated with masses of colorful sponges along the deep water abyss known as the Tongue of the Ocean. Divers position themselves along sand patches among the coral heads in about 50 feet of water as Caribbean reef sharks and an occasional bull or lemon shark cruise midwater in anticipation of a free handout. During the feeding period, the bait is controlled and fed from a polespear by an experienced feeder. There are usually 6 to 12 sharks present, ranging from four to eight feet in length. Some operators make two dives to this site, allowing divers to cruise the wall with the sharks in a more natural way before the feeding dive.

The Shark Buoy, also on the southwest side of New Providence, is tethered in 6,000 feet of water. Its floating surface mass attracts a wide variety of ocean marine life such as dolphin fish, jacks, rainbow runners and silky sharks. The silky sharks are typically small, three to five feet long, but swarm in schools of six to twenty, with the sharks swimming up to the divermasters' hands to grab the bait.

From the operator's standpoint, the only special equipment needed for shark dives is a chain mail diving suit for the feeder's protection, some type of feeding apparatus, and intestinal fortitude. The thrill of diving among sharks is the main attraction for the divers. For the most part, the dives are safe, with only the feeder taking an occasional nick from an excited shark. Divers participating in shark dives are required to sign waivers prior to the actual dive. As the fine print in most life insurance policies notes, claims for any scuba-related accidents are not payable. However, there do exist specialty insurers such as Divers Alert Network.

Wreck Diving

Wreck diving is divided into three levels: nonpenetration, limited penetration, and full penetration. Full penetration and deep wreck diving is normally done only by divers who have completed rigorous training and have extensive diving experience. Nonpenetration wreck diving refers to recreational diving on wrecks without entering an overhead environment that prevents direct access to the surface. Divers with open water certification are qualified for this type of diving without further training as long as they are comfortable with the diving conditions and the wreck's depth. Limited penetration wreck diving is defined as staying within ambient light and always in sight of an exit. Full penetration wreck diving involves an overhead environment away from ambient light and beyond sight of an exit. Safely and extensively exploring the insides of a wreck involves formal training and mental strength. On this type of dive, a mistake can be fatal.

Wall Diving

In a few regions of the world, island chains, formed by volcanos and coral, have been altered by movements of the earth's crustal plates. Extending approximately due east-west across the central Caribbean Sea is the boundary between the North American and Caribbean crustal plates. The shifting of these plates has created some of the most spectacular diving environments in the world, characterized by enormous cliffs

2,000 to 6,000 feet high. At the cliffs, known as walls, the diver experiences the overwhelming scale and dynamic forces that shape the ocean more than in any other underwater environment. It is on the walls that a diver is most likely to experience the feeling of free motion, or flying, in boundless space. Many of the dives in the Bahamas are wall dives.

Reef Diving

Reefs generally are made up of three areas: a reef flat, a lagoon or bay, and a reef crest. The depth in the reef flat averages only a few feet with an occasional deeper channel. The underwater life on a shallow reef flat may vary greatly in abundance and diversity within a short distance. The reef flat is generally a protected area, not exposed to strong winds or waves, making it ideal for novice or family snorkellers. The main feature distinguishing bay and lagoon environments from a reef flat is depth. Caribbean lagoons and bays may reach depths of 60 feet but many provide teaming underwater ecosystems in as little as 15–20 feet. This is excellent for underwater photography and ideal for families or no-decompression-stop diving. The reef's crest is the outer boundary that shelters the bay and flats from the full force of the ocean's waves. Since the surging and pounding of the waves is too strong for all but the most advanced divers, most diving takes place in the protected bay waters.

FAMILY DIVING RESORTS

The current average age of new divers is 36. As the median age of new divers increased, families became a rapidly growing segment of the vacation travel industry. Many parents are busy and do not spend as much time with their children as they would prefer. Many parents who dive would like to have a vacation that would combine diving and spending time with their children. In response to increasing numbers of parents travelling with children, resort operators have added amenities ranging from babysitting services and kids' camps to dedicated family resorts with special facilities and rates. The resort options available have greatly expanded in recent years. At all-inclusive self-contained resorts, one price includes everything: meals, accommodations, daytime and evening activities, and water sports. Many of these facilities offer special activities and facilities for children. Diving is included or available nearby.

For many divers, the important part of the trip is the quality of the diving, not the quality of the accommodations. But for divers with families, the equation changes. Children, especially younger children, may find it difficult to do without a comfortable bed, television, or VCR, no matter how good the diving promises to be. Some resorts, while not dedicated to family vacations, do make accommodations for divers with children. Condos and villas are an economical and convenient vacation option for divers with children. The additional space of this type of accommodation allows parents to bring along a babysitter. Having a kitchen on hand makes the task of feeding children simple and economical. Most diving destinations in the Bahamas, Caribbean and Pacific offer condo, villa and hotel-type accommodations. Some hotels organize entertaining and educational activities for children while parents engage in their own activities.

As the number of families vacationing together has increased, some resorts and dive operators have started special promotions and programs. On Bonaire, part of the Netherlands Antilles, August has been designated family month. During this month, the island caters to families, with a special welcome kit for children and island-wide activities including "eco-walks" at a flamingo reserve, snorkelling lessons, and evening entertainment for all ages. In conjunction, individual resorts and restaurants offer family packages and discounts. Similarly, in Honduras, which has very good diving, one resort started a children's dolphin camp during summer months. While diving family members are out exploring the reefs, children between ages 8 and 14 spend their days learning about and interacting with a resident dolphin population. The program includes classroom and in-water time as well as horseback riding and paddle boating.

One travel company, Rascals in Paradise (1-800-U-RASCAL), specializes in family travel packages. The founders, Theresa Detchemendy and Deborah Baratta, are divers, mothers, and travel agents who have developed innovative packages for diving families. Theresa says, "The biggest concern for parents is their children's safety, and then what the kids will do while they're diving or enjoying an evening on the town." The Rascals people have worked with a number of family-run resorts all over the world to provide daily activities, responsible local nannies, and child-safe facilities with safe balconies, playgrounds, and children's pools.

They have also organized family weeks at popular dive destinations in Belize, Mexico, and the Cayman Islands. Family week packages account for over 50 percent of Rascals' bookings each year. On these scheduled trips, groups of three to six families share a teacher/escort who brings along a fun program tailored for children and serves as activities director for the group. Rascals Special Family Weeks packages are priced based on a family of four (two adults and two children, age 2–11) and include a teacher/escort, one babysitter for each family, children's activities, meals, airport transfers, taxes, services, and cancellation insurance (see Exhibit 4). For example, in 1995, a seven-night family vacation at Hotel Club Akumal, on the Yucatan coast, was $2,080–$3,100 per family.[4] Rascals also packages independent family trips to 57 different condos, villas, resorts, or hotels that offer scuba diving. An independent family trip would not include a teacher/escort (see Exhibit 5). A seven-night independent family trip to Hotel Club Akumal ran $624–$1,779 in 1995.[5]

Rascals' approach is unique in the travel industry because they personally select the resorts with which they work. "We try to work with small properties so our groups are pampered and looked after,' says Detchemendy. "The owners are often parents and their kids are sometimes on the property. They understand the characteristics of kids." Typically, Detchemendy and Baratta visit each destination, often working with the government tourist board in identifying potential properties. If the physical structure is already in place, it is easy to add the resort to the Rascals booking list. If modifications are needed, the two sit down with the management and outline what needs to be in place so that the resort can be part of the Rascals program.

Rascals evaluates resorts according to several factors: (1) Is the property friendly toward children and does it want them? (2) How does the property rate in terms of safety? (3) What are the facilities and is there a separate room to be used as a Rascals Room? (4) Does the property provide babysitting and child care by individuals who are screened and locally known? A successful example of this approach is Hotel Club Akumal, in Akumal, Mexico. Detchemendy and Baratta helped the resort expand its market reach by building a family-oriented resort that became part of the Rascals

---

[4]Lunch and airport transfer not included. Prices reflect seasonal fluctuations and are subject to change. Airfares not included.

[5]Based on a family of four with two adults and two children age 2–11. Rates are to be used as a guide only. Each booking is quoted separately and will be dependent on season, type of accommodation, ages and number of children, meal and activity inclusions. Airfares not included.

EXHIBIT 4   Rascals in Paradise Pricing Guide*: Rascals Special Family Weeks (in U.S. dollars)

Destination	Duration	Price	Notes
Bahamas			
South Ocean Beach	7 nights	$3,120–$3,970	Lunch not included
Small Hope Bay	7 nights	$3,504	Scuba diving included. Local host only.
Mexico			
Hotel Buena Vista	7 nights	$2,150–$2,470	
Hotel Club Akumal	7 nights	$2,080–$3,100	Lunch and airport transfer not included.

*Prices are based on a family of four with two adults and two children aged 2–11. All packages include the following (except as noted): Accommodations, Rascals escort, meals, babysitter, children's activities. airport transfers, taxes & services, and a $2,500 cancellation insurance per family booking. Airfares not included.

EXHIBIT 5   Rascals in Paradise Pricing Guide*: Independent Family Trips (in U.S. dollars)

Destination	Duration	Price	Notes
Bahamas			
South Ocean Beach	7 nights	$1,355–$1,771	
Small Hope bay	7 nights	$2,860–$3,560	All meals, bar service, baby-sitter, and diving included.
Hope Town Harbour Lodge	7 nights	$962–$1,121	
Treasure Cay	7 nights	$875–$1,750	
Stella Maris, Long Island	7 nights	$1,547–$2,597	
Mexico			
Hotel Buena Vista	7 nights	$1,232–$1,548	All meals included
Hotel Club Akumal	7 nights	$624–$1,779	
Hotel Presidente	7 nights	$1,120–$1,656	
La Concha	7 nights	$655–$963	
Plaza Las Glorias	7 nights	$632–$1,017	

*Prices are based on a family of four with two adults and two children aged 2–11. Rates are per week (seven nights) and include accommodations and applicable taxes. These rates are to be used as a guide only. Each booking is quoted separately and varies according to season, type of accommodation, ages and number of children, and meal and activity inclusions. Airfares not included.

program. Baratta explained "In that case, we were looking for a place close to home, with a multilevel range of accommodations, that offered something other than a beach, that was family friendly, and not in Cancun. We found Hotel Club Akumal, but they didn't have many elements in place, so we had to work with them. We established a meal plan, an all-inclusive product and designated activities for kid. We went into the kitchen and created a children's menu and we asked them to install a little kids' playground that's shaded." The resort became one of their most popular family destinations.

Rascals offered two types of services to resort operators interested in creating family vacations. One was a consulting service. For a modest daily fee plus expenses, Baratta or Detchemendy, or both, would conduct an on-site assessment of the resort. This usually took one or two days. They would provide a written report to the resort regarding needed additions or modifications to the resort to make if safe and attractive for family vacations. Possible physical changes might include: the addition of a Rascals room, child-safe play equipment, and modifications to existing buildings and structures, such as rooms, railings, and docks, to prevent child injuries. Rascals always tried to use existing equipment or equipment available nearby. Other nonstructural changes could include: the addition of educational sessions, playtimes, and other structured times for entertaining children while their parents were diving. The report also included an implementation proposal. Then after implementation, the resort could decide whether or not to list with Rascals for bookings.

Under the second option, Rascals provided the consulting service at no charge to the resort. However, they asked that any requests for family bookings be referred back to Rascals. Rascals would then also list and actively promote the resort through its brochures and referrals. For resorts using the Rascals booking option, Rascals would provide premiums such as hats and T-shirts in addition to the escorted activities. This attention to the family was what differentiated a Rascals resort from other resorts. Generally, companies that promoted packages received net rates from the resorts that were from 20 percent to 50 percent lower than "rack" rates. Rascals, in turn, promoted these special packages to the travel industry in general and paid a portion of their earnings out in commissions to other travel agencies.

Rascals tried to work with its resorts to provide packaged and prepaid vacations. This approach created a win-win situation for the resort managers and the vacationer. A packaged or an all-inclusive vacation was a cruise ship approach. It allowed the inclusion of many activities in the package. For example, such a package might include seven nights' lodging, all meals, babysitting, children's activities, and scuba diving. This approach allowed the vacationer to know, up front, what to expect. Moreover, the cost would be included in one set price, so that the family would not have to pay for each activity as it came along. The idea was to remove the surprises and make the stay enjoyable. It also allowed the resort operator to bundle activities together, providing more options than might otherwise be offered. As a result, the package approach was becoming popular with both resort owners and vacationers.

In its bookings, Rascals required prepayment of trips. This resulted in higher revenues for the resort since all activities were paid for in advance. Ordinarily, resorts on their own might only require a two- or three-night room deposit. Then, the family would pay for the rest of the room charge on leaving, after paying for other activities or services as they were used. While vacationers might think they had a less expensive trip this way, in fact, prepaid activities were generally cheaper than a la carte activities. Moreover, they potentially yielded lower revenues for the resorts. Rascals promoted prepaid vacations as a win-win, low stress approach to travel. Rascals had been very successful with the resorts it listed. Fifty percent of their bookings were repeat business, and many inquiries were based on word-of-mouth referrals. All in all, Rascals provided a link to the family vacation market segment that the resort might not otherwise have. It was common for Rascals' listed resorts to average annual bookings of 90 percent.

CORAL DIVERS RESORT

Coral Divers Resort had been in operation 10 years. Annual revenues had reached as high as $554,000. Profits generally had been in the 2 percent range, but for the past two years, losses had been experienced. The expected turnaround in profits in 1994 had never materialized (see Exhibits 6 and 7). While not making them rich, the

EXHIBIT 6   Coral Divers Resorts, Balance Sheets, 1992–1994

	Fiscal Year ending		
	1994	**1993**	**1992**
Assets			
Current assets:			
Cash	$ 5,362	$ 8.943	$ 15,592
Accounts receivable	2,160	8,660	2,026
Inventories	5,519	6,861	9,013
Prepaid expenses	9,065	8,723	8,195
Total current assets	22,106	33,187	34,826
Fixed assets:			
Land	300,000	300,000	300,000
Building	200,000	200,000	200,000
Less: accumulated depreciation	(70,000)	(60,000)	(50,000)
Boats	225,000	225,000	225,000
Less: accumulated depreciation	(157,500)	(135,000)	(112,500)
Vehicles	54,000	54,000	54,000
Less: accumulated depreciation	(32,400)	(21,600)	(10,800)
Diving equipment	150,000	150,000	150,000
Less: accumulated depreciation	(90,000)	(60,000)	(30,000)
Total fixed assets	579,100	652,400	725,700
Total assets	$601,206	$685,587	$760,526
Liabilities and Shareholders Equity			
Current liabilities:			
Accounts payable	$ 1,689	$ 4,724	$ 1,504
Bank loan	20,000	0	2.263
Mortgage payable, current portion	25,892	25,892	25,892
Note payable, current portion	40,895	40,895	40,895
Total current liabilities	88,476	71,511	70,554
Long-term liabilities:			
Mortgage payable, due in 1996	391,710	417,602	443,494
Note payable, 5 year	81,315	122,210	163,105
Total long-term liabilities	473,025	539,812	606,599
Total liabilities	561,501	611,323	677,153
Shareholders' equity			
Jonathan Greywell, capital	44,879	44,879	44,879
Retained earnings	(5,174)	29,385	38,494
Total shareholders' equity	39,705	74,264	83,373
Total liabilities and shareholders's equity	$601,206	$685,587	$760,526

EXHIBIT 7   Coral Divers Resort, Income Statements, 1992–1994

	Fiscal Year ending		
	1994	**1993**	**1992**
Revenue:			
Diving & lodging packages	$482,160	$507,670	$529,820
Day diving	11,680	12,360	14,980
Certifications	5,165	5,740	7,120
Lodging	2,380	1,600	1,200
Miscellaneous	1,523	1,645	1,237
Total revenues	502,908	529,015	554,357
Expenses:			
Advertising and promotion	15,708	15,240	13,648
Bank charges	1,326	1,015	975
Boat maintenance and fuel	29,565	31,024	29,234
Cost of goods sold	762	823	619
Depreciation	73,300	73,300	73,300
Dues and fees	3,746	4,024	3,849
Duties and taxes	11,405	18,352	17,231
Insurance	36,260	34,890	32,780
Interest, mortgage, note, and loan	40,544	40,797	41,174
Management salary	31,600	31,600	31,600
Office supplies	12,275	12,753	11,981
Professional fees	11,427	10,894	10,423
Repairs and maintenance, building	15,876	12,379	9,487
Salaries, wages, and benefits	196,386	194,458	191,624
Telephone and fax	9,926	9,846	7,689
Trade shows	14,523	14,679	14,230
Utilities	20,085	19,986	17,970
Vehicles, maintenance, and fuel	12,753	12,064	11,567
Total expenses	537,467	538,124	519,381
Net income	$ (34,559)	$ (9,109)	$ 34,976
Retained earnings, beginning	$ 29,385	$ 38,494	$ 3,518
Retained earnings, ending	(5,174)	29,385	38,494

Note: Bahama $1 = US $1

business had provided an adequate income for Greywell and his wife, Margaret, and their two children, Allen, age seven, and Winifred, age five. However, revenues had continued to decline. From talking with other operators, Greywell understood that resorts with strong identities and reputations for quality service were doing well. Greywell thought that the Coral Divers Resort had not distinguished itself in any particular aspect of diving or as a resort.

The Coral Divers Resort property was located on a deep water channel on the southwest coast of the island of New Providence in the Bahamas. The property occupied three acres and had beach access. There were six cottages on the property,

EXHIBIT 8   Coral Divers Resort Pricing Guide*

| | | Family Dive Vacations | |
Destination	Duration	Price	Notes
Bahamas			
Coral Divers Resort	7 nights	$1,355–$1,455	Standard accommodations, continental breakfast, and daily two-tank dive included.
Coral Divers Resort	7 nights	$1,800–$1,950	Deluxe accommodations, continental breakfast, and daily two-tank dive included.

*Prices are based on a family of four with two adults and two children aged 2–11. Rates are per week (seven nights) and include accommodations and applicable taxes. Rates varied somewhat based on season, type of accommodation, ages and number of children. Airfares not included. Prices dropped to $600–700 per week for the standard package and $800–900 for deluxe accommodation if diving was excluded.

each having a kitchenette, a full bath, a bedroom with two full-size beds, and a living room with two sleeper sofas. Four of the units had been renovated with new paint, tile floors, microwave, color TV, and VCR. The two other units ranged from "adequate" to "comfortable". Greywell tried to use the renovated units primarily for families and couples, while putting groups of single divers in the other units. Also on the property was a six-unit attached motel-type structure (see Exhibit 8 for prices). Each of these units had two full-size beds, a pull-out sofa, sink, refrigerator, microwave, and TV. The resort had the space and facilities on the property for a kitchen and dining room, but it had not been used. However, there was a small family-run restaurant and bar within walking distance.

Greywell had three boats that could carry from eight to twenty passengers each. Two were 40-foot fiberglass V-hull boats powered by a single diesel inboard with a cruising speed of 18 knots; both had a protective cabin with dry storage space. The third was a 35-foot covered platform boat. Greywell also had facilities for air dispensing, tank storage, and equipment repair, rental, and sale.

Coral Divers Resort, affiliated with PADI and NAUI, had a staff of 11, including four scuba diving instructors. Greywell, who worked full-time at the resort, was a diving instructor certified by both PADI and NAUI. The three other diving instructors had various backgrounds. One was a former U.S. Navy SEAL working for Coral Divers as a way to gain resort experience. One was a local Bahamian whom Greywell had known for many years. The third was a Canadian who had come to the Bahamas on a winter holiday and never left. There were two boat captains and two mates. Given the size of the operation, the staff was scheduled to provide overall coverage, with all of the staff rarely working at the same time. In addition, there was a housekeeper, a groundskeeper, and a person who minded the office and store. Greywell's wife, Margaret, worked at the business on a part-time basis, taking care of administrative activities such as accounting and payroll. The rest of her time was spent looking after their two children and their home.

A typical diving day at Coral Divers for Greywell began around 7:30 AM. He would open the office and review the activities list for the day. If there were any divers that needed to be picked up at the resorts in Nassau or elsewhere on the island, the van driver would need to leave by 7:30 AM to be back for the 9 AM departure.

Most resort guests began to gather around the office and dock about 8:30. By 8:45, the day's captain and mate began loading the diving gear for the passengers.

The boat left at 9 AM. Morning dives were usually "two-tank dives," that is, two dives utilizing one tank of air each. The trip to the first dive site took about 20–30 minutes. Once there, the captain would explain the dive, the special attractions of the dive, and tell everyone when they were expected back on board. Most dives lasted 30–45 minutes, depending on depth. The deeper the dive, the faster the air consumption. A divemaster always accompanied the divers on the trip down. The divemaster's role was generally to supervise the dive. The divemaster was responsible for the safety and conduct of the divers while under water.

Once back on board, the boat would move to the next site. Greywell tried to plan dives that had sites near each other. For example, the first dive might be a wall dive in 60 feet of water, while the second would be a nearby wreck 40 feet down. The second would also last about 40 minutes. If things went well, the boat would be back at the resort by noon. This allowed for lunch and sufficient surface time for divers who might be going back out in the afternoon. Two morning dives were part of the resort package. Whether the boat went out in the afternoon depended on whether enough nonresort guest divers had contracted for afternoon dives. If they had, Greywell was happy to let resort guests ride along and dive free of charge. If there were not enough outside paying divers, there were no afternoon dive trips and the guests were on their own to swim at the beach, go sightseeing, or just relax. When space was available, it was possible for nondivers (either snorkellers or bubble-watchers) to join the boat trip for a fee of $15–$25.

Greywell's Options

Greywell's bookings ran 90 percent of capacity during the high season (December through May) and 50 percent during the low season (June through November). Ideally, he wanted to increase the number of bookings for the resort and dive businesses during both seasons (see Exhibit 9 for comparative costs of diving vs. skiing vacations). Adding additional diving attractions could increase both resort and dive revenues. Focusing on family vacations could increase revenues since families would probably increase the number of paying guests per room. Break-even costs were calculated based on two adults sharing a room. Children provided an additional revenue source since the cost of the room had been covered by the adults, and children under 12 incurred no diving-related costs. However, either strategy, adding adventure diving to his current general offerings or adjusting the focus of the resort to encourage family diving vacations, would require some changes and cost money. The question became whether the changes would increase revenue enough to justify the costs and effort involved.

Emphasizing family diving vacations would probably require some changes to the physical property of the resort. Four of the cottages had already been renovated. The other two also would need to be upgraded. This would run $10,000 to $20,000 each, depending on the amenities added. The Bahamas had duties up to 50 percent, which caused renovation costs involving imported goods to be expensive. The attached motel-type units also would need to be refurbished at some point. He had the space and facilities for a kitchen and dining area, but had not done anything with it. The Rascals in Paradise people had offered to help set up a children's menu. He could hire a chef or cook, attempt to do the cooking and run the dining room himself, or offer the concession to the nearby restaurant or someone else. He would also need to

EXHIBIT 9   A Canadian Vacation Comparison: Diving in Nassau vs. Skiing in Whistler/Banff (in Canadian dollars)

Nassau—7 Nights*

	January 5–11			February 16–22		
	Dbl./Person Range	Child	Family (3)	Dbl./Person	Child	Family (3)
Average cost for 12 packages	$1,201	$711	$3,113	$1,429	$723	$3,582
Range	$919–1,377	$667–737	$2,575–3,461	$1,217–1,687	$707–737	$3,157–4,081

*Includes quotes for select hotels only.
*Includes ground transportation and accommodation (some taxes may be additional) and estimated cost for five two- tank dives ($337.50).

Ski Vacation—7 Nights**

	January 5–11			February 16–22		
	Dbl./Person Range	Child	Family (3)	Dbl./Person	Child	Family (3)
Average for 20 packages	$1,161	$566	$2,888	$1,270	$567	$3,107
Range	$757–1,645	$454–1,166	$2,087–3,845	$824–1,739	$454–1,172	$2,221–4,031

**Includes quotes for select hotels only.
**Includes ground transportation, accommodations, and lift passes; some taxes may be additional.
**Does not include airfare.

EXHIBIT 9   A U.S. Vacation Comparison: Diving in the Caymans/Cozumel vs. Skiing in Vail/Breckenridge/Winter Park (in U.S. dollars)

Caymans/Cozumel—7 nights*	January 5–11			April 16–22		
	Dbl/Person	Child	Family (3)	Dbl/Person	Child	Family (3)
Cayman Islands						
7 Mile Beach Resort	$1,099	free	$1,998	$ 949	free	$1,698
Seaview Hotel	899	free	1,628	799	free	1,428
Hyatt Regency	1,499	free	2,856	1,299	free	2,198
Radisson	1,299	free	2,398	1,149	free	1,998
Cozumel						
Casa del Mar	899	free	1,648	799	free	1,248
Suites Colonia	799	free	1,538	719	free	1,278
Average cost	$ 933	free	$2,011	$ 952	free	$1,641

*Includes quotes for select hotels only.

Ski Vacation—7 Nights**	January 5–11			February 16–22		
	1 to a Room	2 to a Room	3 to a Room	1 to a Room	2 to a Room	3 to a Room
Average for 18 packages (per person)	$945	$678	$659	$1,250	$880	$821
Range (per person)	$420–2,766	$298–1,489	$391–1,215	$830–1,935	$533–1,304	$492–1,304

**Includes quotes for select hotels only.
**Includes lodging and lift passes, some taxes may be additional.
**Does not include airfare, but does include rental car.

build a play structure for children. There was an open area with shade trees between the office and the cottages that would be ideal for a play area. Rascals would provide the teacher/escort for the family vacation groups. It would be fairly easy to find baby sitters for the children as needed. The people, particularly on this part of the island, were very family-oriented and would welcome the opportunity for additional income. In asking around, it seemed that $5 per hour was the going rate for a sitter. Toys and other play items could be added gradually. The Rascals people had said that, once the program was in place, he could expect bookings to run 90 percent of capacity annually from new and return bookings. While the package prices were competitive, the attraction was in group bookings and the prospect of a returning client base.

Adding adventure diving would be a relatively easy thing to do. Shark Wall and Shark Buoy were less than an hour away by boat. Both of these sites offered sharks that were already accustomed to being fed. The cost of shark food would be $10 per dive. None of Greywell's current staff were particularly excited about the prospect of adding shark feeding to their job description. But these staff could be relatively easily replaced. Greywell could probably find an experienced divemaster who would be willing to lead the shark dives. He would also have to purchase a special chain mail suit for the feeder at a cost of about $10,000. While there were few accidents during the feeds, Greywell would rather be safe than sorry. His current boats, especially the 40-footers, would be adequate for transporting divers to the sites. The other shark dive operators might not be happy about having him at the sites, but there was little they could do about it. Shark divers were charged a premium fee. For example, a shark dive would cost $100 for a two-tank dive, compared to $25–$75 for a normal two-tank dive. He figured that he could add shark dives to the schedule on Wednesdays and Saturdays without taking away from regular business. He needed a minimum of four divers on a trip at regular rates to cover the cost of taking out the boat. Ten or twelve divers was ideal. Greywell could usually count on at least eight divers for a normal dive, but he did not know how much additional new and return business he could expect from shark diving.

A third option was for Greywell to try to improve his current operations and not add any new diving attractions. This would require him to be much more cost efficient in his operations. Actions such as strictly adhering to the minimum required number of divers per boat policy, along with staff reductions, might improve the bottom line by 5–10 percent. He would need to be very attentive to materials ordering, fuel costs, and worker productivity in order to realize any gains with this approach. However, he was concerned that by continuing as he had, Coral Divers Resort would not be distinguished as unique from other resorts in the Bahamas. He did not know what would be the long-term implications of this approach.

As Greywell reached the office, he turned to watch the sun sink into the ocean. Although it was a view he had come to love, a lingering thought was that perhaps it was time to relocate to a less crowded location.

FEDEX VS. UPS: THE WAR IN PACKAGE DELIVERY

Lane Crowder, *University of Virginia*

Robert E. Spekman, *University of Virginia*

Robert Bruner, *University of Virginia*

It seemed in January 1995 that the intense rivalry between Federal Express (FedEx) and United Parcel Service (UPS) would continue unabated. Although the two firms were expected to report increases in profits for calendar year 1994, analysts were concerned about the sustainability of this performance. Both firms had expanded their service offerings dramatically, reengineered operations, transformed corporate cultures, and wrung major productivity improvements from their organizations. Additionally, they had ventured boldly into the application of new technology, and committed massive amounts of new capital to acquire firms, routes, and equipment. The rapid pace of corporate transformation continued, with no time for digestion or reflection. Analysts wondered whether these efforts would create stronger firms, delighted customers, and higher performance and value, or whether the competitive strategies would ultimately be self-destructive. What motivated the torrid pace of transformation at these two firms? What might account for the *path* that their rivalry had taken? What changes had their rivalry imposed on the two firms internally, in their organizations, and operations? Were the firms *flexible* enough to withstand the unforeseen shocks that lay ahead? Would either firm, or both, succeed?

CORPORATE HISTORY

UPS History and Corporate Culture

In 1980, with profits of $189 million on sales of $4 billion, UPS delivered its 1.5 billionth package.[1] Founded by Jim Casey in 1907 as a bicycle messenger service in Seattle, Washington, UPS had grown to become the leading carrier service in the United States. UPS acquired a small company with common-carrier rights in Los Angeles in 1922, and by 1953 had expanded its services to provide contract delivery for retail stores in major cities throughout the United States. It was not until 1953, however, that the company decided to compete directly with the United States Postal Service (USPS) in the common-carrier business. That same year UPS introduced its two-day air service. Its early success was based on the maintenance of low overhead costs. Following George D. Smith's appointment as chief executive officer in 1962, the company experienced tremendous growth, doubling its sales and profits and earning $31.9 million on sales of $548 million in 1969.

UPS's success was also attributed to its ownership structure. Casey believed strongly that the company should belong to its managers and their families—the only shareholders were 3,700 employees. As a result, company executives could tightly control long-term goals and could strictly limit the flow of information about the company to outsiders, helping to protect against potential competition. Executives could not be interviewed, and advertising and news coverage were kept to a minimum.[2]

The absence of public investors, however, did not insulate UPS from all problems. Throughout its history, UPS blamed the Teamsters Union, which had represented UPS drivers since 1916, for rate hikes due to salary increases included in each labor contract. Other UPS employees, including mechanics and pilots, were also unionized. In 1973, 17,000 UPS workers went on strike to protest a company proposal to replace all full-time workers who sorted packages with part-time workers as the former employees quit.[3] Another major strike in 1994 over the increase in package weight limits from 70 to 150 pounds resulted in the permanent loss of business to FedEx from several major customers, including Spiegel, Inc., and Catalog Shipper.[4]

UPS's growth into a corporate giant was due partially to its overall philosophy that stressed quality and efficiency. Four thousand UPS employees worked each night at the UPS sorting hub in Louisville, Kentucky. They unloaded, sorted, and reloaded approximately 400,000 parcels per night onto 80 airplanes, whose flights were so perfectly timed that the pilots did not need to brake the planes. Each package displayed a bar code to enable accurate sorting.[5] The entire sorting process took

---

[1]*International Directory of Company Histories,* ed. Adele Hast (Detroit, St. James, 1992): Vol V. pp. 553–35.

[2]Ibid.

[3]"The 'Casual' Issue at UPS," *Business Week* (1 November 1976), p. 28.

[4]"UPS Sues Union; Some Customers Switch to other Shipper," *The Houston Chronicle* (10 February 1994).

[5]Todd Vogel and Chuck Hawkins, "Can UPS Deliver the Goods in a New World?" *Business Week* (4 June 1990), p. 80.

about four and a half hours.[6] During peak seasons even top executives participated in the loading, unloading, and sorting processes.[7]

Ground operations were conducted in an equally efficient manner. An army of engineers was constantly researching how to move packages more quickly. As *Business Week* reporter Todd Vogel affirmed, "Every route is timed down to the traffic light. Each vehicle was engineered to exacting specifications. And the drivers, all 62,000 of them, endure a daily routing calibrated down to the minute." As one UPS driver, Mark Dray, stated:

> [D]rivers are expected to keep precise schedules (hours are broken down into hundredths) that do not allow for variables such as weather, traffic conditions, and package volume. If they're behind schedule, they're reprimanded . . . and if they're ahead of schedule, their routes are lengthened. Drivers make 100 to 120 deliveries a day . . .[8]

This quest for efficiency prompted a 1993 Teamsters study that concluded that UPS's drivers were "among the most stressed" workers in the United States. A union survey of 53,000 employees concluded that 70 percent thought that "unjust pressure was applied to the company's quest for productivity."[9] UPS executives questioned the methodology of the Teamster-sponsored study and claimed the annual worker survey showed that 89 percent of workers believed that benefits were good and 70 percent felt UPS paid them well. The company also noted that UPS drivers earned the highest salaries in the industry.[10] Another survey indicated that more than 80 percent of all UPS employees said they were proud to work for the company and would recommend UPS to their friends as a good place to work.

The UPS corporate philosophy was also based on responsibility. UPS created strong company loyalty in its managers; many of UPS's top executives had joined the company as delivery workers and worked their way into executive positions. CEO Kent Nelson commented,

> We give [managers] complete authority to run their operations and do their jobs. We push decision making down to the lowest possible levels . . . The system we have creates a tremendous amount of initiative, responsibility, hard work, and long hours . . . We've never been a company that pays high salaries, even to our chairman. But we are owners. Our lowest-level supervisors own stock in our company.[11]

UPS's mission statement and corporate strategy statement are shown in Exhibit 1.

History of Federal Express

Entrepreneur Frederick W. Smith started FedEx in 1971 with a $4 million inheritance from his father. Smith's idea originated from an economics term paper he wrote while at Yale. He believed that an overnight delivery service could succeed if it owned and operated its own airplanes, rather than depend on the baggage compart-

---

[6]Richard Weintraub, "Delivering a Revolution: The Fierce Rivalry between FedEx and UPS Remakes Global Commerce," *Washington Post* (28 August 1994), p. H1.

[7]Vogel and Hawkins, p. 80.

[8]Jill Hodges, "Driving Negotiations; Teamsters Survey Says UPS Drivers among Nation's Most Stressed Workers," *Star Tribune* (9 June 1993), p. D1.

[9]Kenneth C. Crowe, "Kinder and Gentler On-Time Delivery; Teamsters Seek Less Stress for UPS Jobs," *Newsday* (24 March 1993), p. 41.

[10]Hodges, p. D1.

[11]"Behind the UPS Mystique: Puritanism and Productivity," *Business Week* (6 June 1983), p. 66.

EXHIBIT 1 United Parcel Service's Mission Statement and Corporate Strategy Statement

Our Corporate Mission

We introduced a Corporate Mission Statement in 1991 that re-focused our company objectives on the four constituencies it is intended to serve. The Mission defines our reason for being as an organization, expressed in terms of our commitment to each of those constituencies.

Supporting our Mission is a Corporate Strategy Statement. The Corporate Strategy Statement states our plan for carrying out the Mission. It is our road map into the future. It focuses our attention on aspects of our business that can be further developed in order to accomplish our Mission.

The Mission Statement

Customers	Serve the ongoing package distribution needs of our customers worldwide and provide other services that enhance customer relationships and complement our position as the foremost provider of package distribution services, offering high quality and excellent value in every service.
People	Be a well-regarded employer that is mindful of the well-being of our people, allowing them to develop their individual capabilities in an impartial, challenging, rewarding, and cooperative environment and offering them the opportunity for career development.
Shareowners	Maintain a financially strong, manager-owned company earning a reasonable profit, providing long-term competitive returns to our shareowners.
Communities	Build on the legacy of our company's reputation as a responsible corporate citizen whose well-being is in the public interest and whose people are respected for their performance and integrity.

Corporate Strategy Statement

UPS will achieve worldwide leadership in package distribution by developing and delivering solutions that best meet our customers' distribution needs at competitive rates. To do so, we will build upon our extensive and efficient distribution network, the legacy and dedication of our people to operational and service excellence, and our commitment to anticipate and respond rapidly to changing market conditions and requirements.

ments of passenger airplanes. Packages could also be routed quickly and most efficiently if transported through a single central location. In this manner, Smith believed that he could capture the unfulfilled area of the delivery market—service to smaller U.S. cities—and provide the fastest delivery in the country.

Before the first package could be delivered, planes and facilities needed to be purchased, which contributed to enormous start-up costs. Raising an additional $91 million in venture capital, Smith began building his business around a central facility in Memphis, Tennessee. He acquired 14 Dassault Falcon planes and hired 389 employees. By 1973, the company was flying to and from 25 U.S. cities. Each package came through Memphis, where it was immediately routed to another airport for next-day delivery.

Start-up costs and an expensive ad and direct-mail campaign in 1975 contributed to losses of $29 million. Despite an increase in sales to $43.5 million, the company continued to operate at an $11.5 million loss throughout the year. With investors threatening to oust Smith, company president Arthur Bass stepped in to improve delivery schedules. By the end of 1976, FedEx saw a profit of $3.6 million, transporting 19,000 packages per night.

By 1977, FedEx enjoyed $8 million in profits on sales of $110 million. It had established a niche in the delivery market, servicing 31,000 frequent customers, including IBM and the United States Air Force. It would soon deliver to 130 cities from 75 airports, beating the competition by providing faster service to smaller cities.

The late 1970s proved favorable to FedEx. Government deregulation of the airline industry allowed common carriers to carry over 7,500 pounds of goods—larger planes could now replace smaller planes, reducing the number of trips between cities. FedEx responded with the purchase of several Boeing 727-100Cs.[12] Extra capital was raised through the sale of 650,000 shares at $11.75 per share in 1977, and the following year the company became officially listed on the New York Stock Exchange. By 1979, profits were up to $21.4 million with sales of $258.5 million.

Expansion in the early 1980s had reached 40 percent per year. Nearly 6,700 employees deployed 65,000 packages per night. Thirty-two Falcons, thirty-eight 626s, five 737s, eight DC-10s and 2,000 vans rounded out the company transportation inventory. Smaller, expensive computer and electronic equipment supported customer demand for fast delivery. In addition to two-way radios, computers were installed in delivery vehicles and bar-code scanning was implemented.[13]

The inability of USPS to guarantee quality service contributed to increased public demand for FedEx services. In response, FedEx reduced the cost of its overnight letter in 1981 to $9.50. FedEx soon generated the most revenue of any U.S. air-delivery company, surpassing many older, established companies.

FedEx's Corporate Culture

FedEx adhered to a very simple motto: people, service, profits. Expectations were made clear to employees and each new employee underwent an extensive training and orientation program. The company's overall goal was 100 percent customer satisfaction, and a favorable employee environment helped create a satisfied customer. Employees could move into management positions and were given first priority when filling vacant positions. Only when no one within the company fit the job description were job openings made available to the public. An extensive grievance program included the Open Door Policy, Guaranteed Fair Treatment Procedure, and a Survey, Feedback, and Action Program. An outstanding service program recognized and compensated outstanding employees, and a leadership institute, Leadership Evaluation and Awareness Process, trained employees in management issues.[14]

Traditionally, FedEx avoided hiring employees affiliated with any union and worked hard to improve working conditions. When it bought Flying Tiger International in 1989, however, it acquired 940 Tiger pilots who belonged to the Air Line

[12]*International*, pp. 451–53.

[13]*Federal Express Corporation—Annual Report 1992.*

[14]Patricia A. Galagan, "Training Delivers Results to Federal Express," *Training & Development* (December 1991), p. 26.

Pilots Association (ALPA). In 1993, ALPA began representing FedEx's 2,300 pilots (despite a nonmajority vote) who were concerned about their pension benefits and chances to achieve captain status.[15] Nonetheless, FedEx did not have to contend with the union problems that plagued UPS.

FedEx also had extensive armies of employees who worked into the wee hours of the night to ensure that each package "absolutely, positively" arrived overnight. FedEx driver Sam Koger explained, "In this company, there's no such thing as 'it's not my job.'" At the superhub in Memphis, from 11:00 P.M. until 3:00 A.M., workers unloaded large metal containers (at a rate of 20 packages a minute), loaded packages onto 171 miles of conveyor belts, sorted, and reloaded trucks and aircraft. Approximately 900,000 packages were carried by 105 airplanes from the superhub. Laser scanners read each package at a rate of 29 packages a minute. Conveyor belts moved at 700 feet per minute, and teams could unload a DC-10 in 20 minutes and reload it in 35 minutes. A 1994 analysis estimated that less than 1 percent of packages were routed incorrectly.[16] Approximately 40 workers monitored operations from a large room equipped with computers and a huge TV screen tuned to the Weather Channel.[17]

FedEx took its commitment to quality service seriously. A service quality indicator measured the number of dissatisfied customers in terms of concrete numbers instead of percentages. "We needed to change traditional ways of thinking," explained W. Jack Roberts, vice-president of auditing. "We all grew up thinking that 95 percent was pretty good. But with our tremendous volume, if we were at 99 percent, in the course of a year we would have 3.3 million dissatisfied customers." In 1990, FedEx was awarded the Malcolm Baldridge Award for quality. "Quality was really part of the culture from the outset," commented Smith. "I think it came from the fundamental recognition that in providing time-definite transportation, quality was really all that we were selling,"[18] Exhibit 2 presents FedEx's mission statement. Exhibit 3 contains a fact sheet comparing FedEx and UPS.

Other Competitors in the Overnight-Package Industry

Although FedEx and UPS controlled a large portion of the package-delivery market, other competitors were vying to gain market share. Companies such as Airborne Freight Company. Consolidated Freightways (and its subsidiary, Emery Freight), DHL, and TNT entered the market for express and global deliveries. Deregulation of the trucking industry in the 1980s allowed truck companies to set their own rates, creating intense pricing competition. Many companies went out of business, but the few that remained became stronger.

THE 1980S: THE ONGOING WAR

By the time FedEx had established the successful, new overnight delivery market, UPS realized that it had to address this new form of competition. FedEx's position forced UPS to reexamine its way of doing business; the company had to adapt to

---

[15]Agis Salpukas, "Labor's Showdown at Federal Express," *New York Times* (7 February 1993), p. 1.

[16]Stephanie Strom. "A Wild Sleigh Ride at Federal Express," *New York Times* (20 December 1994), p. D1.

[17]Strom, p. D1.

[18]Peter Bradley, "Making Quality Fly: Federal Express's Quality Control," *Purchasing* (17 January 1991), p. 100.

EXHIBIT 2   Federal Express Mission Statement

Federal Express is committed to our PEOPLE-SERVICE-PROFIT philosophy. We will produce outstanding financial returns by providing totally reliable, competitively superior global air-ground transportation of high priority goods and documents that require rapid, time-certain delivery. Equally important, positive control of each package will be maintained utilizing real time electronic tracking and tracing systems. A complete record of each shipment and delivery will be presented with our request for payment. We will be helpful, courteous, and professional to each other and the public. We will strive to have a completely satisfied customer at the end of each transaction.

People-Service-Profit Philosophy

People-Service-Profit is our underlying philosophy. We believe that by working as a team, we can produce exemplary service for our customers, which in turn will provide outstanding long-term financial returns for our stockholders. This philosophy drives our employees' relationships with our customers and with one another, and has earned for us a reputation as a great place to work.

customers' changing needs. While UPS reexamined its business methods, FedEx realized that it had to stay ahead of any changes that its competitors might make. Over the next 13 years the two companies became embroiled in a fierce competitive struggle that embraced such arenas as service enhancement, technology development, and global expansion.

The Service War

It was not until 1982 that UPS finally responded to FedEx's market challenge, expanding its services to include overnight air delivery service at about half the cost of FedEx's overnight service.[19] Any customer who used UPS daily could call the company by 5 P.M. and request overnight delivery. Many companies who had depended on FedEx for overnight delivery were enticed by the savings they could enjoy through UPS. "We used to give 15 to 20 packages a day to Federal Express," asserted Michael Loscalzo, national manager for parts and traffic at Rolls-Royce Motors, Inc. "Now, with the exception of maybe four or five that miss the regular UPS pickup, everything goes UPS. The service is good, and the price is almost 50 percent less than Federal Express."[20] Other companies seemed to agree. FedEx quickly responded by announcing on October 18, 1982, that it would guarantee overnight delivery by 10:30 A.M., instead of noon. This guarantee cost FedEx an additional $18 million per year and increased its workforce by 1,000 new employees.[21]

In April 1983, FedEx increased its air fleet with the purchase of two new types of airplanes for $100 million. These new aircraft allowed FedEx to establish a "regional delivery hub-and-feeder system" that would increase service from 74 percent to

---

[19]*International,* pp. 533–35.

[20]"Behind the UPS Mystique: Puritanism and Productivity," *Business Week* (6 June 1983), p. 66.

[21]Stuart Auerbach, "Federal Express Still Top Banana of Fly-by-Nights," *Washington Post* (31 October 1982), p. F1.

EXHIBIT 3   Fact Sheet Comparisons, UPS and FedEx, 1994

	United Parcel Service		FedEx	
Started Operations	August 1907		April 1973	
Headquarters	Atlanta, Ga.		Memphis, Tenn.	
Chairman and CEO	Kent C. Nelson		Frederick W. Smith	
1993 Revenue	$17.8 billion		$7.8 billion	
Average Daily Delivery Volume	11.5 million		2 million	
Countries Served	Over 200 including territories		186	
Number of Employees	303,000		98,000	
Aircraft Fleet	757 PFs	47	McDonnell Douglas MD-11s	13
	757 PFs on order	18	Airbus 300	2
	727s	59	Airbus 310 on order	15
	DC-8s	52	Boeing 747s	6
	767s on order	30	McDonnell Douglas DC-10s	30
	747s	15	DC-10s on order	5
	Chartered aircraft	302	Boeing 727s	159
			Cessna 208s	216
			Fokker F-27s	32
Total Aircraft (not including charter)	221		458	
Worldwide Airports Served	610		325	
Air Hubs	Louisville, Ky.		Memphis, Tenn.	
Regional Hubs	Philadelphia, Pa.		Indianapolis, In.	
	Dallas, Tex.		Oakland, Calif.	
	Ontario, Calif.		Newark, N.J.	
	Rockford, Ill.		Anchorage, Alaska	
	Columbia, S.C.		Fort Worth, Tex.	
Worldwide Service Centers	2,400		1,400	
Worldwide Drop Boxes	25,000		29,500	

Sources: UPS and Federal Express.

95 percent of the United States.[22] A senior vice-president, Thomas R. Oliver, admitted that this expansion was a direct response to UPS's entry into the overnight delivery business: "In some respects they [UPS] are clearly an enormous threat. . . . They make more stops every day than we have total customers."[23] UPS's size could indeed seem overwhelming; in 1984 the company transported 7.8 million small boxes a day, making 680,000 stops. The company accounted for 1.9 billion packages delivered by ground transportation and 55.6 million packages delivered by air in 1984 alone; total revenues equaled $7 billion. In contrast, FedEx earned $115.4 million on revenues of $1.44 billion with daily deliveries of 400,000 parcels in 1984.[24]

---

[22]Eugene Kozicharow, "Federal Express Plans Regional Hubs," *Aviation Week and Space Technology* (April 11, 1983), p. 39.

[23]Kozicharow, p. 39.

[24]Joan M. Feldman, "UPS: Bigger than You Think; United Parcel Service," *Air Transport World* (March 1985), p. 28.

Other competitors, such as Emery Freight, also began to imitate FedEx by acquiring their own planes, focusing activity around a central hub, and offering overnight service. In addition, USPS introduced an overnight letter at half the cost of FedEx.

Despite increased competition, FedEx dominated the overnight air delivery market throughout the 1980s. Expansion of its Memphis superhub was accompanied by the establishment of a second major hub in Indianapolis and regional hubs in Newark, New Jersey; Oakland, California; and Anchorage, Alaska.[25] Plans were also made to build a $35 million maintenance facility one-half mile from the Memphis superhub in 1992. In 1994, FedEx planned to construct a new hub at the Fort Worth Alliance Airport and double the size of the Indianapolis hub to 1.14 million square feet at a cost of $210 million.[26]

UPS's inability to break FedEx's stronghold on the overnight delivery market during the late 1980s resulted in several shifts away from traditional ways of conducting business. In an uncharacteristic move, publicity-shy UPS launched a $30 million television campaign in 1987 to announce its lower overnight delivery rates: $8.50 compared with FedEx's $11. UPS also began to make its services more accessible, often imitating FedEx service options: It established 11,500 overnight-letter drop-off stations in office buildings and set up 15 air-express service centers to compete with FedEx's 12,000 overnight-letter boxes, 165 drive-through stations, and 371 express-delivery stores.[27] In 1989, UPS began to offer same-day pickup for new clients, a service that had always been offered to customers by FedEx.[28]

In order to handle increased demand, UPS began its own hub expansion in 1989 with the construction of a facility in Ontario, California, at a cost of $68 million.[29] Over the next five years, UPS would invest in six new hubs, including Philadelphia; Dallas–Fort Worth ($21 million);[30] Grand Rapids, Michigan ($43 million);[31] Louisville (international expansion); Rockford, Illinois;[32] and the Chicago Area Consolidated Hub, the world's largest sorting facility of its kind. With 1.9 million square feet of sorting space, the Chicago hub was projected to handle 2.8 million packages daily by the year 2000.[33] In 1994, UPS opened a logistics center in Singapore[34] and planned to open another regional hub in Columbia, South Carolina ($30 million). Also in 1994, UPS spent $75 million to consolidate its corporate offices in Atlanta.

In response to UPS's lowered rates, FedEx announced its standard overnight service in 1989, which would deliver packages weighing five pounds or less for $8.25, if dropped off at a FedEx center.[35]

---

[25]"Federal Express: AirTransport World Awards—20 Years of Excellence," *Air Transport World* (February 1994), p. 48.

[26]"Federal Express Plans $210 Million Expansion at Indianapolis Hub," *Airports* (9 August 1994), p. 319.

[27]Dean Foust and Resa W. King, "Why Federal Express has Overnight Anxiety," *Business Week* (9 November 1987), p. 16.

[28]"Big Changes at Big Brown Ready it for Future Growth; United Parcel Service," *Chilton's Distribution* (May 1989), p. 16.

[29]"UPS to Build Hub at Ontario International Airport," *Business Wire* (23 February 1989).

[30]"UPS to Build $21 Million Regional Hub at D/FW Airport," *PR Newswire* (4 June 1990).

[31]"UPS Opens New Hub Near Grand Rapids, Mich." *Aviation Daily* (4 September 1991), p. 429.

[32]"UPS to Install New US Hub," *South China Morning Post* (18 February 1994), p. 8.

[33]Hal Dardick, "UPS Putting Hodgkins on Road to Recovery," *Chicago Tribune* (7 September 1994), p. 3.

[34]"UPS to Set up Logistics Centre in Kallang or Loyang," *Straits Times* (29 July 1994), p. 44.

[35]L. Harrington, "UPS, Federal Express Flex their Muscles," *Traffic Management* (May 1989), p. 18.

Unlike FedEx, UPS did not offer reduced rates for frequent corporate users, nor did it deliver on Saturdays. UPS decided it needed to expand some of its services to remain competitive. In 1990, the company matched FedEx's guarantee of morning delivery by 10:30 A.M. Paul Schlesinger, a transportation analyst for Donaldson Lufkin & Jenrette, acknowledged that "as UPS adds features, they increase the number of customers for whom they become a competing alternative."[36]

Although competition between the companies was escalating, evidence showed that the overnight-delivery market was becoming saturated.[37]

The Technology War: Racing to Build New Capabilities

Both FedEx and UPS realized that to stay competitive they needed to use technology to create cutting-edge capabilities. Traditionally slow to implement advanced technology, UPS preferred to focus on quality and efficiency. With the growing popularity of FedEx and overnight delivery, however, UPS faced some serious decisions. Francis Erbrick, vice-president for Information Services at UPS, admitted, "If you went into our information services facility in 1985, you went into 1975 in terms of technology."[38] UPS initiated a $1.4 million five-year program to expand its single IBM mainframe with 600 terminals into an operation of six mainframes with 17,000 terminals. In its quest to upgrade its information systems capabilities, UPS acquired Roadnet Technologies and II Morrow. These two companies developed a system that allowed dispatchers to track the progress of each delivery vehicle along its delivery route on a computer screen, and installed a device to help UPS vehicles avoid breakdowns by regulating engine activity.[39] UPS engineers also began to develop an automatic package-tracking system, similar to the one FedEx had used since the early 1980s.[40]

Unlike UPS, FedEx had been using advanced technology to link its services and operations since 1983. Improvements to tracing and billing systems were a priority, and CEO Smith contended that "for further system enhancements, lower costs, and future opportunities, we have connected our customer service centers with the largest existing private satellite network using Earth stations, dramatically increasing the capacity and reliability of our long-distance communications systems."[41]

In one instance, however, FedEx's quest for technological superiority misfired. Smith realized that fax machines and electronic mail would take over part of the overnight-letter market, and he had wanted to jump into the market before corporate America. Zapmail, a $100-million electronic-mail service that FedEx created to provide customers with fax and e-mail capabilities, failed because of internal problems and machine malfunctions. Customers soon realized, however, that they could save money by installing their own fax machines and operating their own e-mail systems.

In 1989, UPS made a major investment in information technology to upgrade its systems to FedEx's level. An $80-million computer and telecommunications center in Mahwah, New Jersey, was established to link all of UPS's computer networks

---

[36]Ric Manning, "UPS Challenges Federal Express for Overnight Delivery Market," *Gannett News Service* (14 November 1990).

[37]Foust and King, p. 62.

[38]Resa W. King, "UPS Gets a Big Package—of Computers," *Business Week* (25 July 1988), p. A66.

[39]Ibid.

[40]Mary E. Thyfault, "Tracking Technology—The First Nationwide Cellular Data Network Puts UPS Back on the Leading Edge," *Information Week* (18 May 1992), p. 12.

[41]Kozicharow, p. 39.

worldwide,[42] The company also launched its Maxiship that allowed frequent UPS customers to obtain computers, printers, and UPS software to create custom-shipping manifests and management reports.[43]

In a bold move, UPS tried to leapfrog FedEx's information systems capability with its Delivery Information Acquisition Device (DIAD), which combined a bar-code reader for packages with a computer screen for signatures. DIAD allowed couriers to phone in package information directly to the UPS computer system in New Jersey while on their routes, saving tremendous amounts of time. The system allowed UPS to tell customers the exact location of their packages, the delivery time, and who signed for their package, all within a few moments.[44] UPS delivery drivers' computers were connected to a cellular modem/telephone developed by Motorola, Inc., which would immediately connect the driver to the nearest cellular carrier of McCaw Cellular Communications, GTE Mobile Communications, PacTel Cellular, and Southwestern Bell Mobile systems. Under this new "Maxitrac" system, customers with UPS software could call directly into the UPS mainframe system from their computers, and immediately receive information on the status of their packages. UPS officials did not expect the system to be fully functional until 1994,[45] and as of May 1992, customers still had to wait a day to track their packages.[46] FedEx introduced a matching upgrade of its version of the Maxitrac system in 1993.

The International War: The Battle for Global Coverage

In addition to the escalating technology and capabilities war, both companies were engaged in a rapid expansion of overseas operations. In 1984, FedEx entered the international delivery market with its first acquisition—a Minnesota-based company named Gelco Express that delivered to 84 countries. FedEx went on to acquire companies in Britain, the Netherlands, and United Arab Emirates. In 1985, it established an airport hub in Brussels, increasing its European services. By 1988, FedEx offered delivery to 90 countries.[47]

UPS began its foray into the international delivery market in 1975 with service to Canada. In 1976, it expanded into West Germany with 120 delivery vans. The company did not try to break earnestly into the international market, however, until it acquired an Italian delivery company, Alimondo, and nine other European courier services in 1988.[48] The purchase of Asian Courier System expanded UPS operations to Hong Kong, Singapore, Taiwan, Malaysia, and Thailand. To enhance its international delivery systems, UPS contracted with Arthur Andersen to create a system that coded and tracked packages, and automatically billed customers for customs duties and taxes. The company also became the first to implement U.S. Customs Service's Automated Brokerage Interface in April 1988 that would link customs brokers immediately with the Customs Service.[49]

---

[42]Harrington, p. 18.

[43]Frederic Paul and Bob Brown, "Rivals FedEx, UPS Bring Battle to High-Tech Arena; Firms Demo Network-Based Customer Services," *Network World* (7 June 1993), p. 31.

[44]"The Wizard is OZ; Interview with United Parcel Service Chief Executive Officer Kent Nelson," *Chief Executive* (March 1994), p. 40.

[45]Allen Cheng, "UPS Counts on High Tech to Overtake Federal Express," *Gannett News Service* (16 September 1991).

[46]Thyfault, p. 12.

[47]*International*, V. pp. 432–34.

[48]*International*, V, pp. 533–35.

[49]King, p. A66.

In 1989, both UPS and FedEx announced further acquisitions in the United Kingdom. UPS bought Arkstar Ltd. and its divisions, Atlasair Parcel Service Ltd., and Atexco Ltd., increasing UPS's total number in Great Britain to 19 facilities. FedEx bought Home Delivery Service that gave the company 58 parcel distribution centers and eight parcel sorting and freight sorting centers in Great Britain.[50]

On January 17, 1989, UPS announced another British purchase—IMS Air Services Group and its seven subsidiary companies. The acquisition expanded UPS services (which included Europe and the Pacific Rim) to parts of Africa and the Middle East. Simultaneously, UPS bought six other European delivery services in Belgium (Road Air Parcel Service), Denmark (Danish Express Parcel Service), Finland (Nielsen Express), France (TTA Express), the Netherlands (Road Air Parcel Service), and Switzerland (Fracht Air Parcel Service).[51] That same year UPS also acquired Belgium's Seabourne European Express Parcels, and secured landing rights to fly into Tokyo six times weekly.[52] A UPS spokesperson, John Flick, commented that "by acquiring Seabourne, we gained a company with road permits that would have taken UPS years to get together."[53] UPS was establishing its name throughout the world in bits and pieces.

In February 1989, FedEx acquired Tiger International, Inc., for $883 million in an attempt to greatly strengthen its market position and delivery capabilities in the international arena. FedEx, which held landing rights at only five international airports, wanted Tiger's existing delivery routes and landing privileges for instant access to Europe, East Asia, and South America. The acquisition gave FedEx a 7 percent international market share.[54]

The acquisition proved to be more costly and less profitable than expected and pushed the company's debt up to $2.1 billion.[55] FedEx bought Tiger only three weeks after learning it was for sale, claiming that it hurried the transaction to prevent UPS purchase. UPS insisted that it had contemplated, but rejected, the purchase after deciding that it would not be profitable. FedEx had to spend millions of dollars just to upgrade Tiger's aircraft to meet U.S. Federal Aviation standards. By May 31, 1991, FedEx's international losses amounted to $194 million, causing the company's net income to drop 37 percent.[56]

Meanwhile, UPS announced at the end of 1989 that it would expand services to the Soviet Union, Hungary, East Germany, and Poland, giving it delivery capability to 175 different countries. By 1990, it was using its own planes to fly to Hong Kong and South Korea, eliminating a contract it had previously had with Tiger International. Despite its expansion, UPS did not expect to see a profit on its international divisions until 1993.[57] UPS's director of public relations noted that "our losses abroad aren't dissimilar to Federal's, but they have shareholders and Wall Street to answer to. We can take our time and do it right. We know Europe and Japan are the

---

[50]"UPS, Federal Express Complete Acquisitions in the U.K.," *Aviation Daily* (9 January 1989).

[51]"UPS Acquires Seven Foreign Companies as Expansion Continues," *Aviation Daily* (18 January 1989).

[52]Erik Calonius and Sandra L. Kirsch, "Federal Express's Battle Overseas," *Fortune* (3 December 1990), p. 137.

[53]James Aaron Cooke, "Dogfight over Europe: Air Express Companies are Battling for Shippers' Business in Europe as '1992' Approaches," *Traffic Management* (February 1992), p. A97.

[54]Vogel and Hawkins, p. 80.

[55]*International,* V, pp. 432–34.

[56]Calonius and Kirsch, p. 137.

[57]Jill Arabas, "UPS Looks to Rule Global Waters with Shipping's 'Tightest Ship,'" *Chicago Tribune* (8 April 1990), p. B14.

answer to significant profits. It is extremely painful for us in the short term, but we know it's the right thing."[58]

The Other International Competitors

DHL Worldwide Express was the undisputed leader in the international delivery market in the late 1980s with a 45 percent market share.[59] The company had already established its hold on Europe and so far it had not lost market share because of the entry of UPS and FedEx in the international arena. It employed 34,000 people with 1,610 facilities serving 218 countries.[60]

TNT Limited was another international competitor. Based in Australia, the company served Europe, North and South America, Southeast Asia, and New Zealand.[61] TNT had an international market share of about 9 percent.[62]

THE 1990S: THE WAR CONTINUES

Rate Increases

On February 18, 1991, UPS started to charge more for residential delivery than for commercial delivery. It raised its commercial shipping rates by 3.2 percent and its residential shipping rates by 16.1 percent. The company explained the separate rates in a letter to its customers:

> The introduction of separate price has become necessary due to a dramatic increase in residential deliveries during the past few years and the resulting increase in our average delivery cost. Because of the greater number of miles driven and the fewer number of packages per residential stop, these deliveries are more costly for UPS than commercial deliveries.[63]

The cost of UPS next-day letters was also increased from $8.50 to $9.75. On February 24, 1992, the rates went up again; residential delivery rates rose 10.7 percent, while commercial delivery rates rose 3.2 percent. The company blamed the hikes on its new Teamster contract.[64]

In the early 1990s, FedEx decided to compete with UPS in UPS's traditional two-day ground-delivery market. In 1992, FedEx announced its Express Saver service, which was a two-day short-distance shipping service for packages weighing up to 150 pounds; this service offered bulk price reductions for companies shipping large amounts of merchandise.[65] UPS began to offer customer discounts for large shipping needs, but did not alter its policy of not handling packages weighing more than

---

[58]Joan Feldman, "Solid Footing: UPS's International Air-Express Expansion Is Made Possible by its Main Business—Ground Delivery," *Air Transport World* (September 1991), p. 66.

[59]Vogel and Hawkins, p. 80.

[60]Rahita Elias, "DHL Dashes Ahead," *Business Times* (13 June 1994), p. 18.

[61]*International*, pp. 523–25.

[62]Elias, p. 18.

[63]Jerrold Ballinger, "New UPS Rate Schedules Called a 'Terrible Blow' to Catalogers; Commercial, Residential Rates are Split," *DM News* (17 December 1990), p. 1.

[64]Ric Manning, "UPS Upping its Delivering Charges by Average 5%," *Courier-Journal* (6 February 1992), p. B12.

[65]Mark B. Solomon, "Federal Express Takes on UPS with Short-Haul Truck Service," *Information Bank Abstracts* (18 May 1992), p. B2.

70 pounds.[66] To counter the FedEx two-day offer, UPS began to ship hazardous materials by air in early 1993 and launched another ad campaign with the familiar slogan, "We run the tightest ship in the shipping business."[67]

Other, smaller competitors began to challenge the two giants' hold on the market. Airborne Freight's Airborne Express, which had a 12 percent share of the overnight delivery market in 1990, was growing faster than FedEx.[68] With sales of $1.48 billion in 1992, Airborne was the third-largest express delivery carrier. Without funds to launch nationwide ad campaigns, Airborne had attracted corporate clients by maintaining a constant price over four years and engaging in a yearlong price war with FedEx.

UPS attempted to offset its rising prices on several new fronts. It repainted its fleet of trucks with the first logo change in 32 years, to draw attention to the company's global outlook. The company also implemented a new service number (1-800-PICK-UPS) to promote customer accessibility.[69] Saturday delivery was implemented, and by 1993 Saturday pickup service was part of UPS's business. Also in early 1993, in an attempt to attract corporate customers who wanted guaranteed, but not necessarily express, delivery, UPS added a new three-day delivery at a substantially lower price than FedEx's two-day service.[70] In addition, the company began to offer the Prepaid Letter, allowing customers to pay for next-day-air and second-day-air letters in advance.

International Expansion

On the international front, both UPS and FedEx were gearing up for the anticipated union of the European common market, which would take effect on January 1, 1993. UPS acquired its 12th courier company (Prost Transport of France) for $50 million, the most money the company had ever paid for an acquisition. UPS already owned companies in Spain, France, Italy, the United Kingdom, Denmark, Finland, Belgium, Ireland, the Netherlands, and Switzerland; it flew its own planes into Canada, Mexico, and Australia. Meanwhile, FedEx had accumulated 22 foreign subsidiaries, financed mostly with increased long-term debt.[71]

Despite the expansion, both companies were struggling to make their international ventures profitable. Although UPS could afford to lose some money in Europe, FedEx was in more of a financial squeeze because of its debt burden. On March 16, 1992, with European demand for overnight delivery only a fraction of the U.S. overnight demand, FedEx cut back on some of its operations in Europe. FedEx would continue to deliver to Europe, but would depend on its European partners for local deliveries in 16 major cities. DHL purchased FedEx's European sorting center

---

[66]Feldman, "Solid," p. 66.

[67]"New UPS Ads Focus on Service," *Atlanta Journal and Constitution* (19 January 1993), p. F2.

[68]Steve Wilhelm, "Airborne Overnight Deliveries Still Growing—but Slowly," *Puget Sound Business Journal* (10 December 1990), p. 12.

[69]"UPS Rolls Out a New Look: 64,000 Vehicles with New Graphics to Hit the Road across the Country," *PR Newswire* (25 October 1993).

[70]Mark B. Solomon. "UPS, Federal Express Go at Each Other Again," *Information Bank Abstracts* (25 January 1993), p. A17.

[71]Janet Blake, "Expansion Is Part and Parcel of the UPS Plan; Competition: the Company Is in the Midst of a Campaign to Dominate the International Package Delivery Market. Its Efforts in Europe Place Emphasis on Air Express Packages," *Los Angeles Times* (29 December 1991), p. D7.

at the Brussels airport as part of a $1.25-billion five-year capital-improvement plan to increase its competitive edge.[72]

UPS, with no outside shareholders or stock market to answer to, decided to weather its international troubles and hope that its foreign ventures would be profitable in the end. UPS's logistics manager, Ian Chong, asserted, "We're so big in the United States with no real competitors, that we can afford to have an adventure in Europe and the rest of the world."[73] Hoping to take full advantage of FedEx's retrenchment, UPS bought another company in Great Britain, Carryfast Limited. Donald Layden, UPS's international operations manager, commented, "The overall strategy is for us to be the leading provider of package distribution services worldwide. As a matter of fact, it's part of our company's mission statement." UPS hoped its international service would account for one-third of total revenue by the year 2000.[74]

On the domestic front, several other competitors had grown in strength. USPS, trying to attract customers and remain competitive with its reasonably priced Priority Mail, had introduced a sophisticated tracking system known as Comprehensive Tracing and Tracking in 1991 to keep up with the systems already in place at FedEx and UPS.[75] In 1993, in a further attempt to remain competitive, USPS awarded Emery Air Freight Corporation (a subsidiary of Consolidated Freightways) a 10-year contract worth $1.15 billion to deliver USPS Express Mail and Priority Mail.[76] Emery, by concentrating on heavy-freight delivery, had gained the greatest market share of airfreight shipments weighing more than 70 pounds by the second quarter of 1993. Emery accounted for 19 percent of the domestic overnight market, 13 percent of the domestic deferred market, and 8.5 percent of the export heavy-freight market. With facilities in 88 countries. Emery was second in the overall U.S. export market (behind FedEx), with a little more than 7 percent of the market share.[77]

Warehousing and Logistics Services and Technology

During the mid-1990s, FedEx and UPS targeted warehousing and logistics services. Airborne Express had already entered this specialized delivery market when FedEx began its push into this area. Increased use of warehousing services by companies such as IBM prompted FedEx to create a separate business relating to technology and warehousing known as Business and Logistics Services (BLS). This system provided clients with sophisticated technology to give them "far greater inventory control than before. Their information systems will produce customized and standardized services containing one or several functions, among them purchase orders, receipt of goods, order entry and warehousing, inventory

[72]"DHL Acquires FedEx Station; DHL Worldwide Express, Federal Express European Sorting Center," *Air Cargo World* (July 1993), p. D7.

[73]Emma Haughton, "United Picks a Package to Pass the Parcels Around: the US Courier Company United Parcel Service Has Come Late to IT but with a Vengeance," *Computer Weekly* (21 December 1991), p. 34.

[74]"UPS Optimistic about Shipping its Strategy Worldwide," *Los Angeles Times* (4 July 1992), p. D2.

[75]Margaret M. Seaborn, "Postal System Keeps Tabs on Overnight Mail; the US Postal Service's Comprehensive Tracing and Tracking System Gives It an Edge in the Overnight Delivery Business." *Government Computer News* (19 August 1991), p. 124.

[76]"Emery Gets $1.15-Billion Express Mail Pact," *Proprietary to the United Press International* (15 April 1993).

[77]"Emery Returns to Profitability; Emery Worldwide," *Distribution* (February 1994), p. 22.

accounting, shipping, accounts receivable. . . ."[78] This new system attracted business from companies such as National Semiconductor and the London design company Laura Ashley, which awarded FedEx BLS a $260-million contract to store, track, and ship products quickly to individual stores worldwide.[79] BLS also offered two-, four-, and six-hour delivery to some customers.

UPS was not to be outdone in the logistics market. It also established a subsidiary, known as Worldwide Logistics, Inc., to handle shipping and warehousing for customers, including Dell Computer's European delivery area. UPS's Louisville division, Inventory Express, stored and delivered products overnight, such as flowers and medical equipment. However, UPS's logistics system was still two years behind FedEx's system, which was expanding even further. In 1993, FedEx began to completely update its information technology systems to create, in reporter Joan Feldman's words, "what is believed to be the largest object-oriented client-server UNIX system in the commercial world. . . . [It] will replace or integrate 38 different [information technology] systems. . . ."[80]

FedEx also unveiled another technological advancement, PowerShip 3, at the Comdex/Spring '93 computer exhibition. Powership 3 consisted of a desktop shipping system given free to customers who shipped three or more packages a day. The system allowed customers to store frequently used addresses, print address labels, request a courier without a telephone, and trace packages. A Sun Microsystems, Inc., SPARserver connected the user's personal computer to FedEx.[81]

FedEx was also implementing use of new electronic system technologies to decrease delivery time, increase customer service, and decrease operating costs. In addition to the SuperTracker bar-code scanner, FedEx introduced its Advanced Sorting Tracking Routing Assistance, which converted information from Super-Tracker into labels to be used by both people and machines. The Customer Service Workstations, implemented in 1993, increased the number of phone calls each customer-service representative could handle by halving the time spent on each call. Its Command and Control System allowed FedEx engineers to reroute planes and determine the most efficient ways to coordinate landings and takeoffs. From 1983 to 1993, FedEx reduced its per-unit costs by 38 percent, from $19.94 to $12.30.[82]

Although UPS had already invested $1.4 billion in information technology FedEx's efforts to all new capabilities prompted further upgrades in UPS's information systems. "Nineteen ninety-two was the first year we spent more on computers than on vehicles," described UPS CEO Kent Nelson. "Initially that scared me, but information is just as important as packages."[83] In a separate interview one year later Nelson stated, "The thing we had to do to grow in air was to convince the shipping public that we could provide all the services that the leader—Federal Express—has

[78]Joan Feldman, "Now, More Than Ever, Time Is Money; Logistics, Managing Movement and Storage, Is the Newest Concept in the Package-Delivery Business," *Air Transport World* (March 1993), p. 46.

[79]Linda Wilson, "Stand and Deliver—in just Five Years, IS has Become Part and Parcel of UPS's Drive to Recapture Market Leadership and Redefine Its Mission," *Information Week* (23 November 1992), p. 32.

[80]Feldman, "Now," p. 46.

[81]Paul and Brown, p. 31.

[82]*Federal Express Corporation—Annual Report 1993.*

[83]"The Wizard," p. 40.

been able to provide. And that can only be done through technology."[84] UPS planned to spend an additional $3.2 billion on information technology by 1996, including a worldwide computer network known as PRISM to handle customer requests, billing, and package tracing internationally.[85]

Internal systems improvements at UPS included the creation of optical character recognition equipment that could scan address labels or other documents and convert the information into an electronic data file without having to type the information in by hand.[86] Improved efficiencies in aircraft communication links, computer routing systems, and sorting systems also contributed to decreasing costs. An in-vehicle information system (IVIS) was installed in UPS's feeder fleet to streamline driver hours and provide trip information, including fuel and oil usage.[87]

Price Wars

UPS was in danger of losing one of its largest corporate customers, Kodak, in 1990. Kodak had attempted to secure discounts for its large shipments, but UPS refused to change its policies. Kodak found that other competitors would offer discounts and threatened to switch courier services. In response, UPS gave Kodak its own personal full-time service representative to help the corporation lower its shipping costs and awarded discounts to Kodak. Because of the change, Kodak increased the number of packages it sent through UPS to 50,000 (a 15 percent jump).

Despite UPS's attempt to offset rising prices through expanded service options and discounts to professional customers, many companies began to switch from UPS to FedEx, which offered custom-design deals and faster service for the same price.[88] *Catalog Age* reported:

> Nearly a dozen mailers, including Neiman Marcus, Omaha Steaks, L.L. Bean, Biobottoms, and The Sharper Image, say they have shifted over 90 percent of their packages to FedEx two-day economy service at no extra charge to their customers. . . . Federal Express is wooing catalogers with discounted contract rates, a tactic UPS had (until recently) refused to offer. No two FedEx contracts with catalogers are identical. . . .[89]

UPS was forced to alter its strict pricing formulas and began to make deals with big catalogue companies such as Lands' End.[90] Yet, a 1994 rate increase of 3.9 percent resulted in the loss of business from many catalogue companies such as Williams-Sonoma, Inc. "Obviously, UPS is powerful," commented Robert K. Early, senior vice-president of Williams-Sonoma. "But for the longest time they had what I call General Motors disease, which is operating under the illusion that you can say you're the biggest and, therefore, everyone has to do things your way."[91]

---

[84]Juliette Walker, "UPS Introduces Shipping Management Systems," *Business Times* (2 August 1993), p. 20.

[85]Joseph Bonney, "UPS Bets a Billion; United Parcel Service' International Expansion," *American Shipper* (January 1993), p. 26.

[86]*United Parcel Service—1993 Report to Shareholders.*

[87]Ibid.

[88]Larry Jaffee, "Omaha Steaks Assigns MO Delivery to Federal Express, Cutting UPS," *DM News* (6 December 1993), p. 4.

[89]Harry Chevan and Paul Miller, "Shippers Challenge UPS; Federal Express, USPS Gain Volume, Forcing United Parcel Service to Reconsider Its Stance," *Catalog Age* (January 1994), p. 1.

[90]Ibid.

[91]Strom, p. D1.

International Gains and Losses

By mid-1993, UPS's CEO, Kent Nelson, announced that the international-services segment would not make a profit by 1994: "Maybe we'll get there in 1996." Although UPS believed that it could succeed where FedEx had failed, the European market still only demanded delivery of fewer than 200,000 packages per night, while U.S. demand was at two million packages per night.[92] Like FedEx, UPS had misjudged the European market and employees. Employees in Spain did not like UPS's work policies; management in France retired; and UPS had a hard time competing with the cheap rates offered by the Italian postal system.[93]

By mid-1994, FedEx was making a profit on its international services. The company had been able to lower costs and business had doubled within a five-year period, despite dependence on contract agreements with European carriers.[94] FedEx was still expanding globally and began to offer services to South Africa. It had attained 9 percent of the global market. UPS had a 29 percent market share, second only to DHL.[95]

Alliance Wars

UPS and FedEx were waging another war in the fight for service superiority. The two companies began to engage in alliances with other companies in an attempt to become more convenient for their customers. In August 1993, an alliance between FedEx and Kinko's allowed FedEx to place drop-off areas in 600 Kinko's stores across the United States and Canada.[96] In another alliance, FedEx won the business to ship Radio Shack products.[97] In October 1994, FedEx completed arrangements with Wal-Mart to place drop-off stations in more than 400 Sam's wholesale warehouse stores across the country.

In August 1994, UPS bought close to a 29 percent interest in the software firm ConnectSoft; the two companies planned to create a Windows-based software program for UPS's automated shipping and information systems.[98] In November, UPS collaborated with Liberty National Bank and Trust Co. to speed up check processing time for many U.S. banks.[99]

A Saturated Market?

By early 1994, UPS decided to offer delivery service for heavier packages. On February 7 the company announced that it would deliver packages weighing up to 150 pounds, prompting some complaints among workers.[100]

---

[92]Nikki Tait, "UPS Rethinks Its Deliveries of Red Ink from Europe," *Financial Times* (15 June 1993), p. 21.

[93]Tait, "UPS," p. 21.

[94]Weintraub, p. H1.

[95]Elias, p. 18.

[96]"Federal Express, Kinko's in Pact," *The Wall Street Journal* (12 August 1993), p. C10.

[97]"Radio Shack Introduces Gift Express; First Nationwide Electronics Gift Distribution Program Offers Gift Wrapping and Federal Express Service throughout the United States," *Business Wire* (1 June 1994).

[98]"UPS Makes Software Investment; United Parcel Service Buys Stake in ConnectSoft," *Software Industry Report* (22 August 1994), p. 7.

[99]William Armbruster, "UPS, Federal Express Sign Up New Partners," *Journal of Commerce* (14 November 1994), p. C3.

[100]Pam Schancupp, "UPS, Fedex Ship Furniture; United Parcel Service of America Inc., Federal Express Corp," *HFD—The Weekly Home Furnishings Newspaper* (7 February 1994), p. 17.

FedEx was finding it harder to sustain its rapid growth rates of years past. In 1994, annual revenues at FedEx were up 9 percent to $8.5 billion with income at $204.4 million, nearly four times that of the previous year. Despite the good news, CEO Fred Smith conceded that "as the organization matures, we can't do things in the same way. We have to grow fast to offset the escalation of maturity."[101] One of Smith's new initiatives was to augment FedEx's ground service with the purchase of 4,000 new trucks and an investment of $200 million in ground vehicles. One analyst, Greg Smith of the research consulting firm Colography Group, commented, "The more you can do with trucks, the more FedEx will buy and the more they'll become like UPS."[102] With FedEx's expansion into traditional UPS territory, UPS once again raised the ante. On October 10, 1994, UPS announced its Early A.M. service, which guaranteed delivery by 8:30 A.M. This service would cost $40 per letter and $45 per package.[103]

In November, both companies announced on-line client services via the Internet: UPS through CompuServe and Prodigy, and FedEx through America Online. FedEx had collaborated with IBM, Apple Computer, Intuit, America Online, and CommerceNet to create a Windows and Macintosh program that would allow customers to track packages on-line starting in early 1995. UPS customers, while on-line in 1995, would not have the capability to track packages until later. UPS's online services were provided free to frequent customers.

In January 1995, UPS acquired SonicAir for an estimated $60 million. The plan for this acquisition was to use SonicAir's capability to offer same-day delivery in select U.S. locations.[104]

What would happen in the late 1990s? Greg Smith of the Colography Group explained that "the bottom line is that both companies are still moving boxes from point A to point B. . . . The value they're adding with the services is information, which is what continues to differentiate them."[105] UPS's group manager of Business Development observed that "you reach a point where you can't save any more" by improving efficiencies, but he asked, "What else can you do? And that's where we hope technology can truly help us."[106]

But would advancing technology and next-generation information support systems be enough to keep the industry attractive given the specter of market maturity? As early as 1987, *Business Week* reporter Dean Foust was suggesting the "onset of a maturing market." Foust went on to say,

> Admittedly there are no "great" stocks in the cutthroat air-express business. The industry is a classic case of booming profits leading to industry overcapacity, followed by fierce competition. Corporate shippers now are consolidating their business among just a few couriers, usually winning lucrative price breaks in the process.[107]

---

[101]Joan Feldman, "The Price of Success; FedEx Is Solidly No. 1 in Express Shipping and Is Relying on Technology to Stay There Despite the Pressures of Rising Costs; Federal Express Corp.; Company Profile," *Air Transport World* (September 1994), p. 46.

[102]Feldman, "The Price," p. 46.

[103]"UPS to Offer Early Morning Delivery," *Bloomberg Business News* (29 September 1994), p. E2.

[104]Robert Frank, "UPS Agrees to Acquire SonicAir in Plan to Offer Customers Same-Day Delivery," *The Wall Street Journal* (5 January 1995).

[105]Julia King, "FedEx, UPS to Deliver On-line Ship Info to Desktops," *Computerworld* (14 November 1994), p. 62.

[106]Arabas, p. B14.

[107]Foust, p. 62.

A CONTINUOUS TRANSFORMATION

The strategic emphasis on advancing technology, new services, and global expansion were an integral part of UPS's and FedEx's constant efforts to adapt to a shifting market. Moreover, each company reacted to the strategies and new competitive capabilities being put in place by the other. They had shifted resources, developed new competencies and capabilities, imitated each other's actions, and reengineered their value chains in a series of ongoing maneuvers to outflank one another.

Strategy Shifts at UPS

UPS first shifted strategic gears in September 1982 when it decided to compete directly with FedEx in the overnight-express market. UPS's vice-president of customer service admitted that this was "a very hard decision for us" because of the tremendous amount of capital investment for aircraft and sorting hubs.[108] *Business Week* reporter Todd Vogel discussed the shift that UPS experienced in the early 1980s:

> As UPS spent the early 1980s oiling its own mousetrap, Federal Express Corp. invented a better one. Customers wanted overnight service, the ability to track packages en route, and volume discounts. FedEx offered all three. Although UPS Chairman Kent C. "Oz" Nelson admits his company was skeptical at first, "it finally sunk in that Federal was right." UPS was profitable and efficient, but it was losing its grip on the marketplace.[109]

UPS's financial commitment to technology in 1985 signified a second major strategy shift and reallocation of resources. Rino Bergonzi, UPS's vice-president for information services, asserted that "a lot of our customers had begun asking for more information-based, value-added services to supplement their business. Competition and our customers' demands have forced us to change in a lot of ways."[110] UPS entered the technological arena with determination, investing billions of dollars and matching FedEx in many ways and surpassing it in others.

During the early 1990s, UPS initiated a third transformation in strategy. The 1992 UPS report to shareholders announced a new corporate strategy: "You will hear terms that seemed only remotely related to our business until recently. Terms such as: partnership with customers; information technology; customized contracts; global distribution network; logistics solutions; flexibility; decentralized decision-making." *Business Week* reporter Chuck Hawkins asserted, "Gone is the we-know-what's-best-for-you imperiousness that was UPS's hallmark for decades. In its place, UPS stresses customer satisfaction."[111] UPS also implemented other changes in the early 1990s to increase net income. The company decided to put more emphasis on corporate shippers as compared to residential delivery. The company also began putting more resources into marketing, increasing the marketing staff from seven to more than 300. It began stressing customer service more to its managers. Five hundred managers participated in week-long seminars on the issue.[112]

---

[108]Feldman, "UPS," p. 28.

[109]Vogel and Hawkins, "Can UPS," p. 80.

[110]Sharon Kindel, "When Elephants Dance," *Financial World* (9 June 1992), p. 76.

[111]Chuck Hawkins, "After a U-Turn UPS Really Delivers," *Business Week* (31 May 1993), p. 92.

[112]Ibid.

The Evolution of Strategy at Federal Express

Although FedEx had changed tremendously since 1982, it had not undergone the turnabouts in strategic emphasis that UPS had. The big differences at FedEx involved the number of changes in the types of services it provided. By 1994, the company had imitated some of UPS's strategies by using more trucks when possible to reduce costs. FedEx CEO Fred Smith had indicated that he thought the battleground would shift to the two- and three-day delivery arenas. He admitted that "the glamour part of our business is the planes, but I think just as much about our 30,000 trucks."[113] Ted Scherck of the Colography Group expressed the idea of alternative transportation: "You can lower inventory costs without higher transportation costs. That is the revolution we are in right now. Shippers are demanding a menu . . . a mix of air, road and rail."[114] FedEx's biggest strategy change, other than expanding globally, was to expand its offerings beyond the express letter and small package market. In 1991, it introduced its EXPRESSfreighter to parts of Asia and London,[115] and in 1992 it expanded the service to other locations.[116] It also was paying more attention to the residential market from which UPS was retreating. In 1994, Federal Express decided officially to change its logo name to FedEx, a move that accepted customers' slang term for the company.[117] The company was continually trying to improve and add to its service menu, but the initial philosophy of 100 percent customer satisfaction remained the same.

FINANCIAL PERFORMANCE

Since UPS's full-fledged attack on the air-express market in 1982, analysts estimated that UPS had invested over a billion dollars in overseas expansion, which in 1995 had still not made a profit.[118] It had spent countless dollars in acquisitions to help improve delivery systems and advance its technology base. UPS's $60-million acquisition of SonicAir in January 1995 was its most expensive acquisition to date.[119] UPS continued to face problems with unionized employment and eroding residential volume. In its 1993 annual report to shareholders, UPS management admitted that:

> revenue from our ground services increased in 1993, even with a 2 percent decline in volume. . . . Much of the decline in volume occurred in residential packages, which have decreased 15 percent since 1991. Higher rate increases for residential deliveries during the past two years drove some mail-order shippers to the U.S. Postal Service and other carriers.[120]

FedEx had invested an estimated $2.5 billion in its overseas operations since 1982.[121] Analysts were increasingly doubtful about whether FedEx represented a good investment. One analyst asserted in a December 1993 report that

---

[113]Weintraub, p. H1.

[114]Ibid.

[115]*Federal Express Corporation: Annual Report 1991.*

[116]*Federal Express Corporation: Annual Report 1993.*

[117]"New Look for Federal Express," *The Dorfman Report* CNBC (21 June 1994).

[118]" 'Big Brown' Delivers a Challenge to Rivals: United Parcel Service' Purchase of Carryfast Makes It a Major Player in Europe. But Can It Succeed Where FedEx Failed?" *Financial Times* (1 July 1992), p. 23.

[119]Robert Frank, "UPS Agrees to Acquire SonicAir in Plan to Offer Customers Same-Day Delivery," *The Wall Street Journal* (5 January 1995).

[120]*United—1993.*

[121]Tait, "FedEx," p. 19.

average yields are on a long-term decline due to competitive pressures and the maturation of the market. . . . Although Federal Express is the acknowledged service leader in the express package market, the competition is catching up. Volume growth rates at United Parcel Service and Airborne Express have been almost twice Federal Express' volume growth in recent months. . . .[122]

Exhibits 4 through 10 present a variety of financial and operating statistics for the two competitors.

Two big questions remained: Once the two companies had achieved worldwide operations, automated all their systems, and achieved maximum efficiency for the lowest cost, would they both be attractively profitable? And which one would emerge as the industry leader?

Up-to-date statistics on UPS are posted at *www.ups.com*. FedEx's Web address is *www.fedex.com*.

---

[122]H. Perry Boyle Jr., "Federal Express Corporation," *Alex, Brown & Sons Research Transportation Report* (6 December 1993), pp. 1–2.

EXHIBIT 4 Comparative Financial Highlights, FedEx and UPS, 1982–1994 (in thousands of dollars)

	1982	1985	1986	1987	1988	1989	1990	1991	1992	1993	1994
Federal Express											
Year ended May 31											
Revenues ($)	803,915	2,015,920	2,573,229	3,178,308	3,882,817	5,166,967	7,015,069	7,688,296	7,550,060	7,808,043	8,383,235
Operating income ($)	119,466	258,617	344,021	364,743	379,452	424,435	387,355	373,126	276,967	508,455	608,012
Operating margin	14.9%	12.8%	13.4%	11.5%	9.8%	8.2%	5.5%	4.9%	3.7%	4.8%	6.1%
Net income (loss) ($)	78,385	76,077	131,839	(65,571)	187,716	184,551	115,764	105,290	64,560	109,809	185,174
UPS											
Year ended Dec. 31											
Revenues ($)	5,213,226	7,686,719	8,619,703	9,682,155	11,032,075	12,357,918	13,606,344	15,019,830	16,518,621	17,682,353	19,575,690
Operating income ($)	502,627	984,598	1,158,344	945,804	1,045,736	1,215,270	1,052,177	1,251,256	1,277,784	1,457,672	1,556,000
Operating margin	9.6%	12.8%	13.4%	9.8%	9.5%	9.8%	7.7%	8.3%	7.7%	8.2%	7.9%
Net income ($)	331,866	567,627	668,966	734,150	758,723	693,424	596,776	700,170	516,167	809,635	943,000

Sources: Federal Express and UPS annual reports and SEC 10-K filings.

Case 15 • FedEx vs. UPS: The War in Package Delivery

689

EXHIBIT 5 Comparative Prices and Delivery Commitments of Leading Package Delivery Competitors, 1993

Prices shown are for a two-pound package sent from Baltimore to Los Angeles.

Company	Next Morning	Two-Day
Federal Express		
Price	$24.25	$14.00
Commitment	10:30 A.M.	4:30 P.M.
Airborne		
Price	$13.75	$9.00
Commitment	12 noon	3:00 P.M.
United Parcel Service		
Price	$18.50	$10.50
Commitment	10:30 A.M.	
U.S. Postal Service		
Price	$13.95	N/A
Commitment	3:00 P.M.	
DHL		
Price	$24.25[1]	N/A
Commitment	12 noon	

[1]$4.50 extra for pickup.

Source: Alex Brown & Sons, 1993.

EXHIBIT 6   Percentage Composition of Federal Express's Revenues, 1982–1994

	1982	1984	1986	1988	1990	1991	1992	1993	1994
Priority overnight service	85.95%	74.60%	63.66%	60.96%	50.86%	46.44%	44.28%	43.97%	43.73%
Standard overnight service	6.97%	13.44%	22.02%	23.26%	4.69%	7.10%	11.14%	12.97%	13.76%
Economy two-day service	6.08%	10.70%	12.57%	12.85%	8.91%	9.41%	10.42%	12.41%	12.87%
Domestic freight service					0.39%	0.50%	0.98%	1.12%	1.34%
International priority service				8.89%	9.43%	10.91%	13.77%	14.30%	15.54%
International freight service				7.02%	12.31%	10.52%	9.27%	7.30%	5.95%
Charter				1.65%	2.48%	4.84%	2.49%	14.25%	1.34%
FedEx logistics service and other	1.01%	1.27%	1.75%	2.93%	10.94%	10.28%	7.65%	6.49%	5.46%
Total revenue (in thousands)	$803,915	$1,436,305	$2,573,229	$3,882,817	$7,015,069	$7,688,296	$7,550,060	$7,808,043	$8,479,456

Source: Securities and Exchange Commission Form 10-K for Federal Express Corporation for fiscal year ended May 31, 1994.

EXHIBIT 7 Comparative Domestic and Foreign Revenues, Pre-tax Income, and Assets, UPS and Federal Express, 1986–1994 (in thousands)

	1986	1990	1991	1992	1993	1994
United Parcel Service						
Domestic:						
Revenues			$13,694,728	$14,721,686	$15,822,558	$17,297,843
Income before income taxes			1,470,645	1,545,484	1,698,299	1,902,140
Identifiable assets			7,982,387	7,873,398	8,359,395	9,886,634
Foreign:						
Revenues			1,325,102	1,796,935	1,959,795	2,277,847
Loss before income taxes			(253,580)	(276,189)	(266,602)	(326,764)
Identifiable assets			876,174	1,164,419	1,214,436	1,295,770
Consolidated:						
Revenues			15,019,830	16,518,621	17,782,353	19,575,690
Income before income taxes			1,217,065	1,269,295	1,431,697	1,575,376
Identifiable assets			8,858,561	9,037,817	9,573,831	11,182,404
Federal Express						
Domestic:						
Revenues	$2,456,832	$4,784,887	$ 5,057,831	$ 5,194,684	$ 5,667,964	$ 6,199,940
Operating income (loss)	358,267	608,069	671,186	635,872	559,140	559,629
Identifiable assets	3,007,348	3,798,364	4,032,361	3,941,022	4,432,578	4,883,644
Foreign:						
Revenues	116,397	2,230,182	2,630,465	2,355,376	2,140,179	2,279,516
Operating income (loss)	(14,246)	(194,490)	(391,393)	(612,905)	(181,967)	(28,997)
Identifiable assets	2,286,074	1,876,709	1,640,100	1,522,164	1,360,486	1,108,854
Consolidated:						
Revenues	2,573,229	7,015,069	7,688,296	7,550,060	7,808,043	8,479,456
Operating income (loss)	344,021	413,579	279,793	22,967	377,173	530,0632
Identifiable assets	$5,293,422	$5,675,073	$ 5,672,461	$ 5,463,186	$ 5,793,064	$ 5,992,498

Sources: UPS reports to shareholders, Federal Express annual reports, and SEC 10-K reports.

EXHIBIT 8 Comparative Financial Ratios for UPS and FedEx, 1982–1994

	1982	1985	1986	1987	1988	1989	1990	1991	1992	1993	1994
Federal Express											
Profit/sales	9.8%	3.8%	5.1%	−2.1%	4.8%	3.6%	1.7%	0.1%	−1.5%	0.7%	2.4%
Sales/assets	1.10	1.06	1.13	1.27	1.29	0.98	1.24	1.36	0.01	0.01	1.42
Assets/equity	2.08	2.34	2.08	2.33	2.27	3.54	3.44	3.40	3.46	3.47	3.11
Profits/equity	22.4%	9.4%	12.1%	−6.1%	14.1%	12.4%	7.0%	0.3%	−7.2%	3.2%	10.6%
Profits/assets	10.7%	4.0%	5.8%	−2.6%	6.2%	3.5%	2.0%	0.1%	−2.1%	0.9%	3.4%
Earnings per share	$1.85	$1.61	$2.64	−$1.27	$3.56	$3.53	$2.18	$.11	−$2.11	$.98	$3.65
Price/earnings ratio	40.14	37.66	23.91	−31.40	14.22	12.96	15.54	352.27	−25.83	72.32	16.51
Avg. daily package volume	1,125,881	406,049	550,306	704.392	877,543	1,059,882	1,234,174	1,310,890	1,472,642	1,710,561	1,925,105
Avg. revenue per pound	$3.81	$3.45	$3.4	$3.33	$3.1	$3.04	$3.1	$3.07	$2.87	$2.6	$2.48
Avg. revenue per letter	$24.79	$19.19	$17.92	$16.97	$16.32	$16.28	$16.61	$17.19	$16.25	$15.17	$14.95
UPS											
Profit/sales	6.4%	7.4%	7.8%	7.6%	6.9%	5.6%	4.4%	4.7%	3.1%	4.6%	4.8%
Sales/assets	2.54	1.85	1.76	1.66	1.65	2.57	1.66	1.70	1.83	1.861.75	1.75
Assets/equity	0.96	2.05	1.98	1.93	2.11	2.20	2.27	2.29	2.42	2.42	2.41
Profits/equity	30.0%	28.0%	27.1%	25.9%	23.9%	19.3%	16.5%	18.1%	13.9%	20.5%	20.3%
Profits/assets	16.2%	13.6%	13.7%	13.4%	11.3%	8.8%	7.3%	7.9%	5.7%	8.5%	8.4%
Earnings per share	$1.97	$3.36	$3.96	$4.64	$4.69	$1.07	$0.95	$1.14	$0.87	$1.40	$1.63
Price/earnings ratio	4.70	9.82	10.35	10.34	11.41	54.21	64.21	14.04	21.26	15.18	n.a.
Avg. Daily Package Volume		7.5 mil								11.5 mil	

Sources: UPS annual report to shareholders, Federal Express annual report, and SEC 10-K forms.

EXHIBIT 9   Comparative Market Shares of Leading Competitors in Package Delivery Industry, 1987 and 1992

	1987	2nd quarter 1992	
	Express Package	Express Package	Overnight Package
Federal Express	52.8%	29.5%	58.8%
Airborne	6.6	20.0	16.1
UPS	13.2	35.8	11.3
U.S. Postal Service	8.0	3.8	10.4
DHL	2.5	8.0	NA
Others	16.9	2.9	3.4
Total	100.0%	100.0%	100.0%

Note: Express packages are those weighing between 3 and 70 pounds.

Sources: Colography Group and *Business Week* (March 30, 1987).

EXHIBIT 10   Comparison of Federal Express Stock Prices vs. Standard & Poor's 500 Index, 1982–1994

Year	FedEx	S&P 500
1982	$74¼	140.64
1983	46¼	163.55
1984	34½	163.24
1985	60⅝	162.24
1986	63⅛	211.28
1987	39⅞	242.17
1988	50⅝	247.08
1989	45¾	278.97
1990	33⅞	340.36
1991	38¾	417.09
1992	54½	435.71
1993	70⅞	466.45
1994	60¼	459.27

Sources: Bloomberg database and
Standard & Poor's Index.

THE QUAKER OATS COMPANY, GATORADE, AND SNAPPLE BEVERAGE

Arthur A. Thompson, Jr., *The University of Alabama*

John E. Gamble, *University of South Alabama*

In November 1994, Quaker Oats Co. negotiated a deal to acquire iced tea and fruit drink marketer Snapple Beverage Corp. for $1.7 billion in cash, a move that took Quaker off the list of rumored takeover targets and greatly strengthened its position as a producer-marketer of beverage substitutes for soft drinks. Quaker's Gatorade brand commanded 85 percent of the sports drink segment in the United States, generated worldwide sales of almost $1.2 billion, and was Quaker's fastest-growing, most lucrative product. Snapple had 1993 sales of $516 million, up from $95 million in 1991, and was the clear-cut market leader in New Age or alternative beverages, with national distribution capability and growing brand awareness among consumers. Quaker's acquisition of Snapple elevated it into a nonalcoholic beverage powerhouse, with nearly $2 billion in sales, trailing only Coca-Cola and PepsiCo.

Quaker agreed to pay Snapple shareholders $14 a share for the 121,620,000 shares outstanding, a price roughly equal to the $13.75–$14.25 trading range of Snapple stock in the few days before the agreement was announced. Shares of Snapple, which had traded in the $28–$32 range in late 1993 and early 1994, had fallen in recent months when its sales growth during the first three quarters of 1994 slowed significantly and ready-to-drink tea products carrying the Lipton and Nestea brands began to capture almost 50 percent of sales in supermarkets. The Lipton line was jointly produced and marketed by PepsiCo and Unilever's Thomas J. Lipton subsidiary; the Nestea line was the product of an alliance between Coca-Cola and Nestlé (Nestlé was the world's largest food products company and the producer of Nestea-brand teas).

Hours before the Quaker–Snapple agreement was announced, Snapple reported a third-quarter earnings drop of 74 percent, which analysts attributed to oversized inventories and intensifying competition. In NYSE trading on the following day, Quaker's stock fell nearly 10 percent, from $74.50 to $67.125. The drop in price was said to be a combination of Snapple's poor earnings report, the reduced likelihood that Quaker would be a takeover target, and the rich acquisition price Quaker was paying for Snapple. Wall Street analysts regarded the outlook for Snapple's future sales and earnings as very uncertain. Whereas Snapple management indicated in May 1994 that it was comfortable with a 1994 earnings per share projection of 86 cents a share, the confidential business plan Snapple gave Quaker during their negotiations contained a projection of only 55 cents a share; in a filing with the Securities and Exchange Commission in the week following the acquisition announcement, Snapple indicated that 1994 earnings of 40 cents a share appeared more reasonable.[1] The $14 acquisition price represented a multiple of 35 times Snapple's latest 40 cents per share earnings projection and a multiple of nearly 20 times Snapple's estimated 1994 operating earnings (the latter multiple was well above the multiples of 10 and 11 that other recently acquired beverage companies had commanded).[2]

To finance the Snapple acquisition, Quaker borrowed $2.4 billion from NationsBank. Quaker planned to use the loan proceeds to (1) make cash payments of $1.7 billion to Snapple's shareholders for the outstanding 121,620,000 shares, (2) pay off $100 million in Snapple debt, (3) refinance $350 million in Quaker's debt, and (4) retain $250 million for working capital. Quaker management was reportedly seeking buyers for its European pet foods business and Mexican chocolate subsidiary (combined sales of $900 million) as part of an ongoing restructuring of its food products lineup and, presumably, to raise cash to pay down debt associated with the Snapple acquisition.

THE QUAKER OATS COMPANY

In 1994, Quaker Oats was the 12th largest food and beverage company in the United States, with worldwide sales of $6 billion (see Exhibit 1). The company operated 54 manufacturing plants in 16 states and 13 foreign countries and had distribution centers and sales offices in 21 states and 18 foreign countries. Nearly one-third of corporate revenues came from sales outside the United States. Quaker's worldwide grocery product portfolio included such well-known brands as Quaker Oats, Cap'n Crunch, Rice-A-Roni, Gatorade, Aunt Jemima, Ken-L Ration pet foods, and Van Camp's bean products; 81 percent of the company's sales came from brands holding the number one or number two position in their respective categories. Moreover, 82 percent of Quaker's worldwide sales came from brands positioned in categories where sales volumes were

---

[1]Reported in *The Wall Street Journal*, November 7, 1994, p. A4.
[2]*The Wall Street Journal*, November 3, 1994, pp. A3 and A4.

EXHIBIT 1   The 25 Largest Food and Beverage Companies in the
United States (Ranked by 1993 food and beverage sales, in
millions of dollars)

Company	1992	1993
1. Philip Morris	$33,024	$34,526
2. ConAgra Inc.	16,201	16,499
3. PepsiCo	13,738	15,665
4. Coca-Cola	13,039	13,937
5. IBP Inc.	11,128	11,671
6. Anheuser-Busch	10,741	10,792
7. Sara Lee	6,622	7,206
8. H.J. Heinz	6,582	7,103
9. RJR Nabisco	6,707	7,025
10. Campbell Soup	6,263	6,586
11. Kellogg	6,191	6,295
12. Quaker Oats	5,576	5,731
13. CPC International	5,502	5,636
14. General Mills	5,234	5,397
15. Seagram Company	5,214	5,227
16. Tyson Foods	4,169	4,707
17. Ralston Purina	4,558	4,526
18. Borden Inc.	4,056	3,674
19. Hershey Foods	3,220	3,488
20. Procter & Gamble	3,709	3,271
21. Dole Foods	3,120	3,108
22. Hormel Foods	2,814	2,854
23. Chiquita Brands	2,723	2,522
24. Dean Foods	2,220	2,243
25. International Multifoods	2,281	2,224

Source: The Food Institute.

growing. Hot cereals were Quaker's oldest, best-known, and most profitable products. Of the top-25-selling cereal brands, Quaker had four: Instant Quaker Oatmeal, Cap'n Crunch, Old Fashioned and Quick Quaker Oats, and Life Cereal.

Quaker's top management was committed to achieving real earnings growth of 7 percent and providing total shareholder returns (dividends plus share price appreciation) that exceeded the S&P 500 stock index over time. Management also believed it could enhance shareholder value by prudently using leverage. Prior to the Snapple acquisition, Quaker issued $200 million in medium-term notes, increasing total debt to $1 billion. In fiscal 1994, Quaker used its debt proceeds and cash flows from operations to repurchase 3 million shares of common stock, make four small acquisitions, extend the company's record of consecutive dividend increases to 27 years, and make $175 million in capital investments to support growth and efficiency improvements. Exhibit 2 provides a 10-year financial summary of Quaker Oats corporate performance.

EXHIBIT 2 Financial Summary for Quaker Oats Company, 1984–1994 (dollars in millions, except per share data)

Year Ended June 30	5-Year CAGR*	10-Year CAGR*	1994	1993	1992	1991	1990	1989	1988	1987	1986	1985	1984
Operating Results, †													
Net sales	4.1%	7.7%	$5,955.0	$5,730.6	$5,576.4	$5,491.2	$5,030.6	$4,879.4	$4,508.0	$3,823.9	$2,968.6	$2,925.6	$2,830.9
Gross profit	6.3%	10.8%	3,028.8	2,860.6	2,745.3	2,652.7	2,350.3	2,229.0	2,114.6	1,750.7	1,298.7	1,174.7	1,085.7
Income from continuing operations before income taxes and cumulative effect of accounting changes	9.6%	6.0%	378.7	467.6	421.5	411.5	382.4	239.1	314.6	295.9	255.8	238.8	211.3
Provision for income taxes	10.3%	4.0%	147.2	180.8	173.9	175.7	153.5	90.2	118.1	141.3	113.4	110.3	99.0
Income from continuing operations before cumulative effect of account changes	9.2%	7.5%	231.5	286.8	247.6	235.8	228.9	148.9	196.5	154.6	142.4	128.5	112.3
Income (loss) from discontinued operations—net of tax			—	—	—	(30.0)	(59.9)	54.1	59.2	33.5	37.2	28.1	26.4
Income from the disposal of discontinued operations—net of tax			—	—	—	—	—	—	—	55.8	—	—	—
Cumulative effect of accounting changes—net of tax			—	(115.5)	—	—	—	—	—	—	—	—	—
Net income	2.7%	5.3%	$ 231.5	$ 171.3	$ 247.6	$ 205.8	$ 169.0	$ 203.0	$ 255.7	$ 243.9	$ 179.6	$ 156.6	$ 138.7
Per common share:													
Income from continuing operations for cumulative effect of accounting changes	12.3%	9.5%	$ 3.36	$ 3.93	$ 3.25	$ 3.05	$ 2.93	$ 1.88	$ 2.46	$ 1.96	$ 1.77	$ 1.53	$ 1.35
Income (loss) from discontinued operations			—	—	—	(0.40)	(0.78)	0.68	0.74	0.43	0.47	0.35	0.32
Income from the disposal of discontinued operations			—	—	—	—	—	—	—	0.71	—	—	—
Cumulative effect of accounting changes			—	(1.59)	—	—	—	—	—	—	—	—	—
Net income	5.6%	7.2%	$ 3.36	$ 2.34	$ 3.25	$ 2.65	$ 2.15	$ 2.56	$ 3.20	$ 3.10	$ 2.24	$ 1.88	$ 1.67
Dividends declared:													
Common stock	8.1%	12.2%	$ 140.6	$ 136.1	$ 128.6	$ 118.7	$ 106.9	$ 95.2	$ 79.9	$ 63.2	$ 55.3	$ 50.5	$ 44.4
Per common share	12.1%	14.4%	$ 2.12	$ 1.92	$ 1.72	$ 1.56	$ 1.40	$ 1.20	$ 1.00	$ 0.80	$ 0.70	$ 0.62	$ 0.55
Convertible preferred and redeemable preference stock			$ 4.0	$ 4.2	$ 4.2	$ 4.3	$ 3.6	—	—	—	$ 2.3	$ 3.6	$ 3.9
Average number of common shares outstanding (in thousands)			67,618	71,974	74,881	75,904	76,537	79,307	79,835	78,812	79,060	81,492	80,412

*CAGR—compound average growth rate.

EXHIBIT 2 Concluded

Year Ended June 30	1994	1993	1992	1991	1990	1989	1988	1987	1986	1985	1984
Financial Statistics‡, §											
Current ratio	1.0	1.0	1.2	1.3	1.3	1.8	1.4	1.4	1.4	1.7	1.6
Working capital	$ (5.5)	$ (37.5)	$ 168.7	$ 317.8	$ 342.8	$ 695.8	$ 417.5	$ 507.9	$ 296.8	$ 400.7	$ 316.8
Property, plant and equipment—net	$1,214.2	$ 1,228.2	$2,173.3	$1,232.7	$1,154.1	$ 959.6	$ 922.5	$ 898.6	$ 691.0	$ 616.5	$ 650.1
Depreciation expense	$ 133.3	$ 129.9	$ 129.7	$ 125.2	$ 103.5	$ 94.2	$ 88.3	$ 81.6	$ 59.1	$ 56.3	$ 57.4
Total assets	$3,043.3	$ 2,815.9	$3,039.9	$3,060.5	$3,377.4	$3,125.9	$2,886.1	$3,136.5	$1,944.5	$1,760.3	$1,726.5
Long-term debt	$ 759.5	$ 632.6	$ 688.7	$ 701.2	$ 740.3	$ 766.8	$ 299.1	$ 527.7	$ 160.9	$ 168.2	$ 200.1
Preferred stock (net of deferred compensation) and redeemable preference stock	$ 15.3	$ 11.4	$ 7.9	$ 4.8	$ 1.8	—	—	—	—	$ 37.9	$ 38.5
Common shareholders' equity	$ 445.8	$ 551.1	$ 842.1	$ 901.0	$1,017.5	$1,137.1	$1,251.1	$1,087.5	$ 831.7	$ 786.9	$ 720.1
Net cash provided by operating activities	$ 450.8	$ 558.2	$ 581.3	$ 543.2	$ 460.0	$ 408.3	$ 320.8	$ 375.1	$ 266.9	$ 295.5	$ 263.6
Operating return on assets″	19.9%	21.1%	18.9%	18.8%	20.4%	14.4%	18.3%	22.1%	25.8%	24.5%	24.4%
Gross profit as a percentage of sales	50.9%	49.9%	49.2%	48.3%	46.7%	45.7%	46.9%	45.8%	43.7%	40.2%	38.4%
Advertising and merchandising as a percentage of sales	26.6%	25.7%	26.0%	25.6%	23.8%	23.4%	24.9%	22.9%	21.7%	19.4%	18.4%
Income from continuing operations before cumulative effect of accounting changes as a percentage of sales	3.9%	5.0%	4.4%	4.3%	4.6%	3.1%	4.4%	4.0%	4.8%	4.4%	4.0%
Total debt-to-total capitalization ratio#	68.8%	59.0%	48.7%	47.4%	52.3%	44.2%	33.8%	50.2%	35.7%	28.9%	35.4%
Common dividends as a percentage of income available for common shares (excluding cumulative effect of accounting changes)	63.1%	48.9%	52.9%	58.9%	65.1%	46.9%	31.3%	25.9%	31.2%	33.0%	32.9%
Number of common shareholders	28,197	33,154	33,580	33,603	33,859	34,347	34,231	32,358	27,068	26,670	26,785
Number of employees worldwide	20,000	20,200	21,100	20,900	28,200	31,700	31,300	30,800	29,500	28,700	28,400
Market price range of common stock—High	$ 82	$ 77	$ 75 1/4	$ 64 7/8	$ 68 1/8	$ 66 1/4	$ 57 1/8	$ 57 5/8	$ 39 1/4	$ 26 1/8	$ 16 1/8
—Low	$ 61 7/8	$ 56 1/8	$ 50 1/4	$ 41 3/4	$ 45 1/8	$ 42 5/8	$ 31	$ 32 5/8	$ 23 1/2	$ 14 1/4	$ 10 3/4

** Fiscal 1994 results include a pretax restructuring charge of $118.4 million, or $1.09 per share, for workforce reductions, plant consolidations, and product discontinuations and a pretax gain of $9.8 million, or $0.13 per share, for the sale of a business in Venezuela.

† Fiscal 1989 results include a pretax restructuring charge of $124.3 million, or $1.00 per share, for plant consolidations and overhead reductions and a pretax charge of $25.6 million, or $0.20 per share, for a change to the LIFO method of accounting for the majority of U.S. Grocery Products inventories.

‡ Income-related statistics exclude the results of businesses reported as discontinued operations. Balance sheet amounts and related statistics have not been restated for discontinued operations, other than Fisher-Price, due to materiality.

§ Effective fiscal 1991, common shareholders' equity and number of employees worldwide were reduced as a result of the Fisher-Price spinoff.

″ Operating income divided by average identifiable assets of U.S. and Canadian and International Grocery Products.

Total debt divided by total debt plus total shareholders' equity including preferred stock (net of deferred compensation) and redeemable preference stock.

Source: 1994 Annual Report.

Quaker's Corporate Organization and Brand Portfolio

Quaker Oats' worldwide production and sales operations were structured around two broad geographic groups: U.S. and Canadian Grocery Products and International Grocery Products. The U.S. and Canadian Grocery group was subdivided into four product divisions: Breakfast Foods, Gatorade Worldwide, Diversified Grocery Products (pet foods and grain products), and Convenience Foods. The International Grocery Products group had three geographic operating divisions: Europe, Latin America, and Pacific. Exhibit 3 shows the financial performance of the two major product groups. Exhibit 4 shows the brands and sales of the divisional units.

The Gatorade Worldwide Division

Gatorade was developed in 1965 for the University of Florida Gators; it was sold to Stokely-Van Camp in 1967. Quaker acquired the Gatorade brand in 1983 when it bought Stokely-Van Camp. At the time, Gatorade sales were about $100 million.

Since the acquisition, sales of Gatorade had grown at an average annual compound rate of 22 percent, spurred by the addition of flavor and package-size variety as well as wider geographic distribution. Worldwide sales were just over $1.1 billion in 1994, up 21 percent over fiscal 1993. U.S. and Canadian volume increased 19 percent; international volume was up 31 percent. According to Quaker estimates, Gatorade held a 77 percent share of the $1.3 billion U.S. sports beverage category as of mid-1994 (down from 90 percent-plus in 1990–91) and more than 40 percent of the global sports drink market. Quaker management believed that Gatorade's science-based rehydration capability to replace salts and fluids lost during exercise, its strong identity with sports, and its leading position domestically and globally made it an exceptionally profitable growth opportunity worldwide. Gatorade was Quaker's

EXHIBIT 3 Financial Performance of Quaker's Two Major Grocery Products Groups, 1989–1994 (dollars in millions)

| Product Group | Fiscal Year Ended June 30 | | | | | |
	1989	1990	1991	1992	1993	1994
U.S. and Canadian Grocery Products						
Net sales	$3,630	$3,610	$3,860	$3,842	$3,930	$4,253
Operating income	256	373	429	435	447	431
Identifiable assets	2,055	2,150	2,229	1,998	1,877	1,999
Return on net sales	7.1%	10.3%	11.1%	11.3%	11.4%	10.1%
Return on assets	13.1%	17.7%	19.6%	20.6%	23.1%	22.2%
International Grocery Products						
Net sales	$1,250	$1,421	$1,631	$1,734	$1,800	$1,702
Operating income	93	172	104	105	128	106
Identifiable assets	482	638	656	842	745	786
Return on net sales	7.5%	12.1%	6.4%	6.1%	7.1%	6.2%
Return on assets	20.0%	30.7%	16.1%	14.0%	16.2%	13.9%

Source: 1994 Annual Report.

number one growth priority, and the stated mission of the Gatorade Worldwide division was "to quench hot and thirsty consumers in every corner of the world."

Gatorade's Market Scope   In 1994, Gatorade was marketed in 26 countries on five continents and had the leading market position in most locations. The brand's biggest markets in 1994 were the United States, Mexico, South Korea, Canada, Venezuela, Italy, Germany, and Taiwan. In 1994, sales of Gatorade totaled nearly $900 million in the United States and approximately $220 million in the remaining 25 countries where it was marketed. Management's objective was to increase sales in Latin America, Europe, and the Pacific to $1 billion by the year 2000.

In Latin America, Gatorade's sports drink share was about 90 percent in all countries where it was available. Mexico was Gatorade's second largest market after the United States. In 1994, sales in Brazil rose fourfold as Gatorade was successfully relaunched in the Sao Paulo region. Sales volumes were rising in Venezuela and the Caribbean, and Gatorade was introduced into Chile. Quaker was investing in additional production facilities to supply the Latin America market.

Competition in the sports beverage market in Europe was fierce because in a number of important countries the market was already developed. When Gatorade was introduced in these country markets, it had to win sales and market share away from established brands. Quaker had pulled Gatorade out of the competitive U.K. and French markets. Given the varying competitive intensity from country to country, Quaker's Gatorade division was focusing its marketing resources on the most promising European country markets. Sales were currently biggest in Germany and Italy. In 1994, Gatorade was introduced in Holland and Austria. Quaker management anticipated that Gatorade sales in Europe would evolve more slowly than other global locations. In 1994, volume grew 9 percent in Europe but sales revenue was lower because of weaker European currencies against the U.S. dollar.

EXHIBIT 4   Quaker Brands and Sales, by Division, 1989–1994 (dollars in millions)

Division/Category	Brands/Products	Sales in Fiscal Year Ending June 30					
		1989	1990	1991	1992	1993	1994
Breakfast Foods	Quaker Oatmeal, Cap'n Crunch, Life, Quaker rice cakes, Quaker Chewy granola bars, Quaker grits, Aunt Jemima cornmeal	$1,292	$1,280	$1,322	$1,313	$1,425	$1,573
Pet Foods	Ken-L Ration, Gaines, Kibbles 'n Bits, Puss 'n Boots, Cycle	608	518	531	531	529	539
Golden Grain	Rice-A-Roni, Noodle Roni, Near East Golden Grain, Mission	283	275	297	309	269	305
Convenience Foods	Aunt Jemima breakfast products, Celeste frozen pizza, Van Camp's canned beans, Wolf chili, Burry cookies, Maryland Club coffee, Proof & Bake frozen products, Petrofsky's bakery products	857	901	978	953	949	924
Gatorade (U.S. and Canada)	Gatorade	584	630	724	727	750	906
Europe	Quaker cereals, Gatorade, Felix cat food, Bonzo dog food, Cuore corn oil	969	1,085	1,326	1,355	1,336	1,164
Latin America and Pacific	Quaker cereals, Gatorade	281	336	305	380	465	538

Source: 1994 Annual Report.

Throughout most of the Pacific, Gatorade was sold primarily via licensing agreements. Quaker's most successful licensing agreement was with Cheil Foods in South Korea, where Gatorade was a strong second in the sports beverage segment. Gatorade volume in South Korea ranked third, behind the United States and Mexico. In fiscal 1994, Gatorade was introduced in Australia (where the brand was sold through an arrangement with Pepsi-Cola bottlers of Australia), Singapore, and Hong Kong. Although Gatorade was not the first sports drink marketed in Australia, the brand captured the leading share by mid-1994, less than 12 months after it was introduced.

The expense of underwriting Gatorade's entry into new country markets had pinched Gatorade's international profit margins. Quaker's profits from international sales of Gatorade were expected to remain subpar as the company pushed for expanded penetration of international markets. Quaker management believed that increased consumer interest in healthy foods and beverages, growing sports participation, expanded sports competition in the world arena, increasing acceptance of international brands, and a growing population in warm climate countries and in youthful age segments—especially in Latin America and the Asian Pacific—all bode well for Gatorade's continued sales growth in international markets.

The U.S. Market Situation   The Gatorade brand was coming under increased competition pressure in the U.S. market as a number of companies introduced their own sports beverage brand:

Brand	Marketer
Powerade	Coca-Cola Co.
All Sport	Pepsi-Cola Co.
10-K	Suntory (Japan)
Everlast	A&W Brands
Nautilus Plus	Dr Pepper/Seven Up
Snap-Up (renamed Snapple Sport in April 1994)	Snapple Beverage Co.

Soft-drink companies were looking for new market segments because the $47 billion retail soft drink market had grown less than 3 percent annually since 1980. Both Coca-Cola and Pepsi were moving to market their brands directly against Gatorade's well-developed connections to sports teams, coaches, trainers, and celebrity athletes (Michael Jordan was Gatorade's athlete spokesman). Coca-Cola had maneuvered successfully to get Powerade named as the official sports drink of the 1996 Olympic Games in Atlanta and was running Powerade ads to sponsor World Cup Soccer. Coca-Cola's Powerade ads on local TV and radio carried the tag line "More power to ya." Coca-Cola had signed pro basketball–football star Deion Sanders to appear in Powerade ads. Pepsi-Cola's commercials for All Sport touted the theme "Fuel the fire" and showed gritty scenes of youths playing fast-action sports like blacktop basketball. Pepsi had also enlisted pro basketball's Shaquille O'Neal to appear in its ads and was sponsoring telecasts of NCAA basketball games. Snapple's ads for Snap-Up/Snapple Sport featured tennis celebrities Ivan Lendl and Jennifer Capriati. Suntory was seeking to attract preteens to its 10-K brand with ads featuring a 12-year-old boy who played five sports. Gatorade rivals were expected to spend $30 million to $40 million advertising their brands in 1994. Pepsi's All Sport and Coca-Cola's Powerade were considered particularly formidable brands because they were backed by nationwide networks of local soft drink bottlers who delivered daily to major supermarkets (and at least weekly to other soft drink retailers and vending machine outlets) and who typically stocked the shelves of retailers and set up in-store aisle displays. With such distribution muscle both Powerade and All Sport could gain market exposure everywhere soft drinks were available.

To counter rivals' efforts to horn in on Gatorade's market share, Quaker doubled its 1994 ad budget to nearly $50 million and created ads that reduced Michael Jordan's role in favor of product-benefit claims. Quaker also expanded Gatorade's line to eight flavors, compared to four for Powerade and All Sport. Still, Gatorade's estimated market share was 5 percentage points lower in fall 1994 than a year earlier.

In an attempt to develop a new beverage category, the Gatorade division was test-marketing a new product named SunBolt Energy Drink, designed for morning consumption or any time consumers wanted a "pick-me-up." SunBolt contained three carbohydrate sources, caffeine, and vitamin C equivalent to a whole orange; it was offered in four flavors. SunBolt was positioned in juice aisles of grocery stores where Gatorade was shelved.

Despite the entry of other sports beverages, Quaker management regarded water as Gatorade's biggest competitor as a "thirst quencher." Moreover, in many supermarkets, Gatorade was located alongside fruit juices, whereas Powerade and All Sport were often located in the soft drink section, something Gatorade executives believed was an advantage. Gatorade executives also believed that the entry of competing sports drink brands would help grow the category enough so that Gatorade sales would grow despite a declining market share. According to Quaker President Phil Marineau:[3]

> When you have a 90 percent share of a category and competitors like Coke and Pepsi moving in, you're not foolish enough to think you won't lose some market share. But we're going to keep our position as the dominant force among sports drinks. Greater availability is the key to the U.S. success of Gatorade.

Gatorade's Marketing and Distribution Strategies   Quaker executives concluded as of early 1994 that U.S. sales of Gatorade were approaching the limits of its traditional grocery channel delivery system—Gatorade was shipped from plants to retailer warehouses, and stores ordered what they needed to keep shelves stocked. Sustaining Gatorade's sales growth in the United States meant stretching the distribution strategy for Gatorade to include other channels. Donald R. Uzzi, a Pepsi executive, was hired in March 1994 as president of Gatorade's U.S. and Canada geographic unit. Uzzi's top strategic priority was to develop additional sales outlets for Gatorade; the options included fountain service for restaurants and fast-food outlets, vending machines, direct deliveries to nongrocery retail outlets, and point-of-sweat locations such as sports gyms and golf courses. The customary way of accessing such outlets was by building a network of independent distributors who would market to and service such accounts. In 1994, Gatorade's strongest markets were in the South and Southwest.

---

[3]As quoted in "Gatorade Growth Seen Outside U.S.," *Advertising Age*, November 15, 1993, p. 46.

In foreign markets, Gatorade relied on several strategies to establish its market presence:

- Shipping the product in, handling the marketing and advertising in-house, and partnering with a local distributor to sell retail accounts, gain shelf space, and make deliveries. This approach was being utilized in Greece with a food distribution company.

- Handling the marketing and advertising in-house and having a local partner take care of manufacturing, sales, and distribution. This approach was being used in Australia.

- Contracting with a soft drink bottler to handle production, packaging, and distribution, with Gatorade taking care of marketing functions and supervising the contractor. This strategy was used in Spain, where the contractor was a Pepsi-owned bottler.

- Handling all functions in-house—manufacturing, marketing, sales, and distribution. Such was the case in Venezuela where Quaker had built facilities to produce Gatorade.

SNAPPLE BEVERAGE CORP.

Snapple Beverage Corp. originated as a subchapter S corporation in 1972. The company, operating as Mr. Natural, Inc., was the brainchild of three streetwise entrepreneurs: Leonard Marsh, Arnold Greenberg, and Hyman Golden. Marsh and Greenberg were lifelong friends, having gone to grade school and high school together; Golden was Marsh's brother-in-law. Mr. Natural, headquartered in Brooklyn, marketed and distributed a line of specialty beverages for the New York City area; the company's products were supplied by contract manufacturers and bottlers. The company's sales and operating scope grew gradually. Its all-natural products sold well in health food stores; later, delicatessens and convenience stores began to take on the line. By 1988, the company had become a regional distributor and headquarters operations were moved to East Meadow on Long Island (N.Y.) Exhibit 5 summarizes key events in the company's history.

Capitalizing on consumers' growing interest in natural and healthy beverage products, the three entrepreneurs launched an all-natural beverage line under the Snapple name in 1980. Over the years, more flavors and varieties were added; Snapple iced teas were introduced in 1987. Introduction of the Snapple iced tea line was supported with a creative and catchy advertising campaign stressing the message, "Try this, you'll love the taste, and it's good for you." Snapple's recipe for making a good-tasting iced tea involved making it hot and then bottling it; artificial preservatives or colors were avoided. Snapple's strategy was simple: make all-natural beverages that taste great, and keep introducing new and exciting flavors. As sales grew (principally because devoted health-conscious consumers spread the word among friends and acquaintances), company principals Leonard Marsh, Arnold Greenberg, and Hyman Golden plowed their profits back into the Snapple brand. Wider geographic distribution was attained by signing new distributors and granting them exclusive rights to distribute the Snapple line across a defined territory.

By 1991, sales had reached $95 million. Revenues jumped to $205.5 million in 1992 and to $516.0 million in 1993, as distribution widened and more consumers

EXHIBIT 5   Summary of Key Events in Snapple Beverage Corporation's History

1972

Marsh, Golden, and Greenberg formed a company in association with a California juice manufacturer to distribute 100% natural fruit juices in New York City, primarily via health food distributors.

1979

A production plant is purchased in upstate New York to produce a line of pure, natural fruit juices.

1980

The name "Snapple" makes its first appearance when Snapple Beverage Corporation became the first company to manufacture a complete line of all-natural beverages.

1982

Snapple introduces Natural Sodas and pioneers the natural soft drink category.

1986

All Natural Fruit Drinks join the Snapple family, including Lemonade, Orangeade, Grapeade, and more.

1987

Snapple launches its All Natural Real Brewed Ice Tea and revolutionizes the beverage industry with the first tea to be brewed hot instead of mixed from cold concentrate. Snapple's signature wide-mouth bottle also makes its first appearance.

1990

Snapple introduces Snapple Sport, the first isotonic sports drink with the great taste of Snapple.

1991

Snapple recruits its first international distributor in Norway.

1992

The Thomas H. Lee Investment Company buys Snapple and leads an effort to take the company public. The stock triples in the first three months and is listed among the hottest stocks in the country. The three cofounders retain 23.1% of Snapple's common stock and Thomas H. Lee ends up owning 47.5% of Snapple's common shares.

1992/1993

Fruit Drink line expands to include such exotic flavors as Kiwi-Strawberry Cocktail, Mango Madness Cocktail, and Melonberry Cocktail.

1993

Snapple goes international, signing on distributors in the United Kingdom, Canada, Mexico, the Caribbean, Hong Kong, and elsewhere.

1994

Snapple introduces seven new products including Guava Mania Cocktail, Mango Tea, Amazin Grape Soda, Kiwi Strawberry Soda, and Mango Madness Soda as well as new diet versions of some bestsellers—Diet Kiwi Strawberry Cocktail, Diet Mango Madness Cocktail, and Diet Pink Lemonade.

Source: Company promotional materials.

EXHIBIT 6   Snapple's Income Statement, 1992 and 1993

	1992	1993
Net sales	$205,465,595	$516,005,327
Cost of goods sold	127,098,086	298,724,646
Gross profit	78,367,509	217,280,681
Selling, general, and administrative expenses	45,455,818	105,693,741
Nonoperating expenses	10,626,742	9,116,664
Interest expense	19,086,213	2,459,297
Income before tax	3,198,736	100,010,070
Provisions for income taxes	1,262,919	32,387,498
Net income before extraordinary items	1,935,817	67,623,481
Extraordinary item	(2,632,904)	0
Net income	$ (697,087)	$ 67,623,481

Source: Company annual report.

were attracted to try the line. Snapple's sales in 1993 ranked it no. 35 on the top 50 beverage companies list. Exhibits 6 and 7 present Snapple's financial statements. The company went public in December 1992 as Snapple Beverage Corp., with the three founders retaining 23.1 percent of the stock (7.7 percent each). After the initial public offering at a split-adjusted price of $5, the stock traded as high as $32.25 in late 1993 before trading as low as $11.50 in mid-1994. Responding to concerns of investors and Wall Street analysts as to whether the company's rapid growth was sustainable, Leonard Marsh said:

> For those of you who might have heard mumblings that we've grown too far, too fast, I suggest you consider Snapple in the proper context. The average American drank 500 soft drinks last year (1993) . . . and the average American drank only five Snapples last year. That's a 1 percent share of a $64 billion pie.[4]

During the summer months of 1994, Snapple marketed 75 varieties and flavors in five categories (ready-to-drink iced teas, fruit drinks, natural sodas and seltzers, fruit juices, and sports drinks) and had distributors in all 50 states. Despite sales of more than $500 million, Snapple had fewer than 200 employees; production, bottling, packaging, and distribution were handled by contractors and independent distributors. Company activities were focused on marketing, new product development (the company had expertise in flavor technology), and overall management of contractors and distributors. In May 1994, however, management initiated construction of the company's first production facility—a $25 million plant in Arizona, scheduled to begin operations in 1995 and employ 100 people.

Snapple was widely credited with catalyzing a more pronounced consumer trend toward New Age beverages, spurring added sales growth in bottled waters, sports drinks, and juices as well as its own line of flavored teas and fruit drinks. In 1993,

[4]As quoted in Beverage World's *Periscope*, February 28, 1994, p. 21.

EXHIBIT 7 Snapple Beverage Corporation Balance Sheet, 1992 and 1993

	1992	1993
Assets		
Cash	$ 97,486,632	$ 13,396,949
Receivables	17,428,379	53,010,325
Inventories	16,166,183	40,922,888
Other current assets	6,788,585	4,192,759
Total current assets	137,869,779	111,522,921
Net property, plant, and equipment	1,053,399	10,751,597
Deferred charges	3,705,001	18,552,625
Intangibles	82,770,827	97,819,997
Other assets	1,338,166	304,745
Total assets	$ 226,737,172	$ 238,951,885
Liabilities and Shareholders' Equity		
Accounts payable	$ 6,100,345	$ 7,326,411
Current long-term debt	150,469	8,949,665
Accrued expenses	16,999,258	17,573,454
Income taxes	446,892	6,034,860
Other current liabilities	90,000,000	3,860,844
Total current liabilities	113,696,964	43,745,234
Long-term debt	18,226,138	26,218,911
Other long-term liabilities	4,000,000	5,011,000
Total liabilities	135,923,102	74,975,145
Minority interest	0	1,499,717
Common stock	1,213,766	1,216,096
Capital surplus	90,297,391	94,334,533
Retained earnings	(697,087)	66,926,394
Total shareholders' equity	90,814,070	162,477,023
Total liabilities and shareholders' equity	$ 226,737,172	$ 238,951,885

Source: Company annual report.

New Age or "alternative" beverages constituted a $3 billion product category. Exhibit 8 shows trends in the per capita consumption of liquid beverages in the United States during the 1983–94 period.

Snapple's Marketing and Distribution Strategies

In Snapple's early days, the product wasn't selling well; market research revealed consumers thought the bottles were ugly and difficult to store. A packaging redesign followed, resulting in the use of clear wide-mouth 16-ounce glass bottles—a container that management said was "perfectly suited to the hot-brewed process we use to make Snapple beverages." The new bottles were affixed with redesigned labels. Sales perked up quickly, buoyed by an offbeat and catchy media campaign.

EXHIBIT 8 Per Capita Consumption of Liquid Beverages in the United States, 1983–1994 (in gallons)

	1983	1984	1985	1986	1987	1988	1989	1990	1991	1992	1993E	1994P
Soft drinks	37.0	38.8	41.0	42.3	44.3	46.2	46.7	47.6	47.8	48.0	48.9	49.6
Coffee*	26.1	26.3	26.8	27.1	27.1	26.5	26.4	26.4	26.5	26.1	25.9	26.0
Beer	24.3	23.9	23.9	24.2	24.0	23.8	23.6	24.0	23.3	23.0	22.8	22.5
Milk	19.7	19.8	20.0	19.9	19.8	19.4	19.6	19.4	19.4	19.1	18.9	19.1
Tea*	7.2	7.2	7.3	7.3	7.3	7.4	7.2	7.0	6.7	6.8	6.9	7.0
Bottled water	3.4	4.0	5.2	5.8	6.4	7.3	8.1	9.2	9.6	9.9	10.5	11.2
Juices	8.2	7.0	7.9	7.8	8.3	7.7	8.0	7.1	7.6	7.1	7.0	7.0
Powdered drinks	6.5	6.4	6.3	5.2	4.9	5.3	5.4	5.7	5.9	6.1	6.0	5.9
Wine†	2.2	2.3	2.4	2.4	2.4	2.3	2.1	2.0	1.9	2.0	1.7	1.6
Distilled spirits	1.9	1.9	1.8	1.8	1.6	1.5	1.5	1.5	1.4	1.3	1.3	1.3
Subtotal	136.5	137.6	142.6	142.6	146.1	147.4	148.6	149.9	150.1	149.4	149.9	151.2
Imputed water consumption‡	46.0	44.9	39.9	39.9	36.4	35.1	33.9	32.6	32.4	33.1	32.6	31.3
Total	182.5	182.5	182.5	182.5	182.5	182.5	182.5	182.5	182.5	182.5	182.5	182.5

* Coffee and tea data are based on a three-year moving average to counterbalance inventory swings, thereby portraying consumption more realistically.
† Includes wine coolers beginning in 1984.
‡ Includes all others.
E = estimated; P = projected.

Source: John C. Maxwell, "Annual Soft Drink Report," *Beverage Industry Supplement*, March 1994, p. 6.

The company sparked demand for Snapple products with offbeat, witty ads and catchy themes. Snapple had gotten the greatest mileage out of an ad featuring a stereotypical receptionist, "Wendy the Snapple Lady" (who was actually employed in the company's marketing department), responding to customer inquiries. Snapple ads sometimes poked fun at things. Print ads compared Snapple sales to "hot cakes" and "greased lightning" with "more flavors than you can shake a stick at." Ivan Lendl and Rush Limbaugh appeared in Snapple TV ads as celebrity endorsers. Most of Snapple's distributors were local soft drink bottlers/distributors who had third-place or fourth-place market shares (usually behind Coca-Cola and Pepsi) and who were eager to take on product lines where competition was less intense and profit margins were bigger. The average price per case for New Age beverages was around $9 to $11 versus $5 to $6 per case for soft drinks. On average, soft drinks offered bottlers and distributors $1 margin per case compared with about $3 per case for New Age products. These distributors delivered Snapple directly to supermarkets, convenience stores, delicatessen outlets, and up-and-down the street retailers, on trucks carrying an assortment of branded beverages (low-volume soft-drink brands, bottled waters, club soda, tonic water, ginger ale, and perhaps canned Gatorade). Snapple's distributors were responsible for everything—selling retail accounts, keeping shelves stocked, handling point-of-sale displays, and setting prices. Retail prices for a 16-ounce bottle were typically around 75 cents. Snapple's surging sales in 1992 and 1993—a boom that reportedly began in convenience stores and delicatessens where trend-setting consumers bought Snapple from the cooler and drank it straight from the bottle—helped it recruit distributors willing to commit time and resources to the Snapple line. Snapple established a nationwide network of distributors in a matter of months—something few alternative beverage brands had been able to do. The attractive profit margins distributors earned on Snapple sales were a key factor underlying the company's ability to recruit distributors willing to invest time and resources in building the Snapple brand. Snapple's market research showed that half the U.S. population had tried Snapple by the end of October 1993. Snapple's sales were biggest in California and the Northeast; sales were weakest in the South and Southwest. By mid-1994, Snapple had begun introducing its brands in Europe. Launches in Britain, Ireland, and Norway came first, followed by Sweden and Denmark. Test-marketing was under way in France and Spain. As of November 1994, only 1 percent of Snapple's sales were derived from overseas markets.

In April 1994, Snapple announced it had developed an exclusive, glass-front vending machine capable of offering 54 different flavors simultaneously; the machine held 18 cases of the company's 16-ounce wide-mouth bottles. The company expected to place 10,000 units in service by year-end to broaden its distribution beyond supermarkets, convenience stores, and delicatessens.

Competition in the Iced Tea/New Age Segment

Snapple's success in developing consumer interest in ready-to-drink iced teas and teas spiked with fruit juices attracted other competitors quickly. In 1993, Coca-Cola, Pepsi-Cola, Dr Pepper/Seven-Up, and Cadbury Schweppes/A&W Beverages all launched New Age offerings. Several regional products, most notably Arizona Iced Tea (packaged in distinctive tall cans with a Southwestern motif), also entered the market. As of 1994, the major players in the ready-to-drink iced tea segment were:

Brand	Marketer
Snapple	Snapple Beverage Corp.
Lipton	Pepsi-Cola and the Thomas J. Lipton division of Unilever
Nestea	Coca-Cola Nestlé Refreshments (a joint venture of the Coca-Cola Company and Nestlé)
Tetley	A&W Brands and Tetley Tea Co. partnership
Luzianne	Barq's Inc. and Wm. B. Reily partnership
All Seasons	Cadbury Beverages and Omni Industries
Celestial Seasonings	Perrier Group of America and Celestial Seasonings
Arizona	Ferolito, Vultaggio and Sons

Besides the major players, there were 5 to 10 niche brands of bottled teas. In addition, Pepsi-Cola had teamed with Ocean Spray Cranberries, Inc., to introduce a line of juices and lemonade. Minute Maid had announced a new line of juices, Very Fine and Tradewinds were planning lemonade entries, and Gatorade introduced its eighth flavor, Gatorade Iced Tea Cooler. An Information Resources survey of supermarket sales of canned and bottled iced teas during the 12 weeks ended April 17, 1994, showed the following:[5]

Brand	Case Volume (in millions)	Dollar Volume (in millions)
Snapple	2.5	$22.3
Lipton	2.3	14.9
Nestea	1.0	7.8
Arizona	0.5	5.0

Snapple's market share (based on dollars) was 17 percentage points lower in this survey than the comparable year-earlier period. The Arizona brand was gaining share and had edged out Snapple as the market leader in several markets in the West. However, Snapple's market share of convenience store sales was estimated to be in the 75 percent range. Exhibit 9 presents estimated case sales of alternative beverage companies.

Industry analysts estimated that wholesale volume for iced tea flavors grew from $500 million in 1992 to more than $1 billion in 1993. Alternative beverage sales were breaking out into 40 percent take-home purchases and 60 percent single-service and on-premise consumption. Ready-to-drink teas and juice-based drinks were the fastest-growing products in the New Age category, while sales of "clear" products dropped to the 8 to 9 percent range (down from 44 percent growth in 1992). Analysts were divided in their assessments about how long the booming growth in ready-to-

---

[5]As reported in *The Wall Street Journal*, June 9, 1994, p. B6.

EXHIBIT 9	Estimated Case Sales of Alternative Beverage Companies, 1992–1993

| Company/Brand | Case Sales (in millions) | |
	1992	1993
Snapple Beverage Company		
Snapple Iced Tea	28.33	52.63
Snapple drinks	19.73	45.41
Snapple sodas	1.52	3.10
Snapple Snap-Up/Sport	0.51	1.03
Snapple juices	0.51	1.03
Total	50.60	103.20
Coca-Cola Company		
Nestea	14.00	33.00
Powerade	1.20	10.00
Minute Maid Juices-to-Go	5.00	15.00
Total	20.20	58.00
PepsiCo		
Ocean Spray	6.50	16.00
Lipton	—	33.00
All Sport	2.00	3.00
H2 Oh!	0.50	0.63
Total	9.00	52.63
Perrier Group		
15-Brand totals	30.40	36.70
Cadbury beverages/A&W brands		
Tetley	2.90	4.30
Everlast	—	—
Others	17.30	17.30
Total	20.20	21.60
Ferolito, Vultaggio and Sons		
Arizona	—	2.00
All others	169.60	175.37
Segment totals	300.00	449.50

Source: Compiled from "Annual Soft Drink Report," *Beverage Industry Supplement*, March 1994, pp. 22–23.

drink teas and fruit beverages would last. Some analysts believed that teas and fruit drinks would enjoy continued growth because of their healthy, "all-natural" image with consumers and because the proliferation of brands and varieties would help develop greater buyer interest. Others were skeptical, observing that trendy products had comparatively short life-cycles and that three or four growth years were all many product categories ever experienced. While some cola bottlers had derisively referred to Snapple as a member of the "brand of the day" club, unconvinced of its power to sustain broad consumer interest, market research indicated that younger consumers (who had fueled the growth in New Age beverages) had gravitated to Snapple, Arizona, and unusual niche brands with distinctive packaging and a certain mystique. In fall 1994, industry observers saw bottled tea as becoming increasingly complex to market successfully because the market was overcrowded, costs to support a brand were rising, shelf space was harder to obtain, and image was such a dominant factor in a brand's success or failure.

In late August 1994, Coca-Cola and Nestlé unexpectedly announced dissolution of their iced tea alliance; in recent weeks, Nestea sales had been disappointing, falling well behind supermarket sales of both Snapple and Lipton. It was not clear whether Nestlé would continue to market Nestea bottled teas on its own. Meanwhile, Pepsi–Lipton had begun running a series of radio ads attacking Snapple as being "mixed up from a tea powder." The announcer said, "Snapple. Isn't that a cute name. Kinda snappy. I bet they call it Snapple 'cause it's iced tea made in a snap." The spot went on to boast that Lipton Original varieties were "real brewed," a trait that Pepsi–Lipton believed was its best weapon against rivals.[6] Pepsi had also run Super Bowl ads for Lipton Original and promoted Lipton Original heavily in supermarkets, including a 99-cent value pack containing one bottle each of Lipton Original, All Sport, and Ocean Spray Lemonade.

Snapple management indicated its iced teas were made from "the finest tea leaves in India" but wouldn't specify how it was produced. Arnold Greenberg said:

> Pepsi would die to make tea taste so great. People don't care how it's made. They just care that it tastes good.[7]

Snapple management also pointed out that the less expensive Lipton Brisk varieties, sold in cans and 64-ounce bottles, were not "real brewed." Analysts estimated that during the first five months of 1994, about 60 percent of Pepsi's prepared iced teas were Lipton Brisk varieties. To counter the increased competition from rival teas, Snapple more than doubled its 1994 advertising budget and launched a new $65 million media campaign in April 1994.

Quaker Oats Web address is *www.quakeroats.com.*

---

[6]As quoted in *The Wall Street Journal*, June 9, 1994, p. B6.
[7]Ibid.

JIM THOMPSON THAI SILK COMPANY*

Robert A. Pitts, *Gettysburg College*

As he looked back on his 20 years as managing director of Jim Thompson Thai Silk Company (JT), Bill Booth felt considerable pride. The company had grown to become, by 1994, Thailand's leading retailer of native silk, commanding an enviable two-thirds share of the premium tourist market. It had also expanded far beyond its original base of merely retailing products produced by others, to become the country's only fully-integrated producer of native silks.

Recent developments were threatening to undermine this hard-earned success, however. Bangkok's increasing auto congestion, escalating air pollution, and soaring AIDS infection rate were causing foreign tourists—JT's primary customers—to avoid the city as a travel destination. Since JT's shops were all located in Bangkok, its revenue and profitability were falling. Eager to find a way to reverse this decline, Booth had established strategic planning as a major priority for the coming year.

EARLY HISTORY

JT was founded in 1951 by James Thompson, an American who arrived in Thailand at the end of the Second World War as a member of the U.S. Office of Strategic

*This case won the 1995 Curtis E. Tate Outstanding Case Research Award as the best case presented at the 1994 National Case Research Association Annual Meeting. The author thanks company management for their helpful cooperation in developing this material.

Services, predecessor to the Central Intelligence Agency. A member of a prominent Delaware family and a graduate of Princeton University, Mr. Thompson determined to make a career in Thailand following cessation of hostilities. Becoming interested in the commercial potential of native silk, he opened a retail shop in Bangkok to sell retail fabric produced by local weavers. The store's reputation for superb quality and innovative design made it particularly popular among tourists and foreigners stationed in Bangkok—two groups able to afford its prices, which were well above those of most local competitors.

With expansion of tourism and the U.S. troop buildup in South East Asia in connection with the Vietnam War, JT grew rapidly. Then, a strange event occurred. During a 1967 Easter holiday in a Malaysian jungle resort, Mr. Thompson mysteriously disappeared and, despite a lengthy search lasting many months, was never seen again.[1] JT's board appointed as acting managing director an American who had been assistant manager under Mr. Thompson. Seven years later, in 1974, the acting manager died, and Bill Booth was appointed managing director.

Booth had arrived in South East Asia in the early 1960s as a member of the U.S. military in Vietnam. Struck by the beauty and vitality of nearby Thailand, he settled there at the completion of his military assignment. Booth devoted his early months in the country to intensive study of the Thai language, and eventually became very fluent. Following an unsuccessful attempt to enter the local silk business on his own, he joined JT in 1964, where he held a variety of positions before becoming managing director.

EXPANSION

Under Booth's direction, JT expanded into each successive stage of the silk production process. The first step in this process began in 1974, when it established a sewing venture in partnership with a prominent Thai businesswoman. Four years later it acquired a printing plant in partnership with a West German textile printer. In 1979, it entered the weaving business, choosing to establish this activity on a wholly-owned basis rather than through joint venture, and to locate it not in Bangkok, where its sewing and printing plants were situated, but in Northeastern Thailand, where many of its contract weavers lived. Finally, in 1988 JT entered into sericulture (the breeding of silkworms for production of raw silk fiber) and spinning (twisting together of fibers to produce yarn), establishing these operations on a wholly-owned basis and locating them near its weaving mill in Northeastern Thailand. Exhibit 1 is a map of Thailand; Exhibit 2 provides basic facts about the country.

The company's expansion into production had been motivated in part by a desire to improve product uniformity. Booth noted, for example, that this objective had influenced JT's entry into weaving:

> During the early years, we left weaving entirely in the hands of contract weavers. This arrangement worked fine so long as final sales went primarily to tourists buying through our retail outlet. It became a stumbling block to expansion of our home furnishing business, however. Owners of hotels, office buildings, apartments, and condominiums from time to time need to replace wall covering and upholstery fabric, and when they do, they need replacement material that precisely matches the color of original fabric. Our contract

---

[1] For an excellent account of this search, see William Warren, *Jim Thompson: The Legendary American of Thailand,* Jim Thompson Thai Silk Company, 1993.

EXHIBIT 1   Map of Thailand

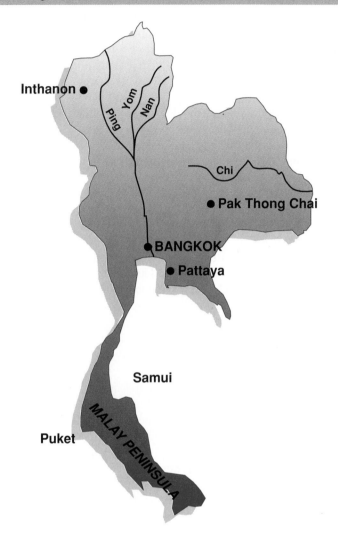

weavers were unable to meet this requirement, so we entered weaving ourselves. We can now replicate orders much more precisely.

Another objective motivating the company's move into weaving had been a desire to improve delivery capability. Booth provided the following details:

Contract weavers are sometimes unreliable about meeting delivery schedules. This posed little difficulty as long as our business was primarily retail, since our well-stocked store always contained plenty of merchandise for tourists to make their selection. It became a problem as we tried to expand our home furnishing business, however. Delay in receipt of wall covering or upholstery material can postpone occupancy of a new building, and late occupancy imposes a serious cost on a building's owner. By bringing weaving under our direct control we have significantly improved our ability to deliver on time.

A third objective motivating JT's expansion into production had been a desire to establish secure sources of supply. During the 1980s, JT experienced increasing

---

EXHIBIT 2   Facts about Thailand

Overview

Size: 198,000 square miles (slightly more than twice the size of Wyoming); 1993 population 59 million; 1993 population growth rate 1.4%; ethnic divisions: Thai 75%, Chinese 14%; religions: Buddhism 95%, Muslim 3.8%; literacy rate 93%; capital city: Bangkok (1993 population 5.9 million); 1992 gross domestic product $103 billion; 1992 per capita gross domestic product $1,800; 1992 annual inflation rate in consumer prices 4.5%.

Government

Until 1932 the country was ruled as an absolute monarchy. Since that date it has experienced a series of relatively bloodless military coups and new constitutions. Though officially a constitutional monarchy, it operates in fact as a benign military dictatorship. It is unique among South Asian nations in never having experienced European rule.

Economy

The economy is relatively free of controls on private enterprise that are common in other developing countries. The dominant sector is private, only 10% of manufacturing output being produced by government-owned entities. The Industries Promotion Act of 1962 provides companies operating in designated industries guarantees against nationalization, and exemptions from import duties, export duties, and many taxes.

Currency

The Thai "baht" is freely convertible into foreign exchange. Its value against the dollar has remained very stable over a long period of time. US$1 = 25.28 baht (April 1993), 25.400 baht (1992), 25.517 baht (1991), 25.585 baht (1990), 25.702 baht (1989), 25.294 baht (1988).

Sources: *Encyclopedia of the Third World,* Volume III, Facts On File (New York, 1992); *The Statesman's Yearbook 1994–1995,* St Martin's Press (New York, 1994); *The World Fact Book 1994–95,* Central Intelligence Agency, Brassey's (Washington, 1994); *The Europa World Yearbook 1994,* Volume III, Europa Publications Limited (Rochester, Kent, England, 1994).

difficulty obtaining raw silk in quantities needed to feed its weaving operation. Shortages were caused in part by a decline in the acreage that Thai farmers devoted to mulberry cultivation. Total acreage devoted to this end fell from about 60,000 hectares in the mid-1970s to less than 40,000 hectares in the early 1990s. (One hectare = 10,000 square meters, or 2.417 acres.) This decline was caused by migration of villagers from the depressed silk-producing regions in the Northeast to Bangkok in search of higher-paying jobs and by conversion on the part of many remaining farmers to other crops—particularly to cassava, the European demand for which was increasing. Since mulberry leaves constitute a silkworm's chief diet, declining mulberry cultivation led to reduction in output of raw Thai silk.

Developments in China, where JT historically had obtained a large share of its silk supply, also contributed to the problem. China produced more than half of the world's raw silk output, and supplied almost 90 percent of world exports. The Chinese government had long encouraged silk production, but in the 1980s began to allow silk producers to cultivate other crops. Thus freed from government constraint, many farmers switched out of mulberry into more lucrative crops such as fruits and vegetables. As silk output fell, prices on the world market climbed, leading remaining producers to skirt official channels and sell their output at elevated prices through Hong Kong's black market.

A fourth factor motivating JT's expansion into production had been a desire to improve technology. The Thai silk industry was dominated by very small producers employing traditional handicraft methods. As a consequence, the technology employed was generally quite rudimentary. Raw silk, for example, was produced mainly by farm women and children in the poor northeast portion of the country, while most weaving was carried out by individuals working in very small family operations. These players lacked resources to underwrite significant improvement in technology. JT had undertaken production in part to bring its substantial resources to bear on this problem.

TECHNOLOGY TRANSFER

Each successive step into silk production had obliged JT to acquire new technology. Generally, needed expertise was not available in Thailand. Consequently, JT had been obliged to seek it abroad. JT had used several approaches over the years to secure foreign technology. One was to form joint ventures with foreign firms. JT had used this method, for example, to secure initial technology for its printing plant. Its joint venture partner in this activity was a small West German textile printer with a reputation for very high quality. This firm had helped select initial equipment for the printing venture, arrange factory layout, and oversee early startup. In addition, the firm had assigned one of its senior engineers—Mr. Czerny—to assist the venture on a continuing basis. Making visits to Thailand four times each year, Czerny had counseled JT not only on printing matters, but on a host of other textile-related issues as well, in the process becoming an integral member of JT's management team.

A second method JT had used to obtain foreign technology was to send company personnel abroad for technical training. It had used this device, for example, to obtain technology for its sericulture operation. During early development of this operation, JT employees had made extended visits to China to receive training at the Chinese Sericulture Research Institute. Employees hired to operate the company's spinning machines had also traveled to China for technical training.

Yet another device JT had used to obtain technology from abroad was to bring foreign experts to Thailand to train company employees. Experts from China's Sericulture Research Institute, for example, had made numerous trips to Thailand to train JT employees in mulberry cultivation, silkworm rearing, and cocoon production techniques, and several of its technicians were in Thailand as late as 1994 providing such training.

The network of relationships which Booth maintained with knowledgeable foreigners had also helped the company obtain foreign expertise. One key individual in this network was Henry Thompson, nephew of Jim Thompson and heir to his interest in the company. A resident of the United States with extensive business experience and a keen interest in JT's welfare, Henry had provided thoughtful counsel on many occasions during the course of the company's development.

PRODUCTION ACTIVITIES

As a result of this expansion, JT by 1994 was no longer simply a retailer of silk fabric made by others, but was involved in each stage of the complex process through which the delicate filament produced by a silkworm is transformed into such products as fabric, articles of clothing such as blouses, and pillowcases. Key activi-

EXHIBIT 3 Vertical Production Flow of JT's Silk Production Activities*

Activity	Output	Internal Supply Capability†	Employees	Location
Sericulture	Cocoons	66%	150†	PTC§
Spinning	Yarn	22%	250	PTC
Weaving	Fabric	100%	1,500	PTC
Printing	Printed fabric	100%	100	Bangkok
Sewing	Accessories	100%	350	Bangkok

*The company also produced small quantities of cotton fabric, but most of the cotton fabric it sold to retail and home furnishing customers was purchased from outside suppliers.
†Percent of JT's requirement supplied internally.
‡JT also utilized approximately 1,500 contract farming families in a broad area surrounding its sericulture facility to raise silkworm eggs to the cocoon stage.
§Pak Thong Chai. Sericulture, degumming, and spinning were carried out in upper Pak Thong Chai Province; weaving was done in the provincial capital and a nearby village.

ties JT performed in bringing about this transformation were sericulture, spinning, weaving, printing, and sewing (see Exhibit 3).

Sericulture

Silk thread is made from a fine, lustrous fiber produced by a silkworm when it forms a cocoon near the end of its life cycle. A silkworm's sole diet is mulberry leaves. Silk production therefore commences with the growing of mulberry trees. JT cultivated mulberry trees on a 900-acre plantation at the upper end of a farming valley in Pak Thong Chai Province, about 150 miles northeast of Bangkok. The 150 workers employed in this operation picked leaves from mulberry trees, conveyed them to a large rearing house, and fed them to silkworms placed there on trays stacked on long racks. Eggs produced by these silkworms were sold to approximately 1,500 contract farming families located in a wide area surrounding the facility. Farmers raised the silkworms hatched from these eggs to the cocoon stage, then sold cocoons back to JT.

This arrangement was theoretically capable of producing 30,000 boxes of eggs annually which, under proper conditions, would yield 800 tons of fresh cocoons, or 120 tons of raw silk fiber. Adverse developments had caused actual results to fall short of these targets, however. An infestation of flying insects and fungi severely reduced egg output in 1991, and drought the following year devastated the mulberry crop, causing contract farmers to demand fewer eggs. This decline in demand forced JT to place a large inventory of unsold eggs in cold storage. A subsequent surge in world supply of raw silk, accompanied by a corresponding drop in price, further eroded contract farmers' demand for JT's eggs. These adverse developments had caused the number of cocoons JT repurchased from contract farmers to decrease from a peak of 290 tons in 1990 to only 173 tons in 1993.

Despite these setbacks in the production area, JT had made progress on the technical front. Its sericulture operation had succeeded in producing several highly resistant crossbreeds of Chinese white and Thai yellow silkworm species. In addition, its extension activities had helped contract farmers improve production yields, and the average number of fresh cocoons produced per box of silkworm eggs increased from 23 kilograms in 1992 to 27 kilograms in 1993.

Spinning

Each cocoon produced by a silkworm consisted of a continuous strand of silk fiber varying in length from 800 to 1200 yards, wound up and bound together by a natural glue. JT released the fiber contained in cocoons by eliminating this glue in a process called "degumming." It then spun the resulting fiber into yarn in a facility adjacent to its sericulture operation. This activity utilized fourteen automated spinning machines and employed 250 operators. Its output in 1993 was 38.5 tons of yarn, down from a peak of 48.5 tons the previous year.

Weaving

Yarn produced by its spinning operation and that procured from outside sources was conveyed to JT's weaving mill located in the town of Pak Thong Chai about 15 miles from the company's sericulture operation. This facility was the largest hand-weaving operation in the country. Yarn entering the mill was first dyed to give it a particular color, then woven into fabric on one of the 537 hand looms installed in the facility. In addition to this mill, JT also operated a satellite weaving mill, containing 277 hand looms, in a nearby village. Looms at both locations had been designed and built by company technicians. Most of the company's 1,500 weavers were women. Hand weaving was a slow, tedious process. During a typical eight-hour shift, a weaver added only two or three meters to the length of the fabric being produced on her loom. Fabric width was generally about one meter.

JT also operated several power looms at its Pak Thong Chai facility, mainly to weave cotton fabric. Total output from these machines amounted to just 38,000 meters of fabric in 1993, compared to 593,000 meters of fabric produced on the company's hand looms.

Printing

A portion of the fabric produced by JT's weaving mills was shipped to its printing joint venture near Bangkok. The latter was equipped with both tables for hand printing and with state-of-the-art machines for high-speed machine printing. In 1993, this facility processed 355,000 meters of hand-printed silk fabric, 191,000 meters of hand-printed cotton fabric, and 984,000 meters of machine-printed cotton and synthetic fabric. Most of this output went for JT's internal use. JT was negotiating to purchase its joint venture partner's 26 percent interest in this operation in exchange for JT stock, with the understanding that the joint venture partner would continue to provide technical help following transfer of ownership. The latter showed interest in this arrangement, but was seeking an increase in the fee it received for technical assistance from the current level of 2 percent of printing revenues to 5 percent. Anticipating favorable conclusion of this negotiation, JT was planning the orderly transfer of printing equipment to a new printing facility it was building adjacent to the company's weaving mill in Pak Thong Chai. The planned move to this facility would enable the company to avoid problems arising from increasingly stringent water pollution regulation in the Bangkok area.

Sewing

A portion of the fabric leaving JT's weaving and printing mills went to its sewing joint venture in Bangkok. In 1993 the joint venture operation employed 350 skilled seamstresses to produce more than 500,000 different pieces of merchandise. High-volume items were neckties, purses, and pillowcases. JT was negotiating to buy out its partner in this venture.

OTHER ACTIVITIES

In addition to the production operations noted above, JT supported activities in finance, purchasing, design, and sales, among others. Exhibit 4 lists JT's management personnel by function for all areas of operation.

Finance

JT's original capital had been supplied by Jim Thompson and two other Americans (49 percent), and 29 Thai weaving families and silk traders (51 percent). Very few of the shares issued to the latter had subsequently changed hands except by inheritance. The widow of one of the original American shareholders had recently sold her 25 percent stake to a large Japanese department store chain for a price reputed to be $25 million. This firm, which operated two stores in Thailand—both located in Bangkok—was now JT's largest shareholder.

EXHIBIT 4   Management of Jim Thompson Thai Silk Company

Managing Director: W. M. Booth

Deputy Managing Director: Pichet Buranastidporn

Division Managers
Production: Surindr Supasavasdebhandu
Purchasing: Supphong Mangkonkarn
Design Advisor: Gerald W. Pierce
Accounting: Mrs. Warunee Tanatammatorn

Department Managers
Executive Secretary: Miss Supaporn Tongperm
                        Miss Nithima Smitharak
Advisor: Chob Pundee
Design: Tinnart Nisalak
Design Liaison: Mrs. Sirilak Sirisant
Merchandise/Warehouse: Mrs. Panya Yothasiri
Marketing: Mrs. Veronique De Champvallier
Retail: Mrs. Jeannie Cho Menge
        Mrs. Lorna M Jarungklin
        Mrs. Aporn Yordmuang
Computer Processing: Sakda Siriphongwatana
Internal Audit: Kosol Jirabunjongkij
Home Furnishing: Mrs. Chidchanok Supavaradom
Dispatching: Mrs. Kanchana Pundee
Personnel: Prachaub Chirakarnphong
            Somchai Apisithwanich

Source: 1993 Annual Report.

JT's growth over the years had been financed largely by retained earnings. As a result, the company had issued very few new shares since its inception, and had resorted to no borrowing on a long-term basis. Despite its recent profit decline and its continued dividend payout, which had averaged 30 percent of earnings in recent years, JT was accumulating funds in excess of the amount needed to operate its business. In early 1994, this excess was invested mainly in short-term certificates of deposit. Exhibit 5 contains a 10-year financial summary.

EXHIBIT 5   Jim Thompson Thai Silk Co., Selected Financial Data, 1984–1993 (Baht in millions)

	1993	1992	1991	1990	1989	1988	1987	1986	1985	1984
Income Statement Data										
Revenues	847	810	914	991	931	774	667	481	382	354
Expenses										
Cost of sales	428	401	462	514	488	400	377	268	213	219
Selling & administrative	160	147	151	156	139	119	88	75	5	51
Interest	2	0	0	0	0	0	0	1	1	1
Income taxes	77	78	106	111	106	89	70	48	44	33
Total expenses	667	626	719	782	734	608	535	392	316	304
Net profit	181	184	195	209	197	167	132	90	66	50
Balance Sheet Data										
Current assets										
Cash & S.T. investment	288	221	232	158	71	82	172	158	131	88
Receivables	53	32	38	55	35	33	26	24	24	20
Inventories	564	531	473	433	476	414	227	152	135	130
Other	21	20	35	53	7	2	8	6	2	2
Total current assets	927	804	778	698	589	531	433	341	292	240
Fixed assets										
Inv. in subsidiaries	28	39	77	77	49	34	33	31	21	26
Property, plant, equipment	406	395	279	226	201	127	77	62	47	40
Other	8	4	3	1	1	0	2	3	3	0
Total fixed assets	442	438	359	304	251	161	112	96	71	66
Total assets	1,369	1,242	1,137	1,002	840	693	545	438	362	306
Current liabilities										
Bank debt	2	2	4	5	4	13	8	12	12	14
Accounts payable	26	15	12	19	10	11	12	19	17	15
Accrued expenses	15	19	31	4	6	5	3	4	3	2
Income tax payable	40	33	58	57	55	47	39	28	23	17
Other current liabilities	8	20	5	22	23	19	9	5	4	3
Total current liabilities	91	89	110	107	98	95	71	68	59	51
Shareholders' equity	1,279	1,153	1,027	895	742	598	474	370	303	256
Total liabilities and shareholders' equity	1,369	1,242	1,137	1,002	840	693	545	438	362	306

Source: Annual Reports (errors due to rounding) $1 U.S. = 25.28 Baht (April 1993).

Purchasing

JT purchased large quantities of silk cocoons from suppliers located in Thailand, and significant amounts of silk fiber and silk yarn from both domestic and foreign sources. It also purchased large quantities of cotton fabric from outside sources. To deal with increasing shortages of domestic raw silk, it had established remote buying stations in various parts of Thailand beginning in the early 1980s. In 1993 these stations purchased a total of 90.5 tons of fresh cocoons and 134 tons of silk yarn.

Design

Creative design was frequently mentioned by JT managers as one of JT's primary strengths, serving to differentiate the firm from competitors and enabling it to command premium prices. In 1994 the design department employed more than 30 people devoted to developing new fibers, new color formulations, new weave patterns, new print designs, and new garments. A weave designer from Ireland and a print specialist from Taiwan had recently joined the group. Having outgrown its former quarters in the company's headquarters building located in downtown Bangkok, the department had recently moved to a new location on the outskirts of the city.

Sales

JT's sales revenues came from three major markets—retail (80 percent of the 1993 total), home furnishing (9 percent), and export (11 percent).

Retail Sales   JT operated five retail outlets, all located in Bangkok. Its flagship store, located next to its headquarters building in the heart of Bangkok's commercial district, was designed to resemble a Siamese palace of an earlier era, with several tiers of sloping tile roofs. The building's sumptuous interior was lined from floor to ceiling with teak shelves containing the largest selection of Thai silk fabric in the world, and its many nooks and crannies contained a vast assortment of colorful purses, neckties, and pillowcases. A mezzanine displayed garments representing the latest ready-to-wear women's fashions. Home furnishing fabrics were displayed on the store's second floor; home decorative merchandise—including sisal carpeting, antique furniture, porcelain vases, hand-painted wall panels, and Oriental room screens—was on the third floor. In addition to its main store, JT operated four "satellite" outlets in other parts of the city. Three of the latter were located in the lobbies of luxury hotels, while the fourth was located on the ground floor of Bangkok's recently opened World Trade Center. All four satellite outlets had been established during the past two years.

JT's retail merchandise was typically priced 15 percent to 20 percent above levels charged by rivals. Popular items were printed neckties (priced at $35.70 in early 1994), head scarfs ($31.00), printed cushion covers ($18.90), and printed silk napkins ($11.00). Retail prices were scrupulously maintained, the only exception to this policy being huge clearance sales which JD held twice a year in the ballroom of a large Bangkok hotel. Prices at these biennial events were typically set 50 percent or more below retail list. These sales lasted three Sundays in a row, and were so popular that JT limited attendance to approximately 5,000 "invitation only" customers.

In early 1994 there were dozens of competitors selling high-priced silk and cotton merchandise to foreign tourists in Bangkok. However, the number of such rivals had decreased over the years, and several powerful competitors of an earlier era had all but collapsed. In the meantime, JT had grown to become the undisputed market leader, commanding an estimated two-thirds of the entire premium market.

Home Furnishing Sales   JT sold drapery, wall covering, and upholstery fabric direct to local hotels, office buildings, condominiums, and housing projects. Its sales effort was focused mainly on interior designers who were chief decision makers in this market. It had recently opened a home furnishing showroom dedicated to such designers on the second floor of its headquarters building. Key purchase considerations in this market were design, price, and delivery. Numerous suppliers, many larger and more highly automated than JT, served the market. Despite this handicap, JT's sales of home furnishing fabric had nevertheless grown in recent years. A sizable portion of these sales consisted of cotton fabric, the bulk of which JT purchased from contract suppliers and sold under its own brand.

Export Sale   JT's export sales were handled by commissioned agents located in more than two dozen countries throughout the globe. Most export sales consisted of home furnishing fabric. Major export markets were the United States, Japan, United Kingdom, Germany, France, Hong Kong, and Singapore. Sales to Europe had declined somewhat in 1993, but were expected to increase in 1994 as a result of the recent appointment of a new distributor in Germany. Initiatives planned for 1994 included an international advertising program, larger than any ever mounted before; a new showroom scheduled to open in London; and increased effort in several growing Asian markets including Korea, Taiwan, and the Philippines.

REASONS FOR SUCCESS

When asked for reasons for the company's success, JT executives cited the following key factors: expertise, innovation, willingness to invest, and leadership.

Outside Experts

Frequent use of outside experts was widely cited as a key contributor to the company's success. Surindr Supasavasdebhandu, production manager, provided two examples:

> Mr. Czerny has helped us enormously over the years—in identifying the most appropriate machinery for our needs (often relatively inexpensive second hand equipment), in installing new equipment, and in adapting machinery to our particular needs. He is very patient and knows how to work with our employees.
>
> At the time we first set up our sericulture operation, two experts from the National Sericulture Institute in China came here to work with us. They provided us a great deal of help getting started. Now, their experts come here for shorter assignments to help us with particular problems as they crop up.

Continual Innovation

Surindr explained that JT had not merely duplicated technology brought in from the outside, but had often significantly adapted it to the company's special needs. He offered the following examples:

> When we first began dyeing we brought in experts from several big organizations in Thailand to advise us on boiler design. We didn't stop there, however. I took a course in thermodynamics so that I could understand what happens inside a boiler. We installed a microprocessor to control the process. As we accumulated knowledge over time, we made continual modifications. I could relate similar stories in our reeling and weaving operations. We are forcing ourselves to continually improve, to compete with ourselves for greater efficiency and higher reliability.

Willingness to Invest

The company's willingness to invest, even in projects which did not appear to show adequate return on investment, was felt to be another important contributor to the company's success. Pichet Buranastidporn, deputy managing director, offered the following example:

> It was hard to justify our silk plantation on straight ROI criteria. However, this facility has provided us important intangible benefits. It gives us protection in the event raw silk prices suddenly rise. It also enhances our reputation by making us a fully integrated producer.

Leadership

Executive leadership was another factor cited as critical to the company's success. Booth pointed to the exceptional capability of his senior managers, all of whom were Thai.

> The textile industry is considered low-tech by most Thai managers—not a very exciting area to be in. Because of this stigma, it's hard to attract really good managers to a company like ours. Another problem is the reluctance of many Thai managers to question higher-ups. Because of this trait, even individuals who are very qualified technically often don't have the independence of mind to become really effective managers. We have been very lucky to avoid these difficulties. Pichet and Surindr, for example, approach their jobs with a great deal of independent judgment. This quality has helped them develop into very capable, imaginative managers. Perhaps their strong roots in Chinese culture, which encourages more independence of mind, fosters this quality. It might also come from the fact that the three of us joined the company at about the same time and have grown up here together, so we just naturally consider ourselves as equals.

Pichet and Surindr, in turn, spoke highly of Booth's contribution. Surindr offered the following details:

> Bill arrives early, and leaves late—seven days a week—setting a good model for the rest of us to follow. He spends much of his time visiting our different operations, raising questions and providing information everywhere he goes. He doesn't try to make decisions for us, but instead helps us think more clearly about the situations we're facing.

Pichet felt that the decision process which had evolved under Booth's leadership had contributed to the company's success.

> We spend a lot of time discussing an issue before a decision is made. Deliberations usually take place in the evening, often over drinks, and are very informal. This kind of setting helps generate a lot of good ideas. It also provides plenty of opportunity for potential obstacles to surface. When obstacles emerge, we go back to the drawing board to study details more carefully. When a decision finally emerges, we have generally thought it through very thoroughly.

A POSSIBLE MARKETING WEAKNESS

While extolling JT's many strengths, several executives felt that the company suffered from weakness in the area of marketing. One described the problem as follows:

> In the past, demand at our retail store was so strong we didn't have to worry much about marketing. Our big challenge was to produce enough to meet demand. The situation is very different today. With retail sales declining, we must now find new customers, decide which ones we can serve most effectively, devise strategies for reaching new segments, and so on.

These are essentially marketing tasks. Since we have never had to look too hard for customers, our marketing skills are not yet very well developed.

The condominium market here in Bangkok illustrates the problem. Bangkok has experienced a phenomenal boom in condominium construction over the past decade. These units need to be furnished, their owners have plenty of money to pay for the very best, and Jim Thompson has an outstanding reputation for design and quality. Yet we have garnered very little of this market.

Another illustration of the problem is our experience at the World Trade Center. When we began opening satellite retail outlets a few years ago, our policy was to confine them to luxury hotels. Consequently, we made no effort to secure space in the World Trade Center which was scheduled to open in 1992. Only after an intense sales campaign by the Center's management were we finally persuaded to open an outlet there. To our great surprise, results at the Center have been spectacular.

BOOTH'S ROLE

Close observation of Booth's interactions with staff and others showed him performing a variety of different roles in managing the company.

Booth frequently brought together key people whose interaction could benefit the company. He performed this role, for example, during a day-long visit to the company's production operations in Pak Thong Chai. Accompanying him on this visit were a young Thai male named Tamrong who managed the company's printing joint venture, Czerny, and Surindr. A major purpose of the visit was to provide these three an opportunity to plan a proposed move of printing equipment from its current location in Bangkok to the new facility being prepared at Pak Thong Chai. During much of the day the three discussed the logistics of this move.

Since Czerny spoke no Thai and Surindr and Tamrong spoke no German, discussions among the three took place in English. For the most part this procedure worked fairly well. However, there were occasions when one of the three became confused. At such moments, Booth would interject a brief clarifying comment—in English to Czerny, in Thai to the other two.

Also accompanying Booth on this trip was the representative of a major Brazilian raw silk producer. He had been invited to visit Pak Thong Chai in part to comment on the company's procedures for buying raw silk. He spent the better part of an hour examining raw silk fiber piled on tables in JT's receiving area. During his inspection, he asked numerous questions about location of suppliers, storage procedures, treatment of incoming material, etc. Since he spoke no Thai and JT's purchasing personnel spoke no English, Booth played the role of interpreter.

Booth's input to conversations most frequently took the form of questions posed to clarify specific points. For example, during a discussion of spinning defects which took place on the floor of the spinning room in Pak Thong Chai, Booth asked whether the source of the problem might be insufficient maintenance frequency. This question in turn led to extensive discussion of the plant's equipment maintenance procedures.

Yet another role which Booth performed on a regular basis was that of gracious host. He took obvious pleasure in treating his Pak Thong Chai visitors to lunch at an outdoor restaurant, and later in the afternoon, during a meeting in the weaving factory's conference room, to cold beverages and appetizers. He also graciously received the steady stream of visitors who arrived at his well-appointed office on the top floor of the company's headquarters building in Bangkok. Visitors included department managers, lower-level employees, suppliers, customers, and directors. Each was cordially received, offered coffee or tea (in the evening, beer), and engaged in pleasant conversation. Not infrequently, several visitors were seated around the table in his office, engaged in lively discussion of topics ranging from developments in European weaving technology to hazards of restoring antique Thai houses.

RETAIL MARKETING PROBLEMS

Dollar sales at JT's flagship retail outlet had declined 11 percent since the peak level reached in 1990, and unit sales had fallen even further. While these declines had been offset somewhat by increases at the company's new satellite outlets, the company's overall retail sales had dropped in recent years.

JT managers attributed this decline to a variety of adverse environmental developments occurring in Bangkok. Rapid industrialization was destroying many of the charms which once attracted tourists to the city—its easygoing pace, distinctive Asian architecture, and vast network of canals. Auto congestion was becoming so severe that several hours were sometimes needed to travel just a short distance within the city. This development was of special concern to JT because most customers traveled by taxi to reach its flagship store. Air pollution had reached an alarming level. The city's AIDS infection rate, particularly among the bar girls who constituted an attraction for some male visitors to the city, had received unfavorable publicity in the international press. Recessions in Japan and Europe, which historically supplied a large proportion of JT's customers, also played a role.

These developments, together with the Iraq war and a brief military coup occurring in Bangkok in 1991, caused the number of tourists visiting Thailand to decline that year for the first time in many years (see Exhibit 6). While tourist activity had recovered somewhat since then, visitors were beginning to skirt Bangkok and travel directly to resorts elsewhere in the country. An article appearing in a recent issue of the *Bangkok Post* provided the following details about this trend.

> One of the major areas of concern is visitor arrivals from Japan which have tapered off. Although Japan's economic woes are said to be partly responsible, the TAT [Tourist Authority of Thailand] is also blaming a spate of adverse publicity over sex, AIDS, and environmental problems in Thailand. The main turnoff appears to be more Bangkok than Thailand. Visitor arrivals in January–September 1993 (by nationality) showed a total of 433,485 Japanese visitors to Thailand (down 1.28 percent on the same period in 1992) but 374,138 arrivals at Bangkok airport (down 14.21 percent duing Jan–Sept 1992).
>
> This indicates that more Japanese are bypassing Bangkok and taking advantage of the increasing number of direct flights to Puket [a popular resort on Thailand's southwest coast]. Japanese tour operators note that the environment-and-safety conscious Japanese are showing strong signs of general disgust with the capital city's traffic problems. Strong marketing by new Puket developments like the Pacific Islands Club and the new Sheraton Grande [Puket is an island off the south coast, in the Indian Ocean] are also diverting the Japanese from Bangkok.[2]

OPTIONS FOR IMPROVEMENT

In light of these developments, JT managers were seeking ways to reduce the company's dependence on Bangkok's tourist market. During the early weeks of 1994, four options for achieving this objective were under consideration.

---

[2]*Bangkok Post*, December 30, 1993, p. 45.

EXHIBIT 6   Jim Thompson Thai Silk Company

I. International Tourist Arrivals in Thailand (in thousands)

	1986	1987	1988	1989	1990	1991	1992	1993
Malaysia	653	765	868	736	752	808	729	830
Japan	259	342	449	556	652	560	570	582
Taiwan	111	195	189	400	503	454	407	525
Singapore	194	240	249	290	336	320	324	364
Germany	119	148	190	222	243	257	276	320
U.S.A.	196	236	258	267	285	248	274	278
Korea	31	37	65	112	148	180	204	271
Hong Kong	84	132	154	396	383	341	291	265
China	—	—	—	—	61	75	129	262
U.K.	147	184	280	200	238	198	236	250
Australia	95	111	138	219	252	203	208	205
France	100	132	157	187	194	173	194	202
Others	829	961	1,234	1,225	1,252	1,270	1,294	1,407
Total	2,818	3,483	4,231	4,810	5,299	5,087	5,136	5,761

II. Tourist Expenditures in Thailand (% of total)

	1986	1990	1993
Shopping	27.4	39.0	42.8
Accommodations	26.6	23.1	23.0
Food and beverages	16.9	15.1	15.1
Local transit	15.6	13.3	10.7
Entertainment	10.0	7.6	5.1
Other	3.5	1.9	3.3
Total	100.0	100.0	100.0

Source: Tourism Authority of Thailand.

1. Develop a mail order catalogue displaying accessories such as neckties, purses, blouses, etc., and target the catalogue to foreigners who had already purchased JT products during visits to Bangkok.

2. Open a retail store in a major foreign city such as New York, Paris, or Tokyo.

3. Open a retail shop at a Thai beach resort such as Puket, Samui (an island in the Gulf of Siam), or Pattaya (a resort on the Gulf of Siam's east coast). All three locations were growing very rapidly. Puket and Samui were still relatively unspoiled. Pattaya, however, was beginning to experience its own brand of environmental degradation. An article appearing in a 1991 issue of *The Economist* provided the following details.

> Twenty-five years ago Pattaya was a sleepy fishing village. Then it was discovered by American soldiers on R&R from Vietnam, and the Thai brand of sun, sea, and sex was invented, beginning a boom in tourism. Today Pattaya is a mess. Uncontrolled building

has ruined its shoreline. The sea is coated with a film of raw sewage. Last year so many tourists died in mysterious circumstances that even the shady mafia that controls the town was embarrassed. An alarming proportion of the bar girls, many of whom are in fact transvestites, are HIV positive. Lucky is the hotel with 10 percent of its rooms occupied.[3]

4. Expand sales to the domestic home furnishing market.

JT managers were particularly enthusiastic about the last of these options, for several reasons. The domestic home furnishing market experienced little adverse affect from the city's traffic congestion. Indeed, the market may have actually benefited from such congestion, since an increasing number of people were moving from the outskirts of Bangkok to downtown condominiums near their work locations to avoid traffic jams during commuting hours. A heady construction boom was taking place in the city, and new units being built needed furnishing. And JT's reputation for creative design and good quality were highly prized by interior decorators, who acted as prime decision makers in the market.

The home furnishing market presented JT a major challenge, however. Most home furnishing sales consisted of relatively low-priced cotton fabric produced by suppliers utilizing high-speed mechanical looms. JT's weaving expertise, by contrast, lay in hand weaving. To compete more effectively in the home furnishing market, JT would need to significantly improve its high-speed mechanical weaving capabilities.

In an effort to improve its ability in this area, JT had purchased six secondhand high-speed mechanical looms over the past several years from a German company, Rohleder GMBH. JT's personnel had experienced difficulties operating the equipment, however, and trained operators were not available in Thailand. To overcome this obstacle, JT had sent several of its operators to Germany to receive training from Rohleder. Rohleder was the world's eighth largest, and Germany's second largest, manufacturer of upholstery fabric used for couches, chairs, etc. When difficulties persisted following the trainees' return to Bangkok, JT had approached Rohleder for further assistance. Ensuing conversations revealed that Rohleder was interested in establishing its own weaving facility in Asia in order to gain access to low-cost Asian labor and to better serve its growing base of Asian customers. Lacking operating experience in the region, it hoped to secure an Asian partner, and inquired whether JT would consider joining it in constructing a jointly-owned weaving mill in Thailand.

Investigation revealed that Rohleder's existing weaving mill, located near Frankfurt, was one of the most technically advanced in the world. Its entire output of fabric was sold to wholesalers who in turn sold, often under their own brands, to interior decorators and furniture manufacturers. Wholesalers generally gave Rohleder very high marks for quality and technical sophistication. Though more than 70 years old, Rohleder was still controlled by its founding family.

While Rohleder's skill in mechanical weaving—the very capability JT needed to improve its position in the home furnishing market—made the proposed venture with Rohleder attractive, Booth felt that the other options under consideration also offered promise. He hoped that the planning effort scheduled for the coming weeks would help clarify the pros and cons of all the options open to the company, so that he and his managers could make an optimal decision regarding the company's future direction.

---

[3]*The Economist*, July 6, 1991, p. 78.

CASE
18
WHIRLPOOL CORPORATION

Arthur A. Thompson, *The University of Alabama*

Bryan Fuller, *The University of Alabama*

In 1995, Whirlpool Corporation was the world's leading producer and marketer of major home appliances. The company had manufacturing plants in 12 countries and marketed products in over 120 countries under such brands as Whirlpool, KitchenAid, Roper, Estate, Bauknecht, Ignis, Laden, Inglis, Brasemp, Consul, and Semer. Whirlpool was also the principal supplier to Sears Roebuck and Co. of many major home appliances that Sears sold under it own private-label Kenmore brand.

Since 1988, Whirlpool had embarked on a strategy to globalize its home appliance business and to lead the industry's transformation from a collection of national markets and national competitors to a global market with global competitors. The strategy was the product of an assessment by Whirlpool's management of the appliance industry worldwide, of Whirlpool's current position as a North America-only producer and marketer, and of what Whirlpool's long-term strategic direction should be. The assessment, led by newly appointed CEO David Whitwam in 1987, produced several conclusions. First, profitable growth opportunities in the North American market were scarce. Competition was fierce and margins wafer-thin. Where once there had been several dozen North American appliance manufacturers, now there were four large, dominant players—Whirlpool, General Electric, Maytag, and White/Frigidaire, all positioned to do battle in a price-driven market characterized by relatively high saturation rates for major household appliances and up-and-down annual sales volumes.

Second, to continue to grow and flourish in the major home appliance business, Whirlpool would have to enter foreign markets and eventually become a global competitor. Just as had occurred in North America, the appliance industry in Europe was starting to consolidate, thus presenting Whirlpool with opportunities to enter the European market via acquisition. Moreover, with the advent of the European Common Market, management thought it was probable that the European market for appliances would evolve toward a single market with similar home appliances and away from its present state as a group of individual country markets with distinctly different home appliances. Latin America was seen as a region with enormous growth potential, given the low saturation rates of major home appliances. And Asia, by the year 2000, was expected to become the world's largest market for home appliances. Hence, to participate in the industry's future growth, management argued, Whirlpool would have to be a global player.

Third, Whirlpool's management concluded that global success would require a strong customer focus combined with best-cost, best-quality production and that Whirlpool's North American home market would have to be profitable enough to provide much of the financial means for Whirlpool to invest in a long-term strategy to build a globally competitive position. Since the 1987 assessment, Whirlpool's management had not wavered in its commitment to an aggressive global strategy.

THE WORLD MARKET FOR HOME APPLIANCES

Major home appliances (often referred to as "white goods") consisted of kitchen appliances (ranges, cooking tops, ovens, refrigerators, freezers, garbage disposals, dishwashers, compactors, and microwaves), laundry appliances (washers and dryers), and to a lesser extent comfort appliances (room air conditioners and dehumidifiers). Appliance manufacture represented one of the world's largest consumer goods industries. Worldwide shipments of home appliances totaled about 194 million units in 1994, equal to a wholesale market of $55 to $60 billion. Market conditions varied significantly across the appliance industry's four most important geographic regions: North America, Europe, Latin America, and Asia.

The North American Appliance Market

Total appliance shipments in North America approximated 50 million units annually, recently accounting for between 25 and 30 percent of the world total. Exhibit 1 shows shipments by product category. Except for Mexico, the market was mature, growing less rapidly on average than the economy. Shipments were projected to increase 1 to 3 percent annually through the year 2000. Overall appliance demand varied from year to year depending on saturation levels, replacement needs, housing starts, and general economic conditions. Each of these sales-determining factors affected the various appliance product categories differently. Sales of ranges, dishwashers, compactors, and built-in ovens and microwaves, for example, were heavily affected by changes in new housing starts. Refrigerators, which had the highest saturation rate of any appliance (some households had more than one), were minimally affected by housing starts and depended chiefly on the decisions of households to replace their present refrigerator. Washer and dryer sales were least dependent on housing starts but washers had a much higher saturation rate than dryers, making replacement decisions a bigger sales driver for washers than for dryers. Since household saturation rates for dishwashers, laundry appliances, and freezers were lower

EXHIBIT 1 Shipments of Major Household Appliances in North America, 1990–1994 (in thousands of units)

Product Category	1990	1991	1992	1993	1994
Kitchen appliances, total	30,218	29,019	31,226	32,597	35,839
Cooking, total	13,862	12,630	13,685	14,222	16,057
Electric ranges	3,444	3,309	3,574	3,848	4,159
Gas ranges	2,429	2,401	2,614	2,755	2,951
Microwave ovens/range	8,126	7,012	7,588	7,703	9,030
Food waste disposers	4,137	4,002	4,195	4,436	4,789
Trash compactors	185	129	126	125	120
Automatic dishwashers	3,637	3,571	3,820	4,099	4,572
Freezers	1,296	1,414	1,639	1,609	1,690
Refrigerators	7,101	7,273	7,761	8,109	8,611
Laundry appliances, total	10,512	10,510	11,232	11,867	12,325
Dryers, total	4,320	4,313	4,717	5,074	5,332
Electric	3,318	3,295	3,563	3,853	4,033
Gas	1,002	1,018	1,154	1,229	1,299
Washers	6,192	6,197	6,515	6,793	6,993
Total appliances	40,730	39,529	42,457	44,463	48,164

Source: *Appliance Manufacturer,* 1995.

than for other appliances (ranges or refrigerators), there was an initial purchase market for them independent of replacement demand and new housing starts. Low saturation levels sometimes resulted in big gains in sales volumes; for example, in the 1980s, when consumers decided microwaves were a "must have" appliance, unit volume soared. Exhibit 2 shows saturation rates by product type. General economic conditions were a driver of appliance sales because of their effects on housing starts, the current ability of households to afford either initial or replacement purchases, and the tendency of households to postpone buying discretionary items like appliances during recessions—home appliances were the epitome of a cyclical durable goods industry.

Each appliance category had its own life span. According to the Association of Home Appliance Manufacturers, ranges had a life span of 10 to 30 years, laundry appliances 10 to 16 years, refrigerators and freezers 10 to 20 years, and dishwashers 7 to 14 years—see Exhibit 2 for average life expectancy by appliance type. About 75 percent of all appliance purchases in North America were made to replace another appliance. While appliance purchases could be accelerated or postponed, their functional necessity in the lifestyle of households limited the deferral period. Except when they had had a bad experience, U.S. consumers exhibited strong brand loyalty on replacement purchases.

While there were no major new home appliance products in the development stage, appliance manufacturers were introducing a variety of new features to stimulate faster replacement and spur new demand. Such features included user-friendly electronic controls that were more durable and easier to see, easier to clean components, quieter operation, greater energy efficiency, programmable controls, larger capacity, more efficient use of space, and the cosmetics of color and styling.

In the United States, recently enacted federal standards called for 25 percent increases in the energy efficiency of appliances; the Department of Energy's goal was

EXHIBIT 2	Major Appliance Product Saturation Levels in the United States, 1973–1994 (percent of households with appliance)							

Product	1973	1983	1990	1991	1992	1993	1994	Average Life Expectancy (years)
Kitchen appliances								
Dishwasher	34	45	52	48	50	51	52	9
Microwave oven	1	3	84	85	85	86	89	10
Electric range	47	58	61	57	57	58	59	15
Gas range	52	43	45	46	46	45	45	18
Disposer	35	50	52	47	50	51	52	9
Freezer	31	43	44	33	38	40	40	12
Refrigerator	100	100	100	100	99	99	100	15
Laundry appliances								
Electric dryer	41	49	49	51	51	53	54	13
Gas dryer	10	15	17	16	18	17	18	14
Washer	68	74	73	73	74	74	75	13

Source: Standard & Poor's Industry Surveys: *Appliance,* September 1995.

to reduce energy usage in appliances by 25 percent every five years. Manufacturers were beginning to promote the reduced energy usage of their new appliances because the energy cost savings were significant enough in some cases to pay for early replacement. For instance, refrigerators purchased in the 1960s and 1970s could use as much as $15 to $20 of electricity per month; those purchased in 1995 used as little as $5 per month. Federal regulations regarding the phase-out of ozone-depleting chlorofluorocarbons had also had an impact on the design of refrigerators and freezers; however, when a few manufacturers moved early to introduce models with CFC-free technology in 1994, rivals quickly followed and the new standards were being met ahead of schedule.

Wholesale and Retail Distribution During the past two decade there had been major consolidation among appliance distributors and retailers. In 1995, about 50 percent of total appliance volume was accounted for by the 10 leading retailers. Sears, with a 25 percent market share, was the biggest of the appliance mega-retailers, followed by Montgomery Ward, Circuit City, and Silo. A number of smaller retailers and distributors had exited the business because of inability to match the prices and bargaining power of large-volume dealers and because manufacturers were bypassing distributors with factory-direct strategies. Large chain retailers had increased their demands for service from manufacturers in addition to wrangling price concessions.

To meet these demands and still eke out a profit, appliance manufacturers were revamping their shipping and warehousing systems to shorten delivery times, streamline order processing, and reduce the need for large retailer inventories. Whirlpool, for example, had begun replacing its system of independent distributors with a factory-direct distribution system that would permit delivery of all its products to retailers within 24 hours. General Electric had instituted a "Direct Connect" program for its retail dealers that allowed stores to operate with virtually zero inventory.[1] With Direct Connect, GE dealers utilized computer software giving them on-line access to GE's distribution warehouse inventories 24 hours a day; they could use the system to check model availability and place orders for next-day delivery. Dealers got GE's lowest prices, regardless of order size, plus consumer financing through GE Credit with the first 90 days free of interest. In exchange, GE dealers agreed to (1) promote sales of nine different GE appliances, while stocking only microwaves and air conditioners for customer carryout, (2) guarantee that GE products account for at least 50 percent of sales, and (3) pay GE through electronic funds transfer on the 25th of the month. With Direct Connect, dealer profit margins on GE products increased since dealer costs for inventory were virtually eliminated and dealers did not have to order full-truckload lots to get GE's best price. Manufacturers' efforts to speed delivery and streamline distribution activities not only permitted dealers to function as appliance showrooms but also facilitated the creation of manufacturer–dealer partnerships that cut both partners' costs and improved the service provided to household appliance buyers.

Competition   Since 1980, the manufacturing portion of the North American appliance industry had gone through several rounds of merger/acquisition activity that reduced the field from 15 competitors to a market dominated by 5 major players:

Company	Major Brands	Overall Market Share
Whirlpool	Whirlpool, KitchenAid, Roper, Estate, Inglis	33.6%
General Electric	General Electric (GE), Hotpoint	27.7
Electrolux/ Frigidaire	Frigidaire, Tappan, Kelvinator, White-Westinghouse, Gibson	16.9
Maytag	Maytag, Jenn-Air, Magic Chef, Admiral, Norge, Hardwick	14.6
Raytheon/Amana	Amana, Speed Queen, Caloric/Modern Maid	5.5
		98.3%

There were several other participants that competed in specialized segments: the Japanese and Korean producers in microwave ovens (Matsushita/Panasonic, Sharp, Sanyo, Toshiba, Samsung, and Goldstar), Emerson Electric (In-Sink-Erator waste disposals and Emerson room air conditioners), Thermador-Waste King (high-end ranges, ovens, refrigerators, compactors, and garbage disposals), and a few makers of room air conditioners and dehumidifiers. Industry consolidation had been driven by the competitive needs to provide distributors and dealers with a broad product line (in terms of both price ranges and appliance categories) and to achieve volume-related operating economies. Given the maturity of the North American appliance market and continuing inability to increase prices (fierce competition had kept appli-

---

[1]Michael Treacy and Fred Wiersema, *The Discipline of Market Leaders* (Reading, MA: Addison-Wesley Publishing, 1995), pp. 33–34.

ance price flat for almost a decade), manufacturers saw revenue and volume growth as being dependent on a wider product line, acquisition, and a larger market share.

GE and Whirlpool had been the overall market share leaders in North America for over two decades. Market share by appliance category varied among the major competitors—see Exhibit 3. Competition centered around price, the introduction of attractive new product features, product performance and quality, appearance and styling, the range and caliber of services offered to distributors and dealers, and brand-name reputation. Exhibit 4 provides a profile of Whirlpool's North American competitors.

While GE and Whirlpool were generally regarded as the overall lowest-cost U.S. appliance manufacturers, in 1995 virtually all of the remaining U.S. producers operated comparatively efficient, cost-competitive plants. The minimum efficient scale plant for ranges, refrigerators, dishwashers, and washer-dryers was about 500,000 units annually. The recent wave of mergers had permitted companies to consolidate production into an efficient number of plants, combine purchasing activities and gain more bargaining leverage with suppliers, share technology and R&D across plant and product categories, and eliminate costly excess capacity. While cost differences still remained, the gaps were narrower and related more to differences in design, quality, performance feature, and degree of vertical integration (in-house manufacture of parts and components versus outsourcing) than to differences in plant efficiency.

Manufacturing was essentially an assembly-line operation. Labor costs were typically under 10 percent of total costs. Parts and components averaged 30 to 45 percent of total costs, depending on the appliance. Cost fluctuations were chiefly a function of changes in the prices of raw materials and components; unit costs also depended on the percentage utilization of manufacturing capacity. High-volume manufacturers often had significant purchasing power leverage with parts and components suppliers and, in recent years, had been able to procure needed supplies from outside parts specialists with world-scale plants at better prices than appliance manufacturers who had integrated backward into parts and components manufacture.

High-end appliances carried greater profit margins than medium- and low-priced models. Company profit margins were thus a reflection of a more or less profitable product mix, as well as operating efficiency. For instance, Maytag's overall margins eroded slightly when it purchased Magic Chef, a maker of medium- and low-end appliance products. And Whirlpool's margins benefited from its acquisition of KitchenAid, a producer of high-end appliances.

All manufacturers were experiencing pressure on profit margins. Appliance prices had risen less than 10 percent on average since the early 1980s. By way of comparison, the consumer price index had risen 40 percent during the same period.

The European Appliance Market

Total appliance shipments across all of Europe were around 50 million units annually, up from 44 million units in 1988 and 35 million units in the early 1980s. The five best-selling appliances were refrigerators, washers, cooking equipment, microwave ovens, and freezers. In general, appliance saturation rates were lower in Europe than in the United States (see Exhibits 2 and 5), but rates varied significantly from country to country even for the same appliance. Whereas nearly all West European households had refrigerators, in many countries in Eastern Europe refrigerators were a luxury. Only 1 in 3 European households had dishwashers, ranging from 2 in 5 in Germany and France to just 1 in 10 in Britain. Appliance sales were expected to

EXHIBIT 3   U.S. Market Shares of Major Appliance Manufacturers by Product Category, 1988–1994

Product/Manufacturers	Market Share (%)				Product/Manufacturers	Market Share (%)			
	1994	1992	1990	1988		1994	1992	1990	1988
Washers					**Ranges (Gas)**				
Whirlpool	52	52	52	50	Maytag	24	27	21	24
GE	17	16	15	17	Electrolux (Frigidaire)	24	25‡	20‡	7
Maytag	17	17	17	16	Raytheon (Caloric)	20	22	20	15
Electrolux (Frigidaire)	12	10	9	10	GE	27	19§	34§	‖
Raytheon (Speed Queen)	2	4	4	4	Brown	2	3	1	4
Others	—	3	3	3	Perrless-Premier	2	3	1	3
					Tappan	—	—	—	25
Dryers (gas)					Roper	—	—	—	15
Whirlpool	53	53	55	52	Others	1	1	3	7
Maytag	15	17	16	12					
GE	14	14	13	16	**Ranges (Electric)**				
Electrolux (Frigidaire)	12	10	9	11	GE	37	30§	47§	30
Raytheon (Speed Queen)	5	4	3	3	Whirlpool	25	30	15	13
Norge	—	—	—	2	Maytag	14	17	11	10
Others	1	2	4	4	Electrolux (Frigidaire)	17	15‡	19‡	15
					Raytheon (Caloric)	6	7	6	7
Dryers (electric)					Thermador	1	1	2	n.a.
Whirlpool	52	52	52	52	Roper	—	—	—	14
GE	17	18	19	16	Tappan	—	—	—	7
Maytag	15	15	15	12	Others	—	—	—	4
Electrolux (Frigidaire)	14	12	8	11					
Raytheon (Speed Queen)	2	3	4	3	**Microwave Ovens**				
Norge	—	—	—	2	Sharp	25	20	15	17
Others	—	—	2	4	Samsung	21	18	18	18
					Matsushita	15	17	12	13
Refrigerators					Electrolux	7	10	7	5
GE	35	35	36	35	Goldstar	10	10	18	19
Whirlpool	25	25	27	28	Sanyo	5	7	7	5
Electrolux (Frigidaire)	18	17	19	21	Maytag	8	6	5	2
Maytag (Admiral)	13	13	7	10	Raytheon	2	4	4	6
Raytheon (Amana)	7	8	9	5	Whirlpool	1	3	2	2
Others	2	2	2	1	Toshiba	—	1	3	2
					Others	6	4	9	11

Note: Market share figures include units made for private-label retailers as well as those sold under manufacturers' brand names.   (*continued*)

n.a.—not available.

*No longer makes freezers.

†Includes sales of Design and Manufacturing (acquired by Electrolux).

‡Includes Tappan, an Electrolux unit.

§Includes Roper, a GE unit.

‖Did not manufacture gas ranges at this time.

Sources: *Appliance Manufacturer,* April 1990–94.

EXHIBIT 3   Concluded

Product/Manufacturers	Market Share (%)				Product/Manufacturers	Market Share (%)			
	1994	1992	1990	1988		1994	1992	1990	1988
Freezers					**Disposers**				
Electrolux (Frigidaire)	73	76	32	32	In-Sink-Erator	65	65	62	60
W.C. Wood	17	14	n.a.	n.a.	Electrolux	17	17	23	30
Maytag (Admiral)	*	*	22	22	Waste King	10	10	8	5
Raytheon (Amana)	5	5	6	6	Whirlpool (KitchenAid)	3	2	n.a.	n.a.
Whirlpool	5	5	38	36	Maytag	1	2	1	1
Others	—	—	4	4	Watertown Metal	2	2	5	2
					Others	2	2	1	2
Dishwashers									
GE	40	40	35	40	**Compactors**				
Whirlpool	31	31	34	19	Whirlpool	82	70	74	67
Electrolux (Frigidaire)	20†	20†	19†	7	GE	—	14	16	14
Maytag	8	8	11	7	Brown	18	14	5	6
Thermador	1	1	1	1	Thermador	—	1	3	3
Design and Manufacturing	—	—	—	20	Emerson	—	—	—	8
Emerson	—	—	—	5	Others	—	1	2	2
Others	—	—	—	1					

n.a.—not available.
*No longer makes freezers.
†Includes sales of Design and Manufacturing (acquired by Electrolux).
‡Includes Tappan, an Electrolux unit.
§Includes Roper, a GE unit.
||Did not manufacture gas ranges at this time.
Sources: *Appliance Manufacturer,* April 1990–94.

grow 2 to 3 percent annually in Europe throughout the 1990s. Sales in the former communist block of European countries were expected to flourish after 2000, as these countries strengthened their economies and household purchasing power increased; Eastern Europe accounted for 5 to 10 percent of world appliance sales. European consumers paid a higher percentage of household income for appliances than did U.S. households. European consumers often paid up to twice as much for appliances as U.S. consumers when cost was measured by number of hours worked.

The European appliance market was complex because of varying consumer preferences in choosing appliances, varying mechanical differences, and varying electrical standards. The French preferred top-loading washing machines, whereas front-loading washers were preferred in most other European countries. German and U.K. washing machines spun at a faster rate during the spin cycle than those in Italy and other southern European countries because drying clothes took longer in Northern climates. Northern Europeans wanted large refrigerators because they tended to shop once a week in supermarkets; southern Europeans got by on small refrigerators because they shopped almost daily in open-air markets. Northern Europeans liked refrigerators with freezer units on the bottom; southern Europeans were accustomed to freezers on the top. British households, which were heavy consumers of frozen

EXHIBIT 4 Profile of Whirlpool's North American Competitors

Maytag

Headquartered in Iowa, Maytag had 1994 sales of $3.4 billion and profits of $148 million. Maytag was best known for its top-quality washers and dryers. To compete more broadly, Maytag in the late 1980s acquired the Magic Chef, Jenn-Air, Norge, and Admiral appliance lines and purchased Chicago Pacific, owner of Hoover vacuum and several European plants that manufactured home appliances sold under the Hoover brand name. Maytag's strategy was to offer a wider selection of brand-name appliances at various price points: Jenn-Air at the high end, Maytag in the middle to upper range, Admiral and Magic Chef in the medium to low range, and Norge on the low end. Maytag expanded Jenn-Air's line of cooking tops and ranges to include refrigerators and dishwashers, the Maytag line of washing equipment to include cooking equipment, dishwashers, and refrigerators, and the Magic Chef line of cooking equipment to include dishwashers and refrigerators. Maytag then developed "focus factories" whereby all brands of the same appliance (dishwashers, refrigerators, and cooking equipment) would be produced at the same plant. By jointly sharing technologies and production facilities, Maytag hoped to improve designs and increase manufacturing efficiencies; Maytag also produced more parts and components in-house than most other appliance makers. Maytag created two sales force organizations to market the five brands: one was responsible for the Jenn-Air line, the Magic Chef line, and the low-end Norge line; the other handled the Maytag line and the medium-priced Admiral line.

The Hoover acquisition included a large European subsidiary that manufactured laundry appliances, dishwashers, and vacuum cleaners and provided a vehicle for entering the European appliance market; as of 1994, over 15 percent of Maytag's sales were derived from foreign markets. In 1995, Maytag consisted of nine company subsidiaries with 22 manufacturing plants in the United States and six European countries. So far, Maytag's foray in Europe had not been profitable.

General Electric

General Electric was the sixth-largest industrial enterprise in the United States, with 1994 sales of $60.1 billion and profits of $4.7 billion. GE was broadly diversified; its biggest businesses were power generation equipment, aircraft engines, lighting products, appliances, TV broadcasting (it owned NBC), medical equipment and services, plastics, and financial and credit services. GE Appliances had 1994 sales of $6 billion and operating profits of $683 million. The division was a low-cost producer; it had modern, efficient manufacturing plants and operated its own distribution network to serve retail dealers. GE's strongest appliance lines were cooking tops, built-in ovens and microwaves, refrigerators, and dishwashers. GE had an extensive network of U.S. retail dealers, plus it had recently begun selling its appliances through Sears's Brand Central store format. GE also supplied its appliances directly to builders for installation in new homes and apartments. In 1994, GE Appliances introduced more than 300 new appliance models, led by a 30-cubic-foot side-by-side refrigerator-freezer (the world's largest capacity) that fit in the same space as 27-cubic-foot models and a new high-performance model that used no ozone-depleting chloroflurocarbons (CFCs) in the compressor refrigerant and had greater storage capacity. The division had made major capital investments in its refrigerator and laundry equipment plants and had a world-class dishwasher plant.

Although sales were heavily concentrated in North America, GE Appliances had recently begun putting more emphasis on export sales to increase its presence in the fastest-growing global markets, particularly India, China, Southeast Asia, and South America. It had developed a number of new models specifically for export to foreign country markets. GE's international strategy had two main parts: export sales of products manufactured in North America and strategic alliances with strong local appliance manufacturers. In 1995, GE appliances were sold on every continent, with domestically produced appliances being exported to more than 50 countries. Export sales were biggest in Europe and Asia; distribution in the Middle East, South America, and Africa was established in 1992. GE had about a 25 to 30 percent share of the U.K. appliance market but was a niche player in most other foreign markets. Its most important strategic alliances were in Mexico (with MABE) and in India (with Godrej and Boyce, India's largest appliance maker). The joint venture with Godrej and Boyce was established in February 1993 to develop, manufacture, and market a range of selected home appliances to meet the growing demands of India's expanding middle-income population. Gondrej-GE's objective was to increase revenues 10-fold by the year 2000.

EXHIBIT 4 Concluded

Electrolux

Swedish-based Electrolux was the world's second-largest manufacturer of white goods. It was the European market leader. It had entered the U.S. market in 1986 when it acquired White Consolidated Industries, the third-largest U.S. producer, for $780 million. White Consolidated was a company recently created by merging the businesses of a number of lesser-known appliance brands; White's biggest-selling appliance lines were Frigidaire refrigerators, freezers, washers, and dryers. Electrolux had also acquired Tappan (best known for its gas cooking ranges) and Design and Manufacturing, the principal supplier of dishwashers sold under Sears's Kenmore label. In 1991, Electrolux had changed the name of its WCI Major Appliance Group to Frigidaire Company. Since the acquisition, Electrolux had invested over $600 million in Frigidaire, improving production methods and equipment, modernizing and expanding existing factories, and building new refrigerator and dishwasher plants. Like Whirlpool, Electrolux was restructuring its appliance business along global lines. Frigidaire's design engineers had been consolidated into a single unit; the unit worked closely with Electrolux's appliance design centers in Sweden and Italy, endeavoring to coordinate and standardize designs where possible. Frigidaire was paring its list of suppliers and establishing long-term relationships with those who could mesh their efforts with Frigidaire's to make a competitive difference. Electrolux was moving to coordinate its procurement worldwide.

Electrolux, Whirlpool's biggest rival in Europe, was broadly diversified and had acquired 200 companies during the 1980s. During the 1990s, Electrolux had focused greater attention on its core appliance business. So far, its Frigidaire division had been only marginally profitable. However, Electrolux's strategic intent was to raise consumer awareness of the Frigidaire brand name to a level equal to GE and Whirlpool and to reposition Frigidaire as a high-end brand. In 1995, Frigidaire introduced its new Gallery line of refrigerator-freezers, ranges, dishwashers, and washer-dryers to appeal to high-end consumers; the expertise of Electrolux's global design center was used to develop the new line. Frigidaire launched a $20 million ad campaign (the biggest national print and TV advertising blitz in the company's history) to launch the Gallery line. Frigidaire management believed that, since all U.S. manufacturers made good-quality appliances, successful differentiation of the Frigidaire brand depended on being a leader on styling and performance features.

Raytheon/Amana

Raytheon was a diversified, technology-based company that ranked among the 100 largest U.S. corporations and was best known as the maker of Patriot missiles. Raytheon consisted of five business groups, one of which was major home appliances. The appliance group had sales of just over $1 billion and consisted of three brands: Amana, Speed Queen, and Caloric/Modern Maid. Amana was positioned in the upper end of the appliance market; the brand's best-selling models were refrigerators, freezers, smooth-top cooking equipment, and microwaves. Caloric was a maker of gas and electric ranges. Speed Queen was the leading supplier of washers and dryers for the coin-operated segment and for hotels, hospitals, prisons, and other commercial operations; it had significant exports, with sales in 95 countries. In 1991, the three brands, which formerly had operated as independent subsidiaries, were consolidated into a single operation under the Amana umbrella. Downsizing, consolidation of marketing and other functions, and plant upgrading ensued. Speed Queen became the laundry equipment supplier for both the Speed Queen and Amana brands; Amana washer-dryer models were positioned in the mid- to high-end segment, and Speed Queen–branded models were targeted to the lower and mid-market segments. Amana washers and dryers offered stainless steel baskets and drums (which the company said were preferable to porcelain or plastic in terms of wear and tear on clothing), were quiet, and carried the longest warranties in the industry; dryer models could be easily adjusted with a screwdriver to open from the right or left and had a moisture sensor that signaled the dryer to stop as soon as the fabric was dry.

foods, insisted on units with 60 percent freezer space. Italian households preferred cooking on elegantly designed gas ranges, whereas German households preferred practical electric cooking equipment. British households used either gas or electric cooking equipment, depending on which tended to be most economical in their community. In France, where cooking practices relied heavily on special sauces and baking, self-cleaning ovens were very popular; in Italy, where much of the food was grilled, the self-clean function was not as popular.

EXHIBIT 5   Estimated Appliance Saturation Rates outside North
America, 1994

Geographic Region	Appliance	Estimated 1994 Saturation Rate
Western Europe	Refrigerators	99%
	Cooking	97
	Washers	82
	Dryers	18
	Dishwashers	30
	Microwave ovens	40
	Freezers	40
Latin America	Refrigerators	70
	Cooking	90
	Washers	40
	Microwave ovens	6
	Room air conditioners	10
Asia	Refrigerators	30
	Washers	20
	Microwave ovens	7
	Room air conditioners	8

Source: Whirlpool's 1994 Annual Report.

Manufacturers coped with the country-to-country differences in sizes, shapes, and styles by developing flexible assembly lines that could handle small runs for many different models and styles in a cost-effective manner. An Italian refrigerator plant, for example, produced 935 variations of 54 basic models. Electrolux produced 1,500 variations of 120 basic appliance designs to accommodate the diverse market conditions in Europe. Some manufacturers believed, however, that as European economic integration proceeded, the fragmented and heterogeneous makeup of the European appliance market would gradually give way to greater homogeneity, reducing the need to produce so many variations of the same appliance. Other producers were skeptical about whether consumer preferences would converge rapidly.

The appliance market in Europe was also more driven by environmental factors. Relatively high electricity prices made the energy efficiency of appliances an important consumer concern. Washers were designed to economize on water usage, a concern in European locations like Germany where water was expensive. European manufacturers were considered to be leaders in energy efficient appliances, low water usage, and built-in models (a desirable feature, given the comparatively small size of European kitchens and living quarters).

Distribution   In Europe, home appliances were retailed through about 40,000 dealers. As in the North American market, the distribution sector was becoming more concentrated. Large retail chains were selling a growing fraction of appliances, both under manufacturers' brands and their own private labels. Many European manufacturers produced appliances for sale under a distributor's own private label. Retail chains in Europe had been able to exert considerable bargaining leverage over manufacturers with idle factory capacity.

Because the European appliance market was so fragmented, many brands were country-specific within Europe. In addition, language and cultural differences made it more troublesome to advertise the same brand across the entire continent. Whirlpool was having difficulty establishing the Whirlpool brand in several European countries because Whirlpool was virtually unpronounceable in certain languages.

Competition Although the manufacturing side of the European appliance market was consolidating, there were still 35 appliance makers in Western Europe and another 50 or so in Eastern and Central Europe. Most were small companies that either specialized in making a single appliance line (stoves or laundry equipment) or competed in just a single country (due to differing product designs, consumer preferences, electrical standards, or trade restrictions). Fewer than eight appliance manufacturers competed broadly across most of Europe with a fairly complete lineup of appliance products. The market leaders in 1995 were:

Company	Major Brands	Overall Market Share
Electrolux	Electrolux, Zanussi, Zoppas, Euroflair, Arthur Martin, Faure, Zanker, Juno	25%
Bosch-Siemens	Bosch, Siemens, Constructa, Neff	15
Whirlpool	Whirlpool, Bauknecht, Ignis, Laden	13
Elfi/Brandt	Brandt, Ocean, eight others	10
Merloni	Ariston, Indesit, Scholtes, New World	9
Candy	Candy, Zerowatt, Rosieres, LEC	7
General Electric	GE, Hotpoint	1
Maytag	Hoover	1

Source: *Appliance Manufacturer,* April 1995; July 1994.

In 1989, the top five manufacturers accounted for 57 percent of the market; in 1994, they had a combined market share approaching 70 percent.

Exhibit 6 provides a profile of Whirlpool's major European competitors. European manufacturers also faced competition from Japanese and South Korean manufacturers in the microwave oven segment. As in the North American market, competition was focused on price, performance features, styling, dealer networks, brand image and reputation, and energy consumption.

Rival appliance manufacturers were pursuing ways to reduce manufacturing costs, improve product quality, add attractive new features, and revamp designs to permit reduced energy and water consumption, recyclability of appliance components, and greater standardization of parts and components. Whirlpool, for example, had introduced a new automatic washer line in Europe that retained fewer than 1 percent of the parts and components of its predecessor.

EXHIBIT 6   Profile of Whirlpool's European Competitors

AB Electrolux (Sweden)

Electrolux was the market share leader in Europe and had made several acquisitions to build its position: Arthur Martin (France, 1976), Zannusi (Italy, 1986), Lehel (Hungary, 1991), and AEG Hausgerate (Germany, 1994). The Zannusi acquisition marked the beginning of Electrolux's strategy to lead the transition from a series of separate country markets for appliances to more of a pan-European market for appliances. Increased penetration of the Eastern European market, which accounted for approximately 10 percent of the global appliance market, was the most recent component of Electrolux's strategy to eventually dominate the European appliance market. The Lehel acquisition provided the vehicle for establishing Electrolux products in Russia, Poland, the Czech Republic, Slovakia, Hungary, and Turkey. The company' goal was to double Eastern European sales by 1999 by establishing wholly or partially owned companies in the region. The AEG Hausgerate acquisition gave Electrolux a market share in Germany roughly equal to Bosch-Siemens (Germany accounted for the largest white goods volume of any European country and was the country where consumers placed the biggest emphasis on styling and sophisticated product features). The AEG Hausgerate acquisition also gave Electrolux market leadership in all of Europe's major geographic segments and allowed the company to offer a comprehensive product range across Europe. Thus, with the addition of the AEG brand, Electrolux had three pan-European brands—AEG's sales were primarily in central Europe, while the Electrolux and Zannusi brands were strong in both southern and northern Europe. The Zannusi brand was also established in every North African country. Electrolux had integrated its three international product divisions and numerous local marketing companies into a single organization to achieve greater scale economies in product development and production and to facilitate coordinated marketing across countries and continents. Electrolux reported $13.8 billion in sales for 1994 and $712 million in operating profits (household appliances accounted for 60 percent of the company's business).

Bosch-Siemens (Germany)

Bosch-Siemens Hausegeraete GmbH was established in 1965 as a 50-50 joint venture between Robert Bosch GmbH and Siemens AG; Siemens was Germany's second-largest industrial enterprise (its main products were power-generation equipment, electrical and electronics products, and telecommunications equipment) and Bosch was the country's eighth-largest industrial manufacturer (its primary businesses were auto parts and communications technology products). As of 1994, Bosch-Siemens had sales of $4.8 billion and profits of $224 million. Sales outside Germany in 1993 accounted for approximately 42 percent of total sales. The company had subsidiaries in 20 countries in Western and Eastern Europe (including Russia) and Scandinavia. Bosch-Siemens had manufacturing facilities in Germany (5), Spain (5), Greece (1), Slovenia (1), and Poland (1). Appliances were marketed under such brands as Bosch, Siemens, Constructa, Balay, Baby, Lynx, Crolls, and Neff. The company was the market leader in Germany with a 30 percent market share. Bosch-Siemens had acquired two Spanish appliance manufacturers in 1989, Balay SA and the Safel Group. Output from a new facility in Poland was expected to increase sales in Eastern Europe from $299 million in 1994 to $359 million in 1999. In Eastern Europe and Russia, Bosch-Siemens had positioned its products in the middle and lower-end segments; elsewhere, it concentrated on the middle and high-end segments where it had developed a reputation for innovation and technological sophistication. Management had planned to grow the company's European market share to 18 percent to 19 percent by 1999, largely through acquisitions in the United Kingdom, France, and Italy where its market shares were low. Bosch-Siemens management had stated that current differences in the appliance preferences of European consumers would be slow to change, and that to be successful, manufacturers would have to offer a large number of regional variations. Bosch-Siemens was also interested in increasing its sales in the Asian market and recently acquired a majority interest in Wuxi Little Swan Co., a leading Chinese manufacturer of laundry appliances. Management was also involved in negotiations to establish a washer production joint venture in China; 1994 export sales to Asia were in the $50 million range.

Elfi/Brandt Electromenager (Italy)

In late 1992, the Italian holding company Elfi (Elletrofinanziaria) acquired the last French domestic appliance group, Thomson Electromenager (TEM). Elfi's management believed TEM's sales outside of France were well below what was possible with TEM's resources. The TEM acquisition gave Elfi a 10 percent share of the European market, roughly the same as Merloni, and marked the first step in Elfi's strategy to establish a pan-

EXHIBIT 6   Concluded

Elfi/Brandt Electromenager (Italy) (*continued*)

European appliance manufacturing and sales group. Shortly after the acquisition, Elfi announced a major restructuring plan that first grouped appliance operations under a new organization, Brandt Electromenager; the move put the brands gained in the TEM acquisition (Brandt, De Dietrich, Sauter, Thermor, Thomson, and Vedette) and Elfi's four brands (Ocean, CGA, Blomberg, and Elektra Bregenz) under common management. Brandt Electromenager was divided into three divisions (washing, refrigeration, and cooking) to consolidate operations across its plants in Italy, Germany, and France. Since the reorganization, Brandt had maintained but not expanded its dominant share of the French appliance market (28 to 30 percent) and was intent on expanding its share of the European market. In 1995, Brandt's management indicated that it was considering entering the Polish appliance market.

Merloni Elettodomestici (Italy)

Based in Fabriano, Italy, Merloni was the fifth-largest European appliance manufacturer with 1994 sales of $1.1 billion. Merloni's sales consisted of washers and dishwashers (35 percent), refrigerators and freezers (34 percent), and ovens/stoves (31 percent). The company had subsidiaries in 11 European countries, as well as in the Cayman Islands and Argentina. As of 1994, Merloni's overseas operations accounted for 9 percent of total sales. European sales were concentrated in Italy (28 percent), France (20 percent), UK (13 percent), and Turkey (11 percent). Since 1980, the company's growth strategy was driven by a need to gain critical mass and access to other European countries as the European market consolidated. Merloni's growth in the European market was largely due to acquisition, namely Indesit and Scholtes in 1988, and several lesser operations in Portugal, Turkey, and Argentina. In 1995, Merloni bought New World Domestic Appliances, a leading U.K. gas range manufacturer. New World had a 24 percent share of the U.K. market for freestanding gas ranges (24 percent), and a 14 percent share of the U.K. market for built-in gas ranges (second only to Whirlpool's 18 percent share). In Western Europe, Merloni's sales had grown an average of 17 percent annually since 1980. The company's brand names included Ariston, Indesit, New World, and Scholtes. Merloni management believed Eastern Europe was key to the company's future success. The company had recently built a refrigerator and freezer manufacturing facility in Russia, as well as a 1.5 million-unit compressor plant. In 1994, Merloni sold over 60,000 appliances in Russia (20 percent share of the import market), generating sales of approximately $25 million. Merloni opened an office in Singapore in 1993 and was developing plans to enter the Chinese market.

Candy Elettrodomestici (Italy)

Candy specialized in the manufacture of washing machines, dishwashers, and refrigerators. In 1993, Candy posted sales of $249 million and profits of $1.7 million. Candy's market share in Italy was 11 percent, trailing only Merloni (21 percent) and Zannusi (26 percent) Almost 50 percent of Candy's total sales were in its home market of Italy, with the remaining half coming from European countries, countries formerly comprising Russia, and North Africa. Candy's cross-border operations had increased its European market share from 2 percent in 1980 to 6 percent in 1993, most of which had been achieved through acquisition: Zerowatt (Italy), Rosieres (France), and LEC (U.K.). In 1992, Candy announced construction of a manufacturing plant in Libya. Candy had also aggressively targeted the Russian market since the collapse of the old communist regime. By early 1995, Candy and Merloni were supplying approximately 50 percent of washing machine sales in Russia.

General Electric

GE's Hotpoint brand commanded a 28 percent share of the U.K. market for cleaning appliances (washers, dryers, dishwashers, and vacuum cleaners) where it had a manufacturing presence. GE was a niche player in the rest of Europe, with most of its sales being supplied from U.S. plants.

Maytag/Hoover

The acquisition of Hoover in 1989 not only gave Maytag a substantial share of the appliance market in the United Kingdom but also manufacturing operations as well. By 1994, Hoover's share of the appliance market in the United Kingdom was 15 percent, second only to Hotpoint. Hoover Europe's 1994 sales totaled $399 million; profits were a meager $420,000 but 1994 was the division's first profitable year since its acquisition. In the rest of Europe, Maytag was a niche player. Maytag formed an alliance in 1992 with Bosch-Siemens to extend its presence in the European market. Maytag's alliance with Bosch-Siemens included technology sharing and collaborative product development.

EXHIBIT 7   The Global Market for Major Home Appliances, by Geographic Region, 1994–2004

Geographic Region	Population	Annual Market Demand (in units)		Estimated Compound Average Growth Rate
		1994	2004 (est.)	
North America	380 million	46 million	63 million	3.6%
Europe (including Eastern Europe, Middle East, and Africa)	1.1 billion	75 million	94 million	2.5
Western Europe only	325 million	51 million	63 million	2.4
Latin America	380 million	17 million	30 million	6.5
Asia	2.9 billion	56 million	120 million	8.8
World total	5.1 billion	245 million	370 million	4.7%

Source: Whirlpool's 1994 Annual Report.

Whirlpool and Electrolux were both employing strategies to compete all across Europe; both believed that a convergence of European lifestyles would ultimately lead to a more uniform appliance market in Europe. Both were pursuing ways to consolidate and integrate their European operating while still accommodating the market imperatives for country-specific product designs in certain locations. According to Leif Johnson, Electrolux's president:

> I want to be a good Frenchman in France and a good Italian in Italy. My strategy is to go global only when I can and stay local when I must.[2]

The Latin American Appliance Market

The Latin American market consisted of 37 South American, Central American, and Caribbean countries with a combined population of 380 million people. In 1994 alone, appliance shipments were up over 15 percent. Brazil accounted for about 8 million of the 17 million appliances sold in Latin America in 1994. Brazil had a relatively young population, with between 600,000 and 700,000 new households expected to be formed before 2000. The five best-selling appliances were automatic washers, microwave ovens, ranges, refrigerators, and room air conditioners; saturation rates for all five were quite low except for ranges (see Exhibit 5). Even though many Latin American countries had low-income economies, the sale of appliances were expected to grow 6 to 7 percent annually as prosperity spread through the region—see Exhibit 7. Recent trade agreements among nine South America countries had made cross-border marketing of home appliances easier, and lower tariffs in Venezuela, Brazil, and Argentina were spurring buyer demand.

With its joint venture partners, Whirlpool was the clear market leader in Latin America, with a market share of about 27 percent. None of its major competitors—Refripar, Continental Dako, and Madosa—had as much as a 10 percent market share. Altogether, there were approximately 65 home appliance manufacturers in the region. Competition in the Latin American region centered around product

[2]As quoted in *Fortune*, September 20, 1993, p. 82.

features, price, product quality and performance, service, warranties, advertising, and dealer promotion.

The Asian Appliance Market

Asia consisted of two very different appliance markets—Japan and the rest of the region (China, Thailand, Indonesia, Malaysia, India, Australia, New Zealand, Taiwan, Hong Kong, and Singapore). The appliance market in Japan was virtually closed to outsiders; Matsushita, Sharp, Toshiba, Sanyo, and a few other Japanese appliance makers accounted for close to 100 percent of the market, and their control over distributor-dealer networks made any foreign incursion into the Japanese market formidable and expensive. But elsewhere, the Japanese manufacturers lacked such a stronghold. Outside Japan, Matsushita was the market leader; yet, its market share was less than 10 percent. Whirlpool was the leading non-Japanese competitor with a market share of just over 1 percent. Other key players outside Japan included Sharp, Sanyo, Samsung, and Goldstar. Exhibit 8 provides profiles of Whirlpool's chief competitors in Asia. Competition was based on local production capabilities, product features, price, product quality, and product performance. Many of the better-known Asian manufacturers had integrated backward, making a sizeable fraction of the parts and component systems needed for their appliances. Whirlpool, however, was following a different path; Lee Ross, manufacturing vice president of Whirlpool's Asian Appliance Group, explained.

> We're going to focus on our core competencies, then outsource the rest. You can't be world-class at everything. I think the rapid expansion of business in Asia is also increasing the number of quality suppliers. So vertical integration is less necessary today than when these other companies started manufacturing.[3]

As a rule, appliance plants in Asia were less automated because low wage rates made it more cost-effective to use labor-intensive production methods to perform many of the work steps.

Asia was the fastest-growing region within the global home appliance industry (Exhibit 7) and had also become the world's largest home appliance market, accounting for nearly 23 percent of shipments in 1994. The best-selling appliances in Asia were refrigerators, washers, microwave ovens, and room air conditioners (see Exhibit 5 for saturation rates). More refrigerators were sold in China in 1994 than in any country worldwide; only about 10 percent of Chinese households had refrigerators. In 1994, appliances sales in China totaled about 20 million units, about 40 percent of the total Asian market and 10 percent of the world market. Demand for major home appliances in China was expected to reach 60 million units annually by 2004, equal to about 50 percent of the Asian market and 20 percent of the world market. Chinese retailers of home appliances preferred to deal with one manufacturer for all the products they carried. Home appliance demand in India, the world's second most populous country, was also rising strongly.

Like other regions in the world, the Asian appliance market had features unique to certain countries, consumer segments, and product categories. The electric power supply in many Asian countries was unreliable; in addition to frequent outages, there were wide swings in voltages and frequencies. In India, for example, appliances had

---

[3]As quoted in *Appliance Manufacturer,* February 1995, p. W-31.

EXHIBIT 8   Profile of Whirlpool's Asian Competitors

Matsushita Electrical Industrial Co. (Japan)

Matsushita, one of the world's largest conglomerates, earned $911 million on consolidated 1994 sales of $70 billion. Since 1989, Matsushita's sales outside Japan had grown from 42 percent to 49 percent of total revenues. Matsushita had manufacturing plants in 38 countries and produced a wide variety of electronics and appliance products. Matsushita's appliance products were sold under the Panasonic brand overseas and the National brand in Japan. Over the years, Matsushita had built a strong domestic retail appliance network that had enabled the company to maintain a market leading position in Japan for many of the product lines, including refrigerators and air conditioning. In 1993, Matsushita opened what was billed as the "largest microwave oven factory in the world" in Chicago, Illinois. Outside of Japan, Matsushita was the acknowledged leader of the appliance market in Asia, although in 1995 its Asian share amounted to less than 10 percent. Management believed that expansion of Matsushita's presence in the Chinese appliance market would increase its leading share of the Asian market. Matsushita participated in 16 Chinese joint ventures and had plans to build 30 appliance manufacturing plants in China.

Sanyo Electric Co., Ltd. (Japan)

The Sanyo Group consisted of 60 manufacturing companies, 33 sales companies, and 15 other companies operating in 28 different countries. Sanyo manufactured a broad range of consumer electronic products, industrial equipment, and household appliances. In the early 1990s Sanyo had formed an equity joint venture in China to produce up to 400,000 washing machines. Sanyo's management expected the Chinese market for washers to grow from 900,000 units in 1994 to 2.4 million units by 1997. Home appliances accounted for almost 20 percent of Sanyo's 1994 sales of $16.4 billion. However, Sanyo's appliance sales were stagnant; its $2.8 billion in appliance sales in 1993 represented a five-year low.

Toshiba Corporation (Japan)

Toshiba was one of Japan's leading producers of semiconductors, electronics, and electrical appliances. Due to the rising value of the yen in the world currency market in the 1990s, Toshiba's management believed that it had become necessary to begin relocating its appliance manufacturing operations outside Japan. In 1993 Toshiba began to develop its manufacturing operations in Thailand and planned eventually to make Thailand Toshiba's primary appliance production base for Indochina. In 1994, Toshiba pulled out of the U.K. microwave oven market despite its 14 percent market share, citing profit margin pressures from cheaper Korean and Chinese products. Toshiba reported consolidated sales of $48.2 billion and profits of $450 million for its fiscal year ending March 31, 1995.

Hitachi Limited (Japan)

Hitachi was one of the world's 15 largest diversified corporations, with 1994 revenues of $76.4 billion, profits of $1.1 billion, and 330,000 employees. Hitachi manufactured telecommunications products, power generation equipment, industrial machinery, appliances, and consumer electronics products. The company's appliance products had captured sizable market shares in several Asian countries, an example being Thailand where Hitachi held a leading 20 percent share of the refrigerator market in 1994. Late in 1994, Hitachi's management announced the introduction of a new low-end appliance brand for its home market to complement the high-end Hitachi brand. The company did not have plans to market the new low-end products outside of Japan. In 1994 Hitachi also entered into the Chinese appliance market by forming a joint venture to produce air conditioners.

Sharp Corporation (Japan)

A private company established in 1912, Sharp manufactured consumer electronics, information and office automation equipment, electrical devices and home appliances. In 1994, the company posted sales of $16.3 billion and profits of $448 million.

Sharp's "New Life" strategy, begun in the mid-1970s, focused on developing products that appealed to diverse consumer tastes. The "New Life" strategy also promoted new consumer lifestyles by emphasizing color and design. The strategy was successful enough that Sharp's appliance business posted growth rates of over 10 percent through the early 1980s (versus an industry average for the same period of 3 percent). The "New Life" strategy continued into the 1990s, and was particularly popular with younger consumers. However, Sharp's appliance group was growing more slowly than other Sharp divisions and accounted for only 17.5 percent of total corporate revenues.

EXHIBIT 8   Concluded

Sharp Corporation (Japan) (*continued*)

In the 1970s Sharp established manufacturing joint ventures in Taiwan, Brazil, Korea, and Malaysia in response to the appreciation of the yen. In the early 1990s, Sharp built more overseas manufacturing plants to reduce its production costs. A market leader in the microwave oven segment, the company had built a microwave oven plant in Thailand with a capacity of 1 million units per year. Sharp also had a subsidiary in China that produced 200,000 air conditioners a year, and the company had plans to initiate a joint venture in Shanghai to produce a variety of household appliances.

Samsung Electronics Company, Ltd. (Korea)

Samsung was South Korea's largest producer of consumer electronics and had 1994 sales of $14.6 billion and profits of $1.2 billion. In the early 1990s Samsung began aggressively expanding its Asian appliance division. In 1994, Samsung formed a joint venture with Trade Import Export Electronics Co. in Vietnam to produce refrigerators and washing machines and committed to investing $500 million in appliance manufacturing facilities in Suzhou, China. Also in 1994, Samsung announced a contract to export approximately $33 million in washing machines to India's Voltas Company and to provide Voltas with Samsung's washer manufacturing technology for an additional $7 million. Samsung and Voltas planned to extend the technology transfer agreement to include microwaves, air conditioners, and refrigerators. In 1995 Samsung expanded its manufacturing operations in Thailand, building a washing machine manufacturing plant (100,000 unit capacity). The company planned to invest an additional $20 million in the Thailand complex to include production of refrigerators and microwave ovens.

Goldstar (Korea)

A multinational conglomerate, Goldstar manufactured a wide variety of products, including consumer electronics, semiconductors, and household appliances. In the 1980s, Goldstar's share of the Korean market had declined and the company had lost its No. 1 position to Samsung. A change of management in 1991 resulted in a reorganization of Goldstar into 9 strategic business units including 29 operating groups that were run by multidisciplinary teams (designers, engineers, factory workers, and marketing people). Production operations were simplified to reduce costs (the average length of a microwave assembly line was reduced from 200 to 65 meters). By 1994 average output per employee had doubled, and Goldstar had regained its dominant position in the Korean appliance market, surpassing Samsung's sales in refrigerators and washing machines. Management then adopted a two-pronged strategy to build its global position: (1) Goldstar began shifting production of low-end products to China and Vietnam, and (2) Goldstar began to develop strategic alliances with leading technology companies (appliances—GE). Three new joint ventures in China were established by Goldstar in 1994. By 1997, Goldstar's management planned for overseas production to account for 25 percent of its total appliance output, up from 10 percent in 1993. As of 1995, Goldstar's 8 percent share of the imported appliance market in Russia was second only to Samsung's (10 percent).

AB Electrolux (Sweden)

Electrolux's management believed expansion of its market share in Asia to be the primary component of its growth strategy heading into the 21st century. The company planned to double its 1994 Asia market revenues by 1999, and was building five new manufacturing facilities in the region. The company planned to compete on quality, technology, and range of product offerings. Electrolux designed new product lines for the Asian market (for instance, cold wash–only washers for countries with limited electric power supplies or populations with low buying power) and set product prices 10 to 15 percent above comparable Japanese products. The company intended to spend approximately $30 million between 1994 and 1997 to introduce and promote the Electrolux brand name in Asia. Electrolux's management believed China was the growth market of the future, and in 1994 opened its second joint venture factory in Tianjin, China.

to be designed to handle anywhere from 170 to 270 volts; this meant adding more windings to motors and other coil components to protect against failure. Much of the region had high humidity and many metropolitan areas were near salty seacoast air, making corrosion resistance and protection of controls from moisture a critical quality issue. The typical Asian residence didn't have the ductwork to accommodate central air conditioning and consumers disliked room air conditioners that took up scarce window space; the preferred product was a split system where the condensing unit was located outside, the evaporating unit with fan was installed high on an outside wall, and remote controls were used to regulate operation.

Clothes dryers and dishwashers were niche market items because Asian incomes were too low for many households to afford them. Because little baking was done in Asia and kitchens were small, there was little demand for ranges with ovens. Most cooking was done on portable two-top burners that could be stored when meals were finished. Asian consumers wanted clothes washers to be portable and easily moved because most residences had no place to keep one permanently hooked up to a water supply and drain; often they were stored in an outside hallway or porch and moved into the kitchen or bathroom for use. A lack of space also affected refrigerator size; some were only four feet high so the top could be used for something else. Moreover, because refrigerators were a status symbol for families rising up the economic ladder, they were sometimes placed in the living room, which led to a preference for stylish designs and colors—in India, for example, refrigerators were sold in bright blue or red. In one part of China, freezer capacity was important; in another part, households preferred large crispers for fresh vegetables. There were technology variations as well. In China, all three types of clothes washers (horizontal-axis, vertical-axis and twin-tub) were being marketed as well as both direct-cool refrigerators (the dominant type in Europe) and forced-air refrigerators (the dominant type in the United States). In Hong Kong there was a preference for compact, European-style appliances, but Taiwan households preferred larger American-style appliances.

WHIRLPOOL'S GLOBAL STRATEGY

Whirlpool's decision in the late 1980s to formulate and pursue a global strategy was based on management's conclusion that the major home appliance industry would, in time, be dominated by a handful of global players and that global expansion was Whirlpool's best route to less cyclical performance, greater shareholder value, and long-term viability. According to Whirlpool's CEO David Whitman:

> Several other possibilities were considered first, including the idea of diversifying away from appliances, forward and backward integration, and a major financial restructuring. But when we looked at the global marketplace, it quickly became clear that the only reason we were defining our industry as "slow growing" was because we were defining the industry as North American. When we looked at the world appliance market, we saw an industry that had significant growth prospects.[4]

Whirlpool's strategic approach quickly evolved into one of not only participating in, but leading, the industry's globalization. Between 1987 and 1995, Whirlpool broadened its stable of brands in North America, established a major position in Europe, entered the Latin American market by partnering with several Latin American producers and constructing plants in Brazil and Argentina, and began building a base for competing aggressively in Asia. Exhibit 9 shows the global presence Whirlpool had developed by 1995. It was the only manufacturer that was an active player in all four regions of the global appliance industry. Exhibit 10 shows Whirlpool's revenues by product category.

---

[4]As quoted in Jay Palmer, "Oh Boy, a Washer," *Barron's.* September 26, 1994, p. 17.

EXHIBIT 9   Whirlpool's Global Presence by Geographic Region, 1994

Geographic Region	Manufacturing Plants	Sales Offices	Subsidiaries, Joint Ventures and Affiliates
North America	13	20	2
Europe	10	20	0
Latin America	5	0	6
Asia	4	6	6

Source: Whirlpool's 1994 Annual Report.

EXHIBIT 10   Whirlpool's Revenues by Product Category, 1992–1994 (in millions of dollars)

Product Category	1992	1993	1994
Laundry appliances (washers and dryers)	$2,489	$2,481	$2,610
Refrigerators, freezers, and room air conditioners	2,525	2,588	2,900
All other home appliances	2,083	2,299	2,439
Total	$7,097	$7,368	$7,949
Whirlpool Financial Services	204	165	155
	$7,301	$7,533	$8,104

Source: Whirlpool's 1994 Annual Report.

Whirlpool's Strategy and Position in North America

To put itself in position to offer consumers a wide selection of brand-name appliances at various price points, Whirlpool made four acquisitions in the late 1980s:

- KitchenAid, a high-end manufacturer of dishwashers and food mixers.
- Roper, a maker of low-end appliances and one of Sears's suppliers of Kenmore brand appliances.
- Inglis, the leading Canadian appliance maker.
- A 49 percent ownership stake in Vitromatic, the second-largest appliance maker in Mexico.

Responsibility for the acquired businesses, along with Whirlpool's other U.S. operations, was then consolidated under a single unit, the North American Appliance Group (NAAG). NAAG had 1994 sales of $5.05 billion and operating profit of $522 million (see Exhibit 11). Sears was NAAG's biggest customer, accounting for about 19 percent of sales each year since 1990.[5]

---

[5]Whirlpool had been Sears's principal supplier of laundry equipment for over 75 years and of room air conditioners for over 30 years. During the three decades following World War II, most of Whirlpool's

EXHIBIT 11   Whirlpool's Revenues and Operating Profits by Geographic Region, 1993 and 1994

	1993	1994
Net Sales Revenue		
North America	$4,559	$5,048
Europe	2,225	2,373
Latin America	303	329
Asia	151	205
Operating Profits		
North America	$ 474	$ 522
Europe	139	163
Latin America	43	49
Asia	(5)	(22)
Operating Profit Margin		
North America	10.4%	10.3%
Europe	6.3	6.9
Latin America	14.2	14.9
Asia	(3.3)	(10.7)

Source: Whirlpool's 1994 Annual Report.

NAAG's strategy was to build market position by giving customers compelling reasons beyond price to select Whirlpool appliances. The objective was to create a "dominant consumer franchise" in home appliances such that consumers would insist on Whirlpool's brands for reasons other than price, view Whirlpool products as clearly superior to other appliances, and demonstrate strong brand loyalty in future purchase decisions. To create this degree of consumer support, management believed that NAAG's appliance lineup would increasingly have to include functional and attractive products, that the company would have to operate from a platform of both high quality and low cost, and that constant product innovation and superior service would have to permeate its operations. To open the door to greater imagination and innovation, management had reconceptualized its business, switching from a product-dominated definition—the refrigerator business, the washing machine business, or the range business—to a functional definition—the food preservation business, the fabric care business, and the food preparation business. David Whitwam believed that the design issues changed dramatically when the business definition was keyed to the function that consumers wanted the product to accomplish:

business consisted of supplying Kenmore appliances to Sears; Sears had a sizable ownership stake in Whirlpool (as it did in several other of its key suppliers). However, Sears elected to divest its Whirlpool ownership stake when it became apparent that Sears could obtain Kenmore appliances from Whirlpool at even lower costs if Whirlpool pursued scale economies by increasing sales of Whirlpool brand appliances at the same time it supplied private-label goods to Sears.

The microwave couldn't have been invented by someone who assumed he or she was in the business of designing a range. Such a design breakthrough required seeing the opportunity as "easier, quicker food preparation," not "a better range."[6]

NAAG was cultivating different images and themes for its three major brands: KitchenAid, style and substance; Whirlpool, products to help people run their home; and Roper, a quality value brand.

The KitchenAid line of food mixers epitomized the sort of dominant consumer franchise that Whirlpool was trying to create all across its major home appliance lines. KitchenAid food mixers dominated the premium end of the category in both North America and Europe, selling for prices substantially above the industry average because they delivered superior styling, performance, reliability, and service. Annual sales had increased fivefold over the past eight years. NAAG had plans to begin introducing the KitchenAid food mixer line in Latin America and Asia.

The Whirlpool refrigerator division was selected by a consortium of electric utilities to produce a chlorofluorocarbon-free, superefficient refrigerator in 1992; the division received a $30 million award for submitting the winning design. The new no ozone-depleting models were introduced in 1994 and not only featured much lower use of electricity but also a new exterior look and new bins, shelves, crispers, and interior controls. To build the new models, Whirlpool used insulation technology from its European operations, compressor technology developed by its Brazilian affiliates, and manufacturing and design expertise supplied by NAAG. Starting in 1995, CFC refrigerants were eliminated from all KitchenAid, Whirlpool, and Roper refrigerators and freezers. Surveys indicated that Whirlpool's new side-by-side refrigerator-freezer was the best in the industry. A new clothes washer that used one-third of the water and energy of conventional washers was scheduled for 1996. Whirlpool's European technology was being used in a line of new, quieter dishwashers.

All told, more than two-thirds of NAAG's product lineup was new in 1995, and hundreds of additional models were scheduled for 1996, NAAG's work in new product development was not confined to North America. The LaVergne (Tennessee) Division had designed and produced a room air conditioner that was being sold in Asia and would eventually be sold worldwide.

The North American Appliance Group's manufacturing plants were all implementing factory master plans that would enable them to produce more models in smaller runs each day, thus allowing production to be matched closely to current dealer sales. Whirlpool, like General Electric, had eliminated independent distributors and was supplying retail dealers factory-direct. Surveys of retail dealers indicated that Whirlpool's "Quality Express" product-delivery system was clearly superior in terms of on-time delivery, driver courtesy, responsiveness, and overall ability to meet dealer needs. The plants were also on track to reduce warranty service rates by 90 percent. A five-year quality improvement plan had been implemented in 1992, and by 1994 Whirlpool's studies showed that interim warranty service targets were being met. Whirlpool's market research indicated that service repair frequencies for its appliances were the lowest in the industry in 1994.

The role of the North American Appliance Group in Whirlpool's global strategy was to maintain sufficient profitability and cash flow to fund the company's expan-

---

[6]"The Right Way to Go Global," *Harvard Business Review,* March–April 1994, p. 143.

sion into markets in the rest of the world. During the 1990s, NAAG had been able to generate between $100 million and $200 million annually to help finance such activities.

Whirlpool's Strategy and Position in Europe

Whirlpool's entry into Europe was accomplished in two stages. In 1989, Whirlpool acquired 53 percent of the major home appliance division of Dutch-based NV Philips's for $470 million; Philips was Europe's third-largest appliance producer, with about $2 billion. In 1991, Whirlpool spent $600 million to buy out the remaining 47 percent interest in Philips's major home appliance business. Whirlpool Europe B.V. (WEBV) was formed to manage Whirlpool's activities in Europe, the Middle East and Africa. Philips's appliance business had been floundering for several years prior to its acquisition by Whirlpool; Philips had employed a multi-country strategy in Europe, with virtually no cross-border coordination. Philips's washing machines made in Germany did not even have one screw in common with the washers made at its Italian plant. WEBV management promptly initiated a Europeanwide approach in all areas of operation: procurement, technology and component standardization, manufacturing, marketing, and dealer support activities. David Whitwam explained the rationale for a uniform strategy even though no one shape or style of appliance would sell in all of Europe's national and regional markets:

> The basic technology and the basic components are still very similar, market to market. The adaptations needed to meet local preferences can be done very late in the production cycle. We can leverage the similarities.[7]

Early on, Whirlpool initiated a brand-transfer program, putting the Philips-Whirlpool brand on all Philips brand appliances and eliminating several of the national brand names Philips used in specific European countries. WEBV earmarked $110 million to promote the Whirlpool name with consumers over a five-year period. Starting in 1995, the Philips was dropped entirely from all labels and advertising. Recent consumer surveys showed that Whirlpool was Europe's most-recognized appliance brand, and in 1994 Whirlpool was the largest-selling appliance brand in Europe.

Product development was carried out at two regional technology centers, both of which worked closely with Whirlpool's other technology centers worldwide. The goal was to achieve more commonality of components and more modularity in assembly. Procurement at the 10 European plants was increasingly being performed by the company's global procurement organization. WEBV maintained a growing database, tracking cost and quality of manufacturing practices at each of its plants to ensure that best practices were recognized and transferred.[8] To reduce costs and improve efficiency, WEBV was planning to eliminate 2,000 positions, realizing cost savings of $80 million annually by 1996. Since 1990, WEBV had improved productivity by 25 percent and reduced first-year warranty service rates by one-third. However, WEBV's operating margin of 5.6 percent was still far from its goal of 10 percent.

As in the North American market, Whirlpool was utilizing a multibrand strategy to cover all price segments. Banknecht brand appliances were positioned in the medium- to high-price range; Whirlpool brand appliances were positioned to appeal to the broad middle market segment, and Ignis brand products were value-priced for

[7]Palmer, "Oh Boy, a Washer," p. 17.

[8]"Around the World with Whirlpool: Europe." *Appliance Manufacturer,* February 1995, p. W-12.

budget-conscious buyers. Laden brand appliances were sold in France, in addition to the other three brands.

To strengthen Whirlpool's brands with the approximately 40,000 European appliance dealers stocking one or more of WEBV's brands, WEBV took a road show across Europe in 1994 to provide dealers with product information, explaining how the benefits of product features could be communicated to consumers, giving product demonstrations, and offering training to dealer salespeople. A major accounts group was created to coordinate sales and marketing to transitional dealer buyer groups (the four largest represented a combined total of nearly 6,000 dealers) and to the major retail appliance chains. As of 1995, WEBV's top 70 accounts represented over half of its sales.

To provide European consumers with service levels comparable to those provided in the United States, WEBV had formed a consumer service operation consisting of 1,000 consumer service representatives and field service technicians at locations throughout Europe. Six customer assistance centers were in operation in Germany, the United Kingdom, Belgium, Holland, Austria, and Switzerland, and five others were planned for Poland, Hungary, Slovakia, Greece, and the Czech Republic. The centers booked repair calls, responded to customer complaints, provided product information, facilitated the ordering and invoicing of spare parts, processed warranty claims, and handled extended service contracts. Through Whirlpool Financial Corporation, WEBV was leasing appliances to consumers in the former communist countries of Central and Eastern Europe.

A new clothes dryer model and a new family of microwave ovens were introduced in 1994. Other whole new generations of Bauknecht, Whirlpool, and Ignis brand appliances were being developed, including six new lines in 1995. By 1998, about 85 percent of sales in Europe were expected to come from models that didn't exist in 1993. WBEV's new automatic washer design retained fewer than 1 percent of the parts and components of its predecessor.

WEBV's 1994 sales were approximately 8 million units, up 1.5 million units since 1990. The division's share of the European market had gone up for five consecutive years. About 10 percent of WEBV's sales were to countries in Central and Eastern Europe. WEBV's line of VIP microwave ovens was the best-selling microwave oven in Europe and the recipient of eight awards for superior performance. Whirlpool executives believed WEBV was in a favorable position relative to competitors because it had an experienced dealer network in Western Europe, balanced sales throughout the Western European market under well-recognized brand names, manufacturing facilities located in different countries, and the ability to customize its products to meet the preferences of diverse buyers in different country and regional markets. According to Jeff Fettig, president of WEBV:

> We are successfully eliminating the geographical borders as the basis for defining our markets. It's the consumer segments and not the borders that are significant.[9]

Whirlpool's Strategy and Position in Latin America

Whirlpool first entered the Latin American market in 1958 when it bought an equity interest in Multibras S.A. of Brazil, a manufacturer of major appliances. By 1995, Whirlpool had expanded its position to include equity interests in Embraco S.A., a

---

[9]As quoted in *Appliance Manufacturer,* February 1995, p. W-6.

EXHIBIT 12   Summary of Whirlpool's Strategic Moves to Establish a
Market Presence in Latin America

1958	Whirlpool invests in Latin America through purchase of an equity interest in Multibras S.A., a part of the Brasmotor holding company in Brazil. Multibras is later renamed Brastemp S.A.
1976	Brasmotor S.A. acquires Consul, a Brazilian manufacturer of refrigerators/freezers and room air conditioners. Consul was founded in 1950 as a manufacturer of kerosene-powered refrigerators.
1976	Whirlpool increases its investment in Brazil through purchases of equity interests in Consul and Embraco S.A., a maker of compressors.
1984	Semer, a Brazilian manufacturer of stoves, is acquired by Brastemp. Semer broadens its product line to include semiautomatic clothes washer/dryers and countertop dishwashers.
1992	Whirlpool acquires the control of SAGAD S.A. from Philips Electronics N.V., and renames it Whirlpool Argentina.
1992	South American Sales Co. (SASCO) is formed as a sales and marketing joint venture with Brasmotor to manage export sales to Latin America.
1993	Whirlpool sells 40 percent of its interest in Whirlpool Argentina to Brasmotor.
1994	Brastemp, Consul and Semer are merged and renamed Multibras S.A.
1994	Embraco acquires Whirlpool's Italian refrigerator-compressor business. The transaction involves a plant in Riva di Chieri, Italy, which manufactures Aspera-brand compressors.

Source: *Appliance Manufacturer,* February 1995, p. W-39.

maker of compressors, and Brasmotor S.A., a Brazilian holding company with interests that included Multibras and Brasmotor. It also bought control of SAGAD S.A. in Argentina, a transaction that completed the acquisition of Philips Electronics' worldwide appliance business; SAGAD was renamed Whirlpool Argentina. In 1995, Whirlpool Argentina was marketing a full line of appliances produced locally and in Brazil by Multibras, as well as by Whirlpool plants in North America and Europe. Whirlpool's Brazilian partners also exported appliances to the Middle East, Africa, and North America. Exhibit 12 summarizes Whirlpool's moves to establish a market presence in Latin America.

While the majority of appliance products made by Whirlpool's Brazilian affiliates and Whirlpool Argentina were for the medium and high ends of the Latin American market, efforts were underway to strengthen Whirlpool's presence in the low end of the price spectrum. Eight brands were currently being sold in the Latin American market. For high-end buyers, there were U.S.-made KitchenAid and Whirlpool models, Brazilian-made Brastemp models, and European-made Bauknecht models. Positioned in the middle of the price spectrum were Brazilian-made Consul models, European-made Ignis models, and Whirlpool Argentina's Eslabon de Lujo brand. At the low end were the Brazilian-made Semer brand and a substantial selection of Eslabon de Lujo brand models. Brastemp offered a full line of appliances and exported its models to Africa and the Middle East. The Consul line included refrigerators, freezers, microwave ovens, and room air conditioners; Consul models were exported to Africa, the Middle East, North America, Singapore, Australia, and Switzerland. The Semer brand included ranges, semiautomatic washers (no spin cycle), dryers, and countertop dishwashers; Semer appliances were sold in 50 countries in Latin America, Africa, and the Middle East. In Brazil, sales of the Brastemp,

Consul, and Semer brands combined resulted in Whirlpool/Multibras having the leading market share. Whirlpool Argentina had an 18 percent share of the 3 million-unit Argentine market; 40 percent of its appliance sales were made locally and sold under the Whirlpool brand name.

Whirlpool utilized 60 distributors in 37 countries to access the large numbers of small independent appliance retailers. Pleasing appliance distributors was a critical success factor because Latin American distributors were typically responsible for servicing and maintaining product warranties, as well as importing, warehousing, and marketing the various product lines to local retailers. Distributors were the main vehicle for educating retailers on product features and benefits; Whirlpool regional sales managers and professional trainers worked closely with the 60 distributors to facilitate dealer training and education.

The region's four Brazilian plants and one Argentinean plant each had factory master plans to incorporate best practice manufacturing methods. Plant teams had visited North American and European plants to study and share manufacturing and quality control approaches. Initiatives to erase operating distinctions between the various Latin American organizations and to more fully connect with Whirlpool worldwide were underway in 1995. Processes, systems, technology, and people were being shared freely among the operating units of Whirlpool's Latin American Appliance Group.

Whirlpool's Strategy and Position in Asia

While Whirlpool had exported appliances to Asia for many years, it did not establish an operating base in Asia until 1989 when several sales offices were opened. Management decided to truly understand Asian consumers preferences and lifestyles and the trade channels to access the marketplace before deciding where to put factories and what products to build in Asia. During the 1990s, as its knowledge of the market increased, Whirlpool added sales locations and began putting together a manufacturing base, usually with local partners, with Whirlpool maintaining a majority interest.

In 1987, Whirlpool entered into a joint venture with a company in India to manufacture automatic and semiautomatic washers and twin-tub washers for the Indian market; the venture, called TVS Whirlpool, sold its products under the brand name of TVS. In 1993, a technology center was established in Singapore to coordinate product development in the region. In early 1994, Whirlpool partnered with Great Teco Trade Co. in Taiwan to form a large distributorship for Whirlpool appliances in Taiwan. Over the next 12 months, a flurry of moves were made to develop Asian manufacturing capability:

- Whirlpool acquired a controlling interest in Kelvinator of India, Ltd., the second largest manufacturer and marketer of refrigerators in India. Kelvinator of India had 3,000 retail dealers handling its product line.

- Whirlpool purchased a majority interest in the largest Chinese producer of microwave ovens; the company had annual sales of 500,000 units in China (about a 50 percent market share) and exported another 500,000 units to Asian, European, and Latin American markets. (This acquisition, together with Whirlpool's microwave operations in Europe, made Whirlpool one of the world's five largest makers of microwave ovens.)

- Whirlpool entered into a joint venture with Beijing Snowflake Electric Appliance Group, a state-owned enterprise that produced refrigerators and freezers. Whirlpool had majority ownership. Beijing Snowflake's operations produced 120,000 units annually, and an expansion was under way to increase production to 500,000 units annually by 1997.

- Discussions for two other joint ventures in China, one to make room air conditioners and the other to make clothes washers, were under way. Both involved partners who were the leading Chinese manufacturers in their respective product categories.

By early 1995, Whirlpool's strategy in Asia had seven key elements: partnering with solid local companies (usually with Whirlpool having a controlling interest), transferring best practices from Whirlpool's other operations worldwide to Asia, developing the manufacturing skills of the workforces at the various Asian plant locations, making the Whirlpool brand the centerpiece of the Asian marketing plan and effectively positioning other brands around it, leveraging the company's global size in procurement of parts and components (the company's best suppliers in other regions were being encouraged to work with Whirlpool in Asia), designing products around a common platform that allowed modifications for specific areas within the Asian market, and concentrating on four specific appliance products—refrigerators, clothes washers, microwave ovens, and room air conditioners. Ranges were not on Whirlpool's product priority list because of small kitchens, less baking of goods, and widespread use of portable, two-burner tabletop units. Where demand for ranges, cooking tops, and ovens existed (Australia and New Zealand, for example), the market was supplied by Whirlpool plants in other global locations.

The company's Asian managers were spending considerable time promoting a one-company vision and developing rapport between once-independent operations. In 1994, Whirlpool sold about 700,000 appliance products in Asia; in 1995, the total was expected to be about 2.8 million units. At the end of 1994, Whirlpool had about 800 employees in the Asia region; management foresaw that it could have close to 10,000 by year-end 1995. Whirlpool executives believed that the most critical driver of success in Asia was having strong local talent, only a small percentage of which could come by transferring people from other Whirlpool operations to Asia.

India and China were the primary targets for locating manufacturing plants. Recent changes in government policy in both countries had made it possible for foreign corporations to own a controlling interest in local manufacturing companies. In many other Asian countries, governments insisted on majority control, exercised strong policy-making roles, or imposed dividend restrictions; in addition, there were significant trade barriers in Asia that made locating large-scale plants in countries with small local markets a risky proposition (since exports were necessary to fully utilize capacity). Robert Frey, head of the Whirlpool Asia Appliance Group, observed:

> In both India and China, you can afford to build a world-class, global scale, million-unit-a-year factory and be fairly certain that the plant can be fully utilized just satisfying the demands of the local market. The size of these markets lets you start operating at a competitive level.
>
> In some places you have to balance your foreign exchange or achieve a certain level of exports. Sometimes there are import tariffs on key components. So you have to understand all the rules and carefully manage all the logistics they require.[10]

---

[10]As quoted in *Appliance Manufacturer*, February 1995, p. W-24.

Whirlpool had ambitious plans for its Asian operations. According to Robert Frey:

First of all, we expect to stay ahead of the pack in terms of Western players. And within 10 years, we expect to achieve a leadership position in Asia. By leadership position, I mean having a strong market share, more than 10 percent, having a presence in all key markets, and having the level of influence such that all major retailers want Whirlpool's products in their stores.

Whirlpool's expansion into Asia was a move that was anticipated nine years ago when the company adopted a vision of world leadership. We need to be a leader in Asia. It is imperative to survival in the appliance industry. We don't believe you will be a major player in the appliance industry in 10 years if you aren't a major player in Asia. So this is a natural next step. This is not just an Asian strategy, but a key part of Whirlpool's global strategy.[11]

The World Washer

In 1990, Whirlpool began production of a "world washer." The concept was to make a compact, affordable washer that handled small loads, that could be built at various locations with local labor and local materials, that required low investment in facilities and equipment, and that could be assembled with flexible manufacturing methods, thereby permitting models to be customized as needed for various markets throughout the world. For the time being, Whirlpool had assigned production of the world washer to Brastemp in Brazil, TVS Whirlpool in India, and Vitromatic in Mexico. The world washer's unique design specifications called for the unit to be built in modules, with 15 to 20 percent fewer parts than conventional washers. Modular components were tested during assembly to ensure a quality end product and to eliminate the need for service bays at the end of the line to rework defective units. Plants were given the authority to utilize different components to cut costs or to satisfy consumer preferences in specific country or regional markets. For instance, stainless steel baskets were used at the plants in Brazil and India because they required no welding and no operator to complete the assembly; while stainless steel was more expensive than porcelain, the two plants were able to avoid investing several million dollars in additional equipment. In Mexico, however, Vitromatic was associated with a porcelain producer and found it more economical to use porcelain baskets instead of stainless steel ones. World washer units sold in areas that lacked sophisticated plumbing were modified so that wash water could be loaded by hand and discharged directly onto the ground.

World washer models were introduced in the United States in 1993. A Whirlpool official explained the strategic thinking behind the move:

The number of persons living alone in this country has more than doubled in the past 20 years. The average number of people in a household has dropped from 3.1 to 2.6. Statistics like this suggest there's a growing number of folks out there who would be interested in buying compact machines that take up less space and handle small loads efficiently. It's not a huge market, but we sure can't afford to ignore it.[12]

All of Whirlpool's design personnel and technology centers were looking increasingly toward global parts, component systems, and products. The goal was to lever-

[11]Ibid.
[12]As quoted in *Dealerscope,* October 1992, p. 61.

age Whirlpool's technological expertise and capabilities on a global scale. Ed Eisele, vice president of technology for Whirlpool's Asian Appliance Group, said:

> There are certain core technologies you want to capitalize on when you design certain products. Obviously you have to differentiate some things . . . but where technologies are similar, you want to borrow on the strong existing experience within the Whirlpool organization rather than start from scratch every time.[13]

Another Whirlpool technology executive noted:

> The world is shrinking. We see Whirlpool globally getting into product platforms that have applicability in a lot of different markets. In some cases, if volumes justify it, a product may be manufactured in more than one region, just like the world washer being manufactured in India, Brazil, and Mexico. In other cases, a product may be made in one location to serve several different world markets. So product design will become more global in nature.[14]

WHIRLPOOL'S FINANCIAL PERFORMANCE

Although senior management exuded confidence that Whirlpool's global strategy was timely and well matched to industry and competitive conditions, the company's financial performance seven years after the strategy's launch was still lackluster at best. Since the beginning of 1988, Whirlpool had invested nearly $2 billion in new capital pursuing its strategy, yet net earnings were lower in 1993 and 1994 than in 1984, 1985, and 1986, the three years immediately preceding the decision to compete globally. The company's 10-year trend in earnings per share was uninspiring. Operating profit margins, return on assets, and return on stockholder's equity were all lower throughout the 1990s than they had been in the mid-1980s—see the 11-year financial review in Exhibit 13. Some Whirlpool shareholders were concerned whether Whirlpool's strategy to become the global market leader in major home appliances was working. When would they begin to see a real bottom-line payoff?

If you wish to do further research on Whirlpool's global appliance strategy, a good starting point is the company's Web site: *www.whirlpool.com.*

---

[13]As quoted in *Appliance Manufacturer,* February 1995, p. W-32.
[14]As quoted in *Appliance Manufacturer,* February 1995, p. W-29.

EXHIBIT 13 Eleven-year, Consolidated Statistical Review, Whirlpool Corp., 1984–1994 (millions of dollars, except share data)

	1994	1993	1992	1991	1990	1989	1988	1987	1986	1985	1984
Consolidated Operations											
Net sales	$7,949	$7,368	$7,097	$6,550	$6,424	$6,138	$4,306	$4,104	$3,928	$3,465	$3,128
Financial services	155	165	204	207	181	136	107	94	76	67	63
Total revenues	8,104	7,533	7,301	6,757	6,605	6,274	4,413	4,198	4,004	3,532	3,191
Operating profit	$ 397	$ 482	$ 479	$ 393	$ 349	$ 411	$ 261	$ 296	$ 326	$ 295	$ 288
Earnings from continuing operations before income taxes and other items	292	375	372	304	220	308	233	280	329	321	326
Earnings from continuing operations before accounting change[1]	158	231	205	170	72	187	161	187	202	182	190
Net earnings[2]	158	51	205	170	72	187	94	192	200	182	190
Net capital expenditures	418	309	288	287	265	208	166	223	217	178	135
Depreciation	246	241	275	233	247	222	143	133	120	89	72
Dividends paid	90	85	77	76	76	76	76	79	76	73	73
Consolidated Financial Position											
Current assets	$3,078	$2,708	$2,740	$2,920	$2,900	$2,889	$1,827	$1,690	$1,654	$1,410	$1,302
Current liabilities	2,988	2,763	2,887	2,931	2,651	2,251	1,374	1,246	1,006	781	671
Working capital	90	(55)	(147)	(11)	249	638	453	444	648	629	632
Property, plant, and equipment—net	1,440	1,319	1,325	1,400	1,349	1,288	820	779	667	514	398
Total assets	6,655	6,047	6,118	6,445	5,614	5,354	3,410	3,137	2,856	2,207	1,901
Long-term debt	885	840	1,215	1,528	874	982	474	367	298	125	91
Total debt—appliance business	965	850	1,198	1,330	1,026	1,125	441	383	194	64	53
Stockholders' equity	1,723	1,648	1,600	1,515	1,424	1,421	1,321	1,304	1,350	1,207	1,096
Per Share Data											
Earnings from continuing operations before accounting change	$ 2.10	$ 3.19	$ 2.90	$ 2.45	$ 1.04	$ 2.79	$ 2.33	$ 2.61	$ 2.72	$ 2.49	$ 2.59
Net earnings	2.10	0.67	2.90	2.45	1.04	2.70	1.36	2.68	2.70	2.49	2.59
Dividends	1.22	1.19	1.10	1.10	1.10	1.10	1.10	1.10	1.03	1.00	1.00
Book value	23.83	22.80	22.67	21.78	20.51	20.49	19.06	18.83	18.21	16.46	14.97
Closing stock price—NYSE	50¼	66½	44⅝	38⅞	23½	33	24¾	24⅜	33⅞	24¹¹⁄₁₆	23¼

EXHIBIT 13 Concluded

	1994	1993	1992	1991	1990	1989	1988	1987	1986	1985	1984
Key ratios											
Operating profit margin	4.9%	6.4%	6.6%	5.8%	5.3%	6.6%	5.9%	7.1%	8.1%	8.4%	9.0%
Pretax margin[3]	3.6%	5.0%	5.1%	4.5%	3.3%	4.9%	5.3%	6.6%	8.2%	9.1%	10.2%
Net margin[4]	2.0%	3.1%	2.8%	2.5%	1.1%	3.0%	3.6%	4.4%	5.0%	5.1%	5.9%
Return on average stockholders' equity[5]	9.4%	14.2%	13.1%	11.6%	5.1%	13.7%	12.3%	14.1%	15.8%	15.8%	18.3%
Return on average total assets[6]	2.8%	4.0%	3.3%	2.9%	1.4%	4.9%	4.9%	6.2%	8.0%	9.1%	10.6%
Current assets to current liabilities	1.0	1.0	0.9	1.0	1.1	1.3	1.3	1.4	1.6	1.8	1.9
Total debt—appliance business as a percent of invested capital[7]	34.4%	31.6%	41.7%	46.1%	37.6%	39.2%	20.5%	19.3%	—	2.8%	2.7%
Price-earnings ratio	23.9	20.8	15.4	15.9	22.6	12.2	18.2	9.1	12.5	9.9	9.0
Fixed charge coverage[8]	3.0	3.2	2.6	2.3	1.8	2.7	3.5	5.4	7.7	10.7	11.9
Other Data											
Number of common shares outstanding (in thousands):											
Average	75,490	72,272	70,558	69,528	69,443	69,338	69,262	71,732	73,831	73,285	73,171
Year-end	73,845	73,068	70,027	69,640	69,465	69,382	69,289	69,232	74,128	73,325	73,234
Number of shareholders (year-end)	11,821	11,438	11,724	12,032	12,542	12,454	12,521	12,128	11,297	11,668	8,912
Number of employees (year-end)	39,016	39,590	38,520	37,886	36,157	39,411	29,110	30,301	30,520	25,573	22,757
Total return to shareholders (five-year annualized)[9]	12.0%	25.8%	17.0%	6.7%	2.8%	11.3%	4.4%	6.2%	26.8%	26.6%	26.6%

[1]Accounting changes: 1993—accounting for postretirement other than pensions, 1987—accounting for income taxes, and 1986—accounting for pensions.
[2]The company's kitchen cabinet business was discontinued in 1988.
[3]Earnings from continuing operations before income taxes and other items, as a percent of revenue.
[4]Earnings from continuing operations before accounting change, as a percent of revenue.
[5]Earnings from continuing operations before accounting change divided by average stockholders' equity.
[6]Earnings from continuing operations before accounting change, plus minority interest, divided by average total assets.
[7]Cash, debt, minority interests, and stockholders' equity.
[8]Ratio of earnings from continuing operations (before income taxes, accounting change, and interest expenses) to interest expense.
[9]Stock appreciation plus reinvested dividends.

PEPSICO, INC.

John E. Gamble, *University of South Alabama*

Richard C. Hoffman, *Salisbury State University*

Going into 1997 PepsiCo was a diversified consumer products company with businesses in three different industries: beverages (Pepsi-Cola), snack foods (Frito-Lay), and restaurants (Taco Bell, KFC, Pizza Hut, California Pizza Kitchens, Chevys Mexican Restaurants, Hot-n-Now, Eastside Mario's and D'Angelo's sandwich shops). PepsiCo had 1996 sales of $31.6 billion and net income of $1.15 billion. About 30 percent of the company's sales came from operations outside the United States, providing the company with geographic market diversification as well as line of business diversification. The company's beverages were available in 194 countries, its snack foods were available in 40 countries, and KFC, Pizza Hut, and Taco Bell restaurants operated in 94 countries.

> "Nothing focuses the mind better than the constant sight of a competitor who wants to wipe you off the map."
>
> **Wayne Calloway**
> *Former CEO, PepsiCo*

Wayne Calloway, PepsiCo's chairman of the board and chief executive officer from 1986 to 1996, believed that a portfolio of beverages, snack foods, and fast-food restaurants offered valuable synergy and strategic fit opportunities because of the similarity of each industry's key success factors. Competitive success in all three industries was, in large part, a function of a company's ability to create a distinctive image and to develop innovative and tasty new products. Under Calloway, PepsiCo made it a regular practice to move its best managers from positions in one business unit to assignments in the other two business units in order to promote the transfer of skills, practices, know-how, and innovative ideas from one business to another. Calloway believed that such shifting of key personnel helped PepsiCo capture strategic fit relationships among its different businesses, build stronger competitive capabilities, and keep managers' thinking fresh and innovative.

Early in 1996, Wayne Calloway announced that he would resign as CEO of PepsiCo because of his ongoing battle with cancer. PepsiCo shareholders had fared well during Calloway's 10-year reign as chairman of the board and CEO. The company's stock price had increased from $4⅜ in 1986 to its year-end 1995 price of $27¹⁵⁄₁₆. PepsiCo's shares appreciated 54 percent in 1995 alone. In 1995 the company was ranked 17th among publicly traded companies in creating shareholder value, as measured by market value added (MVA). PepsiCo's return to its investors was $16.7 billion greater than invested capital. PepsiCo's key rival, Coca-Cola, was ranked first in providing wealth to its stockholders with an MVA of almost $61 billion. Exhibits 1 and 2 present the results of PepsiCo's recent financial performance.

Roger Enrico became PepsiCo's new chief executive officer on April 1, 1996. Enrico was a 25-year veteran of the company and had experience in all three of the company's lines of business. Enrico joined Frito-Lay's marketing department in 1971, where he remained until becoming president and CEO of the PepsiCo's beverage segment in 1983. Enrico left the Pepsi-Cola beverages unit in 1991 to become CEO of Frito-Lay. In 1994 Enrico moved from Frito-Lay to head up the company's restaurant businesses.

Each of the three PepsiCo business segments had prospered under Enrico's leadership. In the 1980s, Enrico initiated and launched Pepsi-Cola's new advertising campaign that was directed primarily at young consumers. The combination of new slogans, taste testing, and endorsements from celebrities like Michael Jackson and Madonna quickly revitalized Pepsi-Cola's stodgy image. Enrico's marketing strategy was credited with enticing Coca-Cola into the disastrous introduction of New Coke in 1985. Enrico detailed the rivalry between the two soft-drink companies and the failure of New Coke in his 1986 book, *The Other Guy Blinked: How Pepsi Won the Cola Wars.*

While at Frito-Lay, Enrico improved the snack food division's performance by dramatically cutting costs and improving the quality of Frito-Lay's products. During his tenure as head of PepsiCo Worldwide Restaurants, Enrico pushed successfully for new product introductions that helped bolster same-store sales. He also instituted a restaurant refranchising plan intended to lessen the restaurant group's dependency on capital and cash infusions from PepsiCo's other business segments to finance the construction of new restaurants.

Within months of taking over as chairman and CEO of PepsiCo in 1996, however, Enrico found himself having to deal with a number of fairly serious problems at PepsiCo. The company's beverage business—although number two in the soft-drink industry—began to fall behind Coca-Cola by a growing margin in both domestic and international markets. Frito-Lay—the only national manufacturer and marketer of salty snacks in the United States—was under investigation by the U.S. Justice Department for alleged anticompetitive business practices. And even though Enrico had made some progress in getting PepsiCo's restaurant businesses rejuvenated with some popular new menu items, the unit as a whole was still plagued with declining same-store sales and narrowing profit margins. The restaurant group's growth was being fueled by the addition of more restaurant outlets rather than sales growth at existing store locations. Investors and Wall Street were clearly concerned about PepsiCo's performance. At year-end 1996, PepsiCo's stock was trading in the same range where it traded in April when Enrico took over the company's top management position.

EXHIBIT 1   Selected Financial Results for PepsiCo's Three Major Lines of Business, 1993–1996 (in millions of $)

	Beverages	Restaurants	Snack Foods	Corporate
North American Sales				
1996	$ 7,725	$9,110	$6,618	
1995	7,400	9,202	5,863	
1994	6,541	8,694	5,356	
1993	5,918	8,026	4,674	
International Sales				
1996	$ 2,799	$2,331	$3,062	
1995	2,982	2,126	2,682	
1994	2,535	1,827	2,908	
1993	2,148	1,330	2,353	
North American Operating Profits				
1996	$ 1,428	$ 370	$1,286	
1995	1,249	726	1,149	
1994	1,115	637	1,043	
1993	804	685	901	
International Operating Profits				
1996	$ (846)	$ 153	$ 346	
1995	117	112	301	
1994	136	86	354	
1993	97	109	285	
Assets				
1996	$ 9,816	$6,435	$6,279	$ 607
1995	10,032	6,759	5,451	1,555
1994	9,566	7,203	5,044	1,684
1993	9,105	6,412	4,995	2,103
Depreciation				
1996	$ 440	$ 546	$ 346	$ 7
1995	445	579	304	7
1994	385	539	297	7
1993	359	457	279	7
Capital Expenditures				
1996	$ 648	$ 657	$ 973	$ 9
1995	566	750	769	34
1994	677	1,072	532	7
1993	491	1,005	491	21

Source: *1996 PepsiCo, Inc. 10-K.*

EXHIBIT 2   Selected Financial Data for PepsiCo, 1990–1996 (in millions of dollars except per share amounts)

	Compound Growth Rate 1991–96	1996	1995	1994	1993	1992	1991	1990
Summary of Operations								
Net sales	10%	$31,645	$30,421	$28,472	$25,021	$21,970	$19,292	$17,516
Operating profit	4%	2,546	2,987	3,201	2,907	2,371	2,112	2,042
Gain on stock offering by an unconsolidated affiliate		—	—	18	—	—	—	118
Interest expense, net		(600)	(555)	(555)	(484)	(472)	(452)	(506)
Income from continuing operations before income taxes and cumulative effect of accounting changes	4%	2,047	2,432	2,664	2,423	1,899	1,660	1,654
Income taxes	1%	898	826	880	835	597	580	563
Income from continuing operations before cumulative effect of accounting changes		1,149	1,606	1,784	1,588	1,302	1,080	1,091
Cumulative effect of accounting changes		—	—	(32)	—	(928)	—	—
Net income	1%	$1,149	$1,606	$1,752	$1,588	$374	$1,080	$1,077
Net income per share	1%	$0.70	$1.00	$1.09	$0.98	$0.23	$0.68	$0.68
Cash dividends per share	14%	$0.45	$0.39	$0.35	$0.30	$0.26	$0.23	$0.19

EXHIBIT 2   Concluded

	Compound Growth Rate 1991–96	1996	1995	1994	1993	1992	1991	1990
Cash Flow Data								
Provided by operating results		$4,194	$3,742	$3,716	$3,134	$2,712	$2,430	$2,110
Capital spending		2,287	104	2,253	1,982	1,550	1,458	1,180
Operating free cash flow	21%	$1,907	$1,638	$1,463	$1,152	$1,162	$972	$930
Dividends paid	14%	$706	$599	$540	$462	$396	$343	$294
Year-end Position								
Total assets	5%	$24,512	$25,432	$24,792	$23,706	$20,951	$18,775	$17,143
Total debt	1%	8,465	9,215	9,519	9,634	8,672	8,034	7,526
Shareholders' equity		6,623	7,313	6,856	6,339	5,356	5,545	4,904
Book value per share	4%	$4.29	$9.28	$8.68	$7.93	$6.70	$7.03	$6.22
Market value per share	12%	$29.58	$27⅝/16	$18⅛	$20¹⁵/16	$21⅛	$16⅞	$12⅞
Shares outstanding		1,606	788	790	799	799	789	788
Employees		486,000	480,000	471,000	423,000	372,000	338,000	308,000

Source: *1996 PepsiCo, Inc. 10-K.*

EXHIBIT 3   U.S. Per Capita Liquid Consumption (in gallons)

Beverage	1980	1990	1991	1992	1993	1994E
Soft drinks	34.2	47.7	47.8	48.0	49.0	50.6
Bottled water	2.7	8.4	9.3	9.9	8.8	9.7
Beer*	24.3	24.0	23.3	23.0	22.8	22.7
Wine*	2.1	2.0	1.9	2.0	1.8	1.8
Distilled spirits*	2.0	1.4	1.3	1.3	1.3	1.3

E—Estimated.
*Based on population age 21 years and over.
Source: *S & P Industry Surveys*

PEPSICO'S BEVERAGE BUSINESS UNIT

Soft-drink beverages were the oldest and largest business in PepsiCo's portfolio lineup. In 1996 the Pepsi-Cola Company was the world's largest manufacturer and marketer of soft drinks. Popular Pepsi-Cola brands included Pepsi, Diet Pepsi, Mountain Dew, Slice, and Mug; in addition, the division owned marketing rights to the 7UP brand outside the United States. PepsiCo's beverage line also included a number of alternative beverage brands such as All-Sport, Lipton's Brew ready-to-drink iced tea, and Aquafina bottled water.

The Beverage Industry

In 1995 soft drink volume in the United States had grown to a record 13.7 billion gallons. The mature $52 billion industry grew at only 1–3 percent per year during the late 1980s and early 1990s, but industry volume increased at a more rapid 4.3 percent in 1994 and 3.6 percent in 1995. Bottled water was the only beverage category that outpaced soft drink growth during 1995. Soft drinks accounted for one quarter of all beverages consumed in the United States, equal to nearly two 12-ounce cans per day for every man, woman, and child in America. Exhibit 3 provides beverage consumption trends in the United States between 1980 and 1994.

The brands fueling the higher industry growth rates in the mid-1990s indicated a shift in soft drink consumer preferences might be in the making. As the baby boomer generation aged and more people became health- and weight-conscious during the late 1980s and early 1990s, diet drinks and caffeine-free diet drinks grew markedly in popularity and fueled industry growth. But growth in the diet category had begun to level off since 1989, and longtime industry-leading brands like Coca-Cola Classic, Pepsi-Cola, and Sprite achieved the greatest growth in 1995. When adjusted for the industry growth rate, volume sales of Coca-Cola Classic grew by 27.4 percent in 1995, Pepsi grew by 9.5 percent, Dr Pepper volume increased 11.5 percent, Sprite's volume increased by 19.4 percent, and Mountain Dew increased volume by 16.0 percent. The sales volumes of less popular brands showed signs of eroding and captured little consumer interest. The tenth best-selling brand—caffeine-free Diet Pepsi—held only 1.1 percent of the market.

The late-1980s trend toward reduced caffeine content appeared to be undergoing some reversal as sales of high-caffeine-content drinks posted strong sales increases in

1996. Mountain Dew (52 milligrams of caffeine per 12-ounce serving) was one of the fastest growing brands of the year. Although Mountain Dew's caffeine content was somewhat higher than popular soft drinks like Pepsi-Cola (38 milligrams of caffeine per 12-ounce serving), its caffeine content was only about one-fourth of that for a similar sized serving of coffee. In late 1996 Coca-Cola introduced Surge, a high-caffeine-content (53 milligrams of caffeine per 12-ounce serving) citrus flavored soft drink, to compete with Mountain Dew. Coca-Cola management budgeted $50 million to advertise the new Surge brand in 1997. Pepsi's 1996 advertising budget for Mountain Dew was $30 million.

The soft drink industry had two major value chain activities: (1) the manufacture of concentrated syrup and (2) bottling and local distribution activities. The concentrated syrup base for soft drinks was produced by the long-time industry leaders—Coca-Cola, Pepsi-Cola, Dr Pepper, and Royal Crown. The bottling and distribution of soft drinks was the most capital intensive part of the industry and had traditionally been handled by local area bottlers—many of whom were independent franchisees of the large concentrate producers. Pepsi-Cola owned and operated most of its U.S. bottling operations (bottling plants, warehouses and distribution centers, and vehicles used for delivery and sales). Coca-Cola had more independent bottlers than Pepsi-Cola, but had for several years been acquiring poor performing bottlers and turning over their operations and franchise territories to Coca-Cola Enterprises—an independent subsidiary of Coca-Cola. Both Pepsi-Cola and Coca-Cola had elected to establish large-scale "anchor bottlers" in markets outside of the United States and make them responsible for distribution within defined geographic areas. Pepsi maintained ownership interests in most of its anchor bottlers.

Coca-Cola was the leader in the industry with a worldwide market share of 46 percent. It led in all but one of the primary distribution channels through which soft drinks were sold in the United States. In food stores, which accounted for an estimated 48 percent of total industry volume, Coca-Cola brands led Pepsi-Cola brands by 33.3 percent to 31.8 percent. Coca-Cola also led Pepsi-Cola by 31.2 percent to 30.0 percent in mass merchandiser channels which accounted for 6 percent of industry sales. Coca-Cola's greatest lead was in fountain sales to restaurants, where it led Pepsi-Cola by a 41 percent to 30 percent margin. Fountain sales accounted for 27 percent of soft-drink industry sales. In convenience stores, however, Pepsi-Cola edged Coca-Cola's brands with a 35.8 percent share in 1995 versus Coca-Cola's 35.4 percent. The convenience store channel represented 9 percent of soft drinks sales in the United States. Exhibits 4, 5, and 6 present statistics on the strength of Pepsi-Cola brands in the U.S. and international markets.

Consolidation among beverage producers and relatively slow growth in established markets like the United States and many parts of Europe had heightened the intensity of competition in the soft drink industry. Creative marketing campaigns involving innovative advertising, promotion, and new packaging were the key to sparking consumer interest and achieving competitive success. In the mid-1980s Pepsi-Cola began using celebrity endorsements as part of its sales and marketing effort, the most notable of which was its $5 million endorsement contract with Michael Jackson. In the first six months of 1996, Pepsi-Cola spent $63.7 million to advertise Pepsi and Diet Pepsi in the United States. Coca-Cola spent $110.5 million to advertise Coke and Diet Coke during the same period. Both Pepsi and Coke had outstanding success with new packaging, like Pepsi's one-liter "Big Slam" and "The Cube" 24-can pack. Coca-Cola's introduction of its 20-ounce and one-liter "contour" bottles, which resurrected the traditional Coke bottle shape,

EXHIBIT 4   Leading U.S. Soft Drink Companies, 1995

Rank	Company	Gallons (millions)	Market Share
1	Coca-Cola	5,915	42.9%
2	Pepsi-Cola	4,202	30.6
3	Dr Pepper/Cadbury/7UP	2,208	16.1
4	Cott (private label brands)	337	2.4
5	Royal Crown	269	2.0
6	National Beverage (Shasta, Faygo)	234	1.7
7	Monarch (NuGrape, Dad's)	148	1.1
8	Double-Cola	52	0.4
9	Big Red	31	0.2
	All others	359	2.6
	Total soft drink industry	13,755	100.0%

Source: *Beverage World,* March 1996.

EXHIBIT 5   Leading U.S. Soft Drink Brands, 1991–1995

Brand	Market Share, in Percent				
	1991	1992	1993	1994	1995
Coca-Cola Classic	19.3	19.3	19.5	19.7	20.0
Pepsi-Cola	16.4	16.1	15.4	15.6	15.4
Diet Coke	10.1	9.8	9.6	9.5	9.5
Dr Pepper	5.0	5.3	5.5	5.8	6.0
Mountain Dew	4.0	4.3	4.6	5.2	5.6
Diet Pepsi	6.1	6.2	5.7	5.6	5.4
Sprite	3.8	3.9	4.1	4.4	4.9
7UP	2.8	2.9	2.8	2.9	2.7
Caffeine Free Diet Coke	2.3	2.2	2.1	2.0	1.9
Caffeine Free Diet Pepsi	1.4	1.3	1.2	1.2	1.1

Source: *Beverage World,* March 1996.

was credited with contributing to Coca-Cola's volume gains during 1995 and 1996. Coca-Cola management had discussed the possibility of introducing a contoured 12-ounce can.

Coca-Cola management believed that its production and distribution capabilities were a source of competitive advantage over its soft-drink rivals. Whereas Pepsi-Cola had relied upon celebrity endorsements and a string of memorable ads to attract customers, Coke had elected to invest in its bottling operations. Coca-Cola CEO Roberto Goizueta believed that his company's investment in facilities, equipment, and systems was more important than catchy marketing campaigns, saying, "You let me have the bottling plants and the trucks and the highly efficient

EXHIBIT 6   1994–1995 Volume Growth and Comparative 1995 Market
             Shares of Coca-Cola and Pepsi-Cola, Selected Country and
             Regional Markets

Top 10 Markets	Volume Growth (1994–1995)	Market Share (1995)	
		Coca-Cola	Pepsi-Cola
United States	+2%	43%	31%
Mexico	+1	61	21
Japan	+10	34	5
Brazil	+55	51	10
East-Central Europe	unknown	40	21
Germany	–2	56	5
Canada	+2	37	34
Middle East	unknown	23	38
China	unknown	20	10
United Kingdom	+12	32	12
Worldwide Averages	+9%	46%	21%

Source: *Beverage World,* March 1996; *Fortune,* October 28, 1996.

systems, and I'll let you have the TV commercials. I'll beat you to a pulp over time."[1]

International markets provided a promising growth opportunity for soft drink companies. Although the per capita consumption was relatively low, the international industry volume was about 70 percent larger than the U.S. market. Per capita consumption in foreign country markets was expected to increase as soft drinks gained broader geographic distribution and were more intensively promoted abroad. International volume grew 9 percent during 1994–1995, whereas growth in the United States during the same time was only 3–4 percent.

Coca-Cola had been the leading soft drink producer worldwide since the end of World War II. Its international sales topped $12.7 billion in 1995, up 15 percent from the previous year; foreign sales represented 71 percent of Coca-Cola's total soft drink sales. Much of Coca-Cola's success in international markets came not only from its two premier brands, Coca-Cola Classic and Diet Coke, but also from country-specific brands that it had developed to appeal to local taste preferences. Coca-Cola introduced 30 new soft drinks in Japan between 1994 and early 1997—most of which were not colas. For example, Coca-Cola vending machines in Japan might only offer three colas among the 25 choices available through the machine. Popular soft drinks sold by Coca-Cola in Japan included Georgia—a coffee-based drink; Lactia—a fermented milk drink; and Sokenbicha—a tea-flavored drink. PepsiCo, a distant second to Coca-Cola in international markets (see Exhibit 6), had far fewer international brands; Pepsi's international sales accounted for only 34 percent of its total soft-drink revenue.

---

[1]*Fortune,* October 28, 1996, p. 78.

THE PEPSI-COLA COMPANY ———————————————————

Pepsi-Cola Company began in 1903 when Caleb D. Bradham, a pharmacist, started to market his beverage invention in North Carolina. In 1995 Pepsi-Cola brands accounted for about $32 billion in worldwide retail sales, equal to about 20 percent of all retail sales of soft drinks. The company was the second largest soft drink producer in the world and Pepsi was ranked 10th among the most recognized brand names in the world (4th in the United States) out of 6,000 brands surveyed by Lander Associates, a San Francisco consulting firm. In 1995 Pepsi-Cola Company's domestic sales grew at a rate of 7 percent versus 3.6 percent for the industry as a whole, while its international sales growth exceeded 19 percent.

Pepsi-Cola brands and their respective shares of worldwide retail sales included: Pepsi ($18.4 billion), Diet Pepsi ($4.1 billion), Mountain Dew ($3.8 billion), 7UP ($2.1 billion—non-U.S. sales only), Miranda ($1.6 billion), Slice ($650 million), and Mug ($160 million). Pepsi-Cola brands were available in 194 countries. Pepsi's product line also included a number of New Age or alternative beverages like ready-to-drink teas, coffee-based drinks, and isotonic sports beverages. Pepsi's isotonic beverage, All-Sport, was a distant third to Gatorade—the original isotonic beverage that still held an 80 percent market share in the United States and 40 percent internationally. The company's Lipton brand of ready-to-drink teas was the best-selling brand in that rapidly growing category. While the alternative beverage category grew 70 percent in 1995 to reach $9.5 billion in U.S. retail sales, Pepsi-Cola's share of the category increased from 1 percent in 1992 to 13 percent in 1995. Some of Pepsi's gain in market share was attributed to new product introductions such as The Radical Fruit Company of New York line of fruit juices, Mazagran, Pepsi Kona, and Frappuccino—all coffee-based drinks—and Josta guarana soda, a high-caffeine drink made with Brazilian guarana berries.

Even though Pepsi-Cola was the world's number two soft drink company, it was competing head-on against a rival whose strategic intent was not just to remain number one but to keep widening the gap between itself and the number two company in the industry. During 1996 Pepsi lost ground to Coke in the United States and in almost every international market. Coke's overall 43 percent to 31 percent market share lead over Pepsi in the United States was the largest lead Coke had achieved in over 20 years. Coca-Cola's objective was to exceed 50 percent market share both internationally and in the United States by 2001. Coca-Cola management believed that it was on track to achieve its long-term strategic objective, having captured approximately 80 percent of total industry expansion in the United States during the first six months of 1996. Coca-Cola's Roberto Goizueta stated in 1996 that he was currently less concerned with PepsiCo's corporate strategy than he was in the past, "As they've become less relevant, I don't need to look at them very much anymore."[2] In fact, some PepsiCo investors believed that the company's management had failed to craft a viable competitive strategy for its beverage business. Analysts and investors criticized management for relying too heavily on advertising to compete against Coca-Cola and that something more was needed. The company had also been criticized for entering too many international markets without adequate capital to support a successful launch of its brands.

—————————

[2]Ibid., p. 71.

Pepsi-Cola's international operations were in some degree of trouble in 1996. Pepsi trailed Coke substantially in most markets around the world and its largest international bottler, BAESA—with operations in Brazil, Argentina, Chile, Uruguay, and Costa Rica—was on the verge of bankruptcy. PepsiCo's 20 percent ownership stake in the bottler forced the company to take a $525 million special charge in 1996 that caused the company's international operations to have a net loss for the year. It was expected that PepsiCo would be forced to invest at least $200 million into the South American bottler during 1997 to avert bankruptcy, correct its operating problems, and put it back on sound competitive footing.

Not all of Pepsi-Cola's problems in international markets were internal. Coca-Cola management dealt Pepsi-Cola's Latin American operations a blow in August 1996 when it acquired a 50 percent interest in Pepsi's Venezuelan bottler. The acquisition put Pepsi out of business overnight in a market where Pepsi had outsold Coke by a 4 to 1 margin. The loss of the bottler was especially disturbing since the local owners were personal friends of PepsiCo CEO Roger Enrico. Enrico stated that Coca-Cola's move was "a new low" and that "the terms of engagement have changed."[3] Craig Weatherup, president of Pepsi-Cola North America, commented on Coca-Cola management, "Their Achilles' heel is their own arrogance, and it eventually will be their downfall. I hope I'm around to see it."[4]

PEPSICO'S RESTAURANT BUSINESS UNIT

PepsiCo's restaurant segment was comprised of three worldwide fast-food franchise systems (Pizza Hut, Taco Bell, and KFC) and a group of five lesser restaurant chains (California Pizza Kitchens, Chevys Mexican Restaurants, Hot-n-Now, Eastside Mario's, and D'Angelo's sandwich shops). In 1995 the combined sales growth of PepsiCo's restaurants was 6 percent domestically and 16 percent internationally.

An Overview of the Restaurant Industry

Over the past 20 years, Americans had spent a rising portion of their food dollars at restaurants. Demographic factors, such as more two-income families, more women in the workforce, and an increase in the number of households made up of singles, along with a growing desire for better-quality leisure time, had combined to make eating out an attractive option to preparing meals at home. In 1995, consumers worldwide spent over $150 billion at fast-food restaurants. U.S. fast-food sales grew at a compounded annual rate of 6 percent between 1990–1996 to reach $100 billion. Americans spent about 50 percent of their food dollars at restaurants in 1996, up from 33 percent in 1980.

An increasing portion of meals purchased at restaurants were for off-premise consumption. This reflected both hurried lifestyles and a desire to avoid food preparation at home. According to the National Restaurant Association, 64 percent of fast-food sales were for off-premise consumption in 1996. Off-premise consumption accounted for only 34 percent of restaurant traffic in 1984. Only 25 percent of Pizza Hut customers and 12 percent of KFC customers chose to dine in. Among PepsiCo's

[3]Ibid., p. 78.
[4]Ibid., p. 84.

restaurants, Taco Bell had the largest percentage of dine-in customers with 55 percent of its customers dining in and 45 percent choosing to carry out or use drive-throughs.

For the past several years, the fast food segment of the restaurant industry had been challenged by market saturation and by the shrinking availability and quality of labor. In seeking to bring food to the customer rather than having the customer come to the food, fast food companies established outlets in such nontraditional locations as sports stadiums, airports, large-scale discount warehouses, shopping malls, university dorms and eating areas, and gasoline stations. There were 191,000 fast-food restaurants in the United States in 1995, up 74 percent over 1980.

It was becoming increasingly difficult for restaurants to attract quality employees since the total number of 16- to 24-year-olds—the primary labor supply for restaurants—had declined by more than 10 percent since 1985. During the same period, the total number of all types of restaurants in the United States had increased nearly 11 percent. A survey conducted by the National Restaurant Association in 1996 indicated that restaurateurs believed that the availability of labor was second only to competitive rivalry as the greatest challenge to the industry. Some franchise chains had adopted a commissary/satellite strategy to reduce on-site labor requirements and food preparation costs. The use of a commissary involved centralizing many of the food preparation activities traditionally performed in each restaurant and capturing scale economies in preparing and cooking select menu items.

Value-conscious consumers and fierce rivalry among the growing numbers of fast-food outlets produced strong price competition among the leading fast-food chains during the mid-1990s. To build customer traffic, most chains began offering bundled value meals that combined a main course, side dish, and a drink for one low price. Management of many restaurants found that the value meals increased volume and often boosted market share, but put a squeeze on margins.

Operating efficiency in restaurants was largely a function of controlling food and labor costs. A 1994 survey of 2,200 restaurants by Deloitte & Touche indicated that the median annual sales for fast-food restaurants was $8,518 per seat and $41,443 per employee. The survey also found that food and beverage costs accounted for 32 percent of each sales dollar at fast food restaurants. Payroll expenses represented about 26 percent of each sales dollar and roughly 2.5 percent more went for employee benefits. Many restaurants had incorporated productivity-boosting computer technology to minimize labor costs and to compensate for the decrease in the labor pool. Computers were used for labor scheduling, seating management, menu planning, and inventory tracking and purchasing. Fixed costs in the restaurant industry such as rent, utilities, and marketing expenses approached 30 percent of sales. The average pretax net profit margin was 9 percent for the firms sampled by Deloitte & Touche.

Franchised restaurants had some advantage in the industry as a result of economies of scale in distribution and purchasing. Franchising also represented an important vehicle for growth in restaurant sales. By offering restaurant franchises, restaurant companies could rapidly expand a brand concept without bearing the full costs of expansion—typically, in a franchising relationship, the costs of land acquisition, building construction, equipment, and fixtures were borne by the franchisee. It was common for the franchisee to pay a royalty of about 3–5 percent of sales to the parent company and also contribute another 4 percent toward corporate advertising. In return, the franchisee received brand-name recognition, a concept menu, recipes, training, and marketing support.

Fast food restaurants had U.S. sales of over $100 billion during 1996. The four most popular fast food concepts based on menu offering were hamburger, pizza,

EXHIBIT 7   Top 10 U.S. Restaurant Chains, 1995

Company	Sales (in Millions)	Number of Units
McDonald's	$29,914	15,205
Burger King	8,400	7,547
Pizza Hut	7,900	10,648
KFC	7,275	9,407
Taco Bell	4,925	5,950
Wendy's	4,500	4,406
Hardee's	3,360	3,456
Subway	3,000	9,893
Domino's Pizza	2,650	5,079
Dairy Queen	2,484	5,540

Source: *Restaurants & Institutions,* July 1, 1996.

chicken, and Mexican restaurants. Chains emphasizing hamburgers represented the largest part of the U.S. franchise restaurant industry (see Exhibit 7). Within this $51 billion segment, McDonald's market share was 58 percent, compared to 16 percent for runner-up Burger King, 8.8 percent for Wendy's, and 6.6 percent for Hardee's. In 1995, McDonald's 11,300 outlets accounted for 19 percent of all sales by U.S. franchise restaurant chains and 10 percent of total U.S. restaurant spending.

The Pizza Segment   Pizza franchise chains had about 24,000 outlets with estimated sales of about $15.6 billion in 1995. Sales were up about 11 percent from 1994. The leading chains—Pizza Hut, Domino's and privately owned Little Caesars—accounted for more than 80 percent of segment sales. Exhibit 8 shows systemwide sales figures for the major competitors in this segment.

The Chicken Segment   Fast-food chains emphasizing chicken had estimated sales of over $10.4 billion in 1995; the segment leader was PepsiCo's KFC division (see Exhibit 8). KFC's combined company-owned and franchised domestic sales represented 70 percent of the chicken entree segment. The second and third largest chains—Church's Fried Chicken and Popeye's Famous Fried Chicken—merged in 1989; their combined systemwide U.S. sales in 1995 were over $1.4 billion. Total sales in the chicken segment actually declined by $100 million from 1994 to 1995.

The Mexican Segment   Mexican chains grew at a rate of 12 percent from 1994 to 1995 as people looked for an alternative to the traditional fast food products. This segment produced roughly $7.2 billion in sales for 1995. PepsiCo's Taco Bell chain dominated the segment (see Exhibit 8). Rival Mexican chains were expanding primarily on a regional basis.

The Growing Emphasis on International Expansion   As the U.S. market became more saturated and competitive, the leading franchised restaurants shifted their attention to international markets as the primary source of growth. While the international fast-food market was approximately half the size of the U.S. market, many countries still

EXHIBIT 8   Sales and Units of Leading U.S. Restaurants in the Chicken, Pizza, and Mexican Segments, 1995

Chicken segment

Company	Sales (in Millions)	Units
KFC	$7,275	5,142
Churchs Chicken	737	1,165
Popeye's Famous Fried Chicken	710	907
Chick-fil-a	502	592
Kenny Rogers Roasters	285	250
El Pollo Loco	200	250
Boston Market	159	1,023
Grandy's	156	184
Lee's Famous Recipe Chicken	152	274
Bojangles' Chicken & Biscuits	101	206

Pizza segment

Company	Sales (in Millions)	Units
Pizza Hut	$7,900	10,648
Domino's Pizza	2,650	5,079
Little Caesars	2,000	4,700
Papa John's	458	632
Round Table Pizza	376	562
Chuck E. Cheese	263	332
Shakey's	250	450
Godfather's	250	522
Pizza Inn	233	475
California Pizza Kitchen	171	70

Mexican segment

Company	Sales (in Millions)	Units
Taco Bell	$4,925	5,950
Chi-Chi's	341	1,375
El-Torito	237	105
Del Taco	216	266
Taco John's	166	420
Taco Cabana	158	127
Chevys Mexican Restaurants	150	54
El Chico	144	94
Taco Time	115	306
Don Pablo's	89	76

Source: *Restaurants & Institutions,* July 1, 1996.

offered faster near-term growth rates and even greater long-term potential as their markets for fast-food developed. Overall, international growth in fast food was approximately 12 percent. Even though foreign markets were attractive to U.S.-based fast-food companies, there were many risks associated with entering international markets. In addition to the challenge of satisfying international taste preferences, fast food companies experienced difficulties in repatriating profits because of local government restrictions. They also had to contend with international currency fluctuations. Frequently, site development costs abroad were higher than in the United States and qualified suppliers were not readily available. Political instability and varying ethical standards were also threats to international operations. In 1996 the Chinese government terminated the 20-year lease on the site of McDonald's 700-seat Beijing location. The company was forced to relocate its largest restaurant after its two-year fight failed to convince the Chinese government to honor the lease. PepsiCo, McDonald's, Burger King, and Domino's Pizza were the only companies to have over 500 international units in 1996. Even though PepsiCo had the greater number of international units, McDonald's had the most successful international fast food business. Almost one-half of McDonald's 1995 revenue of $29.9 billion came from its 7,012 international outlets.

PepsiCo's Restaurant Group

PepsiCo was the largest restaurant conglomerate in the world in 1996. Its three chains combined, KFC, Pizza Hut, and Taco Bell, had over 28,500 units with worldwide sales of $11.3 billion in 1995 (Exhibit 9). All three restaurant chains were ranked among the top five U.S. chains. The company and its franchisees operated over 8,000 international units located in 94 countries and had international system-wide sales of $6.5 billion in 1995. The company's competitive strategy was directed primarily at creating a distinctive, exciting image for each of its restaurant brands and adding innovative items to its menus. PepsiCo management was allocating considerable time and resources to bolster and refresh KFC's image and reputation with consumers. The company changed the name of the business from Kentucky Fried Chicken to KFC, added a number of non-fried chicken items to its menu, added an all-you-can-eat buffet to its menu lineup, and spent heavily to renovate its KFC units.

Pizza Hut, acquired in 1977, was the leading pizza chain in the world and had a 51 percent market share of the $15.6 billion U.S. franchised pizza market. Taco Bell, acquired in 1978, was the leading fast-food chain in the Mexican food segment, with only a few regional competitors. Its systemwide domestic sales of $4.9 billion represented 68 percent of the $7.2 billion Mexican fast food industry segment. KFC, which PepsiCo acquired in 1986, had domestic system sales of about $7.3 billion in 1995 and accounted for 70 percent of the U.S. chicken market. With over 5,000 units, it had more than four times as many U.S. restaurants as the next largest chicken chain.

Whereas PepsiCo's early restaurant acquisition strategy was to acquire established market leaders, the company had recently begun to acquire small, relatively unknown companies. Hot-n-Now, a drive-through-only hamburger concept, was acquired in 1990. California Pizza Kitchen, a joint venture formed in 1992, was a full-service pizza restaurant that featured pizzas cooked in wood-fired ovens. Eastside Mario's, D'Angelo's sandwich shops, and Chevys Mexican Restaurants were all acquired in 1993. Eastside Mario's and D'Angelo's sandwich shops were operated by Pizza Hut management. All D'Angelo's sandwich shops were integrated within Pizza Hut units.

EXHIBIT 9   Financial Statistics for PepsiCo's Restaurant Chains, 1993–1995 (in millions of $)

	United States			International
	Pizza Hut	**Taco Bell**	**KFC**	
Sales				
1995	$3,977	$3,503	$1,722	$2,126
1994	3,712	3,340	1,642	1,827
1993	3,595	2,855	1,576	1,330
Operating profits				
1995	$ 308	$ 105	$ 38	$ (21)
1994	285	273	101	71
1993	338	256	91	93
Amortization of intangible assets				
1995	$ 36	$ 23	$ 18	$ 32
1994	38	27	22	18
1993	35	23	23	25
Depreciation expense				
1995	$ 189	$ 179	$ 101	$ 110
1994	178	153	107	101
1993	159	122	101	75
Identifiable assets				
1995	$1,700	$2,276	$1,111	$1,672
1994	1,832	2,327	1,253	1,791
1993	1,733	2,060	1,265	1,354
Capital spending				
1995	$ 168	$ 305	$ 93	$ 184
1994	225	442	69	338
1993	209	442	106	248

Source: *1995 PepsiCo, Inc. Annual Report.*

Chevys was a full-service Mexican restaurant and, along with Hot-n-Now, was part of the Taco Bell organization.

PepsiCo's restaurants had all introduced new products from time to time to freshen the appeal of their menus, stimulate consumer interest, and boost customer traffic. Pizza Hut introduced Stuffed Crust pizzas and Triple Decker pizzas in the United States and Europe in 1995 and 1996. KFC introduced such new products as Tumble Marinated Original Recipe, Colonel's Crispy Strips, and Chunky Chicken Pot Pies to complement its traditional fried chicken dinners. Taco Bell introduced the Double Decker Taco, the Texas Taco, a line of Sizzlin' Bacon products, and low-fat Border Lights menu items. Although value-priced bundle meals were not offered at Pizza Hut, KFC offered the value-priced Mega Meal and Taco Bell offered Extreme Value Meals. Pizza Hut relied more on coupons, special lunch and evening buffets, and delivery as promotional tactics. Forty-seven percent of Pizza Hut sales were delivered to the customer; Taco Bell did not offer delivery services and KFC only delivered 7 percent of its sales. KFC management did expect to expand delivery beyond the 400 U.S. units offering delivery in 1995.

PepsiCo management was pleased with the performance of its 100 U.S. dual-branded units. The pairing of a Taco Bell unit and KFC unit under the same roof improved operating margins since site development costs, construction costs, and overhead expenses were shared. The pairing worked well since the two brands did not appear to cannibalize each other's sales. KFC traditionally had strong sales and customer traffic during dinner hours, while most of Taco Bell's business was during lunch. Sales for the dual-branded units were 20 percent higher than single unit concepts. The company planned to add an additional 200 dual-branded restaurants during 1996.

Management of the restaurant group was beginning to look for cost-sharing opportunities within the restaurant division in addition to dual-branding as a means to bring down operating costs. The worldwide purchasing and procurement operations and international administrative headquarters of all restaurant concepts were consolidated in 1996. Efforts to consolidate administrative operations (such as payoff and accounts payable) were begun in 1996, but management believed that it would take a number of years to successfully merge the support activities of PepsiCo's restaurants.

In 1996 a number of investors and Wall Street analysts expressed the opinion that PepsiCo should divest or spin off its restaurant businesses. Hot-n-Now and Chevys both experienced operating losses in 1995. PepsiCo management intended to license or refranchise all of its 200 company-owned Hot-n-Now units. However, of the 150 units that the company had licensed or franchised, 42 had been returned to PepsiCo because of the new owners' inability to turn around the restaurants. PepsiCo chose to close all 42 of the returned units. PepsiCo management also hoped to franchise or license poor-performing company-owned Taco Bell, Pizza Hut, and KFC units. While KFC units had steady same store sales in 1996, the same store sales of Taco Bell had been in decline since 1994. Pizza Hut's same store sales had declined more than 10 percent after the novelty of its stuffed crust pizza innovation faded. A Wall Street analyst suspected that PepsiCo's refranchising plan would fail to rid the company of all poor-performing restaurant units. "Pepsi admits these stores they're selling are underperforming. The concern here is that they run out of hard-working, energetic, stupid franchisees to buy these things."[5] In September 1996 a fund manager who controlled over three million PepsiCo shares told Roger Enrico that "No one can understand why you don't just spin this thing off. It diverts management attention, it doesn't fit with the company's other business, and you're not running it well."[6]

PEPSICO'S SNACK FOOD BUSINESS UNIT

PepsiCo's snack food segment primarily manufactured and marketed snack chips under the Frito-Lay brand in the United States and under a number of brands in international markets.

The Snack Food Industry

Snack foods in the United States was a $60 billion industry that included candy, chips, cookies, and crackers. Americans' annual per capita consumption of salty snacks—potato, corn, and tortilla chips, cheese puffs, and pretzels—exceeded 18 pounds in 1995 compared to 9 pounds per capita 15 years earlier. Retail sales of these salty snacks totaled $12.1 billion in 1995. The annual growth rate of the U.S. snack

---

[5]*The Wall Street Journal,* September 30, 1996, p. A1.
[6]Ibid.

EXHIBIT 10   Snack Chip Consumption and Volume Growth for Selected Country Markets, 1995

Country	Consumption Level (pounds per capita)	Growth Rate (1994–1995)
United States	18	+1
United Kingdom	10	+3
Spain	4	+1
Mexico	4	−6
Brazil	2	+4

Source: *1995 PepsiCo, Inc. Annual Report.*

food industry was about 1 percent, while the international snack food industry enjoyed a 9 percent annual rate of growth. International snack chip retail sales totaled $18 billion, with an annual per capita consumption of less than 11 pounds. As with the soft drink and fast food industries, many U.S. companies found success abroad difficult to obtain. The taste preferences of European, South American, and Asian consumers could vary greatly from the taste preferences of U.S. consumers. To gain broad market acceptance, most snack food flavors needed to be customized to the local market. Exhibit 10 presents the consumption levels and growth rates of various international snack food markets.

In 1996 Frito-Lay was the only national manufacturer and marketer of salty snacks in the United States. Anheuser-Busch's Eagle Snacks and Borden had held the industry's second and third positions, respectively, but both companies chose to abandon the market. Both firms had found it difficult to compete against Frito-Lay and make a profit. When it exited the industry in early-1996, Anheuser-Busch had lost over $500 million since it launched Eagle Brand snacks in 1979. The company sold the Eagle Brand trademark and brand name to Procter & Gamble (P&G). P&G—the makers of Pringle's potato chips—had no immediate plans to relaunch the brand. Eagle Brand's five production facilities were sold to Frito-Lay. Exhibit 11 presents Frito-Lay's market shares in snack foods in 1994 and 1996.

Distribution and new product introductions were the keys to success in this industry. Frito-Lay's regional competitors lacked the resources to make their chips as widely available as the Frito-Lay brands. The primary channels of distribution for snack foods were supermarkets and convenience stores. Supermarkets accounted for 43 percent of industry sales that, more or less, belonged to Frito-Lay. The company's established distribution system and wide variety of products were unmatched by the remaining regional snack food companies. Frito-Lay also had an advantage over many regional snack chip makers who were unable to pay supermarket slotting fees—sometimes as much as $100,000 per foot of shelf space. A snack food company executive commented on the difficulty of competing with Frito-Lay in supermarkets. "The traditional retail grocery is Frito-Lay's domain. They've got the trucks, they've got the deep pockets and the products."[7] Regional companies' best approach to gaining access to supermarket customers was by offering highly

---

[7]*Brandweek,* March 18, 1996, p. 34.

EXHIBIT 11 Market Shares of U.S. Potato Chip Producers, 1994 vs. 1996

Company	1994 Market Share	1996 Market Share
Frito-Lay	49.5%	53.9%
Eagle Snacks	11.5	6.5*
Borden	8.4	N/A
Private label	8.1	6.9**
Others	22.5	32.7
Total	100.0%	100.0%

* Prior to the company's exit from the industry.
**Estimated from 1995 sales.
Sources: *Snack Food,* September 1994; *Brandweek,* September 19, 1995; *U.S. News & World Report,* September 16, 1996.

differentiated, niche brands like Bachman's super-premium Black Bean Tortilla Chips with salsa seasoning.

Convenience stores, which accounted for 20 percent of snack food sales, traditionally carried one national brand and one regional brand. The convenience store channel was particularly attractive because it offered high margins and was growing more rapidly than other channels since consumers were eating more meals away from home. Other snack food channels included vending machines, bars, restaurants, warehouse clubs, discounters, and sports stadiums.

U.S. consumers were attracted to low-calorie, low-fat snacks only if they were as tasty and flavorful as their higher fat content counterparts. The per capita consumption of pretzels, which were baked and had a low fat content, increased 100 percent between 1990 and 1996. Other tasty, low-fat snacks were also selling well. Nabisco management was pleased with the performance of its SnackWell's line of low-fat cookies and sweet snacks. Frito-Lay had achieved success with its Baked Tostitos and Tostitos line of salsas. In fact, the Tostitos line of salsas was the top-selling new processed food item in the United States in both 1994 and 1995.

Frito-Lay management hoped that the availability of Olestra, a fat substitute made by Procter & Gamble and marketed under the Oleon brand name, would allow it to introduce new fat-free products that consumers would enjoy. Olestra is a synthetic chemical of sugar and vegetable oil that contains no calories. After 25 years of testing, the product was approved for human consumption by the U.S. Food and Drug Administration (FDA) in early 1996. Later in the year, Frito-Lay purchased the exclusive rights to Oleon through 1999 and had begun test-marketing its Max line of no-fat, reduced-calorie chips in three U.S. cities. A one-ounce bag of the Max line of chips contained zero grams of fat and 70 calories. An equal portion of Lay's chips contained 10 grams of fat and 150 calories.

Frito-Lay and P&G admitted that Oleon could produce mild gastrointestinal discomfort for some individuals who ate chips made with the product. One consumer group, however, claimed that 3 percent of those who consumed the product could expect severe discomfort. The group also claimed that Oleon removed vitamins from the body that were thought to decrease the risk of cancer. In late 1996 the consumer group was urging the FDA to rescind its approval of the product and had asked Frito-Lay to voluntarily discontinue test-marketing Max chips.

PepsiCo's Frito-Lay Division

PepsiCo acquired Frito-Lay in 1965. Frito-Lay was PepsiCo's most profitable division, accounting for 28 percent of company sales and 48 percent of its profits in 1995. Frito-Lay had captured over one-half of the $12.1 billion U.S. salty snack food market. In 1995 Frito-Lay's pound volume grew 10 times faster than the industry. Industry analysts expected Frito-Lay's growth to continue into 1997 since Eagle Brand had liquidated its assets and abandoned the industry. A Frito-Lay executive assessed the company's competitive position in the industry. "Basically, we are the category."[8]

Frito-Lay management attempted to build competitive advantage in snack foods by ensuring high product quality and wide distribution of its established brands, introducing new brands that would appeal to health-conscious consumers, and taking its brands to countries where demand for snack foods was growing. Frito-Lay's best-known products included Doritos, Ruffles, Lay's, Fritos, Tostitos, Chee-tos, and GrandMa's cookies. Doritos was Frito-Lay's largest single selling brand with estimated worldwide retail sales of $1.7 billion for 1995. The Doritos brand faced no single large competitor, but did confront competition from many regional brands—most of which were priced below Doritos. Eight of the top 10 selling snack chips in the United States were made by Frito-Lay. Frito-Lay's worldwide brands, and their estimated worldwide retail sales, are presented in Exhibit 12.

Frito-Lay's international snack food businesses operated in 40 countries with a 30 percent market share of the total international snack chip market. In 1989 PepsiCo/Frito-Lay acquired United Kingdom-based Smiths Crisps Ltd. and Walker Crisps Ltd. for $1.34 billion. These acquisitions made Frito-Lay the leading snack food company in Europe, where it led its nearest competitor in six of the eight major markets where the two companies competed. Frito-Lay's geographic expansion was rapid paced with the division entering 20 new countries between 1989 and 1995. In 1995 alone, Frito-Lay launched snack food operations in Saudi Arabia, South Africa, several Latin American countries, Poland, and four other Eastern European nations. Frito-Lay had been successful in modifying its popular U.S. snack brands to appeal to international taste preferences. In Asian markets, Frito-Lay replaced the cheese flavoring in Chee-tos with fish and steak flavoring to please consumers. The company also added chili and lime flavoring to products marketed in Latin America. Frito-Lay had found that Ruffles and Lay's potato chips were popular around the world without modification.

In 1996 Frito-Lay was the undisputed global leader in snack foods, emerging victorious from its encounter and brief rivalry with Eagle. Several years earlier, when Eagle Brand was consistently gaining ground on Frito-Lay and Wayne Calloway saw Frito-Lay's market share drop to 38 percent, he moved Roger Enrico over to Frito-Lay to try to reverse Frito-Lay's market share slide. Enrico discovered that consumers viewed Frito-Lay products as too greasy and bland and as inferior to Eagle Brand chips. Enrico responded by spending $90 million to improve the company's products and processes. While president of Frito-Lay, Enrico initiated the development of a genetically engineered potato that was superior to potatoes previously purchased by the company. Under Enrico, Frito-Lay also retooled its production facilities with new ovens and fryers to improve the manufacturing process. Enrico took measures to

---

[8]Ibid., p. 33.

EXHIBIT 12   Selected Frito-Lay Snack Food Brands

Brand	Year Acquired/Introduced	1995 Worldwide Sales (in millions)
Doritos	Introduced 1966	$1,700
Ruffles	Acquired 1958	1,600
Lay's Potato Chips	Introduced 1938	1,500
Chee-tos	Introduced 1938	917
Tostitos	Introduced 1981	754
Fritos	Introduced 1932	575
Walkers (Sold outside of U.S. only)	Acquired 1989	540
Rold Gold Pretzels	Acquired 1961	364
Sun Chips	Introduced 1991	199
Funyuns	Introduced 1969	131
Hostess (Sold outside of U.S. only)	Acquired 1992	113
Santitas	Introduced 1986	103

Source: *1995 PepsiCo, Inc. Annual Report.*

improve the company's cost position by laying off more than 1,000 employees and reducing operating expenses by $500 million.

An important element of Frito-Lay's strategy was the continuous introduction of new products. Its "better-for-you" low-fat and no-fat brands like Baked Tostitos tortilla chips, Baked Lay's potato chips, Reduced Fat Ruffles, and Tostitos salsas accounted for over 45 percent of sales growth in 1995. The "better-for-you" category made up over 10 percent of Frito-Lay's 1995 U.S. sales. The company's established brands like Lay's, Ruffles, and Doritos also experienced volume growth, partly due to the introduction of co-branded flavor extensions. Hidden Valley Ranch Wavy Lay's, KC Masterpiece Lay's potato chips, Pizza Hut Doritos, and Taco Bell Doritos were popular with consumers.

Frito-Lay had developed a competitive advantage over rivals by continually building its distribution network and by developing an exceptionally strong 15,000-person sales force. Frito-Lay delivered direct from its manufacturing plants to individual stores, thus eliminating the costs of warehousing operations. Frito-Lay was one of the first companies to introduce handheld computers for its sales force, enabling salespeople to generate daily sales data for a particular store or geographic location. This sales and market tracking data was used by sales managers to evaluate Frito-Lay's competitive performance and was also transmitted to Frito-Lay production facilities to aid in inventory management and production scheduling.

Frito-Lay management intended to reengineer the process for selling and delivering snacks to high-volume accounts like supermarkets, warehouse clubs, and discounters. Traditionally, a route business manager would take orders, deliver products, and stock store shelves. The company believed that it could provide better service to large retailers by subdividing the job so that sales personnel would handle the accounts, drivers would make deliveries to the store, and in-store stockers would keep the product available and neatly displayed on the shelf. Management hoped that this new process would improve service to these large accounts and also help provide the manpower for its "Quantum Leap" initiative. Quantum Leap was intended to double

Frito-Lay's market share in the convenience store channel by 2000. Under Quantum Leap, sales routes would be made much smaller so that route business managers could call on convenience stores more frequently. Also, Frito-Lay management intended to give these route drivers the authority and freedom to negotiate deals with store managers rather than having promotions approved by higher level managers.

Frito-Lay's dominance of the U.S. snack foods industry had drawn the attention of the U.S. Justice Department. The department launched an antitrust investigation into the company's competitive practices in 1996 to determine if the company was engaged in destructive competitive behavior. Specifically, the Justice Department was looking into the practice of slotting in supermarkets. The Grocery Manufacturers of America estimated that food and nonfood manufacturers spent $2.5 billion annually to gain access to U.S. supermarket shelves. Some legal experts questioned the government's concern with Frito-Lay's slotting practices, since the Justice Department had not been concerned with the practice in the past. An investment firm analyst remarked on Frito-Lay's competitive practices and its industry dominance, "They've driven all their competitors out of business by being too successful. There's nothing unethical [about that]. They're just better at product development, marketing and execution."[9]

THE ISSUES CONFRONTING ENRICO AND PEPSICO CORPORATE MANAGEMENT

PepsiCo's stock price had been flat throughout 1996—a time when the market had experienced an increase of over 25 percent and the stock of Coca-Cola, its key rival, had appreciated by 42 percent. There was every indication that Wall Street investors were concerned about the long-term performance potential of PepsiCo's business portfolio. Enrico knew that he and PepsiCo's corporate-level executives would need to arrive at an action plan quickly.

(PepsiCo's Web site address is *www.pepsico.com*.)

---

[9]*Time*, June 10, 1996, Internet report.

BOMBARDIER LTD. (B)

Joseph Lampel, *New York University*

Jamal Shamsie, *New York University*

"I want a company with a continuous flow, that is not subject to the drastic fluctuations of being in just one business."[1] These were the words of Laurent Beaudoin, chairman of Bombardier, during the early 1980s as he contemplated his company's dramatic rise to prominence. The Canadian company's name had been at one point synonymous with snowmobiles. Its pioneering efforts in the development and the launching of the Ski-Doo had been handsomely rewarded. By the late 1960s, Bombardier controlled close to 50 percent of the snowmobile market, about three times as much as its closest competitor.

Notwithstanding this success, Laurent Beaudoin came to believe that the potential of the snowmobile market was limited and that Bombardier should take steps to insulate itself from the uncertainties of the recreational market. Throughout the 1970s and the 1980s, Beaudoin led his company on an aggressive strategy of diversification into other areas of leisure and transportation.

As the company moved into the 1990s, its revenues had grown considerably beyond the $28 million in sales that it had generated from snowmobiles some 30 years earlier. The company had grown into a vast, publicly traded conglomerate with factories in seven countries and a labor force of over 34,000 employees. However, while Bombardier's revenues had grown dramatically, its profits had not kept pace. Each year, solid performances by some of its businesses were insufficient

Note: This case is a revised and thoroughly updated follow-on to a case developed by the same authors in 1988. Copyright © 1994, by the authors.
[1]"Bombardier: Making a Second Leap from Snowmobiles to Mass Transit," *Business Week,* February 23, 1981.

EXHIBIT 1   Bombardier's Income Statements, 1989–1993 (in millions of Canadian dollars)

	For the Year Ended January 31				
	1993	1992	1991	1990	1989
Net sales	$4,448.0	$3,058.6	$2,892.3	$2,143.3	$1,426.0
Cost of sales	4,180.2	2,828.2	2,672.5	1,974.4	1,298.9
Operating income	267.8	230.4	219.8	168.9	127.1
Interest on long-term debt	46.7	28.7	17.3	7.5	5.3
Other interest expenses	32.3	23.9	35.9	51.7	13.0
Other expenses	37.9	56.4	46.1		
Pretax income	150.9	121.4	120.5	117.2	108.8
Income taxes	18.1	13.7	20.4	25.7	39.2
Extraordinary loss	—	—	—	—	1.3
Net income	$ 132.8	$ 107.7	$ 100.1	$ 91.5	$ 68.3

Source: Bombardier annual reports.

EXHIBIT 2   Bombardier's Sales, by Class of Business, 1989–1993 (in millions of Canadian dollars)

	For the Year Ended January 31				
	1993	1992	1991	1990	1989
Aerospace	$2,228.4	$1,519.1	$1,382.9	$ 840.6	$ 630.7
Defense	366.5	366.2	358.3	214.7	143.9
Transportation	1,237.6	725.6	697.1	639.5	311.3
Consumer products	555.8	391.5	398.0	399.0	310.3
Capital group	59.7	56.2	56.0	49.5	29.8
Total	$4,448.0	$3,058.6	$2,892.3	$2,143.3	$1,426.0

Source: Bombardier annual reports.

to compensate for unexpected losses elsewhere (see Exhibits 1 through 5 for Bombardier's financial picture and organization). For example, the transportation group had just reported a loss of $72.6 million, representing the largest one-year loss that any Bombardier business had ever incurred. The stable stream of profits on which Bombardier's strategy depended was proving more elusive than Beaudoin had expected.

GROWING WITH SNOWMOBILES

Birth of the Snowmobile

Work on the snowmobile was first started in the mid-1920s by Joseph-Armand Bombardier in his father's garage at Valcourt, Quebec. But it took until 1935 before

EXHIBIT 3   Bombardier's Profits from Operations, by Class of
             Business, 1989–1993 (in millions of Canadian dollars)

| | For the Year Ended January 31 | | | | |
	1993	1992	1991	1990	1989
Aerospace	$180.6	$137.2	$112.9	$ 69.8	$ 34.8
Defense	6.9	2.0	28.5	17.8	7.4
Transportation	(72.6)	3.5	20.1	16.5	46.3
Consumer products	28.6	(9.1)	(29.5)	10.1	14.6
Capital group	7.4	(12.2)	(11.5)	3.0	5.7
Total	$150.9	$121.4	$120.5	$117.2	$108.8

Source: Bombardier annual reports.

EXHIBIT 4   Bombardier's Balance Sheets, 1989–1993 (in millions of
             Canadian dollars)

| | For the Year Ended January 31 | | | | |
Assets	1993	1992	1991	1990	1989
Cash and term deposits	$ 235.1	$ 179.2	$ 87.5	$ 84.0	$ 150.0
Accounts receivable	380.4	360.1	413.7	428.8	174.0
Financing receivables	942.1	640.8	491.3	458.0	307.5
Inventories	1,803.1	1,215.7	992.7	583.5	220.2
Prepaid expenses	19.6	13.6	9.5	12.2	9.9
Fixed assets	834.5	626.8	533.5	335.7	262.1
Other assets	55.2	34.5	35.3	34.8	27.0
Total assets	$4,270.0	$3,070.7	$2,563.5	$1,937.0	$1,150.7
Liabilities and Shareholders' Equity					
Short-term loans	884.9	640.1	558.2	376.8	153.2
Accounts payable	1,311.6	883.2	818.1	671.1	341.5
Income taxes payable	69.3	18.2	13.7	13.3	5.7
Long-term debt	698.5	381.2	265.9	147.0	70.6
Other liabilities	112.0	54.9	68.0	55.6	54.5
Convertible notes	209.6	193.8	145.4	50.4	—
Preferred shares	34.1	35.7	37.4	157.7	158.3
Shareholders' equity	950.0	863.6	656.8	465.1	366.9
Total liabilities and shareholders' equity	$4,270.0	$3,070.7	$2,563.5	$1,937.0	$1,150.7

Source: Bombardier annual reports.

Joseph-Armand had built the first snowmobile. It consisted of a large plywood body
set on caterpillar tracks and driven by a heavy, conventional internal combustion
engine.

These early snowmobiles were hand-assembled in versions intended to accommodate from 5 to 25 passengers. In each case, the machine was individually adapted for
a specific use according to the wishes of different customers. By 1942, Joseph-

EXHIBIT 5   Bombardier's Business Unit Organization, 1993

Aerospace and Defense	Transportation Equipment	Motorized Consumer Products
Aerospace Group North America	**Transportation Equipment Group North America**	**Motorized Consumer Products Group**
Canadair (Canada)	Transportation Equipment Group (Canada, U.S.)	Sea-Doo/Ski-Doo Division (Canada)
de Havilland (Canada)	UTDC Systems Divsion (Canada, U.S.)	Bombardier-Rotax GmbH (Austria)
Learjet Inc. (U.S.)	Bombardier S.A. de C.V. (Mexico)	Scanhold Oy (Finland)
	Auburn Technology (U.S.)	Industrial Equipment Division (Canada)
Short Group	**Bombardier Eurorail**	
Short Brothers PLC (United Kingdom)	BN Division (Belgium)	
	Societe ANF-Industrie S.A. (France)	
	Bombardier-Wien A.G. (Austria)	
	Bombardier Prorail Limited (United Kingdom)	

Source: Bombardier annual reports.

Armand had incorporated his garage to form Bombardier Snowmobile Limited and was producing snowmobiles to serve doctors, missionaries, woodsmen, foresters, trappers, and farmers in outlying districts of Quebec.

With the advent of World War II, the basic snowmobile design was adapted to produce an amphitrack armored carrier called the Penguin for use by Canadian troops. Subsequently, the demonstrated durability and ruggedness of the snowmobile also led to the development and production of various forms of specialized industrial equipment. These consisted of machines that were especially suited for use in forestry, logging, oil exploration, and snow removal.

Eventually, Joseph-Armand and his son Germain tackled the challenge of developing and producing a smaller and lighter version of the basic snowmobile design intended to carry one or two persons. The key to the new design was the coupling of a recently introduced two-cycle motor-scooter engine with an all-rubber track that had internal steel rods built in for added strength. By 1959, the first snowmobile directed at the individual user was introduced into the market. Initially, Joseph-Armand thought of calling his invention the Ski-Dog, but he decided in favor of a more bilingual name, the Ski-Doo.

Development of the Snowmobile

When he died in 1964, Joseph-Armand left behind a company that had 700 employees and a product that was enjoying increasing popularity—16,500 Ski-Doos had been sold and demand was clearly on the rise. Joseph-Armand's son Germain took over as president but shortly thereafter relinquished his post for reasons of health. The company passed into the hands of son-in-law Laurent Beaudoin, a chartered accountant and one of the first management graduates of the University of Sherbrooke. Beaudoin realized that certain factors were standing in the way of the development of the full potential of the snowmobile:

> There were two fundamental problems arising from the nature of the company's beginnings. First, there was no research and development department because it had all taken place in the mind of Joseph-Armand Bombardier. Second, the company which he created was, very naturally, a production-oriented company. It produced machines to fill a market need, which was mainly for large machines to do practical jobs, rather than creating and seeking out new markets.[2]

Beaudoin introduced an R&D section, set up an integrated marketing system, and geared up facilities for efficient mass production. Extensive research confirmed that an untapped snowmobile market existed not only for transport but also for recreation and sport. Bombardier invested heavily in the development of this potential market. Over the next several years, extensive advertising, the establishment of a dealer network, and the setting up of 18 regional sales groups covering Canada, the United States, and Europe resulted in Bombardier becoming a leader in the snowmobile market and turned the Ski-Doo trademark into a generic term for snowmobiles.

But the success of Bombardier also brought about the entry of new producers of snowmobiles. Most of the new competition came from U.S. companies that had been closely watching the development of the snowmobile business. Beaudoin, however, was not fazed at the prospect of more competition. He was confident about the capabilities of his company to maintain its leadership:

> It's an industry that looks very simple. Everybody looks and says: "Gee, we can get in tomorrow morning and grab everything." But it's not that simple. The advantage we have over all those companies is that we eat snow, we know snow, and are snowmobilers ourselves.[3]

In order to ensure that it could meet this growing competition, Beaudoin also decided to start acquiring almost all of the company's suppliers, most of which were situated within the province of Quebec. These acquisitions led to the development of a series of subsidiaries and affiliates that manufactured parts or accessories related to snowmobile production (see Exhibit 6). This push for acquisitions eventually climaxed in the $30 million purchase of Rotax-Werk. Located in Austria, Rotax-Werk manufactured the two-stroke engine used in the Ski-Doo. By 1970, Bombardier's own production facilities, or those of its subsidiaries and affiliates, were supplying over 90 percent of the 1,400 parts that went into the manufacturing of the Ski-Doo. Beaudoin saw these moves as a necessary precaution against an eventual intensification of competition, in particular the likely outbreak of price wars: "If there is any price war, we will be in a position to face it. This has been our first idea."[4]

Shortly thereafter, Bombardier moved to buy out its largest competitor. In 1971, it finalized the acquisition of Moto-Ski from its U.S. parent Giffin Industries. This acquisition consolidated Bombardier's domination of the snowmobile market. By this time, the achievements and stature of Bombardier were acclaimed as a product of

[2]"Bombardier Skids to Success," *International Management,* January 1972.

[3]"Snow Job?" *Forbes,* February 1, 1970.

[4]Ibid.

EXHIBIT 6   Bombardier's Acquisitions, 1957–1992

Consumer Products	Transportation Equipment	Aerospace and Defense
1957 Rockland Industries* Location: Kingsbury, Quebec Business: Rubber parts	1970 Lohner-Werke Location: Vienna, Austria Business: Streetcars	1973 Heroux# Location: Longueuil, Quebec Business: Aeronautical parts
1968 La Salle Plastic* Location: Richmond, Quebec Business: Plastic parts	1976 Montreal Locomotive Works# Location: Montreal, Quebec Business: Locomotives, diesel engines	1986 Canadair Location: Montreal, Quebec Business: Aerospace
1969 Roski* Location: Roxton Falls, Quebec Business: Fiberglass products	1984 Alco Power Location: Auburn, N.Y. Business: Locomotives, diesel engines	1989 Short Brothers Location: Belfast, Northern Ireland Business: Aerospace
1970 Rotax-Werk Location: Gunskirchen, Austria Business: Engines	1986 BN Construction Location: Bruges, Belgium Business: Mass transit products	1990 Learjet Location: Wichita, Texas Business: Business jets
1970 Walker Manufacturing* Location: Montreal, Quebec Business: Sportswear	1986 Pullman Technology Location: Chicago, Illinois Business: Mass transit products	1992 de Havilland Location: Toronto, Ontario Business: Commuter aircraft
1970 Drummond Automatic Plating† Location: Drummondville, Quebec Business: Chrome plating	1989 ANF-Industrie Location: Paris, France Business: Mass transit products	
1970 Jarry Precision‡ Location: Montreal, Quebec Business: Transmissions	1990 Procor Engineering Location: Wakefield, England Business: Railcars	
1971 Moto-Ski§ Location: LaPocatiere, Quebec Business: Snowmobiles	1992 Carros de Ferrocarril (Concarril) Location: Mexico City, Mexico Business: Mass transit products	
1972 Ville Marie Upholstering‖ Location: Beauport, Quebec Business: Foam seats	1992 UDTC Location: Kingston, Ontario Business: Mass transit products	
1989 Scanhold Oy Location: Rovaniemi, Finland Business: Snowmobiles		

* Disposed of in 1983.
† Disposed of in 1976.
‡ Closed down in 1973.
§ Dissolved in 1975.
‖ Disposed of in 1979.
Disposed of in 1989.

Source: Financial Post Corporation Service.

Canadian imagination and entrepreneurial vigor. An article, published at the beginning of 1972, bestowed praise on the company:

> Not many companies can claim to have started an entirely new industry—fewer still to have done so and stayed ahead of the pack. Bombardier Ltd. has done just that . . . It is a company owned and managed by Canadians, which several foreign companies would dearly love to own. It is the largest Quebec-owned company operating in the province, and is one of the 200 most profitable public companies in Canada.[5]

---

[5]"Bombardier Skids to Success."

The Crunch for Snowmobiles

The early 1970s saw an increasing number of companies competing in the snowmobile market. In addition to new American and Canadian firms, Bombardier had to contend with the entry of Swedish, Italian, and Japanese manufacturers. Yet while the number of competitors was increasing, market growth in snowmobiles was slowing down.

Several reasons were advanced for the softening of snowmobile sales. The main blame was put on the stagnant economy, which was seen as the principal cause of the decline in demand. Snowmobiles constituted a type of purchase that was often postponed by consumers during a downturn in the economy. Other reasons were more peculiar to the snowmobile market. Poor winters, with late snow and unusually low precipitation, reduced the recreational use of snowmobiles. At the same time, newspaper stories of crashes and injured or killed riders led to a mounting concern over safety of snowmobiles. Finally, environmentalists were vocal in their criticism of the high noise levels generated by snowmobiles, particularly in wilderness areas.

There was growing awareness that stricter legislation covering the design and use of snowmobiles was likely to be forthcoming. Bombardier attempted to meet these concerns by trying to design better safety features and special mufflers for their upcoming snowmobile models. It also produced films, slides, and brochures on safety measures and the proper use of the snowmobile. Furthermore, a newly created public relations department tried to involve the various levels of government and different types of businesses in the creation of a system comparable to the one found in the ski industry. This was to include the development of snowmobile trails, snowmobile weekends, and snowmobile resorts.

The market for snowmobiles dropped sharply through most of the 1970s before it began to stabilize at around 100,000 units a year during the 1980s (see Exhibit 7). In order to adjust to these lower level of sales, Bombardier gradually sold off the various subsidiaries that were producing parts and accessories for its snowmobiles. Apart from assembling the snowmobiles, Bombardier's actual manufacture of the vehicle was limited to the engine, which was still supplied by the company's Rotax division in Austria.

Beaudoin attributed the gradual dismantling of the vertically integrated manufacturing operations to the general state of the snowmobile industry. But eventually he acknowledged that Bombardier's position in the depressed snowmobile market had also been slipping. From a 45 percent share during the early 1970s, the company's share had declined to about 25 percent by the late 1980s. The competition had been closing in on Bombardier's leadership, causing it to have second thoughts about the long-term attractiveness of the industry that it had pioneered.

MOVING AWAY FROM SNOWMOBILES

In 1974, Bombardier seized on an opportunity to bid on a four-year $118 million contract to build 423 new subway cars for the proposed extension of the Montreal underground transit system. The bid represented a major departure from the core business of the company. It was not, however, the first time that Bombardier had ventured away from manufacturing and marketing snowmobiles.

Early Diversification Moves

Even before the snowmobile market was developed, Bombardier had been producing all-terrain tracked and wheeled vehicles for different kinds of industrial use. The company had continuously developed and marketed many basic types or sizes of

EXHIBIT 7   Snowmobile Market Statistics, 1971–1992

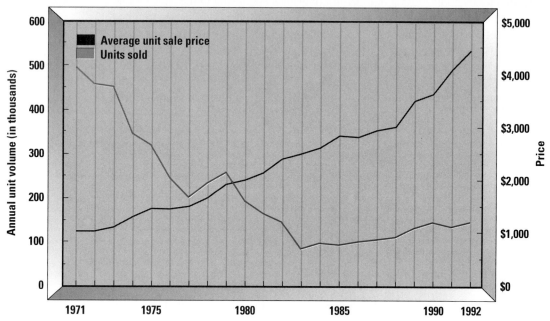

Source: International Snowmobile Manufacturers Association.

vehicles for work in swamps, forests, and snow. The earliest of these were the Muskeg series of carriers, tractors, and brushcutters that were used in logging, construction, petroleum, and mining. Later developments included the SW series for urban snow removal, the Skidozer line for grooming snowmobile trails and ski slopes, and the Bombi carrier for transporting people over snowy or marshy terrain.

A further departure from snowmobiles came as a result of Bombardier's acquisition of suppliers (see Exhibit 6). Originally, the acquisitions were undertaken in order to consolidate the company's position in the snowmobile market. Once made, they presented attractive opportunities. For example, Rotax-Werk was acquired in 1970 because it produced the engines that were used in Ski-Doos. But it also manufactured engines for boats and motorcycles. Another acquired subsidiary proceeded to develop and introduce a new type of fiberglass sailboat, followed by a canoe and a catamaran.

In addition, the success of the snowmobile created other ancillary markets. For instance, traveling on snowmobiles at 40 miles per hour in subfreezing temperatures required specialized clothing. Beaudoin saw this new type of market as a promising opportunity:

> Someone was going to have to supply wet-proof clothing that was warm enough to prevent our customers from freezing to death on our machines. We decided it might as well be us.[6]

Consequently, Bombardier acquired an apparel manufacturer in order to introduce snowmobile clothing. This led the company into the sportswear market because the

---

[6]Ibid.

acquired manufacturer was already engaged in the production and marketing of several other types of sportswear. Said Beaudoin: "We are in the leisure business."[7]

In other instances, Bombardier sought to enter markets not directly related to its core snowmobile business. In 1970, the company introduced a new product called the Sea-Doo, which was a kind of snowmobile on water. This was marketed most heavily in Florida and California. Unfortunately, the Sea-Doo was found to rust in salt water and production was suspended after a couple of years. A more technically successful product was the Can-Am motorcycle, which was test-marketed by Bombardier in 1973. The idea for the motorcycle originated with the development of a new engine by Bombardier's new Rotax subsidiary in Austria. The result was a light, high-performance motorcycle that quickly gained recognition after it won several races in Canada, the United States, and Europe.

A Bold Thrust

It was around this time that Bombardier began to see mass transit as a potentially lucrative market. The decision to move into mass transit was facilitated by overtures to Bombardier from the French-based Compagnie Industrielle de Materiel de Transport (CIMT). CIMT had been involved in a partnership with Canadian Vickers Limited on a previous order for the Montreal subway system. Charles Leblanc, who was vice president, administration, for the company at the time stated:

> CIMT came to us. They said don't be afraid of it. They pointed out that the same manufacturing steps were needed for subway cars as for snowmobiles. So we went ahead and bid.[8]

Winning the award of this substantial contract represented Bombardier's entry into the mass transit market. There were strong doubts whether Bombardier had the necessary capabilities to complete the order. Up to this point, the company's involvement in mass transit products had been limited to trams and streetcars produced by its Austrian subsidiary. But trams and streetcars were substantially different in design from subway cars.

The company moved to convert the Moto-Ski snowmobile plant at La Pocatiere to handle production of subway cars. The complexity of making a subway car proved several orders of magnitude greater than that of a snowmobile. A subway car had 8,000 parts and 14 kilometers of electric wiring, compared to only 2,000 parts in a snowmobile. The shift to producing subway cars required considerable retraining of the labor force. It also required new investment in physical facilities. The estimated cost of conversion was about $5 million, of which $1 million was provided by a grant from the Canadian government.

Bombardier then experienced some problems in production, due in part to a labor strike in its newly converted plant. Nevertheless, the company began to make deliveries of subway cars to the city of Montreal late in 1976. By this time, Bombardier had also won contract awards for commuter cars in the United States and for subway cars in Mexico. But the firm made its biggest splash in 1982, landing a large and prestigious order of about $1 billion for 825 subway cars from the Metropolitan Transportation Authority of New York. The company managed to acquire the tech-

---

[7]Ibid.
[8]"Why Bombardier Is Trying Out Mass Transit," *Business Week*, March 10, 1975.

nology that it needed for these subway cars from Kawasaki, the Japanese firm that had manufactured the previous batch of New York subway cars. A low-interest export financing scheme from the Canadian federal government also helped to clinch the sale.

Encouraged by its success in winning orders, Bombardier bought out the mass transit activities of Pullman and Budd companies. Between them, these companies accounted for the designs of 85 percent of the vehicles operating in the United States and Canada. By 1988, the company had also acquired almost all of the stock of a Belgian mass transit company that had supplied the technology to develop and build the streetcars that it had already delivered to Portland, Oregon. The acquired firm, BN Constructions Ferroviares et Metalliques S. A., had three factories in Belgium, one in England, and one in France. Besides streetcars, BN manufactured subway cars, electric railcars, passenger coaches, and freight cars.

During the next two years, Bombardier followed up with two more acquisitions to increase its presence in Europe. In France, it spent $23.5 million to acquire ANF-Industrie, one of the largest suppliers of railcars and coaches to the French railway industry. ANF was already working with Bombardier's BN subsidiary on a contract worth $650 million for the design and manufacture of shuttle train cars for the English Channel tunnel project. Across the channel from France, Bombardier purchased Procor Engineering Limited, a major British manufacturer of passenger and freight cars for the railway.

During 1992, Bombardier picked up two more manufacturers of mass transit equipment in North America. In Mexico, the company acquired Carros de Ferrocarril (Concarril), the largest manufacturer of rail cars. Besides paying $27 million to the Mexican government, it assumed $55 million of the debt that Concarril had accumulated when operations were suspended a few months earlier. Back home, Bombardier added to its Canadian production capacity by purchasing Toronto-based UTDC from the Ontario government for $34 million. Additionally, it was able to negotiate a $17 million subsidy from the provincial government in return for a commitment to maintain employment and invest up to $30 million in new plant and equipment.

Reflecting back on Bombardier's growing position in mass transportation products, Beaudoin stressed the role of Lohner-Werke, an Austrian manufacturer of tramways that was included with the purchase of Rotax. Bombardier had at one point shopped around for firms that would buy Lohner-Werke but had found few takers. Beaudoin commented:

> Everyone thinks we're great strategists but it was by chance that Bombardier got involved in rail transportation . . . The decision to hold onto the Austrian subsidiary was the turning point. It taught us how to operate a company abroad, and it developed our expertise in the rail sector.[9]

A Stab at Related Diversification

Shortly after its entry into mass transit, Bombardier tried to find new acquisitions that would help it to become a significant competitor in the transportation business. According to Beaudoin, Bombardier's move into mass transit products had done much to moderate the company's dependence on recreational products, particularly

---

[9]"Trains, Planes and Snowmobiles," *CA Magazine,* November 1992.

the snowmobile. He summed up his company's diversification objectives in the following terms:

> Our goal is to develop some equilibrium between transportation and recreation. The transportation and recreation cycles are different. Recreational products are strong when the economy is strong. It's the reverse for transportation because of energy problems.[10]

In 1976, Bombardier succeeded in purchasing the Montreal Locomotive Works (MLW) from its U.S. parent for a cash payment of $16.8 million. Bombardier was given much needed financial help from the Quebec government in finalizing this deal. The diesel-electric locomotives produced by MLW were mostly in the lighter category, ranging from 1,000 to 2,000 horsepower. The main markets for such locomotives were mainly the operators of railways in developing countries.

Bombardier's purchase of MLW was largely motivated by its growing interest in developing the Light, Rapid and Comfortable (LRC) passenger train. Its partners in this project were Alcan and Dofasco. The Canadian government also contributed development grants through its program for the advancement of industrial technology. The new train was designed to run at constant high speeds on existing North American tracks. Both Via Rail in Canada and Amtrak in the United States began to make test runs of the new LRC trains during the late 1970s and early 1980s. Bombardier vice president Henry Valle, who had previously headed MLW, talked about the distinctive features of the LRC:

> We think the LRC is as good or better than anything comparable on the market anywhere. And we don't think anyone anywhere knows any more about high-speed trains than we do.[11]

Bombardier also made substantial investments to upgrade the MLW facilities for the production of diesel locomotives. In 1984, the company sought to expand its capacity and obtain new customers through the $30 million acquisition of Alco Power, located in Auburn, New York. However, Alco's production capabilities were also limited to the lighter category of diesel-electric locomotives that were similar to those offered by MLW.

At the same time, Bombardier was being forced to reevaluate its potential orders for passenger locomotives that would result from the sales of its LRC train. The company had believed that it would eventually make worldwide sales of 150 locomotives and 750 coaches. But by 1986, after the sale of only 31 locomotives and 100 coaches to Canadian-based Via Rail, there were no more orders on hand. Even Via Rail had declined to exercise its options for further orders because of mechanical and electrical problems it had experienced with equipment already delivered.

Bombardier also began to realize that it was not likely to build a viable position in the locomotive market unless it developed and produced locomotives with greater horsepower, such as those presently manufactured by General Electric and General Motors. The company explored the possibility of linking up with existing large competitors such as General Electric or Kawasaki in order to gain better access to the technology that would be required to develop higher powered locomotives. When alliance discussions failed, Bombardier decided to terminate the production of new

---

[10]"Snowmobiles to Subways: Bombardier Maps Out its Route," *Financial Post,* September 13, 1980.

[11]"Bombardier Looks to Amtrak to Open Doors to U.S. Inter-City Market," *Globe & Mail,* November 16, 1977.

locomotives and to focus primarily on the servicing of existing locomotives. Most of this work was subsequently channeled into the Alco facility in New York state. In 1989, the MLW facility was finally sold to the Canadian division of General Electric. Raymond Royer, soon to become Bombardier's president, expressed the company's disappointment over the sale: "It has been very painful for us. It's a major decision to take, but if we can't make a profit, we have to act as good managers."[12]

LEAVING SNOWMOBILES BEHIND

As Bombardier moved into the 1980s, it was becoming increasingly aware of the volatility in the orders for its newly developed mass transit business. As the company was completing deliveries on the large order of subway cars for New York City, it was not sure when other orders of a comparable size would become available. Mass transit orders were sporadic, following no predictable cycles, seasons, or patterns. Consequently, Bombardier began to look for businesses that could insulate it from the uncertainties of the mass transit business. The search led the company to look beyond mass transit to automobiles and aerospace, both of which are industries whose size could provide it with considerable scope for further expansion. However, entry into either of these would represent the first major shift in business focus since Bombardier's entry into mass transit.

Exploration of Entry into Small Car Manufacture

In 1983, Bombardier started actively exploring the possibility of introducing into the North American market a small car designed to carry two persons that would retail for about $7,000. The company negotiated an agreement with Daihatsu Motor Company of Japan to obtain the technology that was going to be used in the design of the car. Daihatsu, which was partly owned by Toyota, was the smallest producer of cars in Japan. Talks between Bombardier and Daihatsu focused on a joint venture framework for development and production of the new car.

As a first step, Bombardier would begin production of the Daihatsu three-cylinder car that was already marketed in Asia and Europe. The next step would be for Bombardier and Daihatsu to jointly design a front-wheel-drive version of this car for the North American market. The car would be produced by Bombardier at Valcourt, where the company had sufficient spare factory space. The facilities were deemed to be sufficient to handle production of about 200,000 cars annually. Sales and service were to be carried out by the 350 snowmobile dealers that Bombardier had developed throughout Canada and the United States.

Supported by generous grants from the various levels of the Canadian government, Bombardier spent about $15 million developing and testing four prototypes. Although prototype testing had gone well, there were still strong doubts within the company about the size of the potential market for such a small car. Since the car was to be powered by a three-cylinder engine, it would offer a maximum speed of about 55–65 miles per hour. It would therefore have to be targeted as a second car, used mainly for driving within the urban and suburban areas.

In 1987, Laurent Beaudoin finally announced that the company had decided to abandon the proposed joint venture to assemble small cars. Among other factors,

---

[12]"Locomotives to Be Dropped," *Globe & Mail,* July 13, 1985.

Beaudoin cited the rising value of the yen, which made the cost of imported parts from Japan—notably the power train—much too expensive to meet the company's profitability objectives. In his words: "We saw there was no realistic way to attain an acceptable profit in the medium term."[13]

Diversifying in Another Direction

Even as Bombardier was getting ready to abandon small cars, it was actively exploring an opportunity that emerged when the Canadian government expressed its intention to sell Canadair, an aerospace company located in Montreal. Canadair had run into difficulty after spending in excess of $1 billion to develop the Challenger, a business jet that earned praise from industry observers for being spacious, quiet, and fuel efficient. Unfortunately for Canadair, projected sales of the aircraft showed that it was unlikely to cover initial development costs.

When the financial condition of Canadair could no longer be concealed from the public, the government decided to absorb the development costs and sell the company. As a Canadian company based in Quebec, Bombardier was favorably positioned to take advantage of the government's predicament. After a brief negotiation period, the Canadian government agreed to sell Canadair to Bombardier for $120 million, provided it continued to develop Canadair's assets. In addition to its highly regarded business jet, these assets also included the CL-215 water bomber. The CL-215 had been the mainstay of the company during the 1970s while the Challenger was being developed. Although it offered excellent firefighting capabilities, Canadair was having difficulty obtaining new orders for the plane.

Immediately after its acquisition, Bombardier moved to turn Canadair around by reducing management hierarchy and cutting operating costs. With the encouragement of Bombardier's top management, Canadair also decided to further exploit its existing technological capabilities. It announced plans to adapt the Challenger design to create an extended 50-seat short-haul regional jet. This commuter version was designed to serve the growing traffic in short-haul routes, particularly in the United States and in Europe. The $300 million development project received substantial financial help from both the federal and provincial levels of the Canadian government.

In 1989, Bombardier expanded its aerospace business to Europe, acquiring Short Brothers PLC from the British government. Bombardier paid $60 million for the company and agreed to continue its operations in Belfast, Northern Ireland, for at least four years. In return, the British government agreed to write off $1.3 billion of the company's debt and provide grants totaling more than $200 million. The deal gave Bombardier control of a firm with $1.5 billion in orders and entry into the lucrative European aviation industry. Short produced Tucano trainer aircraft and C-23 Sherpa aircraft for European military outfits. However, the major share of its revenues came from supplying aircraft components to other aircraft manufacturers such as Boeing and Fokker. Bombardier also began to use Short's expertise to design and manufacture several components for the regional jet under development by Canadair.

Shortly after acquiring Short Brothers, Bombardier launched efforts to acquire Learjet Corporation, a financially troubled U.S. manufacturer of small jets. Learjet was purchased for $75 million in cash and assumption of $38 million of outstanding debt from its parent, which had filed for protection under the bankruptcy code. The

---

[13] "Bombardier, Daihatsu Abandon Venus Project," *Globe & Mail,* June 24, 1987.

company produced several models of light jets such as the 31A and 35A, both of which seated 9 or 10 passengers, compared to the 12 to 19 passengers that could be carried by the Challenger models. By 1991, Learjet had begun to adapt the existing Learjet designs to develop a model 60, which would accommodate more passengers and be able to fly longer distances. Beaudoin commented on Bombardier's strategy to exploit the technology that it had obtained through the Canadair, Short, and Learjet acquisitions: "First acquire the outside technology, then improve on it to become competitive."[14]

In 1992, Bombardier acquired 51 percent of Boeing's ailing de Havilland division, with an option to buy out the rest of the company from the Ontario provincial government after four years. De Havilland produced the Dash 8-100 and Dash 8-300 lines of propeller-driven commuter aircraft seating 37 to 40 passengers each. Beaudoin felt that these would complement the Challenger regional jet that was currently being developed by the company's Canadair division. Although de Havilland had been a consistent money loser for Boeing, Bombardier was protected from any losses during the first four years of operations by a $300 million reserve fund set up by the Canadian federal and provincial governments.

Asked to explain how Bombardier would be able to turn around ailing aerospace companies that others had failed to revive, Beaudoin answered:

> The main difference is we're very close to those operations. We have a very quick decision-making process. We encourage entrepreneurship among our people. We delegate responsibility to them. And we support them in their decision-making process.[15]

Participation in the Defense Market

The acquisition of Canadair also resulted in Bombardier's entry into the defense industry. Canadair was a major producer of airborne surveillance systems, and it also possessed a fully developed capability for servicing military aircraft. Shortly after Bombardier's acquisition of Canadair, the Canadian government awarded the company a lucrative contract for the maintenance of the CF-18 fighter that would eventually result in more than $1 billion of revenues. This contract led to further technical services, including full-scale fatigue tests for the CF-5 and CF-18, as well as maintenance of other aircraft used by the Canadian armed forces.

In addition to these contracts, Canadair was also involved in the design and manufacture of unmanned or remotely piloted air surveillance systems. Its CL-89 surveillance systems had already been purchased by several NATO countries. The company had recently completed work on a more advanced CL-289 system and was planning to start work on a CL-227 Sentinel system.

Bombardier's activities in the defense sector expanded considerably as a result of its subsequent acquisition of Short Brothers. Short Brothers had developed military aircraft, notably the older Tucano military trainer and the more recently developed Sherpa C-23 transport. The company had long-term contracts for providing technical support for the fleets of Tucano trainers and Sherpa cargoes operated by the British Air Force and others.

Furthermore, Short was also engaged in the production and delivery of short-range defense systems for the British armed forces. The first of these systems was the high-velocity Starstreak missile system that had been under development since 1987.

---

[14]"Planes, Trains and Snowmobiles," *Enroute*, March 1991.
[15]"On the Move," *Montreal Gazette*, November 1, 1993.

More recently, this system had been complemented by the introduction of a more advanced laser-guided Starburst missile system. The company was also exploring many possible export markets in Europe, the United States, and the Far East.

BOMBARDIER'S CURRENT BUSINESS PORTFOLIO

By 1993, Bombardier's operations fell into three different business sectors, consisting of 16 different divisions or subsidiaries (see Exhibit 5). While the transportation equipment sector included the largest number of divisions, the bulk of sales came from the aerospace and defense sector. A fourth sector, the Bombardier Capital Group, provided credit and financing services for all other sectors. Although Bombardier was moving to bring its various divisions and subsidiaries under centralized control, they continued to be managed as separate administrative and financial entities. Each division or subsidiary was headed by a chief executive who possessed a considerable degree of autonomy. However, these chief executives were expected to work closely with the member of Bombardier's corporate management team that had lead oversight for their particular business sector.

Bombardier's top management worked mostly out of the company's corporate headquarters in Montreal. Except for a brief period, the position of chairman and chief executive officer had been occupied by Laurent Beaudoin. Joseph-Armand's son Andre Bombardier, and son-in-law Jean-Louis Fontaine, held positions as vice chairmen of the company. Raymond Royer, who was hired away from a rival snowmobile manufacturer by Beaudoin in the early 1970s, was currently president and chief operating officer of the corporation.

Aerospace and Defense Group

Although Bombardier was a relatively new entrant into the aerospace industry, its string of acquisitions quickly elevated it to the status of seventh largest manufacturer of civil aircraft in the world. Furthermore, its extensive range of turboprops and jets made the company one of the most diversified aerospace manufacturers in the world (see Exhibit 8). Over the last three years, revenues from Bombardier's aerospace and defense segment accounted for just over 60 percent of the company's total sales. Aerospace and defense products were also the only significant contributors to the firm's overall pretax profits.

Bombardier's financial performance in the aerospace sector had been achieved in the face of growing difficulties in securing sufficient orders for its products. The shortage of orders was particularly evident in the market for commuter aircraft where the company's Canadair division had recently launched the newly developed Challenger regional jet, the first commercial jet liner on the market with fewer than 70 seats. When the $275 million project was launched with great fanfare in early 1989, it had more than 100 tentative orders. Despite a worldwide marketing offensive, only 36 of these had been converted into firm orders. The company had not received any new orders for well over a year. Regional airlines had been noticeably slow to sign up for a unique jetliner in spite of the fact that it was designed especially with this market in mind.

There was a similar shortage of orders for the lower priced propeller-driven Dash 8 lines of commuter aircraft offered by the newly acquired de Havilland subsidiary. The company was considering shutting down most of its operations for two months in the upcoming summer, temporarily laying off 2,000 of its 2,800 employees. The potential closure stemmed from the cancellation of an order for 22 of the Dash 8 turboprops by an Irish aircraft leasing firm that was experiencing financial difficulties.

EXHIBIT 8   Bombardier's Aerospace Products

Large Business Aircraft

Canadair Challenger

Major competitors: Gulfstream models and Dassault's Falcon business jet line

Small Business Aircraft

Learjet 31 and 35A
Learjet 60

Major competitors: Cessna's Citation line, British Aerospace models, and Beech's BeechJet

Commuter Aircraft

Canadair Regional Jet RJ-100
de Havilland Dash 8 100 and 300

Major competitors: British Aerospace Jetstream lines, Saab, and Fokker's regional aircraft lines

Amphibious Aircraft

Canadair CL-215 and CL-415

Military Aircraft

Short's Sherpa
Short's Tucano

Source: Business and Commercial Aviation 1992 Handbook.

Beaudoin attributed the problems with orders to excess capacity, fare wars, and record losses in the commercial airline industry. He was confident that the sales of commuter jets would pick up as industry conditions improved. A Stanford University study commissioned by Bombardier forecast that there would be demand for 7,000 aircraft in the 20- to 90-seat category between 1994 and 2010, propelled by the growth of smaller, regional airlines, particularly in the United States and Europe. Bombardier management saw only a few aircraft on the horizon that could provide strong competition for its products. Saab of Sweden was planning to introduce a 50-seat turboprop in 1994, and Fokker's new 70-seat jet was expected to be ready for introduction in 1995.

Most of Bombardier's remaining sales in aerospace came from the company's business jets. Canadair's Challenger business jet had managed to gain about 25 to 30 percent of the market for large business jets in spite of strong competition from Gulfstream and Dassault. Canadair had just introduced a longer range version of the Challenger and was hoping to build sales in international markets with a Global Express high-speed business jet that would cover the distance between New York and Tokyo without refueling. This luxury jet would contain a fully equipped office, main cabin, bedroom, and a bathroom with a shower. However, both Gulfstream and Dassault had also begun to develop competing models that were likely to be introduced at around the same time.

With the acquisition of Learjet, Bombardier added small business jets to its product line. The Learjet 31A and 35A models could seat up to 10 people and had a range of just under 1,500 nautical miles. The newly developed model 60 extended that range to almost 3,000 nautical miles, making it comparable in range to the larger Challenger business jets. Nevertheless, Learjet had relatively few orders in a market that was heavily dominated by Textron's Cessna division. With seven different models avail-

EXHIBIT 9   Bombardier's Mass Transit Products

Heavy Rail	**Technology Source**
Rubber-tired subway cars	License from CIMT France
	Acquired through BN and ANF
Steel-wheeled subway cars	License from Kawasaki
Conventional Rail	
Commuter and rail cars	Acquired through Pullman
	Acquired through BN and ANF
Shuttle-train cars	Acquired through BN and ANF
LRC railcars	Developed with Alcan and Dofasco
TGV railcars	License from GEC-Alsthom
Light Rail	
Light rail vehicles	Acquired through BN and UTDC
Streetcars	Acquired through Rotax
Monorail	License from Disney
PeopleMover	License from Disney

Source: Financial Post Corporation Service.

able, Cessna had captured almost 60 percent of the market for small business jets. In order to improve its market position, Learjet had recently announced the development of a new Learjet 45 based on a completely new design offering more cabin space, greater range, and better fuel efficiency at a more competitive price.

Bombardier had tried to use the excess capacity in its aerospace divisions to build components for the larger aircraft manufacturers. However, declining orders for larger aircraft were likely to reduce the work that Short Brothers and Canadair did on components for such companies as Boeing, Airbus, and Fokker. As a result, Bombardier had sought to spread the risk faced by its subsidiaries by reducing each division's reliance on a single product line. Instead of making only the Dash 8, for instance, de Havilland was also doing engine modifications on Canadair-built CL-215T waterbombers, designing the wings for the new Learjet 45, and painting the Challenger regional jet.

Transportation Equipment Group

Bombardier's transportation products included a wide variety of heavy, conventional, and light-rail vehicles. The expansion into different transportation products was achieved through a combination of licensing agreements and related acquisitions (see Exhibit 9). As a result of this product expansion, Bombardier ranked among the top 10 producers of mass transit equipment in the world. During the last three years, revenues from this segment accounted for about 25 percent of the company's total sales. But the sector had shown low levels of profits in recent years, culminating in a loss of $72.6 million before taxes during the last year.

Bombardier's recent acquisitions in Belgium, France, and England had also given the company greater access to the larger European market for mass transit equipment. Its presence in several European countries allowed it to neutralize pressure on governments to award mass transit jobs to local companies. Bombardier had won several large contracts from the Belgian and French railways, but it had only a 7 percent share of the orders for mass transit equipment in Europe. In part, this was the result of stiff competition the company faced from several large multinationals such as Asea Brown Boveri, GEC-Alsthom, AEG-Westinghouse, and Siemens.

Bombardier's European operations had been plagued by chronic cost overruns on several of the contracts that its various divisions had succeeded in winning. The biggest such problem occurred with the $700 million contract by the company's Belgian BN Construction subsidiary to provide 250 high-speed shuttle train cars to the consortium building the English Channel tunnel. Bombardier had filed a lawsuit claiming that repeated changes in design specifications for the rail cars resulted in $450 million of additional costs.

The company's purchase of Concarril from the Mexican government in 1992 was turning out to be a disappointment. Concarril had recently lost on two important subway contracts that it had bid for and was still waiting to hear about the outcome on a third bid. Beaudoin argued that since the acquisition of the Mexican unit was relatively inexpensive, it could afford to be patient in realizing a return on the investment Bombardier had made. He claimed that Concarril gave Bombardier a presence in each of the countries covered by the North American free-trade agreement and a gateway to South America.

In general, Bombardier had fared much better in the North American market north of Mexico. The company believed it had a 30 percent share of the mass transit orders in the U.S. and Canada. It had just delivered the first set of technologically advanced subway cars to the New York City Transit Authority and was presently also working on orders for subway cars for the transit authorities in such other cities as Toronto and Boston. Through its newly acquired UTDC subsidiary based in Toronto, Bombardier had also obtained an order for 108 subway cars for Ankara as part of a fully automated subway project for the Turkish capital.

Beaudoin estimated that North American demand for new subway and rail cars would surpass 4,000 during the next five years, and hundreds more would need to be refurbished. Bombardier's major competition in North America came chiefly from Morris Knudsen and Asea Brown Boveri. However, the company expected to face stiffer competition in the future as leading U.S. defense contractors entered this business as part of their transition to civilian production. Recently, Bombardier had to bid against such new defense-oriented entrants as Lockheed Corporation, Hughes Aircraft, and Rockwell International to obtain a contract supplying mass transportation vehicles for Los Angeles.

Finally, Bombardier was aggressively searching for clients since its acquisition of the exclusive North American rights for France's TGV trains from GEC-Alsthom. It had spent millions trying to persuade governments on both sides of the Canada–U.S. border of the merits of electrified fast trains, but so far it had little to show for this investment. A proposed TGV link joining Dallas and Houston was in limbo, and hopes for an estimated $7 billion TGV line connecting Montreal and Toronto had been dashed by cash-short governments.

Motorized Consumer Products Group

The original lines of snowmobiles and a revived Sea-Doo represented the bulk of the sales of motorized consumer products currently offered by Bombardier. Although the company was still one of the largest manufacturers of snowmobiles in 1993, revenues from this segment accounted for only 13 percent of the company's total sales during the 1990s. Furthermore, consumer products had just rebounded with a pretax profit of $29 million in the last year, after two successive years of losses.

During the 1980s, Bombardier lost the leadership in the snowmobile market that it had originally pioneered. Its market share declined as other competitors continued to develop stronger technological and manufacturing advantages. In the early 1990s, the company moved aggressively to update its product lines, increase its product quality, and reduce its production costs. By 1993, the company had regained some of its lost market share, attaining almost 25 percent of North American sales. But Bombardier was still in second position, just behind U.S.-based Polaris Industries and just ahead of Japanese-based Yamaha.

Bombardier had increased its product line to 20 models of snowmobiles that were geared toward six different types of users. These included family models developed for greater comfort and safety, as well as sporty models designed for higher speed and better performance. It revamped its distribution system to introduce new models earlier in the year and began producing on order rather than for inventories.

In 1992, Bombardier acquired full ownership of Scanhold Oy, producer of the Lynx line of snowmobiles and utility vehicles. While Scanhold already dominated the snowmobile market in the Scandinavian countries, the proximity of its plant to the potentially massive Russian market was promising. Bombardier had hired Soviet hockey legend Vlasislav Tretiak to help promote its machines, after its Ski-Doo and Lynx snowmobiles had finished one-two in an international snowmobile race in Moscow in 1992.

Apart from snowmobiles, the company had experienced considerable success with a revival of its Sea-Doo watercraft. Its launch in 1987 was a result of three years of research and development, including the development of a new Rotax engine. In spite of growing competition, the Sea-Doo had been well received and its market share had grown to almost 37 percent of the sit-down segment of the North American light watercraft market. During 1992, Bombardier added other models, including a three-passenger GTX model and a jet-powered Explorer runabout. Growth prospects for the Sea-Doo looked promising because of increasing popularity of personal watercraft usage.

With the exception of the Rotax engines, most of the company's consumer products were manufactured in a shared production facility in Valcourt where the company was first started. Its assembly line was capable of producing several hundred snowmobiles and watercraft daily. Part of the facilities had been expanded or adapted for the manufacturing of industrial and logistic equipment, with rates of production that could vary from three to six units per day.

LOOKING TOWARD THE FUTURE

> I don't mean to downplay my own contribution but I have always followed the conservative management principle that was behind Joseph-Armand Bombardier's success: Stick to what you know.[16]

Beaudoin had always argued that the change in Bombardier during the 1970s and 1980s was more than merely a shift in the company's products and markets. For him, the expansion in the company's scope was motivated by the need to spread risk. By

---

[16]"Trains, Planes and Snowmobiles."

1993, Bombardier's sales had reached $4.4 billion, up from $1.4 billion of only four years earlier. Its profits had risen to $132.8 million from $68.3 million during the same time period. Furthermore, the company had a backlog of orders worth just over $8 billion. The backlog, which was spread over aerospace and transportation equipment, was at the highest level ever recorded.

In spite of this promising performance, Bombardier chairman Laurent Beaudoin had to reassure stockholders during the company's annual meeting in June 1993. Bombardier's stock had wobbled in recent months, falling under $11.75, well below its 1992 peak of $17.25. The company had also been forced to cancel plans to raise $150 million through the issue of a new class of shares. The souring of the company's stock price and prospective stock offering was attributed to the up-and-down performance of Bombardier's nonaerospace businesses and to the uncertain outlook for sales of its aerospace products.

During his speech to shareholders, Beaudoin stressed that while individual sectors within Bombardier had had good and bad years, the sectors that performed well more than compensated for those that did not. He pointed to the rebound in the consumer products sectors, which had posted profits after the success of the new Ski-Doo and the Sea-Doo models. He also predicted that the transportation sector would reverse its losses in 1994 once the contract dispute over the English Channel project was resolved.

Looking farther ahead, Beaudoin confidently predicted that his transportation giant would double its revenue over the next five years. In addition, he vowed that the growth would come from the businesses that the company presently owned and not though acquisitions of new ones. According to Beaudoin, the company already sold its products in 50 countries around the world and expected to gradually tap into emerging markets in South America, Asia, central and eastern Europe, and the countries of the former Soviet Union.

But analysts who had tracked Bombardier's performance over the years noted the company had largely grown through acquiring companies, often at bargain-basement prices and usually with generous government help. This had led to some serious concerns about the distorting effects that subsidies had on the company's profitability, particularly in the extremely important aerospace sector. Many of these subsidies were expected to run out in 1994.

The company thus faced the challenging task of consolidating its recent string of acquisitions while at the same time generating enough cash to finance the next round of product development. Beaudoin downplayed the problems that some analysts attributed to the diversity and range of businesses in the company's portfolio of investments, commenting:

> What does Bombardier do, essentially? It assembles metal parts. It welds. It uses professionals and trades that revolve around this key activity. If you look at it from this angle, you can see that there isn't a big difference between a railcar and an aircraft fuselage. For a welder or a machinist, in fact, it's simply a question of millimeters or fractions of millimeters.[17]

(Bombardier's Web site address is *www.bombardier.com*)

---

[17]Ibid.

GREENLEY COMMUNICATIONS AND THE WESTERN REGION NETWORK TELEVISION STATIONS*

George M. Puia, *Indiana State University*

Marilyn L. Taylor, *University of Missouri–Kansas City*

Greenley Communications had never before considered selling one of its television properties. However, James Poinset, vice president of the Television Group, needed to make a recommendation to the board concerning the Montana properties comprising Western Region Network Television (WRNT). WRNT consisted of KWRN in Billings and KWGF in Great Falls, and their satellite stations. (Satellite stations rebroadcast the signal from the parent station, but provided little or no local programming.) Of special concern was Great Falls's KWGF and its two low-power satellites, one serving Missoula and the other serving Butte and Helena. Three and a half years earlier, in July 1990, Greenley had acquired these three stations at a fire-sale price. Local television stations had always been profitable ventures for the communications firm. Given the low acquisition cost for Great Falls, the set of three stations should have become profitable within their first two years. They had not, and now, in January 1994, a decision needed to be made. Should Greenley Communications cut its losses and sell the broadcast properties or try to turn the unit around?

*Management cooperated in the field research for this case, which was written solely for the purpose of stimulating student discussion. All events and individuals are real, but the names of individuals and the company's location have been disguised at the organization's request.

Poinset had tried several operational changes in Great Falls to reduce costs and increase revenues. The changes had been moderately successful, but KWGF in Great Falls was not measuring up to the performance of Greenley's other properties. Poinset considered the implications of a possible divestiture. He knew that decisions of this magnitude were difficult to reverse. What would it cost to keep the unit and try to make it profitable? If Greenley decided to sell the Great Falls station, who would be the likely buyers? What should corporate do with the unit until it sold? Poinset knew the decisions would not be easy.

GREENLEY COMMUNICATIONS

In 1994, Greenley Communications was a closely held diversified communications company. The company operated in 15 states, mostly in the Midwest, in the following major business segments:

- *Newspapers.* Publication of daily newspapers and shoppers in 12 states. The major sources of revenue were advertising, circulation, and job printing.
- *Broadcasting.* Operation of television, AM and FM radio stations, and networks in six states. The major source of revenue was advertising.
- *National Media.* Publication of two nationally distributed publications, commercial printing operations, tours, an insurance agency, and book clubs. The major sources of revenues were advertising and circulation, commercial printing, and insurance commissions. Operations located near corporate headquarters.
- *Other.* Operation of retail computer stores; development and sales of computer software; installation and monitoring of alarm systems; sales of small business telephone systems. Locations in three states.

Channels magazine listed Greenley as the U.S. television industry's 86th largest revenue producer. Given the regulations prohibiting a company from owning more than seven radio stations and seven full-power TV stations having a signal radius of more than 60 miles, Greenley considered its national ranking a major accomplishment, especially since the company did not operate in the largest media markets.

Stanton G. Greenley founded the firm in 1919 when he purchased his first newspaper—a small weekly in Joplin, Missouri. He continued to acquire newspapers, adding his first daily paper in 1928. In 1934, Greenley combined the six daily newspapers under his control to form Greenley Publications. In 1981, the firm changed its name to Greenley Communications Inc. to better reflect its broader business interests. By 1994 these activities included 21 daily newspapers; five radio stations; nine television stations; a national weekly magazine; a regional biweekly magazine; a semiweekly newspaper; seven free metropolitan newspapers; a computer software company; two computer retail stores; sports, agricultural, and information radio networks; and a security and telephone systems company. (Exhibits 1 and 2 show financial results for 1992 and 1993.)

Stanton's two sons, Thomas and Louis, had been active in the business from an early age. At the time of Stanton's death in 1986, both his sons were in executive positions. In 1990, Thomas, the older of the two brothers, assumed the role of chairman of the board while Louis took responsibility for operations as president and chief executive officer. Although Louis was intimately familiar with all of Greenley Communications operations, most of his career experience had been in print media.

EXHIBIT 1 Greenley Communications, Selected Financial Data, 1992 and 1993 (dollar amounts in thousands)

	1993	% of Revenues	1992	% of Revenues
Operating revenues:				
Newspaper division	$79,699	60.2%	$74,127	54.4%
Broadcast division*	26,572	20.0	26,872	19.7
National Media division	30,165	22.7	37,859	27.8
Other	3,738	2.8	4,727	3.5
Greenley corporate	34	0.02	4	0.0
Subtotal	$140,208	105.72%	$143,589	105.4%
Less: Intercompany sales and minority interests	7,595	5.7	7,392	5.4
Total	$132,613	100.0%	$136,197	100.0%
Operating profit:		**Margins**		**Margins**
Newspaper division	$14,377	18.0%	$12,742	17.2%
Broadcast division	4,168	15.7%	4,543	16.9%
National Media division	2,487	8.2%	2,722	7.2%
Other	155	4.3%	280	
Greenley corporate	(3,095)	n.a.	(3,538)	
Total	$18,092	12.9%	$16,749	12.3%
Pretax profit:		**Margins**		**Margins**
Newspaper division	$11,788	14.8%	$10,204	13.8%
Broadcast division	1,774	6.7%	2,224	8.3%
National Media division	1,581	5.2%	1,714	4.5%
Other	103	2.8%	218	
Greenley corporate	(6,571)		(7,063)	
Total	$8,675	6.5%	$7,297	5.4%
Identifiable assets:		**Pretax ROA**		**Pretax ROA**
Newspaper division	$60,591	19.4%	$61,584	16.6%
Broadcast division	34,932	5.1%	35,245	6.3%
National Media division	12,484	12.7%	13,243	12.9%
Other	1,407	7.3%	1,633	13.3%
Greenley corporate	6,875	n.a.	3,485	n.a.
Total	$116,289	7.5%	$115,190	6.3%

*Includes WRNT.

Greenley Communications took its mission of providing quality journalism to local communities quite seriously. Indeed, the firm had a long heritage of social responsibility and community involvement. A quote from the founder in a recent company annual report epitomized this sense of personal and firm responsibility:

All of our publications and stations are dedicated to serving the communities in which we are located.

EXHIBIT 2 Greenley Communications, Abbreviated Consolidated Balance Sheet, Years ended December 31, 1992 and 1993, (thousands of dollars)

	1993	1992
Assets		
Current assets	$ 26,682	$ 26,277
Plant and equipment	86,184	81,899
Less: Accumulated depreciation	42,845	39,605
Net plant and equipment	43,338	42,294
Other assets	46,269	46,619
Total assets	$116,289	$115,190
Current Liabilities and Owners' Equity		
Current liabilities	$ 22,862	$ 22,948
Deferred credits and long-term liabilities	11,714	10,734
Long-term debt	13,530	16,072
Minority interest in subsidiaries	25	22
Shareholders' investment		
Paid-in capital	$ 1,833	$ 1,833
Retained earnings	66,325	63,579
Total	$ 68,158	$ 65,412
Total liabilities and shareholders' investment	$116,289	$115,190

The annual report described Greenley Communications as a growing media company. Although pleased with the company's track record, the board was concerned that the company's growth had come largely through acquisitions. Further, most of Greenley's broadcast properties were in communities where little population growth was expected. The board credited much of the company's success to the decentralized management approach that allowed subsidiaries to have control over their news, editorials, and day-to-day operating decisions.

The vice president for broadcast operations was James Poinset. A 20-year veteran of Greenley with all of his experience in broadcasting, Poinset made nearly all of the operating decisions for the Broadcast Division. However, some of the strategic decisions were reserved for Greenley's corporate officers. The corporate officers also established the criteria for evaluation of divisional performance and for capital expenditures. Acquisition decisions were made at the corporate level.

THE MONTANA ACQUISITION

In 1989 Poinset had considered but rejected acquisition of television station KWRN, in Billings, Montana. KWRN, a CBS affiliate, had operated for 30 years as the sole local television station in Billings. Currently, its only competition was KBTV, an independent which began operations in late 1989. (Exhibit 3 shows comparative data for the competing stations in Great Falls and Billings. Figure 1 is a map of the area.) The station had been managed for several years in absentia for a private investor who

EXHIBIT 3 Selected Comparisons of the Three Competing Television Stations in Great Falls and Billings, Montana

	Daily Average No. of Viewers	Rate Card for 60-s Spots*	Date of First Broadcast
Great Falls			
KWGF (Greenley)	23,300	$320	8/12/1985
KRGP (ABC)	15,200	125	10/31/1988
KMMW (NBC)	54,600	325	3/1/1961
Billings			
KWRN (CBS) (Greenley)	35,500	$475	3/22/1958
KBTV	n.a.	200	12/1/1989
KWON	Not on the air		

*Actual rates charged vary according to number of spots purchased, time of day, and target demographics.

Source: *Broadcasting/Cablecasting Yearbook,* 1992.

lived in a distant state and knew little about television. During this period, the station had fallen on hard times. In 1988, the Billings properties had generated $1.1 million operating income on revenues of $3.8 million.

At nearly the same time as the initial Billings proposal, an old acquaintance and station broker offered Poinset the opportunity to buy KWGF in Great Falls, Montana, along with its two satellite stations. The satellite operations were low-power stations, a special category of FCC restricted licenses with a smaller viewing area. Low-power stations had no legal requirement to produce local programming. Great Falls was a much smaller and less lucrative market than Billings. Poinset promptly turned down Great Falls as overpriced.

About a month later, another broker contacted Tom Greenley, the president's brother. Tom, who had worked successfully with this broker in the past, became excited about the property in Great Falls and contacted Poinset. Poinset wasn't enthusiastic about Great Falls or the creation of a Montana network ultimately to be called Western Region Network. However, Poinset was, as he put it, "gently over-ruled." Poinset did agree with one part of Tom's logic. He would not have purchased Great Falls on its own merits, but with the simultaneous acquisition of Billings, Poinset felt he could make Great Falls a viable operation.

As Poinset went over the data on the stations Tom was interested in, he noticed that KWRN in Billings and KWGF in Great Falls had similar histories. Both stations had been owned by investment bankers who had, Poinset put it, "severely molested" the stations to reduce operating costs and make them more profitable in the short run. The Greenley management team investigating the properties noticed a neglect of basic repairs and housekeeping along with more serious problems in programming and production practices. James Poinset felt that with Greenley's experience in broadcasting, the company could program both stations to be more appealing to the local viewer. In prior broadcast acquisitions, Greenley had operated the stations that it purchased for the long term.

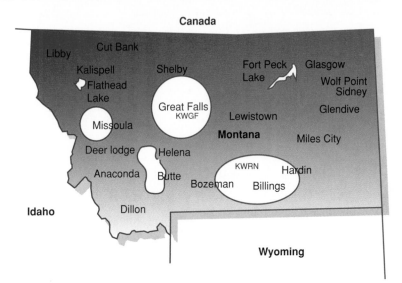

FIGURE 1   Operating Area for Western Region Network Television Stations

The purchase of KWGF in Great Falls was to include two satellite stations, one serving Butte and Helena, the other in Missoula. The acquisition of both Billings and Great Falls with their satellites would clearly give Greenley the dominant media position in Montana. Greenley would have a television signal in virtually every major population center of Montana. Cable television was available in all the communities served by WRNT. However, cablecasters did not usually provide coverage of local news and community events and therefore exercised little local community influence.

Montana had experienced a boom in the early 1980s after years of little or no growth. Rising crude oil prices in the 1970s had caused the United States to take a hard look at its dependence on foreign oil. When oil was $3 a barrel, oil fields like those in Montana were not financially attractive to develop. When oil prices soared to over $30 a barrel, eastern Montana, endowed with oil and natural gas, experienced a boom. Although this was not the first oil boom in Montana history—early settlers to the state had even named one oil-rich county between Billings and Great Falls "Petroleum County"—it was a welcome development. The Northwest was also becoming an increasingly popular tourist attraction, and Montana was striving to win its fair share of tourist dollars. In the 1980s, Montana's population grew from 330,000 to over 470,000, a 41 percent increase.

Great Falls was a small market, but the city's growth potential and statewide influence allowed it to support three broadcast stations, one for each of the competing national networks. The 1990 census put Great Falls's population at 51,000 and Billings's at 47,000. Great Falls residents had more purchasing power, with per capita incomes 25 percent greater than per capita incomes in Billings. In the late 1980s, the economy was expanding very rapidly and generating many opportunities.

COMBINING OPERATIONS

In 1990, Poinset recommended that Greenley Communications's board of directors acquire the Great Falls property KWGF. In his report to the board, Poinset noted it was unlikely that Great Falls would be able to stand alone as a successful station, but it could become profitable if combined into a network with the Billings station. The combined network could achieve economies of scale sufficient to generate the necessary level of return. Poinset based his recommendations on several assumptions:

1. Great Falls could take its news feed from Billings, greatly reducing its news production costs. (News is the most expensive programming for a local television station.)

2. The local economy would expand due to booming oil and natural gas exploration.

3. Both stations were affiliated with the same network, and though the network would not formally commit in advance to any new agreements, it hinted that additional network revenues were available for serving the two markets.

4. There was strong potential for increased advertising sales by "selling Montana as a package," according to Poinset's contacts at the two national agencies active in the area. Both agencies estimated (but did not commit to) a 25 percent increase in national advertising revenues. Poinset had never run a regional network within Greenley Communications. In the past, all stations reported directly to the corporate offices, which were located in a moderate-size city in mid-Missouri. Further, he had never seen an effective centralized sales operation for different local TV markets of the same firm.

5. Both stations had been mismanaged by their investment banker owners. As a result, the final negotiated price was only 60 percent of the asking price. Further, a significant portion of acquisition price was to be paid as a noncompete clause, a device which would improve the tax position of Greenley Communications.

Based on Poinset's recommendations and the usual financial and asset-inventory data, the board approved the Great Falls acquisition in July 1990, only a month after Billings was acquired. The Board left Poinset and his management team to merge Billings, Great Falls, and the satellite operations into an effective regional television network, Western Region Network Television (WRNT). The purchase price for the Great Falls properties was $2.5 million plus an additional $1 million in a noncompete agreement with the seller. Greenley Communications was to pay for the noncompete agreement in installments of $200,000 a year for five years. In his report to the Board, Poinset indicated that the Great Falls property ought to be worth $4.5 to $5.0 million "in the near future."

After the acquisition, Greenley's know-how in TV broadcasting and the company's commitment to quality local television was transferred to the new operations in Montana. Poinset and his staff quickly improved both the appearance of the on-air presentation and the station's market share. The network, however, did not generate a profit in its first year.

INDUSTRY DATA

Local network affiliate television stations had three major sources of revenue:

- A proportionate share of network advertising dollars.
- National advertising sales (often sold by national sales representative firms).
- Local sales of advertising.

A media buyer typically made the decision to purchase advertising on the basis of cost per thousand persons reached. The larger the audience ratings at the time a commercial aired, the greater the revenue. Potential audience size also influenced rates. The potential audiences were ranked in consecutive order from greatest to least. The areas involved were not defined by city boundaries, but by the transmission range of the local broadcaster. These geographic areas were called *areas of dominant influence,* or ADIs. At the time of the acquisition, Billings was the 188th ADI. National advertisers, through their agents, showed little interest in the Great Falls market. Exhibits 4 and 5 present the income statements and balance sheets for KWGF, in Great Falls. Exhibit 6 gives the pro forma income projections for fiscal years 1990 and 1991, as developed at the time of purchase for the Great Falls and Billings stations. Exhibits 7 and 8 provide selected industry data. Exhibit 9 gives the combined results of the three competing stations in Great Falls.

EARLY MOVES

Initially, Greenley attempted to operate Great Falls with a general manager in Great Falls. This organizational arrangement fit very well with the corporate philosophy of decentralization and with the objective of understanding and meeting local market media needs. However, within the short span of 6 months, it became apparent that the Great Falls operation was not going to meet its revenue projections in the near future.

Following the acquisition, Poinset pulled together some of his team to plan the Great Falls operations. Normally, Greenley Communications did not retain any of the management team of the businesses it acquired but replaced them with managers of its own choosing. One of Greenley's veteran station managers was designated to move from another of the company's stations to head Great Western's operations from the Billings divisional office.

However, just before the manager was to move to Billings, he decided to leave Greenley Communications. There was no designated backup for the manager, so Poinset opted to employ an outsider, a local man named Robert Grotino. This was an unusual move for Greenley, but Grotino seemed to present an unusual opportunity. Although Poinset had only known Grotino personally a short time (Grotino was a consultant on the Great Falls project), he knew a lot about the man's background. Grotino had been the manager at Billings before the investment bankers took it over. He was very well connected and well liked in Montana. As Poinset put it "Robert Grotino . . . knew everyone (from) the janitor to the governor. And he was a good manager." Grotino also knew television. At one time, he had even served on the affiliates' national advisory board to the CBS network. On his first day back as WRNT manager, Grotino received seven bouquets of roses and five magnums of champagne from local customers and civic leaders.

THE PLAN FOR WRNT

As WRNT general manager, Grotino was asked to develop a comprehensive plan for the Montana properties, one that focused on reducing operating expenses and increasing revenues. After months of work, Grotino came back with a proposal.

First, Great Falls could save production costs by relying heavily on news from Billings. Billings was a larger, more dynamic city, and Grotino expected the news would be of interest statewide. Second, the Billings office would provide central

EXHIBIT 4   Consolidated Statements of Operations for KWGF in Great Falls, Montana, 1988–1993*

	7 Months thru July 1993		12 Months Ended Dec. 1992†		12 Months Ended Dec. 1991†		12 Months Ended March 1989		12 Months Ended March 1988	
	$	%	$	%	$	%	$	%	$	%
Sales revenues										
Local	$ 424,699	50.4	$ 477,068	42.0	$ 503,110	40.8	$ 651,159	43.6	$ 612,356	41.7
National	215,229	25.5	321,297	28.3	408,093	33.0	460,324	30.8	499,685	34.0
Regional	7,207	.9	62,349	5.5	70,648	5.7	123,312	8.2	122,159	8.3
Political sales	40,475	4.8	38,538	3.4	-0-	-0-	-0-	-0-	-0-	-0-
Total sales revenue	687,610	81.6	899,252	79.1	981,851	79.5	1,234,795	82.6	1,234,200	84.0
Other revenues:										
Network	136,508	16.3	225,071	19.8	241,029	19.5	191,669	12.8	162,711	11.0
Production	6,751	0.8	2,449	0.2	7,737	0.6	41,677	2.8	33,404	2.3
Studio rental	n.a.	-0-	n.a.		n.a.		5,288	0.4	14,272	1.0
Barter revenue net of expense	-0-	-0-	-0-	-0-	-0-	-0-	(18,413)	1.2	9,697	.7
All other	12,204	1.4	9,829	.9	4,687	.4	39,684	2.6	14,383	1.0
Total other revenue	155,463	18.4	237,349	20.9	253,453	20.5	259,905	17.4	234,467	16.0
Total revenue	$ 843,073	100.0	$ 1,136,601	100.0	$ 1,235,304	100.0	$ 1,494,700	100.0	$ 1,468,667	100.0
Operating expenses:										
Agency/representation commission	$ 50,939	6.1	70,121	6.2	75,383	6.1	173,311	11.6	170,374	11.6
Technical	153,950	18.3	273,911	24.1	247,913	20.1	332,881	22.3	199,503	13.6
Program	189,530	22.5	305,859	26.9	306,030	24.8	50,582	3.4	36,296	2.5
Production	-0-	-0-	-0-	-0-	-0-	-0-	60,725	4.1	54,363	3.7
Operations	-0-	-0-	-0-	-0-	-0-	-0-	39,653	2.7	98,315	6.7
Promotions	-0-	-0-	-0-	-0-	-0-	-0-	24,550	1.6	36,715	2.5
News	96,352	11.4	122,984	10.8	177,320	14.3	257,699	17.2	256,151	17.4
Sales	123,159	14.6	186,455	16.4	188,286	15.2	223,006	14.9	233,490	15.9
General and administrative	188,422	22.3	264,476	23.3	308,924	25.0	523,950	35.0	386,215	26.3
Total operating expenses	802,352	95.2	1,223,806	107.7	1,303,856	105.5	1,686,357	112.8	1,471,422	100.2

EXHIBIT 4 (Concluded)

	7 Months thru July 1993		12 Months Ended Dec. 1992†		12 Months Ended Dec. 1991†		12 Months Ended March 1989		12 Months Ended March 1988	
	$	%	$	%	$	%	$	%	$	%
Operating profit (loss)	40,721	4.8	(87,205)	7.8	(68,552)	5.5	(191,657)	(12.8)	(2,755)	(.2)
Miscellaneous nonoperating income	235	-0-	5,376	.5	(2,663)	2	-0-	-0-	-0-	-0-
Other expenses:										
Depreciation and amortization	243,383	32.4	362,826	31.9	349,552	28.3	469,692	31.4	347,186	23.6
Rent	93,476	11.11	28,832	11.3	123,096	10.0	-0-	-0-	607,078	41.3
Interest	n.a.	n.a.	n.a.	n.a.	n.a.	n.a.	494,150	33.1	132,411	9.0
Corporate expenses	n.a.	n.a.	n.a.	n.a.	n.a.	n.a.	32,466	2.2	42,322	2.9
Miscellaneous	8,000	.9	6,646	.6	-0-	-0-	-0-	-0-		
Total	344,859	40.9	498,304	43.8	472,648	38.5	996,308	64.6	1,128,997	87.8
Net (Loss) before the cumulative effect of a change in accounting principle	(303,900)	36.0	-0-	-0-	-0-	-0-	(1,187,965)	(79.5)	(1,132,353)	77.1
Cumulative effect on years prior to March 31, 1987 of changing to a different depreciation method	-0-	-0-	-0-	-0-	-0-	-0-	-0-	-0-	116,936	8.0
Net (Loss)	$ (303,900)	(36.0)	$ (580,137)	(51.0)	$ (543,863)	(44.0)	$ (1,187,965)	(79.5)	$ (1,015,417)	(69.1)

*1990 data not available.

†1991 and 1992 include expenses of $200,000 for amortization of noncompete clause; 1993 included $119,000 for noncompete expense amortization.

EXHIBIT 5　Consolidated Balance Sheets for KWGF, Inc. in Great Falls, Montana, Years Ended March 31, 1993, 1992, 1989, and 1988*

	1993	% of Assets	1992	% of Assets	1989	% of Assets	1988	% of Assets
Assets								
Current assets	$ 303,905	11.0	$ 337,839	11.6	$ 516,731	15.4	$ 416,679	13.4
Deferred charges and other assets	141,835	5.2	79,198	2.7	467,964	14.0	356,253	11.5
Property and equipment (at cost, net of accumulated depreciation)	1,907,034	69.3	1,956,019	67.3	2,368,169	70.6	2,327,221	75.1
Covenant not to compete	400,002	14.5	533,335	18.4	-0-	-0-	-0-	-0-
Total assets	$2,752,778	100.0	$2,906,393	100.0	$ 3,352,864	100.0	$ 3,100,158	100.0
Liabilities and Stockholders' Deficit								
Current liabilities	$ 127,772	4.6	$ 120,501	4.1	$ 471,191	14.0	$ 1,011,276	32.6
Liabilities due after one year	24,568	.8	93,554	3.2	4,077,349	121.6	4,671,482	150.7
Total liabilities	152,340	5.4	214,055	7.4	4,548,540	135.7	5,682,758	181.7
Stockholders' deficit:								
Paid-in capital	n.a.	n.a.	n.a.	n.a.	3,294,889		720,000	
Accumulated deficit	n.a.	n.a.	n.a.	n.a.	(4,490,565)		(3,302,600)	
Total stockholders' deficit	2,600,438	95.0	2,692,338	93.0	(1,195,676)	35.7	(2,582,600)	76.9
Total liabilities and stockholders' deficit	$2,752,778	100.0	$2,906,393	100.0	$ 3,352,864	100.0	$ 3,100,156	100.0

*1990 and 1991 data not available.

Note: The sellers received payment for promising not to compete in the local television market for five years. The total amount due to the sellers for the noncompete agreement was a tax deductible expense that burdened the income statement of WRNT for its first five years of operation. However, payment for a noncompete contract was more tax-advantageous than payment for a like amount of goodwill.

EXHIBIT 6 WRNT Pro Forma Income Projections at Time of Purchase (Dollar Figures in Thousands)

	Actual Operating Results		Pro Forma Projections of Combined Results	
	Great Falls 12 Mo. Ended 3/31/90	Billings 12 Mo. Ended 12/31/89	WRNT 1990*	WRNT 1991†
Revenues				
National	$ 398	$ 1,390		
Local/regional	585	1,367		
Net	199	567		
Miscellaneous	36	132		
Trade	(75)	77		
	$ 1,293	$ 3,533	$4,826	$5,309
Expenses				
Agency	85	242		
News	225			
Sales	263	558		
Tech	238	268		
Programming	273			
G&A	410	670		
	$ 1,494	$ 2,395	$3,889	$3,695
Operating income	$ (201)	$ 1,138	$ 937	$1,614

*Assumes no changes from 1989 rates of activity.
†Assumes 10% revenue increase and 5% expense decrease.

services such as accounting, traffic (scheduling, logging, and invoicing of local commercial spot time), and news wire services. Billings could also handle some of the commercial (nonnews) production and all of the promotion expenses for Great Falls. The revenue plan involved selling advertising on all four stations, including the satellites, as a package. This package created a potential audience comparable to the 146th ADI. Better still, Grotino reported that the purchasing power of the enlarged Montana area would be comparable to the 100th ADI, not the 146th.

By the end of the planning process, Poinset was beginning to feel that WRNT had sufficient potential to attract major clients. As Poinset and Grotino discussed the plan further, it seemed apparent that Great Falls would not require a general manager. Instead, a department manager in Great Falls could serve as a supervisor and report to Grotino in Billings. Grotino could drive the 180 miles from Billings to Great Falls on a regular basis to check the operations.

Poinset approved the basic plan and began to implement it. The cost cuts (e.g., a reduction in the Great Falls payroll from over 20 to 13, with only one employee in Billings devoted to Great Falls activities) immediately improved Great Falls's

	Average Net Revenue	Total Expenses	Total Salaries	Nonsalary Expenses
EXHIBIT 7	Selected Industry Expense Factors for All Stations as a Percent of Net Revenues			
ADI Markets				
1– 10	$35,012,000	70.1%	19.7%	50.4%
11– 20	21,291,900	68.5	21.7	46.8
21– 30	17,238,600	69.2	23.4	45.8
31– 40	10,758,500	73.1	27.8	45.3
41– 50	9,643,400	71.4	25.8	45.6
51– 60	8,347,200	74.2	29.9	44.3
61– 75	6,214,600	81.9	32.3	49.6
76–100	4,935,400	74.1	27.5	46.6
101–125	3,806,500	85.9	33.1	52.8
126–150	3,049,100	82.9	34.1	48.8
151–175	2,398,200	83.9	37.1	46.8
176 and over	1,796,900	88.1	37.8	50.3
Revenue Size				
$50 million and over	$64,591,800	59.0%	13.4%	45.6%
$25–50 million	31,549,000	63.3	22.6	40.7
$20–25	21,604,600	64.0	20.6	43.4
$15–20	17,238,600	70.1	24.2	45.9
$10–15	12,298,600	70.7	25.1	45.6
$8–10	7,789,200	70.3	26.8	43.5
$6–8	6,681,900	76.4	28.4	48.0
$4–6	4,957,800	81.1	28.2	52.9
$2–4	3,049,100	85.9	31.5	54.4
Under $2 million	1,258,700	108.0	42.6	65.4

Source: National Association of Broadcasters.

bottom line. However, several of the key assumptions used to justify the decision did not pan out. First, it turned out there were no economies of scale in news gathering. Indeed, Great Falls citizens showed little interest in Billings news. As Poinset put it:

> The idea of broadcasting news from Billings, we should have known better. The distance was so far that the two cities could care less what happens to the other. It just did not work. So now we are looking at what we are going to do. News is the most expensive item, but it is where you make the most money.

Within just a few months Great Falls needed to increase its news expenses to maintain its competitiveness. News programming was of critical importance for most local TV operations as it was the only locally produced program. News, combined with the programming provided through its network affiliation, usually defined a local station's identity.

EXHIBIT 7   Selected Industry Expense Factors for Affiliate Stations Only as a Percent of Average Affiliate Station Revenues

	Average Net Revenue	Total Expenses	Total Salaries	Nonsalary Expenses
Nationwide	$ 5,760,300	75.8%	28.1%	47.7%
ADI Markets				
1– 10	$42,701,900	59.5%	20.4%	39.1%
11– 20	26,016,100	63.4	23.0	40.4
21– 30	18,123,800	63.2	24.0	39.2
31– 40	13,208,700	68.9	24.5	44.4
41– 50	10,284,400	70.7	26.0	44.7
51– 60	8,774,800	70.3	28.6	41.7
61– 75	6,665,300	79.9	33.1	46.8
76–100	4,957,800	73.7	27.9	45.8
101–125	3,909,700	84.5	32.4	52.1
126–150	3,082,900	80.7	32.4	48.3
151–175	2,398,200	83.9	37.1	46.8
176 and over	1,796,900	88.1	37.8	50.3
Revenue Size				
$40 million and over	$57,180,600	48.7%	15.0%	33.7%
$25–40 million	31,549,000	62.9	23.2	39.7
$15–25	19,245,600	62.8	24.2	38.6
$10–15	12,302,100	69.8	26.2	43.6
$7–10	8,527,400	70.3	27.6	42.7
$5–7	5,940,500	80.0	30.6	49.4
$4–5	4,598,300	74.6	28.7	45.9
$3–4	3,553,200	83.7	32.4	51.3
$2–3	2,499,100	85.1	33.7	51.4
Under $2 million	1,354,900	106.0	40.3	65.7
Regions				
New England	$11,588,400	67.8%	20.1%	47.7%
Middle Atlantic	8,469,700	82.3	29.2	53.1
South Atlantic	6,071,600	70.5	20.1	50.4
East North Central	4,938,300	78.6	25.2	53.4
East South Central	5,205,900	78.3	28.5	49.8
West North Central	3,590,400	86.5	33.6	52.9
West South Central	5,240,600	75.2	26.3	48.9
Mountain	4,695,300	82.5	27.1	55.4
Pacific	6,338,600	83.1	27.2	55.9

Source: National Association of Broadcasters.

EXHIBIT 8 Typical Revenues and Expenses by Type of Station, 1990

	Affiliate Stations		Satellite Stations		Secondary Stations	
Revenues	**Dollars**	**Percent**	**Dollars**	**Percent**	**Dollars**	**Percent**
Network compensation	$ 562,800	8.5%	$ 86,000	10.4%	$ 321,700	9.9%
National and regional advertisers	3,051,700	46.4	288,700	34.8	1,477,700	45.7
Local advertisers	2,968,500	45.1	455,400	54.9	1,434,400	44.4
Total time sales	6,583,000	100.0	830,100	100.0	3,233,800	100.0
Political advertising revenue	11,900		0		4,800	
Trade-outs and barter	122,200		2,600		61,000	
Revenues other than time sales	116,700		21,900		66,600	
Total net revenues	$5,760,300		$ 812,400		$2,865,000	
Expenses						
Engineering	466,200	10.7%	181,800	20.4%	278,900	11.5%
Program and production	1,000,700	22.9	147,800	16.6	515,900	21.2
News	678,000	15.5	109,500	12.3	318,700	13.1
Sales	565,900	13.0	131,500	14.8	365,200	15.0
Advertising and promotion	187,800	4.3	4,900	0.5	78,800	3.2
General and administrative	1,466,400	33.6	316,000	35.4	871,700	35.9
Total expenses	4,365,000	100.0	891,500	100.0	2,429,200	100.0
Pretax profit	$1,395,300		$ (79,100)		$ 435,800	
Profit margin		24.22%		(9.73%)		15.21%

Source: *Television Financial Report,* Washington, D.C.: National Association of Broadcasters.

Further, multistation management was not as effective as hoped. The driving time between stations was much longer under winter conditions, and reduced the amount of time Grotino actually worked with the Great Falls station manager. Poinset also found that managing properties in Montana was not like managing properties in midwestern or southern states. The Great Falls transmitter was located on a mountain nearly 6,000 feet above the city. To service the transmitters required, among other items, a fleet of snowmobiles! Worst of all, few advertising buyers were interested in "buying Montana" as a package. The buyers preferred purchasing Billings without Great Falls. Only political campaigns (which were required by law to pay the lowest advertising rates) and a few regional institutions were interested in advertising on the Billings–Great Falls network.

CHANGING MARKET CONDITIONS

Most seriously, Montana's economy began a severe downturn. By 1993, three years after the acquisition, the net purchasing power of the Great Falls area had declined by 40 percent. Most of the big oil companies had pulled out and had taken their executives with them. Other people had left Great Falls because there just were not sufficient opportunities to make a living. The population had actually decreased by over 18,000 people. The situation had deteriorated so badly that the ABC affiliate,

EXHIBIT 9   Consolidated Financial Information for Great Falls' Three Television Stations (KWGF, KRGP, and KMMW), 1989, 1991, and 1992*

	1992	1991	1989
Network compensation	$ 1,008,679	$ 867,846	$ 739,439
National/regional advertising	1,621,372	1,508,446	1,838,101
Local advertising	1,950,595	1,621,971	1,930,508
Total time sales	4,580,646	3,998,263	4,508,048
Net revenues	4,086,255	3,694,532	4,144,874
Total expenses	7,259,477	6,669,034	4,286,053
Pretax profit	(3,173,222)	(2,974,502)	(141,179)
Profit margin	−77.66%	−80.51%	−3.41%
Trade-outs and barter	35,197		169,761
Political advertising	221,985	-0-	-0-
Stations reporting	3	3	3

*1990 information unavailable because not all stations provided data.

Source: National Association of Broadcasters.

one of the three stations in the area, just shut down its station and let its signal go dark—a highly unusual occurrence in broadcasting.

Despite the moderate success of the Billings station, WRNT was unable to show a net profit. In 1991, the first full year of the Great Falls operation under Greenley ownership, KWGF showed an operating loss of $68,552 (see Exhibit 4 for details). In 1992, the operating loss increased to over $87,000. However, the cost cuts and revenue increases had begun to have some effect, and by May of 1992, Great Falls had produced an operating profit. The problem was that a modest operating profit was not attractive. The company needed to recover its initial investment and generate an additional $200,000 per year just to cover the noncompete portion of the purchase contract. The population of Great Falls had decreased, and so had KWGF's rate card (the price it charged for advertising). KWGF's actual rates were so low that even a dramatic increase in spot sales would not bring operations to a breakeven position. (See Exhibit 3 for comparative data on KWGF and the two other stations in Great Falls.)

WRNT—THE DILEMMA

Poinset was concerned. Relying on experience alone, he would probably admit defeat and cut his losses. But this case was different. The combined stations were generating an operating profit even though it was not sufficient to pay back Greenley's original investment on the anticipated timetable. The profits from KWRN even compared favorably to the profits of other stations its size, according to the NAB (National Association of Broadcasters) annual survey of station performance.

It was also difficult to estimate how much Great Falls's KWGF and its two satellites could bring if sold. To test the market, Poinset had taken a prospective buyer to view the property. The prospect offered $2 million for the Great Falls properties, substantially below the $3.5 million needed to cover the original investment and recent improvements to the equipment. Poinset wondered if he could find a buyer enamored with the idea of owning a television station or if someone else could come up with a better operating plan. Greenley Communications was not interested in selling the Billings station, and Poinset himself would not have been interested in purchasing Great Falls if the Billings station had not been available at the same time. Poinset had bought KWGF when the market was growing and the station had potential for increased operating profits, and he thought it not unlikely that the Great Falls economy would eventually recover. Indeed, an increase in fuel prices would assure its comeback. Yet predicting the state's future economic performance was hardly an exact science. The fact remained that if the Great Falls station was sold on the basis of its present potential, it would currently bring substantially less than Greenley had paid.

Poinset knew several brokers who would aggressively market the station on Greenley's behalf, but he doubted they would have much success in securing an offer near the price Greenley had paid. There were potential competitive and morale problems with a broker lising as well. Once the stations were officially listed with a broker, it would only be a matter of time before both competitors and existing employees heard the news. Damage control might be difficult. Poinset also faced a potential adverse reaction from corporate management at having to sell a broadcast property for the first time—a sale that would surely incur a loss. It was a difficult decision.

ESCORTS, LTD. (A)*

Andrew Delios, *The University of Western Ontario*

Jaideep Anand, *The University of Western Ontario*

In mid-1993, Mr. Rajan Nanda, the chairman and managing director of Escorts Ltd. (Escorts) in Faridabad, India, was reviewing the performance of the company. In the first two years following the introduction of India's economic liberalization program, Escorts' profits had declined while revenues were stagnant (see Exhibit 1). The chairman, concerned about Escorts' performance, had charged the newly created Corporate Strategic Planning Department with formulating a plan of response and charting a new strategic direction for the company.

Escorts, the 18th largest company in India (see Exhibit 2), was founded by H. P. Nanda on October 17, 1944. During its first five decades, the company grew steadily and was either the market leader or the second largest producer in its markets. Escorts was primarily a manufacturing company producing farm and construction equipment, motorcycles and autoparts, though it had recently entered the financial and telecommunication sectors. In 1993, The Escorts group of companies had revenues of Rs. 16.5 billion (US$ 513 million); Escorts Ltd.'s revenues were Rs. 9.82 billion.

COMPANY HISTORY

On October 17, 1944, Escorts Agents Ltd., founded by two brothers, Yudi and Hari Nanda, began operations as a private bus service in Lahore, India. In 1947, during the partition of India in which Lahore became a part of Pakistan, all the assets of the

EXHIBIT 1   Summary of Escorts Ltd.'s Operations, 1984–1993 (in millions of ruples)

	1984	1985	1986	1987	1988–89	1989–90	1990–91	1991–92	1992–93
Total income	3,280	3,780	3,850	4,820	7,830	7,700	9,760	10,930	9,820
Cost of sales	3,070	3,500	3,610	4,500	7,360	7,110	8,910	10,380	9,300
Interest	80	110	160	200	260	240	250	340	430
Profit before tax	130	180	90	130	210	350	530	210	90
Tax	50	10	10	0	30	120	200	80	0
Profit after tax	90	170	80	70	180	230	330	130	90
Dividend	30	30	30	50	90	100	120	100	70
Retained profits	60	140	50	20	100	120	220	30	20

Notes:
1. Exchange rates varied considerably during this 9 year period. At the end of 1993, US$ 1 equaled Rs. 30.77.
2. Escorts Ltd. is the largest company in the Escorts group. In the Escorts group of companies, agribusiness accounted for 46 percent of revenues, two-wheelers for 20 percent, automotive components 22 percent, construction equipment for 8 percent. The remaining 4 percent came from a variety of activities.

Source: Company records.

company were lost. The Nandas reestablished Escorts in Delhi as an agency house serving foreign manufacturers in India. Yudi and Hari Nanda were, respectively, the managing director and chairman of Escorts Agents, as the company was then known. In 1948, Yudi Nanda founded Escorts (Agriculture and Machines) Ltd., a separate entity from Escorts Agents Ltd. After Yudi Nanda's death, the two companies were merged in 1953.

In Escorts' first international alliance, the company served as Westinghouse's franchisee for domestic appliances in India. With the recognition of the opportunities in the Indian rural economy, the company quickly forged a number of additional marketing alliances with German corporations like MAN, AEG, Haniel & Leung, and Knorr Bremse for sophisticated electrical and mechanical engineering equipment. Another series of alliances with American corporations like Minneapolis Moline, Wisconsin, and Massey-Ferguson facilitated entry into agricultural tractors, implements, and engines. Escorts provided the marketing and service activities in these alliances, beginning the development of a strong dealer network across all of India.

In 1954, Escorts participated in its first industrial venture, manufacturing piston rings and liners in partnership with Goetz Werke of Germany. Subsequent collaborations with Mahle of Germany in 1960, for the production of pistons, and with Ursus of Poland, for the assembly of tractors, solidified Escorts' backward integration from distribution to the manufacture of industrial products. In January 1960, Escorts Agents Pvt. Ltd. was incorporated as a public company under the name of Escorts Ltd.

Throughout Escorts' early years, focus was on the company's strength as a broadly based marketing and service network that had extensive access to India's large and widely dispersed population. The tractor business exemplified Escorts' customer focus. In the 1950s, Escorts instituted a policy of on-site service. Escorts offered to repair and service tractors at the customer's farm. To provide this service, dealers were located in small towns near the villages in which the tractors were used.

Escorts stimulated the development of the tractor market through its customer focus. In the 1950s and 1960s, Indian farmers, unaware of the benefits of mechaniza-

EXHIBIT 2 India's Top 25 Companies Based on Sales, 1993

Rank	Company	Industry	1993 Sales	Increase (Decrease) from 1992	1993 Pretax Profit	Increase (Decrease) from 1992
1	ITC	Conglomerate	37,408	26.0%	4,219	31.1%
2	Tata Steel	Steel	33,521	20.3	5,450	(6.8)
3	Reliance Industries	Conglomerate	31,086	35.1	8,809	53.3
4	Tata Engineering (TELCO)	Vehicles	28,758	(4.9)	3,276	(21.2)
5	Hindustan Lever	Consumer products	20,868	17.5	2,177	22.7
6	Larsen & Toubro	Engineering	18,875	34.8	3,058	1.5
7	Grasim Industries	Textiles	17,480	18.8	2,800	5.4
8	Associated Cement	Cement	15,202	7.3	1,807	(39.2)
9	Mahindra & Mahindra	Vehicles	14,252	23.7	1,204	(4.7)
10	Bajaj Auto	Vehicles	12,430	2.4	2,109	2.7
11	Century Textiles	Textiles	11,969	9.0	2,422	(15.3)
12	Southern Petro	Fertilizers	11,676	14.6	1,447	32.1
13	Gujarat State Fertilizer	Fertilizers	10,515	3.1	2,064	6.7
14	JK Synthetics	Textiles	10,142	1.7	1,134	(25.8)
15	Hindalco Industries	Aluminum	9,755	14.0	2,748	35.0
16	Ballapur Ind.	Conglomerate	9,586	9.7	1,604	8.6
17	Ashok Leyland	Vehicles	9,544	(7.4)	1,196	3.9
18	Escorts	Conglomerate	9,385	(11.4)	697	(2.1)
19	MRF	Tyres	8,469	13.9	869	8.5
20	Indian Rayon	Textiles	8,092	22.3	1,772	26.2
21	Bombay Suburban	Utility	7,976	40.3	1,236	66.4
22	Peico	Electronics	7,970	7.0	721	(23.3)
23	Crompton Greaves	Electrical products	7,804	8.3	773	6.1
24	ICI India	Chemicals	7,792	10.1	823	(11.0)
25	Indian Aluminum	Aluminum	7,617	15.6	968	10.4

Note: All monetary values are in millions of rupees.

Source: Economic Times Research Bureau.

tion, were reluctant to adopt tractors. Escorts sought to change this aversion to mechanization. A private Institute of Farm Mechanization was established at Azadpur, Delhi. Customers, many of them newcomers to the use of automated farm machinery, were trained, free of cost, by Escorts when they purchased a tractor.

Escorts combined this service and market orientation with extensive manufacturing capabilities. In 1993, Escorts had 20 manufacturing plants located throughout India. Though the technology employed in these plants was competitive within India, the technical expertise was acquired through a series of international alliances (see Appendix A for a description of an alliance with Yamaha). Company growth during the 1960s and 1970s occurred through product diversification, and the company moved into a number of new industries.

Diversification

In the 1960s and 1970s, Escorts grew in a controlled market: Manufacturers were only able to produce products for which they held a license. A number of acts and policies institutionalized the government's efforts to control production. The Monopoly and Restrictive Trade Practices (MRTP) Act prevented large companies from obtaining exclusive control of any one market. Sales of any one firm in a particular market were limited; thus individual company growth was shunted away from concentration in any one product area. The Foreign Exchange Regulation Act (FERA) controlled the amount of foreign trade, limiting international competition in India's domestic markets.

Finally, a licensing authority controlled growth across sectors in the economy. The licensing authority determined which areas in the economy had the highest priority, and, by the issuance of licenses, who was able to produce in the different markets. Market mechanisms were distorted, and industry became widely known as a system of "know-who, not know-how." To grow and to receive licenses for production, companies had to curry favor with government officials. Companies that possessed the majority of licensed capacity for a product could control prices by restriction of output. Competitors were not free to enter markets because India's licensing system, while professing to prevent the formation of monopolies, resulted in licensees having significant monopoly power and a privileged market position. Escorts' growth during this period was primarily achieved by product line diversification. After growth in the 1970s and 1980s, Escorts' licensed capacity was greater than its productive capacity, and it had a large number of foreign partners. (See Exhibit 3).

A Moment of Crisis

Through the 1970s and 1980s, Escorts' revenues, profits, and share price increased steadily. However, in 1983, the price of Escorts' shares began to climb perceptibly faster on stock exchanges across India. From a January price of Rs. 40, shares doubled to Rs. 80 in May 1983. Hostile takeovers were unheard of at this time in India, and Escorts' managers suspected that they were being green-mailed at this time, though, in fact, a takeover of Escorts was being attempted by Swraj Paul, a London-based nonresident Indian (NRI).

Escorts was susceptible to a stock market raid partly because of the country's expropriatory tax laws. High marginal tax rates, which frequently exceeded 60 percent, left little in retained earnings for the internal financing of growth, and at times, even forced companies to sell shares to meet their tax liabilities. Thus, frequent share issues had diluted the stock holdings of the founding Nanda family. In the 1980s, the Nanda family held just 15 percent of the total equity capital of the company.

Two government-controlled Indian financial institutions, Unit Trust of India and Life Insurance Corporation, jointly controlled over 50 percent of Escorts' equity. The dominant presence of these financial institutions in Escorts was not unusual among Indian companies. Other large companies, such as DCM (a conglomerate), TELCO, and Tata Steel (see Exhibit 2 for India's 25 largest private sector companies), had 40 percent or more of their shares owned by financial institutions.

Investment in Indian companies by financial institutions was an important means of providing capital and financing growth. Generally, these institutions followed a noninterventionist policy, supporting management but not seeking control over management. However, the weak ownership position of the founding families of many of India's larger companies made them vulnerable to hostile takeovers.

NRIs like Swraj Paul were in a favorable position to invest in Indian businesses because of the foreign exchange problems faced by the Indian economy. NRIs were encouraged by the Indian government to invest foreign funds in India to help improve the country's balance of payments position. However, such investments

EXHIBIT 3   A Profile of Escorts' Product Lines (1990s)

Product/Business	Collaboration	Licensed Capacity	Installed Capacity	Quantity Produced (1993)
Agricultural tractors	Fiat Geotech, Italy Ursus, Poland Ford, U.S.	42,500	28,000 15,500	27,876
Harvester combines	Claas OHG, Germany		100	
Motorcycles	Yamaha, Japan			
	Cekop, Poland	500,000	210,000	114,702
Pistons	Mahle GmbH, Germany	3,750,000	4,500,000	3,839,920
Piston rings	Goetze AG, Germany	Delicensed	34,800,000	31,931,587
Shock absorbers	Fichtel & Sach, Germany Aygyst Bilmstein GmbH		2,875,000	1,658,979
Telescopic front fork	Kayaba, Japan	2,781,250		Counted in shocks
Struts	Kayaba, Japan			
Railway ancillaries	Knorr Bremise, Germany	N.A.	N.A.	35,000
Carburetors (for 4-wheeled vehicles)	Mikuni, Japan	N.A.	600,000	N.A.
Clutch assemblies	Fuji, Japan	N.A.	10,000,000	N.A.
CDI magnetos	IIC, Japan	N.A.	100,000 sets	N.A.
Hydraulic products, automatic valves	Herion-Werke, GmbH	N.A.	30,000	N.A.
Cranes	Faun, Germany R & R, Germany	413	200	217
Excavator loaders	J.C. Bamford Excavators Ltd.		900	646
Compactors	Dynapac, Sweden	875	30	16
VSAT satellite communication systems	Hughes Network Systems	N.A.	N.A.	N.A.
Telecommunications	JS Telecom Bosch, France	62,500 lines	62,500 lines	10,750 lines

Source: Company records.

were intended to be passive, long-term investments, rather than to gain management control. Thus, individual NRIs were restricted to a 1 percent ownership position in any one Indian company, although this restriction could be circumvented by purchasing shares through a series of companies and thereby, in a circuitous manner, attain a controlling interest.

Escorts, led by the efforts of H. P. Nanda, resisted Swraj Paul's takeover attempt. Appeals to the government and to other industry leaders to deal with the threat of NRI control of Indian companies did not bring immediate results. Finally, Escorts found an ally in Rajiv Gandhi, the prime minister's son, and, at that time, the general secretary of the Congress Party. Rajiv Gandhi's efforts and influence eventually resulted in total NRI holdings in any Indian company being restricted to 5 percent of the company's outstanding shares. This ruling helped prevent the takeover of Escorts, though the battle between the Nandas, Swraj Paul, the Reserve Bank of India, and the government of India continued for another three years before the situation was finally resolved in Escorts' favor. The Nanda family purchased back Swraj Paul's shares at a premium. These events left an indelible mark on Escorts. Management at Escorts remained sensitive to the possibility of takeover, and later strategies reflected the desire not to increase the company's exposure to this threat. By 1993, equity in Escorts held by financial institutions remained high, but had slipped to 48 percent, while the Nandas' holdings had increased to 20 percent.

ESCORTS: PRELIBERALIZATION

Organizational Structure

Prior to 1991, the Escorts group of companies consisted of a number of subsidiary and associate companies, technical collaborations, and joint ventures. Twenty separate business entities existed in the Escorts group. These entities were organized under a broad directive which divided marketing and manufacturing functions. Each entity had a separate mandate that may or may have not been related to the mandate of another entity. Thus, considerable overlap existed between these business entities. A typical example was tractors.

Historically, Escorts had been India's largest producer of tractors in the 25 to 50 horsepower range. Prior to 1993, tractors were produced by two separate divisions: one was a farm equipment manufacturing division, and the other was a manufacturing joint venture first with Ford, and then with Ford New Holland which was taken over by Fiat-Agri. The first division operated two manufacturing plants, the second, one plant. Both the divisions had complete automony in sourcing, manpower, and other administrative decisions, and acted as profit centers. Both division heads reported directly to H. P. Nanda, then the managing director and chairman of Escorts. The divisions produced tractors under the Escorts and Ford names, and these brands were sold through a third division, the Farm Equipment division, responsible only for the distribution and sale of tractors.

Like the two manufacturing divisions, the farm equipment division acted independently and reported on its own profitability. A fourth division in the broader area of farm equipment, Escorts Claas Limited, a wholly owned subsidiary, was involved in the manufacture of harvester combines. Output from this independent venture was also marketed through the Farm Equipment division.

This system, which separated manufacturing and sales, was utilized in a similar manner across each of Escort's major product areas. Twenty separate entities existed, each with its own division head who reported to the chairman. Under this system, despite the separation and independence of operations, it became difficult to apportion responsibility between divisions for the failure to meet targets.

Collaborations

Escorts had routinely partnered with foreign companies in technical collaborations and equity joint ventures. Foreign participation benefited Escorts in a number of ways. Escorts swiftly acquired manufacturing capability, often gaining the rights to market its products under an internationally recognized brand name like Yamaha or Ford; and Escorts received technology and product feature upgrades as long as the venture was in existence. Escorts' most successful ventures were its 1990 joint venture with Yamaha, Japan, to manufacture of motorcycles; J. C. Bamford, UK, for the manufacture of earthmoving equipment (1979); Ford, the United States, for the manufacture of low-power (less than 50 hp) tractors (1969); Mahle of Germany for piston rings (1959); and Goetze of Germany for the production of pistons (1954).

By the 1980s, through these and other alliances with companies based in England, Germany, Japan, Poland, and the United States, the Escorts group of companies was large. The individual businesses produced or distributed tractors, industrial equipment, two-wheelers, and construction equipment (see Exhibit 3). While each of these products was manufactured for the transport industry, the competitive environments faced by each of these businesses were different and the products were evolving in different ways.

BUSINESSES

Tractors and Farm Equipment

During its three decades of serving the Indian tractor market, Escorts had sold over 500,000 tractors to the farmers of India. Tractors formed the backbone of Escorts' business. Escorts entered the tractor market in the late 1940s, selling tractors manufactured by Minneapolis Moline of the United States. In the 1950s, Escorts moved to the import of Ferguson tractors; Ferguson was subsequently acquired by Massey Harris of Canada, and became Massey-Ferguson. Following this sale, Massey-Ferguson set up an independent company in India called Tractors and Farm Equipment Ltd. (TAFE), and secured a 40 percent share of the tractor market. Massey-Ferguson no longer supplied Escorts with tractors and Escorts was blocked from participation in the tractor market, as only five models, TAFE, Eicher, International Harvester, Zetor, and Harsha, were licensed for manufacture and sale in India.

Faced with permanent exclusion from this market, Escorts lobbied the government to secure an industrial license to manufacture tractors in India. Eventually, a license was obtained, and Escorts began to develop in-house research and development capabilities to improve Poland's Ursus tractor, the prototype for the Escorts tractor. Manufacture of the Escorts tractor line was done wholly in India; no parts or components were sourced from suppliers outside India. However, Escorts did not emerge as the premier manufacturer of tractors until its collaboration with Ford in 1969.

In 1968, the Indian government recognized the need to increase the quantity of domestic tractor manufacture. Escorts identified this as an opportunity to expand its tractor line and supersede TAFE as the number one tractor manufacturer in India. Escorts brand tractors operated in the 25 to 40 hp range, and Escorts approached Ford about producing a higher horsepower tractor. In 1969, a contract was signed with Ford Motor Company to manufacture Tractor Model 3000, a 47 horsepower tractor. The new joint venture was named Escorts Tractors Limited. Escorts had a 60 percent equity share, and Ford owned a 40 percent share.

The joint venture proceeded through stages typical of Escorts' other collaborations. Initially, tractors were sent in a knocked-down condition to Faridabad for assembly. Tractor manufacture was gradually phased into the Faridabad plant, and soon the plant completed all stages of manufacture. The technology transfer was facilitated by the placement of three or four of Ford's technical and management personnel in India.

EXHIBIT 4   Leading Competitors in the Tractor Market in India

Company	Market Share	Market Segment	Collaboration
1. Mahindra	24.9%	3 cylinder engine 30 hp	International Harvester
2. Escorts	21.2	Ford: 50 hp (9.2%) Escorts: 25–45 hp (11.9%)	Fiat-Agri
3. TAFE	17.2	Tractors for paddy farming	Massey-Ferguson
4. Punjab Tractors	14.1	—	Several foreign partners
5. Eicher	11.1	18–25 hp	Formerly had a German collaborator
6. Hindustan Machine Tools	10.2	—	Zetor

Notes:
1. Most companies produced a 2-cylinder engine. Mahindra's 3-cylinder engine was more powerful and enjoyed a better reputation than the standard 2-cylinder engine.
2. Several smaller manufacturers accounted for 1.4 percent of the Indian tractor market.

Source: Company records.

However, by the mid-1970s, after the technology had been transferred, Ford had reduced its managment commitment to one individual. The joint venture was being managed almost solely by Escorts. The joint venture was successful in its initial mandate, to help Escorts displace TAFE as the number one tractor manufacturer in India. The 47 hp tractor became very popular in India and soon outsold TAFE despite its higher price. Escorts and Ford tractors held a leading 26 percent share in the under-50 hp tractor market in 1991, only to be displaced by Mahindra later in the 1990s. (See Exhibit 4 for a list of competitors in India's tractor market.)

During its three decades of serving the Indian tractor market, Escorts had sold over 500,000 tractors. Ford brand tractors accounted for 300,000 units and Escorts brand tractors, 200,000 units. Ford tractors were larger and operated at the 50 hp level. Tractors sold under the Escorts name ranged between 25 and 47 hp. Tractors in India tended to be smaller and less expensive than those sold in North America, Europe, and Australia, making the Indian market unique. The usage patterns of tractors in India differed as well. Tractors purchased in Western markets were usually used exclusively on the farm, and often in conjunction with a variety of application specific implements. In India, a tractor had to be as versatile as a pickup truck. Less than 50 percent of the time, a tractor was used directly for farming purposes; the majority of the time, the tractor acted as a mode of transportation, moving people and goods from one place to another along the nation's rural roads and highways.

The majority of tractors produced by Escorts and other manufacturers in India like Eicher were sold in the north of India. Escorts' tractor sales were concentrated in three northern states: 28.5 percent of tractor sales were in Uttar Pradesh, 16.8 percent in Punjab, and 12.5 percent in Haryana. These states were engaged more in wheat than rice production, and Escorts' tractors were designed for use in the relatively drier fields used in wheat production. For example, the brake systems and horsepower levels on Escort's tractor models made them unsuitable for use in wet paddy fields. However, as agricultural patterns changed in India, Escorts expected tractor requirements to change. Agriculture was becoming more sophisticated, and more market niches were being created, leading to larger markets for more specialized equipment. For example, the wheel base of an Escorts' tractor would have to be widened and clearances increased for it to be suitable for cotton farming. Other agricultural applications would require further modifications. Uniformity in tractors was expected to decrease in the move towards specific end-use designs.

Aside from tractors, Escorts produced other farm equipment. A joint venture, Escorts Class Ltd. (ECL), produced harvester combines for domestic and international markets. Domestic sales accounted for half of the revenues of this subsidiary and were to South Indian markets. Southeast Asian markets were the primary destination for export sales. ECL planned to continue concentrating on these regions with volumes increasing to five times present levels in the coming years. A redesigned model of the current combine was to be introduced to northern Indian markets in 1995–96.

Two-Wheelers

The two-wheeler market was composed of three segments: motorcycles, scooters, and mopeds. In 1993, Escorts participated solely in the motorcycle segment which it had entered in the early 1960s, though the moped segment would be entered in 1994. In the early 1970s, the Escorts (Rajdoot) motorcycle, Escorts GTS, became widely known after being depicted in the 1972 blockbuster movie, *Bobby*. The GTS, ridden by the hero of the film and known as the Bobby, was quite popular among school-boys and university students in 1970s India. The Rajdoot 175cc, the traditional Escorts motorcycle, was, as measured by unit sales, the most successful motorcycle line in India. It was the only motorcycle model in India to have sold more than one million units.

In 1985, Escorts introduced a new 100cc motorcycle. This motorcycle, the Yamaha RX 100, was developed in a collaborative venture with Yamaha of Japan. Yamaha provided the technology for production of the Yamaha RX 100, and Escorts provided the land, factory, and distribution system. In 1990, Yamaha became an active partner in this venture. The partnership, initiated by Escorts in 1981, was one of many collaborations between Indian and Japanese companies to manufacture motorcycles. Also in the mid-1980s, the three other major Japanese motorcycle manufacturers—Suzuki, Kawasaki, and Honda—became active in the Indian market. By the time Escorts' application to produce 100cc motorcycles was sanctioned, several other joint ventures such as Hero Honda, TVS Suzuki and Bajaj Kawasaki were operating and selling motorcycles.

In 1993, Escorts' position in the motorcycle segment was strong. Production of the Yamaha RX 100 cc motorcycle was accomplished with 95 percent Indian parts and labor, and Escorts was searching for a partner to develop a four-stroke engine to counter similar product developments by Hero Honda and Bajaj Kawasaki. Recently, however, there had been an industrywide downturn in sales (see Exhibit 5). Further, with government liberalization of trade policies and foreign investment regulations, foreign investment in the automotive sector was subject to automatic approval and competition was expected to intensify. Escorts was formulating plans to move into the scooter segment in a collaboration with a foreign partner.

Other Businesses

Escorts produced a variety of component parts for automobiles, motorcycles, tractors and construction machinery in its components businesses. This portion of Escorts' business, more than any other, enjoyed substantial and growing overseas demand for its product. A fourth business area was industrial and construction equipment in

EXHIBIT 5   Trends in Unit Sales of Motorcycles in India, 1981–1993

	1981–85	1986–89	1990	1991	1992	1993
Rajdoot 350*	4204	—	—	—	—	—
Rajdoot 175cc*	337,948	331,960	85,516	53,502	46,789	58,310
Escorts HD (GTS)*	6320	—	—	—	—	—
Yamaha RX 100*	0	126,356	68,509	64,100	46,483	56,399
Bajaj KB100/4S	0	65,723	49,083	33,252	34,015	42,134
Ideal Jawa 250cc	150,680	5848	0	630	2519	5866
Enfield/Explorer	111,818	28,185	26,967	17,130	17,677	16,360
Hero Honda	13,292	120,058	135,001	127,803	148,134	183,671
TVS Suzuki AX100	39,482	37,043	33,746	30,085	53,120	87,220
Total**	762,011	1,405,522	471,429	373,417	397,019	466,936

*Indicates products of Escorts Group.
**Total does not include sales of other smaller manufacturers not listed in the table.
Notes:
1. Total motorcycle sales were forecasted to increase by 100,000 units in 1994 and 1995. By 1996, annual sales of motorcycles in India were forecasted to be 700,000 units.
2. Demand for mopeds was similar to that for motorcycles, while demand for scooters was approximately double that of motorcycles.

Source: Company records, Government of India documents.

which Escorts manufactured and marketed a diverse range of construction, road-building, and material-handling equipment.

A variety of other business areas completed the Escorts Group portfolio of businesses. Railway ancillaries, financial services, telecommunications (Escorts was planning to form a joint venture with First Pacific, a Hong Kong–based firm, to provide cellular services), and heath care (included in the group of companies was the Escorts Heart Institute and Research Centre) were a few of Escorts' other business interests.

LIBERALIZATION

The Indian economy had been slowly liberalizing through the 1980s, but it was not until 1991 that changes were initiated to make the market truly accessible and desirable to foreign investors. Changes in India's industrial policy at this time were designed to attract foreign direct investment and to encourage technology collaboration agreements between Indian and foreign firms. The changes substantially abolished industrial licensing, facilitated foreign direct invesment and technology transfer, and opened up areas previously reserved for the public sector to the private sector. The areas still reserved for the public sector were those of national strategic concern such as defense, railways, and atomic energy.

Liberalization in trade policy resulted in the dismantling of the system of export and import licensing, and included a scaling down of tariff barriers. Most goods could now be imported freely, with quantitative restrictions on imports of capital goods and intermediate products almost completely removed. Tariff reductions were substantial. Prior to July 1991, tariff rates were as high as 300 percent. By 1993, the average tariff

EXHIBIT 6   Examples of Multinationals Doing Business in India

Market	Multinational	Brand
Consumer Durables		
Passenger cars	Suzuki	Maruti-Suzuki
	General Motors	Opel-Astra
	Daimler Benz	Mercedes-Benz
	Peugeot	Peugeot 309
Motorcycles	Suzuki	Suzuki
	Kawasaki	Kawasaki Bajaj
	Honda	Hero Honda, Kinetic Honda (scooter)
	Yamaha	Escorts Yamaha
White goods/	General Electric	Godrej-GE
home appliances	Bosch	IFB Bosch
	Sanyo	BPL-Sanyo
	Whirlpool	Whirlpool, National
Consumer Nondurables		
Soaps and detergents	Unilever	Surf, Lux, Le Sancy, etc.
	Proctor & Gamble	Camay, Head & Shoulders, etc.
	Henkel	Henko
Personal care	Colgate-Palmolive	Colgate
	Ciba-Geigy	Cibaco
	Reckitt & Colman	Dettol
	Gillette	Gillette
Food and beverages	Unilever	Lipton, Brooke Bond, Wall's
	Nestlé	Nestlé, Cerelac, Polo
	Cadbury Schweppes	Cadbury
	PepsiCo	Pepsi, Pizza Hut, Kentucky Fried Chicken
	Coca-Cola	Coca-Cola
	Kellogg's	Kellogg's
Apparel	Coats Viyella	Louis Phillippe, Van Heusen
	Benetton	Benetton
	Lacoste	Lacoste

Source: Economic Coordination Unit, Government of India. *India: Business Perspectives,* 1994.

rate was 65 percent. For capital goods, tariff rates were in the 20–40 percent range and were nil for goods and equipment used for export-oriented activities.

The initial results of liberalization were positive. GDP growth increased from less than 1 percent in 1992–92, to a projected 5.3 percent in 1994–95. The dollar value of imports and exports grew by 25 percent in this same period, while foreign direct investment (FDI), led by firms based in the United States, tripled. In addition, numerous multinationals had established a presence in India in the early 1990s (see Exhibit 6). Sectorally, FDI was distributed across many industries, with primary sectors such as fuels, oil refining and power receiving the largest share of FDI.

Shortly after liberalization, interest in the stock market surged. Investors from all walks of life emerged and the Bombay Stock Index more than doubled from its

January 24, 1992, position at 2,200, to its peak of 4,500 in April of the same year. However, the euphoria of investors was smothered under the weight of falling stock prices in the late-April 1992 stock scandal and crash of the Bombay Index. Investors suffered substantial losses in the index's rapid 1,500 point decline. The index continued to decline slowly and rested at the 2,500 level in early 1993.

Many of the investors caught in the crash represented India's large and emerging middle class. These individuals purchased the bulk of consumer products such as white goods, electronic equipment, two-wheelers, and four-wheelers. However, as a result of the crash, their purchasing power was diminished and consumption of these products declined. The poor financial health of these consumers was exacerbated by the reluctance of banks to lend during 1992 when the rupee was devalued and inflation continued to be high. Escorts' managers attributed the poor performance of Escorts to the decline in the stock market, the concomitant decline in purchasing power of middle-class consumers, and a sector specific decline in the automotive industry. Supporting this explanation was the sluggish motorcycle market in 1991–92 (see Exhibit 5), which rebounded in 1993. Overall, the economic picture was positive and strong growth was expected in the mid-1990s.

ESCORTS: POSTLIBERALIZATION

Liberalization in India had stimulated growth across most sectors; however, Escorts suffered through two years of stagnant growth and declining profits immediately following liberalization (see Exhibit 1). Also, Escorts had recently lost its market leader position in the tractor market to Mahindra, a company which had performed well following liberalization (see Exhibit 2). In 1993, the Corporate Strategic Planning Department (CSPD) was created. The department was charged with the task of navigating Escorts through a period of adjustment, and with charting Escorts' future course through the uncertain waters of the Indian economy.

Growth Opportunities

The CSPD recognized that liberalization had created several new opportunities, along with new threats, in the various markets in which Escorts participated. For example, the domestic tractor market was opened to foreign competitors. However, despite the size and growth potential of the agricultural sector in India, Escorts did not expect a large number of new entrants to this industry. New competitors required a distribution system which reached into India's numerous villages and agricultural communities, and they required a product suitable for the small scale of Indian agriculture (see Appendix B for a description of Escorts' unique distribution system). The 25–50 hp tractor models that were sold in India were difficult for foreign competitors from Western markets, who produced 100–125 hp tractors, to emulate. Tractor manufacturers based in countries like Japan and Taiwan produced tractors suitable for rice cultivation on very small, terraced paddy fields. Also, new entrants to the tractor industry had to contend with the considerable goodwill Escorts had created during its years of serving rural agricultural markets.

The two-wheeler segment, already a global industry, was expected to become much more competitive in future years. Escorts had to become more competitive in this sector by better utilizing its distribution system and by developing motorcycles which were technologically competitive with those of similar size sold in world markets. Escorts sold 16,000 to 18,000 motorcycles in international markets, accounting for about 20 percent of this division's sales. However, exports of these motorcycles were restricted by Yamaha, its joint venture partner.

Automotive components was Escorts' most globally competitive business. Growth in this area was expected to come from both domestic and international markets. Telecommunications was also seen as a key growth area by Escorts, though it was a new business area for Escorts. Further, Escorts believed that as it moved through the 1990s, leadership in markets would be related to technical strengths. Accordingly, a Research Center employing 220 engineers and technicians (total employment at Escorts was approximately 25,000 people) had been recently established with the mandate to upgrade existing products and develop new products in anticipation of consumer needs.

A PLAN OF RESPONSE

Management at Escorts' CSPD had evaluated these changes in the Indian economy against Escorts' current position and strategy. Clearly, conditions in India had changed; new opportunities had opened up, and a general sense of optimism pervaded the business community. However, Escorts' recent performance had been poor, and the industries in which it competed were evolving at a faster pace and were evolving in different directions. Escorts had to respond to these diverse changes, and several options existed. The company could choose to consolidate its assorted businesses; it could invest its resources aggressively in new product areas like telecommunications; or it could broaden the scope of its current businesses. While the managers in the CSPD had to select one of these three options, or develop another, they also had to decide on the focus of the company. Whichever of these options was chosen, it would set the company's strategic direction for the years to come.

APPENDIX A: ESCORTS–YAMAHA JOINT VENTURE

Escorts had two plants manufacturing motorcycles. One plant, located in Faridabad, was wholly designed and operated by Escorts. The other plant in Surajpur commenced operations in 1986. Originally, the Surajpur plant was operated by Escorts and produced Yamaha motorcycles under a licensing agreement with Yamaha. In 1990, a new plant was established in the Surajpur location.

Yamaha participated more actively in designing and operating this plant. The plant employed a new, younger workforce and new forms of work organization were introduced. Training was a common theme in this plant. Senior managers, technical personnel, and supervisors underwent extensive training which included short two- to six-weeks stints in Japan. Workers received two-weeks' training prior to going on to the shop floor. Thereafter, a group of new workers would undergo further training in which they were directed by a group of 10 Japanese and 10 Indian trainers. The cycle between shop-floor and off the shop-floor training was repeated for several months. Formal training continued throughout the employment span of the worker, with monetary rewards accompanying the acquisition of new skills.

The plant followed a typical Japanese design with work organized on a cellular basis. Work teams were responsible for each cell, and workers were trained to perform a multitude of tasks within a cell. Each machine operator was cross-trained and assigned to work on a number of machines whereas in the Faridabad plant one worker was assigned to just one machine. Just-in-time practices were also adopted.

TABLE 1   Comparison of Surajpur and Faridabad Plants, 1990

Plant	Annual Output (# of motorcycles)	Number of Workers	Output per worker	Change over Time	Materials Inventory
Surajpur	77,500	625	124	30–60 minutes	15–30 days
Faridabad	96,000	4,000	24	8 hours	3–6 months

Source: Transnational Corporations and Management Division, *Transnational Corporations and the Transfer of New Management Practices to Developing Countries,* New York: United Nations.

The operating performance at the Surajpur plant, in comparison to the Faridabad plant, was far superior (see Table 1). The Surajpur plant produced nearly the same number of motorcycles with a workforce 6.5 times smaller than the Faridabad plant.

APPENDIX B: ESCORTS DEALERS' DEVELOPMENT ASSOCIATION LIMITED

Distribution in India was challenging. The nation's urban population was concentrated in 21 cities with populations greater than one million people. The rural population was less concentrated. Hundreds of millions of people lived in the 640,000 villages that dotted India's countryside. Escorts' distribution channels had to access both rural and urban segments because farm equipment was sold in mainly rural areas and bi-wheelers had greater sales in the urban regions.

Escorts' extensive dealer network had grown incrementally during the company's 50 years of operations. More than 500 dealers serviced the farm equipment customer segment and 700 dealers retailed bi-wheelers. These dealers, dispersed across this large and populous nation, were welded together into a large, cohesive network termed the Escort Dealers' Development Association Limited (EDDAL). This network permitted Escorts to constantly upgrade the quality of tractor and motorcycle dealership while imparting a sense of unity to the dealers.

The philosophy behind the network was one of assistance and mentorship. Larger dealers helped smaller dealers. Through EDDAL, financial assistance, training programs, and managerial education programs were offered to dealers.

Of the 14 directors in this association, 11 were dealers themselves. From the 191 dealer members that comprised EDDAL when it was formed in 1977, membership had increased to 818 by 1993. Funding for EDDAL came from the dealers themselves, who contributed a set amount for each unit sold, and from Escorts, which contributed a larger set amount. Most recently, in response to the increased acceptance of debt purchasing by Indian consumers, Escorts was encouraging EDDAL member dealers to jointly establish refinancing programs to assist with the financing of bi-wheeler purchases.

23

ROBIN HOOD

Joseph Lampel, *New York University*

It was in the spring of the second year of his insurrection against the High Sheriff of Nottingham that Robin Hood took a walk in Sherwood forest. As he walked he pondered the progress of the campaign, the disposition of his forces, the Sheriff's recent moves, and the options that confronted him.

The revolt against the Sheriff had begun as a personal crusade. It erupted out of Robin's conflict with the Sheriff and his administration. However, alone Robin Hood could do little. He therefore sought allies, men with grievances and a deep sense of justice. Later he welcomed all who came, asking few questions and demanding only a willingness to serve. Strength, he believed, lay in numbers.

He spent the first year forging the group into a disciplined band, united in enmity against the Sheriff and willing to live outside the law. The band's organization was simple. Robin ruled supreme, making all important decisions. He delegated specific tasks to his lieutenants. Will Scarlett was in charge of intelligence and scouting. His main job was to shadow the Sheriff and his men, always alert to their next move. He also collected information on the travel plans of rich merchants and tax collectors. Little John kept discipline among the men, and saw to it that their archery was at the high peak that their profession demanded. Scarlock took care of the finances, converting loot to cash, paying shares of the take, and finding suitable hiding places for the surplus. Finally, Much the Miller's son had the difficult task of provisioning the ever-increasing band of Merrymen.

The increasing size of the band was a source of satisfaction for Robin, but also a source of concern. The fame of his Merrymen was spreading, and new recruits poured in from every corner of England. As the band grew larger, their small bivouac became a major encampment. Between raids the men milled about, talking and playing games. Vigilance was in decline, and discipline was becoming harder to enforce. "Why," Robin reflected, "I don't know half the men I run into these days."

The growing band was also beginning to exceed the food capacity of the forest. Game was becoming scarce, and supplies had to be obtained from outlying villages. The cost of buying food was beginning to drain the band's financial reserves at the very moment when revenues were in decline. Travelers, especially those with the most to lose, were now giving the forest a wide berth. This was costly and inconvenient to them, but it was preferable to having all their goods confiscated.

Robin believed that the time had come for the Merrymen to change their policy of outright confiscation of goods to one of a fixed transit tax. His lieutenants strongly resisted this idea. They were proud of the Merrymen's famous motto: "Rob from the rich and give to the poor." "The farmers and the townspeople," they argued, "are our most important allies. How can we tax them, and still hope for their help in our fight against the Sheriff?"

Robin wondered how long the Merrymen could keep to the ways and methods of their early days. The Sheriff was growing stronger and becoming better organized. He now had the money and the men and was beginning to harass the band, probing for its weaknesses. The tide of events was beginning to turn against the Merrymen. Robin felt that the campaign must be decisively concluded before the Sheriff had a chance to deliver a mortal blow. "But how," he wondered, "could this be done?"

Robin had often entertained the possibility of killing the Sheriff, but the chances for this seemed increasingly remote. Besides, killing the Sheriff might satisfy his personal thirst for revenge, but it would not improve the situation. Robin had hoped that the perpetual state of unrest, and the Sheriff's failure to collect taxes, would lead to his removal from office. Instead, the Sheriff used his political connections to obtain reinforcement. He had powerful friends at court and was well regarded by the regent, Prince John.

Prince John was vicious and volatile. He was consumed by his unpopularity among the people, who wanted the imprisoned King Richard back. He also lived in constant fear of the barons, who had first given him the regency, but were now beginning to dispute his claim to the throne. Several of these barons had set out to collect the ransom that would release King Richard the Lionheart from his jail in Austria. Robin was invited to join the conspiracy in return for future amnesty. It was a dangerous proposition. Provincial banditry was one thing, court intrigue another. Prince John had spies everywhere, and he was known for his vindictiveness. If the conspirators' plan failed, the pursuit would be relentless, and retributions swift.

The sound of the supper horn startled Robin from his thoughts. There was the smell of roasting venison in the air. Nothing was resolved or settled. Robin headed for camp promising himself that he would give these problems his utmost attention after tomorrow's raid.

KITTY'S MAIDS*

Tom Hinthorne, *Montana State University—Billings.*

Make Your Home Sparkle & Shine.

"We Give YOU Time!"
   Kitty's business card

It was early May in Billings, Montana (population 84,000), and Kitty was wondering how she was going to improve the profitability of her business. Kitty's Maids was the largest maid service in the Billings market, but part-time competitors were undercutting Kitty's prices by 50 to 60 percent. Gross income had declined, and profits and cash flows had recovered only slightly after a dramatic drop two years ago. In addition, workers' compensation insurance premiums were skyrocketing and employee turnover was high. The income statements (Exhibit 1) and the balance sheet (Exhibit 2) were not encouraging.

Nevertheless, Kitty was a believer in the adage that, "Winners never quit and quitters never win!" A professional employer organization might be able to reduce her workers' compensation premiums and employee turnover. And several people had suggested targeting different market segments.

STRATEGIC ISSUES

Barbara Robbins, a friend and business acquaintance, had encouraged Kitty to think about the following issues:

*This case, which was originally presented at the North American Case Research Association's annual meeting in 1994, is based entirely on field research and was written solely for the purpose of stimulating student discussion. Kitty and her business are real and accurately represented. The financial figures have been simplified and altered slightly, but the trends have been preserved. Copyright ©1996 by the *Case Research Journal* and Tom Hinthorne.

EXHIBIT 1 Kitty's Maids Year-End Income Statement

	Year 1	Year 2	Year 3
Gross income	$160,000	$145,000	$141,000
Operating expenses			
Advertising and promotion	10,000	12,000	9,750
Amortization (original purchase)	3,600	2,400	
Automotive (3 vehicles)	7,550	7,200	11,000
Customer damage	400	700	800
Depreciation	7,500	3,400	2,850
Dues and publications	375	180	500
Employee benefits	800	600	300
Insurance and workers' compensation	5,300	7,150	6,700
Leased equipment	500	700	100
Legal and professional fees	200	1,500	250
Nonrecurring expense	14,000	9,200	3,700
Office expenses	3,650	3,750	3,050
Operating supplies	4,875	5,850	4,800
Payroll	65,700	64,500	62,500
Payroll taxes	5,400	6,000	7,000
Rent	5,700	5,700	5,850
Repairs and maintenance	1,050	2,250	2,400
Travel and entertainment	2,000	2,100	2,400
Training and classes	400	250	1,100
Uniforms	350	1,000	700
Utilities and telephone	3,700	2,400	3,300
Miscellaneous expenses	150	200	200
Total operating expenses	$143,200	$139,030	$129,250
Interest	2,100	2,470	2,000
Miscellaneous expenses	1,000	100	350
Total expenses	$146,300	$141,600	$131,600
Profit before income taxes	13,700	3,400	9,400
Income taxes – 15%	2,055	510	1,410
Net profit	$ 11,645	$ 2,890	$ 7,990

Source: Company records.

1. Is the business economically viable? Why? Why not?
2. What kind of a business do you want to own in three years? Five years?
3. How do you plan to accomplish this objective?

Barbara said, "You need to define your business objectives. Next, you need to develop and implement a strategy that will achieve your objectives. Then, you need to translate the strategy into a monthly operating plan, compare actual performance to plan every month, and act accordingly."

Kitty's response was, "Where do I start?" The suggestion to "develop and implement a strategy" was easier said than done, and managing the business left little time for learning new skills.

EXHIBIT 2 Kitty's Maids Balance Sheet, December 31, Year 3	
Assets	
Current assets	
Cash	$ 7,000
Inventory—supplies	300
Accounts receivable	5,300
Workers' compensation deposit	600
Total current assets	$13,200
Fixed assets	
Equipment	$ 8,700
Automobiles	27,400
Less accumulated depreciation	(15,300)
Total fixed assets	20,800
Total assets	$34,000
Liabilities and Owner's Equity	
Current liabilities	
Accounts payable	$ 3,500
Payroll taxes payable	3,300
Current portion of notes	6,000
Total current liabilities	$12,800
Long-term liabilities	
Note payable—Adams	$11,300
Note payable—bank	2,100
Total long-term liabilities	$13,400
Owner's equity	7,800
Total liabilities and owners' equity	$34,000

Source: Company records.
Note: Income statements were generated monthly, but comparative analyses were done by hand. No balance sheets were available for years 1 and 2.

KITTY

Seven years ago, Kitty had purchased a home cleaning business and renamed it Kitty's Maids. She bought the business only 1 1/2 days after a friend suggested that she look into it. At first, the business was quite successful under Kitty's management (e.g., sales rose 56 percent in one year). In fact, Kitty was so successful that the magazine *Successful Woman in Business* did a full-page profile of her. Gradually, however, the market had become more competitive.

Kitty had earned a Bachelor of Science degree in Business Education about 23 years ago, and since then she had taken several computer classes. Until her divorce, about 10 years ago, she had rarely worked outside the home. Since then, however,. she had worked in insurance, real estate, radio sales, and yellow pages sales. While raising a family, she had coached coed soccer for eight years and worked as a volunteer in many community activities. As a volunteer, she had learned a lot about people and had refined her promotional skills.

Kitty was also very active in the Chamber of Commerce. She had recently acquired a Ceiling Pro dealership, and she wore a 1- by 3-inch yellow nameplate with her name, "Kitty's Maids," and "Ceiling Pro" embossed in purple script, which was a guaranteed conversation starter. (Exhibit 3 is a promotional flier advertising Kitty's Maids and the Ceiling Pro service.) Kitty enjoyed people, and she freely acknowledged that her volunteer work promoted her business. As Kitty explained, "I'm a people person, and I deal with all kinds of personalities." One of Kitty's primary strengths was her engaging personality.

She was sensitive to people's needs and often went out of her way to help others; Kitty gave two examples:

> Tanya's mother and I are friends, but I don't know her very well. We have a mutual friend and see each other socially. Tanya's mother is a single parent with two kids. Both quit high school. Tanya is 16, and I offered to give her a job when she dropped out of high school. I thought that by working here, she could see what kind of job she would have for the rest of her life and what kind of pay she's going to have to live on. Tanya is a good worker, but she's got an attitude problem.
>
> Amy (an employee) has a son in Deer Lodge (a Montana prison) who she hadn't seen in nine months. A friend called and said that Amy could visit him. She would need an I.D., but she had no driver's license or birth certificate. So I called Deer Lodge and found out that she would need a picture and a notarized statement saying that she was the person in the picture. By then, Amy had left for the day. She lives about eight miles from the office. I found her house, met her kids, petted her dog, looked at her flowers, and talked to her about getting an I.D. I took a picture of her with my Polaroid, and the next day we got the notarized statement. She was elated! It took three hours of my time, but she was very happy! She even brought me back a picture of her and her son.

As a business owner, Kitty felt she had an opportunity to help people less fortunate than herself. For Kitty, this was one of the things that made business ownership meaningful.

KITTY'S BUSINESS

Kitty's Maids was centrally located on the ground floor of an attractive, two-story office complex. Kitty used 3- or 4-person teams (10 to 12 people total) to clean homes and two small offices, her only commercial accounts. The flier shown in Exhibit 3 sketches the nature of her business.

Kitty's Maids was bonded and insured; and the company supplied everything to its cleaning crews, including cleaning equipment, insurance, cleaning supplies, transportation (three vehicles), and uniforms. The vehicles were yellow hatchbacks with a purple "Kitty's Maids" logo and telephone number on each side (see Exhibit 3). The uniforms were purple polo shirts and purple sweatpants with a gray apron. Shorts were allowed in the summer.

Customers

Kitty's Maids had about 70 to 75 regular customers. The business specialized in cleaning the homes of elderly people, single professionals, and two-income families. Repeat customers were about 75 percent of her business, and clients that used Kitty's Maids regularly for three to four months generally became long-term customers. The other 25 percent involved special projects (e.g., spring cleanings, weddings, people moving in and out of residences, and so on). Kitty related a recent call from a customer to illustrate what was often involved:

EXHIBIT 3   Kitty's Maids Promotional Flier

"WE PAY ALL TAXES"

Gift Certificates

Kitty's
Maids /Ceiling Pro أعلى

REGULAR MAID SERVICE
- Professional Home Cleaning -
- Clean kitchen counters & sinks
- Damp wipe cabinet doors
- Load dishwasher
- Clean microwave
- Clean outside of all appliances
- Scrub & disinfect tubs & showers
- Clean & disinfect stools & sinks
- Wash non-carpeted floors on hands & knees
- Dust mop wood floors
- Vacuum rugs, carpeting & stairs
- Vacuum upholstered furniture
- Remove cobwebs
- Clean edges & corners
- Dust baseboards
- Dust window ledges & door frames
- Dust furniture, hanging pictures
- Dust books & knick knacks
- Clean mirrors
- Pick up & straighten up
- Empty trash
- *We don't open any doors or drawers*

GUARANTEED WORK - BONDED - INSURED
Dependable, Professional,
Supervised Team Cleaning

SPECIAL PROJECTS
- Oven-Grills
- Refrigerators
- Tile floors
- Vacuum draperies
- Vacuum mattresses
- Carpet cleaning
- Windows
- Walls
- Light fixtures
- Wood paneling

COMMERCIAL
The Ceiling Pro Way
- Acoustic tile and textured ceiling cleaning
- Office cleaning

The Ceiling Pro Advantage
- Removal of nicotine, smoke, cooking grease, soot, and dirt
- Ceiling tile restored to like-new condition
- Savings of 30%-70%, or more over painting & replacing
- No dirty, dusty business interruptions
- Sound absorbing qualities and fire retardancy values maintained

---

Weekly - Every other week
Every 3rd week - Monthly
* Move in - Move out *
* Seasonal Cleans *
* Special Events*

FREE ESTIMATES
256-1400

BILLINGS
AREA CHAMBER OF COMMERCE.
We're members...Join us!

Do You Find Yourself Cleaning What Your Housekeeper Missed?

Are You A Career Person By Day And The Cleaning Person By Night?

IRS Requires Taxes Paid On Housekeepers

WHAT YOU DON'T KNOW ABOUT INDEPENDENT HOUSEKEEPERS CAN REALLY HURT YOU.

It seems simple enough.

You need your house cleaned, the housekeeper needs the money, they clean. You pay. Simple.

Until the housekeeper slips in the bathroom and sues you for medical bills and lost wages.

Until Social Security and the IRS file claims against you for not withholding from the housekeeper's paycheck.

Until the housekeeper accidentally breaks a crystal vase of both great monetary and sentimental value—and you discover she has no insurance.

The housekeeper had a bad day or fails to show up altogether—homeowner has no recourse.

These are just a few of the many and often serious problems you should be aware of before hiring an independent housekeeper. Problems you can avoid entirely by hiring **Kitty's Maids**.

Kitty's Maids (1) Pays all Social Security and Employment Taxes, (2) Pays all Unemployment Benefits, (3) Pays Bonding, Liability, & Workers' Compensation Insurance, (4) Provides Cleaning Products, (5) Guaranteed Satisfaction.

Kitty's Maids—Dependable, Supervised Team Cleaning.

Kitty's Maids /Ceiling Pro   256-1400

1513-14th St. West • Billings, MT 59102

A customer calls in and swears that we stole a *Smithsonian* magazine off the coffee table. What do I do? Just say, "Oh, I'll check," and forget it? I have to check and let her know that I checked. This is the same lady that thought we were eating her M&Ms! . . . We're still cleaning her home.

Service

Kitty's Maids had developed a reputation for excellent service. As Kitty noted,

We can clean a 2,000-square-foot house in an hour. We're dependable, and we guarantee our work. I send in a team of four people who are in our uniforms; and they're trained, bonded, and insured. They bring everything they need to clean, and if a customer isn't satisfied, within 24 hours they go back and redo.

A regular customer—a woman in her eighties—called and complained that the "guy" [Steve] had done a lousy job of cleaning. In fact, no one had done a good job, except for Mary. The lady was unhappy! I talked to her. Come to find out, someone had given her a book on how to take charge of her life, and she was letting everyone have it today! I asked her if she wanted us to come back and reclean. She said no, it really wasn't that bad. By then, we were both laughing about it.

Another elderly woman, on seeing Steve, said to the supervisor, "Why do you have a guy here? They don't know how to clean!" Steve heard the comments and was upset. The woman watched him work the whole time and in the end grudgingly acknowledged that he had done a good job. On hearing this, I laughed. Isn't that a reversal? I mean, women are kind of used to hearing these comments; but he finds the stereotypes uncomfortable! The guys don't last long.

Pricing

The home and office cleaning markets were fairly price-sensitive. Kitty charged $20 per hour (per person) for first-time customers and about $16 per hour (per person) for repeat customers. Thus, a four-person team would cost a regular customer $64 per hour. Customers typically paid from $40 to $100 every two weeks. The average customer paid $65 every two weeks. And her best customer paid $100 every week.

Marketing

Kitty marketed the business. She did not clean except on the rare occasion when she overbooked a team. Kitty was proud of her 65 percent closure rate on telephone inquiries. She advertised her maid services on the radio and in fliers, newspapers, and the yellow pages. However, her cars were her best advertisement. As Kitty explained, "I park them near our office on one of the busiest streets in town; and although I do a great deal of print and other media advertising, more often than not it's the cars that bring people to us." Kitty also liked to play golf, and she said that she had "sold off the golf course." Kitty offered a free "home analysis." Her estimate hinged on the square footage of the house and the number of rooms, people, pets, knick-knacks, and smokers.

Commercial Cleaning

As the flier shown in Exhibit 3 indicates, the Ceiling Pro process removed "nicotine, smoke, cooking grease, soot, and dirt" from "acoustic tile and textured" ceilings. The addition of the Ceiling Pro dealership gave Kitty the opportunity to provide a specialized commercial cleaning service.

Employees

Kitty's "cleaning specialists" used professional cleaning procedures and were cross-trained in various jobs. They were also trained to follow standard job safety precautions (e.g., to use kneepads and rubber soled shoes and proper lifting techniques).

Home cleaning jobs varied. Kitty emphasized that "Cleaning is hard work!" A team could clean up to six homes a day. Hence, scheduling and travel time were important issues; and a maid's paid time might vary from 27 to 35 hours a week. Kitty paid her employees from the time they left the office until the time they returned, with the exception of their lunch time. As Kitty noted, "I pay a lot of drive time. Drive time adds about 10 percent to the cost of doing business." The scheduling problems increased when an employee called in sick or had car problems and had to be picked up at home by Kitty; she explained:

Monday. Chris is on vacation for the week. Janet calls from Rapid City (390 miles from Billings). Her car is broken down, and she can't get back to work. Karen calls in and quits. So we're short three people, and we have 13 homes to do today. Luckily none of them are very big. We'll get them all done by working late. Actually, that was the only Monday problem. Except for being short three people, we had to give up a home, which would have been an "initial," so that's losing about $2,000 to $2,500 a year. Just a simple little matter—that's a joke!

The employees were paid every two weeks. The cleaning specialists were paid a base rate of $4.50 per hour plus $0.25 per hour for every two weeks of perfect attendance plus $0.25 per hour for every week of complaint-free work. As Kitty noted, "If a complaint doesn't cost me anything, than it doesn't cost the employee anything." A training supervisor received $6.00 per hour.

Kitty hired her employees through help-wanted advertisements. She required references, which she checked; and she required prospective employees to bring their police records to the interview. However, privacy laws restricted the screening process. For example, the applicant was not required to divulge any misconduct (e.g., theft) or prior workers' compensation claims.

The employees ranged from 16 to 46 years of age. Most of them did not have a high school diploma. Some had worked as motel maids or in home health care. And, as Kitty explained, "These people don't think much of themselves. Society looks down on this kind of work." Kitty, however, was very supportive. For example, she had an employee that was preoccupied with getting a divorce. The employee's productivity had dropped, but Kitty's empathy for the person's situation kept her from terminating the individual. Kitty encouraged her employees to improve their skills (e.g., to complete high school) and to develop positive attitudes, modeled after her own. However, friction between employees was an ongoing problem.

Okay, it's Monday morning and we have eight regular homes to do and an "initial," which means they will become a "regular," so we have to do a really good job! Well, we have to do a good job anytime! But we do extra work in an "initial" home. We have eight people that show up for work. Janet says that her teeth are hurting her really badly, and I'm sure that they do. She is going to have them out next week, and she wants to go home. So that puts us with a really long day. Plus we have one brand new person, and one person has worked here for two days.

Tanya is having a problem. She does not want to work with Marla. She does not like the way that Marla is treating her. Marla is putting her down. Marla is 40 years old and is on work release for dealing drugs. Tanya is 16 years old and is a high school dropout. I think Tanya has a very valid point. So I bring Tanya and Marla together to talk things out. This leaves two teams waiting for them because they were both on the same team and now the teams have to be reorganized. We sit down and talk, and they get a few things straightened out. Then we agree to finish the conversation later tonight, which we do. Okay, that's one Monday morning.

It's Monday morning, and we have two teams. We normally have this day off. (Every other Monday is usually a day off.) I have scheduled both teams to work, so nobody is very happy. Everybody is pretty grumpy, and they have really hard jobs to do today. They have some houses that are really, really, really, really dirty!

I'm sending Tanya with Chris because of Tanya's attitude. Chris won't put up with it. Chris calls me later and tells me what's going on with Tanya. I asked Chris if she wants me to come get Tanya, send her home, and fire her. I'm sick of Tanya. Chris says she'll work with her that day.

I send Angie with Stacey's team. Angie is Chris's daughter and usually is on either Chris's or Mary's team. She doesn't smoke. The rest of the team smokes. Their attitude seems to be that you're sending her with us to check up on us. Angie seems to think I'm punishing her.

Stacey calls me about 3:00 P.M., calling Angie "that girl." Stacey says Angie doesn't know how to work and that the other two people on the team agreed that all she does is hang around and that she did a lousy job on her bathroom. Before the conversation was over, Stacey admitted that it was the worst bathroom that we have ever done. It was a two-hour shower. Stacey said that it had probably not been cleaned in the five years since the wife had died. I told her that I would come up and check Angie's work.

Needless to say, there is a big screw-up when Chris comes in. Chris is the training supervisor. I always tell her when we're having problems with somebody, and I tell her about Angie's shower. Then I go out to check the home. Chris waits at the office for her daughter.

When we return to the office, Chris—in front of everybody—lights into Stacey for the way she'd treated Angie. So now we have a major battle on our hands. Stacey is screaming back, and I am sitting there dumbfounded and wondering what do I do now. Stacey is quitting. Chris is screaming, and I pull them into another room. It is 6:00 P.M., but we start talking things over.

Kitty continued with several other employee-related incidents:

Stacey has been very angry for the last month. She thinks that she is being picked on, so she was picking on Chris's daughter. I told Chris that she was out of line, that we needed to sit down and talk about it and not yell. Stacey's still yelling. I yell at Stacey to quit yelling and have to apologize. Stacey wants to just walk out and leave, and it's one of the biggest messes I've ever been in in my life. Later, Chris apologizes for blowing up at Stacey in front of everyone. Angie comes in and talks to Stacey, and they straighten things out. It was a comedy of errors with one misunderstanding after another on everyone's part. Finally, by 7:30 P.M. we seemed to have talked it all out. That was today!"

Tanya has a 5:30 P.M. nail appointment that I told her I hoped that she got to. She is telling Chris that I said she would be at her 5:30 appointment, which is not what I said. And I'm out of town.

Tanya refused to do the last home because of her nail appointment. So I have a homeowner who is probably furious with me. I haven't called her today to find out how mad she is, because I haven't had time to call. She was a last-minute add-on. I had told her that we were trying to work her in, but I had also called her back and told her that we would work her in.

So do I fire Tanya for refusing to work and for having a lousy attitude at the last home because she thought she was going to be late for her nail appointment? She says she's being made the scapegoat because none of them wanted to do the last house. I wish I knew the answers in these situations. So we had a really scrumptious day!"

Kitty's training supervisor had been with her for nearly three years; but most of her employees tended to leave within a few weeks to three months. (The business mailed an average of fifty W-2 forms every year.) Exit interviews showed that people left for a variety of reasons. Some left for a better job. Others said that they could make more money on welfare. Some did not want to work anymore, while others said the work was too hard or their boyfriend did not want them to work. Finally, as Kitty explained, "You can't pay day care and work as a maid. This is a pass-through job."

KITTY'S COMPETITORS

The home cleaning market in Billings was serviced by six professional maid services. Kitty's Maids was the dominant maid service with about 30 percent of the market. Kitty's two largest competitors each held market shares of about 17 percent. However, there were also many "shadow" competitors, generally individuals or members of a family. They had relatively few customers, and they undercut Kitty's price by 50 to 60 percent. Since the same people cleaned the place every time, they offered a sense of privacy and security and a continuity of service that the maid services could not match. Some also offered additional services (e.g., ironing, laundry, and nanny services).

These "shadow" competitors were variously obligated by law to pay many of the same income- and payroll-related assessments that the maid services had to pay (e.g., withholding for income taxes, Social Security taxes, and workers' compensation insurance premiums). Yet they seldom paid these charges, allowing them to price their services for less. They and their employers ran some risk of being caught, but the risks were low. As Kitty noted, "The playing field isn't level." But as the flier in Exhibit 3 indicates, Kitty was striking back against these "independent housekeepers."

As Kitty explained, "The Zoe Baird affair was one of the best things that ever happened to me. Ever since then, one of the first things that people ask me is, 'Do you pay the taxes?' " [Ms. Baird, President Clinton's first choice for attorney general, lost her chance at the top Justice Department job after it was revealed that she and her husband had hired an illegal immigrant to provide live-in child care and had not paid Social Security taxes for the woman and her husband, who was the family's driver.] As Kitty liked to say, "If Zoe Baird had been our customer, she would have been attorney general today!"

THE WORKERS' COMPENSATION INSURANCE SITUATION

Workers' compensation insurance was a state-mandated insurance requirement that provided wage loss and medical benefits to employees injured on the job. In addition, it protected employers from legal action for damages from work-related injuries suffered by their employees. Neither general liability nor health and accident insurance policies could be substituted for workers' compensation insurance.

The state required all employers to cover their full-time, part-time, seasonal, or occasional employees with workers' compensation insurance. Kitty said that individual homeowners that hired "independent housekeepers" were obligated to pay the state a minimum of $194 per year or a percentage of the wages paid, whichever was more.

Employees were first classified according to an occupational-risk code. Then, the employer paid a premium that was based on: (1) a legislated base rate for each occupational-risk code; (2) an additional premium or discount based on the employer's safety record over the last three years; and (3) a volume discount based on the employer's total premium payment.

Kitty's Premiums

Kitty's Maids was in a relatively costly occupational-risk code. Maids did a lot of bending and lifting, which in some cases led to medical and loss-of-work claims. Unfortunately, Kitty's cleaning specialists had filed several claims, and Kitty's insurance premiums had risen from 4.7 percent of total wages to 17.4 percent in the last 4 1/2 years. Recently, Kitty had been told that the premium would go to 29.1 percent in July, and the July premium had to be paid by June 1.

Given the labor-intensive nature of the business, the 24.4 percent increase (from 4.7 to 29.1 percent) was equivalent to a 10 percent increase in total cost. Moreover, Kitty's highest claims had occurred last year, and on the three-year moving average system of figuring costs, last year would not be dropped from the calculations for another two years.

Worker Exploitation of the Claims System

Montana's workers' compensation insurance program had been plagued by worker exploitation. Some claims were difficult to disprove, and state officials did little to dispute them. In early May, the local newspaper, the *Billings Gazette*, had run a story on the situation and had featured Kitty's business. During the last three years, a total of $31,000 in claims had been filed by Kitty's employees. Kitty had disputed three in particular, including:

- $4,000 in disability payments and $7,000 in medical bills for a 37-year-old employee who hit her elbow on a towel rack.
- $500 in disability payments and $3,000 in medical bills for an employee who had surgery for carpal tunnel syndrome after three weeks on the job.
- $15,000 in disability and medical payments to an employee who claimed she bruised her lower back when she threw a bag of garbage over her shoulder.

In the first instance, workers' compensation officials agreed that they could have disputed the claim; but they argued that it would have cost $5,000 to $7,000 to dispute the $11,000 claim in court and they chose to pay it—so Kitty pays. In the second instance, Kitty learned that by law the last employer is responsible for the claim—so Kitty pays. In the last instance, Kitty was told that the employee was "an accident waiting to happen." Apparently, state officials felt that the claim may have been fraudulent but chose not to dispute it—so Kitty pays. Workers' compensation officials were reluctant to challenge the medical judgments of doctors, and some people felt that a few doctors and lawyers may have been taking advantage of the workers' compensation process for their own financial ends.

The filing of a fraudulent claim was a criminal offense. However, the program was designed to provide—without regard to fault—wage loss and medical benefits to workers suffering from a work-related injury or occupational disease.

Over the last year, Kitty had complained to various state officials and legislative representatives. She had met with the state director of workers' compensation, the chair of the worker's compensation board of directors, and the governor. While people were generally sympathetic, they did not and perhaps could not provide any relief. Their suggestion to Kitty was, "Close your business. You cannot pay these rates." Kitty felt she was caught in a web of bureaucratic insensitivity and irresponsibility.

In Kitty's view, the intent of the workers' compensation legislation was being subverted by the administrative process. Even worse, the administrative process was jeopardizing the existence of the businesses and the jobs that the legislation was intended to protect and encourage. Kitty was not alone in her feelings.

Legislative Change

During the last session of the Montana Legislature, several bills had been passed to improve Montana's troubled workers' compensation fund, which had been overwhelmed by rising costs. Employers were complaining about rising premiums, and employees were complaining about unsafe work practices. Both were complaining about poor service.

Historically, the administration of the workers' compensation program had tended to be reactive rather than proactive. As a result, businesses had not dealt aggressively with safety issues. In the event of an accident, medical assistance was given to the injured worker, the accident was investigated, the workers' compensation claim was processed, and the matter was closed. However, Kitty said the accident was investigated only by the attending physician. The employer could find out what disability and medical payments had been awarded but only after the fact and only if the employer called the state agency that administered workers' compensation and asked for the information.

The new laws required every employer to establish, implement, and maintain educational safety programs that met specified standards (e.g., regarding general employee safety, job safety training, refresher training, and periodic self-inspection). The intent of the new legislation was to make employers and employees more accountable for safety in the workplace. Kitty had asked for government help twice. The first time she was told to be more careful in hiring people and was given some hiring guidelines. The second time she received no further guidance.

Historically, the administration of the workers' compensation program had also been relatively lax on the investigation and substantiation of claims. The new laws tightened these controls, and the Department of Justice aggressively pursued their enforcement. The raids, prosecutions, and convictions received extensive media coverage. The incentive to file a fraudulent claim was said to be dropping rapidly.

While it would take some time to assess the effects of the new legislation, the initial reactions were positive. Although Kitty's efforts and the efforts of others seemed to be paying off, there was no retroactive compensation for any employer.

Using a Professional Employer Organization (PEO)

Kitty had recently received a promotional booklet from a human resources management firm with branches in several states. It outlined the services provided by a relatively new and rapidly growing type of business called a professional employer organization (PEO).

A PEO could contract with Kitty to do her payroll, meet all her federal and state withholding requirements (i.e., Social Security, unemployment, and workers' compensation), provide her and her employees with benefits (e.g., medical, dental, and retirement), and provide a variety of human resource functions (e.g., employee safety training). The PEO offered a menu of services, and Kitty could choose those that best met her needs. Kitty could see several potential benefits:

1. A PEO would pay her employees. It would also pay her federal and state withholding obligations and prepare her employees' W-2 statements. Finally, it would be accountable to the various regulatory agencies for everything it did. In turn, Kitty would write one check each pay period to the PEO. The cost of this service would be 5 percent of the payroll plus a setup fee of $50 per person. Kitty would have to supply the PEO with each employee's hours and wage rates every pay period. Kitty would still be able to hire and fire employees and direct their activities. Thus, a PEO would allow her to spend more time on developing her business, which could lead to an increase in revenues and perhaps a reduction in costs.

2. A PEO would significantly reduce her workers' compensation premiums. The PEO's premium—7 percent—was much lower than Kitty's premium, which would rise to 29.1 percent in July.

3. A PEO could provide benefits to Kitty and her employees that Kitty was unable to provide (e.g., medical and dental). The PEO would also provide an employee's manual, a safety manual, and guidance on safety and other issues.
4. A PEO would be able to advise Kitty on regulatory changes and her obligations under, for example, the Occupational Safety and Health Act, the Fair Labors Standards Act, the Americans with Disabilities Act, and the Family Medical Leave Act.

Kitty wanted to think about the proposal. She was also concerned about retaining a reputable firm. The representative of the PEO that had contacted her was polite and persuasive, but she wanted to see what other firms had to offer and what the licensing authorities in Montana might have to say about these firms.

A year ago, a workers' compensation official had told Kitty that PEOs were illegal in Montana and that, if she contracted with a PEO, the state could sue her. More recently, the chair of the workers' compensation board of directors had told her that she could legally contract with a PEO. There seemed to be mixed views on the legality of contracting with a PEO in Montana. As Kitty reflected on these developments, it seemed to her that every opportunity raised a new set of problems.

SOME BUSINESS OPTIONS

As Kitty discussed her situation with different people, she found that they freely dispensed advice, but had no real answers. At one extreme was Barbara Robbins, with her suggestions for a complete strategic evaluation. At the other were those who thought she should sell the business.

At one point, Kitty called Dave Krueger, the director of Montana Business Connections at Montana State University in Billings, and asked for some help with her business. Dave directed her to a management professor, who in turn suggested that Kitty's Maids might make a good case study.

The case was tested in several classes, ranging from introduction to management classes to information systems classes to business policy classes. Most of the students were nontraditional students and some were familiar with her business. After the classes had discussed the case, Kitty met with the students and discussed the issues. Some results are presented below.

The Real Estate Market

A student who was a realtor suggested that Kitty target the real estate market. New homes needed to be cleaned before they could be sold. There was also the resale market. Buyers wanted to move into clean homes. They were not interested in moving into or cleaning up someone else's mess. A clean home generally meant a clean bathroom(s), a clean kitchen, and clean windows. At times, the carpets and/or draperies needed cleaning, or the prior occupant's debris had to be removed. Sometimes the grass needed mowing, the flower beds needed weeding, and the shrubs needed trimming. While Kitty did not provide many of these services, she could engage reputable people to perform them; and a job well-done might lead to a permanent cleaning arrangement with the new occupant.

The price for providing such services was said to range from $200 to $1,500. For several reasons, the market was less price-sensitive as the value of the property increased. First, the cost of cleaning was a one-time charge. Second, employers often paid for an employee's cost of moving, including the cost of cleaning. Third, few people wanted to move into someone else's dirty house or clean it themselves. Finally, the cleaning cost was a relatively minor expense when compared to the closing costs, which might range from $2,000 to $5,000, and the down payment, which might range from $5,000 to $30,000.

Although the turnover in housing was both seasonal and cyclical, local real estate records indicated that single-family residential closings had risen from 1,200 to 2,700 over the last four years. New home completions had risen from 140 to 410 over the same period. The supply of houses was quite limited, and the cost of housing was rising. Unemployment levels in the general area hovered at 4 percent compared to the national average of about 6.5 percent.

The Commercial Market

A student who had been responsible for a night janitorial team at the airport in Laramie, Wyoming, suggested that Kitty bid for janitorial contracts with public service organizations, such as city, county, or federal government offices, hospitals, libraries, and schools. Reductions in funding were encouraging many of these organizations to operate more efficiently. Contracting for selected services was one way to reduce costs.

Kitty was not receptive to the suggestion. Her response was, "That's night work, and I'm working 50 to 60 hours a week now." Someone suggested that she could hire a night supervisor or perhaps promote her training supervisor. To the last suggestion, Kitty's response was, "My training supervisor doesn't want any more responsibility." Kitty also said that she did not have the equipment to do the night work (e.g., floor polishers, etc.) and that commercial cleaners had the same problems with employee turnover that she had. The questions continued until finally Kitty said, "I don't want to go down the learning curve in the commercial market! I want to grow the Maids! I don't want to start a new business!"

The Home Cleaning Market

Kitty asked, "Why do people hire maids? Is it to save time? To avoid cleaning? To acquire status? How can I market maid services to upper-income people (e.g., dentists, doctors, and lawyers)?" In response, a student suggested that she needed to do some market survey research; but the person cautioned that the survey design was critical. The survey design had to be statistically valid, and the survey had to respect people's civil rights. (Market demographics for Yellowstone County are shown in Exhibit 4).

Another student also noted that the commercial market was a composite of many different market segments. For example, Kitty was already cleaning two small offices. Why not target, say, small professional offices as a means of entering the upper-income home cleaning market? The yellow pages indicated that there were more than 80 dentists, 250 physicians and surgeons, and 320 lawyers in Billings. Alternatively, why not target successful small businesses as a means of entering the upper-income home cleaning market?

Employee Turnover

Several people thought that the work teams were a good idea but perhaps Kitty was not realizing their full motivational potential. Granted, they were cleaning up to six homes a day and the quality of the work was good; but the turnover must be

EXHIBIT 4   Market Demographics—Yellowstone County, Montana

Population	Number	Percent of total
Billings	83,600	70.8%
Yellowstone County	118,000	
Household Income (breakdown #1)		
<$40,000	32,900	73.5%
$40,000–$60,000	7,600	17.0%
$60,000–$75,000	2,100	4.6%
>$75,000	2,200	4.9%
	44,800	
Household Income (breakdown #2)		
<$35,000	29,500	65.8%
$35,000–$50,000	8,100	18.1%
$50,000–75,000	5,000	11.2%
>$75,000	2,200	4.9%
	44,800	
Employment by Occupation		
Administrative/managerial	6,900	
Professional	7,000	
Elderly (number of households headed by elderly)		
60–64 years of age	4,600	
65–74	8,100	
75+	5,100	

Source: Billings Chamber of Commerce and U.S. Census data.

devastating. However, they were not specific on what should be done, although there was some reference to "need satisfaction."

It was also suggested that Kitty give more thought to incentive compensation to increase worker productivity and retention as well as the quality of service. One student, who was retraining after an industrial accident, said, "Good people won't stay with you for $5.00 an hour." Another said that she made $12.00 per hour cleaning a dentist's office, but she had been a dental assistant and knew how to handle the equipment and waste.

Market Image

On a different tack, one student thought that the business lacked a credible, distinctive image. He argued that the yellow cars were ugly, the slogan on Kitty's business card was nonsensical ["We give YOU (you mean "we charge YOU for"?) Time!"], and the Maids was just a high-cost business in a highly competitive market (see Exhibit 5). Kitty laughed and replied, "Most men think the cars are ugly! Women just want them in the driveway—ugly or not!" A lady who heard the conversation argued that Fred's comment was not only tacky but ignorant. She liked the yellow cars! She said that Kitty *was* giving people time! She agreed with Kitty's statement, "To walk into a clean house after you've been at work all day—that really feels good!"

EXHIBIT 5   Kitty's Maids Stationery and Business Card

Make Your Home Sparkle & Shine.

"We Give You Time!"

Make Your Home Sparkle & Shine.

"We Give You Time!"

Kitty Pugh
1513 - 14th Street West
Billings, Montana 59102
256-1400

Professional Home
Cleaning
BONDED & INSURED

Clean Kitchen Counters & Sinks
Damp Wipe Cabinet Doors
Load Dishwasher
Clean Outside of All Appliances
Wash Kitchen & Entry Floors
Clean & Disinfect Tubs & Showers
Clean & Disinfect Stools & Sinks
Wash Bathroom Floors & Counters
Dust Mop Hard Surface Floors
Vacuum Rugs & Carpeting
Vacuum Carpeted Stairs
Vacuum Upholstered Furniture
Remove Cobwebs
Clean Edges & Corners
Dust Baseboards
Dust Window Sills & Door Ledges
Dust Furniture
Dust Books & Knickknacks
Dust Hanging Pictures & Clean Mirrors
Pick Up & Straighten Up
Empty Trash

Kitty Pugh
1513 - 14th Street West
Billings, Montana 59102
256-1400

Database Management

A student majoring in information services said that Kitty needed a database management system to monitor and selectively access customer profiles and needs. This would enable her to better serve her existing clientele and to develop new clients. Kitty's response was that she "hates sitting at computers!" (Kitty had owned a computer for six years, but it was used primarily by a part-time office assistant.) Kitty had also said earlier that she did not know how much each customer cost her. With 70 to 75 regular customers and a desire to grow the business, Kitty admitted that a database management system might be a good idea; but she also said the benefits were unclear.

THE NEXT FEW MONTHS

Kitty found the students' suggestions somewhat frustrating and lacking in specifics. For example, it was all very well to suggest that she develop a database management system, but Kitty found herself responding to such advice by saying, "Fine, I agree! Now, how do I do it? Where do I start?" Managing the business was emotionally and physically exhausting, and there was little time for learning new skills. But Kitty was not a quitter, and by mid-May she was back on the offensive. Her new stationery and cards (Exhibit 5) were out, and she appeared buoyant.

Kitty's attention was focused on reducing the workers' compensation premiums that were, in her words, "taking everything I have." In fact, on May 17 she was going to Helena, the state capital, to meet again with workers' compensation officials. This time she was taking a bag of garbage similar to the one that had produced the $15,000 in disability and medical payments. The employee had stated that she had bruised her lower back when she threw a bag of garbage over her shoulder. The employee claimed that, unbeknownst to her, the bag of garbage had contained boards. Kitty had since learned that the "boards" in question were computer control modules (panels), which weighed perhaps 1 to 2 pounds apiece! The bags themselves, which contained discarded paper products, typically weighed only 2 or 3 pounds.

In addition, when she returned from Helena, Kitty was going to look into using a PEO. Finally, Barbara Robbins had called two days ago to ask how things were going. She had asked Kitty, "Have you given any more thought to the strategic issues that we discussed sometime ago?" Kitty had responded, "Yes, I have. Where do I start?" In response, Barbara had said, "There are no easy solutions. It's going to take a lot of your time, and it's going to be a long process."

Kitty reflected on the Tanya situation:

Tanya called at 8:45 this morning. She said she was sick, and she wouldn't be in today. I said, "Tanya, it's Friday; and your friends have the day off from school! Right?" She said no, she was sick. I didn't believe her, so I told her to get to work or she was not working here any more. She was here in 20 minutes, and she didn't seem to be sick! They'll push you as far as they can, but at some point you have to draw a line! But it's hard to know where to draw the line and how to get them to cooperate.

And so it went:

Tanya didn't come because her back was hurting. She didn't call in until 8:50 A.M. . . . Tanya didn't come in because she had a court date. She called in at 7:15 A.M. . . . Over the last six weeks, Tanya was absent four full days and three half days. One day, Tanya came to work, but I didn't send her out with the teams. I told her to make up her mind—either she works every day all day or she doesn't have a job. She told me I was extremely unfair. I told her to call me by 2:00 P.M. that afternoon with her decision. She never called back.

I found out later that her mother is thinking about taking me to court because Tanya had been with me for more than three months and I didn't have a good reason to fire her. My point of view is that I didn't fire her. But I worry a lot about the legalities because you hear horror stories, and once you've been through "work comp" like I have, you know that those horror stories are really true. So I may end up in court over this. I hope not, but it's a possibility.

Later, in looking back on these experiences, Kitty had these thoughts:

Management is about listening, working things out. You talk with employees individually, and then you talk with them together. No one has all the necessary skills. You learn to work things out! I tell my teams, "Mistakes are something you learn from. What are we learning?" I try to learn from every complaint and compliment from clients and employees. I want to grow personally too!

BAMA PIE, LIMITED

Raymond E. Belford, *Oklahoma City University*

Bama Pie, Limited's phenomenal growth over the past 24 years of its 65-year history was due directly to the growth of its major customer, McDonald's, and a fanatical commitment to quality. As the single-source supplier of pies to McDonald's U.S. operations, Bama was testimony to how a small, aggressive, and creative company could succeed competing with much larger organizations. By providing top-quality pie products and "never missing an order," Bama had been able to expand its core pie business by landing 50 percent of McDonald's oven-ready, prebaked frozen biscuit needs. Its new role as a supplier of McDonald's breakfast biscuit requirements was expected to allow Bama to increase total sales to approximately $100 million in 1992. Bama Pie's actual financial information was closely guarded since it was a privately held, family-owned limited partnership; the company's CEO was 38-year-old Paula Marshall-Chapman, who had succeeded her father and grandfather as head of the business.

Bama Pie produced more than 1 million pies per day from facilities in Tulsa, Oklahoma, for McDonald's. In 1968, the firm was producing only 500 pies per day. In 1991, the company completed a $38 million facility in Tulsa to produce the biscuits for McDonald's, arranging the bank financing within about six weeks. The new facility, in early 1992, was producing more than 120,000 biscuits per hour.

Other major customers included Pizza Hut (for which Bama was producing approximately 25 percent of its bread stick requirements), TCBY, and Braum's (an Oklahoma-based ice cream chain).

The company, in an effort to lessen its dependence on McDonald's, had begun seeking business with other major fast-food and convenience food companies. In 1992, more than 70 percent of Bama's business was with McDonald's. Less than 10 percent of the company's revenues came from products carrying the Bama Pie brand, the best-known of which was a 3-inch pecan pie. Of the McDonald's business, about

EXHIBIT 1   Bama Pie, Ltd., Mission Statement

Bama Pie, Ltd., is an international company in business to develop, produce, and market fresh, frozen, and ready-to-prepare food products generally described as convenience foods, snacks, and other bakery items. We shall serve our products to food service and retail customers and are dedicated to developing new markets as well as serving our major customer, McDonald's. All our products will conform to specific requirements which will ensure our name represents QUALITY to ourselves, our customers, and our suppliers. This will provide continued growth and a fair return to the partners on their investment.

We shall continue to operate as a privately held and fiscally responsible company, and shall be oriented to serving our customer's needs.

In support of this, we are committed to:

• Being flexible and responsive to our customers.
• Ensuring that product requirements are adhered to throughout our processes.
• Maintaining a high degree of employee motivation by providing an environment of equal opportunity, fair treatment, and growth opportunities. This includes fair and equitable compensation, involvement, recognition, and rewards.
• Operating and establishing "partnership relationships" with our suppliers.
• Providing management with information and controls which empowers the planning and decision-making process.
• Being a "Corporate Good Citizen" by active and responsible involvement in our community.

4 percent was exported to McDonald's operations in Hong Kong and Taiwan. In early 1992, Bama was working toward establishing a joint venture in Hong Kong to provide pies to McDonald's in Hong Kong, the People's Republic of China, and Taiwan. Bama also had a licensing arrangement in Canada with a Canadian baker that provided pies to McDonald's Canadian operations.

The firm considered itself responsible for McDonald's pies worldwide. Marshall-Chapman's father, Paul Marshall, began providing technical assistance to McDonald's in the early days as he, Ray Kroc (McDonald's founder), and Fred Turner (early president of McDonald's) worked together. The technical assistance in helping establish local bakeries in McDonald's global enterprise had always been provided at no cost to McDonald's. "We see it as part of our service," said Marshall-Chapman.

In 1991, Bama competed in the national Baldrige awards for quality and made the fourth cut. The companies that reached the fifth cut were chosen for the prestigious award. The company was under consideration in 1992 for the award. Marshall-Chapman was named Quality Fanatic of the Year in 1989 by Philip Crosby of the Quality College.

The word most often heard around Bama Pie headquarters in Tulsa was *quality*. Paula Marshall-Chapman had attended numerous quality conferences and had spoken to international groups about the company's commitment to quality. The company had dropped its traditional mission statement (see Exhibit 1) in favor of a diagram depicting "Bama's Quality Circle" (see Exhibit 2). According to Marshall-Chapman, "We had a very nice mission statement of a traditional nature—very wordy, very flowery, like most progressive companies. If you've read most mission statements, they tend to be written for Wall Street or people outside the organization. We felt the mission should be written for our employees. Our Quality Circle is very simple and keeps us focused."

EXHIBIT 2   Bama's Quality Circle

BUZZINGS

The Busy B's • Bama Pie Ltd. • BTC • Bama Pailet • Base Inc. • Bama Sweets • Bama Foods • January 1992

BAMA'S QUALITY CIRCLE	OUR QUALITY FUTURE

OUR QUALITY FUTURE

1991 was a transition year for our Quality culture. You may have not been aware it was because "Quality" is a way of life at Bama—but subtle changes have been occurring. As a company, in our sixth year involved with the Quality process, our needs are very different. We have matured with Crosby's principles and now is the time to adopt our own values. In 1992 we will be building a solid quality foundation based on these principles.

➤ People
➤ Products
➤ Services
➤ Profits
➤ Continuous Improvement

Our mission is to consistently strive to improve all processes, through continuous improvement, to ensure total customer satisfaction.

—Paula Marshall-Chapman

The company also had a values statement (Exhibit 3) that reinforced "quality as a way of life" at Bama. The company's quality statement was read before every meeting held in the company. "It helps keep us focused," Marshall-Chapman explained.

COMPANY HISTORY

The origins of Bama Pie dated back to 1927 when Henry C. Marshall decided to utilize the pie-baking talents of his wife, Cornelia Alabama Marshall (who went by the name Bama), to provide employment for himself after a lengthy period of being out of work. Bama Marshall began baking pies for the lunch counter at the Woolworth's in Dallas. Her talents created a market for her pies that topped 75 per day (including take-home purchases), and the local owner of Woolworth's expanded his lunch counter to 75 stools to handle customer volume.

Bama was soon baking up to 300 pies per day for Woolworth's, and business at the lunch counter was booming. Bama was spending so much time at her work, Henry began to think she was being unfaithful to him and was "carrying on" with the owner of the Woolworth's. He sent his son, Paul, down to "spy" on Bama. When Paul reported back that the reason the owner "liked Mama so much is because of the pies she was making," Henry came up with an idea.

The following passage from *A Piece of the Pie* by Paul Marshall describes the event:[1]

---

[1] Paul Marshall with Brian and Sandy Miller, *A Piece of the Pie* (Tulsa: Walsworth Press, 1987).

EXHIBIT 3   The Bama Pie Values Statement

Customers

Bama will provide our customers with products and services that conform to their requirements and deliver them on time, at a competitive price.

Suppliers

Bama will encourage open and honest communication with our "partners" and reward those who have adopted and demonstrated use of the continuous improvement process. We will also encourage the sharing of ideas.

Passion

Bama will conduct our business with integrity and professionalism and with a strategy of continuous improvement. This will provide increased profits and create worldwide awareness of our products. We will continue to focus on being a "Corporate Good Citizen" by being active in our community.

Quality

Products and Services

Product quality and product safety will be the responsibility of every employee. We will sell quality products and services at a fair value. We will anticipate and react to our customers' needs. We will take pride in all products and services which we perform.

People

Bama will attract result-oriented people, provide a safe work environment, operate as an equal opportunity employer, focus on employee development and retention, develop mutual trust and respect for each other, and support promotion from within. We will inspire new ideas and innovation by creating the environment whereby we create employee satisfaction.

Through continuous improvement our name will represent QUALITY to our customers, our suppliers, and ourselves. We believe that if we live by these values we will establish the Bama Companies as world class and will achieve our long-range objectives.

I heard Papa ask Mama something that made me cringe.

"Blanchie, how are things at Woolworth's?"

That question sounded innocent enough, but I knew Papa was fishing for an answer that would drive him into the rage which he had been holding in for weeks. (Paul still thought his father believed his mother was having an affair.) I looked over at Mama and saw her relaxed manner. She had no idea what was happening with Papa.

"I'm working harder these days, that's for sure. A man from the head office came down this week."

She stopped talking there. I guess she wanted to see if Papa was interested in her news or just making conversation.

Papa looked over at Mama and said, "So?"

"So he told me what a good job I was doing and how he wished more employees worked as well as I did. Then he asked me if I would be willing to move to Amarillo and be in charge of the lunch counter at the new store there."

I got even more worried right then. Papa didn't say anything right at first. I must have held my breath for at least 10 minutes waiting for Papa to blow.

But he never did. When he finally broke the silence, he spoke in a soft voice. "Blanchie, if you can make pies for Mr. Tanner to sell, why can't you make pies for me to sell?"

Mama looked over at him, surprised like.

"What do you mean?" she asked.

"Just that. If Mr. Tanner can make money on your pies, why can't we? I've been thinking about this for weeks now. I'm not talking foolishness. You make some pies and I'll carry them around the area here and sell them."

Mama just rolled her head back, shut her eyes, and moaned a sigh. It was more like she was tired than anything else.

Papa didn't pay her any mind. He just kept on talking. "I've been looking at those Hubig pies in the stores. They make the smaller seven-inch pies thin so they look larger. They could cost a quarter of what the big nine-inch family pies cost," Papa's voice was getting stronger. He wasn't looking at Mama anymore, but looking out above the rooftops across the street.

"I've checked on prices. Dried fruit runs about 5 cents a pound and that's the most expensive part of the pie. How many pies could you make with a pound of dried fruit?"

Mama didn't answer. Papa didn't seem to be expecting an answer, either, because he just kept talking and even started gesturing with his arms, swinging this way and that.

"Your pies taste a hundred times better than Hubig's. Why, before long we'll be selling pies all over Dallas, then the whole country."

Papa stopped suddenly and turned to Mama who was wilted next to him. I think she must have been wishing he'd calm down and start talking about the smell of fresh cut grass or something.

"I've even come up with a name for the company." It was too dark to tell, but his voice sounded like there must have been a gleam in his eyes.

"Now you know I've always called you Blanchie because I didn't like Cornelia Alabama, or even 'Bama' like your family called you. But for a company, 'Bama' is just fine. In fact, I like it real good. 'The Bama Pie Company,' how does that sound Blanchie?"

I couldn't see Mama right then, but hearing the swing squeaking, I figured she sat up in her seat before she answered Papa.

"Well, I . . . "

I think Mama was surprised at how excited Papa was at the idea of starting a business selling her pies. From hearing her hesitate, I knew Papa would be selling Mama's pies before long.

"The idea sounds all right. But we don't have much of a place to make pies or enough pans and equipment. We . . . "

"Don't worry about a thing, Blanchie. Tell me what you need and I'll get it for you."

"Well, I'll have to think about it for a while. I . . . "

"Fine," Papa said. "We'll start tomorrow."

Thus, the Bama Pie Company was born, according to Paul Marshall's recounting of the event. The next day, Henry took $1.67 and went out to obtain what was needed. He talked a bakery goods supplier into granting credit with the $1.67 paid down on an order that totaled more than $25. He obtained the rest of what was needed on credit from the grocery store where the family had shopped and was known. That evening, the family pitched in to make pies, and the following day, Henry set out to sell the first Bama Pies. The first day's sales far exceeded expectations, and the company began to grow.

Soon the sales route had expanded to the delivery of two baskets of pies per day. When sales were slow, Henry Marshall would walk farther and extend the route until all the pies were sold each day. One day, as evening was approaching and he had a few pies left, he spotted a grocery store across the street from where he was. He approached the grocer and asked if he could leave the pies on consignment, promising to service the store daily with fresh products. The grocer agreed and thus began a new phase; Bama Pie became a wholesale distributor.

Soon a car was purchased and modified to carry the pies; and the company established routes in the Dallas area. All the Marshall children became involved in the business, including Paul. The company tried to expand into Waco in 1931, but was unsuccessful because of the Depression.

In the mid-1930s, Paul Marshall observed the operation of Bama's major competitor, Hubig Pies. He was overwhelmed with the modern, high-volume, machine-aided production. Seeing the operation made him aware of how small and old-fashioned Bama was. He attempted to convince his father of the need to purchase new equipment, but to no avail. The company continued to produce pies in a highly labor-intensive process. Paul's dream had become bigger than his father's; he saw the need to change to high-volume, machine-production methods as the way to expand the company. This conflict became a source of disagreement over the years between Paul and his father.

During the next few years, the older Marshall children opened other Bama Pie operations, including one in Oklahoma City started by Paul's sister Grace and her husband. In a move for independence, Paul moved to Oklahoma City and began working for his sister as a route salesman. It was in Oklahoma City that Paul met and eventually married Lilah Drake, who worked in the kitchen of the pie company. Both had the dream of opening their own Bama Pie shop and looked toward Tulsa as a potential market; they began saving for the future.

In the meantime, Paul's brother, Henry, who had reopened the Bama Pie store in Waco, decided to leave the Waco operation and move to Tulsa. While Paul understood his dad's rule that whoever established a territory first had rights to it, he was disappointed that Tulsa would be taken. When Paul and Lilah discovered Henry was simply going to walk away from the Waco business, they decided to take over the Waco operation. Within a year, Waco was profitable and expanding. In January 1937, Paul's father told him his brother would like to return to Waco, which was closer to his wife's family. Paul and his brother agreed to trade operations, and on February 6, 1937, Paul and Lilah, with their new son John, arrived in Tulsa.

The company struggled through 1937, and a decision to buy a large quantity of new "soft wheat flour" from General Mills nearly did the company in. The new flour was developed for pies, but the formula worked best with baked pies, not the fried pies that made up the bulk of Bama's sales. After discovering the problem and restoring lost customer confidence, the company had grown to six drivers and 14 women assisting Lilah in the bakery by the spring of 1938.

The company continued to prosper as the United States entered World War II, and Paul was given a draft classification of 4-F (which exempted him from being called to duty) since the company was a major supplier to the military.

In December 1943, the owner of Mrs. Marshall's Pies offered to sell his company to Paul Marshall. Paul recounted the meeting in his book:

> "Paul, I just wanted to meet another damned fool named Marshall who was in the pie business."
>
> I laughed and decided I liked Archie Marshall.
>
> We talked shop for a while, then Archie asked. "Would you like to buy my business?"
>
> My eyes popped wide open. Who did he think I was, Rockefeller or something? I was almost embarrassed to answer him. But I wanted him to know who he was dealing with from the beginning. I wasn't going to play the high roller. "Archie," I said, "I couldn't buy the spare tire off of your Cadillac."
>
> Archie didn't look at me right then. He just swung his feet back and forth under the table and stared out the window for a few seconds. Then he turned to me and said, "I didn't ask you if you *could* buy my business. I asked you if you would *like* to buy my business."
>
> Well, it was a fact that I would love to have his business, but I didn't understand what he was talking about. "Sure, Archie, I'd like to have your business, but I don't have the kind of money you're looking for. I can tell you that right now."
>
> "I'll work that out," Archie said.

They worked out a deal, and Bama Pie Company acquired Mrs. Marshall's Pies. One of the major contributions of the acquisition was an understanding of quality.

Paul Marshall said, "The most valuable asset we acquired was a 10-cent calendar advertising Karo syrup. On that calendar was a phrase that became our slogan, 'Keep your eye on the key to success, QUALITY.' "

By the end of 1945, Bama Pies was a well-established and profitable operation. But over the next few years, the company was beset with major union organizing problems that left Paul Marshall with a bitter resentment of unions. He fought the union's attempt to unionize his company despite threats on his life and the members of his family. He endured beatings of his drivers, threatening calls at 2 AM, stink bombs that ruined products, smashed pies in the grocery stores, boycotts, and other forms of harassment.

He called national attention to his plight when he had a welder friend create a rotating track with a department store manikin fitted to it to put on the front of his bakery as a "counter-picket." He dressed the manikin in a suit and placed an American flag in its hands. The manikin moved continuously back and forth on a track above the street while the union's live picket walked back and forth below. Since the bakery was on heavily traveled U.S. Route 66, the counter-picket attracted national attention with photos appearing in *Life* and other magazines. One day a group of kids who had gathered to watch Duke (as the manikin was called) started calling the live union picket a "dummy." The union picket picked up a rock and threw it at one of the kids. This brought a barrage of rocks from the kids and he was driven off. That ended the picketing, but not the harassment.

As the union eroded Bama Pie's markets among grocery stores and hotel restaurants, Paul Marshall began to look for new markets immune from union pressures. At a Chicago bakery equipment auction in 1951, he encountered a refrigerated truck carrying frozen pies. In May 1953, he got into the frozen pie business when he contracted to provide pies for five new Howard Johnson's restaurants being constructed on the new Turner Turnpike linking Tulsa with Oklahoma City. Once in the frozen pie business, he quickly saw that the future of Bama Pies was in frozen pies—with frozen pies there were no stale pies to pick up, no more waste.

Bama supplied the Howard Johnson's restaurants until mid-1955, when Marshall was informed by the head office that Howard Johnson's was going to begin making its own pies. Bama Pie then trained its efforts on large supermarkets. By the late 1950s, the company was working on a frozen turnover fried pie that could be sold in restaurants. By the beginning of 1960, all the other Bama Pie operations owned and operated by Paul's brothers and sisters had gone out of business, leaving only the Tulsa operation.

Another major turning point for Bama Pies occurred in 1965 when Paul Marshall landed the account of Sandy's restaurant chain (later purchased by Hardee's). In his book, Paul describes the event as follows:

> I couldn't wait to get back to Tulsa so I could tell our employees about the orders we'd have coming in.
>
> For 30 miles I nearly broke my arm patting myself on the back for landing the Sandy's account. I thought over what we had said in our meeting and grinned to myself. Then suddenly the sobering truth of our agreement hit home.
>
> During my chat with Mr. Andres (president of Sandy's) he had pointed out all of the Sandy's locations on a wall map. And like some dunce, I was only thinking of the pies we would be selling to all those locations. The little red pins on the map were spread out over the midwest, from Arizona to Ohio. But I only saw inches between pins.
>
> The reality of what those pins meant hadn't registered on me at the time, but now it was hitting me full force. Our trucks would have to drive 100 to 500 miles between stops!

There wouldn't be any way my company could survive with shipping costs gobbling our profits.

By the time I was on the outskirts of Bloomington, I had come up with a plan to make it all work. I decided the only way to justify delivering pies to such spread-out markets was to acquire more fast-food customers and establish distribution points. The thought never occurred to me to call off the deal with Sandy's.

It was 11 o'clock when I reached Bloomington. The McDonald's hamburger store had just opened so, after I parked in their lot, I grabbed one of our sample frozen pies out of the dry-ice cooler in the trunk and then walked in and ordered coffee.

"You got any pie?" I asked the manager as he served my coffee.

"No, but I wish we did," he said.

Marshall discovered that individual McDonald's units were not allowed to make menu decisions and was told he needed to go to McDonald's headquarters in Chicago. He decided to make a cold call immediately and headed his car toward Chicago with his remaining frozen pies. Surprisingly, he was able to see the frozen-food buyer and arranged to leave some samples for a dinner of McDonald's executives that evening. He then headed back to Tulsa.

When he called to see how the pies fared, he was told they weren't bad, but were not what McDonald's was looking for. He convinced Al Bernardin, the McDonald's buyer, to allow him to attempt to develop a pie that McDonald's would want.

Bernardin told Marshall, "Well, Paul, we'd be willing to work with you on developing a good pie. But I'm certainly not going to promise anything. And I'll warn you, if you work for 10 years trying to come up with a pie that fits our needs, you still might not get the order."

The next attempt to make a pie that McDonald's would accept brought an unexpected response. The quality wasn't good enough. He was told the crust needed to be lighter and the apples needed to be sliced, rather than chipped.

"We want a quality product, not a cheap one. I promise you that we will pay the price for quality," Bernardin told him. Marshall was surprised that a low-priced, high-volume restaurant chain would be more interested in quality than price, but he was happy for the opportunity to develop the high-quality product McDonald's demanded.

For more than a year, Marshall traveled almost weekly between Tulsa and Chicago until he finally produced a product that McDonald's was satisfied with.

The pies were test-marketed in Joplin and Springfield, Missouri, and soon amounted to nearly 7 percent of each store's sales. Soon, Marshall was called to Chicago to meet with the top executives of McDonald's. To supply McDonald's more than 600 restaurants on a national basis would require a significant investment for Bama Pies, and Marshall was concerned about coming up with the $250,000 he estimated would be needed.

When Fred Turner, McDonald's president, asked him if he was ready to begin supplying McDonald's on a national basis, Marshall had to tell the truth and admit he probably couldn't.

In his book, he describes the event:

"How much money would you need to get ready to supply McDonald's?" Turner asked.

I was glad I had done some figuring on that question already. "It would cost us $250,000 to build a line that would produce 20,000 pies an hour."

"Can you get that kind of money?" he asked, his eyes never wavering from mine.

Mr. Turner was questioning me like a judge who wanted to know if I was guilty or not—there was no discussion called for.

"I don't know," I said, feeling weak in the pit of my stomach. I figured Mr. Turner was wondering why we Oklahoma hicks were wasting his time. I had hoped our meeting would be real casual, just friends sitting down to talk over what would be needed to make McDonald's pies. I wasn't prepared for the rapid-fire questions and piercing eyes of Mr. Turner.

"How long have you been doing business at your bank?" Mr. Turner asked.

"Probably 25 years or so," I replied, hoping he wasn't going to ask our credit limit.

"Do you owe them anything?"

"Not much. Our mortgage is paid down quite a bit."

"Fine," he said. "I'll send a couple of men down to Tulsa to talk with your banker and see if we can make this pie business work."

"Thank you, sir."

"What kind of contract would you like?" Mr. Turner asked.

"If we can't give you the quality and service you need, Mr. Turner, a contract won't help either of us. But if we can, we won't need one."

"I like your way of thinking, Paul," Mr. Turner said. He reached out and shook my hand, then Johnny's hand and marched out the door.

A couple of days later, two McDonald's executives visited Marshall's bank, and the next day one of the bank's officers called and said, "Paul, I understand you could use a quarter of a million dollars?"

Thus began a long-term relationship with McDonald's that allowed Bama Pies to grow along with McDonald's as one of its key suppliers. During the 1970s and 1980s, Paul and Lilah traveled worldwide with McDonald's officials as consultants to assist local bakers in supplying fruit pies for McDonald's far-flung global enterprise. In 1987, Bama Pies received an award for being a 20-year vendor to McDonald's.

PAULA MARSHALL-CHAPMAN

Paula Marshall-Chapman succeeded her father in 1985 as chief executive officer of the company and immediately made quality her top priority. "To be honest, we almost lost the account in the mid-80s because we had let our quality fall a bit as we struggled to keep up with our growth," Marshall-Chapman said. She said her father was ready to retire and was almost becoming a problem. "Someone would call from McDonald's about a problem, and he might tell them just what they could do with it. He really didn't relate to the younger technical staff that McDonald's was sending around. He might tell one of them that they didn't know anything about the pie business and that he was 'buddies with Ray Kroc and had been making pies since before they were in diapers.'"

"When I took over, I spent a lot of time just listening," she said.

Taking over the company was not an automatic thing for Marshall-Chapman—she had to earn her way to the top. Paula first joined the company in 1970; she recalled: "My ideas of going off to college were sidetracked when I was a senior in high school. I got pregnant. I first went to work in the thrift stores (Bama Pie's retail operation for picked up and damaged products) and began learning about the business. I learned how to meet and talk to customers, how to display merchandise, how I could increase sales by providing samples, and I also learned how much poor quality costs. We were selling pies for a nickel in the thrift store that could be sold for 50 cents if the product had not been damaged."

After a few years, Paula moved to the central office and learned how to manage the company's fleet of 35 trailer trucks. (The company in 1992 operated more than 90 trucks through Bama Pie Trucking, a subsidiary.) She said that job provided a learning experience in the areas of government regulation, fuel costs, and record keeping and generally broadened her view of the company.

In the mid-1970s, Bama decided to computerize, and Paula was selected to make the purchase. As a result, she was the person trained to run the new system, and in that capacity she learned the value of training people and helping people solve problems. Since she also had to set up the company's systems on the computer, she learned about costs, payables, invoicing, and again expanded her knowledge about the company. "In my position, I got to be known as Bama's problem solver," she recalled.

Her father noticed her management talents but had been grooming her older brother, Johnny, to take over the company. Paula remembered, "Dad began to say things to me like: 'You really like this business, don't you?' 'Why don't you want to do more?' 'Women probably don't need to be in a CEO role.' Like most kids, when a parent says you can't do something, that's what you decide you want to do just to show them they are wrong."

Paula began her college education during this time, attending Tulsa Junior College and working full time. In 1982, her older brother had a serious illness and her other brother "got into a fight" with her father, so her father came to her and said, "You're going to have to be the one, or we're going to have to sell the company."

For the next three years, she traveled with her father everywhere. She said when her father first presented her as the future CEO to some of the McDonald's officials, they laughed. "During that time I learned a lot," she says. Some of the best advice her father gave her included: "Always have a good work ethic. Be committed to what you are doing. Commitment is what gets through hard times and there will always be hard times."

In 1985, Paul Marshall handed over the reins of the company to Paula and retired to Naples, Florida. According to other Bama executives, when he left, he left. He let Paula run the company and stayed out of the way. The company, which had been incorporated, was reorganized as a partnership in 1985 to allow Paula's parents to cash out their equity. Paula then became a general partner.

Between 1985 and 1992, Paula reshaped the company. She recruited a young, professional executive staff. She also completed a bachelor's degree through Oklahoma City University's Competency Based Degree Program and was recognized as a distinguished alumna of that program in 1989.

Employees described Paula as a "unique chief executive." One marketing representative who had previously worked for Pizza Hut in the PepsiCo organization was asked to compare what it was like at Pizza Hut and Bama. He said:

> At PepsiCo, everything was numbers driven. You either made the numbers, or you were gone. You didn't feel like you were treated as a person. Big companies are like that. You worked for an organization. Here you work for a human being who treats you as a human being. Paula is more concerned about long term. She doesn't look for someone to blame when a problem arises, she only wants to look for what caused the problem and find a way to fix the problem. I've never seen her blame anyone for anything.

MANAGEMENT IN 1992

Marshall-Chapman reshaped the management team significantly after she took control of the company and assembled a highly professional staff with an average age under 40.

John Davsco, 45, was vice president of operations. He joined Bama Pie in 1989 after 19 years of high-level operations management with Pillsbury. A graduate of St. Louis University in 1968, he also had a brief career as a major league baseball pitcher with the St. Louis Cardinals and Cincinnati Reds.

William L. Chew, 35, vice president of finance, joined the firm in 1987 after two years as controller of a real estate management and development company and seven years with Price Waterhouse in Chicago. He was a 1978 graduate of the University of Illinois and a certified public accountant.

Kay White, 46, vice president of human resources, joined Bama Pie in 1976 as a line worker in production. She was promoted to supervisor and then plant manager and served 2½ years as operations director.

Brenda Rice, 31, vice president for quality assurance systems, joined the company in 1989. She previously was employed in McDonald's R & D Division and worked with Bama Pies in developing the biscuit for McDonald's. She also worked as product development technologist with Magic Pantry Foods (Canada). She received an associate degree in food science from Humber College, Toronto, Canada, in 1981.

With more than 70 percent of the company's business coming from McDonald's, Bama had never developed a fully functioning marketing department. During 1991, the company began establishing a marketing strategy and hired Lynn Dickson, previously associated with Pizza Hut, to begin developing a professional marketing function within the company. Exhibit 4 presents an organization chart for the company.

PRODUCTS

The products Bama Pies produced included 3-ounce pies and 3-inch biscuits for McDonald's, bread sticks for Pizza Hut, 9-inch graham cracker pie shells, 3-inch and 9-inch pecan pies, and soft cookies.

The 3-ounce pies supplied to McDonald's were provided frozen as either ready to fry or bake, with the bulk of the volume having apple or cherry fillings. The company could also produce pies with lemon, peach, and apricot fillings. The original pies supplied to McDonald's were fried turnovers. The baked product was an optional choice in the restaurants in the McDonald's organization and had been increasing in popularity.

The 3-inch biscuit was processed in the new 135,000-square-foot facility in Tulsa and was prebaked to a ready-to-bake stage, frozen, and then baked off in the individual restaurant. The product took several years to develop, with McDonald's, Bama Pies, and Quaker Oats (the other 50 percent supplier) jointly working on the project. Currently, Bama supplied operations west of the Mississippi, and Quaker supplied restaurants east of the Mississippi. During the development of the product, the group experimented with more than 200 recipes.

According to Marshall-Chapman, the reason McDonald's wanted a ready-to-bake product was to ensure a consistent product at all its units. When biscuits first began appearing in restaurants, they were made from mixes. "Our customer has 8,000 domestic restaurants and, thus, 8,000 biscuit bakers. That means a lot of variation is possible," Marshall-Chapman said.

The long development time resulted from McDonald's insistence that the frozen product be equal in quality to fresh-baked, made-from-scratch products. To provide the product, a carefully controlled process was developed. The biscuits were essentially 90 percent baked, frozen, and then shipped to distribution centers for delivery to the restaurants. The product, packaged in a baking bag, was then finished off in

EXHIBIT 4 Bama Pie Ltd., Corporate Organization as of September 1990

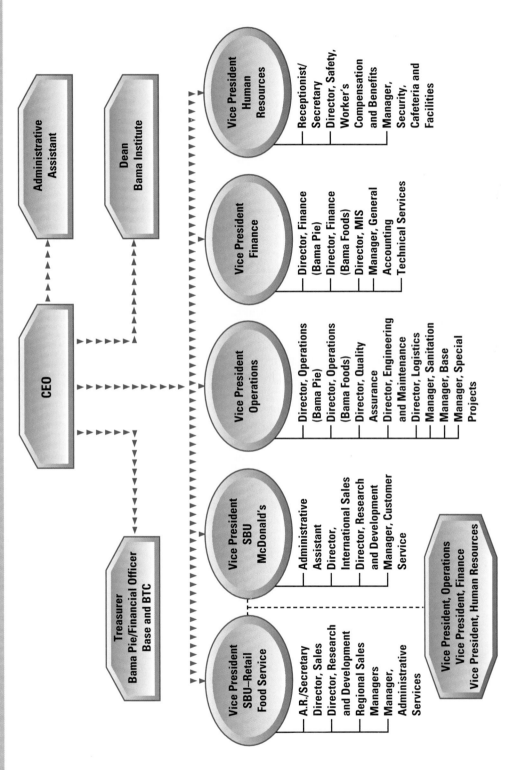

EXHIBIT 5	Bama Pie's Use of Ingredients in Its Products, 1984 versus 1991	

Description	1984 Pounds (in millions)	1991 Pounds (in millions)
Frozen apples	3.5	9.2
Frozen cherries	3.0	1.6
Flour	2.0	11.0
Shelled pecans	2.0	0.3
Shortening	1.5	4.2
Sugar	1.0	2.6
Shelled eggs	0.9	0.4

Note: Reduction in cherries is because the cherry pie is now optional at McDonald's restaurants. In 1984, it was a required menu item. Reduction in pecans and eggs is due to reduced number of pecan pies being sold, an outcome attributed to increased weight and health concerns.

convection ovens at the local restaurant to give that "just baked" appearance, taste, and texture.

The bread sticks were produced in the 11th Street plant of Bama Pies and were a frozen dough product, made under a confidential agreement with Pizza Hut with the recipe kept secret. The dough was processed, rolled to a specific thickness, and shipped frozen in flat pieces about 9 inches by 12 inches. The dough was thawed and the sticks cut at the restaurant before baking.

The 3-inch and 9-inch pecan pies were a mainstay of Bama Pies and had been produced for almost the entire 65 years of operation. The recipe was virtually unchanged from the original developed by Marshall-Chapman's grandmother. The pies were fully baked, packaged in single wraps, and then boxed in a variety of quantities. Customers included Wal-Mart and Sam's Wholesale Clubs.

The 9-inch graham cracker shells were produced for retail sale and were also provided to TCBY and Braum's. The shells came in an aluminum pie pan ready to be filled with a customer's own filling. The shells were often used for cheesecake and ice box pies or could be filled with ice cream or yogurt to provide an ice cream pie product.

The cookies were soft products that competed directly with the large soft cookies produced under the Grandma's label by Frito-Lay, a PepsiCo subsidiary. The cookies were packaged individually and boxed for retail sale. See Exhibit 5 for listings of the ingredients Bama Pie used in its products.

OPERATIONS

McDonald's Pies

The 3-ounce pies for McDonald's were processed in the 11th Street Plant. Ingredients were mixed in two different areas. The dough was prepared in large mixers that fed a moving conveyor system that rolled the dough out on two separate belts approximately 24 inches wide. The filling was prepared in large, heated mixing bowls with real fruit added. This mixture was pumped through seven separate hoses that streamed filling on the bottom conveyor of dough. The top layer was then placed on top of the filling, and the pies were then cut and sealed in a two-step operation. The pies were sent to a spiral freezer where they were frozen. The process was basically the same whether the pie was a fried product or a baked product. The dough mixture was different for each product, and the baked product had slits cut in the top of each pie.

After freezing, the pies were processed slightly differently. The fried product was dipped in a liquid that immediately froze to the pie and caused the finished pie to have a bubbly, flaky texture. The pies were hand-packed 12 to a tray, and six trays were then boxed together in an automated operation. Four boxes were shrunk wrapped together before moving into the storage freezer. The baked pies were processed similarly, but instead of being dipped when exiting the freezer, they were sprayed with water and dusted with cinnamon before packaging.

Each hour, samples were taken from the production process to the test kitchen where the same ovens and fryers used by McDonald's were installed. The product was finished off and tested to ensure specifications were being met. Each line was capable of producing 40,000 pies per hour, and more than 1 million pies were produced daily at the plant.

McDonald's Biscuits

The McDonald's biscuit was produced in a new facility that *Baking & Snack* magazine called "world class."[2] The facility contained two parallel production lines that included 250-foot ovens. The dough was mixed and laid down on a flour-dusted conveyor belt that transferred the dough through a series of rollers until it was a 50-inch-wide sheet. The dough was then cut and passed through a metal detector before dropping into the baking pans. The biscuit pans passed three wide through the oven where modular construction and nine heating zones transformed the dough into a biscuit ready for freezing in about 15 minutes. The highly automated line removed the pans, cleaned them, re-oiled them, and returned them for reuse. The biscuits were then cartoned and put through a spiral freezer after cooling to 90 degrees. After freezing, the biscuits were wrapped and passed through another metal detector before being boxed for shipment and moved into the storage freezer.

Graham Shells

The graham shells were produced on a highly automated line that was installed in 1991 and put into operation in early 1992. The graham meal was mixed and fed into a hopper that dumped an exact measurement of meal into an aluminum pie pan and was then automatically pressed and formed. The shell moved through a process where the clear plastic cover was pressed into place and sealed to the pan. Next, the shells were automatically stacked and boxed for shipment.

Pizza Hut Bread Sticks

Using the secret recipe from Pizza Hut, the dough was mixed and fed onto a conveyor belt into a series of rollers that reduced the sheet of dough to the proper thickness and width. The dough was then run through a cutter that produced sheets of

---

[2]Laurie Gorton. "World Class: Bama Creates a Flexible Plant Dedicated to Making Ready-to-Bake Biscuits," *Baking & Snack*, November 1991.

dough approximately 9 inches by 12 inches. These sheets were then frozen in a spiral freezer before packaging and boxing. The bread stick line was located in the 11th Street plant.

Pecan Pies

The 3-inch and 9-inch pecan pies were also produced in the 11th Street plant. The dough was prepared and rolled and fed onto a conveyor line where it was cut and dropped into the aluminum pie shell. The dough was then automatically formed inside the shell. The pies continued on and were filled with pecans and pie filling before entering an oven approximately 200 feet long. Once the pies were baked, they were conveyed back to packaging by passing through a cooling tunnel where they went through automated packaging machines and were hand-packed and boxed.

Cookies

The soft-batch cookies were processed in much the same manner as the pecan pies. The batter was measured and dropped onto a conveyor belt that took the cookies through the oven and returned them through a cooling tunnel for packaging.

THE MCDONALD'S RELATIONSHIP

The relationship with McDonald's was unusual in that Bama had been the company's principal supplier of pies for 24 years and had never had a contract. Moreover, Bama did not sell directly to McDonald's. McDonald's selected and approved suppliers, but the actual sales were made to independently owned distribution centers that supplied the McDonald's restaurants around the country.

The company did not have a contract for the biscuit product either. "When a couple of banks heard we wanted to borrow $40 million to build a biscuit plant and didn't have a contract to even buy one biscuit, they ran away," Marshall-Chapman said. McDonald's put the company in touch with Texas Commerce Bank in Houston, and Bama found a bank that was actively seeking to develop a business relationship with McDonald's. In fact, the bank had formed a team to function as McDonald's specialists. The bank understood that McDonald's developed "partnership arrangements" with suppliers and that contracts were not a part of the business. "They (both the bank and McDonald's) were eager to help, and we completed the deal at extremely favorable rates," Marshall-Chapman said.

COMMITMENT TO QUALITY AND STAYING PRIVATE

Favorable lending rates were extremely important to Bama Pie, since the company and Marshall-Chapman were committed to remaining private. Marshall-Chapman believed going public would ruin the company: "Public companies have to run the business for Wall Street. They have to think quarterly. I want to run our business for my customers and my employees. I want to concentrate on developing the business, not worrying about what is happening to my stock price."

Decisions were made based on what the management team thought was best. A commitment to quality was evident in everything the company did. Marshall-Chapman believed that not having to answer to stockholders allowed the company to focus on quality; she indicated the company was ahead of the people who were teaching total quality management: "They (the Quality College and others) are now calling us and asking us what we've done new and what we're currently working on."

Bama insisted on quality from its suppliers. Suppliers were expected to ship random samples of product runs due for Bama in advance so they could be pretested. "We want to know if there is a problem before the shipment leaves their plant," Marshall-Chapman said. Vendors were willing to cooperate because it was much less expensive to provide the samples and get preapproval for shipment than to risk having a whole order rejected after shipment and returned.

The company had installed a total quality arrangement discipline in its approximately 600 employees through extensive training and educational programs offered through the in-house Bama Institute. Getting employees involved in all aspects of quality permeated everything, including internal record keeping. Within a year's time, inventory adjustments based on physical counts had dropped from between $50,000 and $70,000 per month to less than $3,000 per month and was still improving. "One month we'd have a negative adjustment, the next a positive adjustment," William Chew, vice president of finance said. At a time when the company was attempting to refine its cost system and implement standard costs under an activity-based cost system, the inventory problem was major. Chew commented, "Even our fork truck operators have gotten involved in helping solve the inventory adjustments problem."

To support the quality program and refine data for decision making, the company purchased a new computer system using Prism software on an IBM AS/400 mainframe. The conversion was implemented within one year. "We were able to do it because Paula released people from some of their regular jobs and put them on the project," Chew said. According to the consultants working with Bama, no company had ever been able to accomplish such a conversion in such a short period. The result was a system with world-class manufacturing software that supported an activity-based standard cost accounting system and electronic data interchange transactions.

DRUG POLICIES

Bama was a "drug-free" workplace: All applicants for employment were screened for drugs. According to company officials, approximately one in five applicants tested positive. In addition, all employees (including Paula) had been drug tested and random drug testing was administered within the company. The random sampling for drug tests was determined by a computer program. Urine samples were taken and tested in a lab. A positive result was grounds for immediate dismissal.

According to Marshall-Chapman, the company's drug policy was mainly aimed at reducing accidents. Since the program had been implemented, accidents had declined significantly. Any employee involved in an accident at work was automatically drug tested.

BEBOPP

In 1990, Bama instituted the Bama Employees' Bonus on Profit Plan (BEBOPP) to provide bonus incentives to all employees in the company. The plan was based on an annual return on sales objective that was established by Marshall-Chapman. The goal was expressed as a percentage, and for each 0.5 percent above the target all employees shared in a bonus pool. The pool began at 2 percent of payroll and increased for each 0.5 percent above the target. For example, if Bama's return on sales topped the goal by 2 percent, the bonus pool would equal 3.5 percent of payroll. Even though the program was based on annual sales, quarterly payments were made to employees. All eligible employees received equal dollar amounts from the pool.

FUTURE PROSPECTS

The company was attempting to decrease its reliance on McDonald's. The biscuit plant, which was also capable of producing cookies and other bread-type products, had underutilized capacity plus room for expansion. The main plant also had open capacity.

Opportunities for new business were coming in faster than the company could deal with them. John Davsko, vice president of operations, said, "We have people calling us all the time asking if we are interested in developing a product for them. Our reputation is bringing business. We had one potential customer referred to us by one of our suppliers."

However, there were problems with expansion. Management believed any expansion had to come mainly from new product development. Bama believed it could not seek additional customers for its fast-food pie product without putting its McDonald's account at risk. Likewise, it would be unwise to seek another customer for biscuits or bread sticks. According to Marshall-Chapman, about the only negative thing Paul Marshall had said regarding how Paula had handled the business since he left is, "He thinks we're expanding too fast, and he doesn't like us borrowing money."

NOVOTEL

Brian Hunt, *City University Business School, London*

Charles Baden-Fuller, *City University Business School, London*

Roland Calori, *Groupe ESC Lyon*

The Novotel story began in 1967 when Paul Dubrule and Gerard Pelisson, neither of whom came from a hotel background, opened the first Novotel adjacent to the airport in Lille, France. Once established, the two principals began to develop their business. Driven by an ambitious entrepreneurial spirit, they expanded their empire by building new hotels and buying existing hotel chains.

The period from 1972 to 1977 saw expansion into other European countries. Novotel International was created in 1970 and in 1973 Novotel opened its first hotel outside France. Also in 1973, the company launched the two-star Ibis hotel chain and in 1974 bought the three-star Mercure hotel chain. One senior manager recalls these early days:

> Novotel, Ibis and Formule I were the chains created by Gerard Pelisson and Paul Dubrule. They had an approach where they said "there is a need for three-star hotels," and they created Novotel; "there is a need for two-star hotels," and they created Ibis; "there is a need for one-star hotels," and they created Formule 1.

In 1983, a merger with the Jacques Borel hotel and restaurant group added the Sofitel chain of luxury hotels. In the same year the group was named Accor, with Paul Dubrule and Gerard Pelisson as co-presidents. The Novotel name was retained for

EXHIBIT 1   Novotel in the Accor Group

Brand	Rating	Founded (or acquired)
Sofitel	4 star (deluxe)	1980 (1985)
Novotel	3 star	1967
Mercure	3 star	1974
Ibis	2 star	1973
Formule 1	1 star (budget motel)	1985

Source: Company documents and interviews.

the group's three-star hotel chain. In 1985 the group launched the Formule 1 budget hotel chain.

The Accor group now employs over 144,000 people and operates in 132 countries. It owns 50 trademarks in six fields of activity in businesses related to the travel and hospitality. Accor operates 2,183 hotels with over 2 million guest rooms and has over 53,000 employees in this sector.

The place occupied by the Novotel chain in the Accor Group's hotels is shown in Exhibit 1.

In 1985, the Academie Accor was created as "the first European corporate university for employee training" and its inception emphasizes the Group's commitment to staff training and development. Located next to Accor Head Office in Evry, southeast of Paris, the Academie is responsible for coordinating, managing, and teaching training courses to Accor Group personnel. Courses last from one day to several weeks and cover a range of managerial and operational topics. The Academie's summer university program is particularly popular and successful, and brings together managers from a wide range of disciplines throughout the Accor organization.

The Development of Novotel

During the 1970s, Novotel expanded at an average rate of one hotel every month. By the end of 1977, Novotel had 76 hotels throughout Europe. From 1978 to 1983, the Novotel division decelerated its growth in France to focus more on expansion in other European countries. Expansion in neighboring countries created another 28 hotels, 19 in Germany alone. In 1984 Novotel expanded operations in Great Britain, building 13 hotels between 1987 to 1994. Today, Novotel is the market leader in Europe with 214 Novotels in 18 European countries.[1]

This case study focuses on Novotel in Europe. However, Novotel is a worldwide group with operations in Africa, North and South America, the Middle East, Asia, and the Pacific. Worldwide, Novotel has 280 hotels in 46 countries with a total of 43,035 rooms and employs over 33,000 people.

---

[1]There are 111 Novotels in France, 32 in Germany, 17 in Great Britain, 8 in Belgium, 7 in the Netherlands and 39 Novotels in 14 other European countries. There are 6 Novotels in overseas departments of France. Novotel's European network has 30,258 hotel rooms.

While ownership is a predominant characteristic of Novotel, some Novotels are operated on the basis of a franchised contract. In comparison with its competitors, Novotel owns a greater portion of its hotels and most Novotels in Europe[2] are wholly owned subsidiaries.

Franchise Novotels are obliged to follow head office procedures on product policy (e.g., room size, furnishings) and pricing policy (e.g., room rates, Novotel card holder benefits, conference rates). Novotel informs franchisees of human resource policies and evolving management tools. Franchisees have more flexibility in these areas but usually choose to adopt Novotel policies and systems.

During the period of growth, Novotel was an exciting place to be. The rapid expansion program created a need for more GMs to manage the new hotels and for personnel to occupy other positions. People who enjoyed a fast-paced working environment found themselves on an accelerated promotion track and it was not unusual for some people to have a meteoric career path, as two senior managers describe:

> Your career in Novotel took off like a rocket. You could begin as a *Maitre d' hotel* in a hotel restaurant and four or five years later you could be a general manager. Two years after that you could be a regional manager. All you needed was to be faithful, to have a lot of energy, to be very motivated, and to do things with good common sense.
>
> Former Novotel managers have progressed to become the presidents of Motel 6, Formule 1, Ibis, Mercure, and Sofitel. Novotel is where everyone grew in the '70s.

To this day, Novotel continues to offer employees a dynamic career. Company literature stresses that Novotel is a school for life. The following tenet encapsulates the ideal career path within the Accor group:

> Communicate in two languages,
> work in two countries,
> work for two respected brands,
> gain experience in two professional areas,
> that's the ideal career path at Accor.

The Novotel Recipe

From the beginning when they opened their first hotel, Paul Dubrule and Gerard Pelisson approached hotel management differently from their competitors. In an industry ridden with hierarchy, where employees are conscious of job titles and conform closely to their job descriptions, the two hoteliers tried to organize and manage their business creatively. The current co-president explains:

> One of the reasons for Paul Dubrule's and Gerard Pelisson's success was that they didn't know the industry and they had a different mind-set.

Several distinctive innovations stood out. First the founders realized that the standardized hotel concept then becoming increasingly popular in the USA could be imported into Europe.[3] At the time, hotel industry practice decreed that hotels should somehow reflect the local area, and most European hotels stressed the differences

---

[2]149 hotels providing 20,173 rooms.

[3]For a description of the American model of hotels see Peter Barge, "International Management Contracts" in Jones, P. and Pizam, A. (eds), *The International Hospitality Industry: Operational Issues* (Pitman, 1993); see also Yvonne Guerrier, "The Development of a 'Corpus of Knowledge' for Hotel and Catering Managers," Paper presented to 11th EGOS Colloquium, Paris, July 1993.

between their hotels from one location to another. In this climate, Dubrule and Pelisson's belief that uniformity would be a profitable formula must have seemed nonsensical to existing hoteliers in Europe.

Second, Novotel was a pioneer for the hotel industry in Europe. It led the industry in introducing a number of innovative practices that have since become standard. Novotel claims to be the first European hotel chain to install a bathroom in every guest bedroom, to provide telex facilities, to build swimming pools, to install self-dial telephones in every guest bedroom, and to provide shoe polishing machines for guests.

Third, the founders wanted to develop a team of flexible people who could work together, and trained to do a variety of tasks. Their idea was to train staff to be multifunctional and flexible (*polyvalence* in French). On the front desk, for example, staff would be taking reservations, checking in guests, handing out room keys, and orienting guests to the amenities of the hotel and the surrounding area. Such staff flexibility diverged from the traditionally accepted functional organization of other hotels.[4]

The founders maintained a strategy of siting their hotels out-of-town. Here, in the absence of other interested investors, they could buy land very cheaply. In this way they were able to obtain large plots of land that later became prime sites. Over time, land prices increased making it expensive for competitors to build their hotels near existing Novotels. Moreover, the large plots enabled Novotel to expand existing hotel sites and to construct easily a range of outdoor amenities such as free parking zones, landscaped gardens, terraces, barbecue areas, swimming pools, and children's play areas. Many Novotels offer several such amenities for the enjoyment and convenience of guests.

Novotel's marketing director believed that location was one of the chain's major sources of competitive advantage. Since the first Novotel was created adjacent to Lille airport subsequent Novotels was usually been located in one of two prime locations: near international airports or adjacent to motorway junctions. Some Novotels were conveniently near both locations. When its network of out-of-town sites was well-established, Novotel built up a network of center-city hotels.

Many employees indicated that Novotel gained and subsequently retained guests by offering guests a blend of features from three- and four-star hotels. Traditionally four-star hotels were too expensive for the average business or family traveler, and many three-star hotels were often not so comfortable. Novotel bridged a gap by providing rooms and other amenities associated with four-star hotels, yet avoiding the costs of too high a provision of some other four-star services.

The Novotel Product

The Novotel product was, and still is, standardized worldwide, irrespective of location. In Europe, all Novotel guest bedrooms measure 24 metres square.[5] The room is furnished to provide suitable accommodation for both business travelers and fami-

---

[4]According to the industry researchers cited above, each of these strategies was truly innovative and broke contemporary hotel industry practices.

[5]In some countries, for example in the USA and Asia, the size of the standard Novotel guest room is 26 metres square. In some Novotels guest bedrooms may be furnished with two double beds instead of one double bed and a sofa.

lies. The first group provided business from Monday to Thursday, the second from Friday to Sunday and during vacation periods.

Guest bedrooms are furnished and decorated with identical furniture, fixtures and fittings. These include a double bed, a sofa, a large desk area, two chairs, table and bedside lights, and a television. Differences are minimal. A framed print may be the only distinctive feature from room to room, location to location, or even country to country.

When Novotel entered the hotel industry, hotels rooms at all price levels were rather imposing, darkly decorated with heavy fabrics, and contained heavy traditional furniture. Novotel's product standardization was extremely innovative in France, and indeed in Europe.

A Novotel guest bedroom decorated in pastel shades with white standard-designed furniture provided guests with a clean, airy ambience and space. These features strongly distinguished Novotel from rival hotel chains. Over time, changes to this standard product have been minimal and are mainly technology-related, for example, the additional electrical outlets for computer terminals and the latest model of television.

Guest bedroom standardization made a facility easier and more economical to operate. Cleaning and other housekeeping functions could be simplified and training procedures standardized. To some extent, there were economies of scale in purchasing various room fixtures and furnishings. Standardization also allowed a common worldwide marketing strategy for guests, especially those who were regular Novotel guests or who expected universal standards.

Quality Control

In its formative years, Novotel was managed as an entrepreneurial enterprise, tightly controlled from the administrative center. However, as the Novotel network expanded, control became problematic. In spite of training programs and quality control procedures, standards were slipping. The chain encountered difficulty in delivering consistent service on a worldwide basis.

In 1987 the Operations Department introduced a customer-oriented system to monitor and maintain standard procedures. Known as the *95 Boulons* [95 Bolts], these consisted of 13 steps [*etapes*] covering all aspects of a Novotel employee's interaction with guests from reservation to check-out. These steps were each divided into a number of compulsory directives for staff.[6] For example, how to greet guests, how to lay out a place setting in the restaurant, how and where bedroom furnishings should be set out. Co-president Gilles Pelisson explained the rationale behind *les Boulons;*

> Novotel had people joining from other hotel groups and needed to make sure that they didn't manage Novotel in the same way that they managed their former hotel. The introduction of the Bolts gave the GMs and their staff a quality programme and references and standards.

The *95 Boulons* were listed in a booklet entitled *'95 Boulons-Zero defaut* which was issued to all Novotel employees. New recruits received their booklet as part of the

---

[6]A *Boulon* was defined as *"une exigence de qualite qui contribue a l'attachement de notre client a notre enseigne."* The 13 *Boulons* were: reservation, arrival-access, parking, check-in, hall, bedroom, bathroom-WC, evening meal, breakfast, shops, bar, outdoor games-swimming pool, check-out.

EXHIBIT 2   Examples of Bolts from the *95 Boulons* Booklet

Check In

19. The receptionist is standing when the guest arrives. He/she smiles and says: "Good morning/afternoon/evening, Sir (Madam)".
20. Smoking in reception is not allowed.
21. Indicate the number and the location of the guest bedroom and how to get there.
22. Outline the principal services of the hotel (restaurant and bar open until midnight)

Source: Novotel company documents.

induction and orientation procedure. Exhibit 2 shows an excerpt from the *'95 Boulons* booklet.

In order to monitor and sustain quality, inspection teams visited Novotels on average twice annually. Known as *Ambassadeurs de Qualite*, two or more inspectors would make reservations anonymously, check in unannounced, and stay as *incognito* guests for one or two days. Their task was to monitor each department's performance from a guest's viewpoint. Their stay completed, *Ambassadeurs de Qualite* would identify themselves and ask for a short meeting with the general manager. They would hand over their written report based on their visit and invite the GM's comments. Identified shortcomings in the hotel would be graded on a percentage point scale, with recommendations for improvement.

Not surprisingly, some GMs and their staff regarded with apprehension an inspection visit, especially as their performance bonuses were directly linked to *Ambassadeurs de Qualite* reports. Starting in 1987, *Ambassadeurs de Qualite* used the *95 Boulons* booklet as a reference for their checklist and subsequent report.

According to a number of GMs and staff, *les Boulons* were an appropriate system of quality control for its time. They were introduced at a time when the Novotel network had become very large and staffing needs meant that new employees (often with differing backgrounds) were entering the organization at a range of different levels. Co-president Gilles Pelission explained:

> Novotel tried to really organize its product in the best way, They really tried to tighten everything and make each rivet work. For example, they thought that a receptionist should be standing up when a guest comes to reception.

However, for all their contribution to management and control, *les Boulons* encouraged overrigidity and uniformity to the exclusion of creativity and initiative. Over a period of time, many Novotel staff came to resent the ways in which *les Boulons* stifled spontaneous responses to local situations. Some people disliked being treated in what one person described as "an adult-child relationship" and another compared to "treating people like robots." Pelission reflected:

> At the time the concept was to be very controlled in the way we operated, but without authority and without adding layers of management.
>
> Somehow, we got into too much detail. There was a sentence that everybody should say at the end of a telephone conversation: "Thank you for choosing Novotel." After a while this became a pain in the neck for everybody. There was a lot of resentment by the staff at

EXHIBIT 3   Simplified View of Novotel's Management and Reporting
             Structure in the 1980s

Head Office

Ninth level:	President of Accor
Eighth level:	President of Novotel
Seventh level:	Directors of Operations
Sixth level:	Regional Managers
Fifth level (sometimes):	*Directeurs delegues*

Novotel Hotel Units

Fourth level:	General Managers
Third level:	*Sous-Directeurs*
Second level:	Heads of Department
First level:	Novotel Staff

Source: Novotel company documents and interviews.

having been forced to say precise words—this is where, I guess, we went overboard and
overdid it.

This is not to say that all staff felt inhibited by the introduction of *les Boulons*. There
was sometimes a disparity between the imposed rigidity of *les Boulons* and the
working styles of newly recruited managers and staff. Many of these employees took
a fresh approach. One GM, recruited to Novotel from his previous employment as a
manager in Accor's chain of motorway restaurants, described his initial impressions:

> When I came here I saw the situation in the hotel with new eyes because I had never sold a
> room before, never. I came as manager and I asked my staff some questions such as "Why
> are we doing it like this?" Everybody reflected and answered "Well, we can't do it any
> differently . . . because it's the system."

A number of GMs noticed that the situation experienced by the Novotel division was
replicated in a microcosm in some Novotel units. Some GMs reported that a widespread attitude was, "Our hotel is in a good economic situation, there are no competitors, we have a lot of guests, we post good results; why change anything?"

Management Structure

By the late 1980s Novotel had grown immensely. In order to manage the large
number of geographically dispersed hotels, a nine-layered management structure had
evolved. Exhibit 3 shows the reporting hierarchy between the head office and individual Novotels in the late 1980s.

Each Novotel was headed by a general manager (GM). GMs reported to their
regional manager, who was responsible for eight or nine, sometimes more, hotels in an
area. On the next tier of the reporting hierarchy was the director of operations who
reported to the president of Novotel. Like his counterparts in other divisions of the
Accor group the president of Novotel reported to the president of Accor. This nine-
layer-structure was the minimum; in some areas, there was another layer of directors,

called *Directeurs delegues,* between the general manager and the regional manager. Typically a *Directeur delegue* was a GM in charge of coordinating three to five hotels.

There were also many layers of management within each hotel. Formally, there were three layers between the staff and their general manager, but in some hotels more layers of management and supervision existed.

NOVOTEL IN 1990–1992

New Competition

After the heady days of the late 1980s, the beginning of the 1990s brought a period of changing fortunes for Novotel. The hospitality industry was expanding rapidly, particularly the leisure and travel segment. Seemingly high profits—enhanced partly by Novotel's publicized success, encouraged new enterprises, sometimes with little or no prior hotel experience, to enter the industry.

For a number of years, Novotel faced almost no competition from hotels on adjacent properties. But then things began to change. According to two GMs of Novotels in France:

> As far as my hotel is concerned, four years ago we were alone in the area, no other hotels around. Now there are five hotels and a big restaurant.

> I manage a Novotel adjacent to an international airport. A couple of years ago when I arrived here, there were five hotels in the area with 1,500 rooms. These were mainly Accor. We had Sofitel, Mercure, Ibis, plus Holiday Inn. Today, 18 months later, we've got 10 hotels and over 3,000 rooms. The new competitors today are Hyatt, Copthorne, Quality Inn, Hilton. Nor has it stopped. Sheraton is arriving soon, followed by Campanile, Bleu Marine. So the competition is tough, very tough.

Apart from increased competition, Novotel and its rivals faced pressure from another direction. The onset of the recession in Europe in the early 1990s encouraged companies to be more cost conscious. Many companies were more frugal about travel and entertainment expenses. For the hotel industry, the effect was twofold. On the one hand, there were fewer business travelers; on the other, many businesspeople who continued to travel were conservative in their spending. Some stayed in cheaper accommodation.

In the autumn of 1990, Iraq invaded Kuwait. The ripples of the Gulf crisis and the subsequent buildup of Western coalition forces were felt throughout Europe. It caused a major upheaval as many people avoided international travel.

For some Novotels in Europe, paradoxically 1989, 1990, and 1991 were good revenere years. The bicentennial celebrations in France in 1989 and high tourist levels the following year provided unexpectedly high revenues. In certain Novotels, the impending Gulf crisis seemed to pass unnoticed. Although package tours canceled prearranged bookings, their places were taken by individual guests. As individual guests paid premium room rates rather than the discounted rates enjoyed by tour groups, some Novotels enjoyed windfall profits. These contributed towards high annual profits for the group for 1991.

Over the years, Novotel rooms rates had increased at a rate faster than those of competitors. To some observers, Novotel's rates were spiraling out of control, and top management and staff seemed oblivious to the competitive risks.

In addition, there were signs that a succession of good annual results had induced complacency. Perceptive observers noticed subtle changes in the culture of various Novotels. A long-serving senior manager described his perception of the changing ambience:

> Customers were saying: "I want to make a meeting," or "I want to book rooms and I can get a better price elsewhere." Our reservations people were saying "Take it or leave it." In the hotels, if things were not happening quite so well, for example if breakfast was at the wrong time or just forgotten, they would say, "We are sorry but if you don't want to use Novotel next time there are plenty of people who do because you are occupying a room in place of others." I'm exaggerating a little but that was the feeling at that time.

As Novotel had grown in size, the staff flexibility [*polyvalence*] encouraged by co-founders Dubrule and Pelisson had diminished. Monitoring and control procedures such as *Les Boulins* had achieved quality objectives but stifled individual initiative. The hierarchial management structures lengthened response times and sensitivity to changing customer preferences and competitive circumstances. Some company personnel believed that the Novotel culture was becoming increasingly self-satisfied and out of touch with its guests and the marketplace.

As time passed, it became clear that the creative spirit of the founders had become diluted by rapid expansion and the addition of many new employees. The pace of innovation, a strong factor in the growth and success of Novotel, was slowing down. A buoyant market had supported the company's success and blinded management to the need to adapt and change. Favorable market conditions had also masked internal shortcomings.

In Europe, the absence of a concerted program of renovation and refurbishment resulted in existing properties becoming run-down. Some Novotels were impersonal and lacked warmth. These factors accumulated to reduce Novotel's strong lead over competitors.

Signs of Trouble

A series of routine meetings in 1992 saw the beginnings of vigorous internal debate. Exhibit 4 shows the sequence of events.

The first signs that top management was starting to recognize and be concerned about Novotel's problems occurred in January 1992 at a meeting in Lisbon attended by 52 regional managers and GMs. Although they did not express their opinions openly, many participants were guardedly discussing what was wrong at Novotel. One participant reflected on what transpired:

> The Novotel brand, the product, had become stale, depasse. We thought that we were the best. We were the leader. We were innovators. But every company copied Novotel—Accor even profited from our success, our results.

After years of record-breaking results, profits were waning. Novotel monitored financial results on a month-by-month basis so that the previous month's revenues could be analyzed within six weeks. In the spring of 1992, there were signs of a profit decline.

However, there were disagreements over the reasons for the slowdown. Optimists believed that external, rather than internal, factors were the source of Notovel's problems. Proponents of this argument reasoned that the whole hospitality industry was transitioning to a new phase. This much was evident from insider gossip and reports in newspapers and trade journals. Furthermore, in the hotel industry seasonal

EXHIBIT 4   Calendar of Events, 1991–92

1991
January	Gulf crisis.
December	Novotel posts record profits of 500m francs.

1992
January	Lisbon meeting.
April	"Open Space" meeting of hotel managers in Novotel Fontainebleau. Managers say they want freedom to make decisions and try new ideas.
August	Philippe Brizon named vice-president with responsibilities for marketing.
Late November	Committee meeting in Fontainebleau draws up final list of objectives. Philippe Brizon and Gilles Pelisson are asked by co-presidents of Accor to present ideas for future development of Novotel.
December	Claude Moscheni becomes President of Pullman International Hotels. Gilles Pelission and Philppe Brizon named Novotel co-presidents. Novotel profits fall to one-half of 1991.

fluctuations were a fact of life. Business would pick up, eventually. After all, in spite of a poor start, the previous year had produced excellent results—even though a little less than the exceptional profits enjoyed develop during the period 1989-90.

Claude Moscheni (Novotel president since 1983) took the position that something *was* wrong, arguing that Novotel's problems were as much internal as external. He responded by making some changes to the management structure and altering decision making practices.

In April of the same year, opinions were more overtly stated at an "Open Space" meeting in Novotel Fontainebleau, France. (The "Open Space" format allowed participants to propose discussion topics. Participants were free to move from forum to forum, or leave if they so wished.) At this meeting, GMs raised the important theme that regional managers did not allow them decision-making freedoms. They were frustrated that an unwieldy number of managerial levels stifled creativity and initiative. They complained that too much paperwork kept them office-bound and restricted face-to-face contact with staff and guests. Claude Moscheni responded by stating publicly to his regional directors, "Let your managers breathe."

In August 1992, Philippe Brizon, then president of Ibis, was appointed vice-president of Novotel with marketing responsibilities. He was asked to assist the president and to identify Novotels problems. Moscheni and Brizon then invited all directors of operations (DOPs) in Europe to a series of meetings. One recalls:

> In '92 there were meetings to reflect why the economic results were going down. They asked us to reflect what had happened and what we had to do to return to good profits.

During the last part of 1992, Philippe Brizon and Gilles Pelisson (director of operations for the Paris region since 1991) were asked to reflect on these discussions and to propose a viable action plan for Novotel. Their plan was presented to the two co-presidents of Accor and ultimately became the basis for the project *Retour vers le Futur*.

In December, a number of Accor divisions were reorganized. Claude Moscheni, longtime president of Novotel, became president of Pullman International. Pullman International was the Accor Group's four-star deluxe hotel chain that included such internationally renowned hotels brands as Sofitel, Pullman, Mercure, and Altria Hotels. Over 10 years, Moscheni's skills had helped build the Novotel chain into the crown jewel of the group. His managerial skills were openly acknowledged and his expertise would bring a valuable asset to his new post. However, within Novotel, many felt it was time for a change.

Philippe Brizon and Gilles Pelisson were named as the two new co-presidents of Novotel, and given a clear mandate to introduce major changes. By now it was clear to Group headquarters that there was a profits slippage. Profits posted for 1992 were half those for 1991.

The Original Brizon-Pelisson Plan

The original plan proposed by Philippe Brizon and Gilles Pelisson attempted to address Novotel's fundamental problems. The final plan looked somewhat different. The core of the plan was simple: to "Re-Novotelize" Novotel. This was to be achieved by refocusing on three aspects: *clients, personnel,* and *gestion* (guests, staff, and administration). These themes interrelated to form the tripod on which the revitalization of Novotel's operations were based.

The plan envisaged that the customer was more important than the product and recognized this fact as the basis of future initiatives. Under the plan, Novotel would become more sensitive to changes in the marketplace; in particular, it would become more responsive to changing consumer tastes and preferences.

The Novotel brand was to be repositioned strategically. This would include refurbishing Novotels, altering and freshening the Novotel logo and brand identity, and increased advertising and marketing efforts to reestablish the Novotel brand image in the mind of the consumer. The strategy also suggested the need for a new Novotel image for the year 2000.

In order to give more autonomy to Novotel staff, the plan called for reorganizing the personnel and management structure. Accor advisers would be temporarily assigned to Novotel to overhaul the human resources structure. The roles of GMs would be redefined, as would be payment and reward systems for all staff. Management teams would be encouraged. In line with these changes, improvements would be made to various management accounting procedures. A significant number of changes related to cost management, with the ultimate aim of cost reduction.

Suggested changes to the administrative systems included initiatives to improve productivity. Novotels and their restaurants were to be reorganized. The structure of Head Office was to be streamlined. The information system was to be upgraded. Particular attention was given to improving the 5 to 10 underperforming Novotels.

The New Co-Presidents

According to many senior managers and GMs, one of Novotel's assets during this turbulent period was the complementary personalities of the new co-presidents, Philippe Brizon and Gilles Pelisson.

Philippe Brizon was a graduate of the prestigious French Grand Ecole, HEC, and he had had a long career in Accor. He rose to being president of the *Courte Paille* fast-food restaurant chain and was president of the Ibis hotel chain from 1984–88. A number of senior managers described him as an intellectual with an artistic mind. Very marketing-oriented, he was excellent with figures. Acknowledged by colleagues as a "visionary," one GM remarked, "It appears he's already thinking twenty-five years hence."

Giles Pelisson came with a very different background. Nephew of the cofounder, he graduated from the French Grande Ecole, ESSEC, and held an MBA from Harvard, after which he worked in the USA for several years, initially in a New York bank. He subsequently joined Accor and worked in the group's restaurant operations and other subsidiaries on both the East and West Coasts. He was regarded as very operations-minded and an effective implementer of strategies. In 1991, he joined Novotel as director of operations for the Paris region. Colleagues said that he enjoyed working with his managers. The two men reportedly discussed every major decision.

Once in place, the two new co-presidents acted swiftly to organize their management team and set their plan in motion.

EARLY 1993: BUILDING A NEW TEAM

Choosing the Top Team

With approval for their outline plan, and aware that they would become co-presidents in 1993, Brizon and Pelisson began to assemble their core management team. They moved fast. As one senior manager recalls,

> I got my phone call at home on Christmas Day. That's when Gilles Pelisson phoned me to say "do you want to come or not?" It's not normal in this company that you get telephoned on Christmas Day, but I suppose it was urgent. Two days before he had phoned me to say: "Claude Moscheni is leaving. I'm taking the co-presidency with Philippe Brizon. I'm thinking about you coming to Paris. I'll give you 48 hours to decide if you would like to come."

The two co-presidents decided on a flat organization structure, centered around 12 directors of operations (DOPs) and supported by a few key functional heads such as finance, marketing, and human resources. Local GMs would report to the 12 DOPs with no intermediate layers of management. In practice, this meant that a typical European DOP had some 20 to 25 reports, far more than previously, some covering several countries.

The new structure took effect immediately, sending a signal of change to all managers in the system. A number of people found themselves in new positions. Some of the previous regional heads, many of whom were long-serving managers with Novotel, were persuaded to move to other openings in Accor. The new top team had more women than in the past.

The new structure eliminated one and a half layers of management and changed the role of the senior managers. With so many reports it was not possible for the senior managers to be so intimately involved in their GM's operational details as had previously been the case.

In addition to these changes at senior levels, all *Directeurs Delegues* were reassigned back to their old positions. One general manager commented:

> It was quite a shock. One moment I had been given a promotion to be in charge of three hotels as well as manager of my own hotel, and I felt important and rewarded. Then, a few

months later, my new responsibility was taken away from me. I admit that I was shocked and depressed. Now, I see the reason why, and can understand.

The effect of these changes was to reduce the size of the head office and create a tighter, leaner operational center.

The top team met together for the first time at a three-day seminar on February 9, 1993, where they decided how they would function.

The Anthropologists' Work

Simultaneous with these organizational changes, the two co-presidents recruited consultants to help them. Avoiding the large well-known consulting groups, they chose two leading anthropologists and asked them to document the Novotel culture. The idea to use anthropologists to help the team discover Novotel's cultural history was seen as inspirational in achieving new ideas and accord.

Through intensive interviews across the organization, the anthropologists began to identify Novotel's roots or *genes*. This helped them to identify and recommend future directions for the organization. Open-space meetings among the top team complemented the anthropologists' work and helped further refine the issues confronting the organization.

The team identified the need to place the hotel guest at the top of the organization. The relationship of the Novotel structure to the guests and the employees was symbolized by a flower—a marguerite—and the sun. The sun represented the guests. The center of the flower represented the general manager stimulating the efforts of his team. The petals represented the support for the GM including management and staff teams in his Novotel, various interfunctional groups, and relationships with other Novotel GMs.

The Working Parties

In late February, the top team identified three issues they felt were of major concern and needed greater exploration—communication (marketing and image), management, and commercial. They established three working parties to examine the three issues and make recommendations. For the first time, the groups involved people outside the very top team. Several members of the team emphasized the importance of the consultants' work. The communications group was typical of how the three groups tackled their assignment.

Membership of the communications group consisted of eight senior managers: the managers of marketing and public relations; two directors of operations, two GMs (both French), and the two co-presidents. The anthropologists were also present as facilitators to encourage brainstorming sessions. For several weeks the group examined all aspects of Novotel's image, particularly the notion that Novotel was faithful to guests. The group also identified the need to improve Novotel's hotel facilities. Using the image of a lighthouse in the night, they identified various improvements to make guests more welcome. These proposals were later made part of a one billion Franc refurbishment and investment program.

Later, the group's work led to the redesign of the Novotel logo. The new logo had a softer look that conveyed a feeling of hospitality and a warm welcome. The new logo was subsequently used by all Novotels and featured in a major advertising campaign launched later the same year.

The two other working parties also generated many new ideas. One was to reduce prices and costs as a means of bolstering Novotel's competitive position in the market. The decision was made to cut prices by 5 percent across the board, a move that was seen as vitally urgent and necessary. While the price cut was risky (since it would boost profits only if the trend of falling occupancy was reversed), occupancy ended up rising by several percentage points *and* the average cost per room rented dropped significantly. Meanwhile, actions were also taken to increase cost flexibility. Hotel occupancy can swing unpredictably, not only from week to week, but also from day to day. Novotel was felt to be less responsive to such swings than was desirable.

The work groups further proposed that GMs needed a simplified set of performance measures. In the past, Novotel had relied on complex measures such as the Bolts, with financial results being one of the most important. In the future, it was decided to abolish the Bolts. It was also decided that financial targets were still vital, but that managers should be evaluated on the three parameters of customers, management, and people. The idea of simplified performance measures reinforced the vision of restoring Novotel to its entrepreneurial roots.

Between March and April 1993, each director of operations organized three-day meetings with their general managers in order to make a diagnosis and suggest improvements, and to refine the new approaches proposed by the top management team.

Concerned that success of the change effort depended on involving as many people in the organization as possible, Philippe Brizon and Gilles Pelisson took their show "on the road" to hotel locations throughout Europe. During March and April they attended the 19 sessions organized by the DOPs.

At about this time, it was decided to establish a *war room* at the headquarters in Evry, where each hotel in the European network could be regularly monitored. The walls in this room were lined with charts, each representing one Novotel, grouped by regional director. Each chart contained about five simple performance measures under each of the main headings of customers, management, and people. Colored adhesive paper stars indicated improvement programs and degrees of progress. Anyone in the room could easily see how each Novotel location was progressing, and how the regional directors were developing their group of hotels. All key meetings were held in the *war room*, symbolically emphasizing the importance of continuous improvement.

By March 1993, it was clear to everyone in the whole Accor Group that Novotel's financial results were deteriorating. Not only was the year 1992 poor in comparison to 1991, but all 1993 forecasts looked bleak. Monthly returns showed some steep declines. This was largely shared throughout the organization.

In the early months of 1993, although most people in Novotel knew that a change program was imminent, they were unaware of what the actual changes would be. They had already seen the arrival of two new co-presidents and were adjusting to a new reporting structure.

Selecting General Managers

During the late spring/early summer of 1993, all DOPs were asked to assess their general managers. One explained:

> I was asked to select my new managers. I had freedom of choice. Of course, I consulted Gilles and Philippe. It was difficult, and in the end there were four who did not stay.
>
> All my remaining managers went away for three days together. On the first day we addressed the past. "We must change, and to change we must know what is wrong and

EXHIBIT 5   The Written Statement of the Novotel Spirit

> ### THE NOVOTEL SPIRIT
> The NOVOTEL chain is both a reference and a preference for people
> whose lifestyle or business takes them all over the world.
>
> NOVOTEL maintains a loyal commitment to its guests.
>
> For them, NOVOTEL had developed a simple dependable concept; a single
> identical room design in every hotel, complemented by meeting facilities,
> restaurants, and convenient parking. Behind these similarities is a wide variety
> of locations (at airports, close to major routes, in city centers, by the sea, etc.) and
> extra touches, thanks to the sense of hospitality and service shared by all
> NOVOTEL staff, becoming true <<maitre de maison>>.
>
> And there's always something new at NOVOTEL!
> This year brings a new visual identity, lower prices, renovations, greater
> regional adaptation, the establishment of a Minitel service in France 36.15.
>
> NOVOTEL, a chain and staff that's always on the move!

Source: Novotel corporate literature.

what is right. We must keep what is right and deal with what is wrong." On the second and third days we created projects. It was very difficult. People were always coming back to the past and saying this or that would not work.

We had to create a climate of change, to inspire the general managers in charge of the hotels to go back to their teams and make things happen. We discussed all the ideas that the working parties discussed: the new values, the spirit of *Maitre de Maison*, the new structure, the new ideas of communication. In every case, I was asking my managers how they were going to implement it.

Although the meetings were fraught with difficulty, they were highly constructive. It was apparent that many of the ideas set out in the earlier working parties needed modification and alteration. It was becoming apparent that the project's original emphasis leaned too much towards cost and price cutting, to the detriment of creating new corporate values. As the change effort continued, it became more and more evident that Novotel needed to identify ways of creating new values for guests and reinforcing its product differentiation.

One of the constructive outcomes was the decision to adopt *Retour vers le Futur* as the slogan for the Novotel change program.

The *Retour vers le Futur* project aimed at instilling the Novotel spirit [*l'esprit Novotel*] into all Novotel staff. The tenets of the Novotel spirit were an entrepreneurial spirit, a commitment to colleagues and guests, and a pride in the Novotel brand image (see Exhibit 5).

The Assessment Center

It was apparent to all concerned that the new organization would require new kinds of behavior from general managers. It was also evident that many GMs would need considerable help in implementing changes and ensuring that changes were permanent. Novotel recognized on the one hand that it would have to invest in training for the GMs, but on the other that it did not know which GMs had weaknesses. An assessment center was therefore set up.

The assessment center was designed to identify weaknesses of GMs and pinpoint where appropriate training would be needed. In spite of its title, the assessment center was not used to select managers; that had already been done. GMs were told the assessment center intended to help correct skills deficiencies, and that poor performance in the assessment center would not (directly) jeopardize jobs.

The assessment activity was conducted over a long day. Each GM undertook a series of role plays in managing the operations of an employment agency. These roles involved resolving conflicts, assessing subordinates, and making presentations to superiors. Scored results and informal feedback were given to the manager at the end of the assessment. It was followed up by specific training provided by Novotel and the Accor Academie.

Initially, many managers who took the assessment were very apprehensive. Some said the process was very stressful. As time went on, the assessors become more able to alleviate apprehensions, and participants were reassured that the program was as constructive as intended.

The October Convention

In October 1993, Novotel held a major three-day convention, entitled *Les Recontres de Futur* (Meeting the Future). This was the largest gathering of its kind in the history of Novotel. It brought together all the Novotel top team and all general managers. In all, more than 300 people attended.

The event was both a celebration and a serious working function. Philippe Brizon and Gilles Pelisson welcomed participants in 25 languages. Two Benedictine monks addressed the assembly and explained the nature of hospitality and welcome according to the 25 centuries tradition of their monastic order. They described the relationship of their monastery and their brethren towards their guests and explained their hospitality duties and procedures.

Paul Dubrule and Gerard Pelisson, Novotel cofounders and now co-presidents of Accor, chaired lunches during which they made speeches and answered questions about the original precepts of Novotel and their ideas about its future. Co-Presidents Brizon and Pelisson led many of the discussions and debates. The new logo was unveiled and its message explained to the participants.

The activities during the convention dealt with many aspects of the proposed changes, and reexamined the group's future directions. As a symbolic act, each participant painted a section of a huge mural painting that represented the history and renovation of Novotel. The painting was later cut into 378 pieces and a piece given to each participant. In order to facilitate the dissemination of information from the convention, the various sessions were video recorded, edited, and distributed as three videocassettes. These were translated into other European languages (the convention proceedings were in French) and sent to GMs to facilitate training sessions related to the project.

CHANGING THE HOTELS

Breaking the Structure

The *Retour vers le Futur* project changed the structure and operations of the administrative corporate center. Additionally, it significantly transformed operations and work routines in every Novotel. Not all hotels needed to change equally, nor were all changing at exactly the same time, but, in general, the whole group marched in lockstep. This was evident from interviews with head office managers, with various staff in seven hotels in three countries and from details on the walls of the war room in Evry.

Changes in Internal Structure

The first and most obvious change was the reduced number of supervisory levels in the internal structure in a Novotel unit. This reduced costs and improved cost flexibility. Before the introduction of the project, each Novotel generally had four formal management layers; in practice, some hotels had more. Within this structure the need for each of the levels to be informed and consulted impeded the rapid movement of information and slowed down decision making. A restaurant manager in France recalls that this was the system in operation when she first joined Novotel:

> Under our old way of working there were too many people who worked without saying anything. You had the waiter and the head waiter and the people who are higher than them and so on. There were about four or five steps, from the lower levels to the boss. If you wanted to speak to the head of department you had too many people to ask first.

This situation was particularly noticeable if a staff member needed to respond immediately to a guest's request or problem. The lengthy delay needed to provide a satisfactory answer sometimes became embarrassing. A receptionist at a Novotel in Germany said:

> Before, there was one person responsible for each department. There was a food and beverages manager, there was a rooms division manager, there was a deputy general manager, there was a general manager and an assistant and too many people, who were responsible but still they didn't work with each other. They worked in the same hotel but said, "This is my department" and they didn't help each other.

The *Retour vers le Futur* project reduced the internal management structure by one layer. Now there are only three steps between staff and GM: staff, heads of departments, and the GM. Heads of departments include *Maitres d'Hotel* (in food and beverage departments), housekeeping, and heads of the front desk.

One immediate consequence of this delayering was a reduction in the numbers employed in a hotel, sometimes by a considerable amount. Flattening the traditional hierarchial structure brought all members of the staff closer together, facilitated information and communication flows, and accelerated decision making. According to one restaurant manager:

> Now we ask people to give their opinion and to ask if there's a problem or a question. It's better to have everybody's opinion; this is very important. We have no more steps now. Only one step between the boss and the heads of departments and after that you have all the staff.

There were also changes in the flow of information from Novotel headquarters. GMs were no longer inundated with memos and requests from many departments. Headquarters staff collated instructions on administrative matters and sent these simultaneously to the various Novotels. In the hotel these were collected in a reference file called the Pilot Case, so-called because it resembled an airline pilot's document case.

Introducing the Changes

Initially, general managers were responsible for informing their staff about the *Retour vers le Futur* project and introducing its principles into their Novotel. No formal training program was available to the hotels to help them manage the change process. GMs were given only broad guidelines to follow.

Some GMs collaborated in training their staff and organized "cross-meetings" to advise and help each other. Shared training sessions had an additional advantage of not depleting the number of staff in a Novotel at any one time. Some GMs held their training seminars in a neutral environment, such as a different hotel in the area.

One method of training used by some GMs was to replicate the brainstorming activities they had experienced in the consultants' focus groups. In a similar way in which the consultants had stimulated discussions, GMs asked their staff to reflect on their work, their perspective on Novotel's problems, and how Novotel could change. With an opportunity to reflect on and discuss these topics, staff members were usually able to make suggestions for changing work routines in their hotel. However, initially, staff members who were interested in the project were a minority, and some of their colleagues remained skeptical. One GM quantified the response from his staff to the new project:

> I think immediately a few were very motivated, and a few were very negative. The rest said, "We'll wait and see and do it afterwards."

A receptionist in France describes her initial confusion:

> Well, at first we didn't understand the project because we didn't know what it was and we didn't know what people would like to do. After six months, we started to see what it was. The project came very slowly. Then we started to understand that we had to do things by ourselves, it was not necessary to ask your *chef*. People started to do things by themselves. Well, after that, the project went faster, and we started to move very quickly between the work that we have to do here and the extra work we've got to do.

In this Novotel, those staff members who greeted the project with enthusiasm signed an undertaking describing how they would change their own work routines. To get the project moving, the motivated people pressed ahead with their ideas for change and tried to encourage colleagues to contribute. This sometimes divided the staff, a consequence that conflicted with the spirit of the project. In their enthusiasm, mistakes were made and sometimes relationships became strained. One GM spent four months to resolve the situation to everyone's satisfaction.

> The organizers were beginning to be regarded by others as moving towards a supervisory role in which it was assumed that they would be telling others what to do and be promoted sooner than similarly qualified colleagues. Fortunately, I noticed the situation occurring and assured everyone that the *Retour vers le Futur* project was intended to help eliminate hierarchies, not create them. However, it was a slow process convincing people that this was so.

In order to sensitize his team to the project and its expectations, this GM asked his staff to make a *Blazon* [badge] for their hotel. This prompted the hotel staff to think about and depict their vision for the future. The anthropologists had used this activity with great success to encourage focus groups of general managers to reflect on the Novotel culture.

While hotel staff were managing aspects of the project, guests became aware of changes in staffing and routines. A restaurant manager in France described his experience:

> We've got some customers who come to the hotel every month, and it was very difficult for them in particular. They saw new faces and they said, "Well, its not like usual." They said, "What's the matter, everything is changing around here?" They didn't like this. After about six months they continued coming, and they said "Yes, it's better now."

New Roles for General Managers

A significant part of the project envisaged a transformed role for the Novotel general manager. Traditionally, in many hotels, GMs occupied the pinnacle of a hierarchial structure. From this position as a figurehead the GM made all decisions, but was remote from staff and guests.

The new Novotel structure saw the role of the GM differently. The GM was a coach, responsible for advising staff and encouraging them to develop their professional and personal competencies. He, or she, animated the hotel team to optimize the service and facilities offered to guests. The GM was seen as the skipper of a boat, choosing the right team members, assigning them to the right place, and leading so that teams performed in the best possible way.

The *Retour vers le Futur* project resulted in the hotel staff having increased autonomy and being empowered to make a broad range of decisions. A GM in France explained his role as coach:

> Everybody knows today that they have to make decisions. They have the possibilities to express themselves and move ahead. If they need me, I'm there; if they don't need me, I'm not there.

In order to pass on instructions and to keep abreast of developments in each functional area, GMs held regular meetings with their heads of department. In these meetings, information was bidirectional and heads of departments briefed GMs on work within their department.

As far as guests were concerned, the traditional manager was distant and unapproachable. In the new era, the general manager was designated as *Maitre de Maison* [Mine Host], a title which signified a new image with responsibilities for making the guest the most important person in Novotel's relationships for putting the *Maitre de Maison* in closer contact with guests. A GM in France outlined his perception of this new role:

> It's a new spirit. Today, we say a guest of Novotel doesn't like the manager to wear a tie. He prefers to have people to speak to him, to drink something with him. I bring two people together, I introduce one to the other to create an ambience signified by our motto: *"Bienvenue vous etes chez vous."*

Not all GMs were comfortable with their new role. They were expected to generate increased business from limited resources and to use their initiative to seek out new business opportunities. GMs were thus forced to become even more attuned to the preferences and needs of their core customers [*fond de clientele*]. One GM explained how his strategy favored regular guests over other guests:

> You would think in an airport hotel that you have people staying for a short stay, only one night. But there are people coming once, twice, three times, ten times a month sometimes.

Those are my regular customers. The people for the air show are coming for the air show only once every two years and these people are prepared to pay—if the room rate was a thousand francs a night, for example those people wouldn't say anything. But if you keep space for your regular customers, they'll come back next time to you. Incidentally, those regular customers are not all paying the full price: you've got corporate rates, you've got people paying 10 percent, 15 percent less than the rack rate. I could sell all the [rooms in the] hotel at the full rate to those people who come only for the exhibitions, but what do I do with my regular customers, with the core of customers? They'd go somewhere else, forever. And I've seen that with the other hotels. Some people have gone to those hotels for one, two or three nights. But they've come back to us afterwards. Because during this air show, during this or that exhibition they found out by phoning our competitor that there was no room for them. Our competitor had given them a special price when they'd needed them, but afterwards there was no space for them when they needed a room.

New Layouts

In the past, all Novotels had standardized public areas such as the lobby, bar, and restaurant. The change process initiated during 1993 permitted differences. Within broad guidelines, GMs were allowed to exercise their own discretion over the style and decoration. For example, one GM installed a television set in the bar area where businesspeople, who tend to travel alone, wanted something to watch. On vacation routes, where the majority of guests were families with children, GMs were more likely to install a pool table, a miniature basketball net, or a table of building bricks.

Changing Work Routines

GMs and their staff believed that one of the stimulating aspects of the *Retour vers le Futur* project was the way it prompted changes in work routines. The project had driven some form of change in most, if not all, jobs. One head of reception described the new responsibilities for the reception team:

Take cashing up, for example. Before, we took the cash and checked it, and then we'd make a new cash-book for the following week or for two or three days. Now that's finished. Each person has their own till and their own responsibility for their cash for the bank. Each person also has many things to do which, before, were done by the head of reception. For example, before, all the invoices which we send to companies went to the head's desk and he would send off the invoice. Now, reception staff make their own invoices and one person is responsible for sending out the bills.

Flattening the Novotel structure and encouraging greater autonomy and responsibility gave heads of reception new responsibilities, including training staff in how the hotel procedures worked. One head of reception compared current work procedures to former routines:

Before, people knew only one part of the things we do at the back. Now, each person does the job from the beginning to the end; and they now know why they are doing this. I give each person a range of things to do and they take responsibility for them.

In addition to encouraging staff to assume greater responsibility, the project broadened the outlook of staff and enabled people to see a greater part of the whole operation in their hotel. A restaurant manager in Germany explained how efficient ordering of supplies affected customer service:

The work is allocated out and we each have a lot of new responsibilities. For example, in the restaurant we have people who order the kitchen supplies: the bread, tableware, and all the plates, glasses, and things. Take bread for example, when you order too much there is waste; when you order too little then you have people sitting and waiting for this. It makes you realize how important it is to order the right quantities. Of course, occasionally mistakes happen, but it is necessary to understand why it is very important to order things at the right time and in the right quantities. At the beginning, mistakes were made. But now people are aware of each part of the system.

The project also prompted changes in the way in which staff members worked with each other. Reduced levels of staffing, job flexibility, cross-functional discussion and project groups helped generate empathy for colleagues' work. Staff members were beginning to see how their colleagues' work affected the work of others and contributed to the whole operation. A receptionist outlined the changes that had taken place:

Before, everybody worked in each separate section of the hotel and we didn't ask them to think about their work. Everybody worked separately, for example, as the boss or as the head of a department. Now we all work together. This is very important because they have some ideas. We want them to invest themselves to work in the same direction.

One result of greater responsibility was increased autonomy that benefitted both staff member and guest. For example, receptionists were given some autonomy to discuss the room rate with the guest. In Germany, a Novotel receptionist said:

When a client comes in at ten o'clock in the evening and he asks for the room rate, what do you do when you tell him the rack rate and he says, "That's too expensive for me, could you do it for a lower price?" Well before, I would have said, "No, I'm sorry, sir, I'm not allowed to deal with prices for you." But, now, as a receptionist I can say I can go down on the price 10 percent.

The autonomy to negotiate prices did not solely apply to guests who arrive late. The same receptionist could also negotiate prices for group bookings, a task previously handled by her manager.

However, there were still some decision areas where staff had to confer with their GM. These related mainly to policy matters or long-term operating decisions. Periodic consultation usually resulted in agreed guidelines. A banqueting manager in Germany related how she and her general manager met in July, December, and April, to decide promotional rates for her customers. Once agreed, the banqueting manager decided specific rates according to room availability and customers' needs:

I have decisions on the number of rooms I can sell and at what particular period, but I always ask the other managers of the reception. We do it altogether, I don't have to ask the general manager for this. I go to reception and ask for 20 or 50 rooms for this period, and we speak about the price. If we don't agree, which sometimes happens, maybe then we go and see the general manager and he will tell us what he thinks about it. It's the same for the price of the menu I sell and for the kind of menu. I go and see the *chef de cuisine*, I ask him: "Do you think that for 50 persons, I could sell it at this price. I think I could have the business if I sell it at that price. Can you manage your business at that price?" And he says "Yes" or "No, please increase it."

Another GM related his efforts to create a painstakingly complex computer analysis to track guests' food and beverage spending in the hotel restaurant and bar. He decided that this would help more effective staff scheduling and thus improve the service provided to guests. He created his own project and tested out his theories. After much work at the end of his normal working day, he came up with a satisfactory system. He was using the results of his tracking analysis to help him and his team better predict room bookings, staff costs, and HR planning. "Since the project *Retour vers le Futur*," he said, "you can try out what you think you need to try."

Hotel Teams

The teamwork initiative encouraged staff to help other departments during busy periods. In some cases, teams operate only in their own functional area such as the restaurant, reception, housekeeping. Teams are informal and generally meet every day to discuss with the head of department issues arising that day—for example, the level of hotel occupancy and how this will affect the work of the department, any business that needs special attention, planning for future events in the department.

However, while people were willing to help, lack of specialized training and insufficient time to attend relevant training precluded staff from certain departments from helping colleagues as much as they would like. To help resolve this problem, an initiative called *Progres Novotel* was launched to support the newly introduced system of team work in each Novotel.

The change program allowed people to transfer to different departments by arrangement with their GM and department head. Generally, this worked to everyone's benefit and satisfaction: individuals could challenge themselves with a new work area and develop their skills; Novotel gained an employee who was pursuing the spirit of *polyvalence* [flexibility]; guests dealt with an employee who was informed and competent in two or more work areas.

Astonishing the Guests

Management was encouraging Novotel staff to astonish hotel guests with their actions and treatment. Some reception staff at one hotel in France dressed in clown costumes at *Mardi Gras*:

> For *Mardi Gras* we decided to dress up as clowns. At the reception we worked in our clown costumes, and it was very funny to see the guests arriving at reception. We had a very good time that day. First, the guests were very surprised: they didn't know where they had arrived. It was very funny. Afterwards they laughed and said we had to dare, and it's important for us to be daring. We enjoy our guests; we have no limits and that's very important.

Another hotel in France celebrated the opening week of *La Chasse* [the hunting season] with a suitably decorated restaurant whose staff wore hunting costumes. Yet another hotel had a Quebec theme with receptionists dressed in Canadian attire (checkered shirts, neckerchiefs, jeans, and boots). The lobby exhibited Canadian paintings and guest singers performed in the bar.

Some staff give free rein to their imaginations. The hotel that celebrated *Mardi Gras* thought that Easter should be celebrated too:

> We met local chocolate makers and they made for us a special big boat made of chocolate. We made a special presentation of that big boat with flamingos and sugar. It was very big and very important looking. And then we had some rabbits and some eggs.

The organizers of such activities saw them as a way of capturing the imagination of guests and showing guests that they cared about them. They also believed that doing things to entertain guests was an effective way of competing with other hotels. Such diversions were especially effective for guests who attended conferences and seminars. The GM of the hotel which celebrated *Mardi Gras* explained:

> It's easy to receive a guest in a beautiful room, with a good bed. We have more than most: we have air-conditioning, they haven't. We have the biggest room: it's 25 metres. But, we are more expensive. If we want to be different, we have to astonish the guests with the wine tasting, the barbecue party, and everything different. These are things you find usually in a long stay hotel, in a place where you stay four, five, six, seven days. But in some hotels when you sleep only one night, you arrive at two or three in the afternoon and you leave at six or seven the following morning. Usually you sleep, have a drink, eat, and then you go away. Here we want to give something different to that. We do a lot of things to—the best word is "*il faut etonner.*" We have to astonish our guests to see them again.

Reflective Clubs

In order to identify opportunities where improvements could be made, some hotels created reflective clubs (*Clubs de Reflexion*). These were informal groups of staff meeting together to suggest initiatives. The general manager was not necessarily involved; one GM said, "I am invited sometimes when they want to invite me." This GM described two reflective clubs which had started in his hotel. One involved managing costs more efficiently; the second, called *Club action clients*, was addressing guest-related issues.

Club members were drawn from every service area and made suggestions relating to the service provided by the hotel as a whole rather than club members' specific functions. Suggestions made included making a *terrain de boules* (a playing area for *boules*) and organizing a barbecue party for guests. The cost management club made a proposal for coordinating purchasing and supply of cleaning products to benefit from bulk buying discounts. This club also suggested that when a member of staff broke a piece of glassware or crockery, a fine should be deducted from the person's salary. With a fine of 10 francs per item, staff became more careful about avoiding breakages.

Reflective clubs were seen as yet another way in which staff members became sensitive to the operating issues and challenges faced by colleagues in other departments. Furthermore, they helped employees appreciate how the work of different departments combined to provide an aggregate service to guests. As the manager explained:

> They feel the difference because they tell me, "Before, we have just to do our work; we haven't to say something about our work. Today, we are obliged to say what we think about our work." It's a big difference and they feel it.

NETWORKING BETWEEN HOTELS

In addition to the initiatives stimulated by the *Retour vers le Futur* project, there were a number of cross-country initiatives intended to cement new working styles and abet further unification of the Novotel culture.

More Clubs

In the past, networking between Novotels was limited; any links were often formally sanctioned and structured. Beginning in 1993, general managers were encouraged to form spontaneous clubs to examine common problems that hotels shared.

These clubs consisted of Novotels that had similar profiles (location and organization) and interests (busy periods, business opportunities, business clients). One such club was the European Airports club, whose membership consisted of general managers of Novotels that were situated close to major European airports—Berlin, Brussels, London Heathrow, Milan, Madrid, Charles de Gaulle, and Orly in Paris. Another airport club consisted of GMs from regional airports such as Birmingham International, Lille, Lyon. Other personnel joined club meetings according to the topic under consideration.

One GM was selected as club leader and was responsible for the organization of meetings, preparing agendas, and distributing minutes of meetings. The leader of the club was not the chairperson; topics were discussed in a "round table" format. Airport clubs met once every two or three months, with the location rotating according to membership. Airport club meetings were attended by approximately 10 people. The two airport clubs met together once a year to discuss common problems and issues.

There was a club of city center Novotels whose operational and managerial problems were quite different from those in airport hotels. Members of this club included the large metropolitan Novotels situated in such city centers as Bagnolet and Les Halles in Paris, and Hammersmith in London. Hotels that had a major proportion of their business coming from seminars and meetings also formed a club.

While busy work schedules precluded all GMs from attending every meeting of their club, minutes circulated by the club leader informed all members of topics and progress. A copy of the minutes of each meeting was sent to Novotel headquarters; still, clubs were autonomous decision-making bodies and had authority to launch their own initiatives.

Progress Groups

Progress groups [*Groupes de Progres*] made a significant contribution to maintaining momentum.

Progress groups were formal "committees" that functioned at the level of country managers and DOPs. Each group has approximately six or seven members chosen by the *Committee de Direction* (management committee). Groups met regularly, on average once per month, and were not specific to the GMs in one country. A progress group leader was responsible for organizing meetings and circulating minutes. Meeting sites rotated among group members' hotels.

Progress group members discussed themes relating to the *Retour vers le Future* project and helped give continued impetus and direction to the project. Progress groups had been responsible for a number of significant initiatives currently being instigated.

One of these initiatives was a productivity project to investigate more efficient practices in food and beverage (F&B) departments. So far, this initiative had had two phases. Phase 1 was concerned with cost control and reducing F&B prime costs by 5–10 percent. Revising the content of menus had enabled reductions in the amount of supplies in store. Close scrutiny of the ways in which meals were prepared helped eliminate waste. Phase 2 of the project was concentrating on better purchasing and storage procedures.

Another progress group investigated potential improvements to the service provided by the housekeeping department. The group examined all housekeeping practices and procedures. A human resources consultant was engaged to analyze room-cleaning routines in detail. Close examination of how rooms were cleaned indicated potential savings. Dividing the work differently reduced time taken for the task. Eventually, the time needed to clean a room was reduced from an average of 35–40 minutes to 28 minutes, a reduction of approximately 10 minutes per room per person. Extended to a 150-room hotel, this represented a considerable time saving.

Better planning of the housekeeping department also provided a better service for the guest, since reduced room-cleaning time allowed cleaning work to begin later. The absence of room-cleaning staff in the early morning left corridors free of cleaning carts at the time when guests were going down to breakfast or checking out. Postponing cleaning times until after 9:00 A.M. also meant that guests were not disturbed by vacuum cleaner noise in the early morning.

Reexamining the housekeeping function brought about improvements in the equipment used for housekeeping. One improvement involved redesigning the cart used to transport cleaning utensils, bed linen, and other supplies from room to room. The new model was smaller and slimmer, allowing it to fit inside the door alcove of a guest room rather than cluttering the hallway.

The newly designed room cleaning process was made into a training video. One training video showed staff *how* guest rooms should be cleaned; another explained *why* the rooms were cleaned.

The next stage of the housekeeping project, scheduled for 1995, was to be aimed at cost control.

Marketing Initiatives

Since the start of the revitalization of the chain in 1993, a number of groupwide marketing initiatives had been taken. Two of these were the Dolphi Club and the Novotel cardholder club. In Europe, some 400,000 children, accompanied by their parents, stayed at Novotel annually. Children represented approximately 10 percent of the 5 million guests who stay annually at Novotel. Under the company's family policy, children under 16 years old sharing their parents' room received free accommodation and breakfast.

The Dolphi Club [*le Club Dolfi*] was a children's club whose mascot was a smiling dolphin. A sales manager who worked on *le Club Dolfi* project explained how the club operated:

> When children come to reception, we give them balloons. When they go to the restaurant, we give them a small dolphin toy and a special place mat and colored pens to draw with. Dolfi recommends special dishes for his young friends from our special lunch or dinner menu. We also give children nice straws for their soft drinks.

Novotel was the first international hotel chain to offer a membership card for frequent visitors. Called *la Carte NOVOTEL partner,* it gave cardholders a number of benefits. A quarterly newsletter was sent to all members. Cardholders received a room in any Novotel without prior booking. Cardholders also were entitled to a 15 percent discount on the regular room rate. In addition, members were entitled to preferential treatment and discounts when using any of the services within the Accor group.

Training: *Progres Novotel*

In recent months, a progress group had completed work on *Progres Novotel*, a program designed to change the way in which staff were trained and assessed.

Early on, top management realized that training was a crucial element of reinforcing and cementing the changing routines and work practices of the organization. The *Progres Novotel* project was designed to ensure that staff became competent employees with recognized steps in their training and development. A new formal training package was introduced in France in December 1993, and was being introduced into neighboring countries in phases. Plans called for it to be introduced to all Novotel employees before the end of 1995.

The team working on *Progres Novotel* analyzed the skills needed to work in a Novotel and further subdivided this work into three stages. Each of the three stages represented a stage of competence based on degree of difficulty: bronze [*bronze*], silver [*argent*], and gold [*or*]. A fourth category, platinum [*platin*], involved the skills and preparation necessary to be a department head. In all, the *Progres Novotel* project consisted of approximately 300 competencies needed by various Novotel staff members.

It was expected that people would move through the four stages, in some cases simultaneously, as they became more competent in their own work and, possibly, gained experience in a different department. The first stage took a person no longer than two months from the time they began working at a Novotel. The second level of competency-building was captured in the phrase, "I know my work and I now take some autonomy; I am able to take some decisions and I don't need a supervisior nearby." The third level entailed enough expertise that a staff member could say, "I know my work, I am autonomous, and I am able to train a new colleague."

As they progressed through the stages, employees received salary increments and the satisfaction of knowing that their progress was noted on their employment records. General managers kept a personal record book and each employee's competence was denoted by an evaluation indicator [*methode de mesure*]. Heads of department evaluated the progress of their staff using an evaluator's guide [*guide des evaluateurs*] for each competence. By design, each competence level included work from a different department. For example, kitchen staff were expected to know how to serve a table.

Progres Novotel project members insisted that such procedures were not a reversion to a hierarchy of jobs, but rather were a "hierarchy of knowledge" aimed at ensuring that Novotel trained its employees as an investment for their future.

MAINTAINING MOMENTUM

So far, Novotel management believed the *Retour vers le Futur* project was on course. Those in the center were keen to keep up the pressure to ensure that momentum was maintained and the ideas of the project were seen through. They saw their work as having just begun, not finished. One of the co-presidents said:

> The first step was to change in our heads, in order to manage differently, but while most people expect the "Back to the Future" project to have a beginning and an end, our greatest challenge is now to make them understand that change is, from now on, a permanent way of Novotel strategic thinking.

THE LINCOLN ELECTRIC COMPANY, 1996

Arthur Sharplin, *University of Texas at Austin*

John A. Seeger, *Bentley College*

It was February 29, 1996. The Lincoln Electric Company, a leading producer of arc welding products, had just celebrated its centennial year by reporting record 1995 sales of over $1 billion, record profits of $61.5 million, and record employee bonuses of $66 million. This performance followed two years of losses—the only losses in the company's long history—stemming from a seemingly disastrous foray into Europe, Asia, and Latin America. (Exhibits 1 and 2 present operating results and ratios for recent years.)

Headquartered in the Cleveland suburb of Euclid, Ohio, the company was widely known for its incentive management system. According to the *New York Times*, thousands of managers visited Lincoln's headquarters each year for free seminars on the system, which guaranteed lifetime employment, paid its production people only for each piece produced, and paid profit-sharing bonuses that reportedly averaged 90 percent of annual wages or salary for the 60-year period from 1934–94.[1] James Lincoln, the main architect of the incentive management system, had been dead 30 years by 1995, but he remained a dominant influence on the company's policies and culture.

The authors thank Richard S. Sabo of Lincoln Electric for help in the field research for this case. Management exerted no editorial control over content or presentation of the case. All events and individuals are real.

[1]Barnaby J. Feder, "Rethinking a Model Incentive Plan," *New York Times*, September 5, 1994, Section 1, p. 33.

| EXHIBIT 1 | Five-Year Operating Results (In thousands of dollars, except per share data) |

| | Year Ended December 31 | | | | |
	1995	1994	1993	1992	1991
Net sales	$1,032,398	$906,604	$845,999	$853,007	$833,892
Income (loss) before cumulative effect of accounting change	61,475	48,008	(40,536)	(45,800)	14,365
Cumulative effect of accounting change			2,468		
Net income (loss)	$ 61,475	$ 48,008	$(38,068)	$(45,800)	$ 14,365
Per share:					
Income (loss) before cumulative effect of accounting change	$2.63	$2.19	$(1.87)	$(2.12)	$0.67
Cumulative effect of accounting change			.12		
Net income (loss)	$2.63	$2.19	$(1.75)	$(2.12)	$0.67
Cash dividends declared	$0.42	$0.38	$0.36	$0.36	$0.30
Total assets	$617,760	$556,857	$559,543	$603,347	$640,261
Long-term debt	$93,582	$194,831	$216,915	$221,470	$155,547

Record sales and profits, however, were not of themselves cause for complacence. Lincoln Electric had gone public during 1995 in order to reduce the substantial debts it had run up during its two money-losing years; now the company was subject to public scrutiny, and such publications as the *New York Times* and *Business Week* questioned whether the famous incentive management system was consistent with the firm's obligations to its public stockholders. Dividends for 1995 amounted to $9.1 million, while bonuses had totaled $66 million. Even at $66 million, however, bonuses equaled only 56 percent of employees' annual pay. Some workers complained loudly that the average $21,000 payment in December was far short of what it should have been.

Lincoln's hometown newspaper, the Cleveland *Plain Dealer*, saw the worker complaints as a sign of increasing strain between management and workers. Characterizing Lincoln's work pace as "brutal, a pressure cooker in which employees are constantly graded and peer pressure borders on the fanatical," reporter Thomas Gerdel said Lincoln "faces growing discontent in its workforce."[2] *Business Week* said, "Lincoln increasingly resembles a typical public company. With institutional shareholders and new, independent board members in place, worker bonuses are getting more of a gimlet eye." Chairman and CEO Donald F. Hastings had set up a committee and hired Price Waterhouse to study the bonus program and the company's productivity.

"If Lincoln can adapt to new times without sacrificing employee goodwill," said *Business Week*, "another model pay plan may yet emerge."[3]

---

[2]Thomas W. Gerdel, "Lincoln Electric Experiences Season of Worker Discontent," *Cleveland Plain Dealer*, December 10, 1995.

[3]Zachary Schiller, "A Model Incentive Plan Gets Caught in a Vise," *Business Week*, January 22, 1996, p. 89.

EXHIBIT 2   Selected Financial Ratios for Lincoln Electric, 1992–1995

Fiscal Year Ending December 31	1995	1994	1993	1992
Quick ratio	0.89	0.95	0.74	0.89
Current ratio	2.12	2.17	1.85	2.16
Sales/cash	102.35	86.97	41.51	41.35
SG&A/sales	0.28	0.29	0.33	0.35
Receivables: turnover	7.33	7.19	7.66	7.66
Receivables: days of sales	49.11	50.04	47.02	46.98
Inventories: turnover	5.65	5.84	5.89	4.98
Inventories: days of sales	63.77	61.66	61.14	72.27
Net sales/working capital	5.48	5.35	5.65	4.94
Net sales/net plant & equipment	5.02	4.92	4.99	4.09
Net sales/current assets	2.89	2.89	2.60	2.66
Net sales/total assets	1.67	1.63	1.51	1.41
Net sales/employees	$172,066	$159,249	$140,159	$134,714
Total liability/total assets	0.46	0.64	0.73	0.64
Total liability/invested capital	0.67	0.92	1.13	0.92
Total liability/common equity	0.87	1.90	3.01	2.13
Times interest earned	9.07	6.09	−1.66	−0.84
Current debt/equity	0.00	0.01	0.07	0.07
Long-term debt/equity	0.28	1.00	1.51	1.11
Total debt/equity	0.29	1.02	1.58	1.19
Total assets/equity	1.87	2.87	3.90	3.04
Pretax income/net sales	0.10	0.09	−0.06	−0.04
Pretax income/total assets	0.16	0.14	−0.08	−0.06
Pretax income/invested capital	0.24	0.21	−0.13	−0.08
Pretax income/common equity	0.31	0.43	−0.35	−0.19
Net income/net sales	0.06	0.05	−0.04	−0.05
Net income/total assets	0.10	0.09	−0.07	−0.08
Net income/invested capital	0.15	0.12	−0.11	−0.11
Net income/common equity	0.19	0.26	−0.28	−0.25

Source: Disclosure, Inc. Dow-Jones On-Line News Service.

A HISTORICAL SKETCH

In 1895, having lost control of his first company, John C. Lincoln took out his second patent and began to manufacture an improved electric motor. He opened his new business with $200 he had earned redesigning a motor for young Herbert Henry Dow (who later founded the Dow Chemical Company). In 1909, John Lincoln made his first welding machine (Exhibit 3 describes the welding process). That year, he also brought in James, his younger brother, as a salesman. John preferred engineering and inventing to being a manager, and in 1914 he appointed James vice president and general manager. Exhibit 4 shows a condensed history of the firm.

James Lincoln soon asked the employees to form an "advisory board." At one of its first meetings, the advisory board recommended reducing working hours from 55 per week, then standard, to 50. This was done. In 1934, the famous Lincoln bonus

EXHIBIT 3   What Is Arc Welding?

Arc welding was the standard joining method in shipbuilding for decades and remained so in 1996. It was the predominant way of connecting steel in the construction industry. Most industrial plants had their own welding shops for maintenance and construction. Makers of automobiles, tractors, and other items employed arc-welding. Welding hobbyists made metal items such as patio furniture and barbecue pits. The popularity of welded sculpture was growing.

Arc welding employs electrical power, typically provided by a "welding machine" composed of a transformer or solid-state inverter connected to a building's electrical system or to an engine-driven generator. The electrical output may vary from 50 to 1,000 amps at 30–60 volts (for comparison, a hair dryer may use 10 amps at 120 volts) and may be alternating or direct current (AC or DC) of varying wave patterns and frequencies. The electrical current travels through a welding electrode and creates an arc to the item being welded. This melts the actual surface of the material being welded, as well as the tip of the electrode, resulting in deposit of the molten metal from the electrode onto the surface. When the molten metal refreezes, the pieces being joined are fused into one continuous piece of steel.

Welding electrodes—called "consumables" because they are used up in the welding process—are of two main types, short pieces of coated wire (called "stick" electrodes or "welding rods") for manual welding and coils of solid or tubular wire for automatic and semiautomatic processes. The area of the arc must be shielded from the atmosphere to prevent oxidation of the hot metal. This shielding is provided by a stream of inert gas which surrounds the arc (in "MIG," or metallic-inert gas welding) or by solid material called "flux" which melts and covers the liquefied metal surface. Flux often contains substances that combine with the molten metal or catalyze chemical reactions. The flux may be affixed as a coating on welding rods, enclosed inside tubular welding wire, or funneled onto the weld area from a bin (in "submerged arc" welding). Arc welding produces sparks, heat, intense light, and noxious fumes, so operators usually wear face, body, and eye protection and, if ventilation is inadequate, breathing devices.

Other types of welding include oxy-fuel welding, which uses a flame to melt metals together; tungsten-inert gas (TIG) welding, which employs a tungsten electrode to create an arc to melt a welding rod; induction welding, which uses electrical coils to induce currents in the metal being welded thereby heating it; resistance welding, which heats the weld joint by passing current directly through it; and plasma-arc welding, which is similar to arc welding but involves higher temperatures and a more tightly constrained arc. Related processes include cutting metals with oxy-fuel torches, laser beams, and plasma-arc systems.

plan was implemented. The first bonus averaged 25 percent of base wages. By 1940, Lincoln employees had twice the average pay and twice the productivity of other Cleveland workers in similar jobs. They also enjoyed the following benefits:

- An employee stock purchase plan providing stock at book value.
- Company-paid life insurance.
- An employees association for athletic and social programs and sick benefits.
- Piece rates adjusted for inflation.
- A suggestion system with cash awards.
- A pension plan.
- A policy of promotion from within.
- A practice, though not in 1940 a guarantee, of lifetime employment.

EXHIBIT 4   Condensed History of Lincoln Electric Company

1895	Company founded by John C. Lincoln.
1909	James Lincoln joins as salesman. (General Manager, 1914)
1934	Bonus plan implemented, at 25 percent of base earnings.
1940	Employees earning double the area's average wage.
1942–45	Factories built in South Africa (later closed), England (later sold to employees), and Australia. Motor production discontinued.
1951	Main factory built in Euclid, Ohio.
1955	Motor production resumed.
1958	Historic guaranteed employment policy formalized.
1965	James Lincoln's death. William Irrgang president.
1970	Annual revenues reach $100 million for the first time.
1972	Irrgang named chairman/CEO. Ted Willis becomes president.
1977	New electrode factory built in Mentor, Ohio.
1982–83	Recession slashes revenues. Employees on 30-hour weeks. ESAB begins global expansion.
1986	Willis named chairman/CEO. Don Hastings becomes president. International operations include five plants in four countries.
1992	Foreign operations include 21 plants in 15 countries. Long-term debt at $220 million. Hastings named Chairman/CEO. Fred Mackenbach named president.
1992–93	Global recession. First losses in Lincoln's history. International retrenchment begins.
1995	International operations include 16 plants in 11 countries. Public stock issue provides funds for debt reduction. New motor factory built.

- Base pay rates determined by formal job evaluation.
- A merit rating system which affected pay.
- Paid vacations.

During World War II the company suspended production of electric motors as demand for welding products escalated. Employee bonuses averaged $2,250 in 1942 (about $20,000 in 1995 dollars). Lincoln's original bonus plan was not universally accepted: the Internal Revenue Service questioned the tax deductibility of employee bonuses, arguing they were not "ordinary and necessary" costs of doing business, and the Navy's Price Review Board challenged Lincoln's high profits. But James Lincoln overcame the objections, loudly refusing to retract the firm's obligations to its workers. Also during World War II, Lincoln built factories in Australia, South Africa, and England.

In 1951, Lincoln completed a new main plant in Euclid, Ohio; the factory remained essentially unchanged in 1995. In 1955, Lincoln again began making electric motors, but they represented only a small percentage of the company's revenue through 1995.

Executive Succession

William Irrgang, an engineer and longtime Lincoln protégé, became president when James Lincoln died in 1965. By 1970, Lincoln's annual revenues had grown to $100 million and bonuses were averaging about $8,000 per employee each year (about

EXHIBIT 5   Lincoln Electric Company's Bonus History, 1981–1995

Year	Total Bonus Payments (in millions)	Number of Employees	Avg. Gross Bonus per Worker	Bonus as a % of Wages	W-2 Avg. Earnings per Factory Worker
1981	$59.0	2,684	$22,009	99.0	
1982	41.0	2,634	15,643	80.1	
1983	26.6	2,561	10,380	55.4	
1984	37.0	2,469	15,044	68.0	
1985	41.8	2,405	17,391	73.2	
1986	37.7	2,349	16,056	64.8	
1987	44.0	2,349	18,791	70.5	
1988	54.3	2,554	21,264	77.6	
1989	54.5	2,633	20,735	72.0	$47,371
1990	56.2	2,701	20,821	71.2	47,809
1991	48.3	2,694	17,935	65.0	39,651
1992	48.0	2,688	17,898	61.9	40,867
1993	55.0	2,676	20,585	63.9	48,738
1994	59.0	2,995	19,659	60.2	55,757
1995	64.4	3,396	*21,168	55.9	57,758

*Employee with more than 1 year on service

Source: Lincoln Electric Company document.

$30,000 in 1995 dollars). Irrgang was elevated to chairman in 1972 and Ted Willis, also an engineer and protégé of James Lincoln, became president. In 1977, Lincoln completed a new electrode plant a few miles from Euclid, in Mentor, Ohio, doubling its capacity for making welding wire and rods.

Lincoln's net sales were $450 million in 1981 and employee bonuses averaged $20,760 (about $34,000 in 1995 dollars) that year. But sales fell by 40 percent in the next two years owing, Lincoln management said, to "the combined effects of inflation, sharply higher energy costs, and a national recession." By 1983, the firm's net income and bonuses had collapsed to less than half their 1981 levels. Exhibit 5 lists bonus amounts from 1981 to 1995.

But there was no layoff. Many factory workers volunteered to do field sales work and customer assistance. Others were reassigned within the plants, some repairing the roof of the Euclid factory, painting, and cleaning up. The workweek, previously averaging about 45 hours, was shortened to 30 hours for most nonsalaried workers. Several new products, which had been kept in reserve for just this kind of eventuality, were brought to market. Sales, profits, and bonuses began a slow recovery.

Bill Irrgang died in 1986. Ted Willis took over as chairman and Don Hastings became president, taking primary responsibility for domestic operations.

THE LINCOLN PHILOSOPHY

Throughout the tenures of these CEOs, the business philosophies first articulated by James Lincoln remained in effect, forming the foundation of the company's culture and providing the context within which the incentive management system worked.

Lincoln's own father had been a Congregationalist minister, and the biblical Sermon on the Mount, with Jesus's praise of meekness, mercifulness, purity of heart, and peacemaking, governed his attitudes toward business. James never evangelized his employees, but he counseled truthfulness in speech, returning evil with good, love of enemies, secret almsgiving, and quiet trust and confidence.[4]

Relationships with Customers

In a 1947 speech, James Lincoln said, "Care should be taken . . . not to rivet attention on profit. Between 'How much do I get?' and 'How do I make this better, cheaper, more useful?' the difference is fundamental and decisive." He later wrote, "When any company has achieved success so that it is attractive as an investment, all money usually needed for expansion is supplied by the customer in retained earnings. It is obvious that the customer's interests, not the stockholder's, should come first." He added,

> The Christian ethic should control our acts. If it did control our acts, the savings in cost of distribution would be tremendous. Advertising would be a contact of the expert consultant with the customer, in order to give the customer the best product available when all of the customer's needs are considered. Competition then would be in improving the quality of products and increasing efficiency in producing and distributing them; not in deception, as is now too customary. Pricing would reflect efficiency of production, it would not be a selling dodge that the customer may well be sorry he accepted. It would be proper for all concerned and rewarding for the ability used in producing the product.

Lincoln's pricing policy, often stated, was "Price on the basis of cost and keep downward pressure on cost." C. Jackson Graham, founder of The American Productivity Institute, said prices of Lincoln products, on average, grew at only one-fifth the rate of inflation in the decades after 1930. Some prices actually went down. For example, Lincoln welding electrodes that sold for $0.16 per pound in 1929 were $0.05 in 1942. And Lincoln's popular SA-200 welder decreased in price from 1958 to 1965.

Until the 1990s, Lincoln was the dominant U.S. producer of arc welding products and was able to keep market prices low, especially for consumables. That changed after Miller Welding Co. grew to match Lincoln in U.S. sales of machines and ESAB became the world's largest supplier of welding consumables and materials. In 1984, Don Hastings said,

> Right now we are paying the price of not having enough capacity in Mentor [Ohio] to supply our customer demand. We are spending money now. But if we had spent it last year, we would not be having the shortages that we're having right now. We're also allowing our competition to raise prices because there's nothing we can do about it without more capacity.

Lincoln quality was legendary. In the refinery and pipeline industries, where price was seldom the main consideration in purchasing, Lincoln welders and electrodes were almost universally specified for decades. Warranty costs at Lincoln typically averaged under 1/4 percent of sales. A Lincoln distributor in Monroe, Louisiana, said he had sold hundreds of Lincoln welders and had never had a warranty claim.

Lincoln sold its products directly to major customers and indirectly through distributors, most of which were welding supply stores. Lincoln also licensed hundreds of service centers and trained their personnel to do maintenance and

---

[4]F. C. Eiselen, E. Lewis, and D. G. Downey, eds., *The Abingdon Bible Commentary* (Nashville, TN: The Abingdon Press, Inc., 1929), pp. 960–69.

warranty work on Lincoln machines. The company maintained a system of regional sales offices, which serviced both direct customers and distributors. In keeping with James Lincoln's principle that salespersons should be "expert consultants," sales jobs at Lincoln were only open to graduate engineers until about 1992, when Hastings changed the policy; he began to recruit majors in liberal arts, business, and other disciplines into the sales force.

Hastings instituted Lincoln's Guaranteed Cost Reduction (GCR) program in 1993. Under GCR, Lincoln sent teams of engineers, technical representatives, and distributors to customer facilities with a goal to "find ways to improve fabrication procedures and product quality as well as methods to increase productivity." Hastings promised, "The Lincoln Electric Company will guarantee in writing that your company's annual arc welding fabrication costs will be reduced by a specified amount. If you don't save that amount, a check will be written for the difference." Lincoln cited these "successes" in its literature promoting GCR:

> A fabricator of steel buildings found GCR savings of $25,000/year and, as a result of the program, developed an improved welding cost analysis system. A manufacturer of heavy grading equipment verified savings in excess of $50,000/year and productivity gains from 50% to 90%. An automotive manufacturer produced productivity increases, in specific welding operations, exceeding 20%. Resultant savings totaled over $1,000,000 a year.

Relationships with Employees

The company professed to still adhere to the basic precepts James Lincoln set down early in his development of the incentive system:

> The greatest fear of the worker, which is the same as the greatest fear of the industrialist in operating a company, is the lack of income . . . The industrial manager is very conscious of his company's need of uninterrupted income. He is completely oblivious, evidently, of the fact that the worker has the same need.
>
> He is just as eager as any manager is to be part of a team that is properly organized and working for the advancement of our economy . . . He has no desire to make profits for those who do not hold up their end in production, as is true of absentee stockholders and inactive people in the company.
>
> If money is to be used as an incentive, the program must provide that what is paid to the worker is what he has earned. The earnings of each must be in accordance with accomplishment.
>
> Status is of great importance in all human relationships. The greatest incentive that money has, usually, is that it is a symbol of success . . . The resulting status is the real incentive . . . Money alone can be an incentive to the miser only.
>
> There must be complete honesty and understanding between the hourly worker and management if high efficiency is to be obtained.

"I don't work for Lincoln Electric; I work for myself," said Lester Hillier in the 1994 *New York Times* article. "I'm an entrepreneur," added Hillier, a welder at Lincoln for 17 years. Other workers, asked in April of 1995 about why people worked so hard and what motivated them, responded:

Joe Sirko, machine operator since 1941:

People want their bonus. And a decent job. No layoffs. I wanted a job where I could spend all the money I make all year and then I get the bonus. I still do that. I go out and live it up. I go to the races. I go everywhere.

When I came here—under James Lincoln—the jobs were given to family. Almost everybody in here was family. My brother got me in. Somebody else's brother got them in or their dad got them in. It was all family. And J. F. backed that a hundred percent. Family, right on down. If you had someone in your family, they were in. Now, they have three different interviewers down there. They all interview.

They hired a lot of people once, to reduce the overtime, remember, and they had all them people when it slowed down. They were sweeping and cleaning—and they didn't know what to do with them. When James Lincoln was alive, he always got up when he gave the bonus and told them—they would be complaining about overtime—he told them that they would either work, because he didn't want to over hire all them extra people. He believed in all the overtime.

Kathleen Hoenigman, wiring harness assembler hired in 1977:

I worked in factories before and the factories I worked at either went out of business or moved to another state. I will have to say that my money is more here, but I did always make good money. This is much more, because of the bonus. I invest. I also bought a house. Right now, I give my mother money.

I feel that people here that are making all this money, they work so hard for it that they don't want to spend it stupidly and what they do is invest, for the future. And they also, you know, take care of their family.

I like the challenge. I also like the money and the fact that the money is tied to my own output. You have to be motivated yourself. You want the company to succeed, so you want to do better. By having guaranteed employment, the company has to be strong. To me, guaranteed employment means if there's a slowdown you always have a job. Like they'll always take care of you. Back in 1982, when sales slumped, they put me on the roof carrying buckets of tar.

Scott Skrjanc, welder hired in 1978:

Guaranteed employment is in the back of my mind. I know I'm guaranteed a job. But I also know I have to work to get paid. We don't come in and punch a card and sit down and do nothing.

Linda Clemente, customer service representative hired in 1986:

Well, I guess the biggest thing is guaranteed employment. And I think most people want to be the best that they can be. For other people, maybe the motivation is the money, because they are putting kids through college and things like that. I mean, it's definitely a benefit and something everybody works for.

Relationships with Unions

There had never been a serious effort to organize Lincoln employees. While James Lincoln criticized the labor movement for "selfishly attempting to better its position at the expense of the people it must serve," he still had kind words for union members. He excused union excesses as "the natural reactions of human beings to the abuses to which management has subjected them." He added, "Labor and management are properly not warring camps; they are parts of one organization in which they must and should cooperate fully and happily."

Several of the plants Lincoln acquired during 1986–92 had unions and the company stated its intention to cooperate with them. No major Lincoln operation had a union in 1995, although 25 of the Ohio employees did attend a union presentation by the United Auto Workers in December, after the announcement of the 1995 bonus rate. "The attendance, out of a total of 3,400 workers, was disappointing even to organizers," said the Cleveland *Plain Dealer*. Lincoln spokesman Bud Fletcher said, "The secret to avoiding those types of situations is that management has to work twice as hard to provide all the elements that membership in an organization like a union would have. We've got to listen, we've got to sit down, we've got to take our time."

Relationships with Stockholders

Through 1992, Lincoln shareholders received dividends averaging less than 5 percent of share price per year and total annual returns averaged under 10 percent. The few public trades of Lincoln shares before 1995 were at only a small premium over book value, which was the official redemption price for employee-owned stock.

"The last group to be considered is the stockholders who own stock because they think it will be more profitable than investing money in any other way," said James Lincoln. Concerning division of the largess produced by incentive management, he wrote, "The absentee stockholder also will get his share, even if undeserved, out of the greatly increased profit that the efficiency produces."

Under Hastings, Lincoln gave shareholders more respect. Dividends, while limited under certain credit agreements, were increased in 1994 in preparation for the public issue, and again in 1995. And the presence of new outside directors on the Lincoln board (see Exhibit 6) seemed to protect public shareholder interests.

THE LINCOLN INCENTIVE MANAGEMENT SYSTEM

Lincoln's incentive management system was defined by the firm's philosophy and by the rules, regulations, practices, and programs that had evolved over the 60 years since its origination.

Recruitment Every job opening at Lincoln was advertised internally on company bulletin-boards and any employee could apply. In general, external hiring was permitted only for entry-level positions. Often, applicants were relatives or friends of current employees. Selection for these jobs was based on personal interviews—there was no aptitude nor psychological testing and no educational requirement—except for engineering and sales positions, which required a college degree. A committee consisting of vice presidents and supervisors interviewed candidates initially cleared by the personnel department. Final selection was made by the supervisor who had a job opening. Out of over 3,500 applicants interviewed by the personnel department in 1988, fewer than 300 were hired. The odds were somewhat better in 1995, as Lincoln scrambled to staff its new electric motor factory and to meet escalating demand for its welding products.

Training and Education New production workers were given a short period of on-the-job training and then placed on a piecework pay system. Lincoln did not pay for off-site education, unless specific company needs were identified. The idea behind this policy was that not everyone could take advantage of such a program, and it was unfair to spend company funds for a benefit to which there was unequal access. Recruits for sales jobs, already college graduates, were given an average of six months on-the-job training in a plant, followed by a period of work and training at a regional sales office.

Sam Evans, regional manager for international, described the training program when he joined Lincoln in 1953 as an electrical engineering graduate:

> A few months into the training, I decided to move to sales. During those days, the training program was about a year—several months learning to weld, several months on the factory floor, and in other departments. I got the MBA while I was working in Buffalo as a sales engineer.

Merit Rating Each manager formally evaluated subordinates twice a year using the cards shown in Exhibit 7. The employee performance criteria—"quality," "depend-

EXHIBIT 6   Officers and Directors of Lincoln Electric Company, 1995

Directors

Donald F. Hastings, 67, *1980
Chairman of the Board and Chief Executive Officer

Frederick W. Mackenbach, 65, *1992
Retired President and Chief Operating Officer

Harry Carlson, 61, *1973
Retired Vice Chairman

David H. Gunning, 53, *1987
Chairman, President and Chief Executive Officer of
Capitol American Financial Corp.

Edward E. Hood, Jr., 65, *1993
Former Vice Chairman of the Board and Executive
Officer of The General Electric Co.

Paul E. Lego, 65, *1993
President of Intelligent Enterprises

Hugh L. Libby, 70, *1985
Retired Chairman of the Board and Chief Executive
Officer of Libby Corp.

David C. Lincoln, 70, *1958
Retired Chairman of the Board and Chief Executive
Officer of Lincoln Laser Co. and President of Arizona
Oxides LLC

Emma S. Lincoln, 73, *1989
Retired
Formerly an Attorney in private practice

G. Russell Lincoln, 49, *1989
Chairman of the Board and Chief Executive Officer of
Algan, Inc.

Kathryn Jo Lincoln, 41, *1995
Vice President of The Lincoln Foundation, Inc. and Vice
Chair/Secretary of The Lincoln Institute of Land Policy

Anthony A. Massaro, 52, *1996
President and Chief Operating Officer

Henry L. Meyer III, 46, *1994
Chairman of the Board of Society National Bank and
Senior Executive Vice President and Chief Operating
Officer of KeyCorp

Lawrence O. Selhorst, 63, *1992
Chairman of the Board and Chief Executive Officer of
American Spring Wire Corporation

Craig R. Smith, 70, *1992
Former Chairman and Chief Executive Officer of
Ameritrust Corporation

Frank L. Steingass, 56, *1971
Chairman of the Board and President of Buehler/
Steingass, Inc.

*Date elected as a director.

Officers

Donald F. Hastings, 67, *1953
Chairman and Chief Executive Officer

Anthony A. Massaro, 52, *1993
President and Chief Operating Officer

David J. Fullen, 64, *1955
Executive Vice President, Engineering and Marketing

John M. Stropki, 45, *1972
Executive Vice President
President, North America

Richard C. Ulstad, 56, *1970
Senior Vice President, Manufacturing

H. Jay Elliott, 54, *1993
Senior Vice President, Chief Financial Officer and
Treasurer

Frederick G. Stueber, 42, *1995
Senior Vice President, General Counsel and Secretary

Frederick W. Anderson, 43, *1978
Vice President, Systems Engineering

Paul J. Beddia, 62, *1956
Vice President, Government and Community Affairs

Dennis D. Crockett, 53, *1965
Vice President, Consumable Research and Development

James R. Delaney, 47, *1987
Vice President
President, Lincoln Electric Latin America

Joseph G. Doria, 46, *1972
Vice President
President and Chief Executive Officer, Lincoln Electric
Company of Canada

Paul Fantelli, 51, *1970
Vice President, Business Development

Ronald A. Nelson, 46, *1972
Vice President, Machine Research and Development

Gary M. Schuster, 41, *1978
Vice President, Motor Division

Richard J. Seif, 48, *1971
Vice President, Marketing

S. Peter Ullman, 46, *1971
Vice President
President and Chief Executive Officer, Harris Calorific
Division of Lincoln Electric

Raymond S. Vogt, 54, *1996
Vice President, Human Resources

John H. Weaver, 57, *1961
Vice President
President, Lincoln Africa, Middle East and Russia

*Year joined the company.

EXHIBIT 7   Lincoln's Merit Rating Cards

Increasing Output ➤ ➤

Days Absent ◯   **OUTPUT**

This card rates HOW MUCH PRODUCTIVE WORK you actually turn out.

It also reflects your willingness not to hold back and recognizes your attendance record.

This rating has been done jointly by your department head and the Production Control Department in the shop and with other department heads in the office and engineering.

EM-629A Rev. 1988

Increasing Ideas and Cooperation ➤ ➤

IDEAS AND COOPERATION

This card rates your Cooperation, Ideas and Initiative.

New ideas and new methods are important to your company in our continuing effort to reduce costs, increase output, improve quality, work safely and improve our relationship with our customers. This card credits you for your ideas and initiative used to help in this direction.

It also rates your cooperation – how you work with others as a team. Such factors as your attitude towards supervision, co-workers, and the company; your efforts to share your expert knowledge with others; and your cooperation in installing new methods smoothly, are considered here.

This rating has been done jointly by your department head and the Time Study Department in the shop and with other department heads in the office and engineering.

EM-629B Rev. 1988

Increasing Dependability ➤ ➤

DEPENDABILITY

This card rates how well your supervisors have been able to depend upon you to do those things that have been expected of you without supervision.

It also rates your ability to supervise yourself including your work safety performance, your orderliness, care of equipment, and the effective use you make of your skills.

This rating has been done by your department head.

EM-629C Rev. 1988

Increasing Quality ➤ ➤

QUALITY

This card rates the QUALITY of the work you do.

It also reflects your success in eliminating errors and in reducing scrap and waste.

This rating has been done jointly by your department head and the Quality Assurance Department in the shop and with other department heads in the office and engineering.

EM-629D Rev. 1988

ability," "ideas and cooperation," and "output"—were considered independent of each other. Marks on the cards were converted to numerical scores, which were forced to average 100 for each specified group, usually all the subordinates of one supervisor or other manager. Thus, any employee rated above 100 would have to be balanced off by another rated below 100. Individual merit rating scores normally ranged from 80 to 110. Any score over 110 required a special letter to top management. Scores over 110 were not considered in computing the required 100 point average for each evaluator. Point scores were directly proportional to the individual's year-end bonus.

Welder Scott Skrjanc seemed typical in his view of the system, "You know, everybody perceives they should get more. That's natural. But I think it's done fairly."

Under Lincoln's initial suggestion program, employees were given monetary awards of one-half of the first year's savings attributable to their suggestions. Later, however, the value of suggestions was reflected in merit rating scores. Supervisors were required to discuss performance marks with the employees concerned. Each warranty claim was traced to the individual employee whose work caused the defect, if possible. The employee's performance score was reduced, or the worker could repay the cost of servicing the warranty claim by working without pay.

Compensation Basic wage levels for jobs at Lincoln were determined by a wage survey of similar jobs in the Cleveland area. These rates were adjusted quarterly in response to changes in the Cleveland Area Wage Index, compiled by the U.S. Department of Labor. Wherever possible, base wage rates were translated into piece rates. Practically all production workers—even some fork truck operators—were paid by the piece. Once established, piece rates were changed only if there was a change in the methods, materials, or machinery used in the job. Each individual's pay was calculated from a daily Piecework Report, filled out by the employee. The payroll department, responsible for paying 3,000 employees, consisted of four people; there was no formal control system for checking employees' reports of work done.

In December of each year, bonuses were distributed to employees. Incentive bonuses from 1934 to 1994 averaged about 90 percent of annual wages; the total bonus pool typically exceeded after-tax (and after-bonus) profits. Individual bonuses were determined by merit rating scores. For example, if the board of directors authorized a bonus equal to 80 percent of total base wages paid, a person whose performance score averaged 95 in the two previous evaluation periods received a bonus of 76 percent (0.80×0.95) of base wages.

Because of company losses in 1992 and 1993, the bonus was about 60 percent of base wages and management was forced to borrow $100 million to pay it. After Lincoln's turnaround in 1994, the 60 percent bonus rate was continued as $63 million was used to repay principal and interest on the borrowed money. Average compensation of Lincoln's Cleveland employees in 1994 was about $36,000 before bonuses, so the average bonus was $10,000–$12,000 less than if the 90 percent average had applied. Some felt that employees were paying for management's mistakes.

Continuous Employment In 1958 Lincoln formalized its guaranteed continuous employment policy, which had unofficially been in effect for many years. Starting in 1958, every worker with over two years' longevity was guaranteed at least 30 hours per week, 49 weeks per year. The requirement was changed to three years' longevity in the recession year of 1982, when the policy was severely tested. In previous recessions the company had been able to avoid major sales declines. However, sales plummeted 32 percent in 1982 and another 16 percent the next year. Management cut most of the nonsalaried workers back to 30 hours a week for varying periods of time. Many employees were reassigned and the total workforce was slightly reduced through normal attrition and restricted hiring. The previous year had set records, and some employees grumbled at their unexpected misfortune, to the surprise and dismay of some Lincoln managers.

Among employees with a year or more of service, employee turnover ran only 4 percent at Lincoln Electric. Absenteeism, too, was extremely low; critics in the press noted this was understandable, since workers were not paid for sick days. They noted, too, that 25 to 30 percent of new hires quit in their first six months of work, in spite of Lincoln's intensive interview process. In 1995, Lincoln's Cleveland workers were averaging over 45 hours a week on the job. Employee turnover after the first year was under 1 percent per year, excluding retirements. "The vast majority that quit do so before their first bonus," said Dick Sabo, director of corporate communications. "Once they see the dollars, they realize they are extremely well paid for their efforts." The average length of service of Lincoln's Cleveland workers in 1995 was about 14 years.

Stock Ownership by Employees   James Lincoln said that financing for company growth should come from within the company—through initial cash investment by the founders, through reinvestment of earnings, and through stock purchases by those who work in the business. He claimed this approach gave the following advantages:

1. Ownership of stock by employees strengthens team spirit. "If they are mutually anxious to make it succeed, the future of the company is bright."

2. Ownership of stock provides individual incentive because employees feel they will benefit from company profitability.

3. "Ownership is educational." Owner-employees "will know how profits are made and lost; how success is won and lost."

4. "Capital available from within controls expansion." Unwarranted expansion would not occur, Lincoln believed, under his financing plan (which did not allow for borrowing capital for growth).

5. "The greatest advantage would be the development of the individual worker. Under the incentive of ownership, he would become a greater man."

6. "Stock ownership is one of the steps that can be taken that will make the worker feel that there is less of a gulf between him and the boss."

Under Lincoln's employees' stock purchase plan, each employee could buy a specified number of shares of restricted common stock from the company each year, with company financing. The stock was priced at "estimated fair value" (taken to be book value) and the company had an option to repurchase it. Lincoln had always exercised its option to repurchase shares tendered by employees and many employees felt it was obligated to do so. In 1992, approximately 75 percent of the employees owned over 40 percent of the total stock of the company. Lincoln family members and former Lincoln executives owned about half the remainder.

As Lincoln was preparing to report its first quarterly loss in August 1992, the directors voted to suspend repurchases under the stock purchase plan, in order to prevent wholesale tendering of shares by employees at a time when Lincoln was short of cash. The change in policy meant that employees could sell their stock in the open market as unrestricted stock if they wished to convert it to cash. At that time, book value (and therefore market value) was about $19 per share. As it turned out, only 11 percent of the unrestricted shares were converted.

In preparation for the public issue of stock in 1995, the employees' stock purchase plan was terminated on March 30, automatically converting all shares issued under it to unrestricted stock. Market value of the shares at that time was about $40. After the public issue, shareholders approved a new stock purchase plan permitting employees to purchase up to $10,000 per year in open-market shares without brokers' commissions.

Vacations   Lincoln's plants were shut down for two weeks in August and two weeks during the Christmas season for vacations, which were unpaid. Employees with over 25 years of service got a fifth week of vacation at a time acceptable to superiors. When Lincoln was unable to meet its customers' orders in 1994, most employees agreed to work overtime through the August vacation period. Some of these employees were given vacations at alternate times.

Fringe Benefits   Lincoln sponsored a medical plan (whose cost was deducted from the annual bonus pool) and a company-paid retirement program. At the main plant, a cafeteria operated on a break-even basis, serving meals at about 60 percent of outside prices. The Employee Association, to which the company did not contribute, provided disability insurance and social and athletic activities. Dick Sabo commented,

> The company maintains traditional fringe benefits which include life insurance, health care, paid vacations, an annuity program (401K), and a variety of employee participation activities. All of these programs, of course, reduce the amount of money which otherwise could be received by the employees as bonus. Each employee is, therefore, acutely aware of the impact of such benefit items on their overall earnings in each year.

He also cautioned,

> When you use "participation," put quotes around it. Because we believe that each person should participate only in those decisions he is most knowledgeable about. I don't think production employees should control the decisions of the chairman. They don't know as much as he does about the decisions he is involved in.

The primary means of employee participation beyond an employee's immediate work environment were the suggestion program and the advisory board. Members of the advisory board were elected by employees and met with President Fred Mackenbach every two weeks. Unlike James Lincoln and Bill Irrgang, CEOs Willis and Hastings did not regularly attend these meetings. Responses to all advisory board items were promised by the following meeting. Exhibit 8 provides excerpts from minutes of the advisory board meeting of March 14, 1995 (generally typical of the group's deliberations).

The advisory board could only advise, not direct, although its recommendations were taken seriously. Its influence was shown on December 1, 1995, when Lincoln reversed a two-year-old policy of paying lower wages to new hires. Veteran workers had complained loudly. *Business Week* quoted Joseph Tuck, an inspector with 18 years' service: "If an individual shows he can handle the workload, he should be rewarded" with full pay.[5]

---

[5]Schiller, "A Model Incentive Plan."

EXHIBIT 8   Excerpts from Advisory Board Minutes, March 14, 1995

Mr. Mackenbach opened the meeting by welcoming three new members to the Board. He called on Mr. Beddia to inform the Board about the Harvest for Hunger food drive.

Prior Items

1. Could all air-cooled engines be covered when we receive them? Answer: The Material Handling Department will cover the top pallet of each stack when the engines are unloaded.

2. Could the 401K contributions from bonus be included in the year-to-date totals on the remaining regular December pay stubs. Answer: Yes, it will be.

3. An employee was almost hit by a speeding electric cart in Bay 16. Could a slow speed sign be posted? Answer: Signs cautioning pedestrians regarding Towmotor traffic have been installed. Additional changes are being reviewed.

New Business

1. Why was an employee of the Motor Division penalized for a safety issue when he performed his job as instructed? Answer: Referred to Mr. Beddia.

2. Has our total percent of market share increased? Answer: In the past, we could provide a precise answer. Some of our competitors no longer provide the required information to NEMA. However, in our judgment, we are increasing our percent of market share in both consumables and equipment.

3. Could an additional microwave unit be installed in Bay 24 vending area? Answer: Referred to Mr. Crissey.

4. Could we consider buying an emergency vehicle instead of paying between $300 and $500 per ambulance run to the hospital? Answer: When we use the services of the Euclid Fire and Rescue Squad, there is a charge of approximately $350. While in general this charge is covered by hospitalization insurance, we will ask Mr. Trivisonno to review this with city officials.

5. When will the softball field be completed? Answer: A recreational area on the EP-3 site will become a reality, although certain issues with the city must be resolved first. We will show the preliminary layout at the next meeting.

6. Is a member of the Board of Directors being investigated for fraud? Answer: We are not aware of any investigation of this type.

7. Is our investment in Mexico losing value? Could we have an update as to how our Mexican operation is doing? Answer: Yes. An update will be provided at the next meeting.

8. Could something be done to eliminate the odor created when the septic tank is cleaned? Answer: Referred to Mr. Hellings.

INTERNATIONAL EXPANSION

Internationally, the welding equipment industry was highly fragmented but consolidating. No global statistics reported total economic activity or companies' market shares in various countries, but many developed economies had local suppliers. Two U.S. producers—Lincoln and Miller Electric—and one European firm, ESAB (the largest welding firm in the world by 1996), had the capability to supply their products to users in most markets of the world. Exhibit 9, adapted from the 1995 annual report, shows Lincoln's recent sales by region.

Until 1986, Lincoln Electric held to James Lincoln's original policy toward international ventures, according to Sam Evans, Regional Manager of International and a 40-year Lincoln veteran. James Lincoln had felt his company could manufacture in any English-speaking country. Otherwise, he let others promote Lincoln products internationally. Evans described the approach:

We dealt with Armco International, which was a division of Armco Steel. Lincoln licensed Armco to manufacture and market our products in Mexico, Uruguay, Brazil, Argentina,

EXHIBIT 9 Lincoln Electric's Financial Results by Geographic Sector, 1993–1995 (in thousands of dollars)

	United States	Europe	Other Countries	Total*
1995				
Net sales to unaffiliated customers**	$711,940	$201,672	$118,786	$1,032,398
Pretax profit (loss)	79,737	10,171	10,956	99,584
Identifiable assets	404,972	194,319	80,921	617,760
1994				
Net sales to unaffiliated customers	$641,607	$156,803	$108,194	$ 906,604
Pretax profit (loss)	68,316	7,891	4,062	80,168
Identifiable assets	350,012	165,722	76,129	556,857
1993				
Net sales to unaffiliated customers	$543,458	$211,268	$ 91,273	$ 845,999
Pretax profit (loss)	42,570	(68,865)	(22,903)	(46,950)
Identifiable assets	389,247	172,136	69,871	559,543

* Totals for profit/loss and identifiable assets will not cross-add due to elimination of intercompany transactions.
** Net sales reported for the United States include materials exported to unaffiliated customers, amounting to $81,770,000 in 1995; $64,400,000 in 1994; and $58,100,000 in 1993. Net sales excludes intracompany sales to Lincoln's overseas branches.

and in France. It was electrodes, but included assembly of machines in Mexico. Armco also marketed Lincoln products along the Pacific Rim and in a few other areas of the world. At one point, we also had a joint venture with Big Three Corporation in Scotland.

In 1986, Lincoln Electric faced a newly aggressive Scandinavian competitor, ESAB Corporation, a subsidiary of the Swiss-Swedish engineering/energy group Asea Brown Boveri. ESAB had acquired a number of welding products manufacturers throughout the world during the industry downturn of 1982–85. Starting in 1986, ESAB entered the U.S. market, buying several U.S. welding products companies (trade names acquired by ESAB included Oxweld, Genuine Heliarc, Plasmarc, Allstate Welding Products, Alloy Rods, and the former Lindy Division of Union Carbide). ESAB opened an electrode plant less than a mile from Lincoln's Cleveland headquarters.

In the global recession of the early 1980s, ESAB's acquisitions put it in position to have a volume base large enough to capture economies of scale in its research and development programs. Dick Sabo said Lincoln's CEO, Ted Willis, was concerned about the mounting market threat that ESAB posed and met with the chairman of ESAB in 1986, hoping "that we could work together." The relationship soon soured, however, and Willis decided to challenge ESAB internationally.

During the 1986–92 period, Lincoln purchased controlling interests in manufacturing and marketing operations in 16 countries. It took over most of the operations previously licensed to Armco and Big Three. It put a factory in Brazil, where ESAB had an estimated 70 percent market share. Lincoln expanded into gas welding and cutting by buying Harris Calorific Corporation, which made oxyacetylene cutting and welding equipment in the United States, Italy, and Ireland. Lincoln's largest new investment was the purchase of Messer Griesheim's welding products business in Germany, considered ESAB's most profitable territory. Altogether, Lincoln opened or expanded plants in

England, France, the Netherlands, Spain, Norway, Mexico, Venezuela, and Japan. The expansion required heavy borrowing; for the first time, James Lincoln's conservative financial policies were discarded. Long-term debt rose from zero in 1986 to over $220 million in 1992. Exhibit 10 summarizes Lincoln financial statements for 1986–94.

Separate Lincoln-type incentive management plans remained in place at the company's factories in Australia, Mexico, and the United States, but attempts to implement such plans in other countries were largely unsuccessful. Sabo said the main problem was that Europe lapsed into recession. He added, "Germany started to fail within two months after we purchased Griesheim. The country had 27 percent unemployment. So we didn't implement the system at all. We didn't get a chance to." In Brazil, Willis learned that regulations defined incentive bonuses to be part of base salaries, which could not be reduced during downturns, so the Lincoln system was not installed there.

Welder Scott Skrjanc, a 17-year veteran of the production force, had another idea about why the system did not work out overseas:

> Their culture, as I understand it, was so much different from ours. Their work ethic and work habits, I guess, aren't like the United States. They have a saying in German that means, "slowly, slowly, but good." And I guess that's how they perceive it. Here, we do high-quality work, but we work fast—and smart. As you get older, you get wiser and work smarter.

Sam Evans, who had run Lincoln's operations in Eastern Europe until cancer forced his return to Cleveland for successful treatment, gave his view of CEO Willis's performance in the international expansion:

> Ted Willis's belief—and I think it was a very good belief, although he is often criticized by Lincoln people—was that we needed a stronger world organization. The welding industry was consolidating in the world market, much like the steel industry did in the 1930s. He felt we needed this larger sales base so that we could invest in the research and development to maintain our position in the industry. I think that has succeeded. Even though we have had failures internationally, we have grown with our base.
>
> We are coming out with a lot of new items—the new square-wave machines, which control the actual wave form, the new stainless products, the inverter technology in motors and machines. We are moving rapidly ahead of the industry. That was Mr. Willis's vision, and it was a good one. His financial vision wasn't so good—perhaps.

Retrenchment and Turnaround under Hastings

Willis retired in 1992 and Don Hastings became chief executive officer. Hastings set about "consolidating and reorganizing" the foreign operations. An agreement was negotiated with ESAB to close the Lincoln factory in Brazil and to license ESAB to make Lincoln products there; in return, ESAB closed its Spanish electrode plant and Lincoln used its excess capacity in that country to supply ESAB's needs. Lincoln mothballed its German plant, losing an estimated $100 million there. It also shut down factories in Venezuela and Japan. Practically all of Lincoln's international operations that were not closed were scaled back. By 1996 ESAB, now owned by Britain's Charter Group, was recognized as the largest welding vendor in the world, with key markets in East and Western Europe, South America, and the Far East; it had the "leading position in stick electrodes (a declining market) and an even bigger position in fluxed core wires (a rapidly growing market)."[6]

---

[6]*N. Utley, et al*, Grieg Middleton & Co., report number 1674211, 12/12/95; Investext 02/23/96.

EXHIBIT 10 Highlights of Lincoln Electric's Financial Performance, 1986–1994 (in millions of dollars)

Balance Sheet Data	1986	1987	1988	1989	1990	1991	1992	1993	1994
Assets									
Cash and equivalents	$ 47.0	$ 61.0	$ 23.9	$ 19.5	$ 15.5	$ 20.3	$ 20.6	$ 20.4	$ 10.4
Receivables	46.0	61.7	90.9	100.8	127.3	118.0	111.3	110.5	126.0
Inventories	52.3	74.7	116.3	120.5	164.4	206.3	171.3	143.7	155.3
Other current assets	9.4	9.1	12.0	14.4	14.5	17.5	18.0	51.1	21.7
Total current assets	154.8	206.4	243.1	255.1	321.7	362.1	321.2	325.7	313.4
Gross plant	153.2	195.7	274.8	328.2	387.7	422.9	435.2	406.7	444.5
Accumulated depreciation	93.4	121.2	148.6	170.2	193.1	213.3	226.8	237.0	260.3
Net plant	59.8	74.5	126.3	158.0	194.7	209.6	208.4	169.7	184.2
Long-term investments	11.5	0.3	0.0	0.0	0.0	0.0	0.0	0.0	0.0
Intangible and other assets	13.1	13.4	33.8	42.6	55.9	68.6	73.7	64.1	59.2
Total assets	$239.2	$294.7	$403.2	$455.8	$572.2	$640.3	$603.3	$559.5	$556.9
Liabilities and Stockholders' Equity									
Short-term debt	$ 4.6	$ 6.6	$ 39.2	$ 41.6	$ 40.6	$ 50.7	$ 27.1	$ 33.4	$ 18.1
Accounts payable	11.2	23.4	36.8	40.0	44.3	46.6	44.2	43.5	54.8
Other current liabilities	25.1	32.7	38.1	41.0	52.4	61.3	77.2	99.0	71.2
Total current liabilities	41.0	62.7	114.2	122.6	137.3	158.6	148.5	175.9	144.1
Long-term debt	0.0	5.7	17.5	30.2	109.2	155.5	221.5	216.9	194.8
Other long-term liabilities	11.7	9.7	15.3	16.6	24.0	20.3	17.8	15.3	17.0
Minority interests	4.0	11.9	31.4	42.6	47.4	41.7	16.8	7.9	6.8
Total liabilities	56.7	90.0	178.4	211.9	317.9	376.1	404.6	416.0	218.6
Common equity	182.6	204.7	224.8	243.8	254.3	264.1	198.7	143.5	194.1
Total equity capital	182.6	204.7	224.8	243.8	254.3	264.1	198.7	143.5	194.1
Total liabilities & capital	$239.2	$294.7	$403.2	$455.8	$572.2	$640.3	$603.3	$559.5	$556.9
Income Statement Data									
Net sales	$370.2	$443.2	$570.2	$692.8	$796.7	$833.9	$853.0	$846.0	$906.6
Cost of goods sold	245.4	279.4	361.0	441.3	510.5	521.8	553.1	532.8	556.3
Gross profit	124.8	163.8	209.2	251.5	286.2	312.1	299.9	313.2	350.3
SG&A expense	100.3	119.7	165.2	211.1	259.2	270.5	280.3	273.3	261.7
Operating profit	24.5	44.1	44.0	40.4	27.0	41.6	19.6	39.9	88.6
Restructuring charge	0	0	0	0	0	0	(23.9)	(70.1)	2.7
Nonrecurring operating expense	0	0	0	0	0	0	(18.9)	(3.7)	0
Other income	6.1	7.1	14.4	15.7	14.4	8.5	7.5	4.5	4.5
Earnings before interest and taxes	30.6	51.2	58.4	56.1	41.4	50.1	(15.7)	(29.4)	95.9
Interest expense	1.0	1.3	2.6	7.6	11.1	15.7	18.7	17.6	15.7
Income taxes	13.7	22.3	21.5	21.0	19.3	20.0	11.4	(6.4)	32.2
Accounting charge	0	0	0	0	0	0	0	2.5	0
Net income	$ 15.8	$ 27.6	$ 34.4	$ 27.6	$ 11.1	$ 14.4	$ (45.8)	$ (38.1)	$ 48.0

Source: McDonald and Company and SEC reports.

In 1992 and 1993, Lincoln wrote off about $130 million of its foreign assets and reported its first-ever net losses—$46 million and $38 million respectively. Citing the profitable performance of the firm's U.S. workers, Hastings convinced the board of directors to give them incentive bonuses at 60 percent of wages each year in spite of the overall losses. Dividends were cut by nearly 40 percent from the 1991 level. In 1994, Hastings told the U.S. employees, "We went from five plants in four countries in 1986 to 21 plants in 15 countries in 1992. We did it too fast, we paid too much, we didn't understand the international markets or cultures, and then we got hit by a tremendous global recession." By mid-1995, Lincoln was down to 16 plants in 11 countries. Dick Sabo described the company's new relationship with ESAB:

> So the animosity has ended. We're still competitors, but we are more like the U.S. competitors. In the U.S. we've always had a competitive situation, but we're friendly competitors. So, overall, the strategy that Ted Willis originated was good. The implementation was poor. That's where the problem was.

Rank-and-file employees commented on the results of the attempt at international expansion. Stenographer Dee Chesko, a 27-year employee, said she had heard no bitterness voiced about the losses:

> What I was hearing was people were disappointed—that they felt upper management should know, per se, what they're doing. You know, how could this happen? Not bitterness . . . a little frustration. But, if companies are to expand and be global, this has to be expected.

Assembler Kathleen Hoenigman, hired in 1977, added:

> They say, "We want to be number one. We want to be number one." So we are going to keep buying and buying and buying. I think we will be investing more overseas. And I think we are going to be number one internationally, not just in the U.S., but the manufacturing will be done here. The expansion helped. We lost money, but I think it helped. You know what, if we didn't do as we did, we wouldn't be known as well as we are right now. Because we were staying just like a little . . . a little pea, while everybody was building up around us.

Sabo said Lincoln expected to continue expanding internationally, "But we're going at it a little differently." He explained:

> Under Willis, we bought a manufacturing site with the intent of creating the marketing demand. Under Hastings, we're developing the marketing demand with the anticipation that we'll build the manufacturing site to meet the demand. So what we're trying to do is take the existing facilities that we have and sell a lot of product and create enough demand so that we have to buy—or build—more facilities to service that demand.
>
> We're just getting there in terms of being global. We're global to the extent that we market in 123 countries. We're global to the extent that we have distributors in 86 different countries. We're global because we have manufacturing sites in 10 countries. Are we global in our management style? No. We're just starting to develop that.

THE U.S. WELDING PRODUCTS INDUSTRY IN 1995

The welding products market of the mid-1990s was classified as "mature and cyclical." In the United States, annual sales volume had ranged between $2.5 and $2.7 billion since 1988 (see Exhibit 11). The main arc welding products were power sources and welding machines; consumable items such as welding electrodes; acces-

EXHIBIT 11   Trends and Forecasts in the Welding Apparatus Industry, 1987–1994 (dollars in millions except for average hourly earnings)

	1987	1988	1989	1990	1991	1992[1]	1993[2]	1994[3]
Industry Data								
Value of shipments[4]	$2,105	$2,498	$2,521	$2,684	$2,651	$2,604	$2,576	—
Total employment (000)	18.7	19.7	19.0	19.2	19.5	19.4	19.5	—
Production workers (000)	11.5	12.3	11.6	12.0	11.8	11.7	11.7	—
Average hourly earnings	$ 12.10	$ 12.45	$ 12.67	$ 13.15	$ 13.07	—	—	—
Capital expenditures	$ 45.4	$ 49.3	$ 59.1	$ 67.7	$ 50.5	—	—	—
Product Data								
Value of shipments[5]	$1,918	$2,263	$2,298	$2,475	$2,434	$2,374	$2,340	—
Value of shipments (1987 $)	1,918	2,135	2,077	2,154	2,034	1,935	1,874	1,954
Value of imports	—	—	$ 480	$ 365	$ 478	$ 381	$ 458	$ 458
Value of exports	—	—	491	566	597	621	661	671

		Percent Change				
	1988–89	1989–90	1990–91	1991–92	1992–93	1993–94
Industry Data						
Value of shipments[4]	0.9%	6.5%	(1.2)%	(1.8)%	(1.1)%	—
Value of shipments	(3.3)	2.5	(5.2)	(4.1)	(3.0)	3.9%
Total employment	(3.6)	1.1	1.6	(0.5)	0.5	—
Production workers	(5.7)	3.4	(1.7)	(0.8)	0.0	—
Average hourly earnings	1.8	3.8	(0.6)	—	—	—
Capital expenditures	19.9	14.6	(25.4)	—	—	—
Product Data						
Value of shipments[5]	1.5	7.7	(1.7)	(2.5)	(1.4)	—
Value of shipments	(2.7)	3.7	(5.6)	(4.9)	(3.2)	4.3
Value of imports	—	(24.0)	31.0	(20.3)	20.2	0.0
Value of exports	—	15.3	5.5	4.0	8.1	11.3

[1]Estimate, except exports and imports.
[2]Estimate.
[3]Forecast.
[4]Value of all products and services sold by establishments in the welding apparatus industry (SIC 3548).
[5]Value of products classified in the welding apparatus industry produced b.
Source: U.S. Department of Commerce: Bureau of the Census; International U.S. Industrial Outlook January, 1994.

sories such as protective clothing; automated wire feeding systems; and devices to manipulate or position the electrodes, such as robots.

After the downturn in 1982–83, when industry sales fell 30–40 percent, the U.S. welding products industry consolidated. By 1995, at least 75 percent of machine and consumables sales was accounted for by just four companies: Lincoln, Miller Electric Company (which did not sell consumables), ESAB Corporation, and Hobart Brothers. ESAB had recently been sold to Britain's Charter Group; both Miller and Hobart had recently been acquired by Illinois Tool Works, Inc. Lincoln and Miller were thought to have about equal unit sales of machines and power supplies, about double Hobart's volume. Hundreds of smaller companies marketed various niche products, and several international firms sold limited lines of transformer- and inverter-based machines in the United States and elsewhere. Over 600 exhibitors were registered to show their wares at the 1996 annual Welding Show in Chicago, where 25,000 potential customers would attend.

Starting in the early 1990s, Lincoln, Miller, and Hobart each began buying similar articulated-arm robots and adapting them to welding applications. The size of the robotics segment of the welding products market was unclear in 1995, but Chet Woodman, head of Lincoln Automation, said his unit had robotics sales of about $7 million in 1994 and predicted $50 million annual revenue by the year 2000.

ESAB, Lincoln, and Hobart each marketed a wide range of continuous-wire and stick electrodes for welding mild steel, aluminum, cast iron, and stainless and special steels. Most electrodes were designed to meet the standards of the American Welding Society (AWS) and were thus essentially the same as to size and composition from one manufacturer to another. Price differences for similar products among the three companies amounted to only a percent or two. Competitively priced foreign products were well represented in the market, however, as imported consumables that purported to meet AWS standards were commonly available. There was no testing system to confirm a product's conformance to the standards.

Every electrode manufacturer had a limited number of proprietary products, but these typically constituted only a small percentage of its total sales. There were also many producers of specialized electrodes for limited applications, such as welding under water and welding space-age alloys, and several international companies marketed general-purpose electrodes. Wire for gas-shielded (MIG) welding was thought to be the biggest-selling welding consumable. ESAB claimed to have the largest share of the global welding consumables and materials market.

LINCOLN'S MANUFACTURING PROCESSES

Lincoln made about twice as many different products in 1995 as it had 10 years earlier. Its net sales per employee in 1994 were $159,248. For U.S. employees only, the number was about $225,000. About two-thirds of Lincoln's net sales were products made in the Cleveland area.

Fortune magazine declared Lincoln's Euclid operation one of America's ten best-managed factories, and compared it to a General Electric plant also on the list:

> Stepping into GE's spanking new dishwasher plant, an awed supplier said, is like stepping "into the Hyatt Regency." By comparison, stepping into Lincoln Electric's 33-year-old, cavernous, dimly lit factory is like stumbling into a dingy big-city YMCA. It's only when one starts looking at how these factories do things that similarities become apparent. They have found ways to merge design with manufacturing, build in quality, make wise choices about automation, get close to customers, and handle their work forces.[7]

As it had for decades, Lincoln required most suppliers to deliver raw materials just in time for use on its production line. James Lincoln had counseled producing for stock when necessary to maintain employment. For many years after his death, however, the firm manufactured only to customer order. In the late 1980s, Hastings decided to resume maintaining substantial finished goods inventories and Lincoln purchased a finished goods warehouse.

---

[7]Gene Bylinsky, "America's Best-Managed Factories," *Fortune*, May 28, 1984, p. 16.

Outsourcing

It was James Lincoln's policy to keep Lincoln as insulated as possible from work stoppages in supplier plants, especially unionized ones. He also felt Lincoln quality was higher than that most suppliers could provide. So instead of purchasing most components from outsiders, Lincoln made them from basic industrial raw materials such as coils of steel sheet and bar, pieces of metal plate, spools of copper and aluminum wire, and pallets of paints and varnishes. Lincoln even made its own electronic circuit boards to assure their performance in outdoor, cold, dirty conditions; commercial suppliers were accustomed to making circuits boards for warm, clean computers. At one point, the firm had contemplated buying its own steel rolling mill. President Ted Willis, however, was concerned over the mill's union affiliation, and the purchase was not completed.

As an exception to on-site manufacture of components, gasoline and diesel engines for the engine-driven machines were purchased. Like its main competitors, Lincoln used Wisconsin-Continental, Perkins, and Deutz engines in 1995.

Welding Machine Manufacture

In the welding machines portion of Lincoln's manufacturing plant in Euclid, most engine-driven welders, power supplies, wire feeders, and so forth were assembled, tested, and packaged on conveyor lines. Almost all components were made by numerous small "factories within a factory." Various of these small factories—mostly open work areas—made gasoline tanks, steel shafts, wiring harnesses, and even switches, rheostats, and transformers. The shaft for a certain generator, for example, was made from round steel bar by two men who used five machines. A saw cut the bar to length, a digital lathe machined different sections to varying diameters, a special milling machine cut a slot for the key way, and so forth, until a finished shaft was produced. The operators moved the shafts from machine to machine and made necessary adjustments and tool changes. Nearby, a man punched, shaped, and painted sheet metal cowling parts. In another area, a woman and a man put steel laminations onto rotor shafts, then wound, insulated, and tested the rotors. Many machines in the factory appeared old, even obsolete; James Lincoln had always insisted on a one-year payback period for new investments, and it appeared the policy was still in effect.

Consumables Manufacture

The company was secretive about its consumables production and outsiders were barred from the Mentor, Ohio, plant (which made only electrodes) and from the electrode area of the main plant. Electrode manufacture was highly capital intensive and teams of Lincoln workers who made electrodes shared group piece rates. To make electrodes, rod purchased from metals producers, usually in coils, was drawn down to make wire of various diameters. For stick electrodes, the wire was cut into pieces, most commonly 14 inches long, and coated with pressed-powder "flux." Dick Sabo commented,

> The actual production of a stick electrode has not changed for at least 40 years. Bill Irrgang designed that equipment. As to the constituents which make up the electrodes, that may change almost daily. There are changes in design from time to time. And every new batch of raw material has a little different consistency, and we have to adjust for that. We make our own iron oxide [a main ingredient of many fluxes]. We have had that powder kiln in operation since about the 1930s. We may have the largest production facility for iron oxide

pellets in the world. At first, we contemplated selling the pellets. But we decided not to give our competition an edge.

Stick electrodes were packaged in boxes weighing 2 to 50 pounds. Continuous wire electrode, generally smaller in diameter, was packaged in coils and spools, also 2 to 50 pounds each, and in drums weighing up to half a ton. Some wire electrode was coated with copper to improve conductivity. Lincoln's Innershield wire, like the "cored" wire of other manufacturers, was hollow and filled with a material similar to that used to coat stick electrodes.

The New Electric Motor Factory

In 1992, Lincoln saw an opportunity to become a major factor in the electric motor business by purchasing the assets of General Motors' AC-Delco plant in Dayton, Ohio. New government regulations prescribing the energy efficiency of electric motors made it necessary to redesign whole product lines; GM decided instead to exit the industry. Lincoln's intent was to combine AC-Delco's technology and product line with Lincoln's manufacturing expertise and cost structure in the Dayton plant. Don Hastings offered to involve the existing union in its operation of the plant provided Lincoln's incentive compensation system was adopted. Dick Sabo described what happened:

> We asked the AC-Delco employees if they wanted to adopt the Lincoln Incentive System and keep their plant open—and their jobs. They voted overwhelmingly not to adopt the system. And they knew all about us. We put a lot of effort into telling them about Lincoln, even brought some employees up here to tour our plant and talk to Lincoln people. What struck Mr. Hastings as odd was that people would vote themselves out of work rather than knuckle down and put in the effort that it takes to be in the motor business. That was sort of an eye opener for Lincoln Electric.

The Dayton plant was closed. In mid-1995, Lincoln's new electric motor factory, close to its main Euclid plant, was near completion and in partial operation. The plant was designed to make motors from 1/3 to 1,250 horsepower, in custom configurations as well as standard specifications, with shipment six days after customer orders. Lincoln's electric motor sales in 1994 totaled about $50 million, and the goal was $100 million in sales by the year 2000. U.S. total motor sales in 1994 were about $2.8 billion.

Robotics

Adjacent to the electric motor factory was a smaller building housing Lincoln's Automation unit. There, work teams of two or three put together robotic welding units that combined Fanuc (Japanese) articulated arms with Lincoln automatic welders. In operation, the robot arm manipulated the wire electrode much as a human operator would, but faster and more accurately. The system, priced at about $100,000, could be purchased with a laser "eye" to track irregular seams and could be programmed to follow any three-dimensional path within the arm's reach. Chet Woodman, head of Lincoln Automation, was a former Hobart executive with over a decade of experience in robotics manufacturing and marketing.

MANAGEMENT ORGANIZATION

James Lincoln stressed the need to protect management's authority. "Management in all successful departments of industry must have complete power," he said, "Management is the coach who must be obeyed. The men, however, are the players who alone can win the game." Examples of management's authority were the right to transfer workers among jobs, to switch between overtime and short time as required, and to assign specific parts to individual workers. There were no executive perks—management offices were crowded and austere; there were no executive washrooms or lunchrooms or automobiles, and no reserved parking spaces, except for visitors. Normally, executives ate in the employee cafeteria.

James Lincoln never allowed preparation of a formal organization chart, saying this might limit flexibility. Irrgang and Willis continued that policy. During the 1970s, Harvard Business School researchers prepared a chart reflecting the implied management relationships at Lincoln. It became available within the company, and Irrgang felt this had a disruptive effect. Only after Hastings became CEO was a formal chart prepared. Exhibit 12 shows the official organization chart in 1995 and Exhibit 6 lists officers and directors. Two levels of management, at most, existed between supervisors and Mackenbach. Production supervisors at Lincoln typically were responsible for 60 to over 100 workers. Hastings, who was 67, had recruited experienced managers from outside the company and appointed a number of new, young vice presidents, mainly from the field, so they could compete for the top jobs.

Promotion from Within

Until the 1990s, Lincoln had a firm policy of promotion from within and claimed to hire above the entry level "only when there are no suitable internal applicants." In 1990, all senior managers at Lincoln were career Lincoln employees—and all directors were present or former employees or Lincoln family members. However, when Lincoln purchased Harris Calorific in 1992, its CEO, Paul F. Fantelli, was retained and later became vice president of business development of Lincoln. A number of other acquired company officials were integrated into Lincoln's management structure.

Lincoln's CFO in 1996, H. Jay Elliott, came from Goodyear in 1993; General Counsel Frederick Stueber came from a private law firm in 1995; and Anthony Massaro, the nominated successor to Fred Mackenbach as president, joined Lincoln from his position as group president of Westinghouse Electric Co. in 1993. Several outside directors were also elected, including the CEO of Capital American Financial Corporation, a former vice chairman of General Electric, a former CEO of Westinghouse, and the CEO of Libby Corporation. Still, there were no announced plans to hire more managers from outside. Company executives and Lincoln family members had a clear majority of the seats on Lincoln's board of directors.

Lincoln managers received a base salary plus an incentive bonus. The bonus was calculated in the same way as for workers. The only exceptions to this method of compensation were the three outsiders Hastings hired as managers in 1993–95 and the company's chief executive officer. The former outsiders had special employment contracts. Sabo explained how the CEO was compensated:

> James Lincoln set the chairman's salary at $50,000 plus 0.1 percent of sales. After Willis became chairman, it was based on a percentage of sales plus a percentage of profit. It became apparent that when the company started losing money it was difficult to pay someone based on losses. So they changed the approach for Don Hastings. [Through the lean years] Don was paid somewhere around $600,000 base salary plus incentives.

For 1995, Hastings was paid $1,003,901.[8]

---

[8]Baltimore, MD, Disclosures, Inc. (via Dow Jones News Service).

EXHIBIT 12 Lincoln Electric's Organization Chart, 1995

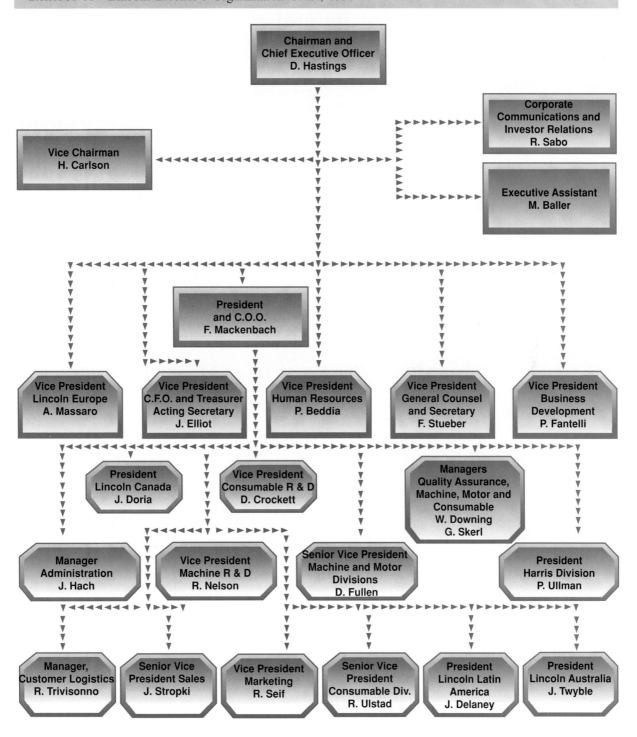

LOOKING TO THE FUTURE

When Lincoln in the spring of 1995 announced plans to raise capital with a public issue of stock, Dick Sabo said certain Lincoln family members were afraid the family would lose control of the company. "Paranoid, I guess, is the proper term," he remarked. Sam Evans added,

> I hope the public issue is handled in such a manner that those public owners understand that the success of this company is based on the incentive system. For 60 or 70 years, that has been our success—through the contribution of the employees. We have succeeded because we had a good product, good R and D, and excellent management for most of that period. But we've also had great contribution from the employees.

In early 1996, with the public stock issue accomplished and a record year in both sales and profits just completed, a *Business Week* article said:

> . . . executives are now considering ways to move toward a more traditional pay scheme and away from the flat percentage-bonus formula. "The bonus is a good program, and it has worked well, but it's got to be modified some," says Director David C. Lincoln, whose father John C. Lincoln founded the company in 1895. Adds Edward E. Lawler, who heads the University of Southern California's Center for Effective Organizations: "One of the issues with Lincoln is how [its pay plan] can survive rapid growth and globalization."

(The company's Web address is *www.lincolnelectric.com*.)

WAL-MART STORES, INC.

Arthur A. Thompson, *The University of Alabama*

Kem Pinegar, *Birmingham-Southern College*

Tracy Robertson Kramer, *George Mason University*

In 1994, Wal-Mart seemed well on its way toward achieving Sam Walton's vision of becoming a $125 billion company by the year 2000. Wal-Mart's three-person leadership team, consisting of Chairman of the Board S. Robson Walton (Sam and Helen Walton's oldest son), Vice Chairman and Chief Operating Officer Donald G. Soderquist (a veteran Wal-Mart executive whose role went back to the company's formative years), and President and CEO David D. Glass (handpicked by Sam Walton to succeed him as CEO), could look with justifiable pride on the company's remarkable climb to having become the world's largest discount retailer:

	1960	1970	1980	1990	1994
Sales	$1.4 million	$31 million	$1.2 billion	$26 billion	$67 billion
Profits	$112,000	$1.2 million	$41 million	$1 billion	$2.3 billion
Stores	9	32	276	1,528	2,136

In the months since Walton's death in 1992, Wal-Mart's sales had grown from $44 billion annually to over $67 billion annually. Every week, more than 40 million people shopped in a Wal-Mart store. Each year, Wal-Mart sold 55 million sweatsuits, 27 million pairs of jeans, and nearly 20 percent of all the telephones bought in the United States. Procter & Gamble supplied more goods to Wal-Mart than it sold in all of Japan.

Wal-Mart had made *Fortune*'s list of the 10 most admired corporations several times and in late 1989 was named "Retailer of the Decade" by *Discount Store News*. No company in the world could match Wal-Mart's revenue growth of over $65 billion in 14 years. Owners of Wal-Mart's stock had fared spectacularly well: a 100-share $1,650 investment in Wal-Mart stock in 1970, when shares first began trading, was worth $2.7 million in 1994; a 100-share investment at $47 per share in 1983 had become, after stock splits, a 3,200-share investment worth $91,000 in 1994. The market value of Wal-Mart's common stock (equal to the stock price times the number of outstanding shares) was the sixth highest of all U.S. companies as of March 1994. The Walton family owned about 35 percent of Wal-Mart's stock, worth about $23 billion.

Exhibit 1 provides a summary of Wal-Mart's financial and operating performance for fiscal years February 1984 through January 1994.

SAM WALTON

Sam Walton graduated from the University of Missouri in 1940 with a degree in economics and took a job as a management trainee at J.C. Penney Co. His career with Penney's ended with a call to military duty in World War II. When the war was over, Walton decided to open a Ben Franklin retail variety store in Newport, Arkansas, rather than return to Penney's. Five years later when the lease on the Newport building was lost, Walton decided to relocate his business in Bentonville, Arkansas, where he bought a building and opened Walton's 5 & 10 as a Ben Franklin-affiliated store. By 1960 Walton was the largest Ben Franklin franchisee, with nine stores.

In 1961 Walton started to become concerned about the long-term competitive threat to variety stores posed by the emerging popularity of giant supermarkets and discounters. An avid pilot, he took off in his plane on a cross-country tour studying the changes in stores and retailing trends, then put together a plan for a discount store of his own. Walton went to Chicago to try to interest Ben Franklin executives in expanding into discount retailing; when they turned him down, he decided to go forward on his own. The first Wal-Mart Discount City opened July 2, 1962, in Rogers, Arkansas.

Sam Walton's talent for discount retailing surfaced early. Although he started out as a seat-of-the-pants merchant, he had great instincts, was quick to learn from other retailers' successes and failures, and was adept at garnering ideas for improvements from employees and promptly trying them out. As the company grew, Sam Walton proved an effective and visionary leader. His folksy manner and his talent for motivating people, combined with a very hands-on management style, produced a culture and a set of values and beliefs that kept Wal-Mart on a path of continuous innovation and rapid expansion. Wal-Mart's success and Walton's personable style of leadership generated numerous stories in the media that cast the company and its founder in a positive light and soon made both famous. As Wal-Mart emerged as the premier discount retailer in the United States, an uncommonly large cross-section of the American public came to know who Sam Walton was and to associate his name with Wal-Mart.

WAL-MART'S STRATEGY

The hallmarks of Wal-Mart's strategy were low everyday prices, wide selection, a big percentage of name-brand merchandise, a customer-friendly store environment, low operating costs, disciplined expansion into new geographic markets, innovative merchandising, and customer satisfaction guarantees. On the outside of every Wal-Mart store in big letters was the message "We Sell for Less." The company's advertising tag line reinforced the low-price theme: "Always the low price. Always." Its low-price image was bolstered with ads urging customers to bring in "any competitor's local ad—we'll match it." Major merchandise lines included housewares, consumer electronics, sporting goods, lawn and garden items, health and beauty aids, apparel, home fashions, paint, bed and bath goods, hardware, automotive repair and mainte-nance items, toys and games, and groceries (mostly nonperishable items such as packaged products, household supplies, snack foods, and canned goods). As of 1994, store sizes averaged about 84,000 square feet, with a range of 40,000 to 180,000 square feet. In-store fixtures were basic, but the atmosphere was bright, cheery, and fresh, with ample aisle space and attractively presented merchandise displays. Store personnel were friendly and helpful; the aim was to make each shopper's experience pleasant and satisfying. In 1993 Wal-Mart announced plans to replace 100 of its standard snack bars with franchise-owned McDonald's restaurants.

Penny-pinching cost consciousness pervaded every part of Wal-Mart's opera-tions—from store construction to pressuring vendors and suppliers for low prices on every item Wal-Mart stocked to supplying stores via an efficient distribution system to keeping corporate overhead costs down. The cost savings Wal-Mart achieved were passed on to customers in the form of lower retail prices.

Wal-Mart's Geographic Expansion Strategy

One of the most distinctive features of Wal-Mart's business strategy was the manner in which it expanded outward into new geographic areas. Whereas many chain retailers achieved regional and national coverage quickly by entering the largest metropolitan centers before trying to penetrate less populated markets, Wal-Mart always expanded into *adjoining* geographic areas, saturating each area with stores before moving into new territory. New stores were usually clustered within 200 miles of an existing distribution center so that deliveries could be made cost effectively on a daily basis; new distribution centers were added as needed to support store expan-sion into additional states. But the really unique feature of Wal-Mart's geographic strategy involved opening stores in small towns surrounding a targeted metropolitan area *before* moving into the metropolitan area itself—an approach Sam Walton termed "backward expansion." Wal-Mart management believed that any town with a shopping area population of 15,000 or more persons was big enough to support a Discount City store. Once stores were opened in towns around the most populous city, Wal-Mart would locate one or more stores in the metropolitan area and begin major market advertising.

By clustering new stores in a relatively small geographic area, the company's advertising expenses for breaking into a new market could be shared across all the area stores, a tactic Wal-Mart used to keep its advertising costs under 1 percent of sales (compared to 2 or 3 percent for other discount chains). Don Soderquist ex-plained why the company preferred its backward expansion strategy.[1]

> Our strategy is to go into smaller markets first before we hit major metro areas because you've got a smaller population base to convince over. So you begin to get the acceptance in smaller markets and the word begins to travel around and people begin to travel further and further to get to your stores.

---

[1]*Discount Store News*, December 18, 1989, p. 162.

EXHIBIT 1 Financial and Operating Summary for Wal-Mart Stores, Inc., Fiscal Years 1984–1994 (Dollar amounts in thousands except per share data)

	1994	1993	1992	1991
Operating Results				
Net sales	$67,344,574	$55,483,771	$43,886,902	$32,601,594
Net sales increase	21%	26%	35%	26%
Comparative store sales increase	6%	11%	10%	10%
Rentals from licensed departments and other income—net	640,970	500,793	402,521	261,814
Cost of sales	53,443,743	44,174,685	34,786,119	25,499,834
Operating, selling, and general and administrative expenses	10,333,218	8,320,842	6,684,304	5,152,178
Interest costs:				
Debt	331,308	142,649	113,305	42,716
Capital leases	185,697	180,049	152,558	125,920
Provision for federal and state income taxes	1,358,301	1,171,545	944,661	751,736
Net income	$2,333,277	$1,994,794	$1,608,476	$1,291,024
Per share of common stock*:				
Net income	$1.02	$0.87	$0.70	$0.57
Dividends	0.13	0.11	0.09	0.07
Financial Position				
Current assets	$12,114,602	$10,197,590	$8,575,423	$6,414,775
Inventories at replacement cost	11,483,119	9,779,981	7,856,871	6,207,852
Less LIFO reserve	469,413	511,672	472,572	399,436
Inventories at LIFO cost	11,013,706	9,268,309	7,384,299	5,808,416
Net property, plant, equipment, and capital leases	13,175,366	9,792,881	6,433,801	4,712,039
Total assets	26,440,764	20,565,087	15,443,389	11,388,915
Current liabilities	7,406,223	6,754,286	5,003,775	3,990,414
Long-term debt	6,155,894	3,072,835	1,722,022	740,254
Long-term obligations under capital leases	1,804,300	1,772,152	1,555,875	1,158,621
Preferred stock with mandatory redemption provisions	—	—	—	—
Shareholders' equity	10,752,438	8,759,180	6,989,710	5,365,524
Financial Ratios				
Current ratio	1.6	1.5	1.7	1.6
Inventories/working capital	2.3	2.7	2.1	2.4
Return on assets**	11.3%	12.9%	14.1%	15.7%
Return on shareholders' equity**	26.6%	28.5%	30.0%	32.6%
Other Year-End Data				
Number of Wal-Mart stores	1,953	1,850	1,714	1,568
Number of Supercenters	68	30	6	5
Number of Sam's Clubs	419	256	208	148
Average Wal-Mart store size (square feet)	83,900	79,800	74,700	70,700
Number of associates	528,000	434,000	371,000	328,000
Number of shareholders	257,946	180,584	150,242	122,414

*Reflects the two-for-one stock split distributed February 1993.
**On beginning of year balances.

Source: Company annual report for 1994. (The company's fiscal year ends in January.)

In the small towns Wal-Mart entered, it was not unusual for a number of businesses that carried merchandise similar to Wal-Mart's lines to fail within a year or two after Wal-Mart's arrival. Wal-Mart's low prices tended to attract customers away from apparel shops, general stores, pharmacies, sporting goods stores, shoe stores,

EXHIBIT 1 (*continued*)

1990	1989	1988	1987	1986	1985	1984
$25,810,656	$20,649,001	$15,959,255	$11,909,076	$8,451,489	$6,400,861	$4,666,909
25%	29%	34%	41%	32%	37%	38%
11%	12%	11%	13%	9%	15%	15%
174,644	136,867	104,783	84,623	55,127	52,167	36,031
20,070,034	16,056,856	12,281,744	9,053,219	6,361,271	4,722,440	3,418,025
4,069,695	3,267,864	2,599,367	2,007,645	1,485,210	1,181,455	892,887
20,346	36,286	25,262	10,442	1,903	5,207	4,935
117,725	99,395	88,995	76,367	54,640	42,506	29,946
631,600	488,246	441,027	395,940	276,119	230,653	160,903
$1,075,900	$837,221	$627,643	$450,086	$327,473	$270,767	$196,244
$0.48	$0.37	$0.28	$0.20	$0.15	$0.12	$0.09
.06	.04	.03	.02	.02	.01	.01
$4,712,616	$3,630,987	$2,905,145	$2,353,271	$1,784,275	$1,303,254	$1,005,567
4,750,619	3,642,696	2,854,556	2,185,847	1,528,349	1,227,264	857,155
322,546	291,329	202,796	153,875	140,181	123,339	121,760
4,428,073	3,351,367	2,651,760	2,030,972	1,388,168	1,103,925	735,395
3,430,059	2,661,954	2,144,852	1,676,282	1,303,450	870,309	628,151
8,198,484	6,359,668	5,131,809	4,049,092	3,103,645	2,205,229	1,652,254
2,845,315	2,065,909	1,743,763	1,340,291	992,683	688,968	502,763
185,152	184,439	185,672	179,234	180,682	41,237	40,866
1,087,403	1,009,046	866,972	764,128	595,205	449,886	339,930
—	—	—	—	4,902	5,874	6,411
3,965,561	3,007,909	2,257,267	1,690,493	1,277,659	984,672	737,503
1.7	1.8	1.7	1.8	1.8	1.9	2.0
2.4	2.1	2.3	2.0	1.8	1.8	1.5
16.9%	16.3%	15.5%	14.5%	14.8%	16.4%	16.5%
35.8%	37.1%	37.1%	35.2%	33.3%	36.7%	40.2%
1,399	1,259	1,114	980	859	745	642
3	—	—	—	—	—	—
123	105	84	49	23	11	3
66,400	63,500	61,500	59,000	57,000	55,000	53,000
271,000	223,000	183,000	141,000	104,000	81,000	62,000
79,929	80,270	79,777	32,896	21,828	14,799	14,172

and hardware stores operated by local merchants. The "Wal-Mart effect" in small communities was so big that it had spawned the formation of consulting firms specializing in advising local retailers how to survive the opening of a Wal-Mart.

Experimentation with New Store Formats

A second element of Wal-Mart's growth strategy involved employing different store formats to build market share within a given area. Sam's Wholesale Club marked Wal-Mart's first major venture in expanding its merchandising reach. The company saw excellent strategic fit between its Wal-Mart discount operations and the concept of wholesale club merchandising.

Sam's Wholesale Club   Sam's Wholesale Clubs were membership-only, cash-and-carry warehouses, approximately 100,000 square feet in size, which carried frequently used, brand-name items in bulk quantities as well as some big-ticket merchandise (TVs, tires, household appliances, computers, and electronic equipment). To qualify for membership, one had to be the owner of a business, self-employed, a government employee (federal, state, or local), a Wal-Mart stockholder, or be buying on behalf of a civic or community service organization; a federal tax I.D. or a business license was often used to establish an applicant's membership eligibility. The annual membership fee was $25. Sam's catered to the needs of small businesses for general merchandise and supplies for internal use. The advertising tag line for Sam's was "Our business is your business."

Most goods at Sam's were displayed in the original cartons stacked in wooden racks or on wooden pallets. Where feasible, incoming merchandise was premarked and palletized, allowing it to be moved from delivery trucks into the selling/display area by forklifts. In the greatly downscaled apparel department, merchandise was displayed on tables, in boxes, and hanging from metal racks. Many items stocked were sold in bulk quantity (five-gallon containers, bundles of a dozen or more, and economy-size boxes). Prices tended to be 10 to 15 percent below the prices of Discount City stores since merchandising costs and store operation costs were substantially lower.

The first Sam's was opened in 1983 and by 1994 there were 419 Sam's Clubs open in 49 states. Sales in fiscal year 1993 exceeded $12.3 billion, averaging just over $48 million per unit. Wal-Mart was experimenting with several modifications of the Sam's Wholesale Club format, including increasing the size from 100,000 to 130,000 square feet, creating more excitement in merchandise presentation, and offering such service and merchandise enhancements as a bakery, a butcher shop, a produce department, an optical facility, and an express shipping service.

The Supercenter Format   Wal-Mart's newest store variation was the Supercenter, a format that Wal-Mart began testing in 1987. Supercenters were intended to give Wal-Mart improved drawing power in its existing markets by providing a one-stop shopping destination. Supercenters had the full array of general merchandise found in Wal-Mart stores, plus a full-scale supermarket, deli, fresh bakery, and such specialty/convenience shops as a hair salon, portrait studio, dry cleaners, and optical wear department. Supercenters were about 125,000 to 150,000 square feet in size and were targeted for locations where sales per store of $30 to $50 million annually were thought feasible.

Wal-Mart management believed the Supercenter format was quite promising; numerous experiments were under way in the 68 Supercenters already open and the company was planning to open 50 additional Supercenters in the remaining months of 1994. In trying to perfect the Supercenter concept, Wal-Mart management was focusing on improving merchandise layouts and displays and on learning all it could about grocery marketing and grocery distribution. To enhance its knowledge of the supermarket business and develop the organizational ability to execute the Supercenter concept with a high degree of proficiency, Wal-Mart had acquired a grocery distribution company in Texas, McLane Company, which had nationwide distribution capabilities and also operated food processing facilities. McLane was a

EXHIBIT 2   Wal-Mart Retailing Locations, February 1994

	Wal-Mart Stores	Sam's Clubs	Supercenters	Distribution Centers	McLane's	Western
Alabama	70	8	4	1		
Alaska		3				
Arizona	29	6		1	1	
Arkansas	66	4	11	6		
California	66	26		1	2	
Colorado	34	8		1	1	1
Connecticut	2	3				
Delaware	2	1				
Florida	124	36	1	1	1	
Georgia	83	14		1	1	1
Hawaii		1				
Idaho	7	1				
Illinois	101	24	1		1	
Indiana	69	14		2		
Iowa	45	4		1		
Kansas	42	7	1			
Kentucky	67	4	1			
Louisiana	72	9	2			
Maine	14	3				
Maryland	13	9				
Massachusetts	7	5				
Michigan	30	21				
Minnesota	29	8				
Mississippi	52	3	5	1	1	
Missouri	91	12	14			
Montana	4	1				
Nebraska	17	3				

major supplier to The Southland Corporation's 7-Eleven chain of convenience stores and to independent grocers. In 1993 McLane had sales of $2.9 billion.

In addition, Wal-Mart had a small number of Bud's Warehouse Outlets, which specialized in close-out goods, and was experimenting with a new concept called vendor stores that involved selecting key suppliers in a major category and giving them wide latitude in merchandising their products; suppliers participating in the vendor store trials included Rubbermaid, Black & Decker, Cannon, Pioneer, Gitano, Toshiba, and Wrangler. In 1993 Wal-Mart had opened a farm, home, and garden store called County Farms that focused on the business needs of farmers; the stores had refrigerated vaccines to treat animal ailments, selected farm and garden equipment, a market quote board for commodity prices, a conference room 4H clubs could use for meetings, a small-engine parts and service center, and an array of lawn, garden, and feed products.

Exhibit 2 shows the number of Wal-Mart stores in each state as of 1994.

	Wal-Mart Stores	Sam's Clubs	Supercenters	Distribution Centers	McLane's	Western
EXHIBIT 2 Wal-Mart Retailing Locations, February 1994 (*continued*)						
Nevada	6	2				1
New Hampshire	11	4				
New Jersey	9	5				
New Mexico	19	3				
New York	28	14			1	
North Carolina	79	12				
North Dakota	8	2				
Ohio	49	21		1		
Oklahoma	72	6	9			
Oregon	15					
Pennsylvania	37	12		1		
Puerto Rico	3	2				
Rhode Island	2	1				
South Carolina	49	6		2		
South Dakota	8	1				
Tennessee	84	8	2			
Texas	214	52	17	4	3	2
Utah	11	4		1	1	
Virginia	41	8		1	1	
Washington	3	2			1	
West Virginia	12	4				
Wisconsin	48	10		1		
Wyoming	9	2				
USA Total	**1,953**	**419**	**68**	**27**	**15**	**5**
Mexico	14*	7	2		1	
Grand Total	**1,967**	**426**	**70**	**27**	**16**	**5**

*Includes 2 Superamas, 10 Boedegas, and 2 Aurreras.

Merchandising Innovations

Wal-Mart was unusually active in experimenting with and testing new merchandising techniques. From the beginning, Sam Walton had been quick to imitate good ideas and merchandising practices employed by other retailers. According to the founder of Kmart, Sam Walton "not only copied our concepts, he strengthened them. Sam just took the ball and ran with it."[2] Wal-Mart prided itself on its "low threshold for change" and much of management's time was spent talking to vendors, employees, and customers to get ideas for how Wal-Mart could improve. Suggestions were

---

[2]As quoted in Bill Saporito, "What Sam Walton Taught America," *Fortune*, May 4, 1992, p. 105.

EXHIBIT 3 Comparative Financial Performance of Sears (Merchandise Group Operations only), Kmart and Wal-Mart, 1980–1993

Year	Sales (In millions of dollars)			Net Income (In millions of dollars)			Net Income as a Percentage of Sales		
	Sears*	Kmart	Wal-Mart**	Sears*	Kmart	Wal-Mart**	Sears*	Kmart	Wal-Mart**
1980	$18,675	$14,118	$ 1,643	$ 229	$ 429	$ 56	1.2%	3.0%	3.4%
1981	20,202	16,394	2,445	285	311	83	1.4	1.9	3.4
1982	20,667	16,611	3,376	432	408	124	2.1	2.5	3.7
1983	25,089	18,380	4,667	781	859	196	3.1	4.7	4.2
1984	26,508	20,762	6,401	905	835	271	3.4	4.0	4.2
1985	26,552	22,035	8,451	766	757	327	2.9	3.4	3.9
1986	27,074	23,812	11,909	736	1,028	450	2.7	4.3	3.8
1987	28,085	25,627	15,959	787	1,171	627	2.8	4.6	3.9
1988	30,256	27,301	20,649	524	1,244	837	1.7	4.6	4.1
1989	31,599	29,533	25,811	647	1,155†	1,076	2.1	3.9	4.2
1990	31,986	32,070	32,602	257	1,146	1,291	0.8	3.6	4.0
1991	31,433	34,580	43,887	486	1,301	1,608	1.5	3.8	3.7
1992	31,961	31,031	55,484	(2,977)	941	1,995	(9.3)	2.7	3.6
1993	29,565	34,156	67,345	752	(328)	2,333	2.5	(1.0)	3.5

*Sears' data represents Merchandise Group Operations only; revenues and income for other Sears' businesses (insurance, finance, and so on) have been eliminated so that data will be comparable across companies.
**Wal-Mart's fiscal year ends January 31 of each year; data for the period January 31, 1980 through January 31, 1981 are reported in Wal-Mart's annual report as 1981 results. Because Wal-Mart's fiscal year results really cover 11 months of the previous calendar year, this exhibit shows Wal-Mart's 1981 fiscal results in the 1980 row, its 1982 fiscal results in the 1981 row, and so on. This adjustment makes Wal-Mart's figures correspond more to the same time frame as the calendar year data for Sears and Kmart.
†Before a pre-tax provision of $640 million for restructuring.

Source: Company annual reports, 1980–1993.

actively solicited from employees. Almost any reasonable idea was tried; if it worked well in stores where it was first tested, then it was quickly implemented in other stores. Experiments in store layout, merchandise displays, store color schemes, merchandise selection (whether to add more upscale lines or shift to a different mix of items), and sales promotion techniques were always under way. Wal-Mart was regarded as an industry leader in testing, adapting, and applying a wide range of cutting-edge merchandising approaches.

THE COMPETITIVE ENVIRONMENT

Discount retailing was an intensely competitive business. Wal-Mart's two closest competitors were Kmart and Sears. Both firms had comparable strategies and store formats but throughout the 1980s Wal-Mart had grown far faster than Kmart (see Exhibit 3). In 1989 Sears, concerned with lagging sales and Wal-Mart's rise to industry leadership, switched to an everyday-low-price strategy and started stocking leading brand-name merchandise to complement its own private-label goods. In 1994, nearly all discounters were using some form of everyday low pricing.

Competition among discount retailers centered around pricing, store location, variations in store format and merchandise mix, store size, shopping atmosphere, and image with shoppers. Wal-Mart was the only top-10 discount retailer that located a majority of its stores in rural areas. Surveys of households comparing Wal-Mart with Kmart and Target indicated that Wal-Mart had a strong competitive advantage. According to *Discount Store News*:[3]

> When asked to compare Wal-Mart with Kmart and Target, the consensus of households is that Wal-Mart is as good or better. For example, of the households with a Wal-Mart in their area, 59 percent said that Wal-Mart is better than Kmart and Target; 33 percent said it was the same. Only 4 percent rated Wal-Mart worse than Kmart and Target. . . . When asked why Wal-Mart is better, 55 percent of the respondents with a Wal-Mart in their area said lower/better prices. . . . Variety/selection and good quality were the other top reasons cited by consumers when asked why Wal-Mart is better. Thirty percent said variety; 18 percent said good quality.

Wal-Mart's reputation extended to areas where it did not have stores, reducing the costs of pushing outward into new geographic areas. Numerous stories in the media about Sam Walton and Wal-Mart's merchandising prowess had given the company a favorable image and name recognition among consumers.

The Warehouse Club Segment

The two largest competitors in the warehouse club segment were Price/Costco and Sam's Wholesale Clubs. These two accounted for a combined total of 80 percent of total sales among wholesale clubs and 55 percent of total store outlets (see Exhibit 4). In November 1990, Wal-Mart acquired Wholesale Club in a $172 million transaction, a move that increased the size of the Sam's chain to 168 stores by adding 27 stores in six midwestern states. The per-store cost of the acquisition was just over $6 million compared to $5.5 million to build and open a new Sam's. Analysts said the acquisition cut a year off the time it would have taken to enter these states and, at the same time, provided an established customer base. With the acquisition, Sam's became the undisputed leader of the warehouse club segment.

There was an industrywide effort among wholesale club competitors to differentiate themselves on the basis of service. Service differentiation was intended to make club membership appealing to a broader segment of the market. Prior to the late 1980s, none of the major warehouse clubs operated in the same geographic markets. However, the success of the club concept had fueled geographic expansion by all competitors. As competitors saturated the geographic areas surrounding their initial stores, they were expanding outward to increase market coverage and were trying to beat rival clubs to the most attractive market areas. By the 1990s, warehouse club competitors had moved into rivals' markets and were competing head-on for the first time, forcing mergers and producing slowdowns in sales growth. In 1994, the wholesale club market in the U.S. was regarded as mature.

WAL-MART'S APPROACHES TO STRATEGY IMPLEMENTATION

To implement its strategy, Wal-Mart put heavy emphasis on forging solid working relationships with both suppliers and employees, paying attention to even the tiniest

---

[3]*Discount Store News*, December 18, 1989, p. 168.

details in store layouts and merchandising, capitalizing on every cost-saving opportunity, and creating a high-performance spirit. The characteristics that often stalled the growth and success of large companies—too many layers of management, lack of internal communication, and an unwillingness or inability to change—were absent at Wal-Mart.

The Everyday-Low-Price Theme

While Wal-Mart did not invent the everyday-low-price strategy, it had done a better job than any other discount retailer in executing the concept. The company had the reputation of being the everyday-lowest-priced general-merchandise retailer in its market. In areas where Wal-Mart had a store, consumer surveys showed 55 percent of the households considered Wal-Mart's prices as lower or better than competitors; an impressive 33 percent of the households not having a Wal-Mart store in their area had the same opinion.[4] Wal-Mart touted its low prices on its store fronts ("We Sell for Less"), in advertising, on signs inside its stores, and on the logos of its shopping bags.

Advertising

Wal-Mart relied less on advertising than any of its competitors. The company distributed only one or two circulars per month (versus an average of one per week at Kmart) and ran occasional TV ads, relying primarily on word-of-mouth to communicate its marketing message. As a percentage of sales, Wal-Mart's advertising expenditures were the lowest in the discount industry, several percentage points below what Kmart spent. Wal-Mart's spending for radio and TV advertising was so low that it didn't register on national ratings scales. Most Wal-Mart broadcast ads appeared on local TV and local cable channels. However, Wal-Mart had been successful in supplementing its low ad expenditures with media publicity concerning several programs it had initiated. Wal-Mart's policy of giving preferential treatment to products made in the United States generated thousands of local newspaper articles, nearly all of which quoted Wal-Mart statistics that its Buy American plan had saved or created thousands of American jobs. Wal-Mart had also gotten free media publicity with its program to spotlight products with environmentally safe packaging. The company often allowed charities to use its parking lots for their fund-raising activities.

Distribution

Over the years, Wal-Mart management had turned the company's centralized distribution systems into a competitive edge. David Glass said, "Our distribution facilities are one of the keys to our success. If we do anything better than other folks that's it."[5] Wal-Mart got an early jump on competitors in distribution efficiency because of its rural store locations. Whereas other discount retailers relied upon manufacturers and distributors to ship directly to their mostly metropolitan-area stores, Wal-Mart found that its rapid growth during the 1970s was straining suppliers' ability to use independent trucking firms to make frequent and timely deliveries to its growing number of rural store locations. To improve the delivery of merchandise to its stores, the company in 1980 began to build area distribution centers and to supply stores from these centers with its own truck fleet. Wal-Mart added new distribution centers

---

[4]Ibid.

[5]Ibid., p. 54.

EXHIBIT 4   Comparative Statistics for Leading Membership Warehouse Retailers, 1991–92

Chain, Parent, Headquarters	Revenues[a] (in millions)		Percent Change	Operating Income (in millions)		Percent Change
	1992	1991		1992	1991	
Sam's Club Wal-Mart Stores Bentonville, AR	$12,339	$ 9,430	30.8%	$270*	$233	15.9%
Price Club[1] The Price Co., San Diego, CA	7,480	6,740	10.9	223	213	4.7
Costco Wholesale[2] Costco Wholesale Corp. Kirkland, WA	6,620	5,305	24.8	184	136	35.3
Pace Membership Warehouse Kmart Corp., Aurora, CO	4,358	3,646	19.5	30*	39	(23.1)
BJ's Wholesale Club Waban Inc., Natick, MA	1,760	1,432	22.2	30*	17	76.5
Smart & Final Smart & Final Inc. Santa Barbara, CA	752*	683	13.4	21*	18	16.7
Mega Warehouse Foods Megafoods Stores, Inc. Mesa, AZ	293	245	19.6	3.5*	3	16.7
Warehouse Club[3] Warehouse Club Inc., Skokie, IL	241	250	(3.6)	0.2	(0.4)	—
Wholesale Depot Wholesale Depot Inc. Natick, MA	200*	100*	100	NA	NA	—
Club Aurrora[4] Wal-Mart Stores/Cifra S.A. Mexico City	60*	—	—	—	—	—
Price Club de Mexico[5] Price Club de Mexico S.A. de C.V. Mexico City	40*	—	—	—	—	—
Total:	$34,143	$27,811	23.2%	—	—	—

[a]Sales and membership fees where applicable. *DSN estimate. ( ) decrease. NA: not available or not applicable.
[1]Includes sales from 17 Canadian clubs; revenues include membership fees and other income of $160M in 1992 and $142M in 1991; excludes real estate income. Merged with Costco in 1993.
[2]Includes sales from 12 Canadian clubs; revenues include membership fees and other income of $121M in 1992 and $90M in 1991. Merged with Price in 1993.
[3]Revenues included membership fees and other income of $7M in 1992 and 1991.
[4]Revenues, club count not included in Sam's Club statistics.
[5]Revenues, club count not included in Price Club statistics.
Sam's Club fiscal year ended Jan. 31, 1993.
Price Club fiscal year ended Aug. 31, 1992.
Costco Wholesale fiscal year ended Aug. 30, 1992.
Pace Membership Warehouse fiscal year ended Jan. 27, 1993.
BJs Wholesale Club fiscal year ended Jan. 30, 1993.

Smart & Final fiscal year ended Jan. 4, 1993.
Mega Warehouse Foods fiscal year ended Dec. 31, 1992.
Warehouse Club fiscal year ended Oct. 3, 1992.
Wholesale Depot fiscal year ended Dec. 31, 1992.

Source: *Discount Store News*, March 1, 1993, p. 18.

EXHIBIT 4 *(continued)*

Number of Stores			Average Club Size	Membership	Merchandise
1/92	1/93	1/94*			
208	256	305	115,000	Paid; restricted	General merchandise/food
88	94	102	117,000	Paid; restricted	General merchandise/food
91	100	110	115,000	Paid; restricted	General merchandise/food
87	115	137	115,000	Paid; restricted	General merchandise/food
29	39	54	110,000	Paid; restricted	General merchandise/food
116	125	139	16,00	Free; unrestricted	Food/janitorial/packaging
14	22	31	52,000	Free; unrestricted	Food/household and business consumables/
10	10	10	100,000	Paid; restricted	General merchandise/food
4	8	15	64,000	Paid; restricted	General merchandise/food
2	3	8	75,000	Paid; restricted	General merchandise/food
8	1	3	100,000	Paid; restricted	General merchandise/food
649	773	914	—	—	—

when new, outlying stores could no longer be reliably and economically supported from an existing center. In 1994, the company had 22 distribution centers covering 21.5 million square feet. Together the centers employed 16,000 workers who handled over 850,000 truckloads of merchandise annually with a 99 percent accuracy rate on filling orders. Wal-Mart's distribution centers made extensive use of automated systems:[6]

---

[6]Ibid.

The conveyor system starts with walk-pick modules where order selection occurs. The cartons move on a conveyor to a central merge where an operator releases cartons onto a sortation system. A laser scanner reads a bar code and tells the automatic sorter where to divert cartons at rates in excess of 120 per minute. The cartons are diverted to various shipping doors.

A study of 1988 data indicated Wal-Mart's distribution cost advantage over Sears and Kmart was significant:

	1988 Sales (in millions)	Distribution Costs (in millions)	Distribution Costs as a Percent of Sales
Sears	$30,256	$ 2,513	5.0%
Kmart	27,301	956	3.5
Wal-Mart	20,649	263	1.3

Source: *Discount Store News*, December 18, 1989, p. 201.

Whereas Wal-Mart had the capability to make daily deliveries to nearly all its stores, Kmart delivered to its stores about once every four to five days and Target delivered every three to four days.

The Use of Cutting-Edge Technology

Wal-Mart was aggressive in applying the latest technological advances to increase productivity and drive costs down. The company's technological goal was to provide employees with the tools to do their jobs more efficiently and to make better decisions. Technology was not used as a means of replacing existing employees. Moreover, Wal-Mart's approach to technology was to be on the offensive—probing, testing, and then deploying the newest equipment, retailing techniques, and computer software programs ahead of most, if not all, other discount retailers.

In 1974 the company began using computers to maintain inventory control on an item basis in distribution centers and in its stores. In 1981, Wal-Mart began testing point-of-sale scanners and committed itself to chainwide use of scanning bar codes in 1983—a move that resulted in a 25 to 30 percent faster checkout of customers. In 1984, Wal-Mart developed a computer-assisted merchandising system that allowed the product mix in each store to be tailored to its own market circumstances and sales patterns. Between 1985 and 1987 Wal-Mart installed the nation's largest private satellite communication network, which allowed two-way voice and data transmission between headquarters, the distribution centers, and the stores and one-way video transmission from Bentonville's corporate offices to distribution centers and to the stores; the system was less expensive than the previously used telephone network. The video system was used regularly by company officials to speak directly to all employees at once.

In 1989 Wal-Mart established direct satellite linkage with about 1,700 vendors supplying close to 80 percent of the goods sold by Wal-Mart; this linkup allowed the use of electronic purchase orders and instant data exchanges. Wal-Mart had also used the satellite system's capabilities to develop a credit card authorization procedure that took five seconds, on average, to authorize a purchase, speeding up credit checkout by 25 percent compared to the prior manual system. The company had exemplary data processing and information systems. Not only had the company developed the computer systems to provide management with detailed figures on almost any aspect of Wal-Mart's operations, but the company was also regarded as having one of the lowest-cost, most efficient data processing operations of any company its size in the world. The company's rapid adoption of cutting-edge retailing technologies across many areas of its business had given Wal-Mart a technology advantage over most other discounters.

Construction Policies

Wal-Mart management worked at getting more mileage out of its capital expenditures for new stores, store renovations, and store fixtures. Ideas and suggestions were solicited from vendors regarding store layout, the design of fixtures, and space needed for effective displays. Wal-Mart's store designs had open-air offices for management personnel that could be furnished economically and featured a maximum of display space that could be rearranged and refurbished easily. Because Wal-Mart insisted on a high degree of uniformity in the new stores it built, the architectural firm Wal-Mart employed was able to use computer modeling techniques to turn out complete specifications for up to 12 new stores a week. Moreover, the stores were designed to permit quick, inexpensive construction as well as to allow for low-cost maintenance and renovation. All stores were renovated and redecorated at least once every seven years. If a given store location was rendered obsolete by the construction of new roads and highways and the opening of new shopping locations, then the old store was abandoned in favor of a new store at a more desirable site. As of 1994, Wal-Mart was expanding or relocating stores at the rate of 100 per year.

In keeping with the low-cost theme for facilities, Wal-Mart's distribution centers and corporate offices were also built economically and furnished simply. The offices of top executives were modest and unpretentious. The lighting, heating and air-conditioning controls at all Wal-Mart stores were connected via computer to Bentonville headquarters, allowing cost-saving energy management practices to be implemented centrally and freeing store managers from the time and worry of trying to hold down utility costs. Wal-Mart mass-produced a lot of its displays in-house, not only saving money but also cutting the time to roll out a new display concept to as little as 30 days.

Relationships with Suppliers

Wal-Mart was noted for driving a hard bargain with its suppliers, bringing all of its considerable buying power to bear. The company's purchasing department was austere and utilitarian. Purchasing agents were dedicated to getting the lowest prices they could, and they did not accept invitations to be wined or dined by suppliers. The marketing vice president of a major vendor told *Fortune* magazine:[7]

> They are very, very focused people, and they use their buying power more forcefully than anybody else in America. All the normal mating rituals are verboten. Their highest priority is making sure everybody at all times in all cases knows who's in charge, and it's Wal-Mart. They talk softly, but they have piranha hearts, and if you aren't totally prepared when you go in there, you'll have your ass handed to you.

Even though Wal-Mart was tough in negotiating for absolute rock-bottom prices, the company worked closely with suppliers to develop mutual respect and to forge long-term partnerships that benefited both parties. Vendors were invited to tour Wal-

---

[7]*Fortune*, January 30, 1989, p. 53.

Mart's distribution centers to see firsthand how things operated and to learn what kinds of problems Wal-Mart had in achieving greater efficiency. Vendors were also encouraged to voice any problems in their relationships with Wal-Mart and to become involved in Wal-Mart's future plans. For example, in 1987 after Sam Walton asked Procter & Gamble executives to view a focus group of Wal-Mart executives talking about their prickly relationship with P&G, P&G responded by stationing a team of people near Wal-Mart headquarters to work with Wal-Mart on a continuing basis.[8] One top-priority project involved an effort to supply more P&G items in recyclable packaging to meet Wal-Mart's publicly stated goal of selling products that were environmentally safe. Another concerned linking the two companies' computers to set up a just-in-time ordering and delivery system for many products P&G supplied to Wal-Mart stores; when Wal-Mart's stocks reached the reorder point, a computer automatically sent a resupply order by satellite to the nearest P&G factory, which then shipped more of the item to a Wal-Mart distribution center or, in the case of disposable diapers, directly to the store. P&G and Wal-Mart saw the automatic reordering arrangement as a win-win proposition because with better coordination P&G could plan efficient manufacturing runs, streamline distribution, and lower its costs, passing some of the savings on to Wal-Mart.

Wal-Mart looked for suppliers who were dominant in their categories (thus providing strong brand-name recognition), who could grow with the company, who had full product lines (so that Wal-Mart buyers could both cherry-pick and get some sort of limited exclusivity on the products it chose to carry), who had the long-term commitment to R&D to bring new and better products to retail shelves, and who had the ability to become more efficient in producing and delivering what they supplied. As one supplier remarked, "Wal-Mart wants suppliers who can keep up." Several suppliers described Wal-Mart's approaches to doing business with them:[9]

> They challenge us constantly. Can we do this? How about if we tried that? They're constantly on the lookout for ways to improve themselves.
>
> They approach problems as opportunities, not as complaints. They're completely genuine in meetings . . . all cards are on the table.
>
> No matter how good your products are, if they don't tell the story on the shelf, they won't do well at Wal-Mart. They're looking for dynamic, creative packaging that will act as a salesman.
>
> They know their stores, their products, and their markets, and they have an uncanny ability to predict what their customer wants. Their advice about products is valuable to us.
>
> We have to do what we say we're going to do . . . Wal-Mart's demands can be staggering, like when they need many thousands of VCRs for a promotion. If we can't be sure that we can have the stock *in their warehouses* on a given day, we let them know that, [and] suggest moving the promotion back a month.
>
> They honor their commitments and they expect the same in return. If we gear up for a promotion, and the circular gets cancelled, they'll still take the goods. That's how they do business.

Wal-Mart's "Buy America" Policy

In a March 1985 letter sent to about 3,000 domestic suppliers, Sam Walton discussed the serious threat of the nation's balance of trade deficit and conveyed the company's desire to carry more U.S.-made goods in Wal-Mart's stores:

---

[8]Saporito, "What Sam Walton Taught America," p. 104.
[9]*Discount Store News*, December 18, 1989, pp. 109 and 156.

> Our Wal-Mart company is firmly committed to the philosophy of buying everything possible from suppliers who manufacture their products in the United States. We are convinced that with proper planning and cooperation between retailers and manufacturers many products can be supplied to us that are comparable, or better, in value and quality to those we have been buying offshore . . . Wal-Mart believes our American workers can make the difference if management provides the leadership.

Walton then sent a now-famous edict to Wal-Mart buyers and merchandise managers: "Find products that American manufacturers have stopped producing because they couldn't compete with foreign imports." Wal-Mart kicked off its Buy America program publicly with newspaper and TV ads featuring the slogans "We Buy American Whenever We Can So You Can, Too" and "Wal-Mart—Keeping America Working and Strong." Wal-Mart's stores displayed "Bring It Home to the USA" banners hanging from store ceilings; special "Made in America" posters and small placards citing job-creating statistics were put on fixtures that held American-made goods—see Exhibit 5. In the company's 1993 annual report, management explained the Buy America program and cited instances of products that were now being made in U.S. plants:

> The Buy America program demonstrates a long-standing Wal-Mart commitment to our customers that we will buy American-made products whenever we can *if* those products deliver the same quality and affordability as their foreign-made counterparts. It also exemplifies a *partnership* that we have developed with our American vendors and suppliers to seek out products that can be manufactured here competitively and to help facilitate their reintroduction to the American marketplace.
>
> We have never said that we always buy American. We wish we could. But many times we have paid a premium to get products that were previously made overseas to be manufactured here.
>
> Last year, Wal-Mart challenged Kalikow Brothers, a long-time vendor-partner, to move production of popular men's shorts back from the Orient to the States. By working together, we were able to relocate the manufacturing to a plant in Lake Butler, Florida. Over 125 jobs were added. A second plant has been rejuvenated in the process.
>
> A maker of ladies' foundation garments in Blackwell, Oklahoma, Southwest Cupid, adapted modular concepts introduced at a seminar sponsored by Wal-Mart and one of the vendor's fabric suppliers. As a result of these efforts, they were able to bring production back from Haiti and Jamaica. Because of our increased orders for their Lady Manhattan brand, they are opening a new plant in concert with the Native American community located in Hominy, Oklahoma.
>
> These are just two examples of conversions that Wal-Mart has helped facilitate from offshore to domestic manufacturing. There are many more.
>
> Whatever can be competitively made in the USA, should be. It won't happen overnight. It might not happen in every industry and every category. But to keep trying is the right thing to do, and Wal-Mart will not let up in its efforts.

Wal-Mart claimed the program had resulted in its reducing its purchases of foreign-made goods from about 35 percent to about 30 percent of everything it sold. According to industry analysts, however, Wal-Mart still imported about twice as much of what it sold as Kmart. Yet because of the manner in which Wal-Mart had implemented and communicated its Buy America policy, consumer awareness of Wal-Mart's efforts was high in comparison with awareness of other companies' efforts that had followed Wal-Mart's lead in promoting American-made products.

Wal-Mart's Environmentally Safe Policy

In 1989 Wal-Mart became the first major retailer to embark on a program urging vendors to develop products and packaging that would not harm the environment.

EXHIBIT 5   Examples of Wal-Mart's Signs and Ads Advocating American-Made Products and
Environmental Consciousness

Management negotiated with its suppliers of signs, shopping bags, and other such items to convert them to environmentally safe products. It started posting shelf signs beside merchandise with environmentally safe features. The company took its campaign public with full-page ads in *USA Today* and *The Wall Street Journal* using the theme "We're Looking for Quality Products That Are Guaranteed Not to Last." The policy was implemented because Wal-Mart's top management saw the environment as a top-priority national issue; David Glass, Wal-Mart's president, told an audience:[10]

> I believe that retailers and suppliers must now be socially conscious in a way that we haven't before. Those of you who don't believe that we have a terrible problem with the environment are naive. We are running out of land to bury things. We are quickly spoiling our drinking water and eroding the ozone layer. . . .
>
> We need to take a responsibility for the role we play and for our own actions. What we will do is identify these products in our showrooms and ask our customers to buy those rather than other products that are not safe for the environment. . . . We believe we can bring [environmentally safe products] to market at the same kind of price.

The company further described its policy and efforts in its 1993 annual report:

> As serious as environmental challenges are becoming—pollution, waste of resources and others—the real hurdle is the mistaken collective belief that we simply can't do anything about them.
>
> At Wal-Mart, we *know* we can do something, because we know our people. They have *proven* they can make a difference. So all of us are working harder to understand the environmental issues, to communicate them more effectively, and to do the right things in all of our stores across America.
>
> It is important to note that our program was not designed to sell a particular product, promote a private label, or capitalize on a politically correct cause. The truth is reason enough: The health of our planet is at stake. Our customers know it, and we know it.
>
> Last year our stores together with their communities recycled approximately 442,000 tons of paper and plastic. In partnership with our vendors, we now print *all* of our circulars on recycled paper. Each year, we buy more products made of recycled materials, and we challenge our vendor-partners to find alternatives that are more environmentally responsible. These efforts have resulted in hundreds of product or packaging improvements.
>
> Our customers want to help, too. So we help them by collecting motor oil and batteries and establishing neighborhood recycling centers, often placing bins in our store parking lots until permanent centers can be established. To encourage environmental efforts by our schoolchildren, we are involved with programs like Kids for a Clean Environment. To date, this international organization has over 30,000 members in local clubs across America. We print and distribute materials and newsletters, and we help fund an 800 number. In one of our most ambitious efforts, we are building an experimental Wal-Mart store of the future.
>
> Opening in the spring of 1993 in Lawrence, Kansas, this unique store is designed to be environmentally friendly in every way possible. We believe it will create new markets for recycled products and construction techniques. It will serve as a working laboratory for students. It will become a dynamic experiment in testing new environmental ideas.
>
> We realize we have barely begun. But with the support of Wal-Mart's customers, shareholders, and our vendor-partners, we are certain we can create a cleaner and a safer environment for our children.

Despite some cynical observations that Wal-Mart's policy was a publicity and marketing ploy, Wal-Mart had succeeded in influencing suppliers to spend more on R&D to develop products with more environmentally safe ingredients and to find ways to use recyclable packaging materials. Procter & Gamble was among the first suppliers to be responsive to Wal-Mart's environmental program; by 1990 all of P&G's soap and detergent packages had been converted to 100 percent recycled cartons, and its plastic containers were being coded so they could be efficiently

---

[10]*Discount Store News*, December 18, 1989, pp. 109 and 156.

separated for recycling. The head of P&G's team servicing the Wal-Mart account commented, "They're trying to do the right thing and to educate the consumer."

Wal-Mart's Approach to Providing Superior Customer Service

Wal-Mart tried to put substance behind its pledge of "Satisfaction Guaranteed" and do things that would make customers' shopping experience at Wal-Mart pleasant. A "greeter" was stationed at store entrances to welcome customers with a smile, thank them for shopping at Wal-Mart, assist them in getting a shopping cart, and answer questions about where items were located. Clerks and checkout workers were trained to be courteous and helpful and to exhibit a 'friendly, folksy attitude." All store personnel took an oath of friendliness: "I solemnly promise and declare that every customer that comes within ten feet of me, I will smile, look them in the eye, and greet them, so help me Sam." Wal-Mart's management stressed five themes in training and supervising store personnel:

1. Think like a customer.
2. Sell the customer what they want to buy.
3. Provide a genuine value to the customer.
4. Make sure the customer has a good time.
5. Exceed the customer's expectations.

One of the standard Wal-Mart chants drilled into all employees was

> Who's number one? The customer.
> The customer is the boss.

Wal-Mart's newest stores had wider aisles and significantly more customer space. In all stores, efforts were under way to present merchandise in easier-to-shop shelving and displays. Floors in the apparel section were carpeted to make the department feel homier and to make shopping seem easier on customers' feet. Store layouts were constantly scrutinized to improve shopping convenience and make it easier for customers to find items. Store employees wore blue vests to make it easier for customers to pick them out from a distance. Fluorescent lighting was recessed into the ceiling, creating a softer impression than the exposed fluorescent lighting strips used at Kmart stores. Management stressed making the decor of Wal-Mart's stores convey feelings of warmth and freshness as a way of signaling customers that Wal-Mart was a bit more upscale and carried a little better quality merchandise than rivals. Yet nothing about the decor conflicted with Wal-Mart's low-price image; retailing consultants considered Wal-Mart very adept at sending out an effective mix of vibes and signals concerning customer service, low prices, quality merchandise, and friendly shopping environment.

Wal-Mart's management believed that the attention paid to all the details of making the stores more user-friendly and inviting caused shoppers to view Wal-Mart in a more positive light. A reporter for *Discount Store News* observed:[11]

> The fact is that everything Wal-Mart does from store design to bar coding to lighting to greeters—regardless of how simple or complex—is implemented only after carefully considering the impact on the customer. Virtually nothing is done without the guarantee

---

[11]Ibid., p. 161.

that it benefits the customer in some way. . . . As a result Wal-Mart has been able to build loyalty and trust among its customers that is unparalleled among other retail giants.

SAM WALTON'S LEADERSHIP STYLE AND BUSINESS PHILOSOPHY

Mr. Sam, as he was fondly called and remembered, was not only Wal-Mart's founder and patriarch but also its spiritual leader. Despite great wealth, he was a man of simple tastes and genuine affection for people. His folksy personality, unpretentious manner, and interest in people and their feelings caused people inside and outside the company to hold him in high esteem. Regarded by many as "the entrepreneur of the century" and "a genuine American folk hero," he enjoyed a reputation for being concerned about employees, being community-spirited, and being a devoted family man who epitomized the American dream and demonstrated the virtues of hard work. Casewriter interviews with Wal-Mart associates in 1986 indicated how he was regarded by the rank-and-file:

> He's a beautiful man. I met him when this store opened. He came back two and one-half years later and still remembered me. He walked over to this department and said, "Grace, you and I have been around a long time, I'm gonna hug your neck."

> I was just . . . I was thrilled [to meet him]. He's a very special person. He is a very outgoing person, and it kind of motivates you just to sit and listen to him talk. He listens— that's another thing.

> He's just an everyday person . . . When you meet him he's just like one of us. You can talk to him. Anything you want to ask him—you can just go right up and ask.

> He's really down-to-earth. He'll put his arm around you, hug you, and tell you you're doing a good job.

> Mr. Walton cares about his employees. You get the feeling that you're working for him instead of Wal-Mart. And although he may not need the money, he's good to us and we try to be good to him.

Four key core values and business principles underpinned Sam Walton's approach to managing the company:[12]

- Treat employees as partners, sharing both the good and bad about the company so they will strive to excel and participate in the rewards.
- Build for the future, rather than just immediate gains, by continuing to study the changing concepts that are a mark of the retailing industry and be ready to test and experiment with new ideas.
- Recognize that the road to success includes failing, which is part of the learning process rather than a personal or corporate defect or failing. Always challenge the obvious.
- Involve associates at all levels in the total decision-making process.

He practiced these principles diligently in his own actions and insisted other Wal-Mart managers do the same. Until his health failed badly in 1991, he spent several days a week visiting the stores, gauging the moods of shoppers, listening to employ-

---

[12]Ibid., p. 29.

ees discuss what was on their minds, learning what was or was not selling, gathering ideas about how things could be done better, complimenting workers on their efforts, and challenging them to come up with good ideas. Charles Cates, a former manager of the second store Wal-Mart opened, described what happened on a typical Sam Walton visit to a Wal-Mart store:[13]

> First, you get a telephone call from Sam. He says, "Charlie, can you pick me up at the airport?" Then, in the car, he wants to know who your assistant managers are . . . the names of their children, wives, and what's happening in their lives. So you brief him on your assistants and their families.
>
> When he gets to the store, he wants to take a tour. He goes to each department manager. He'll says, "The department looks good," and ask, "Why are we out of merchandise? What are your sales this year? What's your markup? What's your best-selling item?
>
> He pats them on the back, shakes their hands, and thanks them for doing a good job. He's always motivating people. The associates feel like they're working directly for Sam Walton.
>
> After the tour, he'll meet with the associates in the store lounge. He commends them for the store's sales increases and he talks about merchandise. He has contests with merchandise. He'll tell a department manager: "You all find an item and I'll find an item and we'll see which item sells better."
>
> He's always challenging us. He'll look at another item and ask, "It's priced at $5. How many more can we sell at $4?"

Following Walton's lead, it became established practice for Wal-Mart managers at all levels to spend much time and effort motivating employees to achieve excellence, motivating them to offer ideas, to get involved, and to function as partners. A theme reiterated over and over again was that every cost counted and every worker had a responsibility; the slogan that every employee heard repeatedly was, "The customer is boss and the future depends on you." David Glass explained the philosophy underlying this approach:[14]

> Wal-Mart is unique because we require involvement. There's a pressure to get involved. Whatever level you're at, you'll perform far better if you're involved and believe that you can make a difference.

Wal-Mart fostered the concept of involvement by referring to all employees as "associates," a term Sam Walton had insisted on from the company's beginnings because it denoted a partnerlike relationship.

The values, beliefs, and practices that Sam Walton tried to instill in Wal-Mart's culture were reflected in statements made in his autobiography, completed weeks before his death in April 1992:[15]

- Everytime Wal-Mart spends one dollar foolishly, it comes right out of our customer's pockets. Everytime we save a dollar, that puts us one more step ahead of the competition—which is where we always plan to be.

- One person seeking glory doesn't accomplish much; at Wal-Mart, everything we've done has been the result of people pulling together to meet one common goal.

---

[13]Ibid., p. 235.

[14]Ibid., p. 83.

[15]Sam Walton with John Huey, *Sam Walton: Made in America* (New York: Doubleday, 1992), pp. 10, 12, 47, 63, 115, 128, 135, 140, 213, 226–29, 233, 246, 249, 254, and 256.

- I have always been driven to buck the system, to innovate, to take things beyond where they've been.

- We paid absolutely no attention whatsoever to the way things were supposed to be done, you know, the way the rules of retail said it had to be done.

- My role has been to pick good people and give them the maximum authority and responsibility. . . . I'm more of a manager by walking and flying around, and in the process I stick my fingers into everything I can to see how it's coming along. . . . My appreciation for numbers has kept me close to our operational statements and to all the other information we have pouring in from so many different places.

- The more you share profit with your associates—whether it's in salaries or incentives or bonuses or stock discounts—the more profit will accrue to your company. Why? Because the way management treats the associates is exactly how the associates will then treat the customers. And if the associates treat the customers well, the customers will return again and again.

- The real challenge in a business like ours is to become what we call servant leaders. And when they do, the team—the manager and the associates—can accomplish anything.

- There's no better way to keep someone doing things the right way than by letting him or her know how much you appreciate their performance.

- I like my numbers as quickly as I can get them. The quicker we get that information, the quicker we can act on it.

- The bigger we get as a company, the more important it becomes for us to shift responsibility and authority toward the front lines, toward that department manager who's stocking the shelves and talking to the customer.

- We give our department heads the opportunity to become real merchants at a very early stage of the game . . . we make our department heads the managers of their own business . . . we share everything with them: the costs of their goods, the freight costs, the profit margins. We let them see how their store ranks with every other store in the company on a constant, running basis, and we give them incentives to want to win.

- We're always looking for new ways to encourage our associates out in the stores to push their ideas up through the system. . . . Great ideas come from everywhere if you just listen and look for them. You never know who's going to have a great idea.

- A lot of bureaucracy is really the product of some empire builder's ego . . . we don't need any of that at Wal-Mart. If you're not serving the customers, or supporting the folks who do, we don't need you.

- I believe in always having goals, and always setting them high . . . the folks at Wal-Mart have always had goals in front of them. In fact, we have sometimes built real scoreboards on the stage at Saturday morning meetings.

- You can't just keep doing what works one time, because everything around you is always changing. To succeed, you have to stay out in front of that change.

- I feel like it's up to me as a leader to set an example.

Walton's success flowed from his cheerleading management style, his ability to instill the principles and management philosophies he preached into Wal-Mart's culture, the close watch he kept on costs, his relentless insistence on continuous improvement, and his habit of staying in close touch with both consumers and associates. It was common practice for Walton to lead cheers at annual shareholder meetings, store visits, managers' meetings, and company events. His favorite Wal-Mart cheer was

> Give me a W!
> Give me an A!
> Give me an L!
> Give me a squiggly! (Here, everybody sort of does the twist.)
> Give me an M!
> Give me an A!
> Give me an R!
> Give me a T!
> What's that spell?
> Wal-Mart!
> Who's number one?
> The CUSTOMER!

He observed, "If I'm leading the cheer, you'd better believe we do it loud." Walton was also noted for his rendition of "calling the hogs"—the University of Arkansas Razorbacks' cheer. The company had a number of cheers and chants, and Walton used them to create a "whistle while you work" atmosphere, loosen everyone up, inject fun and enthusiasm, and get sessions started on a stimulating note.

Soliciting Ideas from Associates

Associates at all levels of the company were challenged to come up with ideas and suggestions to make the company better. An assistant store manager explained:[16]

> We are encouraged to be merchants. If a salesclerk, a checker, or a stockman believes he can sell an item and wants to promote it, he is encouraged to go for it. That associate can buy the merchandise, feature it, and maintain it as long as he can sell it.

That same assistant store manager, when he accidentally ordered four times as many Moon Pies for an in-store promotion as intended, was challenged by the store manager to be creative and figure out a way to sell the extra inventory. The assistant manager's solution was to create the first World Championship Moon Pie Eating Contest, held in the store's parking lot in the small town of Oneonta, Alabama. The promotion and contest drew thousands of spectators and was so successful that it became an annual store event.

Listening to employees was a very important part of each manager's job. All Wal-Mart executives relied on MBWA (management by walking around); they visited stores, distribution centers, and support facilities regularly, staying on top of what was happening and listening to what employees had to say about how things were going. It was a practice Sam Walton initiated and ardently believed in:[17]

> The folks on the front lines—the ones who actually talk to the customer—are the only ones who really know what's going on out there. You'd better find out what they know. This really is what total quality is all about. To push responsibility down in your organization, and to force good ideas to bubble up within it, you must listen to what your associates are trying to tell you.

---

[16]*Discount Store News*, December 18, 1989, p. 83.
[17]Sam Walton with John Huey, *Sam Walton: Made in America*, p. 248.

Walton always insisted that most of the company's best ideas came from Wal-Mart associates and that visiting stores and listening to associates was a valuable use of his time. Wal-Mart's use of people greeters at the entrance of each store was one of those ideas; according to Wal-Mart's Tom Coughlin:[18]

> Back in 1980, Mr. Walton and I went into a Wal-Mart in Crowley, Louisiana. The first thing we saw as we opened the door was this older gentleman standing there. The man didn't know me, and he didn't see Sam, but he said, "Hi! How are ya? Glad you're here. If there's anything I can tell you about our store, just let me know."
>
> Neither Sam nor I had ever seen such a thing so we started talking to him. Well, once he got over the fact that he was talking to the chairman, he explained that he had a dual purpose: to make people feel good about coming in, and to make sure people weren't walking back out the entrance with merchandise they hadn't paid for.
>
> The store, it turned out, had had trouble with shoplifting, and its manager was an old-line merchant named Dan McAllister who knew how to take care of his inventory. He didn't want to intimidate the honest customers by posting a guard at the door, but he wanted to leave a clear message that if you came in and stole, someone was there who would see it.
>
> Well, Sam thought that was the greatest idea he'd ever heard of. He went right back to Bentonville and told everyone we ought to put greeters at the front of every single store. A lot of people thought he'd lost his mind.
>
> Our folks felt that putting someone at the door was a waste of money. They just couldn't see what Sam and Dan McAllister were seeing—that the greeter sent a warm, friendly message to the good customer, and a warning to the thief. They fought him all the way on it. Some people tried hard to talk him out of it. They tried to ignore it.
>
> Sam just kept pushing and pushing and pushing. Every week, every morning, he'd talk about greeters. He'd throw fits whenever he went into a store and didn't find one. Gradually, he wore everyone down and got his way. I'd say it took about a year and a half because they really resisted it. But Sam was relentless.
>
> I guess his vindication had to be the day in 1989 when he walked into a Kmart in Illinois and found that they had installed people greeters at their front doors.

A Wal-Mart store manager told one of the casewriters that up to 90 percent of his day was spent walking around the store communicating with the associates—praising them for a job well done, discussing how improvements could be made, listening to their comments, and soliciting suggestions. Task forces to evaluate ideas and plan out future actions to implement the ideas were common, and it was not unusual for the person who developed the idea to be appointed the leader of the group. Store managers asked each associate what she or he could do individually and what could be changed to improve store operations. Associates who believed a policy or procedure detracted from operations were encouraged to challenge and change it.

The company had a fleet of 12 airplanes that enabled Wal-Mart executives to make weekly visits to the field and regularly tour all company facilities.

THE WORK ATMOSPHERE AT WAL-MART

Throughout company literature, comments could be found referring to Wal-Mart's "concern for the individual." Such expressions as "Our people make the difference," "We care about people," and "People helping people" were used repeatedly by Wal-Mart executives. According to one of the company's management recruiters,

---

[18]Ibid., pp. 229–30.

It's a special feeling you get when you walk into a Wal-Mart store. And when you're working there is when you really notice it because the people care about each other. It's like being with a successful football team, that feeling of togetherness, and everyone is willing to sacrifice in order to stay together.

Wal-Mart associates at a rural store location told the casewriters about how they liked working at Wal-Mart and about the family-oriented atmosphere that prevailed among store associates:

There is no comparison between Wal-Mart and other places I've worked. Wal-Mart is far above. They just treat customers and associates really nice.

It's more of a family-oriented place than anywhere I've worked. They seem to really care about their employees. It's not just the money they're making, but a true concern for the people working here.

We're just like a family. Everybody cares for each other. The management is fantastic. You can go to them for anything and feel free to contradict them if you want to.

I care about my responsibilities. You're just more proud of it. You're more apt to care about it. You'll want people to come in and see what you've done. I guess the pats on the back let you know what you've done is appreciated. And when they show their appreciation you're going to care more and do better.

We're a united group. We may be from different walks of life but once we get here we're a group. You may leave them at the door, but when you're in here you're part of a family. You help each other; you try to be everybody's friend. It's a united feeling.

Yet, Wal-Mart still had vestiges of some "old-fashioned" beliefs and employment practices that seemed out of step in an otherwise progressive company. Restrictions on hiring persons over 65 were not formally lifted until Sam Walton himself approached the mandatory retirement age of 65. There were relatively few women in store management positions even though the majority of the employees in many stores were female. Only three of the company's top 113 executives were women. Associates were not allowed to date one another without authorization from the executive committee, a requirement that had resulted in several lawsuits against the company.

At the close of interviews with Wal-Mart associates at two Alabama stores, the casewriters asked associates to relate what made Wal-Mart special from their perspective:

They tell us that we are the best.

I like working at Wal-Mart better than any other place. I'm freer to handle the work better . . . I can go at my own speed and do the work the way I want to do it.

I enjoy Wal-Mart; I've been here eight years. Of course, we work, but that's what we're here for. You've got potential with Wal-Mart.

I think Wal-Mart is one of the best companies there is. I wouldn't want to work for anyone else.

The editors of the trade publication *Mass Market Retailers* paid tribute to Wal-Mart's associates in 1989 by recognizing them collectively as the "1989 Mass Market Retailers of the Year." They summed up the contributions and efforts of Wal-Mart's employees:

The Wal-Mart Associate. In this decade that term has come to symbolize all that is right with the American worker, particularly in the retailing environment and most particularly at Wal-Mart.

Compensation and Incentives

Wal-Mart had installed an extensive system of incentives that allowed associates to share monetarily in the company's success.

The Profit-Sharing Plan   Wal-Mart maintained a profit-sharing plan for full- and part-time associates; individuals were eligible following one year of continuous employment provided they had worked 1,000 hours or more. Annual contributions to the plan were tied to the company's profitability and were made at the sole discretion of management and the board of directors. Wal-Mart's contribution to each associate's profit-sharing account became vested at the rate of 20 percent per year beginning the third year of participation in the plan. After seven years of continuous employment the company's contribution became fully vested; however, if the associate left the company prior to that time, the unvested portions were redistributed to all remaining employees. Most of the profit-sharing contributions were invested in Wal-Mart's common stock, with the remainder put into other investments. Associates could begin withdrawals from their accounts upon retirement or disability, with the balance paid to family members upon death. Company contributions to the plan totaled $98.3 million in 1991, $129.6 million in 1992, and $166 million in 1993. In early 1994 the value of the profit-sharing fund exceeded $2 billion and the plan included approximately 300,000 participants.

Stock Purchase Plan   A stock purchase plan was adopted in 1972 to allow eligible employees a means of purchasing shares of common stock through regular payroll deduction or annual lump-sum contribution. Prior to 1990, the yearly maximum under this program was $1,500 per eligible employee; starting in 1990 the maximum was increased to $1,800 annually. The company contributed an amount equal to 15 percent of each participating associate's contribution. Long-time employees who had started participating in the early years of the program had accumulated stock worth over $100,000. About one-fourth of Wal-Mart's employees participated in the stock purchase plan in 1993.

In addition to regular stock purchases, certain employees qualified to participate in stock option plans; options expired 10 years from the date of the grant and could be exercised in nine annual installments. At year-end 1993 there were nearly 29 million shares reserved for issuance under stock option plans. The value of options granted in recent years was substantial: $96 million (1990), $128 million (1991), $143 million (1992), and $235 million (1993).

Base Compensation and Benefits   Although only full-time associates were eligible to participate in Wal-Mart's benefits programs, Wal-Mart did not deliberately use large numbers of part-time employees to avoid having to pay benefits. Part-time jobs were most common among salesclerks and checkout personnel in the stores where customer traffic varied appreciably during days of the week and months of the year.

Associates at Wal-Mart were hired at higher than minimum wage and could expect to receive a raise within the first year at one or both of the semiannual job evaluations. An associate told a casewriter that at least one raise was guaranteed in the first year if Wal-Mart planned to keep the individual on the staff. The other raise depended on how well the associate worked and improved during the year. At Wal-Mart only the store managers were salaried. All other associates, including the department managers, were considered hourly employees.

Sales Contests and Other Incentive Programs   One of Wal-Mart's most successful incentive programs was its VPI (Volume Producing Item) contests. In this contest, departments within the store were able to do a special promotion and pricing on items they themselves wanted to feature. Management believed the VPI contests boosted sales, breathed new life into an otherwise slow-selling item, and helped keep associates thinking about how to bolster sales; two sales associates commented on the VPI incentive scheme:

> We have contests. You feature an item in your department and see how well it sells each week. If your feature wins, you get a half day off.
>
> They have a lot of contests. If you're the top seller in the store you can win money. For four weeks in a row I've won money. That gives you a little incentive to do the very best you can. You kind of compete with other departments even though we're a big family in the long run. You like a little competition, but not too much.

Associate incentive plans were in place in every store, club, distribution center, and support facility. Associates received bonuses for good ideas, such as how to reduce shoplifting or how to improve merchandising. Wal-Mart instituted a shrinkage bonus in 1980. If a store held losses from theft and damage below the corporate goal, every associate in that store was eligible to receive up to $200. As a result, Wal-Mart's shrinkage ran about 1 percent compared to an industry average of 2 percent.

Another motivational tactic that Wal-Mart employed involved dress-up days in which associates dressed according to a theme (for instance, Western days or Halloween); these added fun and excitement for associates, and the festive mood carried over to the customer.

Training

> At Wal-Mart we guarantee two things: Opportunity and hard work.
>
> **Bill Avery,**
> *Wal-Mart management recruiter*

Management Training   Wal-Mart managers were hired in one of three ways. Hourly associates could move up through the ranks from sales to department manager to manager of the check lanes into store management training. Second, people with outstanding merchandising skills at other retail companies were recruited to join the ranks of Wal-Mart managers. And third, Wal-Mart recruited college graduates to enter the company's training program.

Casewriter interviews with Wal-Mart associates revealed a positive attitude concerning advancement opportunities and the company's work climate:

> You have the option to go as far as you want to go if you do a good job.
>
> It's up to you; if you do the work, you'll get the raises. I think it's a good place to work. There's a lot here (as far as advancement) if you want to work for it. It's a good open relationship with management. The benefits are good and the pay is above average for most discount stores.

The management training program involved two phases. In the first phase the trainee completed a 16-week on-the-job training program:

Phase I

Week 1	Checkouts/service desk
Week 2	Cash office
Weeks 3 & 4	Receiving
Week 5	Invoicing
Weeks 6, 7, & 8	Hard goods merchandising
Weeks 9 & 10	Merchandise office
Weeks 11, 12, & 13	Home and seasonal merchandising
Weeks 14, 15, & 16	Apparel merchandising

At designated times during Phase I, trainees were tested and evaluated by the store managers. During this time, the individual was encouraged to complete a self-critique of his/her own progress and also a critique of the caliber of guidance being received from the training effort. At the end of Phase I, the trainee moved at once into Phase II.

The initial three weeks of Phase II were structured to cover such management topics as internal/external theft, scheduling, store staffing, retail math, merchandise replenishment, and the Wal-Mart "Keys to Supervision" series, which dealt with interpersonal skills and personnel responsibilities. After completion of the first three weeks of Phase II, the trainee was given responsibility for an area of the store. The length of time during the remainder of Phase II varied according to the rate at which each trainee progressed. After showing good job performance, demonstrated leadership, and job knowledge, the trainee was promoted to an assistant manager. As an assistant manager, training continued with the retail management training seminar, which was designed to complement the in-store training with other vital management fundamentals. With the quickly paced growth rate of Wal-Mart stores, an above-average trainee could progress to store manager within five years. Through bonuses for sales increases above projected amounts and company stock options, the highest performing store managers earned around $70,000 to $100,000 annually.

To further promote management training, in November 1985 the Walton Institute of Retailing was opened in affiliation with the University of Arkansas. Within a year of its inception every Wal-Mart manager from the stores, the distribution facilities, and the general office was expected to take part in special programs at the Walton Institute to strengthen and develop the company's managerial capabilities.

Associate Training   Wal-Mart did not provide a specialized training course for its hourly associates. Upon hiring, an associate was immediately placed in a position for on-the-job training. From time to time, training films were shown in the Friday morning associates' meetings, but no other formalized training aids were provided by Wal-Mart headquarters. Store managers and department managers were expected to train and supervise the associates under them in whatever ways were needed.

A number of associates commented on the Wal-Mart training programs:

Mostly you learn by doing. They tell you a lot; but you learn your job every day.

They show you how to do your books. They show you how to order and help you get adjusted to your department.

We have tapes we watch that give us pointers on different things. They give you some training to start off—what you are and are not supposed to do.

The training program is not up to par. They bring new people in so fast—they try to show films, but it's just so hard in this kind of business. In my opinion you learn better just by experience. The training program itself is just not adequate. There's just not enough time.

We have all kinds of films and guidelines to go by, department managers' meetings every Monday, and sometimes we have quizzes to make sure we're learning what we need to know.

The most training you get is on the job—especially if you work with someone who has been around awhile.

Meetings

The company used meetings both as a communication device and as a culture-building exercise. Wal-Mart claimed to hold the largest annual stockholders' meeting in the world. Shareholders' meetings were held in the University of Arkansas Razorback basketball arena and were usually attended by 5,000 to 8,000 people, including associates and vendors. The necessary formalities of the meeting were typically conducted very promptly; the remainder of the meeting typically resembled a two-hour corporate pep rally featuring company cheers, skits, and a parade of vendors and associates who were cited for special accomplishments. Vendors were recognized for having met tight delivery deadlines, for having lowered prices, or for having cooperated extensively. Associates who had exceeded goals, helped people in distress, or written new cheers or songs were brought up and recognized on stage, with scenes of their accomplishments appearing on the screens behind them.

The Year-End Managers' Meetings Held in February in a convention hall set up like a Wal-Mart store with new displays and product lines, these three-day meetings brought together Wal-Mart managers from the store department level on up. Geography and numbers had recently forced Wal-Mart to have four meeting sessions held at two different sites. Everyone, including wives, wore Wal-Mart name tags with first names in big letters and last names in fine print. The meetings included presentations by managers and vendors, discussions of expansion plans and company goals, training videos, achievement awards, Wal-Mart cheers, a banquet, and entertainment. Wal-Mart's senior executives viewed these meetings as a way to reinforce the bonds of teamwork within the management ranks.

The Saturday Morning Headquarters Meetings At 7:30 A.M. every Saturday morning since 1961, the top officers, the merchandising staff, the regional managers who oversaw the store districts, and the Bentonville headquarters' staff—over 100 people in all—had gathered to discuss the week's sales, store payroll percentages, special promotion items, and any current problems. Reports on store construction, distribution centers, transportation, loss prevention, information systems, and so on were also given to keep everyone up-to-date. In his autobiography, Sam Walton reflected on the meetings and their role in Wal-Mart's culture:[19]

---

[19]Ibid., pp. 62 and 164.

From the very start we would get all our managers together and critique ourselves. . . . We would review what we had bought and see how many dollars we had committed to it. We would plan promotions and plan the items we intended to buy. Really, we were planning our merchandising programs. And it worked so well . . . it just became part of our culture. . . . We wanted everybody to know what was going on and everybody to be aware of the mistakes we made. When somebody made a bad mistake—whether it was myself or anybody else—we talked about it, admitted it, tried to figure out how to correct it, and then moved on to the next day's work.

The Saturday morning meeting is where we discuss and debate much of our philosophy and our management strategy; it is the focal point of all our communication efforts. . . . Its purpose is to let everyone know what the rest of the company is up to. If we can, we find heroes among our associates in the stores and bring them in to Bentonville, where we praise them in front of the whole meeting. . . . For the meeting to work, it has to be something of a show.

The meetings were deliberately very informal and relaxed. Those attending might show up in tennis or hunting clothes so that when the meeting was over they could go on to their Saturday activities. The meetings tended to be upbeat and usually began with several Wal-Mart cheers.

The Friday Morning Store Meetings

On Friday morning, general store meetings were held in each Discount City store and wholesale club. Associates at every level could ask questions and expect to get straightforward answers from management concerning department and store sales and cost figures, along with other pertinent store figures or information. The meeting might also include information on new company initiatives, policy change announcements, and perhaps video training films. Often, the meeting would begin or end with one or more Wal-Mart cheers.

Each week, department and store figures were posted in the meeting area. That way associates could see how their departments ranked against other departments and how the store was doing overall. If the figures were better than average, associates were praised verbally and given pats on the back; associates in departments that regularly outperformed the averages could expect annual bonuses and raises. When departmental performances came out lower than average, then the store manager would talk with department associates to explore ways to improve. On the door leading into the employee area in each store was a sign that said, "Today's stock price is _____, tomorrow's depends on you."

The Friday Merchandising Meeting

Another Wal-Mart tradition was a weekly meeting of the buyers and merchandising staff headquartered in Bentonville and the regional managers who directed store operations. David Glass explained the purpose:[20]

In retailing, there has always been a traditional, head-to-head confrontation between operations and merchandising. You know, the operations guys say, "Why in the world would anybody buy this? It's a dog, and we'll never sell it." Then the merchandising folks say, "There's nothing wrong with that item. If you guys were smart enough to display it well and promote it properly, it would blow out the doors." So we sit all these folks down together every Friday at the same table and just have at it.

We get into some of the doggonedest, knock-down drag-outs you have ever seen. But we have a rule. We never leave an item hanging. We will make a decision in that meeting even if it's wrong, and sometimes it is. But when the people come out of that room, you

---

[20]Ibid., pp. 225–26.

would be hard-pressed to tell which ones oppose it and which ones are for it. And once we've made that decision on Friday, we expect it to be acted on in all the stores on Saturday. What we guard against around here is people saying, "Let's think about it." We make a decision. Then we act on it.

Another technique Wal-Mart used to keep buyers in touch with customers and attuned with store operations involved sending each buyer out to a different store every three months to act as manager for two to three days in the department he or she bought merchandise for—referred to by Wal-Mart as the Eat What You Cook program.

All these meetings plus the in-the-field visits by Wal-Mart management created a strong bias for action. A *Fortune* reporter observed, "Managers suck in information from Monday to Thursday, exchange ideas on Friday and Saturday, and implement decisions in the stores on Monday."[21] General Electric CEO Jack Welch described his experiences at Wal-Mart:

> Everybody there has a passion for an idea and everyone's ideas count. Hierarchy doesn't matter. They get 80 people in a room and understand how to deal with each other without structure. I have been there three times now. Every time you go to that place in Arkansas, you can fly back to New York without a plane. The place actually vibrates.[22]

WAL-MART'S FUTURE

In 1988 Sam Walton, at the age of 70, reduced his role in active day-to-day management, relinquishing the title of chief executive officer to David Glass, but nonetheless retaining the title of chairman of Wal-Mart's board of directors. Until his death in April 1992, Walton continued to make appearances at major company events and to serve as company patriarch, but the task of leading the company into the 1990s was turned over to Glass and his next-in-command, Donald Soderquist, who functioned as chief operating officer. Both were highly regarded inside and outside the company, and both were seen as having the full complement of retailing savvy and management skills to follow in Walton's footsteps. The management team under Glass and Soderquist was believed by retailing experts to be very talented and very deep in the skills needed to sustain Wal-Mart's success.

At Wal-Mart's 1990 annual stockholders' meeting, Sam Walton expressed his belief that by the year 2000 Wal-Mart should be able to double the number of stores to about 3,000 and to reach sales of $125 billion annually. At the time, some retailing analysts were even more bullish on Wal-Mart's long-term prospects, predicting that the number of stores, clubs, and Supercenters could number over 4,300 and could generate nearly $200 billion in sales by the turn of the century. Wal-Mart's four biggest sources of growth potential were seen as (1) expanding into states where it had no stores, (2) continuing to saturate its current markets with new stores, (3) perfecting the Supercenter format to expand Wal-Mart's retailing reach into the whole grocery and supermarket arena—a market with annual sales of about $375 billion, and (4) moving into international markets. Wal-Mart had recently begun opening stores in Mexico. In 1994, the company was operating 18 stores in Mexico in a joint venture with CIFRA, Mexico's largest retailer, and two Wal-Mart

---

[21]Bill Saporito, "What Sam Walton Taught America, p. 105.
[22]Ibid.

Supercenters. Wal-Mart had plans for aggressive expansion of its CIFRA joint-venture operations as well as opening additional Wal-Mart Supercenters in Mexico City, Monterrey, and other major population centers in Mexico. In early 1994, Wal-Mart announced plans to acquire 120 Woolco stores in Canada and spend $100 million to revamp them to the Wal-Mart format.

However, in early 1994 there were signs of an impending slowdown in Wal-Mart's growth, and in addition the company had suffered through a series of embarrassing events that cast a dubious light on some of its operating practices. Throughout much of 1993, sales gains at Wal-Mart stores that had been open more than a year ran in the 4 to 7 percent range, compared to historical annual gains of 10 to 15 percent (see line 3 of Exhibit 1); sales at some Sam's Wholesale outlets actually declined from levels a year earlier. Companywide, sales grew only 22 percent in 1993 versus revenue growth of 25 to 35 percent annually in earlier years.

A report on CBS's *60 Minutes* showed instances of Wal-Mart stores' posting Made in America signs on racks of apparel that actually came from foreign sources: the *60 Minutes* program also told of instances where Wal-Mart had sourced merchandise from foreign manufacturers that utilized child labor and sweatshop tactics in their factories to hold down costs and meet the price levels that Wal-Mart's buyers insisted on. Gitano, a major Wal-Mart supplier headquartered in Italy, was under investigation for racketeering, falsifying corporate records, and numerous other criminal and civil violations. An Arkansas Chancery Court in October 1993 ordered Wal-Mart to stop selling health and beauty care products and over-the-counter drugs below cost at its Conway Supercenter. The suit was brought by the owners of three Conway drugstores who contended Wal-Mart was trying to injure competition and drive them out of business. In depositions taken in 1992 Wal-Mart employees said the chain set prices based on how much competition it faced—for strong competition, lower prices, and for weak competition, higher prices. At the trial, David Glass acknowledged that Wal-Mart sold some merchandise below cost but he denied that the reason was to drive competitors out of business. Wal-Mart had appealed the judge's verdict. Because 22 other states had statutes similar to the one in Arkansas barring pricing practices that could injure competitors, observers speculated that any retailer who discounted and/or underpriced competitors to draw shoppers or who used different prices in different areas based on market conditions and competition could be accused of predatory pricing.

In Vermont several communities had resisted giving store construction permits to Wal-Mart following strong protests by local residents and businesspeople that the opening of a Wal-Mart in their communities was inconsistent with preserving Vermont's rural character and that such stores would (1) adversely impact both local shopkeepers and the environment (due to added traffic, visual pollution, and soil erosion) and (2) impair the state's ability to attract tourists seeking a peaceful rural get-away. Wal-Mart's stock price, which had historically risen each year, fell 13 percent during 1993 and in early 1994 was trading in the $23 to $28 range—substantially below the record high of $33 reached in early 1993.

(Wal-Mart's Web address is *www.wal-mart.com*)

KMART CORPORATION

John E. Gamble, *University of South Alabama*

In 1997 Kmart Corporation was the second largest full-line discount retailer in North America—operating more than 2,200 stores in the United States, Canada, Puerto Rico, Guam, and the U.S. Virgin Islands. But the company was struggling, having lost $200 million on sales of $33.5 billion in 1996, and having posted losses in two of the three previous years. Revenues had only grown at a modest 4.5 percent annually since 1992. So far, the company's turnaround strategy, initiated in 1995 and directed at eliminating the company's operating inefficiencies and making it more competitive with Wal-Mart—the discount chain industry leader, had not produced positive bottom-line results. Wal-Mart still led Kmart on every one of the discount retail industry's important performance indicators during 1996 (sales growth, net profit margins, and sales per square foot), just as it had during the entire 1990s when it became obvious that Kmart was struggling.

In March 1995 Kmart's CEO, Joseph Antonini, facing mounting criticism from investors and pressure from board members, resigned. In June 1995, the company's board of directors recruited Floyd Hall away from Grand Union Supermarkets and appointed him as chairman, chief executive officer, and president. The board charged Hall with turning around the ailing company. Hall and his top management team promptly launched a number of new initiatives to restore the company to profitability and to compete more effectively with Wal-Mart. However, the main hurdle for Hall and his management team was the effective execution of their plan, since in years past, Kmart had established a reputation for poorly implementing strategies crafted by its previous managers.

COMPANY HISTORY AND BACKGROUND

In 1897 Sebastian S. Kresge and John McCrory formed a partnership to own and operate two five-and-dime stores—one in Detroit, Michigan, and the other in

Memphis, Tennessee. Sebastian Kresge operated the partnership's store in downtown Detroit while McCrory operated the company's Memphis store. The two men, failing to see any advantage to the partnership after two years, dissolved their business relationship in 1899 and went their own ways—Kresge assuming sole ownership of the Detroit store and McCrory the Memphis store. By 1912, Sebastian Kresge had expanded his five-and-dime variety store operation into a chain of 85 stores with annual sales of more than $10 million, making the S. S. Kresge Company the second largest chain of variety stores in the United States at the time.

In 1929, S. S. Kresge expanded into Canada, opening 19 Canadian five-and-dime stores. That same year, the company opened a Kresge five-and-dime in the world's first suburban shopping center—the Country Club Plaza in Kansas City, Missouri. When suburban shopping started to grow dramatically during the 1950s, and shoppers became increasingly attracted to full-line discount stores that carried a wider variety of household items and apparel at lower prices than five-and-dimes, Kresge responded by opening 18 Kmart full-line discount department stores in 1962. At the time of Sebastian Kresge's death in 1966, the S. S. Kresge Company operated 735 Kresge variety stores and 162 Kmart full-line discount stores with combined annual sales of over $1 billion. Throughout the remainder of the 1960s and 1970s, Kresge management increased the number of Kmart stores and replaced existing Kresge stores with Kmart stores. The company's name was changed to Kmart Corporation in 1977, a reflection of the fact that over 95 percent of the company's sales were generated by Kmart units. In 1981 the company opened its 2,000th Kmart location.

Diversification into Other Types of Retail Businesses

During the 1980s and early 1990s, Kmart management began to diversify the company into other businesses rather than continue to emphasize and rely on growing simply by expanding the number of Kmart locations and boosting sales at existing store locations. Kmart purchased two cafeteria chains in 1980 and 1983, but divested both of them in 1986 because of disappointing results. In 1984 Kmart acquired Builders Square (a chain of warehouse-style home centers) and Walden Book Company, which operated Waldenbooks stores in all 50 states. PayLess Drug Stores and Bargain Harold's Discount Outlets (a Canadian retailer) were acquired in 1985. In 1988 three start-up businesses—American Faire hypermarts (giant stores carrying a huge variety of household, apparel, and supermarket merchandise), Pace Membership warehouse clubs, and Office Square warehouse-style office supply stores—were added to the corporation's portfolio of retail chain businesses.

The Sports Authority (a 10-store chain of sporting goods superstores) was acquired in 1990 to complement and strengthen Kmart's own Sports Giant stores started in 1989; the Sports Giant stores were subsequently renamed and integrated into The Sports Authority chain. Kmart also acquired a 22 percent interest in OfficeMax office supply superstores in 1990 and increased its interest in the business to over 90 percent in 1991. In 1992, Kmart management acquired Borders, Inc. (a chain of 22 book superstores in the Midwest and northeast United States), purchased a chain of 13 discount stores in the Czech Republic and Slovakia, acquired Bizmart (a 105-store chain of office supply stores), and announced that it would open up to 100 Kmart stores in Mexico in a 50-50 joint venture with Mexican retailer El Puerto de Liverpool. The company also entered into a joint venture with Metro Limited to open discount stores in Singapore in 1994. Exhibits 1–3 present statements of Kmart's recent financial performance.

EXHIBIT 1 Selected Financial and Operating Statistics, Kmart Corporation, 1992–1996
(Dollars in millions, except per share data)

	1996	1995	1994	1993	1992
Summary of Operations					
Sales	$31,437	$31,713	$29,563	$28,039	$26,470
Cost of sales, buying, and occupancy	24,390	24,675	22,331	20,732	19,087
Selling, general and administrative expenses	6,274	6,876	6,651	6,241	5,830
Interest expense, net	453	434	479	467	411
Continuing income (loss) before income taxes	330	(313)	102	(306)	1,142
Net income (loss) from continuing operations	231	(230)	96	(179)	745
Net income (loss)	$(220)	$(571)	$296	$(974)	$941
Per Share of Common Stock					
Net income (loss) from continuing operations	$0.48	$(0.51)	$0.19	$(0.41)	$1.63
Dividends declared	—	0.36	0.96	0.96	0.92
Book value	10.51	10.99	13.15	13.39	16.64
Financial Data					
Total assets	$14,286	$15,033	$16,085	$15,875	$16,769
Long-term debt	2,121	3,922	1,989	2,209	2,995
Long-term capital lease obligations	1,478	1,586	1,666	1,609	1,612
Capital expenditures	343	540	1,021	793	1,187
Depreciation and amortization	654	685	639	650	566
Ending market capitalization	5,418	2,858	6,345	9,333	10,837
Weighted average share outstanding (millions)	486	460	457	457	456
Number of Stores					
United States	2,134	2,161	2,316	2,323	2,281
Canada	123	127	128	127	127
Other	4	22	37	36	27
Total Stores	2,261	2,310	2,481	2,486	2,435
Selling Space and Sales per Square Foot					
U.S. Kmart selling space (millions of sq. ft.)	156	160	166	182	181
U.S. Kmart store sales per comparable selling square foot	$201	$195	$181	$160	$152

Source: 1996 Kmart Corporation Annual Report.

OVERVIEW OF THE U.S. DISCOUNT RETAIL INDUSTRY

The U.S. discount retail industry grew 6 percent in 1996, accounting for an estimated $332 billion in sales. The industry included full-line discount stores (e.g., Wal-Mart, Kmart, and Target); specialty discounters (e.g., Toys "R" Us and Office Depot); warehouse clubs (e.g., Sam's and PriceCostco); off-price apparel chains (e.g., T. J. Maxx and Marshalls); jewelry and hard line discount retailers (e.g., Service Merchandise and Best Products); and discount mass merchants (e.g., Sears and Montgomery Ward). Exhibit 4 shows the sales for each of these segments for 1994–1996.

The specialty discount segment was the fastest growing segment of the retail discount industry, with a projected sales increase of almost 15 percent in 1996. In 1995 the

EXHIBIT 2 Consolidated Statement of Operations for Kmart Corporation, 1994–1996 (Dollars in millions, except per share data)

	Fiscal Year Ended January		
	1996	**1995**	**1994**
Sales	$31,437	$31,713	$29,563
Cost of sales, buying and occupancy	24,390	24,675	22,331
Gross margin	7,047	7,038	7,232
Selling, general and administrative expenses	6,274	6,876	6,651
Other (gains) losses	(10)	41	—
Continuing income before interest, income taxes, and dividends on convertible preferred securities of subsidiary	783	121	581
Interest expense, net	453	434	479
Income tax provision (credit)	68	(83)	6
Dividends on convertible preferred securities of subsidiary, net of income taxes of $16	31	—	—
Net income (loss) from continuing operations before extraordinary item	231	(230)	96
Discontinued operations, net of income taxes of $(3), $(139), and $64	(5)	(260)	83
Gain (loss) on disposal of discontinued operations, net of income taxes of $(240), $88, and $282	(446)	(30)	117
Extraordinary item, net of income taxes of $(27)	—	(51)	—
Net income (loss)	$ (220)	$ (571)	$ 296
Earnings (loss) per common share:			
Continuing retail operations	$ 0.48	$ (0.51)	$ 0.19
Discontinued operations	(0.01)	(0.57)	0.19
Gain (loss) on disposal of discontinued operations	(0.92)	(0.06)	0.25
Extraordinary item	—	(0.11)	—
Net income (loss)	$ (0.45)	$ (1.25)	$ 0.63
Weighted average shares (millions)	486.1	459.9	456.6

Source: 1996 Kmart Corporation Annual Report.

specialty segment grew by 22.5 percent, with many categories within the segment growing much more rapidly. For example, sales at book superstores grew 45.9 percent; pet supply chains grew 38.4 percent; office supplies superstores grew by 33.7 percent; computer chains grew 34.5 percent; baby superstores grew 29.1 percent; consumer electronics chains grew 27.7 percent; and the sales of home furnishings chains grew by 27.7 percent. Two categories, crafts and sporting goods, grew at a rate substantially lower than that of other specialty categories, but still at a rate faster than the overall discount retail industry.

The growth in specialty discount chains was attributed to the wide selection of merchandise that the stores carried in their one specialty category and to their attractive everyday-low-pricing strategy. Home furnishing stores such as Waccamaw, Bed Bath & Beyond, and Linens 'n Things experienced growth rates that approached 40 percent in 1996. Full-line chains looked upon specialty chains as "category killers" because full-

EXHIBIT 3   Kmart's Consolidated Balance Sheets, Fiscal Years 1995 and 1996 (in millions of dollars)

	January 29, 1997	January 31, 1996
Assets		
Current assets:		
Cash and cash equivalents	$ 406	$ 1,083
Merchandise inventories	6,354	6,022
Other current assets	973	894
Net current assets of discontinued operations	—	554
Total current assets	7,733	8,553
Property and equipment, net	5,740	5,365
Property held for sale or financing	200	434
Other assets and deferred changes	613	526
Net long-term assets of discontinued operations	—	55
Total assets	$14,286	$15,033
Liabilities and Shareholders' Equity		
Current liabilities:		
Long-term debt due within one year	$ 153	$ 7
Trade accounts payable	2,009	1,793
Accrued payrolls and other liabilities	1,298	1,019
Taxes other than income taxes	139	176
Total current liabilities	3,602	2,995
Long-term debt and notes payable	2,121	3,922
Capital lease obligations	1,478	1,586
Other long-term liabilities	1,013	1,250
Company obligated mandatorily redeemable convertible preferred securities of subsidiary trust holding solely 7¾% convertible junior subordinated debentures of Kmart (Redemption value of $1,000 at January 29, 1997).	980	—
Shareholders' equity:		
Common stock	486	486
Capital in excess of par value	1,608	1,624
Retained earnings	3,105	3,326
Treasury shares and restricted stock	(37)	(92)
Foreign currency translation adjustment	(70)	(64)
Total shareholders' equity	5,092	5,280
Total liabilities and shareholders' equity	$14,286	$15,033

Source: 1996 Kmart Corporation Annual Report.

line chains with their wide-ranging merchandise lineup could not devote the same amount of shelf space and square footage to any one product category. Research indicated that many consumers believed they were more likely to find what they were looking for at a specialty store, with its wide-ranging selection of brands, styles, colors, and so on, than they would at full-line discount stores having a more limited selection of brands and styles in any one product category.

EXHIBIT 4   Retail Discount Industry Sales by Type of Store, 1994–1996
(in billions of dollars)

	1994	1995	1996[4]
Full-line discount stores[1]	$138.3	$151.1	$157.3
Specialty discounters[2]	55.6	68.1	77.7
Warehouse clubs	39.0	41.1	42.3
Other discount mass merchants[3]	33.3	31.4	32.6
Off-price apparel chains	17.0	15.4	15.5
Jewelry/hard lines retailers	7.2	6.9	6.8
Total market	$290.4	$314.0	$332.2

[1]Includes full-line discount department stores, supercenters, closeout liquidators, and single-price retailers.
[2]Includes home, automotives, crafts, toys office supplies, book, computer superstores, baby superstores, pet supplies, consumer electronics and sporting goods specialty stores.
[3]Includes Sears, Ward, QVC, HSN, and variety stores.
[4]Estimated.

Source: *Discount Store News*, July 1, 1996, p. 38.

The full-line discount segment was the only retail segment, other than the specialty discount segment, that was growing faster than the U.S. economy. The full-line discount segment was projected to grow by 4.1 percent in 1996, following growth of 9.2 percent in 1995. The full-line discount segment and the entire discount retail industry were both rapidly consolidating through merger and acquisition, liquidation, and bankruptcy. From January 1995 through June 1996, 9 regional full-line discount chains and 13 chains competing in other segments were liquidated, an additional 20 discount chains were either acquired or merged with another chain, and 23 discount retail chains filed for Chapter 11 bankruptcy protection. Regional chains with annual sales of less than $500 million were expected to become casualties of industry consolidation in the near future.

Competitive success within the full-line discount segment of the industry hinged primarily upon store location, store appeal and shopping atmosphere, merchandise selection and availability, and everyday low pricing. Everyday low pricing squeezed store profit margins, but the industry's leading practitioners of everyday low pricing, Wal-Mart, Kmart and Target, were adding consumables (such as food) to boost store traffic and were adding more high-margin items (better grades of apparel and ready-to-assemble furniture) to bolster store margins. Full-line discount stores had to monitor buyer preferences carefully and respond quickly to changing buying patterns, stocking new items growing in favor and giving less shelf and display space to slower-selling items; otherwise, store sales languished and shopper interest waned. Exhibit 5 lists the sales, growth rates, gross margins, and percentage of store sales for major merchandise categories carried by full-line discount stores.

Wal-Mart, Kmart, and Target were all adding to their selection of lawn and garden equipment and power tools. Sears dominated these merchandise categories with its Craftsman line of hand tools and power tools and its selection of professional-grade power tools such as Makita, Milwaukee, and DeWalt. Kmart and Wal-Mart carried primarily Black & Decker power tools and their own private-label brands of power tools. Wal-Mart had licensed the names of three magazines to add name appeal to its own merchandise lines—it was selling tools under the *Popular Mechanics* brand name,

EXHIBIT 5 Full-Line Discount Store Sales, by Product Category, 1995

Category	Sales (in billions)	Growth rate (1994–1995)	Gross Margin	Percent of Store Sales
Apparel	$ 38.0	1.7%	33.6%	25.1%
Food	13.1	38.0	19.2	8.6
Consumer electronics	11.9	23.3	16.5	7.8
Housewares	10.7	15.7	29.1	7.1
Health and beauty care	9.3	18.3	19.8	6.2
Domestics	8.1	6.8	33.9	5.4
Toys	7.8	0.0	28.1	5.2
Lawn and garden	6.1	34.4	28.2	4.0
Sporting goods	5.4	12.5	27.2	3.6
Stationery	5.3	18.5	40.4	3.5
Pharmacy	4.8	0.0	24.6	3.2
Furniture	4.7	40.3	32.2	3.1
Household cleaners	4.6	19.6	19.6	3.0
Hardware	4.5	18.0	34.2	3.0
Automotives	4.0	15.5	22.0	2.7
Miscellaneous*	3.5	7.7	40.4	2.3
Jewelry/watches	2.6	(1.5)	41.5	1.7
Cosmetics	2.5	14.9	25.0	1.7
Photo	2.3	(11.3)	16.9	1.5
Crafts	1.9	(1.6)	38.0	1.3
Total	$151.1			100.0%

*Includes snack bar, video rental and other categories not listed.

Source: *Discount Store News*, August 5, 1996, p. 46.

its better paint line was branded *House Beautiful*, and its lawn and garden products were sold under the *Better Homes and Gardens* brand name. Generally, private-label brands offered consumers lower prices and retailers higher margins than national brands.

Successful discount stores were most likely to be located near a major highway or interstate—to make the store readily accessible to shoppers over a wide retail trade area. The major trend among full-line discount retailers was to build larger stores stocked with a broader line of merchandise, particularly groceries and traditional supermarket items. Newly constructed discount stores were often double the size of stores constructed in the 1980s. Wal-Mart Supercenters and Super Kmart Centers were as large as 180,000 square feet and included products typically found in full-line grocery stores, department stores, auto supply stores, and hardware stores. In rural areas, the supercenter-type stores generally offered a wider selection of food items than competing supermarkets.

Aside from just carrying a wider selection of merchandise, Wal-Mart Supercenters, Super Kmart Centers, and other full-line merchandisers were giving food items a more prominent placement in their stores, selling a growing number of food items under their own private-label brands—Wal-Mart's "Sam's American Choice," Kmart's "American

Fare," and Target's "Archer Farms." Kmart had recently developed a store-within-a-store concept for both its traditional stores and its supercenter stores that allocated 8,700 square feet to convenience items; the new area was located near the store entrance to make it convenient for shoppers to stop in and get a few items. Both regional and national chains had begun to experiment with meals-to-go that were intended to appeal to two-income families who did not have time to cook at home.

Kmart UNDER JOSEPH ANTONINI, 1987–1995

Antonini's Strategy to Grow Kmart

Kmart's strategy of growth via diversification into a variety of retail businesses was initiated by Bernard Fauber, the company's chief executive officer from 1980 to 1987. However, most of Kmart's acquisitions were orchestrated by Joseph Antonini, who succeeded Fauber as Kmart's chairman, CEO, and president in 1987. Both Fauber and Antonini believed that entry into specialty retail stores would provide the company with greater growth opportunities than would be possible with only the Kmart chain of discount stores. The move to expand Kmart's scope of retail operations was intended to position the company in such faster growing product categories as drugstore merchandise, office supplies, books, building materials, and sporting goods. Antonini also believed it made good strategic sense for Kmart to be involved in warehouse clubs and hypermarts because such stores were simply a larger-scale and slightly modified version of the retailing format that traditional discount stores like Kmart were already operating. Antonini saw the purchase of the discount stores in the Czech Republic and Slovakia and the joint ventures in Mexico and Singapore as valuable ways to begin positioning Kmart more aggressively in international retail markets.

Antonini's second strategic initiative to stimulate revenue growth focused on a $3.5 billion "renewal" program in 1991 to modernize, expand, or relocate Kmart's 2,435 discount stores. Most of these stores were built during the company's dramatic growth period in the 1960s and 1970s and had undergone little or no remodeling or renovation since they were constructed. Antonini wanted to increase the size of Kmart stores from a typical 80,000 square feet to about 100,000 square feet so that a wider variety of merchandise could be offered to consumers. The modernized Kmart stores provided brighter lighting, wider aisles, more modern and colorful interior signs, and more attractive merchandise displays. In 1992 he announced that the company would launch as many as 500 Super Kmart Centers that, like American Fare, would include both a discount store and a grocery store in a 160,000–180,000 square-foot building. By 1994 the sales of the renovated and new Super Kmart Centers were 23 percent above the sales of the chain's older, unrefurbished stores.

Antonini also initiated efforts to increase the volume of apparel sold in Kmart stores. He believed that increased sales of high-margin apparel would provide the stores with better operating margins and allow the company to offer lower everyday pricing on nonapparel items, like household items and health and beauty products. The company improved the styling and quality of its private-label apparel and began to include more natural fibers and less polyester in its garments. Kmart used endorsements from Jaclyn Smith and Kathy Ireland to create private-label-branded lines of apparel to appeal to fashion-conscious and designer-conscious shoppers. Antonini also added national brands of apparel and footwear like Wrangler, Hanes, L.A. Gear, and Britannia to the company's merchandise mix.

Attempts to Cure Kmart's Longstanding Inventory Management Problems

Joseph Antonini also believed that the company needed to correct its long-running inability to maintain proper inventory levels in its stores. Kmart had been confronted with this problem for years, but the company had never really been able to resolve it. Most Kmart stores either stocked out of popular-selling items relatively frequently and/or were burdened with excess stocks of slow-moving items that eventually had to be marked down significantly to clear the items from the stores. Antonini believed that Kmart's decentralized buying and merchandising process was at the root of the company's poor inventory management practices. Typically, Kmart buyers negotiated purchases with manufacturers, distribution people shipped products to stores, advertising specialists coordinated the company's advertising, and a separate marketing staff was responsible for promotions. Additionally, the company's store managers were authorized to purchase merchandise specific to their geographic locale and to place special ads in local area newspapers.

Antonini and Chief Information Officer David Carlson implemented a number of state-of-the-art information systems to correct the inventory management problems in the company's 2000-plus stores. In 1990 Kmart launched the GTE Spacenet satellite-based network that linked individual Kmart stores with the Kmart corporate office in Troy, Michigan, and some suppliers. The system allowed Kmart management to eliminate its traditional decentralized inventory management process and adopt a centralized process that was intended to reduce escalating inventory costs while meeting local preferences and price sensitivities. The GTE Spacenet communication system allowed management to implement its Central Merchandising Automated Replenishment (CMAR) system that was jointly developed by Kmart's information systems staff and Electronic Data Systems, a leading supplier of data-processing services. The CMAR system allowed Kmart's corporate office to keep track of every sale in each store. All scanner data was transmitted via a local area network to a UNIX server in the back room of each individual store. At the end of every day, the server transmitted sales data to the corporate headquarters via the GTE Spacenet satellite.

The next morning Kmart product-category managers studied the sales data from each store and later that day placed orders with vendors to replenish each store's inventory. Vendors that were members of Kmart's Partners in Merchandise Flow Program were allowed to monitor the scanner data themselves and ship to Kmart distribution centers when they determined it was necessary to maintain Kmart's desired inventory levels. The distribution centers used a cross-docking system that helped keep inventory levels at the distribution center to a minimum. A senior executive at Kmart explained how centralized category management allowed the company to reduce expenses and keep products that consumers wanted on the shelves.[1]

> Category management has been very successful for us. It's shifted our entire focus to the front door. Years ago we were busy with shipments—looking at what was coming in the back door from our suppliers. Today we have a front-door focus in that we are focusing on the consumer and what the register tape tells us she's taking out the front door. We've seen

---

[1]"Kmart's Category Approach," *Discount Merchandiser*, May 1994, p. 118.

dramatic improvements in turnover. In fact, we used to call our distribution centers "warehouses" because products would come in and sometimes just sit there. Now they are truly distribution centers with goods flowing in and right out, often within a day or two.

Kmart identified about 1,500 hard lines categories and several hundred soft lines categories and selected managers to make all buying and merchandising decisions, including pricing, assortments, and promotions, for their assigned category of products. Each category manager used the scanner data available from CMAR and demographic profiles and consumer purchasing behavior data provided by third parties such as Nielsen Marketing Research to make their purchasing decisions. Each category manager was required to develop a sales plan, a gross margin plan, and a turnover plan that was presented to the senior marketing executives at the beginning of the financial year.

Kmart spent about $160 million annually to create and implement information systems like CMAR technology and other state-of-the-art computer systems during Antonini's tenure as Kmart's top executive. The company implemented electronic data interchange (EDI) systems with some suppliers that attempted to reduce the company's dependence on paper-based transaction processing. The company also developed the ShopperTrack system, utilized in its newest stores, that used backroom computers and ceiling-mounted sensors to monitor how many customers were in each department throughout the day. The system used the tracking data to project store and department customer counts at 15-minute intervals. Store managers were instructed to use this information to schedule employee staffing at the store's checkout stations and merchandise departments.

Difficulties in Implementing and Executing Antonini's Strategy

At the outset, both Wall Street and Kmart investors reacted favorably to Antonini's moves to diversify the corporation into a number of attractive discount retail segments, to renovate and enlarge Kmart stores, to improve merchandise selection, quality and availability, and to improve information systems. The consensus was that these moves would allow the company to grow faster and to compete more effectively against its major rivals. However, as efforts to implement the strategy continued to unfold, events made it increasingly clear that Kmart was being outmaneuvered by its rivals; Wal-Mart, in particular, was leaving Kmart far behind (see Exhibits 6 and 7). Kmart's sales per store continued to run close to $185 per square foot in 1992, 1993, and 1994, despite the merchandising efforts initiated by Antonini and other Kmart executives. Kmart's pricing continued to average 10 to 15 percent above its chief competitors, as Kmart sought to boost its subpar store margins and make up for the higher selling, general, and administrative expenses brought on by relatively low sales volumes per square foot of selling space.

Moreover, while Fauber and Antonini built Kmart's retailing portfolio far beyond its core discount store base, Kmart management never was able to transform any of its acquisitions into enterprises able to compete successfully against key segment rivals in terms of sales, net income, or efficient inventory management. In almost every retailing business that Kmart diversified into, it trailed the industry leader by a considerable distance. Builders Square stores achieved sales volumes only one-third the per-store sales volume of industry leader, Home Depot. The company's Pace warehouse clubs never were able to match the selection and pricing of Sam's warehouse clubs and, in the end, many of Pace's store locations were eventually sold to Wal-Mart. Knowledgeable retail analysts attributed the failure of Kmart's American

EXHIBIT 6   Comparative Financial Performance of Sears, Kmart, and Wal-Mart, 1980, 1985, 1987–1996

Year	Sales (in millions of dollars)			Net Income (in millions of dollars)			Net Income as a Percentage of Sales		
	Sears*	Kmart	Wal-Mart**	Sears*	Kmart	Wal-Mart**	Sears*	Kmart	Wal-Mart**
1980	$18,675	$14,118	$ 1,643	$ 229	$ 429	$ 56	1.2%	3.0%	3.4%
1985	26,552	22,035	8,451	776	757	327	2.9	3.4	3.9
1987	28,085	25,627	15,959	787	1,171	627	2.8	4.6	3.9
1988	30,256	27,301	20,649	524	1,244	837	1.7	4.6	4.1
1989	31,599	29,150	25,811	647	261†	1,076	2.1	3.9	4.2
1990	31,986	28,607	32,602	257	673	1,291	0.8	2.4	4.0
1991	31,433	29,488	43,887	486	752	1,608	1.5	2.6	3.7
1992	31,961	26,470	55,484	(2,977)	941	1,995	(9.3)	2.8	3.6
1993	29,565	28,039	67,345	752	(974)††	2,333	2.5	(0.8)	3.5
1994	29,608	29,563	82,494	875	296	2,681	2.7	0.3	3.2
1995	31,188	31,713	93,627	1,025	(571)	2,740	2.9	(1.4)	2.9
1996	33,512	31,437	104,859	1,271	(220)	3,056	3.8	(0.7)	2.9

*Sears' data represents Merchandise Group Operations only.

**Wal-Mart's fiscal year ends January 31 of each year; data for the period January 31, 1980 through January 31, 1981, are reported in Wal-Mart's annual report as 1981 results. Because Wal-Mart's fiscal year results really cover 11 months of the previous calendar year, this exhibit shows Wal-Mart's 1981 fiscal results in the 1980 row, its 1986 results in the 1985 row, and so on. This adjustment makes Wal-Mart's figures correspond more to the same time frame as the calendar year data for Sears and Kmart.

†After a pretax provision of $640 million for restructuring.

††After a pretax provision of $904 million for restructuring.

Source: Company annual reports, 1980, 1985, 1987–1996.

EXHIBIT 7　Selected Operating Statistics for the Leading North American Discount Retailers, 1995

Top Discount Department Stores and Discount Mass Merchants

Rank	Company	Sales (in millions)			Net Profit Margin			1995 Sales per Square Foot	SG&A as a Percent of 1995 Sales	Number of Stores as of Dec. 1995
		1995	1994	Percent Change	1995	1994	Percent Change			
1	Wal-Mart Stores[a]	$54,330	$53,350	1.8%	2.9%	3.25%	(10.0)%	$379	16.0%	2,943
2	Sears[b]	31,188	29,608	5.3	2.9	2.7	7.4	261	21.7	810
3	Kmart[a]	26,779	26,986	(0.8)	(1.65)	0.90	(283.0)	185	21.8	2,326
4	Target[a]	15,807	13,600	16.2	*	*	*	282	*	670
5	Montgomery Ward[b]	6,219	6,218	0.0	0.2	2.0	(90.0)	141	25.5	340

[a]Discount department store
[b]Discount mass merchandiser
*Data unavailable.

Top Supercenter Chains

Rank	Company	Sales (in millions)			Number of Stores			1995 Sales per Square Foot	1996 Average Store Size (in square feet)
		1995	1994	Percent Change	January 1995	January 1996	January 1997 (Projected)		
1	Wal-Mart Supercenters	$11,500	$4,650	147.3%	143	247	350	$314*	188,000
2	Meijer	5,600	5,600	0.0	99	99	109	283	200,000
3	Super Kmart Centers	3,650	1,400	160.7	67	93	104	285*	160,000
4	Fred Meyer	3,429	3,128	9.6	131	136	142	237	109,000
5	Smitty's	675	670	0.8	28	29	28	358	65,000

*Estimated by dividing 1995 sales by the average number of stores between January 1995 and January 1996.

Source: Discount Store News, July 1, 1996; company annual reports.

Fare stores in part to poor store design and poor store management. Payless Drugs, Waldenbooks, and OfficeMax were all weak-performing businesses under Kmart's management, posting either operating losses or minimal operating profits.

Joseph Antonini attributed some of Kmart's difficulties in the apparel segment of its core retail discount business to rapidly shifting market conditions rather than weak strategy on Kmart's part. For example, while, as the company had planned, the Kathy Ireland and Jaclyn Smith apparel lines were successfully positioned as national brands in the minds of shoppers, the initial success proved short-lived. By 1994, sales of the two apparel lines were sagging because of changing buyer preferences. Antonini, whose background and experience had been largely in apparel and soft lines, explained the reasons for the downturn: "Substantial shifts are taking place. For example, clothes just don't mean as much as they did five years ago, focus groups tell us. Designer names are not driving shoppers to stores, but in many ways have the opposite effect. Today, Mom is usually the last family member to get a new outfit. She is sacrificing for her family."[2] Antonini, in a 1994 *Forbes* interview, said that the U.S. economy played a role in undermining some of Kmart's merchandising efforts: "The economy is hurting, disposable income is down, and people are spending money only on essential products. The fringe items—and I consider apparel to be a fringe item—aren't selling anywhere across the country like they used to."[3]

Antonini's expectation that sales of higher-margin apparel items would allow the company to offer lower prices on thousands of other items sold in Kmart stores didn't pan out either. As it turned out, Kmart was at a cost disadvantage relative to Wal-Mart and was not able to meet Wal-Mart's pricing on many items. In addition, Wal-Mart management was intent on being the low-price leader and chose not to allow competitors to price popular items below what Wal-Mart charged. A Wal-Mart executive gave the following explanation of the importance of the company's five-point operating cost advantage and its pricing strategy: "It's very simple. We're not going to be undersold. What that means is, that in an all-out price war, [our competitors] will go broke 5% before we will."[4]

When asked about Wal-Mart's meteoric climb to the top of the full-line discount industry, Antonini stated that Wal-Mart management, who he at times referred to as "snake oil salesmen,"[5] came across as successful largely because Wal-Mart was new to the industry and consumers were inclined to try out a new store. In 1994 he commented that, "They have enjoyed the advantage of being the new show in town in many of our markets."[6] Antonini suggested that Wal-Mart's newcomer advantage was very similar to the new retail shopping excitement that Kmart was able to create during its period of rapid growth in the 1960s and 1970s.

Kmart's Super Kmart Centers   Kmart's new Super Kmart Centers were having marginally greater success competing against Wal-Mart's Supercenters than older Kmart stores were having in competing with Wal-Mart's regular discount stores. Super Kmart Centers were approximately the same size as Wal-Mart Supercenters and, like Wal-Mart Supercenters, included a full-line grocery, discount store, and specialty departments like automobile service, photo centers, pharmacies, video rentals, floral departments, and

---

[2]"Antonini, On Changes in the Marketplace," *Discount Merchandiser*, December 1994, p. 12.
[3]"The Best-Laid Plans. . . . " *Forbes*, January 3, 1994, p. 44.
[4]"The High Cost of Second Best," *Fortune*, July 26, 1993, p. 99.
[5]Ibid.
[6]"Kmart's Agenda for Recovery," *Discount Merchandiser*, July 1994, p. 14.

hair salons. Super Kmart Centers were developed as a response to Wal-Mart's Supercenters, with little originality or creativity on the part of Kmart headquarters, and had their own unique culture and policies. When the first group of Super Kmart Center stores were opened, employees were proud of the stores' open "no walls" management style and culture that facilitated free and open communication; moreover, they saw their stores as Wal-Mart killers and worked hard to deliver better customer service than Wal-Mart. However, a manager of a rival to Super Kmart Centers noted that the impressively strong and vibrant entrepreneurial spirit of Super Kmart Center store employees (evident in the first group of stores opened) had waned because such cultures had not been firmly implanted in the nearly 100 new Super Kmart Centers that were opened between 1992 and 1995.

Kmart management indicated that annual sales per square foot at Super Kmart Centers were almost 60 percent greater than the annual sales at the company's regular Kmart discount stores. (see Exhibit 7). However, the profitability of the supercenter stores was not materially different than that of the traditional stores, since as much as 40 percent of the sales at the supercenters consisted of low-margin grocery items.

Kmart's Image with Consumers   Surveys of U.S. discount store shoppers commissioned by *Chain Store Age Executive* found three consistent negative images that customers attributed to Kmart: out-of-stock merchandise, poor housekeeping, and indifferent service. Additionally, the consumers surveyed found Wal-Mart's locations more convenient and believed that Wal-Mart offered better pricing and product selection than Kmart. Antonini's store renovation and remodeling strategy was directed at eliminating Wal-Mart's pricing and selection advantage. However, in 1995—the company's fourth year into its renovation, relocation, and remodeling strategy—sales per square foot at Kmart remained flat at around $185, resulting in S, G, & A expense ratios that were far above Wal-Mart's because the typical Wal-Mart store had sales per square foot of over $375. The higher expense ratios kept Kmart's bottom-line performance from materially improving.

Kmart's Store Renovation and Renewal Program   Wall Street analysts were very critical of Kmart's efforts at upgrading its stores. Many investors were displeased with Kmart management's use of the proceeds of a $1 billion equity issue in 1991. At the time the new shares of stock were sold, management had indicated that the capital was to be used to renovate and refurbish older Kmart stores. As it turned out, a sizable portion of the money spent in its "renewal" program went into acquiring new specialty retail stores rather than renovating older Kmart stores. Wall Street analysts made the following comments about Kmart's store renewal efforts.[7]

> They aren't doing full renovations, just repainting or putting in new linoleum instead of gutting the stores entirely and redesigning them. And that has hurt them. It's back to the old Kmart culture where it's better to spend money on new stores and expand the chain.
>
> Even Betty Crocker got a new hair-do. I just drove by a Kmart store sign and it looked like a Howard Johnson should be next to it, circa 1957. They have a long way to go before getting rid of the popcorn smell when you walk in the door.
>
> It's not as if they started their remodeling program six months ago. We should have seen a more positive effect on earnings by now.
>
> By the time they're done, it will be time to start all over again.

[7]"Attention Bottom Fishers," *Financial World*, March 28, 1995, p. 31.

Some shareholders and industry analysts suggested that the lack of management commitment to the store "renewal" program was a result of the company's past strategies. Kmart had achieved great success during the 1960s and 1970s as a result of its rapid addition of stores. The company's stock jumped from $0.50 per share when the first Kmart store was opened in 1962 to $32 in 1972. Some investors believed that the era of store growth at Kmart helped mold a managerial mind-set that favored putting more emphasis on store expansion than on proper management of existing stores and on merchandising efforts to boost annual sales at each existing store.

Continuing Inventory Problems   Even though Kmart had invested far more than its industry rivals on developing systems and procedures to correct its inventory-related problems, the problems still existed. Kmart stores still were faced with frequent stockouts of merchandise and some of Kmart's vendors had criticized Kmart's buying procedures, stating that the corporate office frequently placed orders for merchandise and then later canceled the orders. A Kmart executive explained the difficulties of implementing its centralized merchandising strategy:[8]

> Bringing this decision-making power to the desktop is a hurdle. Category management evolved with computer systems, but it's still a challenge to get these high-powered PCs on everyone's desktops and to have them linked together via local area networks. Furthermore, some buyers may not be computer literate or used to dealing with scanner and syndicated data. So it can be an educational process as well as a hardware installation process. Most of our buyers started out as store managers, so to them it's attractive to think, "Oh, I'll call my old store to see how this product is doing." We have to get them additionally looking at and relying on this internal computer data, syndicated third party data, and quantitative information. It also takes a certain kind of person, someone who knows merchandising, who knows computer processing, who knows about financing, who knows a little about advertising—someone who knows enough about everything, as opposed to being a specialist in just one area. The information and the software available are just tools. You still need an experienced person who can tie it all together.

Customer Service Problems   Some Kmart stores were plagued with unresponsive customer service. A 1994 *Forbes* article cited customer complaints of indifferent Kmart employees who, when asked for a specific item in the store, would wave their hand in a general direction. Another disgruntled shopper complained that, "At the superstores in Farmington Hills or Southfield, the help is surly and uncooperative and you can never find the products that you need and have to have."[9] Commenting to the *Forbes* reporter on that particular complaint, Antonini said:

> Last year Kmart did $34 billion in sales. We had 180 million shoppers come through our doors. We had 1.3 billion transactions. Kmart's fine. We did the business. We did the sales. Now obviously this one shopper wasn't happy, but the store you're referring to is the Super Kmart store, I imagine. That store will do $80 million. Unfortunately this customer wasn't happy and obviously we don't like that. But when you get the amount of customers we get into a store, obviously we're not going to please everybody, but we try, we try.[10]

Morale Problems   Under Antonini, Kmart had continuing internal morale problems. Some employees believed these problems stemmed from the way that Antonini

---

[8]Ibid., pp. 119–20.
[9]"The Antonini Transcript," *Discount Store News*, April 17, 1995, p. 12.
[10]Ibid.

treated subordinates. One Kmart employee told *Forbes* reporters that frequently Antonini would publicly berate other senior executives and use epithets like "stupid," "jerk," or "inept" when addressing them. The Kmart employee also stated that Antonini would tell store personnel that they disgusted him and would frequently tell executives that they weren't worth the salaries they were paid. Antonini denied the charges cited by *Forbes*. "Remember, we're changing culture, and not everyone is happy with change. Am I a tough taskmaster? Yes. Do I challenge people? Yes. Am I demanding? Yes. But to say I'm abusive is an outright lie."[11]

Growing Pressure for Better Performance   In January 1994, rumors were circulating that Kmart's board was pressuring Antonini to show more progress in improving Kmart's competitiveness and financial performance. Responding to queries about whether the board had given him a deadline to get things turned around and had urged revisions in the company's strategy. Antonini said, "Absolutely not true. Because of two down quarters, people would say that? It's unequivocally not true . . . While the economy is going to be difficult, while competition will continue to be fierce, we feel our strategy is right for the future."[12]

In March 1995, following eight consecutive quarters of lower earnings, Antonini resigned as Kmart's chairman of the board, CEO, and president.

FLOYD HALL'S TURNAROUND EFFORTS, JUNE 1995–MARCH 1997

Kmart's board of directors appointed Floyd Hall as the company's new chairman, chief executive officer, and president in June 1995. Hall, who was recruited from Grand Union Supermarkets, had engineered Target's growth during the 1980s and had recently gotten Grand Union back on track. Floyd Hall accepted the position with the intention of turning around Kmart within three years and then moving on to other ventures. "I'm just trying to build a team . . . get a good succession plan and new policies and practices in place. By the way, I do expect to go out on top."[13] Hall and the board quickly assembled a new top-level management team—with 12 new vice-presidents in marketing and product development; strategic planning, finance, and administration; merchandising; information systems; and other key areas. The 12 new vice presidents had an average of 27 years of retail experience. When Hall asked his new management team to review and evaluate Kmart's competitive position, he found that Kmart trailed Wal-Mart by a considerable distance on every key performance indicator. Wal-Mart's customers averaged 32 store visits per year, while Kmart's customers averaged 15 visits per year. Kmart's sales per square foot in 1994 were $185, compared to Wal-Mart's $379 and Target's $282. Only 19 percent of Kmart shoppers considered themselves loyal to the chain, while 46 percent of Wal-Mart shoppers considered themselves loyal Wal-Mart shoppers. Hall stated, "The most devastating news I saw in all the research was that 49 percent of Wal-Mart's shoppers drive past a Kmart to get to Wal-Mart."[14]

---

[11]"The Best-Laid Plans . . . ," p. 45.

[12]Ibid.

[13]"Kmart Is Down for the Count," *Fortune*, January 15, 1996, p. 103.

[14]Ibid., p. 102.

Hall believed that Kmart must be fixed "department by department" and that management must not try to "put a Band-Aid on our problems. This requires surgery."[15] Hall's first priority was to close nearly 400 Kmart stores and divest all noncore businesses from the company's portfolio between 1995 and 1997. Hall also initiated over $900 million in cost reductions during 1995 and 1996 by consolidating the company's Canadian operations with its U.S. operations, consolidating the company's payroll functions (payroll was previously handled by two companies), clearing out $700 million in old inventory, and using the company's volume buying power to reduce the cost of benefits for its 300,000 employees.

Some of the portfolio restructuring actually had taken place in the months just before Antonini's departure. Kmart sold Payless Drugs in 1993 and spun off OfficeMax and Sports Authority as independent stand-alone companies in late 1994. The initial public offerings of stock in Office Max and in Sports Authority were completed in December 1994, with Kmart retaining a 25 percent equity ownership in OfficeMax and a 30 percent equity ownership in Sports Authority. In addition, the company's 21.5 percent interest in Cole Myer, an Australian retailer, was sold in 1994. These transactions provided the company with an approximate after-tax gain of $250 million.

In 1995 and 1996, Hall and Kmart's new management team sold the company's Czech and Slovak stores for $115 million; completed public offerings of stock to divest the company's remaining interests in OfficeMax and Sports Authority (netting the company an after-tax gain of $155 million); sold the assets of the Kmart auto centers to Penske for $84 million; completed a public stock offering of Border's Bookstores group (that resulted in an after-tax loss of $185 million); and sold the Rite Aid drugstore chain for $257 million. The company also discontinued its joint ventures in Singapore and Mexico and entered into a strategic alliance with Cardinal Health to manage the pharmacies in all Kmart and Super Kmart stores.

While Kmart executives believed that these divestitures, store closings, and cost-cutting efforts gave Kmart a stronger balance sheet, more business focus, and improved cost-competitiveness versus Wal-Mart, they were well aware that long-term success in turning Kmart around hinged on dramatically boosting sales and bringing shoppers into Kmart stores more frequently. In late-1996 Marv Rich, Kmart's executive vice-president of strategic planning and finance, stated "Our problem is not expenses—and we're getting a better handle on them. Our real problem is sales. If we had double the sales, our expense ratio would be half of what it is today, all things being equal."[16]

Kmart's Financial Crisis

Floyd Hall and the other members of Kmart's top management team were confronted with a potentially devastating financial crisis during the last half of 1995 that was a result of Kmart's poor cash flow and the financial decisions made by previous Kmart management. As was common with most retailers, Kmart management had a long-standing preference for financing new store construction off of the company's balance sheet. Groups of newly constructed stores were sold to such organizations as pension funds and insurance companies, who then leased the stores back to Kmart on

---

[15]"Kmart: Who's in Charge Here?" *Business Week*, December 4, 1995, p. 107.

[16]"Leaner, Meaner, Cleaner: Nearly $1 Billion in Cost Cutting Has Goosed Earnings and Improved Efficiencies," *Discount Store News*, December 9, 1996, p. 28.

long-term lease agreements. This was a hidden financial obligation, since long-term lease payment obligations were not required, under accounting rules then prevailing, to be shown as a long-term liability on Kmart's balance sheet; the company only had to report current-year lease payments as an operating expense on its annual income statement.

In the early-1990s, Kmart's financial officers had agreed to special "put provisions" in a number of Kmart's store-leasing agreements in exchange for better lease terms from the financing organizations. The "put provisions" stipulated that if Kmart's bond rating was downgraded to junk-bond status, then Kmart would immediately be obligated to buy back the leased stores from the lease-owner and eliminate any risk of potential default on the remaining years of the leasing agreement. In July 1995—just one month after Hall became Kmart's CEO—Kmart was placed on credit watch by various credit-rating agencies as an indication that they were considering downgrading Kmart's bond rating. The credit watch placement had the effect of preventing Kmart from borrowing on 30-to-60-day commercial paper over the October–November period to pay suppliers for shipping the volume of goods needed to build its Christmas inventory. In order to have ample warehouse and store inventories for the Christmas season, Kmart was forced to activate a $2 billion backup revolving line of credit held by a consortium of 70 banks, adding interest costs and further straining Kmart's already precariously thin profit margins and cash flows.

In October 1995, rumors began on Wall Street that Kmart would consider bankruptcy protection because of the pending bond rating downgrade and the put provisions agreed to during the Antonini era; a number of stories concerning the company's financial difficulties appeared in *The Wall Street Journal* in October 1995. As the rumors took hold, many Wall Street analysts began to debate whether the leaseholders would exercise their "put options" and require Kmart to buy back the leased stores, thus triggering a financial catastrophe for Kmart and forcing it to declare bankruptcy. Kmart's store buyback obligation with leaseholders amounted to $600 million—money that it did not have and might well not be able to raise, according to Wall Street speculation. To make matters worse, the covenants of Kmart's $2 billion revolving line of credit stated that if the leaseholders exercised their put options, any borrowings under the line of credit would immediately become due and payable. Kmart's accounts payable to its vendors already exceeded $3.5 billion for its purchases for Christmas inventory. The potential for Kmart to be faced with obligations to its vendors and creditors totaling $6 billion, compounded by swirling rumors, drove the company's stock price down to $5¾ per share—50 percent of its book value.

As Wall Street expected, Kmart's long-term debt was downgraded to junk bond status in January 1996. Hall and Kmart financial officers had already visited with the leaseholders in late December 1995 and negotiated an agreement for them not to immediately exercise the put options and demand payment. Hall and Kmart financial executives knew from past experiences of other troubled retailers that vendors would not ship Kmart additional merchandise if they were not paid for what had already been shipped. Hall also knew that the company would not survive if there was a broad pullback by vendors and Kmart had to go without merchandise in its stores, so the decision was made to use the available cash to pay vendors in a manner sufficiently timely to ensure continued shipments.

As Kmart paid its suppliers, management continued talks with the 70 banks that funded Kmart's line of credit. The negotiations were difficult, since Kmart did not have sufficient cash to make the required repayments on its revolving line of credit, and the banks' primary concern was how quickly their exposure on the outstanding loans could be covered. Kmart's creditors agreed to allow the company to suspend principal payments on its debt for 18 months while Hall and Kmart's financial officers negotiated a new financing proposal with a consortium of banks led by Chemical Bank. Chemical Bank agreed to put a consortium of lenders together to provide Kmart with $3.7 billion to refinance its obligations under the revolving line of credit and the leased-store debt associated with "put options"—contingent on the company's ability to raise $750 million through an equity issue.

The crisis came to an end in June 1996, when Kmart issued $1 billion in convertible preferred shares and signed a new $3.7 billion financing agreement with Chemical Bank. Because these funds were essential to keeping Kmart from declaring bankruptcy, Hall and Kmart's financial officers agreed to attractive interest rates on the bank loans and to substantial fees for the investment brokers to ensure that buyers were found for the $1 billion in convertible preferred stock.

Attracting Customers to Kmart

Floyd Hall and his new management team determined that there were a number of underlying problems that made it difficult for the company to compete against Wal-Mart:

- Items in high demand were frequently out of stock in Kmart stores.
- The company's pricing was above that of Wal-Mart.
- Kmart had a limited selection of merchandise in some categories.
- Some merchandise stocked in Kmart stores was of inferior quality.
- Many Kmart stores had very poor housekeeping and customer service.

Hall's management team concluded that a combination of new strategies and improved implementation of existing strategies were required to correct Kmart's shortcomings.

A New Merchandising and Distribution Strategy   Kmart had been confronted with serious inventory management problems as far back as the early 1980s, and the new management team saw inventory management as the single biggest problem that had to be corrected. A big part of the solution, they believed, lay in eliminating many slow-selling items and unpopular brands and reducing the number of vendors. Under Antonini's centralized merchandising strategy, Kmart carried one or two national brands, an assortment of second- and third-tier brands, and some private-label brands. The new top management team found that many of the second- and third-tier brands cluttered store shelves and frequently did not sell without deep markdowns.

Kmart's new merchandising executives eliminated some second-tier brands and most third-tier brands and began to develop its private-label brands to fill the gaps in its merchandise mix left by the removal of the lesser-known brands. Kmart reengineered its buying process so that category managers were no longer making buying decisions in isolation from those in other functional areas. Under the reengineered process, Kmart set up buying teams made up of specialists in merchandising, planning, finance, inventory control, logistics, distribution, and advertising. The new process was designed to ensure that merchandise was available when demanded and would sell without regular or deep markdowns.

Studies indicated that most customers shopped in Kmart stores primarily during weekend sales and only occasionally at other times. Management decided that store traffic during nonsale times could be increased by stocking a wider variety of popular national brands like Rubbermaid and Wrangler. Kmart's sales of Rubbermaid products increased by 25 percent after it began to carry a wider assortment of the company's products. To fill gaps left by eliminated brands, Kmart extended its BenchTop do-it-yourself hardware line, began offering a wider variety of American Fare food products, introduced its new line of Route 66 denim apparel, and increased the number of K-Gro horticultural products available in its stores.

Kmart also completely redesigned the Martha Stewart Everyday bed and bath collection and planned a relaunch of the brand in 1997. The Martha Stewart private-label line of linens, towels, and other bed-and-bath products had been created during the Antonini era; however, under Antonini, the brand had not done particularly well because of inadequate promotion and a limited product line. The reintroduced Martha Stewart bed-and-bath collection included a wider variety of products—linens, bath towels, beach towels, draperies, pillows, blankets, and paint. The collection was manufactured by WestPoint Stevens and Springs and used high-quality materials such as 200-thread-count fabrics. The Martha Stewart paint line was manufactured by Sherwin-Williams and featured 256 colors that were similar to colors available in Martha Stewart's $80 per gallon line of paints offered by high-end retailers.

Stephen Ross, Kmart's general merchandise manager of soft lines, stated that the company would extend the Martha Stewart line to include household items in other store departments so as to allow customers to give their homes a decorator look. "We're going to make a case for her [our customer] to do something to freshen up her home—whether her bedroom or bathroom—give her a reason to do it because we've given her some décor tips and we're making it easy to do."[17] Ross believed that having a coordinated Martha Stewart line across store departments, offering decorator tips, and pricing the line competitively would prompt customers to make multiple purchases of Martha Stewart branded products.

Company management took a series of steps to improve its working relationships with suppliers, to correct out-of-stocks, and to reduce its distribution costs. Warren Flick, Kmart's COO, said, "You can't say enough about the importance of our relationships with our key suppliers in terms of finding efficiencies which are so necessary to take zero-value-added processes out of the system."[18] Kmart began a Collaborative Forecasting and Replenishment program with Warner-Lambert and several technology firms. The program was designed to share Kmart's customer and product information with its suppliers over the Internet. The company also upgraded its IBM Inventory Forecasting and Replenishment Modules system to shorten its replenishment cycle by a full day. Kmart's chief information officer Donald Norman said that the company had reduced the amount of time to replenish some merchandise from 40 hours to 18 hours.

The company also attempted to improve and expand its cross-docking capabilities in its distribution centers. Products that were delivered to its distribution centers were unloaded from suppliers trucks, audited for proper quantity, and then placed on a conveyor belt where they were loaded onto trucks headed for Kmart stores. The improved process was beneficial to both Kmart and its suppliers. The process shortened merchandise delivery time to Kmart stores, reduced inventory held in distribution

---

[17]"The Martha-ization of Kmart's Home," *Discount Store News*, December 9, 1996, p. 4.

[18]"Flick Unveils Plan to Revamp Kmart," *HFN: The Weekly Newspaper for the Home Furnishing Network*, November 11, 1996, p. 2.

centers, and improved the company's cash flow. Suppliers who had previously shipped to individual Kmart stores reduced their shipping costs by delivering to fewer destination points, and they received payment earlier since Kmart paid invoices upon receipt of the order at the warehouses rather than at the time of delivery to its stores.

Improving Kmart's Store Productivity and Relative Cost Position   Despite the efforts of Kmart executives, at year-end 1996 Kmart's store productivity still trailed Wal-Mart's by a wide margin. Kmart had sales of $201 per square foot of retail space compared to sales of $379 per square foot for Wal-Mart. While Kmart's new super-stores achieved higher sales volume than the company's older stores, they did not attract customers in sufficient volume to come close to matching sales per square foot at Wal-Mart. Kmart executives saw increased store traffic as the key to improving store productivity and lowering prices. Increased store traffic meant greater economies of scale in distribution and store operations—cost reductions that could then be passed along to shoppers in the form of lower and more competitive prices.

Hall developed and rolled out a redesign of existing stores that was intended to attract more customers to Kmart stores. The company tested its high-frequency Pantry concept during 1995 in selected stores and announced in January 1997 that it would expand the Pantry concept to 1,800 stores during the next three years. The Pantry concept was a redesign of existing stores that took items typically found in a convenience store and placed them in an 8,700-square-foot-area at the front of Kmart stores. Merchandise that was already sold in Kmart stores like diapers, paper towels, bread, milk, dog food, beverages, and snack foods was gathered and placed in one department, then supplemented by additional dry grocery items. Kmart rearranged remaining store merchandise so that frequently purchased items like small appliances and soft lines (underwear, T-shirts, socks, and fleece products) were placed near the Pantry area.

Kmart management expected that the high-frequency Pantry concept would increase store traffic by more than 10 percent and that many shoppers searching for convenience-store items would purchase other items while at Kmart. Warren Flick argued that the new Pantry concept would successfully increase sales per square foot because, "If you have the consumables, you'll get the customers."[19] Kmart management was attracted to the Pantry concept because convenience-store sales were growing rapidly across the United States and because Kmart could implement the feature in its stores at relatively modest incremental costs. The cost to convert an existing Kmart store to the new Pantry concept was $600,000 versus $10 million for a new 100,000-square-foot Kmart store or $20 million for a new 180,000 Super Kmart Center. One Kmart executive doubted that the strategy would, by itself, boost Kmart's bottom-line performance significantly since most of the high-frequency convenience store items carried very low margins. "The Pantry has all the earmarks of something that can increase our sales. Not our profits."[20]

Changes in Structure, Communications, Culture, and Rewards   Concerned that the attitudes and performance of Kmart store managers and associates were adversely impacting shopper visits and loyalty, Hall brought in every Kmart store manager for a five-day meeting in September 1996. Kmart had never had a store managers' meeting, and Hall wanted to emphasize how important the store managers were to

---

[19]"Kmart's Aim: Steal Market Share Away from Wal-Mart," *Daily News Record*, December 13, 1996, p. 1.

[20]"Kmart is Down for the Count," p. 103.

the company's success, to reiterate the company's strategic themes and initiatives, and to discuss how store managers could do their jobs better. At the meeting, the executive team explained the company's mission and strategy, and what individual store managers' roles were in implementing the strategy. The executive team also made it clear that they intended to end Kmart's historically insular, turf-wary organizational culture and adopt a more team-oriented atmosphere at both corporate headquarters and in the stores. The company also announced its new management development program to help the company develop future store-level and corporate-level managers from within its ranks. The company had always promoted from within, but had never attempted to build career paths for its managerial employees.

Kmart corporate-level managers also used the five-day conference to unveil its new store and field organizational structure and incentive compensation plan for store managers. One feature of the reorganization involved reducing the number of stores that each district manager was responsible for from 28 to 11. This reduction was intended to allow district managers to have the time necessary to visit every store in their districts more frequently and to provide better coaching to store managers. Within the stores, associates no longer had at-large responsibility, but were assigned to departments. Depending on the size of the store, as many as 14 departments and department managers were created in Kmart stores. Kmart executives believed that giving associates defined areas of responsibility would create a feeling of ownership within their department and encourage employees to offer better service in their departments. The establishment of department heads was also intended to improve customer service and to help associates begin a career as a Kmart manager.

A new incentive compensation plan for store managers was developed to replace Kmart's old managerial pay plan. Previously, Kmart managers were paid a salary plus a bonus based on store sales. Under the new compensation plan, store managers were eligible for both bonuses and stock options. The new bonus plan tied 50 percent of a store manager's bonus to meeting the store's budget objectives for the year and 50 percent to the store's customer satisfaction rating. The customer satisfaction rating was determined by the results of independent mystery shoppers who visited each store 28 times per year. Mystery shoppers rated each store on customer service provided in specialty departments, the general product knowledge of associates, associate friendliness and willingness to provide assistance, the speed of the checkout process, and all aspects of store cleanliness—from parking lots to fixtures.

Kmart also initiated efforts to improve communications between corporate-level management and its store managers. The company began weekly satellite feeds to discuss merchandising and operations and to provide training in vendor relations and human resources management. The idea was not so much to communicate frequently with stores, but rather to communicate effectively. Kmart's head of merchandise presentation and communications stated that in the past Kmart management put out so many directives to store managers that few could be implemented with real effectiveness. "There's never been a person in Troy [the company's headquarters] who didn't think that their program wasn't the most important one. But if you add them all up at the end of the day, there are 42 programs, and we're capable of doing two."[21]

Kmart established a corporate-level committee to review proposals for new programs, to determine how much time each program would take to implement, and to determine if individual stores had sufficient staffing to execute the plan successfully.

---

[21]"All Hands On Deck: Teamwork Initiates from the Buyer Level to the Stock Room Focus on Improving Operations," *Discount Store News*, December 9, 1996, p. 25.

Once the corporate-level committee determined that a plan could be implemented, it became the responsibility of a store-level committee to put the plan into place. A new program called All Hands On Deck required each store to have a committee made up of a replenishment manager and all department managers to coordinate merchandise stocking and new program implementation. The All Hands On Deck committee met each morning to determine what was needed to ensure that every department had its displays set up and was properly stocked. The All Hands On Deck committee was empowered to shift associates from departments who had little to do to prepare for the day over to help associates from departments that had to set up new displays or stock large amounts of inventory on its shelves or racks.

KMART'S FUTURE PROSPECTS

As Kmart Corporation approached the second anniversary of Floyd Hall's turnaround strategy in June 1997, Kmart executives could point to improved strategic and financial performance in a number of areas. The new $3.7 billion financing agreement and $1 billion convertible preferred equity issue had restored the company's solvency, the company had eliminated close to $1 billion in non-value-adding expenses, and the company's sales per square foot of floor space had increased modestly to $201 from $185 in 1994. In March 1997, the company was able to repay a $1.2 billion term loan that was part of its $3.7 billion financing arrangement concluded in June 1996. The term loan was paid two years ahead of schedule. The company had successfully divested all of its specialty businesses except Builders Square and was currently attempting to find a buyer for that business after its discussions with Waban, Inc., broke down in March 1997.

The company had also improved its level of customer service and its in-stock position—two areas that Hall and other top-level managers believed to be strategically important to the company's turnaround. Between year-end 1994 and April 1997, the company's customer satisfaction index rating had improved from 68 percent to 87 percent. Its in-stock position on hard lines had improved from 88 percent to 95 percent and from 88 percent to 96.5 percent on soft lines. The company was clearly making progress toward correcting its weaknesses associated with the management of its full-line discount stores and achieving Floyd Hall's vision of operational excellence. Hall commented:

> All I want is a perfect store. The parking lot would be paved, striped and well lit. There would be no chewing gum on the sidewalks and no fingerprints on the doors. And when you stepped inside, the store would be brighter, the sight lines would be low with clear airport-type signage. The merchandise would be more fashion-forward and deliver a strong value message. It would be a place that would be a pleasure to shop in with warm, friendly and knowledgeable people and enough of them to help you when you need it.[22]

Floyd Hall was pleased with his management team's efforts and at year-end 1996 predicted that "1997 is going to be a banner year for Kmart and 1998 will be the [company's] biggest growth year."[23]

(Kmart's Web address is *www.kmart.com*)

---

[22]"O.K.mart Now It's Time for Results," *Discount Store News*, December 9, 1996, p. 25.
[23]Ibid.

JOURNEY TO EXCELLENCE: THE RITZ-CARLTON HOTEL IN SYDNEY, AUSTRALIA*

Supryia A. Desai, *University of Virginia*

Elliott N. Weiss, *University of Virginia*

In mid-1993, Alan Leibman, general manager, The Ritz-Carlton Sydney, and Kim Dutton, quality and training manager, reminisced about a recent conversation they had had in Australia at The Bar, the upscale saloon of Mr. Leibman's property:

"You know, Kim, when I first learned what the Malcolm Baldrige Award meant for The Ritz-Carlton Hotel Company, I never dreamed that I might write an application for a similar award in another country, let alone another hemisphere! It just doesn't seem like its been only a year since we won the Baldrige Award in the U.S.," Alan continued as he sipped his Toohey's Beer. "It certainly doesn't seem like only two years since I had my first glimpse of the Sydney Opera House from a QANTAS airplane."

Kim agreed, "Yes, it is pretty amazing. But we have a great story to tell here in Australia. And think about the reaction of our employees and our customers when we win the Australian National Quality Award!"

"What do you mean '*when*'?" exclaimed Alan. "Do you think we're ready to apply for the award? We've come a long way, but do you really think we've progressed far enough on the journey to excellence here?" The general manager pushed further, "Once we've *successfully* implemented the quality

> "I'll take the group of employees I have, put them in any hotel in the world, and they'll give anyone a run for their money. By empowering employees to move heaven and earth, you are guaranteed a very successful operation.
>
> **—Alan Leibman**
> *General Manager, The Ritz-Carlton Sydney, Director of Operations, Australia*

*The authors would like to thank the Citi-Bank Global Scholars Program for providing funding for the writing of this case.

EXHIBIT 1   Ritz-Carlton Hotel Properties, 1993

U.S. Properties	International Properties
The Ritz-Carlton, Amelia Island, Florida (449 rooms)	The Ritz-Carlton, Sydney, Australia (106 rooms)
The Ritz-Carlton, Atlanta, Georgia (447 rooms)	The Ritz-Carlton, Double Bay, Australia (140 rooms)
The Ritz-Carlton, Boston, Massachusetts (278 rooms)	The Ritz-Carlton, Cancun, Mexico (370 rooms)
The Ritz-Carlton, Buckhead, Georgia (553 rooms)	The Ritz-Carlton, Hong Kong (216 rooms)
The Ritz-Carlton, Cleveland, Ohio (207 rooms)	Hotel Arts, Barcelona, Spain (459 rooms)
The Ritz-Carlton, Dearborn, Michigan (308 rooms)	
The Ritz-Carlton, Houston, Texas (232 rooms)	
The Ritz-Carlton, Huntington, California (383 rooms)	
The Ritz-Carlton, Kansas City, Missouri (373 rooms)	
The Ritz-Carlton, Kapalua, Hawaii (550 rooms)	
The Ritz-Carlton, Laguna Niguel, California (393 rooms)	
The Ritz-Carlton, Marina del Rey, California (306 rooms)	
The Ritz-Carlton, Mauna Lani, Hawaii (550 rooms)	
The Ritz-Carlton, Naples, Florida (463 rooms)	
The Ritz-Carlton, New York, New York (214 rooms)	
The Ritz-Carlton, Palm Beach, Florida (220 rooms)	
The Ritz-Carlton, Pentagon City, Virginia (345 rooms)	
The Ritz-Carlton, Philadelphia, Pennsylvania (290 rooms)	
The Ritz-Carlton, Phoenix, Arizona (281 rooms)	
The Ritz-Carlton, Ranch Mirage, California (240 rooms)	
The Ritz-Carlton, St. Louis, Missouri (301 rooms)	
The Ritz-Carlton, San Francisco, California (336 rooms)	
The Ritz-Carlton, Tysons Corner, Virginia (399 rooms)	
The Ritz-Carlton, Washington, D.C. (245 rooms)	

---

program in Australia, then I will know we are ready to apply for the Aussie award! The problem is, how does one decide if implementation has been successful *enough*?"

THE RITZ-CARLTON HOTEL COMPANY

In 1983, W. B. Johnson Properties, of Atlanta, Georgia, acquired exclusive U.S. rights to the Ritz-Carlton name. W. B. Johnson then formed The Ritz-Carlton Hotel Company to develop and operate luxury, five-star hotels and resorts. Ten years later, The Ritz-Carlton Hotel Company operated close to 30 hotels and resorts worldwide catering to the luxury segment of the hotel industry (see Exhibit 1). In 1993, the company also managed nine international sales offices and employed over 12,000 people to deliver service for a 10,000-room luxury hotel company. The sales offices marketed The Ritz-Carlton luxury hotel rooms and meeting space internationally, while individual hotels marketed their own restaurants and banquet facilities locally. The Ritz-Carlton customer was faithful: Since 1989, its business center hotels had retained 97.1 percent of their key local corporate accounts.[1]

---

[1]The Ritz-Carlton Application Summary, Malcolm Baldrige Award, 1992.

Up to the early 1980s, the U.S. luxury hotel industry was fragmented. Most luxury properties were independently owned and operated, leading to inconsistent service and quality across hotels. Corporate and association meetings, a growing segment of the hotel business in the 1980s, found the service and facilities of most independent hotels and resorts unresponsive and outdated. Other resort properties were skilled in representing the locale in which they operated and offered quality service, but were often limited in success by their single location. Leisure travelers generally found hotels inconsistent, expensive, and offering little value added for the high prices. Because of the industry fragmentation, the travel industry's highest standards were not applied consistently across hotels, leaving much to be desired. W. B. Johnson and The Ritz-Carlton identified this gap in the high-end segment of the hotel industry as well as the insufficient quality and service variability that plagued many of the properties. Through ensuing research, The Ritz-Carlton also identified the most important, yet *least* emphasized, quality within a luxury hotel—consistent, highly personalized, and genuinely caring service delivery.[2] Ritz-Carlton executives believed a company that successfully satisfied the demand of this largely ignored segment could be very profitable.

The Ritz-Carlton Hotel Company early on set a goal of distinguishing its hotels as the very best in each of its markets. The company strove to establish a reputation for excellence for its line of hotels that would make The Ritz the industry benchmark. To do so in one of the most logistically complex service businesses in the world required a focused and aggressive service quality program. Components of the ongoing service quality program included participatory executive leadership, thorough information gathering, detailed planning, coordinated execution, and a well-trained workforce.[3] The last dynamic was the most important since the company's ensuing quality and productivity initiatives would not have succeeded without employees being empowered from the beginning.[4]

The Ritz-Carlton's success over the past decade had been the impetus for a not-so-timid expansion plan. In addition to properties in Hong Kong, Spain and Mexico, two Australian hotels, as well as 25 U.S. properties, top management expected the number of The Ritz-Carlton hotels to double by 1996 to 60 properties.[5] Hotels were slated for Indonesia, Tokyo, and Seoul, as well as for domestic U.S. destinations like New Orleans and Orlando. However, Ritz-Carlton executives realized that the company's continued success depended on service excellence as much as, if not more than, growth.

THE RITZ-CARLTON SERVICE AND THE MALCOLM BALDRIGE AWARD

With the luxury hotel industry so fragmented and intensely competitive in the early 1980s, Ritz-Carlton executives recognized the need to develop and capitalize on a unique competitive advantage to succeed. Management decided that The Ritz-Carlton's competitive edge would be delivering the highest level, most consistent,

---

[2]Ibid.

[3]Ibid.

[4]Horst Schulze, "Top Service Every Time," August 14, 1993.

[5]"Of Luxury and Losses: Many Ritz-Carlton's Are Lacking in Profits," *The Wall Street Journal*, April 22, 1994, Section B, p. 1.

EXHIBIT 2   Summary Explanation of Malcolm Baldrige National Quality Award

The Malcolm Baldrige National Quality Awards are made annually to recognize U.S. companies that excel in quality management and quality achievement. Up to two awards may be given in each of three eligibility categories: Manufacturing companies, service companies, and small businesses.

The Award promotes:
- awareness of quality as an increasingly important element in competitiveness,
- understanding of the requirements for quality excellence, and
- sharing of information on successful quality strategies and the benefits derived from implementation of these strategies.

The core values and concepts are embodied in seven categories, as follows:
- Leadership
- Strategic Quality Planning
- Management of Quality Process
- Customer Focus and Satisfaction
- Information and Analysis
- Human Resource Development and Management
- Quality and Operational Results

The Award Criteria are built upon these core values and concepts:
- Customer-driven quality
- Leadership
- Continuous Improvement
- Full participation
- Fast response
- Design quality and prevention
- Long-range outlook
- Management by fact
- Partnership development
- Public responsibility

---

personal service of any hotel chain and an unmatched reputation as a reliable luxury hotel supplier. As The Ritz-Carlton Hotels developed, the company's senior leadership built a system of service delivery capabilities to meet or exceed individual guest expectations, pacify dissatisfied guests, and prevent further dissatisfaction from occurring. The system was predicated on the fundamental principles of Total Quality Management (TQM): customer focus and continuous improvement.

The Ritz-Carlton built its entire hotel management strategy around integrating TQM-based principles into every aspect of its business and every facet of operating its hotels. Processes traditionally implemented in Japanese manufacturing companies were being introduced in all of The Ritz-Carlton hotels long before TQM became a popular management tool in the United States. The result: In 1992, The Ritz-Carlton was the *first* hotel company ever to be awarded the prestigious Malcolm Baldrige Award. The award was created to recognize U.S. companies excelling in quality management and achievement (see Exhibit 2 for Malcolm Baldrige Award explanation).

Horst Schulze, Ritz-Carlton CEO, believed that the process the company had gone through to apply for the Baldrige Award had made the hotel chain's own TQM systems much more effective. The Malcolm Baldrige criteria were part of a "diagnostic" system designed to highlight strengths and areas for improvement. Because the criteria were comprehensive in scope, covering all operations, processes and work units, The Ritz-Carlton was able to refine its own TQM system and identify areas for further improvement. Integrating the core values and concepts of the award into the entire The Ritz-Carlton service quality program enabled the company to learn how to identify pattern problems, resolve them permanently, and measure each hotel's progress in the areas of quality and productivity (see the Ritz-Carlton's 1992 Malcolm Baldrige Award Application in the Appendix).

The veteran quality programs at The Ritz-Carlton were built around Employee Selection, Orientation and Training Certification, New Hotel Quality Assurance, and The Ritz-Carlton Gold Standards. Corporatewide programs included Strategic Quality Planning, Daily Quality Production Reporting, Quality Engineer Certification, and Supplier Certification. The Gold Standards represented The Ritz-Carlton's definition of service quality. The Credo, The Motto, the Three Steps of Service, and The Ritz-Carlton Basics together made up the Gold Standards (see Exhibit 3). The Gold Standards were communicated aggressively during training and were "a way of life" in departments all across the organization. Throughout The Ritz-Carlton Hotel Company, management stressed The Credo: " . . . the genuine care and comfort of our guests is our highest mission." Executives emphasized that strong employee focus on this aspect of The Credo was in harmony with the customer's perception of Ritz-Carlton employees as being "Ladies and Gentlemen Serving Ladies and Gentlemen," as stated in The Motto.[6] Each hotel promoted employee acceptance of the Gold Standards in its own ways, though employee selection and training was the one method all properties used vigorously.

The Ritz-Carlton employee selection, orientation, and training certification processes were acclaimed in the hotel industry for producing well-trained and skilled employees. Employees were informed that they had been "selected, not hired." The selection process included three or more rigorous interviews, even for line positions in the kitchen and housekeeping departments. At both new and already operational hotels, employees underwent orientation in corporate and hotel-specific principles and values. In the 60 days following selection, employees were rigorously trained for job certification. On average, an employee would be engaged in over 100 hours of education during the course of their employment. The result was that 96 percent of employees rated "excellence in guest services" as their highest priority even though 3,000 new employees had recently been added to the company's operations.[7] Through extensive training and selective recruiting practices, The Ritz-Carlton had succeeded in overcoming the notorious problem that plagued most hotel chains: underskilled employees and high employee turnover ratios.

Virtually from the company's inception, each new hotel was opened under the guidance of senior leadership. The famous "seven-day countdown" was part of the New Hotel Quality Assurance program. During that period, Horst Schulze personally communicated The Ritz-Carlton Hotel Company principles during orientation, senior leaders monitored work areas, and Gold Standards were introduced. Contrary to the industry practice of a "progressive opening" during which a hotel opened in phases, each Ritz-Carlton hotel opened fully prepared for business, with each department fully staffed, motivated, and operational.

To supplement these basic quality programs, Ritz-Carlton management continued to develop additional initiatives aimed at providing the highest level of service. The quality effort focused on measuring daily progress. The Daily Quality Production Report identified trends in defects in certain areas of the hotel(s) and by type of recurring defect. For example, room service delivery time (from time of order) was

---

[6]The Ritz-Carlton Gold Standards, The Credo and The Motto.
[7]The Ritz-Carlton Application Summary, Malcolm Baldrige Award, 1992.

EXHIBIT 3   The Gold Standards

The Motto

"We are Ladies and Gentlemen Serving Ladies and Gentlemen."

The Three Steps of Service:

1. A warm and sincere greeting. Use the guest name, if and when possible.
2. Anticipation and compliance with guest needs.
3. Fond farewell. Give them a warm good-bye and use their names, if and when possible.

The Credo

The Ritz-Carlton Hotel is a place where the genuine care and comfort of our guests is our highest mission. We pledge to provide the finest personal service and facilities for our guests who will always enjoy a warm, relaxed yet refined ambience. The Ritz-Carlton experience enlivens the senses, instills well-being, and fulfills even the unexpressed wishes and needs of our guests.

The Ritz-Carlton Basics

1. The Credo will be known, owned and energized by all employees.
2. Our motto is: "We are Ladies and Gentlemen Serving Ladies and Gentlemen." Practice teamwork and "lateral service" to create a positive work environment.
3. The three steps of service shall be practiced by all employees.
4. All employees will successfully complete Training Certification to ensure they understand how to perform to The Ritz-Carlton standards in their position.
5. Each employee will understand their work area and Hotel goals as established in each strategic plan.
6. All employees will know the needs of their internal and external customers (guests and employees) so that we may deliver the products and services they expect. Use guest preference pads to record specific needs.
7. Each employee will continuously identify defects (Mr. BIV) throughout the Hotel.
8. Any employee who receives a customer complaint "owns" the complaint.
9. Instant guest pacification will be ensured by all. React quickly to correct the problem immediately. Follow up with a telephone call within twenty minutes to verify the problem has been resolved to the customer's satisfaction. Do everything you possibly can to never lose a guest.
10. Guest incident action forms are used to record and communicate every incident of guest dissatisfaction. Every employee is empowered to resolve the problem and to prevent a repeat occurrence.
11. Uncompromising levels of cleanliness are the responsibility of every employee.
12. "Smile—We are on stage." Always maintain positive eye contact. Use the proper vocabulary with our guests. (Use words like—"Good Morning," "Certainly," "I'll be happy to" and "My pleasure").
13. Be an ambassador of your Hotel. Always talk positively. No negative comments.
14. Escort guests rather than pointing out directions to another area of the Hotel.
15. Be knowledgeable of Hotel information (hours of operation, etc.) to answer guest inquiries. Always recommend the Hotel's retail and food and beverage outlets prior to outside facilities.
16. Use proper telephone etiquette. Answer within three rings and with a "smile." When necessary, ask the caller, "May I place you on hold." Do not screen calls. Eliminate call transfers when possible.
17. Uniforms are to be immaculate; wear proper and safe footwear (clean and polished), and your correct name tag. Take pride and care in your personal appearance (adhering to all grooming standards).
18. Ensure all employees know their roles during emergency situations and are aware of fire and life safety response processes.
19. Notify your supervisor immediately of hazards, injuries, equipment or assistance that you need. Practice energy conservation and property maintenance and repair of Hotel property and equipment.
20. Protecting the assets of The Ritz-Carlton Hotel is the responsibility of every employee.

constantly measured and analyzed for potential areas for improvement. Progress was also made with hotel suppliers in the Supplier Certification program. The Ritz-Carlton Company created alliances with key suppliers who consistently provided high-quality goods and services.

However, employee involvement and motivation were seen as the keys to the company's success. Employees were encouraged to take responsibility for their positions and for solving problems brought to their attention. Many Ritz-Carlton hotels had developed procedures and techniques to promote employee involvement in problem prevention. Using the information network and building on the company's proven track record in quality service delivery, management had established a long-term goal to become defect-free, have 100 percent customer retention, and reduce cycle time 50 percent by 1996.[8]

Employees at Ritz-Carlton hotels in the United States had unquestionably been successful in helping the company achieve service quality excellence. Once the company began developing and operating international hotels, however, questions arose as to the transferability of Ritz-Carlton's U.S. service quality program to other cultures. Declining occupancy rates and rising operating costs in many international economies, as well as in the United States, added more pressure and constraints. Moreover, the company's financial performance had been hurt in recent years by a worldwide depressed economy.

THE RITZ-CARLTON HOTEL, SYDNEY

In 1993, the Australian economy was slowly recovering from a severe recession that had begun in mid-1990. By the third quarter of 1993, unemployment had reached an all-time high of 11 percent, though GDP grew at a rate of 3 percent between 1992 and 1993, with inflation steady at 2 percent.[9] Despite some tentative signs of improvement, labor-related and productivity problems were impeding a full recovery (see Exhibit 4). In the early 1990s, wages were on average 10 percent higher in Australia than in the United States, and rising 2.5 percent faster than inflation by the end of 1992.[10] It was common practice to grant four-week, paid vacations, often with a 17.5 percent above-normal salary. Weekend and overtime rates were generally higher when compared to other industrialized nations, and 40-hour or fewer work weeks had become the norm because of union lobbying.[11] This especially affected the Australian hotel industry as labor expenses in Australian hotels were a bigger fraction of a hotel's operating budget than the 35–40 percent existing in the United States.[12]

The Sydney hotel industry was not immune to a depressed economy and lagging growth, despite its importance to Australian economic activity. For three years prior, Aussie hotels had been engaged in an all-out discount war. At the end of 1992,

---

[8]Ibid.

[9]"Australia Labor Trends, 1991–1992," United States Department of Labor, Bureau of International Labor Affairs, Foreign Labor Trends and "Australia Unemployment Rate, Civilian Labor, 1993," same source. "Foreign Economic Trends and Their Implications for the United States," U.S. Department of Commerce International Trade Administration, April 1993.

[10]"World Economic Outlook, October 1993," International Monetary Fund and "Country Report, USA, 2nd quarter 1993," The Economist Intelligence Unit.

[11]Ibid.

[12]"Trends in the Hotel Industry," Pannell Kerr Forster, USA Edition 1991.

EXHIBIT 4   Economic Statistics for Australia, 1990–1993

	1990/91	1991/92	1992/93 (Projected)
Population (millions)	17.5	17.5	17.5
Populations growth (%)	1.3	1.2	1.2
Nominal GDP (A$)	378,413	384,871	407,001
Nominal GDP per capita	16,624	16,627	16,556
Real GDP (A$—% change)	– 0.8	0.4	3.0
Consumer Price Index (% change)	5.4	1.9	2.1
Gov't. budget balance (% of GDP)	0.5	– 2.4	– 3.3
Labor force (000's)	8,522	8,573	8,650
Unemployment rate (avg. %)	8.4	10.4	10.5
Tourism receipts/expenditures (A$)	19,000	19,769	19,800

"Foreign Economic Trends and Their Implications for the United States," U.S. Department of Commerce, International Trade Administration, April 1993.

Australia had the cheapest luxury (five-star) hotel room rates in the world. Images of guests walking into five-star properties and bargaining for room rates made Australian hoteliers nervous. As long as the domestic economy lagged, so would profitability of Australian hotels since poor domestic performance was not being offset by overseas business. Competition had developed in other nearby destinations such as the Far East, Los Angeles, and Hawaii. Lower airfares and greater value made these locations increasingly attractive for business travelers, who made up 60 percent of Australian hotel business. With travel and tourism revenues going elsewhere, Australia entered into the same situation that plagued the American hotel industry in the recent years: oversupply of hotel rooms, guerrilla-type discount price wars, and a depressed economy. In particular, the supply/demand mismatch was caused by overly optimistic occupancy rate and demand projections by industry forecasters in the late 1980s.

In spite of the economic situation in Australia, The Ritz-Carlton Hotel, Sydney continued to display the luxurious excellence for which the company was renowned. Situated in the heart of Sydney's business district and opened in August 1990, the hotel served affluent corporate, convention, and leisure guests. Luxurious appointments and top-of-the-line facilities gave the Sydney property its signature Ritz-Carlton status. Competition came from other downtown luxury hotels such as The Park Hyatt and the Regent. There were 9 other hotels in downtown Sydney and another 15 hotels of competitive significance outside the downtown area.

In January 1993, Alan Leibman was appointed general manager of The Ritz-Carlton Sydney Hotel. Leibman's self-described "vibrant" personality was seen by many colleagues as a key to the future success of a hotel one writer called "so exclusive, [it] had no guests."[13] In light of the fiercely competitive Australian hotel industry, Leibman was charged with increasing productivity, quality, and profitability, while controlling costs. The market had become increasingly demanding and more knowledgeable about hotel quality. Those luxury hotels that chose to cut services and

[13]"Macquarie Street Maverick," *Australian Magazine*, July 1993.

EXHIBIT 5   Article Excerpts about Alan Leibman and The Ritz-Carlton Sydney

The *Australian Jewish News*, "Life at the Ritz," March 12, 1993, p. 1:

"He started at the bottom washing pots. Now he is Director of Operations Australia for The Ritz-Carlton Hotel Company and General Manager of The Ritz-Carlton Sydney. And he is only 26. Alan Leibman is the youngest general manager of a five star hotel in Sydney, if not Australia.

"Leibman said he loves hotels and is passionate about people and servicing guests properly. 'I want top hotels with a wonderful environment for employees to thrive in,' he said."

Australian Magazine, "Macquarie Street Maverick," Deirdre Blayney, July 1993, p. 8:

"Alan Leibman firmly believes that a hotel takes on the personality of it general manager. He describes his own as "vibrant," which augurs well for The Ritz-Carlton, Sydney.

" . . . he says service is still the key. 'I think we're going to have to become superior at service. The Australian consumer is a lot more educated now about what good service is and understands that they've got buying power. I think you'd better, *every* time, deliver what you're promising the guest.' "

Asian Hotelier, "Step One: Ask the Guests," Alan Leibman, 1993, p. 16:

"The success of The Ritz-Carlton Sydney [I] attribute to the ladies and gentlemen who run the hotel, who stuck through the tough times and listened to the customer, took it all in and said we are going to make this a unique experience.

"It is also important that we continue to energize our people, and that we continue with ongoing training. It is very important to make sure people are trained, not just in the technical side of things. We must make sure that continuous education takes place."

quality to remain profitable soon found themselves without the niche clientele they sought. To top it all off, three new five-star properties, totalling 1,200 new rooms, were slated to open in Sydney during the first half of 1993.

Although he was The Ritz-Carlton Hotel Company's youngest general manager and corporate director, Leibman's past experiences in the hotel industry, and in Australia, made him aware of the need for an effective management team to successfully implement The Ritz-Carlton service quality program in Australia (see Exhibit 5 for article excerpts about Leibman). Along with an Executive Committee of eight, he created an Australian strategy for service quality based on the success he had witnessed with The Ritz-Carlton hotels in the U.S. (see Exhibit 6 for the hotel's organization chart). Having recognized the profit potential in repeat and domestic business, Leibman also began shifting Sydney's *marketing* focus to the Australian guest, and the *employee* focus to improved productivity and quality. This was exactly in line with The Ritz-Carlton Hotel Company's efforts to establish a competitive advantage for its U.S. hotels.

Though The Ritz-Carlton Sydney was expected to achieve a level of service consistent with Ritz-Carlton properties worldwide, it operated in a cultural environment much different from the United States and Australian workers had a different lifestyle and work ethic. Many of the service quality programs implemented at Ritz-Carlton hotels in the United States could only be initiated in Australia with modifications and a unique understanding of the challenges to be encountered.

THE QUALITY PROGRAM DOWN UNDER

Alan Leibman recognized that the programs implemented by The Ritz-Carlton Sydney would not be successful without employee "buy in." In order to gain employee

EXHIBIT 6   Organization Chart, The Ritz-Carlton Hotel, Sydney, Australia

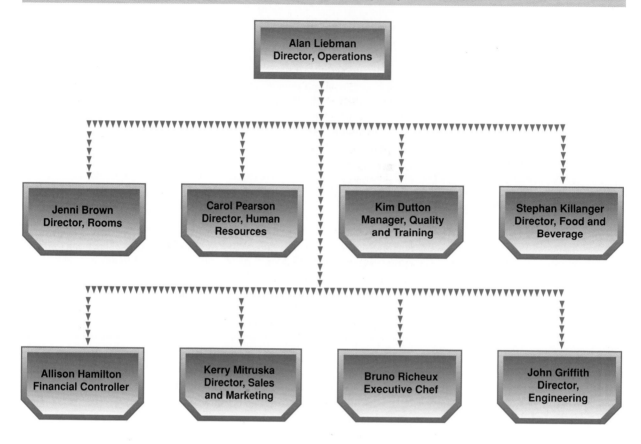

support for the necessity of quality programs, Leibman spent considerable time making employees feel part of the organization and empowering them:

> We used a lot of what we have done for the Baldrige as far as making sure that [the employees] felt part of the organization, that they were making decisions, that there was absolute empowerment—that you were not paying lip service to empowerment. Once they saw that, and they saw that you were pushing and giving to them, and that they were sharing their successes with you, [they felt part of the organization] . . . You have got to go out there and understand what makes the housekeeper tick, you have got to understand what makes the doormen tick. We did that, and I instilled that all the way through to my executives, as well, which is very much what we are about at The Ritz-Carlton: understanding our people and what motivates them.

Leibman found there were distinct cultural differences between Australian employees and their U.S. counterparts. Australian employees were typically less apt to buy "hype" than American workers. To successfully engage sincere "buy-in," an Australian manager had to be straightforward and open. In order to successfully manage the employees and achieve The Ritz-Carlton level quality, Leibman found it necessary to reassess the American-based company's attitude toward doing business in an international setting. His first instinct had been to manage the hotel and its employees as though it were an American hotel with American employees. "We didn't handle it well in the beginning. We came out here as many American companies do and said, 'Ah, they speak English—must just be like doing business in the States.' It's different."[14] He had to ensure employees and customers that The Ritz-Carlton planned to do business in Australia in an Australian way. This change in management style involved what Leibman describes as "softening" the traditional U.S. approach taken with employees. He spent a great deal of time talking one-to-one with employees and promoted an "open door" policy. Leibman also capitalized on the hotel's quality and training manager, Kim Dutton, who had been there since December 1991. She was familiar with Australian employees, and their tendencies to be less self-motivated, and more focused on personal relationships than Americans. Together, Leibman and Dutton tailored The Ritz-Carlton service quality program to the Australian culture, and developed motivational and productivity-improvement programs designed with their values in mind. The Ritz-Carlton Hotel Company's service quality program was officially introduced in the Sydney property immediately preceding Leibman's arrival, in June 1992. While highlighting his emphatic commitment to The Ritz-Carlton service quality program, Leibman simultaneously made some changes in the organization.

The Ritz-Carlton Sydney employed over 230 people when Leibman came on board. Because labor costs were so much higher in Australia than in the United States, Leibman had to reduce the work force by 100 and create a "lateral" service organization. Employees were asked to assume greater responsibility: Doormen often assisted front office clerks or other "front of the house" staff. With a depressed economy and a leaner staff, management at The Ritz-Carlton Sydney had to integrate staff to a greater extent in solving problems in order to maintain a high level of employee motivation and involvement.

During her years with the Australian Ritz-Carlton operations, Kim Dutton realized that problems needed to be prevented, not fixed. With that in mind, Dutton and Leibman created programs and motivated employees to use these programs to improve the hotel's performance in problem identification, resolution, and prevention. They also realized that Australian employees worked differently from their American counterparts, and all programs would not be received as enthusiastically as they had been in the United States. Dutton therefore targeted quality improvement programs for selected areas, instead of introducing a multitude of problem-solving teams, or quality programs at once.

One example of this plan was the self-inspecting housekeeping process. By eliminating room inspection by senior managers, housekeepers became accountable for their work. Responsibility for guest praise and complaints rested with the housekeeper. When Leibman first became general manager, supervisors would extol the virtues of employee empowerment while double-checking a housekeeper's work. The irony in this was quickly identified and addressed through the self-inspecting housekeeping initiative. Initial results were promising: Hotel guests found their rooms were cleaner, and housekeeping staff felt ownership of their job. However, the significant increase in direct responsibility eventually highlighted the need for further training for housekeepers before a self-inspecting program could be completely implemented.

Management also began to circulate hotel profit and loss statements among employees. The objectives in sharing nonpublic financial information with staff were to create

---

[14]"Macquarie Street Maverick," *Australian Magazine*, July 1993, p. 8.

EXHIBIT 7   Internal Defects Report, Sample Form

Your Name: _____

Your Department: _____

Date: _____

What problems or conditions are interfering with your job or with guest satisfaction (i.e. facilities, services, time, training, supplies, security, purchasing)?

PROBLEM: (Be specific as to the date, time and location)

POSSIBLE CAUSE:

RECOMMENDED SOLUTION:

How often does this problem occur? _____ times a day / week / month

****

Received: _____
Followed up: _____
Followed up: _____
Followed up: _____

24–48–30 Rule:

When you complete an Internal Defect Report, within 24 hours an executive committee member will get back with you and thank you for filling out the defect report; he/she will acknowledge that it was received. Within 48 hours a decision will be made as to how the defect can be dealt with. In 30 days, the Quality Leader will follow up to see if the solution is working and/or check on the status of the team's progress with the solution.

---

an opportunity for employees to better understand management's decision-making process, involve employees in the hotel's progress, and create a deeper sense of responsibility. Employees began to prioritize requests based on their order of importance, and developed a clearer understanding of how their actions affected both costs and the bottom line.

Leibman's team also implemented the popular self-managed work team program, which had rapidly become commonplace in most U.S. Ritz-Carlton hotels. For the most part, Australian workers had successfully adapted to this new style of management. However, some employees requested to return to a "supervisor structure" to reduce administrative responsibilities for staff. Employees typically felt that these tasks consumed too much of their time. Management decided to reassess the components of the self-managed work team program that seemed to conflict with the Australian work ethic.

Internal Defect Reports (IDR) were another means of raising employee awareness to increasing problem prevention efforts. IDR's were created to solve the problems initiated by recurring *m*istakes, *r*eworks, *b*reakdowns, *i*nefficiencies, or *v*ariation (Mr. BIV). Employees were trained in the definition of a "recurring problem" and why it was so important to eliminate such complexities. Once an employee identified a "Mr.

EXHIBIT 8   The Daily Quality Production Report

The DQPR is a report that shows the amount of quality the Hotel produces every day. The DQPR itemizes the number of guests registered in the Hotel, the number of guests serviced in our Food & Beverage outlets and the number of defects or problems that were experienced throughout the day with both our external customers (guests) and our internal customers (employees or departments we work with in the Hotel). The DQPR pinpoints opportunities to improve our products or services by showing us what is going wrong, where it's going wrong, and how often. We can then act upon this knowledge and correct problems which will, in turn, improve our services and products and enable the Hotel to become more successful.

Sources of Information for the Daily Quality Production Report includes:

- Guest Incident Action Forms
- F & B Captain's Reports
- Missing Items Report
- Meeting Planner Evaluations
- Guest Complaint Letters
- Engineering Log Sheets

- Accounting Information
- Housekeeping logs
- Concierge Call Sheets
- Guest Complaint Calls
- Internal Defect Reports

- All Log Books
- MOD Log Book
- Comped checks
- Comment Cards
- Security Reports

Daily Quality Production Report Formula for measurement of quality production:

Number of occupied rooms
+ Food & beverage covers   = Total production
− Guest complaints   − Internal customer complaints   = **Total Quality Production**

BIV," he or she would fill out an IDR and submit it to Kim Dutton. IDRs were subsequently integrated into the Daily Quality Production Report, which was reviewed by the Executive Committee every other day. Exhibit 7 shows an example of an Internal Defect Report, and some training material that accompanied it when distributed to employees.

Though 526 IDRs were submitted between 1992 and 1993, there were two main problems with the program. First, Australian employees felt uncomfortable with the program because of the sense of "snitching" on a fellow employee. Second, a follow-up system, which was created to ensure that the Mr. BIV problem was permanently corrected, proved unmanageable in the Australian operations. With responsibility for the service quality programs at two hotels, Dutton was not always able to comply with the "24-48-30" follow-up rule (see Exhibit 7). Though IDRs became an invaluable source of information for hotel management, the Executive Committee reviewed IDRs every *other* day and poor administration of the program may have caused some recurring problems to go unrecognized.

Daily Quality Production Reporting became an essential tool in measuring the progress that was being made through these programs (Exhibit 8). The report identified strengths and weaknesses in hotel processes in over 20 divisions and departments within the Sydney hotel. This comprehensive summary of progress in service quality was an effective management tool in assessing the success of quality improvement programs.

Management actively used information systems to support its efforts to increase efficiency and lower costs while providing the highest quality service. Computer tracking systems were used to monitor human and telephone traffic. The information generated assisted management in scheduling the smaller number of employees more resourcefully. Because Leibman had cut the workforce at the Sydney property, it was

EXHIBIT 9   The Good Ideas Board

Within each department, there is a "Good Ideas Board" upon which employees can write down and track their ideas or suggestions for improvements. These boards are the responsibility of each department and it is up to the individuals in each department to think of and follow up on their ideas. The employee(s) who have an idea own that idea. It is up to the employee who generated the idea to act on and follow up on the idea. Ideas are suggestions for making the department or the hotels run more efficiently, operate more effectively, reduce waste, generate greater profits, or improve morale. The notion is that "NO idea is too big and no idea is too small. There are no stupid ideas." Every month each department votes on a "Departmental Idea of the Month" and turns it in to the Quality Department. Those ideas are then taken to the managers weekly meeting and one "Hotel Idea of the Month" is voted on and sent to our corporate office. All Hotels' ideas are then shared throughout the company. The communal sharing of ideas and lessons learned benefits the entire organization. This sort of shared learning also makes for a stronger and more cohesive organization.

imperative that service not falter because of a lower employee-to-guest ratio. The famous Ritz-Carlton guest history database proved to be a valuable tool for providing the highest level of service quality. When special requests were made at any of The Ritz-Carlton Hotels, that information was entered into the computer. Customer preference data was accessible at all properties internationally via the computer network. "If a guest requested Johnson's Baby Shampoo during their stay at the Ritz-Carlton in Sydney . . . when they check in to The Ritz-Carlton Hong Kong five years later, they'll have Johnson's Baby Shampoo waiting for them in the shower."[15]

Dutton also managed a unique productivity improvement and employee involvement program called the "Good Ideas Board" (Exhibit 9). Over 700 ideas had been submitted by hotel employees for management consideration in just one year. Because of the novelty of the Good Ideas program, and the lack of familiarity with this type of an initiative by Australians, Dutton worked hard to encourage employees to share ideas and suggestions. She taught principles of idea ownership and encouraged employees to take responsibility for and act on their ideas. The Good Ideas Board reflected The Ritz-Carlton Sydney's commitment to employee involvement in hotel operations.

From the beginning, Leibman felt it was imperative to return to the internal customer and start listening to their comments. Employees were encouraged to submit suggestions for improvement based on their knowledge of the native Australian's preferences. Soliciting a high level of input from employees not only benefitted guest service but operational costs as well. Leibman offered examples of employees who, by their own resolve, researched alternative purchases to save $30,000–40,000 on glassware and $3,500 on envelopes. Leibman believed many other costs could be reduced or modified as necessary as hotel operations became more tailored to target market preferences.

---

[15]"Step One: Ask the Guests," *Asian Hotelier.*

The most important element of success, according to Leibman, was employee empowerment. Despite Australia's cultural differences and the merits of tailoring company practices and procedures to fit local circumstances, the results still had to come out the same: an exceptionally high and consistent level of service. One-to-one and roundtable discussions were part of the employee interaction that resulted in increased communication, greater understanding, and, eventually, more authority on the part of employees. Employee recognition and promotions became an integral part of the human resources process at Sydney. When promotions were not possible, it was felt that increased employee involvement and fulfillment would offset whatever financial constraints prevented the hotel from financially rewarding employees. Once employees took greater interest in their jobs, and assumed more responsibility for the results of their work, hotel performance indeed improved significantly. In 1993, The Ritz-Carlton Sydney boasted the highest occupancy rate among all Sydney hotels, with repeat business accounting for over 30 percent of the total.

Leibman believed the Sydney property had successfully implemented corporate principles and values in establishing uncompromising service traditional of The Ritz-Carlton hotel chain, while improving the financial performance of the hotel. Leibman felt more confident in his employees' ability to compete internationally and with other Ritz-Carlton employees worldwide.

THE AUSTRALIAN NATIONAL QUALITY AWARD AND ITS IMPLICATIONS

Alan Leibman was proud of the progress The Ritz-Carlton Sydney had made to date, but he had some doubts about the hotel's position on service quality and TQM systems relative to the other Ritz-Carlton Hotels. As he reviewed the stringent criteria for the Australian Quality Award, similar to those of the Baldrige Award, several questions ran through his mind. The Ritz-Carlton Hotel Company applied for the Malcolm Baldrige Award after eight years of business operation. Was it possible, after only a few months as general manager, for Leibman to consider having Ritz-Carlton Sydney become an applicant for the Australian Quality Award?

Achievements of the Sydney hotel were impressive. Through employee satisfaction surveys, performance evaluations, Phase II of Orientation (follow-up and feedback), roundtable discussions, divisional and departmental meetings, and Daily Quality Production Reports, Leibman was certain that employee morale, motivation and performance had improved significantly (Exhibit 10). Productivity, as measured by P&L statements, payroll cost per occupied room, serving time in restaurants, and other performance measurements had risen rapidly as employees of The Ritz-Carlton Sydney seemed to adjust relatively well to a new style of management and service quality programs. The Ritz-Carlton's training program ensured that employees were motivated by improved service, performance and productivity. But, was all this good enough?

Why had some productivity improvement programs flourished, while other employee involvement initiatives faltered in Australia? Given Australia's progress to date, were companywide goals of Six Sigma quality, 100 percent customer retention, and 50 percent cycle time reduction by 1996 realistic for the Australian operations? How would Leibman further motivate and involve his employees to reach the much greater goal of 100 percent defect-free operations?

EXHIBIT 10   Quotes from Employees of The Ritz-Carlton Sydney

They have allowed me to transfer and explore . . . gain experience in a variety of departments in different areas of the Hotel. This allows me to develop a range of skills and an understanding of the interactions of the various departments in the Hotel. It has showed me how everything works together and has the potential to impact the guest.

—Martina Lyons, Executive Reservations and Group Coordinator

My growth through the Hotel Company has been constant. Within a three-year period, I have moved from a Group Sales Manager at Double Bay [resort] to a Director of Sales & Marketing for both Hotels, to handling projects for the Asia-Pacific region. Reaffirms our commitment to promotion from within and challenging the employees.

—Kerry Mitruska, Director of Sales & Marketing

The Hotel is very flexible and continuously tries to keep ahead of the competition. The environment is positive and I like this because it makes my work more interesting, challenging, and it helps me to grow and improve my skills.

—Marike Ciarns, Administrative Assistant in Human Resources

Developed as an individual, taking on more responsibility which has improved my working and personal life.

—Margaret Best, Human Resources Manager

APPENDIX: SUMMARY OF MALCOLM BALDRIGE AWARD APPLICATION FOR THE RITZ-CARLTON HOTEL COMPANY

The Ritz-Carlton Chronology of Quality

Genesis–1983	Travel Industry and Customer Survey Research
	New Hotel Start-Up Quality Assurance
	The Ritz-Carlton Gold Standards
1988	Employee Selection, Orientation and Training Certification
1989	The Ritz-Carlton Daily Line-Up Meeting
	Baldrige Audits
	Strategic Quality Planning
	Hotel Quality Assurance
	Cost of Quality
	Daily Quality Production Reporting
	Quality Engineer Certification
1992	Supplier Certification
1993	Business Management System
	Six Sigma
	50% Cycle Time Reduction
1996	100% Customer Retention

Leadership

At The Ritz-Carlton, the senior leadership group doubles as the senior quality committee. The senior leaders personally devised the two original quality strategies to broaden the quality leadership of The Ritz-Carlton. The first course of action was new hotel start-up quality assurance. The other initial course of action was the establishment of our Gold Standards. The Gold Standards, in their simplicity, represent an easy-to-understand definition of service quality. Companywide, employees are devoted to our organization's principles.

Lessons Learned: When senior leaders personally instill a strong vision and a set of principles in their employees and then given them the confidence, freedom and authority to act, people take responsibility for their jobs and do whatever is necessary to satisfy their customers.

Information and Analysis

Our approach to capture and use customer satisfaction and quality-related data is real time and proactive because of our intensive personalized service environment. Systems for the collection and utilization of customer reaction and satisfaction are widely deployed and extensively used throughout the organization. Our efforts are centered on various customer segments and product lines. Our approach is the use of systems which allow every employee to collect and utilize quality-related data on a daily basis. These systems provide critical, responsive data which includes: (1) online guest preference information; (2) quantity of error-free products and services; (3) opportunities for quality improvement. Today, the goal of our business management system is to become more integrated, more proactive, and more preventive. The quality, marketing, and financial results of each hotel are aggregated and integrated to determine what quality factors are driving the financial outcome.

Lessons Learned: We needed immediate responses from listening posts, combined with systems accessible to all, just to keep pace with ever-changing individual customer demands.

Strategic Quality Planning

Our primary objective, during our genesis period, was opening new hotels that met the highest travel industry quality ratings by opening day. This required detailed planning and was achieved through our preopening control plan. This continuously improving plan synchronizes all steps leading up to opening day. Today, the quality plan continues to be the business plan. The primary objectives are to improve the quality of our products and services, reduce cycle time, and improve price value and customer retention. At each level of the company—from corporate leaders to managers and employees in the 720 individual work areas of our company—teams are charged with setting objectives and devising action plans, which are reviewed by the corporate steering committee. As we move forward, our plans are based on clear quality and customer satisfaction priorities. All plans center on directing the resources of The Ritz-Carlton—time, money, and people—to the wishes and needs of our guests and travel planners, as well as employees.

Lessons Learned: Action plans developed by each level of the organization must be screened to ensure they (1) have been adequately researched, (2) have been adequately resourced, (3) contain no complexity before they are undertaken.

Human Resources Utilization

A most important resource in any organization is the people. This is especially true in a growing quality organization that provides highly personalized, genuinely caring service to a demanding, prestigious travel consumer. Our commitment to planning and to realizing the full potential of our people begins with our selection process. Once a hotel is open, the training manager and senior hotel executives work as an orientation team, over a period of two days, to personally demonstrate our Gold Standards and methods and to instill these values in all new employees. The next gate review is the responsibility of the work area leader and their department trainer. The new employees undergo a comprehensive training period to master the procedures of the position. Through these and other mechanisms, employees receive over 100 hours of quality education to foster premium service commitment, solve problems, set strategic quality plans, and generate new ideas.

Lessons Learned: A collective quality commitment must be gained from the entire workforce. There is no substitute for selecting employees who believe in the organization's values.

Management of Process Quality

Since The Ritz-Carlton is primarily a professional hotel management company, quality assurance most often begins with a private developer interested in creating a high-quality hotel project in appealing, diverse travel destinations. Our process for assuring the quality of our new hotel products and services has evolved over eight years of benchmarking, development, and improvement. Our product management process has three integral parts: interactive team pyramid, basic product management process, and regional product management process. All new hotel development issues and problems are resolved prior to initial customer occupancy while teams from operating hotels improve the entire process. There are 8 mechanisms used solely to improve the quality of poor processes, products and services: (1) New Hotel Start-Up Improvement Process, (2) Comprehensive Performance Evaluation Process, (3) Quality Network, (4) Standing Problem-Solving Team, (5) Quality Improvement Teams, (6) Strategic Quality Planning, (7) Streamlining Process, and (8) Process Improvement. To make sure we deliver quality products and services, The Ritz-Carlton continually conducts both self audits and outside audits.

Lessons Learned: New products and services that get off to a good start are most reliable and efficient. The major thrust of our quality effort is to prevent difficulties from ever reaching a customer.

Quality and Operational Results

The Ritz-Carlton compares its quality levels with the best competitive products and services in the U.S. and in the world. We subscribe to the services of independent travel and hospitality professionals and rating organizations. The quality performance criteria of these organizations includes over 100 specific quality measurements. Within the past six years, The Ritz-Carlton is the consistent benchmark for quality hotel products and services in the U.S.

Lesson Learned: Never underestimate the value of even 1 idea or quality improvement effort.

Customer Satisfaction

Customer satisfaction is a deeply held belief at The Ritz-Carlton and begins with an absolute understanding of the needs and expectations of our customers. Customer information is gathered in a variety of ways, both internal and external. We integrate customer satisfaction and other quality-related data into our business management system. We make it simple for our customers to voice their needs and expectations to The Ritz-Carlton. When customers do have complaints, we use a customer management system that is largely driven by employees, not managers. At The Ritz-Carlton, our goal is 100% complaint resolution prior to guest departure. Our major method for assessing customer satisfaction has been our guest and travel planner satisfaction system. The objective of our quality effort is: *never lose a single customer*.

ACER COMPUTER PRODUCTS (TAIWAN): SHORTENING THE PRODUCT DEVELOPMENT CYCLE*

Jean-Francois Tremblay, *University of Western Ontario*

John R. Kennedy, *University of Western Ontario*

It was 8:30 P.M. on August 1, 1993, and Brian Chong, Rich Huang, and Jackson Lin, managers in the Product Management department of Acer's Portable Products Division in Taipei, were still at work. Acer wanted to speed up development of new notebook computers by five months, and the trio had been asked to outline problems that should be resolved beforehand. Simon Lin, president of Acer's Computer Products Business Unit, awaited their report the following day.

"It's a good report, but we haven't recommended anything," commented Lin. "Maybe we should just let Simon handle it. They'll probably ask for our input anyway before making any decisions. Our report is quite comprehensive," said Huang.

"Why don't we leave it as is? I have a long drive before getting back home and I have to prepare for my trip to the U.S. the day after," said Chong. "Simon will tell us whether he likes it so far, and if so will tell us to draft the recommendations."

TAIWAN'S COMPUTER INDUSTRY

Ever since the introduction of the IBM PC in 1981, Taiwan-based firms had been highly successful at providing quality, feature-packed, personal computers and peripherals. Taiwan's traditional strengths were ideally suited to the characteristics of the PC industry. Initially, Taiwan's lower wage rates and labor costs played a central role in Taiwan's competitiveness. However, with the appreciation of the NT$[1] in the late 1980s, other factors took on a larger importance. Taiwan had an ample supply of experienced electronics engineers and technicians highly qualified in the design of PC components, PCs, monitors, pointing devices, and other computer-related hardware. Moreover, since Taiwanese companies tended to be small and flexible, they were able to react swiftly to meet fast-changing market requirements. Taiwan computer companies were also able to maintain their overheads at 10 percent of the overall cost of operations; this gave them a considerable cost advantage over companies from other countries that operated with more bureaucratic cost structures.

As demand for PCs and related products increased in the 1980s, Taiwan gained a central position in the worldwide chain of supply for information technology (IT) hardware. In 1993, the island produced 70 percent of the world's PC motherboards, almost half of the monitors, nearly all of the world's handheld-scanners, and with 30 percent of total output, was the third largest producer of notebook computers. Almost all of the world's computer companies sourced a substantial portion of their hardware from Taiwan.

By 1993, Taiwan possessed a valuable pool of human talent skilled in the rapid development of IT hardware. In addition, the suppliers' infrastructure—foreign as well as domestic—and subcontractors could provide anything from a PC casing to an application-specific integrated circuit at prices more attractive than anywhere else. Any component or part necessary for the making of computer products could be manufactured faster in Taiwan than almost anywhere else in the world. And because of its market weight, Taiwan benefited from a very high level of service from worldwide suppliers. Only in the case of severe worldwide shortages of key components (i.e., LCDs DRAMs, CPUs) did Taiwan companies see their supply rationed based on the magnitude of their needs. However, Taiwan's largest computer companies were sufficiently resourceful to weather any component shortage.

ACER INC.

By 1993, Acer sales had reached over US$1.7 billion. The company manufactured a broad array of products, either as components or consumer goods. These included motherboards, PCs and notebooks, monitors, pointing devices, keyboards, multiuser UNIX-based systems, LANs and other communications devices, fax machines, multimedia systems, laser printers, Asics[2], and even DRAMs. Typically, Acer's end-user products came in a wide range of models, with many different options and configurations. Its computers could be equipped with different microprocessors running at various speeds, and fitted with either monochrome or color screens of various degrees of sophistication. In addition, customers could order a keyboard in virtually any language.

Acer had been founded in 1976 with US$25,000 in capital. In a previous company, the founder and CEO, Stan Shih, had directed the development of Taiwan's first pen-watch. He had also managed Taiwan's largest manufacturer of calculators.

---

[1]One US dollar could be traded for 40 New Taiwan dollars (NT$) in the early 1980s. In 1993, the NT$ had appreciated to one US$ yielding only 25NT$.

[2]Asic stands for application specific integrated circuit. An Asic is a chip that can do the work of several chips, as it has been designed to perform a dedicated task. Using Asic chips on electronic boards allows the R&D staff to keep costs down without sacrificing performance. Acer designed its own Asic chips, which it also sold to other Taiwanese manufacturers.

From the outset, Acer had given a high priority to product development; in 1976, the company had devoted about 60 percent of its initial capital to the purchase of R&D equipment. Since then, the company had grown fast. It had pioneered several computer technologies, the most important of which was bilingual systems (Chinese-English). It had also obtained several contracts for OEM[3] production from companies such as Texas Instruments, Unisys, and Apple. Shih's overall strategy for Acer often appeared confusing; the company usually explained that Shih was a fervent player of the ancient game of GO. According to company mythology, Acer did business the same way GO is played. (See Exhibit 1 for an explanation of the game.)

Stan Shih was not a "hands-on" manager. He was more of a visionary leader providing a constant supply of goals and dreams for Acer and Taiwan. As the chairman and CEO of what was referred to as Taiwan's largest computer company (Tatung disputed the title), Shih had a flamboyant style and was famous for his analogies full of imagery. He was seen as one of the leaders in the emergence of Taiwan's computer industry. He had written three books that had sold well among Taiwan's ambitious young people. He saw the future of Taiwan as that of a high-tech island. Like many Taiwanese growing up in the postwar years, Shih had seen and participated in the Taiwan economic "miracle"; in 40 years, Taiwan had risen from wretched poverty to become one of the largest trading nations in the world. For Shih, no goal was too great or too distant to be deemed unreachable. He encouraged his employees to think that way.

Acer was a well-known brand in many countries. It was among the top three players in Taiwan, South Africa, Singapore, Thailand, Malaysia, Chile, among others. Unlike other Taiwanese companies, Acer spent millions of dollars promoting itself around the world. Still, the company was falling far short of its goal of making the Acer brand one of the three top PC brands in North America and Europe.

Among industry insiders in the U.S. and Europe, it was well-known that Acer products were generally well-designed, well-built, and that Acer was, of the world's large PC companies, among the fastest to introduce new products based on new technologies. Its products often received positive reviews in trade magazines. The company was a frequent recipient of awards from Taiwan's Ministry of External Trade. In 1989, Acer had been among the first companies to come up with a PC based on Intel's 80386 CPU running at 33MHz; the unit was later selected for an Editor's Choice award by the influential *PC Magazine* in the United States. More recently, Acer had licensed its ChipUp technology to Intel. The owner of a PC built with a ChipUp motherboard could upgrade to a faster CPU simply by replacing the CPU on the motherboard. The system automatically reconfigured itself to match the faster microprocessor.

In 1993, Acer derived about 40 percent of its revenues from OEM/ODM business. This meant that the company also produced items as diverse as Apple's PowerBook and Canon's new notebook computer with built-in printer. By 1993, Acer had three factories in Taiwan, one in Malaysia, and assembly units in the Netherlands, the USA, Germany, Brazil, Mexico, and several other locations. In 1991, Acer had purchased a U.S. company called Altos, one of the continent's leading manufacturers of multiuser systems. And since 1991, through a joint venture with Texas Instruments, Acer had operated a highly profitable foundry producing 4MB DRAM chips.

---

[3]OEM meant that Acer manufactured products for a client who then sold them under its own brandname. ODM (original design manufacturing) meant that Acer also provided the design of the product as well as the manufacturing.

EXHIBIT 1   Acer and the Game of GO

To understand how five entrepreneurs parlayed $25,000 in 1976 into a worldwide, billion-dollar enterprise, one needs to have a basic knowledge of the ancient Chinese game of GO or "wei-chi." The Mother of all board games, GO developed over several millennia in China. It is similar to the Western game of chess, but requires far more patience and long-term strategies. Since day one, the founders of Acer have uniquely applied the strategies of GO to Acer's business, so much so that GO is reflected in nearly every move Acer has made in its 15 years.

The key buzzword in any game of GO is "long-term." Players must be in for the long haul, or not at all. This has clearly been the hallmark of Acer's business strategies.

GO is played on a 19 line by 19 grid. Players alternately place black and white stones at any of the 361 intersection points on the board. The general objective is to render sections of the board inaccessible to your opponent; the player who controls the most territory when the stones are used up is the winner.

A successful GO players tests his skills in four important strategies of the game. These are "chang chi," or the ability to sustain one's vitality; "hyo yen" (or living eyes), the setting up of strongholds, (e.g. independent, profitable business units) from which to advance; and "huo shih," or the strategy of self-strengthening through strategic alliances. Players spend much of their time in the initial stages preparing for the "bu ju," or setting of the stage for the final victory. Once all the elements are in place, the player with the most successful "bu ju" (strategic preparation) can grab a winning amount of territory (market share).

In September 1991, Acer Chairman and CEO Stan Shih declared that "all the systems are now Go" for Acer to make its move to achieve its corporate mission of becoming a top-five player in the PC industry. Hence the GO strategy theme for The Acer Group in 1991.

From Acer 1991 Annual Report, page 3.

Aside from manufacturing, Acer was also involved in publishing, trading, and owned its distribution channels in Taiwan.

Worldwide distribution of Acer brandname products was done primarily through qualified distributors. Almost from the start, this had been the company's preferred channel. Acer was keen to maintain good relations with its distributors; it perceived them as the gateway to the highly diversified markets in which Acer competed. There were wide differences between countries. For instance, Germany required state-of-the-art machines that met some fairly stringent, government-mandated environment regulations. Meanwhile, countries such as Lithuania or the Philippines cared essentially about price. Acer was usually anxious to be among the first companies to enter new country markets. Recently, efforts had been focused on penetrating the markets of Eastern Europe and Indochina.

In 1992, Acer's top management felt that the company was becoming too complex to manage. Moreover, it felt that the staff was losing the energy and motivation which had led Acer to consistently achieve growth rates of over 100 percent for the first 10 years of its existence. In the 1991 fiscal year, Acer had incurred the first loss since it was founded. As a result, the company's management had laid off 400 employees, 8 percent of its Taiwan workforce at the time. It was later decided to split Acer into 10 Business Units (BUs), operating as independent profit centers. Later on, some of these BUs were to become independent companies listed on the stock market. See Exhibit 2 for the Acer Group's 1993 organizational chart.

DECISION MAKING AT ACER

The decision-making process at Acer was informal, but followed a consistent pattern. A major change was usually the result of extensive discussions among large numbers of employees. In this consultation process, some employees' opinions mattered more than others, and this was not always a reflection of the employee's rank. Usually, actual authority was the result of such factors as seniority, rank, recognized expertise or professionalism, and demonstrated dedication to the company.

Seniority

The most senior title in the company was cofounder. With Stan Shih and his wife, a total of six people had invested in Acer in 1976. These cofounders held the most senior positions in the corporation, regardless of their actual job.

Rank and Job Title

Job title and position on the organization chart mattered only if they were supported by the other factors. A manager who had joined the corporation only recently, and had not yet demonstrated his or her abilities, was unlikely to carry much weight.

Recognized Expertise, Professionalism, and Dedication to Acer

Regardless of rank or any other factor, all employees with advanced technical expertise (engineering, law, marketing, corporate administration systems), or with a reputation for getting things done right, were almost always consulted on major decisions affecting their areas.

Outsiders phoning Acer frequently complained that the Acer employees they were trying to reach were always attending some kind of meeting. There was some truth to that. Acer's decision-making process required that lots of meetings take place. Nevertheless, the numerous meetings helped to create common ground across the company on a number of issues that could otherwise be divisive. It was common practice for senior managers to wait until a broad consensus had emerged at lower echelons before announcing new policies. Since everyone affected understood the reasons behind new decisions, the extensive consultation and concensus-building that went on made it easy to implement new decisions.

The implicit complexity of such a decision-making system was a prime reason for Acer being split into Business Units in 1992. The same decision-making pattern was still being used at the BU level, however. Still, decisions affecting Acer Incorporated as a whole continued to require Stan Shih's and the cofounders' attention.

THE U.S. BATTLEFIELD

Acer had traditionally had the most success in parts of the world it described as ALAP, standing for Africa, Latin America, Asia, Pacific. In recent years, this was where the company had earned most of its profits, and Acer held dominant market shares in many countries in those regions. Nevertheless, top management had decided that for the success of the company in the 1990s, the U.S. market was crucial. Management felt that if Acer didn't build a reasonably strong competitve position in the United States, sooner or later, it would lose ground in other parts of the world.

EXHIBIT 2   The Acer Group Organizational Chart, 1993

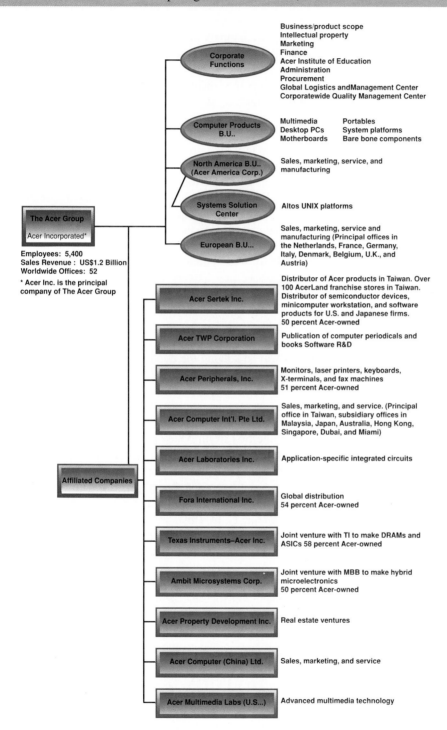

Corporate Functions

Business/product scope
Intellectual property
Marketing
Finance
Acer Institute of Education
Administration
Procurement
Global Logistics andManagement Center
Corporatewide Quality Management Center

Computer Products B.U..

Multimedia	Portables
Desktop PCs	System platforms
Motherboards	Bare bone components

North America B.U.. (Acer America Corp.)

Sales, marketing, service, and manufacturing

Systems Solution Center

Altos UNIX platforms

European B.U...

Sales, marketing, service and manufacturing (Principal offices in the Netherlands, France, Germany, Italy, Denmark, Belgium, U.K., and Austria)

The Acer Group

Acer Incorporated*

Employees: 5,400
Sales Revenue : US$1.2 Billion
Worldwide Offices: 52

* Acer Inc. is the principal company of The Acer Group

Affiliated Companies

Acer Sertek Inc.

Distributor of Acer products in Taiwan. Over 100 AcerLand franchise stores in Taiwan. Distributor of semiconductor devices, minicomputer workstation, and software products for U.S. and Japanese firms. 50 percent Acer-owned

Acer TWP Corporation

Publication of computer periodicals and books Software R&D

Acer Peripherals, Inc.

Monitors, laser printers, keyboards, X-terminals, and fax machines 51 percent Acer-owned

Acer Computer Int'l. Pte Ltd.

Sales, marketing, and service. (Principal office in Taiwan, subsidiary offices in Malaysia, Japan, Australia, Hong Kong, Singapore, Dubai, and Miami)

Acer Laboratories Inc.

Application-specific integrated circuits

Fora International Inc.

Global distribution 54 percent Acer-owned

Texas Instruments–Acer Inc.

Joint venture with TI to make DRAMs and ASICs 58 percent Acer-owned

Ambit Microsystems Corp.

Joint venture with MBB to make hybrid microelectronics 50 percent Acer-owned

Acer Property Development Inc.

Real estate ventures

Acer Computer (China) Ltd.

Sales, marketing, and service

Acer Multimedia Labs (U.S...)

Advanced multimedia technology

The United States had always attracted much of Acer's attention. It was the world's largest market, and had only one official language, which made marketing easier. Early in the 1990s, Acer became keenly aware of the emergence of super-stores and various forms of discount channels in the United States. Sensing that the trend would gather momentum, Acer introduced a new brand of computers named Acros in 1992. Essentially, Acros computers were the same as Acer ones, except that they looked different, sold for less, and the consumer didn't get as much support. The two brands were given different images so as to broaden Acer's appeal to different buyer segments. In 1993, sales of the Acros and Acer brands gave Acer a 3 percent share of the U.S. market.

From 1991 to 1993, T. Y. Lay, Acer's vice president for corporate marketing, had studied the U.S. market and come up with some innovative means of establishing Acer's competitiveness. As a result of his efforts, Acer had changed the way it delivered its products to the United States. By 1993, Acer was airlifting all components subject to quick price changes (especially price cuts). These included hard disks and motherboards. Otherwise, it shipped its "barebone"[4] systems by boat. Components subject to deep price discounting as newer, more advanced versions came on the market, such as DRAMs and CPUs, were purchased and installed at the very last possible moment, ideally a few days before delivery to the end-user. Final assembly was made easy by a new modular design Acer had developed that made it possible to assemble the various parts of a computer in only a few minutes. Even notebook computers made use of this modular design and featured a patented removable key-board and trackball mouse.

These approaches went a long way in solving the two main problems plaguing Acer and other Taiwanese IT companies in the 1990s: faster product cycles and falling prices. The two problems were essentially linked to the supply of components. Margins in the IT industry had attracted an increasing number of players, with the result that competition was now fierce. Competitors tried to outdo each other by lowering prices or skimming the market by being the first to introduce products based on the newest, most advanced generation of components; being late in introducing a product meant that the product would be much less profitable. Meanwhile, high margins in the components industry also had attracted a larger number of players, with the result that component prices were now extremely volatile and that introductions of new genera-tions of components were more frequent. In 1992, a number of Taiwan firms had watched helplessly as notebook prices on the world markets fell 30 percent in the same week, turning forecasted profits into losses on inventories.

In this environment, and given Acer's determination to be successful in the most competitive channels (superstores and discount outlets), time-to-market was becoming the most important strategic consideration for success in the computer industry. Acer believed that Compaq, with some help from Taiwanese engineers, had developed its highly successful Contura notebook line in six months. Even IBM was improving. Notebook development at IBM was now down to the 8 to 10 months range.

THE PORTABLE PRODUCTS BUSINESS DIVISION

The Portable Products Business Division operated as part of the Computer Products Business Unit. In recent years, sales of notebooks at Acer had increased much faster

---

[4]Acer's barebone systems consisted of a casing, power supply, diskette drive, and manuals.

than the other product lines. The division had responsibility for market research, product development, and manufacturing of all notebook computers built by Acer, either its own brands or ODM/OEM products.

Employees of the division had mostly transferred from other operations within Acer. As a result, the division felt that it lacked some expertise in communications technology, which was somewhat of a handicap given the increasing merging of computer and communications technologies, especially in the area of portable computing.

In 1993, division sales were expected to reach NT$5 billion. The division was headed by Haydn Hsieh, who had been with Acer for 13 years. The division was organized around functional departments, covering manufacturing, product management, R&D, and QA/QC.

The product management function was split into three sections that were headed by Brian Chong, Jackson Lin, and Rich Huang.

An engineer and ethnic Chinese from the Philippines, Brian Chong had joined Acer in 1987. He was currently in charge of international market promotion for Acer's portable products, for developing Acer's response to Apple's PDAs[5], for product support, and for a few models of notebooks.

Jackson Lin had been with Acer for four years. He was currently in charge of most models of notebooks. He had worked for AT&T and ITT prior to joining Acer, and thus could provide some expertise in communications technology.

Rich Huang was in charge of the lab pilot-run process and for interfacing with engineers at the factory. He had been with Acer for six years.

Exhibit 3 presents an organization chart of the Portable Products Business Division.

FROM 8-6-2 TO 3-6-1

Simon Lin, president of Acer's Computer Products Business Unit, had announced in the spring of 1993 that the BU had to speed up its product development cycle. The issue became an overall TQM theme, with each business division responsible for developing its own subthemes and campaigns. Since then, TQM has become an important companywide program at Acer.

In the Portable Product Division, Brian Chong, Jackson Lin, and Rich Huang came up with a goal to speed up product developments by five months. Later on, their goal became known as 3-6-1. The table below indicates why.

Step	Prevailing Situation	Goals
Product development process, from design to mass production	8 months	3 months
Time the product remains in the market	6 months	6 months
Phase out	2 months	1 month

---

[5]In 1993, Apple had introduced with great fanfare its Personal Digital Assistant, sold under the Newton brand name. The PDA was an advanced handheld computer, a little larger than an electronic organizer. The user interface consisted of a special pen. The user entered commands in handwriting directly on the screen with this pen. The more advanced models had infrared communications capabilities.

EXHIBIT 3 Organization Chart for Acer's Portable Products Business Division, 1993

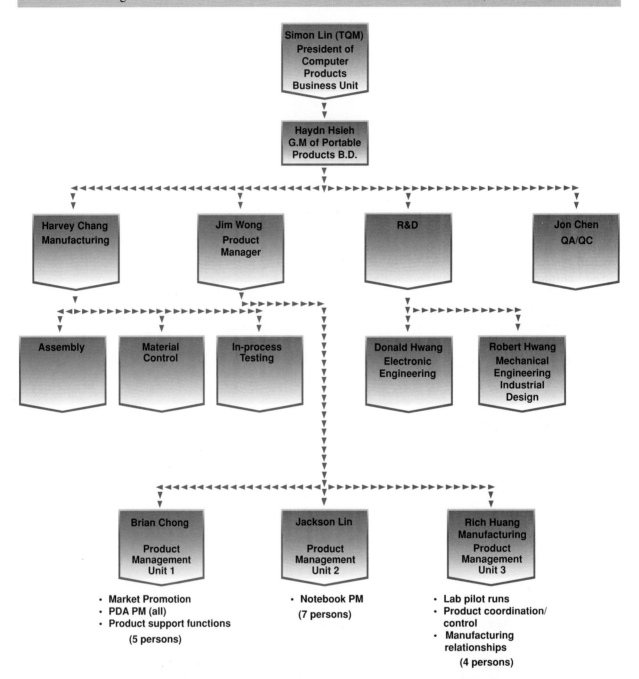

Since developing a new line of notebooks was a complex process, attaining the 3-6-1 goal would also be extremely complex. To make the task more manageable, Lin, Chong, and Huang split the product development process in four areas and together analyzed where improvement would have the greatest impact. They decided that improving the pilot-run process had the greatest potential.

PILOT-RUN PROCESS

Acer on average took eight months to design a new line of notebook computers and put them into production. The pilot run was taking most of the time in this whole process. The pilot-run process included such activities as R&D, materials specification, prototype design, engineering for mass production, and production of samples.

Many people were involved in the pilot-run process. A product manager (PM) was responsible for overall coordination, R&D lab engineers for design, and product engineers for turning the R&D prototypes into mass-produceable designs. Top management, often technically proficient, provided advice and new directions at various stages.[6]

Theoretically, the process started with a product manager issuing market requirement specifications (MRS) to the R&D department. Within a few days, the MRS were translated into external engineering specifications. A preliminary bill of materials (pre-BOM) was sent back to the PM for review. Once the PM approved the pre-BOM, the lab designers went about designing the new machines.

Lab (I) referred to the first attempt by the R&D engineers to come up with a working prototype. For the last few years, computer modeling equipment had been available to simulate how a particular motherboard design would work. In practice however, R&D engineers preferred to manually assemble their prototypes without using the potentially time-saving simulators. After a prototype had been built, there were usually problems with it, so-called "bugs." Engineers spent a lot of time and energy debugging the units. Four times out of five, a first prototype couldn't be debugged satisfactorily, and LAB (I) had to be aborted. In LAB (II), R&D engineers started from scratch again with the design of a new motherboard. Eventually, R&D came up with a working prototype. It then had to assemble a certain number of samples for factory engineers and for marketing purposes. The number of samples to be produced was decided on a case-by-case basis.

Once working units came out of LAB (I) or LAB (II), the pilot-run process moved over to ENG (I). In ENG (I), production engineers (PE) at the Hsinchu factory worked on a test assembly line to arrive at a practical method by which the R&D prototype could be mass-produced. In general, substantial modifications to the LAB design occurred. Moreover, R&D engineers from the Taipei headquarters often had to go to the factory, one and a half hours away, to help out. Often, a modified design from ENG (I) had to be abandoned and the PEs, working with R&D staff from headquarters called in to help out, had to come up with a second engineering design. This was called ENG (II). Before moving on to mass production, PEs were responsible for producing a certain number of samples that Acer sent to its distributors and potential OEM customers or used in trade shows.

The information in Exhibit 4 is representative of the sort of delays that occurred during the pilot-run process. In this table, U386s, V486s, and 750/750C are PC notebooks that Acer had recently developed. "Planned" refers to the number of days that were originally scheduled to complete a particular operation. "Actual" refers to the number of days it actually took to complete the operation. Some models were developed "right the first time," without having to implement LAB (II) or ENG (II).

Before proceeding to mass production, a final BOM was decided on, manuals were produced, and safety, environmental, and software compatibility tests were

---

[6]These interventions by senior managers were partly the result of their being technically proficient, and partly due to the hierarchical values in the Taiwanese culture.

EXHIBIT 4   Planned versus Actual Working Days in Acer's Product Development Activities

	Models					
	U386s		V486s/sc		750/750C	
Item	Planned Days	Actual Days	Planned Days	Actual Days	Planned Days	Actual Days
			LAB (I)			
Materials/PC layout	21	38	28	48	30	52
Prototyping	3	3	4	6	4	4
Debug/testing	14	14	30	46	38	29
	38	55	62	100	72	85
			LAB (II)			
Materials/2nd PC Layout			15	35	14	15
Prototyping			4	4	4	4
Casing			2	3	2	2
Testing			30	48	12	68
			51	90	32	89
			Eng (I)			
Materials/PC layout	7	10	10	15	10	14
Prototyping	3	2	5	8	4	7
Casing	3	3	3	15	2	4
Testing	21	40	21	43	22	56
	34	55	39	81	38	81
			Eng (II)			
Materials/PC layout						7
Prototyping						3
Casing						2
Testing						14
						26

conducted. There was no PERT or Gantt chart describing the sequence in which this occurred. There were usually wide discrepancies between the final BOM and the pre-BOM, a fact usually attributed to the perfunctionary reviews the overworked PMs performed on the pre-BOMs (PMs on average left the office around 8:30 P.M.). On the other hand, production of manuals was one of Acer's strengths; the company had a very experienced staff in this area.

THE REASONS FOR THE DELAYS

In July 1993, Brian Chong, Jackson Lin, and Rich Huang produced their report, written in the form of a TQM story, which documented their efforts in analyzing the pilot-run process and outlining where time could be saved. In short, it showed that the following areas caused problems:

1. A severe lack of control over the whole pilot-run process.
2. Lack of control over the R&D engineers, especially in reviewing their choice of components.
3. Poor communications between the different departments involved.
4. Too many changes while work was in progress.
5. Lack of R&D know-how; the notebook division was unfamiliar with certain technologies, particularly those related to communications.
6. Lack of SMT[7] capacity.
7. Lack of unity in the direction emerging from the top management.
8. A feeling of alienation among the production engineers at the factory, who felt that their jobs were less glamorous than those of the lab engineers.
9. A lack of integration between the R&D engineers and the production engineers. R&D engineers often had to go to a Hsinchu factory (one and a half hours away, depending on traffic) to help in the implementation of their prototypes. This amount of travel time slowed down the development of newer designs.

ALTERNATIVES

The report produced by Lin, Huang, and Chong identified the problems, but omitted any particular recommendations regarding the implementation of a solution. However, the alternatives and the trade-offs involved seemed pretty straightforward to the managers involved:

Tackling the Problems Directly

One possibility was to tackle the problems outlined head-on with a series of actions that would require:

1. Increasing the authority of PMs, and having them act as project managers as well as product managers. PMs would have to use new tools, such as Gantt charts, and closely monitor the product development process. This would require upgrading the management skills of PMs, perhaps by sending them to training programs.
2. Implementing new measures to limit the discretionary authority of R&D engineers, including
   - Closely reviewing their choice of components.
   - Forcing them to use the computer modeling equipment that Acer possessed rather than letting them jump directly into physical assembly.
3. Increasing salaries of the best R&D staff so as not to lose them to competitors.
4. Establishing design freezes, i.e., dates after which upper management would not be allowed to modify new designs.

---

[7]SMT is an abbreviation for Surface Mount Technology. It usually refers to the expensive equipment that is used to automate the process of putting integrated circuits onto boards.

5. Rotating R&D engineers and production engineers to improve the transition between the LAB phase and ENG phase.

6. Recruiting the expertise Acer did not possess in the United States if necessary.

Lin, Huang, and Chong believed that if these measures could be successfully implemented, product development could be dramatically speeded up, quality would improve, and unit production cost would come down. LAB II and ENG II could probably be eliminated. However, although the fifth and sixth measures could probably be implemented without much difficulty, adopting the other measures would be more sensitive. Some of the difficulties were the result of Acer's culture, and others the result of Taiwanese culture.

First of all, top management would probably not go along with a design freeze. Senior managers were very busy, traveled the globe, and would not bother with "minor" administrative considerations until they finally found the time to focus on product development at home.

Second, tightening management of the process would require clarifying the lines of responsibilities and pinning down who exactly had authority over what. This was difficult to implement in Taiwan, partly due to a cultural factor called *"ren-ching-wei."* A discussion of *ren-ching-wei* is presented in Exhibit 5.

Besides *ren-ching-wei*, another factor making implementation of such changes difficult was the fear that increased control could cause engineers to lose their motivation. For many years, Acer had attracted some of Taiwan's brightest graduates to work for its R&D team. Many held advanced degrees from American universities. One of the greatest motivations in their job was to know that they were competing head-on against teams from leading firms in other countries. Their great thrill was to know that they were besting the engineers at Compaq, IBM, or Apple. Increased control could erode this spirit.

Moreover, tight control over employees was against Acer culture. Stan Shih had always said that he believed that every human being was fundamentally good. As a result, control had always been slack at Acer. In Shih's mind, left to themselves, employees always acted in the best interests of the corporation. Acer had traditionally fostered an entrepreneurial culture where employees learned from their mistakes. Practically, Acer did not control how its employees were spending their time, nor did they have to punch time cards. Even direct supervisiors did not control the actions and decisions of their employees tightly. This had the advantage of giving employees a sense that they were in control of their jobs; it was good for morale. On the other hand, it was difficult for management to work out schedules and stay on top of who was doing what.

Finally, it would be difficult to obtain management approval for providing more training to the product manager. With unemployment at 1.3 percent in Taiwan, management believed that improving skills only resulted in increased turnover, with the most capable employees leaving the corporation for better paying jobs with competitors. Moroever, in order to promote a good work atmosphere in the company, Acer's salaries were fixed to a rigid pay scale. Performance bonuses were paid twice a year, but star performers could not expect compensation packages that differed greatly from their colleagues. As a result, many young and bright Taiwanese worked at Acer for a few years to gain experience and to be associated with Acer's prestigious name. They then went on to get better salaries at smaller firms. In this environment, Chong, Lin, and Huang doubted that top management would approve a request for expensive training programs for the product managers.

EXHIBIT 5 *Ren-Ching-Wei:* The Flavor of Human Feelings

Ren-ching-wei permeates all aspects of life in Taiwan and is responsible for much of the harmony found within groups of Chinese people on the island.*

The concept of *ren-ching-wei* is neither a rule nor a code. It refers in a very general way to how Chinese people in Taiwan interact with each other. Westerners have a tendency to simplify *ren-ching-wei* with expressions, such as "Oh, that means I scratch your back and you scratch mine," or "It's about having connections." *Ren-ching-wei* involves spending much time and effort to maintain harmonious relations with co-workers, neighbors, and acquaintances. For example, when an employee marries, he/she typically invites all his/her co-workers to the wedding. These harmonious relations are one reason that implementing a decision is easy in a Chinese company. The existence of *ren-ching-wei* promotes mutual understanding and a blame-free environment in which employees readily accept new challenges.

However, *ren-ching-wei* does not always foster a climate under which making changes is easy. In situations in which a problem cannot be corrected without hurting other people's feelings, or reprimanding or firing someone, it is common for nothing to get changed until it reaches crisis proportions. It is one thing to say: "Punctuality is a problem at this company," and quite another to actually name the employees who come in late, especially in their presence.

Moreover, for the manager, *ren-ching-wei* creates situations in which it is very difficult to attribute responsibility to anyone. A typical "screw-up" in a Taiwanese company has the following scenario. A busy executive accepts, as a favor, a request from the CEO to do a job that falls outside of his jurisdiction. Being too busy, or else to show his trust in a particular employee, the executive delegates the task to someone else with whom he is familiar in another department. As a favor, this employee accepts to do the job, even though he is very busy and has no experience doing this particular kind of task. In the end, if he fails in the task, since he has done his best and didn't turn down the request it is considered inappropriate to place blame on him for the failure. Because of *ren-ching-wei*, it is difficult, and even counterproductive, to turn down requests from co-workers, even when very busy or when the request involves doing something that falls outside one's job responsibility. Also because of *ren-ching-wei*, responsibilities for "screw-ups" cannot be clearly attributed to a particular person.

According to Brian Chong, product managers who had refused to perform favors for their co-workers in the past had more difficulty in completing their projects on time.

*Except for a minor percentage of aboriginals, the vast majority of Taiwanese are ethnic Chinese. Despite Taiwan's advanced level of industrialization, the society adheres to many traditional Chinese customs to a greater extent than China itself. This is partly due to Taiwan's being spared the cultural revolution that raged in China from 1966 to 1976.

On the other hand, change was a way of life at Acer. In 1989, the firm had gone public on the local stock exchange and moved its headquarters to the countryside in the quaint city of Lungtan. In 1991, Acer had split itself up and laid off 400 employees. In 1992, Acer had received ISO 9000 certification. In 1993, headquarters had been moved back to Taipei. Despite some cynicism, employees were used to profound organizational changes occurring once or twice a year.

Leaving Things As Is

Although improving time-to-market was critical, a case could be made for the do-nothing option. To keep on doing things the way they were being done would not upset anyone. Presumably, harmonious relations and high levels of motivation could be maintained. Moreover, as a Taiwanese company that did nearly all of its development work in Taiwan, Acer was still developing its products faster than most foreign firms, if only because Acer suppliers could be depended upon to respond rapidly to Acer requests for next-generation parts and components.

But there were problems with the do-nothing option. First of all, except perhaps in R&D, the atmosphere of high motivation of Acer employees and the entrepreneurial culture seemed to have deteriorated sharply over the last few years. The company was very large now and it was common at Acer for employees not to know the names of the people sitting a few desks away from them.

Moreover, Acer was not the only computer multinational to benefit from Taiwan's capabilities. IBM had had a considerable presence on the island for many years. And Compaq had recently hired several experienced Taiwanese engineers for key positions at its new notebook factory in Singapore. With the do-nothing option, Acer's product development capabilities were soon likely to be outclassed by these competitors.

Not Recommending Anything

Huang, Lin, and Chong were not sure what Simon Lin would decide if they didn't recommend anything. On the one hand, they thought that whether they recommended something or not did not make a very big difference. Given the way decisions were made at Acer, their recommendations were unlikely to be anything more than a basis for consultations. And since they would be heavily involved in these consultations, they would have ample opportunities later on to put their recommendations forward.

According to the trio, the worst outcome would be that upper management would adopt a compromise solution. They were afraid that someone, perhaps a team comprising Lin, Huang, and Chong, would be appointed to make sure that the pilot-run process went along "more smoothly." If such a decision was taken, it was unlikely that the deeper issues would be addressed. The employees appointed to make the process "smoother" would be mere expeditors. The attraction of this compromise solution would be great, given that no fundamental changes would be required.

If the "expedite things along" solution was adopted, the individual(s) appointed were most likely not to have real authority other than their credibility as management's appointees. They would have to continually negotiate with all the individuals involved in the product development process to make sure that the most time-saving way of proceeding was utilized at each step. There probably wouldn't be any funds for additional training of product managers. As to the hiring of expertise in the United States, the matter would probably be referred to Ronald Chwang, a senior VP who had worked extensively in Silicon Valley before joining Acer; Chwang was currently the president of Acer's U.S. subsidiary. Increasing the salaries of the most brilliant R&D staff currently employed by Acer was probably not going to be approved because of the expected stiff resistance from Human Resources.

Sourcing Products Outside

Chong, Huang, and Lin knew that one option that upper management was seriously considering was to source from other companies some of the products in which Acer had less expertise. The most likely candidates were organizers, palmtop computers, and personal digital assistants (PDAs).

The rationale for sourcing outside was that:

- As a Taiwanese company, Acer could source outside more effectively than companies such as IBM, Apple, or Compaq.
- Research firms were predicting that, by 1998, sales of organizers, palmtop computers and PDAs would reach the same level as sales of notebook computers. By sourcing outside, the R&D team of the portable product division could focus solely on developing notebook computers.

CURRENT DEVELOPMENTS

In the summer of 1993, the notebook division produced nine models of Acer notebooks available in a total of 50 basic configurations. When models produced for the OEM were counted in, Acer manufactured hundreds of models of notebooks.[8] Dealers were free to customize the notebooks by adding memory, installing or removing a trackball mouse, an internal modem, and so on. Acer was accepting orders for batches as small as 100 units.

In the summer of 1993, Acer was also in the process of developing six new notebooks. Moreover, one of the top priority projects was a product similar to Apple's PDA. The best selling notebooks in the summer of 1993 were the AcerNote 730 and 750 series. The latter were based on incorporated some version of the 486 family of microprocessors, featured 4MB RAM standard, and had PCMCIA[9] type III slots. A product manager was assigned to each line of notebooks. Chong and Lin oversaw these PMs as well as the product development process.

WHAT NEXT?

After all the work that had gone into producing the report, there was a little bit of anxiety as to what would happen next. According to Brian Chong:

> One of the big problems with Chinese companies is that identifying problems seems relatively easy if they put their hearts into it. Implementing is the biggest problem. I think it's because of the tendency of people to forget about the real long-term implications of what they do. They tend to focus on details. But we have to change. We cannot act like we are a small company anymore. We have to tighten up.
>
> There are two ways really for us to influence the direction the company is taking. One is to convince Simon Lin. That would result in the top down directive approach. Simon would just tell everyone how they have to change. However, I don't think that there would be a lot of buy-in from the employees affected. The other approach is to have a series of meetings with everyone who will be affected by the required changes. That would bring consensus about. The main problem with this approach is that it takes so much time.

(Acer's Web address is *www.acer.com.tw*.)

---

[8]The production line was extremely flexible. Since the casings were standardized for all the models, workers could switch from manufacturing one model to another without even stopping the line.

[9]PCMCIA cards were very popular with notebook and palmtop computers. A little larger than credit cards, PCMCIAs were also referred to as memory cards. Programs and large amounts of information could be stored on these cards. Their main advantages were the small size and that PCMCIA slots consumed less energy than diskette drives, the latter being a critical consideration with notebook and palmtop computers.

CASE 32

FOOD LION AND *PRIMETIME LIVE**

Joseph Wolfe, *University of Tulsa*

On Thursday evening, November 5, 1992, Diane Sawyer of the ABC network's top-rated investigative program *PrimeTime Live* leveled her hazel-eyed gaze into the television cameras and announced,

> Tonight we have a story about what the consumer sees in the supermarket and what goes on behind the scenes . . . a "PrimeTime" investigation.
>
> Food Lion is the fastest-growing grocery chain in the nation, a remarkable success story in an industry where profit margins tend to be perilously low. But six months ago we started talking to current and former employees. Seventy agreed to go on the record, people from different states, who didn't know each other, yet [all] told us similar stories about sanitation and food handling in some departments in their stores.
>
> Before we begin, a word about the Food Lion employees that were filmed with hidden cameras. They're hard working people who care about their jobs. But what this report will show is the kind of thing that *can* happen when the pressure for profit is great and you break the rules.

Following the *PrimeTime* report shown that evening and also the next week, Food Lion was thrown into a maelstrom of negative publicity and market reactions. In Friday trading, the prices of Food Lion's two classes of common stock fell 10.8 percent and 13.8 percent, respectively, and were the NASDAQ's most active over-

*An earlier version of the case was presented at the November 1993 meeting of the North American Case Research Association. Copyright © 1994 by the case author.

the-counter issues. Even before trading opened on Friday morning in New York, the stock price of Food Lion's parent corporation's fell 6.2 percent in very heavy trading on the Brussels stock exchange. As concerned investors bailed out of Food Lion's stock, newspapers and TV stations in cities and towns where Food Lion had stores carried follow-up stories on *PrimeTime Live*'s report. Customer traffic in Food Lion's stores fell off significantly. In March 1993 Standard & Poor's placed up to $500 million of Food Lion's debt on its credit watch list and later that month Moody's Investors Service lowered the chain's senior long-term debt rating. In downgrading Food Lion's bond rating, Moody's cited the *PrimeTime* investigation's negative publicity, the company's falling sales and growth rates, and the fact that the swift recovery Moody's felt would occur after the exposé "isn't happening and further pressures on earnings could occur."

To make matters worse, the televised exposé came at a time when Food Lion was struggling to make a success of its expansion into Texas and Oklahoma. After opening 42 stores in the Dallas/Fort Worth area to disappointing sales in 1991, it was a week away from opening 7 new stores in the Tulsa, Oklahoma, area and trying to make major inroads against strong local and national supermarkets operating in Tulsa. Food Lion officials in both Tulsa and its Salisbury, North Carolina, headquarters tried to minimize the television program's long-term consequences but they admitted the publicity was causing concern. Two months before the *PrimeTime Live* report aired, when Food Lion learned the investigation was under way, it had filed a lawsuit against Capital Cities/ABC Inc. over the methods used in preparing its investigation, and in April, 1993, the suit was amended to include a civil racketeering (RICO) action for damages amounting to at least $30 million.

In the months following the *PrimeTime Live* report, other problems at Food Lion started to surface. The chain's same-store sales had been falling at an increasing rate over recent years and it had made a number of low-growth, defensive expansions to ward off new competition in its home territories. Although Food Lion felt it was both unfairly targeted and blameless regarding the food handling and employment practices detailed in the exposé, various industry observers believed the report merely highlighted the harsh realities of doing business in the supermarket industry and the exploitative practices the company had employed in its quest to expand the number of its stores and gain market penetration across a wider geographic area.

FOOD LION, INC.

Food Lion was started by Ralph Ketner, Brown Ketner, and Wilson Smith in 1957 as a one-store independent called Food Town. The cofounders, all former employees of Winn-Dixie supermarkets, struggled for the next 10 years to build a market base in their home state of North Carolina. A number of stores were opened and closed as the small 16-unit chain fought to win customers and create a successful mechandising format. It was only when Ralph Ketner came up with a strategy of everyday low prices that the chain began to prosper. Food Town went public in 1970. Four years later the Belgium grocery combine of Establissements Delhaize Freres et Cie (Delhaize Le Lion) purchased a controlling stock interest in the company, and shortly thereafter its representatives were elected to half the seats on Food Lion's board of directors. With Delhaize Le Lion's financial backing, rapid expansion ensued. The chain changed its name to Food Lion when in 1983 it expanded into a territory already having a number of stores called Food Town.

DELHAIZE LE LION GROUP

Delhaize Le Lion was Belgium's second largest retailing conglomerate. It was also Belgium's most internationally oriented company, with over 60 percent of its sales coming from outside the country—principally the United States. The company had adopted its overseas diversification strategy mainly because of Belgium's 1975 "loi de cadenas" or padlock law, which attempted to protect the country's small, independent retailers by limiting the domestic expansion of the country's larger retail chains. Speaking to a group of entrepreneurs in June, 1981, Delhaize Le Lion's Guy Beckers described his company's thinking at the time of the law's passage:

> The number of domestic supermarkets could not increase indefinitely and the rate of increase of the revenues of existing supermarkets would diminish some time or another. First, we took it for granted that manufacturing was not our job. We looked at the situation in a number of European countries. Everywhere the same constraints were evident—control by the state, pressure from the trade unions, and not many potential openings as far as sales points were concerned. This made us look toward the United States. We were looking for a region with a growing population and an expanding economy. We chose the Sun Belt, which fulfilled these requirements: (1) lower energy consumption—with air-conditioning there is no problem about heat affecting the quality of work; (2) unemployment—the South is better situated from this point of view than other regions of the United States; (3) the South is the best region for lower wage scales; (4) increase of population—the South comes at the top of the list; (5) the South is at the top of the list for capital investments for equipment and next to the top for nonresidential investments.

Within Belgium, Delhaize Le Lion operated over 100 of its own supermarkets and had 144 franchisees and affiliates, including 64 AD Delhaize supermarkets, 41 neighborhood Delhaize food stores, a number of traditional stores with whom it had long-term supply agreements, a chain of 51 Dial discount stores, and a chain of over 60 DI drug stores. Exhibit 1 summarizes Delhaize Le Lion's holdings and operations in both Western Europe and the United States.

Operating control of Food Lion was delegated to an American group headed by Tom E. Smith, the U.S. company's current CEO. His first affiliation with Food Lion came from working in the company's first store as a bagboy in 1958 when he was 17. After graduating from Catawba College in 1964 with an A.B. in business administration he worked for Del Monte Foods for six years and subsequently became Food Lion's only buyer. In his role as buyer, Smith developed the company's strategy of making mass purchases at discount prices and simplifying store operations by stocking fewer brands and sizes than the chain's competitors. He became the company's vice president for distribution in 1974 and its executive vice president in 1977. In 1981, at the age of 39, Smith was promoted to president of Food Lion and then assumed the added title of CEO in 1986. In 1992 his company-related compensation included dividends on his 1,534,089 shares of Food Lion stock and a base salary of $628,788 (a 20 percent raise from the previous year), plus a $272,955 performance bonus based on record 1991 earnings. In late December, 1991, the company's Class A and B common stocks were both trading in the $24 to $26 range.

FOOD LION'S OPERATING CHARACTERISTICS

Food Lion was a regional supermarket chain operating primarily in the Southeastern section of the United States; it had recently expanded north into Pennsylvania and westward into Louisiana, Texas, and Oklahoma. Average store size approximated 25,000 square feet; the company's older stores were concentrated in rural areas,

---

EXHIBIT 1 Delhaize Le Lion's Business Activities and Holdings

Belgium Retail and Wholesale Operations

106 Delhaize Le Lion company-owned supermarkets
 64 AD Delhaize franchised supermarkets
 41 Delhaize neighborhood food stores
 39 independent stores supplied through food distribution arrangements
 51 Dial discount food stores
 62 DI drug stores
  4 warehouses operated by Delhaize Le Lion Coordination Center SA

Full or Partial Operating Control through Ownership Interests

Delimmo—a real estate company providing long-term leases to 14 of its supermarkets in Belgium. Owned by Delhaize Le Lion SA through a 99.9 percent stock interest.

Delned—a holding corporation 100 percent owned by Delimmo. Through Delned (BV Delhaize The Lion Nederland) Delimmo has a 50 percent interest in Shipp's Corner Shopping Center, Virginia Beach, Virginia, and the Debarry Center, Jacksonville, Florida.

Wambacq & Peeters—a transportation company delivering goods from Delhaize Le Lion's Belgium distribution centers; controlled by Delhaize through a 55 percent stock ownership.

Pingo Doce—a 31-store supermarket chain operating in the Portuguese cities of Lisbon and Porto of which Delimmo has a 38.8 percent stock interest.

Artip SA—an airline ticket reseller 33.14 percent owned by Delhaize Le Lion.

Deficom SA—an affiliate of the Defi holding company in the telecommunications industry of which Delhaize Le Lion has a 10 percent ownership interest.

Food Lion Inc. USA—controlled by Delhaize Le Lion's 50.3 percent ownership of Food Lion's Class A nonvoting shares and a 44.2 percent ownership of its Class B voting shares either directly or indirectly through its wholly owned American subsidiary Delhaize The Lion America Inc. USA.

Delhaize the Lion America—a wholly owned company of Delhaize Le Lion SA (Detla).

Super Discount Markets Inc.—a seven-superstore food chain operating in Atlanta, Georgia, under the name Cub Foods of which Delhaize The Lion America Inc. USA has 60 percent ownership.

Source: Summarized from "Retailer Profile No. 1: Delhaize Le Lion," *Marketing in Europe,* July 1990, pp. 95–99.

---

many serving a trading area of fewer than 7,000 people. The simplicity and standardization of store operations had been a key factor in the company's success. Food Lion stores usually did not carry nongrocery items, shelved approximately 16,000 stockkeeping units (SKUs), and were 20 to 35 percent smaller than the stores of such competitors as Winn-Dixie and Kroger. Because of their smaller size and simple shelf-and-display layouts, Food Lion stores were cheaper to build—about $650,000 each versus $1.5 million for the average supermarket. Exhibit 2 presents data on store operations.

Prior to the 1990s Food Lion had leased stores from local developers. In 1991 the company began assuming ownership of newly constructed stores. Tom Smith attributed the shift in its construction/ownership policy to "a credit crunch that has made it

EXHIBIT 2   Food Lion Stores in Operation, 1988–92

	1992	1991	1990	1989	1988
Number of stores	1,012	881	778	663	567
Total square footage (000)	26,428	22,480	19,424	16,326	13,695
Scanning stores	1,012	801	508	315	130

Source: 1991–92 annual reports, pp. 4–5, and press release, February 11, 1993, p. 3.

difficult, if not impossible, for developers to build Food Lion stores and lease them to us as they have done in the past." Food Lion had financed its Dallas/Fort Worth, Texas, stores with internally generated funds but had indicated it would continue to use debt to finance future store growth. In 1992 Food Lion spent approximately $200 million on new store construction and renovation of older units.

To economize on inbound shipping costs, Food Lion built its regional distribution centers adjacent to rail lines; it got about 25 percent of its goods by rail, a bigger percentage than most rival supermarket chains. In 1991 it opened three new 700,000-square-foot dry/refrigerated facilities, and through an additional expansion in 1992, its total amount of distribution center space amounted to 8.7 million square feet. In 1993 Food Lion operated distribution centers in 9 locations:

- Salisbury, North Carolina
- Dunn, North Carolina
- Prince George County, Virginia
- Elloree, South Carolina
- Green Cove Springs, Florida
- Plant City, Forida
- Greencastle, Pennsylvania
- Roanoke, Texas
- Clinton, Tennessee

Food Lion carefully nurtured its reputation as a low-cost, efficient operation that passed cost savings on to its customers in the form of lower prices. Company lore had it that the firm's name was changed from Food Town to Food Lion because only two letters had to be replaced on store signs. All advertisements were prepared in-house, a practice that helped keep marketing costs to 0.5 percent of sales, compared to the industry's average of about 1.1 percent. Tom Smith appeared in about half of the company's advertisements extolling, "At Food Lion, when we save, you save." The strategy was to attract customers with everyday low prices rather than running costly weekly price-special advertisements in newspapers. As one competitor acknowledged, "They do a good job of promoting their everyday low-price image. They promise to deliver one thing—price—and they do, on groceries and frozens." He also added, however, "Their feature prices on produce are not that dramatic." When resetting or remodeling older stores, Food Lion placed an adhesive covering over its old shelves rather than installing new shelving, a practice that saved up to $10,000 a store. This method also sped up the renovation process by one week, saving an additional $4,000 per renovation. By 1992 Food Lion had installed scanning equipment at the checkout counters in all stores. Store visits by brokers and direct sales representatives were recorded on the store's computer to track whether each store was visited every four weeks as requested. To minimize "shrinkage" or theft, Food Lion was testing an electronic article surveillance (EAS) system in 25 of its stores. Food Lion's director of loss prevention, Clayton Edwards, commented,

> We tagged health and beauty aids, cigarettes, meat, and where applicable, wine. After six months, our gross profits were up nearly 10 percent. The biggest change was in the attitude of store management. With EAS, they feel as if they finally have a way of fighting theft. It makes for a safer shopping environment. We found that once word gets out—and it gets out very quickly—that a particular store is using EAS, the bad apples or undesirables tend to go elsewhere. I think that supermarkets willing to invest in electronic tagging systems will definitely have a competitive advantage in years to come.

At the headquarters level, all buying was centralized and all stores were run in the same fashion, creating a tightly disciplined, consistent, centralized operation. Centralized buying had resulted in both lower procurement costs and food prices for the chain. One vendor said Food Lion has "the best buyers in the business. They will buy a year's worth of product if they can cut a deal and hold the price. Individual buyers have the authority to buy millions of dollars worth of a product with no second opinions needed. There is no buying committee. It's awesome." All stores were relatively small, layouts were almost identical, and store and district managers were told exactly what to do. According to one competitor, Food Lion's "store managers have a checklist of what they should do, and they had better follow it. There's only one way to do things. Managers may have some leeway in supporting local charities, but that's about it. You can go into a Food Lion store in Florida and find the same end displays and plano-grams as in a store in North Carolina." Because of low overhead costs and efficient store operations, a typical Food Lion unit could make a profit on weekly volumes as low as $100,000.

Food Lion had one of the industry's most liberal employee benefits packages. Its stock purchase plan was open to all full-time employees over 18 and all part-timers who had been employed for at least one year. Other benefits included a profit-sharing plan, vision care, and a comprehensive medical and dental plan. Despite the company's progressive benefits, some observers said Food Lion's overall management system encouraged loyalty but discouraged initiative. Many managers had reportedly quit the company after a few years "because they felt the company was cold and impersonal, and they had no real feeling of security there." Others claimed Food Lion saved money by dismissing workers before they were fully vested in the company's profit-sharing plan. One worker, assisted by the United Food and Commercial Workers Union (UFCW), which was engaged in a long-term struggle to organize Food Lion's workers, had filed a civil action suit against Food Lion alleging that the company did not provide dismissed workers with an extension of their health insurance coverage as required by federal law.

Expansion Activities and Plans

During each of the past five years, Food Lion had added over 100 stores per year to its chain. The method Food Lion employed in entering the Jacksonville, Florida, market was typical of how it tried to achieve a foothold in new geographic areas. First the company blanketed the Jacksonville market with ads alerting shoppers "Food Lion is coming to town, and prices will be going down." Then, when its stores opened, Food Lion touted its low prices, often running price comparison ads.

After operating in Jacksonville for one year, Food Lion's five stores had 2.4 percent of the market; by 1991 the company had added 32 more stores and had achieved a 14 percent share. The chain's entry into the market, however, did not go unchallenged. Months before Food Lion's new stores opened in Jacksonville, Winn-Dixie lowered its prices 5 percent across the board; by the time Food Lion opened its stores, food prices in the Jacksonville area were down almost 15 percent. Although Food Lion obtained a 14 percent market share, Winn-Dixie still led with a 28 percent share (down from about 38 percent) after Food Lion completed its Jacksonville expansion.

Given Winn-Dixie's experience with Food Lion, rival chains had begun to learn how to withstand the company's entry into their markets. When Food Lion came to the already crowded Dallas/Fort Worth area in December, 1990, many competitors quickly responded to news announcements of the company's planned entry. Because Food Lion did not emphasize service, many local grocers went to 24-hour operations, promoted home delivery, and added such services as fax machines, Western Union money transfers, and money orders. Some stores emphasized the selection and variety of food offered, especially perishables and deli-bakery selections where Food Lion was felt to be at a competitive disadvantage. Most also lowered prices in one form or another—opting for everyday low pricing, advertising hot specials in weekly shopping guides, running 1-cent sales, or offering triple coupons. Nearly all market participants experienced rising advertising and in-store promotional costs. Some used end-of-aisle displays, banners, and flags to compare their stores' prices to Food Lion's; others advertised they would meet Food Lion's prices on comparable items; and many, such as Tom Thumb Food Stores and Kroger, ran advertisements twice a week rather than weekly. Kroger additionally guaranteed the lowest milk prices in town or triple the difference in cash.

The Organization of Economic Cooperation and Development (OECD), an international agency that promoted mutually beneficial trade practices among countries, began receiving formal complaints against Delhaize/Food Lion in 1985 for not employing fair marketing practices and for operating in ways that threatened the host country's standard of living. The OECD asked its trade union advisory committee to investigate and its summary findings were:

> Food Lion routinely opens a store in a town and launches a competitive war based on lower prices in order to take the market away from the already established supermarkets. The already established grocers are forced into closure or to lower their prices, which they can only do by lowering wages and benefits they pay in line with the level set by Food Lion.

After one year in the Dallas/Fort Worth market, and its attendant price war, Food Lion had garnered a 4 percent market share, less than half its 10 percent objective. Although Food Lion's management expressed initial pleasure with its results, a local real estate broker observed, "In 75 percent of their stores they are extremely pleased, but in 25 percent they are extremely unhappy. They are in some terrible locations." Many of the company's successes were in rural locations and less affluent neighborhoods with less sophisticated shoppers and weaker competition. Vince Watkins, Food Lion's operations vice president, had an explanation for the chain's relatively weak results in Texas. "The competition out there was much better organized in preparing for our entry than perhaps they had been in other areas." Additionally, because of Food Lion's obsession with standardization, its Texas stores ignored local food preferences and stocked popular eastern brands not normally found in the Southwest.

EXHIBIT 3   Population Statistics for States with Existing and Targeted Food Lion Stores

Operations	1990 Per Capita Income	1991 Population (000)	1991 Population Rank	1980–90 Percent Growth	2000 Projected Population* (000)
Current states:					
Delaware	$20,039	680	46	12.1	802
Florida	18,586	13,277	4	32.7	16,315
Georgia	16,944	6,623	11	18.6	8,005
Kentucky	14,929	3,713	24	0.7	3,689
Maryland	21,864	4,860	19	13.4	5,608
North Carolina	16,203	6,737	10	12.7	7,717
Pennsylvania	18,672	11,961	5	0.1	12,069
South Carolina	15,099	3,560	25	11.7	3,962
Tennessee	15,978	4,953	18	6.2	5,424
Texas	16,769	17,349	3	19.4	17,828
Virginia	19,746	6,286	12	15.7	7,275
West Virginia	13,747	1,801	34	−8.0	1,651
Projected states:					
Alabama	$14,826	4,089	22	3.8	4,358
Arkansas	14,218	2,372	33	2.8	2,509
Kansas	17,986	2,495	32	4.8	2,534
Louisiana	14,391	4,252	21	0.3	4,141
Mississippi	12,735	2,592	31	2.1	2,772
Missouri	17,497	5,158	15	4.1	5,473
Oklahoma	15,444	3,175	28	4.0	2,924

*Series A migration assumptions employed.
Sources: *Statistical Abstract of the United States 1992* (Washington, DC: U.S. Department of Commerce, Economics, and Statistics Administration, Bureau of the Census, 1992), pp. 22–23; *Current Population Reports: Population Estimates and Projections,* series P-25 (Washington, DC: U.S. Department of Commerce, Social and Economic Statistics Administration, Bureau of the Census, 1989), p. 13; *Information Please Almanac* 1992 (New York: Dan Golenpaul Associates, 1993), p. 52.

Belatedly, Food Lion management relaxed its standardization policy and allowed its Dallas/Fort Worth stores to stock such regional favorites as ranch beans, various peppers, corn husks, plantain, and a select grade of beef popular with Texans.

Despite these results, Food Lion had designated its "primary expansion areas" for the 1990s as being Kansas, Louisiana, Oklahoma, Missouri, Arkansas, Mississippi, and Alabama. In 1993 Food Lion planned on opening about 110 new stores, primarily in Virginia, Maryland, West Virginia, and Texas. The general mobilizing cry of "2,000 stores by the year 2000" was a common theme throughout the chain. Exhibit 3 presents economic and population growth data for states where the company had existing and planned store locations. Exhibit 4 profiles rival supermarket chains in Food Lion's projected new markets, and Exhibit 5 presents comparative financial and operating data for these same chains.

EXHIBIT 4   Profiles of Selected Actual and Potential Food Lion Competitors

Albertson's Inc.—operates over 650 grocery stores in 19 western and southern states. Store formats include about 250 combination food/drugstores employing approximately 58,000 square feet of selling space per store, 250 superstores of about 42,000 square feet each, 118 27,000-square-ft. conventional supermarkets, and 32 warehouse stores. The company operates 9 full-line distribution centers, which handle about 65 percent of the merchandise carried in its stores. In May 1992, Albertson's acquired 74 Jewel Osco stores. Future sales growth is expected to come from store space expansion planned at about 10% a year and population increases found in its Florida and West Coast markets. The company competes through a strong private brand program, everyday low pricing, and superior service. Albertson's is 40 percent unionized.

Bruno's Inc.—operates more than 250 supermarkets in Alabama, Florida, Georgia, Mississippi, and Tennessee under the names Food World, Consumer Warehouse, Bruno's, Food Max, and Piggly Wiggly. Its stores average about 35,000 square feet each. In 1992 same-store sales fell 1 percent and it has been buffeted by high store opening costs and increased advertising expenditures caused by increased competition in some of its hotly contested markets. Bruno's plans to open 33 new units in 1993 and will be installing in-store computers to reduce inventory shrinkage and increase labor productivity.

Delchamps, Inc.—is affiliated with the Topco cooperative grocery purchasing organization. The chain operates 115 supermarkets along the Gulf coasts of Alabama, Florida, Louisiana, and Mississippi as well as 10 liquor stores in Florida. All stores are leased under long-term agreements and measure about 35,345 square feet each. Sales fell in 1992 due to food price deflation and competitive pressures. Delchamps responded to heavy local competition by doubling the value of coupons up to 60¢ and by making cash donations to schools equalling 1 percent of the cash receipts collected by the schools. The chain has begun to reduce its selling costs by cutting its nighttime store hours and obtaining greater labor productivity.

Giant Food—this is a highly integrated chain of 154 supermarkets concentrated in Washington, DC, Baltimore, and adjoining areas in Virginia and Maryland. It has its own warehouses and distribution network and a construction and maintenance company. Giant Food also produces its own privately labelled ice cream, baked goods, dairy products, soft drinks, and ice cubes. Same-store sales, which have averaged about $22.7 million per store, fell in 1992 but the chain's high degree of vertical integration adds about 1 percent to its overall margins.

The Kroger Co.—America's largest grocery chain with major market shares in the Midwest, South, and West. Kroger operates about 1,265 stores, of which 657 are combination food and drug units and 520 are superstores. The chain also operates over 940 convenience stores. Kroger acquired the Mini-Mart convenience store chain in 1987 and sold its free-standing drug stores in the same year. In October 1988 it accomplished a major restructuring. To foil a takeover bid at that time Kroger declared a special dividend, which left the company with much debt. Much of its current cashflow is now being used to retire that debt. Kroger processes food at 37 plants and offers over 4,000 privately labelled goods. The company is heavily unionized and has faced stiff competition in Houston, Cincinnati, Dayton, and Tennessee.

Weis Markets—has most of its 127 food outlets in southern Pennsylvania but also a few units in Maryland, Virginia, West Virginia, and New York. Other food retailers, including a number of low-price warehouse club chains, have moved into Weis's markets, forcing it to cut prizes. Same-store sales and operating margins have fallen annually for the past few years. Weis owns about 55 percent of its sites, is debt free, and sells nationally branded merchandise plus 1,800 items under its trademarks Big Top, Carnival, and Weis Quality. The company also operates five Amity House Ice Cream Shoppes and the Weis Food Service institutional supply company.

Winn-Dixie Stores—this company is America's fifth largest grocery chain and the largest one in the Sunbelt. It operates about 1,200 supermarkets under the names Winn-Dixie and Marketplace. The chain is nonunionized and has its own distribution centers, processing and manufacturing plants, and a fleet of trucks. In 1990 Winn-Dixie began emphasizing everyday low prices in addition to its usual high service orientation. Store sizes average 31,400 square feet.

EXHIBIT 5   Comparative Statistics for Selected Food Lion Competitors, 1992

	Albertson's	Bruno's	Delchamps	Giant Food	Kroger	Weis Markets	Winn-Dixie
Sales	$10,095.0	$2,618.2	$949.8	$3,550.0	$22,085.0	$1,320.0	$10,074.0
Gross margin	26.0%	22.2%	26.5%	31.5	22.5	27.7%	22.8%
Net profit margin	2.67%	2.34%	.60%	1.85%	.37%	5.90%	2.09%
Inventory turnover	13.0	11.2	10.0	16.0	15.0	14.5	10.9
Long-term debt	$ 575.0	$ 172.2	$ 42.4	$ 255.0	$ 4,250.0	$ 0.0	$ 90.3
Net worth	1,340.0	422.4	112.8	650.0	–2,749.0	692.0	952.2

Note: All data in millions of dollars except for margin percentages and inventory turns per year.

Sources: Value Line company surveys, November 20, 1992, pp. 1498, 1501, 1503–05, 1508, 1515–16.

Company Corporate Responsibility and Community Relations Efforts

Food Lion was proud of its recognition as a good corporate citizen. In 1986 the company received the Martin Luther King Award for its humanitarian efforts. Some of the actions that led to the award included Food Lion's donating trucks to aid southeastern farmers during the 1985 drought to transport hay from Indiana to save farmers' cattle, providing equal-opportunity employment, and establishing express lanes for handicapped customers.

When dealing with controversy, the company had traditionally met the criticism head on. During one attack by Winn-Dixie in Jacksonville, Food Lion produced a television advertisement featuring Tom Smith in his office assuring customers that "Winn-Dixie would have you believe that Food Lion's low prices are going to crumble and blow away. Let me assure you that as long as you keep shopping at Food Lion, our lower prices are to stay right where they belong—in Jacksonville." In 1984 Smith reacted quickly when a number of rumors in eastern Tennessee linked the Food Lion logotype to Satanic worship. Grand Ole Opry star Minnie Pearl was hired by the company to appear in local advertisements until the stories disappeared.

Recent Operating Results

Despite the fallout from the *PrimeTime Live* report, Food Lion stated that its general plans for expansion in 1993 were still in effect (see Exhibit 6). Tom Smith's objective was to double Food Lion's revenues by 1997, even though near-term sales and profit projections had been dampened by recent events—see Exhibits 7 and 8. The company's switch from leasing to owning newly opened stores had pushed long-term debt from 27 percent of capital to 35 percent in 1992, but Smith intended to start selling and leasing back new stores as soon as the real estate market rebounded. Exhibits 9 and 10 present the company's balance sheets and income statements for 1989–92 while Exhibit 11 presents comparative quarterly sales and profit results for comparable periods before and after the *PrimeTime Live* exposé.

EXHIBIT 6   Food Lion's Estimated New Store Expenditures, 1993

Capital Item	Expenditures (000,000)
Construction	$ 60.0
Store equipment	85.0
Land costs and distribution center expansion	10.0
Total	$155.0

Source: Food Lion, Inc. 1992 annual report, p. 15.

EXHIBIT 7   Food Lion's Same-Store Sales Volume Changes, 1989–92

Year	Growth
1989	8.6%
1990	4.5
1991	2.7
1992	−0.4

Source: Food Lion, Inc. 1992 annual report, p. 15.

EXHIBIT 8   Monthly Changes in Same-Store Sales at Food Lion, November 1992–March 1993

Period	Decrease
November, 1992	9.5%
December, 1992	6.2
January, 1993	7.6
February, 1993	5.4
March, 1993	5.7

Source: Food Lion, Inc. 1992 annual report, p. 15.

ABC'S *PRIMETIME LIVE* EXPOSÉ

The food handling and sanitation practices at Food Lion were first brought to *Prime-Time Live*'s attention by the Government Accountability Project, a group that provided support to company whistle-blowers. Subsequently, ABC producer Lynn Neufer-Litt began to gather materials for the exposé by talking to 70 current and past Food Lion employees who had worked at 200 different company stores. To obtain independent confirmation of the various employee claims, several investigators, one of whom was Lynn Neufer-Litt, applied for jobs in over 20 different Food Lion stores. Two were hired and worked in 3 stores in two meat departments and a deli. Via both hidden-camera footage and employee interviews conducted by Diane Sawyer,

EXHIBIT 9 Food Lion Balance Sheets, 1989–92 (in $ millions)

| | Fiscal Year Ending Nearest Saturday to December 31 | | | |
	1992	1991	1990	1989
Assets				
Current assets:				
Cash and cash equivalents	$ 105.1	$ 4.3	$ 10.4	$ 15.7
Receivables	96.0	97.1	77.0	72.9
Income tax receivable	2.2	0.0	0.0	0.0
Inventories	896.4	844.5	673.6	577.9
Prepaid expenses	15.5	36.5	6.7	4.7
Total current assets	1,115.2	982.5	767.6	671.2
Property at cost less depreciation and amortization	1,373.6	1,036.8	791.8	610.5
Total assets	$2,488.8	$2,019.3	$1,559.5	$1,281.7
Liabilities and Shareholders' Equity				
Current liabilities:				
Notes payable	$ 459.6	$ 122.5	$ 127.5	$ 131.7
Accounts payable, trade	324.1	343.2	290.1	237.0
Accrued expenses	196.8	184.0	148.9	104.3
Long-term debt—current	.6	1.1	3.4	12.8
Capital lease obligations—current	5.1	4.1	3.1	3.2
Income taxes payable	0.0	22.0	29.8	21.8
Total current liabilities	986.3	676.9	602.8	510.8
Long-term debt	248.1	247.2	97.9	99.9
Capital lease obligations	245.7	195.2	153.8	95.0
Deferred charges/income	51.4	67.4	36.3	37.4
Deferred compensation	1.7	1.7	0.0	0.0
Total liabilities	1,533.1	1,188.4	890.9	743.2
Shareholder's equity:				
Common stock net common	241.9	161.2	161.1	161.0
Capital surplus	.2	2.0	1.2	.7
Retained earnings	713.6	667.9	506.3	376.6
Total shareholder's equity	955.7	831.1	668.6	538.5
Total liabilities and shareholder's equity	$2,488.8	$2,019.3	$1,559.5	$1,281.7
Dividends paid	$ 53.8	$ 48.0	$ 43.0	$ 32.5

Sources: Company 10-K report; February 11, 1993, press release; company annual reports for 1991–92.

EXHIBIT 10   Food Lion Statements of Income, 1989–92 (in $ millions)

| | Fiscal Year Ending Nearest Saturday to December 31 | | | |
	1992	1991	1990	1989
Net sales	$7,196.0	$6,438.5	$5,584.4	$4,717.1
Cost of goods sold	5,760.0	5,103.0	4,447.2	3,772.5
Gross profit	1,436.4	1,335.5	1,137.2	944.6
Selling and administrative expenses	975.1	855.8	738.7	619.9
Interest expense	49.1	34.4	32.6	29.2
Depreciation and amortization	121.6	104.6	81.4	65.0
Income before taxes	290.6	340.7	284.5	230.5
Provision for income taxes	112.6	135.5	111.9	90.7
Net income	$ 178.0	$ 205.2	$ 172.6	$ 139.8

Source: Company 10-K report and February 11, 1993, press release.

EXHIBIT 11   Quarterly Sales and Income Results at Food Lion before and after the *PrimeTime Live* Report (in $ millions)

Quarter	Sales	Net Income
4/1991	$2,300.0	$60.8
4/1992	2,020.0	27.3
1/1992	1,600.0	49.6
1/1993	1,660.0	21.9

Sources: "Food Lion's Payout Is Delayed Following Fallout of News Story," *The Wall Street Journal*, February 3, 1993, p. B2; and "Firm Posts 56% Decrease in 1st-Quarter Earnings," *The Wall Street Journal*, April 8, 1993, p. C6.

viewers were provided a behind-the-scenes look at Food Lion's food handling methods, labeling practices, actions to protect profit margins, and the kinds of shortcuts employees used to cope with the company's time management system.

Food Freshness and Food-Handling Practices   Razor-thin profit margins and intense price competition made all supermarket chains conscious of ways to trim costs, avoid spoilage, and maintain shelf-life freshness. Since merchandise costs were about 79 percent of total expenses, any savings Food Lion could achieve in this area could prove to be of major importance. Food Lion's upper management went to great lengths to demonstrate frugality and come up with ways to squeeze out cost savings. Area managers and even vice presidents would sometimes get into trash barrels and dumpsters to retrieve discarded food, stating, "You're throwing away profits." Bryan Rogers, an ex-produce manager, told Diane Sawyer, "I've seen them *in* the dumpster, not just leaning over into it, climb *in* it, I mean be up in it," to get merchandise and have it recycled. "Just take a head of cauliflower, for instance, I mean to where it's just got tiny black spots all over the top if it, and they'd bring it back in and want you to take a, like a Brillo pad type of thing, and scrub it to get the little black stuff off and stick it in a tray and reduce it and try to get something for it."

A meat manager stated, "We try to sell everything we can to keep from throwing anything away." Another worker, shown on camera trimming off discolored portions of outdated pork, announced, "OK, these are conversions, they look just as good as fresh." Jean Bull, a meat wrapper who had worked in 12 different Food Lion stores over a 13-year period said,

> I have seen my supervisor take chicken back out of the bone can, make us wash it, and put it back out, and it was rotten. It's just unreal what they'll do to save a dime. They take *that* pork that's already starting to get a slime to it, it gets what they call a halo to it, a kind of green tinge to it, and they take and put that into a grinder with sausage mixture, and they put it back out for anywhere from 7 to 10 days as fresh, homemade sausage. And it's rotten.

Another tale of trimming away spoilage to salvage questionable meat and of the pressures placed on employees to perform was told by Larry Worley, an ex-market manager: "We'd have this pack of cheese, sliced American cheese, and rats would get up on top of that and just eat, eat like the whole corner of it. You'd have to trim it up and put it back out. You *had* to because if we didn't make our gross profit we were out the door.

PrimeTime Live cited other instances of how Food Lion extended the shelf life of outdated products through repackaging or reformulation. Whole ham that was two weeks past the meat packer's "sell-by" date was sliced up, placed in trays, and put on sale as fresh meat. Another worker was observed unwrapping old ground beef and mixing it with fresh ground beef. Bonnie Simpson, a five-year Food Lion veteran meat wrapper, told of the time outdated ham was soaked in bleach to remove its foul odor and then cut into small squares and sold as cubed pork; she also told of how fish was treated to preserve the appearance of freshness:

> Fish has a three-day shelf life, OK? After three days you're supposed to reduce it and sell it or throw it away. But we didn't do that. We soaked the fish in baking soda and then we'd squirt lemon juice on it, then put it back in the case and sell them for three more days. The fish would be so rotten it would crumble in your hand.

In an on-camera segment a manager in the meat department was shown working with some cellophane-wrapped packages of outdated chicken parts, telling workers, "Open them up and put a soaking pad, a couple of them in the tray. This way we can put three days' date on them." He then proceeded to spread barbecue sauce on the chicken parts and sent them to the gourmet section for sale at full price.

Diane Sawyer noted that despite these practices, no cases of food poisoning had been connected to Food Lion or any other grocery chain in North Carolina where these practices were observed. And Johanna Reese, an official of North Carolina's division of environmental health, said Food Lion had an "average to above-average record" regarding health inspections.

Time Management and Unsanitary Work Practices   To try to be as labor efficient as possible, Food Lion utilized a time-management system called "effective scheduling" that was developed by a consulting firm. Under this system all work had been timed and standards established dictating the work's pace. For example, a meat cutter was expected to cut one box of meat every 32 minutes and a meat wrapper was allotted one hour to unload and stock 50 boxes of product. Based on these standards, each store received from headquarters a schedule mandating the work each department should accomplish in 40 hours. Tom Smith was a supporter of controlling labor costs through this means: "We don't work our employees hard. We work them smart."

However, many Food Lion employees found it hard to complete the work in the allotted time and resorted to skipping work breaks and working illegally "off the clock" to complete their assigned workloads. Three workers interviewed by Diane Sawyer on camera said their weekly unpaid work amounted to 10 to 25 hours each week and the work pace was grueling. Mark Riggs, a former manager of two Food Lion stores, said on camera that he felt pressured by higher management to get performance from his employees: "I felt guilty, incredibly guilty, for the things I made people do. It was the biggest reason for me leaving [Food Lion]. I couldn't look at myself in the mirror at the end of the day. You had to push people, push people."

Some Food Lion employees were said to take shortcuts to save time and meet work-load expectations; these shortcuts sometimes resulted in unsanitary workplace conditions. In one meat department the ground beef grinder was not cleaned in either the morning or evening and the department's bandsaw blades and wheels were not disassembled at the end of the workday to eliminate spending time reassembling them the next morning. In these instances, meat residues were later deposited on newly ground meat the next day. In one on-camera scene, a deli clerk, casting a baleful eye around her work station's area, commented after the hidden camera showed dirty trays and baking tins and a meat cutter "ice skating" on a grease-covered floor:

> Well the floor and the meat slicer . . . God, comin' into a place and the glunk on the slicer is thick. The floor's got all kinds of crap all over it. I don't think it's real appealing for a deli.

Another exposé segment pointed out shipping problems associated with Food Lion's advance-purchasing system that was used to obtain discounts from manufacturers. Although Food Lion's centralized advance-purchases and volume buying resulted in lower incoming product costs, occasional shipping delays or problems getting merchandise from distribution centers in a timely manner sometimes resulted in meat products arriving in stores near their "sell-by" dates. In one on-camera sequence the following dialogue transpired:

> **Meat manager:** You *know* that the lamb that you cut on Monday is not gonna run, is not gonna go through Wednesday. Because the damn stuff is old when it comes in.
>
> **"PrimeTime":** What do you mean it's old when it comes in?
>
> **Meat manager:** It's #@!? lamb. I have been on their ass for three years to get some decent lamb, if they want to sell lamb.

Food Lion's Responses

Prior to its broadcast, *PrimeTime Live* provided Food Lion with a report on its investigation and invited a company spokesperson to be an interview subject. Rather than appearing under *PrimeTime*'s conditions, Food Lion immediately began running television advertisements. Tom Smith was shown strolling through a Food Lion store where he mentioned the company's "A" sanitation rating and the chain's pride in its cleanliness standards. On the morning of the telecast, employees in Salisbury held a rally where pro-company petitions and letters were prepared; these expressions were later sent to congresspeople and Capital Cities/ABC Inc. In Tulsa, a newspaper story was published the same morning discussing the program's possible effect on Tulsa's new stores; in the story Vince Watkins was quoted as saying, "It is our understanding that this program will make some very serious and potentially devastating allegations about our company. These allegations will make excellent television but they will not be the truth."

The next day Food Lion distributed a media "fact sheet" outlining its position regarding food handling and employee scheduling practices. The company began visiting each store shown in the segment and interviewing the employees involved. The announcement promised to quickly accomplish the following:

1. Establish more stringent periodic testing of employees to ensure complete and clear understanding of all Food Lion's policies and procedures.

2. Increase internal and external audits and internal inspections by management to ensure that these policies and procedures were rigorously implemented.

3. Continue to ensure that if there ever was any problem in any Food Lion store, anywhere, at any time, it would be fixed.

Other operating procedures were changed immediately. The company's previous meat handling policy had been to open the packages on their "sell-by" date to check for freshness. Any spoiled meat was to be discarded while still-fresh meat would be repackaged and sold at a discount. "So as not to create any further suspicions" about repackaging, Food Lion said price reductions would be taken while the meat remained in the case at which time it could be sold for only one day longer.

Although the chain expressed a belief that the furor would quickly subside, such was not the case. A Food Lion executive admitted, "Out stock price is down, but we expected that to happen and we expect it to go back up to its previous level. The reason Food Lion has been so successful is because our customers are happy with the job we're doing." In an effort to stem the company's sliding stock price, Tom Smith made a 50-minute conference call to Wall Street securities analysts in which he told them most of the program's sources lacked credibility and were union sympathizers. He also made a television commercial where he said, in part, "You've heard some shocking stories about Food Lion. We do have sound policies and procedures. However, occasionally a problem can exist." The headquarters' public relations staff sent 60,000 videotapes of Food Lion's responses to the broadcast out to each employee and urged them to show it to their families, friends, and local groups. It was also suggested that along with showing the tapes employees "might want to have a party with their friends and serve them food from Food Lion's delis."

During the ensuing weeks Food Lion launched a counteroffensive in the press and on television against what it considered unfair, careless, and dishonest reporting on the *PrimeTime Live* segment. As one Food Lion executive put it, "When unwarranted attacks are made on a company, you don't say, 'We'll take our hit and move on.' You come back with the truth." Food Lion questioned whether allegedly out-of-date meat loaf shown on camera was actually nine days old since it would have become visibly black to the television cameras after only four days. Various products were displayed in one televised *PrimeTime Live* sequence, such as Colombo yogurt and Healthy Choice lunch meats, but these items had never been carried by Food

Lion. Also, Beef America products were shown on the *PrimeTime Live* report, but it was Monford beef that had been shipped six to seven weeks old in vacuum sealed packages. The time period on those products was well within the allotted 12 to 14 week freshness period. And in the very damaging barbecue-sauce segment, the chicken products changed from scene to scene.

Additionally, Food Lion management raised questions about the union's integrity, as well as the motivations of three of the program's interviewees. A total of 65 of the 70 people interviewed by *PrimeTime Live* were supplied by the UFCW and 6 of the 7 people identified in the story were involved in UFCW-initiated lawsuits against Food Lion. Joe Sultan, the former perishables manager, was reprimanded for poor conditions in his department and fired for requiring off-the-clock work from his people. Bryan Rogers, while denigrating the company's produce in the telecast, had shopped at a Food Lion the night of the *PrimeTime Live* program. Jean Bull, who talked about selling slime-covered pork, shopped with her family at Food Lion each week; she had been reprimanded for passing bad checks and had a lawsuit pending against Food Lion.

Numerous legal actions were also begun by Food Lion. The company filed a suit charging ABC with fraud because ABC's producers lied to Food Lion to get jobs at its stores. Through this lawsuit, Food Lion gained access to the program's unedited footage as well as the right to question the program's producer. A Food Lion official said, "Some of the things we are finding out from our depositions make it plain to us they engaged in extensive illegal acts and violated state and federal laws in doing so." As a result, Food Lion amended its original suit in April 1993 to include claims the network violated federal racketeering laws in conducting its exposé, alleging that ABC employees engaged in racketeering, trespassing, illicit eavesdropping, and wire fraud; under provisions of the law, Food Lion asked that triple damages be assessed against ABC. ABC's response to this emendation noted that "Food Lion does not challenge the truth of the ABC report. It challenges only the undercover methods used by ABC. We believe Food Lion's charges of racketeering are outrageous. We believe this is a legally baseless complaint."

In another lawsuit filed February 12, 1993 against the UFCW, Food Lion alleged the union had waged a smear campaign in an attempt to unionize the company. In seeking actual and punitive damages, Food Lion charged the union with "abuse of process," use of "economic guerrilla tactics" to tarnish its image, and the filing of frivolous lawsuits to obtain proprietary information about company operations and finances.

Some observers questioned the wisdom of Food Lion's public relations strategy; a Fort Worth retailing consultant said, "From a public relations standpoint, they were their own worst enemy. I would have advised a massive mea culpa as opposed to the defensive posture that they're taking." Food Lion, however, believed it was pursuing the right strategy, citing General Motors' vindication and subsequent network retraction and apology following a flawed NBC *Dateline* report on safety hazards supposedly associated with one of GM's pickup truck models. A Food Lion official said that GM's experience "illustrates that TV tabloid-type programs will go to extraordinary lengths to concoct or stage events."

Although Food Lion had often relied on court actions to defend its business interests, on several occasions the company's practice had been subjected to federal investigation and judicial scrutiny. The company began meeting with the U.S.Labor Department in January 1993 to head off possible federal charges of child-labor and overtime violations; the Labor Department investigation resulted from a 183-person class action suit filed in September 1991 that asked for $388 million in back pay and damages. The suit was filed with the help of UFCW officials; none of the Food Lion workers on behalf of whom the suit was filed were members of the UFCW. Francis D. Carpenter, who claimed to have regularly worked 60- and 70-hour weeks during his seven years at Food Lion's Southern Pines, North Carolina, grocery store, said "It got to the point where I just couldn't take it anymore. My supervisor would always say 'Do what you have to do to get the job done, but don't let me catch you working off the clock.' I took that to mean 'Work off the clock, but don't get caught.'" In its suit the union concluded employees often worked up to 13 hours a week off the clock. Food Lion had already lost one decision of this nature when a North Carolina U.S. District Court judge ordered Food Lion to pay two former employees a total of $53,000 in overtime wages and damages.

Food Lion was also being investigated by the Labor Department regarding some 1,400 incidents of alleged violations of child-labor laws; 1,200 of the incidents involved teenagers working with or near potentially dangerous equipment; the case was one of the largest of its kind involving a single employer. Food Lion believed that about 90 percent of the incidents related to teenagers putting cardboard boxes into package balers that were turned off. A federal ban on teenagers doing that type of work had gone into effect just months prior to the suit's filing and the grocery industry as a whole was fighting the ban's breadth. To help achieve compliance with the new federal requirement, Food Lion had instituted a company policy that required teenage employees to sign statements acknowledging their awareness of the ban. They also wore a blue dot on their name tags identifying themselves as teenagers so that managers would not unknowingly ask underage employees to perform forbidden work. A Food Lion vice president said, "I don't think anybody violated it intentionally and I don't think anyone in management asked them to do it."

Food Lion's Tulsa Operations

Over a short period Food Lion had opened seven stores in the Tulsa metropolitan area. This had virtually coincided with the *PrimeTime Live* report. The stores were built in the city's fastest-growing localities and each faced different combinations of competitors within a two-mile shopping radius. Exhibit 12 lists the major supermarkets operating in the Tulsa market; additional competition came from at least three warehouse clubs and 135 convenience stores.

EXHIBIT 12   Food Lion's Supermarket Competition in Tulsa

Company	Stores
Albertson's	4
Bud's Food Stores	4
Consumer's IGA	2
Homeland	25
Payless Food Store	2
Price Mart	3
Price Rite Reasor's/Reasor's Foods	2
Super H Discount Foods	5
Warehouse Market	12

EXHIBIT 13   Content of Typical Food Lion Price Comparison Advertisement in Tulsa

Comparison reveals:

Food Lion Prices Lower in Tulsa

Food Lion's extra low prices are lower everyday on the items families buy most. Below are just a few examples. These represent thousands of items you can buy for less at Food Lion every day of the week. Visit Food Lion today and discover how much you can save each week on your total food bill.

	Price Mart	Homeland	Food Lion
Libby's lite sliced peaches (16 oz.)	$ .89	$ 1.19	$ .79
Del Monte cut green beans (8 oz.)	.43	.53	.34
Del Monte creamed corn (8.75 oz.)	.43	.53	.34
Veg All (16 oz.)	.59	.59	.48
Del Monte green peas (8.5 oz.)	.43	.53	.30
Bush's baked beans (16 oz.)	.69	.69	.50
Van Camp's Beanee Weenees (7.75 oz.)	.74	.85	.55
Hunt's whole peeled tomatoes (14.5 oz.)	.73	.79	.48
Mahatma yellow rice (5 oz.)	.41	.39	.33
Campbell's vegetable soup (10.5 oz.)	.64	.65	.55
Campbell's cream of chicken soup (10.75 oz.)	.69	.75	.64
Spam deviled spread (3 oz.)	.59	.65	.56
Underwood's deviled ham (4.5 oz.)	1.29	1.39	1.09
Libby's Vienna sausages (5 oz.)	.63	.75	.43
Bush's hot chili beans (16 oz.)	.49	.55	.38
Franco American spaghetti (14.75 oz.)	.65	.69	.50
Franco American Spaghetti O's w/meatballs (14.75 oz.)	1.13	1.16	.89
Chef Boyardee Beef-o-Getti (15 oz.)	1.13	1.16	.89
Chef Boyardee beef ravioli (15 oz.)	1.13	1.16	.79
Chef Boyardee micro. spaghetti w/meatballs (7.5 oz.)	.99	1.09	.79
Prego spaghetti sauce w/mushrooms (30 oz.)	1.89	2.27	1.69
Old El Paso taco dinner (12/9.75 oz.)	2.39	2.59	1.99
Kraft deluxe macaroni (14 oz.)	1.69	1.77	1.39
Crisco shortening (16 oz.)	1.28	1.39	1.23
Totals	$21.95	$24.11	$17.92

America's Fastest Growing Supermarket Chain

This price comparison was made December 17, 1992. Some prices may have changed since that time.

Food Lion's stores were open from 7:00 AM to 11:00 PM and they were clean, well lit, easily accessed, and utilitarian in their appearance. They were 28,000- to 32,000-square-foot stores and cost $1 to $2 million each to construct, depending primarily on the real estate values associated with each unit. All were similarly configured. The company employed its usual low-price strategy which was announced through comparative advertising of the type shown in Exhibit 13. Well in advance of Food Lion's store openings, however, established competitors began cutting prices and featuring cents-off displays and shelf specials. Several reinstituted double redemptions on coupons, a practice that had been previously discontinued in the Tulsa market, and some guaranteed they would match Food Lion's prices on a product-by-product basis.

In addition to the competitive actions taken by other supermarkets, another challenge to Food Lion came immediately from the UFCW's Local 76. John Stone, the local's president, felt the effect of the *PrimeTime Live* exposé would be short-lived and disappear within about three weeks. To keep its own message before the public, and to keep the controversy alive, Stone's UFCW local mailed "informational literature" to households in each Food Lion's store's ZIP-code area and passed out leaflets at each store's parking lot entrance for a number of weeks. Postcard literature mailed to households during the week of December 3, 1992, was headlined "FOOD LION IS FOREIGN OWNED!" and stated, "Every dollar in profit goes overseas to Belgium!" The card said, "Food Lion cheats its employees to gain illegal advantage over American businessmen who obey the law! Don't let a foreign company dump its garbage on American consumers! SHOP AMERICAN! DON'T SHOP AT FOOD LION!" The leaflets passed out at the entrances to store parking lots reiterated the "Buy American" theme and decried the company's abusive labor practices.

What Now?

Addressing shareholders at the company's 1993 annual meeting, Tom Smith acknowledged that problems surrounded its southwestern market expansion, of which Tulsa served only as an example:

> Operating results in this market have been less than originally expected and are significantly below the average for the company's stores in other markets. We will closely monitor and evaluate performance in this market in light of the company's performance objectives and will continue to do all things reasonably necessary to increase performance. However, at the present time, the company does not plan any significant additional growth in the Southwest and is studying alternative strategies for this market.

Asked what Smith's remarks meant, a Food Lion vice president scoffed at any idea of selling the southwestern stores or the 1.1-million-square-foot Roanoke, Texas, distribution center: "We intend to battle hard for market share out there."

Meanwhile the company disclosed in late April 1993 the filing of three shareholder suits against it. One suit alleged Food Lion's top executives conspired to inflate the market price of the company's securities. The second lawsuit maintained executives made misstatements or omissions in its company reports dating back to September 1991, and the third claimed the company's 1992 proxy statement was false and misleading when it failed to disclose the improper food-handling procedures reported by *PrimeTime Live*. During 1993, Food Lion stock traded in the $5 to $8 range on the NASDAQ, far below the $25 to $30 price range that it had traded in during the months preceding the *PrimeTime Live* report.

DESIGNTEX, INC. (A)*

Matthew Mehalik, *University of Virginia*

Michael E. Gorman, *University of Virginia*

Andrea Larson, *University of Virginia*

Patricia H. Werhaue, *University of Virginia*

> The contract textile business is about offering choice, not volume.
>
> **Susan Lyons**

Susan Lyons, vice president of design at DesignTex, a firm specializing in the design and manufacture of textiles for commercial interiors, knew the importance of looking ahead to the next design breakthrough. In February 1991, she had helped launch a new line of fabrics called the Portfolio Collection, a design that evolved out of collaboration with such famous architects as Aldo Rossi, Robert Venturi, Denise Scott Brown, and Richard Meier. This collection was provocative aesthetically and demonstrated that well-designed fabrics could be marketed at reasonable prices.

Although Lyons was proud of the latest collection, she wanted the next design to focus on an issue, not be just a change in aesthetics. The issue of environmental responsibility seemed perfect. "Green" was popular in the trade literature and in the general media, and she had been receiving inquiries from DesignTex's customers about how environmentally responsible DesignTex's products were. Her desire

---

*Partial support for this project was supplied by grants from the Ethics and Values in Science program of the National Science Foundation and the Geraldine R. Dodge Foundation. The conclusions are the responsibilities of the authors, and do not reflect the views of the foundations. Copyright © 1996 by the School of Engineering and Applied Science of the University of Virginia and the University of Virginia Darden School Foundation. All rights reserved.

to pursue an environmental agenda was not, however, simply the result of customer demand. It sprang from deep personal beliefs about environmentalism that reflected her mother's influence. Lyon's mother had been "way ahead of her time." She had been recycling trash and other items and had been conservation minded back in the 1960s when Lyons was growing up. These childhood experiences had made Lyons sensitive to environmental concerns, and she had a strong impulse to act upon them.

Such a breakthrough, thought Lyons, would maintain DesignTex's leadership in the commercial-fabrics design market. DesignTex was vying to be the largest member of the Association of Contract Textiles (ACT), the industry trade organization. Located in New York, DesignTex worked with over 40 textile mills around the world, many of which manufactured the designs created by DesignTex.

DesignTex was also a member of the Steelcase Design Partnership, a group of design firms purchased in 1989 by Steelcase, a giant corporation located in Grand Rapids, Michigan, that manufactured office furniture and supplies. Steelcase formed this partnership to better penetrate a market segment that otherwise had eluded the firm. Although the company was able to turn out huge amounts of products very profitably, its generic product line did not appeal to customers such as architects, who demanded specialty or custom designs. Small, nimble, and entrepreneurial companies were able to meet the demands of the growing custom/specialty niche better than Steelcase, and DesignTex was such a company.

In order to maintain DesignTex's ability to respond to the rapidly changing custom-design market, Steelcase permitted DesignTex's management to operate autonomously. In fact, as a fabric supplier, DesignTex sometimes competed against Steelcase for contracts. Steelcase typically brought in DesignTex as a consultant, however, in matters involving specialty-fabrics design. Susan Lyons summarized the relationship: "DesignTex is very profitable, and Steelcase receives a large amount of money from DesignTex's operation with no oversight, so Steelcase is happy to let DesignTex do its own thing. However, this situation could change if DesignTex's profitability began to decline." By taking the lead in the still volatile environmental market, Lyons hoped DesignTex would boost its profitability and its reputation for innovativeness, thereby maintaining its freedom to operate independent of Steelcase's management influence.

To launch her project, she began surveying the trade literature, contacted yarn spinners who claimed to be environmentally "correct," and monitored competitors who were also attempting to enter this market. The work was difficult because (1) she was also looking at approximately 40 other new designs and design improvements, (2) she wanted the design to look like others in the DesignTex line and (3) she wanted the design to be durable as well as environmentally viable.

Lyons continued her "research" for about two years, from 1991 through 1993. What she found was a jumble of information. As she pointed out, there were "conflicting claims about environmentally safe materials." Cottons were often heavily bleached, and most manufacturers were reluctant to talk about what was in their dyes. She considered using foxfiber with vegetable dyes, but the combination was available in only two colors. She considered using a yarn that was made from recycled plastic soft-drink bottles. In fact, this appeared to be the most promising option, but the vendors were unreliable. These problems seemed difficult to reconcile with her belief that the "contract-textile business is about offering choice, not volume."[1]

---

[1]The information in this section was obtained during an interview with Susan Lyons on 31 July 1995.

THE CLIMATEX OPTION[2]

Because DesignTex also worked with over 40 contract mills around the world, Lyons contacted some of them to investigate their environmental efforts. In December 1992 she became interested in a fabric product called Climatex. Albin Kaelin, managing director of Rohner Textil, a mill located in Switzerland, sent Lyons a sample. He and Rohner Textil had been pursuing an environmental agenda of their own, and he was willing to team up with Lyons and DesignTex in developing a new product based on Climatex.

The fabric, a patented combination of wool, ramie, and polyester, was unique because it wicked away moisture from a person who was in contact with the material over long periods. It was intended to improve comfort in wheelchairs and trucks, since those applications involved extended periods of contact between people and fabrics. Exhibit 1 contains additional information on Climatex.

Lyons also inquired about the possibility of recycling Climatex. Kaelin informed her that recycling fabrics was possible only if the material was pure (e.g., 100 percent wool or cotton), but not if it was a combination of materials. Because Climatex was a blend of wool, ramie, and polyester, no recycling was possible. In addition, Kaelin mentioned that recycling any commercial fabrics was questionable, because they were typically glued as upholstery, and the glue itself made recycling difficult. Nevertheless, he went on to add, "there is a far more important argument on the aspect of ecology to Climatex." Since the fabric was created without any chemical treatments, "the yarn in the fabric can be burned without any damaging chemical reaction and have a good heating factor." By "good heating factor," Kaelin meant that the fabric released a large amount of energy when burned, and he proposed using this energy in the operation of the mill. He also mentioned that Climatex was being tested in Germany by an independent institute, the International Association for Research and Testing in the Field of Textile Ecology (OEKO-Tex).[3]

Both Kaelin and Lyons were pleased when Climatex passed the OEKO-Tex inspections in May 1993. The institute, concerned with human-ecology issues, tested for pH value, content of free and partially releasable formaldehyde, residues of heavy metals, residues of pesticides, pentachorophenole content, carcinogenic compounds, and colorfastness. Having passed these tests, Climatex could bear the OEKO-Tex trademark and was certified to be allergy-free.

By the middle of 1993, Lyons had several options to consider for an environmental design. The most promising one seemed to be the Climatex fabric from Rohner, which was certified to be manufactured within the OEKO-Tex specifications. But she was worried that because the fabric was not recyclable, and because it was difficult to make a grand environmental statement using the OEKO-Tex label, that option might not be as good as it seemed. In addition, the product was not cheap. It was priced competitively within the worsted-wool market niche, but that particular niche was on the expensive end of the overall market. She considered using yarn made from recycled plastic bottles, but she was not confident that the vendors could deliver reliably. Her research uncovered promising options, but each had difficulties and risks.

---

[2]Climatex is a registered trademark of Rohner Textil, AG.

[3]Kaelin quotes from correspondence from Kaelin to Lyons, 3 December 1992, supplemented by the Lyons interview of 31 July 1995.

EXHIBIT 1   Information on Climatex

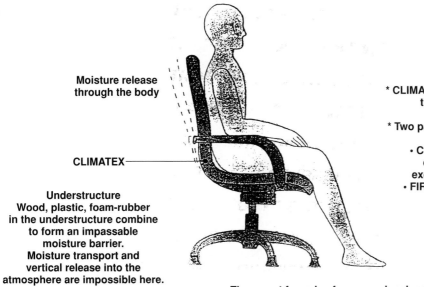

Moisture release through the body

CLIMATEX

Understructure
Wood, plastic, foam-rubber in the understructure combine to form an impassable moisture barrier.
Moisture transport and vertical release into the atmosphere are impossible here.

* CLIMATEX assures an optimal environment through vertical and horizontal moisture transport.
* Two patents assure double security for the discovery of CLIMATEX:
  • CLIMATEX ® as final product with excellent seating comfort and excellent hard-wearing properties.
  • FIRON ® for the unique combination of pure wool and ramie.

The secret formula of pure wool, polyester and ramie (long-fibered plant, native to tropical and subtropical areas)

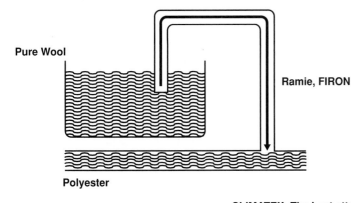

Pure Wool

Ramie, FIRON

Polyester

Pure wool collects up to 1/3 of its own weight in moisture, then "overflows."
Polyester is incapable of taking up this moisture and transporting it.
Now ramie comes into play. The secret of the formula. Ramie absorbs moisture from pure wool and releases it to polyester for transport.
The result: CLIMATEX

CLIMATEX: The best attributes from three different fibers, optimally combined.
Polyester with its high resistance to chafing, minimal creasing, good absorption transport.
Pure wool with its high elasticity, good heat conservation, great moisture absorption.
Ramie with its great absorbency, cooling effect, strong moisture transport acts as a middleman between pure wool and polyester.

In July 1993, DesignTex owner Ralph Saltzman, President Tom Hamilton, Consultant Steve Kroeter, and Lyons met to consider what the next generation of the Portfolio Collection would be. Launched in 1991, Portfolio had been a highly successful major product line. By mid-1993, however, the product's demand had peaked. At this meeting, the team agreed that the next Portfolio collection would have a major impact on the market if its design focused on the green issue.

During that meeting Lyons brought up another factor that could not be neglected: aesthetics. In addition to being environmentally friendly the next Portfolio collection had to be as beautiful as the last. Lyons hoped to collaborate with a prestigious designer in producing beautiful fabrics for the new line, just as she had for the original Portfolio Collection. At the meeting Kroeter suggested that they contact Suzy Tompkins of the Esprit Clothing Company, which had just released a unique line of clothing based on organic cotton. Lyons suggested an architect who was well known for his environmental philosophy and his architectural-design accomplishments, William McDonough. The group agreed that they would contact both designers and invite them to participate in the next generation of Portfolio. Tompkins declined to participate because, as a clothing manufacturer, she rarely worked with commercial-fabric designers. Lyons did, however, receive a more enthusiastic response when she contacted McDonough.

WILLIAM MCDONOUGH

During her environmental literature search, Lyons had come across the name of William McDonough in two places. She had read the March 1993 issue of *Interiors* magazine, which was dedicated entirely to McDonough and his projects. She had also seen an article about him in *The Wall Street Journal*.[4] McDonough had just accepted a job as the dean of Architecture at the University of Virginia. After reading about him, Lyons viewed him as the most high-profile person working with environmental concerns in the design industry.

McDonough had no immediate plans to develop sustainable fabrics, but he responded quite enthusiastically when she made the suggestion to him. He was looking for opportunities to apply his design philosophy. The fabric-design project fit into his plans perfectly.

McDonough came to visit DesignTex in early October 1993. During their meeting, Lyons described the options she had turned up in her literature and marketplace searches and suggested the idea of the recycled plastic bottle fabric to him. In turn, McDonough presented his design philosophy (the elements of this philosophy are outlined in Exhibit 2).

"Two key principles hit home really hard," Lyons said, "the idea that waste equals food and the idea of a cradle-to-cradle design, not a cradle-to-grave design." McDonough stated that in order to meet the waste-equals-food and cradle-to-cradle design criteria, the product had to be able either (1) to compost completely with no negative environmental impact, thereby becoming food for other organisms (organic nutrients) or (2) to become raw material for another industrial product (technical nutrients.) Furthermore, one should not mix the organic and the technical, or one would end up with a product that could be used neither as food for organisms nor as raw materials for technology. "The product should be manufactured without the release of carcinogens, bioaccumulatives, persistent toxic chemicals, mutagens, heavy metals, or endocrine disruptors." McDonough discouraged the use of the term "environmentally friendly" and instead proposed "environmentally intelligent" to describe this method of design, because it involved having the foresight to know that poisoning the earth is not merely unfriendly, but unintelligent.[5]

---

[4]*The Wall Street Journal*, October 23, 1989.

[5]The concepts "cradle-to-cradle," "waste equals food," "current solar income," "environmentally intelligent," and the design protocol discussed above are proprietary to William McDonough and are included in this document with his permission.

EXHIBIT 2 McDonough's Design Philosophy

A CENTENNIAL SERMON:
"DESIGN, ECOLOGY, ETHICS AND THE MAKING OF THINGS"
by
WILLIAM McDONOUGH
THE CATHEDRAL OF ST. JOHN THE DIVINE
NEW YORK, NEW YORK
February 7, 1993
Adapted by
WILLIAM McDONOUGH and PAUL HAWKEN

It is humbling to be an architect in a cathedral because it is a magnificent representation of humankind's highest aspirations. Its dimension is illustrated by the small Christ figure in the western rose window, which is, in fact, human scale. A cathedral is a representation of both our longings and intentions. This morning, here at this important crossing in this great building, I am going to speak about the concept of design itself as the first signal of human intention and will focus on ecology, ethics, and the making of things. I would like to reconsider both our design and our intentions.

When Vincent Scully gave a eulogy for the great architect Louis Kahn, he described a day when both were crossing Red Square, whereupon Scully excitedly turned to Kahn and said, "Isn't it wonderful the way the domes of St. Basil's Cathedral reach up into the sky?" Kahn looked up and down thoughtfully for a moment and said, "Isn't it beautiful the way they come down to the ground?"

If we understand that design leads to the manifestation of human intention, and if what we make with our hands is to be sacred and honor the earth that gives us life, then the things we make must not only rise from the ground but return to it, soil to soil, water to water, so everything that is received from the earth can be freely given back without causing harm to any living system. This is ecology. This is good design. It is of this we must now speak.

If we use the study of architecture to inform this discourse, and we go back in history, we will see that, architects are always working with two elements, mass and membrane. We have the walls of Jericho, mass, and we have tents, membranes. Ancient peoples practiced the art and wisdom of building with mass, such as an adobe-walled hut, to anticipate the scope and direction of sunshine. They knew how thick a wall needed to be to transfer the heat of the day into the winter night, and how thick it had to be to transfer the coolness into the interior in the summer. They worked well with what we call "capacity" in the walls in terms of storage and thermal lags. They worked with resistance, straw, in the roof to protect from heat loss in the winter and to shield the heat gain in summer from the high sun. These were very sensible buildings within the climate in which they are located.

With respect to membrane, we only have to look at the Bedouin tent to find a design that accomplishes five things at once. In the desert, temperatures often exceed 120 degrees. There is no shade, no air movement. The black Bedouin tent, when pitched, creates a deep shade that brings one's sensible temperature down to 95 degrees. The tent has a very coarse weave, which creates a beautifully illuminated interior, having a million light fixtures. Because of the coarse weave and the black surface, the air inside rises and is drawn through the membrane. So now you have a breeze coming in from outside, and that drops the sensible temperature even lower, down to 90 degrees. You may wonder what happens when it rains, with those holes in the tent. The fibers swell up and the tents gets tight as a drum when wet. And of course, you can roll it up and take it with you. The modern tent pales by comparison to this astonishingly elegant construct.

Throughout history, you find constant experimentation between mass and membrane. This cathedral is a Gothic experiment integrating great light into massive membrane. The challenge has always been, on a certain level, how to combine light with mass and air. This experiment displayed itself powerfully in modern architecture, which arrived with the advent of inexpensive glass. It was unfortunate that at the same time the large sheet of glass showed up, the era of cheap energy was ushered in, too. And because of that, architects no longer rely upon the sun for heat or illumination. I have spoken to thousands of architects, and when I ask the question, "How many of you know how to find true South?", I rarely get a raised hand.

EXHIBIT 2   Continued

Our culture has adopted a design stratagem that essentially says that if brute force or massive amounts of energy don't work, you're not using enough of it. We made glass buildings that are more about buildings than they are about people. We've used the glass ironically. The hope that glass would connect us to the outdoors was completely stultified by making the buildings sealed. We have created stress in people because we are meant to be connected with the outdoors, but instead we are trapped. Indoor air quality issues are now becoming very serious. People are sensing how horrifying it can be to be trapped indoors, especially with the thousands upon thousands of chemicals that are being used to make things today.

Le Corbusier said in the early part of this century that a house is a machine for living in. He glorified the steamship, the airplane, the grain elevator. Think about it: a house is a machine for living in. An office is a machine for working in. A cathedral is a machine for praying in. This has become a terrifying prospect, because what has happened is that designers are now designing for the machine and not for the people. People talk about solar heating a building, even about solar heating a cathedral. But it isn't the cathedral that is asking to be heated, it is the people. To solar-heat a cathedral, one should heat people's feet, not the air 120 feet above them. We need to listen to biologist John Todd's idea that we need to work with living machines, not machines for living in. The focus should be on people's needs, and we need clean water, safe materials, and durability. And we need to work from current solar income.

There are certain fundamental laws that are inherent to the natural world that we can use as models and mentors for human designs. Ecology comes from the Greek roots Oikos and Logos, "household," and "logical discourse." Thus, it is appropriate, if not imperative, for architects to discourse about the logic of our earth household. To do so, we must first look at our planet and the very processes by which it manifests life, because therein lie the logical principles with which we must work. And we must also consider economy in the true sense of the word. Using the Greek words Oikos and Nomos, we speak of natural law and how we measure and manage the relationships within this household, working with the principles our discourse has revealed to us.

And how do we measure our work under those laws? Does it make sense to measure it by the paper currency that you have in your wallet? Does it make sense to measure it by a grand summation called GNP? For if we do, we find that the foundering and rupture of the Exxon Valdez tanker was a prosperous event because so much money was spent in Prince William Sound during the clean-up. What then are we really measuring? If we have not put natural resources on the asset side of the ledger, then where are they? Does a forest really become more valuable when it is cut down? Do we really prosper when wild salmon are completely removed from a river?

There are three defining characteristics that we can learn from natural design. The first characteristic is that everything we have to work with is already here—The stones, the clay, the wood, the water, the air. All materials given to us by nature are constantly returned to the earth without even the concept of waste as we understand it. Everything is cycled constantly with all waste equaling food for other living systems.

The second characteristic is that the one thing allowing nature to continually cycle itself through life is energy, and this energy comes from outside the system in the form of perpetual solar income. Not only does nature operate on "current income," it does not mine or extract energy from the past, it does not use its capital reserves, and it does not borrow from the future. It is an extraordinarily complex and efficient system for creating and cycling nutrients, so economical that modern methods of manufacturing pale in comparison to the elegance of natural systems of production.

Finally, the characteristic that sustains this complex and efficient system of metabolism and creation is biodiversity. What prevents living systems from running down and veering into chaos is a miraculously intricate and symbiotic relationship between millions of organisms, no two of which are like.

As a designer of buildings, things, and systems, I ask myself how to apply these three characteristics of living systems to my work. How do I employ the concept of waste equals food, of current solar income, of protecting biodiversity in design? Before I can even apply these principles, though, we must understand the role of the designer in human affairs.

In thinking about this I reflect upon a commentary of Emerson's. In the 1830's, when his wife died, he went to Europe on a sailboat and returned in a steamship. He remarked on the return voyage that he missed the "Aeolian connection." If we abstract this, he went over on a solar-powered recyclable vehicle operated by craftpersons, working in the open air, practicing ancient arts. He returned in a steel rust bucket, spilling oil on the water and smoke into the sky, operated by people in a black dungeon shoveling

EXHIBIT 2   Continued

coal into the mouth of a boiler. Both ships are objects of design. Both are manifestations of our human intention.

Peter Senge, a professor at M.I.T.'s Sloan School of Management, works with a program called the Learning Laboratory where he studies and discusses how organizations learn. Within that he has a leadership laboratory, and one of the first questions he asks CEOs of companies that attend is, "Who is the leader on a ship crossing the ocean?" He gets obvious answers, such as the captain, the navigator, or the helmsman. But the answer is none of the above. The leader is the designer of the ship because operations on a ship are a consequence of design, which is the result of human intention. Today, we are still designing steamships, machines powered by fossil fuels that have deleterious effects. We need a new design.

I grew up in the Far East, and when I came to this country, I was taken aback when I realized that we were not people with lives in America, but consumers with lifestyles. I wanted to ask someone: when did America stop having people with lives? On television, we are referred to as consumers, not people. But we are people, with lives, and we must make and design things for people. And if I am a consumer, what can I consume? Shoe polish, food, juice, some toothpaste. But actually, very little that is sold to me can actually be consumed. Sooner or later, almost all of it has to be thrown away. I cannot consume a television set. Or a VCR. Or a car. If I presented you with a television set and covered it up and said, "I have this amazing item. What it will do as a service will astonish you. But before I tell you what it does, let me tell you what it is made of and you can tell me if you want it in your house. It contains 4,060 chemicals, many of which are toxic, two hundred of which off-gas into the room when it is turned on. It also contains 18 grams of toxic methyl mercury, has an explosive glass tube, and I urge you to put it eye-level with your children and encourage them to play with it." Would you want this in your home?

Michael Braungart, an ecological chemist from Hamburg, Germany, has pointed out that we should remove the word *waste* from our vocabulary and start using the word *product* instead, because if waste is going to equal food, it must also be a product. Braungart suggests we think about three distinct product types.

First, there are consumables, and actually we should be producing more of them. These are products that when eaten, used, or thrown away, literally turn back into dirt, and therefore are food for other living organisms. Consumables should not be placed in landfills, but put on the ground so that they restore the life, health, and fertility of the soil. This means that shampoos should be in bottles made of beets that are biodegradable in your compost pile. It means carpets that break down into CO_2 and water. It means furniture made of lignin, potato peels and technical enzymes that looks just like your manufactured furniture of today except it can be safely returned to the earth. It means that all "consumable" goods should be capable of returning to the soil from whence they came.

Second are products of service, also known as durables, such as cars and television sets. They are called products of service because what we want as customers is the service the product provides—food, entertainment, or transportation. To eliminate the concept of waste, products of service would not be sold, but licensed to the end-user. Customers may use them as long as they wish, even sell the license to someone else, but when the end-user is finished with, say, a television, it goes back to Sony, Zenith, or Philips. It is "food" for their system, but not for natural systems. Right now, you can go down the street, dump a TV into the garbage can, and walk way. In the process, we deposit persistent toxins throughout the planet. Whey do we give people that responsibility and stress? Products of service must continue beyond their initial product life, be owned by their manufacturers, and be designed for disassembly, re-manufacture, and continuous re-use.

The third type of product is called "unmarketables." The question is, why would anyone produce a product that no one would buy? Welcome to the world of nuclear waste, dioxins, and chromium-tanned leather. We are essentially making products or subcomponents of products that no one should buy, or, in many cases, do not realize they are buying. These products must not only cease to be sold, but those already sold should be stored in warehouses when they are finished until we can figure out a safe and non-toxic way to dispose of them.

I will describe a few projects and how these issues are implicit in design directions. I remember when we were hired to design the office for an environmental group. The director said at the end of the contract negotiations, "By the way, if anybody in our office gets sick from indoor air quality, we're going to sue you." After wondering if we should even take the job, we decided to go ahead, that it was our job to find the

EXHIBIT 2   Continued

materials that wouldn't make people sick when placed inside a building. And what we found is that those materials weren't there. We had to work with manufacturers to find out what was in their products, and we discovered that the entire system of building construction is essentially toxic. We are still working on the materials side.

For a New York men's clothing store, we arranged for the planting of 1,000 oak trees to replace the two English oaks used to panel the store. We were inspired by a famous story told by Gregory Bateson about New College in Oxford, England. It went something like this. They had a main hall built in the early 1600s with beams forty feet long and two feet thick. A committee was formed to try to find replacement trees because the beams were suffering from dry rot. If you keep in mind that a veneer from an English oak can be worth seven dollars a square foot, the total replacement costs for the oaks were prohibitively expensive. And they didn't have straight forty foot English oaks from mature forests with which to replace the beams. A young faculty member joined the committee and said, "Why don't we ask the College Forester if some of the lands that had been given to Oxford might have enough trees to call upon?" And when they brought in the forester he said, "We've been wondering when you would ask this question. When the present building was constructed 350 years ago, the architects specified that a grove of trees be planted and maintained to replace the beams in the ceiling when they would suffer from dry rot." Bateson's remark was, "That's the way to run a culture." Our question and hope is, "Did they replant them?"

For Warsaw, Poland, we responded to a design competition for a high-rise building. When the client chose our design as the winner after seeing the model, we said, "We're not finished yet. We have to tell you all about the building. The base is made from concrete and includes tiny bits of rubble from World War II. It looks like limestone, but the rubble's there for visceral reasons." And he said, "I understand, a phoenix rising." And we said the skin is recycled aluminum, and he said, "That's O.K., that's fine." And we said, "The floor heights are thirteen feet clear so that we can convert the building into housing in the future, when its utility as an office building is no longer. In this way, the building is given a chance to have a long, useful life." And he said, "That's O.K." And we told him that we would have opening windows and that no one would be further than twenty-five feet from a window, and he said that was O.K., too. And finally, we said, "By the way, you have to plant ten square miles of forest to offset the building's effect on climate change." We had calculated the energy costs to build the structure, and the energy cost to run and maintain it, and it worked out that 6,400 acres of new forests would be needed to offset the effects on climate change from the energy requirements. And he said he would get back to us. He called back two days later and said, "You still win. I checked out what it would cost to plant ten square miles of trees in Poland and it turns out it's equivalent to a small part of the advertising budget."

The architects representing a major retail chain called us a year ago and said, "Will you help us build a store in Lawrence, Kansas?" I said that I didn't know if we could work with them. I explained my thoughts on consumers with lifestyles, and we needed to be in the position to discuss their stores' impact on small towns. Click. Three days later we were called back and were told, "We have a question for you that is coming from the top. Are you willing to discuss the fact that people with lives have the right to buy the finest-quality products, even under your own terms, at the lowest possible price?" We said, "Yes." "Then we can talk about the impact on small towns."

We worked with them on the store in Kansas. We converted the building from steel construction, which uses 300,000 BTUs per square foot, to wood construction, which uses 40,000 BTUs, thereby saving thousands of gallons of oil just in the fabrication of the building. We used only wood that came from resources that were protecting biodiversity. In our research we found that the forests of James Madison and Zachary Taylor in Virginia had been put into sustainable forestry and the wood for the beams came from their and other forests managed this way. We also arranged for no CFC's to be used in the store's construction and systems, and initiated significant research and a major new industry in daylighting. We have yet to fulfill our concerns about the bigger questions of products, their distribution and the chain's impact on small towns, with the exception that this store is designed to be converted into housing when its utility as a retail outlet has expired.

For the City of Frankfurt, we are designing a day-care center that can be operated by the children. It contains a greenhouse roof that has multiple functions: it illuminates, heats both air and water, cools, ventilates, and shelters from the rain, just like a Bedouin tent. One problem we were having during the design process was the engineers wanted to completely automate the building, like a machine. The engineers asked, "What happens if the children forget to close the shades and they get too hot?" We told

EXHIBIT 2   Continued

them the children would open a window. "What if they don't open a window?" the engineers wanted to know. And we told them that in that case, the children would probably close the shade. And then they wanted to know what would happen if the children didn't close the shade. And finally we told them the children would open windows and close shades when they were hot because children are not dead but alive. Recognizing the importance for children to look at the day in the morning and see what the sun is going to do that day and interact with it, we enlisted the help of teachers of Frankfurt to get this one across because the teachers had told us the most important thing was to find something for the children to do. Now the children have ten minutes of activity in the morning and ten minutes of activity when they leave the building, opening and closing the system, and both the children and teachers love the idea. Because of the solar hot-water collectors, we asked that a public laundry be added to the program so that parents could wash clothes while awaiting their children in school. Because of advances in glazing, we are able to create a day-care center that requires no fossil fuels for operating the heating or cooling. Fifty years from now, when fossil fuels will be scarce, there will be hot water for the community, a social center, and the building will have paid back the energy "borrowed" for its construction.

As we become aware of the ethical implications of design, not only with respect to buildings, but in every aspect of human endeavor, they reflect changes in the historical concept of who or what has rights. When you study the history of rights, you begin with the Magna Carta, which was about the rights of white, English, noble males. With the Declaration of Independence, rights were expanded to all landowning white males. Nearly a century later, we moved to the emancipation of slaves, and during the beginnings of this century, to suffrage, giving the right to women to vote. Then the pace picks up with the Civil Rights Act in 1964, and then in 1973, the Endangered Species Act. For the first time, the right of other species and organisms to exist was recognized. We have essentially "declared" that Homo Sapiens are part of the web of life. Thus, if Thomas Jefferson were with us today, he would be calling for a Declaration of Interdependence which recognizes that our ability to pursue wealth, health, and happiness is dependent on other forms of life, that the rights of one species are linked to the rights of others and none should suffer remote tyranny.

This Declaration of Interdependence comes hard on the heels of realizing that the world has become vastly complex, both in its workings and in our ability to perceive and comprehend those complexities. In this complicated world, prior modes of domination have essentially lost their ability to maintain control. The sovereign, whether in the form of a king or nation, no longer seems to reign. Nations have lost control of money to global, computerized trading systems. The sovereign is also losing the ability to deceive and manipulate, as in the case of Chernobyl. While the erstwhile Soviet Republic told the world that Chernobyl was nothing to be concerned about, satellites with ten-meter resolution showed the world that it was something to worry about. And what we saw at the Earth Summit was that the sovereign had lost the ability to lead even on the most elementary level. When Maurice Strong, the chair of the United Nations Conference on the Environment and Development, was asked how many leaders were at the Earth Summit, he said there were over 100 heads of state. Unfortunately, we didn't have any leaders.

When Emerson came back from Europe, he wrote essays for Harvard on Nature. He was trying to understand that if human beings make things and human beings are natural, then are all the things human beings make natural? He determined that Nature was all those things which were immutable. The oceans, the mountains, the sky. Well, we now know that they are mutable. We were operating as if Nature is the Great Mother who never has any problems, is always there for her children, and requires no love in return. When you think about Genesis and the concept of dominion over natural things, we realize that even if we want to get into a discussion of stewardship versus dominion, in the end, the question is, if you have dominion, and perhaps we do have dominion, isn't it implicit that we have stewardship too, because how can you have dominion over something you've killed?

We must face the fact that what we are seeing across the world today is war, a war against life itself. Our present systems of design have created a world that grows far beyond the capacity of the environment to sustain life into the future. The industrial idiom of design, failing to honor the principles of nature, can only violate them, producing waste and harm, regardless of purported intention. If we destroy more forests, burn more garbage, drift-net more fish, burn more coal, bleach more paper, destroy more topsoil, poison more insects, build over more habitats, dam more rivers, produce more toxic and radioactive waste, we are creating a vast industrial machine, not for living in, but for dying in. It is a war, to be sure, a war that only a few more generations can surely survive.

EXHIBIT 2   Concluded

When I was in Jordan, I worked for King Hussein on the master plan for the Jordan Valley. I was walking through a village that had been flattened by tanks and I saw a child's skeleton squashed into the adobe block and was horrified. My Arab host turned to me and said, "Don't you know what war is?" And I said, "I guess I don't." And he said, "War is when they kill your children." So I believe we're at war. But we must stop. To do this, we have to stop designing everyday things for killing, and we have to stop designing killing machines.

We have to recognize that every event and manifestation of nature is "design," that to live within the laws of nature means to express our human intention as an interdependent species, aware and grateful that we are at the mercy of sacred forces larger than ourselves, and that we obey these laws in order to honor the sacred in each other and in all things. We must come to peace with and accept our place in the natural world.

William McDonough

"The key to the project," McDonough stated, would be "getting the fabric mills to open up their manufacturing processes to inspection to see where problems arise." In addition, the mills would have to examine the processes of the mill partners—the farms, yarn spinners, twisters, dyers, and finishers—so that they could also meet the design protocol. McDonough suggested that his close colleague, Dr. Michael Braungart of the Environmental Protection Encouragement Agency (EPEA) in Germany, could help with this project. Braungart's profession was chemistry and he had led the chemistry department of Greenpeace. He had collaborated before with McDonough in implementing McDonough's design protocols.

In addition to the environmental criteria, McDonough's proposal addressed the aesthetic component of the fabrics.[6] "The fabrics need to be incredibly beautiful as well." He suggested that they use the mathematics of fractals to generate the patterns. Fractals were appealing to McDonough because "they are like natural systems . . . the smallest component is the same as the whole." He was interested in harmonic proportions throughout nature, and he felt that the new designs should reflect natural harmonies in the protocols and in the esthetics.

FORMING THE NETWORK

The day following the McDonough meeting, Lyons contacted Rohner Textil to see if Kaelin would be willing to participate in this project. He was encouraged by Lyon's report and looked forward to meeting McDonough, who traveled to Rohner a fortnight later. McDonough was encouraged by the Climatex project. Nevertheless the Climatex fabric was far from compostable, because the OEKO-Tex standards did not exclude all harmful chemicals that would be released during composting. In addition, McDonough was concerned about the use of polyester because it came from a fossil fuel. He explained to Kaelin his design protocols, which, according to Lyons, was like asking Kaelin to "reinvent his mill." Kaelin responded enthusiastically to McDonough's ideas and eagerly awaited Braungart, who would help begin the assessment of the manufacturing processes.

---

[6]The material in this section was developed from interviews conducted with William McDonough on June 29, 1995, August 16, 1995, and September 21, 1995, and with Susan Lyons on July 31, 1995.

Braungart traveled to the mill in December 1993. He examined it closely to determine the changes needed to meet McDonough's design protocol. Braungart was "pleasantly surprised" by Climatex and its OEKO-Tex approval. He was also impressed with the mill, which, he thought, had dealt with ecology issues in a manner far ahead of everything he had seen up to that point. Braungart's early suggestions were, as expected, in agreement with McDonough's: produce the Climatex product without using polyester so that all-natural materials would be used, which would make the fabric compostable. The problem with Climatex, from McDonough's perspective, was that it mixed organic and technical nutrients, so the fabric could not be composted, yet the technical nutrients could not be recovered.

Braungart's evaluation required him to examine all stages of the fabric-construction process. Because the mill was involved with the fabric weaving, he also inspected the mill's suppliers: farmers, yarn spinners, yarn twisters, dyers, and finishers. Yarn spinners created a cord of yarn/thread from the pieces of individual material fibers, such as wool. Yarn twisters took two or more cords of thread/yarn and twisted them together, producing a much thicker, stronger piece of yarn. Dyers added the colors to the yarn. Finishers added chemicals to the finished weave to make it more durable, flame resistant, static resistant, and stain resistant, if these qualities were required.

Lyons was the main project coordinator and was responsible for creating the "construction," or generalized set of weaving patterns and color palette based on McDonough's designs. "Everyone on the project," she said, "knew that getting the mill contractors to open their books for Braungart's inspection would be difficult, and keeping track of the fabric's production would involve complex management well beyond the normal levels of supervision." Consequently, the team had concluded that the more they could do themselves, the easier it would be to produce the new fabrics. Acting on this philosophy, they intended to have the mill perform the role of dyer as well as of weaver. Kaelin agreed: "We need as few members in the pool as possible.[7]

THE PROJECT UNDER WAY?

By the end of January 1994, Kaelin had eliminated polyester from Climatex, producing a new blend of ramie and wool that preserved the fabric's moisture-wicking properties. He called this new fabric Climatex Lifecycle. Using this fabric seemed easier than using material that reclaimed and reused polyester and other technical nutrients.

By the end of January, Kaelin had sent Braungart all of the security data sheets and production details pertaining to the chemicals and dye substances used in the manufacturing of Climatex Lifecycle. The team hoped that this information would be enough for Braungart to make recommendations on how to proceed by the end of February 1994. They wanted Braungart's examination to be totally complete by the end of March 1995.

At the beginning of March 1994, Braungart had some bad news. The chemicals used in the dye materials did not meet the design protocol. Furthermore, questions about the manufacture of the dye chemicals could not be answered by examining the security data sheets, even though they had passed the OEKO-Tex standards. DesignTex's next Portfolio Collection, McDonough's fractal patterns and design

---

[7]Interviews with Lyons on July 21, 1995.

protocols, and Rohner's next generation of Climatex depended on Braungart's ability to gain access to the manufacturing processes of the dye suppliers, which meant the dye suppliers had to open their books to Braungart. Kaelin contacted Rohner's dye suppliers and asked them to cooperate with Braungart's inspection and answer his questions. By the end of March, however, it was clear that cooperation was not forthcoming. Braungart had contacted over 60 chemical companies worldwide, none of which had agreed to open their books for his inspection.

Another concern was the project's cost. Someone needed to pay Braungart and the EPEA as he studied the manufacturing processes. Kaelin agreed to hire Braungart and the EPEA, because Rohner expected to acquire the patent rights for the next generation of Climatex. By the end of April, however, Braungart had already spent the funds Rohner had provided and needed an extension. Rohner was willing to consider an additional payment, but only after the product had been introduced into the marketplace. None of the team were sure how much money Braungart would require.

Lyons reflected on the situation. DesignTex had made a large commitment to this project, hoping it would propel the firm into the lead of the commercial-fabric market. It had already been three years since DesignTex had launched the first Portfolio Collection, and she was aware of the pressure to get a product out the door. Waiting for Braungart to gain access to the dye process risked the whole project and would dramatically increase its cost, even if he succeeded. On the one hand, perhaps it would be better to relax McDonough's and Braungart's standards a little and test the results of the manufacturing process without inspecting the dye suppliers' dye-protection processes. After all, Climatex Lifecycle was already a major improvement over currently available environmental designs. On the other hand, the whole project was about making a breakthrough in environmental design, and it was not clear that anything short of the McDonough/Braungart approach would represent a sufficient leap forward.

THE BETASERON DECISION (A)*

Ann K. Buchholtz, *University of Georgia*

On July 23, 1993, the United States Food and Drug Administration (FDA) approved interferon beta-1b (brand name Betaseron), making it the first treatment for multiple sclerosis to get FDA approval in 25 years. Betaseron was developed by Berlex Laboratories, a United States unit of Schering AG, the German pharmaceutical company. Berlex handled the clinical development, trials, and marketing of the drug, while Chiron, a biotechnology firm based in California, manufactured it. The groundbreaking approval of Betaseron represented not only a great opportunity for Berlex but also a difficult dilemma. Available supplies were insufficient to meet initial demand and shortages were forecasted until 1996. With insufficient supplies and staggering development costs, how would Berlex allocate and price the drug?

THE CHALLENGE OF MULTIPLE SCLEROSIS

Multiple sclerosis (MS) is a disease of the central nervous system that interferes with the brain's ability to control such functions as seeing, walking, and talking. The nerve fibers within the brain and spinal cord are surrounded by myelin, a fatty substance that protects the nerve fibers in the same way that insulation protects electrical wires. When the myelin insulation becomes damaged, as in demyelinating diseases such as

---

MS, the ability of the central nervous system to transmit nerve impulses to and from the brain becomes impaired. Although the cause of MS remains unknown, much evidence supports the classification of MS as an autoimmune disease in which the immune system mistakenly attacks the myelin sheath, causing sclerosed (i.e., scarred or hardened) areas in multiple parts of the brain and spinal cord.

The symptoms of MS depend to some extent upon the location and size of the sclerotic areas. Symptoms include numbness, slurred speech, blurred vision, poor coordination, muscle weakness, bladder dysfunction, extreme fatigue, and paralysis. There is no way to know how the disease will progress for any individual because the nature of the course it takes can change over time. Some people have a relatively benign course of MS with only one or two mild attacks, nearly complete remission, and no permanent disability. Others have a chronic progressive course resulting in severe disability. The most typical pattern is one in which relatively short periods of exacerbation of symptoms alternate with periods of remission, when the symptoms recede. People with MS live with an exceptionally high degree of uncertainty because the course of their disease can change from one day to the next. Dramatic downturns as well as dramatic recoveries are not uncommon.

THE PROMISE OF BETASERON

Interferon beta is a naturally occurring protein that regulates the body's immune system. Betaseron is a genetically engineered, laboratory manufactured recombinant product composed of interferon beta-1b. In large-scale clinical trials, Betaseron had been shown to reduce the frequency and severity of exacerbations in ambulatory MS patients with a relapsing-remitting form of the disease. It did not reverse damage already done, nor did it completely prevent exacerbations from occurring. However, Betaseron could dramatically improve the quality of life for the person with MS; for example, people taking Betaseron were shown to have fewer and shorter hospitalizations. Other interferons (i.e., alpha and gamma) had been tested, but beta interferon was the first and only drug to have an effect on the frequency of exacerbations. Because it is an immunoregulatory agent, it was believed to combat the immune problems that make MS worse. However, the exact way in which it works had yet to be determined.

Betaseron is administered subcutaneously (under the skin) every other day by self-injection. In order to derive the most benefits from the therapy, it was important that the MS patient maintain a regular schedule of the injections. Some flulike side effects, as well as swelling and irritation around the injection, had been noted; however, they tended to decrease with time on treatment. In addition, one person who received Betaseron committed suicide, while three others attempted to kill themselves. Because MS often leads to depression, there was no way to know whether the administration of Betaseron had been a factor in these deaths. Lastly, Betaseron was not recommended for use during pregnancy.

THE BETASERON DILEMMA

In July of 1993, FDA approval for Betaseron allowed physicians to prescribe the drug to MS patients who were ambulatory and had a relapsing-remitting course of MS. An estimated one-third of the 300,000 people with MS in the United States fell into that category, resulting in a potential client base of 100,000. However, because of an expedited FDA review process for new drug applications, it had taken only one